THE MEDIA STUDIES

The Media Studies Reader is an entry point into the major theories and debates that have shaped critical media studies from the 1940s to the present. Combining foundational essays with influential new writings, this collection provides a toolbox for understanding old and new media as objects of critical inquiry. It is comprised of over forty readings that are organized into seven sections representing key concepts and themes covered in an introductory media studies course: culture, technology, representation, industry, identity, audience, and citizenship. Critical introductions frame each section to help students place each reading in context and within a broader scholarly dialogue. Rather than relegating the issue of difference to just one section, each section includes scholarship that foregrounds the politics of gender, ethnicity, race, class, sexuality, and geopolitics. Longer readings have been selectively edited for conciseness and accessibility, and to maximize breadth of coverage. A map of a rapidly growing—and changing—field, *The Media Studies Reader* is an invaluable resource for students and established scholars alike.

Laurie Ouellette is Associate Professor in Communication Studies at the University of Minnesota, Twin Cities, where she teaches Critical Media Studies. She is also affiliated with the American Studies Department and the Graduate Minor in Moving Image Studies.

THE MEDIA STUDIES READER

Edited by
LAURIE OUELLETTE

Routledge
Taylor & Francis Group

NEW YORK AND LONDON

First published 2013
by Routledge
711 Third Avenue, New York, NY 10017

Simultaneously published in the UK
by Routledge
2 Park Square, Milton Park, Abingdon, Oxon OX14 4RN

Routledge is an imprint of the Taylor & Francis Group, an informa business

Library of Congress Cataloging in Publication Data
The media studies reader / edited by Laurie Ouellette.
   p. cm.
   Includes bibliographical references and index.
   1. Mass media.   I. Ouellette, Laurie.
   P91.25.M3755 2012
   302.23—dc23

2012001172

ISBN: 978–0–415–80124–9 (hbk)
ISBN: 978–0–415–80125–6 (pbk)

Typeset in Amasis
by RefineCatch Limited, Bungay, Suffolk

My gratitude to Matt Byrnie for suggesting this collection and to the editorial team at Routledge, especially Erica Wetter and Sioned Jones, for overseeing its development and publication in an efficient and gracious manner. Thanks are also due to my graduate students at the University of Minnesota-Twin Cities and to James Hay for his helpful suggestions on the introductory material. Finally, kudos to Henry for his quirky insights and patience with this project.

CONTENTS

SECTION III
MEDIA/REPRESENTATION

SECTION IV
MEDIA/INDUSTRY

SECTION V
MEDIA/IDENTITY

SECTION VI
MEDIA/AUDIENCE

SECTION VII
MEDIA/CITIZENSHIP

INTRODUCTION: MAPPING MEDIA STUDIES

Marshall McLuhan, an English professor who wrote famously about the impact of media on human consciousness in the 1960s, is reported to have once said: "We don't know who discovered water, but we know it wasn't the fish." His comment is interpreted to mean that just as the fish has no awareness of an existence outside water, the people of modern societies are so thoroughly immersed in media that we don't realize how much it shapes us. For years, the quotation was widely used as a pedagogical device to encourage students to think critically about the advertising, television, films, newspapers and magazines that permeated their everyday lives. McLuhan's remarks were evoked to introduce the provocative possibility that media influence our understandings of ourselves, and the social world, in profound ways that are often unrecognized. While the need to think critically about media is surely as crucial in 2012 and beyond, McLuhan's parable now seems somewhat dated.

Since McLuhan's time, traditional mass media have converged with increasingly niche-oriented, specialized and customized media platforms and technologies. The commercial media environment of the 21st century is considerably more fragmented, mobile and interactive than it was in the 1960s. At the same time this has occurred, scholarship on media has burgeoned and splintered along lines of specialization and critical perspective. Just as it is no longer possible to speak of the media, or even a particular medium such as television, as a singular entity, many scholars would question the universality of the fish, historicize its world, and bring more specificity to issues of place,

difference, and reception. Contrary to the passive aquatic creative conceived by McLuhan, they might argue that today's fish plays an increasingly active and productive role in media culture, involving proficiency in a range of digital and mobile technologies as well as the constant labor of customizing a personal schedule of "on demand" media consumption.

The point is not really to compare media culture to a fish bowl, but rather to emphasize the extent to which the interdisciplinary field of *critical media studies*, like media, is dynamic and shaped through specific historical, economic and geographical contexts. While McLuhan is one of the most widely recognized proponents of critically "understanding media" of his time, critical media studies developed through a much wider range of questions and theories, many preoccupied with the issue of power. While the origins of media studies can be traced to the rise of mass communication scholarship of the 1920s, the field (as distinct from positivist social scientific approaches) did not emerge as a focal point of research and teaching until the 1970s. Even then, this scholarship was interdisciplinary and eclectic, incorporating scholarly influences as diverse as literary studies, social and political theory, adult education, cultural studies, linguistics and film studies. What connected these influences—and continues to bring coherency to critical media studies—is a concern with the conditions and power relations of the societies in which media operate. While scholars now study a dizzying range of media objects (print, television, film, music, advertising, brands, the Internet, digital games, computers, mobile phones) from multiple methodological and theoretical vantage points, they share a concern with understanding not just media themselves but their changing role in social and power relations.

To approach the study of media critically involves situating media within economic, political, cultural and social contexts and addressing its relationship to capitalism, labor, citizenship, gender, race and class dynamics, inequalities, sexuality, globalization and other issues that are both larger than media, and intertwined with the production, circulation and use of media texts, images, sounds, spaces, artifacts, technologies and discourses. Doing so is not a singular process, but rather a pluralistic and historical inquiry. This is the critical orientation of *The Media Studies Reader*. Cutting across the many subjects, methods and approaches presented here is a critical engagement with media's relationship to the particularities and futures of the societies we live in. While the authors do not always agree about what this engagement entails, all approach the study of media as an endeavor with stakes well beyond the pursuit of knowledge for its own sake. To the extent that McLuhan, in his own way, shared this view, his oft-cited parable is perhaps not so dated after all.

What is Media? What are Media Studies?

The goal of *The Media Studies Reader* is to introduce foundational contributions to the study of media, as well as newer approaches to the media landscape of the 21st century, many of which continue to be engaged with, or build on, early assumptions about media. The collection is not inclusive, but it does provide an entry point into the major theories and debates that have shaped critical media studies from the 1940s to the present. *The Media Studies Reader* provides both a toolbox for making sense of media culture and a genealogy of media as an object of critical inquiry. This is not a progress narrative, in which each new-and-improved theory overcomes the limits of earlier approaches, but rather an attempt to situate the shifting concerns of media studies within historical contexts. These contexts are the backdrop for distinct (but overlapping) "stages" of media, broadly characterized as *mass, niche* and *interactive*.

These stages of media did not evolve spontaneously, but rather closely intersect with parallel developments in the capitalist economy and social relations. As both societies and media have changed, new questions have been asked, new methods have been tried out, and new critical frameworks have gained currency in media studies. Rather than seeing this evolution as the replacement of flawed approaches with better ones, we might follow Lynn Spigel's understanding of waves of critical scholarship as "discursive formations" (2004). Following Michel Foucault (1972) Spigel suggests that different ways of criticizing media constitute the "truths" available to scholars. While we can and should "trace their genealogy across time," discursive formations do not "necessarily follow a neat historical outline or revolution." Nor are discursive formations exhaustive: out of "all the possible statements one could make about media," Spigel writes, these are the "limited groups of statements that are spoken at a specific historical moment" and that circulate among media scholars (Spigel, 2004, p. 1213). Of course, as Foucault pointed out, discourse is never fixed for all time. If the discursive practices collected in this book exemplify existing "knowledge and expectations" about media and media studies, new discursive practices will emerge.

It is important to recognize how waves of media studies intersect with the media landscapes of different eras. The earliest scholarship responded to the rise of mass-produced communication and culture. The expansion of industrial capitalism and the modern changes it set into motion (urbanization, a demarcation of work and leisure, mobile privatization, loss of traditional community, the spread of consumer culture) set the stage for the emergence of national magazines, movies, radio, and television addressed to a broad audience. This development provoked a range of concerns about the industrial origins, centralized attributes and potential impact of the new systems of communication. The critical discourse on mass communication, mass culture and the culture industry rarely specified the formal distinctiveness of particular mediums. Rather, the critique—exemplified within the social sciences by the Payne Foundation's research on child movie audiences in the 1920s and within critical discourse by the Frankfurt School's assessment of the culture industry and its products in the 1940s (1944/2002)—addressed the implications of manufacturing culture as an industrial commodity and mass culture's capacity to reach and influence millions of people. The monopolistic tendencies of the industries involved in the production and distribution of mass communication and mass culture also became a pressing issue. Many formative writings emerged from this stage of media studies, from the political economic research of scholars like Herb Schiller (1989) to characterizations of the "society of the spectacle" influenced by Guy Debord (1967/2000).

In the post-war period, the generalized critique of mass culture gave way to a gradual emphasis on the specific attributes of specific mediums. For example, Marshall McLuhan's *Understanding Media* (1964) is organized around such distinctions, as illustrated by his famous description of mediums as either "hot" or "cool." The application of semiotics to film also occurs around this time, with scholarship such as Christian Metz's *Film Language* (1974) emphasizing the formal, language-like attributes of film and rendering it a distinct and "worthy" object of study. As it developed, screen theory drew from linguistics as well as anthropology, Marxism, feminism and psychoanalysis to theorize the power dynamics of cinema (and later television) as a cultural "apparatus." Such approaches coalesced around a critical reading of visual conventions and texts, rarely placed within broader sociohistorical contexts. Over time, however, scholars began to question the explanatory power of screen theory. The emergence of British cultural studies played an important role in this critique. The work of Raymond Williams, Stuart Hall, Angela McRobbie and other scholars affiliated with the Birmingham Centre for Contemporary Cultural Studies paved the way for a more historicized approach to the "social construction" of media technologies (see Hall, 1980/1991). Cultural studies scholars also raised new questions about the contradictory meanings, pleasures, desires and uses of dominant and subcultural media culture. In nations such as Australia and the United States, complementary approaches were developed by cultural theorists (Grossberg, 1982), cultural historians (Lipsitz, 1988), television scholars (Fiske and Hartley 1989) and feminist scholars (Radway, 1984).

By the 1980s, the audience and everyday life were central to critical media studies in ways they hadn't

been before. In an attempt to understand media's relationship to power, resistance and social change in light of these concerns, scholars turned to new theoretical perspectives (some of which had only been recently translated into English). Antonio Gramsci's theory of hegemony (1971), which emphasizes the sometimes unpredictable contradictions and power struggles of rule by consent rather than force, proved enormously helpful, as did Michel de Certeau's work on the tactics of oppressed groups (1984) and Mikhail Bakhtin's writing on the inversions of power made temporarily possible in the space of the carnival (1984). This work pushed media studies beyond its earlier emphasis on visual languages to a fuller consideration of other media forms (such as music) and bodily sensibilities and affects that are not easily mapped onto ideological processes and looking relations. The rise of conservative political regimes (such as the administrations of Margaret Thatcher and Ronald Reagan) promoting free market policies in the name of the "common person" during this period lent a sense of urgency to these projects. A wave of audience research grounded in theory as well as interviews, ethnography and participant observation emerged, influenced by Stuart Hall's influential essay "Encoding/Decoding" (1980). While their findings varied considerably, the concept of the "active" audience gained visibility as a general descriptor of this work within media studies. This became the catalyst for contestation and reflection, with some scholars questioning the extent to which capitalist-produced media could be empowering and advocating a renewed focus on critical approaches that highlighted the highly concentrated, market-based and increasingly global operations of media industries.

The turn to varied audience negotiations and practices coincided, increasingly, with a gradual de-centering of the mass media and the emergence of a more fragmented, niche-oriented and customized media landscape. Lizabeth Cohen (2003) situates the impetus for narrowcasting within the rapid expansion of postwar consumer capitalism. The quest for profit maximization, she suggests, led to a search for new markets that included other nations as well as untapped populations and lifestyle clusters within the United States. Just as consumer goods were customized for increasingly differentiated markets, so too were films, magazines, radio and television. Within this context, the mass market and its corollary, the mass audience, were reconceived as an array of consumer niches that could be further refined through specialized content and market research. Marginalized groups such as African Americans were embraced as market subsets, while emergent social identities (such as the "independent woman") made possible by the social movements of the 1960s and 1970s were rapidly sold back to consumers as specialized consumer choices. As Michael Curtin (1996) points out, this development emerged as the Fordist mode of production named after automobile manufacturer Henry Ford was giving way to more dispersed, flexible and customized modes of production and culture and information were becoming increasingly central to, not merely reflective of, the post-Fordist capitalist economy. As information, communication, culture and brands became the leading "immaterial" commodities produced by capitalism in the West, what sociologists call individualization (Beck and Beck-Gernsheim, 2002) or the further decline of traditional social networks and the rising imperative to "choose" and express one's own lifestyle and identity, intensified. Not surprisingly, as Lynn Spigel points out (2001), increasingly mobile technologies began to appear around this time, including the first portable televisions, advertised with the promise that each family member would now be granted the "freedom" to customize his or her own viewing rather than watching the same programming together in the family circle.

As with the fragmentation of consumer culture in general, the proliferation of commercial magazines, music, radio stations, and television and cable channels became a highly visible resource for defining identity and lifestyle. At this stage, deregulation was promoted and implemented by politicians and policymakers as a solution to the homogeneity ascribed to mass culture, particularly in the United States. Within this context, the identity politics of the 1960s, which had partly informed Great Society social welfare programs, became a basis for liberalizing media policy through private cable, satellite and new technologies that embraced difference as a commodity and lifestyle choice. In the wake of these intersecting developments scholars have brought new questions and approaches to bear on the study of representation

and identity. The analysis of "positive" and "negative" images had long been challenged by post-structuralist paradigms emphasizing the social construction of reality in more complex terms. However, the rising visibility of difference and the accompanying presumption of an already achieved racial, sexual and gender empowerment across contemporary media culture led many scholars to engage more fully with the intricacies of commodification and media's role in constituting "subjects of capacity" (McRobbie, 2008) and "posting" feminism and civil rights initiatives (Banet-Weiser, 2007).

Also in the 1990s, the global circulation of "image-centered and narrative strips of reality," or what Arjun Appadurai (1990) calls mediascapes, became a focal point of media analysis. As free trade policies expanded the markets of increasingly transnational media industries, cost-cutting measures and risk-minimizing strategies from co-production to the circulation of formats (or templates) on a global scale have become more prevalent. The emergence in the 1980s of private, advertising-based television networks (such as Rupert Murdoch's Sky TV channels) competed with older national broadcasting companies through the purchase of foreign (particularly Hollywood-produced) fare. Co-productions and Hollywood's search for cheaper labor markets also intensified (Miller et al, 2008), changing the dynamics of global media culture. This new stage of globalization intersected with the new interplay between mass culture and niche media, and between the intensification of cultural imperialism and attempts to theorize the hybrid aspects of global media culture (Kraidy, 2005). The rise of global franchises that may originate outside Hollywood, and trade in generic formats, which are localized across national contexts, has intensified these debates (Moran and Malbon, 2006).

Today, scholarship in critical media studies often tends to address the increasingly interactive nature of contemporary media culture, a mode of engagement facilitated in part through the "convergence" of old and new media. Scholars attempt to understand the economic and social shifts associated with convergence and interactivity, as well as the possibilities and limits of these developments as catalysts for social change. The critical debate over interactivity is exemplified at one end by Henry Jenkin's optimistic view of "participatory culture" and its capacity to thrive in a converged, transmedia environment encompassing traditional mass media (such as films and television programs) as well as new technologies (such as computers and cell phones) that allow users to remix content, follow content across platforms and practice new forms of collective intelligence with like-minded fans (2005).

For Jenkins, this new "prosumer" experience broadens the terms of our access to media, and may serve as a springboard for more explicitly political activities. On the other end of the debate is Mark Andrejevic's (2009) more cautious account of the interactive digital capitalist economy, its reliance on dispersed forms of surveillance, and its "offloading" of the labor of customizing and marketing onto consumers. For Andrejevic, filling out a survey online, participating in an online fan forum, or remixing mainstream media content is less an indication of democratization, than evidence of the refinement of media to meet the needs of a current stage of capitalism.

The emergence of 500 channels, flexible viewing platforms and recording devices, online blogs, social networking sites and reality TV shows soliciting the participation of ordinary people, are also part of the interactive stage of media. The emphasis on individual choice, participation and agency is not driven by industry or capitalism alone, but also intersects with social transformations (such as the intensification of mobility) and ways of thinking about democracy and post-welfare citizenship. While the public sphere has long been a key concept in critical media studies, many scholars now find it less useful in light of feminist and critical race critiques of its historically white, masculine biases and blurring boundaries between public and private, factual and fictional, and political culture and "entertainment only."

The narrowcasting of niche media to diasporic groups and political subcultures, and the rise of new forms like talk radio and fake news shows, among other developments, have triggered a turn to other models of analysis, and the convergence of lifestyle media and normative citizenship in the current epoch have encouraged the application of theories of dispersed governmentality and self-fashioning as the basis of citizenship to media studies (Ouellette and

Hay, 2008). There is an uncanny parallel between the active consumer and the active citizen heralded by today's neoliberal political culture, as many scholars have pointed out. Such are the concerns of unfolding contributions to the critical discourse on media and power in the 21st century.

The Media Studies Reader: Key Concepts and Debates

The Media Studies Reader is organized around seven key concepts: culture, technology, representation, industry, identity, audience and citizenship. Each section traces ways of theorizing these concepts in relation to media, as well as major conceptual developments and breaks in critical scholarship around them. There are of course other key concepts and ways of slicing what has become a quite voluminous body of literature. The modest hope of this collection is to consolidate foundational and emergent critical work on related subjects and debates. Doing so highlights the historical development of the field and the critical discourse available to contemporary and future scholars. I have also tried to address two shortcomings of existing readers of this nature.

First, rather than relegating the issue of difference to just one section, I have included critical scholarship that foregrounds the politics of gender, ethnicity, race, class, gender and geopolitics in every section. This means that difference is not theorized only in relation to representation and identity, but is also a thread in the theorization of industry, citizenship and other topics that have historically assumed a universal perspective or a normative (white, male, educated middle class) subject.

The second thing I have done is present a wide range of critical perspectives. Of course, no collection can include every important book or article; there is enough worthwhile scholarship on media to fill libraries, let alone single books. The economics of book publishing also shape the selection process, particularly in cases where important contributions are simply too expensive to reproduce. Nevertheless, I have sought to include a broad spectrum of critical approaches influenced by investments in semiotics, discourse analysis, post-structuralism, Marxism, visual theory, historical analysis, feminism, critical race studies, the critique of empire, hegemony theory, political economy, cultural studies, ethnography and queer theory. I have also included multiple perspectives (which sometimes conflict) on contemporary issues such as media convergence, interactivity and "ordinary people" in the media.

Section One, Media/Culture, introduces theories of mass culture and mass media, beginning with the foundational scholarship of the Frankfurt School and tracing the influence of niche marketing, globalization and new technologies on the mass culture debate in more recent years. Section Two, Media/Technology, introduces critical scholarship on media technologies and debates over technological determinism. Section Three, Media/Representation, introduces critical approaches to representation and meaning, from semiotics and looking relations to commodity fetishism and post-structuralism, through scholarship in which scholars explain these terms and apply them to media-related examples. Section Four, Media/ Industry, addresses the political economy of old and new media, covering private ownership and commercialism, intellectual property, niche marketing, global cultural flows and late capitalism's nourishing of "free labor."

Section Five, Media/Identity, introduces scholarship on media and identity, tracing the analysis of subjectivity and self-fashioning from Marxist and psychoanalytic theories of subjectivity to more recent work on performativity and "presentational" media. Section Six, Media/Audience, explores the audience as an object of analysis, from the emergence of cultural studies scholarship as a response to screen theory and positivist social scientific approaches to newer debates over interactivity. Finally, Section Seven, Media/ Citizenship, examines the way scholars have conceived media's relationship to democracy and citizenship, from debates over the public sphere to work on cultural citizenship, media policy and governmentality.

While the writings collected here provide a map of critical studies, understanding media also involves being open to what is unsettled and unfinished about media and their analysis. My hope is that the reader will use this collection as a springboard for exploring other writings, and not let existing assumptions (and politics) run too far ahead of discovering (to use McLuhan's expression) the media in which we swim.

References

Adorno, Theodor and Max Horkheimer, "The Culture Industry: Enlightenment as Mass Deception," in *Dialectic of Enlightenment* (Stanford: Stanford University Press, 2002), p. 94–156.

Andrejevic, Mark, *iSpy: Surveillance and Power in the Interactive Era* (Lawrence, KS: University of Kansas Press, 2009).

Arjun Appadurai, "Disjuncture and Difference in the Global Cultural Economy," *Theory, Culture & Society*, Vol. 7 (1990), p. 295–310.

Banet-Weiser, Sarah, "What's Your Flava: Race and Postfeminism in Media Culture," in *Interrogating Postfeminism: Gender and the Politics of Popular Culture*, ed. Yvonne Tasker and Diane Negra (Durham, NC: Duke University Press 2007), p. 201–226.

Bakhtin, Mikhail, *Rabelais and His World*, trans. Helene Iswolsky (Bloomington, IN: Indiana University Press, 1968/1984).

Beck, Ulrich and Elizabeth Beck-Gernsheim, *Individualization: Institutionalized Individualism and Its Social and Political Consequences* (Thousand Oaks, CA: Sage, 2002).

Cohen, Lizbeth, *A Consumer's Republic: The Politics of Mass Consumption in Post War America* (New York: Vintage, 2003).

Debord, Guy, *Society of the Spectacle* (Detroit: Black and Red Publishing, 1967/2000).

De Certeau, Michel, *The Practice of Everyday Life* (Berkeley: University of California, 1984).

Michael Curtin, "On Edge: Culture Industries in the Neo-Network Era," in *Making and Selling Culture*, ed. Richard Ohmann (Hanover, NH: Wesleyan University Press, 2006), p. 181–202.

Fiske, John and John Hartley, *Reading Television* (London: Routledge, 1989).

Foucault, Michel, *The Archeaology of Knowledge*, trans. A.M. Sheridan Smith (New York: Pantheon, 1972).

Gramsci, Antonio, *Selection from the Prison Notebooks* (New York: International Publishers, 1971).

Grossberg, Lawrence, "Experience, Signification, and Reality: The Boundaries of Cultural Semiotics," *Semiotica*, Vol. 42 No. 1–4 (1982), p. 73–106.

Jenkins, Henry, *Convergence Culture: Where Old and New Media Collide* (New York: NYU Press, 2005).

Kraidy, Marwan, *Hybridity, or the Cultural Logic of Globalization* (Philadelphia: Temple University Press, 2005).

Lipsitz, George, "This Ain't No Sideshow: Historians and Media Studies," *Critical Studies in Mass Communication*, Vol. 5, No. 2 (1988), p. 147–161.

McRobbie, Angela, *The Aftermath of Feminism: Gender, Culture and Social Change* (Thousand Oaks, CA: Sage, 2008).

Metz, Christian, *Film Language* (Cambridge: Oxford University Press, 1974).

Hall, Stuart, "Encoding/Decoding," in *Culture, Media, Language*, ed. Stuart Hall, David Rowe and Dorothy Hobson (New York: Routledge, 1980), p. 128–138.

Hall, Stuart, "Introduction to Media Studies at the Centre," in *Culture, Media, Language: Working Papers in Cultural Studies 1972–1979* (New York: Harper Collins, 1980).

McLuhan, Marshall, *Understanding Media* (New York: McGraw Hill, 1964).

Miller, Toby, Nitin Govil, John McMurria, Ting Wang and Richard Maxwell, *Global Hollywood: No. 2* (London: British Film Institute, 2008).

Moran, Albert, *Understanding the Global TV Format* (Bristol: Intellect, 2006).

Radway, Janice, *Reading the Romance: Women, Patriarchy and Popular Literature* (Durhan, NC: University of North Carolina Press, 1991).

Ouellette, Laurie and James Hay, *Better Living Through Reality TV: Television and Post-Welfare Citizenship* (Malden, MA: Blackwell, 2008).

Herbert Schiller, *Culture Inc: The Corporate Takeover of Public Expression* (New York: Oxford University Press, 1989).

Spigel, Lynn, "Theorizing the Bachelorette: Waves of *Feminist Media Studies*," *Signs*, Vol. 30, No. 1 (Autumn 2004), p. 1209–1221.

Spigel, Lynn, *Welcome to the Suburbs: Popular Media and Postwar Suburbs* (Durhan, NC: Duke University Press, 2001).

SECTION I

MEDIA/CULTURE

Introduction

This section introduces theories that link media (initially described as mass media or mass communication) and culture, and explore the aesthetics and politics of commercial media. If the term mass media has lost some of its resonance in the era of 500 channels, iPods and Facebook, the specter of mass-produced media has loomed large historically. Since the late 1800s, reformers and critics have accused virtually every mass circulation medium of lowering cultural standards, promoting the wrong values and pandering to uneducated audiences. Social scientists joined the conversation by the 1920s, when they began studying the effects of mass media on human behavior and levels of popular taste. Many of the foundational texts of critical media studies are also concerned with the consequences of manufacturing culture as an industrial commodity.

The rise of mass media coincided with the expansion of industrial capitalism and the social transformations it wrought, including urbanization, the bifurcation of work and leisure (for employed males), and the merchandising of consumer goods previously unimagined or produced at home. Just as factories churned out identical products from breakfast cereal to automobiles, the Fordist mode of production (named after the automobile manufacturer Henry Ford) also put its stamp on emerging forms of media, subjecting recorded music, films, magazines, radio and television to the tenets of centralized production, standardization, economies of scale and profit-maximization. Mass produced and circulated media objects and artifacts (programs, songs, images, texts) took shape in tandem with the modernization of capitalist democracies and (particularly in the United States) the expansion of consumer culture as a corollary of the factory system. Critical and cultural theorists (unlike earlier reformers and social scientists) take these broader socio-economic forces into account when theorizing the cultural attributes and power dynamics of mass culture and the transition from old to new media.

The first major theoretical critique of the culture industry and its products was Theodor Adorno and Max Horkheimer's 1944 essay "The Culture Industry: Enlightenment as Mass Deception," presented in excerpted form here. Members of the Frankfurt School, an esteemed group of German intellectuals who moved to the United States on the cusp of World War II, Adorno and Horkheimer approached the mass media of industrial capitalist societies from the vantage point of critical theory, a philosophical tradition influenced by Marxism, psychoanalysis and German social theory. Their experience as Marxist, Jewish refuges made them particularly critical of industrialized culture's potential to produce social and political uniformity, as in Nazi Germany.

Like other critical German scholars who wrote about mass culture, including Siegfried Kracauer, Walter Benjamin and later Herbert Marcuse, Adorno and Horkheimer saw modernity, under processes of industrialization and capitalism, as having destroyed an older, rural sense of community. This is what the German sociologist Ferdinand Tonnies described as the distinction between *Gemeinschaft* (old organic community) and *Gesellschaft* (modern society/alienation). Upon arriving in the United States, Adorno and

Horkheimer also became increasingly alarmed by the homogeneity and formulaic nature of culture produced factory-style, tendencies barely concealed by what they termed the "pseudo-individuality" of competing cultural products.

While scholars do not always agree with everything that Adorno and Horkheimer wrote, few would dispute their enormous influence on critical media studies. The first scholars to introduce theories of manipulation and exploitation to the study of media, they paved the way for Marxist theories of ideology, even as their arguments were critiqued by feminist and cultural scholars. Perhaps the most trenchant criticism waged against the Frankfurt School concerned their reliance on socially constructed cultural hierarchies. In pointing out the simplicity and repetitiveness of mass culture, and the "narcotic" fixes it offered to belabored workers, Adorno and Horkheimer seemed to conflate commodification and control with assumptions about cultural value. They valued less commonly available, and thus difficult forms of culture (such as classical music and avant-garde art) for its capacity to inspire critical thinking, but one suspects that they never questioned their own pre-disposition to these forms of culture as educated intellectuals. Directly or not, critical media studies has continued to engage with their analysis of the culture industry, by extending and updating its concerns, defending popular media against it, or taking its assessment of mass culture as a benchmark for theorizing the evolving media landscape and the changing political and social implications of mass industrialized culture and communication.

Such is the case with "Mass-Produced Fantasies for Women" by feminist literary scholar Tania Modleski, the lead chapter from her 1982 book *Loving With a Vengeance: Mass Produced Fantasies for Women*. This selection represents an early attempt to better understand the complexities and possibilities of mass culture, particularly for women. Noting that the denigration of mass culture is implicitly gendered, Modleski cites Horkheimer and Adorno when arguing that "It is one of the great ironies in the development of mass culture theory that the people who were first responsible for pointing out the political importance of Modleski (1982).

Drawing from literary critic Fredric Jameson's important 1979 essay "Reification and Utopia in Mass Culture," Modleski argues that some of the critical functions the Frankfurt School attributed to high culture could also apply to devalued women's genres such as gothic novels and soap operas. Her insistence on valuing the mass culture consumed by millions of women, and exploring the anxieties, fantasies and contradictions contained within denigrated forms of mass media, echoed arguments being made in British cultural studies, most especially Angela McRobbie's work on magazines for women and girls (1978). While she ultimately differentiated between "symbolic" and real satisfactions, and in so doing affirmed the importance of unconscious and ideological processes, Modleski's efforts to recuperate the mass culture of women nonetheless anticipated a wave of critical scholarship on the pleasurable and potentially subversive aspects of commercial media in the 1980s and 1990s. "The price women pay for their popular entertainment is high," she explained in a passage that aptly sums up the basic argument of this scholarship, "but they may still be getting more than anyone bargained for."

In "Popular Culture: This Ain't No Sideshow," a chapter from his 2001 book *Time Passages: Collective Memory and American Popular Culture*, George Lipsitz situates the contradictions of mass culture within a longer history of commercialized leisure, from vaudeville and variety shows to movies and television. In so doing he shows how stage performances and their electronic equivalents perpetuated capitalist objectives, but as is the case with most cultural studies scholars, Lipsitz also emphasizes the social nature of taken-for-granted aesthetic hierarchies and the dynamic nature of cultural power. This selection represents a cultural turn in critical media studies in its uptake of Pierre Bourdieu's theories of participation and investment in popular culture, Mikhail Baktin's notion of carnival as an inversion of social order, and Antonio Gramsci's account of hegemony as a struggle over power played out, according to Lipsitz, in the popular media. While Lipsitz is especially concerned with the place of popular memory in these struggles, his survey also exemplifies the search for theoretical alternatives to the pessimism of the Frankfurt School. However invested in the capitalist economy, he contends, the messages of the mass media "retain memories of the past and contain hopes for the future that rebuke the industries and inequities of the present."

While the contributions by Modleski and Lipsitz exemplify an impetus to nuance theories of mass culture, developments from globalization to the fragmentation of the audience to the rise of new technologies have also come to bear on the media landscape. In "Eyes Wide Shut: Capitalism, Class and the Promise of Black Media," a chapter from her 2007 book *Pimpin Ain't Easy: Selling Black Entertainment Television*,

Beretta Smith-Shomade theorizes the intersection of race, media and capitalism, providing an historical perspective on diversification and the rise of niche media. Focusing on Black-owned commercial media, from early newspapers to the cable network Black Entertainment Television (BET), Smith-Shomade reminds us that media produced by and for marginalized groups is not necessarily progressive: private ownership and profit-making have profoundly impacted Black media, she contends, with implications that have intensified in the current niche-oriented media landscape.

Smith-Shomade rejects the equation of consumer recognition with authenticity and empowerment and suggests instead that aims of equality, connection and progress have been subsumed by the imperatives of profit-maximization. Black-owned media have participated in muckraking and crusading for change but they have also promoted class hierarchies and the acquisition of wealth; more importantly, venues like BET trade in "selling blackness," so that race is less an identity, a community or a struggle than a commodity. Integrating critical race theory and political economy, Smith-Shomade's intervention suggests that the emergence of more channels for specialized groups is not a solution to mass culture, but rather an extension of capitalism through difference.

Arjun Appadurai's much-cited 1990 essay "Disjunctures and Difference in the Global Cultural Economy" rethinks issues of commercial media and cultural homogenization on a global scape. To make sense of transnational cultural and economic flows, Appadurai emphasizes less the seamless extension of Western mass culture as a form of cultural imperialism, than the unpredictable "disjunctures" between economy, culture and politics and the indigenization that always occurs when forces from one society are brought into new ones. Rejecting the lumping of all media culture into a singular force (as in the concept of the culture industry), he suggests the term "scape" to emphasize the fluid and irregular shape of the imagined worlds in which people now live. The mediascapes of the global economy provide "image-centered and narrative-based strips of reality" that can form the basis for fantasies and desires, but these do not always map neatly onto the political ideologies circulated by ideascapes or the economic imperatives of financescapes. Indeed, the possibility of disjuncture is what drives change in the global politics of cultural sameness and difference.

The final selection, digital media scholar Lev Manovich's 2010 essay "The Practice of Everyday (Media) Life: From Mass Consumption to Mass Cultural Production" considers the extent to which digital technologies and user-generated content have spawned a new media universe. In this timely essay, Manovich cautions against celebrating user generated content or equating it with alternative or progressive developments. Much of what people post on YouTube and the Web, he points out, follows the conventions of the entertainment industry, suggesting that people's "identities and imaginations" may now be more "colonized by commercial media" than they were when Adorno and Horkheimer first characterized the culture industry. What has changed, Manovich suggests, is that cultural products are now geared to expectations of consumer activity and customization by users. Cultural production intersects with the practice of everyday life, and directly incorporates what Michel de Certeau has called "tactics" (the ways people build their worlds and identities out of ready-made objects through practices of bricolage, customization, assembly and remix).

What does it mean when tactics, long celebrated by cultural studies scholars for affirming ordinary people's creativity and resistance, are structured into the manufacture of commercial culture? In a fascinating conclusion, Manovich indirectly circles back to the Frankfurt School and its hope that art could be a catalyst for critical thinking. Noting that sites like YouTube and Facebook, much like modern art, take the form of a conversation in which one participant responds to (or against) the other, Manovich proposes that the "energy and innovation" at work in user generated content rivals that of modern art, no matter the specific content. In this respect, he brings the long-running debate over mass media full circle.

References

Jameson, Fredric, "Reification and Utopia in Mass Culture," *Social Text* No. 1 (Winter 1979), p. 130–148.
McRobbie, Angela, *Jackie: An Ideology of Adolescent Femininity* (Birmingham, UK: Centre for Contemporary Cultural Studies, 1978).

1.
THE CULTURE INDUSTRY

Enlightenment as Mass Deception

Theodor Adorno and Max Horkheimer

The sociological view that the loss of support from objective religion and the disintegration of the last precapitalist residues, in conjunction with technical and social differentiation and specialization, have given rise to cultural chaos is refuted by daily experience. Culture today is infecting everything with sameness. Film, radio, and magazines form a system. Each branch of culture is unanimous within itself and all are unanimous together. Even the aesthetic manifestations of political opposites proclaim the same inflexible rhythm. The decorative administrative and exhibition buildings of industry differ little between authoritarian and other countries. The bright monumental structures shooting up on all sides show off the systematic ingenuity of the state-spanning combines, toward which the unfettered entrepreneurial system, whose monuments are the dismal residential and commercial blocks in the surrounding areas of desolate cities, was already swiftly advancing. The older buildings around the concrete centers already look like slums, and the new bungalows on the outskirts, like the flimsy structures at international trade fairs, sing the praises of technical progress while inviting their users to throw them away after short use like tin cans. But the town-planning projects, which are supposed to perpetuate individuals as autonomous units in hygienic small apartments, subjugate them only more completely to their adversary, the total power of capital. Just as the occupants of city centers are uniformly summoned there for purposes of work and leisure, as producers and consumers, so the living cells crystallize into homogenous, well-organized complexes. The conspicuous unity of macrocosm and microcosm confronts human beings with a model of their culture: the false identity of universal and particular. All mass culture under monopoly is identical, and the contours of its skeleton, the conceptual armature fabricated by monopoly, are beginning to stand out. Those in charge no longer take much trouble to conceal the structure, the power of which increases the more bluntly its existence is admitted. Films and radio no longer need to present themselves as art. The truth that they are nothing but business is used as an ideology to legitimize the trash they intentionally produce. They call themselves industries, and the published figures for their directors' incomes quell any doubts about the social necessity of their finished products.

Interested parties like to explain the culture industry in technological terms. Its millions of participants, they argue, demand reproduction processes which inevitably lead to the use of standard products to meet the same needs at countless locations. The technical antithesis between few production centers and widely dispersed reception necessitates organization and planning by those in control. The standardized forms, it is claimed, were originally derived from the needs of the consumers: that is why they are accepted with so little resistance. In reality, a cycle of manipulation and retroactive need is unifying the system ever more tightly. What is not mentioned is that the basis on which technology is gaining power over society is the power of those whose economic position in society is strongest. Technical rationality today is the rationality of domination. It is the compulsive character of a society alienated from itself. Automobiles, bombs, and films hold the totality together until their leveling element demonstrates its power against the very system of injustice it served. For the present the technology of the culture industry confines itself to standardization and mass production and sacrifices what once distinguished the logic of the work from that of society. These adverse effects, however, should not be attributed to the internal laws of technology itself but to its function within the economy today. Any need which might escape the central control is repressed by that of individual consciousness. The step from telephone to radio has clearly distinguished the roles. The former liberally permitted the participant to play the role of subject. The latter democratically makes everyone equally into listeners, in order to expose them in authoritarian fashion to the same programs put out by different stations. No mechanism of reply has been developed, and private transmissions are condemned to unfreedom. They confine themselves to the apocryphal sphere of "amateurs," who, in any case, are organized from above. Any trace of spontaneity in the audience of the official radio is steered and absorbed into a selection of specializations by talent-spotters, performance competitions, and sponsored events of every kind. The talents belong to the operation long before they are put on show; otherwise they would not conform so eagerly. The mentality of the public, which allegedly and actually favors the system of the culture industry, is a part of the system, not an excuse for it. If a branch of art follows the same recipe as one far removed from it in terms of its medium and subject matter; if the dramatic denouement in radio "soap operas" is used as an instructive example of how to solve technical difficulties—which are mastered no less in "jam sessions" than at the highest levels of jazz—or if a movement from Beethoven is loosely "adapted" in the same way as a Tolstoy novel is adapted for film, the pretext of meeting the public's spontaneous wishes is mere hot air. An explanation in terms of the specific interests of the technical apparatus and its personnel would be closer to the truth, provided that apparatus were understood in all its details as a part of the economic mechanism of selection. Added to this is the agreement, or at least the common determination, of the executive powers to produce or let pass nothing which does not conform to their tables, to their concept of the consumer, or, above all, to themselves.

If the objective social tendency of this age is incarnated in the obscure subjective intentions of board chairmen, this is primarily the case in the most powerful sectors of industry: steel, petroleum, electricity, chemicals. Compared to them the culture monopolies are weak and dependent. They have to keep in with the true wielders of power, to ensure that their sphere of mass society, the specific product of which still has too much of cozy liberalism and Jewish intellectualism about it, is not subjected to a series of purges. The dependence of the most powerful broadcasting company on the electrical industry, or of film on the banks, characterizes the whole sphere, the individual sectors of which are themselves economically intertwined. Everything is so tightly clustered that the concentration of intellect reaches a level where it overflows the demarcations between company names and technical sectors. The relentless unity of the culture industry bears witness to the emergent unity of politics. Sharp distinctions like those between A and B films, or between short stories published in magazines in different price segments, do not so much reflect real differences as assist in the classification, organization, and identification of consumers. Something is provided for everyone so that no one can escape; differences are hammered home and propagated. The hierarchy of serial qualities purveyed to the public serves only to quantify it more completely. Everyone is supposed to behave spontaneously according to a "level" determined by indices and to select the category of mass product manufactured for their type. On the charts of research organizations, indistinguishable from those of political propaganda, consumers are divided up as statistical material into red, green, and blue areas according to income group.

The schematic nature of this procedure is evident from the fact that the mechanically differentiated products are ultimately all the same. That the difference between the models of Chrysler and General Motors is fundamentally illusory is known by any child, who is fascinated by that very difference. The advantages and disadvantages debated by enthusiasts serve only to perpetuate the appearance of competition and choice. It is no different with the offerings of Warner Brothers and Metro Goldwyn Mayer. But the differences, even between the more expensive and cheaper products from the same firm, are shrinking—in cars to the different number of cylinders, engine capacity, and details of the gadgets, and in films to the different number of stars, the expense lavished on technology, labor and costumes, or the use of the latest psychological formulae. The unified standard of value consists in the level of conspicuous production, the amount of investment put on show. The budgeted differences of value in the culture industry have nothing to do with actual differences, with the meaning of the product itself. The technical media, too, are being engulfed by an insatiable uniformity. Television aims at a synthesis of radio and film, delayed only for as long as the interested parties cannot agree. Such a synthesis, with its unlimited possibilities, promises to intensify the impoverishment of the aesthetic material so radically that the identity of all industrial cultural products, still scantily disguised today, will triumph openly tomorrow in a mocking fulfillment of Wagner's dream of the total art work. The accord between word, image, and music is achieved so much more perfectly than in *Tristan* because the sensuous elements, which compliantly document only the surface of social reality, are produced in principle within the same technical work process, the unity of which they express as their true content. This work process integrates all the elements of production, from the original concept of the novel, shaped by its side-long glance at film, to the last sound effect. It is the triumph of invested capital. To impress the omnipotence of capital on the hearts of expropriated job candidates as the power of their true master is the purpose of all films, regardless of the plot selected by the production directors.

Even during their leisure time, consumers must orient themselves according to the unity of production. The active contribution which Kantian schematism still expected of subjects—that they should, from the first, relate sensuous multiplicity to fundamental concepts—is denied to the subject by industry. It purveys schematism as its first service to the customer. According to Kantian schematism, a secret mechanism within the psyche preformed immediate data to

fit them into the system of pure reason. That secret has now been unraveled. Although the operations of the mechanism appear to be planned by those who supply the data, the culture industry, the planning is in fact imposed on the industry by the inertia of a society irrational despite all its rationalization, and this calamitous tendency, in passing through the agencies of business, takes on the shrewd intentionality peculiar to them. For the consumer there is nothing left to classify, since the classification has already been preempted by the schematism of production. This dreamless art for the people fulfils the dreamy idealism which went too far for idealism in its critical form. Everything comes from consciousness—from that of God for Malebranche and Berkeley, and from earthly production management for mass art. Not only do hit songs, stars, and soap operas conform to types recurring cyclically as rigid invariants, but the specific content of productions, the seemingly variable element, is itself derived from those types. The details become interchangeable. The brief interval sequence which has proved catchy in a hit song, the hero's temporary disgrace which he accepts as a "good sport," the wholesome slaps the heroine receives from the strong hand of the male star, his plain-speaking abruptness toward the pampered heiress, are, like all the details, ready-made clichés, to be used here and there as desired and always completely defined by the purpose they serve within the schema. To confirm the schema by acting as its constituents is their sole *raison d'être*. In a film, the outcome can invariably be predicted at the start—who will be rewarded, punished, forgotten—and in light music the prepared ear can always guess the continuation after the first bars of a hit song and is gratified when it actually occurs. The average choice of words in a short story must not be tampered with. The gags and effects are no less calculated than their framework. They are managed by special experts, and their slim variety is specifically tailored to the office pigeonhole. The culture industry has developed in conjunction with the predominance of the effect, the tangible performance, the technical detail, over the work, which once carried the idea and was liquidated with it. By emancipating itself, the detail had become refractory; from Romanticism to Expressionism it had rebelled as unbridled expression, as the agent of opposition, against organization. In music, the individual harmonic effect had obliterated awareness of the form as a whole; in painting the particular detail had obscured the overall composition; in the novel psychological penetration had blurred the architecture. Through totality, the culture industry is putting an end to all that. Although operating only with effects, it subdues their unruliness and subordinates them to the formula which supplants the work. It crushes equally the whole and the parts. The whole confronts the details in implacable detachment, somewhat like the career of a successful man, in which everything serves to illustrate and demonstrate a success which, in fact, it is no more than the sum of those idiotic events. The so-called leading idea is a filing compartment which creates order, not connections. Lacking both contrast and relatedness, the whole and the detail look alike. Their harmony, guaranteed in advance, mocks the painfully achieved harmony of the great bourgeois works of art. In Germany even the most carefree films of democracy were overhung already by the graveyard stillness of dictatorship.

The whole world is passed through the filter of the culture industry. The familiar experience of the moviegoer, who perceives the street outside as a continuation of the film he has just left, because the film seeks strictly to reproduce the world of everyday perception, has become the guideline of production. The more densely and completely its techniques duplicate empirical objects, the more easily it creates the illusion that the world outside is a seamless extension of the one which has been revealed in the cinema. Since the abrupt introduction of the sound film, mechanical duplication has become entirely subservient to this objective. According to this tendency, life is to be made indistinguishable from the sound film. Far more strongly than the theatre of illusion, film denies its audience any dimension in which they might roam freely in imagination—contained by the film's framework but unsupervised by its precise actualities—without losing the thread; thus it trains those exposed to it to identify film directly with reality. The withering of imagination and spontaneity in the consumer of culture today need not be traced back to psychological mechanisms. The products themselves, especially the most characteristic, the sound film, cripple those faculties through their objective makeup. They are so constructed that their adequate comprehension requires a quick, observant, knowledgeable cast of mind but positively debars the spectator from thinking, if he is not to miss the fleeting facts. This kind of alertness is so ingrained that it does not even need to be activated in particular cases, while still repressing the powers of imagination. Anyone who is so absorbed by the world of the film, by gesture, image, and word, that he or she is unable to supply that which would have made it a world in the first place, does not need to be entirely transfixed by the special operations of the machinery at the moment of the performance. The required qualities of attention have become so familiar from other films and other culture products already known to him or her that they appear automatically. The power of industrial society is imprinted on people once and for all. The products of the culture industry are such that they can be alertly consumed even in a state of distraction. But each one is a model of the gigantic economic machinery, which, from the first, keeps everyone on their toes, both at work and in the leisure time which resembles it. In any sound film or any radio broadcast something is discernible which cannot be attributed as a social effect to any one of them, but to all together. Each single manifestation of the culture industry inescapably reproduces human beings as what the whole has made them. And all its agents, from the producer to the women's organizations, are on the alert to ensure that the simple reproduction of mind does not lead on to the expansion of mind. [. . .]

The belief that the barbarism of the culture industry is a result of "cultural lag," of the backwardness of American consciousness in relation to the state of technology, is quite illusory. Prefascist Europe was backward in relation to the monopoly of culture. But it was precisely to such backwardness that intellectual activity owed a remnant of autonomy, its last exponents their livelihood, however meager. In Germany the incomplete permeation of life by democratic control had a paradoxical effect. Many areas were still exempt from the market mechanism which had been unleashed in Western countries. The German educational system, including the universities, the artistically influential theatres, the great orchestras, and the museums were under patronage. The political powers, the state and the local authorities who inherited such institutions from absolutism, had left them a degree of independence from the power of the market as the princes and feudal lords had done up to the nineteenth century. This stiffened the backbone of art in its late phase against the verdict of supply and demand, heightening its resistance far beyond its actual degree of protection. In the market itself the homage paid to not yet marketable artistic quality was converted into purchasing power, so that reputable literary and musical publishers could support authors who brought in little more than the respect of connoisseurs. Only the dire and incessant threat of incorporation into commercial life as aesthetic experts finally brought the artists to heel. In former times they signed their letters, like Kant and Hume, "Your most obedient servant," while undermining the foundations of throne and altar. Today they call heads of government by their first names and are subject, in every artistic impulse, to the judgment of their illiterate principals. The analysis offered by de Tocqueville a hundred years ago has been fully borne out in the meantime. Under the private monopoly of culture tyranny does indeed "leave the body free and sets to work directly on the soul. The ruler no longer says: 'Either you think as I do or you die.' He says: 'You are free not to think as I do; your life, your property—all that you shall keep. But from this day on you will be a stranger among us.' "[1] Anyone who does not conform is condemned to an economic impotence which is prolonged in the intellectual powerlessness of the eccentric loner. Disconnected from the mainstream, he is easily convicted of inadequacy. Whereas the mechanism of supply and demand is today disintegrating in material production, in the superstructure it acts as a control on behalf of the rulers. The consumers are the workers and salaried employees, the farmers and petty bourgeois. Capitalist production hems them in so tightly, in body and soul, that they unresistingly succumb to whatever is proffered to them. However, just as the ruled have always taken the morality dispensed to them by the rulers more seriously than the rulers themselves, the defrauded masses today cling to the myth of success still more ardently than the successful. They, too, have their aspirations. They insist unwaveringly on the ideology by which they are enslaved. The pernicious love of the common people for the harm done to them outstrips even the cunning of the authorities. It surpasses the rigor of the Hays Office, just as, in great epochs, it has inspired renewed zeal in greater agencies directed against it, the terror of the tribunals. It calls for Mickey Rooney rather than the tragic Garbo, Donald Duck rather than Betty Boop. The industry bows to the vote it has itself rigged. The incidental costs to the firm which cannot turn a profit from its contract with a declining star are legitimate costs for the system as a whole. By artfully sanctioning the demand for trash, the system inaugurates total harmony. Connoisseurship and expertise are proscribed as the arrogance of those who think themselves superior, whereas culture distributes its privileges democratically to all. Under the ideological truce between them, the conformism of the consumers, like the shamelessness of the producers they sustain, can have a good conscience. Both content themselves with the reproduction of sameness.

Unending sameness also governs the relationship to the past. What is new in the phase of mass culture compared to that of late liberalism is the exclusion of the new. The machine is rotating on the spot. While it already determines consumption, it rejects anything untried as a risk. In film, any manuscript which is not reassuringly based on a best-seller is viewed with mistrust. That is why there is incessant talk of ideas, novelty and surprises, of what is both totally familiar and has never existed before. Tempo and dynamism are paramount. Nothing is allowed to stay as it was, everything must be endlessly in motion. For only the universal victory of the rhythm of mechanical production and reproduction promises that nothing will change, that nothing unsuitable will emerge. To add anything to the proven cultural inventory would be too speculative. The frozen genres—sketch, short story, problem film, hit song—represent the average of late liberal taste threateningly imposed as a norm. The most powerful of the culture agencies, who work harmoniously with others of their kind as only managers do, whether they come from the ready-to-wear trade or college, have long since reorganized and rationalized the objective mind. It is as if some omnipresent agency had reviewed the material and issued an authoritative catalog tersely listing the products available. The ideal forms are inscribed in the cultural heavens where they were already numbered by Plato—indeed, were only numbers, incapable of increase or change.

Amusement and all the other elements of the culture industry existed long before the industry itself. Now they have been taken over from above and brought fully up to date. The culture industry can boast of having energetically accomplished and elevated to a principle the often inept transposition of art to the consumption sphere, of having stripped amusement of its obtrusive naiveties and improved the quality of its commodities. The more all-embracing the culture industry has become, the more pitilessly it has forced the outsider into either bankruptcy or a syndicate; at the same time it has become more refined and elevated, becoming finally a synthesis of Beethoven and the Casino de Paris. Its victory is twofold: what is destroyed as truth outside its sphere can be reproduced indefinitely within it as lies. "Light" art as such, entertainment, is not a form of decadence. Those who deplore it as a betrayal of the ideal of pure expression harbor illusions about society. The purity of bourgeois art, hypostatized as a realm of freedom contrasting to material praxis, was bought from the outset with the exclusion of the lower class; and art keeps faith with the cause of that class, the true universal, precisely by freeing itself from the purposes of the false. Serious art has denied itself to those for whom the hardship and oppression of life make a mockery of seriousness and who must be glad to use the time not spent at the production line in being simply carried along. Light art has accompanied autonomous art as its shadow. It is the social bad conscience of serious art. The truth which the latter could not apprehend because of its social premises gives the former an appearance of objective justification. The split between them is itself the truth: it expresses at least the negativity of the culture which is the sum of both spheres. The antithesis can be reconciled least of all by absorbing light art into serious or vice versa. That, however, is what the culture industry attempts. The eccentricity of the circus, the peep show, or the brothel in relation to society is as embarrassing to it as that of Schönberg and Karl Kraus. The leading jazz musician Benny Goodman therefore has to appear with the Budapest String Quartet, more pedantic rhythmically than any amateur clarinetist, while the quartet play with the saccharine monotony of Guy Lombardo. What is significant is not crude ignorance, stupidity or lack of polish. The culture industry has abolished the rubbish of former times by imposing its own perfection, by prohibiting and domesticating dilettantism, while itself incessantly committing the blunders without which the elevated style cannot be conceived. What is new, however, is that the irreconcilable elements of culture, art, and amusement have been subjected equally to the concept of purpose and thus brought under a single false denominator: the totality of the culture industry. Its element is repetition. The fact that its characteristic innovations are in all cases mere improvements to mass production is not extraneous to the system. With good reason the interest of countless consumers is focused on the technology, not on the rigidly repeated, threadbare and half-abandoned content. The social power revered by the spectators manifests itself more effectively in the technically enforced ubiquity of stereotypes than in the stale ideologies which the ephemeral contents have to endorse.

Nevertheless, the culture industry remains the entertainment business. Its control of consumers is mediated by entertainment, and its hold will not be broken by outright dictate but by the hostility inherent in the principle of entertainment to anything which is more than itself. Since the tendencies of the culture industry are turned into the flesh and blood of the public by the social process as a whole, those tendencies are reinforced by the survival of the market in the industry. Demand has not yet been replaced by simple obedience. The major reorganization of the film industry shortly before the First World War, the material precondition for its expansion, was a deliberate adaptation to needs of the public registered at the ticket office, which were hardly thought worthy of consideration in the pioneering days of the screen. That view is still held by the captains of the film industry, who accept only more or less phenomenal box-office success as evidence and prudently ignore the counterevidence, truth. Their ideology is business. In this they are right to the extent that the power of the culture industry lies in its unity with fabricated need and not in simple antithesis to it—or even in the antithesis between omnipotence and powerlessness. Entertainment is the prolongation of work under late capitalism. It is sought by those who want to escape the mechanized labor process so that they can cope with it again. At the same time, however, mechanization has such power over leisure and its happiness, determines so thoroughly the fabrication of entertainment commodities, that the off-duty worker can experience nothing but after-images of the work process itself. The ostensible content is merely a faded foreground; what is imprinted is the automated sequence of standardized tasks. The only escape from the work process in factory and office is through adaptation to it in leisure time. This is the incurable sickness of all entertainment. Amusement congeals into boredom, since, to be amusement, it must cost no effort and therefore moves strictly along the well-worn grooves of association. The spectator must need no thoughts of his own: the product prescribes each reaction, not through any actual coherence—which collapses once exposed to thought—but through signals. Any logical connection presupposing mental capacity is scrupulously avoided. Developments are to emerge from the directly preceding situation, not from the idea of the whole. There is no plot which could withstand the screenwriters' eagerness to extract the maximum effect from the individual scene. Finally, even the schematic formula seems dangerous, since it provides some coherence of meaning, however meager, when only meaninglessness is acceptable. Often the plot is willfully denied the development called for by characters and theme under the old schema. Instead, the next step is determined by what the writers take to be their most effective idea. Obtusely ingenious surprises disrupt the plot. The product's tendency to fall back perniciously on the pure nonsense which, as buffoonery and clowning, was a legitimate part of popular art up to Chaplin and the Marx brothers, emerges most strikingly in the less sophisticated genres. Whereas the films of Greer Garson and Bette Davis can still derive some claim to a coherent plot from the unity of the socio-psychological case represented, the tendency to subvert meaning has taken over completely in the text of novelty songs, suspense films, and cartoons. The idea itself, like objects in comic and horror films, is massacred and mutilated. Novelty songs have always lived on contempt for meaning, which, as both ancestors and descendants of psychoanalysis, they reduce to the monotony of sexual symbolism. In crime and adventure films the spectators are begrudged even the opportunity to witness the resolution. Even in non-ironic examples of the genre they must make do with the mere horror of situations connected in only the most perfunctory way.

Cartoon and stunt films were once exponents of fantasy against rationalism. They allowed justice to be done to the animals and things electrified by their technology, by granting the mutilated beings a second life. Today they merely confirm the victory of technological reason over truth. A few years ago they had solid plots which were resolved only in the whirl of pursuit of the final minutes. In this their procedure resembled that of slapstick comedy. But now the temporal relations have shifted. The opening sequences state a plot motif so that destruction can work on it throughout the action: with the audience in gleeful pursuit the protagonist is tossed about like a scrap of litter. The quantity of organized amusement is converted into the quality of organized cruelty. The self-elected censors of the film industry, its accomplices, monitor the duration of the atrocity prolonged into a hunt. The jollity dispels the joy supposedly conferred by the sight of an embrace and postpones satisfaction until the day of the pogrom. To the extent that cartoons do more than accustom the senses to the new tempo, they hammer into every brain the old lesson that continuous attrition, the breaking of all individual resistance, is the condition of life in this society. Donald Duck in the cartoons and the unfortunate victim in real life receive their beatings so that the spectators can accustom themselves to theirs.

The enjoyment of the violence done to the film character turns into violence against the spectator; distraction becomes exertion. No stimulant concocted by the experts may escape the weary eye; in face of the slick presentation no one may appear stupid even for a moment; everyone has to keep up, emulating the smartness displayed and propagated by the production. This makes it doubtful whether the culture industry even still fulfils its self-proclaimed function of distraction. If the majority of radio stations and cinemas were shut down, consumers probably would not feel too much deprived. In stepping from the street into the cinema, they no longer enter the world of dream in any case, and once the use of these institutions was no longer made obligatory by their mere existence, the urge to use them might not be so overwhelming. Shutting them down in this way would not be reactionary machine-wrecking. Those who suffered would not be the film enthusiasts but those who always pay the penalty in any case, the ones who had lagged behind. For the housewife, despite the films which are supposed to integrate her still further, the dark of the cinema grants a refuge in which she can spend a few unsupervised hours, just as once, when there were still dwellings and evening repose, she could sit gazing out of the window. The unemployed of the great centers find freshness in summer and warmth in winter in these places of regulated temperature. Apart from that, and even by the measure of the existing order, the bloated entertainment apparatus does not make life more worthy of human beings. The idea of "exploiting" the given technical possibilities, of fully utilizing the capacities for aesthetic mass consumption, is part of an economic system which refuses to utilize capacities when it is a question of abolishing hunger.

The culture industry endlessly cheats its consumers out of what it endlessly promises. The promissory note of pleasure issued by plot and packaging is indefinitely prolonged: the promise, which actually comprises the entire show, disdainfully intimates that there is nothing more to come, that the diner must be satisfied with reading the menu. The desire inflamed by the glossy names and images is served up finally with a celebration of the daily round it sought to escape. Of course, genuine works of art were not sexual exhibitions either. But by presenting denial as negative, they reversed, as it were, the debasement of the drive and rescued by mediation what had been denied. That is the secret of aesthetic sublimation: to present fulfillment in its brokenness. The culture industry does not sublimate: it suppresses. By constantly exhibiting the object of desire, the breasts beneath the sweater, the naked torso of the sporting hero, it merely goads the unsublimated anticipation of pleasure, which through the habit of denial has long since been mutilated as masochism. There is no erotic situation in which innuendo and incitement are not accompanied by the clear notification that things will never go so far. The Hays Office merely confirms the ritual which the culture industry has staged in any case: that of Tantalus. Works of art are ascetic and shameless; the culture industry is pornographic and prudish. It reduces love to romance. And, once reduced, much is permitted, even libertinage as a marketable specialty,

purveyed by quota with the trade description "daring." The mass production of sexuality automatically brings about its repression. Because of his ubiquity, the film star with whom one is supposed to fall in love is, from the start, a copy of himself. Every tenor now sounds like a Caruso record, and the natural faces of Texas girls already resemble those of the established models by which they would be typecast in Hollywood. The mechanical reproduction of beauty—which, admittedly, is made only more inescapable by the reactionary culture zealots with their methodical idolization of individuality—no longer leaves any room for the unconscious idolatry with which the experience of beauty has always been linked. The triumph over beauty is completed by humor, the malicious pleasure elicited by any successful deprivation. There is laughter because there is nothing to laugh about. Laughter, whether reconciled or terrible, always accompanies the moment when a fear is ended. It indicates a release, whether from physical danger or from the grip of logic. Reconciled laughter resounds with the echo of escape from power; wrong laughter copes with fear by defecting to the agencies which inspire it. It echoes the inescapability of power. Fun is a medicinal bath which the entertainment industry never ceases to prescribe. It makes laughter the instrument for cheating happiness. To moments of happiness laughter is foreign; only operettas, and now films, present sex amid peals of merriment. But Baudelaire is as humorless as Hölderlin. In wrong society laughter is a sickness infecting happiness and drawing it into society's worthless totality. Laughter about something is always laughter at it, and the vital force which, according to Bergson, bursts through rigidity in laughter is, in truth, the irruption of barbarity, the self-assertion which, in convivial settings, dares to celebrate its liberation from scruple. The collective of those who laugh parodies humanity. They are monads, each abandoning himself to the pleasure—at the expense of all others and with the majority in support—of being ready to shrink from nothing. Their harmony presents a caricature of solidarity. What is infernal about wrong laughter is that it compellingly parodies what is best, reconciliation. Joy, however, is austere: *res severa verum gaudium*. The ideology of monasteries, that it is not asceticism but the sexual act which marks the renunciation of attainable bliss, is negatively confirmed by the gravity of the lover who presciently pins his whole life to the fleeting moment. The culture industry replaces pain, which is present in ecstasy no less than in asceticism, with jovial denial. Its supreme law is that its consumers shall at no price be given what they desire: and in that very deprivation they must take their laughing satisfaction. In each performance of the culture industry the permanent denial imposed by civilization is once more inflicted on and unmistakably demonstrated to its victims. To offer them something and to withhold it is one and the same. That is what the erotic commotion achieves. Just because it can never take place, everything revolves around the coitus. In film, to allow an illicit relationship without due punishment of the culprits is even more strictly tabooed than it is for the future son-in-law of a millionaire to be active in the workers' movement. Unlike that of the liberal era, industrial no less than nationalist culture can permit itself to inveigh against capitalism, but not to renounce the threat of castration. This threat constitutes its essence. It outlasts the organized relaxation of morals toward the wearers of uniforms, first in the jaunty films produced for them and then in reality. What is decisive today is no longer Puritanism, though it still asserts itself in the form of women's organizations, but the necessity, inherent in the system, of never releasing its grip on the consumer, of not for a moment allowing him or her to suspect that resistance is possible. This principle requires that while all needs should be presented to individuals as capable of fulfillment by the culture industry, they should be so set up in advance that individuals experience themselves through their needs only as eternal consumers, as the culture industry's object. Not only does it persuade them that its fraud is satisfaction; it also gives them to understand that they must make do with what is offered, whatever it may be. The flight from the everyday world, promised by the culture industry in all its branches, is much like the abduction of the daughter in the American cartoon: the father is holding the ladder in the dark. The culture industry presents that same everyday world as paradise. Escape, like elopement, is destined from the first to lead back to its starring point. Entertainment fosters the resignation which seeks to forget itself in entertainment.

Amusement, free of all restraint, would be not only the opposite of art but its complementary extreme. Absurdity in the manner of Mark Twain, with which the American culture industry flirts from time to time, could be a corrective to art. The more seriously art takes its opposition to existence, the more it resembles the seriousness of existence, its antithesis: the more it labors to develop strictly according to its own formal laws, the more labor it requires to be understood, whereas its goal had been precisely to negate the burden of labor. In some revue films, and especially in grotesque stories and "funnies," the possibility of this negation is momentarily glimpsed. Its realization, of course, cannot be allowed. Pure amusement indulged to the full, relaxed abandon to colorful associations and merry nonsense, is cut short by amusement in its marketable form: it is disrupted by the surrogate of a coherent meaning with which the culture industry insists on endowing its products while at the same time slyly misusing them as pretexts for bringing on the stars. Biographies and other fables stitch together the scraps of nonsense into a feeble-minded plot. It is not the bells on the fool's cap that jingle but the bunch of keys of capitalist reason, which even in its images harnesses joy to the purpose of getting ahead. Every kiss in the revue film must contribute to the career of the boxer or hit-song expert whose success is being glorified. The deception is not that the culture industry serves up amusement but that it spoils the fun by its business-minded attachment to the ideological clichés of the culture which is liquidating itself. Ethics and taste suppress unbridled amusement as "naïve"—naivety being rated no more highly than intellectualism—and even restrict its technical possibilities. The culture industry is corrupt, not as a sink of iniquity but as the cathedral of higher gratification. At all its levels, from Hemingway to Emil Ludwig, from Mrs. Miniver to the Lone Ranger, from Toscanini to Guy Lombardo, intellectual products drawn ready-made from art and science are infected with untruth. Traces of something better persist in those features of the culture industry by which it resembles the circus—in the stubbornly purposeless expertise of riders, acrobats, and clowns, in the "defense and justification of physical as against intellectual art."[2] But the hiding places of mindless. artistry, which represents what is human against the social mechanism, are being relentlessly ferreted out by organizational reason, which forces everything to justify itself in terms of meaning and effect. It is causing meaninglessness to disappear at the lowest level of art just as radically as meaning is disappearing at the highest.

The fusion of culture and entertainment is brought about today not only by the debasement of culture but equally by the compulsory intellectualization of amusement. This is already evident in the fact that amusement is now experienced only in facsimile, in the form of cinema photography or the radio recording. In the age of liberal expansion amusement was sustained by an unbroken belief in the future: things would stay the same yet get better. Today, that belief has itself been intellectualized, becoming so refined as to lose sight of all actual goals and to consist only in a golden shimmer projected beyond the real. It is composed of the extra touches of meaning—running exactly parallel to life itself—applied in the screen world to the good guy, the engineer, the decent girl, and also to the ruthlessness disguised as character, to the sporting interest, and finally to the cars and cigarettes, even where the entertainment does not directly serve the publicity needs of the manufacturer concerned but advertises the system as a whole. Amusement itself becomes an ideal, taking the place of the higher values it eradicates from the masses by repeating them in an even more stereotyped form than the advertising slogans paid for by private interests. Inwardness, the subjectively restricted form of truth, was always more beholden to the outward rulers than it imagined. The culture industry is perverting it into a barefaced lie. It appears now only as the high-minded prattle tolerated by consumers of religious bestsellers, psychological films, and women's serials as an embarrassingly agreeable ingredient, so that they can more reliably control their own human emotions. In this sense entertainment is purging the affects in the manner once attributed by Aristotle to tragedy and now by Mortimer Adler to film. The culture industry reveals the truth not only about style but also about catharsis.

The more strongly the culture industry entrenches itself, the more it can do as it chooses with the needs of consumers—producing, controlling, disciplining them; even withdrawing amusement altogether: here, no limits are set to cultural progress. But the tendency is immanent in the principle of entertainment itself, as a principle of bourgeois enlightenment. If the need for entertainment was largely created by industry, which recommended the work to the masses through its subject matter, the oleograph through the delicate morsel it portrayed and, conversely, the pudding mix through the image of a pudding, entertainment has always borne the trace of commercial brashness, of sales talk, the voice of the fairground huckster. But the original affinity between business and entertainment reveals itself in the meaning of entertainment itself: as society's apologia. To be entertained means to be in agreement. Entertainment makes itself possible only by insulating itself from the totality of the social process, making itself stupid and perversely renouncing from the first the inescapable claim of any work, even the most trivial: in its restrictedness to reflect the whole. Amusement always means putting things out of mind, forgetting suffering, even when it is on display. At its root is powerlessness. It is indeed escape, but not, as it claims, escape from bad reality but from the last thought of resisting that reality. The liberation which amusement promises is from thinking as negation. The shamelessness of the rhetorical question "What do people want?" lies in the fact that it appeals to the very people as thinking subjects whose subjectivity it specifically seeks to annul. Even on those occasions when the public rebels against the pleasure industry it displays the feebleness systematically instilled in it by that industry. Nevertheless, it has become increasingly difficult to keep the public in submission. The advance of stupidity must not lag behind the simultaneous advance of intelligence. In the age of statistics the masses are too astute to identify with the millionaire on the screen and too obtuse to deviate even minutely from the law of large numbers. Ideology hides itself in probability calculations. Fortune will not smile on all—just on the one who draws the winning ticket or, rather, the one designated to do so by a higher power—usually the entertainment industry itself, which presents itself as ceaselessly in search of talent. Those discovered by the talent scouts and then built up by the studios are ideal types of the new, dependent middle classes. The female starlet is supposed to symbolize the secretary, though in a way which makes her seem predestined, unlike the real secretary, to wear the flowing evening gown. Thus she apprises the female spectator not only of the possibility that she, too, might appear on the screen but still more insistently of the distance between them. Only one can draw the winning lot, only one is prominent, and even though all have mathematically the same chance, it is so minimal for each individual that it is best to write it off at once and rejoice in the good fortune of someone else, who might just as well be oneself but never is. Where the culture industry still invites naïve identification, it immediately denies it. It is no longer possible to lose oneself in others. Once, film spectators saw their own wedding in that of others. Now the happy couple on the screen are specimens of the same species as everyone in the audience, but the sameness posits the insuperable separation of its human elements. The perfected similarity is the absolute difference. The identity of the species prohibits that of the individual cases. The culture industry has sardonically realized man's species being. Everyone amounts only to those qualities by which he or she can replace everyone else: all are fungible, mere specimens. As individuals they are absolutely replaceable, pure nothingness, and are made aware of this as soon as time deprives them of their sameness. This changes the inner composition of the religion of success, which they are sternly required to uphold. The path *per aspera ad astra*, which presupposes need and effort, is increasingly replaced by the prize. The element of blindness in the routine decision as to which song is to be a hit, which extra a heroine, is celebrated by ideology. Films emphasize chance. By imposing an essential sameness on their characters, with the exception of the villain, to the point of excluding any faces which do not conform—for example, those which, like Garbo's, do not look as if they would welcome the greeting "Hello, sister"—the ideology does, it is true, make life initially easier for the spectators. They are assured that they do not need to be in any way other than they are and that they can succeed just as well without having to perform tasks of which they know themselves incapable. But at the same time they are given the hint that effort would not help them in any case, because even bourgeois success no longer has any connection to the calculable effect of their own work. They take the hint. Fundamentally, everyone recognizes chance, by which someone is sometimes lucky, as the other side of planning. Just because society's energies have developed so far on the side of rationality that anyone might become an engineer or a manager, the choice of who is to receive from society the investment and confidence to be trained for such functions becomes entirely irrational. Chance and planning become identical since, given the sameness of people, the fortune or misfortune of the individual, right up to the top, loses all economic importance. Chance itself is planned; not in the sense that it will affect this or that particular individual but in that people believe in its control. For the planners it serves as an alibi, giving the impression that the web of transactions and measures into which life has been transformed still leaves room for spontaneous, immediate relationships between human beings. Such freedom is symbolized in the various media of the culture industry by the arbitrary selection of average cases. In the detailed reports on the modestly luxurious pleasure trip organized by the magazine for the lucky competition winner—preferably a shorthand typist who probably won through contacts with local powers-that-be—the powerlessness of everyone is reflected. So much are the masses mere material that those in control can raise one of them up to their heaven and cast him or her out again: let them go hang with their justice and their labor. Industry is interested in human beings only as its customers and employees and has in fact reduced humanity as a whole, like each of its elements, to this exhaustive formula. Depending on which aspect happens to be paramount at the time, ideology stresses plan or chance, technology or life, civilization or nature. As employees people are reminded of the rational organization and must fit into it as common sense requires. As customers they are regaled, whether on the screen or in the press, with human interest stories demonstrating freedom of choice and the charm of not belonging to the system. In both cases they remain objects.

[. . .]

It is not only the standardized mode of production of the culture industry which makes the individual illusory in its products. Individuals are tolerated only as far as their wholehearted identity with the universal is beyond question. From the standardized improvisation in jazz to the original film personality who must have a lock of hair straying over her eyes so that she can be recognized as such, pseudoindividuality reigns. The individual trait is reduced to the ability of the universal so completely to mold the accidental that it can be recognized as accidental. The sulky taciturnity or the elegant walk of the individual who happens to be on show is serially produced like the Yale locks which differ by fractions of a millimeter. The peculiarity of the self is a socially conditioned monopoly commodity misrepresented as natural. It is reduced to the moustache, the French accent, the deep voice of the prostitute, the "Lubitsch touch"—like a fingerprint on the otherwise uniform identity cards to which the lives and faces of all individuals, from the film star to the convict, have been reduced by the power of the universal. Pseudoindividuality is a precondition for apprehending and detoxifying tragedy: only because individuals are none but mere intersections of universal tendencies is it possible to reabsorb them smoothly into the universal. Mass culture thereby reveals the fictitious quality which has characterized the individual throughout the bourgeois era and is wrong only in priding itself on this murky harmony between universal and particular. The principle of individuality was contradictory from the outset. First, no individuation was ever really achieved. The class-determined form of self-preservation maintained everyone at the level of mere species being. Every bourgeois character expressed the same thing, even and especially when deviating from it: the harshness of competitive society. The individual, on whom society was supported, itself bore society's taint; in the individual's apparent freedom he was the product of society's economic and social apparatus. Power has always invoked the existing power relationships when seeking the approval of those subjected to power. At the same time, the advance of bourgeois society has promoted the development of the individual. Against the will of those controlling it, technology has changed human beings from children into persons. But all such progress of individuation has been at the expense of the individuality in whose name it took place, leaving behind nothing except individuals' determination to pursue their own purposes alone. The citizens whose lives are split between business and private life, their private life between ostentation and intimacy, their intimacy between the sullen community of marriage and the bitter solace of being entirely alone, at odds with

themselves and with everyone, are virtually already Nazis, who are at once enthusiastic and fed up, or the city dwellers of today, who can imagine friendship only as "social contact" between the inwardly unconnected. The culture industry can only manipulate individuality so successfully because the fractured nature of society has always been reproduced within it. In the ready-made faces of film heroes and private persons fabricated according to magazine-cover stereotypes, a semblance of individuality—in which no one believes in any case—is fading, and the love for such hero-models is nourished by the secret satisfaction that the effort of individuation is at last being replaced by the admittedly more breathless one of imitation. The hope that the contradictory, disintegrating person could not survive for generations, that the psychological fracture within it must split the system itself, and that human beings might refuse to tolerate the mendacious substitution of the stereotype for the individual—that hope is vain. The unity of the personality has been recognized as illusory since Shakespeare's Hamlet. In the synthetically manufactured physiognomies of today the fact that the concept of human life ever existed is already forgotten. For centuries society has prepared for Victor Mature and Mickey Rooney. They come to fulfill the very individuality they destroy.

The heroizing of the average forms part of the cult of cheapness. The highest-paid stars resemble advertisements for unnamed merchandise. Not for nothing are they often chosen from the ranks of commercial models. The dominant taste derives its ideal from the advertisement, from commodified beauty. Socrates' dictum that beauty is the useful has at last been ironically fulfilled. The cinema publicizes the cultural conglomerate as a totality, while the radio advertises individually the products for whose sake the cultural system exists. For a few coins you can see the film which cost millions, for even less you can buy the chewing gum behind which stand the entire riches of the world, and the sales of which increase those riches still further. Through universal suffrage the vast funding of armies is generally known and approved, if *in absentia*, while prostitution behind the lines is not permitted. The best orchestras in the world, which are none, are delivered free of charge to the home. All this mockingly resembles the land of milk and honey as the national community apes the human one. Something is served up for everyone. A provincial visitor's comment on the old Berlin Metropoltheater that "it is remarkable what can be done for the money" has long since been adopted by the culture industry and elevated to the substance of production itself. Not only is a production always accompanied by triumphant celebration that it has been possible at all, but to a large extent it is that triumph itself. To put on a show means to show everyone what one has and can do. The show is still a fairground, but one incurably infected by culture. Just as people lured by the fairground crier overcame their disappointment inside the booths with a brave smile, since they expected it in any case, the moviegoer remains tolerantly loyal to the institution. But the cheapness of mass-produced luxury articles, and its complement, universal fraud, are changing the commodity character of art itself. That character is not new: it is the fact that art now dutifully admits to being a commodity, abjures its autonomy and proudly takes its place among consumer goods, that has the charm of novelty. Art was only ever able to exist as a separate sphere in its bourgeois form. Even its freedom, as negation of the social utility which is establishing itself through the market, is essentially conditioned by the commodity economy. Pure works of art, which negated the commodity character of society by simply following their own inherent laws, were at the same time always commodities. To the extent that, up to the eighteenth century, artists were protected from the market by patronage, they were subject to the patrons and their purposes instead. The purposelessness of the great modern work of art is sustained by the anonymity of the market. The latter's demands are so diversely mediated that the artist is exempted from any particular claim, although only to a certain degree, since his autonomy, being merely tolerated, has been attended throughout bourgeois history by a moment of untruth, which has culminated now in the social liquidation of art. The mortally sick Beethoven, who flung away a novel by Walter Scott with the cry: "The fellow writes for money," while himself proving an extremely experienced and tenacious businessman in commercializing the last quartets—works representing the most extreme repudiation of the market—offers the most grandiose example of the unity of the opposites of market and autonomy in bourgeois art. The artists who succumb to ideology are precisely those who conceal this contradiction instead of assimilating it into the consciousness of their own production, as Beethoven did: he improvised on "Rage over a Lost Penny" and derived the metaphysical injunction "It must be," which seeks aesthetically to annul the world's compulsion by taking that burden onto itself, from his housekeeper's demand for her monthly wages. The principle of idealist aesthetics, purposiveness without purpose, reverses the schema socially adopted by bourgeois art: purposelessness for purposes dictated by the market. In the demand for entertainment and relaxation, purpose has finally consumed the realm of the purposeless. But as the demand for the marketability of art becomes total, a shift in the inner economic composition of cultural commodities is becoming apparent. For the use which is made of the work of art in antagonistic society is largely that of confirming the very existence of the useless, which art's total sub-sumption under usefulness has abolished. In adapting itself entirely to need, the work of art defrauds human beings in advance of the liberation from the principle of utility which it is supposed to bring about. What might be called use value in the reception of cultural assets is being replaced by exchange value; enjoyment is giving way to being there and being in the know, connoisseurship by enhanced prestige. The consumer becomes the ideology of the amusement industry, whose institutions he or she cannot escape. One has to have seen *Mrs. Miniver*, just as one must subscribe to *Life* and *Time*. Everything is perceived only from the point of view that it can serve as something else, however vaguely that other thing might be envisaged. Everything has value only in so far as it can be exchanged, not in so far as it is something in itself. For consumers the use value of art, its essence, is a fetish, and the fetish—the social valuation which they mistake for the merit of works of art—becomes its only use value, the only quality they enjoy. In this way the commodity character of art disintegrates just as it is fully realized. Art becomes a species of commodity, worked up and adapted to industrial production, saleable and exchangeable; but art as the species of commodity which exists in order to be sold yet not for sale becomes something hypocritically unsaleable as soon as the business transaction is no longer merely its intention but its sole principle. The Toscanini performance on the radio is, in a sense, unsaleable. One listens to it for nothing, and each note of the symphony is accompanied, as it were, by the sublime advertisement that the symphony is not being interrupted by advertisements—"This concert is brought to you as a public service." The deception takes place indirectly *via* the profit of all the united automobile and soap manufacturers, on whose payments the stations survive, and, of course, *via* the increased sales of the electrical industry as the producer of the receiver sets. Radio, the progressive latecomer to mass culture, is drawing conclusions which film's pseudomarket at present denies that industry. The technical structure of the commercial radio system makes it immune to liberal deviations of the kind the film industry can still permit itself in its own preserve. Film is a private enterprise which already represents the sovereign whole, in which respect it has some advantages over the other individual combines. Chesterfield is merely the nation's cigarette, but the radio is its mouthpiece. In the total assimilation of culture products into the commodity sphere radio makes no attempt to purvey its products as commodities. In America it levies no duty from the public. It thereby takes on the deceptive form of a disinterested, impartial authority, which fits fascism like a glove. In fascism radio becomes the universal mouthpiece of the *Führer*, in the loudspeakers on the street his voice merges with the howl of sirens proclaiming panic, from which modern propaganda is hard to distinguish in any case. The National Socialists knew that broadcasting gave their cause stature as the printing press did to the Reformation. The *Führer's* metaphysical charisma, invented by the sociology of religion, turned out finally to be merely the omnipresence of his radio addresses, which demonically parodies that of the divine spirit. The gigantic fact that the speech penetrates everywhere replaces its content, as the benevolent act of the Toscanini broadcast supplants its content, the symphony. No listener can apprehend the symphony's true coherence, while the *Führer's* address is in any case a lie. To posit the human word as absolute, the false commandment, is the immanent tendency of radio. Recommendation becomes command. The promotion of identical commodities under

different brand names, the scientifically endorsed praise of the laxative in the slick voice of the announcer between the overtures of *La Traviata* and *Rienzi*, has become untenable if only for its silliness. One day the *Diktat* of production, the specific advertisement, veiled by the semblance of choice, can finally become the *Führer's* overt command. In a society of large-scale fascistic rackets which agree among themselves on how much of the national product is to be allocated to providing for the needs of the people, to invite the people to use a particular soap powder would, in the end, seem anachronistic. In a more modern, less ceremonious style, the *Führer* directly orders both the holocaust and the supply of trash.

Today works of art, suitably packaged like political slogans, are pressed on a reluctant public at reduced prices by the culture industry; they are opened up for popular enjoyment like parks. However, the erosion of their genuine commodity character does not mean that they would be abolished in the life of a free society but that the last barrier to their debasement as cultural assets has now been removed. The abolition of educational privilege by disposing of culture at bargain prices does not admit the masses to the preserves from which they were formerly excluded but, under the existing social conditions, contributes to the decay of education and the progress of barbaric incoherence. Someone who in the nineteenth or early twentieth century spent money to attend a drama or a concert, paid the performance at least as much respect as the money spent. The citizen who wanted a return for his outlay might occasionally try to establish some connection to the work. The guidebooks to Wagner's music dramas or the commentaries on *Faust* bear witness to this. They form a transition to the biographical glaze applied to works of art and the other practices to which works of art are subjected today. Even when the art business was in the bloom of youth, use value was not dragged along as a mere appendage by exchange value but was developed as a precondition of the latter, to the social benefit of works of art. As long as it was expensive, art kept the citizen within some bounds. That is now over. Art's unbounded proximity to those exposed to it, no longer mediated by money, completes the alienation between work and consumer, which resemble each other in triumphant reification. In the culture industry respect is vanishing along with criticism: the latter gives way to mechanical expertise, the former to the forgetful cult of celebrities. For consumers, nothing is expensive any more. Nevertheless, they are dimly aware that the less something costs, the less it can be a gift to them. The twofold mistrust of traditional culture as ideology mingles with that of industrialized culture as fraud. Reduced to mere adjuncts, the degraded works of art are secretly rejected by their happy recipients along with the junk the medium has made them resemble. The public should rejoice that there is so much to see and hear. And indeed, everything is to be had. The "screenos" and cinema vaudevilles, the competitions in recognizing musical extracts, the free magazines, rewards, and gift articles handed out to the listeners of certain radio programs are not mere accidents, but continue what is happening to the culture products themselves. The symphony is becoming the prize for listening to the radio at all, and if the technology had its way the film would already be delivered to the apartment on the model of the radio. It is moving towards the commercial system. Television points the way to a development which easily enough could push the Warner brothers into the doubtless unwelcome position of little theatre performers and cultural conservatives. However, the pursuit of prizes has already left its imprint on consumer behavior. Because culture presents itself as a bonus, with unquestioned private and social benefits, its reception has become a matter of taking one's chances. The public crowds forward for fear of missing something. What that might be is unclear, but, at any rate, only those who join in have any chance. Fascism, however, hopes to reorganize the gift-receivers trained by the culture industry into its enforced adherents.

Culture is a paradoxical commodity. It is so completely subject to the law of exchange that it is no longer exchanged; it is so blindly equated with use that it can no longer be used. For this reason it merges with the advertisement. The more meaningless the latter appears under monopoly, the more omnipotent culture becomes. Its motives are economic enough. That life could continue without the whole culture industry is too certain; the satiation and apathy it generates among consumers are too great. It can do little to combat this from its own resources. Advertising is its elixir of life. But because its product ceaselessly reduces the pleasure it promises as a commodity to that mere promise, it finally coincides with the advertisement it needs on account of its own inability to please. In the competitive society advertising performed a social service in orienting the buyer in the market, facilitating choice and helping the more efficient but unknown supplier to find customers. It did not merely cost labor time, but saved it. Today, when the free market is coming to an end, those in control of the system are entrenching themselves in advertising. It strengthens the bond which shackles consumers to the big combines. Only those who can keep paying the exorbitant fees charged by the advertising agencies, and most of all by radio itself, that is, those who are already part of the system or are co-opted into it by the decisions of banks and industrial capital, can enter the pseudomarket as sellers. The costs of advertising, which finally flow back into the pockets of the combines, spare them the troublesome task of subduing unwanted outsiders; they guarantee that the wielders of influence remain among their peers, not unlike the resolutions of economic councils which control the establishment and continuation of businesses in the totalitarian state. Advertising today is a negative principle, a blocking device: anything which does not bear its seal of approval is economically suspect. All-pervasive advertising is certainly not needed to acquaint people with the goods on offer, the varieties of which are limited in any case. It benefits the selling of goods only directly. The termination of a familiar advertising campaign by an individual firm represents a loss of prestige, and is indeed an offence against the discipline which the leading clique imposes on its members. In wartime, commodities which can no longer be supplied continue to be advertised merely as a display of industrial power. At such times the subsidizing of the ideological media is more important than the repetition of names. Through their ubiquitous use under the pressure of the system, advertising techniques have invaded the idiom, the "style" of the culture industry. So complete is their triumph that in key positions it is no longer even explicit: the imposing buildings of the big companies, floodlit advertisements in stone, are free of advertising, merely displaying the illuminated company initials on their pinnacles, with no further need of self-congratulation. By contrast, the buildings surviving from the nineteenth century, the architecture of which still shamefully reveals their utility as consumer goods, their function as accommodation, are covered from basement to above roof level with hoardings and banners: the landscape becomes a mere background for signboards and symbols. Advertising becomes simply the art with which Goebbels presciently equated it, *l'art pour l'art*, advertising for advertising's sake, the pure representation of social power. In the influential American magazines *Life* and *Fortune* the images and texts of advertisements are, at a cursory glance, hardly distinguishable from the editorial section. The enthusiastic and unpaid picture story about the living habits and personal grooming of celebrities, which wins them new fans, is editorial, while the advertising pages rely on photographs and data so factual and lifelike that they represent the ideal of information to which the editorial section only aspires. Every film is a preview of the next, which promises yet again to unite the same heroic couple under the same exotic sun: anyone arriving late cannot tell whether he is watching the trailer or the real thing. The montage character of the culture industry, the synthetic, controlled manner in which its products are assembled—factory-like not only in the film studio but also, virtually, in the compilation of the cheap biographies, journalistic novels, and hit songs—predisposes it to advertising: the individual moment, in being detachable, replaceable, estranged even technically from any coherence of meaning, lends itself to purposes outside the work. The special effect, the trick, the isolated and repeatable individual performance have always conspired with the exhibition of commodities for advertising purposes, and today every close-up of a film actress is an advert for her name, every hit song a plug for its tune. Advertising and the culture industry are merging technically no less than economically. In both, the same thing appears in countless places, and the mechanical repetition of the same culture product is already that of the same propaganda slogan. In both, under the dictate of effectiveness, technique is becoming psychotechnique, a procedure for manipulating human beings. In both, the norms of the striking yet familiar, the easy but catchy, the worldly wise but straightforward hold good; everything is directed at overpowering a customer conceived as distracted or resistant.

Through the language they speak, the customers make their own contribution to culture as advertising.

For the more completely language coincides with communication, the more words change from substantial carriers of meaning to signs devoid of qualities; the more purely and transparently they communicate what they designate, the more impenetrable they become. The demythologizing of language, as an element of the total process of enlightenment, reverts to magic. In magic word and content were at once different from each other and indissolubly linked. Concepts like melancholy, history, indeed, life, were apprehended in the word which both set them apart and preserved them. Its particular form constituted and reflected them at the same time. The trenchant distinction which declares the word itself fortuitous and its allocation to its object arbitrary does away with the superstitious commingling of word and thing. Anything in a given sequence of letters which goes beyond the correlation to the event designated is banished as unclear and as verbal metaphysics. As a result, the word, which henceforth is allowed only to designate something and not to mean it, becomes so fixated on the object that it hardens to a formula. This affects language and subject matter equally. Instead of raising a matter to the level of experience, the purified word exhibits it as a case of an abstract moment, and everything else, severed from now defunct expression by the demand for pitiless clarity, therefore withers in reality also. The outside-left in football, the blackshirt, the Hitler Youth member, and others of their kind are no more than what they are called. If, before its rationalization, the word had set free not only longing but lies, in its rationalized form it has become a straightjacket more for longing than for lies. The blindness and muteness of the data to which positivism reduces the world passes over into language itself, which is limited to registering those data. Thus relationships themselves become impenetrable, taking on an impact, a power of adhesion and repulsion which makes them resemble their extreme antithesis, spells. They act once more like the practices of a kind of sorcery, whether the name of a diva is concocted in the studio on the basis of statistical data, or welfare government is averted by the use of taboo-laden words such as "bureaucracy" and "intellectuals," or vileness exonerates itself by invoking the name of a homeland. The name, to which magic most readily attaches, is today undergoing a chemical change. It is being transformed into arbitrary, manipulable designations, the power of which, although calculable, is for that reason as willful as that of archaic names. First names, the archaic residues, have been brought up to date either by stylizing them into advertising brands—film stars' surnames have become first names—or by standardizing them collectively. By contrast, the bourgeois, family name which, instead of being a trademark, individualized its bearers by relating them to their own prehistory, sounds old-fashioned. In Americans it arouses a curious unease. To conceal the uncomfortable distance existing between particular people they call themselves Bob and Harry, like replaceable members of teams. Such forms of interaction reduce human beings to the brotherhood of the sporting public, which protects them from true fraternity. Signification, the only function of the word admitted by semantics, is consummated in the sign. Its character as sign is reinforced by the speed with which linguistic models are put into circulation from above. Whether folksongs are rightly or wrongly called upper-class culture which has come down in the world, their elements have at least taken on their popular form in a long, highly mediated process of experience. The dissemination of popular songs, by contrast, is practically instantaneous. The American term "fad" for fashions which catch on epidemically—inflamed by the action of highly concentrated economic powers—referred to this phenomenon long before totalitarian advertising bosses had laid down the general lines of culture in their countries. If the German fascists launch a word like "intolerable" [*Untragbar*] over the loudspeakers one day, the whole nation is saying "intolerable" the next. On the same pattern, the nations against which the German *Blitzkrieg* was directed have adopted it in their own jargon. The universal repetition of the term denoting such measures makes the measures, too, familiar, just as, at the time of the free market, the brand name on everyone's lips increased sales. The blind and rapidly spreading repetition of designated words links advertising to the totalitarian slogan. The layer of experience which made words human like those who spoke them has been stripped away, and in its prompt appropriation language takes on the coldness which hitherto was peculiar to billboards and the advertising

sections of newspapers. Countless people use words and expressions which they either have ceased to understand at all or use only according to their behavioral functions, just as trademarks adhere all the more compulsively to their objects the less their linguistic meaning is apprehended. The Minister of Public Education speaks ignorantly of "dynamic forces," and the hit songs sing endlessly of "reverie" and "rhapsody," hitching their popularity to the magic of the incomprehensible as if to some deep intimation of a higher life. Other stereotypes, such as "memory," are still partly comprehended, but become detached from the experience which might fulfill them. They obtrude into the spoken language like enclaves. On the German radio of Flesch and Hitler they are discernible in the affected diction of the announcer, who pronounces phrases like "Goodnight, listeners," or "This is the Hitler Youth speaking," or even "the *Führer*" with an inflection which passes into the mother tongue of millions. In such turns of phrase the last bond between sedimented experience and language, which still exerted a reconciling influence in dialect in the nineteenth century, is severed. By contrast, in the hands of the editor whose supple opinions have promoted him to the status of *Schriftleiter*,* German words become petrified and alien. In any word one can distinguish how far it has been disfigured by the fascist "folk" community. By now, of course, such language has become universal, totalitarian. The violence done to words is no longer audible in them. The radio announcer does not need to talk in an affected voice; indeed, he would be impossible if his tone differed from that of his designated listeners. This means, however, that the language and gestures of listeners and spectators are more deeply permeated by the patterns of the culture industry than ever before, in nuances still beyond the reach of experimental methods. Today the culture industry has taken over the civilizing inheritance of the frontier and entrepreneurial democracy, whose receptivity to intellectual deviations was never too highly developed. All are free to dance and amuse themselves, just as, since the historical neutralization of religion, they have been free to join any of the countless sects. But freedom to choose an ideology, which always reflects economic coercion, everywhere proves to be freedom to be the same. The way in which the young girl accepts and performs the obligatory date, the tone of voice used on the telephone and in the most intimate situations, the choice of words in conversation, indeed, the whole inner life compartmentalized according to the categories of vulgarized depth psychology, bears witness to the attempt to turn oneself into an apparatus meeting the requirements of success, an apparatus which, even in its unconscious impulses, conforms to the model presented by the culture industry. The most intimate reactions of human beings have become so entirely reified, even to themselves, that the idea of anything peculiar to them survives only in extreme abstraction: personality means hardly more than dazzling white teeth and freedom from body odor and emotions. That is the triumph of advertising in the culture industry: the compulsive imitation by consumers of cultural commodities which, at the same time, they recognize as false.

Notes

1. A. de Tocqueville, *De la Démocratie en Amérique*, Paris 1864, Vol. II, p. 151.
2. Frank Wedekind, *Gesammelte Werke*, Munich 1921, Vol. IX, p. 426.

2.
MASS-PRODUCED FANTASIES FOR WOMEN
Tania Modleski

I

Although Harlequin Romances, Gothic novels, and soap operas provide mass(ive) entertainment for countless numbers of women of varying ages, classes, and even educational backgrounds, very few critics have taken them seriously enough to study them in any detail. The double critical standard, which feminists have claimed biases literary studies, is operative in the realm of mass-culture studies as well. One cannot find any writings on popular feminine narratives to match the aggrandized titles of certain classic studies of popular male genres ("The Gangster as Tragic Hero") or the inflated claims made for, say, the detective novel which fill the pages of the *Journal of Popular Culture*. At a time when courses on popular culture have become semirespectable curricular offerings in the universities, one is often hard put to find listed on the syllabi a single novel, film, or television program which makes its appeal primarily to women. As Virginia Woolf observed some time ago, "Speaking crudely, football and sport are 'important'; the worship of fashion, the buying of clothes 'trivial.' And these values are inevitably transferred from life to fiction"—to popular fiction no less than to the fiction in the "great tradition."[1]

However, this is *not* to advocate that criticism of female popular culture should simply "plug into" categories used in studies of male popular culture, categories which are themselves often secondhand, having been borrowed from "high culture" criticism in an effort to gain respectability. Such a task would be impossible even were it desirable. As Joanna Russ has argued, the positive cultural myths are mostly male ones; role reversal (for example, "The Scheming Little Adventuress as Tragic Hero") is an impossibility, involving a contradiction in terms.[2]

There are no doubt a number of reasons why female protagonists and female popular fiction cannot claim for themselves the kind of status male heroes and male texts so often claim. This kind of aggrandizement, occurring both in fiction and in criticism, would appear to be a masculine mode, traceable, at least in part, to the male oedipal conflict. This conflict, it is important to note, is resolved at the expense of woman and necessitates her devaluation. For the male gains access to culture and the symbolic first by perceiving the "lack" of the once all-powerful mother and then by identifying with the "superior" male, the father. Recently, critics, following Roland Barthes, have plausibly argued that most popular or "classic" narratives reenact the male oedipal crisis.[3] We need not list here the dreary catalogue of devices used in the male text to disable the female and thus assert masculine superiority (the grapefruit mashed in the woman's face by one "tragic hero"). At the end of a majority of popular narratives the woman is disfigured, dead, or at the very least, domesticated. And *her* downfall is seen as anything *but* tragic. There are other ways in which male texts work to insist implicitly on their difference from the feminine. Sometimes this is done through language: for instance, through rigorous suppression of "flowery" descriptions or the tight-lipped refusal to employ any expression of emotion other than anger.

Criticism, too, finds it necessary to enhance the superiority of its objects: the male hero and the male text. The temptation to elevate what men do simply because men do it is, it would seem, practically irresistible. (Freud himself succumbed to it. As Kenneth Burke points out, Freud, in his efforts to deflate the ego's pretensions, to show what ignoble fears and shameful desires lurk beneath the beauties of civilization, wound up glorifying these fears and desires by invoking Oedipus, one of the most grandiose figures of Western myth: The-Little-Man-Fearing-For-His-"Widdler" as Tragic Hero.)[4] Further, criticism, like the text itself, often raises its object at the expense of the feminine. Not only does the critical equation of pen and penis, discussed by Sandra Gilbert and Susan Gubar in *The Madwoman in the Attic*, suggest that women lack the necessary equipment to write, or at least to write well, but the feminine text itself is often used as a standard by which other products are measured and found to be not wanting. How often have we seen soap operas used in this way? Even as serious and sensitive a critic of mass culture as Raymond Williams can write, "Since their origins in commercial radio in the thirties, many serials have been dismissed as 'soap opera'. Yet . . ." And the implication, borne out in the rest of the paragraph, is that a necessary if not a sufficient criterion for the worth of serials is their difference from the (utterly dismissable) soap operas.[5]

Given this pervasive scorn for all things feminine, it is hardly surprising that since the beginnings of the novel the heroine and the writer of feminine texts have been on the defensive, operating on the constant assumption that men are out to destroy them. In the earliest plots the heroine was forced to protect her social reputation against the seducer who would rob her of this most prized possession. Similarly, the woman writer worked to protect her literary reputation against the dastardly critics. To aid her heroine in the protection of her virtue the writer, like male authors but for different reasons, had to disable her: e.g. to render her entirely ignorant of the most basic facts of life so that the man, finally impressed by her purity, would quit trying to destroy her and would, instead, reward and elevate her—i.e. marry her. What is worse, in her anxiety to ward off critical scorn, the woman writer had to disable *herself*, to proclaim her weakness and

ignorance loudly and clearly, hoping to be "mercifully spared." One fairly typical preface reads:

> When I attempt to interest an impartial Public in favour of the following Work, it is not from a vain hope, that it is deserving of the *approbation* of the *judicious.*—No, my hopes are better founded; a candid, a liberal, a generous Public will make the necessary allowances for the *first* attempt of a young female Adventurer in Letters.[6]

Thus, if self-aggrandizement has been the male mode, self-abasement has too frequently been the female mode.

As if this were not enough, the criticism written by women has long been in the habit of denigrating what George Eliot called "Silly Novels by Lady Novelists."[7] Of course, plenty of male critics spurn silly novels written by either sex, but their criticism never seems to be so personally motivated. Eliot, for example, wrote her essay out of concern that men would find in these novels proof of the universal inability of women to write anything *but* silly works. Thus women's criticism was also often written out of self-defensiveness and the fear of men's power to destroy.

Heroines of contemporary popular narratives for women continue to act defensively, and if their writers are no longer apologizing for their activity, women critics are more than ever uncomfortable with these narratives. Such discomfort is, to a certain extent, justified, but what is most striking is that it too seems to manifest a defensiveness which has not been felt through. Whereas the old (and some of the new) heroines have to protect themselves against the seductions of the hero, feminist critics seem to be strenuously disassociating themselves from the seductiveness of the feminine texts. And whereas the heroine of romance, as we shall see, turns against her own better self, the part of her which feels anger at men, the critic turns against her own "worse" self, the part of her which has not yet been "liberated" from shameful fantasies.

Thus women's criticism of popular feminine narratives has generally adopted one of three attitudes: dismissiveness; hostility—tending unfortunately to be aimed at the consumers of the narratives; or, most frequently, a flippant kind of mockery.[8] This is the tone used by Eliot, with whom one does not usually associate it. It is, significantly, indistinguishable from the tone men often use when they mention feminine popular art. Again, the ridicule is certainly to some extent justified (though no more justified than it would be if aimed at much male popular art), but it often seems to betray a kind of *self*-mockery, a fear that someone will think badly of the writer for even touching on the subject, however gingerly. In assuming this attitude, we demonstrate not so much our freedom from romantic fantasy as our acceptance of the critical double standard and of the masculine contempt for sentimental (feminine) "drivel." Perhaps we have internalized the ubiquitous male spy, who watches as we read romances or view soap operas, as he watched Virginia Woolf from behind the curtain (or so she suspected) when she delivered her subversive lectures at "Oxbridge," or as he intently observes the romantic heroine just when she thinks she is alone and free at last to be herself.

The present work was conceived and undertaken out of concern that these narratives were not receiving the right kind of attention. I try to avoid expressing either hostility or ridicule, to get beneath the embarrassment, which I am convinced provokes both the anger and the mockery, and to explore the reasons for the deep-rooted and centuries-old appeal of the narratives. Their enormous and continuing popularity, I assume, suggests that they speak to very real problems and tensions in women's lives. The narrative strategies which have evolved for smoothing over these tensions can tell us much about how women have managed not only to live in oppressive circumstances but to invest their situations with some degree of dignity.

Although there have been few serious or detailed studies of contemporary mass art for women, popular feminine narratives of the eighteenth and nineteenth centuries have received much more attention. Some scholars have pointed to the enormous influence of these older narratives on contemporary life and letters. Ann Douglas, for example, holds the nineteenth-century novels by and for women responsible for many of the evils of mass culture. Discussing Little Eva of *Uncle Tom's Cabin* as a typical "narcissistic" heroine, Douglas says, "Stowe's infantile heroine anticipates that exaltation of the average which is the trademark of mass culture." And further, "The pleasure Little Eva gave me provided historical and practical preparation

for the equally indispensable and disquieting comforts of mass culture."[9] Although I think this is going a bit far, the more modest claim that early popular novels for women anticipate the narratives which women find compelling in the twentieth century is certainly demonstrable. Therefore, the debates which even now surround the early narratives (what was their worth? what function did they serve?) are of relevance to any consideration of the later ones.

II

To introduce an admittedly overschematized lineage for the three forms under consideration. Harlequins can be traced back through the work of Charlotte Brontë and Jane Austen to the sentimental novel and ultimately, as I shall have more than one occasion to note, to the novels of Samuel Richardson, whose *Pamela* is considered by many scholars to be the first British novel (it was also the first English novel printed in America); Gothic romances for women, also traceable through Charlotte Brontë, date back to the eighteenth century and the work of Ann Radcliffe; and soap operas are descendants of the domestic novels and the sensation novels of the nineteenth century. In turn, the "antecedants" of the domestic novels, according to Nina Baym, "lay . . . in the novel of manners, with its 'mixed' heroine as developed by Fanny Burney, and even more in the fiction of the English women moralists—Mrs. Opie, Mrs. Barbauld, and especially Maria Edgeworth, with her combination of educational intention, moral fabulating, and description of manners and customs."[10]

My classification is, as I say, overschematized, for the genres do overlap. Thus the plot of the sentimental novel, which often depicts a young, innocent woman defending her virginity against the attacks of a rake, who might or might not reform, would frequently find its way into the domestic novel, which tended to center around women's activities in the home. The following is a description of the routine of the heroine of Susan Warner's enormously popular *Queechy*:

By the most conservative estimate, Fleda performed the parts of three hired men, cook, dairy manager, nurse, and teacher. Up before dawn to do the chores and to care for the livestock, she found time before breakfast to study the latest agricultural methods by which she turned a run-down farm into the show place of the county. The produce from her truck garden commanded the highest prices at market and her new method of haying resulted in the banner crop of the year. In addition to the cares involved in these enterprises, she blacked the boots of her numerous guests, revived the drooping health of an ailing family, and improved her mind by reading and study. Her leisure moments, which were necessarily limited, were spent in dodging the persistent efforts of the villainous Thorn, who devoted his full time to plotting her seduction![11]

Here is a very potent feminine fantasy, common to most nineteenth-century novels and to their twentieth-century counterparts. The man, whether he is plotting the woman's seduction or, as in soap operas, endlessly discussing his marital woes with his coworkers at the hospital, spends all his time thinking about the woman. Even when he appears most indifferent to her, as he frequently does in Harlequin Romances, we can be sure he will eventually tell her how much the thought of her has obsessed him. Thus, women writers have always had their own way of "evening things up" between men and women, even when they seemed most fervently to embrace their subordinate status.

The sentimental novel flourished in America at the end of the eighteenth and in the early nineteenth century. It was, however, an English import rather than an indigenous American product. Like the Harlequins of the present day, the novels repeatedly insisted on the importance of the heroine's virginity. In the classic formula, the heroine, who is often of lower social status than the hero, holds out against his attacks on her "virtue" until he sees no other recourse than to marry her. Of course, by this time he wants to marry her, having become smitten with her sheer "goodness." The early women novelists became pre-occupied, not to say obsessed, with the morality of this plot. Whether or not a rake would really reform was a burning question: some novelists said no, some said yes, and many said no and yes—i.e. put themselves on record as being opposed to the idea that a rake would ever improve his morals and then proceeded to make an exception of their hero.

In these debates, however, the sexual double standard was seldom seriously challenged; very few women went so far as one female character, who, in any case, is not the heroine of the novel: "I could never see the propriety of the assertion [that reformed rakes make the best husbands]. Might it not be said with equal justice, that if a certain description of females were reformed, they would make the best wives?"[12] Rather, the inequality between the sexes was dealt with in other ways. According to J.M.S. Tompkins, for instance, the effect of the "cult of sensibility," the belief that people are innately good and that this goodness is demonstrated in elaborate displays of feeling, "was to induce some measure of approximation in the ethical ideals and emotional sensitiveness of the two sexes." Approval was therefore given to the hero who exhibited an "almost feminine sensibility."[13] In Harlequins, the battle continues to be fought out not in the sexual arena, but in the emotional and—stretching the term—the ethical one. If the Harlequin heroine never questions the necessity of remaining a virgin while the man is allowed to have had a variety of sexual experiences, there is a tacit insistence that the man share her "values." In other words, "speaking crudely," the novels literally reverse the hierarchy pointed out by Virginia Woolf, for "the worship of fashion, the buying of clothes" are important—to both the woman and the man, who is usually even capable of identifying a material as "tulle." More, in novel after novel, the man is brought to acknowledge the preeminence of love and the attractions of domesticity at which he has, as a rule, previously scoffed.

Another typical, but far more somber plot, dealt with the woman who gave in to the libertine, and at the end of the novel died a penitent and often excruciating death. This is essentially the story of the two most popular women's novels of the period, Susanna Rowson's *Charlotte: A Tale of Truth* and Hannah Webster Foster's *The Coquette*. If the reformed-rake plot is borrowed from *Pamela*, the novel of seduction is indebted to *Clarissa*, though, significantly, the women novelists allowed their heroines some measure of conscious choice in their 'fall,' whereas Clarissa, after her initial error of leaving the family, remained pure and had to be drugged to be deprived of her "virtue." The emotional force of these novels seems often to lie less in the act of sin, the "elope-ment," than in the death scenes themselves, a fact which has disturbed and puzzled many critics. But death is too convenient to women fantasists to be easily relinquished, for it can serve a variety of func-tions. On the one hand, it endows the woman with something like "tragic hero" status: "What can a her-oine do?" asks Joanna Russ in pointing out that men have taken all the active plots.[14] She can die. And in dying, she does not have to depart from the passive feminine role, but only logically extend it. On the other hand, death can be a very powerful means of wreaking vengeance on others who do not properly "appreciate" us, and it is in this form that the fantasy of death can be found in Harlequin Romances, which, with their happy endings, seem on the surface to have nothing in common with the tragic *Clarissa* plot.

From one point of view nothing could be easier than to ridicule the prevalence of the seducer in these early novels, and scholars, especially male scholars, have not been behindhand in doing so. Carl Van Doren writes, "Modern readers might think that age one of the most illicit on record if they did not under-stand that Richardson's Lovelace is merely being repeated in different colors and proportions."[15] But even in popular literature, it is never a question of "mere" repetition; why, for example, did women writ-ers not choose to "repeat" Tom Jones or Humphrey Clinker? The figures of Mr. B. in *Pamela*, Lovelace in *Clarissa*, together with their numerous successors, enhanced the importance of women (for the men spend their full time "plotting the seductions" of the heroines) and at the same time provide the means by which women can localize their diffuse and general sense of powerlessness.

In giving vent to this sense of powerlessness, the sentimental novels look forward to the themes, fanta-sies, and preoccupations of both the domestic novels and the Gothic novels. The "reformed-rake" plot and the debate which raged around it pointed to women's sense of vulnerability in regard to marriage and hence foreshadowed the critique of the family which would be the covert project of the so-called "domestic" nov-elists. As Foster's *The Coquette* makes clear, one of the great attractions of the rake was that he seemed to provide an exciting alternative to the staid domestic "pleasures" which were all good women were

supposed to want. Eliza Warton, the ultimately ruined heroine, continually puts off her rather dull clerical suitor in the hopes of receiving a more interesting offer from the lively and witty libertine, Peter Sanford. She complains:

> I recoil at the thought of immediately forming a connection, which must confine me to the duties of domestic life, and make me dependent for happi-ness, perhaps too, for subsistence, upon a class of people, who will claim the right of scrutinizing every part of my conduct; and by censuring those foibles, which I am conscious of not having prudence to avoid, may render me completely miserable.[16]

But, of course, marrying a rake could lead to even more serious domestic disasters; thus, a number of novels showed women marrying men of less than "sound moral principle" and subsequently portrayed the husbands "dragging their families into debt and disgrace and violently closing the scene with sui-cide."[17] At their extreme, such fears inevitably lead to paranoia: "God bless you, my child," exclaims the mother of one "sentimental" heroine, "be careful, cir-cumspect, and wary; suspect every one of a design on you till you are convinced of the contrary. You must think all men knaves and all women treacherous, and then you will avoid many troubles. Trust no one. . . ."[18] As we shall see, Gothic novels most fully express this paranoid sense of the world and, further-more, help women to come to terms with the mothers who (as in the above quotation) seem to be responsi-ble for passing on this paranoia to their daughters in a world ruled by men.

The Gothic novels of Horace Walpole, Ann Radcliffe, and Matthew Lewis achieved their peak of popularity in America at about the same time as the sentimental novel. Critics often attribute their immense popularity to the public's desire for "mere" entertain-ment. James Hart's *The Popular Book: A History of America's Literary Taste* succinctly concludes that many people found in these novels "a new form of escape from their own humdrum lives, allowing them vicari-ously to experience thrilling adventures. From the middle class of America to the Middle Ages of Europe was a wonderfully exciting journey, when made through the medium of a Gothic novel."[19] However, it

is possible to see the exotic settings of Gothics as possessing a much more important function: because the
novels so radically displace reality by putting the action
in distant times and strange and ghostly lands, they are
uniquely equipped to become a site for the displacement of repressed wishes and fears. In other words,
Gothics can present us with the frighteningly familiar
precisely because they make the familiar strange—
which is, it will be recalled, the way Freud said the
uncanny sensation in literature is produced. Thus, set
in a remote place, in a faraway time, the female Gothic
as created by Ann Radcliffe in *The Mysteries of Udolpho*
expresses women's most intimate fears, or, more precisely, their fears about intimacy—about the exceedingly private, even claustrophobic nature of their
existence. So it is that the house, the building itself, to
which women are generally confined in real life,
becomes the locus of evil in an entirely make-believe
sixteenth-century Italian mountain setting.

Furthermore, female Gothics provide an outlet for
women's fears about fathers and husbands, fears which
are much more pronounced than the sentimental heroine's. The plot of Radcliffe's *The Mysteries of Udolpho*,
on which the later Gothic novels are based, has a villainous Montoni carrying off the heroine Emily and
her aunt, whom Montoni marries for her fortune, to a
castle in the mountains where he imprisons the aunt
and persecutes the niece in order to gain control of
her fortune. I will argue that this plot became popular
at a time when the nuclear family was being consolidated in part because it portrayed in an extremely
exaggerated form a family dynamic which would
increasingly become the norm. It spoke powerfully to
the young girl struggling to achieve psychological
autonomy in a home where the remote, but all-powerful father ruled over an utterly dependent wife.

In a sense, then, Gothics are "domestic" novels
too, concerned with the (often displaced) relationships among family members and with driving home
to women the importance of coping with enforced
confinement and the paranoid fears it generates.
Thus, although nineteenth-century readers soon
dropped Gothic novels in favor of the "domestic novels," it could be argued that the later novels are somewhat continuous with the earlier ones. Indeed, Jane
Austen, preeminent among novelists of manners,
who antedated the domestic novelists, began her

career not simply burlesquing the Gothic tradition,
but extracting its core of truth: her mercenary and
domineering General Tilney of *Northanger Abbey*
may not be capable of imprisoning his wife in a turret,
but, like the Gothic villain, he *is* capable of rendering
her existence entirely miserable, and of coldly ruining
the heroine's hopes for happiness.

After dying out for over a century, Gothic novels
again became popular upon publication in 1938 of
Daphne Du Maurier's *Rebecca*, a novel about a woman
marrying a man whom she subsequently suspects of
still being in love with his (dead) first wife, but who, it
turns out, has actually murdered the wife out of anger
at her promiscuity. Significantly, this second "Gothic
revival" took place at the same time that "hard-boiled"
detective novels were attracting an unprecedented
number of male readers. While Dashiell Hammett
and Raymond Chandler were persistently scapegoating women (in Chandler's *Farewell, My Lovely*, a
woman named Helen Grayle is at the bottom of the
whole sordid affair!), the paranoid fears of women
were receiving new life. In the forties, a new movie
genre derived from Gothic novels appeared around
the time that hard-boiled detective fiction was being
transformed by the medium into what movie critics
currently call "film noir." Not surprisingly, film noir has
received much critical scrutiny both here and abroad,
while the so-called "gaslight" genre has been virtually
ignored. According to many critics, film noir possesses the greatest sociological importance (in addition to its aesthetic importance) because it reveals
male paranoid fears, developed during the war years,
about the independence of women on the homefront.
Hence the necessity in these movies of destroying or
taming the aggressive, mercenary, sexually dynamic
"femme fatale" whose presence is indispensable to
the genre. Beginning with Alfred Hitchcock's 1940
movie version of *Rebecca* and continuing through and
beyond George Cukor's *Gaslight* in 1944, the gaslight
films may be seen to reflect *women's* fears about losing their unprecedented freedoms and being forced
back into the homes after the men returned from
fighting to take over the jobs and assume control of
their families. In many of these films, the house seems
to be alive with menace, and the greedy, sadistic men
who rule them are often suspected of trying to drive
their wives insane, or to murder them as they have

murdered other women in the past. The fact that after the war years these films gradually faded from the screen probably reveals more about the changing composition of movie audiences than about the waning of women's anxieties concerning domesticity. For Gothic novels have continued to this day to enjoy a steady popularity, and a few of their authors, like Victoria Holt and Mary Stewart, reliably appear on the best-seller list.

By far, the most popular form of literature for women throughout most of the nineteenth century were the "domestic novels." These novels and the sensation fiction of the 1860s, mostly from England, come together to form the prototypes of the modern soap opera. Elaine Showalter credits sensation writers with a subversive appeal, claiming that they inverted "the stereotypes of the domestic novel." Certainly the sensationalists "expressed female anger, frustration, and sexual energy more directly than had been done previously."[20] Nevertheless, several important studies by women scholars have shown that the domestic novel itself was subversive, thus challenging the orthodox view of the genre, advanced by Herbert Brown: "The domestic novels in which these writers sought to glorify the American home were as limited in scope as the narrow sphere of interests of the women readers for whom they were designed. . . . Domestic fiction records few instances of discontent with this circumscribed life."[21] James Hart corroborates Brown's assessment when he speaks of the women novelists as "middle-class ladies . . . busy fashioning their homes into the land of the heart's content."[22] In sharp contrast, Helen Waite Papashvily characterizes the novels as "handbooks . . . of feminine revolt," encouraging "a pattern of feminine behavior so quietly ruthless, so subtly vicious that by comparison the ladies at Seneca appear angels of innocence."[23] How is it possible for people to read the same group of books and come up with such wildly divergent ideas about them? The answer, I believe, is that many critics tend to take at face value the novelists' endorsement of the domestic ideal and ignore the actual, not very flattering portraits of domesticity which emerge from their works. To be sure, as Brown notes, the novelists tended strenuously to affirm the sacredness of the marriage tie, but they were concerned primarily to show how far short of the ideal many marriages in real life tended to

fall. Some of the very titles of the fiction of Mrs. E.D.E.N. Southworth, one of the most prolific and popular writers of the age, suggest the grievances against marriage, fathers, and husbands Brown says are nowhere to be found: *The Fatal Vow, The Discarded Daughter, The Deserted Wife.* Nina Baym, who is more moderate than Papashvily in her account of the novels, even takes issue with the term "domestic," which she says reinforces the stereotyped idea that the novelists wallowed in domestic bliss. On the contrary, in this fiction

> home life is presented, overwhelmingly, as unhappy. There are very few intact families in this literature, and those that are intact are unstable or locked into routines of misery. Domestic tasks are arduous and monotonous; family members oppress and abuse each other; social interchanges are alternately insipid or malicious.[24]

In much "domestic" fiction men are the culprits responsible for the intense suffering of wives and daughters. Mrs. Southworth, in particular, delighted in portraying men as tyrannical, foolish, un-trusting and untrustworthy. In a typical Southworth plot, the heroine is forced to fend for herself because a guardian, father, or husband persecutes or neglects her, and she manages splendidly until at the end she gets a mate worthy of her, or, alternatively, the mate she has finally comes to appreciate her virtues and abilities, and is transformed into a model husband. Similarly, Fleda's astonishing activities in *Queechy* are necessitated by her guardian's abdication of responsibility; failing in business he becomes increasingly morose, helpless, and tyrannical and ultimately abandons his family and lands them in debt.

Soap operas continue the tradition of portraying strong women who, if they no longer single-handedly run large farms, nevertheless must struggle to keep intact the worlds which the weakness and unreliability of men threaten to undermine. However, men in soap operas tend not to be the bullying tyrants frequently found in domestic fiction. The evil "villain" in soap opera is generally female, and in this respect soap opera closely resembles the nineteenth-century sensation novels written by and for women. In the fiction of Mary Louise Braddon and the recently discovered "thrillers" of Louisa May Alcott, the happiness of the "good" woman is jeopardized by the infernal machinations of a clever and beautiful temptress who gains control over the hapless man with ridiculous ease. In the chapter on soap operas I will explore the appeal of such a character and show that this plot is not really the "inversion" of the "domestic" plot but its complement. Soap operas may also be indebted to the sensation novels for the emphasis on violence, crime, and sexual scandal.

The so-called woman's film of the 1930s and 40s clearly derived from domestic fiction while it added some new themes. The stock figures of domestic fiction—the strong and brave heroines, the weak, often dissolute men—abound in the woman's film. In *Letter from an Unknown Woman*, to cite a famous example of the genre, Joan Fontaine has a brief affair with Louis Jordan, conceives a child by him, and continues to love him over the years though she marries someone else. When the two come together after a long time, he has forgotten her completely, having meanwhile been casually involved with many women. Only when she dies does he become aware of the magnificence of her nature. In *Now, Voyager* Bette Davis falls in love with Paul Henreid, who is trapped in a marriage with a selfish, hypochondriacal woman. Davis rejects a suitor and, relinquishing any hope for "a home of her own, a man of her own, a child of her own," devotes herself entirely to bringing up Henreid's child. A new twist has been given to a typical theme of domestic fiction: in the nineteenth-century novels, women had been preoccupied with children, especially children who died young. This preoccupation has been attributed to the relatively high infant mortality rate and the need of writers like Stowe, the creator of Little Eva, to make perfect martyrs out of the doomed infants. In the woman's film, on the other hand, it is the mothers or the mother-surrogates who are the martyrs, sacrificing everything for their (often ungrateful) children. This shift in attitude may be explained by the fact that women in the twentieth century, much more than their nineteenth-century counterparts, have had to depend on their children for fulfillment, since the "support networks" of women have virtually disappeared. This increased dependency generates increased resentment, a dilemma reflected in the child obsession of the woman's film as well as in soap operas.

Not only did the domestic novels call into question the felicity women were supposed to experience in making home-life the center of their existence, but they also revealed, as Papashvily shows, covert longings for power and revenge. Papashvily devotes a whole chapter of her book to "The Mutilation of the Male," a device which allows the heroine to lead a more active life than would be possible if she had a whole and healthy male to protect her, and which moreover, one suspects, served as a covert expression of feminine anger at male power. Another common device was to have the heroine married off to a man towards whom she felt nothing, but who loved her ardently, passionately, constantly. Sometimes, self-mutilation brought about the desired masculine punishment: in the Elsie Dinsmore books, Elsie, commanded by her father to play the piano on the Sabbath, "sat at the piano until she fainted, striking her head as she fell. Her father's repentence and grief was abject enough to please the most demanding."[25]

Clearly these methods are not, as we say today, the "healthiest" means of venting anger. On the other hand, it should be heartening to feminists to know that, contrary to many male critics, women writers of popular fiction have indeed registered protest against the authority of fathers and husbands even while they appeared to give their wholehearted consent to it. Critics like Papashvily have thus performed in the realm of popular art a liberating task akin to the one engaged in by feminist critics of "high" art. Elaine Showalter beautifully describes this critical activity:

> There is an optical illusion which can be seen as either a goblet or two profiles. The images oscillate in their tension before us, one alternately superseding the other and reducing it to meaningless background. In the purest feminist literary criticism we are similarly presented with a radical alteration of our vision, a demand that we see meaning in what has previously been empty space. The orthodox plot recedes, and another plot, hitherto submerged in the anonymity of the background, stands out in bold relief like a thumbprint.[26]

Not surprisingly this hidden plot often reveals buried anger or hostility (for example, Jane Eyre's fury at Rochester's highhandedness), but it is not simply the obtuseness of male critics which has prevented the discernment of the alternate plots; these plots have had to be "submerged" into more orthodox ones just as feminine rage itself, blocked in direct expression, has had to be submerged, subterranean, devious.

In the following chapters, I will show that even the contemporary mass-produced narratives for women contain elements of protest and resistance underneath highly "orthodox" plots. This is *not* to say that the tensions, anxieties, and anger which pervade these works are solved in ways which would please modern feminists: far from it. Indeed, just as the eighteenth- and nineteenth-century popular novels for women despised and caricatured the "new woman," so too do the contemporary narratives tend to ridicule the "woman's libber" who rejects the adequacy of Bette Davis's "home of her own, man of her own, child of her own" (demanding first and foremost a "room of her own" apart from the man and the child). But, significantly, Bette Davis ultimately rejected them too, if not in favor of a career, then at least for the sake of an emotion and an ideal that transcended the alleged desires of the majority of women. If the popular-culture heroine and the feminist choose utterly different ways of overcoming their dissatisfaction, they at least have in common the dissatisfaction.

III

Objections will arise. Many critics will argue that there are crucial differences between the popular art of the nineteenth century and the mass-produced art consumed by millions today. The division between popular art and great art was not absolute then, as it is now, and popular writers not as severely controlled; hence a writer like Harriet Beecher Stowe could protest the conditions of her age in a way no longer imaginable. Today, the argument runs, only two types of art exist: mass art, which is used by its producers to manipulate the people and to "colonize" their leisure time[27]—in short, to keep them contented with the "status quo"— and high art, which is the last preserve of an autonomous, critical spirit. Since mass art is completely dominated by the "consciousness industry"[28] and since high art alone resists such domination, it follows that the responsible, socially concerned critic must continually focus his or her attention upon

the differences between the two types of art. "The division itself is the truth," Max Horkheimer and T.W. Adorno asserted.[29]

This argument, first advanced by the Marxist-oriented members of the Frankfurt School (notably, Horkheimer, Adorno, and Herbert Marcuse) is especially pernicious because it makes contempt for mass art a politically progressive attitude. It is one of the great ironies in the development of mass-culture theory that the people who were first responsible for pointing out the political importance of mass art simultaneously provided the justification for slighting it. Fortunately, some recent Marxist critics have begun to challenge the assumptions of the Frankfurt School; and many of their theoretical insights inform the pages of this book.[30] Fredric Jameson's important essay, "Reification and Utopia in Mass Culture," makes a two-pronged attack on some of the main ideas of the Frankfurt School. In the first place, he shows that high art—the "modernism" valorized by the Frankfurt School and, more recently, by the *Tel Quel* group in France—has not remained apart from the processes of the "commodification of art." For instance, although modernism may have arisen out of a desire "not to be a commodity," the very effort of avoiding the repetition and "standardization"[31] characteristic of mass art means that modernism must stress "innovation and novelty," must, therefore, capitulate to the "pressure ... to 'make it new' " and thus act in accordance "with the ever swifter historicity of consumer society, with its yearly or quarterly style and fashion changes."[32]

More important for our purposes is the other half of Jameson's argument, which is the one he most fully develops. If, on the one hand, high art does not represent an absolute, uncompromised alternative to mass art, on the other hand, mass art may be said to possess some of the negative, critical functions the Frankfurt School and its numerous followers have attributed to high art alone. This is true on the most general level. As Hans Robert Jauss points out in a critique of Adorno's theories, every work of art presupposes "an aesthetic distance on the part of the spectator; that is, it presupposes a negation of the immediate interests of his everyday life."[33] But as Jameson shows, mass art often contains many specific criticisms of everyday life, in addition to this rather global "negation" (which, however, was of the utmost importance in the Frankfurt School's philosophy of art). As opposed to those critics who claim that mass art is designed to create "false anxieties," manipulate "false needs," and impose "false consciousness," Jameson argues that mass culture performs "a transformational work on [real] social and political anxieties and fantasies which must then have some effective presence in the mass cultural text in order subsequently to be 'managed' or repressed." He invokes the theories of Norman Holland, who in *The Dynamics of Literary Response* describes the operations of the text in producing aesthetic gratification: at the same time that the text symbolically fulfills our wishes, it must protect against the fears which "powerful archaic desires" always threaten to call forth from the unconscious. Jameson concludes:

> Hence Holland's suggestive conception of the vocation of art to *manage* this raw material of the drives and the archaic wish or fantasy material. To rewrite the concept of a management of desire in social terms now allows us to think repression and wish-fulfillment together within the unity of a single mechanism which gives and takes alike in a kind of psychic compromise or horse-trading, which strategically arouses fantasy content within careful symbolic containment structures which defuse it, gratifying intolerable, unrealizable, properly imperishable desires only to the degree to which they can be laid to rest.[34]

Jameson is right to claim that his discussion leads us some distance away from the concept of mass art as "manipulation," as "sheer brainwashing." Nevertheless, there are problems with this part of his essay, specifically with his notion of the social "management of desire," which suggests that there is someone doing the managing. Indeed, in his remarks on *The Godfather*, which Jameson uses as a test case for his theory, he speaks of the "intent to mystify," thus conjuring up, like the text itself, a sort of "Godfather" on whom to project blame.[35] Jameson and other left-wing critics of mass culture are the latest heirs to the old reformist/Populist belief in a group of conspirators ruthlessly holding us back from the attainment of a golden age. Ironically, it is the politically conservative mass-culture critic who

has on occasion warned against the tendency, as Leo Spitzer puts it, to "oversimplify the psychology of the advertiser [and, by extension, of any other so-called captain of consciousness[36]]—who is not only a businessman but a human being: one who is endowed with all the normal potentialities of emotion and who finds expression of these in the exercise of his profession."[37] More recently, European Marxists like Louis Althusser have opposed the facile assumption that there are two groups of people—those within ideology (the masses of people) and those on the outside who, without illusions themselves, manage to control the others by feeding them illusions. We are all "inside" ideology, Althusser has persuasively argued.[38]

Therefore, while my analyses support Jameson's theory that mass-cultural texts both stimulate and allay social anxieties, both arouse and symbolically satisfy the "properly imperishable" desires and fantasies of women, I avoid imputing to, for example, the board of directors of the Harlequin Company, an omniscience about the nature and effects of their product. I sincerely doubt that the men on the board, cynical as they may be about feminine romance, actually possess a total awareness of where "mystification" leaves off and "truth" begins. Indeed, I am quite sure that any cynicism they feel is derived from a mystification of what it means to be a male: *viz.* a "superior" being with "higher" interests and values. This masculine attitude may in fact drive women to Harlequins for a "false" solution to the anxieties it creates, but that is because it is an attitude shared by most men.

The work of Althusser, itself influenced by the psychoanalytic thought of Jacques Lacan, has spurred renewed interest in psychoanalysis among other Marxists. For, if the production of ideology is not the work of any identifiable group, it must be located elsewhere. Rejecting the notion of "false consciousness," many Marxists have turned to a study of the unconscious, as it is structured in and by the family. This emphasis has the merit of beginning to explain why people cling to oppressive conditions even after it is pointed out to them that their own best interests lie elsewhere. It helps explain, for example, why the sales of Harlequin Romances have not simply remained steady in recent years but have actually increased along with the growth of feminism. Only by taking psychoanalytic insights into account, by understanding how deep-rooted are the anxieties and fantasies contained in (and by) popular narratives for women can we begin to explain why women are still requiring what Jameson calls the "symbolic satisfactions" of the texts instead of looking for "real" satisfactions.

But this is easier said than done. Jameson can speak of "desires" and "anxieties" as if the terms were self-evident, but when they are applied to women and women's situation they become extremely problematic. Early followers of Freud tended to characterize women's desire as masochism, a masochism thought to be biologically ordained, for, according to Helene Deutsch, if women did not "naturally" love pain they would neither consent to sexual intercourse nor suffer the difficulties of childbearing.[39] In a classic Freudian psychological manoeuvre, women's very anxieties about pain which they revealed, for instance, in nightmares about rape, were construed by Deutsch as "proof" of women's repressed wish to be physically overpowered. We may smile at the doctrine of women's masochism when it is thus baldly stated, but it survives in milder forms to this day, and is implicitly invoked even by feminist critics when they try to explain the attractions of popular feminine texts. Here is how Ann Douglas describes the Harlequin readers: "[The] women who couldn't thrill to male nudity in *Playgirl* are enjoying the titillation of seeing themselves, not necessarily as they are, but as some men would like to see them: illogical, innocent, magnetized by male sexuality and brutality."[40] It is an important part of my project to show that the so-called masochism pervading these texts is a "cover" for anxieties, desires and wishes which if openly expressed would challenge the psychological and social order of things. For that very reason, of course, they must be kept hidden; the texts, after arousing them, must, in Jameson's formula, work to neutralize them.

When applied carefully, then, a psychoanalytic approach to mass cultural texts can have some of the same value Herbert Marcuse claimed for high art and for psychoanalysis itself. In *Eros and Civilization* Marcuse argues that Freudianism contains a hidden, liberating tendency because it encourages people to explore the sources of their repression and to discover in their dreams and fantasies the long-hidden wishes which ultimately constitute a critique of repressive civilization.[41] In this sense, psychoanalysis by looking

backward enables us to look forward in imagination to a "utopian" world. It is important not to overlook the utopian component of *mass* dreams and fantasies, as Jameson, Hans Magnus Enzensberger, and others have recently pointed out.[42] The Frankfurt School strenuously denied this component, insisting that only "great" art could give us foreshadowings of a better world to come. As Herbert Marcuse, waxing poetical, puts it:

> There is no work of art which does not, in its very structure, evoke the words, the images, the music of another reality, of another order repelled by the existing one and yet alive in memory and anticipation, alive in what happens to men and women, and in their rebellion against it.[43]

But Jameson accurately notes that precisely in order to legitimatize the status quo, the works of mass culture must "deflect … the deepest and most fundamental hopes … of the collectivity to which they can therefore … be found to have given voice."[44] To commit ourselves to a search for the utopian promises of mass art for women, or as I put it in the final chapter, to a "search for tomorrow," is to put ourselves in the way of answering the great vexed question of psychoanalysis first posed by Freud: "What do women want?"

Freud himself did not spend a whole lot of time trying to answer the question, although feminists are beginning to realize that what he did have to say about feminine psychology is of enormous interest and significance.[45] Many recent studies of psychoanalysis and women have expanded Freud's ideas most fruitfully. This work forces us to reconsider some of the generally accepted notions about psychoanalysis and literature. For if, as Freud admitted, the female's psychic development does not parallel the male's then obviously studies of literature based upon masculine psychology will prove inadequate to an understanding of "the dynamics of feminine literary response." When Norman Holland in *The Dynamics of Literary Response* discusses the psychology of the reader, he actually means the *male* reader. And Freud himself was an offender in this respect, as a look at his discussion of the uncanny sensation in literature clearly shows.[46] Freud posits fear of castration as one of the main sources of this sensation. Now, clearly women cannot have the same dread of castration that men do. In Freud's view, women, upon becoming aware that they lack a penis, accept their "castration" as a fait accompli; rather than fearing for the fate of the penis, women at most suffer feelings of inadequacy because of the male's superior penis. If this is so, it would follow that the sensation of the uncanny would be less powerful in women than in men (just as Freud, following similar logic, concluded that the superego is less developed in women[47]). But, as we shall see, Gothic novels for women continually exploit the sensation of the uncanny as it was defined by Freud to a far greater extent than any other type of mass fiction and hence point to the weakness of the classic psychoanalytic model.

I see my work in part as an early contribution to a psychology of the interaction between feminine readers and texts. Analyzing Harlequins, Gothics, and soap operas seems a good way to begin: first, because the works are aimed predominantly or exclusively at a female audience; and secondly, because these fantasies, as complex as we shall find them to be, do not employ as elaborately as "high" art the psychological and formal devices for distancing and transforming the anxieties and wishes of their readers.

IV

To this end—the end of determining what constitutes narrative pleasure for women—each of the following chapters has a different emphasis. While the three forms under consideration are by no means entirely dissimilar, each seems to satisfy particular psychological needs, and each is importantly different from the others in its narrative form.

I will begin my investigation by studying the oldest type of women's narrative, the romance, which is also the most rigid of the three forms in terms of its narrative structure. In 1793, Susanna Rowson, a writer of the "sentimental novel," remarked, "I wonder that the novel readers are not tired of reading one story so many times, with only the variation of its being told different ways."[48] While Rowson's observation could, with even more justice today, be applied to most popular novels, which are, of course, deeply conventional, it pertains most forcibly to Harlequin Romances, for the company which produces them requires its writers to follow a strict set of rules and even dictates the point of view from which the narrative must be told.

The peculiar result is that the reader who reads the story *already knows the story*, at least in all its essentials. I will show that this situation both reflects and contributes to a mild "hysterical" state—using this term in its strict psychoanalytic sense. In his famous case study of Anna O., Josef Breuer, who, with Freud, worked with female hysterics, discusses the way the patient's early "habit of daydreaming" to escape from her "monotonous family life" prepared the way for the extreme hysteria she was to develop.[49] Eventually, she began to experience a kind of "double conscience," as Breuer calls it, which, among other symptoms, was manifested in a need to tell stories about herself in the third person and in a feeling that even when she was at her most "insane," "a clear-sighted and calm observer sat . . . in a corner of her brain and looked on at all the mad business."[50] This kind of duality exists, as we shall see, at the very core of romances, particularly in the relation between an "informed" reader and a necessarily innocent heroine.

Another characteristic of Anna O.'s hysteria consisted of her reliving in the present experiences which had happened in the past. Harlequins too involve the reader in regressive fantasies—both angry fantasies and fantasies of being wholly protected and cherished. But the flight into the past is perhaps most marked in the Gothic text, in which the reader is drawn into a kind of "family romance," as the heroine, on the brink of marriage, confronts early "separation anxieties" and "oedipal difficulties." I said earlier that Roland Barthes and his many followers consider classical narrative to be based on the male oedipal drama; what I want to demonstrate in the chapter on Gothics is that there is at least one kind of story which closely follows the *female* oedipal drama. For this reason I rely more exclusively on a psychoanalytic approach in this chapter than in either of the others. We shall see that the phobias and persecution fears contained within the texts are crucially bound up with "normal" feminine psychological development. Thus, if Harlequin Romance may be called the "hysterical text," we could perhaps think of the Gothic as the "paranoid text."

Despite the significant differences, however, both texts share in common a sense of the insufficiency of female selfhood. The reader of Harlequin Romances finds herself, in "hysterical" fashion, desiring the subversion of the heroine's attempts at self-assertion; and the reader of Gothics identifies with a heroine who fears hereditary madness or who feels literally possessed by the spirits of other women from out of the past. However, feminine selflessness reaches its extreme in the "family romances" of soap operas. And this not so much because the women portrayed on these programs embody it as an ideal; rather, because of the special narrative form of soap operas (because it has no end, because, properly speaking, it has no center), the spectator is invited to disperse herself into a variety of situations which never come to a full and satisfactory conclusion. The spectator becomes the ideal woman, emptied of self, preoccupied by the perennial problems of "all her children." Moreover, in directing the spectator's hostility towards the one woman who repeatedly tries to gain control over feminine powerlessness, soap operas further insure against the possibility of women's becoming more self-assertive. The "villainess" often figures largely as a character in Harlequins and Gothics too, but I postpone a full discussion of her character until the last chapter because the emotional energy the audience invests in it appears to be most extreme in soap operas. This emotion cannot be defined as one of simple loathing, however; it consists of a complex mixture of anger, envy, and sneaking admiration.

Current film theory, even feminist film theory, assumes that the addressee of narrative film is necessarily male; indeed, this is the explicit point of Laura Mulvey's extremely influential essay, "Visual Pleasure and Narrative Cinema," in which she argues that the spectacle and the story work together in order to stimulate masculine pleasure and alleviate basic masculine psychological insecurities. But soap operas are one visual, narrative art uniquely adapted to the psychology of the woman in the home. As we shall see, it can even be said that soap operas train women to become, like women in the home, "ideal readers"—not of texts but of people. The necessity of "reading" people, especially men, is tacitly acknowledged in the other two types of narratives as well. In both Harlequins and Gothics, the heroines engage in a continual deciphering of the motives for the hero's behavior. The Harlequin heroine probes for the secret underlying the masculine enigma, while the reader outwits the heroine in coming up with the "correct" interpretation of the puzzling actions and attitudes of the man. In Gothics the heroine, in the classic

paranoid manner, broods over the slightest fluctuation in the hero's emotional temperature or facial expression, quick to detect in these alterations possible threats to her very life. Carolyn Heilbrun remarks that in popular literature, in the literary classroom, and in life, women have always had to "read" men, and she notes with irony that the only time men "read" women is "in the world of commerce," where "publishers have spent fortunes analyzing what women want, trying to discover those elements in a romance necessary to move the books fast off the shelf of the supermarket." She concludes "that women may be 'read,' their responses deciphered, only if the process reinforces woman's role as consumer, consoler, conquest."[51] It is time to begin a feminist reading of women's reading, for it is possible that even those men whose livelihood depends on deciphering women's responses have remained largely ignorant of the "evils" lurking behind the most orthodox plots. The price women pay for their popular entertainment is high, but they may still be getting more than anyone bargained for.

Notes

1. Virginia Woolf, *A Room of One's Own*, p. 77.
2. Joanna Russ, "What Can A Heroine Do? Or Why Women Can't Write."
3. Roland Barthes, *Roland Barthes*, p. 121. Film theory, in particular, seems to have taken this idea most seriously. See, for example, Janet Bergstrom, "Alternation, Segmentation, Hypnosis: Interview with Raymond Bellour," p. 93.
4. Kenneth Burke, *Language as Symbolic Action*, pp. 352–53.
5. Raymond Williams, *Television*, p. 61.
6. The author of *The Example; or the History of Lucy Cleveland*, quoted in J.M.S. Tompkins, *The Popular Novel in England 1770–1800*, p. 117.
7. George Eliot, "Silly Novels By Lady Novelists."
8. For an example of an article expressing extreme hostility, see Ann Douglas, "Soft-porn Culture." Germaine Greer's chapter on "Romance" in *The Female Eunuch*, pp. 167–85, is a good example of the flippant approach. Most of the many newspaper articles describing women's popular literature are also written in this vein.
9. Ann Douglas, *The Feminization of American Culture*, pp. 2–3.
10. Nina Baym, *Women's Fiction*, p. 29.
11. Herbert Ross Brown, *The Sentimental Novel in America 1789–1860*, p. 289.

12. Eliza Vicery, *Emily Hamilton*, quoted in Brown, p. 38.

13. Tompkins, *The Popular Novel in England*, p. 148.

14. Russ, "What Can a Heroine Do?" p. 7.

15. Quoted in Brown, p. 49.

16. Hannah Webster Foster, *The Coquette* (1797) (New York: Columbia Univ. Press, 1939), p. 41.

17. Tompkins, p. 149.

18. Susanna Rowson, *The Fille de Chambre*, quoted in Brown, p. 48.

19. James Hart, *The Popular Book*, p. 64.

20. Elaine Showalter, *A Literature of Their Own*, p. 160.

21. Brown, p. 282.

22. Hart, p. 106.

23. Helen Waite Papashvily, *All the Happy Endings*, p. xvii.

24. Baym, p. 27.

25. Papashvily, p. 171.

26. Elaine Showalter, "Review Essay: Literary Criticism," p. 435.

27. The term "colonized leisure" is Stanley Aronowitz's. See his *False Promises*, pp. 51–133.

28. The phrase is Hans Magnus Enzensberger's. See *The Consciousness Industry*.

29. Max Horkheimer and Theodor W. Adorno, *Dialectic of Enlightenment*, p. 135.

30. An interesting Marxist critique of the Frankfurt School's position is also advanced by Lillian S. Robinson in her chapter "Criticism: Who Needs It?" in *Sex, Class and Culture*, pp. 69–94.

31. For a full explication of the term "standardization" as it was used by the Frankfurt School, see Theodor W. Adorno, "On Popular Music."

32. Fredric Jameson, "Reification and Utopia in Mass Culture," p. 136.

33. Hans Robert Jauss, "Levels of Identification of Hero and Audience," p. 286.

34. Jameson, p. 141.

35. Jameson, p. 146.

36. The phrase is Stuart Ewen's. See his *Captains of Consciousness*.

37. Leo Spitzer, "American Advertising Explained as Popular Art," in his *Essays on English and American Literature*, p. 263.

38. Louis Althusser, "Ideology and Ideological State Apparatuses," in his *Lenin and Philosophy and Other Essays*, pp. 127–86.

39. Helene Deutsche, *The Psychology of Women*, Vol. II, pp. 105, 245.

40. Douglas, "Soft-porn Culture," p. 28.

41. Herbert Marcuse, *Eros and Civilization*, pp. 127–43.

42. See Enzensberger, p. 110.

43. Herbert Marcuse, *Counterrevolution and Revolt*, p. 92.

44. Jameson, p. 144.

45. Juliet Mitchell's is probably the most extended discussion of Freud's revelance to feminism. See her *Psychoanalysis and Feminism*.

46. Sigmund Freud, "The 'Uncanny.' "

47. See "The Dissolution of the Oedipus Complex."

48. Quoted in Brown, p. 25.

49. Josef Breuer and Sigmund Freud, *Studies on Hysteria*, p. 41.

50. Breuer, p. 46.

51. Carolyn Heilbrun, "Hers," p. C2.

3.
POPULAR CULTURE

This Ain't No Sideshow

George Lipsitz

In this great future, you can't forget your past.
—Bob Marley

The late jazz musician Rahsaan Roland Kirk used to preface his performances with an unusual word of advice for the audience. A burly black man who often wore a stovepipe hat with a feather in it, and who frequently carried two saxophones (which he sometimes played simultaneously), Kirk would peer out at the crowd through dark sunglasses and growl, "This ain't no sideshow." Invariably people would laugh at the incongruity of this consummately theatrical individual denying his theatricality. Yet once Kirk began to play, discerning listeners grasped his point.

There was a show going on when Roland Kirk played music, but it was not a sideshow. Nearly everything that Kirk did and said, nearly everything that he played and sang called attention to his role as a black musician in a society controlled by whites. With bitingly satiric renditions of hymns like "The Old Rugged Cross," Kirk related the forms and conventions of popular music to their origins within the historical struggles of the Afro-American past. With mischievous wordplay his song "Blacknuss" called attention to the unequal relationship between the black keys and the white keys on the piano. Kirk's attire and stage behavior subverted conventional expectations about performance, and his aggressive humor exposed the tension between music as a commodity and music as an expression of lived experience.

What distinguished Rahsaan Roland Kirk's "show" from a "sideshow" was history. All his eccentricities called attention to his identity as a historical subject, a descendant of slaves and a victim of white racism, a human being forced to disguise his pain and anger within the outward appearances of a sideshow. In songs like "The Old Rugged Cross" and "Blacknuss," Kirk translated his experiences and aspirations into art, just as his ancestors had done when they fashioned spirituals, blues, and jazz out of the clash between Afro-American values and Euro-American racism. His stage antics played against the expectations of the audience because they revealed a sedimented layer of historical knowledge and historical critique beneath the surface appearance of novelty and performance. Within the commercial context of commodified mass culture, Rahsaan Roland Kirk created a history that could be hummed, a story of the past that relied on sharps and flats instead of on footnotes, and one that testified to the historicity of experience even while avoiding the linearity and teleology generally associated with historical narratives.

The elements of historical inquiry and explanation encapsulated in Rahsaan Roland Kirk's stage performance present both possibilities and problems. They testify to the importance of historical thinking as an organic and necessary way of understanding human experience, a mode of organizing ideas and interpretations that is as indispensable in everyday life as it is in scholarly research. Yet its location within popular culture gives Kirk's "history" an impressionistic, interpretive, and allegorical aspect. His art contained multilayered and heavily coded covert messages about the past, but for a large part of his audience, Kirk's music inevitably appeared as just another novelty and diversion within the seemingly autonomous realms of commercialized leisure.

Kirk's problem is our problem. The powerful apparatuses of contemporary commercial electronic mass communications dominate discourse in the modern world. They supply us with endless diversion and distraction mobilized to direct our minds toward advertising messages. They colonize the most intimate and personal aspects of our lives, seizing upon every possible flaw in our bodies, minds, and psyches to increase our anxieties and augment our appetites for consumer goods. Culture itself comes to us a commodity. The artistry and historical consciousness of a Rahsaan Roland Kirk becomes obscured by our contexts of reception. We buy records and attend concerts, watch films and television commercials as a matter of course. Rarely do we ask about the origins and intentions of the messages we encounter through the mass media; sometimes we forget that artists have origins or intentions at all, so pervasive are the stimuli around us.

Yet mass communications also embody some of our deepest hopes and engage some of our most profound sympathies. People ingeniously enter those discourses to which they have access; the saxophone or the guitar, the stage or the camera can offer precious and unique opportunities for expression. For some populations at some times, commercialized leisure is history—a repository of collective memory that places immediate experience in the context of change over time. The very same media that trivialize and distort culture, that turn art into commodities, and that obscure the origins and intentions of artists also provide meaningful connection to our own pasts and to the pasts of others. But they do so only indirectly, constrained by the nonlinear biases of the electronic media as well as by a commercial matrix hostile to the kinds of empathy, inquiry, and analysis basic to historical thinking.

The presence of sedimented historical currents within popular culture illumines the paradoxical relationship between history and commercialized leisure. Time, history, and memory become qualitatively different concepts in a world where electronic mass communication is possible. Instead of relating to the past through a shared sense of place or ancestry,

consumers of electronic mass media can experience a common heritage with people they have never seen; they can acquire memories of a past to which they have no geographic or biological connection. This capacity of electronic mass communication to transcend time and space creates instability by disconnecting people from past traditions, but it also liberates people by making the past less determinate of experiences in the present

History and commercialized leisure appear to be polar opposites—the former concerned with continuities that unite the totality of human experience, the latter with immediate sense gratifications that divide society into atomized consumers. But both the variants of history and the forms of commercialized leisure familiar to us originated at the same time and for the same reasons. Both developed in the nineteenth century in response to extraordinary technological and social changes. Recognition of the common origins of history and commercialized leisure can explain the seemingly paradoxical tensions within Roland Kirk's music, while also helping to explain how the "remembering" of history and the "forgetting" of commercialized leisure form parts of a dialectical totality.

Commercialized Leisure and the Crisis of History

As literary critic Richard Terdiman has demonstrated, nineteenth-century industrialization and state-building entailed a massive disruption of traditional forms of memory. The instrumental mentality capable of building the political and industrial machines of that century had to countenance the destruction of tradition—the enclosure of farm lands, massive migrations to industrial cities, the construction of an interchangeable work force, and a consumer market free from the constraints of tradition. A sense of disconnection from the past united an otherwise fragmented and stratified polity, and consequently the study of the past took on new meaning. Terdiman notes that "history became the discipline of memory," whose task was to uncover "the crisis which inevitably entailed disconnection with the past as a referent."[1] Michelet, Dilthey, Bancroft, and the other great historians of the nineteenth century emerged to provide a sense of continuity and connection with the past in societies riddled with the ruptures and dislocations of modernity.

The beginnings of the electronic mass media in the form of the telegraph exacerbated the nineteenth-century crisis of memory. The telegraph enabled simultaneous communication for the first time, dissolving previous barriers of time and space. But that very simultaneity favored the agenda of ascendant industrial capitalism. The telegraph innately privileged the transmission of isolated facts like prices or recent events; it did little to convey context or continuity. Newspapers took on a new role with the stimulus of the telegraph, but it was a role geared toward commerce and change rather than to the preservation of cultural memory. The daily newspaper naturalized a kind of confusion in which the world seemed structured by isolated and discrete events; news became synonymous with change and more important than tradition.

A new kind of commercialized leisure emerged as a corollary to the telegraph in the United States during the late nineteenth century. Previously, churches, lodge halls, and community centers had served as sites for theatrical productions designed to mark festive occasions like weddings and holidays. But urban taverns, dance halls, amusement parks, and theaters brought new meanings to culture. The new, commercial theaters, and later variety, vaudeville, and motion-picture halls, needed no special occasions and no association with ritualized activities to justify plays, skits, and music They carved away a new kind of social space for working-class people—buildings devoted exclusively to leisure activities. Theatrical performances became commodities sold to strangers for an agreed-upon price rather than collective creations by communities enacting rituals essential to group identity and solidarity.[2]

Of course, commercialized theater had existed since the sixteenth century in Europe. Jean-Christophe Agnew, among others, has delineated the complicated connections between the assumptions of theater and the values central to the capitalist marketplace, but in nineteenth-century America, theater, medicine shows, circuses, taverns, dance halls, amusement parks, and vaudeville-variety houses intervened in culture and society in especially important ways. They helped Americans make a decisive break with

Victorian restraints, while at the same time blending an ethnically diverse working class into an "audience" with a unified language and sign-system.

The success of popular theater in nineteenth-century America aggravated the crisis of historical memory by further detaching culture from tradition. It institutionalized a kind of dissembling, one feared by philosophers as far back as Plato. To speak someone else's words or to wear someone else's clothes meant hiding one's own identity. In a world where ancestry, locality, and vocation determined social status and identity, the inherent disguise of acting threatened core values. Role playing in the theater suggested that identities could be changed, that one was not bound by bloodlines, nationality, or occupation. This contained the essence of egalitarian and utopian thought by challenging the legitimacy of static identities inherited from the past, but it also threatened a sense of authentic self-knowledge and created the psychic preconditions for the needy narcissism of consumer desire. On stage, actors deliberately speak and act inauthentically, off stage everyone learns to act, because everyone needs to take on ever-changing roles as a consumer and worker. As literary scholar Michael Bristol points out about the cultural crises posed by theater in Elizabethan England, "An actor is not just someone whose speech is 'dissembling'; the deeper problem is that he is most valued for his ability to dissemble convincingly."[3] As commercialized theaters in nineteenth-century America helped destroy connections to the past, historical tableaux and dramas became common features within them, offering a fictive representation of what was being destroyed in reality. Thus the contents of theatrical productions sometimes ministered to the very wounds that their forms had helped to open.

Along with the telegraph and the daily newspaper, the theater helped reshape cultural memory and consciousness. Its role on behalf of the emergent industrial order helped mold a diverse population into a unified working and consuming force, but it also raised anxieties about the moral costs of disconnection from the past. To many critics, the "dissembling" of theater presented a challenge to established order and morality. These critics feared that nothing genuine or refined could come from a sphere of activity devoted to false representations and masked identities. Furthermore, they recognized that theatrical "time" presented an alternative to work time, pitting the pleasures of lei-sure against the responsibilities of labor. Theater attendance enabled individuals to play out fictive sce-narios of changed identities, to escape from the sur-veillance and supervision of moral authorities and institutions. The fantasy world of the theatrical stage encouraged audiences to pursue personal desires and passions at the expense of their socially prescribed responsibilities.

Yet audiences embraced the new possibilities pre-sented by commercial theater with enthusiasm. Unlike the wedding celebration or the community fes-tival, the theater assembled an audience with no shared history, with no reciprocal responsibilities and obligations. Theatergoers in nineteenth-century America shared intimate and personal cultural moments with strangers. The unfamiliarity of the crowd with each other provided a kind of protective cover—a "privacy in public" whereby personal feel-ings and emotions could be aired without explanation or apology.[4] Women especially utilized the new popu-lar culture as a way of escaping parental surveillance and patriarchal domination.[5] Using the borrowed legitimacy of theater's status as a form of cultural refinement, audiences flocked to the melodramas, vaudeville and variety shows, and later to motion pic-tures for decidedly unrefined productions and perfor-mances. In the theater, they encountered a world momentarily liberated from the sexual and emotional repressions of the nineteenth century. Theatrical per-formances provided an outlet for expression of the needs and desires for pleasure long suppressed by the normative constraints of Victorian America.[6]

The sexual repressions of the Victorian era cre-ated powerful anxieties and tensions that could not be confronted directly by "respectable" citizens. But the-ater productions offered audiences an opportunity to view the forbidden and to contemplate the unthink-able. This "freedom" came less in the form of true sexual emancipation, however, than through a re-direction of frustrations. The unfilled desires and unconsummated lusts of theater audiences made them good customers for sexually suggestive images, no matter how coded, coy, or indirect The theater offered immediate but transitory gratification. It turned sexual impulses and desires into symbolic commodities to be purchased from others. One

bought a theater ticket to see a performance that depicted happiness and pleasures missing from one's own life. Pleasure itself could not be purchased as a commodity—at least not legally—but the image of pleasure represented in the theater could be obtained for a small price. Similarly, theatrical productions evoked other desires—for intimacy, for recognition, for connection to the past. But the very forms of commercial theater aggravated rather than salved me wounds they pretended to heal.

Yet the theater did encompass a kind of free space for the imagination—an arena liberated from old restraints and repressions, a place where desire did not have to be justified or explained. By establish-ing commodity purchases as symbolic answers to real problems, the theater also helped lay the groundwork for the consumer-commodity culture of our own day wherein advertisers and entrepreneurs offer products that promise to bring pleasure and fulfillment. The nineteenth-century theater may have emerged in part as a rebellion against sexual repression, but its great-est long-term significance lay in shaping the psychic and material preconditions for Americans to shift from a Victorian industrial economy to a hedonistic consumer-commodity economy. It would not be the last time that the commercial matrix in which popular culture was embedded worked to undermine its potential for educational or social transcendence.

Melodramas, vaudeville and variety shows, and motion pictures taught Americans to make a break with the discipline, sobriety, thrift, and sexual repres-sion that formed the core of Victorian culture. Appropriate to an industrializing economy, Victorian values provided necessary preconditions for economic growth during the nineteenth century. They stressed the work ethic, personal responsibility, punctuality, and willingness to defer gratification necessary for life as an industrial worker. But by the 1890s, it appeared that Victorian culture had done its work all too well. The hard-working Americans who internalized Victorian values helped build a powerful industrial economy that produced more products than the domestic market could consume. Overproduction and underconsump-tion threatened the very survival of industrial capital-ism in the 1880s and 1890s, as business failures led to massive unemployment and repeated financial panics. The "false promise" of the Victorian code, that sober self-management would lead to upward mobility, helped provoke general strikes and other forms of "aggressive festivity" among workers. To solve their many problems, business leaders had to move away from the production of capital goods like railroads and locomotives and start producing consumer goods for the domestic market. But as long as Victorian repressions inhibited desires for immediate gratification, consumers lacked the psychological makeup necessary for an economy oriented around ever-increasing purchases of commodities by individuals.

Commercialized leisure evolved out of the contradictions in late nineteenth-century capitalism. As I. C. Jarvie notes, motion pictures not only served as renewable commodities in themselves, but they also helped legitimate the consciousness necessary for purchasing other renewable commodities. The specialization of industrial capitalism requires individuals "detachable from tradition, family, and ascription." Jarvie argues that motion pictures encouraged people to see themselves as detached and autonomous consumers by replacing ritualistic community celebrations with leisure that could be purchased as a commodity and shared with strangers.[7] Between 1890 and 1930 American society underwent extraordinary changes, from a Victorian culture of thrift to a consumer-oriented culture of spending. By the 1920s, production of renewable commodities like automobiles and appliances played a more important role in the U.S. economy than production of nonrenewable capital goods like heavy equipment and machinery. Economic historians have long understood the logic of this change for the interests of capital; building factories and locomotive engines brought enormous immediate profits, but the market for them became saturated rather quickly. Consumer goods did not need to last—indeed advertisers worked very diligently to see to it that considerations of fashion and style would render old goods obsolete and engender a demand for new ones.

Scholars examining the transition from Victorianism to consumerism in the U.S. have concentrated on the idea of leisure as contested terrain. Drawing upon the research of E. P. Thompson and Herbert Gutman, they have emphasized the ways in which the transition from agrarian to industrial life gave new meanings to work and play. In pre-industrial

society, agrarian labor could be done at one's own pace and for one's own benefit. In the industrial workplace, factory time replaced natural time, and unremitting labor measured by the time-clock replaced the task-oriented work of the farm. No longer could leisure be mixed in with work, and work itself became a more prominent and a more alienating part of human existence. Just as the centralized industrial work site replaced home labor, so commercial establishments devoted to leisure-time pursuits replicated in the arena of play the capitalist division of labor. Intense resistance against these practices fueled strikes, sabotage, and other forms of working-class self-activity throughout the era of industrialization, but religious, medical, and legal authorities attempted to prevent revolt by inculcating Victorian values within the character structure of the work force, values championing repression, denial, thrift, chastity, sobriety, and hard work. But like most forms of ideological legitimation, they contained severe internal contradictions. When workers *internalized* Victorian norms, their labor produced a surplus of goods that could not be consumed by a domestic market filled with poorly paid thrifty self-denying individuals like themselves. When workers *resisted* Victorian norms, their repressions and anger drove them toward the only available source of pleasure—the illicit vices offered for sale by the underworld.

Thus commercialized leisure both facilitated the triumphs of industrial capitalism and focused attention on their psychic and emotional costs. Commercial culture sought credibility with its audiences by promising at least the illusion of connection with the past. But the gap between lived experience and the false promises of popular culture always created the possibility for counter-memories, for ethnic, class, and regional music, art, speech, and theater. Culture itself contributed to retraining and reshaping the masses to serve the interests of capital, but also to articulating unfilled desires and expressing disconnection from the past. British cultural studies theorist Stuart Hall notes the contradictions in this process as well as the centrality of tradition as a contested category in the nineteenth century,

Capital had a stake in the culture of the popular classes because the constitution of a whole new social order around capital required a more or less continuous, if intermittent, process of re-education. And one of the principal sites of resistance to the forms through which this 'reformation' of the people was pursued lay in popular tradition. That is why popular culture is linked, for so long, to questions of tradition, of traditional forms of life—and why its 'traditionalism' has been so often misinterpreted as a product of a merely conservative impulse, backward looking and anachronistic.[8]

The transformations in behavior and collective memory fueled by the contradictions of the nineteenth century have passed through three major stages in the United States. The first involved the establishment and codification of commercialized leisure from the invention of the telegraph to the 1890s. The second involved the transition from Victorian to consumer-hedonist values between 1890 and 1945. The third and most important stage, from World War II to the present, involved extraordinary expansion in both the distribution of consumer purchasing power and in the reach and scope of the electronic mass media. The dislocations of urban renewal, suburbanization, and deindustrialization accelerated the demise of tradition in America, while the worldwide pace of change undermined stability elsewhere. The period from World War II to the present marks the final triumph of commercialized leisure, and with it an augmented crisis over the loss of connection to the past. Popular culture has played an important role in creating this crisis of memory, but it has also been one of the main vehicles for the expression of loss and the projection of hopes for reconnection to the past.

What Is Popular Culture?

As historian Ramon Gutierrez observes, the term "popular culture" is a description crafted exclusively from the outside. The creators of popular culture do not think of themselves as operating within an endeavor called "popular culture"; they see themselves merely creating signs and symbols appropriate to their audiences and to themselves. It is only from the vantage point of Enlightenment ideals of "high culture" that something called popular culture can be

seen to exist. In recent years, scholars have increasingly challenged the divisions between "high" and popular culture, and rightly so. Yet it is also clear that what we call popular culture differs markedly in its aims and intentions from the Enlightenment culture of "beauty and truth" idealized in the nineteenth century by Matthew Arnold, as well as from the isolated "folk" cultures studied by anthropologists and folklorists. In general, we have a better idea of what commercial culture *is not* (high art and folklore) than what it is. But we can identify some aspects of commercialized leisure that have come to define its conditions of possibility.[9]

Popular culture has no fixed forms: the historical circumstances of reception and appropriation determine whether novels or motion pictures or videos belong to a sphere called popular culture. Similarly, individual artifacts of popular culture have no fixed meanings: it is impossible to say whether any one combination of sounds or set of images or grouping of words innately expresses one unified political position. Images and icons compete for dominance within a multiplicity of discourses; consumers of popular culture move in and out of subject positions in a way that allows the same message to have widely varying meanings at the point of reception. Although cultural products generally reflect the dominant ideology of any given period, no cultural moment exists within a hermetically sealed cultural present; all cultural expressions speak to both residual memories of the past and emergent hopes for the future.

Rather than looking for innately emancipatory or hegemonic forms and meanings within popular culture, we would do better to study its "transformations," which Stuart Hall defines as

"the active work on existing traditions and activities, their active reworking so that they come out a different way: they appear to 'persist'—yet, from one period to another, they come to stand in a different relation to the ways working people live and the ways they define their relations to each other, to 'the others' and to the conditions of life."[10]

In the United States since World War II, these transformations have coalesced around identifiable conditions of possibility. These conditions are not an "aesthetic," or a finite set of rules guiding artistic production and reception; they are not inherently "progressive" practices guaranteed to advance struggles against exploitation and hierarchy wherever they appear; they are not pure, authentic, or transcendent by themselves. They are historically specific elements within commercial culture that allow for the expression of collective popular memory and the reworking of tradition. Participation and investment, carnival, and a struggle for hegemony have provided significant conditions of possibility within American commercial culture since World War II. At times, all of these have created frames of reception consistent with dominant ideology, but they have also worked to hone and sharpen collective popular memory.

Sociologist Pierre Bourdieu's categories of participation and investment accurately characterize audience expectations from American popular culture since World War II.[11] Unlike "high culture" where a dogmatic formalism privileges abstraction over experience, the effectiveness of popular culture depends on its ability to engage audiences in active and familiar processes. Tania Modleski has demonstrated how television soap operas and game shows win credibility with viewers by turning into play the everyday work of nurturing families and making purchases, much as rodeo events or car customizing do for cowboys and mechanics.[12] Fredric Jameson describes popular songs as copies for which there exist no originals, texts whose popularity depends less on innovation or imagination than upon a sense of familiarity conducive to immediate audience appropriation.[13]

Traditions of participation and investment, combined with the internal biases of electronic mass media, tend to privilege forms of communication emanating from aggrieved and marginal communities. Sociolinguists Basil Bernstein, Leonard Schatzman, and Anselm Strauss have identified empathy, immediacy, and emotion as core components of working-class speech, and they have demonstrated how working-class speakers subordinate linear, individualistic, and analytic ways of speaking to stress nonlinear effects and collective emotions.[14] Rhetorician Kathleen Hall Jamieson points out that television favors a style of speaking that historically has been associated with women—an unself-conscious sense of self-disclosure about one's private self and an ability to integrate others into one's discussions—and that, conversely, the medium works against speech styles traditionally associated with men, which favor projection of the self against the environment.[15] The ever changing meanings and deliberate indeterminacies of subcultural slang undercut the authority of the word, replacing it with an appreciation of the inevitable metaphoricity of language. Such usage entails a break with the logocentric world of the Enlightenment in which univocal utterances and precise descriptions serve to fix final meanings and identities; at the same time it foregrounds a sense of language so new that it resembles postmodern poetry and so old that it echoes the ancient Nahaud poet who insisted that "no one among us truly and finally speaks here."[16]

Melodrama presents a particularly significant form of participation and investment within American commercial culture since World War II. Melodrama emerged out of the same nineteenth-century dislocations responsible for the problem of historical memory and the rise of popular culture itself. It emerged as an expression of the inadequacies of Enlightenment language and art, displacing conventional narratives and reasoned discourse with broad physical gestures, tableaux, simple binary oppositions between good and evil, and plots resolved more by fate and sudden reverses than by human action. A precursor to film noir, the gothic romance, and the television night-time serial, melodrama established important subtexts within American popular culture. Television critic Jane Feuer points out that melodrama's unsatisfying endings resist the unproblematic closures of dominant narratives, while cinema scholar Laura Mulvey demonstrates how melodrama contains a critique of the cinematic apparatus itself by subjecting its protagonists to "the curious and prurient gaze of intrusive community, neighbors, friends, and family so that the spectator's own look becomes self-conscious and awkward."[17]

Carnival traditions have provided another important frame of reception for American popular culture since World War II. Bourdieu speaks of popular forms that "satisfy the taste for and sense of revelry, the free speaking and hearty laughter which liberate by setting the social world head over heels, overturning conventions and proprieties."[18] Literary critic Mikhail Bakhtin identifies these sensibilities as the essence of carnival—ritualized celebrations oriented around the passions of plenitude, inversions of the social order, and mocking laughter designed to "uncrown power." The dangerous "dissembling" that so troubled nineteenth-century opponents of popular theater, the anarchic anti-authoritarianism of the Marx Brothers, and the sense of entitlement to the good life enshrined in popular music and television all build upon the oppositional possibilities of carnival. Practices within popular culture like constituting the body as a site for decoration and style, valorizing the street as a locus of sociality and creativity, and inverting dominant icons to affirm a prestige from below also resonate with the legacy of carnival.[19] For Bakhtin, retentions of carnival laughter and display evidence a "materials memory," by which words themselves contain ideological traces from the past that take on renewed significance when they are appropriated in the present.[20]

Like participation and investment, carnival privileges certain social dispositions, but it has no intrinsic political meaning. Only in the context of a struggle for hegemony can the latent possibilities of collective memory be activated. The idea of "a struggle for hegemony" originates with the Italian Marxist Antonio Gramsci, who maintains that elites rule not merely by force but by "managed consent" as well, that they form "historical blocs" with other groups that make existing power relations appear natural and just. Some scholars emphasize the ways in which Gramsci's formulations explain how elites impose their will on society and turn potential rebels into unwitting accomplices in their own victimization. But hegemony is not just imposed on society from the top; it is struggled for from below, and no terrain is a more important part of that struggle than popular culture.

Cultural forms create conditions of possibility, they expand the present by informing it with memories of the past and hopes for the future; but they also engender accommodation with prevailing power realities, separating art from life, and internalizing the dominant culture's norms and values as necessary and inevitable. Politics and culture maintain a paradoxical relationship in which only effective political action can win breathing room for a new culture, but only a revolution in culture can make people capable of political action. Culture can seem like a substitute for politics, a way of posing only imaginary solutions to real problems, but under other circumstances culture can

become a rehearsal for politics, trying out values and beliefs permissible in art but forbidden in social life. Most often, however, culture exists as a form of politics, as a means of reshaping individual and collective practice for specified interests, and as long as individuals perceive their interests as unfilled, culture retains an oppositional potential. Fredric Jameson argues that the dominant culture can only presume to ease anxieties like disconnection from the past by calling attention to them in the first place, thereby running the risk of re-opening the very ruptures it seeks to close.[21] For Jameson, the best cultural creations present contemporary social contradictions in such a way as to suggest eventual resolutions of them, but even works that fall short of that goal retain the potential to play a role in the struggle for hegemony.[22]

The complicated relationship between historical memory and commercial culture, between the texts of popular culture and their contexts of creation and reception, resist conventional forms of cultural criticism. The coded, indirect, and allegorical aspects of popular culture, its inversions of speech and ideology, and its refusal to isolate art from lived experience (a source of corruption as well as social connection) baffle and frustrate critics trained in traditional Western aesthetics and criticism. Neil Postman indicts television as a force debasing public discourse in America because its claims are made with images rather than language. For Postman, the eclipse of language renders empirical tests and logical analysis "impotent."[23]

In a similar vein, Allan Bloom assures us that rock and roll music's entire meaning rests in its rhythm (as if there were only one), which he confidently explains is the "rhythm of sexual intercourse" (as if here, too, there were only one).[24] The equally uninformed Robert Pattison contends that rock music represents the "triumph of vulgarity," through mindless celebration of a debased primitivism. The nadir of Pattison's slipshod argument comes in his dismissal of the Silhouettes' 1958 hit record "Get a Job" as solipsism rejoicing "in the conclusion that language is meaningless." In actuality, the record became a hit during the recession of 1958, and the song's lyrics described the anxieties of looking for work when there are no jobs available. The scat singing of "nonsense" syllables that leads Pattison to see the song as meaningless plays upon well understood conventions within black music of imitating musical instruments with the human voice, a tactic that Louis Armstrong (to use just one example) employed brilliantly to punctuate some of the lyrics in his songs. In fact, Afro-American poets and writers including Bob Kaufman and Ishmael Reed have long drawn on the creative wordplay of scat singing as a vital source for their poetry and prose.[25] Like the anthropologist some years back who decided that the *penitente* cults of New Mexico were "mired in webs of iconographic confusion" because their iconography made no sense to her, Pattison assumes that "Get a Job" has no meaning because it is not expressed in language that he understands. But like the many other errors of fact and interpretation in Pattison's and Bloom's criticisms, these are beside the point because they stem from a larger conceptual error. Like Postman, Pattison and Bloom are so eager to tell us what popular culture does *not* do (advance me agenda of the Enlightenment) that they fail to tell us what popular culture actually *does* or how it is shaped by the economic and social matrix in which it is embedded.

Television provides an important test case for critics of popular culture. As David Marc quips, the number of people who condemn television are exceeded only by the number of people who watch it, but it is difficult to understand or evaluate television's popularity from most of the critical literature about the medium. This is not to call for uncritical approval of everything or anything within popular culture; it is merely to say that questions of connoisseurship and aesthetics need to follow rather than precede an understanding of how the medium does its work within larger social contexts. Even if we could safely dismiss every program on television as artistically worthless, we would still need to understand the ways in which television presents the illusion of intimacy, how it intervenes in family relations, how it serves the consumer economy, and how its hold on the viewing audience relates to the disintegration of public resources, the aggravations of work, and the fragility of interpersonal relations that characterize our lives. Furthermore, to function as a mechanism of escape, television and other forms of popular culture often recuperate the very history that their content appears to erase. Certainly the reach and content of commercial television provide ample grounds for criticism. Television is both an advertising mechanism and the primary discursive medium of our culture; it irreparably inscribes consumer desire and commercialism into the fabric of entertainment, news, and sports. Television colonizes intimate areas of human sexuality and personality, exacerbating anxieties and fears to sell more products. Its penetration into the home helps order domestic space, leisure time, and family identity, while its seemingly endless flow reduces complex ideas and images to a melange of distraction and trivilization. By addressing viewers as atomized consumers, the medium obscures experiences of race, region, class, and gender. By turning politics into entertainment, television transforms citizens into spectators and turns politicians into performers. Television critic Arthur Kroker may be unique in describing Ronald Reagan's State of the Union addresses as more like "Presidential holograms," than political speeches, but Kroker is hardly alone in noticing the ways in which artistic "representation" defined as the depiction of images has superseded political "representation" defined in relation to the distribution of power and resources.

Yet responding to television's popularity with blanket condemnation of its content misses the point; questions of connoisseurship focus too much on how television fails to meet critical expectations at the expense of understanding how television succeeds at intervening in the everyday life of the society it addresses. Like many popular music critics, television's detractors condemn the medium because they feel it debases an otherwise successfully functioning society. Without discounting the shallow vulgarity of the medium, it is important to note that television also reflects an already ongoing unraveling of social relations in society; its needy narcissism serves as a salve for the wounds of everyday life.

Guided by emotion and empathy, working through ritual and repetition, television's core vocabulary reflects its role as a therapeutic voice ministering to the open wounds of the psyche. As a "close-up" medium whose dramatic and social locus is the home, television addresses the inner life by minimizing the heroic while maximizing the private and personal aspects of existence. Where motion pictures favor the panoramic shot, television privileges the zoom shot, looking *in* rather than out. To represent conversation, film directors use the "shot-counter-shot" effect while television directors employ the tightly constructed "two faces east." Thus motion-picture conversation emphasizes the separations between people, while television depicts people as closely linked to one another. This vocabulary of television lends itself to certain kinds of representation—the empathetic nurturing of others that viewers feel while watching a soap opera or a game show, the nonlinear quick cuts and distractions of action/adventure and comedy programs, and the situation comedy's fixation on stars mugging for the camera which stresses individual moments rather than teleological closure. These all focus attention inward and undermine the psychic prerequisites for a public life, but they also reflect a society already turned inward by the rise of consumerism and the demise of a healthy public life.

For all of their triviality and frivolity, the messages of popular culture circulate in a network of production and reception that is quite serious. At their worst, they perform the dirty work of the economy and the state. At their best, they retain memories of the past and contain hopes for the future that rebuke the injustices and inequities of the present. It might be thought a measure of the inescapable irony of our time that the most profound intellectual questions emerge out of what seem to be ordinary and commonplace objects of study. It may well be that such a paradox exposes the decline of intellectual work and the eclipse of historical reason. But there is another possibility. Perhaps the most important facts about people and about societies have always been encoded within the ordinary and the commonplace. Rahsaan Roland Kirk had an eminently serious agenda, but little access to the arenas in which "serious" decisions about power and resources are contested. However, every time he picked up the saxophone (or saxophones), he made a statement about the past, present, and future. By examining the relationship between collective popular memory and commercial culture, we may be on the threshhold of a new kind of knowledge, one sensitive to contestations over meaning and capable of teaching us that a sideshow can sometimes be the main event.

Notes

1. Richard Terdiman, "Deconstructing Memory: On Representing the Past and Theorizing Culture in France Since the Revolution," *Diacritics* (Winter), 1985, 14, 19.

2. I am indebted to Bruce Lincoln for pointing out to me that itinerant actors, lecturers, medicine salesmen, and circus performers lacked direct ties of kinship, propinquity, business, or history with their audiences, thus gaining special privileges to perform, but losing certain protections from the consequences of their performances.

3. Michael Bristol, *Carnival and Theater* (New York: Methuen, 1985), 113.

4. For a discussion of the concept of "privacy in public" see John F. Kasson's social history of Coney Island, *Amusing the Million* (New York: Hill and Wang, 1978).

5. See Kathy Peiss, *Cheap Amusements* (Philadelphia: Temple University Press, 1986).

6. Of course, temporary liberation from sexual repression often mandated a re-problematization of sexuality as well in, for example, the melodrama.

7. I. C. Jarvie, *Thinking about Society: Theory and Practice* (Norwell, MA: Kluwer Academic Press, 1986), 372.

8. Stuart Hall, "Notes on Deconstructing 'the Popular,'" in Raphael Samuel, ed., *People's History and Socialist Theory* (London: Routledge and Kegan Paul, 1981), 227.

9. Here I wish to avoid the debates about "popular" vs. "mass" culture, in which popular describes voluntary bottom-up creation and mass refers to top-down, massmarketed commercial culture. These polarities obscure the important grass-roots creation that takes place within "mass culture," as well as the manipulated "mass" aspects of "popular culture."

10. Stuart Hall, "Notes on Deconstructing 'the Popular,'" 228.

11. Pierre Bourdieu, "The Aristocracy of Culture," *Media, Culture, and Society* n. 2 (1980), 237.

12. Tania Modleski, "The Rhythms of Reception: Daytime Television and Women's Work," in E. Ann Kaplan, ed., *Regarding Television* (Los Angeles: University Publications of America, 1983), 67–75.

13. Fredric Jameson, "Reification and Utopia in Mass Culture," *Social Text* v. 1, 1979.

14. See George Lipsitz, *Class and Culture in Cold War America: A Rainbow at Midnight* (South Hadley, MA: Bergin and Garvey, 1982), 187–88.

15. Kathleen Hall Jamieson, *Eloquence in an Electronic Age* (New York: Oxford University Press, 1988), 81.

16. Quoted by Willard Gingerich, "Heidegger and the Aztecs: The Poetics of Knowing in Pre-Hispanic Nahuatl Poetry," in Brian Swann and Arnold Krupat, *Recovering the Word* (Berkeley: University of California Press, 1987), 100–101.

17. Jane Feuer, "Narrative Form in American Network Television," in Colin McCabe, ed., *High Theory/Low Culture* (New York: St. Martin's, 1986), 112. Laura Mulvey, "Melodrama in and out of the Home," in Colin McCabe, ed., *High Theory/Low Culture*, 96.

18. Pierre Bourdieu, "The Aristocracy of Culture," 239.

19. Stuart Hall, "The Economy of Prestige," Minneapolis, Minnesota, April 9, 1988, author's notes,

20. See Richard Terdiman, "Deconstructing Memory."

21. Fredric Jameson, "Reification and Utopia in Mass Culture."

22. See Hayden White, *The Content of the Form* (Baltimore and London: Johns Hopkins University Press, 1987), 157.

23. Neil Postman, *Amusing Ourselves to Death* (New York: Penguin, 1985), 127.

24. Allan Bloom, *The Closing of the American Mind* (New York: Simon and Schuster, 1987).

25. Maria Damon, " 'Unmeaning Jargon'/Uncanonized Beatitude: Bob Kaufman, Poet," *The South Atlantic Quarterly* 87:4 (Fall) 1988, 708–9.

4.
EYES WIDE SHUT

Capitalism, Class, and the Promise of Black Media

Beretta Smith-Shomade

Capitalism—the system of pimps and hoes
I'm sorry that's the way it goes
In this particular system everyone's a slave
Racist is how they want us to behave
White Johnny be fighting black Michael
Both are blind to the system's sick cycle
In a circle psychotically they slay each other
With a grin because of color of a skin
Pick up that money hoe!
　　　　—"Who Are the Pimps?" Boogie Down
　　　　　　　　　　　　　Productions (1992)

Why talk about capitalism in a book ostensibly about Black Entertainment Television? One of the foundational conundrums raised in this book is the work and understanding of capitalism by and for African-Americans. The capitalist system undergirds all media, image making, and ideas of prosperity in the U.S., and BET, in many ways, represents the quintessential example of black television success. Yet for African-Americans, both the implementation and articulation of capitalism has posed the greatest divisions and hardships. Thus, it is necessary to begin with a discussion of capitalism as an increasingly global system and one in which the commodification of African-American blackness makes it available to all.

　The intellectual father of capitalism, economist Adam Smith, theorized the nature of capital and its variant uses in his 1776 tome *An Inquiry into the Nature and Causes of the Wealth of Nations*. The modern textbook *The Capitalist System* gives flesh to his theoretical framework. In this work, economic scholars Richard C. Edwards, Michael Reich, and Thomas E. Weisskopf defined capitalism and its operation this way:

> Capitalist relations of production are characterized by the complete separation of the producers (wage-workers) from the means of production. Capitalists as a class have a monopoly on the means of production while workers have only their labor-power, which they must sell to the capitalists for a wage if they are to subsist . . . *In respect to control of the work process and ownership of the means of production, capitalism resembles slavery* and differs from feudalism and petty commodity production. The objective of the capitalists is to expand their initial capital by combining labor and means of production and selling the resultant commodities, which are their property, for a profit. *Hence, capitalist production is for exchange, not for use* (Edwards et al.: 41).[1]

Phrased in a more contemporary vernacular, sociologist James Fulcher wrote that capitalism "involves the investment of money to make more money . . . [It] depends on the exploitation of wage labour, which also fuels the consumption of the goods and services produced by capitalist enterprises" (Fulcher: 18). Beyond strict definitions, different types of capitalism enjoy ideological currency and influence the way citizens process the system.

For example, the pro-capitalist writings of philosopher Ayn Rand linked capitalism to free markets, individual rights, and most especially, liberty. Her work claimed capitalism as a progressive, ethical, and objective ideal because it allows "men" the freedom to pursue their own happiness and be moral. Natural capitalism is a system based on strategies that help "enable countries, companies, and communities to operate by behaving as if all forms of capital were valuable" (www.smartcommunities.ncat.org). The offshoot crony capitalism poses the idea of business success as heavily dependent on friendships and family rather than on market forces and open competition. When asking my focus groups of young people (junior high schoolers through collegiate) for their definition of capitalism, responses ranged from "trying to get money as profit" to "supply and demand" to "I dunno." It seems their definitions, when they could articulate them, hinged strictly on the ability to acquire capital—and spend it excessively at will.

All of these definitions—academic and everyday—treat profit, exploitation, and satisfaction as mutually exclusive entities, thereby ignoring the invisible hand of economics that links them together. Thinking through these viable, (though certainly not all-inclusive), definitions of capitalism and applying them to daily living experiences in the U.S. allows for a fuller appreciation of Boogie Down's employment of the pimps-and-hoes metaphor in this chapter's epigraph, especially insofar as it concerns American capitalism and its adherents. The lyrics are an especially apt observation with regard to African-Americans and their introduction to the capitalistic means of production. Most African-Americans' preamble to America's capital system is as manual laborers and as property. While definitions of capitalism are extensive and continually expanding, this book uses the definition that situates capitalism as a system that privileges and demands accumulation of capital (money) for the sake of the individual. For the media industry, it rewards producers, creates and requires consumers, and mandates the existence of poor folks in order to operate successfully. As this chapter will show, this definition works well in connecting the bling, banter, and Black Star Power of BET. However, it is first necessary to work through the ways capitalism has evolved with and resonated in the lives of African-Americans.

Capitalism Manifest

From approximately 1550 to 1850, the Atlantic slave trade existed as one of the most lucrative and successful business ventures in world history. Many scholars who study the founding of the U.S. agree that the presence and work of enslaved Africans "made the flowering of capitalism possible . . ." (Frazier: 15). One of the earliest ways that capitalism circulated was through the missionary impulse. England, Spain, and Portugal (later the Dutch, Arabs, and French) all sent traders and Christian and Islamic missionaries to the African continent—to do business and to proselytize about the wonders of Jesus and Muhammad. Thus alongside their admonition of these deities they introduced the practices of monopoly capitalism—first looking at the continent as a treasure of raw materials, later as a market.[2] Slavery and later the mantra of Manifest Destiny allowed the U.S. to establish a solid economic foundation by exploiting free labor, usurping occupied lands, and murdering its prior inhabitants, aka the natives who didn't work out as laborers. Furthermore, as business scholar Juliet E.K. Walker so persuasively argued, the U.S. government partnered with business to create success—in direct contradiction to the principles of laissez-faire (Walker 1998: xix).

The slave trade's commercial imperatives made the Negro an "article of commerce" or an "animate tool."[3] Enslaved Africans, who later became Americans, were actively involved in the slave trade. However, for the most part, they failed to benefit from its profits or have any say in the direction of slavery as a business. The enterprise operated alongside the developing mythology that defined the American Dream as democracy, freedom, and capitalism. The flourishing practice of enslaving Africans and ideologies of the American Dream shaped capitalism's growth and dictated how African-Americans interpreted their place and participation in this system—an interpretation that called for blacks to engage in said system wholeheartedly, despite the seeming contradiction of this move given their history with capitalism.

As president of the Freedmen's Savings Bank (1874), Frederick Douglass suggested:

[t]he history of civilization shows that no people can well rise to a high degree of mental or even

moral excellence without wealth. A people uniformly poor and compelled to struggle for barely a physical existence will be dependent and despised by their neighbors and will finally despise themselves. While it is impossible that every individual of any race shall be rich—and no man may be despised for merely being poor—yet no people can be respected which does not produce a wealthy class.[4]

Ideas such as these circulated through nineteenth century America. Thus, the mantra to "toil and save" flowed through the teachings to newly emancipated slaves.

Freed black folks were focused on respectability. This idea of respectability, grounded in the economics of individual thrift, enterprise, and savings, existed in the surrounding dominant community. Prior to emancipation, it already manifested itself in the life of the free Negro, as in that of the white working class. And as has been asserted by scholars, "white philanthropists sought to indoctrinate the freedmen with this ideal through the missionary schools and the Freedmen's Bank" (Harris: 46). Making way for progress, the capitalist system transformed African-Americans from the consumed to consumers, at least at that point in history. For many, engaging capitalism appeared to be the only way up and out of poverty.

Resultantly, in the short history of the U.S., the racist system of capitalism has triumphed. This triumph seems clear with the continued perpetuation and inundation of global capitalism—touted by the U.S. across the globe—and implemented by trade agreements, the IMF, the World Bank, and waged war. Conflated with the mythology of the American Dream, capitalists exploit the economic systems' underpinnings to keep power confined to certain racialized (and gendered) groups. Philosopher Karl Marx critiqued this system in his *Capital: A Critique of Political Economy*, (more commonly known as *Das Kapital)*, with a theory of exploitation of the proletariat, an exposition of the labor theory. He criticized Adam Smith (and others) for not realizing that their economic concepts reflected capitalist institutions, not innate natural properties of mankind. And while black (mostly male) leaders and scholars such as W.E.B. Du Bois, Marcus Garvey, Elijah Muhammad,

Angela Davis, and the Black Panthers have offered ways to append capitalism, no serious attempt has ever been made to undermine capitalism's flawed foundation by any U.S. marginalized or mainstream group. However, the value of capitalism for black folks has not proceeded completely uncontested either.

Debate of this system came from many black activists and scholars who considered (and still talk about) themselves as either socialist or communist—in some ways, fighting the evils of capitalism by denying it. Revolutionary psychiatrist Frantz Fanon, economist Abram L. Harris, political theorist Manning Marable, and cultural scholar bell hooks, all provided powerful critiques of capitalism and the need for African-Americans to consider alternative means of progress. The socialism piece in particular reverberated quite acutely in black discourses due to the communal legacy of African ways of being—still manifested in most African-American communities. In other words, capitalism calls for an individualist state of being—a state that has traditionally been foreign to communities of color. These communities are organized around the family—with everything else, economics and politics, flowing from that foundation.[5] However, agreeing with hooks, desegregation has altered the way African-Americans think about community. She argued:

> Desegregation was the way to weaken the collective radicalization of black people that had been generated by militant civil rights and black power movement . . . After years of collective struggle . . . liberal individualism [has become] more the norm for black folks, particularly the black bourgeoisie, more so than the previous politics of communalism, which emphasized racial uplift and sharing resources, (hooks 2000: 92)

Moreover, cultural critic Paul Gilroy argued that even beyond critical cynicism, in the past people like Toni Cade Bambara and Amiri Baraka possessed a righteous anger "about the violence of [capitalism] and the way it delimits people's choices" (Gilroy, interviewed by hooks April 1996). Many of these same scholars and others acknowledge that even the minimal serious critiques of capitalism that once existed have virtually disappeared in favor of the global economy, especially in the United States. From the World Bank and the war on Iraq to the functioning of the Internet and Coca-Cola, capitalism reigns as the virtually uncontested authority of the new world order.

Capitalism does not value extended family support, collective engagement, or community gardens. Psychologist Na'im Akbar argued that at least a part of African-American attitudes toward capital comes from a slave mentality. Specifically, he maintained "... material objects or dregs of property became equated in the African-Americans' thinking with the full power of freedom and self-determination which the master enjoyed" (Akbar 1984: 13). Thinking about the impact of a slave mindset alone makes clear that a more crucial conflict emerges at the very outset of African-Americans relationship with capitalism. And whether or not one agrees with the assessment, one must concede that for whatever reason, African-Americans and capitalism make awkward dance partners. Beyond this observation, some scholars have suggested that the debate of blacks and capitalism is the wrong one anyway.

In his seminal text, *How Capitalism Underdeveloped Black America*, political theorist Manning Marable argued that people forget (or choose to ignore) the racist nature of capitalism. As I maintain, whether talking about capitalism for the masses or black capitalism, the structure retains a hierarchy and fixity that allows only a few to accumulate capital or "make it"—not altering in the least its built-in inequalities. In revisiting his work some years later, Marable remained firm in saying that the "U.S. capitalist state, in the final analysis, will never be cajoled or persuaded to reform itself through appeals of moral suasion. Fundamental change will require a massive democratic resistance movement largely from below and anchored in the working class and among oppressed minority groups" (Marable 2000: xxxviii)—what he called "non-reformist reform."

Historian John Henrik Clarke suggested that investment in any economic or political system was not as crucial as survival and progression of African people. While espousing socialism himself, Clarke believed in black ownership of black communities as an "economic means to effect social change in our favor" (Clarke 1991:10). Activist Malcolm X concurred with Clarke's position stating: "Our economic philosophy is that we should gain economic control over the economy of our own community, the businesses and the other things which create employment so that we can provide jobs for our own people instead of having to picket and boycott and beg someone else for a job" (X 1964: 272–273). Mantras such as these continue to encourage and hold sway over black entrepreneurial efforts.

Yet others such as historian Chancellor Williams suggest that blacks need not "wholly accept [capitalism], but they should reject 'black capitalism' as a solution of the economic bondage problems of the masses ... [instead, they should focus] on a system that *directly* benefits the people lower down, the great common people, and not just the further enrichment of Blacks who are already well-off and far ahead" (Williams 1971: 332). He argued further that both capitalism and communism were here to stay despite groups shouting 'destroy the system.' Economist Julianne Malveaux constantly indicts the U.S. government for its misuse of capitalists' tools. And lest we forget, capitalism is intimately linked to most other ridiculous operating isms—sexism, racism, and classism—isms that are taken to task regularly in academic communities, even if the capitalist elephant in the room often gets a pass. Regardless of the stance, in many areas of African-American scholarship, one can find a critique of capitalism. All of these scholarly observations are particularly implicated in a business like BET through its appeal to black consumers.

And beyond academia, discussions about capitalism within African-American communities yield insights into the psychic platform of BET's foundation and launch. Some argue that blacks are capitalists in the surest sense of the system; what's the problem? Others say that blacks are oppressed by capitalism and should relinquish its trappings. While still others believe that it's all about the money, and things will be bought and sold regardless of the seller's race. So, it might as well be a black man (or woman) who makes the dollars—C.R.E.A.M., "get the money, dollar, dollar bill yaw'll."[6]

Journalist/writer Cora Daniels argued that the post-Civil Rights generation sees capitalism as a movement. She wrote: "The post-civil rights generation has known no other kind of Black power but that of the business world" (Daniels 2004: 145). In the same vein, focus group participant and college student Fred Walker concluded, "I had to make a realization, a strong realization . . . that I am a capitalist. I like making money. I want to make money. And I'm not talking about this gross materialism either" (U of Houston focus group February 2003). One of the central flaws with both of these notions is that they either ignore or pervert the meaning and function of capitalism. Capitalism is not—cannot be—a power movement nor is having the desire to make money capitalism. Moreover, their ideas belie capitalism's central tenet of individualism—an individualism that receives limited manifestation in terms of African-Americans as they endure constant group identification.[7] Or, as cultural critic Greg Tate eloquently mused, ". . . maybe in a virtual America like the one we inhabit today, the only Black culture that matters is the one that can be downloaded and perhaps needs only business leaders at that. Certainly it's easier to speak of hip hop hoop dreams than of structural racism and poverty, because for hip hop America to not just desire wealth but demand power with a capital P would require thinking way outside the idiot box" (Tate 2005). Being trapped within or catering to a specific "idiot box"—in the case of BET television—is exemplified quite well in Spike Lee's *Bamboozled* (2000). As television executive Pierre Delacroix (Damon Wayans) agonized over what to feed the television (the idiot box) in order to continue working, he led audiences to circulating judgments about capitalism in popular media culture.

In the media realm, critiques of capital abound beside often hypocritical examples of its benefits. The black music industry offers ample and sustained review of capitalism, (although most lyrics hoist up getting money as a really, really good thing). In the 1970s, for example, The O'Jays sang about the evil people perpetuate "For the Love of Money" (1974); later, Tina Turner bemoaned what many women do as "Private Dancer[s]" to get money (1984); Tracy Chapman was "Talkin About a Revolution" against the system (1988); and of course, Boogie Down Production's "Who Are the Pimps," cited at the beginning of the chapter, all overtly attack the system of capital.

Yet, the lyrics and images within music videos, the staple of BET no less, serve up near naked women draped over Bentleys in front of mansions as examples of music business success (see any past Jay-Z, 50 cent, Big Tymers, or even Lil' Kim video for proof). Having or acquiring money serves as the primary motivation in many black film narratives as well. For example, films ranging from *Let's Do It Again* (Sidney Poitier, 1975) to *Barbershop* (Tim Story, 2002) illustrate the need and schemes necessary to possess capital—whether or not it is in service to a larger black community.

The Hughes brothers' *Dead Presidents* (Allen and Albert Hughes, 1995) foregrounds the psychological detriments of having no money; and hip hop gangsta films like *New Jack City* (Mario Van Peebles, 1991), *Clockers* (Spike Lee, 1995), *Set It Off* (F. Gary Gray 1996), *Sugar Hill* (Leon Ichaso, 1999), and *Paid in Full* (Charles Stone III, 2002), all revolve around the acquisition of capital.[8] Assertions of capitalist dreams and deferrals abound. And it cannot be overlooked that an obvious link exists between capitalism and sexism—owning capital is seen as congruent with owning women in almost all visual and aural media formats.[9]

Furthermore, regardless of whatever common evaluations surface about the viability and legitimacy of capitalism, alternate ways of acquiring capital are also sanctioned in most U.S. communities. Both legal and under-the-table means of acquiring capital receive validation, as long as money is made. The same person who condemns the drug trade will participate in insider trading or buy, download, or somehow acquire a bootleg copy of music or a film still playing in the theater. Both *Barbershop* and the Wayans brothers' "Homeboy Shopping Network" from *In Living Color* (FOX 1990–1994) illustrate this underground capitalism well with the slogan, "mo' money, mo' money, mo' money!"

But for all the decrying of and debate over illegality and legality, the centrality of capital operating in a way antithetical to humanity—especially black humanity—receives rare attention. Plus, living in the U.S. prevents anyone from escaping the machinations of capitalism altogether. It also virtually precludes any serious consideration of any other type of economic order. Yet, the arguments for and against capitalism advanced by black economists of the early twentieth century reverberate still. These debates are articulated in writings by members of the National Editorial Board of the News & Letters Committees, a

Marxists/Humanists organization committed to the abolition of capitalism. Using the 1992 Los Angeles Riots/Rebellion as a foundation, they argued:

> Black masses today continue to be engaged in both a struggle against capitalism and an internal struggle against their own Black middle class, which is ideologically and economically integrated into the crevices of capitalism ... while Black masses in practice do challenge and show that the bourgeois theory of the state is a mere mask that hides the class rule of capitalism, the Black leader will follow capitalism and say it's only through the bourgeois state that African Americans can be emancipated (National Editorial Board October 2003).

Can we give a shout out to black mega-church leaders, hip hop moguls, and Jesse 'nem? Furthermore, the observations of an essay on millennium capitalism resonate here: "The return on capital has suddenly become more spiritually compelling and imminent ... than the return of Christ" (Eric Kramer quoted in Comaroff and Comaroff 2001: 24). This framework of raging internal paradox provides an opportunity to move from a discussion of capitalism and its impact in the U.S. to one about class construction and the development of black media businesses—thus, moving more closely to the emergence of BET.

The Wages of Class

"No Class"—the Cosby Kids, *Fat Albert and the Cosby Kids* (1972–1984)

Class divisions are a long-standing reality of black life—in all of American life, truth be told. Beyond master's romp through the slave house (as Me'Shell NdegéOcello penned), the separation of folks via income, education, status, ability, and shading harkens back to the African continent and other continents and peoples. However, the articulation of class in African-American communities has taken a less well-paved route. Class is not talked about, at least not directly, in everyday discourses. Assumptions of class are coded in words, looks, behaviors, dress. Community members on all sides of the class prism

know how "no home training," "bougie," "keeping it real," "ghetto," and "siddity" translate. They are covert ways to separate and distinguish folks, one from another; rich (or at least having a white collar or entertainment job) versus poor; educated (from college) versus street cred; haute couture versus ghetto fabulous; Lenox versus Greenbriar. Cultural critic bell hooks called the contemporary iteration of class distinction among youth the wrath of the "me-me" class, the young and the ruthless.

So what does the term class mean? Like capitalism, class is an idea that employs multiple and varied definitions. Clearly philosophers Karl Marx and Friedrich Engels played an influential role in bringing the ideas and value of class study and struggle to the forefront of scholarly and political consciousness. Others such as historian E. P. Thompson made the lives of the working class worthy of study. In a summary of some of the central ways class analysis has developed, political scientist R.J. Rummel wrote:

> Classes have been defined by property ownership (Marx), position or role (Mosca 1939; Pareto 1963), status rank (Warner 1960; Lenski 1966), prestige (Barber 1957); or by intermarriage (Schumpeter 1951) ... class membership is not biologically determined, but is a form of social stratification based on laws, esteem, wealth, or power. ... In all cases ... class is a vertical division into superior-inferior. ... Class is a division in privileges ... [C]lass is a dividing line between different kinds of behavior. What these behaviors are depends on the actual definition, but nonetheless all definitions assume that different classes can be separated empirically according to different patterns of behavior, such as intermarriages, social mixing, organizational memberships, travel, etiquette, and mannerisms (Rummel 1976).

As should be evident by Rummel's assessment of class definitions, the term is not only wide-ranging but also contested among scholars. But why is it important to talk about class along with capitalism, race, media, and BET? Look no further than the devastation of the 2005 Hurricane Katrina in New Orleans and Gulf Port, Mississippi where the preponderance of the residents are poor and black. U.S. President

George W. Bush stepped in four days after the disaster and flaunted his ineffectualness and complete disconnection from those unlike himself—wealthy and white. As the bodies continued to be gathered and the stench swelled, fingers point dexterously at one another. But I assert, along with many others, that as the smoke has cleared, the displaced "evacuees," (aka looters or refugees depending on what you watched and read), found themselves in the same, impoverished position—in other cities with their own ignored and impoverished populations. So when producer and rapper Kanye West stated matter-of-factly that among other things, "George Bush doesn't care about Black people," he's talking as much about racist animosity as class divisions.[10]

The relevance of class distinctions for African-Americans is a relatively new development given black folks' historic positioning. Internally, African-American-class differences are so emotionally raw that it is often painful to even address underlying and systematic shared concerns. Yet business scholar Juliet E.K. Walker believed that class fails to play any role in the development of black enterprises. She surmised that between slavery, debt peonage, and the "deliberate, systematic, and institutionalized actions of whites to exclude blacks from free access to and participation in the American business community during the age of slavery—almost 250 years," racism has been the primary barrier to black business success (Walker 1998: xviii).

African-Americans know race and recognize racist thoughts, behaviors, and most manifestations. Racism is confronted daily on jobs, on the street, watching television, in classrooms, and at the grocery store. Racism is so much apart of the fabric of the U.S. that it doesn't surprise and rarely excites (O.J., Rodney King, Amadou Diallo, Jasper, Texas, Michael Jackson, Columbine, and Kanye's comments notwithstanding). So while I do not disagree with Walker's assessment of the severity of racist affects on African-Americans and black business, I believe that a strong connection exists between race, class, black entrepreneurship, and media. Class is significant in understanding how the demands of capitalism have shaped African-American consciousness and enterprises—especially in the business of image-making.

Let me offer an example from my own biography to emphasize the African-American class commdrun. My mother's family grew up dirt poor in Smith County, Texas, just outside of Tyler—eleven children, a farmer and laborer father and a home-making and early-deceased mother, poor.[11] The family's saving grace beyond a hard-work mandate was education and extended familial support. Not unlike many black families in the early part of the twentieth century, education (or the military)[12] was touted in my family as a way out of no way. This foundation accorded a certain status upon the family—poor but respectable and respected in the community, Buoyed by several family teachers, entrepreneurs, and one lawyer, my mother and most of her siblings found ways to move economically beyond their upbringing. In this case, the manifestation of class allowed the promise and fallacy of boot straps and efforts to distinguish folks—one from another—hard workers from the so-called lazy. Black success was thus used to deny systematic forms of racism that keep the masses of black folks subordinate.

In my generation, the class dilemma becomes evident as an adult with a Ph.D. People assume a certain class status and mindset for me—for both my past and my present—based on those three letters after my name. Far from the poverty of my parents' upbringing, I grew up and flourished in a predominately black working class North Omaha community. Housing projects were as much a part of the community landscape as single-family homes. In a *Christian Science Monitor* story about blacks returning to their roots, a high school classmate, Kenny Cowan, remembered being inspired by living next door to doctors and lawyers in our neighborhoods. He said these were "the kind of people you dreamed of growing up to be" (Axtman 29 April 2004).

Unlike Kenny, I remember older, retired black folks who looked out for me. I have no idea how they earned a living. I remember friends' mothers who worked as teachers and some sorts of administrative personnel and who exposed their children to classes of dance, music, 4-H, softball, and of course, church. I remember the less well-off and the okay (us) engaging one another on our school bus (part of Omaha's desegregation plan), on the softball field, and in the cafeteria, (both with those who had government subsidized meal tickets and those who paid cash—me having both at different points of my schooling). Folks were always proud when you achieved and encouraged you to do so. They held you accountable to certain classist standards. "Liberal individualism" failed to play in my household—in my family and larger family and friend circles. Fortunately for my friends and me, communalism was a way of life. These "old school" class-less communities and ways of thinking were what BET counted on, reaffirmed with subscribers, and sold to advertisers. The usage of class is also one of the reasons why what transpired with the development of BET serves as an oxymoron—community capitalism. Recognizing this, the interplay of class, race, and media cannot be negated or ignored.

Ironically, however, complex narratives like mine, and of other class disparities, rarely appear in visual culture—not in film, not on radio, (except in a very problematic way on the *Tom Joyner Morning Show*)[13], and certainly not on mainstream television. When class conflict appears, it is generally in a television episode—a snippet of its actual existence—that quickly disappears and is almost always shown as humor. Several examples illustrate this point. In a filmic example, Sidney Poitier's *Uptown Saturday Night* (1974) provides a scene where the protagonists Wardell Franklin (Bill Cosby) and Steve Jackson (Sidney Poitier) enter Madame Zenobia's (Lee Chamberlin) world of black elegance and exclusivity—a place where black people possess wealth, privilege, and correct behavior and consumption habits (or at least appear to)—very unlike the manual labor status for Franklin and Jackson.

In the extremely popular and profitable mainstream series *Sex and the City* (Darren Star, creator, HBO, 1998–2004), class emerges as a side thought. The episode "The Caste System" brings visual attention to the lack of class dialogue (or even consciousness) to the four white female protagonists as they chat with one another during their spa pedicures. Literally sitting at their feet we see the backs of presumably, four Asian women. The women can only nod sheepishly when Charlotte (Kristin Davis) points out the fact that class disparities live as evidenced by their pedicurists. And in a second, this moment of consciousness is gone as they quickly move on to talk about class and wealth through one of their

paramour's servants. Yet in George C. Wolfe's *Colored Museum* (as presented on PBS, 1991), he revealed the life of black models as reflective of any black folks on display. During "The Photo Session" exhibit, Female Model (Suzzanne Douglass) and Male Model (Victor Love) pose their way into the consciousness of black America proclaiming:

Female: The world was becoming too much for us.
Male: We couldn't resolve the contradictions of our existence.
Female: And we couldn't resolve yesterday's pain (pain).
Male: So we gave our lives, and now we live inside *Ebony* magazine. (We're fabulous.)
Female: Yes, we live inside a world where everyone is beautiful and wears fabulous clothes.
Male: And no one says anything profound.
Female: Or meaningful.
Male: Or contradictory.
Female: We just smile and show off our cheekbones.

Perhaps it is as communications scholar Jennie L. Phillips argues: "[S]ocial class, particularly any semblance of the upper-middle class, is so firmly entrenched in television programming that its complete normalization masks its presence. It is not that class is absent from television, but rather that it appears as virtually transparent" (Phillips 2004: 1–2).

In the black version of *Sex and the City, Girlfriends* (Mara Brock Akil, creator, 2000), class surprisingly enters the narrative as a fairly central issue with the four female black protagonists but here, as the butt of humor and through a racialized subtext. For example, one of the early running gags in the program is Lynn's (Persia White) hi-racial status and how that makes her a quasi-outsider of these four girlfriends. Bi-racialness confirms a particular form of class consciousness for African-Americans—derived straight from the house nigger/field nigger foundation of early American history. Lynn's white half accords her a privilege, mindset, and pass for inadequacies that "full-blood" black women are not accorded. Meaning, Lynn's constant joblessness, lack of responsibility, and relish in promiscuity are attributes associated with white girls in black communities—rightly or wrongly. Ironically, the actor Tracee Ellis Ross who serves as the main character Joan, is biologically biracial but positioned as having or living 100% black blood lines and culture—making her more authentic, more black. Her class status, along with their friend Toni's (Jill Marie Jones), gets a pass.[14]

In a different example from the same series, the episode "New York Bound" finds Maya (Golden Brooks)—the community college attending, remarried to the same man, teenaged mother of one—selling her book, *Oh, Hell Yes*, from the trunk of her car on Crenshaw Boulevard. This action initiates a whole lot of class confrontation in the episode.

In one way her efforts highlight the black entrepreneurial spirit that hip hop advocates. In another way, however, *Oh, Hell Yes* and Maya's approach to book distribution reek with black recognition of lack as she is already positioned as lower class throughout the series as shown through her dress, job, friends, and speech.[15] Furthermore, as boss and secretary for the better part of the series, Joan and Maya must negotiate a difficult and awkward friendship. Class tensions pervade all of these women's relationships—albeit in humorous and quickly resolved ways.[16]

The significance of class in this book about BET lies in its invisibility and its normalization of wretched inequalities and disparities. Sociologist William Julius Wilson's first major book, *The Declining Significance of Race: Blacks and Changing American Institutions* (1978), caused a stir in academic communities because of its assertion that class divisions are more damaging than racial ones. Historian Robin D.G. Kelley waxed eloquently about the ways in which folks deemed "underclass" negotiate their identity and real-lived positioning as working class in *Race Rebels: Culture, Politics, and the Black Working Class* (1994). Others write about the ways in which class shapes our desires and goals. In *Pimpin Ain't Easy*, economic and social class function as significant tools in constructing consumers. By the twenty-first century, possessing the ability to consume (or at least the access to credit) translated into having equitability and power. When people look to Puffy's white party and who attends as a measure of influence, it is clear that the myth of classlessness conversion is complete—the twistedness of the dress color code making this myth all the more striking. Yet recognizing and calling class out in a class conscious-less, image-making society is necessary to fully digest the

paradox of Black Entertainment Television and to begin visioning and thinking through the worth and measure of African-American representation. The circulating understanding of and relationship African-Americans have to class both perpetuate and resist racist underpinnings. These underpinnings traverse both capitalism and class to inform and shape the ideas and goals of black business development.

Black Business

> Look at those Korean motherfuckers across the street. I betcha they haven't been a year off da motherfucking boat before they opened up their own place . . . A motherfucking year off the motherfucking boat and got a good business in our neighborhood occupying a building that had been boarded up for longer than I care to remember, and I've been here a long time . . . Now for the life of me, I haven't been able to figure this out. Either dem Koreans are geniuses or we Blacks are dumb.
> —ML (Paul Benjamin), *Do the Right Thing* (Spike Lee 1989)

According to many, the confluence of blacks and business is oxymoronic. Whether it comes from in-house critiques by academics like Thomas Sowell who believed: "Race does not change the fundamental principles of economics" (Sowell 1994: 81), E. Franklin Frazier who called "Negro Business: A Social Myth" (Frazier 1957: 129) or outside assessments by people like Gunnar Myrdal who labeled black businesses marginal (1944), a continuing mindset suggests that African-Americans' biological and cultural make-up make them ill-equipped to do business. Yet quiet as it's kept, black businesses existed even in Colonial America—service businesses such as restaurants, hairdressers, and trading posts. Business scholar Juliet E.K. Walker's books on the history of African-American businesses lay out the ways in which blacks have always been interested and successful business people. Economist Abram L. Harris maintained: "Like the white working men of the eighteenth century, the free Negroes were 'men on the make' hoping to escape the wage-earning class through business enterprise and by accumulating wealth" (Harris 1936: 3). Most black enterprises developed post-emancipation and included endeavors like lumbering, life insurance companies, real estate, catering, and tailoring. The largest number of successful black business ventures were in the field of personal services. In these businesses, racial discrimination became more general. Thus, they wetre often described as "defensive enterprises,"—businesses that somewhat shielded the owner against overt, more specified racism—"the product of racial segregation" (Harris 1936: 54).

From the 1880s, the so-called Negro lumpenproletariat, urged by black leaders, placed increasing faith in business and property as a way of escaping poverty and achieving economic independence. "Although ostensibly sponsored as the means of self-help or racial cooperation ... Negro business enterprise was motivated primarily by the desire for private profit and looked toward the establishment of a Negro capitalist employer class" (Harris 1936: 49–50), Yet, Madam C.J. Walker, the nation's first self-made female millionaire, not only adhered to the dogma of money-making but also to community needs and expectations with her beauty business. The dichotomous assertions by Harris and illustrated through Walker can be supported by looking at the writings and speeches of the culture-defining men of the times, Booker T. Washington and William Edward Burghardt Du Bois.

Booker T. Washington encouraged the colored man to proceed with conciliation, to start at the bottom, work hard, and earn the trust of the white man. While his speech at the 1895 Atlanta Cotton States' International Exposition propelled him to leading spokesman for his people, (at least in the minds of whites), it also yielded castigation from black scholars like W.E.B. Du Bois. Distilled, Washington suggested: "No race that has anything to contribute to markets of the world is long in any degree ostracized. It is important and right that all privileges of the law be ours, but it is vastly more important that we be prepared for the exercise of these privileges. The opportunity to earn a dollar in a factory just now is worth infinitely more than the opportunity to spend a dollar in an opera house" (Washington 1895). In a nutshell, Washington believed in both working your way up and in black entrepreneurship. His problematic stance regarding civil rights notwithstanding, Washington's economic plan presented a viable blueprint for black

progress (even if propelled in large measure by white politicians and businessmen). Political theorist Manning Marable evaluated Washington's stance when he wrote, "Washington devoutly believed that corporate capitalism would usher in a wave of prosperity to the black peasantry and working class ... [His] program was the origin of what we call today 'black capitalism'" (Marable, "History", 1998). It is indeed Washington's admonition that African-American entrepreneurs followed despite sustained criticism of this philosophy.

W.E.B. Du Bois, on the other hand, was a twentieth century privileged scholar and activist. He believed in an ideology and group of people that he dubbed the Talented Tenth—the top ten percent of all blacks who will lead the masses of uneducated and uncultured Negroes to prosperity and better standards of living via the tenth's acquisition of professional occupations and business development. In direct rebuke to the industrial proposals of Washington, Du Bois founded the unsuccessful but significant Niagara Movement in 1905 to demand civil rights for blacks and later, initiated conferences at Atlanta University on the progress of black businesses. With Du Bois at its helm, several resolutions pertaining to the development of black businesses were adopted at the 1898 Fourth Atlanta University Conference. Two of those resolutions are salient to this work: 1) business men should be congratulated and patronized, and 2) agitation for the necessity of business careers for young people should continue in churches, schools, newspapers, and by all other avenues (Harris 1936: 52–53). The different approaches that these men offered for black folks' progress resonate contemporarily. In fact, their works' relevance to BET makes understanding their assertions crucial. Through the codes of contemporary understanding, Robert L. Johnson usurped salient aspects of both Washington and Du Bois's trajectories to make the case for the necessity of his BET.

Much later in his life, Du Bois repudiated the viability of capitalism for American Negroes in favor of socialism writing: "I myself long stressed Negro private business enterprise but I soon saw a 'group economy' was necessary for protection" (1957). He also modified his position on the viability of the Talented Tenth saying: "Willingness to work and make personal sacrifice for solving these problems was, of course, the first prerequisite and sine qua non. I did not stress this, I assumed it . . . I assumed that with knowledge, sacrifice would automatically follow. In my youth and idealism, I did not realize that selfishness is even more natural than sacrifice" (1948). But Du Bois's original notion of the Talented Tenth and both he and Washington's advocacy for black business development stuck and became a part of the perceived best path for African-American progress. Their mantras give insight into the veneration Robert L. Johnson received during his reign at BET (or most of it) and the role of the black press in making BET prominent.

Proliferating alongside the efforts of men such as Frederick Douglass, Washington, and Du Bois's encouragement of black business are a number of critics who published work questioning these philosophies. E. Franklin Frazier believed that Du Bois's black elite fostered a "myth" about the significance of black ownership. He suggested that the rise of industrial schools under the encouragement of Washington (business included), trained students to not only become a part of the capitalist operating system but also to predict and forward its perpetuation. This very idea made the 1933 monumental work, *The Mis-Education of the Negro*, that much more powerful. In this text, educator Carter G. Woodson made assertions that remain valid, some seventy plus years later. He observed: ". . . Negroes are trained exclusively in the psychology and economics of Wall Street and are, therefore, made to despise the opportunities to run ice wagons, push banana carts, and sell peanuts among their own people. Foreigners, who have not studied economics but have studied Negroes, take up this business and grow rich" (Woodson 1933: 5). Woodson's observation gives credence to both the phenomenon and incredulity of M.L.'s comments within the narrative of *Do the Right Thing* cited earlier.

Furthermore, in a contemporary example of these philosophies, management scholar Salmon A. Shomade reflected upon his transformation from a black college radical to a corporate suit. Pursuing an MBA degree in part because it sounded professional, he became quickly disappointed in his black (and white) classmates as issues of race in the business world were deemed unimportant. At the beginning he said, "I could care less about what white folks did."

However over the course of his two-year tenure, his interest in radicalism subsided. This transformation was fueled by a defining classroom discussion on the 1987 stock market crash. While everyone gushed about the craziness of the market, Shomade wanted to discuss all the people who lost their jobs. His classmates looked at him as if he were crazy. He concluded: "In corporate America, you are more worried about what people put on your desk. I was muted because there was no fuel to keep the fire [of radicalism] burning. . . . My arguments shifted from black versus white to rich versus poor" (Shomade).

Shomade's observations fall in line with an earlier assessment of Frazier. In it, he maintained "business education is given professional status and is glorified because of the myth of Negro business as a way to economic salvation for the Negro in American society" (Frazier 1957: 137). In the past, he argued, poor students believed that accessing business education would put them squarely in the middle class. "For they have been taught that money will bring them justice and equality in American life, and they propose to get money" (Frazier 1957: 76). Contemporary MBA degree pursuers seek a more advanced goal—riches.

In partial response to both Du Bois and the 1944 study conducted by Gunnar Myrdal, *An American Dilemma*—a report that called the situation of the Negroes in America "pathological," Frazier wrote:

> One of the most striking indications of the unreality of the social world which the black bourgeoisie created is its faith in the importance of 'Negro business,' i.e., the business enterprises owned by Negroes and catering to Negro customers. Although these enterprises have little significance either from the standpoint of the American economy or the economic life of the Negro, a social myth has been created that they provide a solution to the Negro's economic problems. Faith in this social myth and others is perpetuated by the Negro newspapers . . . (Frazier 1957: 27)

His last statement finds concrete support when looking at the most popular twenty-first century publications targeting African-American audiences. The top five magazines, *Essence, Ebony, Jet, Black Enterprise*, and *Vibe*, highlight professional lifestyles (business, entertainment, sports), monetary acquisition, professional firsts, and the status conferred with these elements. Beyond pride, these magazines suggest that the lives of those featured in their pages are the exemplar of black success and the new millennial Moses—they illustrate what can be if you play the game correctly. As has been shown in countless studies, black-owned businesses succeed by catering primarily to African-American consumers. In fact, most ethnically-defined businesses work this way. Economist Andrew F. Brimmer maintained: "Segregation served as a kind of protective tariff to black-owned businesses ... That was harsh for black consumers, but it provided a shield for black businesses" (quoted in Hoffer 1987). Thus, black business was born out of the necessity for goods and services as well as the capitalist impulse.

BET capitalized (literally) on several circulating ideas about and beliefs in black business as a source of racial uplift and pride; the lack of black television presence; the racialized realization of President Ronald Reagan's policies, and the belief in "black capitalism" (as found in the 1960s with SNCC and Stokely Carmichael's "communal economic effort," the SCLC's "Operation Breadbasket," and the Nation of Islam and Elijah Muhammad's "Economic Blueprint"). Many of these programs merged the tenets of capitalism with social or communal tendencies of African-Americans as both a progressive stance and a legacy of Washington, Garvey, and Du Bois. Like most businesses that rely on perceived and actual lack as an appeal, black businesses harp on these tendencies of African-Americans. Thus, I turn finally to an examination of the businesses most closely allied with Black Entertainment Television—communications businesses—in order to bring full circle this introduction to BET's foundation.

And the Promise . . .

From early on, African-Americans understood the potential and sought to harness the power of mass communications. Many believed that through this vehicle, equality, connection, and progress could be advanced and measured. It could serve also as a potentially lucrative, black business venture. So beyond the businesses and approaches, the communications industry attracted a variety of black capitalists. With this impetus, Marable suggested that ties to black business development made the "Black press . . . the chief vehicle to control and to exploit the Black consumer market, as well as to promote the ideology of Black Capitalism to the masses" (Marable 2000: 146).

In the nineteenth century, black newspapers, magazines, and other printed media-flourished and were noted for their crusading tenor. These publications "shined a bright spotlight on the ugly legacy of America's racially segregated past" (Walker 1999: 1). The U.S.'s first black newspaper, *Freedom's Journal*, began in 1827 with Samuel E. Cornish and John B. Russwurm reporting on foreign and domestic news, missions to Africa, and memoirs—with the credo that for "too long others have spoken for us."

In the early twentieth century, publisher Robert Sengstacke Abbott's *Chicago Defender* grew to be one of the largest black-owned newspapers in the country and the first with mass circulation. He pioneered the idea of the paper existing on circulation rather than advertising dollars.[17] Within its pages, Abbott encouraged the migration of African-Americans from the south to Chicago for better-paying jobs. While he certainly had his detractors, the proof of his acumen lies in both the number of papers that subsequently flourished under his model and more importantly, the existence of the *Chicago Defender* still in 2007. In the same Windy City, publisher John H. Johnson achieved millionaire status with the publication of *Negro Digest* (1942), *Ebony* (1945-Present), and *Jet* beginning in 1951 (Walker 1998: 300). The company currently stands as a wholly-owned family conglomerate and the second largest black-owned business in the U.S. It achieved this status by Johnson's "steady insistence in his company's mission—delivering positive portrayals of African-Americans, and securing value from advertisers for the audience he delivered" (Smikle 2005). Scholar and journalist George Sylvie found that into the twentieth century, more than 300 black newspapers continue to serve black communities in the U.S. and the larger business community despite their lack of adequate technology and access to capital (Sylvie 2001).

Yet it seems that the crusading image that enticed blacks to the communications industry has shifted to concentrate on the ethos of money-making. For example, Walker noted that Motown developed into the nation's first black multimillion dollar, multimedia entertainment company. Berry Gordy founded the company in 1959 and was influenced by both John H. Johnson in terms of self discipline and individuality but also by the Ford Motor company's example of producing a consistent product. Yet its sale in 1988 seemed to "[represent]" more than a business decision; it was a symbolic loss, a transfer of an institution important in the economic advancement of black America" (Walker 1998: 302). Furthermore, when *Essence* Magazine was sold to Time, Inc. in 2005, co-founder Edward Lewis remarked, ". . . we're looking forward to aggressively broadening the scope of the *Essence* brand and penetrating new markets around the world. It will give me great pride and comfort to know that *Essence* will be secure for generations to come and that its prospects for even greater success will be brighter now than ever" (*Jet* 25 January 2005). The same thoughts seemed to flow behind the actions of owner and producer Quincy Jones as he sold *Vibe* magazine in July 2006. This new "forward" thinking of contemporary media moguls suggests (and seems to predict) the wave of the future. It is significant that while many prominent African-American communication and entertainment businesses are now being courted by and selling to large, multi-media corporations, others refuse to do so.[18] Yet both responses illustrate the continued belief in black entrepreneurship and capitalism.

Beyond the relationship between capitalism and business, communications-entertainment industries also offer the opportunity to transform black life and the way the larger society views African-Americans. In 1960, personal services and retailing accounted for more than half of all minority enterprises. Between 1960 and 1980, however, growth in minority enterprises occured outside of traditional lines of business. Communication was one of those businesses (Jaynes and Williams 1989: 315). Initially, cinema stood as the ground by which transformation was thought to take place. Whether it was filmmaker Oscar Micheaux's prolific creative career as a filmmaker and novelist, early film production companies like the Lincoln Brothers, or later, the impulse of Melvin Van Peebles' film *Sweet Sweetback's Baadasssss Song* (1971), communications media have taken a leading role in its

perceived ability to illuminate, subvert, and possibly overturn the devastating and lingering effects of slavery, racism, and exclusion from capitalistic progress.

Examples bear this idea out with Elijah Muhammad's 1963 Economic Blueprint plan. In it, technology and communication garnered its own line item—with the newspaper *Muhammad Speaks* at the top of the list. Since the early 1980s, educational consultant and entrepreneur Jawanza Kunjufu used his publication house, African American Images, as a platform for proselytizing on everything black—from the raising of black boys to business development for African-Americans. And broadcaster and scholar Tony Brown employs his long-running syndicated television program, *Tony Brown's Journal* and book publication as a platform for the value of black capitalism.

As should be evident, Robert L. Johnson's idea for BET followed in a long tradition of black business acumen and information dissemination. While the name Black Entertainment Television expressed its intention, the company's marketing relied on the legacy and impetuses of the black press for black communities' support. Johnson's entrepreneurship and vision developed with an assumption of capitalism's value for and within black communities and with knowledge of this population's craving for representation. Moreover, as cultural critic bell hooks argued, Johnson (and others) make "selling blackness" their biggest commodity. "They make sure they mask their agenda so black capitalism looks like black self-determination" (hooks 2000: 94). Examining the confluence of capitalism, class, and black media provides needed background into both the ideological foundation and impulse of BET's business development and consumer-defining goals. BET benefits from and depends upon circulating black binaries of power and wealth, representation and invisibility. In its quest for existence and then prominence, BET has developed into the leading provider of U.S. black imagery.

Notes

1. Italics are mine.
2. See Frantz Fanon's *Wretched of the Earth* (1963: 65), where he talked about the connections between colonialism, capitalism, and violence. Many African countries

used the system of barter as a means of facilitating commerce—always aware of the value in their agriculture and crafts. Furthermore, let me be clear here. Africans from all parts of the continent possessed their own spiritual belief systems—well before the missionaries came.

3. Frazier 1957; 113. See also C.L.R. James, "The Atlantic Slave Trade and Slavery: Some Interpretations of Their Significance in the Development of the United States," *Amistad 1; Writings in Black History and Culture*, eds. John, A. Williams and Charles F. Harris (New York: Vintage Books, 1970).

4. As found in Harris 1936: 26. See U.S. Senate, 46th Congress, 2nd session, Report 440—as found in Circular #1 issued by Douglass.

5. See John Hope Franklin, *From Slavery to Freedom: A History of Negro Americans*, 4th Edition, New York: Alfred A. Knopf, 1974, for a larger exploration of the black family.

6. It is important here to call attention to the emphasis of man-dome as the conduit by which progress is to be obtained for African-Americans. This mindset pervades all facets of society—politics, education, economics. Thus when discussions of "the Man" (the white man) surfaced in the 1970s, they were juxtaposed against an imagined parallel universe in the black community with "the man" there, meaning the black man. See Mark Anthony Neal's *New Black Man* (New York: Routledge, 2005) for a contemporary grappling with black masculinity. Furthermore, Wu-Tang Clan offered this version of the significance of money for young people with their rap C.R.E.A.M.—cash rules everything around me (1993).

7. See Todd Boyd's *The New H.N.I.C.* for a discussion on group identity and young black folks.

8. For a look at how capitalism infuses and directs black culture in film, see my "Rock-a-Bye, Baby!: Black Women Disrupting Gangs and Constructing Hip-Hop Gangsta Film" *Cinema Journal* 42: 2 (2003). Additionally, nearly all of Urban Entertainment's titles involve capitalists' conflicts.

9. I thank Deborah Elizabeth Whaley for reminding me of this reality.

10. In fact in his longer comments West said, "I hate the way they portray us in the media. You see a black family, it says, 'They're looting.' You see a white family, it says, 'They're looking for food.' And, you know, it's been five days because most of the people are black. And even for me to complain about it, I would be a hypocrite because I've tried to turn away from the TV because it's too hard to watch. I've even been shopping before even giving a donation, so now I'm calling my business manager right now to see what is the biggest amount I can give; and just to imagine if I was down there, and those are my people down there. So anybody out there that wants to do anything that we can help—with the way America is set up to help the poor, the black people, the less well-off, as slow as possible. I mean, the Red Cross is doing everything they can. We already realize a lot of people that could help are at war right now, fighting another way—and they've given them permission to go down and shoot us! [Back to Mike Myers, who after saying something stupid, tosses it back to West] George Bush doesn't care about black people!"

11. My father's family developed pretty much the same way in Smith County, Texas—only just outside of Lindale.

12. In fact, many argue for the U.S. military as being more progressive than society in general in its opening of opportunities for African-Americans, due in part to its rigid structure—see John Sibley Butler and Charles Moskos, *All That We Can Be: Black Leadership and Racial Integration the Army Way* (New York: Basic Books, 1997).

13. The *Tom Joyner Morning Show* features Myra Jay, "the poster child for single moms," who represents the single mother—but not in a way that questions the classist implication of what she offers up and her representation thereof.

14. Toni grows up dirt poor in a farming area of Fresno, California. She completely buys into the capitalist discourse of material success as a panacea to the taint of poverty.

15. While Maya dresses similar to all of the other characters, her attire periodically grounds issues of appropriateness and taste as shown most easily in the episode "Never a Bridesmaid" (UPN, initial airdate 27 November 2000).

16. Interestingly too, since 2003, *Girlfriends* is one of the acquired series running on Black Entertainment Television.

17. Unfortunately, this approach has led to the "rollercoaster" success of many black newspapers. See Walker 1999: 2.

18. John H. Johnson (now Linda Johnson Rice's) Johnson Publishing Company, Earl G. Graves Sr. who publishes *Black Enterprise*, Tom Joyner's Reach Media, Byron Allen's Entertainment Studios, Tavis Smiley's "The Smiley Group," Percy Sutton's Inner City Broadcasting, and Spike Lee's Forty Acres & a Mule Filmworks are all still family- or family majority-owned and helmed.

References

Akbar, Na'im. *Chains and Images of Psychological Slavery*, Jersey City, NJ: New Mind, 1984.

Clarke, John Henrik. *Africans at the Crossroads: Notes for an African World Revolution*. Trenton, NJ: Africa World Press, 1991.

Comaroff, Jean and John L. Comaroff. *Millennial Capitalism and the Culture of Neoliberalism*. Durham, NC: Duke University Press, 2001.

Daniels, Cora. *Black Power Inc.: The New Voice of Success*. New York: John Wiley & Sons 2004.

Du Bois, W.E.B. "Negroes and Socialism." *National Guardian* 29 (April 1957): online.

——."Negroes and the Crisis of Capitalism in the United States." *Monthly Review* 4 (April 1953): 478–485. In *W.E.B. Du Bois: A Reader*, edited by David Levering Lewis. New York: Henry Holt and Company, 1995: 624.

——."The Talented Tenth: Memorial Address." *Boulé Journal* 15 (October 1948); 3–13.

Edwards, Richard C., Michael Reich, and Thomas E. Weisskopf. *The Capitalist System: A Radical Analysis of American Society*, 2nd Edition. Englewood Cliffs, NJ: Prentice-Hall, 1978.

Fanon, Frantz. *Wretched of the Earth*. New York: Grove Weidenfeld, 1963.

Frazier, E. Franklin. *Black Bourgeoisie*. New York: Free Press, 1957 first printing, edition cited, London: Collier Books, 1969.

Fulcher, James. *Capitalism: A Very Short Introduction*. New York: Oxford University Press , 2004.

Fusfeld, Daniel R. *Economics: Principles of Political Economy*. Illinois, Scott, Foresman and Company, 1982.

Hall, Stuart, Ed. *Representation: Cultural Representations and Signifying Practices*. London: Sage, 1997.

Harris, Abram L. *The Negro as Capitalist: A Study of Banking and Business Among American Negroes*. College Park, MD: McGrath. 1936.

Hoffer, William. "Black Entrepreneurship in America." *Nation's Business*, June 1987, online, (18 November 2002).

hooks, bell. *Where We Stand: Class Matters*. New York: Routledge, 2000.

hooks, bell. "Thinking about Capitalism: A Conversation with Cultural Critic Paul Gilroy," *Z Magazine* April 1996 (accessed 21 November 2002).

Jaynes, Gerald David and Robin M. Williams, Jr., Eds. *A Common Destiny: Blacks and American Society*. Washington, DC: National Academy Press, 1989.

Kelley, Robin D.G. *Race Rebels: Culture, Politics, and the Black Working Class*. New York: Free Press, 1994.

Marable, Manning. "History, Liberalism, and the Black Radical Tradition." *Radical History Review*, 71 (Spring 1998). http://chnm.gmu.edu/rhr/marable.htm (28 April 2004).

——*How Capitalism Underdeveloped Black America*. Boston: South End Press, 2000.

Myrdal, Gunnar. *An American Dilemma: The Negro Problem and Modern Democracy*. New York: Harper & Bros., 1944.

Phillips, Jennie L. "Unpacking the Transparency of Social Class." Paper presented at the annual conference of the International Communication Association, New Orleans, LA, May 27–31, 2004.

Rummel, R.J. *Understanding Conflict and War, Vol. 2: The Conflict Helix*. Beverly Hills, CA: Sage, 1976.

Smikle, Ken. "Johnson Publishing Company: An Empire Built on Valuing Black Consumers." *Chicago Defender*, 9 August, 2005.

Sowell, Thomas. *Race and Culture: A World View*. New York: Basic Books, 1994.

Sylvie, George. "Technology and African American newspapers: Implications for Survival & Change." In *The Information Society and the Black Community*, edited by John T. Barber and Alice A. Tait. Westport, CT: Greenwood, 2001 77–93.

Tate, Greg. "Hiphop Turns 30: Whatcha Celebratin' For?" *Village Voice*, 4 January 2005, online, (26 August 2005).

Walker, Juliet E. K., Ed. *Encyclopedia of African American Business History*. Westport, CT: Greenwood Press, 1999.

——*The History of Black Business in America: Capitalism, Race, Entrepreneurship*. New York: Macmillan Library Reference, 1998.

Washington, Booker Taliaferro. "Atlanta Exposition Speech." 18 September 1895, Library of Congress. <http://memory.loc.gov/ammem/aaohtml/exhibit/aopart6.html> (27 April 2004).

Williams, Chancellor. *The Destruction of Black Civilization: Great Issues of a Race from 4500 B.C. to 2000 A.D.* Dubuque, IA: Kendall/Hunt, 1971.

Woodson, Carter Godwin. *The Mis-Education of the Negro*. Washington, DC: Associated Publishers, 1933.

X, Malcolm. "Black Revolution." In *I Am Because We Are: Readings in Black Philosophy*, edited by Fred Lee Hord (Mzee Lasana Okpara) and Jonathan Scott Lee. Amherst: University of Massachusetts Press, 1995: 272–273.

5.
DISJUNCTURE AND DIFFERENCE IN THE GLOBAL CULTURAL ECONOMY

Arjun Appadurai

The central problem of today's global interactions is the tension between cultural homogenization and cultural heterogenization. A vast array of empirical facts could be brought to bear on the side of the 'homogenization' argument, and much of it has come from the left end of the spectrum of media studies (Hamelink, 1983; Mattelart, 1983; Schiller, 1976), and some from other, less appealing, perspectives (Gans, 1985; Iyer, 1988). Most often, the homogenization argument subspeciates into either an argument about Americanization, or an argument about 'commoditization', and very often the two arguments are closely linked. What these arguments fail to consider is that at least as rapidly as forces from various metropolises are brought into new societies they tend to become indigenized in one or other way: this is true of music and housing styles as much as it is true of science and terrorism, spectacles and constitutions. The dynamics of such indigenization have just begun to be explored in a sophisticated manner (Barber, 1987; Feld, 1988; Hannerz, 1987, 1989; Ivy, 1988; Nicoll, 1989; Yoshimoto, 1989), and much more needs to be done. But it is worth noticing that for the people of Irian Jaya, Indonesianization may be more worrisome than Americanization, as Japanization may be for Koreans, Indianization for Sri Lankans, Vietnamization for the Cambodians, Russianization for the people of Soviet Armenia and the Baltic Republics. Such a list of alternative fears to Americanization could be greatly expanded, but it is not a shapeless inventory: for polities of smaller scale, there is always a fear of cultural absorption by polities of larger scale, especially those that are near by. One man's imagined community (Anderson, 1983) is another man's political prison.

This scalar dynamic, which has widespread global manifestations, is also tied to the relationship between nations and states, to which I shall return later in this essay. For the moment let us note that the simplification of these many forces (and fears) of homogenization can also be exploited by nation-states in relation to their own minorities, by posing global commoditization (or capitalism, or some other such external enemy) as more 'real' than the threat of its own hegemonic strategies.

The new global cultural economy has to be understood as a complex, overlapping, disjunctive order, which cannot any longer be understood in terms of existing center-periphery models (even those that might account for multiple centers and peripheries). Nor is it susceptible to simple models of push and pull (in terms of migration theory) or of surpluses and deficits (as in traditional models of balance of trade), or of consumers and producers (as in most neo-Marxist theories of development). Even the most complex and flexible theories of global development which have come out of the Marxist tradition (Amin, 1980; Mandel, 1978; Wallerstein, 1974; Wolf, 1982) are inadequately quirky, and they have not come to terms with what Lash and Urry (1987) have recently called 'disorganized capitalism'. The complexity of the current global economy has to do with certain fundamental disjunctures between economy, culture and politics which we have barely begun to theorize.[1]

I propose that an elementary framework for exploring such disjunctures is to look at the relationship between five dimensions of global cultural flow which can be termed: (a) ethnoscapes; (b) mediascapes; (c) technoscapes; (d) finanscapes; and (e) ideoscapes.[2] I use terms with the common suffix scape to indicate first of all that these are not objectively given relations which look the same from every angle of vision, but rather that they are deeply perspectival constructs, inflected very much by the historical, linguistic and political situatedness of different sorts of actors: nation-states, multinationals, diasporic communities, as well as sub-national groupings and movements (whether religious, political or economic), and even intimate face-to-face groups, such as villages, neighborhoods and families. Indeed, the individual actor is the last locus of this perspectival set of landscapes, for these landscapes are eventually navigated by agents who both experience and constitute larger formations, in part by their own sense of what these landscapes offer. These landscapes thus, are the building blocks of what, extending Benedict Anderson, I would like to call 'imagined worlds', that is, the multiple worlds which are constituted by the historically situated imaginations of persons and groups spread around the globe (Appadurai, 1989). An important fact of the world we live in today is that many persons on the globe live in such imagined 'worlds' and not just in imagined communities, and thus are able to contest and sometimes even subvert the 'imagined worlds' of the official mind and of the entrepreneurial mentality that surround them. The suffix scape also allows us to point to the fluid, irregular shapes of these landscapes, shapes which characterize international capital as deeply as they do international clothing styles.

By 'ethnoscape', I mean the landscape of persons who constitute the shifting world in which we live: tourists, immigrants, refugees, exiles, guestworkers and other moving groups and persons constitute an essential feature of the world, and appear to affect the politics of and between nations to a hitherto unprecedented degree. This is not to say that there are not anywhere relatively stable communities and networks, of kinship, of friendship, of work and of leisure, as well as of birth, residence and other filiative forms. But it is to say that the warp of these stabilities is everywhere shot through with the woof of human motion, as more persons and groups deal with the realities of having to move, or the fantasies of wanting to move. What is more, both these realities as well as these fantasies now function on larger scales, as men and women from villages in India think not just of moving to Poona or Madras, but of moving to Dubai and Houston, and refugees from Sri Lanka find themselves in South India as well as in Canada, just as the Hmong are driven to London as well as to Philadelphia. And as international capital shifts its needs, as production and technology generate different needs, as nation-states shift their policies on refugee populations, these moving groups can never afford to let their imaginations rest too long, even if they wished to.

By 'technoscape', I mean the global configuration, also ever fluid, of technology, and of the fact that technology, both high and low, both mechanical and informational, now moves at high speeds across various kinds of previously impervious boundaries. Many countries now are the roots of multinational enterprise: a huge steel complex in Libya may involve interests from India, China, Russia and Japan, providing different components of new technological configurations. The odd distribution of technologies, and thus the peculiarities of these technoscapes, are increasingly driven not by any obvious economies of scale, of political control, or of market rationality, but of increasingly complex relationships between money flows, political possibilities and the availability of both low and highly-skilled labor. So, while India exports waiters and chauffeurs to Dubai and Sharjah, it also exports software engineers to the United States (indentured briefly to Tata-Burroughs or the World Bank), then laundered through the State Department to become wealthy 'resident aliens', who are in turn objects of seductive messages to invest their money and know-how in federal and state projects in India. The global economy can still be described in terms of traditional 'indicators' (as the World Bank continues to do) and studied in terms of traditional comparisions (as in Project Link at the University of Pennsylvania), but the complicated technoscapes (and the shifting ethnoscapes), which underlie these 'indicators' and 'comparisions' are further out of the reach of the 'queen of the social sciences' than ever before. How is one to make a meaningful comparision of wages in Japan and the United States, or of real estate costs in New York and Tokyo, without taking sophisticated account of the very complex fiscal and investment flows that link the two economies through a global grid of currency speculation and capital transfer?

Thus it is useful to speak as well of 'financscapes', since the disposition of global capital is now a more mysterious, rapid and difficult landscape to follow than ever before, as currency markets, national stock exchanges, and commodity speculations move megamonies through national turnstiles at blinding speed, with vast absolute implications for small differences in percentage points and time units. But the critical point is that the global relationship between ethnoscapes, technoscapes and finanscapes is deeply disjunctive and profoundly unpredictable, since each of these landscapes is subject to its own constraints and incentives (some political, some informational and some techno-environmental), at the same time as each acts as a constraint and a parameter for movements in the other. Thus, even an elementary model of global political economy must take into account the shifting relationship between perspectives on human movement, technological flow, and financial transfers, which can accommodate their deeply disjunctive relationships with one another.

Built upon these disjunctures (which hardly form a simple, mechanical global 'infrastructure' in any case) are what I have called 'mediascapes' and 'ideoscapes', though the latter two are closely related landscapes of images. 'Mediascapes' refer both to the distribution of the electronic capabilities to produce and disseminate information (newspapers, magazines, television stations, film production studios, etc.), which are now available to a growing number of private and public interests throughout the world; and to the images of the world created by these media. These images of the world involve many complicated inflections, depending on their mode (documentary or entertainment), their hardware (electronic or pre-electronic), their audiences (local, national or transnational) and the interests of those who own and control them. What is most important about these mediascapes is that they provide (especially in their television, film and cassette forms) large and complex repertoires of images, narratives and 'ethnoscapes' to viewers throughout the world, in which the world of commodities and the world of 'news' and politics are profoundly mixed. What this means is that many audiences throughout the world experience the media themselves as a complicated and interconnected repertoire of print, celluloid, electronic screens and billboards. The lines between the 'realistic' and the fictional landscapes they see are blurred, so that the further away these audiences are from the direct experiences of metropolitan life, the more likely they are to construct 'imagined worlds' which are chimerical, aesthetic, even fantastic objects, particularly if assessed by the criteria of some other perspective, some other 'imagined world'.

'Mediascapes', whether produced by private or state interests, tend to be image-centered, narrative-based accounts of strips of reality, and what they offer to those who experience and transform them is a series of elements (such as characters, plots and textual forms) out of which scripts can be formed of imagined lives, their own as well as those of others living in other places. These scripts can and do get disaggregated into complex sets of metaphors by which people live (Lakoff and Johnson, 1980) as they help to constitute narratives of the 'other' and proto-narratives of possible lives, fantasies which could become prologemena to the desire for acquisition and movement.

'Ideoscsapes' are also concatenations of images, but they are often directly political and frequently have to do with the ideologies of states and the counter-ideologies of movements explicitly oriented to capturing state power or a piece of it. These ideoscapes are composed of elements of the Enlightenment world-view, which consists of a concatenation of ideas, terms and images, including 'freedom', 'welfare', 'rights', 'sovereignty', 'representation' and the master-term 'democracy'. The master-narrative of the Enlightenment (and its many variants in England, France and the United States) was constructed with a certain internal logic and presupposed a certain relationship between reading, representation and the public sphere (for the dynamics of this process in the early history of the United States, see Warner, 1990). But their diaspora across the world, especially since the nineteenth century, has loosened the internal coherence which held these terms and images together in a Euro-American master-narrative, and provided instead a loosely structured synopticon of politics, in which different nation-states, as part of their evolution, have organized their political cultures around different 'keywords' (Williams, 1976).

As a result of the differential diaspora of these keywords, the political narratives that govern communication between elites and followings in different parts of the world involve problems of both a semantic and a pragmatic nature: semantic to the extent that words (and their lexical equivalents) require careful translation from context to context in their global movements; and pragmatic to the extent that the use of these words by political actors and their audiences may be subject to very different sets of contextual conventions that mediate their translation into public politics. Such conventions are not only matters of the nature of political rhetoric (viz. what does the aging Chinese leadership mean when it refers to the dangers of hooliganism? What does the South Korean leadership mean when it speaks of 'discipline' as the key to democratic industrial growth?).

These conventions also involve the far more subtle question of what sets of communicative genres are valued in what way (newspapers versus cinema for example) and what sorts of pragmatic genre conventions govern the collective 'readings' of different kinds of text. So, while an Indian audience may be attentive to the resonances of a political speech in terms of some key words and phrases reminiscent of Hindi cinema, a Korean audience may respond to the subtle codings of Buddhist or neo-Confucian rhetorical strategy encoded in a political document. The very relationship of reading to hearing and seeing may vary in important ways that determine the morphology of these different 'ideoscapes' as they shape themselves in different national and transnational contexts. This globally variable synaesthesia has hardly even been noted, but it demands urgent analysis. Thus 'democracy' has clearly become a master-term, with powerful echoes from Haiti and Poland to the Soviet Union and China, but it sits at the center of a variety of ideoscapes (composed of distinctive pragmatic configurations of rough 'translations' of other central terms from the vocabulary of the Enlightenment). This creates ever new terminological kaleidoscopes, as states (and the groups that seek to capture them) seek to pacify

populations whose own ethnoscapes are in motion, and whose mediascapes may create severe problems for the ideoscapes with which they are presented. The fluidity of ideoscapes is complicated in particular by the growing diasporas (both voluntary and involuntary) of intellectuals who continuously inject new meaning-streams into the discourse of democracy in different parts of the world.

This extended terminological discussion of the five terms I have coined sets the basis for a tentative formulation about the conditions under which current global flows occur: *they occur in and through the growing disjunctures between ethnoscapes, technoscapes, finanscapes, mediascapes and ideoscapes.* This formulation, the core of my model of global cultural flow, needs some explanation. First, people, machinery, money, images, and ideas now follow increasingly non-isomorphic paths: of course, at all periods in human history, there have been some disjunctures between the flows of these things, but the sheer speed, scale and volume of each of these flows is now so great that the disjunctures have become central to the politics of global culture. The Japanese are notoriously hospitable to ideas and are stereotyped as inclined to export (all) and import (some) goods, but they are also notoriously closed to immigration, like the Swiss, the Swedes and the Saudis. Yet the Swiss and Saudis accept populations of guestworkers, thus creating labor diasporas of Turks, Italians and other circum-mediterranean groups. Some such guestworker groups maintain continuous contact with their home-nations, like the Turks, but others, like high-level South Asian migrants tend to desire lives in their new homes, raising anew the problem of reproduction in a deterritorialized context.

Deterritorialization, in general, is one of the central forces of the modern world, since it brings laboring populations into the lower class sectors and spaces of relatively wealthy societies, while sometimes creating exaggerated and intensified senses of criticism or attachment to politics in the home-state. Deterritorialization, whether of Hindus, Sikhs, Palestinians or Ukranians, is now at the core of a variety of global fundamentalisms, including Islamic and Hindu fundamentalism. In the Hindu case for example (Appadurai and Breckenridge, forthcoming) it is clear that the overseas movement of Indians has been exploited by a variety of interests both within and outside India to create a complicated network of finances and religious identifications, in which the problems of cultural reproduction for Hindus abroad has become tied to the politics of Hindu fundamentalism at home.

At the same time, deterritorialization creates new markets for film companies, art impressarios and travel agencies, who thrive on the need of the deterritorialized population for contact with its homeland. Naturally, these invented homelands, which constitute the mediascapes of deterritorialized groups, can often become sufficiently fantastic and one-sided that they provide the material for new ideoscapes in which ethnic conflicts can begin to erupt. The creation of 'Khalistan', an invented homeland of the deterritorialized Sikh population of England, Canada and the United States, is one example of the bloody potential in such mediascapes, as they interact with the 'internal colonialisms' (Hechter, 1974) of the nation-state. The West Bank, Namibia and Eritrea are other theaters for the enactment of the bloody negotiation between existing nation-states and various deterritorialized groupings.

The idea of deterritorialization may also be applied to money and finance, as money managers seek the best markets for their investments, independent of national boundaries. In turn, these movements of monies are the basis of new kinds of conflict, as Los Angelenos worry about the Japanese buying up their city, and people in Bombay worry about the rich Arabs from the Gulf States who have not only transformed the prices of mangoes in Bombay, but have also substantially altered the profile of hotels, restaurants and other services in the eyes of the local population, just as they continue to do in London. Yet, most residents of Bombay are ambivalent about the Arab presence there, for the flip side of their presence is the absence of friends and kinsmen earning big money in the Middle East and bringing back both money and luxury commodities to Bombay and other cities in India. Such commodities transform consumer taste in these cities, and also often end up smuggled through air and sea ports and peddled in the gray markets of Bombay's streets. In these gray markets, some members of Bombay's middle-classes and of its lumpenproletariat can buy some of these goods, ranging from cartons of Marlboro cigarettes, to Old Spice shaving cream and tapes of Madonna. Similarly gray routes, often subsidized by the moonlighting activities of sailors, diplomats, and airline stewardesses who get to move in and out of the country regularly, keep the gray markets of Bombay, Madras and Calcutta filled with goods not only from the West, but also from the Middle East, Hong Kong and Singapore.

It is this fertile ground of deterritorialization, in which money, commodities and persons are involved in ceaselessly chasing each other around the world, that the mediascapes and ideoscapes of the modern world find their fractured and fragmented counterpart. For the ideas and images produced by mass media often are only partial guides to the goods and experiences that deterritorialized populations transfer to one another. In Mira Nair's brilliant film, *India Cabaret*, we see the multiple loops of this fractured deterritorialization as young women, barely competent in Bombay's metropolitan glitz, come to seek their fortunes as cabaret dancers and prostitutes in Bombay, entertaining men in clubs with dance formats derived wholly from the prurient dance sequences of Hindi films. These scenes cater in turn to ideas about Western and foreign women and their 'looseness', while they provide tawdry career alibis for these women. Some of these women come from Kerala, where cabaret clubs and the pornographic film industry have blossomed, partly in response to the purses and tastes of Keralites returned from the Middle East, where their diasporic lives away from women distort their very sense of what the relations between men and women might be. These tragedies of displacement could certainly be replayed in a more detailed analysis of the relations between the Japanese and German sex tours to Thailand and the tragedies of the sex trade in Bangkok, and in other similar loops which tie together fantasies about the other, the conveniences and seductions of travel, the economics of global trade and the brutal mobility fantasies that dominate gender politics in many parts of Asia and the world at large.

While far more could be said about the cultural politics of deterritorialization and the larger sociology of displacement that it expresses, it is appropriate at this juncture to bring in the role of the nation-state in the disjunctive global economy of culture today. The relationship between states and nations is everywhere an embattled one. It is possible to say that in many societies, the nation and the state have become one another's projects. That is, while nations (or more properly groups with ideas about nationhood) seek to capture or co-opt states and state power, states simultaneously seek to capture and monopolize ideas about nationhood (Baruah, 1986; Chatterjee, 1986; Nandy, 1989). In general, separatist, transnational movements, including those which have included terror in their methods, exemplify nations in search of states: Sikhs, Tamil Sri Lankans, Basques, Moros, Quebecois, each of these represent imagined communities which seek to create states of their own or carve pieces out of existing states. States, on the other hand, are everywhere seeking to monopolize the moral resources of community, either by flatly claiming perfect coevality between nation and state, or by systematically museumizing and representing all the groups within them in a variety of heritage politics that seems remarkably uniform throughout the world (Handler, 1988; Herzfeld, 1982; McQueen, 1988). Here, national and international mediascapes are exploited by nation-states to pacify separatists or even the potential fissiparousness of all ideas of difference. Typically, contemporary nation-states do this by exercising taxonomical control over difference; by creating various kinds of international spectacle to domesticate difference; and by seducing small groups with the fantasy of self-display on some sort of global or cosmopolitan stage. One important new feature of global cultural politics, tied to the disjunctive relationships between the various landscapes discussed earlier, is that state and nation are at each's throats, and the hyphen that links them is now less an icon of conjuncture than an index of disjuncture. This disjunctive relationship between nation and state has two levels: at the level of any given nation-state, it means that there is a battle of the imagination, with state and nation seeking to cannibalize one another. Here is the seed-bed of brutal separatisms, majoritarianisms that seem to have appeared from nowhere, and micro-identities that have become political projects within the nation-state. At another level, this disjunctive relationship is deeply entangled with the global disjunctures discussed throughout this essay: ideas of nationhood appear to be steadily increasing in scale and regularly crossing existing state boundaries:

sometimes, as with the Kurds, because previous identities stretched across vast national spaces, or, as with the Tamils in Sri Lanka, the dormant threads of a transnational diaspora have been activated to ignite the micro-politics of a nation-state.

In discussing the cultural politics that have subverted the hyphen that links the nation to the state, it is especially important not to forget its mooring in the irregularities that now characterize 'disorganized capital' (Lash and Urry, 1987; Kothari, 1989). It is because labor, finance and technology are now so widely separated that the volatilities that underlie movements for nationhood (as large as transnational Islam on the one hand, or as small as the movement of the Gurkhas for a separate state in the North-East of India) grind against the vulnerabilities which characterize the relationships between states. States find themselves pressed to stay 'open' by the forces of media, technology, and travel which had fueled consumerism throughout the world and have increased the craving, even in the non-Western world, for new commodities and spectacles. On the other hand, these very cravings can become caught up in new ethnoscapes, mediascapes, and eventually, ideoscapes, such as 'democracy' in China, that the state cannot tolerate as threats to its own control over ideas of nationhood and 'peoplehood'. States throughout the world are under siege, especially where contests over the ideoscapes of democracy are fierce and fundamental, and where there are radical disjunctures between ideoscapes and technoscapes (as in the case of very small countries that lack contemporary technologies of production and information); or between ideoscapes and finanscapes (as in countries, such as Mexico or Brazil where international lending influences national politics to a very large degree); or between ideoscapes and ethnoscapes (as in Beirut, where diasporic, local and translocal filiations are suicidally at battle); or between ideoscapes and mediascapes (as in many countries in the Middle East and Asia) where the lifestyles represented on both national and international TV and cinema completely overwhelm and undermine the rhetoric of national politics: in the Indian case, the myth of the law-breaking hero has emerged to mediate this naked struggle between the pieties and the realities of Indian politics, which has grown increasingly brutalized and corrupt (Vachani, 1989).

The transnational movement of the martial-arts, particularly through Asia, as mediated by the Hollywood and Hongkong film industries (Zarilli, forthcoming) is a rich illustration of the ways in which long-standing martial arts traditions, reformulated to meet the fantasies of contemporary (sometimes lumpen) youth populations, create new cultures of masculinity and violence, which are in turn the fuel for increased violence in national and international politics. Such violence is in turn the spur to an increasingly rapid and amoral arms trade which penetrates the entire world. The worldwide spread of the AK-47 and the Uzi, in films, in corporate and state security, in terror, and in police and military activity, is a reminder that apparently simple technical uniformities often conceal an increasingly complex set of loops, linking images of violence to aspirations for community in some 'imagined world'.

Returning then to the 'ethnoscapes' with which I began, the central paradox of ethnic politics in today's world is that primordia (whether of language or skin color or neighborhood or of kinship), have become globalized. That is, sentiments whose greatest force is in their ability to ignite intimacy into a political sentiment and turn locality into a staging ground for identity, have become spread over vast and irregular spaces, as groups move, yet stay linked to one another through sophisticated media capabilities. This is not to deny that such primordia are often the product of invented traditions (Hobsbawm and Ranger, 1983) or retrospective affiliations, but to emphasize that because of the disjunctive and unstable interplay of commerce, media, national policies and consumer fantasies, ethnicity, once a genie contained in the bottle of some sort of locality (however large) has now become a global force, forever slipping in and through the cracks between states and borders.

But the relationship between the cultural and economic levels of this new set of global disjunctures is not a simple one-way street in which the terms of global cultural politics are set wholly by, or confined wholly within, the vicissitudes of international flows of technology, labor and finance, demanding only a modest modification of existing neo-Marxist models of uneven development and state-formation. There is a deeper change, itself driven by the disjunctures between all the landscapes I have discussed, and constituted by their continuously fluid and uncertain interplay, which concerns the relationship between production and consumption in today's global economy. Here I begin with Marx's famous (and often mined) view of the fetishism of the commodity, and suggest that this fetishism has been replaced in the world at large (now seeing the world as one, large, interactive system, composed of many complex subsystems) by two mutually supportive descendants, the first of which I call production fetishism, and the second of which I call the fetishism of the consumer.

By production fetishism I mean an illusion created by contemporary transnational production loci, which masks translocal capital, transnational earning-flows, global management and often faraway workers (engaged in various kinds of high-tech putting out operations) in the idiom and spectacle of local (sometimes even worker) control, national productivity and territorial sovereignty. To the extent that various kinds of Free Trade Zone have become the models for production at large, especially of high-tech commodities, production has itself become a fetish, masking not social relations as such, but the relations of production, which are increasingly transnational. The locality (both in the sense of the local factory or site of production and in the extended sense of the nation-state) becomes a fetish which disguises the globally dispersed forces that actually drive the production process. This generates alienation (in Marx's sense) twice intensified, for its social sense is now compounded by a complicated spatial dynamic which is increasingly global.

As for the fetishism of the consumer, I mean to indicate here that the consumer has been transformed, through commodity flows (and the mediascapes, especially of advertising, that accompany them) into a sign, both in Baudrillard's sense of a simulacrum which only asymptotically approaches the form of a real social agent; and in the sense of a mask for the real seat of agency, which is not the consumer but the producer and the many forces that constitute production. Global advertising is the key technology for the worldwide dissemination of a plethora of creative, and culturally well-chosen, ideas of consumer agency. These images of agency are increasingly distortions of a world of merchandising so subtle that the consumer is consistently helped to believe that he or she is an actor, where in fact he or she is at best a chooser.

The globalization of culture is not the same as its homogenization, but globalization involves the use of a variety of instruments of homogenization (armaments, advertising techniques, language hegemonies, clothing styles and the like), which are absorbed into local political and cultural economies, only to be repatriated as heterogeneous dialogues of national sovereignty, free enterprise, fundamentalism, etc. in which the state plays an increasingly delicate role: too much openness to global flows and the nation-state is threatened by revolt — the China syndrome; too little, and the state exits the international stage, as Burma, Albania and North Korea, in various ways have done. In general, the state has become the arbiter of this *repatriation of difference* (in the form of goods, signs, slogans, styles, etc.). But this repatriation or export of the designs and commodities of difference continuously exacerbates the 'internal' politics of majoritarianism and homogenization, which is most frequently played out in debates over heritage.

Thus the central feature of global culture today is the politics of the mutual effort of sameness and difference to cannibalize one another and thus to proclaim their succesful hijacking of the twin Enlightenment ideas of the triumphantly universal and the resiliently particular. This mutual cannibalization shows its ugly face in riots, in refugee-flows, in state-sponsored torture and in ethnocide (with or without state support). Its brighter side is in the expansion of many individual horizons of hope and fantasy, in the global spread of oral rehydration therapy and other low-tech instruments of well-being, in the susceptibility even of South Africa to the force of global opinion, in the inability of the Polish state to repress its own working-classes, and in the growth of a wide range of progressive, transnational alliances. Examples of both sorts could be multiplied. The critical point is that both sides of the coin of global cultural process today are products of the infinitely varied mutual contest of sameness and difference on a stage characterized by radical disjunctures between different sorts of global flows and the uncertain landscapes created in and through these disjunctures.

Notes

A longer version of this essay appears in *Public Culture* 2 (2), Spring 1990. This longer version sets the present

formulation in the context of global cultural traffic in earlier historical periods, and draws out some of its implications for the study of cultural forms more generally.

1. One major exception is Fredric Jameson, whose (1984) essay on the relationship between postmodernism and late capitalism has in many ways, inspired this essay. However, the debate between Jameson (1986) and Ahmad (1987) in *Social Text* shows that the creation of a globalizing Marxist narrative, in cultural matters, is difficult territory indeed. My own effort, in this context, is to begin a restructuring of the Marxist narrative (by stressing lags and disjunctures) that many Marxists might find abhorrent. Such a restructuring has to avoid the dangers of obliterating difference within the 'third world', of eliding the social referent (as some French postmodernists seem inclined to do) and of retaining the narrative authority of the Marxist tradition, in favor of greater attention to global fragmentation, uncertainty and difference.
2. These ideas are argued more fully in my book, *Modernity At Large: Cultural Dimensions of Globalization* (Minneapolis: University of Minnesota Press, 1996).

References

Ahmad, A. (1987) 'Jameson's Rhetoric of Otherness and the "National Allegory" ', *Social Text* 17: 3–25.

Amin, S. (1980) *Class and Nation: Historically and in the Current Crisis.* New York and London: Monthly Review.

Anderson, B. (1983) *Imagined Communities: Reflections on the Origin and Spread of Nationalism.* London: Verso.

Appadurai, A. (1989) 'Global Ethnoscapes: Notes and Queries for a Transnational Anthropology', in R.G. Fox (ed.), *Interventions: Anthropology of the Present.*

Appadurai, A. and Breckenridge, C.A. (1990) *A Transnational Culture in the Making: The Asian Indian Diaspora in the United States.* London: Berg.

Barber, K. (1987) 'Popular Arts in Africa', *African Studies Review* 30(3).

Baruah, S. (1986) 'Immigration, Ethnic Conflict and Political Turmoil, Assam 1979–1985', *Asian Survey* 26 (11).

Chatterjee, P. (1986) *Nationalist Thought and the Colonial World: A Derivative Discourse.* London: Zed Books.

Feld, S. (1988) 'Notes on World Beat', *Public Culture* 1(1): 31–7.

Gans, Eric (1985) *The End of Culture: Toward a Generative Anthropology.* Berkeley: University of California.

Hamelink, C. (1983) *Cultural Autonomy in Global Communications.* New York: Longman.

Handler, R. (1988) *Nationalism and the Politics of Culture in Quebec.* Madison: University of Wisconsin.

Hannerz, U. (1987) 'The World in Creolization,' *Africa* 57(4): 546–59.

Hannerz, U. (1989) 'Notes on the Global Ecumene', *Public Culture* 1(2): 66–75.

Hechter, M. (1974) *Internal Colonialism: The Celtic Fringe in British National Development, 1536–1966*. Berkeley and Los Angeles: University of California.

Herzfeld, M. (1982) *Ours Once More: Folklore, Ideology and the Making of Modern Greece*. Austin: University of Texas.

Hobsbawm, E. and Ranger, T. (eds) (1983) *The Invention of Tradition*. New York: Columbia University Press.

Ivy, M. (1988) 'Tradition and Difference in the Japanese Mass Media', *Public Culture* 1(1): 21–9.

Iyer, P. (1988) *Video Night in Kathmandu*. New York: Knopf.

Jameson, F. (1984) 'Postmodernism, or the Cultural Logic of Late Capitalism', *New Left Review* 146 (July–August): 53–92.

Jameson, F. (1986) 'Third World Literature in the Era of Multi-National Capitalism', *Social Text* 15 (Fall): 65–88.

Kothari, R. (1989) *State Against Democracy: In Search of Humane Governance*. New York: New Horizons.

Lakoff, G. and Johnson, M. (1980) *Metaphors We Live By*. Chicago and London: University of Chicago.

Lash, S. and Urry, J. (1987) *The End of Organized Capitalism*. Madison: University of Wisconsin.

McQueen, H. (1988) 'The Australian Stamp: Image, Design and Ideology', *Arena* 84 Spring: 78–96.

Mandel, E. (1978) *Late Capitalism*. London: Verso.

Mattelart, A, (1983) *Transnational and Third World: The Struggle for Culture*. South Hadley, MA: Bergin and Garvey.

Nandy, A. (1989) 'The Political Culture of the Indian State', *Daedalus* 118(4): 1–26.

Nicoll, F. (1989) 'My Trip to Alice', *Criticism, Heresy and Interpretation (CHAI)*, 3: 21–32.

Schiller, H. (1976) *Communication and Cultural Domination*. White Plains, NY: International Arts and Sciences.

Vachani, L. (1989) 'Narrative, Pleasure and Ideology in the Hindi Film: An Analysis of the Outsider Formula', MA thesis, The Annenberg School of Communication. The University of Pennsylvania.

Wallerstein, I. (1974) *The Modern World-System* (2 volumes). New York and London: Academic Press.

Warner, M. (1990) *The Letters of the Republic: Publication and the Public Sphere*, Cambridge, MA: Harvard.

Williams, R. (1976) *Keywords*. New York: Oxford.

Wolf, E. (1982) *Europe and the People Without History*. Berkeley: University of California.

Yoshimoto, M. (1989) 'The Postmodern and Mass Images in Japan', *Public Culture* 1(2): 8–25.

Zarilli, P. (1995) 'Repositioning the Body: An Indian Martial Art and its Pan-Asian Publics' in CA. Breckenridge (ed.) *Consuming Modernity: Public Culture in a South Asian World*, Minneapolis: University of Minnesota Press, 183–215.

6.
THE PRACTICE OF EVERYDAY (MEDIA) LIFE
From Mass Consumption to Mass Cultural Production
Lev Manovich

The explosion of user-created media content on the web (dating from, say, 2005) has unleashed a new media universe. (Other terms often used to refer to this phenomenon include *social media* and *user-generated content*.) On a practical level, this universe was made possible by free web platforms and inexpensive software tools that enable people to share their media and easily access media produced by others, cheaper prices for professional-quality devices such as HD video cameras, and the addition of cameras and video capture to mobile phones. What is important, however, is that this new universe is not simply a scaled-up version of twentieth-century media culture. Instead, we have moved from *media* to *social media*.[1] What does this shift mean for how media functions and for the terms we use to talk about media? What do trends in web use mean for culture in general and for professional art in particular? These are the questions this essay will engage with.

Today *social media* is often discussed in relation to another term, *web 2.0* (coined by Tim O'Reilly in 2004). This term refers to a umber of different technical, economic, and social developments; for our purposes, two commonly held ideas about web 2.0 are most relevant, but, as we will see, only the second is borne out by statistics. First, in the 2000s, we are supposedly seeing a gradual shift from the majority of internet users accessing content produced by a much smaller number of professional producers to users increasingly accessing content produced by other nonprofessional users. Second, if in the 1990s the web was mostly a publishing medium, in the 2000s it

has increasingly become a communication medium. (Communication between users, including conversations around user-generated content, takes place through a variety of forms besides email: posts, comments, reviews, ratings, gestures and tokens, votes, links, badges, photos, and video.)[2]

But these trends do not mean that every user has become a producer or that every user consumes mostly amateur material. According to 2007 statistics, only between 0.5 percent and 1.5 percent of users of the most popular social media sites (Flickr, YouTube, Wikipedia) contributed their own content. Others remained consumers of the content produced by this 0.5–1.5 percent. Further, in commercial media sites we have seen a fundamental shift in cultural consumption, referred to as the long-tail phenomenon. Not only the so-called Top 40 sites but most of the content available online—including content produced by amateurs—finds an audience.[3] These audiences can be tiny, but they are not zero. In the middle of the 2000s every track out of a million or so available through iTunes sold at least once a quarter. In other words, every track no matter how obscure found at least one listener. This translates into a new economics of media. As researchers who have studied the long-tail phenomena have demonstrated, in many industries the total volume of sales generated by such low-popularity items exceeds the volume generated by the Top 40.[4]

The second idea often expressed about web 2.0—the use of the web for social communication—is indeed supported by statistics. The numbers of people participating in some way in social networks, whether by accessing, discussing, or sharing media that they created themselves, are astonishing—at least from the perspective of early 2008. (It is likely that in 2012 or 2018 they will look trivial in comparison to what will be happening then.) MySpace: 300,000,000 users. Cyworld, a Korean site similar to MySpace: 90 percent of South Koreans in their twenties or 25 percent of the total population of South Korea. Hi5, a leading social media site for Central America: 100,000,000 users.[5] Facebook: 14,000,000 photo uploads daily. The number of new videos uploaded to YouTube every twenty-four hours (as of July 2006): 65,000.[6]

Clearly, in the 2000s we are going through a fundamental shift in modern media culture. So what does media mean after web 2.0?

The Practice of Everyday (Media) Life: Tactics as Strategies

For different reasons, media, businesses, consumer electronics, web industries, and academics celebrate content created and exchanged by web users. Academics, in particular, give disproportional attention to certain genres such as youth media, activist media, and political mashups, which are indeed important but do not represent more typical usage by hundreds of millions of people.

In celebrating user-generated content and implicitly equating *user-generated* with *alternative* and *progressive*, academic discussions often stay away from asking certain basic critical questions. For instance, to what extent is the phenomenon of user-generated content driven by the consumer electronics industry—the producers of digital cameras, video cameras, music players, laptops, and so on? or to what extent is the phenomenon of user-generated content also driven by social media companies themselves, who after all are in the business of getting as much traffic to their sites as possible so they can make money by selling advertising and their usage data?

Given that a significant percentage of user-generated content either follows the templates and conventions set up by the professional entertainment industry or directly reuses professionally produced content, does this mean that people's identities and imaginations are now even more firmly colonized by

commercial media than they were in the twentieth century? In other words, is the replacement of mass consumption of commercial culture in the twentieth century by mass production of cultural objects by users in the early twenty-first century a progressive development? or does it constitute a further stage in the development of the culture industry as analyzed by Adorno and Horkheimer in *The Culture Industry: Enlightenment as Mass Deception* (1944)? Indeed, if twentieth-century subjects were simply consuming the products of the culture industry, twenty-first century prosumers and "pro-ams" are passionately imitating it. That is, they now make their own cultural products that follow the templates established by the professionals and/or rely on professional content.

A case in point is anime music videos (AMV). My search for *anime music videos* on YouTube on 7 February 2008 returned 250,000 videos. Animemusicvideos.org, the main web portal for AMV (before the action moved to YouTube), contained 130,510 AMVs as of 9 February 2008. AMVs are made by fans who edit together clips from one or more anime series and put the resultant video to music, which comes from, say, a professional music video. Sometimes, AMVs also use footage cut from video games. In the last few years, AMV makers also increasingly started to add visual effects available in software such as After Effects. But regardless of the particular sources used and their combination, in the majority of AMVs all video and music comes from commercial media products. AMV makers see themselves as editors rather than as filmmakers or animators.[7]

To help us analyze AMV culture, let's put to work the categories set up by Michel de Certeau in *The Practice of Everyday Life.*[8] De Certeau makes a distinction between strategies used by institutions and power structures and tactics used by modern subjects in their everyday lives. The tactics are the ways in which individuals negotiate strategies that were set for them. For instance, to take one example discussed by de Certeau, a city's layout, signage, driving and parking rules, and official maps are strategies created by the government and corporations. The ways an individual moves through the city—taking shortcuts, wandering aimlessly, navigating through favorite routes—are tactics. In other words, an individual can't physically reorganize the city, but he or she can adapt it to his or her needs by choosing how to move through it. A tactic "expects to have to work on things in order to make them its own, or to make them 'habitable.' "[9]

As de Certeau points out, in modern societies most of the objects that people use in their everyday lives are mass-produced goods; these goods are the expressions of strategies of designers, producers, and marketers. People build their worlds and identities out of these readily available objects by using different tactics: bricolage, assembly, customization, and—to use a term that was not a part of de Certeau's vocabulary but that has become important today—remix. For instance, people rarely wear every piece from one designer as they appear in fashion shows; they usually mix and match different pieces from different sources. They also wear pieces of clothing in different ways than they were intended, and they customize the clothes themselves with buttons, belts, and other accessories. The same goes for the ways in which people decorate their living spaces, prepare meals, and in general construct their lifestyles.

While the general ideas of *The Practice of Everyday Life* still provide an excellent intellectual paradigm for thinking about vernacular culture, changes have occurred since its publication, though not dramatically in the area of governance; yet even there we see moves towards more transparency and visibility. But in the consumer economy the changes have been quite substantial. Strategies and tactics are now often closely linked in an interactive relationship, and often their features are reversed. This is particularly true for born-digital industries and media, such as software, computer games, web sites, and social networks. Their products are explicitly designed to be customized by users. Think, for instance, of the original graphical user interface (popularized by Apple's Macintosh in 1984), which allows the user to customize the appearance and functions of the computer and the applications. The same applies to recent web interfaces—for instance, iGoogle, which allows the user to set up a custom home page selecting from many applications and information sources. Facebook, Flickr, Google, and other social media companies encourage others to write applications, which mash up data and add new services (as of early 2008, Facebook hosted over 15,000 applications written by outside developers).

The explicit design for customization is not limited to the web; for instance, many computer games ship with a level editor that allows users to create their own levels of play.

Although the industries dealing with the physical, rather than the digital, world are moving much slower, they are on the same trajectory. In 2003 Toyota introduced Scion cars. Scion marketing was centered on the idea of extensive customization. Nike, Adidas, and Puma have all experimented with allowing consumers to design and order their own shoes by choosing from a broad range of shoe parts. (In the case of the Puma Mongolian Shoe Barbeque concept, a few thousand different shoes can be constructed.)[10] In early 2008 Bug Labs introduced what they called "the Lego of gadgets": an open-sourced consumer electronics platform consisting of a minicomputer and modules such as a digital camera or LCD screen.[11] The recent celebration of DIY practice in various consumer industries is another example of this growing trend. In short, since the publication of *The Practice of Everyday Life*, companies have developed strategies that mimic people's tactics of bricolage, reassembly, and remix. The logic of tactics has now become the logic of strategies.

The web 2.0 paradigm represents the most dramatic reconfiguration to date of the relationship between strategies and tactics. According to de Certeau's original analysis from 1980, tactics do not necessarily result in objects or anything stable or permanent: "Unlike the strategy, it [the tactic] lacks the centralized structure and permanence that would enable it to set itself up as a competitor to some other entity. . . . It renders its own activities an 'unmappable' form of subversion" *("PEL")*. Since the 1980s, however, consumer and culture industries have started to systematically turn every subculture (particularly every youth subculture: bohemians, hip-hop and rap, Lolita fashion, rock, punk, skinhead, goth, and so on)[12] into products. In short, people's cultural tactics were turned into strategies now sold to them. To oppose the mainstream, you now have plenty of lifestyles—accompanied by every subcultural aspect, from music and visual styles to clothes and slang—available for purchase.

However, in the 2000s, the transformation of people's tactics into business strategies went in a new direction. The developments of the previous decade—the web platform, the dramatically decreased costs of media capture and playback, increased global travel, and the growing consumer economies of many countries that after 1990 joined the "global world"—led to the explosion of user-generated content available in digital form: web sites, blogs, forum discussions, short messages, digital photos, video, music, maps, and so on. Responding to this explosion, web 2.0 companies created powerful platforms designed to host this content. MySpace, Facebook, Live Journal, Blogger, Flickr, YouTube, hi5, Cyworld, Wretch (Taiwan), Orkut (Brazil), Baidu (China), and thousands of other social media sites make this content instantly available worldwide (except, of course, in those countries that block or filter these sites). Thus, not just particular features of particular subcultures but the details of the everyday lives of hundreds of millions of people who make and upload their media or write blogs became public.

What was ephemeral, transient, unmappable, and invisible became permanent, mappable, and viewable. Social media platforms give users unlimited space for storage and plenty of tools to organize, promote, and broadcast their thoughts, opinions, behavior, and media. You can already directly stream video using your laptop or mobile phone, and it is only a matter of time before constant broadcasting of one's life becomes as common as email. If you follow the evolution from the MyLifeBits project (2001–) to Slife software (2007–) and the Yahoo! Live personal broadcasting service (2008–), the trajectory towards constant capture and broadcasting of one's everyday life is clear.

According to de Certeau's theory, strategy "is engaged in the work of systematizing, of imposing order." "Its ways are set. It cannot be expected to be capable of breaking up and regrouping easily, something which a tactical model does naturally" *("PEL")*. The strategies used by social media companies today, however are the exact opposite; they are focused on flexibility and constant change. (Of course, all businesses in the age of globalization had to become adaptable, mobile, flexible, and ready to break up and regroup, but they rarely achieved the flexibility of web companies and developers.)[13] According to O'Reilly, one important feature of web 2.0 applications is "design for 'hackability' and remixability."[14] Thus,

most major web 2.0 companies—Amazon, eBay, Flickr, Google, Microsoft, Yahoo!, and YouTube—make available their programming interfaces and some of their data to encourage others to create new applications.[15]

In summary, today strategies used by social media companies often look more like tactics in the original formulation by de Certeau while tactics look like strategies. Since the companies that create social media platforms make money from having as many users as possible visit them (they do so by serving ads, by selling data about usage to other companies, by selling add-on services, and so on), they have a direct interest in having users pour as much of their lives into these platforms as possible. Consequently, they give users unlimited storage space for all their media and the ability to customize their online lives (for instance, by controlling what is seen by whom) by expanding the functionality of the platforms themselves.

This, however, does not mean strategies and tactics have completely exchanged places. If we look at the actual media content produced by users, here the relationship between strategies and tactics is different. As I already mentioned, for many decades companies have been systematically turning the elements of various subcultures into commercial products. But these subcultures themselves rarely develop completely from scratch; rather, they are the result of the cultural appropriation and/or remix of earlier commercial culture.[16] AMV subculture is a case in point. On the one hand, media content exemplifies the new strategies-as-tactics phenomenon; AMVs are hosted on mainstream social media sites such as YouTube, so they are not exactly "transient" or "unmappable" (since you can search them, see how other users rated them, and so on). On the other hand, on the level of content, they very much exemplify de Certeauvian everyday life; the great majority of AMVs consist of segments lifted from commercial anime shows and commercial music. This does not mean that the best AMVs are not creative or original, but their creativity is different from the romantic and modernist model of making it new. To use de Certeau's terms, we can describe the process of creating new web content as a tactical creativity, which "expects to have to work on things in order to make them its own, or to make them 'habitable.' "

Conversations through Media

So far I discussed social media using the old familiar terms. However, these very terms—*content, cultural object, cultural production*, and *cultural consumption*—are redefined by web 2.0 practices. We see new kinds of communication where factual content, opinion, and conversation often can't be clearly separated. Blogs are a good example of this; lots of blog entries consist of comments about an item copied from another source. Or think about forums or comments below a web site entry in which an original post may generate a long discussion that goes into new and original directions, with the original item long forgotten.

Often *content, news*, or *media* become tokens used to initiate or maintain a conversation. Their original meaning is less important than their function as tokens. I am thinking here of people posting pictures on each other's pages on MySpace or exchanging gifts on Facebook. What kind of gift you get is less important than receiving a gift or the act of posting a comment or a picture. Although it may appear that such conversations simply foreground Roman Jakobson's emotive and/or phatic communication functions described in 1960,[17] it is also possible that a detailed analysis will show them to be a genuinely new phenomenon.

The beginnings of such an analysis can be found in the work of social media designer Adrian Chan. As he points out, "All cultures practice the exchange of tokens that bear and carry meanings, communicate interest and count as personal and social transactions." Token gestures "cue, signal, indicate users' interests in one another." While the use of tokens is not unique to networked social media, some of the features pointed out by Chan do appear to be new. For instance, as Chan notes, the use of tokens is often "accompanied by ambiguity of intent and motive (the token's meaning may be codified while the user's motive for using it may not). This can double up the meaning of interaction and communication, allowing the recipients of tokens to respond to the token or to the user behind its use."[18]

Consider another very interesting new communication situation: a conversation around a piece of media—for instance, comments added by users below somebody's Flickr photo or YouTube video that respond not only to the media object but also to

other comments."[19] (The same is often true for comments, reviews, and discussions on the web in general; the object in question can be software, a film, a previous post, and so on.) Of course, such conversation structures are also common in real life; think of a typical discussion in a graduate film studies class, for instance. However, web infrastructure and software allow such conversations to become distributed in space and time; people can respond to each other regardless of their location, and the conversation can in theory go forever. (The web has millions of such conversations taking place at the same time.) These conversations are quite common; according to a report by the Pew Internet and American Life Project, among U.S. teens who post photos online, 89 percent reported that people comment on these photos at least some of the time.[20]

Equally interesting is a conversation that takes place through images or video—for instance, responding to a video with a new video. This, in fact, is a standard feature of the YouTube interface.[21] (Note that all examples of interfaces, features, and common uses of social media sites refer to early 2008; obviously details may change by the date of this essay's publication.) Though social media sites contain huge numbers of such conversations through media, for me the most interesting case so far is a five-minute theoretical video, "Web 2.0 . . . The Machine Is Us/ing Us," posted by a cultural anthropologist, Michael Wesch, on 31 January 2007.[22] A year later this video had been watched 4,638,265 times. It had also generated twenty-eight video responses ranging from short thirty-second comments to equally theoretical and carefully crafted long videos.

Just as is the case with any other feature of contemporary digital culture, some precedents can be found for any of these communication situations. For instance, modern art can be understood as conversations among different artists, artistic schools, critics, and curators. That is, one artist or movement is responding to the work produced by another artist or movement. Thus, modernists in general reacted against classical nineteenth-century culture, Jasper Johns and other pop artists reacted to abstract expressionism, Jean-Luc Godard reacted to Hollywood-style narrative cinema, and so on. To use the terms of YouTube, we can say that Godard posted his video response to one huge clip called classical narrative cinema. But the Hollywood studios did not respond—at least not for another thirty years.

Typically, conversations among artists and artistic schools were not full conversations. One artist or school produced something, another artist or school later responded with their own productions, and this was all. The first artist or school usually did not respond. But, beginning in the 1980s, professional media practices began to respond to each other more quickly, and conversations no longer are one-way. Music videos affect the editing strategies of feature films and television; similarly, today noncinematic motion graphics are employing narrative features. Cinematography, which before only existed in films, is used in video games. But these conversations are still different from the communication between individuals through media in a networked environment. In the case of web 2.0, individuals, rather than only professional producers, directly talk to each other using different media, and the exchange can happen within hours.

Because of their two-way nature, conversations between people conducted through and around visual and/or sound objects can also be related to exchanges between professional critics. Through the medium of a journal, modern art critics were able to respond to each other relatively quickly—if not in hours, then at least in weeks. In fact, such exchanges between critics (and sometimes modernist artists who also acted as critics and theorists) played a key role in the development of modern art. Think of the battles between different modern isms in the 1910s and 1920s conducted in journals such as the Russian *LEF*, Michael Fried's essay "Art and Object-hood" with its attack on minimalism in the 1960s, or the establishment of postmodern doctrine in *October* in the first half of the 1980s. Certainly, very few if any of the conversations between users and fans today have the same length, theoretical grounding, or role as these professional critical exchanges in the past. They do, however, play increasingly important roles in shaping professionally produced media. Game producers, musicians, and film companies try to react to what fans say about their products, implement fans' wishes, and even shape story lines in response to conversations among cultural consumers.

Is Art after Web 2.0 Still Possible?

Do professional artists benefit from the explosion of media content online and the easily available media publishing platforms? Does the fact that we now have such platforms, where anybody can publish their videos and charge for the downloads, mean that artists have a new distribution channel for their works? Or does the world of social media—hundreds of millions of people daily uploading and downloading video, audio, and photographs; media objects produced by unknown authors getting millions of downloads; media objects fluently and rapidly moving between users, devices, contexts, and networks—make professional art irrelevant? In short, while modern artists have so far successfully met the challenges of each generation of media technologies, can professional art survive the extreme democratization of media production and access?

On one level, this question is meaningless. Surely, never has modern art been so commercially successful. No longer a pursuit for a few, contemporary art has become another form of mass culture. Its popularity is often equal to that of other mass media. Most importantly, contemporary art has become a legitimate investment category, and, with all the money invested in it, it is unlikely that this market will ever collapse. (Of course, history repeatedly has shown that even the most stable political regimes do eventually collapse.)

In a certain sense, since the beginnings of globalization in the early 1990s, the number of participants in the institution called contemporary art has grown, an increase that parallels the rise of social media in the 2000s. Since the early 1990s, many new countries have entered the "global world" and adopted Western values in their cultural politics; they have supported, collected, and promoted contemporary art. Thus, today Shanghai already has not just one but three museums of contemporary art plus more large-size spaces that show contemporary art than New York or London. A number of starchitects such as Frank Gehry and Zaha Hadid are now building museums and cultural centers on Saadiyat Island in Abu Dhabi. Rem Koolhaas is building a new museum of contemporary art in Riga.

In the case of social media, the unprecedented growth in the number of people who upload and view each other's media has led to lots of innovation. While the typical diary video or anime on YouTube may not be that special, enough are. In fact, in all media where the technologies of production are democratized (video, music, animation, graphic design, and so on), I have come across many projects that not only rival those produced by most well-known commercial companies and most well-known artists but also often explore areas not yet touched by those with lots of symbolic capital.

While some of these projects come from proto-typical amateurs, prosumers, and pro-ams, most are done by young professionals or professionals-in-training. The emergence of the web as the new standard communication medium in the 1990s means that today in most cultural fields every professional or company, regardless of its size and physical location, has a web presence and posts new work online. Perhaps most importantly, young design students can now put their work before a global audience. They can see what others are doing, and they can develop new tools together; consider, for example, the processing.org community.

Note that we are not talking about "classical" social media or "classical" user-generated content here, since, at least at present, many such portfolios, sample projects, and demo reels are being uploaded on company web sites and specialized aggregation sites known to people in the field. Here are some examples of such sites that I consult regularly: xplsv. tv (motion graphics, animation), coroflot.com (design portfolios from around the world), archinect.com (architecture students' projects), and infosthetics.com (information visualization). In my view, the significant percentage of works you find on these web sites represents the most innovative cultural production done today. Or, at least, they make it clear that the world of professional art has no special license on creativity and innovation.

But perhaps the most important conceptual innovation has been happening in the development of the web 2.0 medium itself. I am thinking about all the new creative software tools—web mashups, Firefox plug-ins, Facebook applications, and so on—coming from both large companies such as Google and from individual developers. Therefore, the true challenge posed to art by social media may not be all the excellent cultural work produced by students and nonprofessionals, although I do think this is also important. The real challenge may lie in the dynamics of web 2.0 culture—its constant innovation, its energy, and its unpredictability.

Notes

1. See Adrian Chan, "Social Media: Paradigm Shift?" www.gravity/.com/paradigm_shift_1.html
2. See ibid.
3. "The long tail" was coined by Chris Anderson in 2004. See Chris Anderson, "The Long Tail," *Wired* 12 (Oct. 2004): www.wired.com/wired/archive/12.10/tail.html
4. More long-tail statistics can be found in Tom Michiels, "The Long Tail of Search," 17 Sept. 2007, www.zoekmachine-marketing-blog.com/artikels/white-paper-the-long-tail-of-search
5. See www.pipl.com/statistics/social-networks/size-growth/
6. See Wikipedia, s.v. "MySpace," "Cyworld," "Facebook," and "YouTube," en.wikipedia.org/wiki/MySpace, en.wikipedia.org/wiki/Cyworld, en.wikipedia.org/wiki/Facebook, and en.wikipedia.org/wiki/Youtube
7. Conversation with Tim Park, 9 Feb. 2009.
8. See Michel de Certeau, *The Practice of Everyday Life*, trans. Steven Rendall (1980; Berkeley, 1984).
9. Wikipedia, s.v. "*The Practice of Everyday Life*," en.wikipedia.org/wiki/The_Practice_of_Everyday_Life; hereafter abbreviated "*PEL*."
10. See www.puma.com/secure/mbbq/
11. See buglabs.net/
12. See Wikipedia, s. v. "The History of Western Subcultures in the Twentieth Century," en.wikipedia.org/wiki/History_of_subcultures_in_the_20th_century
13. Here is a typical statement coming from the business community: "Competition is changing overnight, and product lifecycles often last for just a few months. Permanence has been torn asunder. We are in a time that demands a new agility and flexibility: and everyone must have the skill and insight to prepare for a future that is rushing at them faster than ever before" (Jim Carroll, "The Masters of Business Imagination Manifesto aka The Masters of Business Innovation," www.jimcarroll.com/10s/10MBI.htm).
14. Tim O'Reilly, "What Is Web 2.0: Design Patterns and Business Models for the Next Generation of Software," www.oreillynet.com/pub/a/oreilly/tim/news/2005/09/30/what-is-web-20.html?page=4
15. See Wikipedia, s.v. "Mashup (Web Application Hybrid)," en.wikipedia.org/wiki/Mashup_%28web_application_hybrid%29

16. A very interesting feature in *Wired* describes a creative relationship between commercial manga publishers and fans in Japan. One story quotes Keiji Takeda, one of the main organizers of fan conventions in Japan, as saying, "This is where [the convention floor] we're finding the next generation of authors. The publishers understand the value of not destroying that" (Daniel H. Pink, "Japan, Ink: Inside the Manga Industrial Complex," *Wired* 15 [Oct. 2007]: www.wired.com/techbiz/media/magazine/15–11/ff_manga?currentPage=3).

17. See Louis Hébert, "The Functions of Language," *Signo* (2006), www.signosemio.com/jakobson/a_fonctions.asp

18. Chan, "Social Media."

19. According to a survey conducted in 2007, 13 percent of internet users who watch videos also post comments about the videos. This number, however, does not tell how many of these comments are responses to other comments. See Mary Madden, "Online Video: 57 Percent of Internet Users Have Watched Videos Online and Most of Them Share What They Find with Others," 25 July 2007, www.pewinternet.org/pdfs/PIP_Online_Video_2007.pdf

20. See Amanda Lenhart et al., "Teens and Social Media: The Use of Social Media Gaining a Greater Foothold in Teen Life as They Embrace the Conversational Nature of Interactive Online Media," 19 Dec. 2007, www.pewinternet.org/pdfs/PIP_Teens_Social_Media_Final.pdf

21. The phenomenon of conversation through media was first noted by Derek Lomas in 2006 in relation to comments on MySpace pages.

22. See youtube.com/watch?v=6gmP4nkoEOE

SECTION II

MEDIA/TECHNOLOGY

Introduction

This section considers the role of technology in media culture as theorized by leading scholars in the field. The issue of determination is at the center of critical analysis of media technologies, with some scholars suggesting that different media forms—such as print versus television broadcasting—shape human consciousness and societies in particular ways. While communication scholars have convincingly situated the time and space shifting capacities and "biases" of technologies within historical contexts, critical media studies has more or less rejected the notion that media technologies emerge spontaneously and fully formed, each with their own innate properties.

The suggestion that technology drives societal change is also suspect. Following the cues of Raymond Williams and others who have situated the shape and timing of new technologies within the tensions and contradictions of different stages of capitalism, cultural historians have been especially keen to situate the march of technological "progress" within historical contexts marked by the reconfiguration of public and private, tensions related to gender, race and class, new leisure patterns and the transition from Fordism to a more flexible and dispersed mode of capitalist production.

At the same time, the surge of digital media technologies in recent decades has been accompanied by an impetus to fetishize gadgets and gizmos at the expense of critical analysis, and a touch of technological determinism as well. The aim of this section is to provide a wider perspective, taking scholarship on old media technologies when they were new as an opportunity to historicize the present and featuring influential authors who ask different questions about particular mediums and move discussion beyond a static concern with assumed properties, "advances" and effects.

We begin with Susan Douglas' 2006 essay "The Turn Within: The Irony of Technology in a Globalized World," a reassessment of formative writing on media and technology. Douglas considers the relevance of Marshall McLuhan, best known for his 1964 book *Understanding Media*. As much an intellectual celebrity as a scholar, McLuhan made frequent television appearances, and many of his books crossed over into public discourse and became bestsellers. While his arguments have been updated and advanced by other scholars such as Neil Postman, McLuhan has lost much of his currency in critical media studies, with the notable exception of Canada, where retrospectives on the importance of his work are more common. More often, McLuhan's breezy catch phrases and over-the-top technological determinism often serve as a foil for other approaches. His famous characterization of mediums as "hot" or "cold" is often dismissed as reductive and simplistic, and his assumptions about the media of modern Western and "backward" non-Western societies reveal his own unacknowledged racist and imperialist biases.

However, McLuhan was one of the first to point out how media technologies were reshaping global culture with his enduring metaphor of the "global village." Douglas revisits his prediction that a "new, electronic nervous system" would connect people around the globe in the context of post-9/11 media culture. While Douglas rejects any notion that media operate independently of economic and corporate restraints, she suggests that McLuhan was right to suggest that communications technologies do have particular properties. Calling for a more nuanced understanding of "soft determinism," Douglas argues that rather than forming a global village, new media technologies (including television) have led to a fusion of "ethnocentrism and narcissism, best cast as a 'turn within."

While Douglas synthesizes long-running debates from the vantage point of the present, Walter Benjamin's 1936 essay "The Work of Art in the Age of Mechanical Reproduction" is a much earlier, groundbreaking account of the possibilities of photography and moving images. Benjamin brought Marxist theory and a concern with industrialist capitalist production to bear on his analysis of the new visual technologies of reproduction, including photography and especially film. Benjamin also recognized the narcotic potential of art that does not demand concentration but rather tolerates and indeed encourages "reception in a state of distraction." While Benjamin shared some of the concerns about alienation and loss of organic community articulated by other critical German intellectuals of the period, his scholarship has also been interpreted as being more ambivalent and optimistic about the possibilities of mass cultural production than his contemporaries.

Perhaps the most influential aspect of his essay was his suggestion that the ability to copy and distribute images en mass destroyed the unique "aura" of the original, and thus rendered art far less controllable by rituals grounded in aristocratic and religious practices and more available to practices of leisure and politics. Benjamin was ambiguous on the extent to which mechanical reproduction democratized culture or facilitated a powerful new means of guiding and perhaps manipulating the masses. Perhaps his own uncertainty is partly responsible for the endurance of his arguments, as Benjamin's essay remains one of the foundational texts of critical media studies.

The new technology of recorded sound is the subject of Lisa Gitelman's 1997 essay "Reading Music, Reading Records, Reading Race: Musical Copyright and the Act of 1909." Her historical study shows how recorded sound (phonographs, wax recordings, pianolas and paper music rolls) confounded both copyright law (which was based on the "readability" of print culture) and the visual habits of audiences accustomed to looking at performers instead of pieces of machinery. For Gitelman, technology does not determine social change or possess any "transcendental truths or divine omnipotence." Rather, her scholarship illustrates the value of institutional history, mapped onto "social practices and hierarchies," including racial hierarchies and discrimination. Instead of being colorblind media, she writes, the phonograph and later radio entered into the existing politics of policing racial distinction in ways that informed efforts to define recorded sound as intellectual property. If the new technology partly destabilized the visuality of music including "societal norms of visually apprehending racial and other differences," technology alone was unable to overcome racism or impetus to "own" and control culture as private property.

In "The Domestic Economy of Television Viewing in Postwar America," which was republished in her enormously influential 1990 book *Make Room for TV: Family and Television in Postwar America*, historian Lynn Spigel traces what she calls the social construction of broadcast television in the 1950s. Also rejecting theories of technological determinism, Spigel builds on Raymond Williams' pioneering work on mobile privatization (1974/1992), which situates the emergence of broadcasting at a particular historical juncture (the 1940s and 1950s) in a particular form (centralized distribution, broadest possible reception) within the contradictory requirements of industrial capitalism. Williams argued that broadcasting facilitated virtual mobility and access to public worlds, at a time when social life outside work was increasingly contained within the domestic space of the private home. Spigel adds gender to the picture, and shows how the new medium of television developed in tandem with women's domestic labor practices in the home.

Spigel, following Williams, approaches television as a cultural technology whose birth cannot be fully explained by technological experimentation or centralized public and private institutions. To understand more fully the medium's relationship to a changing way of life, she traces the discursive construction of television and TV watching in popular magazines and other venues. Revisiting the popular discursive contexts in which television was defined and debated enables Spigel to access uncertainty and ambivalence about television's cultural value and impact on family life. These debates, she suggests, spoke to long-running concerns about leisure and labor in the home, as well as burgeoning tensions associated with suburbanization and the nuclear family. Spigel also emphasizes the spatial aspects of media technologies, attending to the place of television in the home and the way in which the privatized domestic space of television reception (a space that was not natural but rather the consequence of broader social and economic configurations) differentiated the medium from cinema and other public recreations.

Anna McCarthy's complimentary 2001 essay "From Screen to Site" introduces a materialist alternative to philosophical accounts of technology that perpetuate a more subtle form of technological determinism. She questions the focus on television as a technology of space and time binding, not because the medium does not provide networked access to distant periods and lands, but because so few scholars have considered how television matters to more localized registers of scale and place. Taking aim at scholars who characterize the television apparatus as an encroaching force of "placelessness," McCarthy argues that television is an object, and like all objects it "shapes its immediate space through its material form."

For her, the "banal and quotidian" materiality of the TV set, whether as a piece of domestic furniture or as part of the visual architecture of gyms, retail stores and bars, is the crucial issue—one she addresses by bringing theories of cultural geography to bear on media studies. Moving away from universal accounts of television's capacity to spectacularly reorganize space and time and from understandings of television as an inherently domestic medium, she explores the multiple "sites" of the televisual, from art installations in shopping centers to the placement of TV sets in airports and bars. In this way, McCarthy opens up new ways of thinking about how the screen "interlaces with the relations of power and everyday practices that define its place." While her contribution to this collection is mainly theoretical, her site-specific approach is the basis for the case studies examined in her book *Ambient Television: Visual Culture and Public Space* (2001) and other work that explores television's move outside the home—a development that has intensified and changed since the 1990s as mobile viewing platforms from iPads to mobile phones have taken hold.

While McCarthy focuses on the materiality of the TV set and its place, Leopoldinia Fortunati argues for a need to explicate the role of each instrument in major societal transformations. Her 2002 essay "The Mobile Phone: Towards New Categories of Social Relations" does not ascribe innate properties to cellular phones, but rather attempts to theorize what the mobile phone "changed that had not already been changed by fixed telephony." So for example, many technologies modified the relationship of modern citizens to time and space, and people have long used technologies to increase time and space as a means to increased social productivity. However, the mobile phone has a privileged role in this technological transformation of time and space, Fortunati suggests.

Mobile phones took shape in the context of privatization and the collapse of the public sector in many capitalist democracies, and the intensification of an enterprising work ethic. By enabling multi-tasking, the ability to exist in two spaces simultaneously, and identification with one's communicative networks more than public spaces (as exemplified by the commuter to chats on her phone rather than talking with fellow travelers), mobile phones seem particularly in sync with the imperatives and tensions of modern societies, much as television was central to an earlier stage of privatization and industrial capitalism according to Williams. By focusing on the relationship between the mobile phone and society, Fortunati provides a template for moving beyond the celebration or dismissal of new technologies to the more complex work of situating the future of new media with the changing contours of social life.

References

McCarthy, Anna, *Ambient Television: Visual Culture and Public Space* (Durhan, NC: Duke University Press, 2001).
Williams, Raymond, *Television: Technology and Cultural Form* (Hanover NH: Wesleyan University Press, 1992).

7.
THE TURN WITHIN

The Irony of Technology in a Globalized World

Susan J. Douglas

It is the first decade of the twenty-first century. The homes of millions are pulsating with some combination of advanced communication technologies: satellite dishes or cable TV, DVD and VCR players, desktop computers, laptops, modems, CD players, streaming video, cell phones, palm pilots, instant messaging, voice mail. Supposedly we are now part of a "global village": all these technologies compose a new, electronic nervous system that radiates out around the world, connecting people and cultures in unprecedented and more intimate ways. A jolt to this nervous system in one part of the world can now be felt instantly halfway around the planet. Marshall McLuhan, who coined the term "global village" in 1964, argued that these new sensory linkages, these "extensions of man," were destined to bind the world together. But McLuhan's assertion was not just about the flow of information. Embedded in it were assumptions about the emergence of a new subject position, one enabled by technology, in which people possessed (and welcomed) a more curious and empathetic global awareness of other cultures and people. "It is no longer possible," insisted McLuhan, "to adopt the aloof and dissociated role of the literate Westerner" because the new communications technologies have "heightened human awareness of responsibility to an intense degree."[1]

But if you were a resident of the United States in the early twenty-first century, did television, with its technically enabled global reach and instantaneity, hail you as a member of this so-called global village? Is the subject position this webwork of satellites, videophones, cameras, and cables seeks to constitute a globally empathetic one? After 9/11, when one would have expected the nightly news programs to provide a greater focus on international news, attention to the rest of the world was fleeting, with the exception of the war in Iraq. After a precipitous decline in celebrity and lifestyle news in the immediate aftermath of the 9/11 catastrophe, a year later the percentages of these stories in the nightly news were back to where they had been pre-9/11. In 2004, despite the war, the percentage of stories about foreign affairs on the commercial nightly news broadcasts was lower than it had been in 1997.[2] In the print media, there has been an explosion in the number of celebrity magazines—here the technologies of telephoto lenses and cell phone cameras are used to capture television stars walking their dogs or taking out the trash.

In entertainment programming, the proliferation, especially after 9/11, of nonscripted television has brought viewers into private realms—apartments, houses, resorts, or made-for-TV camps set up on remote islands—where dramas about relationships, personal behavior, and people's "confessions" urge viewers to look inward, not outward. On ABC, a bachelor sampled the wares of twenty-five very pretty women over a period of weeks before he decided which one he liked best. On MTV, five buff twentysomethings in a preposterously swanky apartment in Las Vegas or San Diego obsessed about which one of them was inconsiderate, "a bitch," or a lout. On The Learning Channel, couples redecorated each others' houses: here people lived for window treatments and flooring options. On the Food Network, we zeroed in on the deep fulfillment that comes from mincing, dicing, and pureeing. From *The Swan* to *Queer Eye for the Straight Guy* to *The Apprentice*, the cameras zoomed in on narcissistic, consumerist obsessions in which the contestants, and we, were to focus on our bodies, ourselves. Here was the antithesis of the global village.

Because McLuhan was a technological determinist, he envisioned only a one-way trajectory for the media, independent of economic or corporate constraints. He failed to anticipate that technologies that enable us to look out beyond our borders can also encourage us to gaze at our navels, and it has turned out that the latter use is more profitable and cost effective than the former. All communications technologies are scopic technologies: as instruments of viewing, listening, and observing, they can slide our perceptions outward or inward. But they do not, cannot, do so on their own.

This essay argues that, at least in the United States, these new communications technologies have not created a global village but have, ironically, led to a fusion of ethnocentrism and narcissism, best cast as a "turn within." While I reject McLuhan's blanket "the medium is the message" aphorism, as well as his monolithic bifurcation of communications technologies as being either (and only) "hot" or "cool," I argue in this essay that communication technologies do have particular, intrinsic properties; they are simply not unidirectional. Thus, we need to consider how the "soft determinism" of technologies interacts with corporate imperatives, producing often ironic and unintended consequences. It is their scopic capabilities, their ability to zoom in or zoom out, interacting with corporate exigencies and consumer desires that can, at times, produce effects quite contrary to what pundits and the public initially thought they were likely to produce. And this, so far, has been true for McLuhan's prediction that communications technologies would create a global village.

American isolationism is nothing new, but it is striking that during this particular period, when technological capabilities and geopolitical exigencies should have interacted to expand America's global vision, just the opposite occurred. The turn within rests on four conditions: what I am calling the irony of technology; the refining of narcissism and the

economies of ethnocentrism, both of which rely on narrative and journalistic story telling conventions; and the triumph of youth demographics. And while the turn within is a dominant trend promoted and reinforced by corporate media, it has not gone completely uncontested, as this essay will later note.

I want to bring together several trends not usually discussed side by side: the crisis in American journalism, particularly television journalism and the decline of the reporting of international news, the explosion in reality TV shows in the immediate post-9/11 period, and the metastasizing of celebrity culture. These trends put the lie to the supposed inevitability of faster, more portable, less expensive communications technologies producing a global village and the globally empathetic subjects who inhabit it. The relative expense of covering international stories and the ratings-driven push for "news you can use" have exacerbated ethnocentrism and parochialism in the news; the relative cheapness of producing unscripted television, in which everyday people act out or compete with each other in apartments or boardrooms, has exacerbated the self-scrutinizing narcissism of reality TV; and the comparable cheapness and profitability of celebrity media have produced a glut of PR and gossip that insist entertainment personalities are more important to focus on than anything else.

There is a powerful and underappreciated synergy between these seemingly disparate genres, between the ethnocentrism in the news and the narcissism of so much entertainment media, that propels a further spiraling within in American culture. By the spring of 2006 the reality TV boom was beginning to attenuate as the networks in particular returned to scripted programming, yet it is worth noting the important ideological work reality TV did during the immediate post-9/11 era. If television news, in particular, bears especial responsibility for squandering its ability to enhance a global awareness despite its ever-augmented capabilities to do so, reality TV, colonizing television as it did between 2001 and 2005, insisted that the most productive way to use communications technologies was to focus them on individual Americans in confined and controlled spaces hermetically sealed from foreign peoples and cultures.

I'd like to suggest that the consequences of the turn within are especially serious for young people.

Let's take just one piece of evidence. In a widely reported and somewhat embarrassing survey done by the National Geographic Society in 2002, more young Americans (aged 18–24) knew that a recent season of *Survivor* was located in the South Pacific than could find either Israel or New Jersey on a map. Only 13 percent could find Iraq (although they probably didn't do worse here than most adults). But in what one would think would have been a giveaway question, fewer than half could find France, Japan, the United Kingdom, or India on the globe. Fewer than 25 percent could name four countries that officially acknowledge having nuclear weapons. Geographic illiterates, American young people came in next to last of all the countries surveyed, doing better than only youth in Mexico.[3] Of course, the United States' own geographical isolation, the underemphasis on geography in the country's schools, and the fact that the United States remains, for the time being, the world's only superpower, with others wanting and needing to know more about us than we seem to want to know about them, all contribute to this illiteracy. In *Tuned Out: Why Americans Under 40 Don't Follow the News*, David Mindich also documents young people's ignorance about current affairs, despite the passion many of them feel for promoting social justice.[4] Media industries, focusing on certain broad trends among young Americans, such as their declining newspaper readership and their concentration on personal concerns, deploy and privilege the microscopic versus the telescopic properties of communications technologies to maximize profits.

None of this scopic calibration is occurring in a vacuum. Despite the increasing mobility, portability, and reach of communications technologies that can help cultivate a global village, television news organizations chose not to use these tools in this way. Celebrity and scandal journalism dominated the 1990s—the O. J. Simpson case, the Lewinsky scandal, the JonBenet Ramsey murder—and relative peace and prosperity did not compel people to look outward. Nor is it surprising that in the wake of 9/11, some Americans wanted to hide under a collective quilt. Concerns about the consequences of outsourcing, and a forced but superficial engagement with the foreign— particularly the Middle East—may also exacerbate the isolationism that fuels cultural narcissism. But this very same context could have—and indeed, many feel

should have—led to a turn outward. The technology is not an obstacle here. On the contrary, the new wireless, digital media provide an instantaneity and reach that McLuhan could only have dreamed of. The question is, why did just the opposite occur?

Scholars have put it this way: Do machines make history?[5] This overly simplified question has been asked for decades now, in American studies, in media studies, and in the history of science and technology. And a tension has persisted between the academic response to this question and what circulates in the popular press. Consistently, most academics have argued against what has come to be called "hard determinism," in which inventions and technological systems have primary agency. But technological determinism is a rather large stream in the journalistic reservoir of how to explain societal change.[6] Too often in the press, communication technologies— television, the Internet, video cameras, cell phones— are cast as the prime movers and shakers. Television has made politics more about image than substance: television and video game violence cause school shootings, the Internet has reactivated grassroots politics, MySpace gives rise to stalkers, and so forth. And, of course, such maxims are not totally wrong.

It would be flattering, but foolish, to think that such determinism does not also at times enter academic work. And it would also be mistaken to think that scholars sometimes do not give technology its due, that in our resolve to avoid technological determinism we can underestimate how socio-technical systems help create and sustain social change. Indeed, what has come to be called "soft determinism," in which technologies are seen not as the prime movers, but as having some agency in the mix of how individuals, institutions, and political-economic systems respond to and shape technological change, has gained some credence. As Leo Marx and Merritt Roe Smith pointed out, even if technology is demoted from the primary agent of historical change to an agent whose effects are determined by socioeconomic, political, and cultural forces, the fact remains that technology may still powerfully direct the course of events. Thus, they redefine technological determinism: "it now refers to the human tendency to create the kind of society that invests technologies with enough power to drive history."[7] Yet most scholars remain quite wary of technological determinism in any form.

Witness, for example, the high ambivalence surrounding Marshall McLuhan and his various gambits in his 1964 best seller, *Understanding Media*. Here, pure and simple, communications technologies changed history, often suddenly and cataclysmically, and these media could, according to McLuhan, be easily divided up into those that were "hot" and those that were "cool." Media content was irrelevant to McLuhan; for him, the medium was the message: the technology's properties, how it engaged people cognitively and emotionally, were much more important than whatever representations or information it conveyed. McLuhan coined the term "the global village" to capture how he saw new media technologies transforming the world.

After his initial success as a media guru in the 1960s and early 1970s, McLuhan fell into serious disfavor among media studies scholars, displaced by neo-Marxist theorists who saw capitalism, not machines, as the prime shaper of media systems. The social constructivism school in science-technology studies emphasized the often complex process of negotiation and conflict among competing inventors, institutions, early adapters, and consumers that together shaped the ultimate form and uses of technology that were often a major mutation of, even at odds with, the machine's initial design and application.[8] In cultural studies, there was also an emphasis on human agency and political economy, on how people used and adapted communications technologies and their content, although admittedly in circumstances not of their own making. Thus, McLuhan's mechanistic determinism seemed simplistic and, well, historically and sociologically inaccurate. And, with the rise of ideology studies, his dismissal of media content also seemed politically naive.

The most recent rejection of McLuhan has come from the British scholar Brian Winston, who has argued against communications technologies producing "revolutions," and emphasized their long scientific gestation periods. Winston argues that "supervening social necessity" propels the diffusion of some technologies while the "suppression of radical potential," typically by self-interested corporations, thwarts the development and diffusion of others. Yet, Winston has been criticized for lumping all sorts of restraints on technological change into his notion of suppression, and in his efforts to counter McLuhanesque determinism may have underplayed some important determining features of the technologies he reviews.[9]

In fact, in recent years, and particularly with the rise of radio studies, and the impact of e-mail and the Web, some scholars, myself included, have been reconsidering McLuhan's insistence that particular media have different consequences than other media because of the inherent properties of that medium. And McLuhan became the "patron saint" of *Wired* precisely because of his vision of a technologically enabled global village and his notions about how new media cannibalize and repurpose existing media, rendering some aspects of them obsolete while amplifying others. At first the Internet's Web-based structure and many-to-many information exchange capabilities seemed to ensure a flattening of hierarchies; new, potentially more democratic relationships could result from the technology itself, it was hoped. So it is not surprising that McLuhan began to enjoy a revived following in the 1990s.

Nonetheless, while most scholars will not go all the way with his "medium is the message" aphorism, some of us have argued that a medium that denies sight to its audience, like radio, might cultivate a different sort of cognitive and psychic engagement than would television, or e-mail, which privileges print but denies tone of voice and facial cues to its users. Hence the rise of "soft-determinism." And despite the rejection of many of McLuhan's assertions, the term "global village" has become such a part of our collective common sense that it seems everyone takes it for granted: of course all these new media have created a smaller world and enhanced mutual knowledge and understanding.

I am suggesting that "the global village" is a myth, at least in the United States. There is much evidence to refute, or at least to seriously undermine, the teleological conceit that increasingly sophisticated media technologies have led automatically to increased awareness of and sympathy for other cultures. On the contrary, one could argue that the great irony of all these media extensions—satellite transmission, cable, video technology, even the Internet—is that they have, instead, promoted even more isolationist and ethno-centric views. I am particularly interested here in exploring how these communications technologies, or, more accurately, the uses they have been put to, have enabled the turn within in the United States. Drawing from the notion of "soft determinism," we can see how portability, miniaturization, low cost, the proliferation of media outlets, and speed of transmission, which indeed could have promoted the "extensions of man," have instead led to the "implosion of culture."

This leads us to one of the conditions on which the turn within rests: the irony of technology. What does this mean? While each communication technology does have its own individual properties, especially regarding which of the human senses it privileges and which ones it ignores, that can shape the transmission and reception of content in particular ways, the economic and political system in which the device is embedded almost always trumps technological possibilities and imperatives. And ideological structures trump technological systems.

Thus, communications technologies can often have the exact *opposite* consequences of what we think and hope they might be. The great irony of our time is that just when a globe-encircling grid of communications systems indeed makes it possible for Americans to see and learn more than ever about the rest of the world, Americans have been more isolated and less informed about global politics. Two historical moments stand out as absolute exemplars of this irony. The first is in the 1980s when the refinement of satellite, cable, and video technology came together to make McLuhan's "extensions of man" a technical reality but a corporate problem. The second was after 9/11 when these "extensions of man" were most needed but had their capabilities inverted. As a result, our media are not telescopes, searching outward, as McLuhan insisted. They have become microscopes, trained inside.

Of course there is an important caveat here—one does not want to substitute technological determinism with economic determinism, nor with a linear declension narrative. There has always been resistance to the one-to-many, center-to-periphery model of communications preferred by U.S. media industries. Insurgent uses of communications technologies have existed at least since the early days of wireless telegraphy, and historically such rebelliousness has become most pronounced (and destabilizing of the status quo) when corporate control has seemed most complete. Ham operators in the first two decades of the twentieth century sought to use radio for lateral communication among peers and groups in defiance of top-down efforts aimed at military and corporate control of the airwaves. In the late 1960s, counterculture disc jockeys disgusted by the hypercommercialism and banality of AM radio developed a new format and ethos, "underground" or "progressive" radio on FM. Today, bloggers seek to circumvent the gatekeepers of the mainstream media to convey alternative accounts of a variety of events, and everyday people broadcast their own videos online. Of course, these oppositional uses are then often quickly co-opted for corporate gain: witness the transformation of great swaths of the Web into strip malls and the co-optation of Napster by services such as iTunes. So corporate definitions of how to use media technology are never final, uncontested, or complete; they are, however, dominant.

Nor do I mean to idealize some allegedly mythic past in which the airwaves were filled with rich, impartial, informative international news. Scholars as diverse as Herbert Gans and Edward Herman and Noam Chomsky documented the ethnocentric, anti-communist filters that framed the news about the former Soviet Union, Eastern Europe, and Latin America.[10] The point is not to compare today with a nostalgic past that did not exist. The point is to compare what the technology permits with how it is used. Let's remember that in 1963, at the height of the civil rights movement, television news expanded from fifteen to thirty minutes so more stories could be covered in more depth. A comparable decision to expand the nightly network news in the wake of 9/11 did not occur.

In the 1970s, a series of technological advances, most notably the expanded use of geosynchronous satellites to transmit television signals and the replacement of film with video, meant that news and events from around the world could be broadcast as they were happening, live, into people's homes in real time. It was this "liveness," this "you are there" immediacy, that fueled visions of the global village and the more attuned, empathetic subject position it was seen to cultivate.

But we should also consider what the new communications technologies of the 1970s and beyond, technologies that were faster, that brought "liveness" to us, laid before Americans in our living rooms and dens.[11] The irony of technology points to the profound contradiction between the technical capabilities of these space eradicating technologies and the news values and routines that have guided their use. For example, in the United States, newsworthiness is defined first and foremost by conflict or disaster. Thus, with a few notable exceptions, since the coming together especially of satellite transmission, videotape, and cable in the late 1970s—which meant that international news could be covered and transmitted live into people's living rooms—what American viewers have had laid before their feet are famine, floods, hijackings, bloody military coups, terrorist attacks, civil wars, and genocide. Americans saw defeat. American humiliation. We watched helpless as people hung off of helicopters, struggling to get out of Saigon. The news showed us a wild, irrational-seeming anti-Americanism. Plane hijackings we couldn't control. Furious masses of people in the streets of Tehran, shaking their fists at us. Everywhere, a loss of control. Everywhere, a wound.

Later, during Desert Storm, designed, in part, to exorcise the "Vietnam syndrome," the new communications technologies brought viewers a video game war, distant and sanitized from its human toll. Simulated views from the cockpit of "smart bomb" attacks, complete with cross hairs, nighttime infrared photography of bombings, and computer graphics flash cards of the military's preferred armaments all fetishized the weaponry, placed viewers in the position of the pilots or military strategists and rendered invisible, or erased, the living targets.[12] Newsman Garrick Utley, in an article in *Foreign Affairs*, also notes that video technology and satellite transmission, with their capabilities for instant communications, "left little time for developing expertise in a specific country. Reporters became known as 'firemen,' flying from one international conflagration to the next."[13] In other words, the speed and new mobility of news reporting technology, and the graphics in the newsroom, worked in opposition to depth, and thus in opposition to global awareness and empathy.

After 9/11, despite some fleeting and pioneering explorations by Christiane Amanpour and a few others

into the reasons for the attacks, the media focused almost exclusively on the heroism of American police and firefighters and repeated the assertion that the reason for the attacks was that "they hate our freedoms" rather than "probing in depth into the geopolitical situation that might have fueled the terrorism."[14] More recently, the images from the invasion in Iraq showed the initial fireworks of "shock and awe," shaky-cam images of embedded reporters whose low-definition videophone-transmitted faces seemed to come from Mars, or staged events like the toppling of the Saddam statue. Images that would have produced empathy with or sympathy for the Iraqi people were censored, as were images of the toll taken on U.S. soldiers and Iraqis alike. As the coverage evolved and the government's grip on news management faltered, Americans learned about beheadings, bombings, and an incipient civil war. So what these technologies brought over the years were, first, representations of American impotence and, then, representations of distant, supposedly triumphant conquests followed by distant, unfathomable chaos. News routines interacting with increasingly orchestrated and rigid government news management and the battle for ratings powerfully governed the scopic range of what communications technologies could show people, and thus, in fact, blunted what these technologies could permit people to see and feel.

McLuhan was writing in the 1960s when the industrial and regulatory framework of television was quite stable and appeared fixed. There were three national networks regulated by the FCC, and in exchange for having control of the nation's airways they were obliged to supply public affairs programming, much the same structure as had governed radio since 1934. For the networks, especially CBS and NBC, news divisions were a source of prestige, especially given their roles in covering the Kennedy assassination and the civil rights movement. By the mid- to late 1960s, these news divisions, using their gradually expanding arsenal of visual technologies, brought the Vietnam War, Soviet tanks rolling into Prague, and men landing on the moon into people's living rooms. It was the technology, not the institutional structures, that was changing: the conversion, by the mid-1960s, to color broadcasts, the rise of electronic newsgathering and the use of the mini-cam to bring live, on-the-spot news to people, cameras aboard spacecraft beaming images back to earth, all indeed pointed to the inevitability of a global village. McLuhan, seemingly gripped by that uncritical ideology of progress that dominated some scholarship and popular thinking in the early 1960s, could not foresee a time when corporate imperatives and financial constraints would thwart what all this new technology could actually deliver.

The high point in the irony of technology occurred not long after McLuhan's death in 1980. Just as outward-reaching media technologies continued to proliferate in the 1980s and beyond, the three broadcast networks, facing competition from the cable networks and pressure to increase their profit margins, spun off their news divisions from their entertainment divisions (which had previously partially subsidized the news), insisted that news divisions become profitable and support themselves, and, thus, downsized them. So, at the very same time—the early to mid-1980s—when the convergence of new media technologies meant that the war in the Falklands, for example, could be brought to viewers around the globe live via CNN—the broadcast networks began cutting costs in their news divisions. All the networks scaled back on international reporting and eliminated a host of foreign news bureaus. International news was replaced by less expensive entertainment news, mayhem news, lifestyle and other human-interest stories, celebrity journalism, and news about health and fitness. By 2000, new news segments devoted to personal health, such as CBS's "Health Watch" and NBC's "Life Line" were embedded news beats in the network news lineups. While those on the right and the left continue to fight over whether the news is dominated by a liberal or conservative bias, few have emphasized that the greatest bias in the news today that emerged from these decisions is the narcissism bias.

Various studies of the news media have documented the turn within in journalism. Between 1971 and 1982, foreign news in newspapers dropped from 10.2 percent to 6 percent of what journalists call the newshole.[15] In 1989, only 2.6 percent of the nonadvertising space in ten leading U.S. newspapers was devoted to international news. The percentages are dramatic as well in the newsweeklies. In *Time*, international news dropped from 24 percent to 14 percent between 1985 and 1995, and in *Newsweek* from 22 percent to 12 percent during the same time period. In 1987 *Time* featured eleven cover stories on international news; by 1997, that number had dropped to one.[16] The decline seems even more precipitous in TV news. The time there devoted to international news has, according to one study, dropped from 45 percent in the 1970s to 13.5 percent by 1995, or, in other words, a whopping 70 percent fall off.[17]

In their critique of the news media, *The News About the News*, Leonard Downie and Robert Kaiser, both top editors at the *Washington Post*, sat down separately with Peter Jennings, Dan Rather, and Tom Brokaw. They showed each anchor a broadcast from his news show in the early 1980s, just as each man had taken over as anchor. "This is amazing, truly amazing," they quote Rather as saying, responding to how few graphics and how much international news the 1981 broadcast he saw contained. All three anchors affirmed that they could never get that much international news in today. The networks had cut back on international news by cutting bureaus and foreign correspondents that are deemed too expensive.[18]

Certainly there were some historical reasons for this. In the early 1970s, the United States was still involved in Vietnam, still enmeshed in the cold war, and those two factors alone could account for the increased coverage back then. The cold war in particular provided an ongoing, us-versus-them, good-versus-evil story in which Vietnam and other international stories could be framed. Likewise, in 1979, the Iranian hostage crisis "became one of the most widely covered stories in television history"; it inaugurated *Nightline*, and Walter Cronkite, by then voted the most trusted man in America, closed every broadcast with an announcement of how many days the hostages had been in captivity.[19] It's not surprising then, one might argue, that international news coverage has dropped from such highs.

But certainly there's more to it than this. And let's examine another set of figures collected after the events in the 1970s. "total foreign coverage on network nightly news programs has declined precipitously," from nearly 3,800 minutes in 1989 to just over 1,800 minutes in 1996 at ABC (the leader) and from 3,350 minutes to 1,175 minutes at NBC.[20] In 1988, ABC featured 1,158 foreign bureau reports; by 1996, that was down to 577 reports. As media critics and disappointed journalists themselves have pointed out, the ongoing press for higher profits and lower costs continued to target international news coverage, the most expensive news to gather despite the new technology. Given that, as Garrick Utley reports, to send a correspondent and a production team plus 600 pounds of equipment to a new locale cost, in 1997, $3,000 a day plus excess baggage fees, international coverage has come to be seen as an expendable expense. In addition, many network executives believed Americans were completely uninterested in foreign news, so why bother? According to Mort Zuckerman, editor in chief of *U.S. News and World Report*, and Maynard Parker of *Newsweek*, "featuring a foreign subject on the cover of the magazine results in a 25 percent drop in newsstand sales."[21] Americans, the conventional wisdom went, wanted "news you can use."

It wasn't just commercial pressures that undercut the possibility for a global village; the entrenched narrative and filmic conventions of the network news also, with some exceptions, worked against constituting an empathetic global village subject. If ideological structures trump technological systems, one of the main ways that they do so is through dominant storytelling practices. News routines in most international stories lead to people in foreign countries being represented in highly conventional, often stereotypical ways that make them seem not at all like "us," but, as that overused word emphasizes, "other." As Herbert Gans's still classic study of the news documented, and as many developing countries have complained, foreign countries become newsworthy in the United States when they are afflicted by natural disasters, wars, coups d'etat, or terrorist attacks.[22]

Thus, the people American viewers see most frequently are victims or combatants. Those we see in the streets of Gaza or Jerusalem or Baghdad are mostly featured in long shots or medium shots, as undifferentiated members of groups or masses. They are furious protestors, masked guerillas, soldiers, or grief-stricken victims. They are "tribal," masses of them gather in the streets shaking their fists, screaming and chanting; they chop each others' limbs off; they are mute, poverty-stricken victims; they wear too many clothes, or not enough; they are antimodern. They are objects of journalistic scrutiny, lacking a subjectivity except one filled with rage or the most desperate sorrow. Occasionally, of course, viewers get a sound-bite from a person in the street, but news programs are more likely to give airtime to official spokespeople. And the sound-bites are all too brief. (The length of the average sound-bite for presidential candidates in the 1996 election was down to 7.2 seconds; why would a person on the streets of China, Sudan, or Iraq get any more?[23]) These were all snapshots, flipping on after the other, and not contextualized, embedded in narratives that made sense or garnered empathy. Why turn outward, toward them? There is nothing to understand, much to reject.

At the same time that industry decisions were blunting the "global village" capabilities of communications technologies, other industrial imperatives began to privilege their narcissistic and domestic surveillance capabilities. Two dominant media trends in the first decade of the twenty-first century, the juggernaut of reality TV between 2000 and 2005, and the explosion in celebrity-based entertainment and journalism magnified the importance of personality, the interpersonal, surveillance of behavior and the body, and an even more insistent consumerism. Video technology made shows such as *COPS, America's Most Wanted*, and *Rescue 911* inexpensive to produce; *America's Funniest Home Videos* made the viewer the producers. MTV's *Real World*, which premiered in 1991, pioneered in using video technology to record the everyday interactions and relationship melodramas of a small group of people. But the turning point came in the summer of 2000, when *Big Brother* and *Survivor* premiered on American television, became rating success stories, and inaugurated a new programming era characterized by minimal writing and the use of everyday people instead of actors. As Susan Murray and Laurie Ouellette point out, the genre almost instantly metastasized to produce subgenres: the gamedoc (*Survivor* and *Fear Factor*), the dating shows (*Joe Millionaire* and *The Bachelor*), makeover/lifestyle shows (*Extreme Makeover, Queer Eye for the Straight Guy*), the docusoap (*Real World, Sorority Life*), talent shows (*American Idol*), and reality sitcoms (*The Osbournes, The Newlyweds*). "Not since the quiz show craze of the 1950s," they write, "have nonfictional entertainment programs so dominated the network prime-time schedule ... By January 2003, one-seventh of all programming on ABC was reality based."[24]

Reality TV came to replace, in particular, the lineup of TV newsmagazines that had dominated various network schedules in the 1990s.[25] Programs such as *Dateline, 20/20* and *48 Hours* offered a mix of investigative reports, typically about domestic issues, and human interest stories that often focused on individuals. While these programs did little to expand people's global horizons they did provide a mix of hard and soft news. On unscripted TV shows, by contrast, the outside world, in the form of magazines, newspapers, books, and TV news (all of which would be part of everyday people's actual environments) is expunged from the bubble of the reality TV world. In the hands of reality TV producers and network executives, cheap, portable, interactive communications technology in the service of this genre privileges self-absorption, self-scrutiny, the intricacies of interpersonal interactions and an obsession with the private and personal at the expense of any broader public issues.

Narcissism sells, not only because it celebrates, even elevates, the quotidian aspects of our everyday lives into weighty theater, but also because narcissism—the desperate desire for the approval of others—also sells products, legions of them. Christopher Lasch's 1977 best seller, *The Culture of Narcissism*, was incredibly prescient in analyzing the role that the media, and especially advertising, played in constituting the "narcissistic personality of our time," a person utterly reliant on the approval of others, desperate to make a good first impression, filled with a deep self-loathing, terrified of aging and death, and having no core, independent self. But even Lasch didn't anticipate this televisual refining and cultivating of narcissism.

The filmic and narrative practices of reality TV are especially designed to promote intimacy and scrutiny of others and the self, quite different from the distance and objectification encouraged by the visual conventions on the nightly news. This stylistic gap also reinforces the bond between the ethnocentrism cultivated by the news and the narcissism cultivated by reality TV. So the news and its storytelling frameworks do not stand alone, they operate in relation to others that dominate in the media. As viewers, we learn who we are supposed to identify with, and who we are supposed to distance ourselves from and see as alien through both genres.

Unlike how we view the long shots of groups and crowds on the news, consider how we meet the participants in most reality shows. Of course there are the seemingly "real" group dynamic shots in the boardroom or jungle or apartment. But then the different participants are shot alone, sitting in a chair, talking to the camera, telling us their reactions, their judgments, concerns. They are subjects of their own lives, *with* inner lives. The structure of the show invites us to empathize with them, judge them, or both.

Having said that, however, let's also consider what is meant to stand for a rich inner life on reality TV. What do the participants in these shows ponder? Who dissed whom, who didn't wash the dishes, who seems sincere, who took responsibility and who shirked it, who has the hots for whom. "She's the party girl–sister I never had," opines one young woman on *The Real World* while another offers the bracing observation that "we've all been put here for a reason." The inner lives viewers get to see consist primarily of banalities, shallow personal bleatings about other people's behaviors. Inner life here consists of reactions and attitudes, in which you don't have to really know much of anything except how you feel. Inner life here is not occupied by concerns about the environment, world hunger, politics, philosophy, or the meaning of life. So, in the overall televisual experience, as we move between news and reality TV, we are invited to distance ourselves from people abroad and, instead, to insert ourselves deeply into the interpersonal relations of a group of preselected, mostly young, mostly white people whose major concerns are staged as highly narcissistic and vapid.

The point is not to single out reality TV as the latest and possibly worst example of television schlock. Rather, by exploding on the scene when it did, between 2000 and 2005, and by insisting through its televisual and narrative conventions that portable, barely noticeable cameras are best deployed, and most effectively reveal the richness of human experience, when trained on preselected people in confined, often domestic spaces, reality TV served as the validating pivot for the turn within in the news and elsewhere. The preferred discourse of the whole genre is one that celebrates a determined isolationism, a luxuriant self-absorption. It was the discourse of reality TV in particular that legitimated, after the initial aftermath of 9/11, a preference for the microscopic rather than the telescopic properties of communications technologies.

The turn within has not gone uncontested, nor is it a uniform turn. A 2002 poll conducted by the Pew Research Center for the People and the Press reported that 63 percent of respondents felt it was very important for the news to cover foreign events and that interest in international news, especially the Middle East, had increased since 2000. For college graduates, international news had become a top news subject.[26] The business press, whose readers require international news and information, provides this service to its audience. Blogs by soldiers in Iraq, freelance journalists, and academics challenge the superficiality or official line proffered by the network news. Especially in the run-up to the U.S.-led invasion of Iraq, and during the occupation and insurgency, e-mail Listservs have offered reports and commentary from international news sources, and BBC.com reported a major increase in hits from U.S. readers. The upstart network Current TV features stories by young people using small digital video cameras to cover everyday life in Iraq, dangerous methods of transport used by illegal immigrants into the United States, and the ongoing war in Afghanistan.

Thus, the turn within has contributed, at least for a subset of the U.S. population, to a hegemonic crisis for the mainstream news media. It is held in widespread disregard, with viewers on the right and the left perceiving bias, and many feeling they are not getting accurate or complete information.[27] So despite powerful industry imperatives, the life span and dominance of the turn within remains unclear, especially given the ongoing threat of terrorism and the rise of other economies, most notably those of India and China, and other nuclear powers, that may cause the spotlight to shift.

In this era in which the word *globalization* is used so constantly, and profligately, and is linked to an automatic assumption that communications technologies undergird the shrinking of the world, we need to address the scopic capabilities of these devices, and analyze which political and economic structures encourage their microscopic versus their telescopic capabilities. This calls, in part, for more policy analysis on our parts, more attention to political economy, more linking of textual analysis with that political economy. And the way state-corporate systems interact with scopic technologies changes over time, so historicizing these relationships is key.

For example, wars, colonial and postcolonial relations, economic relationships, geographic proximity and form of government, from autocratic to neoliberal, all influence different societies to different degrees regarding whether the lenses of their communications systems will zoom out and let the world in or zoom in and keep it at bay. In the United States, wars that involved large sectors of the population, from the Civil War to World War II and the Vietnam War, deployed and often enhanced the telescopic capacities of communications technologies. Just one striking example was radio's—and CBS Radio's in particular—use and refinement of transatlantic shortwave broadcasts to bring the Blitz, or the fall of France, or D-Day directly into people's homes. Yet in the United States, unlike in Europe, geographic proximity matters for naught here, as evidenced by the virtually nonexistent attention news programs give to Canada or Mexico (except when the latter's citizens cross U.S. borders). As government regulation of the broadcast media has weakened in the United States, coverage of international affairs has also declined. And the United States, being, for the moment, the world's only superpower, has meant that others need to learn more about the United States than many feel we need to learn about them. Future research and theorizing needs to itemize, schematize, and analyze these different historical and political articulations comparatively so we can move beyond blanket technological or economic determinism.

When many of us threw McLuhan out in the 1970s, we repudiated the notion that communications technologies could make history on their own, and that rejection stands today, even given how so many communication technologies—the Internet, e-mail and cell phones—have transformed daily life. But it now appears that communication scholars were too quick in our wholesale rejection of "the medium is the message." Communications technologies do have some inherent capabilities that privilege some senses—and thus some cognitive and behavioral processes—over others. As we in American studies consider the ways technology and society affect each other in the digital age, we need to examine how these inherent capabilities are enhanced or thwarted by the institutional structures that regulate, profit from, or are even surprised and destabilized by scopic technologies.

In thinking through soft determinism and the turn within, we should keep in mind Thomas Misa's "middle-level theory" of technological determinism. Misa notes that those who adopt a more "macro" view of history and society tend to give technology a much more causal role (e.g., McLuhan), while scholars doing more "micro-level" analyses, who examine the multiple and often contingent factors shaping technological innovation and diffusion, tend to give technology itself minimal agency. "Middle-level theory" seeks to find an intermediate level of analysis in which technology is seen as both socially constructed and as society shaping.[28] It is at the middle level that we can best analyze the articulations between the scopic capabilities of communications technologies and the industrial decisions about when and why to zoom out and when and why to zoom in.

Today, the economies of ethnocentrism are trumping the telescopic capabilities of communications technologies, particularly on television. With news organizations becoming increasingly small divisions of large entertainment behemoths, the economic incentives for ethnocentric programming are overwhelming. In addition, the triumph of youth demographics means that advertisers want the eighteen to forty-nine demographic, but especially the eighteen to thirty-four demographic. Today's young people rarely watch the network news or read newspapers; in part, they don't trust the news. They see the news as not about or for them but for an older audience, and many are focused on their own lives rather than on current affairs. The mass media pander to all of this and offer fare obsessed with sex, relationships, self-surveillance, physical challenges, voyeurism, the humiliation of others, and incessant celebrity psychodramas.

Without imposing some false taxonomy on communications technologies, we should think more about which ones are telescopic, microscopic, and cinemascopic. They do not fall neatly into categories, as most are multivalent. If we think about satellite transmissions and the new videophones as being telescopic, bringing distant events and peoples into view, their zoom-in images can also isolate these events and peoples from their sociopolitical contexts. Telephoto resolution is often low. The same video technology that brought us *Big Brother* also revealed the beating of Rodney King and, through tourists' own cameras, the first news footage of the 2004 tsunami. And there may be some communications technologies, in isolation or in combination with each other, that we would consider cinemascopic, providing a wide, panoramic view and encompassing the viewer as well as the viewed. Such tableaus have existed primarily in the world of cinema, in which fictional stories about other parts of the world are meant to reveal the actual, "real" truth we don't see on the news. In other words, if we take what is most important from McLuhan—that communications technologies do have inherent properties that we need to take seriously without giving them total deterministic power—then there is still much work to do in thinking through their multiple and at times paradoxical powers.

So we must also keep in mind that the uses and effects of communications technologies are not pat; they are often, as Claude Fischer reminds us in his terrific book about the telephone, *America Calling*, contradictory. The telephone allowed for the invasion of people's privacy from the outside, which many hated; it also allowed for more immediate contact with friends and family, especially important in emergencies, which people embraced.[29] The example I know best is radio, so often cited as "bringing the nation together" during the Great Depression and WWII. Through national entertainment programs that attracted 40 million listeners, Roosevelt's fireside chats, sporting events, and coverage of the war, of course radio enabled (much more than newspapers ever could or did) the construction of an imagined nation.[30] But radio also broadcast local programs that promoted more regional identifications sometimes in opposition to such homogenized national affiliations. Just because the networks and the advertisers who supported them (and, later, the government) wanted to construct a national market with a national self-concept and loyalties does not mean that their success was complete.

Media coverage of new communications technologies either suggests some unilinear trajectory or lapses into a utopian versus dystopian framework (the Internet will produce a thriving new public sphere; the Internet will allow child pornographers to stalk our kids). As we in American studies struggle in our own lives with the multiple, contradictory consequences of the digital revolution and with the rapid but unequal global diffusion of communications technologies, we must always remember the irony of technology, and the ongoing gaps and tensions between technological capabilities on the one hand, and the not insignificant power of ideological frameworks and corporate-state interests on the other. It is at this nexus, in this struggle and mess at the middle levels, that we will find the most interesting and important stories to tell about technology and modern life in the twenty-first century.

Notes

1. Marshall McLuhan, *Understanding Media: The Extensions of Man* (New York: Signet, 1964), 19–20.
2. "The State of the News Media 2005," Project for Excellence in Journalism, online at Journalism.org (accessed July 11, 2006).
3. Survey available at www.nationalgeographic.com/geosurvey (accessed July 11, 2006).
4. David T. Z. Mindich, *Tuned Out: Why Americans Under 40 Don't Follow the News* (New York: Oxford University Press, 2005).
5. The classic article here is Robert L. Heilbroner's "Do Machines Make History?" *Technology and Culture* 8 (July 1967): 335–45.
6. Leo Marx and Merritt Roe Smith, "Introduction," in *Does Technology Drive History?* ed. Leo Marx and Marrit Roe Smith (Cambridge, Mass.: MIT Press, 1994), xi.
7. Marx and Smith, "Introduction," xiv.
8. The flagship book here is *The Social Construction of Technological Systems: New Directions in the Sociology and History of Technology*, ed. Wiebe Bijker, Thomas P. Hughes, and Trevor Pinch (Cambridge, Mass.: MIT Press, 1989).
9. Brian Winston, *Media, Technology, and Society: A History from the Telegraph to the Internet* (New York: Routledge, 1998).
10. Herbert Gans, *Deciding What's News* (New York: Vintage Books, 1979); Edward S. Herman and Noam Chomsky, *Manufacturing Consent* (New York: Pantheon, 1988).
11. Robert Stam, "Television News and Its Spectator," in *Film and Theory*, ed. Robert Stam and Toby Miller (New York: Blackwell, 2000).
12. Susan J. Douglas, "Camouflaging Reality with Faux News, Clever Decoys," *In These Times*, February 13–19, 1991.
13. Garrick Utley, "The Shrinking of Foreign News," *Foreign Affairs*, March–April 1997, 4.
14. S. Elizabeth Bird, "Taking It Personally: Supermarket Tabloids after September 11," in *Journalism After September 11*, ed. Barbie Zelizer and Stuart Allen (New York: Routledge, 2002), 145. See also Michael Traugott and Ted Brader, "Explaining 9/11" in *Framing Terrorism: The News Media, the Government, and the Public*, ed. Pippa Norris, Montague Kern, and Marion Just (New York: Routledge, 2003).
15. James F. Hoge, "Foreign News: Who Gives a Damn?" *CJR*, November–December 1997. The newshole is the amount of time or space devoted to reporting the news, as opposed to the entire paper or broadcast, which also includes advertising.
16. W. Lance Bennett, *News: The Politics of Illusion* (New York: Longman, 2003), 14–15.
17. Hoge, "Foreign News."
18. Leonard Downie Jr. and Robert G. Kaiser, *The News About the News* (New York: Alfred A. Knopf, 2002), 111.
19. Melanie McAlister, *Epic Encounters: Culture, Media, and U.S. Interests in the Middle East, 1945–2000* (Berkeley: University of California Press, 2004), 198.
20. Utley, "The Shrinking of Foreign News," 2.
21. Hoge, "Foreign News."
22. Gans, *Deciding What's News*, 35–37.
23. Bennett, *News*, 34–35.
24. Susan Murray and Laurie Ouellette, eds., *Reality TV: Remaking Television Culture* (New York: New York University Press, 2004), 3–4.
25. I am grateful to Amanda Lotz for this point.
26. "Public's News Habits Little Changed by September 11," Pew Research Center for the People and the Press, online at people-press.org/reports/display.php3?ReportID=156 (accessed July 11, 2006).
27. See the Pew Center's Study, *Media: More Voices, Less Credibility*, at http://people-press.org/commentary/display.php3?AnalysisID=105 (accessed July 11, 2006).
28. Thomas J. Misa, "Retrieving Sociotechnical Change from Technological Determinism," in *Does Technology Drive History?* ed. Marx and Smith, 115–41.
29. Claude S. Fischer, *America Calling: A Social History of the Telephone to 1940* (Berkeley: University of California Press, 1994).
30. See Susan J. Douglas, *Listening In: Radio and the American Imagination* (Minneapolis: University of Minnesota Press, 2004).

8.
THE WORK OF ART IN THE AGE OF MECHANICAL REPRODUCTION
Walter Benjamin

"Our fine arts were developed, their types and uses were established, in times very different from the present, by men whose power of action upon things was insignificant in comparison with ours. But the amazing growth of our techniques, the adaptability and precision they have attained, the ideas and habits they are creating, make it a certainty that profound changes are impending in the ancient craft of the Beautiful. In all the arts there is a physical component which can no longer be considered or treated as it used to be, which cannot remain unaffected by our modern knowledge and power. For the last twenty years neither matter nor space nor time has been what it was from time immemorial. We must expect great innovations to transform the entire technique of the arts, thereby affecting artistic invention itself and perhaps even bringing about an amazing change in our very notion of art." *

—Paul Valéry, PIÈCES SUR L'ART,
"La Conquète de l'ubiquité," Paris.

Preface

When Marx undertook his critique of the capitalistic mode of production, this mode was in its infancy. Marx directed his efforts in such a way as to give them prognostic value. He went back to the basic conditions underlying capitalistic production and through his presentation showed what could be expected of capitalism in the future. The result was that one could expect it not only to exploit the proletariat with increasing intensity, but ultimately to create conditions which would make it possible to abolish capitalism itself.

The transformation of the superstructure, which takes place far more slowly than that of the substructure, has taken more than half a century to manifest in all areas of culture the change in the conditions of production. Only today can it be indicated what form this has taken. Certain prognostic requirements should be met by these statements. However, theses about the art of the proletariat after its assumption of power or about the art of a classless society would have less bearing on these demands than theses about the developmental tendencies of art under present conditions of production. Their dialectic is no less noticeable in the superstructure than in the economy. It would therefore be wrong to underestimate the value of such theses as a weapon. They brush aside a number of outmoded concepts, such as creativity and genius, eternal value and mystery—concepts whose uncontrolled (and at present almost uncontrollable) application would lead to a processing of data in the Fascist sense. The concepts which are introduced into the theory of art in what follows differ from the more familiar terms in that they are completely useless for the purposes of Fascism. They are, on the other hand, useful for the formulation of revolutionary demands in the politics of art.

I

In principle a work of art has always been reproducible. Manmade artifacts could always be imitated by men. Replicas were made by pupils in practice of their craft, by masters for diffusing their works, and, finally, by third parties in the pursuit of gain. Mechanical reproduction of a work of art, however, represents something new. Historically, it advanced intermittently and in leaps at long intervals, but with accelerated intensity. The Greeks knew only two procedures of technically reproducing works of art: founding and stamping. Bronzes, terra cottas, and coins were the only art works which they could produce in quantity. All others were unique and could not be mechanically reproduced. With the woodcut graphic art became mechanically reproducible for the first time, long before script became reproducible by print. The enormous changes which printing, the mechanical reproduction of writing, has brought about in literature are a familiar story. However, within the phenomenon which we are here examining from the perspective of world history, print is merely a special, though particularly important, case. During the Middle Ages engraving and etching were added to the woodcut; at the beginning of the nineteenth century lithography made its appearance.

With lithography the technique of reproduction reached an essentially new stage. This much more direct process was distinguished by the tracing of the design on a stone rather than its incision on a block of wood or its etching on a copperplate and permitted graphic art for the first time to put its products on the market, not only in large numbers as hitherto, but also in daily changing forms. Lithography enabled graphic art to illustrate everyday life, and it began to keep pace with printing. But only a few decades after its invention, lithography was surpassed by photography. For the first time in the process of pictorial reproduction, photography freed the hand of the most important artistic functions which henceforth devolved only upon the eye looking into a lens. Since the eye perceives more swiftly than the hand can draw, the process of pictorial reproduction was accelerated so enormously that it could keep pace with speech. A film operator shooting a scene in the studio captures the images at the speed of an actor's speech. Just as lithography virtually implied the illustrated newspaper, so did photography foreshadow the sound film. The technical reproduction of sound was tackled at the end of the last century. These convergent endeavors made predictable a situation which Paul Valéry pointed up in this sentence: "Just as water, gas, and electricity are brought into our houses from far off to satisfy our needs in response to a minimal effort, so we shall be supplied with visual or auditory images, which will appear and disappear at a simple movement of the hand, hardly more than a sign" (*op. cit.,* p. 226). Around 1900 technical reproduction had reached a standard that not only permitted it to reproduce all transmitted works of art and thus to cause the most profound change in their impact upon the public; it also had captured a place of its own among the artistic processes. For the study of this standard nothing is more revealing than the nature of the repercussions that these two different manifestations—the reproduction of works of art and the art of the film—have had on art in its traditional form.

II

Even the most perfect reproduction of a work of art is lacking in one element: its presence in time and space, its unique existence at the place where it happens to be. This unique existence of the work of art determined the history to which it was subject throughout the time of its existence. This includes the changes which it may have suffered in physical condition over the years as well as the various changes in its ownership.[1] The traces of the first can be revealed only by chemical or physical analyses which it is impossible to perform on a reproduction; changes of ownership are subject to a tradition which must be traced from the situation of the original.

The presence of the original is the prerequisite to the concept of authenticity. Chemical analyses of the patina of a bronze can help to establish this, as does the proof that a given manuscript of the Middle Ages stems from an archive of the fifteenth century. The whole sphere of authenticity is outside technical—and, of course, not only technical—reproducibility.[2] Confronted with its manual reproduction, which was usually branded as a forgery, the original preserved all its authority; not so *vis à vis* technical reproduction. The reason is twofold. First, process reproduction is more independent of the original than manual reproduction. For example, in photography, process reproduction can bring out those aspects of the original that are unattainable to the naked eye yet accessible to the lens, which is adjustable and chooses its angle at will. And photographic reproduction, with the aid of certain processes, such as enlargement or slow motion, can capture images which escape natural vision. Secondly, technical reproduction can put the copy of the original into situations which would be out of reach for the original itself. Above all, it enables the original to meet the beholder halfway, be it in the form of a photograph or a phonograph record. The cathedral leaves its locale to be received in the studio of a lover of art; the choral production, performed in an auditorium or in the open air, resounds in the drawing room.

The situations into which the product of mechanical reproduction can be brought may not touch the actual work of art, yet the quality of its presence is always depreciated. This holds not only for the art work but also, for instance, for a landscape which passes in review before the spectator in a movie. In the case of the art object, a most sensitive nucleus—namely, its authenticity—is interfered with whereas no natural object is vulnerable on that score. The authenticity of a thing is the essence of all that is transmissible from its beginning, ranging from its substantive duration to its testimony to the history which it has experienced. Since the historical testimony rests on the authenticity, the former, too, is jeopardized by reproduction when substantive duration ceases to matter. And what is really jeopardized when the historical testimony is affected is the authority of the object.[3]

One might subsume the eliminated element in the term "aura" and go on to say: that which withers in the age of mechanical reproduction is the aura of the work of art. This is a symptomatic process whose significance points beyond the realm of art. One might generalize by saying: the technique of reproduction detaches the reproduced object from the domain of tradition. By making many reproductions it substitutes a plurality of copies for a unique existence. And in permitting the reproduction to meet the beholder or listener in his own particular situation, it reactivates the object reproduced. These two processes lead to a tremendous shattering of tradition which is the obverse of the contemporary crisis and renewal of mankind. Both processes are intimately connected with the contemporary mass movements. Their most powerful agent is the film. Its social significance, particularly in

its most positive form, is inconceivable without its destructive, cathartic aspect, that is, the liquidation of the traditional value of the cultural heritage. This phenomenon is most palpable in the great historical films. It extends to ever new positions. In 1927 Abel Gance exclaimed enthusiastically: "Shakespeare, Rembrandt, Beethoven will make films . . . all legends, all mythologies and all myths, all founders of religion, and the very religions . . . await their exposed resurrection, and the heroes crowd each other at the gate."* Presumably without intending it, he issued an invitation to a far-reaching liquidation.

III

During long periods of history, the mode of human sense perception changes with humanity's entire mode of existence. The manner in which human sense perception is organized, the medium in which it is accomplished, is determined not only by nature but by historical circumstances as well. The fifth century, with its great shifts of population, saw the birth of the late Roman art industry and the Vienna Genesis, and there developed not only an art different from that of antiquity but also a new kind of perception. The scholars of the Viennese school, Riegl and Wickhoff, who resisted the weight of classical tradition under which these later art forms had been buried, were the first to draw conclusions from them concerning the organization of perception at the time. However far-reaching their insight, these scholars limited themselves to showing the significant, formal hallmark which characterized perception in late Roman times. They did not attempt—and, perhaps, saw no way—to show the social transformations expressed by these changes of perception. The conditions for an analogous insight are more favorable in the present. And if changes in the medium of contemporary perception can be comprehended as decay of the aura, it is possible to show its social causes.

The concept of aura which was proposed above with reference to historical objects may usefully be illustrated with reference to the aura of natural ones. We define the aura of the latter as the unique phenomenon of a distance, however close it may be. If, while resting on a summer afternoon, you follow with your eyes a mountain range on the horizon or a branch which casts its shadow over you, you experience the aura of those mountains, of that branch. This image makes it easy to comprehend the social bases of the contemporary decay of the aura. It rests on two circumstances, both of which are related to the increasing significance of the masses in contemporary life. Namely, the desire of contemporary masses to bring things "closer" spatially and humanly, which is just as ardent as their bent toward overcoming the uniqueness of every reality by accepting its reproduction.[4] Every day the urge grows stronger to get hold of an object at very close range by way of its likeness, its reproduction. Unmistakably, reproduction as offered by picture magazines and newsreels differs from the image seen by the unarmed eye. Uniqueness and permanence are as closely linked in the latter as are transitoriness and reproducibility in the former. To pry an object from its shell, to destroy its aura, is the mark of a perception whose "sense of the universal equality of things" has increased to such a degree that it extracts it even from a unique object by means of reproduction. Thus is manifested in the field of perception what in the theoretical sphere is noticeable in the increasing importance of statistics. The adjustment of reality to the masses and of the masses to reality is a process of unlimited scope, as much for thinking as for perception.

IV

The uniqueness of a work of art is inseparable from its being imbedded in the fabric of tradition. This tradition itself is thoroughly alive and extremely changeable. An ancient statue of Venus, for example, stood in a different traditional context with the Greeks, who made it an object of veneration, than with the clerics of the Middle Ages, who viewed it as an ominous idol. Both of them, however, were equally confronted with its uniqueness, that is, its aura. Originally the contextual integration of art in tradition found its expression in the cult. We know that the earliest art works originated in the service of a ritual—first the magical, then the religious kind. It is significant that the existence of the work of art with reference to its aura is never entirely separated from its ritual function.[5] In other words, the unique value of the "authentic" work of art has its basis in ritual, the location of its original use

value. This ritualistic basis, however remote, is still recognizable as secularized ritual even in the most profane forms of the cult of beauty.[6] The secular cult of beauty, developed during the Renaissance and prevailing for three centuries, clearly showed that ritualistic basis in its decline and the first deep crisis which befell it. With the advent of the first truly revolutionary means of reproduction, photography, simultaneously with the rise of socialism, art sensed the approaching crisis which has become evident a century later. At the time, art reacted with the doctrine of *l'art pour l'art*, that is, with a theology of art. This gave rise to what might be called a negative theology in the form of the idea of "pure" art, which not only denied any social function of art but also any categorizing by subject matter. (In poetry, Mallarmé was the first to take this position.)

An analysis of art in the age of mechanical reproduction must do justice to these relationships, for they lead us to an all-important insight: for the first time in world history, mechanical reproduction emancipates the work of art from its parasitical dependence on ritual. To an ever greater degree the work of art reproduced becomes the work of art designed for reproducibility.[7] From a photographic negative, for example, one can make any number of prints; to ask for the "authentic" print makes no sense. But the instant the criterion of authenticity ceases to be applicable to artistic production, the total function of art is reversed. Instead of being based on ritual, it begins to be based on another practice—politics.

V

Works of art are received and valued on different planes. Two polar types stand out: with one, the accent is on the cult value; with the other, on the exhibition value of the work.[8] Artistic production begins with ceremonial objects destined to serve in a cult. One may assume that what mattered was their existence, not their being on view. The elk portrayed by the man of the Stone Age on the walls of his cave was an instrument of magic. He did expose it to his fellow men, but in the main it was meant for the spirits. Today the cult value would seem to demand that the work of art remain hidden. Certain statues of gods are accessible only to the priest in the cella; certain

Madonnas remain covered nearly all year round; certain sculptures on medieval cathedrals are invisible to the spectator on ground level. With the emancipation of the various art practices from ritual go increasing opportunities for the exhibition of their products. It is easier to exhibit a portrait bust that can be sent here and there than to exhibit the statue of a divinity that has its fixed place in the interior of a temple. The same holds for the painting as against the mosaic or fresco that preceded it. And even though the public presentability of a mass originally may have been just as great as that of a symphony, the latter originated at the moment when its public presentability promised to surpass that of the mass.

With the different methods of technical reproduction of a work of art, its fitness for exhibition increased to such an extent that the quantitative shift between its two poles turned into a qualitative transformation of its nature. This is comparable to the situation of the work of art in prehistoric times when, by the absolute emphasis on its cult value, it was, first and foremost, an instrument of magic. Only later did it come to be recognized as a work of art. In the same way today, by the absolute emphasis on its exhibition value the work of art becomes a creation with entirely new functions, among which the one we are conscious of, the artistic function, later may be recognized as incidental.[9] This much is certain: today photography and the film are the most serviceable exemplifications of this new function.

VI

In photography, exhibition value begins to displace cult value all along the line. But cult value does not give way without resistance. It retires into an ultimate retrenchment: the human countenance. It is no accident that the portrait was the focal point of early photography. The cult of remembrance of loved ones, absent or dead, offers a last refuge for the cult value of the picture. For the last time the aura emanates from the early photographs in the fleeting expression of a human face. This is what constitutes their melancholy, incomparable beauty. But as man withdraws from the photographic image, the exhibition value for the first time shows its superiority to the ritual value. To have pinpointed this new stage constitutes the

incomparable significance of Atget, who, around 1900, took photographs of deserted Paris streets. It has quite justly been said of him that he photographed them like scenes of crime. The scene of a crime, too, is deserted; it is photographed for the purpose of establishing evidence. With Atget, photographs become standard evidence for historical occurrences, and acquire a hidden political significance. They demand a specific kind of approach; free-floating contemplation is not appropriate to them. They stir the viewer; he feels challenged by them in a new way. At the same time picture magazines begin to put up signposts for him, right ones or wrong ones, no matter. For the first time, captions have become obligatory. And it is clear that they have an altogether different character than the title of a painting. The directives which the captions give to those looking at pictures in illustrated magazines soon become even more explicit and more imperative in the film where the meaning of each single picture appears to be prescribed by the sequence of all preceding ones.

VII

The nineteenth-century dispute as to the artistic value of painting versus photography today seems devious and confused. This does not diminish its importance, however; if anything, it underlines it. The dispute was in fact the symptom of a historical transformation the universal impact of which was not realized by either of the rivals. When the age of mechanical reproduction separated art from its basis in cult, the semblance of its autonomy disappeared forever. The resulting change in the function of art transcended the perspective of the century; for a long time it even escaped that of the twentieth century, which experienced the development of the film.

Earlier much futile thought had been devoted to the question of whether photography is an art. The primary question—whether the very invention of photography had not transformed the entire nature of art—was not raised. Soon the film theoreticians asked the same ill-considered question with regard to the film. But the difficulties which photography caused traditional aesthetics were mere child's play as compared to those raised by the film. Whence the insensitive and forced character of early theories of the film.

Abel Gance, for instance, compares the film with hieroglyphs: "Here, by a remarkable regression, we have come back to the level of expression of the Egyptians. . . . Pictorial language has not yet matured because our eyes have not yet adjusted to it. There is as yet insufficient respect for, insufficient cult of, what it expresses."* Or, in the words of Séverin-Mars: "What art has been granted a dream more poetical and more real at the same time! Approached in this fashion the film might represent an incomparable means of expression. Only the most high-minded persons, in the most perfect and mysterious moments of their lives, should be allowed to enter its ambience."† Alexandre Arnoux concludes his fantasy about the silent film with the question: "Do not all the bold descriptions we have given amount to the definition of prayer?"‡ It is instructive to note how their desire to class the film among the "arts" forces these theoreticians to read ritual elements into it—with a striking lack of discretion. Yet when these speculations were published, films like *L'Opinion publique* and *The Gold Rush* had already appeared. This, however, did not keep Abel Gance from adducing hieroglyphs for purposes of comparison, nor Séverin-Mars from speaking of the film as one might speak of paintings by Fra Angelico. Characteristically, even today ultra-reactionary authors give the film a similar contextual significance—if not an outright sacred one, then at least a supernatural one. Commenting on Max Reinhardt's film version of *A Midsummer Night's Oream*, Werfel states that undoubtedly it was the sterile copying of the exterior world with its streets, interiors, railroad stations, restaurants, motorcars, and beaches which until now had obstructed the elevation of the film to the realm of art. "The film has not yet realized its true meaning, its real possibilities . . . these consist in its unique faculty to express by natural means and with incomparable persuasiveness all that is fairylike, marvelous, supernatural."*

[. . .]

XI

The shooting of a film, especially of a sound film, affords a spectacle unimaginable anywhere at any time before this. It presents a process in which it is impossible to assign to a spectator a viewpoint which would exclude from the actual scene such extraneous accessories as camera equipment, lighting machinery, staff assistants, etc.—unless his eye were on a line parallel with the lens. This circumstance, more than any other, renders superficial and insignificant any possible similarity between a scene in the studio and one on the stage. In the theater one is well aware of the place from which the play cannot immediately be detected as illusionary. There is no such place for the movie scene that is being shot. Its illusionary nature is that of the second degree, the result of cutting. That is to say, in the studio the mechanical equipment has penetrated so deeply into reality that its pure aspect freed from the foreign substance of equipment is the result of a special procedure, namely, the shooting by the specially adjusted camera and the mounting of the shot together with other similar ones. The equipment-free aspect of reality here has become the height of artifice; the sight of immediate reality has become an orchid in the land of technology.

Even more revealing is the comparison of these circumstances, which differ so much from those of the theater, with the situation in painting. Here the question is: How does the cameraman compare with the painter? To answer this we take recourse to an analogy with a surgical operation. The surgeon represents the polar opposite of the magician. The magician heals a sick person by the laying on of hands; the surgeon cuts into the patient's body. The magician maintains the natural distance between the patient and himself; though he reduces it very slightly by the laying on of hands, he greatly increases it by virtue of his authority. The surgeon does exactly the reverse; he greatly diminishes the distance between himself and the patient by penetrating into the patient's body, and increases it but little by the caution with which his hand moves among the organs. In short, in contrast to the magician—who is still hidden in the medical practitioner—the surgeon at the decisive moment abstains from facing the patient man to man; rather, it is through the operation that he penetrates into him.

Magician and surgeon compare to painter and cameraman. The painter maintains in his work a natural distance from reality, the cameraman penetrates deeply into its web.[10] There is a tremendous difference between the pictures they obtain. That of the painter is a total one, that of the cameraman consists of multiple fragments which are assembled under a new law. Thus, for contemporary man the representation of reality by the film is incomparably more significant than that of the painter, since it offers, precisely because of the thoroughgoing permeation of reality with mechanical equipment, an aspect of reality which is free of all equipment. And that is what one is entitled to ask from a work of art.

XII

Mechanical reproduction of art changes the reaction of the masses toward art. The reactionary attitude toward a Picasso painting changes into the progressive reaction toward a Chaplin movie. The progressive reaction is characterized by the direct, intimate fusion of visual and emotional enjoyment with the orientation of the expert. Such fusion is of great social significance. The greater the decrease in the social significance of an art form, the sharper the distinction between criticism and enjoyment by the public. The conventional is uncritically enjoyed, and the truly new is criticized with aversion. With regard to the screen, the critical and the receptive attitudes of the public coincide. The decisive reason for this is that individual reactions are predetermined by the mass audience response they are about to produce, and this is nowhere more pronounced than in the film. The moment these responses become manifest they control each other. Again, the comparison with painting is fruitful. A painting has always had an excellent chance to be viewed by one person or by a few. The simultaneous contemplation of paintings by a large public, such as developed in the nineteenth century, is an early symptom of the crisis of painting, a crisis which was by no means occasioned exclusively by photography but rather in a relatively independent manner by the appeal of art works to the masses.

Painting simply is in no position to present an object for simultaneous collective experience, as it was possible for architecture at all times, for the epic poem in the past, and for the movie today. Although this circumstance in itself should not lead one to conclusions about the social role of painting, it does constitute a serious threat as soon as painting, under special conditions and, as it were, against its nature, is confronted directly by the masses. In the churches

and monasteries of the Middle Ages and at the princely courts up to the end of the eighteenth century, a collective reception of paintings did not occur simultaneously, but by graduated and hierarchized mediation. The change that has come about is an expression of the particular conflict in which painting was implicated by the mechanical reproducibility of paintings. Although paintings began to be publicly exhibited in galleries and salons, there was no way for the masses to organize and control themselves in their reception.[11] Thus the same public which responds in a progressive manner toward a grotesque film is bound to respond in a reactionary manner to surrealism.

[. . .]

XIV

One of the foremost tasks of art has always been the creation of a demand which could be fully satisfied only later.[12] The history of every art form shows critical epochs in which a certain art form aspires to effects which could be fully obtained only with a changed technical standard, that is to say, in a new art form. The extravagances and crudities of art which thus appear, particularly in the so-called decadent epochs, actually arise from the nucleus of its richest historical energies. In recent years, such barbarisms were abundant in Dadaism. It is only now that its impulse becomes discernible: Dadaism attempted to create by pictorial—and literary—means the effects which the public today seeks in the film.

Every fundamentally new, pioneering creation of demands will carry beyond its goal. Dadaism did so to the extent that it sacrificed the market values which are so characteristic of the film in favor of higher ambitions—though of course it was not conscious of such intentions as here described. The Dadaists attached much less importance to the sales value of their work than to its uselessness for contemplative immersion. The studied degradation of their material was not the least of their means to achieve this uselessness. Their poems are "word salad" containing obscenities and every imaginable waste product of language. The same is true of their paintings, on which they mounted buttons and tickets. What they intended and achieved was a relentless destruction of the aura of their creations, which they branded as reproductions with the very means of production. Before a painting of Arp's or a poem by August Stramm it is impossible to take time for contemplation and evaluation as one would before a canvas of Derain's or a poem by Rilke. In the decline of middle-class society, contemplation became a school for asocial behavior; it was countered by distraction as a variant of social conduct.[13] Dadaistic activities actually assured a rather vehement distraction by making works of art the center of scandal. One requirement was foremost: to outrage the public.

From an alluring appearance or persuasive structure of sound the work of art of the Dadaists became an instrument of ballistics. It hit the spectator like a bullet, it happened to him, thus acquiring a tactile quality. It promoted a demand for the film, the distracting element of which is also primarily tactile, being based on changes of place and focus which periodically assail the spectator. Let us compare the screen on which a film unfolds with the canvas of a painting. The painting invites the spectator to contemplation; before it the spectator can abandon himself to his associations. Before the movie frame he cannot do so. No sooner has his eye grasped a scene than it is already changed. It cannot be arrested. Duhamel, who detests the film and knows nothing of its significance, though something of its structure, notes this circumstance as follows: "I can no longer think what I want to think. My thoughts have been replaced by moving images."* The spectator's process of association in view of these images is indeed interrupted by their constant, sudden change. This constitutes the shock effect of the film, which, like all shocks, should be cushioned by heightened presence of mind.[14] By means of its technical structure, the film has taken the physical shock effect out of the wrappers in which Dadaism had, as it were, kept it inside the moral shock effect.[15]

XV

The mass is a matrix from which all traditional behavior toward works of art issues today in a new form. Quantity has been transmuted into quality. The greatly increased mass of participants has produced a change in the mode of participation. The fact that the new mode of participation first appeared in a disreputable

form must not confuse the spectator. Yet some people have launched spirited attacks against precisely this superficial aspect. Among these, Duhamel has expressed himself in the most radical manner. What he objects to most is the kind of participation which the movie elicits from the masses. Duhamel calls the movie "a pastime for helots, a diversion for uneducated, wretched, worn-out creatures who are consumed by their worries . . ., a spectacle which requires no concentration and presupposes no intelligence . . ., which kindles no light in the heart and awakens no hope other than the ridiculous one of someday becoming a 'star' in Los Angeles."* Clearly, this is at bottom the same ancient lament that the masses seek distraction whereas art demands concentration from the spectator. That is a commonplace. The question remains whether it provides a platform for the analysis of the film. A closer look is needed here. Distraction and concentration form polar opposites which may be stated as follows: A man who concentrates before a work of art is absorbed by it. He enters into this work of art the way legend tells of the Chinese painter when he viewed his finished painting. In contrast, the distracted mass absorbs the work of art. This is most obvious with regard to buildings. Architecture has always represented the prototype of a work of art the reception of which is consummated by a collectivity in a state of distraction. The laws of its reception are most instructive.

Buildings have been man's companions since primeval times. Many art forms have developed and perished. Tragedy begins with the Greeks, is extinguished with them, and after centuries its "rules" only are revived. The epic poem, which had its origin in the youth of nations, expires in Europe at the end of the Renaissance. Panel painting is a creation of the Middle Ages, and nothing guarantees its uninterrupted existence. But the human need for shelter is lasting. Architecture has never been idle. Its history is more ancient than that of any other art, and its claim to being a living force has significance in every attempt to comprehend the relationship of the masses to art. Buildings are appropriated in a twofold manner: by use and by perception—or rather, by touch and sight. Such appropriation cannot be understood in terms of the attentive concentration of a tourist before a famous building. On the tactile side there is no counterpart to contemplation on the optical side. Tactile appropriation is accomplished not so much by attention as by habit. As regards architecture, habit determines to a large extent even optical reception. The latter, too, occurs much less through rapt attention than by noticing the object in incidental fashion. This mode of appropriation, developed with reference to architecture, in certain circumstances acquires canonical value. For the tasks which face the human apparatus of perception at the turning points of history cannot be solved by optical means, that is, by contemplation, alone. They are mastered gradually by habit, under the guidance of tactile appropriation.

The distracted person, too, can form habits. More, the ability to master certain tasks in a state of distraction proves that their solution has become a matter of habit. Distraction as provided by art presents a covert control of the extent to which new tasks have become soluble by apperception. Since, moreover, individuals are tempted to avoid such tasks, art will tackle the most difficult and most important ones where it is able to mobilize the masses. Today it does so in the film. Reception in a state of distraction, which is increasing noticeably in all fields of art and is symptomatic of profound changes in apperception, finds in the film its true means of exercise. The film with its shock effect meets this mode of reception halfway. The film makes the cult value recede into the background not only by putting the public in the position of the critic, but also by the fact that at the movies this position requires no attention. The public is an examiner, but an absent-minded one.

Epilogue

The growing proletarianization of modern man and the increasing formation of masses are two aspects of the same process. Fascism attempts to organize the newly created proletarian masses without affecting the property structure which the masses strive to eliminate. Fascism sees its salvation in giving these masses not their right, but instead a chance to express themselves.[16] The masses have a right to change property relations; Fascism seeks to give them an expression while preserving property. The logical result of Fascism is the introduction of aesthetics into political life. The violation of the masses, whom Fascism, with its *Führer* cult, forces to their knees, has its counterpart in the violation of an apparatus which is pressed into the production of ritual values.

All efforts to render politics aesthetic culminate in one thing: war. War and war only can set a goal for mass movements on the largest scale while respecting the traditional property system. This is the political formula for the situation. The technological formula may be stated as follows: Only war makes it possible to mobilize all of today's technical resources while maintaining the property system. It goes without saying that the Fascist apotheosis of war does not employ such arguments. Still, Marinetti says in his manifesto on the Ethiopian colonial war: "For twenty-seven years we Futurists have rebelled against the branding of war as antiaesthetic. ... Accordingly we state: ... War is beautiful because it establishes man's dominion over the subjugated machinery by means of gas masks, terrifying megaphones, flame throwers, and small tanks. War is beautiful because it initiates the dreamt-of metalization of the human body. War is beautiful because it enriches a flowering meadow with the fiery orchids of machine guns. War is beautiful because it combines the gunfire, the cannonades, the cease-fire, the scents, and the stench of putrefaction into a symphony. War is beautiful because it creates new architecture, like that of the big tanks, the geometrical formation flights, the smoke spirals from burning villages, and many others. ... Poets and artists of Futurism! ... remember these principles of an aesthetics of war so that your struggle for a new literature and a new graphic art ... may be illumined by them!"

This manifesto has the virtue of clarity. Its formulations deserve to be accepted by dialecticians. To the latter, the aesthetics of today's war appears as follows: If the natural utilization of productive forces is impeded by the property system, the increase in technical devices, in speed, and in the sources of energy will press for an unnatural utilization, and this is found in war. The destructiveness of war furnishes proof that society has not been mature enough to incorporate technology as its organ, that technology has not been sufficiently developed to cope with the elemental forces of society. The horrible features of imperialistic warfare are attributable to the discrepancy between the tremendous means of production and their inadequate utilization in the process of production–in other words, to unemployment and the lack of markets. Imperialistic war is a rebellion of technology which collects, in the form of "human material," the claims to which society has denied its natural material. Instead of draining rivers, society directs a human stream into a bed of trenches; instead of dropping seeds from airplanes, it drops incendiary bombs over cities; and through gas warfare the aura is abolished in a new way.

"*Fiat ars–pereat mundus*," says Fascism, and, as Marinetti admits, expects war to supply the artistic gratification of a sense perception that has been changed by technology. This is evidently the consummation of "*l'art pour l'art.*" Mankind, which in Homer's time was an object of contemplation for the Olympian gods, now is one for itself. Its self-alienation has reached such a degree that it can experience its own destruction as an aesthetic pleasure of the first order. This is the situation of politics which Fascism is rendering aesthetic. Communism responds by politicizing art.

Notes

* Quoted from Paul Valéry, *Aesthetics*, "The Conquest of Ubiquity," translated by Ralph Manheim, p. 225. Pantheon Books, Bollingen Series, New York, 1964.
* Abel Gance, "Le Temps de l'image est venu," *L'Art cinématographique*, Vol. 2, pp. 94 f, Paris, 1927.
* Abel Gance, *op. cit.*, pp. 100–1.
† Séverin-Mars, quoted by Abel Gance, *op. cit.*, p. 100.
‡ Alexandre Arnoux, *Cinéma pris*, 1929, p. 28.
* Franz Werfel, "Ein Sommernachtstraum, Ein Film von Shakespeare und Reinhardt," *Neues Wiener Journal*, cited in *Lu* 15, November, 1935.
* Georges Duhamel, *Scènes de la vie future*, Paris, 1930, p. 52.
* Duhamel, *op. cit.*, p. 58.
1. Of course, the history of a work of art encompasses more than this. The history of the "Mona Lisa," for instance, encompasses the kind and number of its copies made in the 17th, 18th, and 19th centuries.
2. Precisely because authenticity is not reproducible, the intensive penetration of certain (mechanical) processes of reproduction was instrumental in differentiating and grading authenticity. To develop such differentiations was an important function of the trade in works of art. The invention of the woodcut may be said to have struck at the root of the quality of authenticity even before its late flowering. To be sure, at the time of its origin a medieval picture of the Madonna could not yet be said to be "authentic." It became "authentic" only during the succeeding centuries and perhaps most strikingly so during the last one.
3. The poorest provincial staging of *Faust* is superior to a Faust film in that, ideally, it competes with the first performance at Weimar. Before the screen it is unprofitable to remember traditional contents which might come to mind before the stage–for instance, that Goethe's friend Johann Heinrich Merck is hidden in Mephisto, and the like.
4. To satisfy the human interest of the masses may mean to have one's social function removed from the field of vision. Nothing guarantees that a portraitist of today, when painting a famous surgeon at the breakfast table in the midst of his family, depicts his social function more precisely than a painter of the 17th century who portrayed his medical doctors as representing this profession, like Rembrandt in his "Anatomy Lesson."
5. The definition of the aura as a "unique phenomenon of a distance however close it may be" represents nothing but the formulation of the cult value of the work of art in categories of space and time perception. Distance is the opposite of closeness. The essentially distant object is the unapproachable one. Unapproachability is indeed a major quality of the cult image. True to its nature, it remains "distant, however close it may be." The closeness which one may gain from its subject matter does not impair the distance which it retains in its appearance.
6. To the extent to which the cult value of the painting is secularized the ideas of its fundamental uniqueness lose distinctness. In the imagination of the beholder the uniqueness of the phenomena which hold sway in the cult image is more and more displaced by the empirical uniqueness of the creator or of his creative achievement. To be sure, never completely so; the concept of authenticity always transcends mere genuineness. (This is particularly apparent in the collector who always retains some traces of the fetishist and who, by owning the work of art, shares in its ritual power.) Nevertheless, the function of the concept of authenticity remains determinate in the evaluation of art; with the secularization of art, authenticity displaces the cult value of the work.
7. In the case of films, mechanical reproduction is not, as with literature and painting, an external condition for mass distribution. Mechanical reproduction is inherent in the very technique of film production. This technique not only permits in the most direct way but virtually causes mass distribution. It enforces distribution because the production of a film is so expensive that an individual who, for instance, might afford to buy a painting no longer can afford to buy a film. In 1927 it was calculated that a major film, in order to pay its way, had to reach an audience of nine million. With the sound film, to be sure,

a setback in its international distribution occurred at first: audiences became limited by language barriers. This coincided with the Fascist emphasis on national interests. It is more important to focus on this connection with Fascism than on this setback, which was soon minimized by synchronization. The simultaneity of both phenomena is attributable to the depression. The same disturbances which, on a larger scale, led to an attempt to maintain the existing property structure by sheer force led the endangered film capital to speed up the development of the sound film. The introduction of the sound film brought about a temporary relief, not only because it again brought the masses into the theaters but also because it merged new capital from the electrical industry with that of the film industry. Thus, viewed from the outside, the sound film promoted national interests, but seen from the inside it helped to internationalize film production even more than previously.

8. This polarity cannot come into its own in the aesthetics of Idealism. Its idea of beauty comprises these polar opposites without differentiating between them and consequently excludes their polarity. Yet in Hegel this polarity announces itself as clearly as possible within the limits of Idealism. We quote from his *Philosophy of History:*

   "Images were known of old. Piety at an early time required them for worship, but it could do without *beautiful* images. These might even be disturbing. In every beautiful painting there is also something nonspiritual, merely external, but its spirit speaks to man through its beauty. Worshipping, conversely, is concerned with the work as an object, for it is but a spiritless stupor of the soul. . . . Fine art has arisen . . . in the church . . ., although it has already gone beyond its principle as art."

   Likewise, the following passage from *The Philosophy of Fine Art* indicates that Hegel sensed a problem here.

   "We are beyond the stage of reverence for works of art as divine and objects deserving our worship. The impression they produce is one of a more reflective kind, and the emotions they arouse require a higher test. . . ."–G. W. F. Hegel, *The Philosophy of Fine Art*, trans., with notes, by F. P. B. Osmaston, Vol. 1, p. 12, London, 1920.

   The transition from the first kind of artistic reception to the second characterizes the history of artistic reception in general. Apart from that, a certain oscillation between these two polar modes of reception can be demonstrated for each work of art. Take the Sistine Madonna. Since Hubert Grimme's research it has been known that the Madonna originally was painted for the purpose of exhibition. Grimme's research was inspired by the question: What is the purpose of the molding in the foreground of the painting which the two cupids lean upon? How, Grimme asked further, did Raphael come to furnish the sky with two draperies? Research proved that the Madonna had been commissioned for the public lying-in-state of Pope Sixtus. The Popes lay in state in a certain side chapel of St. Peter's. On that occasion Raphael's picture had been fastened in a nichelike background of the chapel, supported by the coffin. In this picture Raphael portrays the Madonna approaching the papal coffin in clouds from the background of the niche, which was demarcated by green drapes. At the obsequies of Sixtus a pre-eminent exhibition value of Raphael's picture was taken advantage of. Some time later it was placed on the high altar in the church of the Black Friars at Piacenza. The reason for this exile is to be found in the Roman rites which forbid the use of paintings exhibited at obsequies as cult objects on the high altar. This regulation devalued Raphael's picture to some degree. In order to obtain an adequate price nevertheless, the Papal See resolved to add to the bargain the tacit toleration of the picture above the high altar. To avoid attention the picture was given to the monks of the far-off provincial town.

9. Bertolt Brecht, on a different level, engaged in analogous reflections: "If the concept of 'work of art' can no longer be applied to the thing that emerges once the work is transformed into a commodity, we have to eliminate this concept with cautious care but without fear, lest we liquidate the function of the very thing as well. For it has to go through this phase without mental reservation, and not as noncommittal deviation from the straight path; rather, what happens here with the work of art will change it fundamentally and erase its past to such an extent that should the old concept be taken up again–and it will, why not?–it will no longer stir any memory of the thing it once designated."

10. The boldness of the cameraman is indeed comparable to that of the surgeon. Luc Durtain lists among specific technical sleights of hand those "which are required in surgery in the case of certain difficult operations. I choose as an example a case from oto-rhinolaryngology; . . . the so-called endonasal perspective procedure; or I refer to the acrobatic tricks of larynx surgery which have to be performed following the reversed picture in the laryngoscope. I might also speak of ear surgery which suggests the precision work of watchmakers. What range of the most subtle muscular acrobatics is required from the man who wants to repair or save the human body! We have only to think of the couching of a cataract where there is virtually a debate of steel with nearly fluid tissue, or of the major abdominal operations (laparotomy)."–Luc Durtain, *op. cit.*

11. This mode of observation may seem crude, but as the great theoretician Leonardo has shown, crude modes of observation may at times be usefully adduced. Leonardo compares painting and music as follows: "Painting is superior to music because, unlike unfortunate music, it does not have to die as soon as it is born. ... Music which is consumed in the very act of its birth is inferior to painting which the use of varnish has rendered eternal." (Trattato I, 29.)

12. "The work of art," says André Breton, "is valuable only in so far as it is vibrated by the reflexes of the future." Indeed, every developed art form intersects three lines of development. Technology works toward a certain form of art. Before the advent of the film there were photo booklets with pictures which flitted by the onlooker upon pressure of the thumb, thus portraying a boxing bout or a tennis match. Then there were the slot machines in bazaars; their picture sequences were produced by the turning of a crank.

Secondly, the traditional art forms in certain phases of their development strenuously work toward effects which later are effortlessly attained by the new ones. Before the rise of the movie the Dadaists' performances tried to create an audience reaction which Chaplin later evoked in a more natural way.

Thirdly, unspectacular social changes often promote a change in receptivity which will benefit the new art form. Before the movie had begun to create its public, pictures that were no longer immobile captivated an assembled audience in the so-called *Kaiserpanorama*. Here the public assembled before a screen into which stereoscopes were mounted, one to each beholder. By a mechanical process individual pictures appeared briefly before the stereoscopes, then made way for others. Edison still had to use similar devices in presenting the first movie strip before the film screen and projection were known. This strip was presented to a small public which stared into the apparatus in which the succession of pictures was reeling off. Incidentally, the institution of the *Kaiserpanorama* shows very clearly a dialectic of the development. Shortly before the movie turned the reception of pictures into a collective one, the individual viewing of pictures in these swiftly outmoded establishments came into play once more with an intensity comparable to that of the ancient priest beholding the statue of a divinity in the cella.

13. The theological archetype of this contemplation is the awareness of being alone with one's God. Such awareness, in the heyday of the bourgeoisie, went to strengthen the freedom to shake off clerical tutelage. During the decline of the bourgeoisie this awareness had to take into account the hidden tendency to withdraw from public affairs those forces which the individual draws upon in his communion with God.

14. The film is the art form that is in keeping with the increased threat to his life which modern man has to face. Man's need to expose himself to shock effects is his adjustment to the dangers threatening him. The film corresponds to profound changes in the apperceptive apparatus–changes that are experienced on an individual scale by the man in the street in big-city traffic, on a historical scale by every present-day citizen.

15. As for Dadaism, insights important for Cubism and Futurism are to be gained from the movie. Both appear as deficient attempts of art to accommodate the pervasion of reality by the apparatus. In contrast to the film, these schools did not try to use the apparatus as such for the artistic presentation of reality, but aimed at some sort of alloy in the joint presentation of reality and apparatus. In Cubism, the premonition that this apparatus will be structurally based on optics plays a dominant part; in Futurism, it is the premonition of the effects of this apparatus which are brought out by the rapid sequence of the film strip.

16. One technical feature is significant here, especially with regard to newsreels, the propagandist importance of which can hardly be overestimated. Mass reproduction is aided especially by the reproduction of masses. In big parades and monster rallies, in sports events, and in war, all of which nowadays are captured by camera and sound recording, the masses are brought face to face with themselves. This process, whose significance need not be stressed, is intimately connected with the development of the techniques of reproduction and photography. Mass movements are usually discerned more clearly by a camera than by the naked eye. A bird's-eye view best captures gatherings of hundreds of thousands. And even though such a view may be as accessible to the human eye as it is to the camera, the image received by the eye cannot be enlarged the way a negative is enlarged. This means that mass movements, including war, constitute a form of human behavior which particularly favors mechanical equipment.

9.
READING MUSIC, READING RECORDS, READING RACE

Musical Copyright and the U.S. Copyright Act of 1909

Lisa Gitelman

I wish to relate an incident which occurred in our store this evening, which I considered the highest compliment that has ever been paid to a talking machine. I was exhibiting a Home [phonograph], with a 24-inch silk horn. Among other Records, I put on No. 8656, The Flogging Scene from "Uncle Tom's Cabin." When the Record was ended, a man sprang out of his chair, wiped the tears from his eyes, and said, "I'd give ten dollars for the privilege of hitting that damned slave driver just once."

—from the Buckeye Music Co., Rudolph, Ohio. Edison *Phonograph Monthly*, February 1905

At the end of the nineteenth century the new technology of recorded sound helped to challenge the visual habits of musical practice. Audiences who were accustomed to watching performers who might themselves be eyeing a printed score could now hear music with nothing to look at but a piece of machinery. Phonographs, wax records, pianolas, and paper music rolls were all new commodities troubling the established musical trade, in part by questioning the visual norms of intellectual property. The phonograph record and the music roll had to be contextualized, to be located against the legible, copyrighted texts of lyrics and notation, which comprised the inviolable units of protected musical writings under article 1, section 8 of the Constitution. Legislative hearings and judicial decisions questioned the nature of reading in an effort to rearticulate the definition of protected "writings." Congressional debate centered around the issue of whether phonograph records and piano rolls could be "read," in what became an early and elaborate exploration of textuality in the new age of machine-readable text. And while Congress tinkered amid the essentialism of American copyright law, honing its application to materially new cultural forms, the shifting optics of popular music brought pressure to bear on other visual habits, including associations between racial difference and skin color. By removing the performer from view, the technology of recorded sound also removed the most keenly felt representation of the performer's race. American musical culture engaged difference in new ways, provoked at once by the enormous popularity of racist "coon" songs during the late 1890s, by early attempts to delimit and commodify authenticity in so-called Negro music, and by the phonograph itself, a mimetic machine that had not failed to accumulate its own parcel of racial associations in the several decades since its invention by Thomas Edison in 1877.

The anecdote received from the Buckeye Music Company (quoted above), which appeared in an Edison trade publication, provides some access to the less familiar elements of musical culture at the turn of the century. Music stores like the Buckeye were distribution points for sheet music, song books, and musical instruments and supplies, as well as phonographs and records. Phonographs occupied an ambiguous position as "self-playing" musical instruments. Without the benefit of radio broadcasting, potential customers had to hear phonographs and records in public in order to know and desire them, so that exhibitions and demonstrations like the one described were frequent and necessary events in showrooms everywhere. The man who jumped up and offered ten dollars to hit Simon Legree was paying the "highest compliment" to the phonograph because the ten dollars he offered to pay so exceeded the thirty-five cents that an Edison record of "The Flogging" really cost. Embedded in this narrative of paying compliments and paying ten dollars are a host of implications about mimesis, culture, and commercialism. The impassioned listener of "The Flogging" might or might not have been mistaking fiction for reality. He did seem to know *Uncle Tom's Cabin*, whether from reading the original or from experiencing some of the plethora of adaptations that had appeared in print and on stage in the half century since Stowe's novel was published in 1852. Either way, the Buckeye proprietor felt complimented because his recording provoked such a powerful emotional response, the way reading the novel might, while the Home phonograph and its record cylinder remained relatively unattended components of the listener's experience. The man did not hear the phonograph, and he did not hear the record; he heard through them to Simon Legree whipping Uncle Tom, and it was this selective hearing that the Buckeye proprietor recognized as the highest compliment that could be paid to any communicative or inscriptive medium, including the talking machine.

The proprietor's anecdote plays off of an important trope resident in Anglo-American constructions of race and class, the familiar narrative of the alien naif who mistakes mimetic representation for reality. In the fictions of Dickens and Twain it is the uncultured bumpkin who takes theatrical production literally, and many "true" anecdotes of the same sort circulated during the nineteenth century. There was the Baltimore man who objected "to an assault on Coriolanus because 'three against one' was not a fair fight," and the man from New Orleans who suggested "to Othello, grieving over the loss of his handkerchief, 'Why don't you blow your nose with your fingers and let the play go on.'" The full truth of these anecdotes cannot be gauged, but the blurring of reality and mimetic action that the anecdotes relate is likely of equal consequence to the circulation and persistence of the anecdotes themselves. With each telling they present and assert culture as an exclusive activity for those who have it and "get it."[1] New technical cultures seem to have relied upon similar anecdotes in their construction of male technocratic expertise. Telegraph and engineering publications of the nineteenth century exhibit a rhetoric of exclusion on the bases of class, race, and gender. Their pages are filled with anecdotes about bumpkins who shimmied up telegraph poles to hear the messages go by and about women who made similar errors with regard to new communications technology.[2]

The same exclusionary trope extends into constructions of racial difference in exploration literature and ethnographic accounts, where racially distanced "natives" play the bumpkin's part, fooled by their own reflections in a mirror or, in a type-scene in the same tradition, by voices emanating from a phonograph. From the 1880s through the 1920s versions of this type-scene filtered into travel narratives, trade publications, and newspapers, into cartoons and comic films as well as serious documentaries. The politics of these interracial encounters was characterized by the self-congratulatory aggression of Western technological achievement and colonial dominance. They seem geared to provide an accessible "comic relief" against which Anglo-American culture could receive the less accessible accounts of its resolute ethnographers, who bundled up phonographs and motion picture cameras for journeys to even less accessible climes, to record the curious natives (in the double, us-and-them, sense of "curious"), all in the name of science. Phonographic and cinematic inscriptions fit the logic of ethnography exactly. The recording phonograph and the camera interceded between the ethnographer and his subject, offering a rhetorically valuable sense of technological impartiality and receptivity. The resulting records and films concretized what is now called the "ethnographic present" tense of anthropological description, freezing the ethnographic subject in time, providing "live" recordings as specimens for further study at home.[3] If the proprietor of the Buckeye Music Company only hinted in these directions, then the Edison and Victor phonograph companies did too, making mimetic confusion a matter of kitsch in their respective promotional images of a well-dressed toddler breaking open a phonograph ("Looking for the Band") and the more famous dog listening to one ("His Master's Voice"). These trademarks tone down and make "cute" and commercial the exclusionary trope by substituting children and pets for the aliens who were elsewhere fixtures of distancing between classes and races. As Michael Taussig explains, the images succeed because they continue "to reinstall the mimetic faculty as mystery in the art of mechanical reproduction, re-invigorating the primitivism implicit in technology's wildest dreams, therewith creating a surfeit of mimetic power" (208). Edison's National Phonograph Company briefly offered its agents multiple electro-type versions of "Looking for the Band" to promulgate its own mimetic prowess; one was the familiar toddler and another was a pair of bug-eyed, black-skinned caricatures.

I am suggesting that intimations of class and race politics lie embedded in the Buckeye proprietor's anecdote as published by the *Edison Phonograph Monthly* and that similar intimations of question and conflict over matters of identity and cultural hierarchy lay buried at different depths in the emergent culture of recorded sound in America. This should be an unremarkable claim by now, the requisite extension of politics differently recognized in popular music by Theodor Adorno and other theorists. At the same time that the technology of recorded sound provoked a reconsideration of statutory authors and readers in debates over copyright, recorded sound helped to modulate the already Gordian politics of popular music. Recordings further complicated the identities of musical authors and musical performers, and the new, hungry mimesis of the recording phonograph itself came to market larded with assumptions about sameness and difference, about a cultural appropria-tion and cultural assimilation. Consider the impact of the phonograph (Dave Laing calls it "a voice without a face") on the tradition of blackface minstrelsy in its twentieth-century survival, the "coon" song. What happens to the "love and theft" of blackface when there is no face?[4] Questions like this one never made it into the debates over copyright, but they comprise the context within which music and musical authorship had to make sense. In tracing the legislative history of musical copyright in the pages below, I assume that neither changes to law nor changes to technology can be isolated from contextual and reciprocally change-able parameters of identity and perception. The tech-nology of recorded sound tempered what I call the visuality of music, the sum of visual experiences that bolster and accompany musical practice and that extend to the societal norms of visually apprehending racial and other differences. Changing visuality meant changing already complex notions of text and perfor-mance at a time when other features of twentieth-century music were also taking shape, among them the transnational reach of American popular culture and the economic structures of the recording industry.

The impassioned listener in the Buckeye Music store was eager to do what many Americans had wanted to and what a few had actually done—stop the sadistic Simon Legree. Stowe's novel had endured half a century of pillaging by melodramatists, paro-dists, and then even the first film companies when the Edison Manufacturing Company tapped it in 1903. It had endured just as many years of piracy by unau-thorized publishing houses and translators, and Stowe had been battered in the courts when she tried to stop them. More than a few versions had indeed foiled Simon Legree, offering their audiences a "Tom show" with a happy ending. By 1905 and Edison record no. 8656, Stowe was almost ten years dead, and her copy-right (as insufficient as it had proven) had expired. When Stowe's longtime neighbor from Hartford, Connecticut, Mark Twain, addressed the joint con-gressional committee that convened in 1906 to revise the copyright code, he had Stowe in mind. Twain came representing authors and had only unkind words for publishers, despite his own checkered career as one. He spoke in favor of extending the term of copy-right to the life of the author plus fifty years. He saved his humor for the end of his statement, when he alluded to the arts included in the proposed law, which extended to cover the mechanical reproduction of sound and images. Twain confessed that he himself had nothing to do with such matters, but he was will-ing, he said, to support copyrights for people in those arts, because he felt for them the same benign interest as a drunkard who, arriving home after a debauch, finds "his house weaving and weaving and weaving around" before him, and when, after some struggle, he gains entrance, stumbles up, and tumbles down the stairs, he exclaims, "God pity a poor sailor out at sea on a night like this." The pious Stowe might have been nonplussed by Twain's analogy, but she and her novel had tried to weather just such storms.[5]

By 1906 the tempest Twain envisions was particularly intense for the producers of music and the means of its mechanical reproduction, since records were increasingly a musical form. The Edison company persisted with "The Flogging," with vaudevillian dialogues and oratory, but "the industry," as it had now become, grew more and more musically oriented through the 1890s, dominated in the new century by three patent-holding phonograph companies, American Graphophone (later Columbia), Victor Talking Machine (later Victor/RCA), and Edison's National Phonograph.[6] With representatives of all three companies in attendance, most of the congressional hearings of 1906 and 1908 were spent wrangling over clause G of the proposed copyright bill, which extended an author's intellectual property to include the rights "To make, sell, distribute, or let for hire any device, contrivance, or appliance especially adapted in any manner whatsoever to reproduce to the ear the whole or any material part of any work published and copyrighted after this act shall have gone into effect" (5). Such a provision would require phonograph record and piano roll manufacturers to obtain licenses from (and pay royalties to) composers, or to obtain licenses from the sheet-music publishers, who frequently obtained the composer's copyright when they published her or his music.

Copyright had been extended to new media before, and both photographs and motion pictures offer points of comparison Photographs were first included in the Act of 1865, and the courts importantly affirmed their eligibility for copyright in the so-called Sarony case of 1884, on the grounds that photographs "are representatives of original intellectual conceptions of the author."[7] The case had involved a "decorative" photograph by Napoleon Sarony of Oscar Wilde, about which—or whom—the men at the 1906 hearings were still giggling.[8] As Jane Gaines indicates, the Sarony decision was important in that it defined authorship's ground zero. The author was merely the "originator" of some work of authorship, and the act of origination became an inference based on the work produced. What this meant by extension "is that Oscar Wilde's own subjecthood in the photograph secures Sarony's copyright in the photograph."[9] The original personality that Wilde displayed in the photograph vouched for the personal originality of Sarony as an author-photographer. The photograph made the photographer. Wilde responded to this new dynamic in his "Canterville Ghost" (1887). Published after his return to Britain from his American tour and after the Sarony decision, Wilde's comic story has the beleaguered Canterville ghost reduced to "amusing himself by making satirical remarks on the large Saroni [sic] photographs of the United States Minister and his wife, which had now taken the place of the Canterville family pictures." Long a subject in the Canterville house, the manorial ghost finds himself as decisively displaced as the Canterville family. The doodling ghost, Sarony, and the minister's family all vie for what Gaines calls "subjecthood."

New media did not always inspire new articulations of the author-subject. Motion picture films were deemed eligible for copyright by the courts in *Edison v. Lubin*.[10] The reasoning behind the Lubin decision involved something like Xeno's paradox: Because individual frames on a film of Kaiser Wilhelm's yacht were more and more similar as they were positioned on the film closer and closer together, until adjacent frames were indistinguishable from one another, the film had to be considered a single photograph, not a new entity, and hence eligible for protection in accordance with the Sarony precedent and the Act of 1865. Authoring a film was the same as authoring a still photograph. Less straightforward were the bureaucratic mechanics of obtaining copyrights on new representational products. Some film producers scratched out the word "author" on copyright registration forms and substituted the word "proprietor." Film companies like the Edison Manufacturing Company puzzled over what object to deposit with the Library of Congress in order to register their rights. Literary authors simply sent copies of their printed works (200,000 of them in 1905 alone), and photographers like Sarony could deposit a photographic print. Should the Edison studio send a positive print of its films, a photographic negative, a "paper" or "bromide print," or some other object?[11] If, like books, films had to carry a warning label indicating their protected status, how and where should such a label be affixed? Did original film "scenarios," as screenplays were then called, require separate copyright protection? Could scenarios be adaptations of copyrighted works? These details took some time to iron out.

Questions of intellectual property rights proved particularly difficult in the case of music and its mechanical reproduction, in part because of the complexities of what Jaques Attali calls "noise," or the "political economy of music," and in part because the legal standards of intellectual property were written, published works or visually apprehended works that the courts could construe as constitutionally protected "writings" in a very broad sense. The combination of pliable uses and new forms made music hard to pin down. The varied economy of American music at the end of the nineteenth century was perched on the edge of mass culture: it relied on noninstitutional as well as institutional means of creating markets for its principal commodity, printed sheet music, while it proved less able to commodity musical performances, phonograph records, and piano rolls in a rational or universal way.[12] It was a heterogeneous and multimillion-dollar economy challenged by market shifts, new patterns of consumption, new products, and a changing clientele.

An 1890s song like "On the Banks of the Wabash," for instance, made its composer, Paul Dresser, rich when it sold more than 500,000 sheets of published, copyrighted musical notation and lyrics, for which he received a royalty. So popular music was "popular" at least in the sense that people wanted to buy, read, and sing or play it, not because they wanted to listen to it. When they did listen to it, they saw it performed in either a public or a domestic setting. Dresser's song, a ballad with improbably romantic lyrics written with his naturalist younger brother, Theodore Dreiser, was popular in the additional sense that it partook of a musical tradition distinct from conservatory or "classical" music. Dresser was successful and prolific within the incipient musical culture of Tin Pan Alley. He was what one critic called an "all-round song writer," who wrote everything from coon songs to ballads. He was also recognizably an expert at "so-called 'mother' songs," conservative and schmaltzy ballads; the word "mother" was one he used "in about all his songs."[13] "On the Banks of the Wabash" achieved its popularity in a calculated if seemingly haphazard way. According to Theodore Dreiser, 5,000 copies were probably distributed for free in New York City, aimed at singers who might elect to perform the work in public. When performed, free handbills were distributed

with the lyrics on them, so that the audience could read along and learn the song, "the sooner [to] hum and whistle it on the streets." Rowdies were hired to sing along in the music hall or to applaud and cheer wildly. Organ grinders were encouraged to play "On the Banks of the Wabash" all over the city. And the publisher manipulated a network of music stores, using discount wholesale/retail agreements and trade advertising to push sales all over the country.[14] A network of music teachers covered the same territories, and various commercial relationships, including payola, kept the distribution networks in place.[15]

When anyone purchased a copy of the sheet music, it came with permission to perform the work before an audience, understood and every so often made explicit in the form of a notice stamped on the printed score. Phonograph and player piano companies bought one copy of the sheet music, ostensibly rendering their royalty unto Dresser, and manufactured thousands of records and music rolls. Edison's phonograph company issued two different versions of "Banks of the Wabash" on wax cylinders, both before the turn of the century, and recorded the song on its celluloid "amberol" cylinder well after Paul Dresser's untimely death in 1906. Composers and their publishers of course decried the situation, and the congressional hearings of 1906 included statements by Victor Herbert and John Philip Sousa arguing for author's rights. Sousa, a remarkably durable commodity in the bandstand circuit, depended for part of his income, as did Dresser, on the royalties that his compositions earned through sheet-music sales. Sousa testified that in using his "copyrighted copy" to make "what they claim is a noncopyrighted copy," the record and music roll companies "take my property" (23). More prescient than most, Sousa also saw the damage phonographs and pianolas were doing to the whole sheet-music industry. "You hear these infernal machines going day and night," he said, and joked that the human vocal chords might soon become vestigial organs and could ultimately disappear forever, casualties of disuse and natural selection. Fewer and fewer people read music; fewer and fewer homes contained musical instruments other than phonographs and "self-playing" pianos. "Popular" music was becoming something people listened to, not something they read, played, or watched. Then

Victor Herbert extended Sousa's corporal fancy. The phonograph and music roll companies, he accused, "are reproducing part of our brain" (26). Ironically, Thomas Edison had no quarrel with Herbert's metaphor; phonograph records did indeed "embody" the composer's conception, they bodied forth his idea, and it was material embodiment, not the mere conception, that ensured both copyrights and patent rights. Musicians received copyrights when their conceptions were embodied in the printed score. Only that material expression or copytext was protected, Edison argued; as anyone familiar with patent law knew, "If the conception is carried out by a different mechanism they lose their monopoly."[16] But the question remained whether phonograph records and music rolls really did constitute a substantially "different mechanism" as such, or whether they represented some new sort of performance, a use, to be taxed by authors according to their rights.

Battle lines were drawn according to the issue of whether records and music rolls could be construed as copies of "writings" protected by article 1 of the Constitution. Writings in this case meant written musical scores, copied and distributed as sheet music. Case law offered a context for the debate. The courts had decided in *White-Smith Music Publishing Co. v. Apollo Co.* that perforated music rolls were performances, not copies according to the law, so that in buying just one piece of sheet music, the Apollo company had paid its due. Despite their decisions, both the lower courts and then the Supreme Court had lamented the letter of the law. In his assenting opinion, Justice Holmes chided, "On principle anything that mechanically reproduces the [original] collocation of sounds ought to be held a copy, or if the statute is too narrow ought to be made so by a further act."[17] Rarely was a legislative mandate so clear. The very terms of the court decisions and the ensuing copyright debate reveal a tentative reassessment of reading and writing. Writing was an activity pursued by composers and publishers, not recording artists or record companies, who were only readers. The question at hand was whether the production of records and music rolls created any nonwritten, readable copy. The courts, Congress, composers, and publishers all wanted to sever writing from reading in a new way. By implication they allowed that machinery—phonographs and pianolas—could read.

In the course of the debate, representatives of phonograph companies and music roll manufacturers assured members of Congress that their products were not copies of "writings" because they could not be "read," urging no damage to the present law. Frank L. Dyer, Edison's patent attorney, CEO, and sometime biographer, testified to this effect in 1906 and again in 1908. According to Dyer, Edison himself had once spent many long hours in his laboratory trying to read phonograph records. After recording the letter "*a*," "He examined with a microscope each particular indentation and made a drawing of it, so that at the end of two or three days he had what he thought was a picture of the letter '*a*.'" But when he compared two records of the letter "*a*," he found that "the two pictures were absolutely dissimilar" (286). Dyer needed to assume that reading was a human activity, not a mechanical one, and if even Edison, their illustrious inventor, could not read phonograph records, then they could not be read. Dyer argued that what Congress proposed was to copyright sound itself, leaving behind the visual nature of all previous copyrights. By analogy, Dyer asked, why not make it possible to copyright perfumes, extending to the nose the same privilege as the ear and the eye (288)? Dyer insisted that changing the nature of reading meant changing the nature of writing.

Musical culture at large continued to wrestle with similar issues, if not exactly in these terms. The *White-Smith v. Apollo* case had involved the sheet music for a coon song entitled "Little Cotton Dolly," and like the anecdotal account of the Buckeye Music Company, the recorded coon song offers a point of access to some of the more neglected features of the emerging industry. With its increasing diffusion, recorded sound destabilized the connections between hearing music and seeing it performed (Laing, 7–8). "Seeing music" extended to a wide range of social practices, including parlor piano playing, amateur and professional concerts, vaudeville and music hall performances, church singing, and revival meetings. The experienced terms of this destabilization must have differed according to these practices and are notoriously hard to pin down. But the most acute destabilization, I would argue, took place around the recorded coon song, since the coon song was a complex, late-nineteenth-century survival of an already intricate and naggingly visual experience, the midcentury minstrel show. As if a harbinger of all copyright quarrels to come, blackface minstrelsy was rooted in a confusion of origins. Minstrelsy had real and mythic antecedents in the antebellum slave culture of the Southern plantation, yet was by definition a Northern, urban form. As Eric Lott explains, it functioned in part by offering audiences commodified "blackness" as a way to engage—subliminally and not—the conjunctive class and race politics of the nation.[18] The white construction of minstrelsy's "blackness" possessed inherent contradictions and played off a contrived sense of authenticity at the same time it relied upon counterfeiting. The form reinforced racial boundaries by denigrating blacks, and it also defiantly transgressed those boundaries for pleasure and profit in what had become marked as a low-brow, "popular" form of entertainment for the white working class. Minstrelsy subverted the questions of racial essentialism on which it fed, providing a raucous catharsis for matters that seemed so pressing elsewhere in the American national scene: slavery, abolition, and Dred Scott helped form the context and complexion of the minstrel shows; *Plessy v. Ferguson* (1896) would be context for the recorded coon song.[19]

The orientation of blackface minstrelsy was visual and performative, even if a large measure of its dubious authenticity was its supposed appropriation of an oral culture it constructed as "blackness." Seeing a white man with his face smeared in burnt cork was the perceptual and the visceral center of blackface for fans and critics alike, though there were black minstrel troops too. Yet just as developments within the music industry tested the persistently visual orientation of copyright law, similar developments challenged the visual orientation of minstrelsy. One challenge came in the popular freestanding coon song, which was performed outside the minstrel show, if well within the minstrel tradition. Another challenge arrived with the player piano and the phonograph. According to the publishers of sheet music, the coon song reached the height of its popularity in the late 1890s, when large numbers of songwriters like Paul Dresser (who had once been a minstrel) churned out more than six hundred coon songs to cash in on the vogue.[20] By then the immense popularity of minstrelsy had passed; the minstrel show was an antebellum form that lasted through Reconstruction and lingered into

vaudeville. What this meant was the sound of white-constructed "blackness" survived without the sight of minstrel blackface, as performers of coon songs could go without burnt cork, particularly as recognizable "coon" elements were incorporated into a variety of different songs and formats. Whereas minstrelsy had been an acknowledged white, working-class form, the coon song allowed middle-class penetration of its tradition, and coon songs were played in middle-class parlors, concerts, syndicated vaudeville, and the other bourgeois venues where sheet music was increasingly consumed. Class lines were doubly enforced and transgressed just as racial boundaries were, as middle-class musical practices picked up and dusted off the threads of a working-class form. Some unblackened white performers were seen to "sound 'black,' " and when music roll and record companies set out to record coon songs, sounding black went colorblind.

Like Frank Dyer insisting that the Committee on Patents and Copyrights was trying to protect sound itself, records and music rolls of "Little Cotton Dolly" seemed to assert that white-constructed blackness was a matter of sound, not skin color. On the heels of the *Plessy* decision, which had determined blackness to be a matter of blood, not skin color, the meaning of music thickened. The American judiciary deemed white-skinned Homer Plessy black by dint of his African blood, and popular culture now interrogated music as another possible substance of intrinsic racial difference. Music rolls even seemed to make sounding black an instrumental matter more than a vocal one, depending on the sound of a piano more than the sound of any singer, and the same aural associations were affirmed with the contemporary ascendance of syncopation as a black-identified musical feature.[21] Of course the sound of blackness was not monolithic; it was never wholly white constructed and was complicated by other black sounds, by recorded black spirituals, the works of well-known black songwriters and performers, a range of black musical theater, ragtime, the stirrings of jazz, and the longstanding tradition of ethnic and racist dialect humor in America. In the same month that Edison's phonograph company recorded its third version of Dresser's "On the Banks of the Wabash," its selections included a "romping coon song" and two "negro dialect poems," one by the late Paul Lawrence Dunbar.

Earlier record catalogs had been as varied, and while the major record companies kept white groups on hand for minstrel-influenced burlesques and coon songs, between them Victor and Columbia recorded nearly eighty songs by the African-American vocalist Bert Williams, who broke the color barrier at Ziegfeld's *Follies* during his tenure with Columbia. All of this recorded blackness without the sight of black, white, or blackened skins was new and uncomfortable, and, I would argue, an unadmitted counterpart to the legislative debate over separating visible "writings" from the sounds of reading. In both contexts the technology of recorded sound helped to displace the visuality of music. Musical composition and the creative agency of performance became complicated within new and less visually rooted features of the entertainment industry.

A few months after publishing its anecdote from the Buckeye Music Company, the *Edison Phonograph Monthly* signaled some of the trade's discomfort in another compliment submitted to jobbers and dealers, this item under the headline "Mr. Collins Is Not a Negro": "Possibly because of his great success in singing coon and rag-time songs for the Edison Phonograph some people seem to have gained the impression that Arthur Collins is a colored man. Such an impression is naturally amusing to Mr. Collins. It is complimentary, however, to imitate the colored race so closely as to be mistaken for the real article."[22] This paragraph again resuscitates a well-worn trope, one resident in anecdotes about audience members who mistook blackface for black. The mistake had been part fulcrum and part safety valve within minstrelsy (as well as imaginably part fact and part fiction) ridden with the racial anxieties it helped diffuse theatrically, anxieties regarding the supposed risks of racial contiguity, "passing," and miscegenation. Music publishers, apparently fearing the same mistake, had sometimes published minstrel songs with pictures of their blackface performers both in and out of makeup (Lott, 20). The *Edison Phonograph Monthly* was doing the same thing in vouching for the distinction between "close" imitation and "the real article." Yet in "Mr. Collins Is Not a Negro," the quickest safety valve proved more elusive than it had before. Unlike the Buckeye Music Company anecdote, this anecdote could not be trumpeted as a compliment to the talking machine, only as an

"amusing" compliment to the performer Arthur Collins, all because the talking machine had redoubled the problem (part horror, part delight) of identifying "the real article." In this sense race, like racism, differs according to its aural and visual forms.[23] Like Thomas Edison intently trying to discern the letter "*a*" within the grooves of a record, listeners who tried to discern skin color in Arthur Collins's records were up against something new. Edison had been interrogating the essential nature of records as inscribed texts. Popular audiences were confronting an incomplete, aural essentialism to the degree that they interrogated records as racialized performances. There was no single, uncomplicated sound for skin color.

It was an interesting historical moment for what is now debated as "black music." Clearly if the crassest technological determinism had pertained or ever could pertain, the phonograph and then radio would have been colorblind media. But technology does not drive history that narrowly, and the observation that the early recording industry was nondiscriminatory because trade publications seem to have paid black musicians their due (Sanjek, 297), needs to include the caveat that the politics of defining and policing racial distinctions has always been a lot more involved than the related now-you-see-it-now-you-don't of discrimination. Paying black songwriters their due carried the baggage of needing to tell which songwriters were black; in whichever order and for whatever matrix of reasons, good and ill, paying and needing to tell became conscious desires and cultural necessities.

As if to emphasize the changing visuality of music, phonograph advertisements from the 1890s to the 1920s picture listeners watching the machine. They stare vacantly at unseen and newly reracialized performers, as if by some collective premonition, keeping their gaze steady for radio and then television. The gaze itself is oddly communal, fraught with unlikely assumptions about the democratic power of mass media. One Edison advertisement from 1908 has a mixed-race group of servants staring appreciatively at their employers' phonograph. Below, the caption simultaneously enrolls western music and the phonograph in the cause of democracy: "One touch of harmony makes the whole world kin". Such rhetoric coincided with Edison's personal expectations for the phonograph, which was an instrument of social leveling in his ken, since it would allow poor and rural audiences to hear opera. The inventor seems not to have appreciated the anarchic potential of the device as a means for class crashing or racial ventriloquism.[24] But Edison and many of his contemporaries were sure that they lived in a world of visible certainties when it came to human identity: the inventor interviewed prospective employees while taking notes on the shapes of their heads. And the author Henry James remarked pointedly on Edison's "street boy" face after the two men met in 1911.[25]

A different sort of essentialism was at stake in legislative chambers during 1906–8, where congressmen and witnesses debated how to handle recorded music. Defining and policing authorship, though certainly less inflammatory, proved almost as nettlesome as defining and policing race or class, all because similarly visual habits of definition did not apply as they had before. American copyright law remained dependent upon material forms, so that new forms always caused new problems. And constitutionally protected "writings" were going to be something altogether different if they could be copied out into purely audible forms, without some sort of visible expression. To members of Congress and many other participants in the hearings, it simply seemed intuitive that phonograph records and music rolls—the latter even inscriptions on paper—were copied writings and could be read. As for visible expression, anyone could see the grooves on a record or the holes in a music roll, even if seeing them did not mean anything musically. Witnesses made analogy to hieroglyphics, which resisted reading for a long time yet were certainly legible. "It is a curious fact," one witness pointed out, "that the earliest known writing, the Assyrian hieroglyphic, was made by an instrumentality very similar to the phonographic needle of to-day impressing itself upon plastic material" (78). Edison would probably have regretted this turn in the debate if he were following it closely. The analogy to hieroglyphics was unhelpful to his cause, yet he himself had made the same comparison with great satisfaction back in 1888. In an essay entitled "The Perfected Phonograph," he gloried in his work: "It is curious to reflect that the Assyrians and Babylonians, 2,500 years ago, chose baked clay cylinders inscribed with cuneiform characters, as their medium for perpetuating records; while

this recent result of modern science, the phonograph, uses cylinders of wax for a similar purpose, but with the great and progressive difference that our wax cylinders speak for themselves, and will not have to wait dumbly for centuries to be deciphered."[26] Here the inventor at once co-opted ancient tradition and assumed the mantle of modern science. The symbolist, nineteenth-century context of his hieroglyph metaphor made using the metaphor in discussions of recorded sound both familiar and extremely powerful. Edison's essay immodestly boosted the inventor to God's place at the same time that it hinted at the profound centrality of technology in American relations with nature. When the same figure surfaced in the congressional debates over copyright, its appeal was slightly different. Invoking the example of cuneiform meant acknowledging that phonograph records could be read without actually having to read them. The complimentary acts of writing and reading could theoretically be separated by centuries, and there was no need to admit so hastily that phonograph records and music rolls could not be deciphered. Meanwhile the traditional object of the hieroglyph metaphor, nature, jibed well with contemporary appeals to music as a natural, universal language, the spiritual residuum of pre-Babel days. Laden with this metaphorical weight records could be celebrated as what Adorno would later call "delicately scribbled, utterly illegible writing." The precision and the delicacy with which they were scribbled vouched for the meaning they contained, and proof positive emerged from the mouth of a phonograph horn. Members of the joint committees of Congress were only less keenly aware than Adorno would be of the cultural implications of such a mouth.[27] The illegibility of recorded music troubled them as little as the dual nature of patent documents did, both actively concealing just the thing they reveal.

Sensing that the day was lost, opponents of clause G marshaled every argument they could think of to show the ill-advised and even unconstitutional nature of the musical copyright provision. Inventors argued that the wording of clause G directly transgressed their rights "to make, sell, distribute, or let for hire" the devices and processes they had patented (97). Albert H. Walker, a patent expert who had appeared as an attorney in *White-Smith v. Apollo*, assured the committee that the bill was unconstitutional for a long list of reasons (106). And many witnesses raised the specter of unfettered monopoly, alleging that the Aeolian music-roll company, ever since its own early involvement in *White-Smith v. Apollo*, had executed exclusive agreements with almost every publisher of sheet music in America, so that in the event of the copyright bill's passing, Aeolian would control all new American music ("a complete monopolistic octopus," 98). Defending against the accusation that they formed a "phonograph trust" themselves, other witnesses pointed out that composers and sheet-music publishers actually benefitted from current conditions. Letters were produced to show the way that phonograph companies were solicited by composers and publishers, who sought to stimulate sheet-music sales by having records made.

A number of witnesses invoked international competitiveness, noting the fact that musical copyright provisions had not succeeded fully in any European country but Italy, where, as of March 1908, the matter still had not reached the court of last resort (157). In France, musical copyright provisions had been advocated by composers, only to be overturned in the courts. In England, Edison's lawyers had embarrassed one copyright holder in court by asking him under oath if he could understand or read what was on a phonograph record; "He answered, 'Of course not.' "[28] None of the witnesses mentioned Mexico, where all three major American phonograph companies had become embroiled in copyright suits, and a lawyer for the American Graphophone Company was wont to complain, "It is exceedingly difficult for the American and English mind to foretell how the foreign mind (and particularly a Latin American mind) will work; and it is also difficult to forecast satisfactorily the outcome of litigation in a foreign country."[29] Not surprisingly, American record companies were trying to forge or maintain the qualities of statutory authorship abroad with the same unattended paternalism that they pursued in their domestic capitalization of coon songs. Lobbyists appealed to western European models, while developments in Mexico vouched for the newly global and frequently colonialist entertainment economy as well as the precocity of cultural capital in breaching national boundaries.

Even in western Europe, however, the matter of musical copyright was far from settled. Representatives of the Berne Convention countries met in Berlin during the autumn of 1908 with the mechanical reproduction of music on their agenda. In an early and important instance of such internationalization, Victor Talking Machine, Columbia, and Edison's National Phonograph companies, all of which variously possessed shares of European markets and relied upon European composers and performers, joined British and German record companies in trying to stymie any change in the articles of the convention. Paul H. Cromelin, a Columbia executive who had already appeared in the Washington hearings, struggled to draw the three American competitors into cooperation with each other and then with their European rivals. The three American companies urged the secretary of state to press their case, even though America was not a member of the Berne Convention. Cromelin had limited success coordinating other efforts, and his work behind the scenes in Berlin was to no avail. On 13 November 1908, revised articles of the Berne Convention were signed in Berlin and sent back to member nations for consideration and the emendation of domestic statues. The new article 13 extended a composer's authorial rights to cover mechanical reproductions. Frank Dyer would testify once more, this time before the copyright committee of the British Parliament, but Britain would go along with the Berne Convention.

The United States Copyright Act of 1909 passed a few months after the new Berne Convention; it was signed by outgoing President Theodore Roosevelt and went into effect in July. The earlier article G, now article *E*, protected composers against unlicensed mechanical reproductions, which were thus deemed copies of writings and, by implication, readable. The new law applied only to musical compositions published after the act, so that it enforced a new industry distinction between new music (which cost money to record) and old music (which could be recorded for free), with the resulting, ironic split between "the popular domain" and "the popular." From between the two peeked the modern consumer, with changing appetites and mercurial tastes, with resident notions of race, class, gender, and nationality as (some of) the data of culture. Another provision of article *E* was called the compulsory license clause. It ensured that once a composer licensed one mechanical reproduction, she or he was compelled to license all other proposed mechanical reproductions for a guaranteed royalty fee of two cents per copy. This arrangement vitiated the exclusive contracts held by the Aeolian Company and added another shade of meaning to the "mass" in "mass culture," since mechanical reproduction became in some sense self-perpetuating. One recording opened the floodgates for multiple recordings as mechanical re-reproduction followed any potentially successful record or music roll. Compulsory license provided only for musical compositions, not musical performances, and the result was an even more heightened sense of "the talent" as a commodity. The record companies intensified their battles for exclusive contracts with celebrated performers. Anyone could record Victor Herbert's compositions after they had been recorded once, but Victor Herbert's Orchestra performed only on Edison records after Herbert signed his exclusive contract with National Phonograph in the summer of 1909; Sousa's band signed an Edison contract one month later. Far from showing Edison's approval of musical copyright,[30] Herbert's contract demonstrates that National Phonograph and other record companies could not afford to be sore losers. They quietly opened composers' royalty accounts in their corporate ledgers. The success of ASCAP and other societies of authors would be later responses to the law.

Clause *E* had been rewritten to avoid any direct conflict with patent rights, but the two forms of intellectual property were closer in 1909 and 1910 than they had been or ever would be again. The context and the content of the 1906 and 1908 hearings accounted for some of their proximity, as did current commercial practices of tying and price fixing. The Supreme Court decision in *Leeds and Caitlin v. Victor Talking Machine* was nearly simultaneous with the new act, and it drew the differing logics of patents and copyrights onto the same plane for the eight years that it stood. The compulsory license provision made musical compositions available to record companies without exclusion; in its *Leeds and Caitlin* decision the Supreme Court regulated what that availability meant, deciding that Victor's patent rights extended to cover which records were played on Victor machines. Leeds and Caitlin, notorious record pirates, had been duplicating Victor records and then competing to supply

Victrola owners. The Court now made duplicating illegal by allowing Victor to dictate (to "tie") which records were played on its patented phonographs. So while the compulsory license provision allowed any recording to be remade, *Leeds and Caidin* assured that remaking would entail live performance, not just "duping" from one record to another. Copyright law made records into copies of protected writings, and patent law briefly protected those copies against duplication. Mechanical reproduction of sound was one thing, mechanical duplication of the same sound was another. Still further contiguity between patent and copyright was established in an early court decision by Learned Hand. In 1910 Hand found in *Hein v. Harris* that the copyright for the composition "The Arab Love Song" had been infringed by "I Think I Hear a Woodpecker Knocking at My Family Tree." Infringement existed, according to Hand, "whether or not the defendant, as he alleges, had never heard the complainant's song, when he wrote his chorus." What this meant was that novelty, not origination or authoring, was the substantial requirement for copyright, just as it had always been for patent rights.[31] Sounding the same meant copying in music. This alliance of patents and copyrights was fleeting. In later interpretations of the law Learned Hand reversed himself, and copyrights diverged from patents accordingly.

In 1909 and 1910 the renegotiated boundary between things and texts had stretched a little thinner. The very lateral groove on a gramophone record, or the up and down engravings of a phonograph needle, were patentable inventions that contained, in some hieroglyphic and as yet undecipherable way, performances of copyrighted sheet music. By extension, phonographs and gramophones were "reading machines" more properly than they were "talking machines," and for the first time reading out loud was explicitly severed from the human subject. Humans could not read wax cylinders or discs, but machinery could. The reader was less replaced than displaced, pushed aside to make room for the new apparatus. As instruments, too, recording phonographs and musical roll perforators could not be authors in the sense that musical composers like Sousa and Herbert were. They produced aural copies of writings, they performed, and they did so until the copyright code was revised again in the 1970s. Then copyright was extended to cover recordings; readings under the 1909 act were made into writings.

While it is unlikely that this new, mechanical kind of reading decisively changed the American experience of reading type or reading music, it did possess some broad implications both for the emerging culture industries and for America's ongoing reconnaissance of the machine in modern life. The legislative construction of the reading machine acknowledged ongoing reformulations of the "popular" and of popularity in music. For example, the two related skills of reading music and playing an instrument were indeed under assault, as Sousa recognized, in part because reading and playing could now be done mechanically. Mechanical process extended to yet more human functions, and in doing so continued the often remarked colonization of the body by the machine. The new colonial purpose of the machine was amusement. Both the technology of recorded sound and the surrounding debate challenged existing visual receptor sites within culture, including elaborate practices of experiencing racial difference in and through performance. These receptor sites survived in modified form, colored by a new inscrutability, their visual orientation technologically challenged and then, ironically, modified in adaptations of a tired nineteenth-century metaphor for nature. America's new hieroglyphics, the grooves on a record, were the works of man and machine, not God and nature. The universality that these potent new symbolic actions possessed derived not from any transcendental truths or divine omnipotence, but rather from the questionable universality of music, as well as from the penchant of westerners for lugging their machinery around the globe, and from the eager adaptability of cultural capital, which inserted itself abroad into new markets on every continent as the American phonograph industry established commercial outposts and sent recording engineers to Europe, Asia, and South and Central America.

Notes

1. Alexandra Mullen pointed me toward many such anecdotes, these from David Grimsted, *Melodrama Unveiled: American Theatre and Culture, 1800–1850* (Chicago: University of Chicago Press, 1968), 60. See also

Lawrence W. Levine, *Highbrow/Lowbrow: The Emergence of Cultural Hierarchy in America* (Cambridge: Harvard University Press, 1988), 30.

2. See Carolyn Marvin, *When Old Technologies Were New: Thinking About Electric Communication in the Late Nineteenth Century* (New York: Oxford University Press, 1988), on the anecdotes and constructed expertise of telegraphy and engineering publications. Of course, popular culture fed and reinforced the same exclusionary rhetoric; recall the spectacularly racist second verse to Stephen Foster's "Oh! Susanna" (1848), performed by the African-American troupe, Christy's Minstrels: "I jumped aboard de telegr[a]ph/And trabbelled down de river,/De Lectric fluid magnified/And Killed five Hundred Nigger"; *Democratic Souvenirs: An Historical Anthology of 19th-century American Music*, ed. Richard Jackson (New York: C. F. Peters Corporation for the New York Public Library, 1988), 104.

3. There is much work still to do on ethnicity and the phonograph. On the ethnographic present see Johannes Fabian, *Time and the Other: How Anthropology Makes Its Object* (New York: Columbia University Press, 1983), and James Clifford and George E. Marcus, eds., *Writing Culture: The Poetics and Politics of Ethnography* (Berkeley: University of California Press, 1986). Examples of the type-scene appear in the *Music Trade Review*, 21 Dec. 1907, in Robert Flaherty's *Nanook of the North* (1922), and elsewhere. For a discussion of type-scenes as such, see Mary Louise Pratt, "Fieldwork in Common Places," in Clifford and Marcus, 27–50. See also Michael Adas, *Machines as the Measure of Men: Science, Technology, and Ideologies of Western Dominance* (Ithaca: Cornell University Press, 1989), and William Peitz, "The Phonograph in Africa: International Phonocentrism from Stanley to Sarnoff," in *Post-Structuralism and the Question of History*, ed. Derek Attridge, Geoff Bennington, and Robert Young (Cambridge: Cambridge University Press, 1987). Michael Taussig explains that bringing a victrola to the jungle or the arctic "proved an easy way for making an intercultural nexus, a new cultural zone . . . for [mutually] discovering strangeness and confirming sameness"; *Mimesis and Alterity: A Particular History of the Senses* (New York: Routledge, 1993), 195 (further references cited in the text). Lizbeth Cohen has noticed that the Victrola was in one sense an instrument for maintaining ethnic identity in the face of "Americanizing" pressures; *Making a New Deal: Industrial Workers in Chicago, 1919–1939* (Cambridge: Cambridge University Press, 1990), 105. I would like to thank Jerry Fabris for sharing his thoughts on the phonograph and the early history of ethnomusicology.

4. See Eric Lott, *Love and Theft: Blackface Minstrelsy and the American Working Class* (New York: Oxford University

Press, 1993); my debt to Lott's readings of minstrelsy will be clear below. See also Dave Laing, "A Voice Without a Face: Popular Music and the Phonograph in the 1890s," *Popular Music* 10 (1991): 1–9. Further references to Lott and Laing are cited by page number in the text.

5. *Arguments Before the Committees on Patents, December 7,8,10 and 11; 59th Congress* (Washington: GPO, 1906), vol. 4 of *Legislative History of the 1909 Copyright Act*, 6 vols., ed. E. Fulton Brylawski and Abe Goldman (South Hackensack: Fred B. Rotheman, 1976), 120–21. This volume is cited by page number in the text; the different hearings are paginated individually.

6. Like early motion pictures, phonograph records partook of the culture of vaudeville, thriving on the same heterogeneity of participants and a similar variety of acts, rooted in the dynamics of performance and a tumult of oral forms. Edison's National Phonograph established its New York offices on Union Square, in the heart of the vaudeville district. See Robert W. Snyder, *The Voice of the City: Vaudeville and Popular Culture in New York* (New York: Oxford University Press, 1989), 58–59; on the class and racial heterogeneity of the vaudeville, variety experience, 106.

7. *Burrow-Giles Lithographic Co. v. Sarony*, 111 U.S. 53 (1884).

8. June 6 hearing; see "laughter," 165. Attendance was all male; Wilde was by then disgraced and dead.

9. See Jane M. Gaines, *Contested Culture: The Image, The Voice, and the Law* (Chapel Hill: University of North Carolina Press, 1991), 56, 68–69, 82.

10. 122 F.R. 240 (1902); Edison won on appeal in 1903, the same year another important precedent was set in one of the *Edison v. American Mutoscope and Biograph Co.* cases; see Charles Musser, *Before the Nickelodeon: Edwin S. Porter and the Edison Manufacturing Company* (Berkeley: University of California Press, 1991), 238.

11. See registration form for Thomas Crahan's "Artistic Glimpses of the Wonder World," 1900. On the matter of deposits see "Copyright" folders, 1908–10, Edison Document File record group, Edison National Historic Site, West Orange, N.J. (elsewhere ENHS), forthcoming in *Thomas A. Edison Papers: A Selective Microfilm Edition*, ed. Thomas E. Jeffrey et al. (Bethesda: University Publication of America). See also Patrick George Loughney, "A Descriptive Analysis of the Library of Congress Paper Print Collection and Related Copyright Materials" (Ph.D. diss., George Washington University, 1988) 60 ff. The number of deposits in 1905 was given by the Librarian of Congress, Herbert Putnam, during his statement in *Arguments before the Committees on Patents . . .* (14).

12. The United States Census reported in 1905 that the annual value of American sheet music had risen from $1.69 million in 1890 to $2.27 million in 1900 and to $4.15 million in 1905. In the same scheme, American pianos produced for 1905 were valued at $69.6 million, while the annual value of phonographs and supplies had surged to $10.2 million in their two decades on the market. These figures were repeated into the record of the congressional copyright hearings as evidence of the vigor that different segments of the music industry possessed.

13. This is from an Edison record catalogue for Blue Amberol record No. 2147, "On the Banks of the Wabash, Far Away," performed by baritone and chorus with orchestra. See Ronald Dethlefson, *Edison Blue Amberol Recordings, 1912–1914* (Brooklyn: APM Press, 1980).

14. See Theodore Dreiser, "Birth and Growth of a Popular Song," *Metropolitan* 8 (1898): 497–502, reprinted in *Selected Magazine Articles of Theodore Dreiser: Life and Art in the American 1890s*, ed. Yashinobu Hakutani, 2 vols. (Rutherford: Fairleigh Dickinson University Press, 1987). See also Paul Dresser, "Concerning the Author of These Songs," *The Songs of Paul Dresser* (New York: Boni and Liveright, 1927), v–x.

15. See Russell Sanjek, *American Popular Music and Its Business: The First Four Hundred Years, Volume 2: From 1790 to 1909* (New York: Oxford University Press, 1988), chap. 11. Further references to this work will be cited by page number in the text. Richard Middleton's methodological reflections on popular music were helpful to these several pages, particularly regarding the varied meaning of "popular" in studies of popular music; of related interest is George H. Lewis's article on popular music as "symbolic communication"; Richard Middleton, *Studying Popular Music* (Milton Keynes: Open University Press, 1990); George H. Lewis, "The Meanings in the Music and the Music's in Me: Popular Music as Symbolic Communication," *Theory, Culture & Society* 1 (1983): 133–41.

16. Edison undated memoranda, covered by Frank L. Dyer letter of 26 Feb. 1908; Edison Document File, ENHS. For a cultural history of Sousa, see Neil Harris, "John Philip Sousa and the Culture of Reassurance," in *Cultural Excursions: Marketing Appetites and Cultural Tastes in Modern America* (Chicago: University of Chicago Press, 1990), 198–232.

17. 209 U.S. 1 (1908); see also 147 F.R. 226 (1902).

18. In the post-minstrelsy age, popular music in general seems to fulfill this role in another way; I am thinking of Paul Gilroy's sensitive polemic, *The Black Atlantic: Modernity and Double Consciousness* (Cambridge: Harvard University Press, 1993), chap. 3, entitled " 'Jewels Brought from Bondage': Black Music and the Politics of Authenticity."

19. On contemporary questions of essentialism I have been particularly influenced by Michael O'Malley and Nell Irvin Painter's *American Historical Review* Forum on race, money, and "intrinsic value" in nineteenth-century America: O'Malley, "Specie and Species: Race and the Money Question in Nineteenth-Century America," *American Historical Review* 99 (1994): 369–95; Painter, "Thinking About the Languages of Money and Race: A Response to Michael O'Malley, 'Specie and Species,'" *American Historical Review* 99 (1994): 396–404. The visuality of racial difference came up with special force in *Plessy v. Ferguson*, in which white-skinned Homer Plessy was confirmed "black," establishing the doctrine of separate but equal; "Facing the possibility that men such as Plessy could renegotiate racial value . . . the court responded with irrational theories of intrinsic racial difference" (O'Malley, 395).

20. See James H. Dormon, "Shaping the Popular Image of Post-Reconstruction American Blacks: The 'Coon Song' Phenomenon of the Gilded Age," *American Quarterly* 40 (1988): 450–71; see also Sanjek, chap. 9.

21. According to Riis, in the period "just before jazz," "'Negro' music seems to have meant syncopated tunes or dialect songs on a nostalgic, Old South theme"; Thomas L. Riis, *Just Before Jazz: Black Musical Theatre in New York, 1890–1915* (Washington: Smithsonian Institution, 1989), 154.

22. *Edison Phonograph Monthly* 3, no. 5 (July 1905): 10.

23. See for example, Patricia A. Turner, *Ceramic Uncles & Celluloid Mammies: Black Images and Their Influence on Culture* (New York: Anchor Books, 1994), 20, 22, for an observation of the differing modes of aural and visual racism.

24. Here I am indebted to Miranda Paton's unpublished work on the iconography of the phonograph, "Seeing How to Listen: Constructing Fidelity for the Musical Phonograph, 1915–1925," and to an e-mail exchange with David W. Stowe about what he calls "racial ventriloquism." Interestingly enough, phonographs and records remain tenaciously visual artifacts for collectors; see Arnold Schwartzman, *Phono-graphics: The Visual Paraphernalia of the Talking Machine* (San Francisco: Chronicle Books, 1993).

25. Edison's notes are in "Employment" folders, Edison Document File, ENHS. James and Edison met on a steamer for Europe; *The Complete Notebooks of Henry James*, ed. Leon Edel and Lyall H. Powers (New York: Oxford University Press, 1987), 329.

26. Thomas Edison, "The Perfected Phonograph," *North American Review* (1888): 641–50. For a rich and extended analysis of the hieroglyph metaphor, see John T. Irwin, *American Hieroglyphics: The Symbol of the Egyptian Hieroglyphics in the American Renaissance* (New Haven: Yale University Press, 1980).

27. Thomas Y Levin, "For the Record: Adorno on Music in the Age of Its Technological Reproducibility," *October* 55 (1990): 23–66; "For the Record" includes translations of Adorno's "The Curves of the Needle," "The Form of the Phonograph Record" (quoted here, 56), and "Opera and the Long-Playing Record." The imagined universality of (usually Western) music jibed with other attempts at universal language. Esperanto (1887) had a grand launch during the Paris exposition of 1900; Richard D. Mandell, *Paris 1900: The Great World's Fair* (Toronto: University of Toronto Press, 1976), 68. There were other stabs at the same thing: IDO (described by L. De Beaufront), the Master Language (described by Stephen Chase Houghton), Word-English (by Alexander Melville Bell), and Tutonish (Elias Molee), all examples from pamphlets in the New York Public Library general collections.

28. On France see, Jaques Attali, *Noise, The Political Economy of Music*, trans. Brian Massumi (Minneapolis: University of Minnesota Press, 1985), 97–98. Some European developments are documented in the records of the National Phonograph Company at ENHS. The British case, *Neumark v. National Phonograph Ltd.*, is described in a letter of 10 April 1907, from G. Croyden Marks to William E. Gilmore, available via *The Thomas A. Edison Papers* (http://edison.rutgers.edu) with the other ENHS sources cited here.

29. C. A. L. Massie to H. C. Kennedy, letter, 19 July 1907, regarding *Jose Elizondo v. Jorge Alcade*; Legal Department Records, ENHS. The copyright in question was a selection from a comic opera entitled "El Chin Chun Chan."

30. Oliver Read and Walter L. Welch, *Tin Foil to Stereo: Evolution of the Phonograph*, 2d ed. (Indianapolis: Howard W. Sams, 1976), 393.

31. 175 F.R. 875 (1910). On Hand, see Benjamin Kaplan, An *Unhurried View of Copyright* (New York: Columbia University Press, 1967), 41; and Ronald Cracas, "Judge Learned Hand and the Law of Copyright," American Society of Composers, Authors, and Publishers, *Copyright Law Symposium* 7 (1956): 55–90.

10.
THE DOMESTIC ECONOMY OF TELEVISION VIEWING IN POSTWAR AMERICA

Lynn Spigel

In 1952, the Western-Holly Company marketed a new design in domestic technology, the TV-stove. The oven included a window through which the housewife could watch her chicken roast. Above the oven window was a television screen which presented an even more spectacular sight. With the aid of this machine the housewife would be able to prepare her meal, but at the same time she could watch television. Although it was clearly an odd object, this TV-stove was not simply a historical fluke. Rather, its invention is a reminder of the concrete social, economic, and ideological conditions that made this contraption possible. Indeed, the TV-stove was a response to the conflation of labor and leisure time at home. If it now seems strange, this has as much to do with the way in which society has conceptualized work and leisure as it does with the machine's bizarre technological form.[1]

In this essay, I examine television viewing in terms of a history of ideas concerning gendered patterns of work and leisure in the home. Based on a study of popular media from the postwar era (especially middle class women's magazines), this essay considers how television was introduced to the American housewife. Television's innovation after World War II occasioned a multitude of responses and expectations voiced in films, magazines, newspapers, and on television itself. These popular discourses were replete with ambivalence about television's relationship to family life. As the TV-stove so dramatically suggests, there was a profound uncertainly about television's place and function in the home, an uncertainty that gave rise to a fierce debate on the cultural and social value of this new domestic object and entertainment form.

Indeed, as other historians have shown, this kind of ambivalence has characterized America's response to a host of household technologies, including television's most obvious predecessor, radio (Covert, 1984; Davis, 1965). In this respect, the popular debates about television should be seen not as an aberrant phenomenon but rather as a specific manifestation of a larger history of ideas about household technology, ideas which were firmly inscribed in gendered patterns of labor and leisure in domestic space. It is these patterns, as they were described to the first wave of television viewers, that I consider in the following pages. To do so, I first briefly describe the historical roots of the domestic ideology and some theoretical questions to which they give rise.

Gender, Work, and Leisure

Since the nineteenth century, middle class ideals of domesticity had been predicated on divisions of leisure time and work time. This doctrine of two spheres represented human activity in spatial terms: the public world came to be conceived of as a place of productive labor, while the home was seen as a site of rejuvenation and consumption. By the 1920s, the public world was still a sphere of work, but it was also opened up to a host of commercial pleasures like movies and amusement parks that were incorporated into middle class family life styles. The ideal home, however, remained a place of revitalization and, with the expansion of convenience products that promised to reduce household chores, domesticity was even less associated with production.

As feminists have argued, this separation has served to justify the exploitation of the housewife whose work at home simply does not count. Along these lines Nanev Folbre (1982) claims that classical economics considers women's work as voluntary labor and therefore outside the realm of exploitation. In addition, she argues, even Marxist critics neglect the issue of domestic exploitation since they assume that the labor theory of value can be applied only to efficiency-oriented production for the market and not to "inefficient" and "idiosyncratic" household chores.

But as feminist critics and historians have shown, the home is indeed a site of labor. Not only do women do physical chores, but also the basic relations of our economy and society are reproduced at home, including the literal reproduction of workers through child rearing labor. Once the home is considered as a work place, the divisions between public/work and domestic/leisure become less clear. The ways in which work and leisure are connected, however, remain a complex issue.

Henri Lefebvre's studies of everyday life offer ways to consider the general interrelations among work, leisure, and family life in modern society. In his foreword to the 1958 edition of *Critique de la Vie Quotidienne*, Lefebvre argues that.

> Leisure . . . cannot be separated from work. It is the same man who, after work, rests or relaxes or does whatever he chooses. Every day, at the same time, the worker leaves the factory, and the employee, the office. Every week, Saturday and Sunday are spent on leisure activities, with the same regularity as that of the weekdays' work. Thus we must think in terms of the unity "work-leisure," because that unity exists, and everyone tries to program his own available time according to what his work is—and what it is not.
>
> (1958/1979, p. 136)

While Lefebvre concentrated on the "working man," the case of the housewife presents an even more pronounced example of the integration of work and leisure in everyday life.

In the absence of a thoroughgoing critique of the issues surrounding work and leisure, it has been difficult for television critics and historians to deal with the central importance of domestic labor for television spectatorship. Recent British ethnographic research suggests that men and women tend to use television according to their specific position within the distribution of leisure and labor activities inside and outside the home (Gray, 1987; Morley, 1986). In the American context, two of the most serious examinations come from Tania Modleski (1983) and Nick Browne (1984), who theorize the way television watching fits into a general pattern of everyday life where work and leisure are intertwined. Modleski suggests that the soap opera might be understood in terms of the "rhythms of reception," or the way women working at home relate to the text within a specific milieu of distraction: cleaning, cooking, child rearing, etc. Browne concentrates not on the individual text but rather on the entire television schedule, which he claims is ordered according to the logic of the workday of both men and women. As he writes, "the position of the programs in the television schedule reflects and is determined by the work-structured order of the real social world. The patterns of position and flow imply the question of who is home, and through complicated social relays and temporal mediations, link television to the modes, processes, and scheduling of production characteristic of the general population" (p. 176).

Women's Magazines and Television

The fluid interconnection between leisure and labor at home presents a context for exploring the ways women use and understand television programming in their daily lives. In the following pages, I focus on a moment in American history, specifically the years 1948–1955, when women were first learning how to accommodate television, both as a domestic object and as an entertainment form. During these years, more than half of all American households installed television, and the basic patterns of daytime television emerged as a distinct cultural form which entailed a particular set of female viewing practices. While most women might not have had the elaborate mechanism offered by the TV-stove, they were in the process of adapting themselves to—or else resisting—a new and curious entertainment machine.

How can we understand the way people integrated television into their lives some 30 years ago? How can we discover a history of everyday life that was not recorded by the people who lived it at the time? The women's home magazines I examine illuminate the reception of television as it was registered in popular media of the postwar period. These magazines included graphics, articles, cartoons, and illustrations depicting television's relationship to family life.[2] While they cannot tell us how television was actually received by people at the time, popular magazines do reveal an intertextual context through which people could make sense of television and its relation to their lives.

The debates about television drew upon and magnified the more general obsession with the reconstruction of family life and domestic ideals after World War II. The 1950s was a decade that placed an enormous amount of cultural capital in the ability to form a family and to live out a set of highly structured gender roles. Although people at the time might well have experienced and understood the constraining aspects of this domestic dream, it nevertheless was a consensus ideology, promising practical benefits like security and stability to people who had witnessed the shocks and social dislocations of the previous two decades. As Elaine Tyler May (1988) suggests, while people acknowledged the limitations of postwar domesticity, they nevertheless often spoke of their strong faith in the overall project of being in a family. In this social climate, television was typically welcomed as a catalyst for renewed familial values. Indeed, television, in many popular discussions, was depicted as a panacea for the broken homes and hearts of wartime life: not only was it shown to restore faith in family togetherness, but as the most sought-after appliance for sale in post-war America, it also renewed faith in the splendors of consumer capitalism. By the same token, however, television was also greeted in less euphoric terms, and as I have argued elsewhere (1988a; 1988b), the discourses on television typically expressed profound doubts about domesticity—especially, gender roles in the home.

Women's home magazines were the primary venue for this debate on television and the family. Yet, apart from the occasional reference, these magazines have been disregarded in television histories. Rather than focusing on the social and domestic context, broadcast history has continually framed its object of study around questions of industry, regulation, and technological invention: that is, around spheres where men have participated as executives, policy makers, and inventors. Women, on the other hand, are systematically marginalized in television history. According to the assumptions of our current historical paradigms, the woman is simply the receiver of the television text, the one to whom the advertiser promotes products. This is not to say industrial history necessarily fails to explain gender relations. Indeed, as other feminist critics have shown, the very notion of femininity itself is in part constructed through and by mass media images as they are produced by the "culture industries." But industrial history clearly needs to be supplemented by methods of investigation that will better illuminate women's subjective experiences and the way those experiences, in turn, might have affected industry output and policies.

By looking at women's magazines as a source of historical evidence, we find another story, one that tells us something (however partial and mediated) about the way women might have experienced the arrival of television in their own homes. These magazines, through their debates on television's place in the domestic sphere, provided women with opportunities to negotiate rules and practices for watching television at home. In addition, they addressed women not simply as passive consumers of promotional rhetoric but also as producers within the domestic sphere. In fact, even the television manufacturers, who used women's magazines to promote the sale of television sets, seem to have recognized this productive role. For, as I will show, rather than simply offering women the passive consumer luxury of total television pleasure, the manufacturers tailored their messages to the everyday concerns of the housewife; they typically acknowledged the conflicts between household chores and television leisure, and they offered their products as solutions to these conflicts.

In this sense, I emphasize the importance of looking at advertisements in relation to the wider media context in which they appear. A popular assumption in advertising history and theory is that ads are the voice of big industry, a voice that instills consumer fantasies into the minds of the masses. But advertising is not simply one voice; rather it is necessarily composed of multiple voices. Advertising adopts the voice of an imaginary consumer—it must speak from his or her point of view, even if that point of view is at odds with the immediate goals of the sales effort. In this respect, television advertisers did not simply promote ideas and values in the sense of an over-whelming "product propaganda." Rather, they followed certain *discursive rules* found in a media form that was popular with women since the nineteenth century. Advertisers often adjusted their sales messages to fit with the concerns voiced in women's magazines, and they also used conventions of language and representation that were typical of the magazines as a whole.

The common thread uniting the ads, editorial content, and pictorial representations was mode of address. The discourses of middle class women's magazines assumed, a priori, that women were housewives and that their interests necessarily revolved around cleaning, cooking, child rearing, and, less explicitly, love making. Indeed, even though the 1950s witnessed a dramatic rise in the female labor force—and, in particular, the number of married women taking jobs outside the home rose significantly (Chafe, 1972; Gatlin, 1987)—these magazines tacitly held to an outdated model of femininity, ignoring the fact that both working class and middle class women were dividing their time between the family work space and the public work space. In this sense, the conventions formed for viewing television arose in relation to this housewife figure; even if the actual reader was employed outside the domestic sphere, her leisure time was represented in terms of her household work. Representations of television continually presented women with a notion of spectatorship that was inextricably intertwined with their useful labor at home.

These magazines offered women instructions on how to cope with television, and they established a set of viewing practices based around the tenuous balance of labor and leisure at home. They told women of the utopian possibilities of fantasy and romantic transport that television might bring to their relatively "unglorious" lives as homemakers, but they also warned that television might wreak havoc on the home and therefore had to be carefully managed and

skillfully controlled. Indeed, these magazines offered women an ambivalent picture of television; the television set appeared less as a simple consumer luxury than as a complex set of problems that called for women's rational decisions and careful examination. In the discussion below, I consider the industrial solution to the working/viewing continuum, then detail the concerns which circulated in magazines, and finally address some of the implications these popular discourses had for gender dynamics in general.

The Industry's Ideal Viewer

Unlike the many household appliances which, since the nineteenth century, have promised to simplify women's work, the television set threatened to disrupt the efficient functioning of the household. And while other home entertainment media such as the phonograph could be enjoyed while doing household tasks, pleasure in television appeared to be fundamentally incompatible with women's productive labor. As William Boddy (1979) argues, the broadcasting industry recognized this conflict when radio was first introduced to the public. But overcoming its initial reluctance, the industry successfully developed daytime radio in the 1930s, and by the 1940s housewives were a faithful audience for soap operas and advice programs.

During the postwar years, advertisers and networks once more viewed the day-time market with skepticism, fearing that their loyal radio audiences would not be able to make the transition to television. The industry assumed that, unlike radio, television might require the housewife's complete attention and thus disrupt her work in the home (Boddy, 1985). Indeed, while network prime time schedules were well worked out in 1948, both networks and advertisers were reluctant to feature regular daytime television programs.

The first network to offer a regular daytime schedule was DuMont, which began operations on its New York station WABD in November 1948. It seems likely that DuMont, which had severe problems competing with CBS and NBC, entered the daytime market to offset its economic losses in prime time during a period when even the major networks were losing money on television. Explaining the economic strategy behind the move into daytime, one DuMont executive claimed, "WABD is starting daytime programming because it is not economically feasible to do otherwise. Night time programming alone could not support radio, nor can it support television" ("DuMont Expansion," 1949, p. 23). In December 1949, DuMont offered a two-hour afternoon program to its nine affiliate stations, and it also made kinescopes available to its non-interconnected affiliates. DuMont director Commander Mortimer W. Loewi reasoned that the move into daytime would attract small ticket advertisers who wanted to buy "small segments of time at a low, daytime rate" ("Daytime Video," 1949, p. 3).

It was in 1951 that the major networks aggressively attempted to colonize the housewife's workday with advice programs, soap operas, and variety shows. One of the central reasons for the networks' move into daytime that year was the fact that prime time hours were fully booked by advertisers and that, by this point, there was more demand for television advertising in general. Daytime might have been more risky than prime time, but it had the advantage of being available—and at a cheaper network cost. Confident of its move into daytime, CBS claimed. "We aren't risking our reputation by predicting that daytime television will be a solid sell-out a year from today . . . and that once again there will be some sad advertisers who didn't read the tea leaves right" (*Sponsor*, 1951, p. 19). Alexander Stronach Jr., ABC vice president, was equally certain about the daytime market, and having just taken the plunge with the *Frances Langford-Don Ameche Show* (a variety program budgeted at the then steep $40,000 a week), Stronach told *Newsweek* (1951, p. 56). "It's a good thing electric dishwashers and washing machines were invented. The housewives will need them."

The networks' faith in daytime carried through to advertisers. In September 1951, the trade journal *Televiser* (p. 20) reported that "47 big advertisers have used daytime network television during the past season or are starting this Fall." Included were such well-known companies as American Home Products, Best Foods, Proctor and Gamble, General Foods, Hazel Bishop Lipsticks, Minute Maid, Hotpoint, and the woman's magazine *Ladies' Home Journal.*

But even after the networks and advertisers had put their faith in daytime programming, they had not resolved the conflict between women's work

and television. The industry still needed to construct program types conducive to the activities of household work. The formal that has received the most critical attention is the soap opera, which first came to network television in December, 1950. As Robert C. Allen (1985) demonstrates, early soap opera producers like Irna Philips of *Guiding Light* were skeptical of moving their shows from radio to television. By 1954, however, the Neilsen Company reported that the soaps had a substantial following; *Search For Tomorrow* was the second most popular daytime show, while *Guiding Light* was in fourth place. The early soaps, with their minimum of action and visual interest, allowed housewives to listen to dialogue while working in another room. Moreover, their segmented story lines (usually two a day), as well as their repetition and constant explanation of previous plots, allowed women to divide their attention between viewing and household work.

Another popular solution to the daytime dilemma was the segmented variety format which allowed women to enter and exit the text according to its discrete narrative units. One of DuMont's first programs, for example, was a shopping show (alternatively called *At Your Service* and *Shopper's Matinee*) which consisted of 21 entertainment segments, all revolving around different types of "women's issues." For instance, the "Bite Shop" presented fashion tips while "Kitchen Fare" gave culinary advice ("Daytime Video," 1949; "DuMont Daytime," 1949). While DuMont's program was short lived, the basic principles survived in the daytime shows at the major networks. Programs like *The Gary Moore Show* (CBS), *The Kate Smith Show* (NBC), *The Arthur Godfrey Show* (CBS) and *Home* (NBC) catered to housewife audiences with their segmented variety of entertainment and/or advice. Instituted in 1954 by NBC President Sylvester Pat Weaver (also responsible for the early morning *Today Show*), *Home* borrowed its narrative techniques from women's magazines with segments on gardening, child psychology, food, fashion, health, and interior decor. As *Newsweek* reported, "The program is planned to do for women on the screen what the women's magazines have long done in print" ("For the Girls," 1954, p. 92).

As NBC began to adapt narrative strategies from women's periodicals, it also initiated an advertising campaign that instructed housewives on ways to watch the new programs while doing household chores. In 1955, *Ladies' Home Journal* and *Good Housekeeping* carried ads for NBC's daytime lineup which suggested that not only the programs but also the scheduling of the programs would suit the content and organization of the housewife's day. The ads evoked a sense of fragmented leisure time and suggested that television viewing could be conducted in a state of distraction. But this was not the kind of critical contemplative distraction that Walter Benjamin (1936/1969) suggested in his seminal essay, "The Work of Art in the Age of Mechanical Reproduction." Rather, the ads implied that the housewife could accomplish her chores in a state of "utopian forgetfulness" as she moved freely between her work and the act of watching television.

One ad that is particularly striking in this regard includes a sketch of a housewife and her little daughter at the top of the page. Below this, the graphic layout is divided into eight boxes composed of television screens, each representing a different program in NBC's daytime lineup. The caption functions as the housewife's testimony to her distracted state. She asks, "Where Did the Morning Go? The house is tidy ... but it hasn't seemed like a terribly tiring morning.... I think I started ironing while I watched the *Sheila Graham Show*." The housewife goes on to register details of the programs, but she cannot with certainty account for her productive activities in the home. Furthermore, as the ad's layout suggests, the woman's daily activities are literally fragmented according to the pattern of the daytime television schedule, to the extent that her everyday experiences become imbricated in a kind of serial narrative. Most significantly, her child pictured at the top of the ad is depicted within the contours of a television screen so that the labor of child rearing is itself made part of the narrative pleasures offered by the NBC daytime lineup (*Ladies' Home Journal*, 1955, p. 130).

Negotiating with the Ideal Viewer

Although industry advertisements offered television as spiritual transportation for the housewife/spectator, popular media were not complicit with distraction as a remedy for the television/labor problem. Women's magazines warned of television's thoroughly negative

effect on household chores and suggested that a careful management of domestic space might solve the problem. In 1950, *House Beautiful* warned of television: "It delivers about five times as much wallop as radio and requires in return five times as much attention.... It's impossible to get anything accomplished in the same room while it's on." The magazine offered a spatial solution, telling women "to get the darn thing out of the living room," and into the TV room, cellar, library, "or as a last resort stick it in the dining room" (Crosby, p. 125).

An ad for Drano (*American Home*, 1955a, p. 14) provided a solution to television's obstruction of household chores: The housewife is shown watching her afternoon soap opera, but this nonproductive activity is sanctioned only insofar as her servant does the housework. As the maid exclaims, "Shucks, I'll never know if she gets her man 'cause this is the day of the week I put Drano in all the drains!'" The Drano Company thus attempted to sell its product by giving women a glamorous vision of themselves enjoying an afternoon of television. But it could do so only by splitting the function of leisure and work across two representational figures: the lady of leisure and the domestic servant.

If the domestic servant was a fantasy solution to the conflict between work and television, the women's magazines suggested more practical ways to manage the problem. As *Better Homes and Gardens* suggested, the television set should be placed in an area where it could be viewed, "while you're doing things up in the kitchen" (Adams & Hungerford, 1949, p. 38). Similarly, *American Home* (1954, p. 39) told readers to put the television set in the kitchen so that "Mama sees her pet programs...." Via such spatial remedies labor would not be affected by the leisure of viewing, nor would viewing be denied by household chores. In fact, household labor and television were continually condensed into one space designed to accommodate both activities. In one advertisement this labor-viewing condensation provided the basis of a joke. A graphic depicted a housewife tediously hanging her laundry on the outdoor clothesline. The drudgery of this work is miraculously solved as the housewife brings her laundry into her home and sits before her television set while letting the laundry dry on the antenna (*American Home*, 1955b, p. 138).

This spatial condensation of labor and viewing was part of a well-entrenched functionalist discourse. The home had to provide rooms that would allow for a practical orchestration of "modern living activities" which now included watching television. Functionalism was particularly useful for advertisers who used it to promote not just one household item but an entire product line. An ad for the Crane Company (*House Beautiful*, 1952a, p. 59) displayed its kitchen appliance ensemble, complete with ironing, laundering, and cooking facilities. Here the housewife could do multiple chores at once because all the fixtures were "matched together as a complete chore unit." One particularly attractive component of this "chore unit" was a television set built into the wall above the washer and dryer.

While spatial condensations of labor and leisure helped to soothe tensions about television's obstruction of household chores, other problems still existed. The magazines suggested that television would cause increasing work loads. Considering the cleanliness of the living room, *House Beautiful* told its readers: "Then the men move in for boxing, wrestling, basketball, hockey. They get excited. Ashes on the floor. Pretzel crumbs. Beer stains." The remedy was spatial: "Lots of sets after a few months have been moved into dens and recreation rooms" (Ward, 1948, p. 220).

In a slight twist of terms, the activity of eating was said to be moving out of the dining area and into the television-sitting area. Food stains on upholstery, floors, and other surfaces meant extra work for women. Vinyl upholstery, linoleum floors, tiling, and other spill-proof surfaces were recommended. In addition, the magazines showed women how to be gracious TV hostesses, always prepared to serve family and friends special TV treats. These snack-time chores created a lucrative market for manufacturers who offered a new breed of "made for TV objects" including TV trays, tables, china sets, and, in 1954, the TV dinner.

While magazines presented readers with a host of television-related tasks, they also suggested ways for housewives to ration their labor. Time-motion studies, which had been integral to the discourses of feminism and domestic science since the progressive era, were rigorously applied to the problem of increasing work loads. All unnecessary human movement which the television set might demand had to be minimized.

Again, this called for a careful management of space. The magazines suggested that chairs and sofas be placed so that they need not be moved for watching television. Alternatively, furniture could be made mobile. By placing wheels on a couch, it was possible to exert minimal energy while converting a sitting space into a viewing space. More typically, the television was mobilized. Casters and lazy Susans were suggested for the heavy console models, but the ideal solution was the easy-to-handle portable set.

More radically, space between rooms could be made continuous in order to minimize the extra movements of household labor which the television set might demand. An ad for *House Beautiful* (1952b, p. 138) suggested a "continuity" of living, dining, and television areas wherein "a curved sofa and a folding screen mark off [the] television corner from the living and dining room." Via this carefully managed spatial continuum, "it takes no more than an extra ten steps or so to serve the TV fans."

Continuous space was also a response to a more general problem of television and family relationships. Popular women's magazines discussed television in the context of domestic ideals that can be traced back to the Victorian period—ideals that were organized around the often contradictory goals of family unity and gender/social hierarchies. By incorporating notions of gender and social place within its structural layout, the middle class homes of Victorian America intended to construct a classically balanced order where ideals of family unity and division were joined in a harmonious blend of formalized rules that governed the residents' behavior. While, for example, the back parlor provided for family bonding during leisure time pursuits, individual bedrooms ensured difference among men, women, and children who were expected to carry out their own essential functions in private spaces. In the twentieth century, and certainly in the postwar era, the ideals of unity and division still pertained—even if domestic architecture had gone through a number of drastic revisions.

Women's household work presented a special dilemma for the twin ideals of family unity and social divisions because household chores demanded a more fluid relation to space than that provided by the formalized settings of the Victorian ideal. This problem became particularly significant by the early decades of the twentieth century when middle class women became increasingly responsible for household chores due to a radical reduction in the number of domestic servants.[3] As Gwendolyn Wright (1981, p. 172) has observed, women were now often cut off from the family group as they worked in kitchens designed to resemble scientific laboratories and far removed from the family activities in the central living areas of the home. Architects did little to respond to the problem of female isolation but continued instead to build kitchens fully separated from communal living spaces, suggesting that labor-saving kitchen appliances would solve the servant shortage.

In the postwar era when the continuous spaces of ranch-style architecture became a cultural ideal, the small suburban home placed a greater emphasis on interaction among family members. The "open plan" of the postwar home eliminated some of the walls between the dining room, living room, and kitchen, and thus it was associated with a higher degree of family bonding and recreational activity. With the help of this new design for living, postwar Americans were meant to rediscover the domestic bonding and personal security that was threatened during wartime. The new "family togetherness" (a term first coined by *McCalls* in 1954) served as a convenient spatial metaphor that offered a soothing alternative to the vast economic, residential, and social dislocations of the postwar world. As Roland Marchand (1982) argues, the ranch-style home and the values placed on domestic cohesion promised a last gasp at cultural "dominion" in a world increasingly structured by bureaucratic corporations and the anonymity of suburban landscapes. But even if the fantasy of dominion was a potent model of postwar experience, the new family home never functioned so idyllically in practice, nor was the domestic ideal itself so simple. Just as the Victorian idea of domesticity was rooted in a fundamental contradiction between family unity and social/sexual hierarchy, the postwar notion of family togetherness was itself based on rigid distinctions between gender lines and social function. The domestic architecture of the period is a testimony to this tenuous balance between unity and division. Even in the continuous ranch-style homes, space was often organized around the implicit differences in the everyday lives of men, women, and children. In the model

homes of postwar suburbia, the woman's work area was still zoned off from the activity area, and the woman's role as homemaker still worked to separate her from the leisure activities of her family.

Women's magazines suggested intricately balanced spatial arrangements that would mediate the tensions between female integration and isolation. Here, television viewing became a special topic of consideration. *House Beautiful* placed a television set in its remodeled kitchen which combined "such varied functions as cooking, storage, laundry, flower arranging, dining, and TV viewing" (Conway, 1951, p. 121). In this case, as elsewhere, the call for functionalism was related to the woman's ability to work among a group engaged in leisure activities. A graphic showed a television placed in a "special area" devoted to "eating" and "relaxing," one "not shut off by a partition." In continuous space, "the worker . . . is always part of the group, can share in the conversation and fun while work is in progress."

While this example presents a harmonious solution, often the ideals of integration and isolation resulted in highly contradictory representations of domestic life. Typically, illustrations that depicted family groups watching television showed the housewife to be oddly disconnected from her family members who were huddled together in a semicircle pattern. Sentinnel Television organized its advertising campaign around this pictorial convention. One ad, for example, depicted a housewife holding a tray of beverages, standing off to the side of her family which was gathered around the television set (*Better Homes and Gardens*, 1952a, p. 144). Another ad showed a housewife cradling her baby in her arms and standing at a window, far away from the rest of her family which gathered around the Sentinnel console (*Better Homes and Gardens*, 1953, p. 169). In an ad for Magnavox Television, the housewife's chores separated her from her circle of friends. The ad was organized around a U-shaped sofa that provided a quite literal manifestation of the semicircle visual cliché (*House Beautiful*, 1948, p. 5). A group of adult couples sat on the sofa watching the new Magnavox set, but the hostess stood at the kitchen door, holding a tray of snacks. Spatially removed from the television viewers, the housewife appeared to be sneaking a look at the set as she went about her hostess chores.

This problem of female spatial isolation gave way to what I call a "corrective cycle of commodity purchases." An article in *American Home* about the joys of the electric dishwasher is typical here (Ramsay, 1949, p. 66). A graphic depicting a family gathered around the living room console included the caption. "No martyr banished to kitchen, she never misses television programs. Lunch, dinner dishes are in an electric dishwasher." An ad for Hot point dishwashers used the same discursive strategy (*House Beautiful*, 1950, p. 77). The illustration showed a wall of dishes that separated a housewife in the kitchen from her family which sat huddled around the television set in the living room. The caption read, "Please … Let Your Wife Come Out Into the Living Room! Don't let dirty dishes make your wife a kitchen exile! She loses the most precious hours of her life shut off from pleasures of the family circle by the never-ending chore of old-fashioned dishwashing!"

This ideal version of female integration in a unified family space was contested by the competing discourse on divided spaces. Distinctions between work and leisure space remained an important principle of household efficiency. The magazines argued that room dividers or separate television corners might help to sanction off the work place from the viewing place and thus allow housewives the luxury of privacy from the television crowd. General Electric used this notion of family division to support the sale of a second television (*Better Homes and Gardens*, 1955, p. 139). The ad depicted a harried housewife who was able to find peace on her new GE kitchen portable. As the split-screen design of the layout showed, Mother and Daughter were able to perform their household work as they watched a cooking show, while Dad enjoyed total passive relaxation as he watched a football game on the living room console.

Television, Gender, and Domestic Power

The bifurcation of sexual roles, of male (leisure) and female (productive) activities served as an occasion for a full consideration of power dynamics between men and women in the home. Typically, the magazines extended their categories of feminine and masculine viewing practices into representations of the body. For men, television viewing was most often depicted in terms of a posture of repose. Men were typically shown to be sprawled out on easy chairs as they watched the set. Remote controls allowed the father to watch in undisturbed passive comfort. In many ways, this representation of the male body was based on Victorian notions of rejuvenation for the working man. Relaxation was condoned for men because it served a revitalizing function, preparing them for the struggles of the work-a-day world. But for women the passive calm of television viewing was simply more problematic. Although women were shown to relax in the home, as I have shown, the female body watching television was often engaged in productive activities.

Sometimes, representations of married couples became excessively literal about the gendered patterns of television leisure. When the Cleavelander Company advertised its new "T-Vue" chair, it told consumers "Once you sink into the softness of Cleavelander's cloud-like contours, cares seem to float away…" (*House Beautiful*, 1954, p. 158). Thus, not only the body but also the spirit would be revitalized by the television chair. But this form of rejuvenation was markedly gendered. While the chair allowed the father "to stretch out with his feet on the ottoman," the mother's television leisure was nevertheless productive. For as the caption stated, "Mother likes to gently rock as she sews." An advertisement for Airfoam furniture cushions used a similar discursive strategy (*Better Homes and Gardens*, 1952b, p. 177). The graphic showed a husband dozing in his foam rubber cushioned chair as he sits before a television set. Meanwhile, his wife clears away his snack. The text read, "Man's pleasure is the body coddling comfort" of the cushioned chair while "Woman's treasure is a home lovely to look at, easy to keep perfectly tidy and neat," with cushioning that "never needs fluffing."

In such cases, the man's pleasure in television is associated with passive relaxation. But for women pleasure is derived through the aesthetics of a well-kept home and labor-saving devices which promise to rationalize the extra labor that television brings to domestic space. Although on one level these representations are compatible with traditional gender roles, subtle reversals of power ran through the magazines as a whole. Even if there was a certain degree of privilege attached to man's position of total relaxation—his right to rule from the easy chair throne—this power was in no way absolute, nor was it stable. Instead, it seems to me, the most striking thing about this gendered representation of the body is that it was at odds with the normative conception of masculinity and femininity. Whereas Western society associates activity with maleness, representations of television attributed this trait to women. Conversely, the notion of feminine passivity was transferred over to the man of the house.[4]

Indeed, it might be concluded that the cultural ideals which demanded that women be shown as productive workers also had the peculiar side effect of "feminizing" the father. As Andreas Huyssen (1986, p. 47) argues, this notion of feminization has been a motif in the discourse on mass culture since the nineteenth century. "Mass culture," Huyssen claims, "is somehow associated with women while real, authentic culture remains the prerogative of men." Indeed, mass culture has repeatedly been figured in terms of patriarchal ideas of femininity and represented in tropes of passivity, consumption, penetration, and addiction. In this way, it threatens the very foundations of so-called "authentic" or high culture that is represented in terms of masculine tropes of activity, productivity, and knowledge.

In 1941, this gendered conception of mass culture reached a dramatic pitch when Philip Wylie wrote his classic misogynist text, *Generation of Vipers*, which was reprinted 16 times. In this book, Wylie connected the discourse on mass culture and women to broadcasting. In general, Wylie argued, women had somehow joined in a conspiracy with big industry and, with the aid of advanced technology, had supplanted the need for men altogether. Women, along with the technocratic world, had stripped men of their masculine privilege and turned them into cowering sissies. In his most bitter chapter entitled "Common Women," Wylie argued that women had somehow gained control of the airwaves. Women, he suggested, made radio listening into a passive activity which threatened manhood and, in fact, civilization. As Wylie (pp. 214–215) wrote,

> The radio is mom's final tool, for it stamps everybody who listens with the matriarchal brand.... Just as Goebbels has revealed what can be done

with such a mass-stamping of the public psyche in his nation, so our land is a living representation of the same fact worked out in matriarchal sentimentality, goo, slop, hidden cruelty, and the foreshadow of national death.

In the annotated notes of the 1955 edition, Wylie (pp. 213–214) updated these fears, claiming that television would soon take the place of radio and turn men into female-dominated dupes. Women, he wrote, "will not rest until every electronic moment has been bought to sell suds and every program censored to the last decibel and syllable according to her self-adulation—along with that (to the degree the mom-indoctrinated pops are permitted access to the dials) of her de-sexed, de-souled, de-cerebrated mate." Although Wylie's rhetoric might seem to be the product of a fevered mind, this basic blend of misogyny and technophobia was common to representations of television and everyday life in the postwar period.

Men's magazines offered tongue-in-cheek versions of the situation, showing how television had turned men into passive homebodies. The fashionable men's magazine *Esquire* and the working man's magazine *Popular Science* presented ironic views of the male sloth. In 1951, for example, *Esquire* (p. 10) showed the stereotypical husband relaxing with his shoes off, beer in hand, smiling idiotically while seated before a television set. Two years later, the same magazine referred to television fans as "televidiots" (O'Brien, p. 24).

If these magazines provided a humorous look at the man of leisure, they also offered alternatives. In very much the same way that Victorians like Catherine Beecher sought to elevate the woman by making her the center of domestic affairs, the men's magazines suggested that fathers could regain their authority through increased participation in family life. As early as 1940, Sydnie Greenbie called for the reinstitution of manhood in his book titled *Leisure for Living*. Greenbie reasoned that the popular figure of the male "boob" could be countracted if the father cultivated his mechanical skills. As he wrote (p. 210), "At last man has found something more in keeping with his nature, the workshop, with its lathe and mechanical saws, something he has kept as yet his own against the predacious female.... And [it becomes] more natural . . . for the man to be a homemaker as well as the woman."

After the war, this reintegration of the father became a popular ideal.[5] As *Esquire* told its male readers, "your place, Mister, is in the home, too, and if you'll make a few thoughtful improvements to it, you'll build yourself a happier, more comfortable, less back-breaking world . . ." ("Home is for Husbands," 1951, p. 88). From this perspective, the men's magazines suggested ways for fathers to take an active and productive attitude in relation to television. Even if men were passive spectators, when not watching they could learn to repair the set or else produce television carts, built-ins, and stylish cabinets. Articles with step-by-step instructions were circulated in *Popular Science*, and the *Home Craftsman* even had a special "TV: Improve Your Home Show" column featuring a husband and wife, Thelma and Vince, and their adventures in home repairs.

Popular Science also suggested hobbies for men to use television in an active and productive way. The magazine ran several articles on a new fad—television photography. Men were shown how to take still pictures off their sets, and in 1950 the magazine even conducted a readership contest for prize winning photos that were published in the December issue ("From Readers' Albums," p. 166).

Conclusion

The gendered division of domestic labor and the complex relations of power entailed by it were thus shown to organize the experience of watching television. While these early representations cannot tell us how real people actually used television in their own homes, they do begin to reveal a set of discursive rules that were formed for thinking about television in the early period. They begin to disclose the social construction of television as it is rooted in a mode of thought based on categories of sexual difference.

Recent ethnographic studies conducted by David Morley (1986), Ann Gray (1987), James Lull (1988), and others reveal the continued impact of gender (and other social differences) on the ways families watch television. Gray's work on VCR usage among working class families in Britain especially highlights how gender-based ideas about domestic technology and productive labor in the home circumscribe women's use of the new machine. Such ethnographic work provides compelling evidence for the intricate relations of television and gender as they are experienced in the viewing situation.

For historians, questions about the television audience pose different problems and call for other methods. The reconstruction of viewing experiences at some point in the past is an elusive project. By its very nature, the history of spectatorship is a patchwork history, one that must draw together a number of approaches and perspectives in the hopes of achieving a partial picture of past experiences. The approach I have taken here provides insights into the way television viewing has been connected to larger patterns of family ideals and gender construction within our culture.

Women's magazines depicted a subtle interplay between labor and leisure at home, and they offered the postwar housewife ways to deal with television in her daily life. These popular discourses show that television was not simply promoted as a pleasure machine; rather, the media engaged women in a dialogue about the concrete problems television posed for productive labor in the home. If our culture has systematically relegated domestic leisure to the realm of nonproduction, these magazines reveal the tenuousness of such notions. Indeed, for the postwar housewife, television was not represented as a passive activity, but rather it was imbricated in a pattern of everyday life where work is never done.

Notes

1. This stove was mentioned in *Sponsor* (1951, p. 119) and *Popular Science* (1952, p. 132). Interestingly, *Popular Science* did not discuss the television component of the stove as a vehicle for leisure but rather showed how "A housewife can follow telecast cooking instructions step-by-step on the TV set built into this electric oven." Perhaps in this way, this men's magazine allayed readers' fears that their wives would use the new technology for diversion as opposed to useful labor.

2. This essay is based on a sample that includes four of the leading middle class women's home magazines, *Better Homes and Gardens, American Home, Ladies' Home Journal,* and *House Beautiful*. I examined each of these magazines for its entire run of issues, 1948–1955. For purposes of comparison, I have also researched general magazines, men's magazines, and women's magazines

aimed at a less affluent reader. For more on sources and method, see my dissertation (1988a).

3. I do not mean to ignore the fact that domestic servants were themselves detached from the family activities through the Victorian model of space and its elaborate separation of servant quarters from central living areas.

4. This is not to say that television was the only domestic machine to disrupt representations of gender. Roland Marchand (1985) claims that ads for radio sets and phonographs reversed pictorial conventions for the depiction of men and women. Ads traditionally showed husbands seated while wives perched on the arm of a chair or sofa. But Marchand finds that "in the presence of culturally uplifting [radio and phonograph] music, the woman more often gained the right of reposed concentration while the (more technologically inclined) man stood prepared to change the records or adjust the radio dials" (pp. 252–253). In the case of television, Marchand's analysis and interpretation do not seem to apply since men were often shown seated and unable or unwilling to control the technology.

5. The reasons for this warrant a book-length study. Some tentative explanations come from Marchand (1982), who argues that the waning of male authority in the public sphere of corporate life contributed to men's increased participation and quests for dominion" in private life. However, I would add speculatively that the whole category of masculinity was being contested in this period. The "quests for dominion" were accompanied by an equally strong manifestation of their opposite. The down-trodden male heroes of film *noir* and the constant uncertainty about the sexual status of the "family man" in the melodramas and social problem films suggest that American culture was seeking to redefine sexual identity, or at least to give sexual identity meaning in a world where the gendered balance of social and economic power was undergoing change.

References

Adams, W., & Hungerford, E. A. (1949, September). Television: Buying and installing is fun; These ideas will help. *Better Homes and Gardens*, pp 38–39, 152–156, 158.

Allen, R. C. (1985) *Speaking of soap operas*. Chapel Hill: University of North Carolina Press.

American Home. (1954, December), p. 39.

American Home. (1955a, October), p. 14.

American Home. (1955b, May). p. 138.

Benjamin, W. (1969). The work of art in the age of mechanical reproduction. In H. Arendt (Ed.). *Illuminations* (pp. 217–252). New York: Shocken. (Original work published 1936)

Better Homes and Gardens. (1952a, December). p. 144.

Better Homes and Gardens. (1952b, October), p. 177.

Better Homes and Gardens (1953, February) p. 169.

Better Homes and Gardens. (1955, October), p. 139.

Boddy, W. (1979). The rhetoric and economic roots of the American broadcasting industry. *Cinetracts*, *6*(2). 37–54.

Boddy, W. (1985). "The shining centre of the home": Ontologies of television in the "golden age." In P. Drummand & R. Patterson (Eds.), *Television in transition* (pp. 125–133). London: British Film Institute.

Browne, N. (1984). The political economy of the television (super) text. *Quarterly Review of Film Studies*, *9*(3), 175–182.

Chafe, W. (1972). *The American woman: Her changing social, economic, and political roles, 1920–1970*. London: Oxford University Press.

Conway, C. (1951, June). Remodeled thinking made over this kitchen. *House Beautiful*, pp. 121–122.

Covert, C.L. (1984). "We may hear too much": American sensibility and the response to radio, 1919–1924. In C. L. Covert & J. D. Stevens (Eds.), *Mass media between the wars: Perceptions of cultural tension, 1918–1941* (pp. 199–220). Syracuse: Syracuse University Press.

Crosby, J. (1950, February). What's television going to do to your life? *House Beautiful*, pp. 66–67, 125–126.

Davis, R. E. (1965). Response to innovation: A study of popular argument about new mass media (Doctoral dissertation, University of Iowa). *Dissertation Abstracts International*, *26*, 6232.

Daytime video: Dumont plans afternoon programming. (1949, November 28). *Telecasting*, p. 3.

Dumont daytime "shoppers" series starts. (1949, December 12). *Telecasting*, p. 5.

Dumont expansion continues (1949, April 12). *Radio Daily*, p. 23.

Esquire (1951, March), p. 10.

Folbre, N. (1982). Exploitation comes home: A critique of the marxist theory of family labour. *Cambridge Journal of Economics*, *6*, 317–329.

For the girls at home. (1954, March 15). *Newsweek*, pp. 92–93.

From readers' albums of television photos. (1950, December). *Popular Science*, p. 166.

Gatlin, R. (1987). *American women since 1945*. Jackson: University of Mississippi Press.

Gray, A. (1987). Behind closed doors: Video recorders in the home. In H. Bachr & G. Dyer (Eds.), *Boxed in: Women and television* (pp. 38–54). New York: Pandora.

Greenbie, S. (1940). *Leisure for living*. New York: George W. Stewart.

Home is for husbands too. (1951, June). *Esquire*, pp. 88–91.

House Beautiful. (1948, November), p. 5.

House Beautiful. (1950, December), p. 77.

House Beautiful. (1952a, June). p. 59.

House Beautiful. (1952b, May), p. 138.

House Beautiful (1954, November), p. 158.

Huyssen, A. (1986). *After the great divide: Modernism, mass culture, postmodernism.* Bloomington: Indiana University Press.

Ladies' Home Journal. (1955, April), p. 130.

Lefebvre, H. (1979). Work and leisure in daily life. In A. Mattelart & S. Siegelaub (Eds.), M. C. Axtmann (Trans.), *Communication and class struggle* (pp. 135–141). New York: International General. (Reprinted from *Critique de la Vie Quotidienne,* Forward, 1958)

Lull, J. (Ed.). (1988). *World families watching television.* Beverly Hills: Sage.

Marchand, R. (1982). Vision of classlessness, quests for dominion: American popular culture, 1945–1960. In R. H. Bremner & G. W. Reichard (Eds.), *Reshaping America: Society and institutions, 1945–1960* (pp. 163–190). Columbus: Ohio State University Press.

Marchand, R. (1985). *Advertising the American dream: Making way for modernity, 1920–1940.* Berkeley: University of California Press.

Modleski, T. (1983). The rhythms of reception: Daytime television and women's work. In E.A. Kaplan (Ed.), *Regarding television* (pp. 67–75). Los Angeles: University Publications of America.

Morley, D. (1986). *Family television: Cultural power and domestic leisure.* London: Comedia.

Newsweek. (1951, September 24), p. 56.

O'Brien, J. (1953, November). Offsides in sports. *Esquire,* pp. 24, 26.

Popular Science. (1952, May), p. 132.

Ramsay, E. (1949, September). How to stretch a day. *American Home,* pp. 66–67.

Spigel, L. (1988a). Installing the television set: The social construction of television's place in the American home, 1948–55 (Doctoral dissertation, University of California). *Dissertation Abstracts International, 49,* 2283A.

Spigel, L. (1988b). Installing the television set: Popular discourses on television and domestic space, 1948–55. *Camera Obscura, 16,* 11–47.

Sponsor. (1951, June 4), p. 19.

Televiser. (1951, September), p. 20.

Tyler May, E. (1988). *Homeward bound: American families in the cold war era.* (New York: Basic Books).

Warn, W. W. (1948, October). Is it time to buy television? *House Beautiful,* p. 20.

Wright, G. (1981) *Building the dream.* Cambridge Massachusetts Institute of Technology Press.

Wyhe, P. (1955). *Generations of vipers* (annotated ed.) New York: Holt, Rinehart and Winston.

11.
FROM SCREEN TO SITE
Anna McCarthy

Television, Philosophy, Modernity

Like all technologies of "space-binding," television poses challenges to fixed conceptions of materiality and immateriality, farness and nearness, vision and touch. It is both a thing and a conduit for electronic signals, both a piece of furniture in a room and a window to an imaged elsewhere, both a commodity and a way of looking at commodities. It therefore makes sense that TV—understood as a particular form or mediation of inscription, speech, and images—should become a cardinal trope in diverse philosophical texts on modernity's core problematic. Alongside the cinema, though rarely in textual proximity to it, TV serves as a kind of rhetorical toy in numerous acts of writing, and representing, the modern. Martin Heidegger's famous description of television as the "abolition of every possibility of remoteness" in "The Thing" leads smoothly toward Jacques Derrida's coded allusion to television's particular (im)materiality in an essay on a novel by Philippe Sollers: "While we remain attentive, fascinated, glued to what presents itself we are unable to see presence as such, since presence does not present itself, no more than does the visibility of the visible, the audibility of the audible, the medium or 'air' which disappears in the act of allowing to appear."[1] Together, these images bracket a core preoccupation with television as a form of writing across space, as remote inscription that produces—and annihilates—places: the place of the body, the place of the screen, the place of dwelling.[2]

As this suggests, the material aspects of television's specificity as a medium have proven particularly attractive to critics interested in some of the more paradoxical modalities of recording and representation. Samuel Weber both narrates, and participates in, what might initially be termed the "television gesture" in modernity's critical tradition. In an essay entitled "Television: Set and Screen," Weber describes the medium as a "technological novelty" that must be seen as "*both the consummation of a very old tradition* and at the same time the *heightening of its internal ambivalences.*" This tradition, he indicates elsewhere, incorporates both writing and deconstruction; within it, "what television does . . . is to 'materialize' in a relatively immaterial manner, the irreducibility of . . . iterability, in the mode of presentation we call 'vision' and 'audition.' "[3] I will return to the specifics of Weber's engagement with television shortly; for now, note simply that—like Fredric Jameson's description of TV as "surrealism without the unconscious"[4]—Weber invokes television as a spatial and semiotic framework for describing ongoing crises in a dominant organizing logic relating signs to things, and sign-things to each other. This does raise the question of whether critics such as Weber and Jameson are actually interested in television at all. Arguably, they want to learn *from* television while avoiding having to learn *about* it. But because they scrutinize the hybrid technological forms associated with television so closely—the screen and the network, for example—such engagements are more than merely televisual gestures. Their interest in the medium's material, technical entities, understood as giving concrete form to modernity's problems of materiality and disappearance, opens up possibilities for dialogue across discursive realms. Television, a quintessentially interdisciplinary object, brings discourses like geography, political economy, video art, and critical theory into alignment with philosophy. In Weber's case, for example, modern technics in the form of television provides a forum in which to explore Heidegger and Walter Benjamin together. Although we might question particular critics' views on television's relationship to the modern framing of being, to phenomenological problems in fixing the place of the body, to emergent specters of late modern political life, the medium clearly has potential as a window on the way we negotiate modernity in critical writing and practice.

But television can perform this task only if the conceptual models that interweave it with ongoing philosophical projects are sufficiently nuanced. A great deal is at stake, in particular in the way critical invocations of the medium take issues of scale and space into account. The fact that the medium's paradigmatic spatial form is the network means that it embodies the methodological conundrum of scale in a number of different analytical areas. Networks are difficult spatial phenomena to grasp because they exist on more than one scale; as Bruno Latour notes in a sound byte from *We Have Never Been Modern*, "even a long network remains local at all points." Latour's goal here is to render problematic any easy acceptance of the concept of "the global"; as he notes, "the words 'local' and 'global' offer points of view on networks that are by nature neither local nor global, but are more or less long and more or less connected."[5] These issues of scale and connectedness, of regional differences and spatial totalities, are certainly matters for philosophical thought, but they extend beyond this realm too. Indeed, the complex problem designated by the concept of scale is explored perhaps most extensively in the discipline of geography. Scale, as David Harvey sums it up, is a concept "both crucial and problematic" for the study of space, particularly in an era in which the concept of "the global" achieves ascendancy. As he notes, "what looks like a system at one level of analysis (e.g., a city) becomes a part at another level (e.g., a network of cities)."[6] The same principle applies equally to television. Television looks very different, depending on whether one's level of analysis is the microlevel of the network's terminal point—the screen, a particular viewing subject or collectivity—or the standard, centralizing transmissions that appear on its face. We might choose to emphasize, or argue for, one level over the other when we invoke television in theory and in criticism, but the result is inevitably a simplification, an artificial resolution of the dialectical tensions between the discrepant scales that comprise the phenomenal form of the medium. This scalar complexity can make writing about the medium's relation to places, bodies, and subjects a particularly difficult process.

As I will suggest in the following, TV's value for philosophical inquiry into ongoing transformations in the relation between materiality and technics hinges on the dialectical movement between "global" generality and "local" specificity that the medium embodies. This movement is perhaps most often expressed as a (problematically idealist) distinction between "the real" and "derealization" (television embodying the latter, acting upon and eradicating the former).[7] But it is also sometimes invoked in terms of "space," and more crucially, "place." Television becomes a force of *placelessness*—as in one sociologist's description of TV as "no sense of place."[8] Now, such characterizations have value as ways of thinking about the medium's historical role within the economic geography of American culture. TV's commercial emergence coincides with the "golden age" of Fordism, and television advertising was crucial for the rise of the national brand economy within which the Fordist wage contract took shape. Arguably, this rise of national brands and retailing chains at the expense of local ones is the eradication of regional specificity and, by extension, a form of placelessness.[9] But the idea that the television *apparatus* is itself an encroaching force of placelessness is a flawed, dangerously fetishistic one. The language of placelessness makes us forget that television is an *object* and, like all objects, it shapes its immediate space through its material form. The term is also quite vague; is placelessness really an adequate description of the range of ways in which we encounter television within spaces of everyday life, from the living room to the departure lounge to the department store?

Thus, rather than focusing solely on the immateriality of the television image, as terms like "placelessness" and "derealization" encourage, a television theory must also take into account the very material *thing*ness of television technology (paradigmatically, the console itself). This involves looking not only at the medium's very *spectacular* reorganizations of space and time—the live broadcast of the media "event," for example—but also the rather more banal and quotidian materiality of the TV *set* itself, the *unremarkable* functions it performs, as a piece of furniture.[10] It means bothering to think about the very basic and barely noticeable physical form of television—inquiring into the assumptions behind the placement of TV sets in hotel bathrooms; wondering why people often decorate TV sets with plastic flowers, or posters, and why they cover them with cloths as if televisions are precious icons.[11] And it means taking into account multiple forms of televisual temporality, too: not only the seemingly instantaneous temporality of live transmissions, but also the routine and redundant cycles of the broadcast day, the endlessly repeating programs that play on the CNN Airport Network, the synchronized flashes of multiple monitors and video walls that constitute the visual architecture of retail stores, bars, and public squares. In short, the philosophical engagement with television's materiality as modern technics must articulate its concern with questions of being and perception with the modern preoccupation with the *everyday* in all of its seeming banality and unreadability.

As I will propose, *site* as well as sight is a crucial conceptual framework for any attempt to think through the televisual as a material scene of representation. Three aspects of TV's technological form in particular can be foregrounded in the intellectual history of the medium, as moments in which television opens up new ways of thinking about place. The first I have already mentioned: it is the indexical force of formal ideologies of television like "liveness" that, through a range of representational and electronic techniques, translates perceived temporal simultaneity into the sense of spatial collapse that Heidegger noted in "The Thing." However, as Jane Feuer has proposed, the ontology of televisual liveness in actual occasions of the transmission and reception of signals from one place to another instantaneously is not a determining aspect of the medium's cultural effects. Rather, it is through the *ideology* of liveness—sustained in ways less spectacular than the "media

event," and filtered through micro-level visual techniques of the broadcast text, whether literally live or not—that television sustains both the intimacy of its direct address to the subject and its claims to documentary truth and historicity.[12] Liveness might thus be seen as a temporal ideology that works to construct two fictive spaces for the viewer simultaneously. On a small scale, it is the space of imagined co-enunciation signified in the direct address of the talking head on-screen; on a larger scale, and in collective terms, this space is the familiar imagined space of the nation looking in on its key sites—a space always constituted, as Benedict Anderson famously noted, via perceived temporal simultaneity.[13] This is the spatial operation of television most often scrutinized in theory: space-binding, the "abolition of every possibility of remoteness."

But another aspect of television that makes it a key heuristic instrument in the philosophical exploration of place, materiality, and technics is far less recognized. This is the fact that its material form is profoundly *site-specific*. As Weber points out, although it is commonplace to note TV's pervasiveness, "for all its ubiquitousness it is not very well understood" (112). I think this is because we have not yet addressed some of the implications of TV's ubiquity—not only that it is constantly available in the home, but also that it is present in other places too, the everyday locations where we shop, eat and drink, wait, and travel in our daily itineraries. What is interesting about this ubiquity is the way it illustrates something specific about TV as a medium: its peculiarly malleable and heterogeneous physical *form*. It can encompass giant video walls and video banks, flat screens that look like illuminated signs, small and large consoles, and all sorts of signal forms, from live transmissions to prerecorded program cycles, to simultaneous mixtures of both. And such divergent forms of television coexist unproblematically; one need only take a cab ride through Times Square, populated with more forms of the televisual apparatus than one could possibly count, to grasp the inadequacy of theoretical models that attempt to address the medium's materiality via an abstracted or idealized sense of its technological manifestation on the level of the everyday. More often than not, such models turn away from the fact of television's multiple phenomenological forms, its ubiquity and difference across a range of spaces, installing instead a more idealist notion of TV and its place: the screen in the home. However, although the home may be economically central to the broadcast television apparatus, this does not mean that critics should accept the pervasive ideological association of television with the domicile as an adequate representation of the actual geography of the medium. When we take the diverse proliferation of material forms and places of television into account, the medium starts to look very different. It becomes impossible to argue that the TV set always organizes relations between, say, public and private, subjects and collectivities, participation and isolation, in identical ways across locations. Rather, television's heterogeneous materiality requires that we accept that its operations upon the subject and its use as a form of communication between individuals must change from site to site, institution to institution. If the flexibility of the technology allows the medium to disappear into the everyday places where it appears, then surely it must simultaneously disappear into the particular relations of public and private, subjects and others, that characterize these places.

The third crucial feature of TV's material relation to space is another form of disappearance, one anticipated in the second: it is the screen's peculiar ability to *dematerialize* at the point of its encounter with philosophy. Despite its integration into everyday life, something we ignore, in Toby Miller's words, "like a pet or a vaguely dotty relative," television embodies technics for philosophers in a total (izing) and aphysical frame. As Weber notes, "the television transmission does not ... as is generally supposed, simply *overcome* distance and separation. (This is the illusion of a 'global village.') It renders them invisible, paradoxically, by transposing them *into* the vision it transmits ... the space defined by the television set is already fractured by the undecideability of that which appears on the screen. Is it taking place here, there, or anywhere?" (122). In this account of television's spatiality the insistent localism and materiality implied in TV's site-specificity, and all the questions raised by this localism, recedes and is replaced by a theoretical model of TV as global epiphenomenon of modernity. The screen here is not a local object we put things on and move around in a space, nor is it even a *network*, really, in a Latourian sense, that is to say, something

that is both global and local, an agent or actor in cultural and scientific definitions of particularity and universality, fetish and fact. It becomes a thing that, in Weber's words, "takes place" and not a thing that makes a place, or a thing that is made *by* a place.

I dwell on Weber's account because his concern with processes of site and place is unusual in philosophical accounts of television. Others read the disappearing acts that TV performs in the place it inhabits as a predictable series of remote operations performed on the subject—operations that have no material form at all, despite the overproduction of material, embodied metaphors to describe such operations, such as "brainwashing," or the expression "glued to" the TV set. A recent, highly nuanced critical account of modern ideas about human perception and mass influence suddenly takes on a paranoid voice when it addresses the topic of television and its immense powers, powers that are systematically denied, even by television's critics:

> Television ... has become so fully integrated into social and subjective life that certain kinds of statements about television (for example, about addiction, habit, persuasion, and control) are in a sense unspeakable, effectively excluded from public discourse. To speak of contemporary collective subjects in terms of effects of passivity and influence is still generally anathema. ... There is usually a tacit a priori conviction that television viewers constitute a hypothetical community of rational and volitional human subjects. The contrary position, that human subjects have determinate psychological capacities and functions that might be susceptible to technological management ... must be disavowed by so-called critics of those same institutions.[14]

The author, Jonathan Crary, breaks here from a careful account of the history of attitudes toward theories of behavior modification via perception into an act of witnessing, of speaking the truth (apparently axiomatic) about television's influence. The problem, of course, is that the statements he describes—statements about viewers as a suggestive mass—are far from excluded from cultural circulation. Rather, such statements fairly constitute the contemporary public discourse on television, *especially* in the media.[15] They form the basis of the media critiques that emerge in popular and academic journalism around violent events like school shootings, for example, critiques that often offer "the influence of the media" as a master hermeneutic. And such fears of manipulation are the basis of a long-standing Hollywood formula, in which media paranoia takes on occult and insidious forms—from the '50s "cult classic" film *The Twonky* [1953] to more "serious" middlebrow critiques, like *A Face in the Crowd* [1957], or more recently *The Truman Show* [1998].

Such free-floating and ever-present ideas about media influence are abetted, on some level, by the conflation of TV's pervasiveness with a sense of dematerialization and derealization. TV's ubiquity makes it possible to speak of its cultural effects and operations of television without having to address its material form, because these operations are so obvious, so clearly already "known," that they are curiously independent of the material place of the screen and the viewing encounter. This tension between materiality and immateriality, what Weber nicely calls TV's "ambivalence," is no doubt what makes the medium attractive as a figure for modernity's spatial ruptures. The ambivalence, as Weber notes, is in part a result of its liveness—ambivalent because liveness is an attribute that applies also to recording, as in the terms "live mic" or "live recording." But it is more centrally, I think, a sign of the conceptual challenge of reconciling the universalizing rhetoric of television (as brainwashing apparatus, as the disappearance of physical space and time) with its myriad site-specific uses and appropriations. It is the challenge of *scale*, in other words. When TV comes to defining modern technics, the sense of extreme material heterogeneity that I have sketched above must somehow conform to an epistemological condition characterized by broad homogeneity. Given this situation, it seems absolutely crucial to move in an alternative direction and *diversify* some of the paradigms through which the materiality of TV may be understood, and its relation to historical subjects best grasped.

Returning to Weber now, and examining his televisual theory in more detail, I want to contribute to the project of expanding our grasp of the material and political forms of television in everyday life, by staging a dialogue between two different theoretical approaches to the medium's spatial ideologies—that is to say, two different ways of thinking about the TV set, and TV images, as material things that shape experience in the sites in which they are viewed and used. Weber marks out these issues as a relationship between the material form of the screen and its *place*, and it is, specifically, the theoretical work that this word *place* is made to do that forms the basis of my own account. A close reading of one particular video-television installation and its relationship to its location over time alerts us to the contrasts between an ontological notion of place and a geographical one. Both, as we shall see, are helpful frameworks for thinking about the quantum and macro forms of the TV set as a material object in social space, though in the end I will prefer the geographical understanding. To my mind, it offers a more complete and historically flexible understanding of materiality, though it does so by building directly on the intellectual lineage that defines the ontological approach.

The Place of the Screen: Heidegger and the Geographers

The ontological conception of place is, simply, the idea of place as dwelling, or, in Heidegger's words, place as "the house of being." Heidegger develops this idea not only in the canonical essay "Building Dwelling Thinking" in which human and environment harmonize at a Black Forest farmhouse, but also in a less-frequently cited piece entitled "An Ontological Consideration of Place."[16] In this essay, Heidegger approaches place as an essential concept for thinking through "the relationship between the ontological dimension of being and the political structure of human existence" (18). He reflects on the idea of place as a human construction and discovers, in the modern separation of political rights from dwelling, "the assumption that 'place' is created and can be created by man" (24). This assumption is dangerous, he proposes, insofar as it neglects the fact that the first experience of place is *being*—"Ontological place . . . precedes the political, social, or economic aspects of existence whose reality lies only in their being adjectival qualifications of being" (26). Philosophical inquiry, therefore, must work to disentangle the place of being from *Gestell*—the setting in place performed by technics, the state, etc.; as a concept, place thus "points both to [the] unique dimensions of being and to the distortion and perversion which arise from its concealment" (26).

Weber offers a provocative theoretical application of Heidegger's ontological notion of place to the relationship between the TV set and its environment. He asks in the introduction to *Mass Mediauras* "how do 'technics,' film and television, the 'setup' and the 'set,' change our relations to places, positions, and emplacements?" (7). Stressing the need for answers that avoid "ontologizing television" and instead recognize its heterogeneity as an apparatus that assumes different forms at moments of production, transmission, and reception, Weber nevertheless proposes that television ultimately "*takes place*"—a term that deftly links the medium's present-tense temporality to its spatial problematic. Invoking the live-transmission's construction of a place for the viewer and its representation of space-binding as a process, he proposes that television upsets the ontology of place because it

> Takes place in at least three places "at once": 1. In the place (or places) where the image and sound are 'recorded'; 2. In the place (or places) where those images and sounds are *received*; and 3. In the places (or places) *in between* ... the unity of television as a medium of presentation thus involves a *simultaneity* that is highly ambivalent. It overcomes spatial distance but only by *splitting the unity* of place and with it the unity of everything that defines its identity with respect to place: events, bodies, subjects. (117)

What is absolutely brilliant about this account is the way it grasps the shape-shifting, scale-busting operations of TV, diversifying rather than ontologizing television technology as a heterogeneous collection of forms and modes of representation and transmission. Television does not simply render the distant present; rather, it intervenes in the experience of space and time via three distinct, relatively autonomous, warping operations.

However there are reasons to take issues with the way Weber renders the concept of place—the site of the TV set in particular. For though he refuses a singular understanding of the screen's discursive and material networks, he presents the place of the screen as an essential kind of unity, a physical and metaphysical phenomenon that is bounded and stable up until the moment that technics enters the picture to order and "re-place" it. "Ever since Aristotle's *Physics*," he notes, "place has been defined in terms of immanence, stability, and containment, as [quoting Aristotle] the 'innermost motionless boundary of what contains.' In the goings on of modern technics ... this innermost boundary is forced, driven out of its motionless state" (70). TV's technological specificity is its ability to alter the fixity of place, to map a "different kind of topography," as Weber describes Heidegger's *Gestell*—a term he translates as *emplacement* over other alternatives like *enframing* and *installation*. Place, in Weber's schema as in Heidegger's, precedes *Gestell* and is *acted upon* by technics. A TV aerial protrudes from the roof of the Black Forest farmhouse, and the fabric of space and time are ripped asunder.

I will return again to the consequences of this way of thinking about site and screen presently, but first I want to outline the geographical alternative. Although it is wholly coherent on its own terms, Weber's description of the Aristotelian notion of place as the dominant one in social thought quite conspicuously oversimplifies the intellectual history of the concept. For several decades, geographers like David Harvey, J. Nicholas Entriken, and Doreen Massey have opposed the ontological understanding of place with a more dialectical view. To some extent, their approaches draw on Heidegger's—recall that the central problematic of his "ontological consideration" is the fact that places are produced in political networks as well as in the ontological networks of being, and he wants to understand what that means. But whereas Heidegger's poetic preoccupations mean that the political production of place is, not surprisingly, a "distortion and perversion" that conceals the aspects of place that reveal being, proponents of geographical concepts of place accept, even promote, what Entriken calls, following Heidegger, its "betweenness." The Marxist geographers' notion of place refuses the Aristotelian formulation of place as bounded ontological plenitude and instead insists that place is *always* a reflection of wider social forces—even, or perhaps especially, in the case of places that are unspoiled, isolated, protected. The long networks of modernity do not enter and interrupt the workings of a previously place-bound world. Rather, they make it possible to historicize the geographical orders that precede them as place-bound ones, and to conceal the forms of interconnection, of external/internal relations, that constructed places in previous eras. From the perspective of the Marxist geographer, both the Black Forest farmhouse and the Mall of America are carved out of the same dynamic, ongoing processes—the specificity of each one is determined by the particular form these processes assume within it. In Harvey's words, "place gets constructed through the working out in that place of interventions and influences from outside." In this respect place exemplifies the principle of dialectic materialism—forces and relations manifest in things.[17] For Harvey, Massey, and others, place is thus not a romantic, timeless sense of communal, ecological belonging, but rather an expression of general space-time relations on all scales as they appear in one particular physical site.

The dialectical strain in geographical approaches to place can strengthen philosophical models of the TV set's material relationship to its location, models exemplified here in the best sense by Weber's schema. Contrasted with an ontological sense of place, the geographical sense of place accounts for, and even measures, spatial *differences* rather than *essences*. Though both the ontological model of place and the geographic one are conceived very specifically as *political* engagements with the philosophical and material consequences of location, the latter, unencumbered by commitments to the concept of being, offers a more thorough account of the viewing, or not-viewing, subject as a historical person, located in a particular social formation. This is because the geographic model allows us to see TV not only as a thing that binds spaces together, as Heidegger himself observes, but also, importantly, as a thing that is place-bound, that is to say *site-specific*, in the way it interweaves with the practices and institutions around it.

Because it is *both* space-binding and site-specific, enmeshed in, and constitutive of, the ambient flow of everyday life in the home and other places, the television set must be seen as a central force in the *dialectical* construction of a place. Indeed, we can learn a lot about the specificity of a place as a snapshot of wider social relations by looking at what the TV set is doing within it. I mean "looking" very literally here. Weber accounts for the political effects of television's material production of space with a deft exploration of the words we use to describe television—farsightedness, remote control, the French word *parasite* for static. But what if we take a different approach, exploring not words but images, and exploiting the materiality of television through another medium defined by a vexed relation between materiality and immateriality—photography? By photographing TV sets in their television settings—something I have been doing for several years now—one can grasp not only what the television set *looks* like in its place, but also how, in its banal appearance in shopping malls, bars, restaurants, and so on, the screen interlaces with the relations of power and everyday practices that define its place. What such an investigation communicates is that, instead of television "taking place," what often happens in such environments is that place "takes television."

Rio (Atlanta)

This possibility is illustrated in the tensions between an ontological and a geographical notion of place that surface in one particular televisual site—a video installation commissioned in 1989, for a shopping mall in Atlanta, by Dara Birnbaum.[18] The mall was designed by the Miami firm Arquitectonica and named Rio in reference to the hit song by the '80s pop-music icons Duran Duran. However, despite this glamour, the mall was located in a poor inner-city neighborhood targeted for gentrification because of its proximity to the city's downtown. It was constructed in the early 1990s on an empty piece of land that had been razed during processes of urban renewal in the 1970s, and intended as a festive entertainment environment for the throngs of young urban professionals predicted to move into the area at any moment. Birnbaum's installation was commissioned as a prestige piece for the mall's wacky-looking atrium, crammed with brass frogs, a reflecting pool, and a perisphere.

The installation was a video wall consisting of twenty-five monitors arranged in a square matrix. The piece's complex system of interactive, "live" image manipulations sought to call attention to the role of mediatized places like shopping malls in the destruction of an ontological sense of place. The twenty-five screens used sophisticated computer circuitry to display layers of imagery from two sources: live news from the Atlanta-based CNN and footage showing the site before the mall was built (a grass slope sparsely dotted with trees). This "lost landscape"—a place "taken" by the mall—would appear on-screen through a random process determined by the movement of shoppers throughout the site. Whenever a shopper entered the visual field of one of several surveillance cameras dotted about the space, a computer-based keying system would digitize his or her image as a silhouette and use it as an electronic video cutout through which one set of footage (the landscape) could be seen in a human outline superimposed on the other (CNN).

As part of a place named after another place, *Rio Videowall* dramatized a set of ideas about how television and consumer culture create, in the words of media critic Joshua Meyrowitz, "no sense of place." The video linked and likened the physical space of the mall to the generalized, abstract space of TV's continual information flows and cycles, and it used the body of the consumer as the point of this articulation. Images of the lost landscape became the repressed other of the "global" CNN newscast with its omnipresent mutterings. The installation was very savvy about television's ability to *take place*, relativizing the eternal present of live news and diminishing its pretensions to realness, liveness, and immediacy by comparing it with the more "live," more "real time," more "present tense" surveillance image of the shopper in the mall. It seemed a canny demonstration of Weber's proposal that "television takes place in taking the place of the body and at the same time transforming both place and body" (117). Similarly, the fact that the video wall's "global" media network, CNN, was a local economic institution employing a large sector of Atlanta's professional class would serve as a reminder of the televisual process "taking place" at the scene of production. This carefully planned relationship between site and screen called attention to technics as a way of ordering, and emplacing, the subject—it seemed designed to signal television's

ability to "split the unity of place." Reading about the piece from afar, and thinking about these issues, I looked forward to visiting Atlanta and experiencing this work in person.

But what I discovered on my first visit to Rio in 1994 was not what I had expected, unfamiliar as I was with the politics of land use in the city of Atlanta (since chronicled in Charles Rutheiser's book *Imagineering Atlanta*).[19] It was a surprise that served as a moment of reckoning in my ongoing evaluation of geographical and ontological perspectives on place and the place assigned to television within them. Around 11 a.m. on a sunny Saturday morning in March, a time when one might expect to encounter throngs of shoppers in an outdoor mall, the open atrium mall was almost completely empty. The video wall was blank and dark, surrounded by stacked plastic chairs and tables. It was not the centerpiece of the mall as much as it was the centerpiece of Hoops, the outdoor sports bar nearby; like most TV sets in bars, it was probably being used to screen sports. From the large speakers attached to the screen, the sound of Black Entertainment Television (BET) echoed throughout the plaza. The stores were, for the most part, deserted shells with "For Lease" signs in the windows. All that was open were two take-out food places, a gym, a vitamin store, and a bar. Of these, all save the gym were closed. In short, Rio was crumbling. I had come to see a video installation "take place" but instead, what I saw was a place that had taken over a video installation. Despite its Mondrianesque postmodern architecture, its perisphere, and its frogs, the mall looked like a failed investment. And indeed, shortly after my visit, the owner filed for bankruptcy. Birnbaum had made an admirable and carefully planned attempt to expose the spatial forms of contemporary consumer culture by juxtaposing television images with an ontological view of the lost pastoral landscape that the video image, as part of the mall, had destroyed. But her attempt was undermined by the very forces she sought to bring to the spectator's awareness.

Yet from another perspective, the mall was quite a "success," albeit not the kind of success that Birnbaum anticipated when she designed the piece as a sly critique of consumer space. Rio may have failed to attract rich white yuppie consumers, but when the mall was purchased later that year by an Atlanta entrepreneur, it became a black business and cultural center. When I revisited the site in 1998, it housed several black-owned businesses, including an art gallery, and a dance studio that served as a performance space for Kwanza celebrations, local theater productions, community-oriented festivals, and United Negro College Fund benefits. The sports bar Hoops, now bought and renamed by a local radio personality named Youngblood, was a particularly popular attraction. The video wall occasionally provided Youngblood's patrons with a source of entertainment, but a representative of the mall's management company told me that it had gradually stopped working, its circuitry deteriorating through exposure to the elements over the years—the place, it seemed, had taken over the TV set and left it to decay.

The very irrelevance of the video wall in the cultural context of Rio after 1993 suggests that Birnbaum's concern for the sense of the "place" destroyed by the mall, while admirable, was in an important sense incomplete. For this concern was rooted in an ontological view of place—the pastoral ideal of the lost natural landscape recovered by video technology. As an ideal, it obscured the fact that this small green place destroyed by Rio only existed because of a prior destruction: that of an inner-city neighborhood, ravaged by urban renewal. Moreover, one might even argue that Birnbaum's use of closed-circuit video to make a critique of commercial culture overlooked certain aspects of inner-city racial politics articulated around consumption. After all, the surveillance cameras she placed around the mall implicated the installation in a racialized visual discourse of crime and visibility, even though their intended use was simply to transform shoppers' images into silhouettes that could be digitized on the video wall's screen. This transformation of the real subject of the camera's gaze into a digitized, featureless outline erased all signs of race and other forms of human specificity. It emptied out identity and installed a standardized, abstracted subjectivity in its place, making the consumer and his or her particularity into a disembodied trace flitting across a screen. Accompanying this ontological notion of place, in other words, was an ahistorical, "ageographic" notion of the subject. Birnbaum's attempt to involve the actual spectator so closely and directly thus simultaneously reduced that consumer to a one-dimensional,

faceless thing—enacting, rather than revealing, his or her "reification."

Had I never visited Rio, remaining content to parse the deft conceptualism of Birnbaum's ontological approach to site and screen from afar, it would have continued to be for me a place perhaps existing *outside of* geography. What I discovered when I went there instead was the fact of the video's place *within* geography—its place in the local patterns of land use and gentrification, the racialized politics of downtown-periphery relations, the vicissitudes of Atlanta's consumer economy. It was designed in some sense to illustrate the process by which modern technics "take" an (ontologized) place, but revealed instead the facts of the video's place in a *geographic* sense. The relationship between site and screen unfolded not on the basis of the site's ontological unity, but rather via its material history and geography of a southern black metropolitan culture. Nothing could have communicated the materiality, and site-specificity, of television's complex spatial operations more effectively than the blank and uncommunicative surface of the video wall. This brief history of *Rio Videowall* shows how the idealist prisms of spatial collapse and virtuality are inadequate as ways of thinking about the relationship between the screen and its place. It suggests instead that approaching place as an active and dynamic form of materiality, quite capable of overpowering technological modes of spatial rupture, adds important nuance to our sense of television's role in the lives of the hypothetical subjects who go about their everyday business in its presence.

In conclusion, I want to suggest a final reason why the philosophical pre-occupation with space-binding in media should be supplemented with an awareness of television's site-specificity. This is the fact that without a model for thinking about the determinations of place, and for describing the material status of the TV set as more than just a window to other worlds, theories of television's spatial processes risk sounding like a technological occult. After all, the language of television theory borrows heavily from the vocabulary of sorcery—one need think only of terms like *materialization* and *dematerialization, manifestation* and *presence*. As Derrida notes, "contemporary technologies like film, television, telephones . . . live on or off of, in some way, a ghostly structure. Film is an art of the ghost, which is to say, it is neither image nor perception. . . . The voice on the telephone also has a ghostly appearance. It is something neither real nor unreal, something which returns, is reproduced—finally, it's the question of reproduction. From the moment when the first perception of an image is linked to a structure of reproduction, we are dealing with the ghostly."[20] However, as Jeffrey Sconce points out, these occult connotations are grounded in particular cultural histories, in anxieties that emerge from material social relations. Without an awareness of these histories, he notes in his own comprehensive account of associations between electronic media and the occult, many theories of contemporary media merely replace "the humanist illusions of traditional metaphysics [with] the technological illusions of electronic presence."[21]

Building on Sconce's point, I cannot think about the occult connotations of space-binding, connotations that lead theorists to characterize the TV set as a piece of furniture endowed with frightening conjuring powers, without recalling Marx's famous discussion of commodity fetishism in *Capital*. Toward the end of chapter 1, he writes:

> The form of wood, for instance, is altered if a table is made out of it. Nevertheless the table continues to be wood, an ordinary, sensuous thing. But as soon as it emerges into a commodity, it changes into a thing which transcends sensuousness. It not only stands with its feet on the ground, but, in relation to all other commodities, it stands on its head, and evolves out of its wooden brain grotesque ideas, far more wonderful than if it were to begin dancing of its own free will.[22]

Here Marx, in one of his best displays of irony, personifies the commodity as a thing that exceeds perception, animated by an unseen force. Perhaps because he feared that his characterization of the table/commodity as a playful, deformed, fairy-tale hybrid sounded fanciful and even supernatural, he added to his description a footnote that underscores his contempt for the immaterialities of superstition. The note reads: "One may recall that China and the tables began to dance when the rest of the world appeared to be standing still—*pour encourager les autres.*" This is a reference to two phenomena of the 1850s: the Taipei revolt of 1853, a proto-Communist rebellion led by a converted Christian farmer, and "the craze for spiritualism which swept over upper-class German society."[23] Marx's point is that European radicals could have found a way out of the stasis and disillusionment that followed the failed revolutions of 1848 by paying attention to the events of China, instead of to the magical hoaxes of the séance table. He turns to spiritualism in this footnote to stress the misapprehensions that occur when we personify things, granting them hidden powers. The commodity's animate "undeadness" must be exposed as a grotesque joke in order to break its hold over us.

The TV set in much media theory is like Marx's dancing table. Its space-binding, scale-shifting effects, and its abolition of remoteness, become mystical, and in the process raise the unwelcome possibility that the theory itself is a form of commodity fetishism. Like the antimedia slogan "Kill Your Television," a slogan which implies that destroying a commodity is a direct action against capitalism, the occult conceptualization of space-binding risks misinterpreting social relations between individuals as social relations among things, and thus reproducing "all the magic and necromancy that surrounds the products of labor on the basis of commodity production" (169). The superstitious treatment of television sets in the material practices of the everyday testifies to the richness of the occult as a resource for thinking about television's omnipresence in consumer culture. For example, I've photographed several interesting attempts to link television and Satan over the past few years. One of the resulting images shows the talismanic placement of Lucifer's image on the TV set of a venerable beatnik institution, the Ear Inn on the far West Side of lower Manhattan, another captures a graffiti writer's invocation of the devil, in response to a transit-car plaque identifying Passaic as the birthplace of television. Despite their occult sensibilities, these anonymous acts of "writing" television display a strongly materialist sense of television as an object that mediates relations among people, in particular places. As I've suggested in the foregoing, this sense of material culture, and place, is one way in which media theory might break the spell of concepts like the immaterial and the unreal in the philosophical encounter with television.

Notes

1. Martin Heidegger, "The Thing," in *Poetry, Language, Thought*, trans. and introduction by Albert Hofsadter (New York: Harper and Row, 1971), p. 165; Jacques Derrida, "Dissemination," in *Dissemination*, trans., with an introduction and additional notes by Barbara Johnson (Chicago: University of Chicago Press, 1981), p. 314.

2. Richard Dienst demonstrates that regardless of what television is taken to be, this sense of simultaneity always serves as a demonstrational optic through which the particularly political dimensions of late modern theoretical projects come into focus. It should be noted that Dienst advances this thesis in relation to temporality, which is subordinated to space in his analytical schema. See Richard Dienst, *Still Life in Real Time: Theory After Television* (Durham, N.C.: Duke University Press, 1994).

3. Samuel Weber, *Mass Mediauras: Form, Technics, Media* (Stanford: Stanford University Press, 1996), pp. 123, 124. Emphasis in original (page numbers in text hereafter).

4. This is the title of the chapter on video art and television in Fredric Jameson, *Postmodernism: Or, The Cultural Logic of Late Capitalism* (Durham, N.C.: Duke University Press, 1991), pp. 67–96.

5. Bruno Latour, *We Have Never Been Modern*, trans. Catherine Porter (Cambridge: Harvard University Press, 1993), p. 122.

6. David Harvey, *Justice, Nature and the Geography of Difference* (London: Blackwell Publishers, 1996), pp. 202, 52.

7. Television haunts anthropologist Marc Augé's somewhat predictable discovery at Disneyland that "we live in a time in which history is staged, made into a spectacle, and derealises reality . . . not only do we enter the screen, inverting the process at play in *The Purple Rose of Cairo* (1985), but behind the screen we find another screen." Marc Augé, "An Ethnologist in Disneyland," *de-, dis-, ex-* 4 (2001), pp. 190–91. See also Margaret Morse, *Virtualities: Television, Media Art, and Cyberculture* (Bloomington: Indiana University Press, 1998).

8. Joshua Meyrowitz, *No Sense of Place: The Impact of Electronic Media on Social Behavior* (New York: Oxford University Press, 1985).

9. On the Fordist economy, see Michel Aglietta, *A Theory of Capitalist Regulation: The U.S. Experience*, trans. David Fernbach (London: NLB, 1979 [2000]) and Alain Lipietz, *Mirages and Miracles: The Crisis in Global Fordism*, trans. David Macey (London: Verso, 1987).

10. On the need for a more thorough understanding of the unremarkable in cultural studies' engagement with everyday life, see Toby Miller and Alec McHoul, *Popular Culture and Everyday Life* (London: Sage: 1998).

11. On such treatments, see John Hartley, *The Politics of Pictures: The Creation of the Public in the Age of Popular Media* (New York: Routledge, 1992); Ondina Fachel Leal, "Popular Taste and Erudite Repertoire: The Place and Space of Television in Brazil," *Cultural Studies* 4, no. 1 (1990), pp. 19–39; Marie Gillespie, "Sacred Serials, Devotional Viewing, and Domestic Worship: A Case Study in the Interpretation of Two TV Versions of The Mahabharata in a Hindu Family in West London," in *To Be Continued: Soap Operas Around the World*, ed. Robert C. Allen (New York: Routledge, 1995); and Svetlana Boym, *Common Places: Mythologies of Everyday Life in Russia* (Cambridge: Harvard University Press, 1994).

12. Jane Feuer, "The Concept of Live Television: Ontology as Ideology," in *Regarding Television: Critical Approaches—An Anthology*, ed. E. Ann Kaplan (Frederick, Md.: University Publications of America, 1983). On the banality of liveness, see Mimi White, "Site Unseen: CNN's War in the Gulf," in *Seeing Through the Media: The Persian Gulf War*, ed. Susan Jeffords and Lauren Rabinovitz (New Brunswick, N.J.: Rutgers University Press, 1994).

13. On direct address and the construction of a fictive national space through the live, or live-coded broadcast, see John Ellis, *Visible Fictions: Cinema, Television, Video*, revised ed. (New York: Routledge, 1992); see also Mimi White, "Site Unseen," and Sasha Torres, "King TV," in *Living Color: Race and Television in the United States*, ed. Sasha Torres (Durham, N.C.: Duke University Press, 1998); and Mary Ann Doane, "Information, Crisis, Catastrophe," in *Logics of Television: Essays in Cultural Criticism*, ed. Patricia Mellencamp (Bloomington: Indiana University Press, 1990).

14. Jonathan Crary, *Suspensions of Perception: Attention, Spectacle, and Modern Culture* (Cambridge: MIT Press, 1999), pp. 71–72. To be fair, Crary's position on the perfidious influence of television is somewhat ambiguous here; in a footnote to this passage he alludes to the uncertainty of "whether or not attention can be controlled or managed" even though the passage itself clearly comes down on the affirmative side of this question.

15. For a full discussion of these cultural fears about communications technology, see Jeffrey Sconce, *Haunted Media: Electronic Presence from Telegraphy to Television* (Durham, N.C.: Duke University Press, 2000).

16. Martin Heidegger, "An Ontological Consideration of Place," in *The Question of Being*, trans, and introduction by William Kluback and Jean T. Wilde (New York: Twayne Publishers, 1958).

17. Harvey, *Justice, Nature and the Geography of Difference*, p. 49.

18. The discussion of Rio in this section draws on chapter 7 of my book *Ambient Television: Visual Culture and*

Public Space (Durham, N.C.: Duke University Press, 2001).

19. Charles Rutheiser, *Imagineering Atlanta: The Politics of Place in the City of Dreams* (London: Verso, 1996).

20. Jacques Derrida, "La danse des fantômes/The Ghost Dance," interview with Andrew Payne and Mark Lewis, *Public* 2, 1989, pp. 61, 68. Quoted in Thomas Keenan, "Have You Seen Your World Today?" *Art Journal* 54, no. 4 (Winter 1995), pp. 102–105. Keenan astutely points out that this is one of several occasions on which Derrida hints at the possibility of a broader engagement with television in his work, although he does not follow up on it. This is surprising, Keenan notes, because "nothing would seem a more tempting target for a deconstructive reading than television—so utterly metaphysical in its presuppositions and its claims, and yet strictly discontinuous in its operations with the experience of subjectivity and representation that defines this metaphysics—and yet it has managed to evade rigorous theoretical scrutiny almost entirely."

21. Sconce, *Haunted Media*, p. 207.

22. Karl Marx, *Capital: A Critique of Political Economy*, vol. 1, trans. Ben Fowkes (London: Pelican Books, 1976), p. 164.

23. Translator's note, ibid.

12.
THE MOBILE PHONE
Towards New Categories and Social Relations[1]
Leopoldina Fortunati

Metamorphosis of Space and Time

That the use of communicative technologies has modified the relationship of modern citizens with space and time is so obvious that it goes without saying. This analysis gives a sense of the old and stale, due not only to its over-inflated use, but also the fact that in most cases it is just a generic statement. The expansion of space and time, the instantaneous nature of communication at a distance, the new ubiquity of human beings, have become dead metaphors.

What has happened is that on the one hand scholars have not been able to take up the thread of the debate developed by the classics on this theme, sometimes very fruitful, on the other, they have not managed to give the various instruments inside these processes their due weight. So it would be very important to make up for these two shortcomings by (a) implementing with the help of the classics the quality of the analysis of the influence of communicative and information technologies on space and time; (b) articulating this analysis, with the purpose of calibrating the role of each instrument (for example, what has the mobile phone changed that had not already been changed by fixed telephony?).

We shall begin to do this by setting out some observations as to how the relation of individuals with space and time has changed with the spread of the mobile phone. Through communicative technologies (including means of transport) modern-day citizens, it has been said, have increased the level of social productivity, not only rationalizing and therefore making

the organization of the world of work and the domestic sphere more productive but also constructing new perceptions and categories of time and space (Harvey 1990; Thompson 199S; Jedlowski 1999; Crang and Thrift 2000). The increase in the capacity to perceive space-time inevitably leads to a metamorphosis inside the psychically active entity and quality of space-time itself (Simmel 1983; Cassirer 1989).

Modern-day citizens 'work' space and time to try to increase them, seeing that they are scarce resources (Luhmann 1988). The attempt is to enlarge the surface of space and the duration of time by means of communicative technologies. Space has widened out horizontally, lengthened out vertically, and at the same time is perceived as a background; while time is experienced in all its extensions and expanded in thickness. Space and time have thus become the new frontiers of increased social productivity. The mobile phone has a privileged role in this technological transformation of time and space, even if it carries the word, that is, mediates an action with a low-energy content such as communication (which makes this power of transformation even more magical and astonishing).

What space and time has the mobile found itself interacting with? With a space that was already transformed before, developing its technological aspect, informative, multicultural, mobile and relational, in short, becoming a complex space, not immediately easy to understand. The increasing difficulty in people's immediate and effective relation with space, which has become increasingly difficult to understand, has been an important element at the base of the spread and success of the mobile phone. This instrument, in fact, has enabled people to somehow attenuate their anxiety and bewilderment in the face of this new quality and dimension of space. The mobile phone is a device that enables people, when they perceive the surrounding environment as extraneous to them, to contact somebody of their intimate circle, that is, to activate the reassuring procedure of recognition. In other words, people react to the lack of informative immediacy of the place, strengthening communicative immediacy with their social networks by means of the mobile. What has happened is that there has been a classic shift, a phenomenon that often takes place in the human psyche, when facing up to something directly is a problem or creates too much suffering. Space has obviously turned out to be devoid of it, de-valorized.

As a consequence, public space, where people meet one another, or the stranger or acquaintance, is becoming less and less univocal with the introduction of the mobile phone (Simmel 1983). The use of the mobile in fact means that the non-univocity of space, already put into crisis by that the ubiquity which the fixed phone ensured, deepens. You have in fact the possibility of choosing more easily between the physical space which you physically go through and the psychological space of the intimacy of your networks of relationships. That is, you have the possibility of choosing between the public space of streets, stations, means of transport and the private space of interpersonal relationships, between chance socialness which may develop with those who happen to be passing by, and chosen socialness (e.g. with the friends you decide to call on your mobile phone). And it is obvious that the choice always falls on the second, if only because it represents the encroaching 'new'.

This phenomenon is evident in means of transport. Compartment conversation, a typical communicative mode in which nothing very important is said, is increasingly often silenced by selected but artificial conversations (that is, by the mobile). The individual is in one place, as a physical presence, but virtually, as an immaterial presence, he or she is elsewhere. An elsewhere that takes on an ever-increasing fascination, because it gives the reality of space a new connotation. Physical space in fact is emptied of significance, becomes less dense as thickness, as the

dimension of virtual space is grafted on to it. This phenomenon has however the implication that more and more distance is created with the unknown. Today it is difficult to surrender oneself to 'unknown lands' because one can face them armed with a mobile, thus defended by the socialness of one's point of departure.

As said above, it is increasingly evident that between chosen and chance sociality the interest is much more on chosen, even if this is virtual. In fact, the more one is forced into mobility, that is, into travelling great distances towards the unknown, the more one has to stress relations with what is familiar. The possibility of choosing the kind of sociality that one wishes to express often leads to the creation of greater distances, or anyway to not creating closeness with strangers or half-strangers. Another element that makes people lean towards chosen socialness, but virtual, is the disparity of information that they have on the person present and on their mobile interlocutor: the person present declares his or her willingness, they are there, it is possible to speak together even a few minutes afterwards, whereas it is not known in what situation the person who telephones finds himself, and whether it will be possible to postpone the conversation, Therefore, at least the first contact, that is, the phatic aspect of mobile conversation, is difficult to avoid.

The consequence is that the public space is no longer covered in full, lived in all its aspects, stimuli and prospects, but is kept in the background of an itinerant cellular 'intimacy'. Thus the possibility of a nomadic intimacy is achieved, but at the same time there is the giving up, discovering and living directly everything that social space can offer. Therefore, public space becomes a background, the public dimension is put into a minority, takes on less importance, and chance socialness becomes less attractive. In this way however the aspects of predictability and uniformity of existence are emphasized. Also in terms of just the communicative aspect, always speaking over the mobile phone with one's own intimate circle of persons, instead of conversing with people met anywhere, outside home, implies remaining closed inside a rigid and inert kind of discourse, because one tends to say the same things, to repeat the same procedures in conversation, and so on.

These sclerotic aspects of communication are also made more acute by the fact that people tend to flee from them, in that they have lost the capacity of mediating reciprocal interests at a social level, empathy towards their interlocutor, negotiation (Fortunati 1998). The reason for this flight is to be seen in the fact that there is a situation of stalemate in fundamental relations, those of man/woman, parents/children and so on. The mobile represents a way of getting round the problem: people recuperate new communicative modes (the somewhere else, ubiquity, the just in time), to valorize communication technologically, which remains however lacking on the plane of meaning. To avoid conflicts, in fact, people learn to be silent or to talk little or to talk about this and that of no importance. From some research (cf. for example Fortunati 1994), it emerges that conversations in the family are rather short and instrumental. The low value of what people communicate in everyday life seems to be reflected also in conversations over the mobile phone, where the communicative mode keeps to the principle of 'maximum fusion'. The contents of mobile calls in fact reveal 'a greater interest in presenting than representing the world, describing experiences rather than exploring their meanings, exhibiting participation rather than analysing' (Minnini 1999: 57). Some limits of 'natural' communication are certainly overcome by means of the mobile, but the semantic aspect remains irremediably in dissolution, in the sense that, as Simmel writes (1991: 38), the transmission speed of communication does not improve the value of what people communicate. On the contrary, mediated communication lowers the quality of the communicative performance, as far as to deprive it of the support afforded by non-verbal language, proxemics, kinesics, etc. (cf. Contarello 2002). The authentic euphoria aroused by telephone techniques, continues Simmel, is the result of a kind of usurpation of the interest in technical modes, which at present are secondary to the problem of value of content, which remains primary. Communication however turns out on the whole to be reinforced by the new performance possible through technology, because, at this point, from being a means in the hands of humankind technology is running the risk of becoming the end (if that has not already happened), starting that overturning of means into ends described by Hegel in *Science of Logic* (1812—16).

Communicative technologies, made, as Gilder (1996) says, of sand, glass and air, and among them especially the mobile phone, have also modified the mental representation of the other structural element that lives in a total inter-penetration with space: time. The mechanical representation of time is more and more unacceptable at a social level. In other words, the abstract, uniform and unitary time of the clock is sinking further and further down in relation to electric and satellite time. With the possibility of perpetual contact, the mobile phone ends in fact by shaping time as a container of potentially continuing connection. Which means that the use of the mobile leads to the application to interpersonal communication of a pattern of connecting times similar to that guaranteed by the world of information, which tends to transmit 24 hours a day.

Time, it has been said, has been stretched out. But in what sense? In the sense that, seeing that its temporal duration cannot be modified, its thickness has expanded. The mobile, much more than the fixed phone, makes it possible to speak and do various actions at the same time as it is being used: walking, driving, and so on. Doing more than one thing at the same time allows you to live a double or triple life, even if this obviously raises your level of stress. The mind gets used to spreading attention in various directions. Certainly it is less brilliant attention, more opaque, but it enables people to cope with multiple actions. As Thrift (2001: 2) points out, 'the ability to register, understand and engineer smaller spaces and times is a critical element of modern organisation'.

The mobile in particular forces people to ask themselves about the compactness of what they are doing. It forces them to single out the pauses in their actions, the pores, the cracks in time, so as to get hold of and to make communicative use of them. More than novice Prousts (in remembrance of things past) people are becoming severe engineers of times and methods of Taylorian memory. But it is no longer a question (or not only) of factory time, so much as the daily time of the social labourer.

The mobile, for example, has definitely saved communicativeness and therefore work, affective and psychological time in traffic hold-ups on the motorway, queues in banks or at the post office, and public offices. The time, that is, that we consider wasted, unproductive. In fact people waste less and less time, in that they use it to speak with their mobile, if only to activate the umbilical cord that enables them to reduce anxiety and uncertainty.

The use of the mobile has also changed the spatialization of time, typical of 'natural' communication, and also telephone communication. The time of physiological disconnection that once regulated the communicative flow inside social relations tends to be drastically reduced. These moments of pause, which were very precious, structured the network of relations inside a rhythm of presence/absence. At the same time, these moments could also be filled with reflection, possible adventures, observation of events, reduction of the uniformity of our existences, and so on. From this angle it is as if the advent of the mobile had obscured the positive aspects of things past, underlining only their negative aspects. What is more, the mobile ends up by supporting social thoughtlessness about time, which is perceived as something to fill up to the very smallest folds.

The loss of diastemic awareness in the administration of time (Dorfles 1980), however, can have very harmful effects on social and above all emotional relations. In the same way as communication also feeds off silence, so seduction needs to cultivate absence: if we eliminate absence and silence, relationships are exposed to premature deterioration, because the rhythmic and aesthetic dimensions of time are lost (Fortunati 2002).

Present Absences: An Increasingly Frequent Oxymoron

The modifications that, armed with the mobile, people bring to space and time are so powerful that they also affect them, and their body, which is the first mode of extension of the individual in space. In the same way as space, people acquire – as will be seen below – the capacity to split themselves into two, to be present and absent at the same time, as well as keeping their body in the background.

With the spread of the mobile, that is, the phenomenology of the presence of individuals in social space also changes, in that individuals apparently present in a given place are actually only half-present. They are present in body, but their attention, mind and senses can at any moment, after a ring of the mobile phone, be drawn elsewhere by their communication network, which can contact them at any moment. If until yesterday the presence of individuals in flesh and blood in social space meant material and immaterial accessibility to their person on the part of those present, today this accessibility has become more limited. On the cultural plane one can observe that the binary opposition presence/absence has undergone the same effect as the opposition life/death, in that in both these oppositions the boundaries between the two concepts are no longer clear. In the same way as people no longer know up to what point an individual is alive and from what point he is to be considered dead (the concept of death, as Baudrillard (1976) writes, has in fact passed from heart attack to flat encephalogram, and tomorrow, we do not know . . .), in the same way people do not quite understand up to where they are present in space or absent. Individuals today, when they are present, are not so completely; they are present, yes, with continuity in their physical part, but discontinuity in the immaterial part. As vampires are alive but not living, or if we prefer, the dead who return to life in certain conditions, in the same way people are present in space, but potentially also absent.

But how is it that people have managed to accept that their presence in space should be emptied out? How is it that artificial communication can have the better of natural communication? We can find an answer to this question in certain historical moments. For example, with the advent of the small screen, people's attention shifted away from natural communication, fragmenting it with TV consumption. Initially people learned to talk while they were watching TV at home. Then with the mobile they developed this tendency even more, learning to answer a call, having no scruple to brusquely interrupt an already-ongoing conversation with somebody. That is, what people got used to doing was diverting attention from interpersonal communication in favour of a virtual conversation, over a distance. In the same way as people hushed their family members so as to be able to watch TV, so in the case of the mobile, they suspend their flesh and blood interlocutor while they talk into the mobile, with the effect that they give the person at the other end more attention than the person in front of them. To respond to that question that we asked at the beginning of this section, it is the previous de-valorization of 'natural' communication that is the element that has implicitly permitted the emptying out of people's presence in space, both as bystanders and as users of the mobile.

The individual's current ambiguous dimension of presence/absence in space means the restructuring also of the sense of belonging to places, which is a main pivot of the sense of belonging. What actually happens is that it becomes transformed into the sense of belonging to one's communicative network. Those affective elements that are lost in the relation with space are transferred to a social level, that is loyalty, the sense of identification, familiarity, stability, security, and so on.

This shift makes it possible, on the other hand, to suffer less from nostalgia, a tormenting feeling which frequently accompanies immigration, mobility, tourism and so on, and which is connected to the sense of loss of one's own relationship with a place. People are also suffering less nostalgia in respect to home, a place where they spend less and less time. The less close relation that people have today with their homes actually lacerates affective equilibrium not only at a generic psychological level, but also at the deep structure of the imagination. The home in fact brings up images of the sacred space and Paradise-like centre inside the constellation of intimacy (Durand 1963). A less firm relation with it cannot help causing on the one hand great pain, and on the other, a greater secularization of space. But this pain of separation from home becomes something that can be borne more easily, as there is a kind of remedy for it through the mobile. This instrument in fact makes the experience of separation less final, and also makes it possible to transform de-sacralized space into social space.

So, the use of the mobile ends up by reinforcing profane space, constructing a space without addresses, without precise localizations, playing down the specifically geographical and anagraphical aspect. Last of all, the use of the telephone, and especially of the mobile phone, ends up by attenuating the social inertia given by the home's being immobile in space (Leonini 1988), to the point that the mobile phone in itself becomes a true mobile home.

However, the partial mode of adhering to a single place is translated at the same time into a sense of more or less potential belonging to many places. Let us analyse this point by point: space expands, vertically, with suffering.

Space, we said, expands. It expands, of course, only at a virtual level, but the expansion is inexorably beyond the horizon that we see and the sense dimensions that we feel. And it expands both horizontally and vertically. On the horizontal plane space widens out on the surface, not easy to read, as a fragmentary juxtaposition of places. In reality, rather than being a real widening out of space, it is a bouncing back and forth from one place to another, interrupting the continuity of space itself. The most interesting widening out is perhaps what happens on the vertical plane. In fact, mobile communications travel in the space above people, in the air, so that the latter end up by occupying and englobing the ether, if only at a communicative level, detaching themselves from space as materiality, as brute matter. Which means that at the mass level people are taking possession, secretly, of the sky, leaving behind the anchorages of worldly reality. This wrapping up of space in a vertical sense means that as the sky is a space of light consistency (difficult to decipher but, even more, to perceive), public social space loses on the whole in consistency, becoming more rarefied. We could say that on a mass level people are trying out a new kind of living, at least as far as communicative means are concerned, halfway up. In a certain sense, they are creating a bridge between living in a terrestrial mode and living in space, in orbit. This widened dimension of the real that people are now living is not only fantastic but real. If the Internet is really creating the conditions for humanity's taking on a planetary consciousness (Longo 1998), the mobile is not far behind. It is the crisis of the sense of belonging to one single place that may be leading people to develop a sense of belonging to an unlimited space. Astronauts, on the other hand, are not only explorers of space, but are also the guinea pigs for the new mass production for the earth. From clothes to food to architecture, to design, furnishing, art: the real is being reshaped starting from the cosmic (Francalanci 1999).

This restructuring of people's sense of belonging to places is not without its suffering, because the change of such an important psychological structure inevitably causes a sense of uncertainty, insecurity and confusion.

Uncontrolled Appropriation of Public Space

The public/private is an opposition whose terms have become rather unclear with time, because the spheres of public and private have produced not a few areas of intersection in their evolution. Think of the feminist slogan of the 1970s 'private is political', the purpose of which was to underline the political, and therefore public, dimension of domestic space and the relations that exist inside it.

In this situation the mobile, already in itself complex, created a little extra confusion. Let us start by considering social space as public space. It is not only the space where processes of coming together and separating of individuals take place, but also that in which these processes have to be based on shared principles and collective norms, as the space in which they happen is subject to the protection of the state. When you telephone from a train compartment or in the street, forcing your own private conversation on to those present, in that moment you are appropriating yourself of the space in which you are present, as if it belonged to you, not to society at large. In that moment, you are erecting around yourself an imaginary fence, but clearly perceptible to those around you, and this is not allowed. Taking possession of the area inside that fence, which is the bubble inside which the conversation with your interlocutor takes place, becomes illegal appropriation of public space. Of course public space also belongs to the absent person with whom you are speaking, but in this situation his right finishes by expropriating those present of the collective property that in that moment they share.

Following on the spread of the mobile, a process has been born, from below, of uncontrolled privatization of entire slices of public space. Public space is increasingly being subjected to temporary dismantling by modern-day citizens who exploit it as if it belonged to them. Now, the fact that this expropriation is temporary and that the space occupied is ethereal attenuates reactions and confounds interpretations. In fact, people find it difficult to understand what is happening, hence their hesitation before taking countermeasures.

What distinguishes this process of privatization of public space from that of the public dimension's penetration of the home, the private place par excellence? It is different in that for the latter access has so far been regulated democratically, seeing that the dimension of the public has so far entered homes only with the consent of those who lived there. The telephone call, for example, could at one time arrive only if someone signed a contract, giving implicit authorization to become the object of contact on the part of anybody. On the contrary, privatization of public space takes place in an uncontrolled way, as its mass practice protects it from precise legislation, and it has involved entire populations.

Public space, subject up to yesterday to the concept of state property, had tacit rules that placed the public good above the individual. At the communicative level, that was transformed into a series of norms and laws that regulated for example permissible behaviour on a communicative plane: not speaking too loud during the night hours, limiting noise so as not to disturb others, and so on.

The use of the mobile in public spaces has taken concepts, norms and laws by surprise, catching them on the completely wrong foot. If up to now the approach developed by sociologists has been to analyse how good manners in social relations had been changed so radically by the use of this communicative instrument (Ling 1998; Ling *et al.* 1998), the time has come to change direction. The problem in fact is much more complex: it is not only a question of aesthetics, of good behaviour, but also an ethical, legal and political problem.

In this uncontrolled appropriation of public space the modal personality strengthened by the mobile also has its importance. It is a personality that is able to govern space in a new way, overcoming inertia and conversing with time, appropriating itself of its fastest extensions. Secondly, it is a personality that has the power to construct a communicative network to its own measure, and to handle it independently of where it happens to be. So, it is a personality that manages to calm anxiety better than previously, as now it is able to re-establish contact with the world of security. If it is true, in fact, that mobility and travelling in general involve a certain precariousness, temporary loss of autonomy and insecurity, it is just as true that the mobile makes it possible to compensate for them through the immediate regaining of one's own stability. Furthermore, this modal personality strengthened by the mobile is a personality that manages to reduce uncertainty. It can never be stressed enough how the phatic function of communication (that is, pure contact), perhaps even more than information, manages to produce this miracle. It is the possibility of contacting its own communicative network at any moment that has the powerful effect of reducing the uncertainty that mobility brings with it.

Lastly, it is a personality that just because of its strong dynamic character is often subject to the dangers of aggressiveness. Like any instrument, the mobile gives the person that possesses and uses it its capability and power, which are progressively losing their magical aspect and becoming standardized abilities usable potentially by any human being. Given its vast spread, this process of strengthening but also standardizing the personality takes place on a large scale, and so this aggressive attitude and behaviour in using it have spread like oil.

As Alberoni (1998) quite rightly says, it is wrong to call the mobile a status symbol. It is no longer an instrument of social distance and distinction, but of equality and closeness to others. From a sociological point of view in particular the mobile has not been a status symbol right from the time of the TACS (Total Access Communication System) boom, which was born with the clear purpose of mass diffusion. So if mobiles are not status symbols, what are they? Alberoni proposes 'mass commodities', or better 'citizenship commodities', that is, a 'must' for modern-day citizens, who no longer have the prestige of those who were the first to use mobiles. Even if mobiles still have to find a mode of use that is respectful of democratic values, as well as good manners.

Cell-Democracy

The modification of one's relation with space through the widespread use of the mobile has become the premise which will also illuminate the role of this instrument in the evolution of democratic society (Dutton 1999). It is evident that the mobile favours the development of democratic relations less than the fixed phone has done and continues to do. It has a less strong role in this sense than the fixed phone, because the possibility of the fixed phone to enter every home, in every place, without differences of race, language and social class, is lost with the mobile. In fact the mobile leaves it up to individuals when, how and who to give their mobile phone number. There does not yet exist in Italy, nor in other countries like France and Great Britain, a mobile phonebook (if ever there will be such a thing in these countries). This means that the mobile enables people to find and be found by those closest to them, in other words by a very limited social network (and often handled by a direct personal contact and controlled by the Caller-ID, cf. Katz 1999). Only this network is given permission to call, while actually reciprocal and official access is not allowed to subscribers as a whole (the mobile with a card is a further complication in this sense).

The fixed phone on the other hand had been implicated very profoundly in the construction of the democratic collocation of the citizens of the world. The more the citizens of this century earned their freedom in social relations and in anonymity – the crowd without a face and without a name – as a *conditio sine qua non* of the attenuation of reciprocal control, the stronger the necessity of having a place that would transmit the memory of their existence. A place that could give further information to those who knew too little to contact them. This place was the telephone directory. The reciprocal pact that citizens agreed upon was that of putting at the community's disposal information about themselves (name, surname, address, phone number, and sometimes profession) to guarantee that they could be found anywhere by anyone, in exchange for the possibility of being able to do the same with others. Despite their endemic errors, telephone directories have served for many years as a repertoire of the knowledge of the population of a country. This situation has partially changed since the possibility, on request, of not appearing in the phonebook has been introduced. The quite numerous requests in some countries (for example the figure of 40 per cent is mentioned for California and about a third for Great Britain) to not be inserted in the telephone directory has ended up by making a large part of the population invisible. As a consequence, the phonebook is more and more incomplete and mutilated. This phenomenon, in which a growing number of subscribers are removing themselves from other people's knowledge, while being able to have access to information about them, is producing an unequal information exchange. This disparity will lead to an ever-greater reluctance on the part of subscribers on the whole to be traceable. Already now we are heading towards a society in which access to subscribers' telephone numbers is beginning to be a problem, causing a democratic involution and great obstacles to the development of traffic. But, evidently, in mature democracies the disadvantages are more numerous (undesired calls from advertisers, or inquiries, disturbers, sex maniacs, etc.) than the advantages that may be obtained for an ever greater number of citizens. The traceability of citizens will remain, however, an open problem that the mobile will certainly not be able to resolve.

The implication of the fixed phone in the construction of the democratic collocation of the citizens of the world has had limits. It has in fact generally privileged the head of the family, that is, the undersigner of the telephone contract. Only his name and surname, in fact, are included in the directory. Wife and children in most cases have remained a hidden presence inside the telephone directory, in that they were not officially traceable, unless indirectly, and always in the context of the family. In fact, if the husband's surname was not known, it was actually impossible to find married women who had kept their maiden names. Likewise, in the case of children, to find them it was necessary to know either their address or their father's name.

However, the fixed phone enabled the mobile to enter into a situation in which it could quite happily give it (the fixed phone) the task of democratic traceability and build for itself (the mobile) a made-to-measure sphere of communication, in which it was the single possessor that decided who to give or not to give their number to. The mobile in fact gives subscribers a strong possibility to promote and organize the communicative network, exactly as they want it (even if it is not rare to receive advertising text messages). The inebriation of being able to construct a communicative network made to measure has been a strong impulse behind the success of the mobile in Europe, and especially in Italy. And it has been so strong, this impulse, that it has driven people to buy more than one mobile, so as to be able to handle various communicative networks which, with their different numbers, could not have intersected.

These further communicative possibilities offered by the mobile phone have been very popular with consumers, because in any case for wide range traceability they could count on the telephone directory. For this reason the fixed phone is widely destined to remain in homes, because only through the fixed phone is it still possible today, but perhaps also in the near and not too distant future, to guarantee oneself wide access to other citizens and social institutions (there does not exist even a public repertory of email sites or addresses!). The mobile, despite its seeming to favour the development of individualism, has also contributed to implementing the development of democratic society in at least two directions: (a) it has extended traceability also during movement in space. Uniting mobility/permanence and mobility/mobility at a communicative level, the mobile has also extended to dynamic space the same communicative prerogatives as static space; (b) it has extended individual access to mobile communication also to members of the family up to yesterday 'invisible' with the fixed phone. That is, the mobile has extended communicative relational space, lighting up areas of darkness, or rather the 'empty spaces' formerly not inhabited by anyone.

As for the first point, in a world in which mobility is high, the mobile has granted the same communicative rights to nomadic persons and those that are sedentary or immobile. Before the mobile, fixed residential persons were forced to lose contact with persons in movement. In fact, when only a small part of the population moved and the rest was residential, only those that moved could contact the residential persons, by using public telephones, as only those that had a fixed phone could be reached. Furthermore, not even persons in movement could contact one another. These two big obstacles, added to the fact that public phones were rigid and difficult to use, were overcome by mobile telephony. And in this sense the mobile has extended the right to communication in the democratic sense.

As for the second point, members of the family that did not appear in the telephone directory – wives and children – have had at least access to their own number with the mobile, and the possibility of handling communicative networks at an individual level. They remain untraceable, on the whole, or traceable with indications given at a personal level, but like all the others (including the head of the family). Also in this sense, the mobile is a 'citizenship commodity', that is, an instrument of democratization, able to extend access to communication.

Conclusions

What seems to emerge quite clearly is the role played by the mobile phone in changes not only and not so much in society, as reality in the wider sense, or better, in its social representation. The use of this instrument has in fact made a notable contribution to modifying the social conception of space and time, determinations capable of integrating, stabilizing and structuring reality. The mobile has been in fact used widely by modern-day citizens, not only to strengthen time and space, resources more and more scarce for humankind, but also to transform social relations with them. The metamorphosis of space and time has consequently modified the statute of the presence and absence of individuals in social space, the relation of citizens with public space, and has interacted notably also in the role played by the mobile in the strengthening of the democratic process.

Note

1. This article is the re-working of a paper presented at the international seminar 'Sosiale Knonsekvenser av Mobiltelefoni', organized by Telenor, Oslo on 16 June 2000.

References

Alberoni, F. (1998) 'Conversazione con Francesco Alberoni', in C.M. Guerci, G. Cervigni, V. Marcolongo and F. Pennarola (eds) *Monopolio e concorrenza nelle telecomunicazioni. Il caso Omnitel*, Milano: Il Sole 24 ore, pp. 130–1.

Baudrillard, J. (1976) *L'échange symbolique et la mort*, Paris: Gallimard.

Cassirer, E. (1923) *Philosophie der Symbolischen Formen, III, Phänomenologie der Erkenntnis*, Oxford (Italian trans. *Filosofia delle forme simboliche. Fenomenologia della conoscenza*, Firenze: La Nuova Italia, 1989).

Contarello, A. (2002) 'Corpo a corpo. Copresenza e comunicazione', in L. Fortunati, J. Katz and R. Riccini (eds) *Corpo futuro. Il corpo umano tra tecnologie comunicazione e moda*, Milano: Angeli.

Crang, M. and Thrift, N. (eds) (2000) *Thinking Space (Critical Geographies)*, London: Routledge.

Dorfles, G. (1980) *L'intervallo perduto*, Milano: Feltrinelli.

Durand, G. (1963) *Les structures anthropologiques de l'Imaginaire*, Paris: PUF.

Dutton, W.H. (1999) Society on the Line (Italian trans. *La società on line. Politica dell'informazione nell'era digitale*, Milano: Baldini & Castaldi, 2001).

Fortunati, L. (1994) 'Conversazioni in famiglia', paper presented at the Internation Conference 'Mutamenti della famiglia occidentale', Bologna, 6–8 October.

Fortunati, L. (ed.) (1998) *Telecomunicando in Europa*, Milano: Angeli.

Fortunati, L. (2002) 'Italy. Stereotypes: true or false', in J. Katz and M. Aakhus (eds) *Perpetual Contact: Mobile Communication, Private Talk, Public Performance*, Cambridge: Cambridge University Press.

Fortunati, L., Katz, J. and Riccini, R. (eds) (2002) *Corpo futuro. Il corpo umano tra tecnologie, comunicazione e moda*, Milano: Angeli. (English trans. *Mediating the Human Body. Technology, Communication and Fashion*, New Brunswick: Erlbaum, 2003).

Francalanci, E.L. (1999) 'Mir-age', in *Arte nello spazio*, Padova: EMB, pp. 11–25.

Gilder, G. (1996) 'L'Europa nel Telecosmo', paper presented at the seminar 'L'età noolitica', Centro Studi San Salvador, 18 March.

Haddon, L. (ed.) (1998) *Communications on the Move: The Experience of Mobile Telephony in the 1990s*, COST248 Report, Farsta: Telia AB, pp. 9–18.

Harvey, D. (1990) *The Condition of Postmodernity*, Oxford: Basil Blackwell (Italian trans. *La crisi della modernità*, Milano: Il Saggiatore, 1997).

Hegel, G.W.F. (1812–16) *Wissenschaft der Logik* (Italian trans. *Scienza della Logica*, Bari: Laterza, 1974).

Jedlowski, P. (1999) 'Le trasformazioni dell'esperienza', in C. Leccardi (ed.) *Limiti della modernità*, Roma: Carrocci, pp. 147–78.

Katz, J. (1999) *Connections. Social and Cultural Studies of the Telephone in American Life*, New Brunswick: Transactions.

Katz, J. (ed.) (forthcoming) *Machines that Becomes Us*, New Brunswick: Transactions.

Katz, J. and Aakhus, M. (eds) (2002) *Perpetual Contact: Mobile Communication, Private Talk, Public Performance*, Cambridge: Cambridge University Press.

Leonini, L. (1988) *L'identità smarrita*, Bologna: Il mulino.

Ling, R. (1998) ' "On peut parler de mauvaises manières!". Le téléphone mobile au restaurant', *Réseaux*, 90: 51–70.

Ling, R., Julsrud, T. and Krogh, E. (1998) 'The Goretex Principle: the Hytte and mobile telephones in Norway', in L. Haddon (ed.) *Communications on the Move: The Experience of Mobile Telephony in the 1990s*, COST248 Report, Farsta: Telia AB, pp. 97–120.

Longo, G.O. (1998) *Il nuovo Golem. Come il computer cambia la nostra cultura*, Roma-Bari: Laterza.

Luhmann, N. (1988) 'Il tempo scarso e il carattere vincolante della scadenza', in S. Tabboni (ed.) *Tempo e società*, Milano: Angeli, pp. 119–37.

McLuhan, M. (1964) *Understanding Media*, New York: McGraw-Hill Book Company.

Meyrowitz, J. (1985) *No Sense of Place. The Impact of Electronic Media on Social Behaviour*, New York: Oxford University Press.

Minnini, G. (1999) *Psicologia del parlare comune*, Bologna: Grasso Editore.

Simmel, G. (1900) 'Die Herrschaft der Technick', in *Philosophie des Geldes*, Leipzig: Duncker und Humblot, pp. 520–35 (Italian trans. 'Il dominio della tecnica', in T. Maldonado (ed.) *Tecnica e Cultura*, Milano: Feltrinelli, 1991, pp. 37–46).

Simmel, G. (1908) *Soziologie. Untersuchungen über die Formen der Vergesellschaftung*, Leipzig: Duncker und Humblot (Italian trans. *Sociologia*, Torino: Edizioni di Comunità, 1983).

Thompson, J.B. (1995) *The Media and Modernity. A Social Theory of the Media*, Cambridge: Polity Press (Italian trans. *Mezzi di comunicazione e modernità*, Bologna: Il Mulino, 1998).

Thrift, N. (2001) 'Timing and Spacing', paper presented to the International Conference 'Spacing & Timing: Rethinking Globalization & Standardization', Palermo, 1–3 November 2001.

SECTION III

MEDIA/REPRESENTATION

Introduction

This section introduces key concepts in the study of representation and meaning—arguably the central domains of critical media studies. The selections offered here chart methods for analyzing media as a language, and culture as a set of conceptual maps for making sense of the world. From an image on a video screen to the décor of a teenager's bedroom to a brand name on a baseball cap to discourse on a particular subject (such as homelessness or madness) symbolic communication is complex, even as we often take the meaning of things for granted. Critical media scholars draw from a range of theories and methods to ascertain not only *what* images, sounds, and clusters represent, as meanings are understood to be arbitrary and socially constructed within contexts—but also *how* meanings are produced, *why* certain meanings emerge at particular times, and how practices of signification intersect with power dynamics.

Stuart Hall's 1996 essay "The Work of Representation" presents a clear and thorough synthesis of the study of representation. Hall, a founding member of the Birmingham Centre for Cultural Studies, does not advocate one approach over another as much as he presents a critical toolbox for analyzing the role of media in the social construction of reality. He traces the advent of semiotics from the work of Ferdinand de Saussure and other linguists who sought to create a "science" of meaning based on fixed principles, to the cultural analysis of the anthropologist Claude Lévi-Strauss and literary critic Roland Barthes. Barthes' influential work on mythologies set the stage for the application of semiotics to popular culture, from wrestling to advertising, and influenced several important books including Dick Hebdige's 1979 classic *Subculture: The Meaning of Style* and Judith Williamson's equally influential 1984 book *Decoding Advertisements*.

Hall also traces the turn to post-structuralist approaches that reject the closed system of meaning presumed by earlier scholars. His treatment of Michel Foucault's contributions to the study of discursive formations situates representation in a more narrow sense, as the production of knowledge (rather than just meaning) through patterns of thinking and speaking about specific topics, from criminality to sexuality. For Foucault, discourse does not reflect or mediate reality as much as it produces the objects of knowledge of which it speaks. Rejecting concepts such as false representation and ideological distortion associated with early Marxism, Foucault is concerned with the intersecting institutions, practices, and the power relations through which discourse constitutes subjects and, through this productivity, makes itself true, as Hall points out.

In "Ways of Seeing," an excerpt from his 1972 book *Ways of Seeing*, art historian John Berger examines the conventions and politics of seeing, an equally important (if less understood) dimension of representation. His groundbreaking chapter on "ways of seeing" women anticipated the critical insights of feminist film theory, most particularly Laura Mulvey's influential 1974 essay "Visual Pleasure and Narrative Cinema," which coined the term the "male gaze." Berger takes the history of Western oil painting as the basis for making several intersecting arguments: that the person assumed to be viewing the painting is male, that the image of woman is designed to flatter him, and that just as men "survey" women, women learn to perpetually survey themselves from a male vantage point. Perhaps his most basic—and yet previously unrecognized—point was that men act, whereas women appear: "This determines not only most relations between men and women but also the relation of women to themselves ... the surveyor of woman in herself is male, the surveyed female," Berger writes. Jumping forward to the mid-1970s, Berger demonstrates remarkably similar relations of looking at work in advertising, suggesting that the dominant ways of seeing were neither invented by nor radically altered by the advent of commercial mass media.

The study of representation, as Berger suggests, is not a purely academic affair but is intimately bound to uneven social relations including hierarchies of gender, race, and class. In the wake of the social and political movements of the 1960s and 1970s, scrutiny of how marginalized and subordinated groups were represented in the media intensified. Activists and academics alike began to monitor stereotypes and misrepresentations of racial minorities, women, the working class, and gay and lesbian people. This is not surprising, considering the media's visible role in the construction of "reality" and sense-making practices. However, as Ella Shohat and Robert Stam argue in "Stereotype, Realism, and the Struggle over Representation," a chapter from their 1994 book *Unthinking Eurocentrism: Multiculturalism and the Media*, the focus on revealing errors and distortions associated with the quest for "progressive realism" can be simplistic as well as unfruitful. Drawing from post-structuralist theory, Shohat and Stam remind us that reality is not self-evidently given and suggest alternatives to the critique of stereotypes understood in terms of mimetic accuracy. Calling for a greater emphasis on voice, discourse, cultural and historical specificity, mode of production, and the role of parody in social critique, they posit a framework for moving beyond a "positive image" approach to representational politics.

In "Soft-Soaping Empire: Commodity Racism and Imperial Advertising," a chapter from her 1995 book *Imperial Leather: Race, Gender and Sexuality in the Colonial Conquest*, Anne McLintock provides an historical case study for understanding the construction of meaning and the multi-layered power dynamics of representation. She examines the process whereby commodities were invested with social and cultural meanings abstracted from the conditions of their manufacture and specifically how a common household good such as soap was invested with "magical, fetish powers" via the emerging sign system of advertising. McLintock's study links the commercial representation of soap to a multidimensional process of commodity fetishism that disavows the domestic labor of British women and colonialized capitalist economies in the arena of empire. Soap advertisements often featured images of colonial conquest, rendering advertising instrumental in the broader colonial discourse of racial hygiene and progress. Her influential study theorizes the stakes of such imagery—and provides a model for tracing the other economies of signs.

Andrew Wernick approaches the current economy of signs as a phenomenon that extends beyond the fetishization of commodities to the collapse of any distinction between promotion and signifying practices. His essay "The Promotional Condition of Contemporary Culture," from his 1992 book *Promotional Culture: Advertising, Ideology and Symbolic Expression*, argues that the logic of promotion has moved beyond advertising to wider processes of cultural commodification that impinge upon personhood. A logic of self-advancing exchange increasingly permeates all communicative acts, he suggests—a claim that is even more convincing in the era of personal branding and new social networking technologies. In advancing the argument that promotion has become a "structuring element in the regime of signification," Wernick exemplifies the cultural economy tradition, noted for its approach to culture and economics as intertwined in opposition to the earlier Marxist model of a determining economic base, with culture and meaning resting on the top. Drawing in part from Jean Baudrillard's theorization of the merger of signs and economic processes (1981), Wernick suggests that the objectives of advanced capitalism have been integrated into processes of signification, such that promotion is now the dominant cultural condition of our time.

The section concludes with Nick Couldry's 2004 essay "Liveness, 'Reality' and the Mediated Habitus from Television to the Mobile Phone," which moves us beyond the study of representation as a language to the constitution of media as the naturalized "center" from which images, information and narratives are distributed and received across space. Couldry is less interested in the unique attributes of particular mediums than in the way that media institutions are the basis of shared experience. One way this is accomplished is through conventions of liveness, exemplified by the journalist on the scene, round the clock coverage of disasters and events "as they are happening," and increasingly the climaxes of popular reality entertainment series. For Couldry, liveness is more than a selling point of television and increasingly digital media as well: liveness is a "category whose use naturalizes the general idea that, through the media, we achieve a shared attention to the realities that matter to us as a society." In this essay as in much of his work, Couldry reminds us that media do more than circulate discourse and images; they also mythologize their own cultural power and necessity to social life through ritualistic conventions such as broadcasting or streaming live.

References

Baudrillard, Jean, *For a Critique of the Political Economy of the Sign* (St. Louis, MO: Telos Press, 1981).
Hebdige, Dick, *Subculture: The Meaning of Style* (London: Routledge, 1979).
Mulvey, Laura, "Visual Pleasure and Narrative Cinema," *Screen* No. 16, Vol. 3 (1975), p 6–18.
Williamson, Judith, *Decoding Advertisements* (London: Marion Boyars Publishers Ltd, 1984).

13.
THE WORK OF REPRESENTATION
Stuart Hall

Representation, Meaning and Language

. . .

The concept of representation has come to occupy a new and important place in the study of culture. Representation connects meaning and language to culture. But what exactly do people mean by it? What does representation have to do with culture and meaning? One common-sense usage of the term is as follows: 'Representation means using language to say something meaningful about, or to represent, the world meaningfully, to other people.' You may well ask, 'Is that all?' Well, yes and no. Representation *is* an essential part of the process by which meaning is produced and exchanged between members of a culture. It *does* involve the use of language, of signs and images which stand for or represent things. But this is a far from simple or straightforward process, as you will soon discover.

How does the concept of representation connect meaning and language to culture? In order to explore this connection further, we will look at a number of different theories about how language is used to represent the world. Here we will be drawing a distinction between three different accounts or theories: the *reflective*, the *intentional* and the *constructionist* approaches to representation. Does language simply reflect a meaning which already exists out there in the world of objects, people and events (*reflective*)? Does language express only what the speaker or writer or painter wants to say, his or her personally intended meaning (*intentional*)? Or is meaning constructed in and through language (*constructionist*)? You will learn more in a moment about these three approaches.

Most of the chapter will be spent exploring the *constructionist* approach, because it is this perspective which has had the most significant impact on cultural studies in recent years. This chapter chooses to examine two major variants or models of the constructionist approach – the *semiotic* approach, greatly influenced by the great Swiss linguist, Ferdinand de Saussure, and the *discursive* approach, associated with the French philosopher and historian, Michel Foucault.

Making Meaning, Representing Things

What does the word **representation** really mean, in this context? What does the process of representation involve? How does representation work?

To put it briefly, representation is the production of meaning through language. The *Shorter Oxford English Dictionary* suggests two relevant meanings for the word:

1. To represent something is to describe or depict it, to call it up in the mind by description or portrayal or imagination; to place a likeness of it before us in our mind or in the senses; as, for example, in the sentence, 'This picture represents the murder of Abel by Cain.'
2. To represent also means to symbolize, stand for, to be a specimen of, or to substitute for; as in the sentence, 'In Christianity, the cross represents the suffering and crucifixion of Christ.'

The figures in the painting *stand in the place of*, and at the same time, *stand for* the story of Cain and Abel. Likewise, the cross simply consists of two wooden planks nailed together; but in the context of Christian belief and teaching, it takes on, symbolizes or comes to stand for a wider set of meanings about the crucifixion of the Son of God, and this is a concept we can put into words and pictures.

Here is a simple exercise about representation. Look at any familiar object in the room. You will immediately recognize what it is. But how do you *know* what the object is? What does 'recognize' mean?

Now try to make yourself conscious of what you are doing – observe what is going on as you do it. You recognize what it is because your thought-processes decode your visual perception of the object in terms of a concept of it which you have in your head. This must be so because, if you look away from the object, you can still *think* about it by conjuring it it up, as we say, 'in your mind's eye'. Go on – try to follow the process as it happens: There is the object ... and there is the concept in your head which tells you what it is, what your visual image of it *means*.

Now, tell me what it is. Say it aloud: 'It's a lamp' – or a table or a book or the phone or whatever. The concept of the object has passed through your mental representation of it to me *via* the word for it which you have just used. The word stands for or represents the concept, and can be used to reference or designate either a 'real' object in the world or indeed even some imaginary object, like angels dancing on the head of a pin, which no one has ever actually seen.

This is how you give meaning to things through language. This is how you 'make sense of' the world of people, objects and events, and how you are able to express a complex thought about those things to other people, or communicate about them through language in ways which other people are able to understand.

Why do we have to go through this complex process to represent our thoughts? If you put down a glass you are holding and walk out of the room, you can still *think* about the glass, even though it is no longer physically there. Actually, you can't think with a glass. You can only think with *the concept of* the glass. As the linguists are fond of saying, 'Dogs bark. But the concept of "dog" cannot bark or bite.' You can't speak

with the actual glass, either. You can only speak with the *word* for glass – GLASS – which is the linguistic sign which we use in English to refer to objects which you drink water out of. This is where *representation* comes in. Representation is the production of the meaning of the concepts in our minds through language. It is the link between concepts and language which enables us to *refer to* either the 'real' world of objects, people or events, or indeed to imaginary worlds of fictional objects, people and events.

So there are *two* processes, two **systems of representation**, involved. First, there is the 'system' by which all sorts of objects, people and events are correlated with a set of concepts or *mental representations* which we carry around in our heads. Without them, we could not interpret the world meaningfully at all. In the first place, then, meaning depends on the system of concepts and images formed in our thoughts which can stand for or 'represent' the world, enabling us to refer to things both inside and outside our heads.

Before we move on to look at the second 'system of representation', we should observe that what we have just said is a very simple version of a rather complex process. It is simple enough to see how we might form concepts for things we can perceive – people or material objects, like chairs, tables and desks. But we also form concepts of rather obscure and abstract things, which we can't in any simple way see, feel or touch. Think, for example, of our concepts of war, or death, or friendship or love. And, as we have remarked, we also form concepts about things we never have seen, and possibly can't or won't ever see, and about people and places we have plainly made up. We may have a clear concept of, say, angels, mermaids, God, the Devil, or of Heaven and Hell, or of Middlemarch (the fictional provincial town in George Eliot's novel), or of Elizabeth (the heroine of Jane Austen's *Pride and Prejudice*).

We have called this a '*system* of representation'. That is because it consists, not of individual concepts, but of different ways of organizing, clustering, arranging and classifying concepts, and of establishing complex relations between them. For example, we use the principles of similarity and difference to establish relationships between concepts or to distinguish them from one another. Thus I have an idea that in some respects birds are like planes in the sky, based on the fact that they are similar because they both fly – but I also have an idea that in other respects they are different, because one is part of nature whilst the other is man-made. This mixing and matching of relations between concepts to form complex ideas and thoughts is possible because our concepts are arranged into different classifying systems. In this example, the first is based on a distinction between flying/not flying and the second is based on the distinction between natural/man-made. There are other principles of organization like this at work in all conceptual systems: for example, classifying according to sequence – which concept follows which – or causality – what causes what – and so on. The point here is that we are talking about, not just a random collection of concepts, but concepts organized, arranged and classified into complex relations with one another. That is what our conceptual system actually is like. However, this does not undermine the basic point. Meaning depends on the relationship between things in the world – people, objects and events, real or fictional – and the conceptual system, which can operate as *mental representations* of them.

Now it could be the case that the conceptual map which I carry around in my head is totally different from yours, in which case you and I would interpret or make sense of the world in totally different ways. We would be incapable of sharing our thoughts or expressing ideas about the world to each other. In fact, each of us probably does understand and interpret the world in a unique and individual way. However, we are able to communicate because we share broadly the same conceptual maps and thus make sense of or interpret the world in roughly similar ways. That is indeed what it means when we say we 'belong to the same culture'. Because we interpret the world in roughly similar ways, we are able to build up a shared culture of meanings and thus construct a social world which we inhabit together. That is why 'culture' is sometimes defined in terms of 'shared meanings or shared conceptual maps [see du Gay, Hall et al., 1997)

However, a shared conceptual map is not enough. We must also be able to represent or exchange meanings and concepts, and we can only do that when we also have access to a shared language. Language is therefore the second system of representation involved in the overall process of constructing meaning. Our shared conceptual map must be translated into a common language, so that we can correlate our concepts and ideas with certain written words, spoken sounds or visual images. The general term we use for words, sounds or images which carry meaning is *signs*. These signs stand for or represent the concepts and the conceptual relations between them which we carry around in our heads and together they make up the meaning-systems of our culture.

Signs are organized into languages and it is the existence of common languages which enable us to translate our thoughts (concepts) into words, sounds or images, and then to use these, operating as a language, to express meanings and communicate thoughts to other people. Remember that the term 'language' is being used here in a very broad and inclusive way. The writing system or the spoken system of a particular language are both obviously 'languages'. But so are visual images, whether produced by hand, mechanical, electronic, digital or some other means, when they are used to express meaning. And so are other things which aren't 'linguistic' in any ordinary sense: the 'language' of facial expressions or of gesture, for example, or the 'language' of fashion, of clothes, or of traffic lights. Even music is a 'language', with complex relations between different sounds and chords, though it is a very special case since it can't easily be used to reference actual things or objects in the world (a point further elaborated in du Gay, ed., 1997, and Mackay, ed., 1997). Any sound, word, image or object which functions as a sign, and is organized with other signs into a system which is capable of carrying and expressing meaning is, from this point of view, 'a language'. It is in this sense that the model of meaning which I have been analysing here is often described as a 'linguistic' one; and that all the theories of meaning which follow this basic model are described as belonging to 'the linguistic turn' in the social sciences and cultural studies.

At the heart of the meaning process in culture, then, are two related 'systems of representation'. The first enables us to give meaning to the world by constructing a set of correspondences or a chain of equivalences between things – people, objects, events, abstract ideas, etc. – and our system of concepts, our conceptual maps. The second depends on constructing a set of correspondences between our conceptual map and a set of signs, arranged or organized into various languages which stand for or represent those concepts. The relation between 'things', concepts and signs lies at the heart of the production of meaning in language. The process which links these three elements together is what we call 'representation'.

Language and Representation

Just as people who belong to the same culture must share a broadly similar conceptual map, so they must also share the same way of interpreting the signs of a language, for only in this way can meanings be effectively exchanged between people. But how do we know which concept stands for which thing? Or which word effectively represents which concept? How do I know which sounds or images will carry, through language, the meaning of my concepts and what I want to say with them to you? This may seem relatively simple in the case of visual signs, because the drawing, painting, camera or TV image of a sheep bears a resemblance to the animal with a woolly coat grazing in a field to which I want to refer. Even so, we need to remind ourselves that a drawn or painted or digital version of a sheep is not exactly like a 'real' sheep. For one thing, most images are in two dimensions whereas the 'real' sheep exists in three dimensions.

Visual signs and images, even when they bear a close resemblance to the things to which they refer, are still signs: they carry meaning and thus have to be interpreted. In order to interpret them, we must have access to the two systems of representation discussed earlier: to a conceptual map which correlates the sheep in the field with the concept of a 'sheep'; and a language system which in visual language, bears some resemblance to the real thing or 'looks like it' in some way. This argument is clearest if we think of a cartoon drawing or an abstract painting of a 'sheep', where we need a very sophisticated conceptual and shared linguistic system to be certain that we are all 'reading' the sign in the same way. Even then we may find ourselves wondering whether it really is a picture of a sheep at all. As the relationship between the sign and its referent becomes less clear-cut, the meaning begins to slip and slide away from us into uncertainty. Meaning is no longer transparently passing from one person to another . . .

So, even in the case of visual language, where the relationship between the concept and the sign seems fairly straightforward, the matter is far from simple. It is even more difficult with written or spoken language, where words don't look or sound anything like the things to which they refer. In part, this is because there are different kinds of signs. Visual signs are what are called *iconic* signs. That is, they bear, in their form, a certain resemblance to the object, person or event to which they refer. A photograph of a tree reproduces some of the actual conditions of our visual perception in the visual sign. Written or spoken signs, on the other hand, are what is called *indexical*.

They bear no obvious relationship at all to the things to which they refer. The letters T,R,E,E, do not look anything like trees in Nature, nor does the word 'tree' in English sound like 'real' trees (if indeed they make any sound at all!). The relationship in these systems of representation between the sign, the concept and the object to which they might be used to refer is entirely *arbitrary*. By 'arbitrary' we mean that in principle any collection of letters or any sound in any order would do the trick equally well. Trees would not mind if we used the word SEERT – 'trees' written backwards – to represent the concept of them. This is clear from the fact that, in French, quite different letters and a quite different sound is used to refer to what, to all appearances, is the same thing – a 'real' tree – and, as far as we can tell, to the same concept – a large plant that grows in nature. The French and English seem to be using the same concept. But the concept which in English is represented by the word, TREE, is represented in French by the word, ARBRE.

Sharing the Codes

The question, then, is: how do people who belong to the same culture, who share the same conceptual map and who speak or write the same language (English) know that the arbitrary combination of letters and sounds that makes up the word, TREE, will stand for or represent the concept 'a large plant that grows in nature'? One possibility would be that the objects in the world themselves embody and fix in some way their 'true' meaning. But it is not at all clear that real trees *know* that they are trees, and even less clear that they know that the word in English which represents the concept of themselves is written TREE whereas in French it is written ARBRE! As far as they are concerned, it could just as well be written COW or VACHE or indeed XYZ. The meaning is *not* in the object or person or thing, nor is it *in* the word. It is we who fix the meaning so firmly that, after a while, it comes to seem natural and inevitable. The meaning is *constructed by the system of representation*. It is constructed and fixed by the *code*, which sets up the correlation between our conceptual system and our language system in such a way that, every time we think of a tree, the code tells us to use the English word TREE, or the French word ARBRE. The code tells us that, in our culture – that is, in our conceptual and language codes – the concept 'tree' is represented by the letters T,R,E,E, arranged in a certain sequence, just as in Morse code, the sign for V (which in World War II Churchill made 'stand for' or represent 'Victory') is Dot, Dot, Dot, Dash, and in the 'language of traffic lights', Green = Go! and Red = Stop!

One way of thinking about 'culture', then, is in terms of these shared conceptual maps, shared language systems and the *codes which govern the relationships of translation between them*. Codes fix the relationships between concepts and signs. They stabilize meaning within different languages and cultures. They tell us which language to use to convey which idea. The reverse is also true. Codes tell us which concepts are being referred to when we hear or read which signs. By arbitrarily fixing the relationships between our conceptual system and our linguistic systems (remember, 'linguistic' in a broad sense), codes make it possible for us to speak and to hear intelligibly, and establish the translatability between our concepts and our languages which enables meaning to pass from speaker to hearer and be effectively communicated within a culture. This translatability is not given by nature or fixed by the gods. It is the result of a set of social conventions. It is fixed socially, fixed in culture. English or French or Hindi speakers have, over time, and without conscious decision or choice, come to an unwritten agreement, a sort of unwritten cultural covenant that, in their various languages, certain signs will stand for or represent certain concepts. This is what children learn, and how they become, not simply biological individuals but cultural

subjects. They learn the system and conventions of representation, the codes of their language and culture, which equip them with cultural 'know-how' enabling them to function as culturally competent subjects. Not because such knowledge is imprinted in their genes, but because they learn its conventions and so gradually *become* 'cultured persons' – i.e. members of their culture. They unconsciously internalize the codes which allow them to express certain concepts and ideas through their systems of representation – writing, speech, gesture, visualization, and so on – and to interpret ideas which are communicated to them using the same systems.

You may find it easier to understand, now, why meaning, language and representation are such critical elements in the study of culture. To belong to a culture is to belong to roughly the same conceptual and linguistic universe, to know how concepts and ideas translate into different languages, and how language can be interpreted to refer to or *reference* the world. To share these things is to see the world from within the same conceptual map and to make sense of it through the same language systems. Early anthropologists of language, like Sapir and Whorf, took this insight to its logical extreme when they argued that we are all, as it were, locked into our cultural perspectives or 'mind-sets', and that language is the best clue we have to that conceptual universe. This observation, when applied to all human cultures, lies at the root of what, today, we may think of as cultural or linguistic *relativism*.

You might like to think further about this question of how different cultures conceptually classify the world and what implications this has for meaning and representation. The English make a rather simple distinction between sleet and snow. The Inuit (Eskimos) who have to survive in a very different, more extreme and hostile climate, apparently have many more words for snow and snowy weather. There are many more than in English, making much finer and more complex distinctions. The Inuit have a complex classificatory conceptual system for the weather compared with the English. The novelist Peter Hoeg, for example, writing about Greenland in his novel, *Miss Smilla's Feeling For Snow* (1994, pp. 5–6), graphically describes 'frazzil ice' which is 'kneaded together into a soapy mash called porridge ice, which gradually forms free-floating plates, pancake ice, which one, cold, noonday hour, on a Sunday, freezes into a single solid sheet'. Such distinctions are too fine and elaborate even for the English who are always talking about the weather! The question, however, is – do the Inuit actually experience snow differently from the English? Their language system suggests they conceptualize the weather differently. But how far is our experience actually bounded by our linguistic and conceptual universe?

One implication of this argument about cultural codes is that, if meaning is the result, not of something fixed out there, in nature, but of our social, cultural and linguistic conventions, then meaning can never be *finally* fixed. We can all 'agree' to allow words to carry somewhat different meanings – as we have for example, with the word 'gay', or the use, by young people, of the word 'wicked!' as a term of approval. Of course, there must be *some* fixing of meaning in language, or we would never be able to understand one another. We can't get up one morning and suddenly decide to represent the concept of a 'tree' with the letters or the word VYXZ, and expect people to follow what we are saying. On the other hand, there is no absolute or final fixing of meaning. Social and linguistic conventions do change over time. In the language of modern managerialism, what we used to call 'students', 'clients', 'patients' and 'passengers' have all become 'customers'. Linguistic codes vary significantly between one language and another. Many cultures do not have words for concepts which are normal and widely acceptable to us. Words constantly go out of common usage, and new phrases are coined: think, for example, of the use of 'downsizing' to represent the process of firms laying people off work. Even when the actual words remain stable, their connotations shift or they acquire a different nuance. The problem is especially acute in translation. For example, does the difference in English between *know* and *understand* correspond exactly to and capture exactly the same conceptual distinction as the French make between *savoir* and *connaitre*? Perhaps; but can we be sure?

The main point is that meaning does not inhere *in* things, in the world. It is constructed, produced. It is the result of a signifying practice – a practice that *produces* meaning, that *makes things mean*.

Theories of Representation

There are broadly speaking three approaches to explaining how representation of meaning through language works. We may call these the reflective, the intentional and the constructionist or constructivist approaches. You might think of each as an attempt to answer the questions, 'where do meanings come from?' and 'how can we tell the "true" meaning of a word or image?'

In the reflective approach, meaning is thought to lie in the object, person, idea or event in the real world, and language functions like a mirror, to *reflect* the true meaning as it already exists in the world. As the poet Gertrude Stein once said, 'A rose is a rose is a rose'. In the fourth century BC, the Greeks used the notion of *mimesis* to explain how language, even drawing and painting, mirrored or imitated Nature; they thought of Homer's great poem, *The Iliad*, as 'imitating' a heroic series of events. So the theory which says that language works by simply reflecting or imitating the truth that is already there and fixed in the world, is sometimes called 'mimetic'.

Of course there is a certain obvious truth to mimetic theories of representation and language. As we've pointed out, visual signs do bear some relationship to the shape and texture of the objects which they represent. But, as was also pointed out earlier, a two-dimensional visual image of a *rose* is a sign – it should not be confused with the real plant with thorns and blooms growing in the garden. Remember also that there are many words, sounds and images which we fully well understand but which are entirely fictional or fantasy and refer to worlds which are wholly imaginary – including, many people now think, most of *The Iliad*! Of course, I can use the word 'rose' to *refer* to real, actual plants growing in a garden, as we have said before. But this is because I know the code which links the concept with a particular word or image. I cannot *think* or *speak* or *draw* with an actual rose. And if someone says to me that there is no such word as 'rose' for a plant in her culture, the actual plant in the garden cannot resolve the failure of communication between us. Within the conventions of the different language codes we are using, we are both right – and for us to understand each other, one of us must learn the code linking the flower with the word for it in the other's culture.

The second approach to meaning in representation argues the opposite case. It holds that it is the speaker, the author, who imposes his or her unique meaning on the world through language. Words mean what the author intends they should mean. This is the **intentional approach**. Again, there is some point to this argument since we all, as individuals, do use language to convey or communicate things which are special or unique to us, to our way of seeing the world. However, as a general theory of representation through language, the intentional approach is also flawed. We cannot be the sole or unique source of meanings in language, since that would mean that we could express ourselves in entirely private languages. But the essence of language is communication and that, in turn, depends on shared linguistic conventions and shared codes. Language can never be wholly a private game. Our private intended meanings, however personal to us, have to *enter into the rules, codes and conventions of language* to be shared and understood. Language is a social system through and through. This means that our private thoughts have to negotiate with all the other meanings for words or images which have been stored in language which our use of the language system will inevitably trigger into action.

The third approach recognizes this public, social character of language. It acknowledges that neither things in themselves nor the individual users of language can fix meaning in language. Things don't *mean*: we *construct* meaning, using representational systems – concepts and signs. Hence it is called the constructivist or **constructionist approach** to meaning in language. According to this approach, we must not confuse the *material* world, where things and people exist, and the *symbolic* practices and processes through which representation, meaning and language operate. Constructivists do not deny the existence of the material world. However, it is not the material world which conveys meaning: it is the language system or whatever system we are using to represent our concepts. It is social actors who use the conceptual systems of their culture and the linguistic and other representational systems to construct meaning, to make the world meaningful and to communicate about that world meaningfully to others.

Of course, signs may also have a material dimension. Representational systems consist of the actual *sounds* we make with our vocal chords, the *images* we make on light-sensitive paper with cameras, the *marks* we make with paint on canvas, the digital *impulses* we transmit electronically. Representation is a practice, a kind of 'work', which uses material objects and effects. But the *meaning* depends, not on the material quality of the sign, but on its *symbolic function*. It is because a particular sound or word *stands for, symbolizes or represents* a concept that it can function, in language, as a sign and convey meaning – or, as the constructionists say, signify (sign-i-fy).

The Language of Traffic Lights

The simplest example of this point, which is critical for an understanding of how languages function as representational systems, is the famous traffic lights example. A traffic light is a machine which produces different coloured lights in sequence. The effect of light of different wavelengths on the eye – which is a natural and material phenomenon – produces the sensation of different colours. Now these things certainly do exist in the material world. But it is our culture which breaks the spectrum of light into different colours, distinguishes them from one another and attaches names – Red, Green, Yellow, Blue – to them. We use a way of *classifying* the colour spectrum to create colours which are different from one another. We *represent* or symbolize the different colours and classify them according to different colour-concepts. This is the conceptual colour system of our culture. We say 'our culture' because, of course, other cultures may divide the colour spectrum differently. What's more, they certainly use different actual *words* or *letters* to identify different colours: what we call 'red', the French call 'rouge' and so on. This is the linguistic code – the one which correlates certain words (signs) with certain colours (concepts), and thus enables us to communicate about colours to other people, using 'the language of colours'.

But how do we use this representational or symbolic system to regulate the traffic? Colours do not have any 'true' or fixed meaning in that sense. Red does not mean 'Stop' in nature, any more than Green means 'Go'. In other settings, Red may stand for, symbolize or represent 'Blood' or 'Danger' or 'Communism'; and Green may represent 'Ireland' or 'The Countryside' or 'Environmentalism'. Even these meanings can change. In the 'language of electric plugs', Red used to mean 'the connection with the positive charge' but this was arbitrarily and without explanation changed to Brown! But then for many years the producers of plugs had to attach a slip of paper telling people that the code or convention had changed, otherwise how would they know? Red and Green work in the language of traffic lights because 'Stop' and 'Go' are the meanings which have been assigned to them in our culture by the code or conventions governing this language, and this code is widely known and almost universally obeyed in our culture and cultures like ours – though we can well imagine other cultures which did not possess the code, in which this language would be a complete mystery.

Let us stay with the example for a moment, to explore a little further how, according to the constructionist approach to representation, colours and the 'language of traffic lights' work as a signifying or representational system. Recall the *two* representational systems we spoke of earlier. First, there is the conceptual map of colours in our culture – the way colours are distinguished from one another, classified and arranged in our mental universe. Secondly, there are the ways words or images are correlated with colours in our language – our linguistic colour-codes. Actually, of course, a *language* of colours consists of more than just the individual words for different points on the colour spectrum. It also depends on how they function in relation to one another – the sorts of things which are governed by grammar and syntax in written or spoken languages, which allow us to express rather complex ideas. In the language of traffic lights, it is the sequence and position of the colours, as well as the colours themselves, which enable them to carry meaning and thus function as signs.

Does it matter which colours we use? No, the constructionists argue. This is because what signifies is not the colours themselves but (a) the fact that they are different and can be distinguished from one another; and (b) the fact that they are organized into a particular sequence – Red followed by Green, with sometimes a warning Amber in between which says, in effect, 'Get ready! Lights about to change.' Constructionists put this point in the following way. What signifies, what carries meaning – they argue – is

not each colour in itself nor even the concept or word for it. It is *the difference between Red and Green* which signifies. This is a very important principle, in general, about representation and meaning. Think about it in these terms. If you couldn't differentiate between Red and Green, you couldn't use one to mean 'Stop' and the other to mean 'Go'. In the same way, it is only the difference between the letters P and T which enable the word SHEEP to be linked, in the English language code, to the concept of 'the animal with four legs and a woolly coat', and the word SHEET to 'the material we use to cover ourselves in bed at night'.

In principle, any combination of colours – like any collection of letters in written language or of sounds in spoken language – would do, provided they are sufficiently different not to be confused. Constructionists express this idea by saying that all signs are 'arbitrary'. 'Arbitrary' means that there is no natural relationship between the sign and its meaning or concept. Since Red only means 'Stop' because that is how the code works, in principle any colour would do, including Green. It is the code that fixes the meaning, not the colour itself. This also has wider implications for the theory of representation and meaning in language. It means that signs themselves cannot fix meaning. Instead, meaning depends on *the relation between* a sign and a concept which is fixed by a code. Meaning, the constructionists would say, is 'relational'. [. . .]

As we said earlier, traffic lights are machines, and colours are the material effect of light-waves on the retina of the eye. But objects – things – can also function as signs, provided they have been assigned a concept and meaning within our cultural and linguistic codes. As signs, they work symbolically – they represent concepts, and signify. Their effects, however, are felt in the material and social world. Red and Green function in the language of traffic lights as signs, but they have real material and social effects. They regulate the social behaviour of drivers and, without them, there would be many more traffic accidents at road intersections.

[. . .]

Representation is the production of meaning through language. In representation, constructionists argue, we use signs, organized into languages of different kinds, to communicate meaningfully with others. Languages can use signs to symbolize, stand for or reference objects, people and events in the so-called 'real' world. But they can also reference imaginary things and fantasy worlds or abstract ideas which are not in any obvious sense part of our material world. There is no simple relationship of reflection, imitation or one-to-one correspondence between language and the real world. The world is not accurately or otherwise reflected in the mirror of language. Language does not work like a mirror. Meaning is produced within language, in and through various representational systems which, for convenience, we call 'languages'. Meaning is produced by the practice, the 'work', of representation. It is constructed through signifying – i.e. meaning-producing – practices.

How does this take place? In fact, it depends on two different but related systems of representation. First, the concepts which are formed in the mind function as a system of mental representation which classifies and organizes the world into meaningful categories. If we have a concept for something, we can say we know its 'meaning'. But we cannot communicate this meaning without a second system of representation, a language. Language consists of signs organized into various relationships. But signs can only convey meaning if we possess codes which allow us to translate our concepts into language – and vice versa. These codes are crucial for meaning and representation. They do not exist in nature but are the result of social conventions. They are a crucial part of our culture – our shared 'maps of meaning' – which we learn and unconsciously internalize as we become members of our culture. This constructionist approach to language thus introduces the symbolic domain of life, where words and things function as signs, into the very heart of social life itself.

[. . .]

Saussure's Legacy

The social constructionist view of language and representation which we have been discussing owes a great deal to the work and influence of the Swiss linguist, Saussure, who was born in Geneva in 1857, did much of his work in Paris, and died in 1913. He is known as the 'father of modern linguistics'. For our purposes, his importance lies, not in his detailed work in linguistics, but in his general view of representation and the way his model of language shaped the

semiotic approach to the problem of representation in a wide variety of cultural fields. You will recognize much about Saussure's thinking from what we have already said about the *constructionist* approach.

For Saussure, according to Jonathan Culler (1976, p. 19), the production of meaning depends on language: 'Language is a system of signs.' Sounds, images, written words, paintings, photographs, etc. function as signs within language 'only when they serve to express or communicate ideas … [To] communicate ideas, they must be part of a system of conventions …' (ibid.). Material objects can function as signs and communicate meaning too, as we saw from the 'language of traffic lights' example. In an important move, Saussure analysed the **sign** into two further elements. There was, he argued, the *form* (the actual word, image, photo, etc.), and there was the *idea or concept* in your head with which the form was associated. Saussure called the first element, the **signifier**, and the second element – the corresponding concept it triggered off in your head – the **signified**. Every time you hear or read or see the *signifier* (e.g. the word or image of a *Walkman*, for example), it correlates with the *signified* (the concept of a portable cassette-player in your head). Both are required to produce meaning but it is the relation between them, fixed by our cultural and linguistic codes, which sustains representation. Thus 'the sign is the union of a form which signifies (*signifier*) … and an idea signified (*signified*). Though we may speak . . . as if they are separate entities, they exist only as components of the sign … (which is) the central fact of language' (Culler, 1976, p. 19).

Saussure also insisted on what in section 1 we called the arbitrary nature of the sign: 'There is no natural or inevitable link between the signifier and the signified' (ibid.). Signs do not possess a fixed or essential meaning. What signifies, according to Saussure, is not RED or the essence of 'red-ness', but *the difference between RED and GREEN*. Signs, Saussure argued 'are members of a system and are defined in relation to the other members of that system.' For example, it is hard to define the meaning of FATHER except in relation to, and in terms of its difference from, other kinship terms, like MOTHER, DAUGHTER, SON and so on.

This marking of difference within language is fundamental to the production of meaning, according to Saussure. Even at a simple level (to repeat an earlier example), we must be able to distinguish, within language, between SHEEP and SHEET, before we can link one of those words to the concept of an animal that produces wool, and the other to the concept of a cloth that covers a bed. The simplest way of marking difference is, of course, by means of a binary opposition – in this example, all the letters are the same except P and T. Similarly, the meaning of a concept or word is often defined in relation to its direct opposite – as in night/day. Later critics of Saussure were to observe that binaries (e.g. *black/white*) are only one, rather simplistic, way of establishing difference. As well as the stark difference between *black* and *white*, there are also the many other, subtler differences between *black* and *dark grey, dark grey* and *light grey, grey* and *cream* and *off-white, off-white* and *brilliant white*, just as there are between *night, dawn, daylight, noon, dusk*, and so on. However, his attention to binary oppositions brought Saussure to the revolutionary proposition that a language consists of signifiers, but in order to produce meaning, the signifiers have to be organized into 'a system of differences'. It is the differences between signifiers which signify.

Furthermore, the relation between the *signifier* and the *signified*, which is fixed by our cultural codes, is not – Saussure argued – permanently fixed. Words shift their meanings. The concepts (signifieds) to which they refer also change, historically, and every shift alters the conceptual map of the culture, leading different cultures, at different historical moments, to classify and think about the world differently. For many centuries, western societies have associated the word BLACK with everything that is dark, evil, forbidding, devilish, dangerous and sinful. And yet, think of how the perception of black people in America in the 1960s changed after the phrase 'Black is Beautiful' became a popular slogan – where the *signifier*, BLACK, was made to signify the exact opposite meaning (*signified*) to its previous associations. In Saussure's terms, 'Language sets up an arbitrary relation between signifiers of its own choosing on the one hand, and signifieds of its own choosing on the other. Not only does each language produce a different set of signifiers, articulating and dividing the continuum of sound (or writing or drawing or photography) in a distinctive way; each language produces a different set of signifieds; it has a distinctive and thus arbitrary way of

organizing the world into concepts and categories' (Culler, 1976, p. 23).

The implications of this argument are very far-reaching for a theory of representation and for our understanding of culture. If the relationship between a signifier and its signified is the result of a system of social conventions specific to each society and to specific historical moments – then all meanings are produced within history and culture. They can never be finally fixed but are always subject to change, both from one cultural context and from one period to another. There is thus no single, unchanging, universal 'true meaning'. 'Because it is arbitrary, the sign is totally subject to history and the combination at the particular moment of a given signifier and signified is a contingent result of the historical process' (Culler, 1976, p. 36). This opens up meaning and representation, in a radical way, to history and change. It is true that Saussure himself focused exclusively on the state of the language system at one moment of time rather than looking at linguistic change over time. However, for our purposes, the important point is the way this approach to language *unfixes* meaning, breaking any natural and inevitable tie between signifier and signified. This opens representation to the constant 'play' or slippage of meaning, to the constant production of new meanings, new interpretations.

However, if meaning changes, historically, and is never finally fixed, then it follows that 'taking the meaning' must involve an active process of interpretation. Meaning has to be actively 'read' or 'interpreted'. Consequently, there is a necessary and inevitable imprecision about language. The meaning we take, as viewers, readers or audiences, is never exactly the meaning which has been given by the speaker or writer or by other viewers. And since, in order to say something meaningful, we have to 'enter language', where all sorts of older meanings which pre-date us, are already stored from previous eras, we can never cleanse language completely, screening out all the other, hidden meanings which might modify or distort what we want to say. For example, we can't entirely prevent some of the negative connotations of the word BLACK from returning to mind when we read a headline like, 'WEDNESDAY – A BLACK DAY ON THE STOCK EXCHANGE', even if this was not intended. There is a constant *sliding of meaning* in all interpretation, a margin – something in excess of what we intend to say – in which other meanings overshadow the statement or the text, where other associations are awakened to life, giving what we say a different twist. So interpretation becomes an essential aspect of the process by which meaning is given and taken. The *reader* is as important as the *writer* in the production of meaning. Every signifier given or encoded with meaning has to be meaningfully interpreted or decoded by the receiver (Hall, 1980). Signs which have not been intelligibly received and interpreted are not, in any useful sense, 'meaningful'.

The Social Part of Language

Saussure divided language into two parts. The first consisted of the general rules and codes of the linguistic system, which all its users must share, if it is to be of use as a means of communication. The rules are the principles which we learn when we learn a language and they enable us to use language to say whatever we want. For example, in English, the preferred word order is subject-verb-object ('the cat sat on the mat'), whereas in Latin, the verb usually comes at the end. Saussure called this underlying rule-governed structure of language, which enables us to produce well-formed sentences, the **langue** (the language system). The second part consisted of the particular acts of speaking or writing or drawing, which – using the structure and rules of the *langue* – are produced by an actual speaker or writer. He called this **parole**. '*La langue* is the system of language, the language as a system of forms, whereas *parole* is actual speech [or writing], the speech acts which are made possible by the language' (Culler, 1976, p. 29).

For Saussure, the underlying structure of rules and codes (*langue*) was the social part of language, the part which could be studied with the law-like precision of a science because of its closed, limited nature. It was his preference for studying language at this level of its 'deep structure' which made people call Saussure and his model of language, **structuralist**. The second part of language, the individual speech-act or utterance (*parole*), he regarded as the 'surface' of language. There were an infinite number of such possible utterances. Hence, *parole* inevitably lacked those structural properties – forming a closed and limited set – which would

have enabled us to study it 'scientifically'. What made Saussure's model appeal to many later scholars was the fact that the closed, structured character of language at the level of its rules and laws, which, according to Saussure, enabled it to be studied scientifically, was combined with the capacity to be free and unpredictably creative in our actual speech acts. They believed he had offered them, at last, a scientific approach to that least scientific object of inquiry – culture.

In separating the social part of language (*langue*) from the individual act of communication (*parole*), Saussure broke with our common-sense notion of how language works. Our common-sense intuition is that language comes from within us – from the individual speaker or writer; that it is this speaking or writing subject who is the author or originator of meaning. This is what we called, earlier, the *intentional* model of representation. But according to Saussure's schema, each authored statement only becomes possible because the 'author' shares with other language-users the common rules and codes of the language system – the *langue* – which allows them to communicate with each other meaningfully. The author decides what she wants to say. But she cannot 'decide' whether or not to use the rules of language, if she wants to be understood. We are born into a language, its codes and its meanings. Language is therefore, for Saussure, a social phenomenon. It cannot be an individual matter because we cannot make up the rules of language individually, for ourselves. Their source lies in society, in the culture, in our shared cultural codes, in the language system – not in nature or in the individual subject.

[. . .]

Critique of Saussure's Model

Saussure's great achievement was to force us to focus on language itself, as a social fact; on the process of representation itself; on how language actually works and the role it plays in the production of meaning. In doing so, he saved language from the status of a mere transparent medium between *things* and *meaning*. He showed, instead, that representation was a practice. However, in his own work, he tended to focus almost exclusively on the two aspects of the sign – *signifier* and *signified*. He gave little or no attention to how this relation between *signifier/signified* could serve the purpose of what earlier we called *reference* – i.e. referring us to the world of things, people and events outside language in the 'real' world. Later linguists made a distinction between, say, the meaning of the word BOOK and the use of the word to refer to a *specific* book lying before us on the table. The linguist, Charles Sanders Pierce, whilst adopting a similar approach to Saussure, paid greater attention to the relationship between signifiers/signifieds and what he called their *referents*. What Saussure called significa-tion really involves *both* meaning and reference, but he focused mainly on the former.

Another problem is that Saussure tended to focus on the *formal* aspects of language – how language actually works. This has the great advantage of making us examine representation as a practice worthy of detailed study in its own right. It forces us to look at language for itself, and not just as an empty, transpar-ent, 'window on the world'. However, Saussure's focus on language may have been too exclusive. The atten-tion to its formal aspects did divert attention away from the more interactive and dialogic features of language – language as it is actually used, as it functions in actual situations, in dialogue between different kinds of speak-ers. It is thus not surprising that, for Saussure, questions of *power* in language – for example, between speakers of different status and positions – did not arise.

As has often been the case, the 'scientific' dream which lay behind the structuralist impulse of his work, though influential in alerting us to certain aspects of how language works, proved to be illusory. Language is *not* an object which can be studied with the law-like precision of a science. Later cultural theorists learned from Saussure's 'structuralism' but abandoned its sci-entific premise. Language remains rule-governed. But it is not a 'closed' system which can be reduced to its formal elements. Since it is constantly changing, it is by definition *open-ended*. Meaning continues to be produced through language in forms which can never be predicted beforehand and its 'sliding', as we described it above, cannot be halted. Saussure may have been tempted to the former view because, like a good structuralist, he tended to study the state of the language system at one moment, as if it had stood still, and he could halt the flow of language-change. Nevertheless it is the case that many of those who have been most influenced by Saussure's radical

break with all reflective and intentional models of representation, have built on his work, not by imitating his scientific and 'structuralist' approach, but by applying his model in a much looser, more open-ended – i.e. 'post-structuralist' – way.

[. . .]

From Language to Culture: Linguistics to Semiotics

Saussure's main contribution was to the study of lin-guistics in a narrow sense. However, since his death, his theories have been widely deployed, as a founda-tion for a general approach to language and meaning, providing a model of representation which has been applied to a wide range of cultural objects and prac-tices. Saussure himself foresaw this possibility in his famous lecture-notes, collected posthumously by his students as the *Course in General Linguistics* (1960), where he looked forward to 'A science that studies the life of signs within society . . . I shall call it semiology, from the Greek *semeion* "signs" . . .' (p. 16). This general approach to the study of signs in culture, and of cul-ture as a sort of 'language', which Saussure foreshad-owed, is now generally known by the term semiotics.

The underlying argument behind the semiotic approach is that, since all cultural objects convey meaning, and all cultural practices depend on mean-ing, they must make use of signs; and in so far as they do, they must work like language works, and be ame-nable to an analysis which basically makes use of Saussure's linguistic concepts (e.g. the signifier/signi-fied and *langue/parole* distinctions, his idea of underly-ing codes and structures, and the arbitrary nature of the sign). Thus, when in his collection of essays, *Mythologies* (1972), the French critic, Roland Barthes, studied 'The world of wrestling', 'Soap powders and detergents', 'The face of Greta Garbo' or 'The *Blue Guides* to Europe', he brought a *semiotic* approach to bear on 'reading' popular culture, treating these activi-ties and objects as signs, as a language through which meaning is communicated. For example, most of us would think of a wrestling match as a competitive game or sport designed for one wrestler to gain victory over an opponent. Barthes, however, asks, not 'Who won?' but 'What is the meaning of this event?' He treats it as a *text* to be *read*. He 'reads' the exaggerated gestures of wrestlers as a grandiloquent language of what he calls the pure spectacle of excess.

In much the same way, the French anthropologist, Claude Lévi-Strauss, studied the customs, rituals, totemic objects, designs, myths and folk-tales of so-called 'primitive' peoples in Brazil, not by analysing how these things were produced and used in the context of daily life amongst the Amazonian peoples, but in terms of what they were trying to 'say', what messages about the culture they communicated. He analysed their meaning, not by interpreting their content, but by looking at the underlying rules and codes through which such objects or practices produced meaning and, in doing so, he was making a classic Saussurean or structuralist 'move', from the *paroles* of a culture to the underlying structure, its *langue*. To undertake this kind of work, in studying the meaning of a television programme like *Eastenders*, for example, we would have to treat the pictures on the screen as signifiers, and use the code of the television soap opera as a *genre*, to discover how each image on the screen made use of these rules to 'say something' (signifieds) which the viewer could 'read' or interpret within the formal framework of a particular kind of television narrative.

In the semiotic approach, not only words and images but objects themselves can function as signifiers in the production of meaning. Clothes, for example, may have a simple physical function – to cover the body and protect it from the weather. But clothes also double up as signs. They construct a meaning and carry a message. An evening dress may signify 'elegance'; a bow tie and tails, 'formality'; jeans and trainers, 'casual dress'; a certain kind of sweater in the right setting, 'a long, romantic, autumn walk in the wood' (Barthes, 1967). These signs enable clothes to convey meaning and to function like a language – 'the language of fashion'.

The clothes themselves are the *signifiers*. The fashion code in western consumer cultures like ours correlates particular kinds or combinations of clothing with certain concepts ('elegance', 'formality', 'casualness', 'romance'). These are the *signifieds*. This coding converts the clothes into *signs*, which can then be read as a language. In the language of fashion, the signifiers are arranged in a certain sequence, in certain relations to one another. Relations may be of similarity – certain items 'go together' (e.g. casual shoes with jeans). Differences are also marked – no leather belts with evening wear. Some signs actually create meaning by exploiting 'difference': e.g. Doc Marten boots with flowing long skirt. These bits of clothing 'say something' – they convey meaning. Of course, not everybody reads fashion in the same way. There are differences of gender, age, class, 'race'. But all those who share the same fashion code will interpret the signs in roughly the same ways. 'Oh, jeans don't look right for that event. It's a formal occasion – it demands something more elegant.'

You may have noticed that, in this example, we have moved from the very narrow linguistic level from which we drew examples in the first section, to a wider, cultural level. Note, also, that two linked operations are required to complete the representation process by which meaning is produced. First, we need a basic *code* which links a particular piece of material which is cut and sewn in a particular way (*signifier*) to our mental concept of it (*signified*) – say a particular cut of material to our concept of 'a dress' or 'jeans'. (Remember that only some cultures would 'read' the signifier in this way, or indeed possess the concept of (i.e. have classified clothes into) 'a dress', as different from 'jeans'.) The combination of signifier and signified is what Saussure called a *sign*. Then, having recognized the material as a dress, or as jeans, and produced a sign, we can progress to a second, wider level, which links these signs to broader, cultural themes, concepts or meanings – for example, an evening dress to 'formality' or 'elegance', jeans to 'casualness'. Barthes called the first, descriptive level, the level of **denotation**: the second level, that of **connotation**. Both, of course, require the use of codes.

Denotation is the simple, basic, descriptive level, where consensus is wide and most people would agree on the meaning ('dress', 'jeans'). At the second level – *connotation* – these signifiers which we have been able to 'decode' at a simple level by using our conventional conceptual classifications of dress to read their meaning, enter a wider, second kind of code – 'the language of fashion' – which connects them to broader themes and meanings, linking them with what we may call the wider *semantic fields* of our culture: ideas of 'elegance', 'formality', 'casualness' and 'romance'. This second, wider meaning is no longer a descriptive level of obvious interpretation. Here we are beginning to interpret the completed signs in terms of the wider realms of social ideology – the general beliefs, conceptual frameworks and value systems of society. This second level of signification, Barthes suggests, is more 'general, global and diffuse ...'. It deals with 'fragments of an ideology ... These signifieds have a very close communication with culture, knowledge, history and it is through them, so to speak, that the environmental world [of the culture] invades the system [of representation]' (Barthes, 1967, pp. 91–2).

Myth Today

In his essay 'Myth today', in *Mythologies*, Barthes gives another example which helps us to see exactly how representation is working at this second, broader cultural level. Visiting the barbers' one day, Barthes is shown a copy of the French magazine *Paris Match*, which has on its cover a picture of 'a young Negro in a French uniform saluting with his eyes uplifted, probably fixed on the fold of the tricolour' (the French flag) (1972b, p. 116). At the first level, to get any meaning at all, we need to decode each of the signifiers in the image into their appropriate concepts: e.g. a soldier, a uniform, an arm raised, eyes lifted, a French flag. This yields a set of signs with a simple, literal message or meaning: *a black soldier is giving the French flag a salute* (denotation). However, Barthes argues that this image also has a wider, cultural meaning. If we ask, 'What is *Paris Match* telling us by using this picture of a black soldier saluting a French flag?', Barthes suggests that we may come up with the message: '*that France is a great Empire, and that all her sons, without any colour discrimination, faithfully serve under her flag, and that there is no better answer to the detractors of an alleged colonialism than the zeal shown by this Negro in serving his so-called oppressors*' (connotation) (ibid.).

Whatever you think of the actual 'message' which Barthes finds, for a proper semiotic analysis you must be able to outline precisely the different steps by which this broader meaning has been produced. Barthes argues that here representation takes place through two separate but linked processes. In the first, the signifiers (the elements of the image) and the signifieds (the concepts – soldier, flag and so on) unite to form a sign with a simple denoted message: *a black soldier is giving the French flag a salute*. At the second stage, this completed message or sign is linked to a second set of signifieds – a broad, ideological theme about French colonialism. The first, completed meaning functions as the signifier in the second stage of the representation process, and when linked with a wider theme by a reader, yields a second, more elaborate and ideologically framed message or meaning. Barthes gives this second concept or theme a name – he calls it 'a purposeful mixture of "French imperiality" and "militariness" '. This, he says, adds up to a 'message' about French colonialism and her faithful Negro soldier-sons. Barthes calls this second level of signification the level of *myth*. In this reading, he adds, 'French imperiality is the very drive behind the myth. The concept reconstitutes a chain of causes and effects, motives and intentions ... Through the concept ... a whole new history ... is implanted in the myth ... the concept of French imperiality ... is again tied to the totality of the world: to the general history of France, to its colonial adventures, to its present difficulties' (Barthes, 1972b, p. 119).

[...]

Discourse, Power and the Subject

What the examples above show is that the semiotic approach provides a method for analysing how visual representations convey meaning. Already, in Roland Barthes's work in the 1960s, as we have seen, Saussure's 'linguistic' model is developed through its application to a much wider field of signs and representations (advertising, photography, popular culture, travel, fashion, etc.). Also, there is less concern with how individual words function as signs in language, more about the application of the language model to a much broader set of cultural practices. Saussure held out the promise that the whole domain of meaning could, at last, be systematically mapped. Barthes, too, had a 'method', but his semiotic approach is much more loosely and interpretively applied; and, in his later work (for example, *The Pleasure of the Text*, 1975), he is more concerned with the 'play' of meaning and desire across texts than he is with the attempt to fix meaning by a scientific analysis of language's rules and laws.

Subsequently, as we observed, the project of a 'science of meaning' has appeared increasingly untenable. Meaning and representation seem to belong irrevocably to the interpretative side of the human and cultural sciences, whose subject matter – society, culture, the human subject – is not amenable to a positivistic approach (i.e. one which seeks to discover scientific laws about society). Later developments have recognized the necessarily interpretative nature of culture and the fact that interpretations never produce a final moment of absolute truth. Instead, interpretations are always followed by other interpretations, in an endless chain. As the French philosopher, Jacques Derrida, put it, writing always leads to more writing. Difference, he argued, can never be wholly captured within any binary system (Derrida, 1981). So any notion of a *final* meaning is always endlessly put off, deferred. Cultural studies of this interpretative kind, like other qualitative forms of sociological inquiry, are inevitably caught up in this 'circle of meaning'.

In the semiotic approach, representation was understood on the basis of the way words functioned as signs within language. But, for a start, in a culture, meaning often depends on larger units of analysis – narratives, statements, groups of images, whole discourses which operate across a variety of texts, areas of knowledge about a subject which have acquired widespread authority. Semiotics seemed to confine the process of representation to language, and to treat it as a closed, rather static, system. Subsequent developments became more concerned with representation as a source for the production of social *knowledge* – a more open system, connected in more intimate ways with social practices and questions of power. In the semiotic approach, the subject was displaced from the centre of language. Later theorists returned to the question of the subject, or at least to the empty space which Saussure's theory had left; without, of course, putting him/her back in the centre, as the author or source of meaning. Even if language, in some sense, 'spoke us' (as Saussure tended to argue) it was also important that in certain historical moments, some people had more power to speak about some subjects than others (male doctors about mad female patients in the late nineteenth century, for example, to take one of the key examples developed in the work of Michel Foucault). Models of

representation, these critics argued, ought to focus on these broader issues of knowledge and power.

Foucault used the word 'representation' in a narrower sense than we are using it here, but he is considered to have contributed to a novel and significant general approach to the problem of representation. What concerned him was the production of knowledge (rather than just meaning) through what he called **discourse** (rather than just language). His project, he said, was to analyse 'how human beings understand themselves in our culture' and how our knowledge about 'the social, the embodied individual and shared meanings' comes to be produced in different periods. With its emphasis on cultural understanding and shared meanings, you can see that Foucault's project was still to some degree indebted to Saussure and Barthes (see Dreyfus and Rabinow, 1982, p. 17) while in other ways departing radically from them. Foucault's work was much more historically grounded, more attentive to historical specificities, than the semiotic approach. As he said, 'relations of power, not relations of meaning' were his main concern. The particular objects of Foucault's attention were the various disciplines of knowledge in the human and social sciences – what he called 'the subjectifying social sciences'. These had acquired an increasingly prominent and influential role in modern culture and were, in many instances, considered to be the discourses which, like religion in earlier times, could give us the 'truth' about knowledge.

Here, we want to introduce Foucault and the *discursive* approach to representation by outlining three of his major ideas: his concept of *discourse*; the issue of *power and knowledge*; and the question of *the subject*. It might be useful, however, to start by giving you a general flavour, in Foucault's graphic (and somewhat over-stated) terms, of how he saw his project differing from that of the semiotic approach to representation. He moved away from an approach like that of Saussure and Barthes, based on 'the domain of signifying structure', towards one based on analysing what he called 'relations of force, strategic developments and tactics':

> Here I believe one's point of reference should not be to the great model of language (*langue*) and signs, but to that of war and battle. The history

which bears and determines us has the form of a war rather than that of a language: relations of power not relations of meaning . . .

(Foucault, 1980, pp. 114–15)

Rejecting both Hegelian Marxism (what he calls 'the dialectic') and semiotics, Foucault argued that:

> Neither the dialectic, as logic of contradictions, nor semiotics, as the structure of communication, can account for the intrinsic intelligibility of conflicts. 'Dialectic' is a way of evading the always open and hazardous reality of conflict by reducing it to a Hegelian skeleton, and 'semiology' is a way of avoiding its violent, bloody and lethal character by reducing it to the calm Platonic form of language and dialogue.

(ibid.)

From Language to Discourse

The first point to note, then, is the shift of attention in Foucault from 'language' to 'discourse'. He studied not language, but *discourse* as a system of representation. Normally, the term 'discourse' is used as a linguistic concept. It simply means passages of connected writing or speech. Michel Foucault, however, gave it a different meaning. What interested him were the rules and practices that produced meaningful statements and regulated discourse in different historical periods. By 'discourse', Foucault meant 'a group of statements which provide a language for talking about – a way of representing the knowledge about – a particular topic at a particular historical moment. . . . Discourse is about the production of knowledge through language. But . . . since all social practices entail *meaning*, and meanings shape and influence what we do – our conduct – all practices have a discursive aspect' (Hall, 1992, p. 291). It is important to note that the concept of *discourse* in this usage is not purely a 'linguistic' concept. It is about language *and* practice. It attempts to overcome the traditional distinction between what one *says* (language) and what one *does* (practice). Discourse, Foucault argues, constructs the topic. It defines and produces the objects of our knowledge. It governs the way that a topic can be meaningfully talked about and

reasoned about. It also influences how ideas are put into practice and used to regulate the conduct of others. Just as a discourse 'rules in' certain ways of talking about a topic, defining an acceptable and intelligible way to talk, write, or conduct oneself, so also, by definition, it 'rules out', limits and restricts other ways of talking, of conducting ourselves in relation to the topic or constructing knowledge about it. Discourse, Foucault argued, never consists of one statement, one text, one action or one source. The same discourse, characteristic of the way of thinking or the state of knowledge at any one time (what Foucault called the *episteme*), will appear across a range of texts, and as forms of conduct, at a number of different institutional sites within society. However, whenever these discursive events 'refer to the same object, share the same style and . . . support a strategy . . . a common institutional, administrative or political drift and pattern' (Cousins and Hussain, 1984, pp. 84–5), then they are said by Foucault to belong to the same **discursive formation**.

Meaning and meaningful practice is therefore constructed within discourse. Like the semioticians, Foucault was a 'constructionist'. However, unlike them, he was concerned with the production of knowledge and meaning, not through language but through discourse. There were therefore similarities, but also substantive differences between these two versions.

The idea that 'discourse produces the objects of knowledge' and that nothing which is meaningful exists *outside discourse*, is at first sight a disconcerting proposition, which seems to run right against the grain of common-sense thinking. It is worth spending a moment to explore this idea further. Is Foucault saying – as some of his critics have charged – that *nothing exists outside of discourse*? In fact, Foucault does *not* deny that things can have a real, material existence in the world. What he does argue is that '*nothing has any meaning outside of discourse*' (Foucault, 1972). As Laclau and Mouffe put it, 'we use [the term discourse] to emphasize the fact that every social configuration is *meaningful*' (1990, p. 100). The concept of discourse is not about whether things exist but about where meaning comes from.

This idea that physical things and actions exist, but they only take on meaning and become objects of knowledge within discourse, is at the heart of the *constructionist* theory of meaning and representation. Foucault argues that since we can only have a knowledge of things if they have a meaning, it is discourse – not the things-in-themselves – which produces knowledge. Subjects like 'madness', 'punishment' and 'sexuality' only exist meaningfully *within* the discourses about them. Thus, the study of the discourses of madness, punishment or sexuality would have to include the following elements:

1. statements about 'madness', 'punishment' or 'sexuality' which give us a certain kind of knowledge about these things;
2. the rules which prescribe certain ways of talking about these topics and exclude other ways – which govern what is 'sayable' or 'thinkable' about insanity, punishment or sexuality, at a particular historical moment;
3. 'subjects' who in some ways personify the discourse – the madman, the hysterical woman, the criminal, the deviant, the sexually perverse person; with the attributes we would expect these subjects to have, given the way knowledge about the topic was constructed at that time;
4. how this knowledge about the topic acquires authority, a sense of embodying the 'truth' about it; constituting the 'truth of the matter', at a historical moment;
5. the practices within institutions for dealing with the subjects – medical treatment for the insane, punishment regimes for the guilty, moral discipline for the sexually deviant – whose conduct is being regulated and organized according to those ideas;
6. acknowledgement that a different discourse or *episteme* will arise at a later historical moment, supplanting the existing one, opening up a new *discursive formation*, and producing, in its turn, new conceptions of 'madness' or 'punishment' or 'sexuality', new discourses with the power and authority, the 'truth', to regulate social practices in new ways.

Historicizing Discourse: Discursive Practices

The main point to get hold of here is the way discourse, representation, knowledge and 'truth' are radically *historicized* by Foucault, in contrast to the rather ahistorical tendency in semiotics. Things meant something and were 'true', he argued, *only within a specific historical context*. Foucault did not believe that the same phenomena would be found across different historical periods. He thought that, in each period, discourse produced forms of knowledge, objects, subjects and practices of knowledge, which differed radically from period to period, with no necessary continuity between them.

Thus, for Foucault, for example, mental illness was not an objective fact, which remained the same in all historical periods, and meant the same thing in all cultures. It was only *within* a definite discursive formation that the object, 'madness', could appear at all as a meaningful or intelligible construct. It was 'constituted by all that was said, in all the statements that named it, divided it up, described it, explained it, traced its development, indicated its various correlations, judged it, and possibly gave it speech by articulating, in its name, discourses that were to be taken as its own' (1972, p. 32). And it was only after a certain definition of 'madness' was put into practice, that the appropriate subject – 'the madman' as current medical and psychiatric knowledge defined 'him' – could appear.

Or, take some other examples of discursive practices from his work. There have always been sexual relations. But 'sexuality', as a specific way of talking about, studying and regulating sexual desire, its secrets and its fantasies, Foucault argued, only appeared in western societies at a particular historical moment (Foucault, 1978). There may always have been what we now call homosexual forms of behaviour. But 'the homosexual' as a specific kind of social subject, was *produced*, and could only make its appearance, within the moral, legal, medical and psychiatric discourses, practices and institutional apparatuses of the late nineteenth century, with their particular theories of sexual perversity (Weeks, 1981, 1985). Similarly, it makes nonsense to talk of the 'hysterical woman' outside of the nineteenth-century view of hysteria as a very widespread female malady. In *The Birth of the Clinic* (1973), Foucault charted how 'in less than half a century, the medical understanding of disease was transformed' from a classical notion that disease existed separate from the body, to the modern idea that disease arose within and could be mapped directly by its course through the human body (McNay, 1994). This discursive shift changed medical practice. It gave greater importance to the doctor's 'gaze' which could now 'read' the course of disease simply by a powerful look at what Foucault called 'the visible body' of the patient – following the 'routes . . . laid down in accordance with a now familiar geometry . . . the anatomical atlas' (Foucault, 1973, pp. 3–4). This greater knowledge increased the doctor's power of surveillance vis-à-vis the patient.

Knowledge about and practices around *all* these subjects, Foucault argued, were historically and culturally specific. They did not and could not meaningfully exist outside specific discourses, i.e. outside the ways they were represented in discourse, produced in knowledge and regulated by the discursive practices and disciplinary techniques of a particular society and time. Far from accepting the trans-historical continuities of which historians are so fond, Foucault believed that more significant were the radical breaks, ruptures and discontinuities between one period and another, between one discursive formation and another.

From Discourse to Power/Knowledge

In his later work Foucault became even more concerned with how knowledge was put to work through discursive practices in specific institutional settings to regulate the conduct of others. He focused on the relationship between knowledge and power, and how power operated within what he called an institutional *apparatus* and its *technologies* (techniques). Foucault's conception of the *apparatus* of punishment, for example, included a variety of diverse elements, linguistic and non-linguistic – 'discourses, institutions, architectural arrangements, regulations, laws, administrative measures, scientific statements, philosophic propositions, morality, philanthropy, etc. . . . The apparatus is thus always inscribed in a play of power, but it is also always linked to certain co-ordinates of knowledge. . . . This is what the apparatus consists in: strategies of relations of forces supporting and supported by types of knowledge' (Foucault, 1980b, pp. 194,196).

This approach took as one of its key subjects of investigation the relations between knowledge, power and the body in modern society. It saw knowledge as always inextricably enmeshed in relations of power because it was always being applied to the regulation of social conduct in practice (i.e. to particular 'bodies'). This foregrounding of the relation between discourse, knowledge and power marked a significant development in the *constructionist* approach to representation which we have been outlining. It rescued representation from the clutches of a purely formal theory and gave it a historical, practical and 'worldly' context of operation.

You may wonder to what extent this concern with discourse, knowledge and power brought Foucault's interests closer to those of the classical sociological theories of ideology, especially Marxism with its concern to identify the class positions and class interests concealed within particular forms of knowledge. Foucault, indeed, does come closer to addressing some of these questions about ideology than, perhaps, formal semiotics did (though Roland Barthes was also concerned with questions of ideology and myth, as we saw earlier). But Foucault had quite specific and cogent reasons why he rejected the classical Marxist problematic of 'ideology'. Marx had argued that, in every epoch, ideas reflect the economic basis of society, and thus the 'ruling ideas' are those of the ruling class which governs a capitalist economy, and correspond to its dominant interests. Foucault's main argument against the classical Marxist theory of ideology was that it tended to reduce all the relation between knowledge and power to a question of *class* power and *class* interests. Foucault did not deny the existence of classes, but he was strongly opposed to this powerful element of economic or class *reductionism* in the Marxist theory of ideology. Secondly, he argued that Marxism tended to contrast the 'distortions' of bourgeois knowledge, against its own claims to 'truth' – Marxist science. But Foucault did not believe that *any* form of thought could claim an absolute 'truth' of this kind, outside the play of discourse. *All* political and social forms of thought, he believed, were inevitably caught up in the interplay of knowledge and power. So, his work rejects the traditional Marxist question, 'in whose class interest does language, representation and power operate?'

Later theorists, like the Italian, Antonio Gramsci, who was influenced by Marx but rejected class reductionism, advanced a definition of 'ideology' which is considerably closer to Foucault's position, though still too preoccupied with class questions to be acceptable to him. Gramsci's notion was that particular social groups struggle in many different ways, including ideologically, to win the consent of other groups and achieve a kind of ascendancy in both thought and practice over them. This form of power Gramsci called hegemony. Hegemony is never permanent, and is not reducible to economic interests or to a simple class model of society. This has some similarities to Foucault's position, though on some key issues they differ radically.

What distinguished Foucault's position on discourse, knowledge and power from the Marxist theory of class interests and ideological 'distortion'? Foucault advanced at least two, radically novel, propositions.

1 Knowledge, Power and Truth

The first concerns the way Foucault conceived the linkage between knowledge and power. Hitherto, we have tended to think that power operates in a direct and brutally repressive fashion, dispensing with polite things like culture and knowledge, though Gramsci certainly broke with that model of power. Foucault argued that not only is knowledge always a form of power, but power is implicated in the questions of whether and in what circumstances knowledge is to be applied or not. This question of the application and *effectiveness* of **power/knowledge** was more important, he thought, than the question of its 'truth'.

Knowledge linked to power, not only assumes the authority of 'the truth' but has the power to *make itself true*. All knowledge, once applied in the real world, has real effects, and in that sense at least, 'becomes true'. Knowledge, once used to regulate the conduct of others, entails constraint, regulation and the disciplining of practices. Thus, 'There is no power relation without the correlative constitution of a field of knowledge, nor any knowledge that does not presuppose and constitute at the same time, power relations' (Foucault, 1977a, p. 27).

According to Foucault, what we think we 'know' in a particular period about, say, crime has a bearing on how we regulate, control and punish criminals. Knowledge does not operate in a void. It is put to

work, through certain technologies and strategies of application, in specific situations, historical contexts and institutional regimes. To study punishment, you must study how the combination of discourse and power – power/knowledge – has produced a certain conception of crime and the criminal, has had certain real effects both for criminal and for the punisher, and how these have been set into practice in certain historically specific prison regimes.

This led Foucault to speak, not of the 'Truth' of knowledge in the absolute sense – a Truth which remained so, whatever the period, setting, context but of a discursive formation sustaining a **regime of truth**. Thus, it may or may not be true that single parenting inevitably leads to delinquency and crime. But if everyone believes it to be so, and punishes single parents accordingly, this will have real consequences for both parents and children and will become 'true' in terms of its real effects, even if in some absolute sense it has never been conclusively proven. In the human and social sciences, Foucault argued:

> Truth isn't outside power. . . . Truth is a thing of this world; it is produced only by virtue of multiple forms of constraint. And it induces regular effects of power. Each society has its regime of truth, its 'general politics' of truth; that is, the types of discourse which it accepts and makes function as true, the mechanisms and instances which enable one to distinguish true and false statements, the means by which each is sanctioned . . . the status of those who are charged with saying what counts as true.
>
> (Foucault, 1980, p. 131)

2 New Conceptions of Power

Secondly, Foucault advanced an altogether novel conception of power. We tend to think of power as always radiating in a single direction – from top to bottom – and coming from a specific source – the sovereign, the state, the ruling class and so on. For Foucault, however, power does not 'function in the form of a chain' – it circulates. It is never monopolized by one centre. It 'is deployed and exercised through a net-like organization' (Foucault, 1980, p. 98). This suggests that we are all, to some degree, caught up in its circulation – oppressors and oppressed. It does not radiate downwards, either from one source or from one place. Power relations permeate all levels of social existence and are therefore to be found operating at every site of social life – in the private spheres of the family and sexuality as much as in the public spheres of politics, the economy and the law. What's more, power is not only negative, repressing what it seeks to control. It is also *productive*. It 'doesn't only weigh on us as a force that says no, but . . . it traverses and produces things, it induces pleasure, forms of knowledge, produces discourse. It needs to be thought of as a productive network which runs through the whole social body' (Foucault, 1980, p. 119).

The punishment system, for example, produces books, treatises, regulations, new strategies of control and resistance, debates in Parliament, conversations, confessions, legal briefs and appeals, training regimes for prison officers, and so on. The efforts to control sexuality produce a veritable explosion of discourse – talk about sex, television and radio programmes, sermons and legislation, novels, stories and magazine features, medical and counselling advice, essays and articles, learned theses and research programmes, as well as new sexual practices (e.g. 'safe' sex) and the pornography industry. Without denying that the state, the law, the sovereign or the dominant class may have positions of dominance, Foucault shifts our attention away from the grand, overall strategies of power, towards the many, localized circuits, tactics, mechanisms and effects through which power circulates – what Foucault calls the 'meticulous rituals' or the 'micro-physics' of power. These power relations 'go right down to the depth of society' (Foucault, 1977a, p. 27). They connect the way power is actually working on the ground to the great pyramids of power by what he calls a capillary movement (capillaries being the thin-walled vessels that aid the exchange of oxygen between the blood in our bodies and the surrounding tissues). Not because power at these lower levels merely reflects or 'reproduces, at the level of individuals, bodies, gestures and behaviour, the general form of the law or government' (Foucault, 1977a, p. 27) but, on the contrary, because such an approach 'roots [power] in forms of behaviour, bodies and local relations of

power which should not at all be seen as a simple projection of the central power' (Foucault, 1980, p. 201).

To what object are the micro-physics of power primarily applied, in Foucault's model? To the body. He places the body at the centre of the struggles between different formations of power/knowledge. The techniques of regulation are applied to the body. Different discursive formations and apparatuses divide, classify and inscribe the body differently in their respective regimes of power and 'truth'. In *Discipline and Punish*, for example, Foucault analyses the very different ways in which the body of the criminal is 'produced' and disciplined in different punishment regimes in France. In earlier periods, punishment was haphazard, prisons were places into which the public could wander and the ultimate punishment was inscribed violently on the body by means of instruments of torture and execution, etc. – a practice the essence of which is that it should be public, visible to everyone. The modern form of disciplinary regulation and power, by contrast, is private, individualized; prisoners are shut away from the public and often from one another, though continually under surveillance from the authorities; and punishment is individualized. Here, the body has become the site of a new kind of disciplinary regime.

Of course this 'body' is not simply the natural body which all human beings possess at all times. This body is *produced* within discourse, according to the different discursive formations – the state of knowledge about crime and the criminal, what counts as 'true' about how to change or deter criminal behaviour, the specific apparatus and technologies of punishment prevailing at the time. This is a radically historicized conception of the body – a sort of surface on which different regimes of power/knowledge write their meanings and effects. It thinks of the body as 'totally imprinted by history and the processes of history's deconstruction of the body' (Foucault, 1977a, p. 63).

Summary: Foucault and Representation

Foucault's approach to representation is not easy to summarize. He is concerned with the production of knowledge and meaning through discourse. Foucault does indeed analyse particular texts and representations, as the semioticians did. But he is more inclined to analyse the whole *discursive formation* to which a text or a practice belongs. His concern is with knowledge provided by the human and social sciences, which organizes conduct, understanding, practice and belief, the regulation of bodies as well as whole populations. Although his work is clearly done in the wake of, and profoundly influenced by, the 'turn to language' which marked the *constructionist* approach to representation, his definition of *discourse* is much broader than language, and includes many other elements of practice and institutional regulation which Saussure's approach, with its linguistic focus, excluded. Foucault is always much more historically specific, seeing forms of power/knowledge as always rooted in particular contexts and histories. Above all, for Foucault, the production of knowledge is always crossed with questions of power and the body; and this greatly expands the scope of what is involved in representation.

The major critique levelled against his work is that he tends to absorb too much into 'discourse', and this has the effect of encouraging his followers to neglect the influence of the material, economic and structural factors in the operation of power/knowledge. Some critics also find his rejection of any criterion of 'truth' in the human sciences in favour of the idea of a 'regime of truth' and the will-to-power (the will to make things 'true') vulnerable to the charge of relativism. Nevertheless, there is little doubt about the major impact which his work has had on contemporary theories of representation and meaning.

[. . .]

Where is 'The Subject'?

We have traced the shift in Foucault's work from language to discourse and knowledge, and their relation to questions of power. But where in all this, you might ask, is the subject? Saussure tended to abolish the subject from the question of representation. Language, he argued, speaks us. The subject appears in Saussure's schema as the author of individual speech-acts (*paroles*). But, as we have seen, Saussure did not think that the level of the *paroles* was one at which a 'scientific' analysis of language

could be conducted. In one sense, Foucault shares this position. For him, it is *discourse*, not the subject, which produces knowledge. Discourse is enmeshed with power, but it is not necessary to find 'a subject' – the king, the ruling class, the bourgeoisie, the state, etc. – for *power/knowledge* to operate.

On the other hand, Foucault *did* include the subject in his theorizing, though he did not restore the subject to its position as the centre and author of representation. Indeed, as his work developed, he became more and more concerned with questions about 'the subject', and in his very late and unfinished work, he even went so far as to give the subject a certain reflexive awareness of his or her own conduct, though this still stopped short of restoring the subject to his/her full sovereignty.

Foucault was certainly deeply critical of what we might call the traditional conception of the subject. The conventional notion thinks of 'the subject' as an individual who is fully endowed with consciousness; an autonomous and stable entity, the 'core' of the self, and the independent, authentic source of action and meaning. According to this conception, when we hear ourselves speak, we feel we are identical with what has been said. And this identity of the subject with what is said gives him/her a privileged position in relation to meaning. It suggests that, although other people may misunderstand us, *we* always understand ourselves because *we were the source of meaning in the first place*.

However, as we have seen, the shift towards a constructionist conception of language and representation did a great deal to displace the subject from a privileged position in relation to knowledge and meaning. The same is true of Foucault's discursive approach. It is discourse, not the subjects who speak it, which produces knowledge. Subjects may produce particular texts, but they are operating within the limits of the *episteme*, the *discursive formation*, the *regime of truth*, of a particular period and culture. Indeed, this is one of Foucault's most radical propositions: the 'subject' is *produced within discourse*. This subject *of* discourse cannot be outside discourse, because it must be *subjected to* discourse. It must submit to its rules and conventions, to its dispositions of power/knowledge. The subject can become the bearer of the kind of knowledge which discourse produces. It can become the object through which power is relayed. But it cannot stand outside power/knowledge as its source and author. In 'The subject and power' (1982), Foucault writes that 'My objective . . . has been to create a history of the different modes by which, in our culture, human beings are made subjects . . . It is a form of power which makes individuals subjects. There are two meanings of the word *subject*: subject to someone else's control and dependence, and tied to his (*sic*) own identity by a conscience and self-knowledge. Both meanings suggest a form of power which subjugates and makes subject to' (Foucault, 1982, pp. 208, 212). Making discourse and representation more historical has therefore been matched, in Foucault, by an equally radical historicization of *the subject*. 'One has to dispense with the constituent subject, to get rid of the subject itself, that's to say, to arrive at an analysis which can account for the constitution of the subject within a historical framework' (Foucault, 1980, p. 115).

Where, then, is 'the subject' in this more discursive approach to meaning, representation and power?

Foucault's 'subject' seems to be produced through discourse in *two* different senses or places. First, the discourse itself produces 'subjects' – figures who personify the particular forms of knowledge which the discourse produces. These subjects have the attributes we would expect as these are defined by the discourse: the madman, the hysterical woman, the homosexual, the individualized criminal, and so on. These figures are specific to specific discursive regimes and historical periods. But the discourse also produces a *place for the subject* (i.e. the reader or viewer, who is also 'subjected to' discourse) from which its particular knowledge and meaning most makes sense. It is not inevitable that all individuals in a particular period will become the subjects of a particular discourse in this sense, and thus the bearers of its power/knowledge. But for them – us – to do so, they – we – must locate themselves/ourselves in the *position* from which the discourse makes most sense, and thus become its 'subjects' by 'subjecting' ourselves to its meanings, power and regulation. All discourses, then, construct **subject-positions**, from which alone they make sense.

This approach has radical implications for a theory of representation. For it suggests that discourses themselves construct the subject-positions from which they become meaningful and have effects. Individuals may differ as to their social class, gendered, 'racial' and ethnic characteristics (among other factors), but they will not be able to take meaning until they have identified with those positions which the discourse constructs, *subjected* themselves to its rules, and hence become the *subjects of its power/knowledge*. For example, pornography produced for men will only 'work' for women, according to this theory, if in some sense women put themselves in the position of the 'desiring male voyeur' – which is the ideal subject-position which the discourse of male pornography constructs – and look at the models from this 'masculine' discursive position. This may seem, and is, a highly contestable proposition. But let us consider an example which illustrates the argument.

How to Make Sense of Velasquez' Las Meninas

Foucault's *The Order of Things* (1970) opens with a discussion of a painting by the famous Spanish painter, Velasquez, called *Las Meninas*. It has been a topic of considerable scholarly debate and controversy. The reason I am using it here is because, as all the critics agree, the painting itself does raise certain questions about the nature of *representation*, and Foucault himself uses it to talk about these wider issues of the subject. It is these arguments which interest us here, not the question of whether Foucault's is the 'true', correct or even the definitive reading of the painting's meaning. That the painting has no one, fixed or final meaning is, indeed, one of Foucault's most powerful arguments.

The painting is unique in Velasquez' work. It was part of the Spanish court's royal collection and hung in the palace in a room which was subsequently destroyed by fire. It was dated '1656' by Velasquez' successor as court painter. It was originally called 'The Empress with her Ladies and a Dwarf'; but by the inventory of 1666, it had acquired the title of 'A Portrait of the Infanta of Spain with her Ladies In Waiting and Servants, by the Court Painter and Palace Chamberlain Diego Velasquez'. It was subsequently called *Las Meninas* – 'The Maids of Honour'. Some argue that the painting shows Velasquez working on *Las Meninas* itself and was painted with the aid of a mirror – but this now seems unlikely. The most widely held and convincing explanation is that Velasquez was working on a full-length portrait of the King and Queen, and that it is the royal couple who are reflected in the mirror on the back wall. It is at the couple that the princess and her attendants are looking and on them that the artist's gaze appears to rest as he steps back from his canvas. The reflection artfully includes the royal couple in the picture. This is essentially the account which Foucault accepts.

[. . .]

The Subject of/in Representation

In his comments, Foucault uses *Las Meninas* to make some general points about his theory of representation and specifically about the role of the subject:

1 'Foucault reads the painting in terms of representation and the subject' (Dreyfus and Rabinow, 1982, p. 20). As well as being a painting which shows us (represents) a scene in which a portrait of the King and Queen of Spain is being painted, it is also a painting which *tells us something about how representation and the subject work*. It produces its own kind of knowledge. Representation and the subject are the painting's underlying message – what it is about, its sub-text.

2 Clearly, representation here is *not* about a 'true' reflection or imitation of reality. Of course, the people in the painting may 'look like' the actual people in the Spanish court. But the discourse of painting in the picture is doing a great deal more than simply trying to mirror accurately what exists.

3 Everything in a sense is *visible* in the painting. And yet, what it is 'about' – its meaning – depends on how we 'read' it. *It is as much constructed around what you can't see as what you can*. You can't see what is being painted on the canvas, though this seems to be the point of the whole exercise. You can't see what everyone is looking at, which is the sitters, unless we assume it is a reflection of them in the mirror. They are both in and not in the picture. Or rather, they are present through a kind of substitution. We cannot see them because they are not directly represented: but their 'absence' is represented – *mirrored* through their reflection in the mirror at the back. The meaning of the picture is produced, Foucault argues, through this complex inter-play between *presence* (what you see, the visible) and *absence* (what you can't see, what has

displaced it within the frame). Representation works as much through what is *not* shown, as through what is.

4 In fact, a number of substitutions or displacements seem to be going on here. For example, the 'subject' and centre of the painting we are looking at seems to be the Infanta. But the 'subject' or centre is also, of course, the sitters – the King and Queen – whom we can't see but whom the others are looking at. You can tell this from the fact that the mirror on the wall in which the King and Queen are reflected is also almost exactly at the centre of the field of vision of the picture. So the Infanta and the Royal Couple, in a sense, share the place of the centre as the principal 'subjects' of the painting. It all depends on where you are looking from – in towards the scene from where you, the spectator, is sitting or outwards from the scene, from the position of the people in the picture. If you accept Foucault's argument, then there are *two* subjects to the painting and *two* centres. And the composition of the picture – its discourse – forces us to oscillate between these two 'subjects' without ever finally deciding which one to identify with. Representation in the painting seems firm and clear – everything in place. But our vision, the way we *look* at the picture, oscillates between two centres, two subjects, two positions of looking, two meanings. Far from being finally resolved into some absolute truth which is *the* meaning of the picture, the discourse of the painting quite deliberately keeps us in this state of suspended attention, in this oscillating process of looking. Its meaning is always in the process of emerging, yet any final meaning is constantly deferred.

5 You can tell a great deal about how the picture works as a discourse, and what it means, by following the orchestration of *looking* – who is looking at what or whom. *Our* look – the eyes of the person looking at the picture, the spectator – follows the relationships of looking as represented in the picture. We know the figure of the Infanta is important because her attendants are looking at her. But we know that someone even more important is sitting in front of the scene whom we can't see, because many figures – the Infanta, the jester, the painter himself – are looking at them! So the spectator (who is also 'subjected' to the discourse of the painting) is doing two kinds of looking. Looking at the scene from the position outside, in front of, the picture. And at the same time, looking out of the scene, by *identifying with* the looking being

done by the figures in the painting. Projecting our-selves into the subjects of the painting help us as spectators to see, to 'make sense' of it. We take up the positions indicated by the discourse, identify with them, subject ourselves to its meanings, and become its 'subjects'.

6 It is critical for Foucault's argument that the painting does not have a completed meaning. It only means something in relation to the spectator who is looking at it. The spectator completes the meaning of the picture. Meaning is therefore con-structed in the dialogue between the painting and the spectator. Velasquez, of course, could not know who would subsequently occupy the position of the spectator. Nevertheless, the whole 'scene' of the painting had to be laid out in relation to that ideal point in front of the painting from which *any* spectator must look if the painting is to make sense. The spectator, we might say, is painted into position in front of the picture. In this sense, the discourse produces a *subject-position* for the spectator-subject. For the painting to work, the spectator, whoever he or she may be, must first 'subject' himself/herself to the painting's discourse and, in this way, become the painting's ideal viewer, the producer of its meanings – its 'subject'. This is what is meant by saying that the discourse constructs the spectator as a subject – by which we mean that it constructs a place for the subject-spectator who is looking at and making sense of it.

7 Representation therefore occurs from at least three positions in the painting. First of all there is us, the spectator, whose 'look' puts together and unifies the different elements and relationships in the picture into an overall meaning. This subject must be there for the painting to make sense, but he/she is not rep-resented in the painting.

Then there is the painter who painted the scene. He is 'present' in two places at once, since he must at one time have been standing where we are now sitting, in order to paint the scene, but he has then put himself into (represented himself in) the picture, looking back towards that point of view where we, the spectator, have taken his place. We may also say that the scene makes sense and is pulled together in relation to the court figure standing on the stair at the back, since he too surveys it all but – like us and like the painter – from some-what outside it.

8 Finally, consider the mirror on the back wall. If it were a 'real' mirror, it should now be represent-ing or reflecting *us*, since we are standing in that position in front of the scene to which everyone is looking and from which everything makes sense. But it does not mirror us, it shows *in our place* the King and Queen of Spain. Somehow the discourse of the painting positions us in the place of the Sovereign! You can imagine what fun Foucault had with this substitution.

Foucault argues that it is clear from the way the discourse of representation works in the painting that it *must* be looked at and made sense of from that one subject-position in front of it from which we, the spec-tators, are looking. This is also the point-of-view from which a camera would have to be positioned in order to film the scene. And, lo and behold, the person whom Velasquez chooses to 'represent' sitting in this position is The Sovereign – 'master of all he surveys' – who is both the 'subject of' the painting (what it is about) and the 'subject in' the painting – the one whom the dis-course sets in place, but who, simultaneously, makes sense of it and understands it all by a look of supreme mastery.

Conclusion: Representation, Meaning and Language Reconsidered

We started with a fairly simple definition of represen-tation. Representation is the process by which mem-bers of a culture use language (broadly defined as any system which deploys signs, any signifying system) to produce meaning. Already, this definition carries the important premise that things – objects, people, events, in the world – do not have in themselves any fixed, final or true meaning. It is us – in society, within human cultures – who make things mean, who signify. Meanings, consequently, will always change, from one culture or period to another. There is no guaran-tee that every object in one culture will have an equiv-alent meaning in another, precisely because cultures differ, sometimes radically, from one another in their codes – the ways they carve up, classify and assign meaning to the world. So one important idea about representation is the acceptance of a degree of *cultural relativism* between one culture and another, a certain lack of equivalence, and hence the need for *translation* as we move from the mind-set or conceptual universe of one culture or another.

We call this the *constructionist* approach to representation, contrasting it with both the *reflective* and the *intentional* approaches. Now, if culture is a process, a practice, how does it work? In the *constructionist perspective*, representation involves making meaning by forging links between three different orders of things: what we might broadly call the world of things, people, events and experiences; the conceptual world – the mental concepts we carry around in our heads; and the signs, arranged into languages, which 'stand for' or communicate these concepts. Now, if you have to make a link between systems which are not the same, and fix these at least for a time so that other people know what, in one system, corresponds to what in another system, then there must be something which allows us to translate between them – telling us what word to use for what concept, and so on. Hence the notion of *codes*.

Producing meaning depends on the practice of interpretation, and interpretation is sustained by us actively using the code – *encoding*, putting things into the code – and by the person at the other end interpreting or *decoding* the meaning (Hall, 1980). But note, that, because meanings are always changing and slipping, codes operate more like social conventions than like fixed laws or unbreakable rules. As meanings shift and slide, so inevitably the codes of a culture imperceptibly change. The great advantage of the concepts and classifications of the culture which we carry around with us in our heads is that they enable us to *think* about things, whether they are there, present, or not; indeed, whether they ever existed or not. There are concepts for our fantasies, desires and imaginings as well as for so-called 'real' objects in the material world. And the advantage of language is that our thoughts about the world need not remain exclusive to us, and silent. We can translate them into language, make them 'speak', through the use of signs which stand for them – and thus talk, write, communicate about them to others.

Gradually, then, we complexified what we meant by representation. It came to be less and less the straightforward thing we assumed it to be at first

– which is why we need *theories* to explain it. We looked at two versions of constructionism – that which concentrated on how *language* and *signification* (the use of signs in language) works to produce *meanings*, which after Saussure and Barthes we called *semiotics*; and that, following Foucault, which concentrated on how *discourse* and *discursive practices* produce knowledge. I won't run through the finer points in these two approaches again, since you can go back to them in the main body of the chapter and refresh your memory. In semiotics, you will recall the importance of signifier/signified, *langue/parole* and 'myth', and how the marking of difference and binary oppositions are crucial for meaning. In the *discursive* approach, you will recall discursive formations, power/knowledge, the idea of a 'regime of truth', the way discourse also produces the subject and defines the *subject-positions* from which knowledge proceeds and indeed, the return of questions about 'the subject' to the field of representation.

Notice that the chapter does *not* argue that the *discursive* approach overturned everything in the *semiotic* approach. Theoretical development does not usually proceed in this linear way. There was much to learn from Saussure and Barthes, and we are still discovering ways of fruitfully applying their insights – without necessarily swallowing everything they said. We offered you some critical thoughts on the subject. There is a great deal to learn from Foucault and the *discursive* approach, but by no means everything it claims is correct and the theory is open to, and has attracted, many criticisms. Again, in later chapters, as we encounter further developments in the theory of representation, and see the strengths and weaknesses of these positions applied in practice, we will come to appreciate more fully that we are only at the beginning of the exciting task of exploring this process of meaning construction, which is at the heart of culture, to its full depths. What we have offered here is, we hope, a relatively clear account of a set of complex, and as yet tentative, ideas in an unfinished project.

References

Barthes, R. (1967) *The Elements of Semiology*, London, Cape.

Barthes, R. (1972) *Mythologies*, London, Cape.

Barthes, R. (1972a) 'The world of wrestling' in *Mythologies*, London, Cape.

Barthes, R. (1972b) 'Myth today' in *Mythologies*, London, Cape.

Barthes, R. (1975) *The Pleasure of the Text*, New York, Hall and Wang.

Barthes, R. (1977) *Image-Music-Text*, Glasgow, Fontaria.

Bryson, N. (1990) *Looking at the Overlooked: four essays on still life painting*, London, Reaktion Books.

Cousins, M. and Hussain, A. (1984) *Michel Foucault*, Basingstoke, Macmillan.

Culler, J. (1976) *Saussure*, London, Fontana.

Derrida, J. (1981) *Positions*, Chicago, IL, University of Chicago Press.

Dreyfus, H. and Rabinow, P. (eds) (1982) *Beyond Stucturalism and Hermeneutics*, Brighton, Harvester.

Du Gay, P. (ed.) (1997) *Production of Culture/Cultures of Production*, London, Sage/The Open University (Book 4 in this series).

Du Gay, P., Hall, S., Janes, L., Mackay, H. and Negus, K. (1997) *Doing Cultural Studies: the story of the Sony Walkman*, London, Sage/The Open University (Book 1 in this series).

Foucault, M. (1970) *The Order of Things*, London, Tavistock.

Foucault, M. (1972) *The Archaeology of Knowledge*, London, Tavistock.

Foucault, M. (1973) *The Birth of the Clinic*, London, Tavistock.

Foucault, M. (1978) *The History of Sexuality*, Harmondsworth, Allen Lane/Penguin Books.

Foucault, M. (1977a) *Discipline and Punish*, London, Tavistock.

Foucault, M. (1977b) 'Nietzsche, genealogy, history', in *Language, Counter-Memory, Practice*, Oxford, Blackwell.

Foucault, M. (1980) *Power/Knowledge*, Brighton, Harvester.

Foucault, M. (1982) 'The subject and power' in Dreyfus and Rabinow (eds).

Freud, S. and Breuer, J. (1974) *Studies on Hysteria*, Harmondsworth, Pelican. First published 1895.

Gay, P. (1988) *Freud: a life for our time*, London, Macmillan.

Hall, S. (1980) 'Encoding and decoding' in Hall, S. et al. (eds) *Culture, Media, Language*, London, Hutchinson.

Hall, S. (1992) 'The West and the Rest', in Hall, S. and Gieben, B. (eds) *Formations of Modernity*, Cambridge, Polity Press/The Open University.

Hoeg, P. (1994) *Miss Smilla's Feeling For Snow*, London, Flamingo.

Laclau, E. and Mouffe, C. (1990) 'Post-Marxism without apologies' in Laclau, E., *New Reflections on the Revolution of our Time*, London, Verso.

Mcnay, L. (1994) *Foucault: a critical introduction*, Cambridge, Polity Press.

Mackay, H. (ed.) (1997) *Consumption and Everyday Life*, London, Sage/The Open University (Book 5 in this series).

Saussure, F. De (1960) *Course in General Linguistics*, London, Peter Owen.

Showalter, E. (1987) *The Female Malady*, London, Virago.

Weeks, J. (1981) *Sex, Politics and Society*, London, Longman.

Weeks, J. (1985) *Sexuality and its Discontents*, London, Routledge.

14.
WAYS OF SEEING

John Berger

Seeing comes before words. The child looks and recognizes before it can speak.

But there is also another sense in which seeing comes before words. It is seeing which establishes our place in the surrounding world; we explain that world with words, but words can never undo the fact that we are surrounded by it. The relation between what we see and what we know is never settled. Each evening we *see* the sun set. We *know* that the earth is turning away from it. Yet the knowledge, the explanation, never quite fits the sight. The Surrealist painter Magritte commented on this always-present gap between words and seeing in a painting called *The Key of Dreams*.

The way we see things is affected by what we know or what we believe. In the Middle Ages when men believed in the physical existence of Hell the sight of fire must have meant something different from what it means today. Nevertheless their idea of Hell owed a lot to the sight of fire consuming and the ashes remaining – as well as to their experience of the pain of burns.

When in love, the sight of the beloved has a completeness which no words and no embrace can match: a completeness which only the act of making love can temporarily accommodate.

Yet this seeing which comes before words, and can never be quite covered by them, is not a question of mechanically reacting to stimuli. (It can only be thought of in this way if one isolates the small part of the process which concerns the eye's retina.) We only see what we look at. To look is an act of choice. As a result of this act, what we see is brought within our reach – though not necessarily within arm's reach. To touch something is to situate onself in relation to it. (Close your eyes, move round the room and notice how the faculty of touch is like a static, limited form of sight.) We never look at just one thing; we are always looking at the relation between things and ourselves. Our vision is continually active, continually moving, continually holding things in a circle around itself, constituting what is present to us as we are.

Soon after we can see, we are aware that we can also be seen. The eye of the other combines with our own eye to make it fully credible that we are part of the visible world.

If we accept that we can see that hill over there, we propose that from that hill we can be seen. The reciprocal nature of vision is more fundamental than that of spoken dialogue. And often dialogue is an attempt to verbalize this – an attempt to explain how, either metaphorically or literally, 'you see things', and an attempt to discover how 'he sees things'.

In the sense in which we use the word in this book, all images are man-made.

An image is a sight which has been recreated or reproduced. It is an appearance, or a set of appearances, which has been detached from the place and time in which it first made its appearance and preserved – for a few moments or a few centuries. Every image embodies a way of seeing. Even a photograph. For photographs are not, as is often assumed, a mechanical record. Every time we look at a photograph, we are aware, however slightly, of the photographer selecting that sight from an infinity of other possible sights. This is true even in the most casual family snapshot. The photographer's way of seeing is reflected in his choice of subject. The painter's way of seeing is reconstituted by the marks he makes on the canvas or paper. Yet, although every image embodies a way of seeing, our perception or appreciation of an image depends also upon our own way of seeing. (It may be, for example, that Sheila is one figure among twenty; but for our own reasons she is the one we have eyes for.)

[...]

According to usage and conventions which are at last being questioned but have by no means been overcome, the social presence of a woman is different in kind from that of a man. A man's presence is dependent upon the promise of power which he embodies. If the promise is large and credible his presence is striking. If it is small or incredible, he is found to have little presence. The promised power may be moral, physical, temperamental, economic, social, sexual – but its object is always exterior to the man. A man's presence suggests what he is capable of doing to you or for you. His presence may be fabricated, in the sense that he pretends to be capable of what he is not. But the pretence is always towards a power which he exercises on others.

By contrast, a woman's presence expresses her own attitude to herself, and defines what can and cannot be done to her. Her presence is manifest in her gestures, voice, opinions, expressions, clothes, chosen surroundings, taste – indeed there is nothing she can do which does not contribute to her presence. Presence for a woman is so intrinsic to her person that men tend to think of it as an almost physical emanation, a kind of heat or smell or aura.

To be born a woman has been to be born, within an allotted and confined space, into the keeping of men. The social presence of women has developed as a result of their ingenuity in living under such tutelage within such a limited space. But this has been at the cost of a woman's self being split into two. A woman must continually watch herself. She is almost continually accompanied by her own image of herself. Whilst she is walking across a room or whilst she is weeping at the death of her father, she can scarcely avoid envisaging herself walking or weeping. From earliest childhood she has been taught and persuaded to survey herself continually.

And so she comes to consider the *surveyor* and the *surveyed* within her as the two constituent yet always distinct elements of her identity as a woman.

She has to survey everything she is and everything she does because how she appears to others, and ultimately how she appears to men, is of crucial importance for what is normally thought of as the success of her life. Her own sense of being in herself is supplanted by a sense of being appreciated as herself by another.

Men survey women before treating them. Consequently how a woman appears to a man can determine how she will be treated. To acquire some control over this process, women must contain it and interiorize it. That part of a woman's self which is the surveyor treats the part which is the surveyed so as to demonstrate to others how her whole self would like to be treated. And this exemplary treatment of herself by herself constitutes her presence. Every woman's presence regulates what is and is not 'permissible' within her presence. Every one of her actions – whatever its direct purpose or motivation – is also read as an indication of how she would like to be treated. If a woman throws a glass on the floor, this is an example of how she treats her own emotion of anger and so of how she would wish it to be treated by others. If a man does the same, his action is only read as an expression of his anger. If a woman makes a good joke this is an example of how she treats the joker in herself and accordingly of how she as a joker-woman would like to be treated by others. Only a man can make a good joke for its own sake.

One might simplify this by saying: *men act* and *women appear*. Men look at women. Women watch themselves being looked at. This determines not only most relations between men and women but also the relation of women to themselves. The surveyor of woman in herself is male: the surveyed female. Thus she turns herself into an object – and most particularly an object of vision: a sight.

In one category of European oil painting women were the principal, ever-recurring subject. That category is the nude. In the nudes of European painting we can discover some of the criteria and conventions by which women have been seen and judged as sights.

The first nudes in the tradition depicted Adam and Eve. It is worth referring to the story as told in Genesis:

And when the woman saw that the tree was good for food, and that it was a delight to the eyes, and that the tree was to be desired to make one wise, she took of the fruit thereof and did eat; and she gave also unto her husband with her, and he did eat.

And the eyes of them both were opened, and they knew that they were naked; and they sewed fig-leaves together and made themselves aprons. . . . And the Lord God called unto the man and said unto him, 'Where are thou?' And he said, 'I heard thy voice in the garden, and I was afraid, because I was naked; and I hid myself. . . .

Unto the woman God said, 'I will greatly multiply thy sorrow and thy conception; in sorrow thou shalt bring forth children; and thy desire shall be to thy husband and he shall rule over thee'.

What is striking about this story? They became aware of being naked because, as a result of eating the apple, each saw the other differently. Nakedness was created in the mind of the beholder.

The second striking fact is that the woman is blamed and is punished by being made subservient to the man. In relation to the woman, the man becomes the agent of God.

In the medieval tradition the story was often illustrated, scene following scene, as in a strip cartoon.

During the Renaissance the narrative sequence disappeared, and the single moment depicted became the moment of shame. The couple wear fig-leaves or make a modest gesture with their hands. But now their shame is not so much in relation to one another as to the spectator.

Later the shame becomes a kind of display.

When the tradition of painting became more secular, other themes also offered the opportunity of painting nudes. But in them all there remains the implication that the subject (a woman) is aware of being seen by a spectator.

She is not naked as she is
She is naked as the spectator sees her.

Often – as with the favourite subject of Susannah and the Elders – this is the actual theme of the picture. We join the Elders to spy on Susannah taking her bath. She looks back at us looking at her.

In another version of the subject by Tintoretto, Susannah is looking at herself in a mirror. Thus she joins the spectators of herself.

The mirror was often used as a symbol of the vanity of woman. The moralizing, however, was mostly hypocritical.

You painted a naked woman because you enjoyed looking at her, you put a mirror in her hand and you called the painting *Vanity*, thus morally condemning the woman whose nakedness you had depicted for your own pleasure.

The real function of the mirror was otherwise. It was to make the woman connive in treating herself as, first and foremost, a sight.

The Judgement of Paris was another theme with the same inwritten idea of a man or men looking at naked women.

But a further element is now added. The element of judgement. Paris awards the apple to the woman he finds most beautiful. Thus Beauty becomes competitive. (Today The Judgement of Paris has become the Beauty Contest.) Those who are not judged beautiful are *not beautiful*. Those who are, are given the prize.

The prize is to be owned by a judge – that is to say to be available for him. Charles the Second commissioned a secret painting from Lely. It is a highly typical image of the tradition. Norminally it might be a *Venus and Cupid*. In fact it is a portrait of one of the King's mistresses, Nell Gwynne. It shows her passively looking at the spectator staring at her naked.

This nakedness is not, however, an expression of her own feelings; it is a sign of her submission to the owner's feelings or demands. (The owner of both woman and painting.) The painting, when the King showed it to others, demonstrated this submission and his guests envied him.

It is worth noticing that in other non-European traditions – in Indian art, Persian art, African art, Pre-Columbian art – nakedness is never supine in this way. And if, in these traditions, the theme of a work is sexual attraction, it is likely to show active sexual love as between two people, the woman as active as the man, the actions of each absorbing the other.

We can now begin to see the difference between nakedness and nudity in the European tradition. In his book on *The Nude* Kenneth Clark maintains that to be naked is simply to be without clothes, whereas the nude is a form of art. According to him, a nude is not the starting point of a painting, but a way of seeing which the painting achieves. To some degree, this is true – although the way of seeing 'a nude' is not necessarily confined to art: there are also nude photographs, nude poses, nude gestures. What is true is that the nude is always conventionalized – and the authority for its conventions derives from a certain tradition of art.

What do these conventions mean? What does a nude signify? It is not sufficient to answer these questions merely in terms of the art-form, for it is quite clear that the nude also relates to lived sexuality.

To be naked is to be oneself.

To be nude is to be seen naked by others and yet not recognized for oneself. A naked body has to be seen as an object in order to become a nude. (The sight of it as an object stimulates the use of it as an object.) Nakedness reveals itself. Nudity is placed on display.

To be naked is to be without disguise.

To be on display is to have the surface of one's own skin, the hairs of one's own body, turned into a disguise which, in that situation, can never be discarded. The nude is condemned to never being naked. Nudity is a form of dress.

In the average European oil painting of the nude the principal protagonist is never painted. He is the spectator in front of the picture and he is presumed to be a man. Everything is addressed to him. Everything must appear to be the result of his being there. It is for him that the figures have assumed their nudity. But he, by definition, is a stranger – with his clothes still on.

Consider the *Allegory of Time and Love* by Bronzino. The complicated symbolism which lies behind this painting need not concern us now because it does not affect its sexual appeal – at the first degree. Before it is anything else, this is a painting of sexual provocation.

The painting was sent as a present from the Grand Duke of Florance to the King of France. The boy kneeling on the cushion and kissing the woman is Cupid. She is Venus. But the way her body is arranged has nothing to do with their kissing. Her body is arranged in the way it is, to display it to the man looking at the picture. This picture is made to appeal to *his*

sexuality. It has nothing to do with her sexuality. (Here and in the European tradition generally, the convention of not painting the hair on a woman's body helps towards the same end. Hair is associated with sexual power, with passion. The woman's sexual passion needs to be minimized so that the spectator may feel that he has the monopoly of such passion.) Women are there to feed an appetite, not to have any of their own.

Compare the expressions of these two women: one the model for a famous painting by Ingres and the other a model for a photograph in a girlie magazine.

Is not the expression remarkably similar in each case? It is the expression of a woman responding with calculated charm to the man whom she imagines looking at her – although she doesn't know him. She is offering up her femininity as the surveyed.

It is true that sometimes a painting includes a male lover.

But the woman's attention is very rarely directed towards him. Often she looks away from him or she looks out of the picture towards the one who considers himself her true lover – the spectator-owner.

There was a special category of private pornographic paintings (especially in the eighteenth century) in which couples making love make an appearance. But even in front of these it is clear that the spectator-owner will in fantasy oust the other man, or else identify with him. By contrast the image of the couple in non-European traditions provokes the notion of many couples making love. 'We all have a thousand hands, a thousand feet and will never go alone.'

Almost all post-Renaissance European sexual imagery is frontal – either literally or metaphorically – because the sexual protagonist is the spectator-owner looking at it.

The absurdity of this male flattery reached its peak in the public academic art of the nineteenth century. Men of state, of business, discussed under paintings like this. When one of them felt he had been outwitted, he looked up for consolation. What he saw reminded him that he was a man.

There are a few exceptional nudes in the European tradition of oil painting to which very little of what has been said above applies. Indeed they are no longer nudes – they break the norms of the art-form; they are paintings of loved women, more or less naked. Among the hundreds of thousands of nudes which make up the tradition there are perhaps a hundred of these exceptions. In each case the painter's personal vision of the particular women he is painting is so strong that it makes no allowance for the spectator. The painter's vision binds the woman to him so that they become as inseparable as couples in stone. The spectator can witness their relationship – but he can do no more: he is forced to recognize himself as the outsider he is. He cannot deceive himself into believing that she is naked for him. He cannot turn her into a nude. The way the painter has painted her includes her will and her intentions in the very structure of the image, in the very expression of her body and her face.

The typical and the exceptional in the tradition can be defined by the simple naked/nude antinomy, but the problem of painting nakedness is not as simple as it might at first appear.

What is the sexual function of nakedness in reality? Clothes encumber contact and movement. But it would seem that nakedness has a positive visual value in its own right: we want to *see* the other naked: the other delivers to us the sight of themselves and we seize upon it – sometimes quite regardless of whether it is for the first time or the hundredth. What does this sight of the other mean to us, how does it, at that instant of total disclosure, affect our desire?

Their nakedness acts as a confirmation and provokes a very strong sense of relief. She is a woman like any other: or he is a man like any other: we are overwhelmed by the marvellous simplicity of the familiar sexual mechanism.

We did not, of course, consciously expect this to be otherwise: unconscious homosexual desires (or unconscious heterosexual desires if the couple concerned are homosexual) may have led each to half expect something different. But the 'relief' can be explained without recourse to the unconscious.

We did not expect them to be otherwise, but the urgency and complexity of our feelings bred a sense of uniqueness which the sight of the other, as she is or as he is, now dispels. They are more like the rest of their sex than they are different. In this revelation lies the warm and friendly – as opposed to cold and impersonal – anonymity of nakedness.

One could express this differently: at the moment of nakedness first perceived, an element of banality enters: an element that exists only because we need it.

Up to that instant the other was more or less mysterious. Etiquettes of modesty are not merely puritan or sentimental: it is reasonable to recognize a loss of mystery. And the explanation of this loss of mystery may be largely visual. The focus of perception shifts from eyes, mouth, shoulders, hands – all of which are capable of such subtleties of expression that the personality expressed by them is manifold – it shifts from these to the sexual parts, whose formation suggests an utterly compelling but single process. The other is reduced or elevated – whichever you prefer – to their primary sexual category: male or female. Our relief is the relief of finding an unquestionable reality to whose direct demands our earlier highly complex awareness must now yield.

We need the banality which we find in the first instant of disclosure because it grounds us in reality. But it does more than that. This reality, by promising the familiar, proverbial mechanism of sex, offers, at the same time, the possibility of the shared subjectivity of sex.

The loss of mystery occurs simultaneously with the offering of the means for creating a shared mystery. The sequence is: subjective – objective – subjective to the power of two.

We can now understand the difficulty of creating a static image of sexual nakedness. In lived sexual experience nakedness is a process rather than a state. If one moment of that process is isolated, its image will seem banal and its banality, instead of serving as a bridge between two intense imaginative states, will be chilling. This is one reason why expressive photographs of the naked are even rarer than paintings. The easy solution for the photographer is to turn the figure into a nude which, by generalizing both sight and viewer and making sexuality unspecific, turns desire into fantasy.*

Let us examine an exceptional painted image of nakedness. It is a painting by Rubens of his young second wife whom he married when he himself was relatively old.

We see her in the act of turning, her fur about to slip off her shoulders. Clearly she will not remain as she is for more than a second. In a superficial sense her image is as instantaneous as a photograph's. But, in a more profound sense, the painting 'contains' time and its experience. It is easy to imagine that a moment ago before she pulled the fur round her shoulders, she was entirely naked. The consecutive stages up to and away from the moment of total disclosure have been transcended. She can belong to any or all of them simultaneously.

Her body confronts us, not as an immediate sight, but as experience – the painter's experience. Why? There are superficial anecdotal reasons: her dishevelled hair, the expression of her eyes directed towards him, the tenderness with which the exaggerated susceptibility of her skin has been painted. But the profound reason is a formal one. Her appearance has been literally re-cast by the painter's subjectivity. Beneath the fur that she holds across herself, the upper part of her body and her legs can never meet. There is a displacement sideways of about nine inches: her thighs, in order to join on to her hips, are at least nine inches too far to the left.

Rubens probably did not plan this: the spectator may not consciously notice it. In itself it is unimportant. What matters is what it permits. It permits the body to become impossibly dynamic. Its coherence is no longer within itself but within the experience of the painter. More precisely, it permits the upper and lower halves of the body to rotate separately, and in opposite directions, round the sexual centre which is hidden: the torso turning to the right, the legs to the left. At the same time this hidden sexual centre is connected by means of the dark fur coat to all the surrounding darkness in the picture, so that she is turning both around and within the dark which has been made a metaphor for her sex.

Apart from the necessity of transcending the single instant and of admitting subjectivity, there is, as we have seen, one further element which is essential for any great sexual image of the naked. This is the element of banality which must be undisguised but not chilling. It is this which distinguishes between voyeur and lover. Here such banality is to be found in Rubens's compulsive painting of the fat softness of Hélène Fourment's flesh which continually breaks every ideal convention of form and (to him) continually offers the promise of her extraordinary particularity.

The nude in European oil painting is usually presented as an admirable expression of the European humanist spirit. This spirit was inseparable from individualism. And without the development of a highly conscious individualism the exceptions to the tradition (extremely personal images of the naked), would never have been painted. Yet the tradition contained a contradiction which it could not itself resolve. A few individual artists intuitively recognized this and resolved the contradiction in their own terms, but their solutions could never enter the tradition's *cultural* terms.

The contradiction can be stated simply. On the one hand the individualism of the artist, the thinker, the patron, the owner: on the other hand, the person who is the object of their activities – the woman – treated as a thing or an abstraction.

Dürer believed that the ideal nude ought to be constructed by taking the face of one body, the breasts of another, the legs of a third, the shoulders of a fourth, the hands of a fifth – and so on.

The result would glorify Man. But the exercise presumed a remarkable indifference to who any one person really was.

In the art-form of the European nude the painters and spectator-owners were usually men and the persons treated as objects, usually women. This unequal relationship is so deeply embedded in our culture that it still structures the consciousness of many women. They do to themselves what men do to them. They survey, like men, their own femininity.

In modern art the category of the nude has become less important. Artists themselves began to question it. In this, as in many other respects, Manet represented a turning point. If one compares his *Olympia* with Titian's original, one sees a woman, cast in the traditional role, beginning to question that role, somewhat defiantly.

The ideal was broken. But there was little to replace it except the 'realism' of the prostitute – who became the quintessential woman of early avant-garde twentieth-century painting. (Toulouse-Lautrec, Picasso, Rouault, German Expressionism, etc.) In academic painting the tradition continued.

Today the attitudes and values which informed that tradition are expressed through other more widely diffused media – advertising, journalism, television.

But the essential way of seeing women, the essential use to which their images are put, has not changed. Women are depicted in a quite different way from men – not because the feminine is different from the masculine – but because the 'ideal' spectator is always assumed to be male and the image of the woman is designed to flatter him. If you have any doubt that this is so, make the following experiment. Choose an image of a traditional nude. Transform the woman into a man. Either in your mind's eye or by drawing on the reproduction. Then notice the violence which that transformation does. Not to the image, but to the assumptions of a likely viewer.

[. . .]

Publicity relies to a very large extent on the language of oil painting. It speaks in the same voice about the same things. Sometimes the visual correspondences are so close that it is possible to play a game of 'Snap!'—putting almost identical images or details of images side by side. It is not, however, just at the level of exact pictorial correspondence that the continuity is important: it is at the level of the sets of signs used.

Compare the images of publicity and paintings, or take a picture magazine, or walk down a smart shopping street looking at the window displays, and then turn over the pages of an illustrated museum catalogue, and notice how similarly messages are conveyed by the two media. A systematic study needs to be made of this. Here we can do no more than indicate a few areas where the similarity of the devices and aims is particularly striking.

The gestures of models (mannequins) and mythological figures.

The romantic use of nature (leaves, trees, water) to create a place where innocence can be refound.

The exotic and nostalgic attraction of the Mediterranean.

The poses taken up to denote stereotypes of women: serene mother (madonna), free-wheeling secretary (actress, king's mistress), perfect hostess (spectator-owner's wife), sex-object (Venus, nymph surprised), etc.

The special sexual emphasis given to women's legs.

The materials particularly used to indicate luxury: engraved metal, furs, polished leather, etc.

The gestures and embraces of lovers, arranged frontally for the benefit of the spectator.

The sea, offering a new life.

The physical stance of men conveying wealth and virility.

The treatment of distance by perspective – offering mystery.

The equation of drinking and success.

The man as knight (horseman) become motorist.

Why does publicity depend so heavily upon the visual language of oil painting?

Publicity is the culture of the consumer society. It propagates through images that society's belief in itself. There are several reasons why these images use the language of oil painting.

Oil painting, before it was anything else, was a celebration of private property. As an art-form it derived from the principle that *you are what you have.*

It is a mistake to think of publicity supplanting the visual art of post-Renaissance Europe; it is the last moribund form of that art.

Publicity is, in essence, nostalgic. It has to sell the past to the future. It cannot itself supply the standards of its own claims. And so all its references to quality are bound to be retrospective and traditional. It would lack both confidence and credibility if it used a strictly contemporary language.

Publicity needs to turn to its own advantage the traditional education of the average spectator-buyer. What he has learnt at school of history, mythology, poetry can be used in the manufacturing of glamour. Cigars can be sold in the name of a King, underwear in connection with the Sphinx, a new car by reference to the status of a country house.

In the language of oil painting these vague historical or poetic or moral references are always present. The fact that they are imprecise and ultimately meaningless is an advantage: they should not be understandable, they should merely be reminiscent of cultural lessons half-learnt. Publicity makes all history mythical, but to do so effectively it needs a visual language with historical dimensions.

Lastly, a technical development made it easy to translate the language of oil painting into publicity clichés. This was the invention, about fifteen years ago, of cheap colour photography. Such photography can reproduce the colour and texture and tangibility of objects as only oil paint had been able to do before. Colour photography is to the spectator-buyer what oil paint was to the spectator-owner. Both media use similar, highly tactile means to play upon the spectator's sense of acquiring the *real* thing which the image shows. In both cases his feeling that he can almost touch what is in the image reminds him how he might or does possess the real thing.

Yet, despite this continuity of language, the function of publicity is very different from that of the oil painting. The spectator-buyer stands in a very different relation to the world from the spectator-owner.

The oil painting showed what its owner was already enjoying among his possessions and his way of life. It consolidated his own sense of his own value. It enhanced his view of himself as he already was. It began with facts, the facts of his life. The paintings embellished the interior in which he actually lived.

The purpose of publicity is to make the spectator marginally dissatisfied with his present way of life. Not with the way of life of society, but with his own within it. It suggests that if he buys what it is offering, his life will become better. It offers him an improved alternative to what he is.

The oil painting was addressed to those who made money out of the market. Publicity is addressed to those who constitute the market, to the spectator-buyer who is also the consumer-producer from whom profits are made twice over – as worker and then as buyer. The only places relatively free of publicity are the quarters of the very rich; their money is theirs to keep.

All publicity works upon anxiety. The sum of everything is money, to get money is to overcome anxiety. Alternatively the anxiety on which publicity plays is the fear that having nothing you will be nothing.

Money is life. Not in the sense that without money you starve. Not in the sense that capital gives one class power over the entire lives of another class. But in the sense that money is the token of, and the key to, every human capacity. The power to spend money is the power to live. According to the legends of publicity, those who lack the power to spend money become literally faceless. Those who have the power become lovable.

Publicity increasingly uses sexuality to sell any product or service. But this sexuality is never free in itself; it is a symbol for something presumed to be larger than it: the good life in which you can buy whatever you want. To be able to buy is the same thing as being sexually desirable; occasionally this is the explicit message of publicity. Usually it is the implicit message, i.e. If you are able to buy this product you will be lovable. If you cannot buy it, you will be less lovable.

[. . .]

The spectator-buyer is meant to envy herself as she will become if she buys the product. She is meant to imagine herself transformed by the product into an object of envy for others, an envy which will then justify her loving herself. One could put this another way: the publicity image steals her love of herself as she is, and offers it back to her for the price of the product.

15.
STEREOTYPE, REALISM, AND THE STRUGGLE OVER REPRESENTATION

Ella Shohat and Robert Stam

Much of the work on ethnic/racial and colonial representation in the media has been "corrective," devoted to demonstrating that certain films, in some respect or other, "got something wrong" on historical, biographical, or other grounds of accuracy. While these "stereotypes and distortions" analyses pose legitimate questions about social plausibility and mimetic accuracy, about negative and positive images, they are often premised on an exclusive allegiance to an esthetic of verisimilitude.[1] An obsession with "realism" casts the question as simply one of "errors" and "distortions," as if the "truth" of a community were unproblematic, transparent, and easily accessible, and "lies" about that community easily unmasked. Debates about ethnic representation often break down on precisely this question of "realism," at times leading to an impasse in which diverse spectators or critics passionately defend their version of the "real."

The Question of Realism

These debates about realism and accuracy are not trivial, not just a symptom of the "veristic idiocy," as a certain poststructuralism would have it. Spectators (and critics) are invested in realism because they are invested in the idea of truth, and reserve the right to confront a film with their own personal and cultural knowledge. No deconstructionist fervor should induce us to surrender the right to find certain films sociologically false or ideologically pernicious, to see *Birth of a Nation* (1915), for example, as an "objectively" racist film. That films are only representations does not prevent them from

having real effects in the world; racist films can mobilize for the Ku Klux Klan, or prepare the ground for retrograde social policy. Recognizing the inevitability and the inescapability of representation does not mean, as Stuart Hall has put it, that "nothing is at stake."

The desire to reserve a right to judgment on questions of realism comes into play especially in cases where there are real-life prototypes for characters and situations, and where the film, whatever its conventional disclaimers, implicitly makes, and is received as making, historical-realist claims. (Isaac Jullen's *Looking for Langston*, 1989, dodges the problem through a generic "end run" by labelling itself as a "mediation" on Langston Hughes.) The veterans of the 1960s civil rights struggle are surely in a position to critique *Mississippi Burning* (1988) for turning the movement's historical enemy – the racist FBI which harassed and sabotaged the movement – into the film's heroes, while turning the historical heroes – the thousands of African-Americans who marched and braved beatings and imprisonment and sometimes death – into the supporting cast, passive victim-observers waiting for official White rescue.[2] This struggle over meaning matters because *Mississippi Burning* might induce audiences unfamiliar with the facts into a fundamental misreading of American history, idealizing the FBI and regarding African-Americans as mute witnesses of history rather than its makers.[3] Thus although there is no absolute truth, no truth apart from representation and dissemination, there are still contingent, qualified, perspectival truths in which communities are invested.

Poststructuralist theory reminds us that we live and dwell within language and representation, and have no direct access to the "real." But the constructed, coded nature of artistic discourse hardly precludes all reference to a common social life. Filmic fictions inevitably bring into play real-life assumptions not only about space and time but also about social and cultural relationships. Films which represent marginalized cultures in a realistic mode, even when they do not claim to represent specific historical incidents, still implicitly make factual claims. Thus critics are right to draw attention to the complacent ignorance of Hollywood portrayals of Native Americans, to the cultural flattening which erases the geographical and cultural differences between Great Plains tribes and those from other regions, which have Indians of the northeast wearing Plains Indians clothing and living in Hopi dwellings, all collapsed into a single stereotypical figure, the "instant Indian" with "wig, war bonnet, breechclout, moccasins, phony beadwork."[4]

Many oppressed groups have used "progressive realism" to unmask and combat hegemonic representations, countering the objectifying discourses of patriarchy and colonialism with a vision of themselves and their reality "from within." But this laudable intention is not always unproblematic. "Reality" is not self-evidently given and "truth" is not immediately "seizable" by the camera. We must distinguish, furthermore, between realism as a goal – Brecht's "laying bare the causal network" – and realism as a style or constellation of strategies aimed at producing an illusionistic "reality effect." Realism as a goal is quite compatable with a style which is reflexive and deconstructive, as is eloquently demonstrated by many of the alternative films discussed in this book.

In his work, Mikhail Bakhtin reformulates the notion of artistic representation in such a way as to avoid both a naive faith in "truth" and "reality" and the equally naive notion that the ubiquity of language and representation signifies the end of struggle and the "end of history." Human consciousness and artistic practice, Bakhtin argues, do not come into contact with the "real" directly but rather through the medium of the surrounding ideological world. Literature, and by extension cinema, do not so much refer to or call up the world as represent its languages and discourses. Rather than directly reflecting the real, or even

refracting the real, artistic discourse constitutes a refraction of a refraction; that is, a mediated version of an already textualized and "discursivized" socioideological world. This formulation transcends a naive referential verism without falling into a "hermeneutic nihilism" whereby all texts become nothing more than a meaningless play of signification. Bakhtin rejects naive formulations of realism, in other words, without abandoning the notion that artistic representations are at the same time thoroughly and irrevocably social, precisely because the discourses that art represents are *themselves* social and historical. Indeed, for Bakhtin art is incontrovertibly social, not because it represents the real but because it constitutes a historically situated "utterance" – a complex of signs addressed by one socially constituted subject or subjects to other socially constituted subjects, all of whom are deeply immersed in historical circumstance and social contingency.

The issue, then, is less one of fidelity to a preexisting truth or reality than one of a specific orchestration of ideological discourses and communitarian perspectives. While on one level film is mimesis, representation, it is also utterance, an act of contextualized interlocution between socially situated producers and receivers. It is not enough to say that art is constructed. We have to ask: Constructed for whom? And in conjunction with which ideologies and discourses? In this sense, art is a representation not so much in a mimetic as a political sense, as a delegation of voice.[5] Within this perspective, it makes more sense to say of *The Gods Must Be Crazy* (1984) not that it is untrue to "reality," but that it relays the colonialist discourse of official White South Africa. The racist discourse of the film posits a Manichean binarism contrasting happy and noble but impotent Bantustan "Bushmen," living in splendid isolation, with dangerous but incompetent mulatto-led revolutionaries. Yet the film camouflages its racism by a superficial critique of White technological civilization. A discursive approach to *First Blood (Rambo)* (1983), similarly, would not argue that it "distorts" reality, but rather that it "really" represents a rightist and racist discourse designed to flatter and nourish the masculinist fantasies of omnipotence characteristic of an empire in crisis. By the same token, representations can be convincingly verisimilar, yet Eurocentric, or conversely, fantastically "inaccurate," yet anti-Eurocentric. The analysis of a film like

My Beautiful Laundrette (1985), sociologically flawed from a mimetic perspective – given its focus on wealthy Asians rather than more typically working-class Asians in London – alters considerably when regarded as a constellation of discursive strategies, as a provocative symbolic inversion of conventional expectations of a miserabilist account of Asian victimization.

That something vital is at stake in these debates becomes obvious in those instances when entire communities passionately protest the representations that are made of them in the name of their own experiential sense of truth. Hollywood stereotypes have not gone unremarked by the communities they portrayed. Native Americans, very early on, vocally protested misrepresentations of their culture and history.[6] A 1911 issue of *Moving Picture World* (August 3) reports a Native American delegation to President Taft protesting erroneous representations and even asking for a Congressional investigation. In the same vein, the National Association for the Advancement of Colored People (NAACP) protested *Birth of a Nation*, Chicanos protested the *bandido* films, Mexicans protested *Viva Villa!* (1934), Brazilians protested *Rio's Road to Hell* (1931), Cubans protested *Cuban Love Song* (1931), and Latin Americans generally protested the caricaturing of their culture. The Mexican government threatened to block distribution of Hollywood films in Mexico if the US film industry did not stop exporting films caricaturing Mexico, Mexican Americans, and the Mexican revolution. More recently, Turks protested *Midnight Express* (1978), Puerto Ricans protested *Fort Apache the Bronx* (1981), Africans protested *Out of Africa* (1985) and Asian-Americans protested *The Year of the Dragon* (1985). Native Americans so vigorously protested the TV series *Mystic Warrior*, based on Ruth Beebe Hill's Ayn Rand-inflected pseudo-Indian saga *Hanta Yo* (1979), that the film version could not be made in the US. One American Indian Movement pamphlet distributed during protests offered ironic guidelines on "How to Make an Indian Movie":

> How to make an Indian Movie. Buy 40 Indians. Totally humiliate and degrade an entire Indian nation. Make sure all Indians are savage, cruel and ignorant ... Import a Greek to be an Indian princess. Introduce a white man to become an "Indian" hero. Make the white man compassionate, brave and understanding ... Pocket the profits in Hollywood.

Critical spectators can thus exert pressure on distribution and exhibition, and even affect subsequent productions. While such pressure does not guarantee sympathetic representations, it does at least mean that aggressively hurtful portrayals will not go unchallenged.

Although total realism is a theoretical impossibility, then, spectators themselves come equipped with a "sense of the real" rooted in their own experience, on the basis of which they can accept, question, or even subvert a film's representations. In this sense, the cultural preparation of a particular audience can generate counter-pressure to a racist or prejudicial discourse. Latin American audiences laughed Hollywood's know-nothing portrayals of them off the screen, finding it impossible to take such misinformed images seriously. The Spanish-language version of *Dracula*, for example, made concurrently with the 1931 Bela Lugosi film, mingled Cuban, Argentine, Chilean, Mexican, and peninsular Spanish in a linguistic hodge-podge that struck Latin American audiences as ludicrous. At the same time, spectators may look beyond caricatural representations to see the oppressed performing self. African-Americans were not likely to take Step'n Fetchit as a typical, synecdochic sample of Black behavior or attitudes; Black audiences knew he was acting, and understood the circumstances that led him to play subservient roles. In the same vein, in a kind of double consciousness, spectators may enjoy what they know to be misrepresentations; Baghdadi spectators could enjoy *The Thief of Baghdad* (1940), for example, because they took it as an escapist fantasy, as a Western embroidery of an already fantastic tale from *A Thousand and One Nights*, with no relation to the "real" historical Baghdad.

The Burden of Representation

The hair-trigger sensitivity about racial stereotypes derives partly from what has been labeled the "burden of representation." The connotations of "representation" are at once religious, esthetic, political, and semiotic. On a religious level, the Judeo-Islamic censure of "graven images" and the preference for abstract representations such as the arabesque cast theological suspicion on directly figurative representation and thus on the very ontology of the mimetic arts.[7] Representation also has an esthetic dimension, in that art too is a form of representation, in Platonic or Aristotelian terms, a mimesis. Representation is theatrical too, and in many languages "to represent" means "to enact" or play a role. The narrative and mimetic arts, to the extent that they represent ethos (character) and ethnos (peoples) are considered representative not only of the human figure but also of anthropomorphic vision. On another level, representation is also political, in that political rule is not usually direct but representative. Marx said of the peasantry that "they do not represent themselves; they must be represented." The contemporary definition of democracy in the West, unlike the classical Athenian concept of democracy, or that of various Native American communities, rests on the notion of "representative government," as in the rallying cry of "No taxation without representation." Many of the political debates around race and gender in the US have revolved around the question of self-representation, seen in the pressure for more "minority" representation in political and academic institutions. What all these instances share is the semiotic principle that something is "standing for" something else, or that some person or group is speaking on behalf of some other persons or groups. On the symbolic battlegrounds of the mass media, the struggle over representation in the simulacral realm homologizes that of the political sphere, where questions of imitation and representation easily slide into issues of delegation and voice. (The heated debate around which celebrity photographs, whether of Italian-Americans or of African-Americans, will adorn the wall of Sal's Pizzeria in Spike Lee's *Do the Right Thing*, 1989, vividly exemplifies this kind of struggle within representation.)

Since what Memmi calls the "mark of the plural" projects colonized people as "all the same," any negative behavior by any member of the oppressed community is instantly generalized as typical, as pointing to a perpetual backsliding toward some presumed negative essence. Representations thus become allegorical; within hegemonic discourse every subaltern performer/role is seen as synecdochically summing up a vast but putatively homogenous community. Representations of dominant groups, on the other hand, are seen not as allegorical but as "naturally" diverse, examples of the ungeneralizable variety of life itself.[8] Socially empowered groups need not be unduly concerned about "distortions and stereotypes," since even occasionally negative images form part of a wide spectrum of representations. A corrupt White politician is not seen as an "embarrassment to the race;" financial scandals are not seen as a negative reflection on White power. Yet each negative image of an underrepresented group becomes, within the hermeneutics of domination, sorely overcharged with allegorical meaning as part of what Michael Rogin calls the "surplus symbolic value" of oppressed people; the way Blacks, for example, can be made to stand for something beside themselves.[9]

This sensitivity operates on a continuum with other representations and with everyday life, where the "burden" can indeed become almost unbearable. It is this continuum that is ignored when analysts place stereotypes of so-called ethnic Americans, for example, on the same level as those of Native Americans or African-Americans. While all negative stereotypes are hurtful, they do not all exercise the same power in the world. The facile catch-all invocation of "stereotypes" elides a crucial distinction: stereotypes of some communities merely make the target group uncomfortable, but the community has the social power to combat and resist them; stereotypes of other communities participate in a continuum of prejudicial social policy and actual violence against disempowered people, placing the very body of the accused in jeopardy. Stereotypes of Polish-Americans and Italian-Americans, however regrettable, have not been shaped within the racial and imperial foundation of the US, and are not used to justify daily violence or structural oppression against these communities. The media's tendency to present all Black males as potential delinquents, in contrast, has a searing impact on the actual lives of Black people. In the Stuart case in Boston, the police, at the instigation of the actual (White) murderer, interrogated and searched as many Black men as they could in a Black neighborhood, a measure unthinkable in White neighborhoods, which are rarely seen as representational sites of crime. In the same way, the 1988 Bush campaign's "allegorical" deployment of the "Black buck" figure of Willie Horton to trigger the sexual and racial phobias of White voters, dramatically sharpened the burden of representation carried by millions of Black men, and indirectly by Black women.

The sensitivity around stereotypes and distortions largely arises, then, from the powerlessness of historically marginalized groups to control their own representation. A full understanding of media representation therefore requires a comprehensive analysis of the institutions that generate and distribute mass-mediated texts as well as of the audience that receives them. Whose stories are told? By whom? How are they manufactured, disseminated, received? What are the structural mechanisms of the film and media industry? Who controls production, distribution, exhibition? [. . .]

The Racial Politics of Casting

Film and theater casting, as an immediate form of representation, constitutes a kind of delegation of voice with political overtones. Here too Europeans and Euro-Americans have played the dominant role, relegating non-Europeans to supporting roles and the status of extras. Within Hollywood cinema, Euro-Americans have historically enjoyed the unilateral prerogative of acting in "blackface," "redface," "brownface," and "yellowface," while the reverse has rarely been the case. From the nineteenth-century vaudeville stage through such figures as Al Jolson in *Hi Lo Broadway* (1933), Fred Astaire in *Swing Time* (1936), Mickey Rooney and Judy Garland in *Babes in Arms* (1939), and Bing Crosby in *Dixie* (1943), the tradition of blackface recital furnished one of the most popular of American pop-cultural forms. Even Black minstrel performers like Bert Williams, as the film *Ethnic Notions* (1987) points out, were obliged to carry the mark of caricature on their own bodies; burnt cork literalized, as it were, the trope of Blackness.

Political considerations in racial casting were quite overt in the silent period. In *The Birth of a Nation* subservient Negroes were played by actual Blacks, while aggressive, threatening Blacks were played largely by Whites in blackface. But after protests by the NAACP, Hollywood cautiously began to cast black actors in small roles. Nevertheless, even in the sound period, White actresses were called on to play the "tragic mulattas" of such films as *Pinky* (1949), *Imitation of Life* (1959), and even of the Cassavetes underground film *Shadows* (1959). Meanwhile, real-life "mulattas" were cast for Black female roles – for example Lena Horne in *Cabin in the Sky* (1943) – although they could easily have "passed" for White roles. In other words, it is not the literal color of the actor that mattered in casting. Given the "blood" definition of "Black" versus "White" in Euro-American racist discourse, one drop of Black blood was sufficient to disqualify an actress like Horne from representing White women.

African-Americans were not the only "people of color" to be played by Euro-Americans; the same law of unilateral privilege functioned in relation to other groups. Rock Hudson, Joey Bishop, Boris Karloff, Tom Mix, Elvis Presley, Anne Bancroft, Cyd Charisse, Loretta Young, Mary Pickford, Dame Judith Anderson and Douglas Fairbanks Jr are among the many Euro-American actors who have represented Native American roles, while Paul Muni, Charlton Heston, Marlon Brando, and Natalie Wood are among those who have played Latino characters. As late as *Windwalker* (1973), the most important Indian roles were not played by Native Americans. Dominant cinema is fond of turning "dark" or Third World peoples into substitutable others, interchangeable units who can "stand in" for one another. Thus the Mexican Dolores del Rio played a South Seas Samoan in *Bird of Paradise* (1932), while the Indian Sabu played a wide range of Arab-oriental roles. Lupe Velez, actually Mexican, portrayed Chinese, "Eskimos" (Inuit), Japanese, Malayans, and American-Indian women, while Omar Sharif, an Egyptian, played Che Guevara.[10] This asymmetry in representational power has generated intense resentment among minoritarian communities, for whom the casting of a non-member of the "minority" group is a triple insult, implying (a) you are unworthy of self-represention; (b) no one from your community is capable of representing you; and (c) we, the producers of the film, care little about your offended sensibilities, for we have the power and there is nothing you can do about it.

These practices have implications even on the brute material level of literal self-representation, that is, the need for work. The racist idea that a film, to be economically viable, must use a "universal" star, reveals the intrication of economics and racism. That people of color have historically been limited to racially designated roles, while Whites are ideologically seen as "beyond ethnicity," has had disastrous consequences for "minority" artists. In Hollywood, this situation is only now changing, with star actors like Larry Fishburne, Wesley Snipes, and Denzel Washington winning roles originally earmarked for White actors. At the same time, even "affirmative action" casting can serve racist purposes, as when the role of the White judge in the novel *Bonfire of the Vanities* (1990) was given to Morgan Freeman in the Brian de Palma film, but only as a defense mechanism to ward off accusations of racism.

Nor does chromatically literal self-representation guarantee non-Eurocentric representation. The system can simply "use" the performer to enact the dominant set of codes; even, at times, over the performer's objection. Josephine Baker's star status did not enable her to alter the ending of *Princess Tam Tam* (1935) to have her North African (Berber) character marry the French aristocrat instead of the North African servant, or to marry the working-class Frenchman played by Jean Gabin in *Zou Zou* (1934). Instead, Zou Zou ends up alone, performing as a caged bird pining for the Caribbean. Despite her protests, Baker's roles were circumscribed by the codes that forbade her screen access to White men as legitimate marriage partners. Their excessive performance styles allowed actresses like Josephine Baker and Carmen Miranda to undercut and parody stereotypical roles, but could not gain them substantive power. Even the expressive performance of the politically aware Paul Robeson was enlisted, despite the actor's protests, in the encomium to European colonialism in Africa that is *Sanders of the River* (1935). In recent years Hollywood has made gestures toward "correct" casting; African-American, Native American, and Latino/a performers have been allowed to "represent" their communities. But this "realistic" casting is hardly sufficient if narrative structure and cinematic strategies remain Eurocentric. An epidermically correct face does not guarantee community self-representation, any more than Clarence Thomas's black skin guarantees his representation of African-American legal interests.

A number of film and theater directors have sought alternative approaches to literally self-representative casting. Orson Welles staged all-Black versions of Shakespeare plays, most notably his "Voodoo Macbeth" in Harlem in 1936. Peter Brook, similarly, cast a rainbow of multicultural performers in his filmic adaptation of the Hindu epic *The Mahabaratha* (1990). Glauber Rocha deliberately confused linguistic and thespian self-representations in his *Der Leone Have Sept Cabecas* (1970), whose very title subverts the linguistic positioning of the spectator by mingling five of the languages of Africa's colonizers. Rocha's Brechtian fable animates emblematic figures representing the diverse colonizing nations, suggesting imperial homologies among them by having an Italian-accented speaker play the role of the American, a Frenchman play the German and so forth.

Such antiliteral strategies provoke an irreverent question: what is wrong with non-originary casting? Doesn't acting always involve a ludic play with identity? Should we applaud Blacks playing Hamlet but not Laurence Olivier playing Othello? And have not Euro-American and European performers often ethnically substituted for one another (for example, Greta Garbo and Cyd Charisse as Russians in *Ninotchka*, 1939, and *Silk Stockings*, 1957)? Casting, we would argue, has to be seen in contingent terms, in relation to the role, the political and esthetic intention, and to the historical moment. We cannot equate a gigantic charade whereby a whole foreign country is represented by players not from that country and is imagined as speaking a language not its own (a frequent Hollywood practice), with cases where non-literal casting forms part of an alternative esthetic. The casting of Blacks to play Hamlet, for example, militates against a traditional discrimination that denied Blacks any role, literally and metaphorically, in both the performing arts and in politics, while the casting of Laurence Olivier as Othello prolongs a venerable history of deliberately bypassing Black talent. We see the possibilities of epidermically incorrect casting in *Seeing Double* (1989), a San Francisco Mime Troupe play about the Israeli-Palestinian conflict, where an ethnically diverse cast takes on shifting roles in such a way as to posit analogical links between communities. An African-American actor plays both a Palestinian-American and a Jewish-American, for example, thus hinting at a common history of exclusion binding Blacks, Jews, and Arabs.

The Linguistics of Domination

The same issues of self-representation arise in relation to language. As potent symbols of collective identity, languages are the foci of deep loyalties existing at the razor's edge of national and cultural difference. Although languages as abstract entities do not exist in hierarchies of value, languages as lived operate within hierarchies of power. Inscribed within the play of power, language becomes caught up in the cultural hierarchies typical of Eurocentrism. English, especially, has often served as the linguistic vehicle for the projection of Anglo-American power, technology, and finance. Hollywood films, for their part, betray a linguistic hybrid bred of empire. Hollywood proposed to tell not only its own stories but also those of other nations, and not only to Americans but also to the other nations themselves, and always in English. In Cecil B. de Mille epics, both the ancient Egyptians and the Israelites, not to mention God, speak English. By ventriloquizing the world, Hollywood indirectly diminished the possibilities of linguistic self-representation for other nations. Hollywood both profited from and itself promoted the world-wide dissemination of the English language, thus contributing indirectly to the subtle erosion of the linguistic autonomy of other cultures.

Since for the colonizer, to be human was to speak the colonizing language, colonized people were encouraged to abandon their languages. Ngũgĩ wa Thiong'o tells of Kenyan children being punished for speaking their own languages, caned or made to carry plaques inscribed with the words "I am stupid."[11] But the colonized, as David Spurr points out, are denied speech in a double sense, first in the idiomatic sense of not being allowed to speak, and second in the more radical sense of not being recognized as capable of speech.[12] It is this historical sense of tying tongues that has provoked protest against countless films, where linguistic discrimination and colonialist

"tact" go hand in hand with condescending characterization and distorted social portraiture. The "Indians" of classic Hollywood westerns, denuded of their own idiom, mouth pidgin English, a mark of their inability to master the "civilized" language. In many First World films set in the Third World, the "word of the other" is elided, distorted, or caricatured. In films set in North Africa, for example, Arabic is an indecipherable murmur, while the "real" language of communication is the French of Jean Gabin in *Pépé le Moko* (1936) or the English of Bogart and Bergman in *Casablanca* (1942). In Lean's *Lawrence of Arabia* (1962), which is pretentiously, even ostentatiously sympathetic to the Arabs, we hear almost no Arabic at all but rather English spoken in a motley of accents, almost all of them (Omar Sharif's being the exception) having little to do with Arabic. And, more recently, Bertolucci's *The Sheltering Sky* (1991), set in North Africa, privileges the English of its protagonists and does not bother to translate Arabic dialog. Given this film history, the relative advance of *Dances with Wolves* (1990), and *Black Robe* (1991), trigger hopes for a sea-change in linguistic representation.

Many Third World filmmakers have reacted against the hegemonic deployment of European languages in dominant cinema. Although English, for example, has become the literary *lingua franca* for postcolonials like Ben Okri, Derek Walcott, Bharati Mukherjee, Salman Rushdie, and Vikram Seth, and in this sense is no longer the possession of its original "owners," it has also been met with the anti-neocolonial demand of return to one's linguistic sources. Ngũgĩ wa Thiong'o's challenge to African writers – that they write in African rather than European languages – has to some extent been taken up by African filmmakers, for whom the use of African languages (with subtitles) is standard procedure. Ousmane Sembene, for example, has filmed in diverse African languages, notably Diola and Wolof. Sembene has also foregrounded the issue of language and power within the colonial situation. His *Xala* (1974), for example, links issues of linguistic and social representation. The protagonist, El Hadji, a polygamous Senegalese businessman, embodies the neocolonized attitudes of the African elite so vehemently denounced by Fanon. Sembene structures the film around the opposition of Wolof and French. While the elite don

African dress and make nationalist speeches in Wolof, they speak French among themselves and reveal European suits beneath their African garb. Many of the characterizations revolve around the question of language. El Hadji's first wife, Adja, representing the precolonial African woman, speaks Wolof and wears traditional clothes. The second wife, Oumi, mimics European fashions, affects French, and wears wigs, sunglasses, and low-cut dresses. Finally, El Hadji's daughter, Rama, representing the progressive hybrid of Africa and Europe, knows French but insists on speaking Wolof to her francophile father, who prefers she seal her lips. Instead, she performs what Gloria Anzaldúa calls "linguistic code-switching" in the face of censorious forces, "transforming silence with (an) other alphabet."[13] Thus conflicts involving language-shifts are made to carry a strong charge of social and cultural tension.

As a social battleground, language forms the site where political struggles are engaged both collectively and intimately. People do not enter simply into language as a master code; they participate in it as socially constituted subjects whose linguistic exchange is shaped by power relations. In the case of colonialism, linguistic reciprocity is simply out of the question. In Sembene's *La Noire de . . .* (Black Girl, 1966), the female protagonist Diouana stands at the convergence of multiple structures of inequality – as Black, as maid, as woman – and her oppression is conveyed specifically through language. Diouana overhears her French employer say of her: "She understands French . . . by instinct . . . like an animal." The colonialist here transforms a defining human characteristic – the capacity for language – into a sign of animality, even though Diouana knows French while her employers, after years in Senegal, know nothing of her language and culture. It is this regime of linguistic non-reciprocity which distinguishes colonial bilingualism from ordinary linguistic dualism. For the colonizer, the refusal of the colonized's language is linked to the denial of political self-determination, while for the colonized mastery of the colonizer's tongue testifies both to a capacity for survival and a daily drowning out of one's voice. Colonial bilingualism entails the inhabiting of conflicting psychic and cultural realms.

The neocolonial situation, in which the Hollywood language becomes the model of "real" cinema, has as its linguistic corollary the view of European languages as inherently more "cinematic" than others. The English phrase "I love you," some Brazilian critics argued without irony in the 1920s, was intrinsically more beautiful than the Portuguese *eu te amo*. The particular focus on amorous language reflects not only the lure of Hollywood's romantic model of cinema projecting glamor and popular stars, but also an intuitive sense of the erotics of linguistic neocolonialism – that is, the sense that the imperializing language exercises a kind of phallic power and attraction. Carlos Diegues' *Bye Bye Brazil* (1980), titled in English even in Brazil, looks at English, as it were, "through" Brazilian Portuguese. The name of the film's traveling entertainment troupe – Caravana Rolidei – phonetically transcribes the Brazilian pronunciation of the English "holiday," in a spirit of creative distortion. This refusal to "get it straight" reveals a typical colonial ambivalence, melding sincere affection and resentful parody. The Chico Buarque theme song features expressions like "bye bye," "night and day," and "OK" as indices of the Americanization (and in this case the multinationalization) of a world where Portuguese-speaking Amazonian tribal chiefs wear designer jeans and backwoods rock groups sound like the Bee Gees, embodying a palimpsestic America. In sum, the issue of linguistic self-representation does not simply entail a return to authentic languages but rather the orchestration of languages for emancipatory purposes.[14]

Writing Hollywood and Race

Important work has already been done on the ethnic/racial representation of oppressed communities within Hollywood cinema. Critics such as Vine Deloria, Ralph and Natasha Friar, Ward Churchill, Annette Jaimes, and many others have discussed the binaristic splitting that has turned Native Americans into bloodthirsty beasts or noble savages. Native American critics have denounced the "redface" convention, the practice of having non-Native Americans – White (Rock Hudson), Latino (Ricardo Montalban), or Japanese (Sessue Hayakawa) – play Native American roles. They have also pointed to the innumerable representational blunders of Hollywood films, which have had Indians perform grotesque dog-eating rituals (*The Battle at Elderbush Gulch*, 1913), and wrist-cutting ceremonies (*Broken Arrow*, 1950), and have misascribed specific ceremonies to the wrong tribes (the Sioux Sun-Dance presented as the *okipa* ceremony of the Mandans). Churchill points out that even "sympathetic" films like *A Man Called Horse* (1970), hailed as an authentic, positive portrayal, depicts a people "whose language is Lakota, whose hairstyles range from Assiniboi through Nez Perce to Comache, whose tipi design is Crow, and whose Sun Dance ceremony ... [is] typically Mandan."[15] The film has the Anglo captive teach the Indians the finer points of the bow, a weapon which had been in use by Native Americans for countless generations, thus demonstrating "the presumed inherent superiority of Eurocentric minds."[16]

How can one account for Hollywood films that show some sensitivity to issues of self-representation? A popular film like *Dances with Wolves* demonstrates the need for a nuanced multivalent analysis. The film did break ground by casting Native Americans to play themselves, yet it was less politically audacious in placing its story in the distant past, cordoned off from the contemporary struggles of living native people. However, a thoroughgoing analysis must see the film as contradictory, affirming at the same time that it (1) constitutes a relatively progressive step for Hollywood in its adoption of a pro-indigenous perspective, and (2) in respecting the linguistic integrity of the Native Americans; yet that (3) this progressive step is in part undermined by the traditional split portrayal of bad Pawnees/good Sioux; that (4) it is further compromised by its elegiac emphasis on the remote past and (5) by the foregrounding of a Euro-American protagonist and his (6) idyll with a non-Indian lover; yet that (7) this Euro-American focalization, given the mass audience's identificatory propensities, also guaranteed the film's wide impact; and (8) that this impact indirectly helped open doors for Native American filmmakers, without (9) introducing major institutional changes within the industry, but also (10) altering the ways in which such films are likely to be made in the future, while (11) still forming part, ultimately, of a capitalist/modernist project that has fostered the destruction of Native American peoples.[17] A textually subtle, contextualized analysis, then, must take into account all these

apparently contradictory points at the same time, without lapsing into a Manichean good film/bad film binaristic schema, the "politically correct" equivalent of "bad object" criticism.[18]

A number of scholars, notably Donald Bogle, Daniel Leab, James Snead, Jim Pines, Jacquie Jones, Pearl Bowser, Clyde Taylor, and Thomas Cripps, have explored how preexisting stereotypes – for example the jiving sharpster and shuffling stage sambo – were transferred from antecedent media to film. In *Toms, Coons, Mulattoes, Mammies and Bucks*, Bogle surveys representations of Blacks in Hollywood cinema, especially foregrounding the unequal struggle between Black performers and the stereotypical roles offered them by Hollywood. Bogle's very title announces the five major stereotypes:

1. the servile "Tom" (going back to Uncle Tom in *Uncle Tom's Cabin*);
2. the "Coon" (Step'n Fetchit is the archetypal example), a type itself subdivided into the "pickaninny" (the harmless eye-popping clown figure) and the Uncle Remus (naive, congenial folk philosopher);
3. the "Tragic Mulatto," usually a woman, victim of a dual racial inheritance, who tries to "pass for White" in such films as *Pinky* and *Imitation of Life*; or else the demonized mulatto man, devious and ambitious, like Silas Lynch in *Birth of a Nation*;
4. the "Mammy," the fat, cantankerous but ultimately sympathetic female servant who provides the glue that keeps households together (the Aunt Jemima "handkerchief head" is one variant), such as Hattie McDaniel in *Gone with the Wind*; and
5. the "Buck," the brutal, hypersexualized Black man, a figure of menace inherited from the stage, whose most famous filmic incarnation is perhaps Gus in *Birth of a Nation*, and which George Bush resuscitated for electoral purposes in the figure of Willie Horton.

Bogle's book goes beyond stereotypes to focus on the ways African-American performers have "signified" and subverted the roles forced on them. For Bogle, the history of Black performance is one of battling against confining types and categories, a battle homologous to the quotidian struggle of three-dimensional Blacks against the imprisoning conventions of an apartheid-style system. It is interesting to compare Bogle's largely implicit theory of performance in film with James C. Scott's anthropology of performance and resistance in everyday life. If we see performance as completely determined from above, Scott argues, we "miss the agency of the actor in appropriating the performance for his own ends."[19] Thus subaltern performance encodes, often in sanitized, ambiguous ways, what Scott calls the "hidden transcripts" of a subordinated group. A kind of "euphemization" occurs when hidden transcripts are expressed within power-laden situations by actors who prefer to avoid the sanctions that a direct statement might bring. At their best, Black performances undercut stereotypes by individualizing the type or slyly standing above it. The "flamboyant bossiness" of McDaniel's "Mammy" in *Gone with the Wind*, her way of looking Scarlett right in the eye, within this perspective, translated aggressive hostility toward a racist system. Bogle emphasizes the resilient imagination of Black performers obliged to play against script and studio intentions, their capacity to turn demeaning roles into resistant performance. Thus "each major black actor of the day managed to reveal some unique quality of voice or personality that audiences immediately responded to. Who could forget Bojangles' urbanity? Or Rochester's cement-mixer voice? Or Louise Beavers' jollity? Or Hattie McDaniel's haughtiness?"[20] Performance itself intimated liberatory possibilities.

Historically, Hollywood has tried to "teach" Black performers how to conform to its own stereotypes. Beavers' voice had no trace of dialect or southern patois; she had to school herself in the southern drawl considered compulsory for Black performers. Robert Townsend's *Hollywood Shuffle* (1987) satirizes these racial conventions by having White directors oblige Black actors to conform to White stereotypes about Blackness. The White directors give lessons in street jive, gestures and mannerisms, all of which the Shakespeare-oriented Black actor-protagonist finds distasteful. The protagonist's own dream, presented in a fantasy sequence, is to play prestigious hero roles such as Superman and Rambo or tragic roles like

King Lear. The desire for dignified and socially prestigious dramatic roles reflects a desire to be taken seriously, not always to be the butt of the joke, to win access to the generic prestige historically associated with tragedy and epic, even if Townsend's film relays this desire, paradoxically, in parodic form.

Apart from studies on Native Americans and African-Americans, important work has also been done on the stereotypes of other ethnic groups. In *The Latin Image in American Film*, Allen Woll points to the substratum of male violence common to Latino male stereotypes – the bandido, the greaser, the revolutionary, the bullfighter. Latina women, meanwhile, call up the heat and passionate salsa evoked by the titles of the films of Lupe Velez: *Hot Pepper* (1933), *Strictly Dynamite* (1934), and *Mexican Spitfire* (1940). Arthur G. Pettit, in *Images of the Mexican American in Fiction and Film* traces the intertext of such imagery to the Anglo "conquest fiction" of writers like Ned Buntline and Zane Grey. Already in conquest fiction, Pettit argues, the Mexican is defined negatively, in terms of "qualities diametrically opposed to an Anglo prototype." Anglo conquest authors transferred to the *mestizo* Mexicans the prejudices previously directed toward the Native American and the Black. They excoriate miscegenation and repeatedly sound the theme of the inevitable decline and degeneracy of Mexicans due to race mixing: "the Spaniards and their 'polluted' descendants have comitted racial and national self-genocide by mixing voluntarily with inferior dark-skinned races."[21] In conquest novels, Mexicans are not called Mexicans but "greasers," "yallers," "mongrels," and "niggers". Hollywood inherited these stereotypes – the bandido, the greaser, the "half-breed" whore – along with the positively connoted elite figures of the Castillian gentleman and the high-caste Castillian woman. Morality, in such works, is color-coordinated; the darker the color, the worse the character.[22]

A number of didactic documentaries address the issue of stereotypes. *The Media Show: North American Indians* (1991) critically dissects the portrayal of "Indians" in Hollywood films (including *Dances with Wolves*). Phil Lucas and Robert Hagopian's *Images of Indians* (1979) examines Hollywood films as purveyors of Native American stereotypes. This documentary is divided into five half-hour segments: "The

Great Movie Massacre" examines the warrior image of the Indian; "Heathen Injuns and the Hollywood Gospel" addresses the misrepresentation of indigenous religion; "How Hollywood Wins the West" focusses on the one-sided representations of history; "The Movie Reel Indians" speaks of industry attitudes toward Native Americans; and "Warpaint and Wigs" speaks of the constructedness and artificiality of the Hollywood Indian. *Black History: Lost, Stolen, and Strayed* (1967), narrated by Bill Cosby, criticizes the historical misrepresentations and stereotypical portrayals of Blacks. Marlon Riggs' *Ethnic Notions* stresses the pain caused by stereotypes incarnated in racist cartoons, toys, and films, and alternates citations of racist materials with interviews with African-American performers and scholars. Gloria Ribe's *From Here, from This Side* (1988) deploys Hollywood films and archival material to communicate a vision of cultural domination from the Mexican side. The Edward Said-narrated *In the Shadow of the West* (1984) critiques orientalist imagery in part through conversations with Palestinians, Lebanese, and Arab intellectuals living in the US. Renee Tajima and Christine Choy's *Who Killed Vincent Chin?* (1988), a film about the murder by White autoworkers of a Chinese-American whom they took to be Japanese, uses media materials in its portrayal of anti-Asian discrimination. Valerie Soe's *All Orientals Look the Same* (1986) undercuts the orientalizing "mark of the plural" by having very diverse Asian-American faces dissolve into one another. Christine Choy's and Renee Tajima's *Yellow Tale Blues* (1990) juxtaposes media imagery with the actual situations of Asian-Americans. Shu Lea Cheang's *Color Schemes* (1989) spoofs American melting-pot ideals through the metaphor of "color wash" to explore the ambiguities of racial assimilation. Twelve performers evoke four ethnic "wash cycles": soak, wash, rinse, extract. Deborah Gee's *Slaying the Dragon* (1987), finally, uses film clips (for example, from *The World of Suzie Wong*, 1960) and interviews to show how Asian women have been stereotyped as docile and exotic.

Riggs' *Color Adjustment* (1991) chronicles the history of Black representation on TV, moving from the caricatural days of *Amos and Andy* through Black sitcoms like *Good Tunes* through *Roots* up to the ultimate Black American family: the Huxtables of *The Cosby Show*. Throughout, *Color Adjustment* speaks less about "authentic" representation than about the fundamental paradigm lurking behind most of the shows – the idealized suburban nuclear family. In one of the quoted programs, *All in the Family*, Edith Bunker praises Black progress: "They used to all be servants, and maids, and waiters, and now they're lawyers and doctors. They've come a long way on television!" But this simulacral meliorism, *Color Adjustment* suggests, is deeply inadequate. Even if TV were peopled exclusively by African-American doctors and lawyers, the concrete situation of African-Americans would not thereby be substantially improved. *Color Adjustment* underlines this contrast between media image and social reality by suggestively juxtaposing sitcom episodes with documentary street footage, sometimes by way of contrast (*The Brady Bunch* versus police attacks on civil rights marches), sometimes by way of comparison (scenes of anti-bussing demonstrators hurling racial epithets juxtaposed with Archie Bunker's racial inanities). *Fade to Black* (1989), finally, aggressively orchestrates very diverse materials: a capsule history of Blacks in films, Althusser-influenced theoretical interventions, clips from feature films (*Vertigo*, 1958; *Taxi Driver*, 1976), rap music and a hard-hitting voice-over commentary. The voice-overs by two Black men contrast White verbal denials of racism with everyday "proxemic" expressions of fear and hostility: the White motorist who clicks the car door lock upon seeing a Black man, the White matron who clutches her purse upon seeing a Black man approach.

The Limits of the Stereotype

We would like both to argue for the importance of the study of stereotyping in popular culture and to raise some methodological questions about the underlying premises of character- or stereotype-centered approaches. (We are not implying that the work of the writers just mentioned is reducible to "stereotype analyis.") To begin, the stereotype-centered approach, the analysis of repeated, ultimately pernicious constellations of character traits, has made an indispensable contribution by:

1. revealing oppressive patterns of prejudice in what might at first glance have seemed random and inchoate phenomena;

2. highlighting the psychic devastation inflicted by systematically negative portrayals on those groups assaulted by them, whether through internalization of the stereotypes themselves or through the negative effects of their dissemination; and

3. signaling the social functionality of stereotypes, demonstrating that they are not an error of perception but rather a form of social control, intended as what Alice Walker calls "prisons of image."[23]

The call for "positive images," in the same way, corresponds to a profound logic which only those accustomed to having their narcissism stroked can fail to understand. Given a dominant cinema that trades in heroes and heroines, "minority" communities rightly ask for their fair share of the representational pie as a simple matter of representational parity.

At the same time, the stereotype approach entails a number of theoretical-political pitfalls. First, the exclusive preoccupation with images, whether positive or negative, can lead to a kind of *essentialism*, as less subtle critics reduce a complex variety of portrayals to a limited set of reified formulae. Such criticism is procrustean; the critic forces diverse fictive characters into preestablished categories. Behind every Black child performer the critic discerns a "pickaninny"; behind every sexually attractive Black actor a "buck"; behind every corpulent or nurturing Black female a "mammy." Such reductionist simplifications run the risk of reproducing the very racial essentialism they were designed to combat.

This essentialism generates in its wake a certain *ahistoricism*; the analysis tends to be static, not allowing for mutations, metamorphoses, changes of valence, altered function; it ignores the historical instability of the stereotype and even of language. Some of the basic terminology invoked by Bogle was not always anti-Black. The word "coon," for example, originally referred to rural Whites, becoming a racial slur only around 1848. At the time of the American revolution, the term "buck" evoked a "dashing, virile young man"; and became associated with Blacks only after 1835.[24] Stereotype analysis also fails to register the ways that imagery might be shaped, for example, by structural changes in the economy. How does one

reconcile the "lazy Mexican" from the "greaser films" with the media's present-day "illegal alien" overly eager to work long hours at half pay? On the other hand, images may change, while their function remains the same, or vice versa. Riggs' *Ethnic Notions* explains that the role of the Uncle Tom was not to represent Blacks but rather to reassure Whites with a comforting image of Black docility, just as the role of the Black buck, ever since Reconstruction, has been to frighten Whites in order to subordinate them to elite manipulation, a device invented by southern Dixiecrats but subsequently adopted by the Republican Party. The positive images of TV sitcoms with Black casts, such as *Different Strokes* and *The Jeffersons*, Herman Gray argues, idealize "racial harmony, affluence, and individual mobility" and thus "deflect attention from the persistence of racism, inequality, and differential power."[25] The Huxtables' success, as Jhally and Lewis put it, "implies the failure of the majority of black people."[26] Contemporary stereotypes, moreover, are inseparable from the long history of colonialist discourse. The "sambo" type is on one level merely a circumscribed characterological instantiation of the infantilizing trope. The "tragic mulatto", in the same vein, is a cautionary figure premised on the trope of purity, the loathing of mixing characteristics of a certain racist discourse. Similarly, many of the scandalously racist statements discussed in the media are less eccentric views than throwbacks to colonialist discourses. Seen in historical perspective, TV commentator Andy Rooney's widely censured remark that Blacks had "watered down their genes" is not a maverick "opinion" but rather a return to the nostrums of "racial degeneracy" theories.

[. . .]

The focus on "good" and "bad" characters in image analysis confronts racist discourse on that discourse's favored ground. It easily slides into *moralism*, and thus into fruitless debates about the relative virtues of fictive characters (seen not as constructs but as if they were real flesh-and-blood people) and the correctness of their fictional actions. This kind of anthropocentric moralism, deeply rooted in Manichean schemas of good and evil, leads to the treatment of complex political issues as if they were matters of individual ethics, in a manner reminiscent of the morality plays staged by the right, in which virtuous American heroes do battle against demonized Third World villains. Thus Bush/Reagan regime portrayals of its enemies drew on the "Manichean allegories" (in the words of Abdul Jan Mohamed) of colonialism: the Sandinistas were portrayed as latter-day bandidos, the *mestizo* Noriega was made to incarnate Anglo phobias about Latino men (violent, drug-dealing, voodoo-practicing), and Saddam Hussein triggered the intertextual memory of Muslim fanatics and Arab assassins.

The media discussion of racism often reflects this same personalistic bias. Mass-media debates often revolve around sensational accusations of *personal* racism; the accusation and the defense are framed in individual terms. Accused of racism for exploiting the image of Willie Horton, Bush advertised his personal animosity toward bigotry and his tenderness for his little brown grandchildren, exemplifying an ideological penchant for personalizing and moralizing essentially political issues. The usual sequence in media accusations of racism, similarly, is that the racist statement is made, offense is expressed, punishment is called for: all of which provokes a series of counter-statements – that the person in question is not racist, that some of the person's best friends belong to the race in question, and so forth. The process has the apparently positive result of placing certain statements beyond the pale of civil speech; blatant racism is stigmatized and punished. But the more subtle, deeper forms of discursively and institutionally structured racism remain unrecognized. The discussion has revolved around the putative racism of a single individual; the problem is assumed to be personal, ethical. The result is a lost opportunity for antiracist pedagogy: racism is reduced to an individual, attitudinal problem, distracting attention from racism as a systematic self-reproducing discursive apparatus that itself shapes racist attitudes. Stereotypic analysis is likewise covertly premised on *individualism* in that the individual character, rather than larger social categories (race, class, gender, nation, sexual orientation), remains the point of reference. Individual morality receives more attention than the larger configurations of power. This apolitical approach to stereotypes allows pro-business "content analysts" to lament without irony the TV's "stereotyping" of American businessmen, forgetting that television as an institution, at least, is permeated by the corporate ethos, that its commercials and even its shows are commercials for business.

The focus on individual character also misses the ways in which social institutions and cultural practices, as opposed to individuals, can be misrepresented without a single character being stereotyped. The flawed mimesis of many Hollywood films dealing with the Third World, with their innumerable ethnographic, linguistic, and even topographical blunders, has less to do with stereotypes *per se* than with the tendentious ignorance of colonialist discourse. The social institutions and cultural practices of a people can be denigrated without individual stereotypes entering into the question. The media often reproduce Eurocentric views of African spirit religions, for example, by regarding them as superstitious cults rather than as legitimate belief-systems, prejudices enshrined in the patronizing vocabulary ("animism," "ancestor worship," "magic") used to discuss the religions.[27] Within Eurocentric thinking, superimposed Western hierarchies work to the detriment of African religions.

[. . .]

A moralistic and individualistic approach also ignores the contradictory nature of stereotypes. Black figures, in Toni Morrison's words, come to signify polar opposites: "On the one hand, they signify benevolence, harmless and servile guardianship and endless love," and on the other "insanity, illicit sexuality, chaos."[28] A moralistic approach also sidesteps the issue of the relative nature of "morality," eliding the question: positive for whom? It ignores the fact that oppressed people might not only have a *different* vision of morality, but even an *opposite* vision of a hypocritical moralism which not only covers over institutional injustice but which is also oppressive in itself. Even the Decalogue becomes less sacrosanct in bitter situations of social oppression. Within slavery, for example, might it not be admirable and therefore "good" to lie to, manipulate, and even murder a slave-driver? The "positive image" approach assumes a bourgeois morality intimately linked to status quo politics. What is seen as "positive" by the dominant group, for instance the acts of those "Indians" in westerns who spy for the Whites, might be seen as treason by the dominated group. The taboo in Hollywood was not so much on "positive images" but rather on images of racial anger, revolt, and empowerment.

The privileging of character over narrative and social structure places the burden on oppressed people to be "good" rather than on the privileged to remove the knife from the back. The counterpart of the "good Black" on the other side of the racial divide is the pathologically vicious racist: Richard Widmark in *No Way Out* (1950) or Bobby Darin in *Pressure Point* (1962). Such films let "ordinary racists" off the hook, unable to recognize themselves in the raving maniacs on the screen. And in order to be equal, the oppressed are asked to be better, whence all the stoic "ebony saints" (Bogle's words) of Hollywood, from Louise Beavers in *Imitation of life* (1934 version), through Sidney Poitier in *The Defiant Ones* (1961), to Whoopi Goldberg in *Clara's Heart* (1988). Furthermore, the saintly Black forms a Manichean pair with the demon Black, in a moralistic schema reminiscent of that structuring *Cabin in the Sky*. Saints inherit the Christian tradition of sacrifice and tend to be desexualized, deprived of normal human attributes, along the lines of the "Black eunuch," cast in decorative or subservient poses.[29] The privileging of positive images also elides the patent differences, the social and moral heteroglossia (Bakhtin's term signifying "many-languagedness"), characteristic of any social group. A cinema of contrivedly positive image betrays a lack of confidence in the group portrayed, which usually itself has no illusions concerning its own perfection. A cinema in which all the Black characters resembled Sidney Poitier might be as much a cause for alarm as one in which they all resembled Step'n Fetchit. It is often assumed, furthermore, that control over representation leads automatically to the production of "positive images." But films made by Africans like *Laafi* (1991) and *Finzan* (1990) do not offer positive images of African society; rather, they offer critical African perspectives on African society. The demand that Third World or minoritarian filmmakers produce only "positive images," in this sense, can be a sign of anxiety. Hollywood, after all, has never worried about sending films around the world which depict the US as a violent land. Rather than deal with the contradictions of a community, "positive image" cinema prefers a mask of perfection.

Image analysis, furthermore, often ignores the issue of function. Tonto's "positive" image, in the *Lone Ranger* series, is less important than his structural subordination to the White hero and to expansionist ideology. Similarly, a certain cynical integrationism simply inserts new heroes and heroines, this time drawn from the ranks of the oppressed, into the old functional roles that were themselves oppressive, much as colonialism invited a few assimilated "natives" to join the club of the "elite." *Shaft* (1971) simply inserts Black heroes into the actantial slot formerly filled by White ones to flatter the fantasies of a certain sector (largely male) of the Black audience. Even the South African film industry under apartheid could entertain with Black Rambos and Superspades.[30] Other films, such as *In the Heat of the Night* (1967), *Pressure Point*, the *Beverly Hills Cop* series with Eddie Murphy (1984, 1987), and, more complexly, *Deep Cover* (1992), place Black characters in highly ambiguous roles as law-enforcers. The television series *Roots*, finally, used positive images as part of a cooptive version of Afro-American history. The series' subtitle – "The Saga of an American Family" – signals an emphasis on the European-style nuclear family (retrospectively projected on to Kunta's life in Africa) in a film which casts Blacks as just another immigrant group making its way toward freedom and prosperity in democratic America. As Riggs' *Color Adjustment* points out, *Roots* paved the way for *The Cosby Show* by placing an upscale Black family in the preexisting "slot" of the idealized white family sitcom, with Cliff Huxtable as benevolent *paterfamilias*, a liberal move in some respects but one still tied to a conservative valorization of family. John Downing, in contrast, finds *The Cosby Show* more ideologically ambiguous, on the one hand offering an easy pride in African-American culture, and on the other celebrating the virtues of middle class existence in order to obscure structural injustice and racial discrimination.[31]

Perspective, Address, Focalization

A "positive image" approach also ignores the question of perspective and the social positioning both of the filmmakers and the audience. We cannot equate the stereotyping performed "from above" with stereotyping "from below," where the stereotype is used as it were "in quotes," recognized as a stereotype and used to new ends. The theater group Culture Clash, for example, invokes stereotypes about Chicanos, but always within a sympathetic Chicano perspective. The notion of positive images disallows this kind of "insider satire," the affectionate self-mockery by which an ethnic group makes fun of itself. Spike Lee's *School Daze* (1988) also applies stereotypes for its own purposes, subverting the segregationist connotations of the all-Black musical in order to explore intraracial tensions within the African-American community. *School Daze* comically stages the ideological and class tensions between White-identified and Black-identified African-Americans. Instead of resorting to the usual community-delegate status of African-Americans, the film liberates narrative space to play out the contradictions of a heterogenous community, demonstrating the confidence of a director who, whatever his notorious blindspots (especially in terms of gender and sexuality), is ready to give voice to a polyphony of conflicting voices. Indeed, questions of address are as crucial as questions of representation. Who is speaking through a film? Who is imagined as listening? Who is actually listening? Who is looking? And what social desires are mobilized by the film?

A "positive image" approach also elides issues of point-of-view and what Gerard Genette calls "focalization." Genette's reformulation of the classic literary question of "point-of-view" reaches beyond character perspective to the structuring of information within the story world through the cognitive-perceptual grid of its "inhabitants."[32] The concept is illuminating when applied to liberal films which furnish the "other" with a "positive" image, appealing dialog, and sporadic point-of-view shots, yet in which European or Euro-American characters remain radiating "centers of consciousness" and "filters" for information, the vehicles for dominant racial/ethnic discourses. Many liberal Hollywood films about the Third World or about minoritarian cultures in the First World deploy a European or Euro-American character as a mediating "bridge" to other cultures portrayed more or less sympathetically. The First World journalists in *Under Fire* (1983), *Salvador* (1986), *Missing* (1982), *The Year of Living Dangerously* (1983), and *Circles of Deceit* (1982) inherit the "in-between" role traditionally assigned to the colonial traveler and later to the anthropologist: the role of the one who "reports back." The mediating character initiates the spectator into otherized communities; Third World and

minoritarian people, it is implied, are incapable of speaking for themselves. Unworthy of stardom either in the movies or in political life, they need a go-between in the struggle for emancipation.

The character whose point-of-view predominates need not be the "carrier" of the "norms of the text." Oswaldo Censoni's *João Negrinho* (1954), for example, is entirely structured around the perspective of its focal character, an elderly ex-slave. But while the film seems to present all its events from João's point of view, apparently to elicit total sympathy with him, what it in fact elicits sympathy for is a paternalistic vision of "good" Blacks leaving their destiny in the hands of well-intentioned White abolitionists. One finds a related ambiguity in liberal films that privilege European mediators over their Third World object of sympathy – the Palestinians in *Hanna K.* (1983), the Indians in *Passage to India* (1984), the African-Americans in *Mississippi Burning*, the Nicaraguans in *Under Fire*, the Indians in *City of Joy* (1990). A recent episode of the TV show *Travel* (April 26, 1992), similarly, glorifies an elderly British woman who helps children in Peru. The *mise-en-scène* foregrounds her as she leads the group singing of "My Bonnie Lies over the Ocean." Throughout she is focalized as a kind of haloed White savior of the oppressed, within an ideology that posits individual altruism as the sole legitimate force for social change. The Third World characters have a subsidiary function in such films and reports, even though their plight is the thematic focus. Media liberalism, in sum, does not allow subaltern communities to play prominent self-determining roles, a refusal homologous to liberal distaste for non-mediated self-assertion in the political realm. In *City of Joy*, what is portrayed as the unrelieved misery of Calcutta – "an inexhaustible object of Christian charity" in the words of Chidananda das Gupta – becomes the scene of Patrick Swayze's personal sacrifice and redemption.[33] The "other" becomes a trampoline for personal sacrifice and redemption.

[. . .]

Cinematic and Cultural Mediations

A privileging of social portrayal, plot and character often leads to a slighting of the specifically cinematic dimensions of the films; often the analyses might as easily have been of novels or plays. A throughgoing analysis has to pay attention to "mediations": narrative structure, genre conventions, cinematic style. Eurocentric discourse in film may be relayed not by characters or plot but by lighting, framing, *mise-en-scène*, music. Some basic issues of mediation have to do with the *rapports de force*, the balance of power as it were, between foreground and background. In the visual arts, space has traditionally been deployed to express the dynamics of authority and prestige. In pre-perspectival medieval painting, for example, size was correlated with social status: nobles were large, peasants small. The cinema translates such correlations of social power into registers of foreground and background, on screen and off screen, speech and silence. To speak of the "image" of a social group, we have to ask precise questions about images. How much space do they occupy in the shot? Are they seen in close-ups or only in distant long shots? How often do they appear compared with the Euro-American characters and for how long? Are they active, desiring characters or decorative props? Do the eyeline matches identify us with one gaze rather than another? Whose looks are reciprocated, whose ignored? How do character positionings communicate social distance or differences in status? Who is front and center? How do body language, posture, and facial expression communicate social hierarchies, arrogance, servility, resentment, pride? Which community is sentimentalized? Is there an esthetic segregation whereby one group is haloed and the other villainized? Are subtle hierarchies conveyed by temporality and subjectivization? What homologies inform artistic and ethnic/political representation?

A critical analysis must also be alive to the contradictions between different registers. For Ed Guerrero, Spike Lee's *Jungle Fever* (1991) rhetorically condemns interracial love, yet "spreads the fever" by making it cinematically appealing in terms of lighting and *mise-en-scène*.[34] Ethic/ethnic perspectives are transmitted not only through character and plot but also through sound and music. As a multitrack audio-visual medium, the cinema manipulates not only point-of-view but also what Michel Chion calls "point-of-hearing" (*point-d'écoute*).[35] In colonial adventure films, the environment and the "natives" are heard as if

through the ears of the colonizers. When we as spectators accompany the settlers' gaze over landscapes from which emerge the sounds of native drums, the drum sounds are usually presented as libidinous or threatening. In many Hollywood films, African polyrhythms become aural signifiers of encircling savagery, acoustic shorthand for the racial paranoia implicit in the phrase "the natives are restless." What is seen within Native American, African, or Arab cultures as spiritual and musical expression becomes in the western or adventure film a stenographic index of danger, a motive for fear and loathing. In *Drums along the Mohawk* (1939), the "bad" Indian drums are foiled by the "good" martial Euro-American drums which evoke the beneficent law and order of White Christian patriarchy. Colonialist films associate the colonized with hysterical screams, non-articulate cries, the yelping of animal-like creatures; the sounds themselves place beast and native on the same level, not just neighbors but species-equals.

Music, both diegetic and non-diegetic, is crucial for spectatorial identification. Lubricating the spectatorial psyche and oiling the wheels of narrative continuity, music "conducts" our emotional responses, regulates our sympathies, extracts our tears, excites our glands, relaxes our pulses, and triggers our fears, in conjunction with the image and in the service of the larger purposes of the film. In whose favor do these processes operate? What is the emotional tonality of the music, and with what character or group does it lead us to identify? Is the music that of the people portrayed? In films set in Africa, such as *Out of Africa* (1985) and *Ashanti* (1979), the choice of European symphonic music tells us that their emotional "heart" is in the West. In *The Wild Geese* (1978), classicizing music consistently lends dignity to the White mercenary side. The Roy Budd score waxes martial and heroic when we are meant to identify with the Whites' aggressivity, and sentimental when we are meant to sympathize with their more tender side. The Borodin air commonly called "This Is My Beloved," associated in the film with the mercenary played by Richard Harris, musically "blesses" his demise with a tragic eulogy.

Alternative films deploy sound and music quite differently. A number of African and Afro-diasporic films, such as *Faces of Women* (1985), *Barravento* (1962), and *Pagador de Promessas* (The Given Word, 1962), deploy drum ouvertures in ways that affirm African cultural values. The French film *Noir et Blanc en Couleur* (Black and White in Color, 1976) employs music satirically by having the African colonized carry their colonial masters on their backs, but satirize them through the songs they sing: "My master is so fat, how can I carry him? . . . Yes, and mine has stinky feet . . ." Films by African and Afro-diasporic directors like Sembene, Cisse, and Faye not only use African music but celebrate it. Julie Dash's *Daughters of the Dust* (1990) deploys an African "talking drum" to drive home, if only subliminally, the Afrocentric thrust of a film dedicated to the diasporic culture of the Gullah people.

Another key mediation has to do with genre. A film like Preston Sturges' *Sullivan's Travels* (1942) raises the question of what one might call the "generic coefficient" of racism. In this summa of cinematic genres, Blacks play very distinct roles, each correlated with a specific generic discourse. In the slapstick land-yacht sequences, the Black waiter conforms to the prototype of the happy-go-lucky servant/buffoon; he is sadistically "painted" with whiteface pancake batter, and excluded from the charmed circle of White sociality. In the documentary-inflected sequences showing masses of unemployed, meanwhile, Blacks are present but voiceless, very much in the left-communist tradition of class reductionism; they appear as anonymous victims of economic hard times, with no racial specificity to their oppression. The most remarkable sequence, a homage to the "all-Black musical" tradition, has a Black preacher and his congregation welcome the largely White prison-inmates to the screening of an animated cartoon. Here, in the tradition of films like *Hallelujah* (1929), the Black community is portrayed as the vibrant scene of expressive religiosity. But the film complicates conventional representation: first, by desegregating the genre; second, by having Blacks exercise charity toward Whites, characterized by the preacher as "neighbors less fortunate than ourselves." The preacher exhorts the congregation not to act "high-toned," for "we is all equal in the sight of God." When congregation and prisoners sing "Let My People Go," the music, the images, and the editing forge a triadic

link between three oppressed groups: Blacks, the prisoners, and the Biblical Israelites in the times of the Pharaoh, here assimilated to the cruel warden. The Sturges who directs the "Black musical" sequence radically complicates the Sturges who directs the slapstick sequence; racial attitudes are generically mediated.

The critique-of-stereotypes approach is implicitly premised on the desirability of "rounded" three-dimensional characters within a realist-dramatic esthetic. Given the cinema's history of one-dimensional portrayals, the hope for more complex and "realistic" representations is completely understandable, but should not preclude more experimental, anti-illusionistic alternatives. Realistic "positive" portrayals are not the only way to fight racism or to advance a liberatory perspective. Within a Brechtian esthetic, for example, (non-racial) stereotypes can serve to generalize meaning and demystify established power, at the same time that the characters are never purely positive or negative but rather are the sites of contradiction. Parody of the kind theorized by Bakhtin, similarly, favors decidedly negative, even grotesque images to convey a deep critique of societal structures. At times, critics have mistakenly applied the criteria appropriate to one genre or esthetic to another. A search for positive images in shows like *In Living Color*, for example, would be misguided, for that show belongs to a carnivalesque genre favoring anarchic bad taste and calculated exaggeration, as in the parody of *West Side Story* where the Black woman sings to her Jewish orthodox lover "Menahem, Menahem, I just met a man named Menahem." (The show is of course open to other forms of critique.) Satirical or parodic films may be less concerned with constructing positive images than with challenging the stereotypical expectations an audience may bring them. The performance piece in which Coco Fusco/ Guillermo Gomez Peña exhibit themselves as "authentic aborigines" to mock the Western penchant for exhibiting non-Europeans in zoos, museums, and freak shows, prods the art world audience into awareness of its own complicity. The question, in such cases, lies not in the valence of the image but rather in the drift of the satire.

What one might call the generic defense against accusations of racism – "It's only a comedy!," "Whites

are equally lampooned!," "All the characters are caricatures!," "But it's a parody!" – is highly ambiguous,
since it all depends on the modalities and the objects
of the lampoon, parody, and so forth. The classic
Euro-Israeli film on Asian and African Jews, *Sallah
Shabbati* (1964), for example, portrays a Sephardi
protagonist, but from a decidedly unSephardi
perspective. As a naif, Sallah on one level exemplifies
the perennial tradition of the uninitiated outsider
figure deployed as an instrument of social and cultural critique or distanciation. But in contrast with
other naif figures such as Candide, Schweik, or Said
Abi al Nakhs al Mutasha'il (in Emil Habibi's
Pesoptimist), who are used as narrative devices to strip
bare the received wisdom and introduce a fresh
perspective, Sallah's naiveté functions less to attack
Euro-Israeli stereotypes about Sephardi Jews than
to mock Sallah himself and what he supposedly
represents – the "oriental," or "black," qualities of
Sephardim. In other words, unlike Jaroslav Hašek,
who exploits the constructed naiveté of his
character to attack European militarism rather than
using it as a satire of Schweik's backwardness, the
director, Kishon, molds Sallah in conformity with
socially derived stereotypes in a mockery of the
Sephardi "minority" (in fact the majority) itself. The
grotesque character of Sallah was not designed, and
was not received by Euro-Israeli critics, as a satire of
an individual but rather as a summation of the
Sephardi "essence." And within the Manichean
splitting of affectivity typical of colonialist discourse,
we find the positive – Sephardim are warm, sincere,
direct, shrewd – and negative poles – they are lazy,
irrational, unpredictable, primitive, illiterate, sexist.
Accordingly, Sallah (and the film) speaks in the
first-person plural "we," while the Ashkenazi characters address him in the second-person plural, "you
all." Kishon's anti-Establishment satire places on
the same level the members of the Establishment
and those outside it and distant from real power.
Social satire is not, then, an immediate guarantor
of multiculturalism. It can be retrograde,
perpetuating racist views, rather than deploying
satire as a community-based critique of Eurocentric
representations.[36]

The analysis-of-stereotypes approach, in its
eagerness to apply an *a priori* grid, often ignores
issues of cultural specificity. The stereotypes of
North American Blacks, for example, are only partly
congruent with those of other multiracial New World
societies like Brazil. Both countries offer the figure of
the noble, devoted slave: in the US the Uncle Tom, in
Brazil the *Pai João* (Father John). Both also offer the
female counterpart, the devoted woman slave or
servant: in the US the "mammy," in Brazil the *mae
preta* (Black mother), both products of a plantation
slavery where the children of the master were
nursed at the Black mammy's breast. With other
stereotypes, however, the cross-cultural analogies
become more complicated. Certain characters in
Brazilian films (Tonio in *Bahia de Todos os Santos*,
1960; Jorge in *Compasso de Espera*, Making Time,
1973) at first glance recall the tragic mulatto figure
common in North American cinema and literature,
yet the context is radically different. First, the Brazilian
racial spectrum is not binary (Black or White) but
nuances its shades across a wide variety of racial
descriptive terms. Although color varies widely in
both countries, the social construction of race and
color is distinct, despite the fact that the current
"Latinization" of American culture hints at a kind of
converging. Second, Brazil, while in many ways
oppressive to Blacks, has never been a rigidly segregated society; thus no figure exactly corresponds to
the North American "tragic mulatto," schizophreni-
cally torn between two radically separate social
worlds. The "passing" notion so crucial to American
films such as *Pinky* and *Imitation of Life* had little
resonance in Brazil, where it is often said that all
Brazilians have a "foot in the kitchen"; in other
words, that they all have a Black ancestor somewhere
in the family. This point is comically demonstrated in
the film *Tendados Milagres* (Tent of Miracles, 1977),
when Pedro Arcanjo reveals his racist adversary Nilo
Argilo, the rabid critic of "mongrelization," to be
himself part Black. The mulatto figure can be seen
as dangerous only in an apartheid system and not
in a system dominated by an official, albeit hypocritical, integrationist ideology like Brazil's. In Brazil, the
figure of the mulatto became surrounded with a
different set of prejudicial connotations, such as that
of the mulatto as "uppity" or pretentious. On the
other hand, this constellation of associations is not
entirely foreign to the US; Griffith's *Birth of a Nation*,

for example, repeatedly pinpoints mixed-race mulattos as ambitious and dangerous to the system.

[. . .]

The Orchestration of Discourses

One methodological alternative to the mimetic "stereotypes-and-distortions" approach, we would argue, is to speak less of "images" than of "voices" and "discourses." The very term "image studies" symptomatically elides the oral and the "voiced." A predilection for aural and musical metaphors – voices, intonation, accent, polyphony – reflects a shift in attention, as George Yudice suggests, from the predominantly visual logical space of modernity (perspective, empirical evidence, domination of the gaze) to a "postmodern" space of the vocal (oral ethnography, a people's history, slave narratives), as a way of restoring voice to the voiceless.[37] The concept of voice suggests a metaphor of seepage across boundaries that, like sound in the cinema, remodels spatiality itself, while the visual organization of space, with its limits and boundaries and border police, forms a metaphor of exclusions and hierarchical arrangements. It is not our purpose merely to reverse existing hierarchies – to replace the demogoguery of the visual with a new demogoguery of the auditory – but to suggest that voice (and sound) and image be considered together, dialectically and diacritically. A more nuanced discussion of race and ethnicity in the cinema would emphasize less a one-to-one mimetic adequacy to sociological or historical truth than the interplay of voices, discourses, perspectives, including those operative within the image itself. The task of the critic would be to call attention to the cultural voices at play, not only those heard in aural "close-up" but also those distorted or drowned out by the text. The analytic work would be analogous to that of a "mixer" in a sound studio, whose responsibility it is to perform a series of compensatory operations, to heighten the treble, deepen the bass, amplify the instrumentation, to "bring out" the voices that remain latent or displaced.

Formulating the issue as one of voices and discourses helps us get past the "lure" of the visual, to look beyond the epidermic surface of the text. The question, quite literally, is less of the color of the face in the image than of the actual or figurative social voice or discourse speaking "through" the image.[38] Less important than a film's "accuracy" is that it relays the voices and the perspectives – we emphasize the plural – of the community or communities in question. While the word "image" evokes the issue of mimetic realism, "voice" evokes a realism of delegation and interlocution, a situated utterance of "speaking from" and "speaking to." If an identification with a community voice/discourse occurs, the question of "positive" images falls back into its rightful place as a subordinate issue. We might look at Spike Lee's films, for example, not in terms of mimetic "accuracy" – such as the lament that *Do the Right Thing* portrays an inner city untouched by drugs – but rather in terms of voices/discourses. We can regret the absence of a feminist voice in the film, but we can also note its repeated stagings of wars of community rhetorics. The symbolic battle of the boomboxes featuring African-American and Latino music, for example, evokes larger tensions between cultural and musical voices. And the final quotations from Martin Luther King and Malcolm X leave it to the spectator to synthesize two complementary modalities of resistance, one saying: "Freedom, as you promised," the other saying: "Freedom, by any means necessary!"

It might be objected that an analysis of textual "voices" would ultimately run into the same theoretical problems as an analysis centered on "images." Why should it be any easier to determine an "authentic voice" than to determine an "authentic image?" The point, we would argue, is to abandon the language of "authenticity" with its implicit standard of appeal to verisimilitude as a kind of "gold standard," in favor of a language of "discourses" with its implicit reference to community affiliation and to intertextuality. Reformulating the question as one of "voices" and "discourses" disputes the hegemony of the visual and of the image-track by calling attention to its complication with sound, voice, dialog, language. A voice, we might add, is not exactly congruent with a discourse, for while discourse is institutional, transpersonal, unauthored, voice is personalized, having authorial accent and intonation, and constitutes a specific interplay of discourses (whether individual or communal). The notion of voice is open to plurality; a voice is never merely a voice; it also relays a discourse, since even an individual voice is itself a discursive sum, a polyphony of voices. What Bakhtin calls "heteroglossia," after all, is just another name for the socially generated contradictions that constitute the subject, like the media, as the site of conflicting discourses and competing voices. A discursive approach also avoids the moralistic and essentialist traps embedded in a "negative-stereotypes" and "positive-images" analysis. Characters are not seen as unitary essences, as actor-character amalgams too easily fantasized as flesh-and-blood entities existing somewhere "behind" the diegesis, but rather as fictive-discursive constructs. Thus the whole issue is placed on a socioideological rather than on an individual-moralistic plane. Finally, the privileging of the discursive allows us to compare a film's discourses not with an inaccessible "real" but with other socially circulated cognate discourses forming part of a continuum – journalism, novels, network news, television shows, political speeches, scholarly essays, and popular songs.[39]

A discursive analysis would also alert us to the dangers of the "pseudopolyphonic" discourse that marginalizes and disempowers certain voices, then pretends to dialog with a puppet-like entity already maneuvered into crucial compromises. The film or TV commercial in which every eighth face is Black, for example, has more to do with the demographics of market research and the bad conscience of liberalism than with substantive polyphony, since the Black voice, in such instances, is usually shorn of its soul, deprived of its color and intonation. Polyphony does not consist in the mere appearance of a representative of a given group but rather in the fostering of a textual setting where that group's voice can be heard with its full force and resonance. The question is not of pluralism but of multivocality, an approach that would strive to culti-vate and even heighten cultural difference while abol-ishing socially-generated inequalities.

Notes

1. Steve Neale points out that stereotypes are judged simultaneously in relation to an empirical "real" (accu-racy) and an ideological "ideal" (positive image). See Neale, "The Same Old Story: Stereotypes and Difference," *Screen Education*, Nos 32–3 (Autumn/ Winter 1979–80).

2. For more on FBI harassment of civil rights activists, see Kenneth O'Reilly, *"Racial Matters": The FBI's Secret File on Black America, 1960–1972* (New York: Free Press, 1989),

3. Pam Sporn, a New York City educator, had her high-school students go to the south and video-interview civil rights veterans about their memories of the civil rights struggle and their reactions to *Mississippi Burning*.

4. See Gretchen Bataille and Charles Silet, "The Entertaining Anachronism: Indians in American Film," in Randall M. Miller, ed., *The Kaleidoscopic Lens: How Hollywood Views Ethnic Groups* (Englewood, NJ: Jerome S. Ozer, 1980).

5. Kobena Mercer and Isaac Julien, in a similar spirit, dis-tinguish between "representation as a practice of depicting" and "representation as a practice of delega-tion." See Kobena Mercer and Isaac Julien, "Introduction: De Margin and De Centre," *Screen*, Vol. 29, No. 4 (1988), pp. 2–10.

6. An article in *Moving Picture World* (July 10, 1911), enti-tled "Indians Grieve over Picture Shows," reports on protests by Native Americans from southern California concerning Hollywood's portrayal of them as warriors when in fact they were peaceful farmers.

7. Religious tensions sometimes inflect cinematic repre-sentation. A German film company plan in 1925 to pro-duce *The Prophet*, with Muhammad as the main character, shocked the Islamic University Al Azhar, since Islam prohibits representation of the Prophet. Protests prevented the film from being made. Moustapha Aaqad's *The Message* (Kuwait, Morocco, Libya, 1976), in contrast, tells the story within Islamic norms, respecting the prohibition of graven images of the Prophet, representation of God and holy figures. The film traces the life of the Prophet from his first revelations in AD 610 to his death in 632, in a style which rivals Hollywood Biblical epics. Yet the Prophet is never seen on the screen; when other characters speak to him they address the camera. The script was approved by scholars from the Al Azhar University in Cairo.

8. Judith Williamson makes a similar point in her essay in *Screen*, Vol. 29, No. 4 (1988), pp. 106–12.

9. See Michael Rogin, "Blackface, White Noise: The Jewish Jazz Singer Finds his Voice," *Critical Inquiry*, Vol. 18, No. 3 (1992), pp. 417–44.

10. Clear social hierarchies also inform the practice of sub-stitutional casting. The evolution of casting in Israeli cinema, for example, reflects changing strategies of representation. The heroic-nationalist films of the 1950s and 1960s, which focussed on the Israeli-Arab conflict, typically featured heroic Euro-Israeli Sabras, played by European Jews (Ashkenazis), fighting

villainous Arabs, while Sephardi Arab-Jewish actors and characters were limited to the "degraded" roles of Muslim Arabs. In most recent political films, in contrast, Israeli-Palestinian actors and non-professionals play the Palestinian roles. Such casting allows for a modicum of "self-representation." And at times the Palestinian actors have actually forced radicalization of certain scenes. In some films Palestinian actors have even been cast as Israeli military officers (for example, Makram Houri in *The Smile of the Lamb* (1986) and in the Palestinian-Belgium film *Wedding in Galilee*, 1987). For more on casting in Israeli cinema, see Ella Shohat, *Israeli Cinema: East/West and the Politics of Representation* (Austin: University of Texas Press, 1989).

11. See Ngũgĩ wa Thiong'o, *Moving the Center: The Struggle for Cultural Freedoms* (London: James Currey, 1993), p. 33.

12. See David Spurr, *The Rhetoric of Empire* (Durham, NC: Duke University Press, 1993), p. 104.

13. Gloria Anzaldua, ed., *Making Face, Making Soul: Hacienda Caras* (San Francisco: Aunt Lute, 1990), pp. xxii, 177.

14. For more on language and power, see Ella Shohat and Robert Stam, "Cinema after Babel: Language, Difference, Power," *Screen*, Vol. 26, Nos 3–4 (May–August 1985).

15. See Ward Churchill, *Fantasies of the Master Race: Literature, Cinema and the Colonization of American Indians* (Monroe, Maine: Common Courage Press, 1992), p. 237.

16. Ibid., p. 238.

17. For a thorough discussion of *Dances with Wolves* from a Native American point of view, see Edward Castillo's essay in *Film Quarterly*, Vol. 44, No. 4 (Summer 1991).

18. See Christian Metz, "The Imaginary Signifier," in *The Imaginary Signifier: Psychoanalysis and the Cinema* (Bloomington: Indiana University Press, 1982).

19. James C. Scott, *Domination and the Arts of Resistance: Hidden Transcripts* (New Haven, Conn.: Yale University Press, 1990), p. 34.

20. Donald Bogle, *Toms, Coons, Mulattoes, Mammies and Bucks* (New York: Continuum, 1989), p. 36.

21. See Arthur G. Pettit, *Images of the Mexican American in Fiction and Film* (College Station: Texas A and M University Press, 1980), p. 24.

22. Analysts have also performed extended analyses of specific films from within this perspective. Charles Ramirez Berg analyzes *Bordertown* (1935), the first Hollywood sound film to deal with Mexican-American assimilation and the film which laid down the pattern for the Chicano social problem film. Among the narrative and ideological features Berg isolates are:

1. stereotypical inversion (that is, upgrading of Chicanos coupled with the denigration of the Anglos, portrayed as oversexed blondes (Marie), materialistic socialites (Dale), and inflexible authority figures (the judge));

2. undiminished stereotyping of other marginalized groups (for example Chinese-Americans);

3. the assimilationist idealization of the Chicana mama as the "font of genuine ethnic values";

4. the absent father (Anglo families are complete and ideal; Chicano families are fragmented and dysfunctional); and

5. the absent non-material Chicana (implying the inferiority of Chicanas to Anglo women).

See Charles Ramirez Berg, "*Bordertown*, the Assimilation Narrative and the Chicano Social Problem Film," in Chon Noriega, ed., *Chicanos and Film* (New York: Garland, 1991).

23. Quoted in *Prisoners of Image: Ethnic and Gender Stereotypes*, (New York: Alternative Museum, 1989).

24. See David R. Roediger, *The Wages of Whiteness: Race and the Making of the American Working Class* (London: Verso, 1991), pp. 88–9.

25. Herman Gray, "Television and the New Black Man: Black Male Images in Prime-Time Situation Comedy," *Media, Culture and Society*, No. 8 (1986), p. 239.

26. See Sut Jhally and Justin Lewis, *Enlightened Racism: The Cosby Show, Audiences and the Myth of the American Dream* (Boulder, Colo.: Westview Press, 1992), p. 137.

27. For a critique of Eurocentric language concerning African religions, see John S. Mbiti, *African Religions and Philosophy* (Oxford: Heinemann, 1969).

28. Toni Morrison, ed., *Race-ing Justice, En-gendering Power: Essays on Anita Hill, Clarence Thomas, and the Construction of Social Reality* (New York: Pantheon, 1992), p. xv.

29. See Jan Pieterse, *White on Black: Images of Africa and Blacks in Western Popular Culture* (New Haven, Conn.: Yale University Press, 1992), p. 207.

30. Ibid., p. 106.

31. On *The Cosby Show*, see John D.H. Downing, "*The Cosby Show* and American Racial Discourse," in Geneva Smitherman-Donaldson and Teun A. van Dijk, eds, *Discourse and Discrimination* (Detroit: Wayne State University Press, 1988); Gray, "Television and the New Black Man," in Todd Gitlin, ed., *Watching Television* (New York: Pantheon, 1987), pp. 223–42; Mark Crispin Miller, "Deride and Conquer," in Gitlin, ed., *Watching Television*; and Mike Budd and Clay Steinman, "White Racism and the Cosby Show," *Jump Cut*, No. 37 (July 1992).

32. See Gerard Genette, *Narrative Discourse: An Essay in Method*, trans. Jane E. Lewin (Ithaca, NY: Cornell University Press, 1980).

33. See Chidananda das Gupta, "The Politics of Portrayal," *Cinemaya*, Nos 17–18 (Autumn–Winter 1992–3).

34. See Ed Guerrero, "Fever in the Racial Jungle," in Jim Collins, Hilary Radner, and Ava Preacher Collins, eds,

Film Theory Goes to the Movies (London: Routledge, 1993).

35. Michel Chion, *Le Son au Cinéma* (Paris: Cahiers, 1985).

36. For more on the fissures between the ethnic-racial and the national in Israeli cultural practices, see Shohat, *Israeli Cinema*.

37. See George Yudice, "Bakhtin and the Subject of Postmodernism," unpublished paper.

38. Two of Clyde Taylor's defining traits of New Black Cinema – the link to the Afro-American oral tradition, and the strong articulation of Black musicality – are aural in nature, and both are indispensable in Black Cinema's search for what Taylor himself calls "its voice." See Clyde Taylor, "Les Grands Axes et les Sources Africaines du Nouveau Cinema Noir," *CinemAction*, No. 46 (1988).

39. James Naremore's analysis of *Cabin in the Sky* deploys this kind of discursive analyis with great precision and subtlety. Naremore sees the film as situated uneasily among "four conflicting discourses about blackness and entertainment in America": a vestigial "folkloric" discourse about rural Blacks; NAACP critique of Hollywood imagery; the collaboration between mass entertainment and government; and the "posh Africanism of high-toned Broadway musicals." See James Naremore, *The Films of Vincent Minnelli* (Cambridge: Cambridge University Press, 1993).

16

SOFT-SOAPING EMPIRE

Commodity Racism and Imperial Advertising

Anne McLintock

Soap is Civilization.

—Unilever Company Slogan

Doc: My, it's so clean.
Grumpy: There's dirty work afoot.

—Snow White and the Seven Dwarfs

Soap and Civilization

At the beginning of the nineteenth century, soap was a scarce and humdrum item and washing a cursory activity at best. A few decades later, the manufacture of soap had burgeoned into an imperial commerce; Victorian cleaning rituals were peddled globally as the God-given sign of Britain's evolutionary superiority, and soap was invested with magical, fetish powers. The soap saga captured the hidden affinity between domesticity and empire and embodied a triangulated crisis in value: the *undervaluation* of women's work in the domestic realm, the *overvaluation* of the commodity in the industrial market and the *disavowal* of colonized economies in the arena of empire. Soap entered the realm of Victorian fetishism with spectacular effect, notwithstanding the fact that male Victorians promoted soap as the icon of nonfetishistic rationality.

Both the cult of domesticity and the new imperialism found in soap an exemplary mediating form. The emergent middle class values – monogamy ("clean" sex, which has value), industrial capital ("clean" money, which has value), Christianity ("being washed in the blood of the lamb"), class control

("cleansing the great unwashed") and the imperial civilizing mission ("washing and clothing the savage") – could all be marvelously embodied in a single household commodity. Soap advertising, in particular the Pears soap campaign, took its place at the vanguard of Britain's new commodity culture and its civilizing mission.

In the eighteenth century, the commodity was little more than a mundane object to be bought and used – in Marx's words, "a trivial thing."[1] By the late nineteenth century, however, the commodity had taken its privileged place not only as the fundamental form of a new industrial economy but also as the fundamental form of a new cultural system for representing social value.[2] Banks and stock exchanges rose up to manage the bonanzas of imperial capital. Professions emerged to administer the goods tumbling hectically from the manufactures. Middle-class domestic space became crammed as never before with furniture, clocks, mirrors, paintings, stuffed animals, ornaments, guns and myriad gewgaws and knicknacks. Victorian novelists bore witness to the strange spawning of commodities that seemed to have lives of their own, and huge ships lumbered with trifles and trinkets plied their trade among the colonial markets of Africa, the East and the Americas.[3]

The new economy created an uproar not only of things but of signs. As Thomas Richards has argued, if all these new commodities were to be managed, a unified system of cultural representation had to be found. Richards shows how, in 1851, the Great Exhibition at the Crystal Palace served as a monument to a new form of consumption: "What the first Exhibition heralded so intimately was the complete transformation of collective and private life into a space for the spectacular exhibition of commodities."[4] As a "semiotic laboratory for the labor theory of value," the World Exhibition showed once and for all that the capitalist system had not only created a dominant form of exchange but was also in the process of creating a dominant form of representation to go with it: the voyeuristic panorama of surplus as spectacle. By exhibiting commodities not only as goods but as an organized system of images, the World Exhibition helped fashion "a new kind of being, the consumer and a new kind of ideology, consumerism."[5] The mass consumption of the commodity spectacle was born.

Victorian advertising reveals a paradox, however, for, as the cultural form that was entrusted with upholding and marketing abroad those founding middle-class distinctions – between private and public, paid work and unpaid work – advertising also from the outset began to confound those distinctions. Advertising took the intimate signs of domesticity (children bathing, men shaving, women laced into corsets, maids delivering nightcaps) into the public realm, plastering scenes of domesticity on walls, buses, shopfronts and billboards. At the same time, advertising took scenes of empire into every corner of the home, stamping images of colonial conquest on soap boxes, matchboxes, biscuit tins, whiskey bottles, tea tins and chocolate bars. By trafficking promiscuously across the threshold of private and public, advertising began to subvert one of the fundamental distinctions of commodity capital, even as it was coming into being.

From the outset, moreover, Victorian advertising took explicit shape around the reinvention of racial difference. Commodity kitsch made possible, as never before, the mass marketing of empire as an organized system of images and attitudes. Soap flourished not only because it created and filled a spectacular gap in the domestic market but also because, as a cheap and portable domestic commodity, it could persuasively mediate the Victorian poetics of racial hygiene and imperial progress.

Commodity racism became distinct from scientific racism in its capacity to expand beyond the literate, propertied elite through the marketing of commodity spectacle. If, after the 1850s, scientific racism saturated anthropological, scientific and medical journals, travel writing and novels, these cultural forms were still relatively class-bound and inaccessible to most Victorians, who had neither the means nor the education to read such material. Imperial kitsch as consumer spectacle, by contrast, could package, market and distribute evolutionary racism on a hitherto unimagined scale. No preexisting form of organized racism had ever before been able to reach so large and so differentiated a mass of the populace. Thus, as domestic commodities were mass marketed through their appeal to imperial jingoism, commodity jingoism itself helped reinvent and maintain British national unity in the face of deepening imperial competition and colonial resistance. The cult of domesticity became indispensable to the consolidation of British national identity, and at the center of the domestic cult stood the simple bar of soap.[6]

Yet soap has no social history. Since it purportedly belongs in the female realm of domesticity, soap is figured as beyond history and beyond politics proper.[7] To begin a social history of soap, then, is to refuse, in part, to accept the erasure of women's domestic value under imperial capitalism. It cannot be forgotten, moreover, that the history of European attempts to impose a commodity economy on African cultures was also the history of diverse African attempts either to refuse or to transform European commodity fetishism to suit their own needs. The story of soap reveals that fetishism, far from being a quintessentially African propensity, as nineteenth-century anthropology maintained, was central to industrial modernity, inhabiting and mediating the uncertain threshold zones between domesticity and industry, metropolis and empire.

Soap and Commodity Spectacle

Before the late nineteenth century, clothes and bedding washing was done in most households only once or twice a year in great, communal binges, usually in public at streams or rivers.[8] As for body washing, not much had changed since the days when Queen Elizabeth I was distinguished by the frequency with which she washed: "regularly every month whether she needed it or not."[9] By the 1890s, however, soap sales had soared, Victorians were consuming 260,000 tons of soap a year, and advertising had emerged as the central cultural form of commodity capitalism.[10]

Before 1851, advertising scarcely existed. As a commercial form, it was generally regarded as a confession of weakness, a rather shabby last resort. Most advertising was limited to small newspaper advertisements, cheap handbills and posters. After midcentury, however, soap manufacturers began to pioneer the use of pictorial advertising as a central part of business policy.

The initial impetus for soap advertising came from the realm of empire. With the burgeoning of imperial cotton on the slave plantations came the surplus of cheap cotton goods, alongside the growing buying power of a middle class that could afford for the first time to consume such goods in large quantities. Similarly, the sources for cheap palm oil, coconut oil and cottonseed oil flourished in the imperial plantations of West Africa, Malay, Ceylon, Fiji and New Guinea. As rapid changes in the technology of soapmaking took place in Britain after midcentury, the prospect dawned of a large domestic market for soft body soaps, which had previously been a luxury that only the upper class could afford.

Economic competition with the United States and Germany created the need for a more aggressive promotion of British products and led to the first real innovations in advertising. In 1884, the year of the Berlin Conference, the first wrapped soap was sold under a brand name. This small event signified a major transformation in capitalism, as imperial competition gave rise to the creation of monopolies. Henceforth, items formerly indistinguishable from each other (soap sold simply as soap) would be marketed by their corporate signature (Pears, Monkey Brand, etc). Soap became one of the first commodities to register the historic shift from myriad small businesses to the great imperial monopolies. In the 1870s, hundreds of small soap companies plied the new trade in hygiene, but by the end of the century, the trade was monopolized by ten large companies.

In order to manage the great soap show, an aggressively entrepreneurial breed of advertisers emerged, dedicated to gracing each homely product with a radiant halo of imperial glamour and racial potency. The advertising agent, like the bureaucrat, played a vital role in the imperial expansion of foreign trade. Advertisers billed themselves as "empire builders" and flattered themselves with "the responsibility of the historic imperial mission." Said one: "Commerce even more than sentiment binds the ocean sundered portions of empire together. Anyone who increases these commercial interests strengthens the whole fabric of the empire."[11] Soap was credited not only with bringing moral and economic salvation to Britain's "great unwashed" but also with magically embodying the spiritual ingredient of the imperial mission itself.

In an ad for Pears, for example, a black and implicitly racialized coalsweeper holds in his hands a glowing, occult object. Luminous with its own inner radiance, the simple soap bar glows like a fetish, pulsating magically with spiritual enlightenment and imperial grandeur, promising to warm the hands and hearts of working people across the globe.[12] Pears, in particular, became intimately associated with a purified nature magically cleansed of polluting industry (tumbling kittens, faithful dogs, children festooned with flowers) and a purified working class magically cleansed of polluting labor (smiling servants in crisp white aprons, rosy-cheeked match girls and scrubbed scullions).[13]

Nonetheless, the Victorian obsession with cotton and cleanliness was not simply a mechanical reflex of economic surplus. If imperialism garnered a bounty of cheap cotton and soap oils from coerced colonial labor, the middle class Victorian fascination with clean, white bodies and clean, white clothing stemmed not only from the rampant profiteering of the imperial economy but also from the realms of ritual and fetish.

Soap did not flourish when imperial ebullience was at its peak. It emerged commercially during an era of impending crisis and social calamity, serving to preserve, through fetish ritual, the uncertain boundaries of class, gender and race identity in a social order felt to be threatened by the fetid effluvia of the slums, the belching smoke of industry, social agitation, economic upheaval, imperial competition and anticolonial resistance. Soap offered the promise of spiritual salvation and regeneration through commodity consumption, a regime of domestic hygiene that could restore the threatened potency of the imperial body politic and the race.

The Pears' Campaign

In 1789 Andrew Pears, a farmer's son, left his Cornish village of Mevagissey to open a barbershop in London, following the trend of widespread demographic migration from country to city and the economic turn from land to commerce. In his shop, Pears made and sold the powders, creams and dentifrices used by the rich to ensure the fashionable alabaster purity of their complexions. For the elite, a sun-darkened skin stained by outdoor manual work was the visible stigma not only of a class obliged to work under the elements for a living but also of far-off, benighted races marked by God's disfavor. From the outset, soap took shape as a technology of social purification, inextricably entwined with the semiotics of imperial racism and class denigration.

In 1838 Andrew Pears retired and left his firm in the hands of his grandson, Francis. In due course, Francis's daughter, Mary, married Thomas J. Barratt, who became Francis' partner and took the gamble of fashioning a middle-class market for the transparent soap. Barratt revolutionized Pears by masterminding a series of dazzling advertising campaigns. Inaugurating a new era of advertising, he won himself lasting fame, in the familiar iconography of male birthing, as the "father of advertising." Soap thus found its industrial destiny through the mediation of domestic kinship and that peculiarly Victorian preoccupation with patrimony.

Through a series of gimmicks and innovations that placed Pears at the center of Britain's emerging commodity culture, Barratt showed a perfect understanding of the fetishism that structures all advertising. Importing a quarter of a million French centime pieces into Britain, Barratt had the name Pears stamped on them and put the coins into circulation— a gesture that marvelously linked exchange value with the corporate brand name. The ploy worked famously, arousing much publicity for Pears and such a public fuss that an Act of Parliament was rushed through to declare all foreign coins illegal tender. The boundaries of the national currency closed around the domestic bar of soap.

Georg Lukács points out that the commodity lies on the threshold of culture and commerce, confusing the supposedly sacrosanct boundaries between aesthetics and economy, money and art. In the mid-1880s, Barratt devised a piece of breathtaking cultural transgression that exemplified Lukács' insight and clinched Pears' fame. Barratt bought Sir John Everett Millais' painting "Bubbles" (originally entitled "A Child's World") and inserted into the painting a bar of soap stamped with the totemic word *Pears*. At a stroke, he transformed the artwork of the best-known painter in Britain into a mass produced commodity associated in the public mind with Pears.[14] At the same time, by mass reproducing the painting as a poster ad, Barratt took art from the elite realm of private property to the mass realm of commodity spectacle.[15]

In advertising, the axis of possession is shifted to the axis of spectacle Advertising's chief contribution to the culture of modernity was the discovery that by manipulating the semiotic space around the commodity, the unconscious as a public space could also be manipulated. Barratt's great innovation was to invest huge sums of money in the creation of a visible aesthetic space around the commodity. The development of poster and print technology made possible the mass reproduction of such a space around the image of a commodity.[16]

In advertising, that which is disavowed by industrial rationality (ambivalence, sensuality, chance, unpredictable causality, multiple time) is projected onto image space as a repository of the forbidden. Advertising draws on subterranean flows of desire and taboo, manipulating the investment of surplus money. Pears' distinction, swiftly emulated by scores of soap companies including Monkey Brand and Sunlight, as well as countless other advertisers, was to invest the aesthetic space around the domestic commodity with the commercial cult of empire.

Empire of the Home

Racializing Domesticity

The Soap

Four fetishes recur ritualistically in soap advertising: soap itself, white clothing (especially aprons), mirrors and monkeys. A typical Pears' advertisement figures a black child and a white child together in a bathroom. The Victorian bathroom is the innermost sanctuary of domestic hygiene and by extension the private temple of public regeneration. The sacrament of soap offers a reformation allegory whereby the purification of the domestic body becomes a metaphor for the regeneration of the body politic. In this particular ad, a black boy sits in the bath, gazing wide-eyed into the water as if into a foreign element. A white boy, clothed in a white apron—the familiar fetish of domestic purity—bends benevolently over his "lesser" brother, bestowing upon him the precious talisman of racial progress. The magical fetish of soap promises that the commodity can regenerate the Family of Man by washing from the skin the very stigma of racial and class degeneration.

Soap advertising offers an allegory of imperial progress as spectacle. In this ad, the imperial topos that I call panoptical time (progress consumed as a spectacle from a point of privileged invisibility) enters the domain of the commodity. In the second frame of the ad, the black child is out of the bath and the white boy shows him his startled visage in the mirror. The black boy's body has become magically white, but his face—for Victorians the seat of rational individuality and self-consciousness—remains stubbornly black. The white child is thereby figured as the agent of history and the male heir to progress, reflecting his lesser brother in the European mirror of self-consciousness. In the Victorian mirror, the black child witnesses his predetermined destiny of imperial metamorphosis but remains a passive racial hybrid, part black, part white, brought to the brink of civilization by the twin commodity fetishes of soap and mirror. The advertisement discloses a crucial element of late Victorian commodity culture: the metaphoric transformation of imperial *time* into consumer *space* – imperial progress consumed at a glance as domestic spectacle.

The Monkey

The metamorphosis of imperial time into domestic space is captured most vividly by the advertising campaign for Monkey Brand Soap. During the 1880s, the urban landscape of Victorian Britain teemed with the fetish monkeys of this soap. The monkey with its frying pan and bar of soap perched everywhere, on grimy hoardings and buses, on walls and shop fronts,

promoting the soap that promised magically to do away with domestic labor: "No dust, no dirt, no labor." Monkey Brand Soap promised not only to regenerate the race but also to magically erase the unseemly spectacle of women's manual labor.

In an exemplary ad, the fetish soap-monkey sits cross-legged on a doorstep, the threshold boundary between private domesticity and public commerce – the embodiment of anachronistic space. Dressed like an organ grinder's minion in a gentleman's ragged suit, white shirt and tie, but with improbably human hands and feet, the monkey extends a frying pan to catch the surplus cash of passersby. On the doormat before him, a great bar of soap is displayed, accompanied by a placard that reads: "My Own Work." In every respect the soap-monkey is a hybrid: not entirely ape, not entirely human; part street beggar, part gentleman; part artist, part advertiser. The creature inhabits the ambivalent border of jungle and city, private and public, the domestic and the commercial, and offers as its handiwork a fetish that is both art and commodity.

Monkeys inhabit Western discourse on the borders of social limit, marking the place of a contradiction in social value. As Donna Haraway has argued: "the primate body, as part of the body of nature, may be read as a map of power."[17] Primatology, Haraway insists, "is a Western discourse ... a political order that works by the negotiation of boundaries achieved through ordering differences."[18] In Victorian iconography, the ritual recurrence of the monkey figure is eloquent of a crisis in value and hence anxiety at possible boundary breakdown. The primate body became a symbolic space for reordering and policing boundaries between humans and nature, women and men, family and politics, empire and metropolis.

Simian imperialism is also centrally concerned with the problem of representing *social change*. By projecting history (rather than fate, or God's will) onto the theater of nature, primatology made nature the alibi of political violence and placed in the hands of "rational science" the authority to sanction and legitimize social change. Here, "the scene of origins," Haraway argues, "is not the cradle of civilization, but the cradle of culture ... the origin of sociality itself, especially in the densely meaning-laden icon of the family."[19] Primatology emerges as a theater for negotiating the perilous boundaries between the family (as natural and female) and power (as political and male).

The appearance of monkeys in soap advertising signals a dilemma: *how to represent domesticity without representing women at work*. The Victorian middle-class house was structured round the fundamental contradiction between women's paid and unpaid domestic work. As women were driven from paid work in mines, factories, shops and trades to private, unpaid work in the home, domestic work became economically undervalued and the middle-class defi-nition of femininity figured the "proper" woman as one who did not work for profit. At the same time, a *cordon sanitaire* of racial degeneration was thrown around those women who did work publicly and visi-bly for money. What could not be incorporated into the industrial formation (women's domestic eco-nomic value) was displaced onto the invented domain of the primitive, and thereby disciplined and contained.

Monkeys, in particular, were deployed to legiti-mize social boundaries as edicts of nature. Fetishes straddling nature and culture, monkeys were seen as allied with the dangerous classes: the "apelike" wan-dering poor, the hungry Irish, Jews, prostitutes, impov-erished black people, the ragged working class, criminals, the insane and female miners and servants, who were collectively seen to inhabit the threshold of racial degeneration. When Charles Kingsley visited Ireland, for example, he lamented: "I am haunted by the human chimpanzees I saw along that hundred miles of horrible country.... But to see white chimpanzees is dreadful; if they were black, one would not feel it so much, but their skins, except where tanned by exposure, are as white as ours."[20]

In the Monkey Brand advertisement, the mon-key's signature of labor ("My Own Work") signals a double disavowal. Soap is masculinized, figured as a male product, while the (mostly female) labor of the workers in the huge, unhealthy soap factories is disavowed. At the same time, the labor of social transformation in the daily scrubbing and scouring of the sinks, pans and dishes, labyrinthine floors and corridors of Victorian domestic space vanishes – refigured as anachronistic space, primitive and bestial. Female servants disappear and in their place crouches a phantasmic male hybrid. Thus, domesticity – seen as the sphere most separate from the marketplace and the masculine hurly-burly of empire – takes shape around the invented ideas of the primitive and the commodity fetish.

In Victorian culture, the monkey was an icon of metamorphosis, perfectly serving soap's liminal role in mediating the transformations of nature (dirt, waste and disorder) into culture (cleanliness, rationality and industry). Like all fetishes, the monkey is a contradic-tory image, embodying the hope of imperial progress through commerce while at the same time rendering visible deepening Victorian fears of urban militancy and colonial misrule. The soap-monkey became the emblem of industrial progress and imperial evolution, embodying the double promise that nature could be redeemed by consumer capital and that consumer capital could be guaranteed by natural law. At the same time, however, the soap-monkey was eloquent of the degree to which fetishism structures industrial rationality.

The Mirror

In most Monkey Brand advertisements, the monkey holds a frying pan, which is also a mirror. In a similar Brooke's Soap ad, a classical female beauty with bare white arms stands draped in white, her skin and clothes epitomizing the exhibition value of sexual purity and domestic leisure, while from the cornuco-pia she holds flows a grotesque effluvium of hobgob-lin angels. Each hybrid fetish embodies the doubled Victorian image of woman as "angel in the drawing room, monkey in the bedroom," as well as the racial iconography of evolutionary progress from ape to angel. Historical time, again, is captured as domestic spectacle, eerily reflected in the frying pan/mirror fetish.

In this ad, the Brooke's Soap offers an alchemy of economic progress, promising to make "copper like gold." At the same time, the Enlightenment idea of linear, rational time leading to angelic perfection finds its antithesis in the other time of housework, ruled by the hobgoblins of dirt, disorder and fetishistic, nonprogressive time. Erupting on the margins of the rational frame, the ad displays the irrational consequences of the idea of progress.

The mirror/frying pan, like all fetishes, visibly expresses a crisis in value but cannot resolve it. It can only embody the contradiction, frozen as commodity spectacle, luring the spectator deeper and deeper into consumerism.

Mirrors glint and gleam in soap advertising, as they do in the culture of imperial kitsch at large. In Victorian middle-class households, servants scoured and polished every metal and wooden surface until it shone like a mirror. Doorknobs, lamp stands and banisters, tables and chairs, mirrors and clocks, knives and forks, kettles and pans, shoes and boots were polished until they shimmered, reflecting in their gleaming surfaces other object-mirrors, an infinity of crystalline mirrors within mirrors, until the interior of the house was all shining surfaces, a labyrinth of reflection. The mirror became the epitome of commodity fetishism: erasing both the signs of domestic labor and the industrial origins of domestic commodities. In the domestic world of mirrors, objects multiply without apparent human intervention in a promiscuous economy of self-generation.

Why the attention to surface and reflection? The polishing was dedicated, in part, to policing the boundaries between private and public, removing every trace of labor, replacing the disorderly evidence of working women with the exhibition of domesticity as veneer, the commodity spectacle as surface, the house arranged as a theater of clean surfaces for commodity display. The mirror/commodity renders the value of the object as an exhibit, a spectacle to be consumed, admired and displayed for its capacity to embody a twofold value: the man's market worth and the wife's exhibition status. The house existed to display femininity as bearing exhibition value only, beyond the marketplace and therefore, by natural decree, beyond political power.

An ad for Stephenson's Furniture Cream figures a spotless maid on all fours, smiling up from a floor so clean that it mirrors her reflection. The cream is "warranted not to fingermark." A superior soap should leave no telltale smear, no fingerprint of female labor. As Victorian servants lost individuality in the generic names their employers imposed on them, so soaps erased the imprint of women's work on middle-class history.

Domesticating Empire

By the end of the century, a stream of imperial bric-a-brac had invaded Victorian homes. Colonial heroes and colonial scenes were emblazoned on a host of domestic commodities, from milk cartons to sauce bottles, tobacco tins to whiskey bottles, assorted biscuits to toothpaste, toffee boxes to baking powder.[21] Traditional national fetishes such as the Union Jack, Britannia, John Bull and the rampant lion were marshaled into a revamped celebration of imperial spectacle. Empire was seen to be patriotically defended by Ironclad Porpoise Bootlaces and Sons of the Empire soap, while Henry Morton Stanley came to the rescue of the Emin of Pasha laden with outsize boxes of Huntley and Palmers Biscuits.

Late Victorian advertising presented a vista of Africa conquered by domestic commodities.[22] In the flickering magic lantern of imperial desire, teas, biscuits, tobaccos, Bovril, tins of cocoa and, above all, soaps beach themselves on far-flung shores, tramp through jungles, quell uprisings, restore order and write the inevitable legend of commercial progress across the colonial landscape. In a Huntley and Palmers' Biscuits ad, a group of male colonials sit in the middle of a jungle on biscuit crates, sipping tea. Moving towards them is a stately and seemingly endless procession of elephants, loaded with more biscuits and colonials, bringing tea time to the heart of the jungle. The serving attendant in this ad, as in most others, is male. Two things happen in such images: women vanish from the affair of empire, and colonized men are feminized by their association with domestic servitude.

Liminal images of oceans, beaches and shorelines recur in cleaning ads of the time. An exemplary ad for Chlorinol Soda Bleach shows three boys in a soda box sailing in a phantasmic ocean bathed by the radiance of the imperial dawn. In a scene washed in the red, white and blue of the Union Jack, two black boys proudly hold aloft their boxes of Chlorinol. A third boy, the familiar racial hybrid of cleaning ads, has presumably already applied his bleach, for his skin is blanched an eery white. On red sails that repeat the red of the bleach box, the legend of black people's purported commercial redemption in the arena of empire reads: "We are going to use 'Chlorinol' and be like de white nigger."

The ad vividly exemplifies Marx's lesson that the mystique of the commodity fetish lies not in its use value but in its exchange value and its potency as a sign: "So far as [the commodity] is a value in use, there is nothing mysterious about it." For three naked children, clothing bleach is less than useful. Instead, the whitening agent of bleach promises an alchemy of racial upliftment through historical contact with commodity culture. The transforming power of the civilizing mission is stamped on the boat-box's sails as the objective character of the commodity itself.

More than merely a *symbol* of imperial progress, the domestic commodity becomes the *agent* of history itself. The commodity, abstracted from social context and human labor, does the civilizing work of empire, while radical change is figured as magical, without process or social agency. Hence the proliferation of ads featuring magic. In similar fashion, cleaning ads such as Chlorinol's foreshadow the "before and after" beauty ads of the twentieth century, a crucial genre directed largely at women, in which the conjuring power of the product to alchemize change is all that lies between the temporal "before and after" of women's bodily transformation.

The Chlorinol ad displays a racial and gendered division of labor. Imperial progress from black child to "white nigger" is consumed as commodity spectacle – as panoptical time. The self-satisfied, hybrid "white nigger" literally holds the rudder of history and directs social change, while the dawning of civilization bathes his enlightened brow with radiance. The black children simply have exhibition value as potential consumers of the commodity, there only to uphold the promise of capitalist commerce and to represent how far the white child has evolved – in the iconography of Victorian racism, the condition of "savagery" is identical to the condition of infancy. Like white women, Africans (both women and men) are figured not as historic agents but as frames for the commodity, valued for *exhibition* alone. The working women, both black and white, who spent vast amounts of energy bleaching the white sheets, shirts, frills, aprons, cuffs and collars of imperial clothes are nowhere to be seen. It is important to note that in Victorian advertising, black women are very seldom rendered as consumers of commodities, for, in imperial lore, they lag too far behind men to be agents of history. Imperial domesticity is therefore a domesticity without women.

In the Chlorinol ad, women's creation of social value through housework is displaced onto the commodity as its own power, fetishistically inscribed on the children's bodies as a magical metamorphosis of the flesh. At the same time, military subjugation, cultural coercion and economic thuggery are refigured as benign domestic processes as natural and healthy as washing. The stains of Africa's disobligingly complex and tenacious past and the inconvenience of alternative economic and cultural values are washed away like grime.

Incapable of themselves actually engendering change, African men are figured only as "mimic men," to borrow V. S. Naipaul's dyspeptic phrase, destined simply to ape the epic white march of progress to self-knowledge. Bereft of the white raimants of imperial godliness, the Chlorinol children appear to take the fetish literally, content to bleach their skins to white. Yet these ads reveal that, far from being a quint-essentially African propensity, the faith in fetishism was a faith fundamental to imperial capitalism itself.

The Myth of First Contact

By the turn of the century, soap ads vividly embodied the hope that the commodity alone, independent of its use value, could convert other cultures to "civilization." Soap ads also embody what can be called *the myth of first contact*: the hope of capturing, as spectacle, the pristine moment of originary contact fixed forever in the timeless surface of the image. In another Pears ad, a black man stands alone on a beach, examining a bar of soap he has picked from a crate washed ashore from a shipwreck. The ad announces nothing less than the "The Birth Of Civilization." Civilization is born, the image implies, at the moment of first contact with the Western commodity. Simply by touching the magical object, African man is inspired into history. An epic metamorphosis takes place, as Man the Hunter-gatherer (anachronistic man) evolves instantly into Man the Consumer. At the same time, the magical object effects a gender transformation, for the consumption of the domestic soap is racialized as a male birthing ritual, with the egg-shaped commodity as the fertile talisman of change. Since women cannot be recognized as agents of history, it is necessary that a man, not a woman, be the historic beneficiary of the magical cargo and that the male birthing occur on the beach, not in the home.[23]

In keeping with the racist iconography of the gender degeneration of African men, the man is subtly feminized by his role as historic exhibit. His jaunty feather represents what Victorians liked to believe was African men's fetishistic, feminine and lower-class predilection for decorating their bodies. Thomas Carlyle, in his prolonged cogitation on clothes, *Sartor Resartus*, notes, for example: "The first spiritual want of a barbarous man is Decoration, as indeed we still see amongst the barbarous classes in civilized nations."[24] Feminists have explored how, in the iconography of modernity, women's bodies are exhibited for visual consumption, but very little has been said about how, in imperial iconography, black men were figured as spectacles for commodity exhibition. If, in scenes set in the Victorian home, female servants are *racialized* and portrayed as frames for the exhibition of the commodity, in advertising scenes set in the colonies, African men are *feminized* and portrayed as exhibition frames for commodity display. Black women, by contrast, are rendered virtually invisible. Essentialist assumptions about a universal "male gaze" elide a great many important historical complexities.

Marx noted how under capitalism "the exchange value of a commodity assumes an independent existence."[25] Toward the end of the nineteenth century, the commodity itself disappears from many ads, and the corporate signature, as the embodiment of pure exchange value in monopoly capital, finds an independent existence. Another ad for Pears features a group of disheveled Sudanese "dervishes" awestruck by a white legend carved on the mountain face: PEARS SOAP IS THE BEST. The significance of the ad, as Richards notes, is its representation of the commodity as a magical medium capable of enforcing and enlarging British power in the colonial world, even without the rational understanding of the mesmerized Sudanese.[26] What the ad more properly reveals is the colonials' own fetishistic faith

in the magic of brand names to work the causal power of empire. In a similar ad, the letters BOVRIL march boldly over a colonial map of South Africa – imperial progress consumed as spectacle, as panoptical time. In an inspired promotional idea, the word had been recognized as tracing the military advance of Lord Roberts across the country, yoking together, as if writ by nature, the simultaneous lessons of colonial domination and commodity progress. In this ad, the colonial map explicitly enters the realm of commodity spectacle.

The poetics of cleanliness is a poetics of social discipline. Purification rituals prepare the body as a terrain of meaning, organizing flows of value across the self and the community and demarcating boundaries between one community and another. Purification rituals, however, can also be regimes of violence and constraint. People who have the power to invalidate the boundary rituals of another people thereby demonstrate their capacity to violently impose their culture on others. Colonial travel writers, traders, missionaries and bureaucrats carped constantly at the supposed absence in African culture of "proper domestic life," in particular Africans' purported lack of hygiene.[27] But the inscription of Africans as dirty and undomesticated, far from being an accurate depiction of African cultures, served to legitimize the imperialists' violent enforcement of their cultural and economic values, with the intent of purifying and thereby subjugating the unclean African body and imposing market and cultural values more useful to the mercantile and imperial economy. The myth of imperial commodities beaching on native shores, there to be welcomed by awestruck natives, wipes from memory the long and intricate history of European commercial trade with Africans and the long and intricate history of African resistance to Europe and colonization. Domestic ritual became a technology of discipline and dispossession.

The crucial point is not simply the formal contradictions that structure fetishes, but also the more demanding historical question of how certain groups succeed, through coercion or hegemony, in foreclosing the ambivalence that fetishism embodies by successfully imposing their economic and cultural system on others.[28] Cultural imperialism does not mean that the contradictions are permanently resolved, nor that they cannot be used against the colonials themselves. Nonetheless, it seems crucial to recognize that what has been vaunted by some as the permanent undecidability of cultural signs can also be violently and decisively foreclosed by superior military power or hegemonic dominion.

Fetishism in the Contest Zone

Enlightenment and Victorian writers frequently figured the colonial encounter as the journey of the rational European (male) mind across a liminal space (ocean, jungle or desert) populated by hybrids (mermaids and monsters) to a prehistoric zone of dervishes, cannibals and fetish-worshippers. Robinson Crusoe, in one of the first novelistic expressions of the idea, sets Christian lands apart from those whose people "prostrate themselves to Stocks and Stones, worshipping Monsters, Elephants, horrible shaped animals and Statues, or Images of Monsters."[29] The Enlightenment mind was felt to have transcended fetish worship and could look indulgently upon those still enchanted by the magical powers of "stocks and stones." But as Mitchell notes, "the deepest magic of the commodity fetish is its denial that there is anything magical about it."[30] Colonial protestations notwithstanding, a decidedly fetishistic faith in the magical powers of the commodity underpinned much of the colonial civilizing mission.

Contrary to the myth of first contact embodied in Victorian ads, Africans had been trading with Europeans for centuries by the time the British Victorians arrived. Intricate trading networks were spread over west and north Africa, with complex intercultural settlements and long stories of trade negotiations and exchanges, sporadically interrupted by violent conflicts and conquests. As John Barbot, the seventeenth-century trader and writer, remarked of the Gold Coast trade: "The Blacks of the Gold Coast, having traded with Europeans since the 14th century, are very well skilled in the nature and proper qualities of all European wares and merchandise vended there."[31] Eighteenth-century voyage accounts reveal, moreover, that European ships plying their trade with Africa were often loaded not with "useful" commodities but with baubles, trinkets, beads, mirrors and "medicinal" potions.[32] Appearing

in seventeenth-century trade lists, among the salt, brandy, cloth and iron, are items such as brass rings, false pearls, bugles (small glass beads), looking glasses, little bells, false crystals, shells, bright rags, glass buttons, small brass trumpets, amulets and arm rings.[33] Colonials indulged heavily in the notion that, by ferrying these cargoes of geegaws and knick-knacks across the seas, they were merely pandering to naive and primitive African tastes. Merchant trade lists reveal, however, that when the European ships returned from West Africa, they were laden not only with gold dust and palm oil but also with elephant tusks, "teeth of sea-horses" (hippopotami), ostrich feathers, beeswax, animal hides and "cods of musk."[34] The absolute commodification of humanity and the colonial genuflection to the fetish of profit was most grotesquely revealed in the indiscriminate listing of slaves amongst the trifles and knick-knacks.

By defining the economic exchanges and ritual beliefs of other cultures as "irrational" and "fetishistic," the colonials tried to disavow them as legitimate systems. The huge labor that went into transporting cargoes of trifles to the colonies had less to do with the appropriateness of such fripperies to African cultural systems than with the systematic undervaluation of those systems with respect to merchant capitalism and market values in the European metropolis.

A good deal of evidence also suggests that the European traders, while vigorously denying their own fetishism and projecting such "primitive" proclivities onto white women, Africans and children, took their own "rational" fetishes with the utmost seriousness.[35] By many accounts, the empire seems to have been especially fortified by the marvelous fetish of Eno's Fruit Salt. If Pears could be entrusted with cleaning the outer body, Eno's was entrusted with "cleaning" the inner body. Most importantly, the internal purity guaranteed by Eno's could be relied upon to ensure male potency in the arena of war. As one colonial vouched: "During the Afghan war, I verily believe Kandahar was won by us all taking up large supplies of ENO's FRUIT SALT and so arrived fit to overthrow half-a-dozen Ayub Khans."[36] He was not alone in strongly recommending Eno's power to restore white supremacy. Commander A. J. Loftus, hydrographer to His Siamese Majesty, swore that he never ventured into the jungle without his tin of Eno's. There was only one instance, he vouched, during four years of imperial expeditions that any member of his party fell prey to fever: "and that happened after our supply of FRUIT SALT ran out."[37]

Fetishism became an intercultural space in that both sides of the encounter appear occasionally to have tried to manipulate the other by mimicking what they took to be the other's specific fetish. In Kenya, Joseph Thomson posed grandly as a white medicine man by conjuring an elaborate ruse with a tin of ENO's for the supposed edification of the Masai: "Taking out my sextant," he records with some glee:

> and putting on a pair of kid gloves – that accidentally I happened to have and that impressed the natives enormously, I intently examined the contents . . . getting ready some ENO'S FRUIT SALT, I sang an incantation – in general something about "Three Blue Bottles" – over it. My voice . . . did capitally for a wizard's. My preparations complete and Brahim [sic] being ready with a gun, I dropped the Salt into the mixture; simultaneously the gun was fired and, lo! up fizzed and sparkled the carbonic acid . . . the chiefs with fear and trembling taste as it fizzes away.[38]

While amusing himself grandly at the imagined expense of the Masai, Thomson reveals his own faith in the power of his fetishes (gloves as a fetish of class leisure, sextant and gun as a fetish of scientific technology and Eno's as a fetish of domestic purity) to hoodwink the Masai. "More amusing," however, as Hindley notes, is Thomson's own naivete, for the point of the story is that "to persuade the Masai to take his unfamiliar remedies, Thomson laid on a show in which the famous fruit salt provided only the 'magic' effects."[39] ENO's power as domestic fetish was eloquently summed up by a General Officer, who wrote and thanked Mr. Eno for his good powder: "Blessings on your Fruit Salt," he wrote, "I trust it is not profane to say so, but I swear by it. There stands the cherished bottle on the Chimney piece of my sanctum, my little idol – at home my household god, abroad my vade mecum."[40] The manufacturers of Eno's were so delighted by this fulsome dedication to their little fetish that they adopted it as regular promotional copy. Henceforth, Eno's was advertised by the slogan: "At home my household god, abroad my vade mecum."

In the colonial encounter, Africans adopted a variety of strategies for countering colonial attempts to undervalue their economies. Amongst these strategies, mimicry, appropriation, revaluation and violence figure the most frequently. Colonials carped rancorously at the African habit of making off with property that did not belong to them, a habit that was seen not as a form of protest, nor as a refusal of European notions of property ownership and exchange value, but as a primitive incapacity to understand the value of the "rational" market economy. Barbot, for example, describes the Ekets as "the most trying of any of the Peoples we had to deal with. . . . Poor Sawyer had a terrible time; the people had an idea they could do as they liked with the factory keeper and would often walk off with the goods without paying for them, that Mr Sawyer naturally objected to, usually ending in a free fight, sometimes my people coming off second best."[41] Richards notes how Henry Morton Stanley, likewise, could not make Africans (whom he saw primarily as carriers of western commodities) understand that he endowed the goods they carried with an abstract exchange value apart from their use value. Since these goods "lack any concrete social role for them in the customs, directives and taboos of their tribal lives, the carriers are forever dropping, discarding, misplacing, or walking away with them. Incensed, Stanley calls this theft."[42]

From the outset, the fetishism involved an intercultural contestation that was fraught with ambiguity, miscommunication and violence. Colonials were prone to fits of murderous temper when Africans refused to show due respect to their flags, crowns, maps, clocks, guns and soaps. Stanley, for one, records executing three African carriers for removing rifles, even though he admits that the condemned did not understand the value of the rifles or the principle for which they were being put to death.[43] Other carriers were executed for infringements such as dropping goods in rivers.

Anecdotes also reveal how quickly colonial tempers flared when Africans failed to be awestruck by the outlandish baubles the colonials offered them, for it wasn't long before the non-Europeans' curiosity and tolerance turned to derision and contempt. In

Australia, Cook carped at the local inhabitants' ungrateful refusal to recognize the value of the baubles he brought them: "Some of the natives would not part with a hog, unless they received an axe in exchange; but nails and beads and other trinkets, that, during our former voyages, had so great a run at this island, were now so much despised, that few would deign so much to look at them."[44]

De Bougainville similarly recalls how a native from the Moluccas, when given "a handkerchief, a looking-glass and some other trifles … laughed when he received these presents and did not admire them. He seemed to know the Europeans."[45] As Simpson points out: "The handkerchief is an attribute of 'civilization,' the tool for making away with the unseemly sweat of the brow, the nasal discharge of cold climates and per-haps the tears of excessive emotion." The white hand-kerchief was also (like white gloves) the Victorian icon of domestic purity and the erasure of signs of labor. The Moluccan's refusal of handkerchief and mirror expressed a frank refusal of two of the central icons of Victorian middle-class consumerism.[46]

In some instances, elaborate forms of mimicry were created by Africans to maintain control of the mercantile trade. As the Comaroffs point out, the Tlhaping, the southernmost Tswana, having obtained beads for themselves, tried to deter Europeans from venturing further into the interior by mimicking European stereotypes of black savagery and portray-ing their neighbors as "men of ferocious habits" too barbaric to meddle with.[47]

In the imperial contest zone, fetishes embodied conflicts in the realm of value and were eloquent of a sustained African refusal to accept Europe's com-modities and boundary rituals on the colonials' terms. The soap saga and the cult of domesticity vividly demonstrates that fetishism was original neither to industrial capitalism nor to precolonial economies, but was from the outset the embodiment and record of an incongruous and violent encounter.

Notes

1. Karl Marx, "Commodity Fetishism," *Capital*, vol. 1, (New York: Vintage Books, 1977), p. 163.

2. See Thomas Richards's excellent analysis, *The Commodity Culture of Victorian Britain: Advertising and Spectacle, 1851–1914* (London: Verso, 1990), especially the introduction and ch. 1.

3. See David Simpson's analysis of novelistic fetishism in *Fetishism and Imagination: Dickens, Melville, Conrad* (Baltimore: Johns Hopkins University Press, 1982).

4. Richards, *The Commodity Culture*, p. 72.

5. Richards, *The Commodity Culture*, p. 5.

6. In 1889, an ad for Sunlight Soap featured the feminized figure of British nationalism, Britannia, standing on a hill and showing P. T. Barnum, the famous circus manager and impresario of the commodity spectacle, a huge Sunlight Soap factory stretched out below them. Britannia proudly proclaims the manufacture of Sunlight Soap to be: "The Greatest Show On Earth." See Jennifer Wicke's excellent analysis of P. T. Barnum in *Advertising Fiction: Literature, Advertisement and Social Reading* (New York: Columbia University Press, 1988).

7. See Timothy Burke, "'Nyamarira That I Loved': Commoditization, Consumption and the Social History of Soap in Zimbabwe," *The Societies of Southern Africa in the 19th and 20th Centuries: Collected Seminar Papers*, no. 42, vol. 17 (London: University of London, Institute of Commonwealth Studies, 1992), pp. 195–216.

8. Leonore Davidoff and Catherine Hall, *Family Fortunes; Men and Women of the English Middle Class* (Routledge: London, 1992).

9. David T. A. Lindsey and Geoffrey C. Bamber, *Soap-Making. Past and Present, 1876–1976* (Nottingham: Gerard Brothers Ltd, 1965), p. 34.

10. Lindsey and Bamber, *Soap-Making*, p. 38. Just how deeply the relation between soap and advertising became embedded in popular memory is expressed in words such as "soft-soap" and "soap opera." For histo-ries of advertising, see also Blanche B. Elliott, *A History of English Advertising* (London: Business Publications Ltd., 1962); and T. R. Nevett, *Advertising in Britain. A History* (London: Heinemann, 1982).

11. Quoted in Diana and Geoffrey Hindley, *Advertising in Victorian England, 1837–1901* (London: Wayland, 1972), p. 117.

12. Mike Dempsey, ed., *Bubbles: Early Advertising Art from A. & Pears Ltd.* (London: Fontana, 1978).

13. Laurel Bradley, "From Eden to Empire: John Everett Millais' Cherry Ripe," *Victorian Studies* 34, #2 (Winter 1991): 179–203. See also, Michael Dempsey, *Bubbles*.

14. Barratt spent £ 2200 on Millais' painting and £ 30,000 on the mass production of millions of individual repro-ductions of the painting. In the 1880s, Pears was spend-ing between £ 300,000 and £ 400,000 on advertising alone.

15. Furious at the pollution of the sacrosanct realm of art with economics, the art world lambasted Millais for

trafficking (publicly instead of privately) in the sordid world of trade.

16. See Jennifer Wicke, *Advertising Fiction*, p. 70.

17. Donna Haraway, *Primate Visions: Gender, Race, and Nature in the World of Modern Science* (London: Routledge, 1989), p. 10.

18. Haraway, *Primate Visions*, p. 10.

19. Haraway, *Primate Visions*, p. 10–11.

20. Charles Kingsley, Letter to his wife, 4 July 1860, in *Charles Kingsley: His Letters and Memories of His Life*, Francis E. Kingsley, ed., (London: Henry S. King and Co, 1877), p. 107. See also Richard Kearney, ed. *The Irish Mind* (Dublin: Wolfhound Press, 1985); L. P. Curtis Jr., *Anglo-Saxons and Celts: A Study of Anti-Irish Prejudice in Victorian England* (Bridgeport: Conference on British Studies of University of Bridgeport, 1968); and Seamus Deane, "Civilians and Barbarians," *Ireland's Field Day* (London: Hutchinson, 1985), pp. 33–42.

21. During the Anglo-Boer War, Britain's fighting forces were seen as valiantly fortified by Johnston's Corn Flour, Pattisons' Whiskey and Frye's Milk Chocolate. See Robert Opie, *Trading on the British Image* (Middlesex: Penguin, 1985) for an excellent collection of advertising images.

22. In a brilliant chapter, Richards explores how the imperial conviction of the explorer and travel writer, Henry Morton Stanley, that he had a mission to civilize Africans by teaching them the value of commodities "reveals the major role that imperialists ascribed to the commodity in propelling and justifying the scramble for Africa." Richards, *The Commodity Culture*, p. 123.

23. As Richards notes: "A hundred years earlier the ship offshore would have been preparing to enslave the African bodily as an object of exchange; here the object is rather to incorporate him into the orbit of exchange. In either case, this liminal moment posits that capitalism is dependent on a noncapitalist world, for only by sending commodities into liminal areas where, presumably, their value will not be appreciated at first can the endemic overproduction of the capitalist system continue." Richards, *The Commodity Culture*, p. 140.

24. Thomas Carlyle, *Sartor Resartus* in *The Works of Thomas Carlyle*, vol. I (London:. Chapman and Hall, 1896–1899), p. 30.

25. Marx, "Theories of Surplus Value," Quoted in G. A. Cohen, *Karl Marx's Theory of History: A Difference* (Princeton: Princeton University Press, 1978), pp. 124–25.

26. Richards, *The Commodity Culture*, pp. 122–23.

27. But palm-oil soaps had been made and used for centuries in west and equatorial Africa. In *Travels in West Africa* Mary Kingsley records the custom of digging deep baths in the earth, filling them with boiling water and fragrant herbs, and luxuriating under soothing packs of wet clay. In southern Africa, soap from oils was not much used, but clays, saps and barks were processed as cosmetics, and shrubs known as "soap bushes" were used for cleansing. Mary H. Kingsley, *Travels in West Africa* (London: Macmillan, 1899). Male Tswana activities like hunting and war were elaborately prepared for and governed by taboo. "In each case," as Jean and John Comaroff write, "the participants met beyond the boundaries of the village, dressed and armed for the fray, and were subjected to careful ritual washing (go foka marumo)." Jean and John Comaroff, *Of Revelation and Revolution: Christianity, Colonialism and Consciousness in South Africa*, vol. 1 (Chicago: University of Chicago Press, 1991), p. 164. In general, people creamed, glossed and sheened their bodies with a variety of oils, ruddy ochres, animal fats and fine colored clays.

28. For an excellent exploration of colonial hegemony in Southern Africa see Jean and John Comaroff, "Home-Made Hegemony: Modernity, Domesticity and Colonialism in South Africa," in Karen Hansen, ed.. *Encounters With Domesticity* (New Brunswick: Rutgers University Press, 1992), pp. 37–74.

29. Daniel Defoe, *The Farther Adventures of Robinson Crusoe*, in *The Shakespeare Head Edition of the Novels and Selected Writings of Daniel Defoe*, vol. 3 (Oxford: Basil Blackwell, 1927–1928), p. 177.

30. For an excellent analysis of commodity fetishism, see W. J. T. Mitchell, *Iconology: Image, Text, Ideology* (University of Chicago Press: Chicago, 1986), p. 193. See also Wolfgang Fritz Haug, *Critique of Commodity Aesthetics: Appearance, Sexuality and Advertising in Capitalist Society*, trans. Robert Bock (Minneapolis: University of Minnesota Press, 1986). See Catherine Gallagher's review essay in *Criticism* 29, 2 (1987): pp. 233–42. On the ritual character of commodities, see Arjun Appadurai, ed., *The Social Life of Things: Commodities in Cultural Perspective* (Cambridge: Cambridge University Press, 1986). See also Sut Jhally, *The Codes of Advertising: Fetishism and the Political Economy of Meaning in the Consumer Society* (London: Routledge, 1990); and, for the language of commodification, see Judith Williamson, *Decoding Advertisements: Ideology and Meaning in Advertising* (London; Marian Boyars, 1978).

31. Cited in Mary H. Kingsley, *Travels in West Africa* p. 622.

32. Simpson, *Fetishism and Imagination*, p. 29.

33. "Trade Goods Used in the Early Trade with Africa as Given by Barbot and Other Writers of the Seventeenth Century," in Kingsley, *Travels in West Africa*, pp. 612–25,

34. Kingsley, *Travels in West Africa*, p. 614.

35. Fetishism was often defined as an infantile predilection. In Herman Melville's *Typee*, the hero describes the people's fetish-stones as "childish amusement . . . like those of a parcel of children playing with dolls and baby houses." *The Writings Of Herman Melville*, The Northwestern-Newberry Edition, Harrison Hayford, Hershel Parker and G. Thomas Tanselle, eds. (Evanston: Northwestern University Press; Chicago: The Newberry Library, 1968), pp. 174–77.

36. D. and G. Hindley, *Advertising in Victorian England*, p. 99.

37. D. and G. Hindley, *Advertising in Victorian England*, p. 98.

38. D. and G. Hindley, *Advertising in Victorian England*, p. 98.

39. D. and G. Hindley, *Advertising in Victorian England*, p. 98.

40. D. and G. Hindley, *Advertising in Victorian England*, p. 99.

41. Kingsley, *Travels in West Africa*, p. 594.

42. Richards, *The Commodity Culture*, p. 125.

43. Richards, *The Commodity Culture*, p. 125.

44. James Cook, vol. 2, *A Voyage to the Pacific Ocean, Undertaken by the Command of His Majesty, for Making Discoveries in the Northern Hemisphere* (James Cook: London, 1784), p. 10.

45. Lewis de Bougainville, *A Voyage Hound the World, Performed by the Order of His Most Christian Majesty, in the Years 1766, 1767, 1768, and 1769*, trans. John Reinhold Forster (London: 1772), p. 360.

46. Barbot admits that the Africans on the west coast "have so often been imposed on by the Europeans, who in former ages made no scruple to cheat them in the quality, weight and measures of their goods which at first they received upon content, because they say it would never enter into their thoughts that white men . . . were so base as to abuse their credulity . . . examine and search very narrowly all our merchandize, piece by piece." It did not take long, it seems, for Africans to invent their own subterfuges to hoodwink the Europeans and win the exchange. By Barbot's account, they would half-fill their oil casks with wood, add water to their oil, or herbs to the oil to make it ferment and thus fill up casks with half the oil. Kingsley, *Travels in West Africa*, p. 582.

47. Jean and John L. Comaroff, *Of Revelation and Revolution*, p. 166.

17.
THE PROMOTIONAL CONDITION OF CONTEMPORARY CULTURE

Andrew Wernick

'There must be some way out of here' said the Joker to the Thief.

—Bob Dylan

The Category of Promotion

In the same breath that cultural theorists, from Adorno to Jameson, have acknowledged the pervasiveness of advertising in the culture of late capitalism, they have limited the force of that insight by assimilating it to a critique of commercialism in general, and by circumscribing what advertising refers to precisely by using that term.

Advertising is commonly taken to mean *advertisements*, paid for and recognizable as such, together with the process of their production and dissemination. In that restricted sense, however vast and ubiquitous a phenomenon, advertising is certainly only one aspect of a wider process of cultural commodification: institutionally, a subsector of the culture industry; textually, a delimited sub-field within the larger field of commercially produced signs. At the same time, the word has a more general meaning. Originally, to animadvert to something was just to draw attention to it; whence to advertise came to mean to publicize, especially in a favourable light. By extension, then, the word refers us not only to a type of message but to a type of speech and, beyond that, to a whole communicative function which is associated with a much broader range of signifying materials than just advertisements *stricto sensu*. Whether as senders, receivers, or analysts of cultural messages we all recognize that

advertising in this second, generic, sense exceeds advertising in the first. But it is hard to grasp the full significance of advertising for contemporary culture unless these meanings are clearly separated. A starting-point for the present study, then, has been to give the functional or expanded sense of advertising a name of its own: *promotion*.

The term has two semantic advantages. The first, reflecting its colloquial usage, is its generality, which directs our attention to the way in which all manner of communicative acts have, as one of their dimensions, and often only tacitly, the function of advancing some kind of self-advantaging exchange. *Promotion* crosses the line between advertising, packaging, and design, and is applicable, as well, to activities beyond the immediately commercial. It can even (as in 'promoting public health') be used in a way which takes us beyond the domain of competitive exchange altogether. For current purposes, though, I have confined it to cases where something, though not necessarily for money, is being promoted for sale – while recognizing that the metaphorical diffusion of the word, wherein it has come to mean any kind of propagation (including that of ideas, causes, and programmes), reflects a real historical tendency for all such discourse to acquire an advertising character. The second advantage stems from the word's derivation. Promotion (as a noun) is a type of sign, and the promoted entity is its referent. From this angle, the triple meaning of the Latin prefix 'pro' usefully highlights the compound and dynamic character of the relationship between promotion and what it promotes. A promotional message is a complex of significations which at once represents (moves in place of), advocates (moves on behalf of), and anticipates (moves ahead of) the circulating entity or entities to which it refers.

Given that definition, the thesis I have been exploring can be simply stated: that the range of cultural phenomena which, at least as one of their functions, serve to communicate a promotional message has become, today, virtually co-extensive with our produced symbolic world.

This may seem hyperbolic, until we start to enumerate the sorts of promotional message, and, associated with them, the circuits of competitive exchange, which are actually swirling about. As we have seen, these include not only advertising in the specific and restricted sense, that of clearly posted 'promotional signs'. They also include the whole universe of commercially manufactured objects (and services), in so far as these are imaged to sell, and are thus constructed as advertisements for themselves. A special case of the latter (in my terminology: 'commodity-signs') is cultural goods. These, indeed, are typically cast in a doubly promotional role. For not only are cultural goods peculiarly freighted with the need and capacity to promote themselves. Wherever they are distributed by a commercial medium whose profitability depends on selling audiences to advertisers they are also designed to function as attractors of audiences towards the advertising material with which they are intercut. In the organs of print and broadcasting, information and entertainment are the flowers which attract the bee. In this sense, too, the non-advertising content of such media can be considered, even semiotically, as an extension of their ads.

But this is not all. The multiply promotional communicative organs constituted by the commercial mass media (and even, via sports sponsorships and the like, by the organs of 'public broadcasting') are also transmissive vehicles for public information and discussion in general. Through that common siting, non-promotional discourses, including those surrounding the political process, have become linked (Bush in Disneyland on prime time news) to promotional ones. It is this complex of promotional media, too, which mediates the communicative activity of all

secondary public institutions – aesthetic, intellectual, educational, religious, etc – to what used to be called 'the general public'. Furthermore, even if not directly commercial themselves, these secondary institutions also generate their own forms of promotional discourse, whether, as in the case of university recruitment campaigns, because they have become indirectly commodified, or, as in the case of electoral politics, because they have a market form which is analogous to the one which operates in the money economy.

There are several respects, finally, in which competition at the level of individuals generates yet a further complex of promotional practices. In part this is an outgrowth of the commodification of labour power, and more particularly, in the professional and quasi-professional sectors of the labour market, of the way in which differentially qualified labour power commands a differential price. Hence the dramaturgical aspects of careers and careerism. In addition, however, as Veblen and many others have described, the promotionalization of the individual also extends into the sphere of consumption, both through fashion and more generally through the way in which status competition is conducted through the private theatre of projected style. At a quite different level of social practice (though, as in the TV ads for Towers department stores, 'everything connects'), the entry, on increasingly symmetrical terms, of (unattached) women and men into free (or non-parentally supervised) socio-sexual circulation has also created a mate/companion/friendship market which generates its own forms of competitive self-presentation. Lastly, when any instance of individual self-promotion spills over from the private realm to become a topic of public communication, whether unintentionally, as a personal drama that makes the news, or deliberately, as the amplified staging of a career (sporting, political, artistic, intellectual, etc), inter-individual competition gives rise to yet a further form of promotional practice: the construction of celebrityhood. This itself enters into the realm of public promotion not just as self-advertising, but as an exchangeable (and promotable) promotional resource both for the individual involved and for other advertisers.

It is tempting to summarize these developments by saying that in late capitalism promotion has become, as Frederic Jameson (appropriating the term from Raymond Williams) has argued of post-modernism (1984: 57), a 'cultural dominant'. Given the provenance of that term, however, and the pecu-liarity of promotion itself as a cultural category, such a formulation will only do if carefully qualified.

Raymond Williams (1982: 204–5) originally devel-oped his distinction between 'dominant', 'residual', 'oppositional' and 'emergent' culture in the context of class-cultural analysis. For him, the interplay of these complexes was conditioned by (and in turn condi-tioned) that of the emergent, dominant, and opposi-tional classes whose positions and sensibilities were expressed in them. In taking over this terminology Jameson gave it a different sociological spin. His problematization of postmodernism focused not on class dynamics, but on the structuring effects of 'third stage' capital on social relations as a whole. This has evident parallels with the approach to the rise of pro-motion being taken here. Still, in Jameson's hands, as in Williams', the notion of 'cultural dominant' remains linked to a notion of culture as (collective) expression. It refers us to the impact of (ascendant) cultural values on the styles, themes, and inflections of artis-tic, pop cultural, architectural, etc, symbolic domains. In late capitalism, he writes (1984: 57), postmodern-ism has replaced modernism as 'a new systemic cultural norm'.

The problem is that promotion – unlike any cul-tural movement – is not only not a class phenomenon, it is not an expressive one either. To be sure, it is embodied in significations, and it is ramified by social-ization practices, psychological strategies and habits, and cultural/aesthetic norms and values. But in the first instance, promotion is a mode of communica-tion, a species of rhetoric. It is defined not by what it says but by what it does, with respect to which its sty-listic and semantic contents are purely secondary, and derived.

I can put the matter more precisely, perhaps, by saying that promotion has become a key structuring element of what Scott Lash (1990: 4–5 and passim) has termed contemporary society's 'regime of signifi-cation'. He defines this as a combinatory structure, parallel to the material economy (conceived of as a 'regime of accumulation'), which comprises two sub-formations. The first is the 'cultural economy', which

itself consists of a combination of four elements: (a) the relations of symbolic production (its property regime), (b) conditions of reception, (c) a mediating institutional framework, and (d) the means of sym-bolic circulation. The second is the 'mode of signifi-cation', involving a determinate set of relations (for example the realist model of representation) between the signifier, signified, and referent of symbolic objects. In general, while allowing for a certain 'rela-tive autonomy', the causal assumption is that the second complex of relations is shaped by the first.

The case of promotion fits the model well. In a promotional message the relation between sign and referent has been (re)arranged in such a way that, first, the former is an anticipatory advocate of the second, and second, within the construction of a promotional image, the boundary between sign and object is blurred. What the suffusion of promotion throughout all levels of social communication has amounted to, then, is a change in the prevalent mode of significa-tion. Moreover, this transformation has itself been associated with changes in the mode of production and circulation of signs (commodification, the rise of the culture industry, and the commercial mass media), that is, with changes in the cultural economy. Indeed, while Lash's model (which he deploys in a fresh attempt to account for the rise of postmodernism) allows for a certain degree of autonomy of the mode of signification from the cultural economy, the causal relation in the case of the late capitalist rise of pro-motion is direct and virtually unmediated.

But here the notion of a 'regime of signification', a structure of structures, definable in itself, which can enter into interactive relations with the (capitalist) economy proper, reveals a limitation. For the rise of commercialized culture, in symbiotic relation with mass media advertising, has itself been intrinsic to a more general process of capitalist development. Not only has culture become a sector of consumer goods production just like any other produced object of human use. Industrialization and mass production have also, and again for purely economic reasons, led to an expansion of the sphere of commodity circula-tion, of which the culture industry, via advertising, has itself become a heavily subsidized adjunct. In addi-tion, and further complicating the picture, the rise of inter-individual and non-commercial promotion has registered the effects of a parallel, and only indirectly related, socio-cultural process in which social life in every dimension has increasingly come to assume a commodity or quasicommodity form.

In trying to locate the place of promotion on the sociological map, in other words, the very distinction between the symbolic and material economies, between the regime of accumulation and the regime of signification, cannot be clearly drawn. And for good reason. Promotional practice is generated exactly on the boundary, a locus which implies the dissolution of the boundary itself.

What the rise of promotion as a cultural force signals, in fact, is not simply a shift to a new mode of producing and circulating signs (cultural commodification), but an alteration in the very relation between culture and economy. Baudrillard (1981), following Debord (1977), has depicted this movement ('the union of sign and commodity')[1] as a merger, although it might be more accurate to depict it as a takeover, since culture has lost its autonomy thereby, while the (market) economy has hypostatized into an all engulfing dynamic. The result is a mutation: still capitalism, but a capitalism transformed. In effect, during the course of advanced capitalist development the globalization and intensification of commodity production have led to a crucial economic modification in which (a) with mass production and mass marketing the moments of distribution, circulation, and exchange have become as strategic as technical improvements in production for profitability and growth and (b) through commodity imaging the circulation and production processes have come to overlap. In which context (with disturbing implications for even an updated Marxism) it has further come about that the ('superstructural') domain of expressive communication has been more and more absorbed, not just as an industry but as a direct aspect of the sale of everything, into the integral workings of the commodified economic 'base'.

This has been a complex transformation, and it evidently did not occur all at once. There have been many phases and stages: from industrialism and the first consumer-oriented urban centres to the radio/film age, coca-colonization and the electronic malls of commercial TV.[2] Whence a further caveat. Besides eschewing an expressionist view of its object, any

thesis about the changed weight of promotion within 'late' capitalist culture must also be careful to avoid too sharp a sense of periodization.

Promotion has culturally generalized as commodification has spread, as consumer goods production has industrialized, leading to the massive expansion of the sphere of circulation, and as competitive exchange relations have generally established themselves as an axial principle of social life. But there has been no catastrophe point, no single historical juncture (for example in the 1950s and 1960s) at which we can say that promotion, having previously been 'emergent', finally became a 'dominant' structuring principle of our culture. It is a question, rather, of a cumulative tendency; a tendency, indeed, of very long standing, since, as Bourdieu (1977: 177) has reminded us, the market as a principle of socio-cultural organization predates capitalism and, even in 'primitive' societies, the symbolic and material economies are to some degree 'interconvertible'. Nor can the process of promotionalization be said to be complete. As with commodification as a whole, the advance of promotion has been uneven, both internationally and also within leading capitalist countries themselves. Even in Baudrillard's America, the mirage runs out at the desert and there are low-intensity zones.

Both for the present and historically, then, all that can be safely asserted is that *pari passu* with the development of the market, promotion is a condition which has increasingly befallen discourses of all kinds; and the more it has done so, the more its modalities and relations have come to shape the formation of culture as a whole. But what condition? What are the characteristics of a culture whose communicative processes have come to be saturated in the medium of promotion? What qualities does it exhibit, more precisely, just by virtue of that fact?

Promotion as a Cultural Condition

The guiding thesis of Horkheimer and Adorno's essay on the culture industry in *The Dialectic of Enlightenment* was that 'culture now impresses the same stamp on everything' (1972: 120). In support, they cited such tendencies as the monopolistic centralization of cultural production, the standardization of cultural produce (which reflects and transmits the rhythms of industrial mass production), the classification of goods and consumers ('Something is provided for all so that none may escape'), the sensate emphasis of style over work, and the promiscuous, mid-market, merging of serious art and distractive entertainment.

In the first instance, their thesis was ironically aimed against conservative laments about the cultural chaos that would ensue from specialization and the decline of organized religion and other ideologically unifying remnants of pre-capitalist society. But it also ran dialectically counter to the analysis of classical sociology. For if, as Durkheim and Weber had asserted, cultural modernity entailed the rational differentiation of social activities and sectors, including, within the cultural sphere, those of art, science, ethics, and religion, then, through the homogenizing impact of commodification, that same movement could be shown to contain the seeds of its own reversal.[3]

Now, implicit in Horkheimer and Adorno's account, though they do not consider it as an independent factor, is that one of the ways in which commodification has been a culturally homogenizing force is through the similar ways in which, whatever the medium and genre, the products of the culture industry present themselves to us as objects and sites of a promotional practice.[4] The point is worth drawing out. It is not just that such diverse vehicles of symbolic expression as pop records, political candidates, philosophical texts, art galleries, news magazines, and sporting events, are all intensively advertised, and that this draws attention to what, as promotables, they all share: the de-sacralized status of publicly circulating, and privately appropriable, items of commercial exchange. The marketing imperative feeds back into their actual construction; so that, for example, the use and build-up of promotional names and the adoption of majoritarian entertainment values have become a common feature of all marketed discourse, regardless of whether its manifest function is to inform, inspire, solidarize or just to entertain. Moreover, this homologous proliferation of self-promotional forms goes beyond the cultural sphere. Not only are the same forms – imaged commodities as advertisements for themselves – to be found throughout the whole world of commercially produced goods. From the clothes we wear, to the parties we vote for at election time, wherever in fact a market of some kind operates, everything mirrors back the same basic signifying mode.

However, the rise of promotion has entailed more than just the boundary-crossing spread of similar rhetorical forms. In a multitude of instances, promotion in one sector has come to dovetail with promotion in another. Bush's campaign appearance at Disneyland advertised that company, just as Disney's $13 million hyping of *Dick Tracy* two years later incidentally boosted the sales of ('Breathless') Madonna's latest album, not to mention audience receipts from the world tour which launched it. In addition, promotional messages borrow their imaging ideas and techniques from one another, whether through direct quotes (in the cola wars), through the logic of positioning wherein a market is segmented into differentially imaged niches, or, more diffusely, by circulating the same stock of promotionally tried-and-tested motifs and social types.

Promotion in different spheres, then, multiply interconnects – both in terms of the common pool of myths, symbols, tropes, and values which it employs, and through the way in which each of the objects to which a promotional message is attached is itself a promotional sign, and so on in an endless chain of mutual reference and implication. Following McLuhan's reference to Poe's sailor (1967: v), I have described the symbolic world which results as a giant vortex in which, for producers and receivers of culture alike, all signifying gestures are swallowed up. But having in mind the *promesse de bonheur* which the discourses of promotion continually proffer, and defer, that vortex can also be thought of as a maze. In fact, an infinite maze: in which there is no final destination, no final reward, and where the walls are pictures (and pictures of pictures) of ever-multiplying varieties of cheese.

Thus, and this is my first point, we can say that the extension of promotion through all the circuits of social life is indeed a force for cultural homogenization, but only if we add the rider that the outcome is not a mere repetition everywhere of the same. For it brings into being a vast web of discourse which is at once continuous from one part to the next, yet asymmetrical with regard to what (and how many) purchasable entities are being aided thereby in their competitive circulation. Overall, then, the sameness of rhetorical form which promotion everywhere installs is counter-balanced by a semiological complexity which makes every point in the flow as intriguing in its formal construction as it is boringly void of deeper content. As Daniel Boorstin has noted, this seductive quality frustrates any merely demystifying critique. 'Information about the staging of a pseudo-event simply adds to its fascination' (Boorstin, 1961: 38).[5]

A second respect in which promotion shapes the signifying materials of a culture in which that mode has generalized is that these materials become pervasively instrumental in character. The point of promotion is to effect a valorizing exchange, and its whole communicative substance is directed to that end.

Again, instrumentalism is a trend about which traditional social theory has had much to say. The notion that in the transition to modernity means-ends rationality became an end in itself, both in the economy, through science-based production, and in the state, through law and bureaucracy, passed from Weber and Heidegger to the Frankfurt thinkers, and thence to Habermas, through whom it has remained a central preoccupation of contemporary thought. For post-war critics of consumer culture, particularly in the United States, the same problematic has framed a corresponding interest in how, through the applications of behavioural psychology, psychoanalysis and the like, the needs and purchasing decisions of consumers are manipulated from above. In that spirit popular writers from Vance Packard to Brian Key have joined with philosophical ones like Marcuse to generate a picture of advertising as the cultural arm of a totally administered society. Such analysis falters, however, when it comes to demonstrating, whether in the case of selling soap or selling politicians, that such manipulation is really scientific, and, more to the point, that it actually works. As Schudson (1986: 210) notes: 'Advertising may shape our sense of values even where it does not greatly corrupt our buying habits.'

In any case, the cultural problem presented by the instrumental character of advertising, or indeed of promotion in any of its forms, is not just a question of the freedom-violating devices through which goods are sold, needs are shaped, or political order maintained. Beyond this external instrumentality, the discourse of promotion is instrumental vis-a-vis itself. If we consider that speech acts have two functions, the performative (aiming at an external change of state in the listener) and the referential (aiming at the communication of a meaning), then what characterizes promotional speech is the thoroughness with which the former is subordinated to the latter. The case is similar to propaganda, though there is a difference. The effectiveness of promotion is not measured by the extent to which its claims and perspectives are actually believed. What matters is simply the willingness of its audience to complete the transaction promotion aims to initiate. And in this, the casualty is not so much 'truth' as the very meaningfulness of the language material (whether verbal, visual or auditory) which promotional messages mobilize to that end.

Because of their calculatedly supporting role, in other words, the ideals and myths conjured up by the words and symbols used to endow a product, institution or personality with imagistic appeal are emotionally, and existentially, devalued. The effect is complementary to the one Roland Barthes (1972) focused on in his analysis of myth. There – for example in the French *lycée* teacher's use of the Latin tag 'ego nominor leo' (my name is lion) to indicate a grammatical rule – a first-order meaning (who cares about the lion?) is effaced before a second-order one (grammatical correctness) conjured up by the first-order sign as a whole. In promotion, these second-order meanings themselves fade in the extrinsic (and profaning) use to which they are put. The Paradise myth evidently packs less of a spiritual punch in a cigarette ad than in an act of worship. In turn, because of the associative responses which advertising itself engenders, this cheapening of the symbolic currency becomes general and feeds back. Even in a church, it is hard to hear 'paradise' without thinking of the multitude of goods – starting with song and film titles – to which that idea, and the many ways of rendering it, have been promotionally linked.

Such devaluation applies, moreover, not only to the plane of the signified, but also to that of that of the signifier. When Billie Holliday's poignant rendition of 'Summertime' is played as the voice-over for a VW ad, its own mystique as a 'classic' performance, which is inextricable from her own as a tragic figure, is diminished in the very act wherein that of the car is associatively enhanced. Fear of a similar effect has led to the banning in British commercials of direct references to royalty. Paradoxically, then, while the vast apparatus of selling uses established social and psychological values to move the merchandise, and thus incidentally serves as an ideological transmitter as well, that very linkage, which makes the rhetoric of ideology itself rhetorical, dis-cathects the moral, political, etc, categories and symbologies of ideological discourse as such.

I have been speaking, so far, about the way that the rise of promotion has been associated with the generation and diffusion of a certain kind of language material. But it is important to consider as well the effect of promotion on the things it promotes. At first sight, promotion stands apart from its object as an external instrument in that object's circulation. However, the (self-interested) exchange of buyer-seller information is an intrinsic aspect of any market. Promotion of some kind – even if it is only a matter of heaping apples on a road-side table to indicate that they are for sale – is necessary to complete an object's instantiation as an item of exchange. In the developed state, moreover, where commodities are designed to have symbolic appeal as part of their own selling operation, the unity of this process is replicated in the very form of the object. There, what is promoted cannot be disentangled from what promotes it, even in principle.

Haug (1986) has coined the term 'commodity aesthetics' to describe this reflexive effect. But, adopting Marx's language of prostitutes and pimps, he still sees the promotional dressing up of commodities as an externality; indeed, as an unnatural embellishment which both mystifies what circulating objects really are – items of human use – and distorts our needing/desiring relation to them. However, for things implicated in a competitive market to be given a self-promotional form is not merely a decorative – and dissimulating – addition. It changes their very being. An object which happens to circulate is converted into one which is designed to do so, and so is materially stamped with that character. In the case, say, of a

Morphy-Richards iron, or even of a Wedgwood vase or a GM car, the distinction between a commodity – only marked as such by its invisible price – and a (self-advertising) commodity-sign may not seem to be of great consequence. For it is only the outward appearance of the latter which is semiotically inscribed, while the bundle of performance characteristics which define what such objects 'really' are remains the same. This cannot be said, though, when the imaged commodity (or quasi-commodity) is already, at the level of its actual use, a complex of signs. When a piece of music, or a newspaper article, or even an academically written book about promotional culture, is fashioned with an eye to how it will promote itself – and, indeed, how it will promote its author and distributor, together with all the other produce these named agencies may be identified with – such goods are affected by this circumstance in every detail of their production.

The necessary and determinate extension of a commodity or quasi-commodity into a promotional sign, and the reincorporation of this into the constitution of the promoted entity itself, manifests, in the clearest fashion, what Derrida has called the logic of the supplement. Promotion is the significative supplement of the commodity. It transforms what it doubles and extends. Furthermore, just as (in Derrida's account) the transformative supplement of writing has been part of language since its oral origins, so too has promotion always been an aspect of even the most undeveloped form of market. The absorption of the circulating object into the circulating sign through 'commodity aesthetics', for all that it has been a real historical process, builds on, develops, and extends a characteristic of the commodity form which is inscribed in its very origin.

Beyond the impact of generalized promotion on the discourses and objects that make up the external aspects of our symbolic world, a few words are needed, finally, on what this development has implied for the subjectivity of those whose communicative activity is mediated by it.

No reflection on the contemporary situation of 'the subject' can avoid reference to the debate which has raged for the last three decades about that category. The initial challenges of structuralism and deconstruction were aimed against radical currents of thought which deployed a vocabulary of history, praxis, and freedom against the alienating and reifying tendencies of a developed capitalism.[6] However, the critique of that humanist vocabulary by Barthes, Althusser, Foucault, and Derrida joined forces with those who used it (against the system) in questioning the inflated individualism which they all took to be an ideological foundation of the established order. As a result, two different kinds of theses about the 'death of the subject' have tended to get confused. The first is a historical thesis, advanced by the early Frankfurt thinkers,[7] to the effect that the (industrial capitalist) organization of production has led to the disorganization of the (classical liberal) subject. At issue, here, is the actual decline, fragmentation, and alienation of the producing and consuming individual in the face of a market-oriented socioeconomic development whose justifying rhetoric falsely promised a moral and political progress predicated on the individual's emancipation as a (responsibly) free being. The second is a philosophical thesis deriving from Nietzsche's reflections on the Cartesian ego. This has questioned whether it is meaningful to talk about the subject at all – especially as an integrated entity which is the real author of its own thought and practice – since, in whatever social and historical situation, the thinking, believing, acting, self, both actually and as a concept, is constituted by, and in the medium of, language.

To propose that contemporary subjectivity is shaped by the cultural determinations I have been describing is evidently to place oneself in the register of the former, that is within a narrative of the (male/bourgeois/Protestant) individual's disautonomizing decline. To which it should be added, however, that the second, poststructuralist, thesis is not irrelevant to the question of how to factor in the mediating implications of promotion, since promotion itself is a communicative phenomenon. Thus the question of what has happened to the subject as a result of the spread of promotion turns, at least in part, on what has happened to the signifying practices and materials by which the individual subject has come to be enveloped.

The literature on advertising has tended to focus on this question from the side of reception, in which the most highlighted effects have been those which derive from the continual interpellation of subjects as consumers. That is: the growing prevalence of an anomic, feed-me, orientation to the world, and a psycho-economy of needs, desires and beliefs which is expressed in a totemic and fetishizing attitude towards branded goods.[8] As many commentators (Reisman, 1950; Reiche, 1970; Lasch, 1976) have noted, the ideological complex represented by consumerism has also been associated with the emergence of a modal character type – anxious, schizoidal, other-directed, oral-dependent, etc – which exhibits the psycho-pathological features of what Freud dubbed the 'narcissistic personality'.

To this catalogue, I would add only one further point. It concerns not the psychology or anthropology of consumption but the impact on individual consciousness of promotional culture as a whole. If we accept that the symbolic universe reconstituted by the rise of promotion has been de-referentialized – a quality which stems, on the one hand, from promotion's instrumentalization of values and symbols, and on the other from its perpetual deferral of the promoted object, together with any closure of the gap of desire which that object's final arrival might bring – then the promotionally addressed subject has been placed in a novel cultural predicament: how to build an identity and an orientation from the materials of a culture whose meanings are unstable and behind which, for all the personalized manner in which its multitudinous messages are delivered, no genuinely expressive intention can be read. Schizophrenic disintegration and the consumerized conformism of the Pepsi Generation are only the most extreme poles of a possible response. More common is a sensibility which oscillates between a playful willingness to be temporarily seduced and a hardened scepticism about every kind of communication in view of the selling job it is probably doing. In that light, cynical privatism and mass apathy – an index of which is the falling participation rate in American elections – can even be construed as a sign of resistance: for Baudrillard, (1983), the only form of resistance still open to the media-bombarded 'silent majority'.

But the envelopment of the individual by promotion must be grasped from both sides of the promotional sign. It is not enough to look at this question only from the side of reception, that is to look at subjects only as readers/listeners addressed by a certain kind of speech. We must also take account of the way in which the contemporary subject has become implicated in promotional culture as a writer/performer of its texts.

Of course, only a minority play a directly authorial role in the imaging and marketing of commercial produce. Fewer still are the named creators or performers of cultural goods, though these have an exemplary importance since media stars are our equivalent of mythic heroes, providing the most salient paradigms of how individual praxis contributes to the shaping of our world. But the list grows if we also include all those playing a more specialist or subordinate role in commercial promotion, as well as those engaged in non- or quasi-commercial forms of promotional practice like electoral politics, or the public relations side of hospitals, schools, and churches. In any case, from dating and clothes shopping to attending a job interview, virtually everyone is involved in the self-promotionalism which overlays such practices in the micro-sphere of everyday life.

At one level or another, then, and often at several levels at once, we are all promotional, subjects. Nor can we practically choose not to be. The penalty of not playing the game is to play it badly; or even, inadvertently, to play it well. Sincerity has become a prized virtue in a society where phoniness is a universal condition. Hence the cult of the natural and unaffected – a cult which is catered to even in the transparently artificial world of show business when, for example, David Bowie in the early 1980s put Ziggy Stardust and the Thin White Duke behind him and reincarnated as himself.

This example illustrates an even more fundamental point. Individuals who self-advertise are doubly implicated in such practice. They are, that is, not only promotional authors but promotional products. The subject that promotes itself constructs itself for others in line with the competitive imaging needs of its market. Just like any other artificially imaged commodity, then, the resultant construct – a persona produced for public consumption – is marked by the transformative effects of the promotional supplement. The outcome is not just the socially adapted self of mainstream social-psychology, a panoply of self-identified roles attuned to the requirements of the social position(s) which a person has come to occupy.

It is a self which continually produces itself for competitive circulation: an enacted projection, which includes not only dress, speech, gestures, and actions, but also, through health and beauty practices, the cultivated body of the actor; a projection which is itself, moreover, an inextricable mixture of what its author/object actually has to offer, the signs by which this might be recognized, and the symbolic appeal this is given in order to enhance the advantages which can be obtained from its trade.

While in other respects their writings are now dated, the social phenomenologists, from Sartre to Goffman, who pondered these matters in the late 1950s (against a drum-beat of concerns about conformism, alienation and anxiety), drew attention to a real issue. The contemporary subject, and nowhere more than in the competitively mediated zones of work and play where our personal self-presentations directly affect our inter-individual rates of exchange, is faced with a profound problem of authenticity. If social survival, let alone competitive success, depends on continual, audience-oriented, self-staging, what are we behind the mask? If the answer points to a second identity (a puppeteer?) how are we to negotiate the split sense of self this implies?[9]

Intersubjectivity, too, is infected by doubt. Knowing how our own promotional moves will be read, how can we make credible to others the imaged egos we want to project as truly our own? And conversely: how can we decipher aright the self-stagings which are similarly projected towards us? To be sure, the result need not be total moral chaos. An ironic distantiation is always possible, and signalling this, or just mutually acknowledging it to be the case, enables us, despite the promotional enactments normally dissimulated on the surface of our discourse, to preserve dialogical respect. Nonetheless, public acts of communication will always be distorted, and properly distrusted, in a social universe in which market forms, and the promotional dynamics to which they give rise, are universally operative. Inauthentic writers are constantly being counterposed to cynical readers: a relationship in which the latter always need to be convinced, while the former must find ways to obviate that resistance when crafting messages for release.

From top to bottom, in short, promotional culture is radically deficient in good faith. For those with sensitive moral digestions, this description will seem too weak. Considering the sugar coating which pastes a personal smile, and a patina of conformist values, over the pervasively self-interested motives which underlie virtually all publicly communicated words and images, the total impression it makes (against which, of course, we screen ourselves through wise inattention) is not merely vacuous, but emetic in its perpetual untruth.

Exit?

The transformist impulse within the tradition of critical social theory from which I have drawn joins with the affirmative conventions of promotional culture itself to direct me to close these reflections on a note, if not of optimism, then at least of openness to what a better future might bring. In so doing, I will not disavow the bleakness of the diagnosis. The spectre of totalitarianism has evidently receded in advanced industrial societies. In two respects, though, a meditation on the place of promotion in contemporary society faces even more difficulties when it comes to thinking our way towards a more liberated, civilized, and organic path of cultural development than was the case for Horkheimer and Adorno when they wrote their gloomy analysis of the culture industry under the shadow of Auschwitz and Mickey Mouse in the early 1940s.

The first is bound up with what both opponents and celebrants of the Thatcher-Reagan era have concurred in describing as the global triumph of liberal capitalism. Not only have the Stalinist regimes of the East collapsed, but also state socialism as a credible project for the Western left. As well, even proponents of a 'third way' – whether cast in the form of socialist democracy, or of a mixed economy with a devolved public sector – have come to seem hopelessly out of touch with a march of events dominated by free trade, the privatization of state enterprise, and the globalization of corporate capital. With markets as with procreation, it seems, you can't be a little bit pregnant.

The correlative development of a culture increasingly made up of endless ads, and driven throughout by the dynamics of commodities and their competitive circulation, has also established itself on a world

scale. And to this, the only alternative which currently presents itself is the type of solution represented, most dramatically, by the revival of Islam. That is: the renewed imposition, in a developmental crisis of modernization, of those traditional/authoritarian blockages to market circulation which a colleague of mine has aptly (and approvingly) characterized as 'atavisms'.[10] It is hard to think of this as more than a temporary (and terroristic) halt. In any case, a reactive fundamentalism, which has its weak First World echoes in born-again Christianity, can have little appeal for those whose vision of social progress has itself emerged from the expectations generated out of the partial freedoms delivered by the market, for example in a more egalitarian and emancipated relation between the sexes.

The second difficulty stems from the very character of the phenomenon under discussion. The way in which the promotional mode has extended to all facets of social communication suggests that commercialism, and the market principle more generally, is an even more engulfing cultural force than was supposed by the Frankfurt thinkers. I can illustrate this with a trivial incident from a recent late night chat show on British TV.[11] The interviewee was a member of the fictional heavy metal band *Spinal Tap*, as featured in the satirical movie of that name. The first half of the interview was 'in character', like an episode from the movie itself. The second half, after a chuckle, got down to the serious business of trade talk. It transpired that *Spinal Tap* (one of the songs from the movie's soundtrack had already been a minor hit) were now really on tour, lip-synching their numbers to live audiences in the midst of the same preposterously exaggerated gothic sets as had graced their equally simulated performances on screen. Having performed in Seattle, they were about to try their hand in London. (The fact that they were not a great success can be attributed to the fact that by the late 1980s heavy metal had been eclipsed by rap as the music of choice for working-class youth, so that the parodic effects were blunted.)

Retroactively, then, the original movie's (pseudo-promotional) savaging of the music business had been turned into actual promotion for an 'act' which was itself designed to promote the re-released video and accompanying record. Echoing this, the interview's mid-point switch from a fake conversation to a real one registered only the transition from the promotional satirization of promotion to promotion itself. Not even satire, then, is immune from a process it may seek to destroy through laughter. And the same can be said of other forms of critique as well. Once we are communicating at all, and especially in public, and therefore in a medium which is promotional through and through, there is no going outside promotional discourse. These very words are continuous with what they are seeking to distance themselves from. To paraphrase what Derrida remarked of textuality in general: there is no *hors-promotion*.

That said, discourse is not the whole of being. And when we look at things in wider perspective, we can see that the extensive and intensive penetration of culture by promotion has not been without its elements of tension and conflict.

Two levels of contradiction can be identified. The first involves what may be termed contradictions of circulation. Here, there is a clash between the promotional imperative inherent in the market's lust-to-expand, and the resistance exercised by the moral, aesthetic or religious mechanisms which, in the interests of the current order, surround certain symbols, entities or sites of potential publicity so as to secure their exclusion from profane processes of circulation. Contradictions of this kind are evident in the uneasiness which, since John Stuart Mill, has attended the development of electioneering, in the clash of campaigns for and against legalizing street prostitution, and in the controversies which break out (though I am not remotely suggesting that this was Rushdie's motive) when an author enhances his name by dancing pirouettes through the revealed truths of a militant world religion. The second type of contradiction is at the level of mass psychology. This concerns the tendency of a promotionalized culture to become depleted of the (existential and cosmological) meaningfulness which those implicated in it, just because it is a culture, seek to derive from its symbolic material. In this direction lie the worried hunches not only of conservative thinkers like Daniel Bell or Robert Nisbet, but also of more liberal ones like Anthony Giddens (1990), that late capitalism is drifting towards a fully fledged spiritual-cum-ideological crisis.

These two sources of tension generate the space and energy for a kind of politics. Normally, as in the instances cited, it is localized and intermittent. However, and without wishing to reduce very complex events and processes to a simple formula, modern history has also shown us, as in inter-war Europe and in North America during the 1960s, that a condensation of the contradictions of circulation and of depleted ideological meaning can create the conditions for a massive cultural revolt. All of which implies that, while history never repeats itself, the spread of commodification is associated with ongoing cultural contradictions which go to the roots of capitalism's processes of social reproduction, and that the activization of these provides a certain room to manoeuvre for those wishing to influence, against the grain of the advancing market, the larger drift of events.

But manoeuvre how? The long-range goal that suggests itself is to enlarge the sphere in which promotion is circumscribed. Even as a gradualist project, it should be emphasized, this is not just a question of restricting bad symbols, but of restricting a bad kind of circulation. At the same time, to speak of restriction alone is not enough. There is an evident danger that any politics of inhibiting promotional circulation can get tangled up in rearguard struggles in which pre-market unfreedoms, associated with repressive-hierarchical definitions of the sacred, are reactively defended or restored. A more radical objective would therefore involve not just rolling back the area of cultural life colonized by competitive exchange, but doing so at the same time as the sacralized categories marking out the boundaries of permissible, competitive circulation were themselves humanistically redefined. This possibility can already be glimpsed in situations of familial or affective intimacy where, against the weight of convention and habit, the creative power of symbolic exchange, and the new forms it can create, can be commonsensically acknowledged and given their due. In the public realm, hemmed in by economic interests, state regulation, and institutional rigidity, a similar recognition would require a transformed consciousness on the part of those who are stewards of socially important institutions and resources, and the translation of such recognition into a transformed practice.

In the long term, any strategy of promotional limitation evidently depends on releasing cultural production from its currently overwhelming commercial imperative. In turn, this implies greater subsidies from taxation for all forms of cultural activity, whether popular, mass or minority, so as to reduce reliance both on advertising revenue and on corporate sponsorships. As well, it implies a sustained effort to revalorize the public realm itself as a space for disinterested expression and communication. That all this is intimately connected to a larger project of restricting the market in favour of cooperation, rehabilitating the public sphere, and dis-alienating secondary institutions, both internally, and vis-a-vis their clients and constituencies, also goes without saying.

At a time of sustained neo-conservative retrenchment, such sentiments will seem dismissibly utopian. If so, I offer no counter-prognoses about when, or whether, contemporary civilization will reopen to buried dreams. Proving the this-sidedness of our (social) thinking is a matter for (political) practice, not theoretical speculation – and who would dare to predict? Meanwhile, in an exercise which has sought merely to depict some of the consequences of blindly pursuing the current market-oriented path, the most that can be hoped for is as modest as the horizons of the time to which it belongs: that while history spins its wheels some hint of what the present dispensation blocks can be kept, at least negatively, alive.

Notes

1. For Baudrillard, however, the crux of the sign-commodity conjunction lies in the totemic and status-differential 'system of objects' which mass-produced consumer goods represent at the point of consumption. Sign-exchange-value doubles exchange-value in the constitution of the commodity, constituting a new term (the sign-commodity) within an expanded, and infinitely commutable, field of 'general exchange'. This model is elaborated throughout Baudrillard's early writings, and receives its most formal treatment in 1981, especially pp 123–9 and 143–63.

2. To which we might now add the promotional conquest of outer space. In saying this I am not just referring to the superpower boosterism of the space race, but to its actual commercialization as a spectacle (logos on spaceships, etc) which the post-Cold War Soviet programme, suddenly starved for cash, has pioneered.

3. Lash, Featherstone, and others have recently taken this argument up again in the context of contemporary discussion about postmodernity and postmodern culture. See Featherstone (1988), and Lash (1990).

4. 'The prevailing taste takes its ideal from advertising, the beauty in consumption. Hence the Socratic saying that the beautiful is the useful has been fulfilled – ironically. The cinema makes propaganda for the culture combine as a whole; on radio, goods for whose sake the cultural commodity exists are also recommended individually' (Horkheimer and Adorno, 1972: 156).

5. That advertisements are creative and can be enjoyed, and judged, in aesthetic terms beyond utilitarian criteria about sales effectiveness, has occurred to many, inside and outside the advertising industry. In a recent article, Nava and Nava (1990) highlight the 'interconnections and overlap between commercial and other forms of art in order to expand our understanding of the ways in which young people exercise critical abilities as audience'. The Cannes Film Festival (whose promotional function is self-evident) includes a competitive section on TV ads. Of course, whether or not advertising has to be regarded (properly speaking) as 'art' depends on whether that category is descriptively and normatively identified with autonomous art, an ideal that rose and fell between the Renaissance and the beginning of this century.

6. For Althusser's decentring assault on humanism and existentialism as the basis for a 'scientific' revolutionary theory, see especially 'Marxism is not a humanism' in Althusser (1969). In a parallel (though not of course identically inspired move) Derrida was equally concerned to rescue Husserl and Heidegger from the left-existentialism to which, through Sartre especially, their work had become linked. See 'The Ends of Man' in Derrida (1986: 109–36).

7. See for example Horkheimer (1972: 235–7).

8. For a discussion of totemism and consumer goods see Leiss et al. (1986), Jhally (1987), and Douglas and Isherwood (1979).

9. The work of Irving Goffman (especially 1959) can be read, in this context, as an interactionist exploration of the promotional self, while that of R.D. Laing and associates can be read as an exploration of the schizophrenogenic consequences.

10. I owe this phrase to my colleague Pradeep Bandyopadhyay, for whom the 'atavisms' however are to be viewed positively, i.e. as a way for non-Western civilizations to assert themselves against the West.

11. The clip was shown shortly after midnight, 22 October 1990, on Channel 3.

References

Barthes, R. (1972) *Mythologies*. New York: Hill and Wang.

Baudrillard, J. (1981) *Towards a Critique of the Political Economy of the Sign*. Translated by C. Levin and A. Younger. St Louis: Telos.

Baudrillard, J. (1983) *In the Shadow of the Silent Majority.* New York: Semiotext(e).

Boorstin, D. (1961) *The Image: or What Happened to the American Dream.* London: Weidenfeld and Nicolson.

Bourdieu, P. (1977) *Outline of a Theory of Practice.* Translated by R. Nice. Cambridge: Cambridge University Press.

Debord, G. (1977) *The Society of the Spectacle.* Detroit: Black and Red.

Giddens, A. (1990) *The Consequences of Modernity.* Cambridge: Polity in association with Basil Blackwell.

Haug, W. (1986) Critique or Commodity Aesthetics: Appearance, Sexuality and Advertising in Capitalist Society. Cambridge: Polity.

Horkheimer, M. and Adorno, T. (1972) *Dialectic of Enlightenment.* New York: Herder and Herder.

Jameson, F. (1984) 'Postmodernism, or the cultural logic of capital', *New Left Review*, No. 146: 55–92.

Lasch, C. (1976) *The Culture of Narcissism: American Life in an Age of Diminishing Expectations.* New York: Norton.

Lash, S. (1990) *The Sociology of Postmodernism.* London: Routledge.

McLuhan, M. (1967) *The Mechanical Bride: Folklore of Industrial Man.* Boston: Beacon.

Reiche, R. (1970) *Sexuality and Class Struggle.* London: New Left Books.

Reisman, D. (1950) *The Lonely Crowd: A Study of the Changing American Character.* Garden City, NY: Doubleday.

Schudson, M. (1986) *Advertising: The Uneasy Persuasion. Its Dubious Impact on American Society.* New York: Basic Books.

Wiliams, R. (1982) *The Sociology of Culture.* New York: Schocken.

18.
LIVENESS, "REALITY," AND THE MEDIATED HABITUS FROM TELEVISION TO THE MOBILE PHONE

Nick Couldry

Liveness should be interpreted as a development within media history as a whole.... At the base, the need to connect oneself, with others, to the world's events, is central to the development of the modern nation.

(Bourdon, 2000, pp. 551–552)

Media belong to the history of the progressive organization of social life across space and time: Media, in other words, are part of governmentality, which is not to deny that they have many other dimensions too (such as expression, pleasure, and imagination). From Durkheim onwards, sociology has been concerned with how social order is enacted, in part, through categories of perception and thought. Liveness can be understood as a category crucially involved in both naturalizing and reproducing a certain historically distinctive type of social coordination around media "centers" from which images, information, and narratives are distributed and (effectively simultaneously) received across space. This general context is helpful for understanding the persistence of "liveness" as a term, and some of the tensions currently surrounding it; even better, understanding mediated "liveness" in this way links media debates to wider questions about how, in media-saturated societies, social "order" is possible to the extent that it is; in particular, it links to the possibility of rethinking one concept of ordering, Pierre Bourdieu's "habitus," for mediated societies, a point to which I return.

This approach questions the way "liveness" in media-studies debates is generally seen as an issue specifically about media texts and the changing conventions and interpretations embedded in media production. It insists that larger questions are at stake, confirming that the curiosity of media scholars in "liveness" has been well-placed, but at the same time detaching that term from an exclusive application to one specific media technology (usually television).

The Forms of Liveness

An important earlier argument which connected television's liveness to wider sociological questions was Jane Feuer's paper on "The concept of live television" (1983). Feuer was interested in the ideology of television as a social technology, not the way other types of ideology (political or commercial) might be transmitted through television: specifically the "ideology" that television connects us "live" to important events, so that we see things as they happen. However, Feuer's article ended (1983, pp. 20–21) with a question about how that ideology is socially reproduced in audiences' use of television texts that remained unanswered. Perhaps this is why analysis of the ideological implications of televisual form ceased, for a while, to be central to media studies in the 1990s (there were other factors, of course, to do with the rethinking of "ideology" itself).

The value of Feuer's work now, however, does not depend on the continued acceptability of the term "ideology"; indeed, things may be clearer without that term. The question instead is whether "liveness" (as applied to television and other media) is purely a descriptive term, whose usefulness depends on matters of fact, or whether it is, in Durkheim's sense, a *category* – a term whose use depends on its place within a wider system or structured pattern of values, which work to reproduce our belief in, and assent to, something wider than the description carried by the term itself: in this case, media's role as a central institution for representing social "reality." In a recent book (Couldry, 2003) I argued that we can develop Feuer's insight by interpreting liveness as a ritual term – that is, a category put to use in various forms of structured action that naturalize wider power relationships. There are many forms of ritualized practice in relation to media. But what follows does not depend on that wider argument. Instead, I will focus on the claim that "liveness" works as a category distinction whose importance is more than purely descriptive.

This is the best way of explaining, I suggest, some striking features of the trajectory of the term "liveness" in discourses about media. I mean, first, the substitutability of the media involved in liveness (originally radio, then television, increasingly the Internet and, in certain respects, the mobile phone); second, the fuzziness permitted over how "simultaneous" transmission and reception have to be for "liveness" to be achieved (White, 2004); and third, the persistence of the term "liveness" notwithstanding challenges to the paradigms of liveness at particular historical moments. These points are connected, so let me explore them in more detail.

In television's early days, when all programs were performances broadcast live, television was entirely a "live" medium in the sense of being broadcast as it was performed. As the proportion of live performance declined, the term "live" switched its reference while remaining in use. Jerome Bourdon (2000) argues that the reference-point of "liveness" shifted to those parts of television which broadcast *real* events as they happen, but this is difficult to fit in with the continued use of "liveness" in relation to fictional or semi-fictional programs such as soap operas or game-docs. Instead, it is more plausible that the decisive criterion of liveness is not so much the factuality of what is transmitted, but the fact of live transmission itself (Ellis, 2000, p. 31).

There is, however, a connection to real events built into "liveness," but an indirect one. Live transmission (of anything, whether real or fictional) guarantees that someone in the transmitting media institution *could* interrupt it at any time and make an immediate connection to real events. What is special, then, about live transmission is the *potential* connection it guarantees with real events. Or at least this is how liveness is now generally constructed. Joshua Meyrowitz put this succinctly:

> There is a big difference between listening to a cassette tape while driving in a car and listening to a radio station, in that the cassette player cuts you off from the outside world, while the radio station ties you into it. Even with a local radio station, you are "in range" of any news about national and world events.
>
> (Meyrowitz, 1985, p. 90)

Liveness – or live transmission – guarantees a potential connection to shared social realities as they are happening.

If understood this way, it is no surprise that the category of liveness continues even as the set of media technologies to which it is applied expands. Not only does television's "liveness" continue to be emphasized as one of its key selling points more than a decade after some argued video recording would mean the end of televisual "liveness" (Cubitt, 1991). Liveness now takes new forms which link television to other media. These media include the Internet – as in the much commented-upon "live" transmission on the *Big Brother UK* Web site of Nick Bateman's expulsion in 2001, hours before edited highlights of the episode could be shown on television (Lawson, 2001) – and the mobile phone, as in U.K. mobile phone companies' marketing strategies during the buildup to the 2001 summer season of reality TV:

> Ultimately the [enhanced] SMS services may all boil down to the quality of the content and characters, not forgetting the giddy excitement that can be generated from a message telling *Big Brother* obsessives of two housemates being in bed together – 'live on the internet now.'
>
> (Vickers, 2001)

Because liveness is not a natural category but a constructed term, its significance rests not on technological fact, but on a whole chain of ideas:

1. that we gain access through liveness to something of broader, "central," significance, which is worth accessing now, not later;
2. that the "we" who gain live access is not random, but a representative social group;
3. that the media[1] (not some other social mechanism) is the privileged means for obtaining that access.

Liveness, in sum, is a category whose use naturalizes the general idea that, through the media, we achieve a shared attention to the "realities" that matter for us as a society.

The connection of liveness to the media's reality-claims is hardly accidental. We could say a great deal more about the reality claims of television, especially about current forms of reality TV which (as we have seen) provide some clear examples of how the reference of "liveness" is being stretched (cf. Couldry, 2003, chapter. 6). Instead, however, I want to discuss how, at the same time that "liveness" is expanding across media, its *categorical* weight is being challenged by potential rival forms of "liveness" which are not (or not unambiguously) linked to a mediated social "centre."

When I say rival "forms" of liveness, I do not mean flows of communication which are necessarily referred to *as* "live" (since liveness is a category, its use is embedded in contexts that are largely habitual), but rather emergent ways of coordinating communications and bodies across time and space which, like "liveness" proper, involve (more or less) simultaneity, yet not an institutional "center" of transmission. Two fundamental shifts in information and communications technologies in the past decade threaten, prima facie, to destabilize liveness in the sense considered so far.

The first is what we could call *online liveness:* social co-presence on a variety of scales from very small groups in chat rooms to huge international audiences for breaking news on major Web sites, all made possible by the Internet as an underlying infrastructure. Often, online liveness overlaps with the existing

category of liveness, for example, Web sites linked to reality TV programs such as *Big Brother* which simply offer an alternative outlet for material that could in principle have been broadcast on television if there had been an audience to justify it. Online liveness here is simply an extension of traditional liveness across media, not a new way of coordinating social experience. But since the communications space of the Internet is effectively infinite, any number of "live" transmissions can go on in parallel without interfering with each other: Alongside live streaming of long-anticipated events on Web sites (major sporting events) and news-site coverage of breaking news exist chat rooms on myriad different sites that link smaller groups of people. All of these involve simultaneous co-presence of an audience, but in the latter case there is no liveness in the traditional sense—that is, a plausible connection to a center of transmission. What if the latter type of online liveness increasingly dominates people's trajectories as media consumers? This "liveness" would involve no central connection mirroring Pierre Levy's (1997) characterization of cyber-culture as "universality *without* totality." It is impossible yet to assess the likelihood of this shift, as the Internet's contrasting tendencies toward fragmentation and concentration are played out. Much, including the Internet's capacity to deliver advertising audiences to fund continued media production, will depend on the outcome.

The second rival form of "liveness" we might call *group liveness* but it would not seem, at first sight, to overlap at all with traditional liveness since it starts from the co-presence of a social group, not the co-presence of an audience dispersed around an institutional center. I mean here the "liveness" of a mobile group of friends who are in continuous contact via their mobile phones through calls and texting. Peer-group presence is, of course, hardly new, but its *continuous mediation* through shared access to a communications infrastructure whose entry points are themselves mobile (and therefore can be permanently open) is new. It enables individuals and groups to be continuously co-present to each other even as they move independently across space. This transformation of social space may override individuals' passage between sites of fixed media access, as when school friends continue to text each other when they get home, enter their bedroom, and switch on their computer. As well as being a significant extension of social group dynamics, group liveness offers to the commercial interests that maintain the mobile telephony network an expanded space for centralized transmission of services and advertising. We return here to the ambiguity of original telephony which served as a limited broadcasting system (Marvin, 1987) before it became exclusively an instrument of interpersonal communication, but mobile phone use may not stabilize toward one use rather than the other in the way fixed telephony did. Whatever happens, the result will affect the context in which traditional liveness—individual communication to a socially legitimated point of central transmission—is understood.

Liveness and Habitus

These last remarks—about how liveness's significance as a category may be changed by other shifts in how communication flows are becoming embedded in social interaction—have been speculative, but in conclusion let me anchor them in some reflections on their empirical consequences. Social categories, in Durkheim's sense, are in one way abstract (they are abstracted in analysis from the flow of social life), but in another they are quite concrete, since they only work by being *embedded* in the thought and action of situated agents. This is especially true of Pierre Bourdieu's development of Durkheim's work through the concept of Mauss, Durkheim's collaborator: habitus. For habitus addresses the level at which embodied dispositions (particularly dispositions to classify the world in social action) are generated by structural features of that same social world. Tracing how the weight of "liveness" as a social category might be changing is part of asking how the "habitus" of contemporary societies is being transformed by mediation itself.

This is, of course, a huge topic, but I hope at least to establish some starting points. Some contextual remarks about Bourdieu's work are necessary, since it has been appropriated in media sociology piecemeal over the years rather than systematically. There are many ways of approaching Bourdieu, but one of the most promising is through a concept neglected in

almost all media sociology: habitus. For it is here that Bourdieu, following a philosophical path out of phenomenology, addresses how agents' dispositions to act are themselves *formed* out of preexisting social contexts, a question that, as Nick Crossley argues, is "one of the most fundamental phenomena that sociology can address" (Crossley, 2001, p. 4).

In recent years habitus has received increasing attention as a concept (Calhoun, 1995; chap. 5; Crossley, 2001; McNay, 1999), although it has also received a fair amount of unsympathetic criticism (Alexander, 1995). It has been most frequently applied, if at all, in media sociology in its form of class-specific habitus in connection with Bourdieu's sociology of taste (Bourdieu, 1984). This, however, is not the most interesting usage of habitus for us here. For habitus is fortunately not tied to Bourdieu's controversial belief that the taste dispositions of social classes are shaped decisively by the early differences in their material conditions of existence; it can also be used more generally to understand the *range* of "generative structures" (McNay, 1999, p. 100) that shape dispositions. Even if a problem with Bourdieu's account of class-specific habitus in the arena of taste is that it ignores how mass media have aided the de-differentiation of taste boundaries (Wynne O'Connor, 1998), there is huge scope for investigating how media might have changed the fundamental conditions under which dispositions of *all* kinds are generated.

Bourdieu's overall neglect of media has often been noted (this is a fundamental issue in assessing his account of how contemporary societies hold together [Calhoun, 1995, p. 155], but it is especially striking when we reflect on his early definition of habitus in this general sense as "a general transposable disposition which carries out a systematic universal application . . . of the necessity inherent in the *learning conditions* [of social action]" (emphasis added) (Bourdieu, 1984, p. 170). Media are clearly relevant to how children learn about the contemporary world, including its temporal and social organization, so mediation should surely be central to rethinking habitus. If we consider one of Bourdieu's best-known analyses of how habitus works in traditional societies, the analysis of the Berber house (Bourdieu, 1990), the mechanism is the structuring of domestic space. But no one can ignore media's role in structuring contemporary domestic space, embedded in the walls of today's living spaces as our "window" onto the distant social world. What is difficult is to capture the sheer breadth and complexity of how media might work as habitus, that is, as a "*materialised* system of classification" (emphasis added) (Bourdieu, 1990, p. 76). Fortunately, in his most developed writing on habitus, Bourdieu is open to the contribution of representations, especially those through which "the group presents itself as such" to itself (1990, p. 108). Media, of course, involve both types of structuring: the prior structuring of the spaces in which we live and become subjects, and the representations in which we recognize ourselves as groups. Liveness, indeed, as a category of media, marks the media's constructed role *as* the access point to what is supposed to be "central" to the "group," that is, the whole society. So the link of liveness to the organization of social behaviour passes quite naturally through the concept of habitus.

This point can be traced to all three types of liveness discussed earlier. Traditional "liveness" is written into daily habits which embody our dependencies on media flows: for example, the regular watching of a television news bulletin at least once every evening or the habit of many, including myself, of being woken daily by an alarm-radio offering the latest live news. The decentralized form of online liveness characterizes Internet use where new forms of public sociality may be emerging, sometimes in circumstances where the existence of relevant "peers" itself has to be generated outside existing social networks (see Orgad [2004] on online self-help groups for breast cancer sufferers). Mobile-phone-based "group liveness"—and its extension into the individual users' sense of themselves as permanently available for contact—is already being translated into embodied forms of responsibility best analyzed in terms of habitus. Take this quotation from an unemployed single mother living in north London:

> I always have my phone with me ... and it is always on. Last week I popped out to the shop on the corner here and forgot my phone. Halfway down [the street] I turned back to get it. The shop is only two minutes away but I still came back ...
> (quoted in Crabtree, Nathan, & Roberts, 2003, p. 29)

The test in all this is to trace how categories of thought come together to organize dispositions and, through them, specific practices. Liveness, in its most general sense of continuous connectedness, is hardly likely to disappear as a prized feature of contemporary media, because it is a category closely linked to media's role in the temporal and spatial organization of the social world. The category "liveness" helps to shape the disposition to remain "connected" in all its forms, even though (as we have seen) the types of liveness are now pulling in different directions. It might seem that, by broadening our consideration of liveness this far, we have lost the specificity that made it such a compelling term in academic writing on media and in everyday media discourse. I hope, however, to have shown that the opposite is true: It is only by understanding the tangled web of social categories in which mediated liveness is lodged that we can understand, in turn, why debates about liveness in media research will continue to have wider resonances for the foreseeable future.

Note

1. On the use of "the media" to refer to those media constructed as society's "central" media, see Couldry (2000, p. 6) and Gitlin (2001).

References

Alexander, J. (1995). *Fin de siecle social theory*. London: Verso.

Bourdieu, P. (1984). *Distinction*. London: Routledge and Kegan Paul.

Bourdieu, P. (1990). *The logic of practice*. Cambridge: Polity.

Bourdon, J. (2000). Live television is still alive. *Media, Culture & Society, 22*(5), 531–556.

Calhoun, C. (1995) *Critical social theory*. Cambridge: Polity.

Couldry, N. (2000). *The place of media power*. London: Routledge.

Couldry, N. (2003). *Media rituals: A critical approach*. London: Routledge.

Crossley, N. (2001). *The social body: Habit, identity and desire*. London: Sage.

Crabtree, J. Nathan, M., & Roberts, S. (2003) *MobileUK: Mobile phone and everyday life*. London: The Work Foundation.

Cubitt, S. (1991). *Timeshift*. London: Routledge.

Ellis, J. (2000). *Seeing things*. London: IBTauris.

Feuer, J. (1983). The concept of live television. in E. Kaplan (ed.), *Regarding television*. Los Angeles: American Film Institute.

Gitlin, T. (2001). *Media unlimited*. New York: Metropolitan Books.

Lawson, M. (2001, August 18). Where were you when Nasty Nick was expelled? *The Guardian,* pp. 2–3.

Levy, P. (1997). *Cyberculture*. London: Sage.

Marvin, C. (1987). *When old technologies were new*. Oxford: Oxford University Press.

McNay, L. (1999). Gender, habitus and field: Pierre Bourdieu and the limits of reflexivity. *Theory, Culture & Society, 16*(1), 95–117.

Meyrowitz, J. (1985). *No sense of place*. New York: Oxford University Press.

Orgad, S. (2004). Just do it! The online communication of breast cancer as a practice of empowerment. In M. Consalvo (Ed.), *Internet research annual, volume 1: Selected papers from the Association of Internet Researchers Conferences 2000–2002*. New York: Peter Lang.

Vickers, A. (2001, May 24). Reality text. *The Guardian*, p. 5.

White, M. (2004). The attractions of television: Reconsidering liveness. In N. Couldry & A. McCarthy (Eds.), *MediaSpace: Place, scale and culture in a media age*. London: Routledge.

Wynne, D., & O'Connor, J. (1998). Consumption and the postmodern city. *Urban Studies, 35* (5/6), 841–864.

SECTION IV

MEDIA/INDUSTRY

Introduction

This section introduces the political economy of old and new media, attending to issues of private owner-ship and commercialism, as well as the structures and practices of increasingly concentrated and transna-tional media corporations. Since Adorno and Horkheimer published their critique of the culture industry, the corporations involved in the manufacture of media have grown substantially, to the point where information and culture are now central to the operations of the global capitalist economy. Deregulation, the rise of new technologies such as cable television, satellites and computers, and increased global trade have also impacted how media industries do business, their production and labor practices, and their cultural output. Keeping pace with these developments, critical scholarship in the political economy tradition examines ownership and regulatory structures, corporate synergy and cross-promotion across proliferating media platforms, intellectual property struggles, niche media, transnational flows, "runaway" production and, as interactive technologies have taken hold, the offloading of value-generating labor onto consumers.

In "The Corporation and the Production of Culture," a chapter from his 1989 book *Culture, Inc.*, Herbert Schiller examines the expansion of the U.S. culture industries and their control by a shrinking number of large transnational corporations following the mergers and acquisitions of the 1980s. Unlike the Frankfurt School, he does not limited his critique to devalued popular media—high culture (including book publishing) has also been subjected to the engines of corporate consolidation and intensified process of commodification, Schiller reports. Culture, moreover, is not the only thing that is commodified: the audience for virtually all cultural and informational goods is also abstracted from social conditions and exchanged on the capitalist market for advertising dollars and corporate profit.

Referencing journalist Ben Bagkidian's declaration of a media monopoly, Schiller identifies a number of consequences of an "awesome concentration of private cultural power" in the 1980s, including dimin-ished diversity of perspective, the corporate appropriation of community and creativity, and perhaps most important the naturalization of corporate control as a reasonable and common sense affair resulting from the generalization of a "corporate voice across the entire range of cultural expression."

Michael Curtin's 1996 contribution "On Edge: Culture Industries in the Neo-Network Era" takes the analysis into the 1990s, and suggests that even as concentrated ownership has further accelerated, the demise of mass media forms (such as general circulation magazines and broadcast television) has opened up new possibilities for "edgy" and oppositional content. Curtin argues that the national mass audience associated with magazines such as *Life* and the major television networks was intimately connected to the Fordist era of mass production and mass consumption, created through government policies that favored the national over the local interests, advertisers seeking broad distribution and corporate lobbies who favored the cost efficiency of national content. He traces the "neo-network" era to rise of specialty maga-zines and cable television in the 1960s and maps the fragmentation of the commercial media landscape and its audiences onto what he calls "neo-Fordism."

While mass production, mass marketing and mass consumption do not disappear, they come to exist side by side with "emerging forms of flexible accumulation" defined by critical geographer David Harvey as encompassing developments such as the dispersion of production, speed, greater reliance on sub-contracting and casual labor, and state policies favoring deregulation and privatization. Curtin's chronology is invaluable for making sense of the partial transition from mass to niche media, and his analysis is far more optimistic than that of Schiller.

Because two tendencies are at work in the culture industries—the focus on mass culture aimed at broad national audiences and forms targeted at niche audiences that pursue specialized interests and intensity, "groups that were at one time oppositional or outside the mainstream have become increasingly attractive to media conglomerates with deep pockets, ambitious growth objectives and flexible corporate structures." Niche markets thus become a testing ground for more diverse, oppositional and innovative content, even as the cultural desires of outliers are commodified, Curtin contends.

In their 2003 essay "When Creators, Corporations and Consumers Collide: Napster and the Development of Online Music Distribution," Tom McCourt and Patrick Burkhart argue that the expansion of an information based New Economy is due to the growth of the industries that trade in intellectual property. Taking the struggle over the peer-to-peer sound file trading site Napster as their example, they show how the recording industry (encouraged by U.S. policy) established and enforced intellectual property rights in an unregulated and communal online platform. If new media technologies have expanded opportunities to bypass corporate gatekeepers and establish alternative economies based on sharing rather than profiteering, these opportunities were curtailed as the consolidated music industry sought a "trans-dimensional extension of copyright law and leak-proof controls of distribution channels through legislation, litigations, mergers and acquisitions and anti-copying technologies".

For McCourt and Burkhart, the Napster case marks a first stage of Old Economy power over online delivery of content—and indeed, since their essay was published television networks, film studios and other culture industries have also sought to control the free distribution of media culture online. The stakes of the commercialization of the Internet are high, the authors contend, as evidenced by the transformation of online music from a "network-enabled community of freely participating individuals to a network delivered community that is relentlessly measured and metered."

The transnational expansion of television is the subject of "The Cultural and Political Economies of Hybrid Media Texts" by Marwan Kraidy, from his 2005 book *Hybridity, or the Cultural Logic of Globalization*. Kraidy argues that television has become a deterritorialized global industry due to intersecting factors including state withdrawal as an active regulator of broadcasting, the growth of multinational corporations and the rise of satellite technologies. His analysis of companies such as Televisa in Mexico and the Lebanese Broadcasting Company shows that media are increasingly treated in economic (rather than educational or social) terms across the globe, and charts some of the risk-minimizing business strategies to result from this shift, including co-productions between companies and the proliferation of low cost reality television genres, many based on globally circulating commercial formats.

What differentiates Kraidy's work from other political economic critiques is his exploration of the cultural hybridization that results when formats are copied, traded and adapted across international contexts. Hybrid texts result where "foreign cultural elements" collide and fuse, producing a "rich text replete with signs and symbols whose intertextual tie-ins subvert the laws of gene." In a global race to maximize profits by reaching as many consumers as possible for the lowest cost and level of risk, co-productions that "cross and fuse cultural differences" are inevitable, and hybridity will be pervasive in media culture worldwide.

Toby Miller and Marie Claire Leger's 2001 essay "Runaway Production, Runaway Consumption, Runaway Citizenship: The New International Division of Cultural Labor" examines the impact of globalization and free trade policies on media production worldwide. They coin the term the New International Division of Cultural Labor when characterizing the importance of flexible cultural labor to the new global cultural economy. The global expansion of Hollywood in the 1990s, coupled with the declining power of organized labor, has encouraged media production companies to move to locations where labor costs are cheap and tax incentives plentiful. In this sense, Miller and Leger remind us that Hollywood currently is, and is not, the center of media production and distribution, a point that is further elaborated in Miller's co-authored books *Global Hollywood* (2001) and *Global Hollywood: No. 2* (2008).

Despite the rubric of globalization, Hollywood industries are still central to the exploitation of below-the-line labor in many parts of the world. At the same time, the turn to runaway production displaces Hollywood's centrality, beginning in the 1950s and accelerating in the 1990s and beyond. If runaway production exemplifies the globalization of the production process, the global flow of cultural goods, along with deregulatory policies that encourage this trend, blur categories of consumption and citizenship. While the tension between the expectation that "audiovisual spaces should be accountable to local viewers as well as far-distant shareholders" is not new, Miller and Leger trace its intensification as free market principles have come to permeate media production on a global scale.

Finally, Tiziana Terranova's 2000 essay "Free Labor: Producing Culture for the Digital Economy" examines the importance of unpaid amateur labor to the digital economy. Her influential essay moves political economic approaches to media into new terrain by tracing the connection between the voluntary actions of media users and what Italian autonomist Marxists call the social factory. When individuals help build commercial web sites by posting content and interacting online, modify software packages or enter their own tastes, preferences and demographic information into digitalized corporate databases, they are also producing value for corporations. Terranova critically explores the nature of a form of immaterial labor which "simultaneously voluntarily given and unwaged, enjoyed and exploited." The current stage of capitalism does not buttress the harsh realities of industrial labor with narcotic entertainment, as argued by the Frankfurt School, but rather nurtures and exploits the creativity and productivity of an unwaged labor force. Free labor, she suggests, has become central to contemporary capitalism, including the media and culture industries.

References

Miller, Toby, Nitin Govil, John McMurria and Richard Maxwell, *Global Hollywood* (London: British Film Institute, 2001).

Miller, Toby, Nitin Govil, John McMurria, Ting Wang and Richard Maxwell, *Global Hollywood: No. 2* (London: British Film Institute, 2008).

19.
THE CORPORATION AND THE PRODUCTION OF CULTURE
Herbert Schiller

The industries that serve as the sites for the creation, packaging, transmission, and placement of cultural messages—corporate ones especially—have grown greatly as their importance and centrality to the corporate economy increases. Many of the largest corporations, whatever their main activity, now possess their own communication facilities for message-making and transmission to local or national audiences. Nevertheless, the industries whose main function is the production of messages and imagery—those that can be seen as cultural industries in their own right—continue to be the main centers of symbolic production. A United Nations Scientific and Cultural Organization (UNESCO) study of these industries defined them in this way:

> Generally speaking, a cultural industry is held to exist when cultural goods and services are produced, reproduced, stored or distributed on industrial and commercial lines, that is to say on a large scale and in accordance with a strategy based on economic considerations rather than any concerns for cultural development.[1]

Included in the cultural industries are publishing, the press, film, radio, television, photography, recording, advertising, sports, and, most recently, the many components that now make up the information industry (data-base creation, production of software for computers, and various forms of salable information).

There is a "second tier" in the category of cultural industries. These activities also provide symbolic goods and services. The services, however, are displayed in relatively permanent installations, instead of being produced serially. Using this measure, museums, art galleries, amusement parks (Disneyland, Sea World—there are more than 600 theme and amusement parks in America), shopping malls, and corporate "public spaces" also function as culture industries.

It is not arbitrary to single out these activities and designate them as cultural industries. It can be maintained with justification that *all* economic activity produces symbolic as well as material goods. In fact, the two are generally inseparable. An automobile, in addition to being a vehicle of transport, is also a striking assemblage of symbols and provides a rich symbolic menu to its owner or aspiring purchaser. A pair of shoes is often much more than foot coverage and protection.

Actually, a community's economic life cannot be separated from its symbolic content. Together they represent the totality of a culture. Still, it is observable in the development of capitalism from its feudal origins that specific categories of symbolic goods and services have been withdrawn from their place in community and individual existence. They have been organized much like other branches of industrial activity, subject to the same rules of production and exchange.

Speech, dance, drama (ritual), music, and the visual and plastic arts have been vital, indeed necessary, features of human experience from earliest times. What distinguishes their situation in the industrial-capitalist era, and especially in its most recent development, are the relentless and successful efforts to separate these elemental expressions of human creativity from their group and community origins for the purpose of *selling them* to those who can pay for them.

In recent centuries, most markedly in the twentieth, cultural creation has been transformed into discrete, specialized forms, commercially produced and marketed. The common characteristics of cultural products today are the utilization of paid labor, the private appropriation of labor's creative product, and its sale for a profit. Jeremy Seabrook has written extensively on the *general process* of commercial production and acknowledges that there is greater efficiency. Productivity is higher and, consequently, the availability of goods is greater. But there is a cost, he notes, a very high cost! "The price paid by working people for the 'successes' of capitalism has been in terms of the breakdown of human associations, the loss of solidarity, indifference between people, violence, loneliness ... and a sense of loss of function and purpose."[2] Describing the same process as it affects a modern cultural product—film—is this appraisal:

> ... the objective character of film is its existence as a comodity. That it is made by wage labor, and that its purpose is exchange value, united it with virtually everything else in capitalism. ... The producer of film is not, in reality, the person whose name flashes on the screen. That person is the surrogate who carries out the generalized logic of the institutional order in which the film industry exists. The ultimate producer of the commodity is the set of property relations that are specific to a historical epoch.[3]

The cultural goods and services of modern American cultural industries, therefore, are not outputs of ahistorical, universalistic creative genius and talent. However much they may be appreciated, imitated, or adopted elsewhere, they remain the specific cultural forms of a particular set of institutional arrangements.

Market control of creativity and symbolic production has developed unevenly since the beginning of capitalism, some creative fields possessing special features or offering greater resistance to their commercial appropriation than others. The amount of money (capital) required to enter a specific cultural

industry has worked either as a constraint—if the amount is considerable—or as an encouragement— if the investment was minimal. Still, by the close of the twentieth century, in highly developed market economies at least, most symbolic production and human creativity have been captured by and subjected to market relations. Private ownership of the cultural means of production and the sale of the outputs for profit have been the customary characteristics. The exceptions—publicly supported libraries, museums, music—are few, and they are rapidly disappearing. The last fifty years have seen an acceleration in the decline of nonmarket-controlled creative work and symbolic output. At the same time, there has been a huge growth in its commercial production.

Parallel with the private appropriation of symbolic activity has been the rationalization of its production. This includes the development of more efficient techniques and the invention of means to expand the market output to a global scale. The production of goods and services in the cultural sphere has indeed been industrialized. It is in this respect that the term "cultural industries" assumes its meaning.

The expanded production and distribution capabilities have increased immeasurably the profitability of cultural production. ... though this is generally left unremarked. Attention is directed instead to the undeniable impressiveness of the new technologies of message-making and transmission and their alleged potential for human enrichment.[4]

Another feature (mostly ignored) of the modern cultural industries is their deeply structured and pervasive ideological character. The heavy public consumption of cultural products and services and the contexts in which most of them are provided represent a daily, if not hourly, diet of systemic values, spooned out to whichever public happens to be engaged. "The typical film from which investors anticipate a profit," writes film analyst Thomas Guback, "may be art or non-art, but it is always a commodity."[5] The same can be said for Broadway musical comedies, best-selling novels, and top-of-the-chart records. They are commodities and ideological products, embodying the rules and values of the market system that produced them. Multi-million-dollar investments in film, theater, or publishing can be relied upon to contain systemic thinkng. In the late twentieth century, those few spaces that have escaped incorporation into the market are being subjected to continuous pressure and, often, frontal attack.

Trends In the Cultural Industries: The New Technologies

Over the course of the last one hundred years, a succession of inventions and technological innovations have produced the means by which certain kinds of cultural production could be expanded enormously. The instantaneous and universal dissemination of cultural outputs is also now technically feasible—though in some instances political factors may operate as limiting conditions.

The improved efficiency of the printing press and the invention of radio, television, cable, fiber optics, the communication satellite, and the computer have transformed communication. Yet the revolutionized instrumentation and the communication process itself remain, for the most part (certainly in the United States), firmly anchored in market relations. Occasionally, there have been some hybrid arrangements, but overall, a market context for the new communication technologies continues to prevail.

This being the case, the great increase in penetrability made possible by the new technologies has created a marketing ideological atmosphere that smothers the senses domestically and is rapidly doing the same globally. The cultural industries have become an integral component of the market economy, and their sales messages, in a remarkable variety of ways, fill public, private, and personal space.

The communication satellite makes message penetrability global. Recent Olympic Games were viewed, it is claimed, by a billion spectators. This is ideological and marketing diffusion beyond the wildest dreams of early twentieth-century prophets of salesmanship—who, by the way, were not shy in their goals and expectations. The cultural industries are booming as their outputs reach domestic audiences of tots to nonagenarians and are exported as well to worldwide markets. The *Wall Street Journal* reports that "The media-blitzed child of the 80's is proving highly brand-conscious.... The interest in labels starts early." Dale Wallenius, publisher of the *Marketing to Kids Report*, says, "Even two-year-olds are concerned about their brand of clothes, and by the age of six are full-out consumers."[6] And, of course, the sales message appears in a variety of ways in addition to standard advertising. This is perhaps the cultural industries' greatest achievement.

The great upsurge in the cultural industries cannot be explained exclusively, however, on the basis of improved technical capabilities. Credit also must be given to social developments that the market economy itself has promoted. As the output of all material goods and services steadily rises, a wide array of supportive activities comes into existence to facilitate their distribution and consumption and even the public awareness of their existence. Advertising, installment credit, personal finance, banking, insurance, retailing, and transport follow closely the expansion of the manufacturing system. In nation after nation, employees in the new fields eventually outnumber workers producing goods. The workers who fill these new occupations now constitute the bulk of the U.S. work force. They have more schooling. They are urban- and suburban-domiciled. They have more time away from the work site. Their families are increasingly, of necessity in many cases, composed of two wage earners.

These conditions combine to bestow an ever-greater importance to the images and messages of the cultural industries. The social "glue," such as it is, of the advanced market economy is provided by a steady diet of news, sports, film, TV comedy and drama, entertainment "parks," tourist excursions, and footage of distant wars and conflicts. The fragmentation and privatization of living arrangements, experience, personal interactions, and total being are alleviated or concealed by "spectaculars" produced by the cultural industries: "Superbowls"; best-sellers; celebrity talk shows; blockbuster movies; and a dizzying cycle of new foods, styles, fashions, and prescriptions for eating, fasting, managing, and succeeding.

In creating and satisfying the huge national appetite for cultural product, the industries engaged in its manufacture exhibit the same economic trends as did the industries in the preceding Industrial era. In that period, the size of the enterprise expanded to take advantage of economies of scale in production, as well as to have on hand the resources needed to exploit opportunities (markets) as they arose, nationally and eventually internationally. The pattern is no different in the cultural industries in the 1980s. A prediction made in the mid-1980s that by 1995 almost 90 percent of all communication facilities (including newspapers, broadcast outlets, cable systems, telephone lines, relays, and satellites) would be in the hands of fifteen companies is close to realization well before that date. Ben Bagdikian, veteran journalist and former dean of the University of California's (Berkeley) Graduate School of Journalism, reported in 1987 how much "progress" to that end had been made:

> In 1982, when I completed research for my book, *The Media Monopoly*, 50 corporations controlled half or more of the media business. By December 1986, when I finished a revision for the second edition, the 50 had shrunk to 29. The last time I counted, it was down to 26.[7]

In the first edition of *The Media Monopoly* (1983), Bagdikian declared that "The fifty men and women [sic] who head these corporations would fit in a large room."[8] In 1987, a much smaller room would have been more than adequate.

These super-aggregations of resources in the cultural-informational sphere are the outcome of internal growth, from spectacular profits (especially in the television, cable, and film branches), and from never-ending consolidations in corporate media and informational activities. The trend is observable in all the industries. *Business Week*, for example, describes Madison Avenue "looking like merger street . . . advertising agencies are gobbling each other up with the ardor they once reserved for bellowing 'new and improved.' "[9]

Mergers in the advertising business are typical of the other cultural industries. They derive from the changing character of the world economy and the growing share of the world market dominated by transnational corporations in general. "Multinationals now account for 20 percent of all advertising and their percentage is growing," notes the president of Young and Rubicam, one of the world's top ad agencies. "You have to be able to serve your client everywhere," he adds.[10]

The one exception—and a qualified one at that—to the transnationalization of the cultural industries is the press. For newspapers especially, it is the national and, even more, the local/regional market that is determining. Here, the objective is exclusivity. Local monopoly is the key to maximum advertising revenues. This explains why "of the 1700 daily papers [in the United States], 98 percent are local monopolies and fewer than 15 corporations control most of the country's daily circulation."[11]

Efforts to start new, competing papers have all but disappeared. And no wonder! The costs are prohibitive. One instance in recent years of a sustained attempt to launch a national newspaper is the *USA Today* undertaking. Since 1982, when *USA Today* first appeared, its operating losses in five years neared half a billion dollars. This figure does not include an additional $208 million for capital costs and the expense of employees borrowed from other papers in the Gannett Company chain, a chain now numbering over 90 newspapers.[12] Who could afford such outlays, other than a billion-dollar media conglomerate with a chairman of the board obsessed with controlling a national organ of opinion? And what does this tell us about the open marketplace for ideas in the 1980s as well as the insistence on First Amendment rights for billion-dollar corporate "individuals"?

Television, a medium with totally different physical characteristics, requires still more gargantuan capital requirements for entry. An independent television station in Los Angeles was sold in 1985 for $510 million. ABC's New York City affiliate with a potential audience in the millions has an estimated price tag of $800 million.

A wave of mergers in the 1980s placed some of the cultural industries at the financial as well as the informational center of the transnational corporate economy. The American Broadcasting company was acquired by Capital Cities, a deal that at the time was the largest merger outside the oil industry in U.S. history. It has since been surpassed. Another already huge conglomerate, Metromedia, itself bought out, sold seven key television stations to Rupert Murdoch and a partner for $2 billion. Murdoch already owned 20th Century-Fox and with the new acquisitions launched a fourth national television network. CBS, regarded by some as the media establishment, has been fighting off one takeover bid after another.

The publishing industry, a less flamboyant branch of the cultural industries, is no less caught up in the merger mania and cross-media combinations. Gulf and Western, already the owner of Paramount Studios and Simon and Schuster, acquired Prentice Hall, the largest textbook publisher in the United States. With these acquisitions, Gulf and Western, among its other activities, is now the largest "publishing house" in the world. The Newhouse publishing chain, owner of innumerable medium-size city newspapers, bought *The New Yorker*, adding it to other publishing holdings that include Random House, Alfred A. Knopf, Pantheon, Villard, Times Books, and Vintage Books.

What it means to function as a cultural industry in publishing—historically a small-scale commercial activity and only recently transformed by industrial conglomeration—is suggested in the evolution of the author-publisher relationship in textbook production. "When I first came into the field," explained David P. Amerman, vice president and director of the college division of Prentice Hall, in 1977, "the way you published a book was to find an academic with a reputation and hope he could write." Amerman observed that then "The book was essentially the author's." Ten years later, "We're exercising our muscle, and telling the author the best way to do it, a lot more than we used to." The *Chronicle of Higher Education*, in which this interview appeared, noted that "While the wholly 'managed' book is still a rarity in publishing, the 'author-assisted' book is a growing phenomenon." Mr. Amerman footnotes this: "We want control over the vocabulary."[13]

But it is not only the author's "vocabulary" that is monitored and managed. The writer's personality as well is now being appropriated and reworked for the marketing effort. The director of publicity for Macmillan, one of the oldest and most prestigious publishing firms, claims that it is not enough for an author to write a book. "Now you also have to sell it."[14] To prepare for this new task, writers are taking lessons on how to talk well to sell well on TV and radio. As talk shows have become a critical factor in the mass marketing of books, the author now has to sell self as well as book.

Contributing still more pressure for commercialization of the book is the growth of a few nationwide book chains—B. Dalton, Walden Books, Barnes & Noble, Crown, and Kroch's & Brentano's, etc. Though their denial of having any influence on the content of what is being published is unanimous, these big retail chains by their choice and promotions largely determine which books will become the big sellers. Their choices, in turn, are finely tuned to selecting works that have the greatest sales potential. While this criterion does not absolutely preclude material that is unfamiliar, socially critical, or seriously antiestablishment, it limits severely the likelihood of its publication—or at least publication by the main commercial houses.

The "Shyness" of the Cultural Industries

In contrast with their willingness to examine *individual* behavior in microscopic detail, the cultural industries—the mass media in particular—are remarkably reticent to examine their own activities. Commentary on the extensive merger movement in the media is illustrative. It receives substantial but essentially unilluminating coverage. Mostly, it is portrayed as entrepreneurial jousting.

Just as round-the-clock "soaps" and happy-talk news shows trivialize life's dilemmas and reduce them to personal strengths and weaknesses, structural changes in the informational system are presented generally in terms of an individual's character and energy. Accordingly, one is asked to consider whether Ted Turner is morally fit to run CBS. Will he endanger that network's status as—what founder and former chairman of the board William Paley called—a public trust? Will S. I. Newhouse quash *The New Yorker*'s vaunted editorial independence? Will Rupert Murdoch's downmarket *New York Post* be taken away from him as a consequence of Senator Kennedy's vendetta against Murdoch's Boston newspaper holding? (It was.)

While the public is asked to reflect on these sideline and basically irrelevant issues, the cultural industries are responding boldly to the uncertainties and opportunities of highly fluid world and national markets. Far from merely reacting, the big media-cultural combines have become major initiators in the rapidly emerging transnational information system. Taking advantage of the pro-profit, anti-union, social accountability-be-damned climate of the Reagan years, media owners and other resource holders are maneuvering freely in the cultural and informational fields. They are concentrating their holdings to better exploit the domestic market and to penetrate the international market with information goods and services, messages and images.

The smell of profits and the lure of global information dominance pervade the media-merger arena.

And so it goes, in film, cable television, network TV, radio, and throughout the cultural industries. In film, for example, "every big studio is now a conglomerate or has been purchased by a conglomerate," writes a Hollywood reporter. "For 1988," he notes, "the buzzword in Hollywood is vertical integration. The major studios—and even some of the minor ones—intend to make and distribute movies, manufacture and sell video cassettes six months later, then syndicate their films to their own television stations, by-passing the networks, and, in the case of Disney, play them on a studio-owned pay-cable channel."[15] The four biggest "studios" are now subordinated to huge conglomerates, which, in turn, own sports teams, movie theater chains, television networks, cable systems, and much else. The president of the Writers Guild of America, for example, describing negotiations for a contract between writers and movie and television producers, noted: "We weren't negotiating with Paramount, but with Coca-Cola."[16]

The recent absorption of movie theaters by the big film companies violates a Supreme Court ruling of the late 1940s that forbade such ownership.[17] Today, indifferent to that forty-year-old injunction, a few studios hold about the same proportion of theaters that was ruled illegal a generation or more ago.[18] One immediate, visible effect of this development has been the practical elimination of art theaters that used to show foreign and domestic films that were not likely to be smash commercial hits. The larger consideration, not unrelated to the former, is that commercial criteria now totally dominate the industry. "The movies have always been an uneasy blend of art and commerce," observes one Hollywood commentator, "but today, commerce is the clear winner."[19]

The late screenwriter and film critic, Lester Cole, experienced the hard commercial side of the film industry firsthand fifty years ago. Running as a central thread throughout his account of the early Hollywood years is the aggressive, anti-union tactics of the egomaniacal moguls of that era. Cole himself was never forgiven for his persistent efforts to organize the film work force. Indeed, it was his militancy on behalf of film workers that put him in jail in the great Hollywood witch-hunt and purge of the 1940s.[20]

The degree of concentration already reached in the cable TV industry, with its multitudinous channels which were supposed to exorcise monopoly control, is striking. "The top four operators now control one-third of cable subscribers," and one company alone, Tele-Communications, has about 18.5 percent of the nation's total subscribers. Additionally, the nation's second-largest cable company, American Television and Communication Corporation, is owned by Time, Inc., the giant magazine conglomerate.[21] At the same time, Geraldine Fabricant reports in the *New York Times* that "cable operators which own the wires and boxes, or hardware, are also gobbling up substantial portions of the software—the shows, movies and sporting events that the cable carries."[22] Meanwhile, the monthly cable connection charges of more than forty-five million subscribers (in 1988) constitute an endless golden flow of revenues to a few super-corporations—who view any effort to make them take into account the social needs of the locales in which they operate as a violation of *their* First Amendment rights.

Radio is described and evaluated by the trade magazine *Radio & Records* as "little more than electronic real estate, and spectrum space is probably the most valuable asset in the United States."[23]

What is the significance of this awesome concentration of private cultural power? For one thing, it means that only the richest groups, nationally and internationally, can afford to own media-informational companies. What follows from this is that these holdings are the means for transmitting the thinking and the perspectives of the dominant, though tiniest, stratum of the propertied class, not only in news but also in entertainment and general cultural product.

At the beginning of the 1980s, well before some of the greatest media consolidations were effected, the UNESCO study already cited reflected on the concentration of control "and the subordination of artists to market forces." It speculated further:

> It is open to question, in order to obtain an accurate portrayal of the system of forces at work in the cultural industries, the assumed symmetry of classical communication theories should not be replaced by a firmly asymmetrical view, *reflecting the predominant influence of the industrial producer of the messages (or the interests backing him), who in*

the end dictates the choice of channel, the content and even the consumer's taste, in the interests of economic or ideological control.[24]

It is precisely this view that is rejected by current communication and media theorists.

In fact, the presence of giantism and concentrated control in the media and allied cultural fields, though hardly a secret, now seems perfectly reasonable to most Americans—and certainly no cause for anxiety. The extent to which the public has been programmed to accept these conditions in the media, and in the economy overall, is remarkable. Especially so when it is remembered that throughout the nineteenth and the first half of the twentieth centuries, powerful antimonopoly social movements flourished in the country. As recently as fifty years ago, an American president, Franklin D. Roosevelt, could touch a responsive populist chord in the country by denouncing the "moneychangers in the temple" and the "economic royalists." In the early years of the century, Theodore Roosevelt attacked "the malefactors of great wealth."[25]

In contrast, in the 1980s, major industrial companies, and the press as well, boast about and insist upon the virtue of their enormous assets. The Hearst Corporation, for example (in an earlier time synonymous with the abuse of press power), now announces in public advertisements:

> The Hearst Centennial. 100 Years of Making Communication History. Hearst is more than 135 businesses, including magazines, broadcasting, newspapers, books, business publishing and cable communications.[26]

Similarly, the Gannett Corporation brazenly assures the public time and again that its ownership of more than 90 newspapers and a clutch of television and radio stations across the country is a guarantor of diversity and pluralism.[27]

The Los Angeles Times Mirror Company, which includes among its holdings, the *Los Angeles Times*, the *Denver Post*, the *Baltimore Sun*, and the *Hartford Courant*, along with other magazines, newspapers, cable and broadcast interests, recently released a plan whereby its chief owners (the Chandler family) and a few other big shareholders could permanently retain control of the company. A spokesperson for the company explained that the maintenance of this control "promote(s) continued independence and integrity of our media operations for the benefit of our shareholders and for the public served by our various media interests."[28] It is not difficult to see that the benefits to the major shareholders, including the Chandler family, will be promoted. It is less easy to see what the public gains from an arrangement that vests control in perpetuity to a tiny group of wealthy stockholders. The notion that "independence and integrity" is guaranteed by such ownership is one of the myths that the media, the press in particular, have cultivated successfully for a very long time.

Rupert Murdoch, another media mogul with international holdings, was exercised because he was ordered to comply with a mild Federal Communications Commission ruling limiting cross-media holdings, i.e., ownership of a TV station and a newspaper by the same interests in one locale. What was seen not so long ago as an elementary and far from sweeping step to assure diversity in a city or region is in the late 1980s treated by arrogant media owners and their political sycophants as arbitrary intervention of the state and as a violation of their First Amendment rights. In this particular case, Murdoch was compelled to sell his New York City newspaper, the *New York Post*.[29]

The two senators from the state of New York argued that this ruling constituted a hardship on the city because jobs would be lost if the *Post* could not be sold and was forced to liquidate. This was a totally unrealistic scenario. The paper was sold. The brand of thinking by Murdoch's defenders discounted media and informational monopoly as long as it offered employment. This is of a piece with the rationale for defense/military expenditures.

Countervailing Pressure on the Cultural Industries?

Despite the pyramiding of assets and combinations of media interests in recent decades, the concentrated cultural industries are not the exclusive players in the message-making business. In many fields (publishing, recording, and, to a much lesser extent, in film and television), numerous small producers do manage to carry on and from time to time produce nationally acclaimed material. This is not, however, a contradiction or an offset to power and in no way diminishes the general dominance of the big players.

Actually, some small-scale production is one means of "managing creativity."[30] It has evolved and been refined to rationalize the handling of a stubbornly recalcitrant yet indispensable resource used in the cultural industries: human creativity. In allowing small-scale and relatively independent activity to continue to exist in cultural work, the big cultural firms insure a constant supply of talent and creativity that otherwise might be ignored or even suffocated in their own bureaucratized, symbol-making factories. The "independents" are continually tapped to replenish exhausted creative energies in the cultural conglomerates. The trick for the latter is to keep the creative juices flowing—but inside channels that reliably lead back to the main conduits.

This objective is achieved primarily by insuring that the cultural production process, monopoly-size or small-scale independent, remains securely anchored in market relations. Privatized message and symbol production binds the producers, large and small, in interdependent relationships in which small players are "more interdependent"—less independent—than the big actors. By the same means, the *content* of the cultural product is no less subject to the market imperative—profitability—wherever it originates.

The ideological component, if marginally more open in independent, smaller-scale productions, overall remains pliable to the corporate voice. Independent producers, as well as executives in the big cultural enterprises, may have *personal* standards and preferences for honest, well-produced subject matter. But whatever the individual inclination, the determining factor in the large majority of decisions about what products and services are made *must be* commercial profitability.

Consider the experience of Pare Lorenz, the director of some of the most powerful social documentaries of the 1930s: *The Plow That Broke the Plains, The River, The Fight for Life*. Lorenz was "saluted" by the Academy of Motion Picture Arts and Sciences in 1981. Yet he made his last film, *The Nuremberg Trials*, in 1946. Since then he has been unable to secure financing for his projects. A documentary attempted in 1948 about the atomic test on the Bikini atoll could not be continued. Lorenz noted simply: "We couldn't

raise two dollars and a half."[31] Lorenz's experience is by no means exceptional. New York City and Los Angeles are filled with independent producers of film and video desperately trying to raise insignificant amounts of money to continue or to begin projects.

If a creative project, no matter what its inherent quality, cannot be viewed as a potential money-maker, salable in a large enough market, its production is problematic at best. This in no way means that all projects that are approved, will, in fact, be money-makers. In a society that fosters consumption, taste and fashion must change rapidly and unceasingly. The larger the cultural enterprise, the greater its resources to finance "mistakes." At the same time, there is also the likelihood of more expensive misjudgments. The cultural industries, no different than the rest of American industry, try to minimize risk. But risk and instability are inherent in capitalist enterprise in general.

To the extent then that the creative process has been absorbed by industries producing for the market, the commercial imperative prevails. General awareness that profitability is the ultimate determinant of cultural production becomes internalized in the creative mindset. Scriptwriters, authors, videomakers, and film directors shape their efforts, consciously or not, with rare exceptions to the deep-structured demands of salability and prospective return.

Even those who may appear to be the last holdouts of individual creativity, the studio artists working alone, find no escape from the market imperative, though the pressure may be brought to bear in less explicit ways. The gallery system, private collectors, art speculators, and the process of museum acquisition constitute a special but in no way fundamentally different commercial framework than television networks that commission shows from TV production companies.

As the cultural industries increasingly occupy pivotal positions of social, political, and even economic power in the latest period of capitalist development, their symbolic outputs, however entertaining, diverting, esthetic, or informative, are essentially elements of corporate expression. Corporate speech, therefore, has become an integral part of cultural production in general. Most imagery and messages, products and services are now corporately fashioned from their origin to their manufacture and dissemination.

Consider, for example, the making and distribution of the successful 1988 movie, *Who Framed Roger Rabbit:*

Walt Disney Co. spent $45 million to make Spielberg's *Who Framed Roger Rabbit* and has committed an additional $10 million to promote it. Coke and McDonald's Corp. will spend an estimated $22 million on ad and promotional campaigns linked to the movie. They hope the hit movie's magic will rub off on diet Coke and Big Mac. Disney, in turn, figures that Roger Rabbit's ubiquity, courtesy of Coke and McDonald's, translates into some $20 million in extra ad exposure for the movie.

Additionally, "some 30 licensees will market toys, jackets and jewelry based on *Roger Rabbit*."[32]

The corporate "voice" now constitutes the national symbolic environment. For this reason, as one artist sees it, "it becomes more and more difficult to maintain the difference between individual and corporate speech. Differences between forms of address become harder to sustain, or even perceive."[33]

It is not so much that one or another corporate giant utilizes the cultural industries to make its preferences known to the public. This, of course, is a continuing and pervasive feature of the domestic cultural landscape. Far more significant is the organic process by which the corporate "voice" is generalized across the entire range of cultural expression. Writing of another place and another time, Henry Glassie's commentary is especially appropriate here:

If people are stripped of the ability to manipulate truth, to make their own things and their own history, they may continue to act properly, but they lose the capacity to think for themselves about their own rightness. They stagnate or surrender. If truth is located beyond the mind's grasp, if it is something that exists but cannot be touched, then culture cannot be advanced or defended. Made consumers, spectators, restrained from voluntary action, people become slaves, willing or not, happy or not, of powers that want their bodies. Those who steal from people their right to make artifacts (in order to sell junk to them) and those who steal their right to make their own history (in order to destroy their will to cultural

resistance)—these can be condemned, for they steal from people the right to know what they know, the right to become human.[34]

Notes

1. UNESCO, *Cultural Industries: A Challenge for the Future of Culture* (Paris: 1982), 21.
2. Jeremy Seabrook, *Unemployment* (London: Grenada, 1983), xiii.
3. Thomas Guback, "Capital, Labor Power and the Identity of Film," conference on culture and communication, Temple University, Philadelphia, March 1985.
4. Laura Landro, "Airing Grievances As Cable-TV Industry Keeps Growing, Rivals Demand Reregulation," *Wall Street Journal*, Sept. 17, 1987.
5. Guback, "Capital."
6. Ellen Graham, "The Children's Hour," *Wall Street Journal*, Jan. 19, 1988.
7. Ben Bagdikian, "The 26 Corporations That Own the Media," *EXTRA!*, the newsletter of F.A.I.R. (Fairness and Accuracy In Reporting), vol. 1, no. 1 (June 1987).
8. Ben H. Bagdikian, *The Media Monopoly* (Boston: Beacon, 1983).
9. "Madison Avenue Is Looking Like Merger Street," *Business Week* (May 12, 1986).
10. Ibid.
11. Bagdikian, *EXTRA!*.
12. Albert Scardino, "USA Today Produces Readers But Not Profits," *New York Times*, July 11, 1988.
13. Karen J. Winkler, "New Approaches Changing the Face of Textbook Publishing," *Chronicle of Higher Education*, vol. XIV, no. 12 (May 16, 1977): 1.
14. Edwin McDowell, "Coaches Help Authors Talk Well to Sell Well," *New York Times*, March 2, 1988. Thomas Whiteside, *The Blockbuster Complex: Conglomerates, Show Business, and Book Publishing* (Middletown, CT: Wesleyan University Press, 1981) provides the "big picture" of conglomeratization in publishing.
15. Aljean Harmetz, "Now Playing: The New Hollywood," *New York Times*, Jan. 10, 1988.
16. Aljean Harmetz, "Movie and TV Writers Go on Strike," *New York Times*, March 8, 1988.
17. Paramount consent decree, May 3, 1948, 334 U.S. 131.
18. Geraldine Fabricant, "2.9 Billion Deal Set for SCI Cable," *New York Times*, Dec. 25, 1987.
19. Aljean Harmetz, "Now Playing."
20. Lester Cole, *Hollywood Red* (Palo Alto: Ramparts Press, 1981).
21. Laura Landro, "Airing Grievances."

22. Geraldine Fabricant, "Is Cable Cornering the Market?" *New York Times*, sec. III, April 17, 1988, p. 1.

23. Andrea Adelson, "Radio Deals Grow Richer in Big Cities," *New York Times*, July 6, 1988.

24. UNESCO, *Cultural Industries*, p. 22 (emphasis added).

25. Franklin D. Roosevelt, first inaugural address, March 4, 1933; Theodore Roosevelt, Aug. 20, 1907. Both quotations in Bohle, *Handbook of American Quotes*.

26. *New York Times*, Jan. 13, 1987.

27. "Freedom Begins at Home," Gannett Corporation advertisement, *New York Times*, June 26, 1979.

28. Richard W. Stevenson, "Times Mirror Plans New Stock Class," *New York Times*, Sept. 4, 1987.

29. Alex S. Jones, "Congress Faces a New Battle Over a 1975 Rule Limiting Media Ownership," *New York Times*, Jan. 11, 1988.

30. I am indebted to Patrice Flichy and Patrick Pajon for this expression.

31. Aljean Harmetz, "Hollywood Hails Lorenz, Documentary Pioneer," *New York Times*, Oct. 21, 1981.

32. Ronald Grover, "Hitching a Ride on Hollywood's Hot Streak," *Business Week* (July 11, 1988), 46–48.

33. Richard Bolton, "Canadian Notes," *Afterimage* (February 1988).

34. Henry Glassie, *Passing the Time in Ballymenone: Culture and History of an Ulster Community* (Philadelphia: University of Pennsylvania Press, 1982).

20.
ON EDGE

Culture Industries in the Neo-Network Era

Michael Curtin

The general-circulation magazine — *Time, Newsweek, Life, Look* — provided a site of popular discourse and imagination throughout the Great Depression, World War II, and the postwar period. These mass magazines were symptomatic of a distinctive moment of national unity, according to publishing executive Mark Edmiston: "We had in this country at that time a sense of shared experience" (136).[1]* Yet in the 1950s, these popular publications would find their status challenged by the rise of television and the fragmentation of the magazine market. Television would then prevail as the primary mediator of national consciousness until the end of the 1970s, only to succumb to its own period of audience fragmentation and industry turmoil. Even worse, says Edmiston, no single medium has emerged as television's successor. "When I put on my citizen hat, I get very worried," he muses. "I think there is clearly a breaking down of any consensus in the country" (141).

Edmiston's concerns are shared by many others, perhaps most notably by author Ken Auletta, whose best-selling book, *Three Blind Mice*, chronicles the decline of the major television networks.[2] Auletta contends that despite their shortcomings, the three majors provided a common hearth where the American people gathered both to be warmed by popular entertainment and to reflect upon the most pressing issues of the day. The fire in this common hearth now appears to be burning low, and many participants in the culture industries see the current era as particularly volatile, marked by contradiction and uncertainty. Of particular concern are the changing technologies of communication, all of which promise to subdivide the national audience and splinter the body politic.

Such dire forebodings about changes in mediated communication are not historically unique. Similar concerns about social coherence and stability have accompanied the introduction of new media technologies in earlier times. Indeed, historian Warren Susman argues that every era of technological innovation has generated dialectic tensions between utopian and dystopian representations of new media.[3] This dialectic is more than a reflection of human ambivalence, however, for it is also an expression of the multiple and conflicting tendencies that arise at any such moment of change.

Perched as we are on the edge of a new era, it is useful to consider the disparate forces that are shaping our cultural environment and to speculate about their impact on public life. A brief analysis of historical trends will not only reveal how the culture industries have sought to organize collective experience through the postwar era but also help us understand the seeming chaos that now confronts media practitioners. I hope to show that the national mass audience is an exceptional blip in the history of humankind and its passing does not mark a decline in societal consensus, much less the demise of the nation. General-circulation magazines and network television were intimately connected to a Fordist era of mass production and mass consumption. Our "shared sense of experience" was less a matter of consensus than it was a manifestation of a particular set of social relations. Changes in the national and global economies over the past two decades help to explain the fragmentation of the national audience and the reorganization of the culture industries. This current period is in fact tied to a set of historical patterns that are fairly coherent, despite a dialectical tension between globalization and fragmentation. By comparing the organization of the culture industries during the Fordist and neo-Fordist eras we can begin to understand some of the shifting forces confronting practitioners in the fields of information and entertainment.

Network TV and National Consciousness

The high network era was in large part a product of explicit government policy that began during television's infancy, the late 1940s and early 1950s, when major corporations in the entertainment and electronics industries wrestled among themselves for control of broadcast licenses and struggled over the technical standards that would guide equipment manufacture. The outcome was a fairly reliable technology based on VHF (very high frequency) transmission. Yet it became clear early on that UHF (ultra high frequency) offered an alternative that promised many more channels, and hence a greater range of choice for the viewer. Rather than encourage this alternative, however, the Federal Communications Commission endorsed the standards promoted by a powerful industry lobby headed by the Radio Corporation of America (RCA), a major electronics manufacturer and owner of the National Broadcasting Company (NBC). The final outcome of the policy process was a "mixed system" that privileged a limited number of VHF stations and created a second-class tier of UHF stations. RCA benefited tremendously from this arrangement since it already was heavily invested in VHF technology and, through its subsidiary NBC, had negotiated affiliation contracts with key VHF stations across the country. Consequently, FCC policy not only anointed RCA's leadership in manufacturing, it also limited the number of stations that might be able to mount a competitive national network.

The FCC's actions were partially motivated by a postwar backlash against New Deal regulators who had tried to rein in RCA's dominance in radio broadcasting during the late 1930s and early 1940s. This postwar favoritism toward powerful broadcast corporations was sustained throughout the fifties by a series of Eisenhower appointees whose predispositions brought about such a cozy period of government-industry cooperation that one former commissioner referred to it as the "whorehouse era" of the FCC.[4] The product of this collaboration was a television system with two-and-a-half national networks: NBC and CBS had affiliates in every market, while ABC could reach viewers in major cities but enjoyed only spotty coverage in smaller markets. Consequently, it would be folly to construe the high network era as an inherent outcome of the technology or primarily as a manifestation of national consensus. It was instead the product of systematic favoritism that allowed powerful elements within the radio industry to limit the development of the technology so as to seal out aspiring competitors from the motion picture, newspaper, and magazine industries.[5]

The network system also was the outcome of a policy process that favored national interests over local interests. During the early years of television, the FCC allowed NBC, CBS, and ABC to own and control stations in five local markets and to seek affiliates in other cities across the nation.[6] All three networks snatched up stations in major urban centers — New York, Chicago, Philadelphia, Los Angeles — hoping to secure control of the largest markets, and then turned their attention to rallying affiliates in other locales. Once they consolidated these alliances across the country, the networks began to pressure local stations to turn over increasing portions of their broadcast day to national programming. Although purportedly owned by local interests, many small stations were only too happy to turn over creative responsibilities so as to lower their own costs and raise their profits. Yet some larger stations, such as those in Chicago, struggled to sustain local television production so as to nurture local interests and to promote the city's sense of identity. In fact, the "Chicago School" of television was so successful during the early years of the medium that many of its programs were also carried regionally and even nationally, thereby competing with producers in New York and Hollywood.[7]

To some extent, this was a replication of the radio era when Chicago was a major center of regional and national program production. Two of the most durable genres of broadcast programming — the soap opera and the domestic comedy — first evolved in Chicago, and *Amos 'n Andy*, the most popular radio program of all time, emerged out of this milieu as well. Nevertheless, Chicago radio lived a conflicted existence throughout its history. Despite the creativity of Chicago producers, they were usually underfunded and often prodded to produce programming that erased the traces of local origin in favor of a more national sound, one closely associated with the networks.[8]

During the television era the same pattern would reemerge. As a result, most of the revenues generated by the Chicago School were skimmed off by the networks rather than reinvested in local production. By the mid-fifties, Chicago TV began to wane as the networks consolidated their operations and began to forge alliances with the creative community in Hollywood.[9] In what was then referred to as a streamlining maneuver, the networks systematically disassembled Chicago television by the end of the decade despite a government regulatory structure explicitly premised on the principle of localism.[10]

Favoritism toward national television was further reinforced by spatial biases in the advertising and consumer products industries as well. As productivity in the civilian economy mushroomed throughout the 1950s, huge corporations pursued the largest possible domestic markets with the enthusiastic encouragement of advertising executives and social scientists. Of the latter, Frank Stanton, who became president of CBS, and A. C. Nielsen, whose firm became synonymous with TV ratings, both portrayed the television audience as a national entity that displayed relatively homogeneous preferences and aspirations. Even on those rare occasions when advertisers reflected on the distinctive motivations of, say, African-American consumers, their rhetoric focused largely on those characteristics that black and white viewers shared.[11] Advertisers saw national television as the greater leveler, smoothing out disparities in life-style and income, making all homes accessible to their products.

The tendencies just outlined bear the unmistakable marks of a Fordist economy in which mass consumption interlocks with systems of mass production, mass marketing, and national regulation.[12] The network television era should therefore be seen less as a product of popular consensus than as a symptomatic expression of a social order built upon a historically specific form of capitalism. By the mid-1950s, when some 60 percent of American families owned a receiver, network television displaced the general-circulation magazine as the preeminent national advertising medium. By the beginning of the following decade, close to 90 percent of American homes owned a television, bringing presidential politics, space exploration, and the antics of Jethro and Granny into the living rooms of almost every American family.

Yet despite this consolidation in the culture industries, the sixties was not necessarily an era of consensus, for television viewing became both a shared experience and an object of sustained social conflict.[13] On some level, almost every major issue of the sixties revolved around questions of televisual representation. Americans watched and argued about what was on; even if they weren't watching, they were arguing about what was on, or what wasn't.

The intensity of the struggle grew so powerful that presidents and vice-presidents lavished tremendous attention on television, perhaps believing that their political fortunes were somehow bound up with those "wires and lights in a box." Reputedly, the medium delivered the presidency into the hands of John Kennedy, while snatching it from the grasp of a less telegenic Richard Nixon. Kennedy's successor, Lyndon Johnson, contended that television also played a significant role in his political fortunes, ultimately driving him from office at the height of the Vietnam War. He was succeeded, of course, by a rehabilitated Richard Nixon who relied on the media savvy of Roger Ailes to help reinvent his public image for the age of television.

But even a more telegenic Nixon never lost his disdain for the small circle of network insiders who controlled access to the national airwaves. This continuing mistrust encouraged the administration to begin promoting cable television as an alternative mode of distribution that promised to undermine the power of network oligarchs and to promote the interests of the so-called silent majority.[14] Nixon was not the only one frustrated with the major networks, however. Enthusiasm for cable television was growing in many quarters, with promoters promising a technological utopia of media plenitude, a "wired nation," which would bypass the centralized circuits of network power. Ironically, Nixon's mistrust of network power was discursively articulated to the utopian aspirations of progressive reformers who also sought an alternative to media oligopoly, one rooted in grass-roots community television.

Yet it would take almost another decade before cable became a commercially profitable technology and began to challenge the concentrated power of the national networks. Neither government policymaking nor technological innovation alone could displace the network oligopoly.[15] Rather, increasing corporate competition among the media industries contributed the final impetus toward change. Cable television would begin to grow in the late 1970s with the emergence of satellite program providers such as Home Box Office (owned by Time-Life), Music Television (owned by Viacom), and Turner Broadcasting. These new services represented the very groups that had been locked out by the FCC in the early days of television regulation — publishers, Hollywood studios, independent program syndicators, and regionally based broadcasters. The software they provided became the core around which new viewer loyalties would be built. In 1980, the prime-time audiences of the three major networks began diminishing by fits and starts, dropping from more than 90 percent of viewers to roughly 50 percent today. As the audience began to fragment, network executives were joined by numerous social critics who made dire predictions about the impact this would have on national consciousness.

Neo-Fordism and the Culture Industries

The temporal pacing of these developments in popular media coincided with profound changes in global capitalism as it moved into a period of crisis during the 1970s and 1980s. Faced with increasing competition and falling rates of productivity, major corporations began to reorganize their operations so as to become more flexible in manufacturing and more responsive to local markets. Although this transition has been described a number of different ways, I refer to it here as neo-Fordism in order to connote a period in which Fordist principles of mass production, mass marketing, and mass consumption exist side-by-side with emerging forms of flexible accumulation.

David Harvey distinguishes four types of flexibility

as characteristic of this new era. The first type involves physical reorganization of the workplace designed to speed up labor processes and enhance productivity. The second level is to be found in labor markets, which are now characterized by the proliferation of subcontracting, part-time employment, and other forms of casual labor. New modes of flexibility also mark a third level, the arena of state policy. For the past two decades, deregulation and/or privatization have been driving the policymaking process in nations around the globe. Besides allowing firms to jettison social responsibilities, this trend has facilitated gigantic corporate mergers and acquisitions. The fourth type of flexibility is the increasing geographic mobility of financial capital, production processes, and people. To these I would add a fifth level of flexibility, one that emphasizes new modes of marketing and distribution, and specifically draws attention to the contested terrain of popular culture. Harvey argues that even though these types of flexibility are not entirely new, they have become central tenets of capitalist strategies since the 1970s.

Such an analysis points to the dialectic relationship between processes of globalization and fragmentation. Rather than a chaotic collapse of national communities and mass consumer markets, Harvey describes this period of transition as marked by the strategic advantages of emerging neo-Fordist principles: "Flexibility has little or nothing to do with decentralizing either political or economic power and everything to do with maintaining highly centralized control *through decentralizing tactics.*" [16] Corporations no longer concentrate their production operations at centralized facilities and they no longer focus their marketing campaigns on a single national audience. Instead, companies like Coca-Cola emphasize a flexible strategy that cultivates indigenous franchise operations around the world. Although the headquarters remain in Atlanta, Ira Herbert is quick to point to the multinational composition of the executive workforce (5). Furthermore, he directs our attention to pattern advertising in which a single concept is spun out in local contexts around the globe. Coca-Cola emphasizes flexibility in its corporate operations and multiplicity in the ways that messages about the product are circulated, both within nations and across national borders. He tells us that each consumer group "should be communicated to in their own way with their own message, with their own sound, with their own visualization. Just as an example, two years ago brand Coca-Cola would create a dozen commercials for the year in North America. [This year] we have just finished producing twenty-six and it is only April" (7). According to Herbert, the ideal outcome of this flexible strategy is for consumers to see Coca-Cola as woven into their local context, an integral part of their everyday world. Yet at the same time, it remains a singular product marketed by a multinational executive workforce that speaks English and is based in Atlanta.[17]

Reorganizing the Culture Industries

This same globalization/fragmentation dialectic is at work throughout the culture industries, and in part it can be attributed to new modes of electronic communication. Since the 1970s, national network broadcasting has been challenged by numerous competitors: satellite, cable, cassette, CD-ROM, Internet, etc. The modes of distribution have become not only more flexible but also less consequential. Broadcasting a program or advertisement in television prime time no longer guarantees broad national exposure. Cultural products now circulate in a variety of media throughout the world, almost regardless of government communications policy, copyright law, or corporate monopoly. The blockbuster film *Waterworld* was, for example, circulated on bootlegged videotapes in the Soviet Union *before* the feature film was officially released to theaters in the United States and more than a year before it would reach network television.

Not only do Hollywood studios have less control over the subterranean circulation of their products but they also recognize that they no longer can dependably construct mass audiences by controlling technology, government regulation, or market economics. Whereas in the past viewers would choose the least offensive program from among the offerings of the three national networks, they now are hailed by a plenitude of choices in a variety of formats. The emergence of "software" as an industry buzzword conveys the recent shift in emphasis away from a few highly regulated channels of exhibition toward multiple circuits of distribution that transcend national borders. In this new environment, audiences will cluster

around a product because it meets their distinctive needs or tastes. In other words, the national/industrial infrastructure that played a crucial role in fostering the high network era of television is becoming less influential, and consequently future audiences/users are more likely to be produced by the cultural forms themselves. In response to these trends and in response to the growing importance of extranational audiences, media conglomerates are developing more flexible strategies that take into account the globalization/fragmentation dialectic.[18]

We can see this new logic at work in the culture industries first by turning our attention to recent developments in television. Both Paramount and Warner Bros. recently launched networks whose viability will primarily hinge on the quality of the programming, according to most industry observers.[19] To some extent these new networks are disadvantaged by their lack of powerful broadcast affiliates in the top one hundred markets, but cable and direct broadcast satellite technology make it possible for them to reach more than 80 percent of U.S. viewers and an even larger percentage of the most affluent households in the nation. Government regulation no longer hampers their ability to address a significant audience across the North American continent, and the reach of their programming is no longer constrained by the geographic diffusion patterns of terrestrial broadcast transmission towers.[20] Just as importantly, ratings data are no longer as reliant on mass circulation figures. Unlike the 1960s, researchers now gather and sell information about demographically defined subsets of the national audience, and advertising agencies now commonly advise their clients that particular groups of viewers are often more important than synchronic national exposure.

Warner Bros. and Paramount therefore hope to follow the example set by the Fox Network, which based its rise to prominence on programming tailored to a young, urban audience.[21] Drawing on some of Hollywood's most talented producers, Fox attracted these viewers with irreverent programs such as *Married with Children, The Simpsons*, and *In Living Color*. These are the programs that television producer David Kendall refers to as having an "edge" (62). They work against Kendall's general principle that television at its best (i.e., most profitable) produces shows with universal values. While it is true that the most powerful networks still rely on mass-appeal programming, new modes of distribution are challenging the axiomatic status of Kendall's assertion. Networks used to focus on maximizing national audiences largely because their competition was limited to one or two other networks that were similarly aiming at mass circulation. Now, however, the major networks find themselves trying to hold together a national audience that is being hailed by a growing variety of niche programmers whose success rides almost exclusively on their appeal to distinctive subsets of viewers.

Here is where we come to a paradox that is peculiar to the current situation. Historically, the popularity of cultural forms has been notoriously difficult to predict. Consequently, large corporations focused most of their efforts on controlling the channels of distribution rather than the creative process itself. They did this through oligopoly, federal regulation, and control over technological development. In the current era, many major media corporations are still trying to operate according to this logic. It therefore makes a lot of sense that huge telephone, cable, computer, and broadcasting firms are now scrambling for partnerships that offer the prospect of controlling future distribution channels. The irony is that these consolidations may prove no more effective than the dominant organizational posture IBM once enjoyed in the computer world. If current economic, political, and technological trends continue, it will become increasingly difficult for large corporations to control the distribution of cultural forms.[22] Thus, like the computer industry, we may be witnessing a shift away from an emphasis upon hardware and limited channels of distribution toward software and flexible corporate conglomerates. Rather than a centralized network structure anchored by New York finance, Hollywood studios, and state-regulated technology, the neo-network era features elaborate circuits of cultural production and reception.

This transformation is not a radical break with the past; rather, it is a transitional phase in which Fordist and neo-Fordist principles exist side by side. For example, studio chieftain Strauss Zelnick claims that the mass market is still at the heart of Fox's movie business. "You make your real money when you have the broadest possible market," says Zelnick. "And you get the broadest possible market by making movies that are great stories" (23). David Kendall agrees with Zelnick by pointing to the fact that the major networks are still looking for series that focus on universal values and concerns. On the other hand, as we have noted, many of the great success stories in television have recently tended to come from niche operators like MTV, Turner, and Fox Television. A similar principle seems to be at work in the radio industry, where Broadcasting Partners regularly outperforms national networks. "Usually, if you have a locally programmed equivalent, it will beat the [national] satellite service," says CFO Nathan Pearson (122). Mark Edmiston also directs our attention to micro markets and the "zine" phenomenon. "As you get narrower in interest," he notes, "you tend to have more intensity of interest [and] the person is more likely to pay the extra money" (137). Thus, success in the magazine business no longer rides on the publication of a general-circulation magazine, but instead relies on the ownership of a collection of specialty publications that profitably manage the relationship between market size and the intensity of consumer interest.

Such an approach engenders a constant search for narrowly defined and underserved markets. Race, gender, and ethnicity have now joined socioeconomic status as potentially marketable boundaries of difference. Edmiston explains, for example, that magazine publishers are currently investigating whether women skiers share a set of needs and interests that are distinctive enough to constitute a commercially viable subscriber base. Similarly, Pearson's Broadcasting Partners fashioned a successful niche by subdividing the African-American radio audience, targeting adults with a pronounced aversion to rap music. In neither case are these niche marketers basing their decisions on allegiances to particular groups at the margins of mass culture; rather, they simply are following a neo-Fordist marketing strategy, one they characterize as strictly capitalistic and generally disinterested in content issues.

The same could be said about Time-Warner, whose music subsidiary Death Row Records specializes in rap music by such popular but controversial artists as Snoop Doggy Dogg, Dr. Dre, and Tupac Shakur.[23] Time-Warner's pursuit of this fragmentary market is complemented, however, by Warner

Television, which is trying to market programs to the major national networks and to international syndicators by employing writers like David Kendall who repeatedly disavow any knowledge of, or concern for, specific subsets of viewers. Indeed, Kendall tells us that the market data he has seen tends to lump Hispanics with other minorities, to ignore differences among international markets, and to turn a blind eye to gay and lesbian viewers. The point for him is to focus on "universals" that will translate to most social contexts. Within the Time-Warner empire itself we therefore can observe a double movement between the global and the local, between the mass market and the niche market.

Similar patterns seem to be operating in the hotel industry, where niche marketer Peter Sonnabend notes, "Our hotels, we like to think, are a special collection — unique properties in unique locations — and those hotels have done pretty well, even in these very tough times" (36). Their successful formula is based on distinguishing the Sonesta experience from the "cookie-cutter" accommodations provided by Marriott, Hilton, and Sheraton. Original artwork, local flavor, and distinctive architecture are all aimed at a specific up-scale clientele that wishes to distinguish its tastes from the mass market and is willing to pay a premium in order to do so. Thus, the hotel industry seems headed in two directions at once: toward consolidation among a handful of megafirms, and toward niche operations that cater to particular tastes.

This trend should not, however, be confused with the emergence of a dual economy. The megafirms are also quite active in niche markets, with firms like Marriott setting up specialty subsidiaries such as Marriott Courtyards and Residence Inns (48). Furthermore, small independent hoteliers like Sonesta do not necessarily travel their route alone. They develop properties in Cambridgeside (next to a major shopping mall development near the heart of Boston) and near Disney World (among the endless clutter of leisure enterprises feeding off the Disney mainstream) (42). Sonesta's very success is based on its relationship to and its distinction from cookie-cutter hotels and mass entertainment sites. The Sonesta experience is not marked by the fact that it offers something intrinsically local or "audientic," but rather by the ways in which it is distinguished from

the competition at each particular site as more local, more authentic, or more tasteful.

This relationship between niche and mass markets directs our attention back to the new modes of corporate organization within the culture industries. Notice that David Kendall works for Warner Bros. Television, which is a relatively autonomous part of the Time-Warner empire, a firm with extensive holdings in film, cable, broadcasting, music, and publishing. The corporation reportedly has been careful to avoid steering its diverse units toward creativity that narrowly conforms to a synergistic imperative. Nevertheless, it has strategically positioned itself to reap the benefits of creative work carried out in a variety of contexts: large-scale, highly integrated enterprises (*Time Magazine*), boutique production operations (TV sitcoms), and seemingly autonomous niche venues (Death Row Records). Note also that each operation targets a different market: the middle-class, college-educated magazine reader; the mass television audience; and the trendy, urban youth culture. Creative synergies are not explicitly mandated between these various operations, but the circulation of creative content among these and the many other divisions of Time-Warner is managed so as to maximize profitability. Rap music, which began as a niche phenomenon, for example, has been leveraged throughout the many distribution circuits of the corporate conglomerate.

Scott Sassa — who is often credited with writing the original business plan for the Fox TV network and is now president of the Turner Entertainment Group — operates in a similar corporate environment.[24] He is responsible for maximizing the "value chain" among Turner Broadcasting, TBS Superstation, TNT, Castle Rock Entertainment, New Line Cinema, Turner Pictures Worldwide, the Cartoon Network, Hanna-Barbera Productions, TNT Latin America, Turner Home Video, Turner Publishing, and Turner Licensing and Merchandising. Sassa says there are two aspects to his job. One is to encourage the creation of popular copyrighted material. The second is to develop a system that leverages content "further, higher, faster than anybody else."[25] The point is to spin out the profitability of all copyrighted material at as many levels as possible. These can be new blockbuster copyrights, such as "Seinfeld" or *Forrest Gump*, or they can be libraries of earlier materials, such as "I Love Lucy" or

Gone with the Wind. Large entertainment conglomerates also leverage niche products such as "Johnny Quest" and "Saved by the Bell," which can be very profitable if marketed through the appropriate channels. This includes not only film, television, cable, music, publishing, and computer software but also ancillary merchandise, franchise agreements, and overseas marketing. "Every copyright that starts out anywhere in the system gets leveraged every which way imaginable," says Sassa.[26] The key to profitability is still distribution, but the distribution system is more diverse and decentered. It also remains highly volatile, given the unpredictable nature of popular responses to new cultural forms. Huge entertainment conglomerates therefore attempt to leverage the profitability of existing products, to counterbalance losses from their many unsuccessful ventures, and to secure copyrights to marginal cultural forms that may prove profitable in the future.

They also try to externalize the risks inherent in the creative aspects of the industry. Movie executive Strauss Zelnick provides useful insights as to how megafirms manage creativity. Zelnick devotes almost all his time to the distribution of cultural products that are produced by a casual labor force that is signed on for each specific film project. Only a handful of the twelve hundred employees at Twentieth Century Fox Film Corporation are directly involved in making motion pictures.[27] The rest come and go, many represented in their contractual negotiations by agencies such as Victoria Traube's firm, International Creative Management. Zelnick describes the creative process as one that is relatively free from corporate calculations. Good stories cannot be churned out by the numbers, we are told. And yet the folklore of the industry unconsciously sets creative boundaries: what themes are hot this season, which audiences use which media, what translates well in overseas markets. It is folklore that members of the casual workforce ignore at their own peril. The informal maxims that circulate at meetings and social gatherings structure the process of seemingly autonomous creative activity.

A similar dynamic is at work in the advertising industry, and Stephen Oakes is the quintessential independent whose creative work is linked to the needs of major corporations through the mediation of a community of animators, producers, and advertising representatives. Many ad agencies, which over the past decade have themselves gone through a period of merger and conglomeration, have cut back their creative staffs and now contract out much of this labor. They set the boundaries for creative labor through a network of personal interactions. Note that Oakes — like Kendall, Zelnick, and Traube — places tremendous significance not on the audience but on the internal networking and communication within this community. It is a site where perceptions of audience tastes are constructed and where creative practitioners strive to bring their distinctive abilities to the attention of other practitioners. "It is very competitive to do the work that we do," says Oakes. "It takes a lot of cold calls and little cliques and friendships to get these prizes because handing out the assignment to do a [television] commercial is a really guarded moment when the creative team at an ad agency is really displaying [its] sense of taste and control of who is going to do these things" (73; also see Oakes: 81, Traube: 95, Kendall: 56, and Kendall: 62). Although not career employees of the same firm, this casual workforce is concentrated in specific creative locales, New York City and Hollywood being the most prominent. Interestingly, many of the most crucial aspects of success revolve around what Anthony Giddens and Erving Goffman have referred to as "facework," those forms of personal interaction that sustain trust between institutional actors.[28] Thus proximity and social interactions are keys to organizing a casual workforce via what David Kendall refers to as the fiction of the industry.

Yet these concentrated creative communities may be undergoing a process of dispersion themselves. In part, this is attributable to the growing phenomenon of telecommuting, something especially popular among those who work in the culture industries. Even more significant may be the emergence of new creative locales: Silicon Valley, the Microsoft campus in Seattle, the South Park neighborhood of San Francisco, the Spokane garage of "Myst" creators Rand and Robyn Miller, and the research institute in Champaign, Illinois, where computer whizzes fashioned the Mosaic software template that now dominates navigation of the World Wide Web.[29] In the past, many culture industries were concentrated around capital-intensive resources in New York City and Hollywood, while less capital-intensive forms – such as music and print fiction – developed multiple and dispersed centers of creative activity.[30] As the costs of film, television, and multimedia production continue to fall, will a similar process of dispersion take place? Can this mean the emergence of new creative locales? During the 1950s or 1960s, it would have been a foregone conclusion that New York and Los Angeles would continue to dominate the national cultural landscape. Yet neo-Fordist principles are reshaping the current geography of social relations at many levels, and much of this change is facilitated by new technologies.

New Locales, New Affinities, New Migrations of Talent

Looked at more broadly, electronic media may be reshaping the cultural landscape in other ways as well. Historically, the telegraph and telephone enabled the geographic separation of blue-collar and white-collar labor during the Fordist era of vertical integration. Headquartered in one location, major corporations knitted together a network of operations throughout the nation as marketing, finance, and planning were increasingly separated from manufacturing operations. Specific cities became renowned for their concentration of corporate headquarters where white-collar workers collaborated not only within their own firms but also with counterparts in related organizations. New communications technologies (computer, fax, teleconference, etc.) are now enabling further dispersal of the corporate workforce as "back office" operations are being moved outside major cities to locations such as New Jersey, while city centers like Manhattan remain the site for "facework" occupations such as corporate law, advertising, and finance.[31]

As part of this transition, local governments are forging cultural policies to enhance the attractiveness and to solidify the distinctive identities of these growing suburban enclaves. As Meadowlands sports promoter Dennis Robinson explains, New Jersey is competing with New York City both through its land development policies and through efforts to position itself as a prominent part of the national and global circuits of entertainment and spectacle. New Jersey

wants to stage major performances that used to be almost exclusively available in urban centers. This growing competition for cultural events is inextricably tied to a competition over the value of local real estate. As Dennis Robinson puts it, "Who ever thought about New Jersey as an entertainment center – internationally, regionally, or nationally – before the existence of the [Meadowlands] sports complex?" (152). Now, however, northern New Jersey is promoting itself as a location to be valued on a par with the Big Apple.

This growing competition between places furthermore registers in Robinson's account of New Jersey's attempt to court the Yankees baseball team, an effort that drew a swift and furious response from corporate leaders in the city. The Rockefellers, who are heavily invested in Manhattan real estate, led the counterattack, no doubt because they understood the economic logic of losing the Yankees to a competitor across the Hudson River. This rivalry over major cultural events revolves around both the immediate economic gains from the events themselves and the long-term value of local real estate, a value determined by the recognizable differences between places.

The spatial objectives of New Jersey's aggressive cultural policies are being complemented by a temporal component as well. The state is trying to promote allegiances to its sports teams as part of a conscious effort to tap youthful enthusiasms that might carry over into the future. New Jersey planners see local sports events as an active form of spectatorship that promotes place-bound affinities across the generations. "In the sports business," says Robinson, "you are really targeting kids, kids that grow up to be fans" (157). These allegiances not only have a tremendous influence on those who grow up and remain in the same area, but as we have seen with championship rounds of major sports events, these allegiances may transcend the local and play a significant role in national and even global impressions of particular places.

The ambitions of New Jersey policymakers are indicative of shifting relationships within the New York metropolitan area, a decentering process that has been described by a number of geographers such as Edward Soja.[32] It also has to do with shifts in the relative power between urban areas across the nation. Thus Charlotte and Phoenix now have NBA basketball teams; Tampa and Denver have NFL football franchises. All four of these cities have emerged as powerful urban centers over the past two decades and are beginning to challenge the economic and cultural dominance of cities like New York. This shifting balance of power helps us understand how migrations of talent may be changing in the neo-network era. As government policymakers and corporate managers develop more flexible, decentralized operations, the geographic allocation of talent must be transformed as well. During the past century, high performance on the job was usually rewarded by a transfer to the corporate headquarters in a major metropolitan locale. But this appears to be changing. Peter Sonnabend and Nathan Pearson work hard to find dynamic staff members to serve their local operations and then have to work even harder to keep them in place (Sonnabend: 52; Pearson: 126). As major corporations become more de-centered, and as communications technologies continue to evolve, we may witness a greater dispersal of talent in both the corporate and cultural domains.

The Neo-Network Era

The national audience was the primary target of culture industries throughout the Fordist era. Companies focused on what David Kendall refers to as the universals of family and workplace, not because these were inherently national constructs but because they proved compatible with the economic, political, institutional, and legal relations that favored national mass markets. Now, new technologies, deregulation, and relentless competition are undermining these national frameworks and reconfiguring the cultural landscape. Although mass markets continue to attract corporate attention and blockbuster copyrights are still a priority, the mass audience no longer refers to one simultaneous experience so much as a shared, asynchronous cultural milieu.[33] That is, culture industries enjoy less control over the daily scheduling of popular entertainments and strive instead for broad exposure through multiple circuits of information and expression. They also seek less to homogenize popular culture than to organize and exploit diverse forms of creativity toward profitable ends. Flexible corporate frameworks connect mass market operations with more localized initiatives.

Therefore, two tendencies are now at work in the culture industries. One focuses on mass cultural forms aimed at broad national or global markets that demand low involvement and are relatively apolitical. Firms that deal in this arena are cautious about the prospect of intense audience responses either for or against the product they are marketing. By comparison, those forms targeted at niche audiences actively pursue intensity. They seek out audiences that are more likely to be highly invested in a particular form of cultural expression. These firms aim not to change niche groups, but to situate products within them. We are therefore witnessing the organization of huge media conglomerates around the so-called synergies that exploit these two movements. MTV identifies itself as hip, young, and alternative, while also conforming to the imperatives of Viacom, a multifaceted corporate parent whose holdings include Paramount studios, United Paramount television network, Blockbuster Video, and Simon & Schuster.[34] The Fox network pursues a similar strategy in its relations with the Wayans family. Their searing critiques of race relations in American society and their risqué sexual humor are ultimately folded into the agenda of the politically conservative Murdoch media empire.

One of the consequences of this new environment is that groups that were at one time oppositional or outside the mainstream have become increasingly attractive to media conglomerates with deep pockets, ambitious growth objectives, and flexible corporate structures. As the channels of distribution have grown more diverse, the oppositional has become more commercially viable and, in some measure, more closely tied to the mainstream. The voracious appetite for innovation in the culture industries means that niche markets are constantly serving as testing and recruiting grounds for new cultural forms. Flexible corporate structures have made it possible to quickly leverage niche artists into major mass phenomena when executives sense a growing audience interest. We have witnessed this pattern with grunge music groups, African-American film directors, and obscure computer software developers. In many ways their work has become mainstream, part of our shared experience. And perhaps they have lost some of their edge. Yet even those niche artists whose work is not leveraged into a mass phenomenon can be profitable if properly exploited through the "value chain" of the conglomerate. They remain outside of the mainstream and yet they have become part of a global/ local dialectic that maintains centralized control through decentralizing tactics. Therefore it is not surprising to read socialist Barbara Ehrenreich's regular commentaries in the pages of *Time* magazine or to learn that some of the most controversial rap singers are signed to "independent" record labels controlled by Time-Warner enterprises. What is surprising perhaps is to hear executives in the culture industries spontaneously disavow their ability to control the creative process and the distribution of popular cultural forms in the neo-network era of post national media.

*Editor's note: page numbers in parentheses refer to the interviews with industry professionals collected in one volume in which this essay originally appeared.

Notes

1. Page numbers in parentheses reference the interviews in this volume. Although Edmiston doesn't mention them, radio and Hollywood film also were major contributors to mass culture during this period. In fact, general-circulation magazines such as *Time* were actually targeted at an educated middle-class reader, whereas film and radio during the height of their popularity tended to address much more diverse audiences.

2. Ken Auletta, *Three Blind Mice: How the TV Networks Lost Their Way* (New York: Random House, 1991). Also see his reflections on the fortunes of television news, "Look What They've Done to the News," *TV Guide*, 9 November 1991, pp. 4–7.

3. Warren I. Susman, *Culture as History: The Transformation of American Society in the Twentieth Century* (New York: Pantheon, 1984).

4. James L. Baughman, *Television's Guardians: The FCC and the Politics of Programming, 1958–1967* (Knoxville: University of Tennessee Press, 1985), p. 13.

5. Among the firms that were frustrated in their attempts to forge competitive regional and national networks were Paramount Pictures, Time-Life, and the *Chicago Tribune*.

6. The networks could own five VHF and two UHF stations, but given the second-class status of the latter, few exercised this option.

7. Joel Sternberg, "Television Town," *Chicago History* 4, no. 2 (Summer 1975): 108–117, and Christopher Anderson and Michael Curtin, "Mapping the Ethereal City:

Chicago Television, the FCC, and the Politics of Place," *Quarterly Review of Film and Video*, 16, no. 3–4 (1997).

8. Les Brown, "When Chi Radio Was in Bloom," *Variety*, 28 March 1962, pp. 61–62; Melvin Patrick Ely, *The Adventures of Amos 'n' Andy: A Social History of an American Phenomenon* (New York: Basic Books, 1991); Robert C. Allen, *Speaking of Soap Operas* (Chapel Hill: University of North Carolina Press, 1985), pp. 101–121; Lester A. Weinrott, "Chicago Radio: The Glory Days," *Chicago History* 3, no. 1 (Spring–Summer 1974):14–22; and Sarajane Wells, "Looking Backward: My Life in Radio," *Chicago History* 7, no. 3 (Fall 1978):179–182.

9. Christopher Anderson, *Hollywood TV: The Studio System in the Fifties* (Austin: University of Texas Press, 1994); Tino Balio, ed., *Hollywood in the Age of Television* (Boston: Unwin Hyman, 1990); and William Boddy, *Fifties Television: The Industry and Its Critics* (Urbana and Chicago: University of Illinois Press, 1990).

10. Throughout the history of the FCC recurrent tensions have existed between the policy discourse of localism – which nostalgically characterizes broadcasting as a surrogate for the New England town meeting or the village green – and the economic realities of commercial network broadcasting. See Anderson and Curtin, "Mapping the Ethereal City."

11. Dwight Brooks, "In Their Own Words: Advertisers' Construction of an African American Consumer Market," *Howard Journal of Communication* 6, no. 2 (October 1995).

12. My use of the term Fordist is not meant to imply the total domination of all aspects of the economy by these modes of operation. Capitalism has always been characterized by internal contradictions and patterns of uneven development. Chicago's regional broadcast operations are a good example of some of the tensions at work in this era. Nevertheless, Fordist principles were at the heart of corporate behavior among the most central actors in the national and global economies during most of this century.

13. Lynn Spigel and Michael Curtin, eds., *The Revolution Wasn't Televised: Sixties Television and Social Conflict* (New York: Routledge, 1996).

14. William E. Porter, *Assault on the Media: The Nixon Years* (Ann Arbor: University of Michigan Press, 1976).

15. Indeed, cable technology has been around since the 1940s and failed to "revolutionize" television until it became the focus of policy debates in the 1970s. See Thomas Streeter, "Blue Skies and Strange Bedfellows," in Lynn Spigel and Michael Curtin, eds., *The Revolution Wasn't Televised*.

16. David Harvey, "Flexibility: Threat or Opportunity?" *Socialist Review* 21 (January 1991):73. Harvey's analysis

is most thoroughly detailed in *The Condition of Postmodernity: An Inquiry into the Origins of Cultural Change* (Cambridge, Mass.: Basil Blackwell, 1989). For another take on this transition see Alain Lipietz, *Mirages and Miracles: The Crises of Global Fordism* (London: Verso, 1987).

17. This kind of thinking is applied to a variety of industries by Kenichi Ohmae's best-seller, *The Borderless World: Power and Strategy in the Interlinked Economy* (New York: Harper Business, 1990). Ohmae is a managing director of McKinsey and Company, one of the world's largest and most influential corporate consulting firms.

18. I use the term extranational to connote social phenomena that are either more local (subnational) or more global (transnational) than those that have dominated the modern era.

19. *Electronic Media*, 2 January 1995, pp. 34–39, and *Variety*, 15 January 1996, pp. 39, 42.

20. The same is true transnationally. Rupert Murdoch's Sky Channel in Europe and Star TV in Asia are reaching vast and growing audiences despite the concerns often articulated by national regulators. The same is true with CNN, whose satellite networks have proven so successful that they have invited competitors. CNN is now locked in a fierce struggle with Televisa, NBC, Reuters, and BBC, each of them vying for the attention of Hispanic-speaking viewers throughout the Western Hemisphere.

21. Interestingly, Fox recently rose from a niche operator to a major network competitor by successfully outbidding CBS for the rights to broadcast National Football League games. This has not only encouraged some CBS affiliates to defect to Fox but also altered the network's attractiveness to Hollywood producers who are shopping around ideas for new programs. Thus, the deep pockets of Fox's corporate parent (Murdoch News Corp.) have allowed the network to pursue a growth strategy primarily based on a heavy investment in programming.

22. The exception here is high-tech, capital-intensive spectacles such as the Super-bowl, the Olympics, and the presidential elections. In these cases, licensing agreements or logistical requirements favor major operators like ABC. But many spectacles, such as the Brown/Simpson tragedy, are remarkable because of their unruliness. During the Simpson trial, the major television networks struggled desperately to compete against each other and against niche services such as Court TV, CNN, and *Hardcopy*.

23. Nisid Hajari, "Looking for Rapprochement," *Entertainment Weekly*, 9 June 1995, pp. 16–17, and Richard Zoglin, "A Company Under Fire," *Time*, 12 June 1995, pp. 37–39. At the time this was written, 1995, Time-Warner still had significant ties to Death Row Records. Due to both internal and external controversies, as well as the continuing success of its music releases, the small record label has gone through a series of ownership and managerial changes too complicated to detail here. Interestingly, however, two of the firms angling for a role in the future of Death Row are Sony and MCA (now owned by Seagram and Matsushita). See Adam Sandler, "Death Row Slapped with $75 Mil Lawsuit," *Variety*, 15 January 1996, p. 38, and "Spirit of Seagram Spreading through MCA," *Variety*, 22 January 1996, p. 8.

24. Indeed, so similar that the two firms seem headed for a megamerger. In this essay, however, I refer to Time-Warner and Turner as separate entities even though they have announced their intentions. I do this because, as of February 1996, the merger has not yet been finalized and Ted Turner has been quoted in the trade press as expressing reservations about going through with the deal. Furthermore, federal regulators have not yet given the go-ahead. As with the proposed Bell Atlantic-TCI deal two years ago, mergers of huge, multifaceted corporate entities can go awry before they are consummated. Nevertheless, the fate of the TWT deal is of little consequence as far as my argument goes. Whether operating as one or two corporate entities, these firms will continue to pursue the strategies discussed in this essay.

25. Interview in *Wired* (March 1995):112.

26. Ibid. Sassa's use of the term "copyright" to refer to cultural forms points to the increasing emphasis on intellectual property law as a means of controlling distribution in a fragmented and globalized market environment. Rosemary Coombe examines the implications of this strategy so far as oppositional and parodic modes of expression are concerned in *Cultural Appropriations: Authorship, Alterity and the Law* (New York: Routledge, 1997).

27. Zelnick: 21. My use of the term casual labor force may seem strange when referring to film stars or popular musicians. Unlike agricultural laborers, temporary office staff, or part-time factory workers, these performers command lavish compensation packages. Yet this top tier of the entertainment industry conceals the far larger pool of creative workers who toil long hours for little pay and no benefits. The key to success for these workers is to convince decision makers in the industry that they understand what it takes to produce hit material. And the key to success for industry executives is to secure an advantageous contract before leveraging a performer's career into the realm of stellar popularity. The success rate on both sides of the equation is extremely low. Nevertheless, the corporate conglomerate can counterbalance its losses, whereas the casual creative worker is particularly vulnerable to market forces. This labor

strategy is not entirely new, of course. Postwar antitrust actions, such as the 1948 Paramount case, sparked the trend toward casual labor in the film industry. Other parts of the culture industries were similarly affected. Yet deregulation since the late 1970s has failed to reverse this trend, largely because of the forces described here. These flexible relationships between creative and administrative talent were first described by Paul M. Hirsch, "Processing Fads and Fashions: An Organization-Set Analysis of Cultural Industry Systems," *American Journal of Sociology* 77 (1972):639–659.

28. Anthony Giddens, *The Consequences of Modernity* (Stanford, Calif.: Stanford University Press, 1990); Erving Goffman, *Behavior in Public Places* (New York: Free Press, 1963).

29. Shortly after Mosaic began to grow in popularity, some of the developers were lured away to join a small entrepreneurial venture called Netscape. By the time of this writing, Netscape had rapidly grown to be the industry standard on the World Wide Web, a matter of intense concern to Microsoft's Bill Gates, who understands the importance of software standards as a way of controlling the distribution of cultural forms. Gates has come up with a competing Web browser, and Netscape is now reportedly looking for a large corporate partner in hopes of bolstering its fortunes in the showdown with Microsoft.

30. Music is an obvious example of dispersed creativity, with the "capitals" of various styles being located in diverse locales: Chicago blues, Nashville country-western, Austin alternative country-western, New Orleans Cajun-pop, Seattle grunge, Athens (Georgia) alternative rock-pop, etc. Entertainment firms are now feverishly in search of new locales and are said to be scouting the garage band scene in such locations as Columbus, Ohio. Ethan Smith and Mike Flaherty, "Local Heroes," *Entertainment Weekly*, 17 March 1995, pp. 28–30.

31. Regarding these changes, see Janet L. Abu-Lughod, *Changing Cities* (New York: Harper Collins, 1991), and Manuel Castells, *The Informational City: Information Technology, Economic Restructuring and the Urban-Regional Process* (Oxford: Basil Blackwell, 1989).

32. Edward W. Soja, *Postmodern Geographies: The Reassertion of Space in Critical Social Theory* (New York: Verso, 1989).

33. National and global media events still pull together huge audiences on an occasional basis, but I am referring here to the more common tendency for large groups of people to share exposure to cultural phenomena in a more temporally diffuse manner. For example, the advertising agency D'Arcy Masius Benton & Bowles conducted a global study of the attitudes and market behaviors of teenagers around the globe in 1994. It argues that a world youth culture does in fact exist based on shared (but not necessarily simultaneous) exposure to specific trends in clothing, media, and popular amusements. "The World's Teenagers," *Sparks!* (A proprietary study from D'Arcy Masius Benton & Bowles, 1994).

34. On MTV, see Andrew Goodwin, *Dancing in the Distraction Factory: Music Television and Popular Culture* (Minneapolis: University of Minnesota Press, 1992).

21.
WHEN CREATORS, CORPORATIONS AND CONSUMERS COLLIDE

Napster and the Development of On-line Music Distribution

Tom McCourt and Patrick Burkart

The development of the information-based 'New Economy' is due in large part to the growth in industries that trade in intellectual property. These industries have been a leading sector in US economic expansion for the past two decades, and currently account for over $40 billion of the US gross national product (Mann, 1998: 41). Intellectual property cases at some law firms have more than quadrupled in the past seven years, with clients now including banks, chemical companies and sports leagues as well as communication companies (Stern, 2000: G12). US public policy has played an active role in shepherding the growth of intellectual property. The 1996 Telecommunications Act encouraged consolidation and cross-ownership within and between telecommunications and media industries, which have since spent billions of dollars to find new markets for their products and services. In addition, the 1998 Digital Millennium Copyright Act (DMCA) extended intellectual property protection to domains previously overlooked by federal copyright law. The US government also has worked aggressively to increase the international copyright interests of US media conglomerates through World Intellectual Property Organization trade negotiations as well as GATT and other agreements.

Despite these frequent and predictable interventions by the US government in matters of commerce and intellectual property, a naive perspective, which we term the Internet Nirvana Theory of intellectual property, pervades domestic public policy discourse on the 'New Economy'. According to this theory, the Internet is an arena of free exchange in which everyone wins. Creators of intellectual property will regain control over copyright while reducing barriers to entry and distributor interference in their productions. Distributors will gain a huge new revenue stream, eliminating material costs, overheads and geographic boundaries while creating opportunities for subscription and licensing systems that require perpetual repurchase of their goods and services. Consumer-electronics and computer companies will sell new recorders, playback systems and auxiliary devices. Technology companies will reap a windfall through patents on anti-copying software and license fees. Service providers like telephone and cable companies will see growing demand for lucrative broadband services. Consumers will find innumerable choices at low cost as the Internet becomes a 'vast intellectual commons' in which 'nothing will ever again be out of print or impossible to find; every scrap of human culture transcribed, no matter how obscure or commercially unsuccessful, will be available to all' (Mann, 2000: 41).

Transaction Cost Economics informs this libertarian vision of 'friction-less capitalism' (cf. Gates, 1996), in which the Internet engenders continual gains in productivity and perfect market equilibrium between producers and consumers. A corollary, the Electronic Market Hypothesis, posits that networked computer technology will match buyers and sellers quickly and at minimal cost in a transparent market space (Kretschmer et al., 2000: 4). However, the dotcom dissolutions of 2000–2, coupled with a growing imposition of Old Economy intellectual property controls on the Internet, seriously challenge Internet Nirvana Theory. Peer-to-peer exchange of audio-visual information is now commercial by mandate, by creating the incentive or requiring host networks to impose subscription, authentication and billing technologies on their users.

These actions are reflected by the means with which the Big Five record companies (EMI, Universal, Sony, Time Warner and BMG [Bertelsmann]) have extended their market dominance to the Internet.[1] The Napster system of peer-to-peer sound file trading posed a serious challenge to the existing recording industry, but the decision in *A&M Records et al.* v. *Napster* firmly established the on-line intellectual property rights of entertainment industry conglomerates and reinforced the Big Five's existing market oligopoly. The defeat of Napster puts an end to one form of unregulated Internet market exchange. The question remains what the new platform for music distribution will be, and what flexibility and sharing of roles between creators, publishers and consumers will be allowed. Relying on news reports and industry analyses in trade publications, we use a political economic perspective to frame a stakeholder analysis of the on-line music market. We conclude that the Big Five seek a transdimensional extension of copyright law and leak-proof control of distribution channels through legislation, litigation, mergers and acquisitions, and anti-copying technologies. These actions have marked the first stage of Old Economy power over on-line delivery of music, video and text. The Napster case began as a lawsuit by the international music oligopoly against an Internet start-up, but results in a regime in which private Internet communities must either police themselves or submit to corporate or state surveillance.

The Music Industry in Transition

The entertainment industry is increasingly central to the domestic and global economies. In 1999, creative industries (film, video, audio, print and software) employed more workers than any other US manufacturing sector (Ziedler, 2000). As Vogel (1998: 132) notes, the recording industry may be the most pervasive and therefore fundamental of the entertainment

industries. It suffered a slump in the mid-1990s as catalog sales reached saturation and the novelty of a new delivery system (compact discs) wore off. The Big Five reinforced their standing through the outright suppression of digital audiotape (which offered higher quality duplication than audio cassettes) for the consumer market, and began phasing out prerecorded cassettes in favor of CDs, which return higher revenues at a lower manufacturing cost per unit. However, attempts at recycling catalogs through new but inferior delivery systems (Digital Compact Cassette and Minidisc) were unsuccessful, and more entertainment alternatives, such as video games, vied for consumer dollars. But after 1997, a strong economic upsurge helped buoy the recording industry and, by June 2000, some entertainment industry leaders, embracing Internet Nirvana Theory, forecast that the Big Five could triple their profits through Internet delivery. Analysts predicted on-line sales of music rising from $836 million in 2000 to $5.36 billion in 2005 (Lyn, 2000: 1; Mathews and Bridis, 2001: A24).

While the Big Five are positioning themselves individually and collectively to maintain their control over music production and distribution, they are also fighting off legal challenges to their dominance. In May 2000, the US Federal Trade Commission (FTC) ruled that the five major record companies illegally discouraged discount pricing of compact discs by retail stores. By withholding cash payments intended for cooperative advertising from retailers that advertised CDs below the suggested 'minimum advertised price', the Big Five artificially inflated CD prices.[2] On 8 August 2000, a coalition of 30 states and US territories also filed suit against the record industry for price fixing (Peers, 2000b: B7). The big five settled this suit in 2002. These legal challenges underscore the fact that Big Five have an obfuscated and multivariate role in the music value chain, depending on what facet of their business (promoter, agent, publisher and/or record company) is involved in a transaction in what role or roles.

Technological developments also have threatened the Big Five's hegemony over music distribution. The earliest form of digital content storage suitable for delivery by modem and PC was the WAV standard; three-minute songs in this format, however, required hours to download. In 1987, the Motion Picture Experts Group (MPEG, a branch of the Geneva-based International Organization for Standardization) developed new digital audio and video compression software. The most powerful version, MPEG-1 Layer 3 (MP3), could compress a 40-megabyte file to one-tenth of its original size. Meanwhile modem speeds increased, and songs could now be downloaded easily onto hard drives. However, MP3 developed outside of the Big Five's control, and offered no intrinsic protections against copying. MP3s therefore threatened the music industry by holding out the 'possibility of a business model that links artists directly to consumers, bypassing the record companies completely' (Garofalo, 1999: 349).

While MP3 undoubtedly will be succeeded by systems that afford greater possibilities for copy protection, it currently has a momentum that diminishes chances for the immediate adoption of a different format. The ubiquity of unprotected MP3 files has set hardware and software divisions of media conglomerates at odds. While consumer electronics divisions want digital music players that would be easy to use and free of restrictions, record companies want a player akin to a 'digital Fort Knox' (Strauss, 1999: B1). These conflicts also underscore the problems of synergy in recent mergers, such as Time Warner and America Online. As the *Wall Street Journal* noted, 'To Time Warner executives producing music, the Web makes stealing pirated copies of their products far too easy. AOL, on the other hand, has grown up in a Web culture that favors the free dissemination of everything from music to movies' (Peers and Wingfield, 2000: B1).

Despite these conflicts, record companies remain attractive to media conglomerates. In December 1998, the number of major recording companies dropped to five when Seagram bought PolyGram Records and merged it into its Universal division. Vivendi (the French wireless company) then purchased Seagram for $34 billion in 2000.[3] Recordings have marginal production costs compared to other electronic media, which can compensate for losses on movies and other costly products across divisions. Record companies also provide immediate cash flow to their parent companies, and their catalogs can generate money for decades through reissues, compilations and licensing. As record companies are absorbed into conglomerates, they are expected to provide predictable revenue streams and have greater quarter-to-quarter accountability. The recording

industry has thus attempted to bolster short-term profits through rapid turnover of new artists and 'blockbuster' releases that can be cross-promoted in other media. Long-term profits have been addressed by extending and deepening intellectual property controls through the strategies we describe below.

Public Actions

Legislation

The recording industry earns profits by controlling intellectual property rights. On the distribution end of the value chain, record companies currently earn revenues from retail sales and the licensing of content for use in other media. On the production end, the business resembles a numbers game. While record companies claim to lose money on most releases, they compensate for failures with huge hits and catalog sales.[4] Although copyright protections are universally justified as incentives for individuals to create, recordings (particularly those of new artists) are often contractually defined as 'work for hire', or collective works akin to films, on grounds that they involve producers, engineers and other personnel in addition to the featured artist. Therefore, these recordings are owned by the companies that finance and market them, not by the artist whose name appears on them. Empirical studies suggest strongly that control of copyright gives rise to collusive behavior and rent-seeking among record companies, creating strong incentives for price fixing (Klaes, in Dolfsma, 2000). Such collusion is correlated with increasing vertical integration in the entertainment industry (Towse, in Dolfsma, 2000).

The Big Five have been instrumental in recent legislation concerning intellectual property. The Audio Home Recording Act of 1992 authorized consumers to make copies of digital music for personal, noncommercial use, yet prohibited serial copies, mandating that consumer CD and DAT recorders incorporate Serial Copy Management System (SCMS) technology, which allows a single digital copy to be made from a digital source but disallows second-generation digital copies.[5] The Digital Performance Rights in Sound Recordings Act of 1995 gave the owners of sound recordings (i.e. the record companies) exclusive control over their music in on-line webcasts. In contrast, radio stations have freedom to use music as they wish after acquiring a license from songwriters' organizations (Krasilovsky and Shemel, 2000: 79).

The two most important legislative acts affecting the content industries, however, were passed in 1998: the Sonny Bono Term Extension Act and the Digital Millennium Copyright Act (DMCA). In the former, Congress, responding to industry pressure, extended existing copyright protection for an additional 20 years. Authored works are covered for the life of the author plus 70 years, corporate-owned 'works for hire' for 95 years.[6] Section 1201(a) of the DMCA made it illegal to circumvent copy-protection technologies; the purpose of bypass is immaterial. The DMCA eliminated 'fair use' provisions of the 1976 Federal Copyright Act, dismissing the tenet that we buy the right to make unlimited copies for personal use after purchasing an original copy.[7] The DMCA also treated Internet service providers and telecommunications networks as publishers, rather than common carriers, with the intent of forcing these networks to bar their users from sharing copyrighted material (Gomes, 2001: B4).

Intellectual property protections are negotiated in a policy environment that responds to the dynamic relationship between technological innovation and industrial interests. Copyright originally covered books; it was extended to maps and charts in 1790, to prints in 1802 and music in 1831, and subsequently to broadcasts, films and software. Mead (1999) finds that:

> [T]he Copyright Act of 1790 stands as the point of divorce between the perceived purposes (which became the protection of authors and publishers) and the methodology of the law (which remained to protect a movable-type based printing industry). The understood goal of the law was set adrift from the actual workings of the law.
>
> (in Chartrand, 2000)

Today, intellectual property rights are bought and sold on the market, independently of creators, by corporate entities largely devoted to promotion and marketing. Dolfsma (2001: 2) claims that the principal function of copyright is now to supply revenues to administrative organizations and intermediaries with little or no creative function, 'such as record companies and music publishers'. Moreover, copyright now covers anything 'fixed in a tangible medium of expression' and reaches anyone who makes a copy or other use of the original work. The result, Lessig (2000: 1) argues, is that '[c]opyright has thus morphed from a short, relatively insignificant regulation of publishers to a restriction that is effectively perpetual, and that regulates anyone with access to a computer or Xerox machine'.

Litigation

The domestic recording industry claims to lose $300 million per year to pirate recordings; a report prepared for the recording industry predicted that by 2002, an estimated 16 percent of all US music sales, or $985 million, would be lost to on-line piracy (Foege, 2000: BU4).[8] The Big Five focused their mounting concerns about piracy in all formats on the legal case against Napster, which was released on the Internet in August 1999. Napster functioned as a music search engine that linked participants to a huge and constantly updated library of user-provided MP3s.[9] Its key architectural feature was an on-line database of song titles and performers, searchable by keyword. The Napster network's MusicShare client provided access to search indices and file lists of those using the service. Its brokered architecture effectively coordinated peers and increased search functionality, and its search and play interface was highly user-friendly. Napster also carried a strong populist appeal, harkening back to the digital bonhomie of the early Internet, in which users traded files directly with each other. From the Napster network's perspective, the larger the connected base of its peer-to-peer system, the greater the value of the network to creators, advertisers and consumers. Devout believers in the Internet Nirvana Theory depicted Napster as a classic 'win-win' proposition.

No sooner had Napster become a 'killer app' than legal woes beset the company. The Recording Industry Association of America (RIAA), a lobbying and trade group representing the Big Five's interests, filed suit against Napster on 7 December 1999, claiming that the free service cut into sales of CDs. Napster's enabling architecture became its legal vulnerability: when a computer with peer-to-peer software is connected to the Internet, it is configured to be both a receiver or client and a sender or server, and its user has become a publisher as well as a consumer. The legal case against Napster turned on the fact that although it did not generate revenue, the service supplied users with peer-to-peer software and provided a brokering service that managed a real-time index of available music files. This combination of marketed products and services, the RIAA argued, effectively turned Napster into a music piracy service. Napster's defenders claimed that its users enjoyed First Amendment protection, so the state could not enforce a prior restraint on the speech of Napster's user/publishers. Its attorneys also argued that the service's 'substantial, non-infringing uses' included allowing users to sample new music and 'space-shift' their collections between delivery systems like CDs and hard drives (Gomes, 2000: A3; M. Lewis, 2000: 1).[10]

Between February and August 2000, the number of Napster users rose from 1.1 million to 6.7 million, making it the fastest-growing software application ever recorded (Media Metrix, 2000). In late July, at the RIAA's request, Federal judge Marilyn Patel ordered an injunction against Napster, finding that the service was used primarily to download copyrighted music and rejecting Napster's arguments. In February 2001, a three-judge panel unanimously upheld the injunction, and Napster soon began filtering its system to block copyrighted material.[11] Napster declared bankruptcy and ceased operations in 2002. Despite the RIAA's claims that Napster-driven piracy was eating into profits, recorded music sales in US reached an all-time high of 785.1 million units in 2000, up 4 percent from 1999. The RIAA claimed that sales of CD singles dropped 39 percent in 2000 and inferred that Napster was to blame, yet fewer CD singles were released as the industry cut production. Some market research suggests that users did not utilize Napster primarily to 'steal' music through non-payment. Instead, they used Napster to 'sample' music before purchasing it. Users also were drawn to the huge array of music it presented, the obscure as well as the popular – a vast catalog (including out-of-print material) that was otherwise inaccessible.[12]

The record industry's legal actions against Napster have increased the prospective transaction costs in e-commerce. Although cybercapitalism in theory should be 'frictionless', eliminating middlemen and cutting overhead costs, the Napster precedent reintroduces friction and increases the legal basis for artificially high consumer prices. We argue that corporate concerns about piracy are a legal and public relations foil for the entertainment industry, and propose that the Big Five's pursuit of the Napster case was not a response to falling profitability due to piracy, but instead a successful counter-strategy to relieve anti-trust pressures while legally securing a claim to the Internet as an alternative delivery system to retail outlets. The timing of the Napster case is critical, as it was initiated at the same time as lawsuits against the Big Five for price fixing by US federal and state agencies.

It is doubtful that on-line distribution will significantly reduce costs to consumers, given the track record for pricing of previous formats. Record companies make higher margins from CDs than they did from vinyl LPs. Despite similar manufacturing costs and royalty payments to artists, CD prices have risen approximately 12 percent since 1998. The industry standard may rise to $18.98 and possibly $20, prices comparable to those in England and Japan (Strauss, 1998: B3).[13] Although on-line distribution eliminates raw materials, storage and shipping, the Big Five have priced downloads of singles between $2 and $4 per song. The cost basis has been calculated by the record industry as the 'expense of encoding the music, royalties for the encryption, maintaining and operating the hardware and additional customer service' (Strauss, 2000: B3).

Private Actions

Mergers and Acquisitions

Despite the RIAA's public claims that no legal means for on-line music-sharing exists, the Big Five have privately hedged their bets through mergers and acquisitions that would allow file-sharing under their exclusive control. Shortly after the Napster decision, Bertelsmann (the only privately held company among the Big Five) broke ranks with the other major record companies on 31 October 2000, and announced that it would loan Napster $50 million to develop a secure file-sharing system that would 'preserve the Napster experience' while compensating copyright holders. Bertelsmann was attracted by Napster's corporate identity, tangible assets and software (including the protocol and interface). In exchange, Bertelsmann retained the right to take a 58 percent interest in Napster when the new service is developed (Gomes et al., 2000: A3).

Bertelsmann's actions regarding Napster follow the example of the Musicbank storage locker service, which obtained licenses for content from Universal, Warner and Bertelsmann only after granting these companies an equity stake. The case of MP3.com is also instructive in this regard. MP3.com's stock was valued as high as $63.61 before the company was hit by a barrage of copyright infringement lawsuits from artists, publishers and record labels against its MyMP3.com storage locker. In May 2001, seven months after winning a $54.3 million judgment from the company, Vivendi purchased MP3.com for $372 million.[14] Vivendi offered $5 per share for MP3.com's stock, which had traded for only $3.01 per share before the acquisition was announced (Sorkin, 2001: C1). Despite its legal liabilities, MP3.com was attractive to Vivendi because it was one of the few firms with the technological infrastructure in place to operate a large-scale on-line distribution service.

In 2000–01, a NASDAQ crash cut the value of the US technology index 60 percent, and effectively burst the speculative bubble surrounding the Internet (Harmon, 2001: C1). As venture capital dried up, the number of e-commerce firms (including those devoted to on-line music recording, distribution and marketing) dropped significantly. This shakeout followed historical patterns of consolidation among new communication and transportation industries that required extensive capitalization, including rail-roads, automobiles, airlines, telephone companies and personal computers (cf. Chandler, 1977). The crash in Internet industrial capitalization was concurrent with the Napster lawsuit, and the Big Five repeatedly used high-profile lawsuits to deter venture capitalists from providing second- and third-round funding to Internet start-up companies. Offering funding and/or content licenses to these start-ups in exchange for equity, the Big Five acquired Internet distribution infrastructure below market value, and also saved research and development costs. Most importantly, they thwarted the creation of independent distribution systems. Alongside the Big Five's use of new template contracts that include on-line distribution rights and Internet domain names, the takeovers of Napster, MP3.com and other services gave the music oligopoly a growth strategy for a newly tamed Internet, as well as a possible way to minimize the delivery bottleneck of retail sales of physical recordings (Kretschmer et al., 2000: 10).

Many observers of the Napster case were surprised at the ease with which entrenched old-economy business interests triumphed over technological innovations that could empower creators and consumers. The legal pullback on Napster, and its subsequent appropriation by the Big Five, has historical precedents. While new communication technologies may initially appear to challenge and undermine pre-existing controls on content and distribution, they can ultimately benefit the status quo. Nearly a century ago, music publishers, alarmed that piano rolls would cut into sales of sheet music, filed a copyright lawsuit against manufacturers of these rolls. The publishers lost their case in the Supreme Court, but they nevertheless persuaded the US Congress to require manufacturers of rolls (and, subsequently, phonograph records) to pay them royalties. Publishers later sued radio stations to stop the widespread practice of broadcasting musical works without paying royalties. These stations countered that their broadcasts increased sales of sheet music, but their argument failed in court, and commercial radio stations have paid to broadcast music ever since (Goldstein, 2000: A25). Live television, and later rebroadcast TV and the home videocassette recorder were all initially perceived as threatening by the film industry. Today, however, studio income from video sales and rentals rivals box-office receipts.

Technology

Despite the global framework developing for intellectual property, the US model for copyright protection is not shared universally. This model makes copyright the financial concern of an industrial group and its stable of artists. In contrast, the European model of moral rights affords creators greater control over the alteration of their works, and assigns pecuniary rights traditionally a secondary or derivative value (Vaver, 1987, in Chartrand, 2000: 231–2). This and other cultural and legal differences have led the European Union to mobilize tariff and non-tariff barriers to free trade with the US in audio-visual products. To circumvent trade conflicts and international disparities in copyright enforcement, the transnational Big Five media firms have united behind Digital Rights Management (DRM) technologies. These technologies 'lock up' content through 'trusted systems' in which copy protection is built into every component sold – the operating system, the artifact and the player.

In December 1998, the Secure Digital Music Initiative (SDMI) was formed by a consortium of record companies, hardware and software manufacturers, and distribution companies to create a universal DRM system. SDMI's 200 members include AOL, AT&T, IBM, Microsoft, Matsushita, Sony, RealNetworks, Liquid Audio, ASCAP, Intel and Napster. Significantly, no consumer or civil rights groups are represented. Based on watermarking technology, SDMI's system is intended to serve as a gate through which content must pass. The system enables time limits on use, restricts the potential number of copies that the purchaser can make from an authenticated original, and permits the tracing of protected content back to the original purchaser.

However, development of the SDMI standard has lagged far behind schedule. Its members have highly divergent and often antagonistic interests, and dissension within its ranks led executive director Leonard Chiariglione to resign in January 2001. These organizational antagonisms were aggravated by a problem intrinsic to software development: every protection scheme can be broken. Shortly after SDMI's founding, the *New York Times* stated, '[SDMI] believes it can do in less than a year what the entire computer software industry has been unable to do in two decades: stop software piracy' (P. Lewis, 1998: D3).[15] Moreover, DRM technologies to date have resulted in products that are complicated to use, and watermarks may degrade sound quality. Since much music is already available for free in some form to gain exposure, and since the Internet's overall lack of central control also reduces the ability to control distribution points, DRM may inadvertently inhibit the popularization of on-line music distribution channels.

Despite these problems, DRM may become a *fait accompli*. On-line rights management was legitimated by the Napster decision, which set a new cost basis for legal claims against infringing parties. DRM technology could therefore become required by law, as was the case with SCMS. Or, equally likely in an environment of industry consolidation and federal anti-regulatory sentiment, DRM could be imposed through private agreements between colluding copyright owners and their related hardware manufacturing divisions, initially beyond the reach of public authority. DRM would impose new costs on consumers by rendering existing formats and hardware obsolete. It also would defeat one of the principles of intellectual property most nettlesome to corporate interests: while copyright is designed to cover works for a limited amount of time, the incorporation of DRM into distribution would copy-protect them forever.

Why Record Companies will Survive

The Napster decision formalizes the implementation of intellectual property controls on the Internet, and consolidates the Big Five's advantages in gatekeeping content and distributing products. Although the Internet in theory allows both creators and distributors to bypass traditional promotional media (print, radio and television) for direct access to consumers, in practice the lockup of the Internet for the Big Five and their parent companies gives them sizeable cross-promotional and cross-industrial channels for marketing products on-line as well as off-line. The Internet provides an enhanced marketplace for record companies, since goods may be copied and transported over the Internet at marginal costs, and unwanted goods may easily be disposed of or delisted. By implementing rights-managed distribution on the Internet, the Big Five will be able to buy, sell and resell audiences and intellectual property in a kind of market arbitrage. This arrangement is possible because, '[w]ithout the material substratum restraining them, commodities may respond instantly to the fractal climate of fashion' (Stallabrass, 1996: 62–3).[16] Envisioning a plethora of on-line packages for consumers, Edgar Bronfman of Seagram predicted: 'You'll be able to program bundles or song packages, compilations, video singles and video compilations. You'll be able to buy or program songs by genre, by era, by the hour or half-hour or minute or day' (Peers, 2000: R14).

The Big Five may find a subscription model to be most lucrative, whereby users pay a flat monthly fee to access record company catalogs via computers, fixed and portable stereos, cell phones and 'Internet appliances'.[17] In April 2001, two subscription systems were announced: Duet (now PressPlay), a project of Universal, Sony and Yahoo; and MusicNet, comprised of BMG, Warner, EMI, AOL and RealNetworks (Markoff, 2001: C1; Wingfield and Ordonez, 2001: B5). These systems have precedents in CD-ROMs and video games, in which users buy a license that allows them to access information. Unlike one-time sales, subscriptions generate steady cash flow and provide a convenient benchmark by which to measure growth. Since subscriptions are usually paid in advance of receiving the product or service, they avoid the volatility of retail sales or pay-per-play. Subscriptions also maximize revenues from those who use the service infrequently, while encouraging increased use among heavy users, and allow the provider to charge higher rates to advertisers (Meyers, 2001: 25). These companies can also harness a growing collection of customer databases derived from Web activity to reduce marketing uncertainty and provide revenues through resale to other vendors (cf. Gandy, 1993).

Subscriptions present new challenges, however. According to one observer:

> [R]evenue generated [by subscription] is contractually considered 'other income'; by federal statute, record companies would have to pay artists a significantly larger cut than what they typically earn from CD sales. If subscription services supplant CD sales, label groups will make less money, paying artists more and making less per song.
>
> (Zisson, 2001: 1)

Subscription prices would need to make up in volume what is lost in profitability, suggesting cost pressures and even price wars among music services. Subscriptions also would penalize chain music stores and retail outlets, which now account for 80 percent of sales in the popular music market. Large catalogs also would require on-line music subscription services to negotiate separate licensing deals with potentially hundreds of record companies, thousands of music publishers, numerous codec license holders, and developers of copy-protection software, all of whom will seek a portion of revenues.

Despite the problems and potential resistance to such a model within the recording industry, no proven alternatives to subscriptions have emerged. Record companies may try to offer their own subscription models, but ultimately will have to license their catalogs to each other to attract the largest number of users. Yet licensing content between the Big Five invites anti-trust action; in 1995, the major record companies dropped their plans to create a competitor to MTV after a Justice Department investigation (Banks, 1996: 82). The Big Five undoubtedly remember their experience with MTV, which asserted marketing controls that conflicted with music industry initiatives, and so may also be wary of allowing third parties to promote and distribute their products over the Internet.

As Kretschmer et al. (2000: 10) state, 'It is always dangerous to open up a new market if it threatens you in the old.' Copyright litigation has been a successful stalling tactic, allowing the Big Five to reorganize their business relationships and sort out on-line delivery systems in a way that will preserve their *de facto* oligopoly of production and distribution. This tendency is evidenced in the growing scope and density of interlocking legal ties and technologies that protect the music industry oligopoly. As they cross the threshold into the era of digital distribution, these ostensibly competitive record companies have united behind the RIAA and SDMI in attempts to control content and distribution. The recent litigation surrounding on-line music delivery is intended to protect the Big Five's intellectual property rights on the Internet and allow it to create additional revenue streams, but the implications of this litigation are much broader. Despite lip service to the rights of creators, entertainment and media companies are increasingly confiscating these rights through what Hugenholtz (2000: 1) terms the 'copyright grab'. Corporate copyright holders seek to maximize the value of their properties by pursuing international copyright protections, by suing for closure of distributors who refuse cooperation on their terms and then absorbing their operations, and by collaborating on DRM technology. The result is that the recording industry oligopoly has systematically extended its lien on intellectual property into new dimensions of social space as well as cyberspace.

The Big Five have expanded their own options for putting more new products into larger and larger markets, but their efforts have also led to what Ronald Bettig views as 'the continuing enclosure of the intellectual and artistic commons', in which 'more and more knowledge and culture are being privately appropriated and submitted to the logic of the marketplace' (P. Lewis, 2000: A17). The Internet Nirvana theorists hoped that Napster would remain exempt from the rest of the intellectual property regime – that a renewed commitment to social regulation based on technological innovation and deregulation, would help the world avoid the fate of cultural enclosure by the culture industries. Dolfsma (2000: 1), writing optimistically before the Napster verdict, stated, 'Currently technological developments and a liberal, free market ideology are working together to create a global economic sphere' – even in acknowledgment of entrenched, anti-competitive conglomerates, industry collusion and the impulse to consolidation enabled by industry deregulation. With few concessions to creators or consumers, the Big Five have disproved Internet Nirvana Theory by successfully using copyright enforcement to tighten their grip on Internet music distribution. The events in the wake of the Napster verdict suggest that, while cyberspace affords new means of packaging and delivery, the ultimate commercial value of music is not an inherent character of the product, but of the manner in which it reaches the user. The commercialization of the Internet transforms the experience of on-line music from a network-enabled community of freely participating individuals to a network-delivered commodity that is relentlessly measured and metered.

Notes

We are grateful to Hugo Burgos, David Bywaters, Cynthia Meyers, Eric Rothenbuhler, and Sharon Strover for comments on earlier drafts of this article. Of course, any faults or errors in this work are our own. Earlier versions of this paper were presented at the 2001 annual meeting of the International Communications Association in Washington, DC and the Global Fusion 2001 Conference in St Louis, Missouri.

1. In 1999, these companies collectively controlled 77.5 percent of the global market in recording sales and 87 percent of recording sales in the US. The 1999 global industrial rankings were as follows: Universal, 21.8 percent; Sony, 19.0 percent; EMI, 12.9 percent; Warner Music Group, 11.9 percent; BMG, 11.9 percent. Domestically, the rankings were Universal, 28.11 percent; Sony, 19.47 percent; BMG, 15.24 percent; Warner, 12.82 percent; EMI, 11.38 percent (Goldsmith et al., 2001. A25).

2. The minimum advertised price strategy was intended to aid local retailers, which were being undercut by electronics 'superstore' chains like Best Buy and Circuit City, which used CDs as 'loss leaders' to entice consumers. The FTC estimated the cost of the minimum advertising price strategy to consumers between 1996 and 1999 at $480 million (Wilke, 1999: A3; Peers and Ramstad, 2000: B1).

3. A proposed joint venture between Warner and EMI would have created a $20 billion colossus that would be the largest music publisher and one of two largest record companies in the world. The proposal was withdrawn when the European Commission threatened to reject a proposed merger of Time Warner and AOL. A subsequent attempt by BMG to purchase EMI failed for similar reasons (Goldsmith and Boston, 2000: B8; Shishkin and Wilke, 2000: A3).

4. In 1999, only 88 recordings accounted for 25 percent of all record sales. This number amounted to three-tenths of 1 percent of all CDs issued (Mann, 2000: 50).

5. The Act also implemented a tax on digital recorders and recording media, with the bulk of proceeds going to the record companies. Given the fact that electronics manufacturers now own record companies, they pay themselves a tax.

6. The 'work for hire' status of recordings has long been disputed between record companies and artists, who see themselves enjoying a status similar to book authors, rather than working as employees of record companies. Although most recordings are works for hire, the 1976 Federal Copyright Act allowed recording artists to reclaim their copyrights after 35 years for all contracts dated after 1 January 1978. In November 1999, an amendment was slipped into an unrelated bill (the Satellite Home Viewer Improvement Act) that would have allowed record companies to retain the rights for the full length of copyright (95 years) (Pareles, 2000: B1). The amendment was defeated in the House and Senate after extensive lobbying by performers.

7. In October 2000, the US Copyright Office allowed only two minor three-year exemptions to the law. One exemption involves Internet filters, which would enable

people to circumvent software encryption and see what sites are being filtered. The other allows users to bypass malfunctioning security features on software they have purchased (Mathews, 2000b: B10).

8. However, some executives acknowledged that the Internet is not a threat to profits. Jay Samit, senior vice-president of EMI, told Reuters news service in June 2000 that 'We've far more to fear from a surplus of CD manufacturing here in Asia, where in some markets 90 percent of CDs are bootlegged, than from the Internet' (Lyn, 2000: 2).

9. Peer-to-peer should not be confused with 'distributed processing', in which sections of large problems are distributed to client computers to achieve collective computational power that exceeds supercomputers. Brokered peer-to-peer networks like Napster use a central indexing server to keep track of files available on the system. More recent peer-to-peer systems like Gnutella and Freenet eliminate the client/server relationship, allowing users to connect directly to each other in constantly mutating networks.

10. Artists were divided over the impact of Napster on music sales. In April 2000, Metallica charged that Napster, along with Yale, Indiana and the University of Southern California, violated copyright laws by enabling students to swap digital music files. The band sought $10 million in damages (in a particularly striking irony, the band issued a free cassette demo tape in the early 1980s and encouraged fans to make copies as a promotional strategy). Rapper Dr Dre also filed lawsuit but other artists rallied to Napster's defense, including Limp Bizkit (who received tour funding from Napster), The Offspring and Public Enemy, whose leader, Chuck D., is one of the most virulent critics of the Big Five.

11. Yet the filtering procedure proved to be more difficult than anticipated as some songs were listed under a variety of names or had their titles misspelled. Additionally, some material not owned by record companies, or approved for Napster's 'Featured Music Program,' was removed without approval of artists (Richtel, 2001: C1).

12. A Yankelovich poll released in June 2000 reported that 66 percent of all respondents who had downloaded music said that 'listening to a song on-line has at least once prompted them to later buy a CD or cassette featuring the same song'. That same month, the Annenberg School at the University of Southern California released a survey finding that 63 percent of students who downloaded MP3s still bought the same number of CDs; 10 percent were buying more CDs; and 39 percent of students who downloaded MP3s purchased CDs that contained the same music due to their superior sound quality (Latonero, 2000: 2; Mathews, 2000a: A3).

13. In contrast, while videotapes were originally priced at $100 when introduced in early 1980s, copying and ubiquity has lowered their prices in some cases to $10, in spite of inflation and no major technological advances.

14. MP3.com had previously settled copyright infringement claims with the other four major record companies for $20 million each.

15. A Microsoft executive belittled the record industry's complaints: 'The software industry loses more money to piracy than the record industry makes' (Shapiro, 1999: B4).

16. This fragmenting tendency was already evident with Napster: Andy Greenwald of *Spin* stated, '[Napster's] very nature – the trading of one song at a time – will place an emphasis on singles. In colleges one song tends to make a hot list, sweep the campus, and then be replaced by another the next week' (Paton, 2000: 1).

17. User authentication and profiling allow a subscription service to regulate access to music through the client software, network feeds, and the use of metadata or computer code attached to MP3 and other files. Metadata encoding of on-line assets permits companies to embed listening and recording restrictions into the media files themselves. A subscriptions-based or pay-per-play payment plan, coupled with metadata tagging of assets, is central to Napster's planned reconfiguration into a secure music delivery network.

References

Banks, J. (1996) *Monopoly Television: MTV's Quest to Control the Music*. Boulder, CO: Westview Press.

Chandler, A. (1977) *The Visible Hand: The Managerial Revolution in American Business*. Cambridge, MA: The Belknap Press.

Chartrand, H. (2000) 'Copyright C. P. U.: Creators, Proprieters, and Users', *Journal of Arts Management, Law, and Society* 30(3): 209–40.

Dolfsma, W. (2000) 'How Will the Music Industry Weather the Globalization Storm?', *First Monday* 5. Available at <http://firstmonday.org/issues/issue 5_5/dolfsma/index.html>.

Foege, A. (2000) 'Record Labels Are Hearing an Angry Song', *New York Times* 11 June: BU4.

Gandy, O. (1993) *The Panoptic Sort: A Political Economy of Personal Information* Boulder, CO. Westview Press

Garofalo, R. (1999) 'From Music Publishing to MP3: Music and Industry in the Twentieth Century', *American Music* 17(3): 318–53.

Gates, W., with N. Myhrvold and P. Rinearson (1996) *The Road Ahead*. New York: Penguin Books.

Goldsmith, C. and W. Boston (2000) 'Bertelsmann Says It May Join Sony in Music Linkup, but No Deal Is Set', *Wall Steet Journal* 2 February: B8.

Goldsmith, C., W. Boston and M. Peers (2001) 'EMI, Bertelsmann Unit End Merger Talks', *Wall Street Journal* 2 May: A25.

Goldstein, P. (2000) 'The Next Napster May Be an Insider', *New York Times* 28 April: A25.

Gomes, L. (2000) 'Napster Is Ordered to Stop the Music', *Wall Street Journal* 27 July: A3.

Gomes, L. (2001) 'Entertainment Firms Target Gnutella', *Wall Street Journal* 4 May: B6.

Gomes, L., W. Boston and A. Mathews. (2000) 'Bertelsmann, Napster Agree on Service', *Wall Street Journal* 1 November: A3.

Harmon, A. (2001) 'What Have E-consultants Wrought?', *New York Times* 13 May: C1.

Hugenholtz, P. (2000) 'The Great Copyright Robbery: Rights Allocation in a Digital Environment', paper presented at 'A Free Information Ecology in a Digital Environment Conference', New York University School of Law, 31 March–2 April 2000. Available on-line at <http://www.ivir.nl/Publicaties/hugneholtz/PBH-Ecology.doc>.

Klaes, M. (1997) 'Sociotechnical Constituencies, Game Theory, and the Diffusion of Compact Discs', *Research Policy* 25(8).

Krasilovsky, M. and S. Shemel (2000) *This Business of Music*, 8th edn. New York: Billboard Books.

Kretschmer, M., G. Klimis and R. Wallis. (2000) 'The Global Music Industry in the Digital Environment: A Study of Strategic Intent and Policy Responses (1996–99)', paper submitted to 'The Long Run: Conference on Long-term Developments in the Arts and Cultural Industries', Erasmus University, Rotterdam, 23–25 February.

Latonero, M. (2000) 'Survey of MP3 Usage: Report on a University Consumption Community', Annenberg School of Communication, University of Southern California, June.

Lessig, L. (2000) 'The Limits of Copyright', *The Standard* 19 June. Available at <http://www/thestandard.com/article/0,1902,16071,00.html>.

Lewis, M. (2000) 'Judge Rules against "Monster"; Napster to Appeal', *Webnoize* 26 July: 1. Available at, <http://news.webnoize.com/item.rs?ID = 9877>.

Lewis, P. (1998) 'Internet Music, to Go', *New York Times* 24 December: D3.

Lewis, P. (2000) 'The Artist's Friend Turned Enemy: A Backlash against Copyright', *New York Times* 8 January: A17.

Lyn, T. (2000) 'Internet to Offer Music Industry Better Returns', Reuters news release, 2 June: 1. Available at, <http://dailynews.yahoo.eom/h/nm/20000602/wr/music profit 1.html>.

Mann, C. (1998) 'Who Will Own Your Next Good Idea?', *Atlantic Monthly* September: 41.

Mann, C. (2000) 'The Heavenly Jukebox', *Atlantic Monthly* September: 41.

Markoff, J. (2001) 'New Venture to Seek Fees for Net Music', *New York Times* 13 April: C1.

Mathews, A. (2000a) 'Music Samplers on Web Buy CDs in Stores', *Wall Street Journal* 15 June: A3.

Mathews, A. (2000b) 'Copyrights on Web Content Are Backed', *Wall Street Journal* 27 October: B1O.

Mathews, A. and T. Bridis (2001) 'Music Labels Urge Congress to Stand by in Online Feud', *Wall Street Journal* 8 March: A24.

Mead, D. (2000) History of Copyright. Available at, <http://www.jps.net/dcm/copyright>.

Media Metrix (2000) 'Press Release', 11 October: 1. Available at <http://www.mediametrix.com/press/releases/20001005.jsp?language = us>.

Meyers, C. (2001) 'Entertainment Industry Integration Strategies', unpublished report, New York University.

Pareles, J. (2000) 'Musicians Take Copyright Issue to Congress', *New York Times* 25 May: B1.

Paton, N. (2000) 'Mom, I Blew Up the Music Industry', *The Observer* 21 May: 1. Available at <http://www.observer.co.uk/review/story/0,6903,223075,00.html>.

Peers, M. (2000a) 'In the Groove', *Wall Street Journal* 20 March: R14.

Peers, M. (2000b) 'States Sue Record Firms Over CD Pricing Policies', *Wall Street Journal* 9 August: B7.

Peers, M. and E. Ramstad (2000) 'Price of CDs Likely to Drop, Thanks to FTC,' *Wall Street Journal* 11 May: B1.

Peers, M. and N. Wingfield (2000) 'Seeking Harmony, AOL and Warner Music Hit Some Dissonant Notes', *Wall Street Journal* 18 April: B1.

Richtel, M. (2001) 'Music Industry and Napster Still at Odds', *New York Times* 21 March: C1.

Shapiro, E. (1999) 'Race Is on to Foil E-music Pirates', *Wall Street Journal* 22 January: B1.

Shishkin, P. and J. Wilke (2000) 'AOL-Time Warner Plan Hits Roadblock', *Wall Street Journal* 19 September: A3.

Sorkin, A. (2001) 'Vivendi in Deal for MP3.com to Lift Online Distribution', *New York Times* 21 May: C1.

Stallabrass, J. (1996) *Gargantua: Manufactured Mass Culture*. New York: Verso.

Stern, C. (2000) 'Copyright Issues Grab Spotlight', *Washington Post* 20 September: G12.

Strauss, N. (1998) 'The Industry vs. Web Pirates', *New York Times* 17 December: B3.

Strauss, N. (1999) 'Pirate-proof Music on Web? So Far, That Does Not Compute', *New York Times* 24 April: B1.

Strauss, N. (2000) 'Digital Music, Chapter 2', *New York Times* 2 August: B3.

Towse, R. (1998) 'The Lottery of Art: Risk and the Artist', paper presented at the ACEI Conference, Barcelona, Spain, June.

Vaver, D. (1987) 'Copyright in Foreign Works: Canada's International Obligations', *Canadian Bar Review* 66 (March).

Vogel, H. (1998) *Entertainment Industry Economics*, 4th edn. New York: Cambridge University Press.

Wilke, J. (1999) 'Music Firms, US Hold Settlement Talks', *Wall Street Journal* 16 December: A3.

Wingfield, N. and J. Ordonez (2001) 'Sony, Universal License Music to Yahoo!', *Wall Street Journal* 6 April: B5.

Ziedler, S. (2000) 'Entertainment and Internet Collision Course Ahead', *Yahoo News* 23 December: 1. Available at <http://www.jang.com.pk/thenews/investors/jan2001/spot.htm>.

Zisson, S. (2000) 'Digital Hollywood: Subscription Models No Longer "S" Word', *Webnoize News* 18 May: 1. Available at <http://news.webnoize.com/item.rs?ID = 9077>.

22.
THE CULTURAL AND POLITICAL ECONOMIES OF HYBRID MEDIA TEXTS

Marwan Kraidy

> The visibility of mimicry is always produced at the site of interdiction.
>
> —Homi Bhabha

The history of broadcasting before the satellite era is one of national systems in which different political outlooks and cultural policies engendered alternate functions for electronic mass communication: broadcasting was a tool of development in much of the non-Western world, a public service in Western Europe, an instrument of direct propaganda under authoritarian regimes, or a commercial enterprise in the United States and elsewhere. National considerations shaped the broadcasting operations inspired by these various media philosophies. Considered an important national asset, broadcasting was harnessed to promote social stability, foster economic development, and consolidate national unity. In addition to national political and socioeconomic factors, the limitations of available technology restricted the expansion of media activities to the confines of the nation-state. National considerations were therefore paramount in determining the agenda, policies, and content of electronic media.

A closer examination, however, suggests that broadcasting's presumed national scope is in effect an ideal type, not a technically accurate description of actual media operations. Since most broadcast signals travel in concentric circles and most countries are not circular in shape, signal spillover has been historically pervasive. Southern Norwegians can watch Swedish television over the air, and denizens of the eastern Mediterranean receive terrestrial signals of varying quality from Egyptian and Greek television stations during hot and humid summer nights. Some countries' public broadcasters, such as Japan's NHK, have committed extraordinary technical and financial assets to achieve universal national coverage of an insular territory that presents enormous physical challenges. It is also evident that many countries have used their national media for transnational influence: in the United States, television has been regarded as a global strategic asset since the emergence of the free flow doctrine during Woodrow Wilson's presidency, and later formulated as policy by Federal Communications Commission head Newton Minow (see Blanchard, 1986; Curtin, 1993). Nasser's Egypt harnessed radio as a redoubtably effective tool for pan-Arab mobilization, compelling the Saudi royal family to develop its own broadcasting operations. Last, cooperation agreements between governments to exchange programming have been a recurring phenomenon, indicating that national media systems are not hermetically sealed entities.

In the last two decades, information technologies have overcome many restraints on terrestrial broadcasting. The advent of geo-stationary satellites, whose orbit is calculated to follow Earth's movements in order to keep the coverage area, or footprint, constant has decreased the technical laboriousness and financial cost of television coverage. Global information networks have mitigated time and space restrictions, albeit selectively and asymmetrically. Faster, less costly, and more efficient information and transportation technologies have made it easier for companies and governments separated by oceans or landmass to cooperate on media ventures. The growing international regime of free trade and decreased government intervention has triggered some of these changes and exacerbated others, as states de facto relinquish the principle of prior consent and cope with a global system based on the free flow precept. These circumstances have inexorably pushed television's transnational and global expansion.

If technology made the transnational expansion of television possible, the neoliberal momentum that peaked in the late 1990s turned television into a largely deterritorialized, global industry. The deregulation of media and telecommunications has entailed the withdrawal of the state as an active manager of national broadcasting, and the concomitant rise in importance of the multinational corporations that now control much of world media activities. These corporations themselves restructured to embrace a post-Fordist modus operandi, as public and national media systems worldwide were thrust into a liberalization frenzy of privatizations, mergers, acquisitions, and vertical and horizontal integration. This transformation became ostensible in the 1990s, as world television screens filled up with internationalized programs, including talk and game shows, reality television, and music videos.

Transnational post-Fordist practices are the undertow of these industry trends. As an economic paradigm, post-Fordism focuses on procedures such as outsourcing, subcontracting, multidivisional competition and collaboration, and joint ventures, caused by a decentralized accumulation of capital. British film and television scholar Michael Wayne argues that political economists of the media have ignored or dismissed post-Fordism because it implies that capitalism's affinity to create monopolies has been at least partly set back. Wayne (2003) argues that post-Fordism is characterized by a "discrepancy between the real [economic] relations and their appearance forms" (p. 84), where industry consolidation is masked by the superficial appearance of pluralism and competition. These practices are "transnational," following Danish media scholar Preben Sepstrup (1990), for whom transnationalization is a primarily economic process which drives sociocultural change.

Another post-Fordist postulate is a belief in regional markets as a counterbalance to the power of global market forces (Wayne, 2003). There is indeed a process of regionalization going on in tandem with media globalization. While the giant conglomerates—Time Warner, Bertelsmann, the News Corporation, Sony, and so on—lead globally, companies such as Televisa and TV Azteca in Mexico and Rede Globo in Brazil continue to strengthen their positions in and beyond Latin America. In the much discussed pan-Arab satellite television industry, dominant companies are emerging amidst a trend toward specialization and consolidation. The privately owned Lebanese Broadcasting Corporation and the Saudi-owned, London-published, Arabic-language daily *al-Hayat* merged newsgathering operations in 2002, and the rise of al-Jazeera in the post-September 11 era has stimulated competitors such as Al-Arabiya and others. In the meantime, U.S. cable company CNBC launched an Arabic service in June 2003, purporting to bring the wonders of personal finance to the nearly three hundred million Arabs in the region and the few million Arabs in North America and Western Europe. The size of this regional audience, in addition to the wealth of Persian Gulf consumers and the demographic youth of the entire area, will undoubtedly continue to attract global players in the near future.

These developments explain why television programs are increasingly hybrid, embedded with signs and symbols with transregional appeal, and executed in line with the imperative of market expansion. It is important to note that since most emerging regional media spheres are commercial, modeled largely in line with U.S. production, promotion, and financing standards, cultural dissimilarities within geocultural regions often require extra production and marketing expenses, which by necessity embed regional processes in global media operations.

Liberalization and consolidation have also triggered a race to the bottom as media companies strive to reach increasingly larger audiences without incurring proportionally higher costs. One result has been that television programs are increasingly designed to appeal to worldwide audiences, a strategy with considerable advantages. Logistically simpler than coproduction, creatively less restrictive than format adaptation, and economically less onerous than both coproduction and format adaptation, program internationalization now pervades television news and entertainment alike, categories that are themselves increasingly blurred. The Cable News Network (CNN) and Music Television (MTV) are textbook cases, the former in news and the latter in entertainment. CNN launched *CNN World Report* in 1987, a unique program that showcased reports on various countries sent in English by local reporters working for local stations. Two presenters in CNN studios introduced the reports, but other than that CNN had no direct production involvement in the content of the program. In the early twenty-first century, executives at CNN International are talking about "de-Americanizing content," according to Chris Cramer, head of CNN International ("The One," 2003, p. 73). Between 1996 and 2001, the percentage of American content on CNN International was reduced from 70 percent to 8 percent, although how to clearly define what is American is arduous, and the most direct definition is content that deals with U.S. issues. Music Television's localization—which in reality means internationalization—strategy relies on segmenting international audiences according to linguistic, cultural parameters in their national or regional contexts. This is conducted through featuring the work of some local artists, hiring local VJs (video jockeys) to host programs, and overall sensitivity to the cultural specificities of the country or region in which MTV operates. Between 2001 and 2003, MTV launched fourteen new channels, including MTV Romania and MTV Indonesia. The total number of worldwide MTV stations stood at twenty-eight in 2003. An MTV executive has even claimed that "[w]e don't even call it an adaptation of American content: it's local content creation. The American thing is irrelevant" ("The One," 2003, p. 73). Becoming more local is, for CNN and MTV, the surest way to become more international.

Another result of global media liberalization is the proliferation of lower-cost, high-impact genres such as the variety show, the talk show—in both its lowbrow and high-brow variations—and more importantly, the now ubiquitous reality genre and its many subtypes. These genres have in common an absence or minimal presence of highly paid talent, low-cost studio or outdoor production, and a tendency toward the raw, bizarre, and sensational. In this environment program-format adaptations and coproductions are increasingly common; the former entail the adaptation to local parameters of tastes and style of a popular program format gleaned from a different culture, whereas the latter involve a partnership between several companies based in multiple countries.

Multinational Partnerships and Cultural Hybridity: The Growth of Coproductions

Coproductions give companies several advantages. Canadian media economists McFadyen, Hoskins, and Finn (1998) include as incentives for entering into coproduction agreements "pooling financial resources," "access to foreign government incentives and subsidies," "access to partner's market," "access to third-country market," "access to particular project initiated by partner," "cultural goals," "desired foreign locations," "cheaper inputs in partner's country," and learning new marketing, production, and management strategies from the partner. These benefits outweigh drawbacks such as "coordination costs," "loss of control over cultural specificity," and "opportunistic behaviour by the foreign partner."

Joining forces allows companies to share equipment, technical staff and know-how, and shooting locations. These benefits, in turn, expand potential sources of funding, including government subsidies and tax breaks, and also spread the risk, so that different entities share the burden of a potential commercial failure. Reducing risk is also related to the bigger markets reached by companies that enter into coproduction arrangements: if a television program or movie fails in a national or regional market somewhere, commercial success in a different market will make up for the losses. These considerable financial, technical, and market incentives have triggered a significant worldwide increase in coproductions. Between 1950 and 1994, there were at least sixty-six bilateral coproduction treaties (P. W. Taylor, 1995), and more than two thousand coproductions took place between 1978 and 1995 (Television Business International, cited in Miller et al., 2001, p. 85). Television documentaries and dramas accounted for the majority of coproductions, and film ventures for the remaining 21 percent (ibid.).

There is a distinction between "equity coproductions" and "treaty coproductions" (Miller et al., 2001,

p. 84). Equity coproductions constitute a strategic and temporary partnership between two or more companies, driven by the search for maximal profits and usually not eligible for treaty status. As purely commercial joint ventures, equity coproductions do not directly involve issues of cultural policy and national identity. Many equity coproductions have included European and Japanese companies contributing to the financing of Hollywood movies. In contrast, treaty coproductions are formal partnerships concluded under the auspices of national governments. This type of coproduction customarily involves artists, technicians, financiers, and the more-or-less active participation of government officials from two or more countries. As a consequence, treaty coproductions are formal affairs that fall in the realm of international relations and involve issues of national identity and cultural policy. Most treaty coproductions come about in the European Union. According to *Screen Digest*, in 1998, out of a total of a 183 movies produced in France, Europe's largest film producer, 81, or 44 percent, were coproductions. The figures were lower for Italy, Germany, and Britain: 14 percent, or 13 out of 92 Italian films; 22 percent, or 11 out of 50 German films; and 28 percent, or 24 out of 87 British movies, were coproduced. Interestingly, that year's figure was significantly lower for the United States, where only 15, or 9 films out of a total of 661, were coproductions (cited in Miller et al., 2001), in contrast to the 1978–1995 period when 14 percent of U.S. television shows were coproduced. This figure during the same time period is 16 percent for France and the United Kingdom, 10 percent for Germany, and 7 percent for Canada (Brown, 1995, cited in ibid., p. 86). While the benefits of coproductions to companies are by now clear, why are governments taking such an interest?

Striving to capitalize on the globalization of media productions, national and regional governments have aggressively pursued and fostered coproductions in order to boost exports and broaden financial "investment in television and film productions. The United Kingdom is a case in point. In the 1990s the then ruling Conservatives decided that the cultural industries had to take advantage of "tremendous export opportunities in a rapidly expanding international market" (Barnett and Curry, 1994, p. 221, cited in Freedman, 2001, p. 3). One of the major obstacles to British and other television-export strategy is the documented prime-time domination of local productions in most domestic markets worldwide. In the United Kingdom itself, for example, *Coronation Street* remains the most popular television program. Despite this recognition, British government support of television exports continued with the rise to power of New Labour. By the late 1990s, Tony Blair's Third Way politics explicitly incorporated free trade in global media products (Blair, 1998). Greg Dyke, who was the chief executive officer of private media conglomerate Pearson before becoming head of the British Broadcasting Corporation, enthusiastically advocated a British strategy for competing in the global television industry. Dyke had made Pearson a world leader in buying, adapting, and selling program formats. "The trick is," he said, "can you globalize and make it local?" (Baker, 1997, cited in Freedman, 2001, p. 4).

In addition to audience preferences for local programs, the entanglement of national and global considerations is another obstacle to television exportation. This snag had been a source of controversy since the 1994 publication of a white paper on the BBC, *Serving the Nation, Competing Worldwide*, which advocated a focus on selling BBC programs worldwide. In an interview with British media researcher Des Freedman in 1997, Harry Reeves, then head of general broadcasting policy, declared international television commerce to be "very high on the list of policy objectives" and not to pose a fundamental contradiction of the BBC's national public service mandate (Freedman, 2001). In this context, the Department of Culture, Media, and Sport (DCMS) commissioned a report to explore areas of improvement in British television exports. The report, *Building a Global Audience: British Television in Overseas Markets* (Graham, 1999), found that the United Kingdom suffered from a substantive deficit in television trade, and that British dramatic productions were too slow, dark, or serious, which hindered their global competitiveness, while British comedy was internationally successful. The report recommended increased liberalization of the domestic British market.

The British example demonstrates the changing relationship between the state and media institutions, in which the mass media are increasingly treated in economic—contra social, cultural, or educational—terms, frequently the media's own economic terms.

From regulator and arbiter, the state has become promoter and cheerleader. The role of government institutions increasingly resembles that of the impresario: they scout opportunities, expedite deals, and reap a portion of the proceeds. Using a mix of financial incentives and cultural appeals, they facilitate access to new markets and coordinate pecuniary transnational partnerships. Even in program-format adaptations, as the next section will demonstrate, the state plays a role.

From *Teletubbies* to *Tele Chobis*: The Unbearable Lightness of Television Programs

The widespread popularity of reality television in the late 1990s accelerated a transnational process of program-format adaptation that Albert Moran (1998) has documented that adaptation as historically pervasive, and current trends indicate that it is poised to increase as the television industry continues to globalize. Like coproduction, format adaptation helps companies reduce risk and uncertainty, in this case by working with a format with demonstrated success. However, formats might not be popular across cultural boundaries. According to Moran: "a television format is that set of invariable elements in a program out of which the variable elements of an individual episode are produced" (1998, p. 13), which means that unlike coproductions, where a program's intellectual property is jointly owned by the partners, the legal ramifications of format adaptation are tricky, and involve the three legal instruments of copyright, breach of confidence, and passing off (Mummery, 1966, cited in ibid., p. 15).

L'affaire Tele Chobis demonstrates the problems that can arise in program-format adaptation and the ill-defined space between adaptation and plagiarism. In the fall of 1999, the leading Mexican network, Televisa, began airing the British and globally popular *Teletubbies*. During the previous summer, marketing executives from Itsy Bitsy Entertainment, the exclusive North American distributors of *Teletubbies*, had been prowling Latin American countries promoting their flagship program. Initially, TV Azteca, Mexico's second-rated television network, was interested and entered into contract negotiations to purchase

Teletubbies. TV Azteca executives changed their minds when Itsy Bitsy insisted that *Teletubbies* must be broadcast without commercials. While advertising before and after the airing of *Teletubbies* was acceptable, the condition that no advertisements appear during *Teletubbies* broadcasts was nonnegotiable and thus a contract breaker. Televisa, on the other hand, agreed to broadcast *Teletubbies* commercial free and as a result purchased the program from Itsy Bitsy. The reaction of TV Azteca executives was swift and surprising: they created a copycat program, which they called *Tele Chobis*. An exploration of the design, promotion, and distribution of *Teletubbies*, followed by an examination of the structural forces and cultural specificities that have shaped *Tele Chobis*, provides a rare vista of the active links that exist between media systems and textuality, and helps us understand the political economy of hybridity.

Anne Wood, a former schoolteacher and founder of Ragdoll Productions Ltd. of Buckinghamshire, U.K., created the original *Teletubbies* with her partner, Andy Davenport, a speech therapist. Since its launch by the British Broadcasting Corporation in 1997, this program has been a watershed event in children's television akin to globally successful classics such as *Sesame Street*. Wildly popular and reaching dozens of countries, it has triggered references to the four "tubbies"—Tinky Winky, Dipsy, Laa Laa, and Po—as the Fab Four, a clear intertextual nod to Beatlemania. It is also routinely controversial, especially in the United States, where a slightly modified version is broadcast by PBS, attracting detractors and supporters from the medical community, religious leadership, and the gay press alike.[1] A typical episode features the four Teletubbies, chubby humanoids dressed in gaudy colors who live in an imaginary space of green nature and friendly animals. They sing, dance, and communicate in a verbal code replete with infantile giggles and playful body movements. The same everyday life and household objects appear with regularity during each episode, and simple stories are repeated several times. The Teletubbies also have screens in their bellies, used to show footage of real children.

An aggressive and wide-ranging marketing campaign centered on successful synergistic deals propelled *Teletubbies* to household-name status. In December 1998, QVC Inc., the world's leading "electronic retailer," broadcast a special Teletubbies program, promoting the newly released home videos "Here Come the Teletubbies" and "Dance with the Teletubbies"; a music CD, "*Teletubbies* the Album"; *Teletubbies* bean-bag characters; and myriad gadgets and accessories ("Teletubby Mania," 1998, December 28). Less than a week later, Ragdoll and Itsy Bitsy announced a deal with Microsoft to create ActiMate Interactive Teletubbies ("Tinky Winky," 1999, January 6). Two months later, FAO Schwarz New York hosted an "International Teletubbies Celebration" to launch the ActiMate Interactive Teletubbies ("International Teletubbies," 1999). In the same year, Burger King's *Teletubbies* promotional campaign was so successful that the fast-food chain found its fifty million finger-puppet Teletubbies depleted within less than a month (Morgan, 1999).

These synergistic retailing agreements have made the juvenile quartet ubiquitous in Western popular culture and highly popular world-wide, triggering a wave of imitation. The Mexican *Tele Chobis* is not the only *Teletubbies* copycat. In March 1999, Ragdoll Productions Ltd. and New York-based Itsy Bitsy Entertainment Company filed a lawsuit in U.S. federal court in Manhattan against Wal-Mart Stores Inc. alleging unauthorized copying. Wal-Mart had been selling Bubbly Chubbies, Teletubbies look-alikes that shared shelf space with the original Teletubbies ("Teletubbies declare," 1999). Wal-Mart argued that the supplier of Bubbly Chubbies had produced a legal opinion by the law firm Buchanan Ingersoll stating that the Bubbly Chubbies "did not infringe upon any trademarks or copyrights" ("Walmart had," 1999). Less than two months after the lawsuit was filed, Wal-Mart agreed to remove from its shelves and destroy the remaining stock of Bubbly Chubbies, ending the legal feud between Wal-Mart and Itsy Bitsy, who continued legal action against the unidentified manufacturer of the Bubbly Chubbies ("Wal-Mart to destroy," 1999).

Publicity for *Teletubbies* also came via the U.S. culture wars. The February 1999 issue of *National Liberty Journal*, edited and published by the Reverend Jerry Falwell, former leader of the Moral Majority, carried the headline "Parents Alert: Tinky Winky Comes Out of the Closet" with an article alleging that purple Tinky Winky was a gay character, and that the "subtle depictions" of gay identity were intentional. Falwell reportedly said: "As a Christian I feel that role modeling the gay lifestyle is damaging to the moral lives of children" (Reed, 1999). This triggered a firestorm of controversy in the U.S. and international media. Across the Atlantic, the BBC sniffed: "the Teletubbies have made the Rev. Falwell, chancellor of Liberty University in Lynchburg, Virginia, hot under the collar" ("Gay Tinky," 1999). The BBC's official response that "Tinky Winky is simply a sweet, technological baby with a magic bag" (ibid.) seemed to be shared by the press and the public alike. The *Washington Post* asked: "Can Mr. Falwell believe that just because Tinky Winky is purple, has a triangle antenna on top of his head and carries a handbag that he's a gay role model for our toddlers? Even Laa Laa, Dipsy and Po must be shaking their heads in disbelief" ("Subliminal Messages?" 1999).

Inevitably, the debate became highly politicized. A February 1999 resolution was introduced at the city council in Berkeley, California, backing the Teletubbies and condemning Falwell's views, leading Ken Viselman, head of Itsy Bitsy Entertainment, to call for leaving politics out of *Teletubbies*. About Tinky Winky, Viselman said: "He's not gay. He's not straight. He's just a character in a children's series. I think that we should just let the Teletubbies go and play in Teletubbyland and not try to define them" ("Calif. Resolution," 1999).[2] A few days later, the March edition of *National Liberty Journal* carried a front-page Falwell article in which he wrote: "Until the recent media explosion accused me of 'outing' Tinky Winky as being gay, I had never heard of this sweet looking character. I certainly have never criticized Tinky Winky in any way" ("Falwell Denies," 1999). However, the conservative reverend stood by his warning about the conjectural dangers of homosexuality (ibid.). Needless to say, this controversy added to the already strong visibility of the program.

The Mexican adaptation, *Tele Chobis*, retained *Teletubbies'* basic structure, but offered variations in terms of the leading characters, the story lines, and the overall content. Instead of Tinky Winky, Dipsy, Laa Laa, and Po, Azteca's copycat featured Nita, Toso, Ton, and Tis. Nita wears green, Toso yellow, Ton blue, and Tis dark pink. Both programs are set in a garden populated with rabbits and replete with toys: the Teletubbies play on a seemingly placeless green hill and live in a bunker under that hill; the Tele Chobis live in a house inside the trunk of a big talking tree that overshadows what looks like a pastoral garden. Like *Teletubbies, Tele Chobis* unfolds in the two spaces of nature and technology (see the analysis of *Teletubbies* in Lemish and Tidhar, 2001), the former represented by the garden, the latter by the nine screens on the wall of the *Tele Chobis* house in the tree. *Teletubbies* and *Tele Chobis* episodes both focus on a limited number of issues and repeat information about them, in addition to circuitous story lines that revisit issues several times during each episode. Also, each installment of both programs includes several familiar objects. For *Teletubbies* these comprise a tittering baby face framed in a sun, a hat, a purse, and a vacuum cleaner. In *Tele Chobis* these encompass the commentators Champi and Ñon *(champiñon* is Spanish for "mushroom"), a sheriff's badge, animals, and the big talking tree. In all these aspects, the similarities between the original and the copycat are straightforward.

Differences between *Teletubbies* and *Tele Chobis* reflect the intended audience. Whereas *Teletubbies* was conceived as a culturally "neutral" text that could be sold across national and cultural borders, *Tele Chobis* was intended for Mexican children. This is manifest in the different placements of real-life children in the two programs. In the British original, sequences of older children appear on screens in the tubbies' abdominal areas, monitors intentionally designed as instruments of localization: different buyers of the program have the ability to insert culturally relevant material in those screens. In contrast, the Mexican copycat incorporates real children in the narrative through parallel editing and montage sequences. One final difference: whereas *Teletubbies* is touted as the only program to have targeted children under the age of two, *Tele Chobis* cast a wider net to include what is probably a two-to-eight age bracket. Unlike the nonlinguistic blabbering of Tinky Winky, Dipsy, Laa Laa, and Po, the Tele Chobis Nita, Toso, Ton, and Tis speak a Mexican-accented Spanish. More importantly, because *Teletubbies* was designed as a "universal" text while *Tele Chobis* was created for the domestic Mexican market from the original and now global format, the latter exhibits a cultural hybridity that is marked, the ensuing analysis will

demonstrate, by incongruent scenes and costumes, a diversity of objects from a variety of geographical and cultural locations, and a hodgepodge of commercials and public service announcements for Mexican and American products and programs.

An episode of *Tele Chobis* ran an hour with six commercial breaks, three to four minutes (six to eight commercials) each. Typical advertisers—oddly, not all targeting children—included clothing companies, technical colleges, computer support, snacks and candy, and Mexican federal government public service announcements on public health, sexual hygiene, the environment, and social development. For example, episode 4, which aired in March 1999, began with the Tele Chobis singing under the talking tree where they live. Then a rapid montage sequence featured the Tele Chobis dancing and walking on waterside alleys, alternating with shots of farm animals. After that, we see Nita, the Tele Chobi dressed in green, waking up in a room inside the tree trunk filled with television monitors, tall glass panels with water bubbles, a yellow cupboard, and a big clock above the door. Nita feels lonely and seeks consolation by talking to the tree. The other three Tele Chobis are then seen having a picnic next to the water, with trees painted white about two feet high. The episode's theme is loneliness, explored in the context of children who are left at home to their own devices. We see testimonies from several real children between the ages of six and three saying what they like to do when they are home alone, one of them a brown-skinned, black-haired boy wearing an NBA T-shirt. Then the Tele Chobis are seen, interspersed with shots of children in gardens and at school, dancing to a song whose lyrics focus on loneliness. Cedar and cypress trees can be glimpsed in some shots, with green mountains reminiscent of *Teletubbies*, but most shots are taken in front of the large tree trunk that serves as the Tele Chobis' abode.

The first break carried advertisements for *Aventuras de Doug* (a Disney cartoon), Hecali clothing, Expertus computer services; public service announcement for the Comisión Nacional de Derechos Humanos (National Human Rights Commission) and La Clave (the telecommunications ministry, promoting new phone services); and finally a promotional preview for the broadcast of an ice-hockey game between Ottawa and Dallas. After the break we are back to the picnic, and a phone number appears on the screen with an invitation for children to call and share their favorite surprise. Nita, Toso, Ton, and Tis initiate a waterside dance, dressed in snow hats, scarves, and earmuffs. After a brief intervention by Champi and Ñon, two tree-perched boorish animal commentators, the scene changes and Ton, the Tele Chobi in blue, comes in dressed as a U.S. sheriff, dancing to a tune of imitation U.S. country-western music. The others have red scarves around their necks, cowboy style, one green, the second dark pink, and the third yellow. The background is interspersed with typically Mexican maguey cacti, and the music shifts from Western line dance to Norteño (Northern Mexican) music, and then settles into a hybrid mix of the two genres. After the dance, the Tele Chobis hug Nita, who tells Ton, Toso, and Tis how lonely he felt waking up without them. After the second commercial break ("Presumed Guilty," a soap opera; Marinela chocolate cakes; environmental and public health PSAs; Elektra electronic appliances store; and a promotional preview for *Los Simpsons*), one's imagination and doing what one likes are introduced by voice-over as palliatives to loneliness, with a children's soccer game providing visuals for a ragtime tune. After the third commercial break, colored balloons cross the screen upward and the Mexican copycat quartet is seen dancing to Norteñas, whose rhythm is enhanced by fluid camera movements and parallel editing of children dancing to the same tune in a school yard.

The hybridity of *Tele Chobis* is manifest on two fronts. First, the set includes many markers of Mexicanness. Unlike their English counterparts, whose abdominal screens project footage of children, in *Tele Chobis* scenes of real children are intrinsically part of the program's structure, which belies *Tele Chobis'* intended national audience. Indeed, markers of Mexicanness are many, the first of which is the use of spoken Mexican Spanish. Second, maguey cacti, whose pulp is the raw material of the quintessentially Mexican pulque or tequila, are prominently featured in the program, often in close-ups. Other markers include the monarch butterflies, identified with the Mexican state of Michoacan, a major resting area for these Monarcas on their seasonal peregrinations, and increasingly associated with Mexico as a country. There is also the Guacamaya parrot, found in Mexico's tropical areas. Also, Norteño music tunes underscore the Mexican identity of *Tele Chobis*. Finally, many of the outdoor scenes are shot in ex-haciendas, whose late colonial architecture is also closely associated with Mexico. These visual and aural markers—most of them naturalistic and therefore highly localized—stamp *Tele Chobis* with Mexicanness, a hybrid identity grafted onto an original and innovative text, product of the imagination of a British schoolteacher and promoted by a U.S. entertainment company.

There is, however, a second, more complex embodiment of hybridity. *Tele Chobis'* odd mixture of icons, signs, and objects underscores a radical intertextuality where foreign cultural elements collide and fuse. NBA T-shirts, country-western music, sheriffs' badges, and promotions for U.S. shows like *The Simpsons* and myriad Disney productions, point to the preponderance of U.S. popular culture as a provider of content and as a source of dialogical connections. Earmuffs, scarves, and wool balaclavas worn by the Tele Chobis while promenading or dancing outdoors are also emblematic of a hibernal northern ethos incongruent with *Tele Chobis'* Mexicanness. The iconic mushrooms, balloons, Jeeps, and other items that swirl vertically across the screen throughout each episode increase the atmosphere of radical cultural diversity characteristic of the show. The carnivalesque nature of the program comes in full focus in a scene where Nita, Toso, Ton, and Tis are dressed like medieval entertainers, in a mise-en-scène that transforms their exaggerated baby faces, protuberant cheeks, and dark-lined eyes into monstrous features.

In keeping in mind the show's intended infantile and juvenile audience, these menacing facial traits are neutralized, as the Tele Chobis use them to scare away insects, especially a bee that is harassing a frightened Toso. At that moment, the voice-over of the tree conveniently intervenes to remind children that insects are good for us and should not be harmed, and a song "*Abejas, Hormigas*" (Bees, Ants), praises the lives of insects and the benefits of insects to humans and the environment. When a butterfly finally lands on Ton's arm, the four humanoids are fascinated and fully converted to friendliness toward insects.

This positive pedagogical turn notwithstanding, the visual monstrosity of that scene, centered on the characters' physical appearance, is symptomatic of a radical cultural openness, a carnival aesthetic. As film scholars Ella Shohat and Stam (1994) write, following Bakhtin: "carnival embraces an anticlassical aesthetic that rejects formal harmony and unity in favor of the asymmetrical, the heterogeneous, the oxymoronic, the miscegenated.... In the carnival aesthetic, everything is pregnant with its opposite, within an alternative logic of permanent contradiction and non-exclusive opposites that transgresses the monologic true-or-false thinking typical of a certain kind of positivist rationalism" (p. 302). Indeed, *Tele Chobis* carries the cross-fertilized debris of variegated cultural influences and aesthetic styles. It may have been a copy of *Teletubbies* from the perspective of modern copyright—an issue I will address shortly— which is why the program was pulled off the air within a few weeks of its first broadcast. To the cultural critic, however, more than a violation of intellectual property laws, it is a rich text replete with signs and symbols whose intertextual tie-ins subvert the laws of genre as the text itself undermines the copyright regime. *Tele Chobis* is therefore an ideal hybrid text, reminiscent of mythological fables, where aesthetic conventions and artistic practices are subverted, where the monstrous cohabitates with the sublime and the universal with the particular, and where the hybridization of cultural forms is not merely an aesthetic attribute of the text, but actually constitutes its texture and pervades its identity.

Tele Chobis can thus be interpreted as a modern version of the fable of ancient mythology. According to Serge Gruzinski, a French anthropological historian of Mexico and author of the ingenious *La pensée métisse* (Gruzinki, 1999), the fable as a genre exhibits "an indifference [to geographical and historical markers" (p. 145, my translation) and a propinquity to embrace disorder and mixtures. Therefore, Gruzinski concludes, the fable is an ideal framework for hybrid cultural forms. As a radically open semiotic system, the fable is a creative space where, Gruzinski wrote in reference to colonial-era Indian paintings in Puebla and Ixmiquilpan, "a centauress can flirt with a Mexican monkey under the eyes of a Spanish cleric" (p. 149).[3] Reeling from Spanish colonial control, native Mexican artists during the Conquista used the fable and grotesque art to effectively subvert colonial aesthetic

conventions, a subversion made possible by the fable's intrinsic tendency toward the foreign, the fabulous, and the fantastic. In sharp contrast with sacred art, where colonial church surveillance would be intense and the borders of the iconographic canon heavily policed, the grotesque arts gave free reign to the imaginative and seditious expressiveness of local artists. Thus Gruzinski demonstrates that the Indian painters of Puebla and Oixmiquilpan appropriated a form, the grotesques, originally conceived in Renaissance Italy, in addition to a native cultural content to create hybrid images that playfully undermined colonial aesthetics. Gruzinski sees the same phenomenon at work in contemporary creations such as Peter Greenaway's *Prospero's Books*, where hybridization "opens the way for all kinds of appropriations: it pokes fun at ordinary logics, scrambles the laws of plausibility, of space and time, ignores the laws of gravity, foils representational conventions" (p. 156).

Arguing for a linear historical correspondence between native Mexican painters of the colonial era, aesthetic innovations in Renaissance Italy, Peter Greenaway's dramatic creations, and *Tele Chobis* would be imprudent. However, as products of a world increasingly characterized by cross-cultural interpenetration, texts from these different periods offer more than simple intertextual traces. Like the fable, children's television offers an extremely flexible creative environment, where the form itself, whether through animated or acted imaginary characters, is a creation, and the content is allowed license (in the use of language, colors, forms, sound, etc.) that would not be tolerated in most other television and film genres (see Kraidy, 1998b, for a treatment of this issue in children's animated film). With its placeless green fields, outlandish characters, invented nonlanguage, and heteroclite content, the original *Teletubbies* embodies this conspicuous openness perhaps more than does any other program for children. As a hybrid offshoot of the already hybrid *Teletubbies, Tele Chobis* thrusts this radical dialogism into new territory, where intertexts jostle in a seemingly random dance of push-and-pull of discordant icons, discrepant musics, dissonant fashions, and incongruous characters.

Unlike hybrid colonial painting, however, which as Gruzinski (1999) evinced, survived and prospered under colonial strictures, the textual excess incarnated in *Tele Chobis* was curbed by the prevailing system of reference and power. Today's global copyright regime, it turns out, is more successful than the colonial Spanish church in bringing overflowing creative energy back into the fold of the permissible. Whereas Indian Mexican painters indulged in aesthetic subversion, the threat of legal action by the U.S. Itsy Bitsy Entertainment and British Ragdoll Productions brought the Mexican *Tele Chobis* to a quick end: as mentioned earlier, the program was taken off the air a few weeks after it was first broadcast. This was facilitated by an environment of stricter intellectual property-law enforcement by Mexican authorities in the wake of the North American Free Trade Agreement (NAFTA), and a transitional period for the Mexican cultural and media sectors.

The *Tele Chobis* affair occurred at a time of fundamental changes in the Mexican audiovisual industries, triggered by their increased integration in global media markets (Lomelí, 2003) and increasing competition between Televisa, the leading media company, and TV Azteca, the creator of *Tele Chobis* and second in Mexican audience ratings. The background of these changes was the liberal economic drive initiated during the Miguel de la Madrid presidency (1982–1988) and culminating in NAFTA. This trend continued after NAFTA, so that by 2000, Mexico had entered twenty-seven free trade agreements ("México en el Mundo," 2000, cited in Sánchez-Ruiz, 2001). In the 1990s, both Televisa and TV Azteca embarked on ambitious global expansion plans. Televisa, which had expanded into the U.S. market in the 1970s and mid-1980s (Sánchez-Ruiz, 2001), in the 1990s pursued a vigorous international strategy to "create a greater dependency on Televisa programming among foreign broadcasters" (Paxman and Saragoza, 2001). The world's leading Spanish-speaking media company also underwent restructuring, cutting costs by U.S. $175 million in 1997 and 1998 ("Televisa Mexico," 1999), which caused its shares to rise by 10 percent ("Mexico's Televisa," 1999).

TV Azteca was privatized during trade negotiations that led to NAFTA, and it was purchased in 1993 for U.S. $643 million ("TV Azteca and Canal," 1998). Its soon-to-be broadened operations consisted of Azteca 7 and Azteca 13, two national stations. In 1997, the company expanded swiftly, issuing U.S.

$425 million in publicly traded bonds in February, and going through an initial public offering of over 20 percent of capital stock in August, also grabbing 32 percent of the U.S. $1.4 billion Mexican advertising market, rising to 36 percent in the first quarter of 1998 (ibid.). This, in addition to several domestic joint ventures and foreign media acquisitions, established TV Azteca as a serious competitor to Televisa. Notably, TV Azteca's joint venture with CNI Canal 40 television gave it access to nearly 100 percent of the Mexico City metropolitan area's 22 million television viewers ("TV Azteca and Canal," 1998). The deal entailed TV Azteca's purchase of 10 percent of Canal 40 shares, giving TV Azteca wider exposure by adding a third channel to its lineup, and providing Canal 40 with content from Azteca's production studios. In late 1998, TV Azteca clinched an exclusive free TV-licensing agreement with Disney for its "Kids and Young Adults" Canal 7 ("TV Azteca Signs," 1998), where *Tele Chobis* was broadcast with commercials for various Disney products. TV Azteca's growth led it to announce that it would raise its advertising rates by 40 percent starting in January 1999 (Barrera, 1998). That same month, TV Azteca became embroiled in a dispute with the Chilean government over the way it managed its acquisition of 75 percent of Chile's Channel 4 television, and faced allegations that it did not comply with Chilean law that mandated top executive positions in television stations to be occupied by Chilean nationals ("TV Azteca Denies," 1999). Nonetheless, TV Azteca's shares rose 10 percent in December 1999 ("Mexico's TV," 1999). Since then, TV Azteca has maintained its number two position, in effect sharing duopolistic control of the Mexican media market with leader Televisa.[4]

Predictably, media liberalization in Mexico involved legal changes. The Mexican Federal Copyright Law (FCL), officially published on December 23, 1996, became effective in March 1997, repealing the 1963 Federal Copyright Law. In the new law, television and broadcasting copyrights are recognized, but "ideas," "formulas," and "concepts" are not legally protected ("Highlights of," 1998). A few years earlier, the Law of Cinematography of 1992 repealed a 1941 law requiring that 50 percent of movies be nationally made. According to the 1992 law, this proportion was to be reduced to 30 percent in 1993, and by five more percentiles yearly until it was down to 10 percent by the end of 1997. The cable television industry was also deregulated to allow up to 49 percent non-Mexican ownership (Sánchez-Ruiz, 2001).

These technological and regulatory changes, coupled with increasing autonomy from government intervention, put enormous pressure on Mexican media companies to provide commercially attractive content. In addition to global expansion and joint ventures elaborated previously, heightened competition led to programming that clashed with prevailing social values, such as talk shows inspired by the "trash" talk-show genre in the United States (LaFranchi, 2000). It was in this environment that TV Azteca created and launched *Tele Chobis*, after deciding that it could neither afford to purchase *Teletubbies* for commercial-free broadcasting, nor let Televisa's acquisition of *Teletubbies* broadcast rights for Mexico go unchallenged. TV Azteca thus resorted to program mimicry, running afoul of intellectual property laws, literally illustrating Homi Bhabha's claim in this chapter's epigraph that "the visibility of mimicry is always produced at the site of interdiction" (1994, p. 89). The *Tele Chobis* story consequently embodies a crossroads of historical, economic, technological, and cultural forces, all of which contributed, at different levels and with various intensities, to the creation of a hybrid, transcultural text.

The hybridity of media texts is explained by the media's transnational political economy. Post-Fordist practices and systemic forces account for the fact that hybrid media texts reflect industry imperatives for targeting several markets at once with the same program or, alternatively, are symptoms of commercially motivated "borrowing." In the absence of the present global structure where interlocking regulatory, financial, political, and cultural forces drive a race to reach the highest number of people for the lowest cost and the minimum amount of risk, therefore entailing creative productions that cross and fuse cultural differences, hybridity would likely not be as pervasive in media texts worldwide. However, as the dissection of the Mexican copycat *Tele Chobis* has shown, both the raison d'être and the kiss of death of hybrid television programs are to be found in political-economic arrangements, which in this case included a Mexican industry in transition, embedded in the North American Free Trade Agreement and the international copyright regime. Granted, media texts, even

before the acceleration of the sector's globalization, have always sought and found inspiration in each other, but the contemporary phenomenon of media programs that carry composite aesthetics and fused cultural elements, in both its breadth and depth, is a product of neoliberalization. Hybrid media texts have the intertextual traces of an increasingly standardized global media industry where successful formats are adapted ad infinitum, hybridized to cater to the proclivities of one audience after another, but always remaining firmly grounded in the same commercial logic where hybrid texts are instruments finely tuned in pursuit of profit.

Notes

Epigraph source: Bhabha, 1994, p. 89.

1. I write "slightly modified" because in the rare instances where there is English speech, such as with the Narrator and Voice Trumpets, it has been converted to an American accent.

2. Viselman's comment reflects a strategic ambiguity on the inherent polysemy of television texts, especially *Teletubbies*, on one hand arguing against trying to define the characters, thus acknowledging multiple meanings, on the other hand rejecting politicized readings of the program, thus attempting to fix the fluidity of the program's meanings.

3. Gruzinski is referring to two sites in Mexico. The first, in the colonial city of Puebla, is the Casa del Deán (literally, house of the dean), which was occupied by a clergyman of high stature between 1564 and 1589 and is considered, at least by Gruzinski, "one of the marvels of the Mexican Renaissance" (1999, p. 112). Its interior is adorned with large and unique paintings, the creation of native Indian Mexican painters, including one tableau of monkeys in playful relation to a centauress, which was one of Gruzinski's main inspiration in his analysis of hybridity, hence the quote I use. The second is an Augustinian church in Ixmiquilpan, a town located around 130 miles northwest of Mexico City. The church contains two very large frescoes that graphically depict bloody war scenes—a highly unusual occurrence in a Catholic church—where European and preconquest Mexican iconic elements mix freely, interpreted by Gruzinski as another manifestation of Mexico's unique hybridity (pp. 116–119). All translations from the French original (Gruzinski, 1999) are mine.

4. According to one source, sales figures for both Televisa and TV Azteca show continued growth. For Televisa, annual sales in $U.S. millions were $1,892.4 in 1999,

$2,163.6 in 2000, $2,147.4 in 2001, and $2,075.4 in 2002. For TV Azteca, the numbers are $564.1 in 2000, $632.6 in 2001, $643.6 in 2002, and $648.0 in 2003 (Hoover's Online, 2004a,b).

References

Barnett, S., and Curry, A. (1994). *The battle for the BBC*. London: Aurum Press.

Barrera, C. (1998, October 7). TV Azteca to raise advertising rates by 40 pct. Mexico city: Reuters.

Bhabha, H. (1994). *The location of culture*. London and New York: Routledge.

Blair, T. (1998). *The third way: New politics for a new century*. Fabian Pamphlet 588. London: Fabian Society.

Blanchard, M. A. (1986). *Exporting the First Amendment: The press-government crusade of 1945–1952*. New York: Longman.

Calif. resolution backs Teletubbie. (1999, February 23). Berkeley, CA: Associated Press.

Curtin, M. (1993, Spring). Beyond the vast wasteland: The policy discourse of global television and the politics of American empire. *Journal of Broadcasting and Electronic Media*. 37(2), 127–145.

Falwell denies "outing" Teletubbies, defends warning. (1999, February 25). Lynchburg, VA: Reuters.

Freedman, D. (2001). Who wants to be a millionaire? The politics of television exports [Paper presented at the International Studies Association Convention, Chicago, February 20–24].

Friedman, J. (1994). *Cultural identity and global process*. London and Thousand Oaks, CA: Sage.

Gay Tinky Winky bad for children. (1999, February 10). *BBC Online*.

Graham, D. (1999). *Building a global audience: British television in overseas markets*. London: Department of Media, Culture, and Sports.

Grossberg, L. (2002). Postscript. *Communication Theory*, 12(3), 367–370.

Gruzinski, S. (1995). Images and cultural *mestizaje* in colonial Mexico. *Poetics Today*, 16(1), 53–77.

Gruzinski, S. (1999). *La pensée métisse*. Paris: Fayard. (Translated as *The Mestizo Mind*. [2002]. [D. Dusimberre, Trans.]. London and New York: Routledge.)

Highlights of the Mexican Federal Copyrights Law (1998). *The U.S.-Mexico Legal Reporter*. Gray Cary Ware and Freidenrich LLP. Retrieved June 10, 2003, from http://library.lp.findlaw.com/articles/file/firms/graycary/gcwf000155.

Hoover's Online (2004a). Grupo Televisa, S.A. Retrieved March 3, 2004, from http://www.hoovers.com/grupo-televisa.-s.a./-ID_51043-/free-co-factsheet.xhtml.

Hoover's Online (2004b). TV Azteca S.A. de C.V. Retrieved March 3, 2004, from http://www.hoovers.com/tv-azteca.-s.a./-ID_53615-/free-co-fin-factsheet.xhtml.

International Teletubbies celebration at FAO Schwartz is fantasy come true for kids. (1999, March 24). [Press release]. New York: Microsoft.

LaFranchi, H. (2000, July 24). Freedom of expression? Jerry Springer-style programs invade Mexico. *Christian Science Monitor*.

Lemish, D., and Tidhar, C.E. (2001). How global does it get? The Teletubbies in Israel. *Journal of Broadcasting and Electronic Media*, 45(4), 558–574.

Lomelí, A. (2003). The internationalization of Mexican television [Paper presented at the Global Fusion 2003 conference, Austin. TX, November 1–3].

McFadyen, S., Hoskins, C., and Finn, A. (1998). The effects of cultural differences on the international co-production of television programs and feature films. *Canadian Journal of Communication*, 23(4).

Mexico's Televisa shares rally on restructure. (1999, February 1). Mexico City: Reuters.

Mexico's TV Azteca shares rise 10 percent. (1999, December 15). Mexico City: Reuters.

Miller, T., Govil, N., McMurria, J., and Maxwell, R. (2001). *Global Hollywood*. London: British Film Institute.

Moran, A. (1998). *Copycat TV: Globalisation, program formats, and cultural identity*. Luton, UK: University of Luton Press.

Morgan, R. (1999, June 7). Teletubbies promo items prove too popular. New York: Reuters.

The one where Pooh goes to Sweden (2003, April 3). *Economist*, p. 73.

Paxman, A., and Saragoza, A.M. (2001). Globalization and Latin media powers: The case of Mexico's Televisa. In V. Mosco and D. Schiller (Eds.), *Continental order? Integrating North America for cybercapitalism* (pp. 64–85). Lanham, MD: Rowman and Littlefield.

Reed, D. (1999, February 10). Falwell's newspaper attempts to label 'Teletubbies' character as gay. Roanoke, VA: Associated Press.

Sánchez-Ruiz, E. E. (2001). Globalization, cultural industries, and free trade: The Mexican audiovisual sector in the NAFTA age. In V. Mosco and D. Schiller (Eds.), *Continental order? Integrating North America for cybercapitalism* (pp. 86–119). Lanham, MD: Rowman and Littlefield.

Sepstrup, P. (1990). *Transnationalisation of television in Western Europe*. London: John Libby.

Shohat, E., and Stam, R. (1994). *Unthinking Eurocentrism: Multiculturalism and the media*. London and New York: Routledge.

Subliminal Messages? (1999, February 16). *Washington Post*, p. A16.

Taylor, P. W. (1995). Co-productions—Content and change: International television in the Americas. *Canadian Journal of Communication*, 20(3).

Teletubbies declare war. (1999, March 23). *BBC Online*.

Teletubby mania on QVC. (1998, December 28). [Press release]. West Chester, PA: Itsy Bitsy Entertainment and QVC.

Televisa Mexico to cut $80 mln in costs in 99/2000. (1999, April 28). Mexico City: Reuters.

Tinky Winky, Dipsy, Laa-Laa, and Po say 'Eh-oh' to Microsoft. (1999, January 6). [Press release]. New York: Itsy Bitsy Entertainment.

TV Azteca and Canal 40 announce joint venture; TV Azteca purchases 10% of Channel 40. (1998, July 29). Mexico City: TV Azteca and S.A. de C.V.

TV Azteca denies wrongdoing in Chile. (1999 January 27). Mexico City: Reuters.

TV Azteca signs exclusive free TV licensing agreement for Disney programming. (1998, November 5). Mexico City: TV Azteca and S.A. de C.V.

Wal-mart had legal ok on Teletubbies look-alikes. (1999, March 23). Chicago: Reuters.

Wal-mart to destroy Teletubby look-alikes. (1999, May 19). New York: Reuters.

Wayne, M. (2003). Postfordism, monopoly capitalism, and Hollywood's media-industrial complex. *International Journal of Cultural Studies*, 6(1), 82–103.Barnett, S., and Curry, A. (1994). *The battle for the BBC*. London: Aurum Press.

23.
RUNAWAY PRODUCTION, RUNAWAY CONSUMPTION, RUNAWAY CITIZENSHIP

The New International Division of Cultural Labor

Toby Miller and Marie Claire Leger[1]

Think of the Mexican entertainment market, with its young population and fast-growing middle class, as a teenager out looking for a good time after being cooped up for too long. For economically emerging peoples all over the globe, Hollywood speaks a universal language — *Forbes*.

(Gubernick and Millman, 1994, p. 95)

Worried that free trade is making their indolent lifestyle less viable, the French are blaming sinister conspiracies and putting quotas on American movies — *Wall Street Journal — Europe*.

(Brooks, 1994, p. 34)

It's not the heat, and it's not the humidity: what's really enervating is day after relentless day of news reports about the G-7 trade negotiations in Tokyo. GATT. Market-share targets. The Uruguay Round. Consultations with the Canadian Prime Minister. Drowsy yet? Part of the problem is that trade talks always focus on desperately unexciting commodities; given the choice between reading about tariffs on non-ferrous metals and, say, Julia Roberts' marriage, many people will skip the trade-barriers story. So here's an age-of-Clinton hybrid: movie stars and arcane trade issues, together in one convenient package — *Time*.

(Anderson, 1993)

Introduction

We inhabit a moment popularly understood as 'the global triumph of the United States and its way of life'

(Hobsbawm, 1998, p. 1). Even Henry Kissinger (1999) states that 'globalization is really another name for the dominant role of the United States.' This state of affairs is both celebrated and feared; while the *Wall Street Journal* gleefully proclaims that America's 'unrivalled dominance' spreads free-market ideology around the world (Murray, 1999), many nations, both developed and undeveloped, fear that the proliferation of US-style capitalism means cultural domination, especially through the audiovisual industries.

US global dominance is the outcome of the 'Washington Consensus.' The ruling *laissez-faire* dogma since the late 1970s, the 'Consensus' favors open trade, comparative advantage, deregulation of financial markets, and low inflation. It has, of course, presided over slower worldwide growth and greater worldwide inequality than any time since the Depression. Job security and real wages are down and working hours are up in the industrialized market economies (IMECS) at the same time as the richest 20% of the world's people earned 74 times the amount of the world's poorest in 1997, up from 60 times in 1990 and 30 times in 1960. But despite the manifold catastrophes of the 'Consensus' across the late 1990s — Mexico, Southeast Asia, Russia, Brazil, and Argentina — it is still hailed as exemplary policy. Repeated failures are deemed aberrations by apologists, who confidently await 'the long run,' when equilibrium will be attained (Palley, 1999, p. 49; Levinson, 1999, p. 21; Galbraith, 1999, p. 13).

The 'Consensus' is animated by neo-liberalism's mantra of business freedom, the marketplace, and minimal government involvement in economic matters. This provides the intellectual alibi for a comparatively unimpeded flow of capital across national boundaries, and the rejection of labor, capital, and the state managing the economy together. The state undermines the union movement on behalf of capital through policies designed to 'free' labor from employment laws. In the process, the Keynesian welfare system, which helped to redistribute funds to the working class, is dismantled. Ralph Nader refers to this as 'a slow motion *coup d'état*,' in which the historic gains to representative discussion and social welfare made by working people and subaltern groups are subordinated to corporate power (1999, p. 7).

This paper investigates the cultural correlatives of the 'Washington Consensus,' the increasing global influence of the United States, and the decreasing power of organized labor and the state. We address these issues through a discussion of screen production, consumption, and citizenship, comparing neoclassical economic theory's account of the sovereign consumer with cultural policy's account of the cultural citizen. As an alternative to those models, we offer a mixture of approaches to consumption derived from social theory, coupled with a theory of the New International Division of Cultural Labor (NICL), which centralizes the importance of 'flexible' cultural labor to the new global cultural economy. We conclude that activists and critical scholars need to expose the contradictions at the center of consumer-citizen rhetorics and strive for democratically accountable forms of intervention. For in an increasingly global division of cultural labor, how citizenship is theorized and practiced matters enormously for working people. How are individual and community rights determined? How *should* they be determined? Should citizenship be granted based on where people live, were born, or work, the temporary or permanent domicile of their employer, or the cultural impact of a foreign multinational on daily life? Such questions form the backdrop to our paper.

Although cries of cultural imperialism were widespread in the 1960s, Hollywood's global expansion in the 1990s was much greater. In 1998, the major US film studios increased their foreign rentals by a fifth from just the year before. Indeed, the overseas box office of \$6.821bn was just below the domestic figure

of \$6.877bn and double the 1990 proportion. International markets in both film and TV are more important now than ever before. Between 1988 and 1993, international box-office receipts for Hollywood increased by 14%, domestic ones by just over half that figure. In contrast, in 1980, the American film industry relied on exports for a third of its annual revenue, the same as 50 years ago. And even though theatrical income as a percentage of a film's overall profit has been steadily declining since 1980, theater release profits remain the benchmark for prices that producers can charge for television exhibition (Segrave, 1997, p. 238). Hollywood's global influence extends beyond what can be measured through the 'legitimate' economy: revenue lost through the illegal international copying of electronic texts was estimated at \$70bn in 1994. This lost revenue became a further incentive for the industry and the US government to redraft the international intellectual property infrastructure (Hills, 1994, p. 185; Hoekman and Kostecki, 1995, p. 127; Mayrhofer, 1994, p. 137).

So this decade has seen a truly foundational change. In 1996, 78% of all cinema tickets sold in the European Union (EU) were for US releases. The most popular 39 films across the world in 1998 came from the United States, and other major filmmaking countries were in decline. The percentage of the box office occupied by indigenous films that year fell to 10% in Germany, 12% in Britain, 26% in France, 12% in Spain, 2% in Canada, 4% in Australia, and 5% in Brazil — all dramatic decreases, to record-low levels in some cases *(The Economist*, 1998b; Groves, 1994, p. 18, and 1999; *Variety*, 1999; Theiler, 1999, p. 575; Woods, 1999a).

While its global cultural dominance is virtually unchallenged, the United States is trying to develop this share of the market still further, by mounting major governmental and business assaults on the legitimacy of national self-determination undertaken by other countries that utilize state support to generate and sustain cultural industries. Relying on the notorious provisions of its 1974 Trade Act, the United States threatens sanctions against those who participate in what it regards as unfair trading practices; Hong Kong, for example, was a particular target for what the United States likes to call screen 'piracy' until it acquiesced with the Trade Office's requirements. Meanwhile, the US government, eagerly eyeing China's 140,000 film theaters, is keen to loosen PRC restrictions on Hollywood imports (USIA, 1997; Barshefsky, 1998; World Trade Organization, 1998; Sullivan, 1999). In 1994, Daniel Toscan du Plantier, then president of the French government's film marketing body stated: 'cinema used to be side salad in world commerce. Now, it's the beef' (quoted in Cohen, 1994, section H23). How are the ownership and control of this 'beef' governed?

The GATT and the WTO

Who can be blind today to the threat of a world gradually invaded by an identical culture, Anglo-Saxon culture, under the cover of economic liberalism? — François Mitterand,

(quoted in Brooks, 1994, p. 35)

If the European Commission governments truly care about their citizens' cultural preferences, they would permit them the freedom to see and hear works of their choosing; if they are really concerned about a nation's cultural heritage, they would encourage the distribution of programming reflecting that heritage — Jack Golodner, President of the Department for Professional Employees, AFL–CIO.

(1994, p. H6)

From its emergence in the late 1940s as one of several new international financial and trading protocols, the General Agreement on Tariffs and Trade (the GATT) embodied in contractual terms the First World's rules of economic prosperity: nondiscrimination; codified regulations policed outside the terrain of individual sovereign-states; and multilateralism. Born under the logic of North American growth evangelism, whereby standardized industrial methods, vast scales of production, and an endless expansion of markets would engineer economic recovery and development for the Western European *detritus* of World War II, simultaneously precluding any turn to Marxism-Leninism, the GATT commenced a long wave of restructuring capitalism. The General Agreement stood for the paradoxically bureaucratic voice of neoclassical economics, rejecting parochial national interests and state intervention in favor of

free trade. Officials worked like puritans ordered by some intellectual manifest destiny to disrupt trading blocs and restrict distortions to the putatively natural rhythms of supply and demand as determined by consumer sovereignty and comparative advantage.

From the early days of GATT in the 1940s, the United States had sought coverage of cinema by the General Agreement, without success. Once TV texts became significant trading commodities, they too came onto the agenda. The Europeans maintained, *contra* the United States, that films and programs were services, not commodities, and hence exempt (Jarvie, 1998, pp. 38–39; McDonald, 1999). The GATT was slow to recognize trade in services (TIS) even though that sector quickly expanded in the postwar era.[2] This was in part because the frequently object-free exchanges that characterize the 'human' side to TIS (restaurants, for example) were not especially amenable to conceptualization and enumeration. But as the Western powers saw capital fly from their manufacturing zones, and sought to become net exporters of services, they discovered ways of opening up the area to bureaucratic invigilation.

Today, TIS accounts for 60% of gross domestic product in the IMECS and more than a quarter of world trade. The Punta del Este Declaration of September 1986 began the seven-year-long Uruguay Round of the GATT. Because of pressure from the United States (always the main player in negotiations) in the service of lobbyists for American Express, Citibank, and IBM, the Uruguay Round put TIS, which includes film, television, and broadcast advertising production and distribution as well as the finance industries, education, tourism, and telecommunications, at the center of GATT negotiations for the first time (Grey, 1990, pp. 6–9; Sjolander, 1992–93, p. 54, n. 5). After the United States failed to have cultural industries incorporated in the 1988 Free Trade Agreement with Canada, its foreign-service and trade officials tried to thwart EU plans for import quotas on audiovisual texts. The Union's 'Television Without [intra-European] Frontiers' directive (adopted in 1989 and amended in 1997) drew particular ire for its 49% limit on texts imported by member nations (McDonald, 1999; Theiler, 1999, p. 558). But attempts to have the Uruguay Round derail such policies were almost universally opposed, with significant participation from India, Canada, Japan, Australia, all of Europe, and the Third

World, in the name of cultural sovereignty. This position equated the culture industries with environmental protection or the armed forces, as beyond neo-classicism: their social impact could not be reduced to price. In 1993, thousands of European artists, intellectuals, and producers signed a petition in major newspapers calling for culture to be exempt from the GATT's no-holds-barred commodification (Van Eiteren, 1996a, p. 47). Western Europe's Community law enshrines freedom of expression through media access — the European Union's alibi for putting quotas on US screen texts, along with the claim that the screen is not a good but a service.[3] The 1993 coalition opposed the idea that the GATT should ensure open access to screen markets, on the grounds that culture must be deemed inalienable (non-commodifiable).

To US critics, this was a smokescreen, with cultural rights secreting the protection of inefficient culture industries and outmoded *dirigiste* statism (Kessler, 1995; Van Eiteren, 1996b; Venturelli, 1998, p. 61). The United States argued from a *laissez-faire* position, claiming that the revelation of consumer preferences should be the deciding factor as to who has comparative advantage in TV and film production — whether Hollywood or Sydney is the logical place to make audiovisual texts. The United States claimed there was no room for the public sector in screen production, because it crowded out private investment, which was necessarily more in tune with popular taste. Both the active face of public subvention (national cinemas and broadcasters) and the negative face of public proscription (import barriers to encourage local production) were derided for obstructing market forces.

The battle waged here between the European Union (against cultural imperialism) and the United States (for unhampered market access) was won by the European Union; the screen was excluded from the GATT in 1993. But this exclusion has not prevented Hollywood from peddling its wares internationally. As noted earlier, half of Hollywood's revenue comes from overseas, with Western Europe providing 55%. The United States supplies three-quarters of the market there, up from half a decade ago. Furthermore, the consolidation of Europe into one market has been a huge boon to Hollywood, along with the deregulation of TV (*Daily Variety*, 1994, p. 16; Van Eiteren, 1996b; *The Economist*, 1998a). And the European screen-trade

deficit with Hollywood grew from \$4.8bn to \$5.65bn between 1995 and 1996 (*Film Journal*, 1994, p. 3; Hill, 1994, p. 2, p. 7, n. 4; *The Economist*, 1998a).

The last gasp of the GATT was the 20,000 page protocol that was agreed in Geneva in 1993, signed in Marrakesh in 1994, and ratified domestically by 125 members and fellow-travelers over the next eight months. In January 1995, the World Trade Organization (WTO) replaced the GATT and bought the latter's *detritus* of GATTocrats. The WTO has a legal personality, a secretariat, and biennial ministerial conferences. This new machinery makes it easier for multinational corporations to dominate trade via the diplomatic services of their home governments' representatives. Environmental concerns and other matters of public interest no longer have the *entrée* that GATT granted via recognition of non-government organizations. Multinationals now find it easier to be regarded as local firms in their host countries, and Third World agricultural production has been further opened up to foreign ownership (Dobson, 1993, pp. 573–576; Lang and Hines, 1993, pp. 48–50). But despite its high-theory commitment to pure/perfect competition, political pressures mean the WTO must nod in the direction of archaeological, artistic, and historic exemptions to free-trade totalizations, as the GATT routinely did (Chartrand, 1992, p. 137).

The WTO's operating protocols favor transparency, most-favored nation precepts, national treatment (identical policies for imported and local commodities), tariffs over other protective measures, and formal methods of settling disputes. Its initial service-industries focus has been on the lucrative telecommunications market, but the Organization is turning to culture. Commodities and knowledges previously excluded from the GATT, such as artworks and international export controls, have been included in the WTO's remit, with extra-economic questions of national sovereignty eluding the written word of trade negotiation but thoroughly suffusing its implementation and consequences (Zolberg, 1995). Even though GATS (the WTO's document that constitutes a binding protocol to the results of the Uruguay Round) states that there must be easy market access and no differential treatment of national and foreign service suppliers, it nevertheless allows 'wiggle room' to exempt certain services from these principles. This margin for maneuver is utilized, for example, by the European Union when it sets quotas for films.

In 1997, the WTO made its first major movement into the culture industries in a case concerning the Canadian version of *Sports Illustrated* magazine. The WTO ruled that Canada could not impose tariffs on the magazine because it was enticing advertisers away from local periodicals, thus beginning the Organization's cultural push (Valentine, 1997; Magder, 1998). In keeping with the *Sports Illustrated* case, the United States seeks to cluster cultural issues under the catch-all rubric of intellectual property and to disavow questions of national sovereignty or meaning (Venturelli, 1998, pp. 62, 66).[4]

Since January 2000, the WTO has been conducting GATS 2000, a round of negotiations that further addresses the liberalization of TIS. One major issue is virtual goods. As audiovisual services are absorbed into concepts such as electronic commerce and information and entertainment services, and the distinction between goods and services begins to blur, the European Union fears that the United States will muscle its way into film and TV through insisting on free-market access to new communication services. As Mark Wheeler states, 'The British Screen Advisory Council (BSAC) has argued that the USA could use the Internet as a Trojan Horse to undermine the Community's "Television Without Frontiers" directive' (2000, p. 258).

This is not a purely economic struggle. For as the 'Washington Consensus' extends to incorporate culture, a rhetorical battle is being waged between two forms of subjectivity: the consumer (championed by the United States) and the citizen (championed by the rest of the world). Civil society is meant to be founded on the individual, but not just on the sovereign consumer. For that craven figure ultimately dies alone, surrounded by rotting goods and spent services: *anomie* is the fate of this isolate, in the lonely hour of the last instance. To avoid such a fate, the individual must also learn sociability and collaboration. In our media-thick era, this dilemma has generated a litany of binary judgements: solo TV-viewing is bad, team bowling is good; gambling on-line is bad, church attendance is good. The liberal individual who can find a way through this thicket of choice and obligation is a magic blend of the selfish and the selfless, the solo and the social. That individual is taken as a model for economic and social

policy throughout the world. Economic models are based on the desire to maximize utility in a selfish way — the consumer as a desiring machine. Social models are based on the preparedness to think beyond oneself, to contribute to social cohesiveness via volunteerism that sidesteps the pitfalls of both business and government. We turn now to the subjects of these models.

Screen Consumption, Screen Citizenship

Entertainment is one of the purest marketplaces in the world. If people don't like a movie or record they won't see it or buy it. The fact that the American entertainment industry has been so successful on a worldwide basis speaks to the quality and attractiveness of what we're creating — Robert Shaye, Chair of New Line Pictures.

(quoted in Weinraub, 1993, p. L24)

FBI + CIA = TWA + Pan Am — graffito written by Eve Democracy in *One + One*.

(Jean-Luc Godard, 1969)

What's the point of saying no to America's nuclear ships when we've said yes, a thousand times yes, to the Trojan Horse of American Culture, dragging it throughout city gates into our very loungerooms. MGM is mightier than the CIA. . . . We are, all of us, little by little, becoming ventriloquial dolls for another society. We are losing our authenticity, our originality, and becoming echoes — *Australian Weekend Magazine*.

(quoted in Pendakur, 1990, pp. 16–17)

There is a complicated relationship between the citizen and its logocentric double, the consumer. The citizen is a wizened figure from the ancient past. The consumer, by contrast, is naive, essentially a creature of the nineteenth century. Each shadows the other, the *national* subject versus the *rational* subject. We all know the popularity of the consumer with neo-classical economists and policy wonks. The market is said to operate in response to this ratiocinative agent, who, endowed with perfect knowledge, negotiates between alternative suppliers and his or her own demands, such that an appropriate price is paid for desired commodities. The supposedly neutral mechanism of market competition sees materials exchanged at a cost that ensures the most efficient people are producing and their customers are content.

This model may occasionally describe life in some fruit and vegetable markets today. But as an historical account, it is of no value: the rhythms of supply and demand, operating unfettered by states, religions, unions, superstitions, and fashions, have never existed as such. Or rather, they have existed as enormously potent prescriptive signs in the rhetoric of international financial organizations, bureaucrats, and journalists, at least since economists achieved their hegemony via the Keynesian end to the Great Depression, and then worked to maintain it, despite 1970s stagflation, via their mass conversion from demand-side to supply-side doctrines. The consumer has become the sexless, ageless, unprincipled, magical agent of social value in a multitude of discourses and institutions since that time. For example, in the screen sector, the decline over the 1990s of non-US film production is often explained away through claims that Hollywood's international success results from the 'narrative transparency' of its continuity story-telling, blended with a vast and internally differentiated internal public of immigrants from diverse cultures, which allegedly makes for a universal means of entertainment that attracts foreign consumers (Olson, 1999). Unmarked in this rationality by their national origins, US audiences are runaways from national culture, animated by individual preferences.

It seems sensible to evaluate the *laissez-faire* rationality introduced above, with consumer interests at its center, as an account of US screen production. This necessitates questioning whether Hollywood is a free market based on consumer demand, and also whether the industry operates under the stated aims of public policy based on the tenets of neo-classical economics — or that relative autonomy from the state, ease of entry by competitors into culture industries, and the resultant diversity of producers guarantee a democratically representative array of textual diversity. We propose four tests of this rationality here, based on the promises and premises of neo-classical economics: (a) freedom of entry into the market for new starters; (b) independence of the culture industries from the state; (c) relationship between the cost of production and consumption; and (d) extent of textual diversity.

Whereas neo-classical economics asserts that there must be freedom of entry into a market for new businesses, this has not been the case in the culture industries. There have been new owners of major Hollywood studios, such as Australia's Channel Seven and News Corporation, Canada's Seagrams, and Japan's Sony, plus a new venture in Dreamworks. But the traditional studios remain as much in charge as ever, as we shall see below in our discussion of flexible specialization.

Another claim of this ideology is that there should not be state subsidies of the industry. Yet the US government endorses trust-like behavior overseas, whilst prohibiting it domestically. The film industry has been aided through decades of tax-credit schemes, the Informational Media Guaranty Program's currency assistance, and oligopolistic domestic buying and overseas selling practices that (without much good evidence for doing so) keep the primary market essentially closed to imports on grounds of popular taste (Guback, 1984, pp. 156–157; Thompson, 1985, pp. 117–118, 122–123; Guback, 1987, pp. 92–93, 98–99; Schatz, 1988, p. 160; Vasey, 1997, pp. 160, 164). After World War II, Hollywood's Motion Picture Export Agency referred to itself as 'the little State Department,' so isomorphic were its methods and contents with Federal policy and ideology. The US Department of Commerce continues to produce materials on media globalization for Congress that run lines about both economic development and ideological influence, problematizing claims that Hollywood is pure free enterprise and that its government is uninterested in blending trade with cultural change (Ferguson, 1992, pp. 83–84; Jarvie, 1998, pp. 37, 40). Meanwhile, the Justice Department is authorized to classify all imported films, which it can prohibit as 'political propaganda' (as it has done with Canadian documentaries on acid rain and nuclear war, for instance) (Parker, 1991, pp. 135, 137; Sorlin, 1991, p. 93). The United States has 196 (count them) state, regional, and city film and TV commissions, hidden subsidies to the screen industries (via reduced local taxes, free provision of police services, and the blocking of public wayfares), State and Commerce Department briefings and plenipotentiary representation (negotiations on so-called video piracy have resulted in PRC offenders being threatened with beheading, even as the United States claims to be watching Chinese human rights as part of most-favored nation treatment) and copyright limitations that are all about preventing the free flow of information (which the United States is forever instructing less-developed countries to permit in order that they might prosper).

Although it is claimed that there is a relationship between the cost of production and consumption, costs are not reflected in the price of tickets or cable fees. They are amortized through a huge array of venues, so reusable is each copy of each text, unlike a car or painting. A gigantic and wealthy domestic English-language market, when added to numerous venues (video, DVD, broadcast networks, cable, and satellite) makes identical, cheaply reproducible texts into profit centers with less depreciation and more potential for transformation and re-sale than conventional goods.

And finally, this ordering of the industry is supposed to lead to greater textual diversity. In the 1960s, imports accounted for 10% of the US film market. In 1986, that figure was 7%. Today, it is 0.75%. Foreign films are essentially excluded from the United States, as never before (*The Economist*, 1997). This is due to the corporatization of cinema exhibition plus increases in promotional costs, to the point where subtitling and dubbing become insupportable for independent distributors. In television, the proliferation of channels in the United States over the past ten years has required companies to change their drama offerings significantly. In 1990, action-adventure, the most expensive TV genre, occupied 20% of primetime on the networks; four years later, the figure was around 1% (Schwab, 1994). Now we are seeing the sudden decline of the soap opera. Reality television, fixed upon by cultural critics who either mourn it as representative of a decline in journalistic standards or celebrate it as the sign of a newly feminized public sphere, should frankly be understood as a cost-cutting measure.

What of the other side to our couplet, the citizen, currently involved in Europe against US demands for a free market? The citizen has also undergone a major revival in the last decade, as social theorists and policymakers have identified citizenship as a magical agent of historical change. More easily identified than class, and more easily mobilized as a justification for state action, citizenship has become a site of hope for a left that has lost its actually existing alternative to international capital. We now address the utility of this move in the context of film and television.

Two accounts of screen citizenship are dominant in academia, public policy, and social activism. In their different ways, each is an effects model, in that they both assume the screen *does* things *to* people, with the citizen understood as an audience member that can be a runaway from both interpersonal responsibility and national culture. The first model, dominant in the United States and exported around the world, derives from the social sciences and is applied without consideration of place. We'll call this the *domestic* effects model, or DEM. It is universalist and psychological. The DEM offers analysis and critique of such crucial citizenship questions as education and civic order. It views the screen as a machine that can either pervert or direct the citizen-consumer. Entering young minds osmotically, it can either enable or imperil learning. And it also drives the citizen to violence through aggressive and misogynistic images and narratives. The DEM is found in a variety of sites, including laboratories, clinics, prisons, schools, newspapers, psychology journals, TV network and film studio research and publicity departments, everyday talk, program classification regulations, conference papers, parliamentary debates, and state-of-our-youth or state-of-our-civil-society moral panics (see Buckingham, 1997 and Hartley, 1996). The DEM is embodied in the nationwide US media theatrics that ensued after the Columbine shootings, questioning the role of violent images (not firearms or straight white masculinity) in creating violent citizens. It is also evident in panics about the impact of TV advertisements on the environment or politics.

The second way of thinking about screen citizenship is a *global* effects model, or GEM. The GEM, primarily utilized in non-US discourse, is specific and political rather than universalist and psychological. Whereas the DEM focuses on the cognition and emotion of individual human subjects via replicable experimentation, the GEM looks to the knowledge of custom and patriotic feeling exhibited by collective human subjects, the grout of national culture. In place of psychology, it is concerned with politics. The screen does not make you a well- or an ill-educated person, a wild or a self-controlled one. Rather, it makes you either a knowledgeable and loyal national subject, or a duped viewer who lacks an appreciation of local custom and history. Cultural belonging, not psychic wholeness, is the touchstone of the global effects model. Instead of measuring responses electronically or behaviorally, as its domestic counterpart does, the GEM looks to the national origin of screen texts and the themes and styles they embody, with particular attention to the putatively nation-building genres of drama, news, sport, and current affairs. GEM adherents hold that local citizens should control local broadcast networks because they alone can be relied upon to be loyal reporters in the event of war, while in the case of fiction, only locally sensitized producers make narratives that are true to tradition and custom. This model is found in the discourse of cultural imperialism, everyday talk, broadcast and telecommunications policy, international organizations, newspapers, cultural diplomacy, post-industrial service-sector planning, and national-cinema discourse. The enumeration of national authenticity in screen texts through fractional ownership has been common in countries concerned to protect their national cultural economies from foreign imports.

Let's run through the problems with these models. The DEM suffers from all the disadvantages of ideal-typical psychological reasoning. Each costly laboratory test of media effects based on 'a large university in the mid-West' is countered by a similar experiment, with conflicting results. As politicians, grant-givers, and jeremiad-wielding pundits call for more and more research to prove that the screen makes you stupid, violent, and apathetic — or the opposite — academics line up at the trough to indulge their hatred of popular culture and ordinary life and their rent-seeking urge for public money. As for the GEM, its concentration on national culture: (a) denies the potentially liberatory and pleasurable nature of different takes on the popular; (b) forgets the internal differentiation of viewing publics; (c) valorizes frequently oppressive and/or unrepresentative local *bourgeoisies* in the name of national culture's maintenance and development; and (d) ignores the demographic realities of its 'own' terrain.

Once we add some history, spatiality, and politics to the DEM/GEM, they become more complicated. Consumption and citizenship have a dynamic relationship to left and right discourse. Citizen-consumers are said to be both constructed and corrupted through popular culture. On one side of the debate, the exercise of choice through purchase is supposed to guarantee the democratic workings of a market-driven society, because the culture industries provide what the public desires. It is also supposed to effect social change — for example, because of racist hiring practices, Denny's restaurant chain is boycotted by some leftists in the United States, some of whom also use the Working Assets long-distance telephone service because it donates a portion of its proceeds to left-wing causes. At certain moments, leftists resisting authoritarian politics may embrace ideologies of liberal individualism and free choice, whereas at other times they may foreground questions of labor rather than consumption in a struggle for collective justice. Nation-building eras see a similar slippage between citizen and consumer, depending on the historical moment and geographical location. For example, state-based modernization projects in Latin America between the 1930s and the 1960s utilized the mass media — song in Brazil, radio in Argentina, and cinema in Mexico — to turn the masses, newly migrated to the cities, into citizens (Martín-Barbero, 1993). Conversely, the 1990s brought a wave of deregulation in the mass media. In lieu of citizen-building, the new logic of the culture industries is the construction of consumers. Néstor García-Canclini notes that this shift in emphasis from citizen to consumer is sometimes linked to the shift of Latin America's dependency on Europe to a dependency on the United States. He summarizes this position as follows: 'We Latin Americans presumably learned to be citizens through our relationship to Europe; our relationship to the United States will, however, reduce us to consumers' (García-Canclini, 2001, p. 1). And in the name of the consumer, ideas of the national popular are eschewed — consumer choice becomes an alibi for structural-adjustment policies imposed by international lending institutions that call for privatization of the media.

In an era of globalized film and television, the idea that audiovisual spaces should be accountable to local viewers, as well as far-distant shareholders, is a powerful one. But how much can be expected from citizenship and consumer ideals when for the first time, trade between corporations exceeds that between states; deregulation sees huge monopoly capitalists converging and collaborating; screen texts are designed to transcend linguistic and other cultural boundaries; textual diversity is a myth; cultural production is not independent of the state; and finally, many of us live in societies that deny or limit our citizenship and consumption claims?

Does this mean that notions of citizenship and consumption are useless in discussing accountability, sovereignty, and democracy with regard to the culture industries? Not exactly. Theorists such as George Yúdice and García-Canclini have elaborated alternative models of citizenship and consumption that go beyond standard leftist critiques of cultural imperialism (watching US drama will turn rural people around the world into Idaho potato farmers) and invectives about socially responsible shopping (purchasing environmentally sound toilet paper and free-range chicken will transform the world, one roll/wing at a time).

Yúdice argues that it may no longer be possible to speak of citizenship and democracy without also considering consumption; indeed, he suggests that consumption can create a new politics of citizenship. First World practices — such as juridical prosecution of discrimination in the private workplace — and practices from Latin America — such as the need to go beyond individual consumer choices in cultural politics to consider the collaboration of local groups, transnational businesses, financial institutions, media, and non-governmental organizations — can be creatively combined with each other. García-Canclini agrees. Although acknowledging that the private takeover of state cultural functions has 'compounded the already existing problems of the inadequate development and instability of our democracies' (2001, p. 2) thus threatening Latin American civil society, he also believes that it is necessary to expand notions of citizenship to include consumption of health, housing, and education.

Both Yúdice and García-Canclini propose a regional federalism that promotes the creation of a specifically Latin American media space. This would be achieved through the state setting quotas for Latin American productions in movie theaters, radio broadcasts, and television programming, the creation of a Foundation for the Production and Distribution of Latin American media, and policies designed to

strengthen Latin American economies and regulate foreign capital in order to foster a citizenship that promotes multiculturalism and democratizes the relationship between the nation and the state (Yúdice, 1995).

García-Canclini (1996) criticizes the widespread neo-liberal dismissal of the state as an inappropriate arbiter of regulation and control. He argues that the market and civil society are not the same thing, thus challenging neo-classical assertions that a free market best serves the interests of society at large. This does not mean a return to the critiques of left-wing cultural commentators that transnational culture perverts pure indigenous traditions — indeed, García-Canclini's (1990) theories of hybridity preclude this kind of analysis. Nor does it elicit more aristocratic complaints that mass dissemination corrupts high art. However, it does challenge neo-liberal policymakers and authors such as Mario Vargas Llosa who assert that the free market finally allows peripherally produced cultural products such as the film *Like Water for Chocolate* to be disseminated around the world. García-Canclini argues instead that without reviving nationalism, there must be a critical state intervention which recognizes that 'culture is too important to be relinquished exclusively to the competition among international markets' (1996, p. 155). Yúdice (2000) states that the creation of regional/continental trading blocs, organized with the intent of moderating US audiovisual dominance and providing space for local cultural expression outside national frameworks, must involve public-private partnerships, including the participation of non-governmental organizations, the state, and industry.

But how can this strategy to create an alternative media space avoid the failings of the European model of regional pan-audiovisual culture? The abiding logic of the European Union's audiovisual cultural policy is commercial: it clearly favors existing large industrial concerns. This has served to bring into doubt the equation of the United States with entertainment and of Europe with education, with art cinema effectively a 'Euro-American' genro in terms of finance and management, and, as was noted earlier, much of Hollywood itself owned by foreigners (Lev, 1993). In this sense, the seeming discontinuity with earlier concerns, when the European Union had a primarily economic personality, is misleading: a notion of cultural sovereignty underpins concerns *vis-à-vis* the United States, but so too does support for European monopoly capital and the larger states inside its own walls (Burgelman and Pauwels, 1992). Meanwhile, the old notions of state cultural sovereignty that were so crucial to Europe's political traditions are being attenuated by the twin forces of 'bruxellois centralization' from outside and separatist ethnicities from within (Berman, 1992, p. 1515).

García-Canclini is critical of the European Union's cultural policies, particularly after the privatization of the communications media in Spain and France. He asserts, however, that the proposal of an audiovisual space is still a good one for Latin America. This is because Latin America has a particular way of being multicultural and modern that is very different from both Europe and the United States. He states that multiculturalism in Latin America is concerned with the need to 'legitimize multiple traditions of knowledge.' It prioritizes forging solidarity rather than the sectarianism he perceives in US and European multiculturalism. Instead, there is a hybridity which precludes each fighting for his own; the Zapatistas in Chiapas, for example, link their regional and ethnic demands to the nation and to globalization, mounting an inclusive critique of modernity that goes beyond the promotion of isolated local interests (García-Canclini, 2001). García-Canclini attributes this to the hybrid ethnic and national identities in Latin America. These hybrid cultures comprise a particularly uneven form of modernity, which includes complicated mixtures of tradition, modernity, and postmodernity. García-Canclini calls this hybridity multi-temporal, stating that it results from Latin America's particular colonial history. That history links the continent in a way that does not apply to Europe, because Latin America is dominated by the Spanish language (with the notable but changing exception of Brazil). The organic unity of this language has been crucial, for example, in the pan-continental and global success of the *telenovela*, which sees production labor and intertextual references drawn from the entire continent, providing a precedent for a broader Latin American linkage in terms of both personnel and cultural signification (Mazziotti, 1996; Mato, 1999, pp. 248–249).

Picking up from this industrial collaboration, we wish to supplement the contributions of Yúdice

and García-Canclini with a labor-theory-of-value approach to media citizenship. For bringing together the economy and textuality of the screen necessitates looking at the terrain of trade and work.

The New International Division of Cultural Labor

> We have created a product that by, say, putting the name of Warner Brothers on it is a stamp of credibility. But that could be an Arnon Milchan film, directed by Paul Verhoeven, starring Gerard Depardieu and Anthony Hopkins, and shot in France and Italy, and made with foreign money —
> John Ptak, Creative Artists Agency of Hollywood.
> (quoted in Weinraub, 1993, p. L24)

The expression 'division of labor' refers to sectoral differences in an economy, the occupations and skills of a labor force, and the organization of tasks within a firm. Life-cycle models of international products suggest they are first made and consumed in the center, in a major industrial economy, then exported to the periphery, and finally produced 'out there,' once technology has become standardized and savings can be made on the labor front. Goods and services owned and vended by the periphery rarely make their way into the center as imports (Keynes, 1957, pp. 333–334; Evans, 1979, pp. 27–28; Cohen, 1991, pp. 129, 133–139; Lang and Hines, 1993, p. 15; Strange, 1995, p. 293).

The idea of a New International Division of Labor (NIDL) derives from retheorizations of economic dependency theory that followed the inflationary chaos of the 1970s. Developing markets for labor and sales, and the shift from the spatial *sen*sitivities of electrics to the spatial *in*sensitivities of electronics, pushed businesses beyond treating Third World countries as suppliers of raw materials, to look on them as shadow-setters of the price of work, competing amongst themselves and with the First World for employment. As production was split across continents, the prior division of the globe into a small number of IMECs and a majority of underdeveloped ones was compromised. Folker Fröbel and his collaborators (1980) christened this the NIDL. The upshot is that any decision by a multinational firm to invest in a particular national formation carries the seeds of insecurity, because companies move on when tax incentives or other factors of production beckon (Fröbel *et al.*, 1980, pp. 2–8, 13–15, 45–48; Allan, 1988, pp. 325–326; Welch and Luostarinen, 1988; Browett and Leaver, 1989, p. 38).

We suggest that just as manufacturing fled the First World, cultural production has also relocated, though largely within the IMECS, as factors of production, including state assistance, lure film and TV producers. This is happening at the level of popular textual production, marketing, information, and high-culture, limited-edition work. Labor market slackness, increased profits, and developments in global transportation and communications technology have diminished the need for colocation of these factors, which depresses labor costs and deskills workers. 'Runaway production' is the common journalistic and industry shorthand for the ensuing exodus of Hollywood production.

How did this globalization of the labor process come about? The standard argument about Hollywood's industrial history is as follows: an artisanal system obtained in New York from the early 1900s until the wholesale shift to California in the 1920s. Vertically integrated industrialization followed, in the form of a studio system that made and distributed films like car manufacturers made jalopies, via rationalized techniques of mass production. In the 1940s, the system was undermined by governmental trust-busting and processes of televizualization and suburbanization: the state called on Hollywood to divest ownership of theaters even as the spread of TV and housing away from city centers diminished box-office receipts. The studios are said by some to have entered a post-Fordist phase of flexible specialization via product differentiation and vertical disintegration, relying on high-end genres and subcontracted independent producers, pre- and post-production companies, and global locations, rather than comprehensive in-house services. But despite this splintering, power remains vested in a small number of companies that resemble the very entities that were supposedly opened to competition 50 years ago via anti-trust. How? They have successfully controlled the gateways to film and TV that make real money for minimal outlay — distribution (Aksoy and Robins, 1992). The

fact of this continued centralized control makes an interrogation of the NICL all the more pressing.

The US film industry has always imported cultural producers, such as the German Expressionists. This was one-way traffic during the classical Hollywood era until the decade from 1946 saw production go overseas. Location shooting became a means of differentiating stories, and studios purchased facilities around the world to utilize cheap labor. Between 1950 and 1973, just 60% of Hollywood films in-production began their lives in the United States. American financial institutions bought foreign theaters and distribution companies, thus sharing risk and profit with local businesses. This was in keeping with the close historic relationship between the film industry and finance capital: as American banks looked overseas for sources of profit through the 1960s, so they endorsed and assisted efforts by Hollywood to spread risk and investment as widely as possible. By the end of the 1980s, overseas firms were crucial suppliers of funds invested in American film or loans against distribution rights in their countries of origin. Joint production arrangements are now well-established between US firms and French, British, Swedish, Australian, and Italian companies, with connections to television, theme parks, cabling, satellite, home video, and the internet. Co-production sees host governments working together or with the United States, as when *JFK* was funded by a Hollywood studio, a French cable network, a German production house, and a Dutch financier, while *The Full Monty*, supposedly the *ur*-British film of its generation, is of course owned by Fox (Wasko, 1982, pp. 206–207; Christopherson and Storper, 1986; Briller, 1990, pp. 75–78; Buck, 1992, pp. 119, 123; Marvasti, 1994; Wasko, 1994, p. 33; Kessler, 1995; Wasser, 1995, p. 424, 431; *The Economist*, 1998c; Wasko, 1998, pp. 180–181; Townson, 1999, p. 9).

Runaway TV and film production from the United States amounted to $500m in 1990 and $2.8bn in 1998. By the end of the 1990s, it was allegedly costing LA another $7.5bn annually in multiplier effects, plus 20,000 jobs. Hollywood's proportion of overseas productions went from 7% of its total to 27%, according to a study undertaken by the Monitor Group for the Directors and Screen Actors Guilds. Eighty-one percent of runaways went to Canada, a total of 232 in 1998 compared to 63 in 1990. Proponents regard the trend as a sign of successful post-Fordist flexible accumulation, whereby Canadian unions work with business and government to operate competitively in a tripartite heaven (Murphy, 1997). The production of high-profile texts like *Mission: Impossible 2* and *The Matrix* in Australia saw savings on LA prices of up to 30% (Waxman, 1999). Other governments covet such successes: between 1990 and 1998, 31 national film commissions were set up across the globe, many of them solely concerned with attracting foreign capital.

The long-term strategy of successive governments in Britain since 1979 has been to break up unions within the media in order to become a Euro-Hollywood by default: the skills generated in a regulated domain of the screen would be retained without the 'inefficiency' of the so-called 'X-factor' — labor. In short, flexibility was to supplant wage stability, and texts were to be oriented towards export. As a consequence, the United Kingdom now has a negative balance of screen trade for the first time in TV history. Associated deregulation produced a proliferation of networks and the inevitable search for cheap overseas content (Cornford and Robins, 1998, pp. 207–209). The British Film Commission (BFC) markets UK production expertise and locations by providing overseas producers with a free service articulating talent, sites, and subsidies and generating a national network of urban and regional film commissions. In 1997, seven Hollywood movies accounted for 54% of expenditure on feature-film production in the United Kingdom. The government opened a British Film Office in Los Angeles to normalize traffic with Hollywood by offering liaison services to the industry and promoting British locations and crews. The BFC announced the Blair government's outlook on cinema: 'set firmly at the top of the agenda is the desire to attract more overseas film-makers' (Guttridge, 1996; Hiscock, 1998; British Film Commission n.d.). The London Film Commission promotes the capital to overseas filmmakers, arranges police permits, and negotiates with local residents and businesses. Its defining moment was *Mission: Impossible*, when the Commissioner proudly said of that film's Hollywood producers: 'They came up with all these demands and I just went on insisting that, as long as they gave us notice, we could schedule it' (Jury, 1996).

In order to keep British studios going, regulations were promulgated in the mid-1990s that meant films entirely made in Britain counted as British, regardless of theme, setting, or stars. So *Judge Dredd* with Sylvester Stallone was 'British,' but *The English Patient* did too much of its post-production work abroad to qualify — until 1998, 92% of a film had to be created in the UK. At the end of that year, the government reduced this requirement to 75% to encourage American companies to make their films in Britain (Woolf, 1998).

After the success of *Titanic*, Mexico also became a key site for offshore production, as had been the case periodically since the 1960s, when *auteurs* such as Sam Peckinpah and John Huston filmed there for the scenery, and Richard Burton plus his attendant *paparazzi* turned Puerto Vallarta into a tourist destination. Restoring Mexico to the Hollywood map gained James Cameron the Order of the Aztec Eagle from a grateful government, which offers Hollywood docile labor, minimal bureaucracy, a dismal *peso*, and a new film commission to provide liaison services. Mexico's film union even maintains an office in LA to reassure anxious industry mavens of its cooperativeness (Sutter, 1998a,b). Perhaps not surprisingly, Rupert Murdoch (1998) welcomes 'new joint ventures between the Hollywood majors and both public and private broadcasting,' citing the numbers of European workers invisibly employed in the making of *Titanic*: 'this cross-border cultural co-operation is not the result of regulation, but market forces. It's the freedom to move capital, technology and talent around the world that adds value, invigorates ailing markets, creates new ones.'

In addition to shooting offshore, there is a second, palimpsestic model of the NICL. In an era when US network television is desperately cutting costs, there are opportunities for outsiders. The trend seems to be towards smaller investments in a larger number of programs for television. Put another way, a huge increase in the number of channels and systems of supply and payment is also producing unprecedented concentration of TV ownership. Some examples of the NICL represent a form of vertical investment, with production processes fragmented across the world. But what may be more significant for the future are the horizontal licensing and joint ventures that mirror domestic retailing systems (Roddick, 1994, p. 30; Schwab, 1994, p. 14).

For the culturalist remit of the GEM, the ability to make locally accented infotainment is one way of nations using the NICL. But there are unintended consequences. Consider the Grundy Organisation. It produced Australian TV drama and game shows from the 1950s that were bought on license from the United States. The company expanded to sell such texts across the world, operating with a strategy called 'parochial internationalism' that meant leaving Australia rather than exporting in isolation from relevant industrial, taste, and regulatory frameworks. Following patterns established in the advertising industry, it bought production houses around the world to make programs in local languages that were based on formats imported from Australia and drew on US models. From a base in Bermuda, the Organisation produced about 50 hours of TV a week in 70 countries across Europe, Oceania, Asia, and North America until its sale in the mid-1990s to Pearson. This exemplified the NICL offshore — a company utilizing experience in the Australian commercial reproduction industry to manufacture American palimpsests in countries relatively new to profit-centered TV. The benefits to Australia, where a regulatory framework birthed this expertise by requiring the networks to support such productions as part of cultural protection, are unclear (Stevenson, 1994, p. 1; Cunningham and Jacka, 1996, pp. 81–87; Moran, 1998, pp. 41–71). In such cases, the GEM is underwriting local cultural *bourgeoisies*.

Nor does this geographically splintered production imply a weakening of US control. It is, for example, certainly true that Vancouver and Toronto are the busiest locations for North American screen production after LA and New York, thanks to a weak Canadian currency and tax rebates of up to 22% on labor costs. But the two Canadian locations' 1998 production slates, of just under $1.5bn, are well behind California's total of $28bn, which incorporated almost 70% of US film production that year. In the 12 years to 1999, the number of culture industry jobs in California rose 137%, while nationwide US employment in entertainment had grown from 114,000 to 240,000 in ten years (Brinsley, 1999; Madigan, 1999c; Ryan, 1999). The hold on foreign capital is always tenuous and depends heavily on foreign exchange rates. The UK government's decision to float the pound and free the Bank of England from democratic consultation contributed to a situation in 1998 where a strengthening currency raised costs for overseas investors and encouraged locals to spend elsewhere, with severe implications for offshore film funds. And so the late 1990s offshore-production boom in Australia and Canada, driven in part by scenery, infrastructure, language, subsidization, and lower pay levels than the United States combined with equivalent skill levels, still depended on weak currencies (Pendakur, 1998, p. 229; Woods, 1999b).

The trend remains for North America to attract talent that has been developed by national cinemas to compete with it. Peter Weir's post-production for *The Truman Show* or *Witness* might take place in Australia, satisfying off-screen indices of localism in order to obtain state financing, but does that make for a real alternative to the United States? What does it mean that Michael Apted — James Bond and 7 *Up* series director — can speak with optimism of a 'Europeanizing of Hollywood' when Gaumont points out that 'a co-production with the Americans … usually turns out to be just another U.S. film shot on location' *(Variety*, 1994; Apted quoted in Dawtrey, 1994, p. 75; Gaumont quoted in Kessler, 1995, n. 143)? Attempts by the French film industry in the 1980s to attract US filmmakers may have the ultimate effect of US studio takeovers, while diplomatic efforts to maintain local screen subsidization continue even as Hollywood producers and networks purchase satellite and broadcast space across Europe (Hayward, 1993, p. 385). AOL-Time Warner, Disney-ABC, Viacom, NBC, and others are jostling their way into the center of the vast and growing Western European industry as sites of production as much as dumping-grounds for old material. The new stations throughout the continent invest in local programming with cost savings from scheduling American filler (Stevenson, 1994, p. 6).

Not all of this cultural work is directly associated with screen production, of course. Disney ensures that it profits from unsuccessful films via merchandizing (46% of annual revenue is from such sales). Much of the manufacturing is undertaken in Third World countries by subcontractors who exploit low-paid women workers. *The Hunchback of Notre Dame* performed poorly at the box-office but sensationally in toy stores, with products made in Taiwan,

Hong Kong, Mexico, Brazil, El Salvador, Thailand, Malaysia, St. Lucia, Colombia, the Philippines, Honduras, the Dominican Republic, India, Bangladesh, Sri Lanka, China, Haiti, the United States, Japan, Denmark, and Canada (Lent, 1998; McCann, 1998; *The Economist*, 1998a; Madigan, 1999a,b; Tracy, 1999).

To summarize, the screen is back where primary and secondary extractive and value-adding industries were in the 1960s, needing to make decisions not just about export, but about the site of production. Advances in communications technology permit electronic off-line editing across the world, but also enable special effects problematizing the very need for location shooting. The trend is clearly towards horizontal connections to other media, global economy and administration, and a break-up of public-private distinctions in ownership, control, and programming philosophy (Marvasti, 1994; Wedell, 1994, p. 325). Screen texts are fast developing as truly global trading forms. This is where the GEM is so influential: US late-night talk show host Jay Leno's promotional spot for NBC's pan-European Super Channel promised 'to ruin your culture just like we ruined our own.' The GATT, the WTO, and the *mythos* of the consumer are the devices of that 'ruination.'

Conclusion

In as labor-intensive an industry as the screen, we know that Leno's promised 'ruination' will involve over a million working people in the United States alone, most of whom have low weekly earnings. These groups have important internal divisions between so-called 'talent' and 'craft' and between heavily unionized film and broadcast workers and non-union cable employees; but their numerical growth and willingness to strike during the dominance of Republican union-busting was a beacon through the 1980s. They stand against virulent anti-union legislation in so-called 'right-to-work' states of the United States, the appeal to capital of the NICL, and pressure for Hollywood workers to deunionize in order to retain employment (Christopherson, 1996, pp. 87, 105–106; Gray and Seeber, 1996a, p. 34; Gray and Seeber, 1996b, pp. 4, 7; Wasko, 1998, p. 179, p. 184, n. 4, pp. 185–186).

Even in the United States, the NICL is a tremendously vexed matter for both economy and

sovereignty. T-shirts with crossed-out maple leaves and 'how 'bout some work, eh?' proliferate among disemployed workers in the LA screen sector (Ryan, 1999). A Film and Television Action Committee was formed in the late 1990s to eliminate runaway production, allying thousands of workers across acting, directing, and technical and support work (*Business Wire*, 1999). Chair Jack Degovia said of the Canadian government and industry: 'They came after us. They got us. The effects companies in Silicon Valley are next' (quoted in Stroud, 1999). Pressure from US workers angered by the flight of screen labor opportunities abroad has seen a proposed Film Protection Amendment in the US Congress to counter Canadian tax incentives that attract Hollywood production. It may be the start of a major backlash against the NICL (Madigan, 1999b). This oppositional voice in the United States characterizes the flight of capital as a reaction to unfair trading that sees state subsidies precluding open competition on the basis of efficiency and effectiveness. There are equivalent culturalist anxieties. The American Film Institute is concerned about any loss of cultural heritage to internationalism and George Quester laments that British costume history crowds out the space for indigenous 'quality' television, claiming there was more Australian high-end drama on US TV in the 1980s than locally produced material (1990, p. 57) — almost a case of GEM-like neuroses! Sean Connery is cast as a Hollywood lead because European audiences love him, while each US film is allotted a hundred generic descriptions for use in specific markets (*Dances with Wolves* was sold in France as a documentary-style dramatization of Native American life, and *Malcolm X* was promoted there with posters of the Stars and Stripes aflame) (Danan, 1995, pp. 131–132, 137; Wasser, 1995, p. 433). Critics question what is happening when US drama is scripted with special attention to foreign audiences and political economists argue that a newly transnational Hollywood no longer addresses its nominal audience.

So where to now for leftist cultural politics? We need to utilize contradictions on each side of the discursive divide between the consumer and the citizen, criticizing both neo-classical accounts of consumers and DEM/GEM takes on citizenship. We must beware falling for the rhetoric of citizenship adopted in discriminatory and exclusionary ways (think always of the non-consumer, the non-citizen, and their fate), and require each part of the consumer-citizen divide to illustrate: (a) the history to their account of either consumption or citizenship; (b) the relationship between multinational capital, democracy, and diversity; and (c) the role of the state in consumption, and of corporations in citizenship. Lastly, we must look to minority, indigenous, and migrant interests any time we are told consumers are unmarked, or that citizens at the center of culture within borders.

If cultural imperialism has lost intellectual *cachet* (even as it has gained diplomatic and political adherents) perhaps the left should go back to where we began, to the person as laborer. The model of citizenship will have to deal with dedomiciled workers, with all the dispossession entailed in that status. And citizenship assumes governmental policing of rights and responsibilities. Does this apply when a NICL is in operation, and deregulation or the protection of retrograde media *bourgeoisies* seem the only alternatives? To whom do you appeal as a person unhappy with the silencing of your local dramatic tradition through TV imports, but demoralized by the representation of ethnic and sexual minorities or women within so-called national screen drama or network news? We have seen first the slow and now the quick dissolution of cultural protectionism in television. That hardly seems an effective place to struggle. We know that globalization of the industry involves a reconfiguration of the labor force, so perhaps that might give a solid material backing to our discussions, alongside the supranationalism proposed by García-Canclini and Yúdice.

Notes

1. With thanks to Nitin Govil.
2. In the mid-1990s, the services sector comprised 70% of gross domestic product in the industrialized nations and 50% in much of the Third World, accounting for $1 trillion a year in trade, perhaps a fifth of the global total (Drake and Nicolaauidis, 1992, p. 37; *The Economist*, 1994, p. 55).
3. As noted above, GATS 2000 promises to problematize this distinction with its new considerations of new communications technology.
4. Ironically, the first case of this nature went against the United States. The WTO found that American copyright law violated global trade rules by permitting large

businesses to play recorded versions of music by foreign artists without paying royalties (Newman and Phillips, 2000).

References

Aksoy, A. and K. Robins (1992) 'Hollywood for the 21st Century: Global Competition for Critical Mass in Image Markets', *Cambridge Journal of Economics*, 16 (1): 1–22.

Allan, B. (1988) 'The State of the State of the Art on TV,' *Queen's Quarterly*, 95 (2): 318–329.

Anderson, K. (1993) 'No Tariff on Tom Cruise,' *Time*, July 19: 67.

Barshefsky, C. (1998) 'Testimony of the United States Trade Representative Before the House Appropriations Committee Subcommittee on Commerce, Justice, State, the Judiciary and Related Agencies,' March 31.

Berman, N. (1992) 'Nationalism Legal and Linguistic: The Teachings of European Jurisprudence,' *New York University Journal of International Law and Politics*, 24 (1): 1515–1578.

Briller, B.R. (1990) 'The Globalization of American TV,' *Television Quarterly*, 24 (3): 71–79.

Brinsley, J. (1999) 'Hollywood's Obsession Over Runaway Production: Eyes Wide Shut,' *Los Angeles Business Journal*, 21 (31): 1.

British Film Commission (n.d.) http://www.britfilmcom.co.uk/content/filming/site.asp.

Brooks, D. (1994) 'Never for GATT,' *American Spectator*, 27 (1): 34–37.

Browett, J. and R. Leaver (1989) 'Shifts in the Global Capitalist Economy and the National Economic Domain,' *Australian Geographical Studies*, 27 (1): 31–46.

Buck, E.B. (1992) 'Asia and the Global Film Industry,' *East-West Film Journal*, 6 (2): 116–133.

Buckingham, D. (1997) 'News Media, Political Socialization and Popular Citizenship: Towards a New Agenda,' *Critical Studies in Mass Communication*, 14 (4): 344–366.

Burgelman, J.-C. and C. Pauwels (1992) 'Audiovisual Policy and Cultural Identity in Small European States: The Challenge of a Unified Market,' *Media, Culture & Society*, 14 (2): 169–183.

Business Wire (1999) 'Presidents of SAG, DGA, TV Academy to Join Edward James Almos, Other Actors, Politicians, Union Leaders and Thousands of Filmworkers at March and Rally in Hollywood on Sunday, Aug. 15,' December 8.

Chartrand, H.H. (1992) 'International Cultural Affairs: A Fourteen Country Survey,' *Journal of Arts Management, Law and Society*, 22 (2): 134–154.

Christopherson, S. (1996) 'Flexibility and Adaptation in Industrial Relations: The Exceptional Case of the U.S.

Media Entertainment Industries,' in L.S. Gray and R.L. Seeber (eds) *Under the Stars: Essays on Labor Relations in Arts and Entertainment*, Ithaca, NY: Cornell University Press, pp. 86–112.

Christopherson, S. and M. Storper (1986) 'The City as Studio; the World as Back Lot: The Impact of Vertical Disintegration on the Location of the Motion Picture Industry,' *Environment and Planning D: Society and Space*, 4 (3): 305–320.

Cohen, R. (1991) *Contested Domains: Debates in International Labor Studies*, London: Zed Books.

Cohen, R. (1994) 'Aux Armes! France Rallies to Battle Sly and T. Rex,' *The New York Times*, January 2: H1, 22–23.

Cornford, J. and K. Robins (1998) 'Beyond the Last Bastion: Industrial Restructuring and the Labor Force in the British Television Industry,' in G. Sussman and J.A. Lent (eds) *Global Productions: Labor in the Making of the 'Information Society'*, Cresskill: Hampton Press, pp. 191–212.

Cunningham, S. and E. Jacka (1996) *Australian Television and International Mediascapes*, Melbourne: Cambridge University Press.

Daily Variety (1994) 'After GATT Pique, Pix Pax Promoted,' June 8: 1, 16.

Danan, M. (1995) 'Marketing the Hollywood Blockbuster in France,' *Journal of Popular Film and Television*, 23 (3): 131–140.

Dawtrey, A. (1994) 'Playing Hollywood's Game: Eurobucks Back Megabiz,' *Variety* March 7–13: 1, 75.

Dobson, J. (1993) 'TNCs and the Corruption of GATT: Free Trade Versus Fair Trade,' *Journal of Business Ethics*, 12 (7): 573–578.

Drake, W.J. and K. Nicolaïdis (1992) 'Ideas, Interests, and Institutionalization: Trade in Services and the Uruguay Round,' *International Organization*, 46 (1): 37–100.

Evans, P. (1979) *Dependent Development: The Alliance of Local Capital in Brazil*, Princeton, NJ: Princeton University Press.

Ferguson, M. (1992) "The Mythology About Globalization,' *European Journal of Communication*, 7 (1): 69–93.

Film Journal (1994) 'Déjà Vu,' Volume 97, Number 6: 3.

Fröbel, F., J. Heinrichs and O. Kreye (1980) *The New International Division of Labor: Structural Unemployment in Industrialised Countries and Industrialisation in Developing Countries*, P. Burgess (trans.), Cambridge: Cambridge University Press; Paris: Éditions de la Maison des Sciences de l'Homme.

Galbraith, J.K. (1999) 'The Crisis of Globalization,' *Dissent*, 46 (3): 13–16.

García-Canclini, N. (1990) *Culturas Híbridas: Estrategias para Entrar y Salir de la Modernidad*, Mexico, DF: Editorial Grijalbo.

García-Canclini, N. (1996) 'North Americans or Latin Americans? The Redefinition of Mexican Identity and the Free Trade Agreements,' in E.D. McAnany and K.T. Wilkinson (eds) *Mass Media and Free Trade: NAFTA and the Culture Industries*, Austin: University of Texas Press, pp. 142–156.

García-Canclini, N. (2001) *Consumers and Citizens: Globalization and Multicultural Conflicts*, G. Yúdice (trans.), Minneapolis: University of Minnesota Press.

Golodner, J. (1994) 'The Downside of Protectionism,' *The New York Times*, February 27: H6.

Gray, L. and R. Seeber. (1996a) 'The Industry and the Unions: An Overview,' in L.S. Gray and R.L. Seeber (eds) *Under the Stars: Essays on Labor Relations in Arts and Entertainment*, Ithaca, NY: Cornell University Press, pp. 15–49.

Gray, L. and R. Seeber. (1996b) 'Introduction,' in L.S. Gray and R.L. Seeber (eds) *Under the Stars: Essays on Labor Relations in Arts and Entertainment*, Ithaca, NY: Cornell University Press, pp. 1–13.

Grey, R. de C. (1990) *Concepts of Trade Diplomacy and Trade in Services*, Hemel Hempstead: Harvester Wheatsheaf.

Groves, D. (1994) 'O'seas B.O. Power Saluted at Confab,' *Variety*, 356 (4): 18.

Groves, D. (1999) 'A Major Force O'seas,' *Variety*, April 12–18: 9.

Guback, T.H. (1984) 'International Circulation of U.S. Theatrical Films and Television Programming,' in G. Gerbner and M. Siefert (eds) *World Communications: A Handbook*, New York Longman, pp. 153–163.

Guback, T.H. (1987) 'Government Support to the Film Industry in the United States,' in B.A. Austin (ed.) *Current Research in Film: Audiences, Economics and Law*, Volume 3, Norwood: Ablex, pp. 88–104.

Gubernick, L. and J. Millman (1994) 'El Sur is the Promised Land,' *Forbes*, 153 (7): 94–95.

Guttridge, P. (1996) 'Our Green and Profitable Land,' *Independent*, July 11: 8–9.

Hartley, J. (1996) *Popular Reality: Journalism, Modernity, Popular Culture*, London: Arnold.

Hayward, S. (1993) 'State, Culture and the Cinema: Jack Lang's Strategies for the French Film Industry,' *Screen*, 34 (4): 382–391.

Hill, J. (1994) 'Introduction,' in J. Hill, M. McLoone and P. Hainsworth (eds) *Border Crossing: Film in Ireland, Britain and Europe*, Belfast: Institute of Irish Studies, pp. 1–7.

Hills, J. (1994) 'Dependency Theory and its Relevance Today: International Institutions in Telecommunications and Structural Power,' *Review of International Studies*, 20 (2): 169–186.

Hiscock, J. (1998) 'Hollywood Backs British Film Drive,' *Daily Telegraph*, July 24: 19.

Hobsbawm, E. (1998) 'The Nation and Globalization,' *Constellations*, 5 (1): 1–9.

Hoekman, B.M. and M.M. Kostecki (1995) *The Political Economy of the World Trading System: From GATT to WTO*, Oxford: Oxford University Press.

Jarvie, I. (1998) 'Free Trade as Cultural Threat: American Film and TV Exports in the Post-War Period,' in G. Nowell-Smith and S. Ricci (eds) *Hollywood and Europe: Economics, Culture, National Identity: 1945–95*, London: BFI, pp. 34–46.

Jury, L. (1996) 'Mission Possible: Red Tape Cut to Boost Film Industry,' *Independent*, July 4: 3.

Kessler, Kirsten L. (1995) 'Protecting Free Trade in Audiovisual Entertainment: A Proposal for Counteracting the European Union's Trade Barriers to the U.S. Entertainment Industry's Exports', *Law and Policy in International Business*, 26, no. 2: 563–611.

Keynes, J.M. (1957) *The General Theory of Employment Interest and Money*, London: Macmillan; New York: St. Martin's Press.

Kissinger, H. (1999) 'Globalization and World Order,' Independent Newspapers Annual Lecture, Trinity College Dublin, October 12.

Lang, T. and C. Hines (1993) *The New Protectionism: Protecting the Future Against Free Trade*, New York: New Press.

Lent, J.A. (1998) 'The Animation Industry and its Offshore Factories,' in G. Sussman and J.A. Lent (eds) *Global Productions: Labor in the Making of the 'Information Society'*, Cresskill: Hampton Press, pp. 239–254.

Lev, P. (1993) *The Euro-American Cinema*, Austin: University of Texas Press.

Levinson, M. (1999) 'Who's in Charge Here?,' *Dissent*, 46 (4): 21–23.

Madigan, N. (1999a) 'Prod'n Headed North,' *Variety*, June 28–July 11: 12.

Madigan, N. (1999b) 'Runaways Inspire Taxing Questions,' *Variety*, August 23–29: 7.

Madigan, N. (1999c) 'Flight or Fight? Industry Gears Up to Keep Production in Area,' *Variety*, November 22–28: L3–4.

Magder, T. (1998) 'Franchising the Candy Store: Split-Run Magazines and a New International Regime for Trade in Culture,' *Canadian-American Public Policy*, Number 34: 1–66.

Martín-Barbero, J. (1993) *Communication, Culture, and Hegemony: From the Media to Mediations*, London: Sage Publications.

Marvasti, A. (1994) 'International Trade in Cultural Goods: A Cross-Sectional Analysis,' *Journal of Cultural Economics*, 18 (2): 135–148.

Mato, D. (1999) 'Telenovelas: Transnacionalización de la Industria y Transformación del Género,' in N. García-Canclini and C.J. Moneta (eds) *Las Industrias Culturales en la Integracion Latinoamericana*, Mexico, DF: Grijalbo, pp. 245–282.

Mayrhofer, D. (1994) 'Media Briefs' *Media Information Australia*, Number 74: 126–142.

Mazziotti, N. (1996) *La Industria de la Telenovela: La Producción de Ficción en América Latina*, Buenos Aires: Paidós.

McCann, P. (1998) 'Hollywood Film-makers Desert UK,' *Independent*, August 14: 7.

McDonald, K. (1999) 'How Would You Like Your Television: With or Without Borders and With or Without Culture — A New Approach to Media Regulation in the European Union,' *Fordham International Law Journal*, 22: 1991–2031.

Moran, A. (1998) *Copycat TV: Globalisation, Program Formats and Cultural Identity*, Luton: University of Luton Press.

Murdoch, R. (1998) 'Presentation Prepared for the European Audiovisual Conference,' Birmingham, April 6–8.

Murphy, D.G. (1997) 'The Entrepreneurial Role of Organized Labour in the British Columbia Motion Picture Industry,' *Industrial Relations*, 52 (3): 531–554.

Murray, A. (1999) 'The American Century: Is it Going or Coming?,' *Wall Street Journal*, December 27: 1.

Nader, R. (1999) 'Introduction,' in L. Wallach and M. Sforza (eds) *The WTO: Five Years of Reasons to Resist Corporate Globalization*, New York: Seven Stories Press, pp. 6–12.

Newman, M. and M.M. Phillips (2000) 'WTO Says U.S. Copyright Law Violates Global Trade Rules on Musical Rights,' *Wall Street Journal*, June 8: A6.

Olson, S.R. (1999) *Hollywood Planet: Global Media and the Competitive Advantage of Narrative Transparency*, Mahwah, NJ: Lawrence Erlbaum.

Palley, T.I. (1999) 'Toward a New International Economic Order,' *Dissent*, 46 (2): 48–52.

Parker, R.A. (1991) 'The Guise of the Propagandist: Governmental Classification of Foreign Political Films,' in B.A. Austin (ed.) *Current Research in Film: Audiences, Economics and Law*, Volume 5, Norwood: Ablex, pp. 135–146.

Pendakur, M. (1990) *Canadian Dreams and American Control*, Toronto: Garamond.

Pendakur, M. (1998) 'Hollywood North: Film and TV Production in Canada,' in G. Sussman and J.A. Lent (eds) *Global Productions: Labor in the Making of the 'Information Society'*, Cresskill: Hampton Press, pp. 213–238.

Quester, G.H. (1990) *The International Politics of Television*, Lexington, MA: Lexington.

Roddick, N. (1994) 'A Hard Sell: The State of Documentary Film Marketing,' *Dox* Number 2: 30–32.

Ryan, J. (1999) 'Action Heats Up in Film Biz War,' *Toronto Sun*, August 29: 50.

Schatz, T. (1988) *The Genius of the System: Hollywood Filmmaking in the Studio Era*, New York: Pantheon.

Schwab, S. (1994) 'Television in the 90's: Revolution or Confusion?,' Tenth Joseph I. Lubin Memorial Lecture, New York University, March 1.

Segrave, K. (1997) *American Films Abroad: Hollywood's Domination of the World's Movie Screens from the 1890s to the Present*, Jefferson: McFarland.

Sjolander, C.T. (1992–93) 'Unilateralism and Multilateralism: The United States and the Negotiation of the GATS,' *International Journal*, 48 (1): 52–79.

Sorlin, P. (1991) *European Cinemas, European Societies 1939–1990*, London: Routledge.

Stevenson, R.W. (1994) 'Lights! Camera! Europe!,' *The New York Times*, February 6: 1, 6.

Strange, S. (1995) 'The Limits of Politics,' *Government and Opposition*, 30 (3): 291–311.

Stroud, M. (1999) 'Valley to Lose Film Jobs?' *Wired News*, June 26: http://www.wired.com/news/news/culture/story/20443.html?wnpg = 2.

Sullivan, M. (1999) 'H.K. Mulls Harsher Piracy Fines,' *Daily Variety*, February 25: 10.

Sutter, M. (1998a) 'Viva Mexico! — Hollywood Heads South of the Border,' *Kempos*, December 21–27: 1, 4–5.

Sutter, M. (1998b) 'Woman on Top in a Macho Man's Union,' *Kempos*, December 21–27: 8.

The Economist (1994) 'A Disquieting New Agenda for Trade,' Volume 332, Number 7872: 55–56.

The Economist (1997) 'Shall We, Yawn, Go to a Film?,' February 1.

The Economist (1998a) 'Culture Wars,' September 12.

The Economist (1998b) 'Foreign Bums on Seats,' August 15.

The Economist (1998c) 'The PolyGram Test,' August 15.

Theiler, T. (1999) 'Viewers into Europeans?: How the European Union Tried to Europeanize the Audiovisual Sector, and Why it Failed,' *Canadian Journal of Communication*, 24 (4): 557–587.

Thompson, K. (1985) *Exporting Entertainment: America in the World Film Market 1907–1934*, London: BFI.

Townson, D. (1999) 'H'wood Techs Migrate North,' *Variety*, August 23–29: 9.

Tracy, J.F. (1999) 'Whistle While You Work: The Disney Company and the Global Division of Labor,' *Journal of Communication Inquiry*, 23 (4): 374–389.

USIA (1997) '1997 National Trade Estimate Report — European Union,' M2 Press Wire.

Valentine, J. (1997) 'Global Sport and Canadian Content: The *Sports Illustrated* Controversy,' *Journal of Sport & Social Issues*, 21 (3): 239–259.

Van Elteren, M. (1996a) 'Conceptualizing the Impact of US Popular Culture Globally,' *Journal of Popular Culture*, 30, (1): 47–89.

Van Elteren, M. (1996b) 'GATT and Beyond: World Trade, the Arts and American Popular Culture in Western Europe,' *Journal of American Culture*, 19 (3): 59–73.

Variety (1994) 'Top 100 All-Time Domestic Grossers,' October 17–23: M60.

Variety (1999) 'H'wood Buries Overseas Pix,' January 25–31: 1, 90–91.

Vasey, R. (1997) *The World According to Hollywood, 1918–1939*, Madison: University of Wisconsin Press.

Venturelli, S. (1998) 'Cultural Rights and World Trade Agreements in the Information Society,' *Gazette*, 60 (1): 47–76.

Wasko, J. (1982) *Movies and Money: Financing the American Film Industry*, Norwood: Ablex.

Wasko, J. (1994) *Hollywood in the Information Age: Beyond the Silver Screen*, Cambridge: Polity Press.

Wasko, J. (1998) 'Challenges to Hollywood's Labor Force in the 1990s,' in G. Sussman and J.A. Lent (eds) *Global Productions: Labor in the Making of the 'Information Society'*, Cresskill: Hampton Press, pp. 173–189.

Wasser, F. (1995) 'Is Hollywood America? The Trans-Nationalization of the American Film Industry,' *Critical Studies in Mass Communication*, 12 (4): 423–437.

Waxman, S. (1999) 'Location, Location: Hollywood Loses Films to Cheaper Climes,' *Washington Post*, June 25: C1.

Wedell, G. (1994) 'Prospects for Television in Europe,' *Government and Opposition* 29 (3): 315–331.

Weinraub, B. (1993) 'Directors Battle Over GATT's Final Cut and Print,' *New York Times*, December 12: L24.

Welch, L.S. and R. Luostarinen (1988) 'Internationalization: Evolution of a Concept,' *Journal of General Management*, 14 (2): 34–55.

Wheeler, M. (2000) 'Research Note: "The Undeclared War" Part II,' *European Journal of Communication*, 15 (2): 253–262.

Woods, M. (1999a) 'That Championship Season,' *Variety*, January 11–17: 9, 16.

Woods, M. (1999b) 'Foreign Pix Bring Life to Biz,' *Variety*, May 3–9: 37, 44, 46, 59.

Woolf, M. (1998) 'Why the Next English Patient Will be British,' *Independent on Sunday*, December 20: 9.

World Trade Organization (1998) 'Audiovisual Services: Background Note by the Secretariat,' S/C/W/40 of June 15.

Yúdice, G. (1995) 'Civil Society, Consumption, and Governmentality in an Age of Global Restructuring An Introduction,' *Social Text*, Number 45: 1–27.

Yúdice, G. (2000) 'The Creation of a Latin American Cultural Space,' Presentation to the Crossroads in Cultural Studies Conference, Birmingham, June 21–25.

Zolberg, V. (1995) 'Museum Culture and GATT,' *Journal of Arts Management, Law and Society*, 25 (1): 5–16.

24.
FREE LABOR

Producing Culture for the Digital Economy

Tiziana Terranova

The real *not-capital* is *labor*.

—Karl Marx, *Grundrisse*

Working in the digital media industry is not as much fun as it is made out to be. The "NetSlaves" of the eponymous Webzine are becoming increasingly vociferous about the shamelessly exploitative nature of the job, its punishing work rhythms, and its ruthless casualization (www.disobey.com/netslaves). They talk about "24–7 electronic sweatshops" and complain about the ninety-hour weeks and the "moronic management of new media companies." In early 1999, seven of the fifteen thousand "volunteers" of America Online (AOL) rocked the info-loveboat by asking the Department of Labor to investigate whether AOL owes them back wages for the years of playing chathosts for free.[1] They used to work long hours and love it; now they are starting to feel the pain of being burned by digital media.

These events point to a necessary backlash against the glamorization of digital labor, which highlights its continuities with the modern sweatshop and points to the increasing degradation of knowledge work. Yet the question of labor in a "digital economy" is not so easily dismissed as an innovative development of the familiar logic of capitalist exploitation. The NetSlaves are not simply a typical form of labor on the Internet; they also embody a complex relation to labor that is widespread in late capitalist societies.

In this essay I understand this relationship as a provision of "free labor," a trait of the cultural economy at large, and an important, and yet undervalued,

force in advanced capitalist societies. By looking at the Internet as a specific instance of the fundamental role played by free labor, this essay also tries to highlight the connections between the "digital economy" and what the Italian autonomists have called the "social factory." The "social factory" describes a process whereby "work processes have shifted from the factory to society, thereby setting in motion a truly complex machine."[2] Simultaneously voluntarily given and unwaged, enjoyed and exploited, free labor on the Net includes the activity of building Web sites, modifying software packages, reading and participating in mailing lists, and building virtual spaces on MUDs and MOOs. Far from being an "unreal," empty space, the Internet is animated by cultural and technical labor through and through, a continuous production of value that is completely immanent to the flows of the network society at large.

Support for this argument, however, is immediately complicated by the recent history of critical theory. How to speak of labor, especially cultural and technical labor, after the demolition job carried out by thirty years of postmodernism? The postmodern socialist feminism of Donna Haraway's "Cyborg Manifesto" spelled out some of the reasons behind the antipathy of 1980s critical theory for Marxist analyses of labor. Haraway explicitly rejected the humanistic tendencies of theorists who see labor as the "pre-eminently privileged category enabling the Marxist to overcome illusion and find that point of view which is necessary for changing the world."[3] Paul Gilroy similarly expressed his discontent at the inadequacy of Marxist analyses of labor to describe the culture of the descendants of slaves, who value artistic expression as "the means towards both individual self-fashioning and communal liberation."[4] If labor is "the humanizing activity that makes [white] man," then, surely, humanizing labor does not really belong in the age of networked, posthuman intelligence.

However, the "informatics of domination" that Haraway describes in the "Manifesto" is certainly preoccupied with the relation between cybernetics, labor, and capital. In the fifteen years since its publication, this triangulation has become even more evident. The expansion of the Internet has given ideological and material support to contemporary trends toward increased flexibility of the workforce, continuous reskilling, freelance work, and the diffusion of practices such as "supplementing" (bringing supplementary work home from the conventional office).[5] Advertising campaigns and business manuals suggest that the Internet is not only a site of disintermediation (embodying the famous death of the middle man, from bookshops to travel agencies to computer stores), but also the means through which a flexible, collective intelligence has come into being.

This essay does not seek to offer a judgment on the "effects" of the Internet, but rather to map the way in which the Internet connects to the autonomist "social factory." I am concerned with how the "outernet"—the network of social, cultural, and economic relationships that criss-crosses and exceeds the Internet—surrounds and connects the latter to larger flows of labor, culture, and power. It is fundamental to move beyond the notion that cyberspace is about escaping reality in order to understand how the reality of the Internet is deeply connected to the development of late postindustrial societies as a whole.

Cultural and technical work is central to the Internet but is also a widespread activity throughout advanced capitalist societies. I argue that such labor is not exclusive to the so-called knowledge workers, but is a pervasive feature of the postindustrial economy. The pervasiveness of such production questions the legitimacy of a fixed distinction between production and consumption, labor and culture. It also undermines Gilroy's distinction between work as "servitude, misery and subordination" and artistic expression as the means to self-fashioning and communal

liberation. The increasingly blurred territory between production and consumption, work and cultural expression, however, does not signal the recomposition of the alienated Marxist worker. The Internet does not automatically turn every user into an active producer, and every worker into a creative subject. The process whereby production and consumption are reconfigured within the category of free labor signals the unfolding of a different (rather than completely new) logic of value, whose operations need careful analysis.[6]

The Digital Economy

The term *digital economy* has recently emerged as a way to summarize some of the processes described above. As a term, it seems to describe a formation that intersects on the one hand with the postmodern cultural economy (the media, the university, and the arts) and on the other hand with the information industry (the information and communication complex). Such an intersection of two different fields of production constitutes a challenge to a theoretical and practical engagement with the question of labor, a question that has become marginal for media studies as compared with questions of ownership (within political economy) and consumption (within cultural studies).

In Richard Barbrook's definition, the digital economy is characterized by the emergence of new technologies (computer networks) and new types of workers (the digital artisans).[7] According to Barbrook, the digital economy is a mixed economy: it includes a public element (the state's funding of the original research that produced Arpanet, the financial support to academic activities that had a substantial role in shaping the culture of the Internet); a market-driven element (a latecomer that tries to appropriate the digital economy by reintroducing commodification); and a gift economy element, the true expression of the cutting edge of capitalist production that prepares its eventual overcoming into a future "anarcho-communism":

> Within the developed world, most politicians and corporate leaders believe that the future of capitalism lies in the commodification of information ... Yet at the "cutting-edge" of the emerging

information society, money-commodity relations play a secondary role to those created by a really existing form of anarcho-communism. For most of its users, the net is somewhere to work, play, love, learn and discuss with other people ... Unrestricted by physical distance, they collaborate with each other without the direct mediation of money and politics. Unconcerned about copyright, they give and receive information without thought of payment. In the absence of states or markets to mediate social bonds, network communities are instead formed through the mutual obligations created by gifts of time and ideas.[8]

From a Marxist-Hegelian angle, Barbrook sees the high-tech gift economy as a process of overcoming capitalism from the inside. The high-tech gift economy is a pioneering moment that transcends both the purism of the New Left do-it-yourself culture and the neoliberalism of the free market ideologues: "money-commodity and gift relations are not just in conflict with each other, but also co-exist in symbiosis."[9] Participants in the gift economy are not reluctant to use market resources and government funding to pursue a potlatch economy of free exchange. However, the potlatch and the economy ultimately remain irreconcilable, and the market economy is always threatening to reprivatize the common enclaves of the gift economy. Commodification, the reimposition of a regime of property, is, in Barbrook's opinion, the main strategy through which capitalism tries to reabsorb the anarcho-communism of the Net into its folds.

I believe that Barbrook overemphasizes the autonomy of the high-tech gift economy from capitalism. The processes of exchange that characterize the Internet are not simply the reemergence of communism within the cutting edge of the economy, a repressed other that resurfaces just at the moment when communism seems defeated. It is important to remember that the gift economy, as part of a larger digital economy, is itself an important force within the reproduction of the labor force in late capitalism as a whole. The provision of "free labor," as we will see later, is a fundamental moment in the creation of value in the digital economies. As will be made clear, the conditions that make free labor an important element of the digital economy are based in a difficult,

experimental compromise between the historically rooted cultural and affective desire for creative production (of the kind more commonly associated with Gilroy's emphasis on "individual self-fashioning and communal liberation") and the current capitalist emphasis on knowledge as the main source of value-added.

The volunteers for America Online, the NetSlaves, and the amateur Web designers are not working only because capital wants them to; they are acting out a desire for affective and cultural production that is nonetheless real just because it is socially shaped. The cultural, technical, and creative work that supports the digital economy has been made possible by the development of capital beyond the early industrial and Fordist modes of production and therefore is particularly abundant in those areas where post-Fordism has been at work for a few decades. In the overdeveloped countries, the end of the factory has spelled out the obsolescence of the old working class, but it has also produced generations of workers who have been repeatedly addressed as active consumers of meaningful commodities. Free labor is the moment where this knowledgeable consumption of culture is translated into productive activities that are pleasurably embraced and at the same time often shamelessly exploited.

Management theory is also increasingly concerned with the question of knowledge work, that indefinable quality that is essential to the processes of stimulating innovation and achieving the goals of competitiveness. For example, Don Tapscott, in a classic example of managerial literature, *The Digital Economy*, describes the digital economy as a "new economy based on the networking of human intelligence."[10] Human intelligence provides the much needed value-added, which is essential to the economic health of the organization. Human intelligence, however, also poses a problem: it cannot be managed in quite the same way as more traditional types of labor. Knowledge workers need open organizational structures to produce, because the production of knowledge is rooted in collaboration, that is, in what Barbrook defined as the "gift economy":

The concept of supervision and management is changing to team-based structures. Anyone responsible for managing knowledge workers knows they cannot be "managed" in the traditional sense. Often they have specialized knowledge and skills that cannot be matched or even understood by management. A new challenge to management is first to attract and retain these assets by marketing the organization to them, and second *to provide the creative and open communications environment where such workers can effectively apply and enhance their knowledge.*[11]

For Tapscott, therefore, the digital economy magically resolves the contradictions of industrial societies, such as class struggle: while in the industrial economy the "worker tried to achieve fulfillment through leisure [and] . . . was alienated from the means of production which were owned and controlled by someone else," in the digital economy the worker achieves fulfillment through work and finds in her brain her own, unalienated means of production.[12] Such means of production need to be cultivated by encouraging the worker to participate in a culture of exchange, whose flows are mainly kept within the company but also need to involve an "outside," a contact with the fast-moving world of knowledge in general. The convention, the exhibition, and the conference—the more traditional ways of supporting this general exchange—are supplemented by network technologies both inside and outside the company. Although the traffic of these flows of knowledge needs to be monitored (hence the corporate concerns about the use of intranets), the Internet effectively functions as a channel through which "human intelligence" renews its capacity to produce.

This essay looks beyond the totalizing hype of the managerial literature but also beyond some of the conceptual limits of Barbrook's work. It looks at some possible explanation for the coexistence, within the debate about the digital economy, of discourses that see it as an oppositional movement and others that see it as a functional development to new mechanisms of extraction of value. Is the end of Marxist alienation wished for by the manager guru the same thing as the gift economy heralded by leftist discourse?

We can start undoing this deadlock by subtracting the label *digital economy* from its exclusive anchorage within advanced forms of labor (we can start then by

depioneering it). This essay describes the digital economy as a specific mechanism of internal "capture" of larger pools of social and cultural knowledge. The digital economy is an important area of experimentation with value and free cultural/affective labor. It is about specific forms of production (Web design, multimedia production, digital services, and so on), but is also about forms of labor we do not immediately recognize as such: chat, real-life stories, mailing lists, amateur newsletters, and so on. These types of cultural and technical labor are not produced by capitalism in any direct, cause-and-effect fashion; that is, they have not developed simply as an answer to the economic needs of capital. However, they have developed in relation to the expansion of the cultural industries and are part of a process of economic experimentation with the creation of monetary value out of knowledge/culture/affect.

This process is different from that described by popular, left-wing wisdom about the incorporation of authentic cultural moments: it is not, then, about the bad boys of capital moving in on underground subcultures/subordinate cultures and "incorporating" the fruits of their production (styles, languages, music) into the media food chain. This process is usually considered the end of a particular cultural formation, or at least the end of its "authentic" phase. After incorporation, local cultures are picked up and distributed globally, thus contributing to cultural hybridization or cultural imperialism (depending on whom you listen to).

Rather than capital "incorporating" from the outside the authentic fruits of the collective imagination, it seems more reasonable to think of cultural flows as originating within a field that is always and already capitalism. Incorporation is not about capital descending on authentic culture but a more immanent process of channeling collective labor (even as cultural labor) into monetary flows and its structuration within capitalist business practices.

Subcultural movements have stuffed the pockets of multinational capitalism for decades. Nurtured by the consumption of earlier cultural moments, subcultures have provided the look, style, and sounds that sell clothes, CDs, video games, films, and advertising slots on television. This has often happened through the active participation of subcultural members in the production of cultural goods (e.g., independent labels in music, small designer shops in fashion).[13] This participation is, as the word suggests, a voluntary phenomenon, although it is regularly accompanied by cries of sellouts. The fruit of collective cultural labor has been not simply appropriated, but voluntarily *channeled* and controversially *structured* within capitalist business practices. The relation between culture, the cultural industry, and labor in these movements is much more complex than the notion of incorporation suggests. In this sense, the digital economy is not a new phenomenon but simply a new phase of this longer history of experimentation.

Knowledge Class and Immaterial Labor

In spite of the numerous, more or less disingenuous endorsements of the democratic potential of the Internet, the links between it and capitalism look a bit too tight for comfort to concerned political minds. It has been very tempting to counteract the naive technological utopianism by pointing out how computer networks are the material and ideological heart of informated capital. The Internet advertised on television and portrayed by print media seems not just the latest incarnation of capital's inexhaustible search for new markets, but also a full consensus-creating machine, which socializes the mass of proletarianized knowledge workers into the economy of continuous innovation.[14] After all, if we do not get on-line soon, the hype suggests, we will become obsolete, unnecessary, disposable. If we do, we are promised, we will become part of the "hive mind," the immaterial economy of networked, intelligent subjects in charge of speeding up the rhythms of capital's "incessant waves of branching innovations."[15] Multimedia artists, writers, journalists, software programmers, graphic designers, and activists together with small and large companies are at the core of this project. For some they are its cultural elite, for others a new form of proletarianized labor.[16] Accordingly, the digital workers are described as resisting or supporting the project of capital, often in direct relation to their positions in the networked, horizontal, and yet hierarchical world of knowledge work.

Any judgment on the political potential of the Internet, then, is tied not only to its much vaunted capacity to allow decentralized access to information but also to the question of who uses the Internet and how. If the decentralized structure of the Net is to count for anything at all, the argument goes, then we need to know about its constituent population (hence the endless statistics about use, income, gender, and race of Internet users, the most polled, probed, and yet opaque survey material of the world). If this population of Internet users is largely made up of "knowledge workers," then it matters whether these are seen as the owners of elitist cultural and economic power or the avant-garde of new configurations of labor that do not automatically guarantee elite status.

As I argue in this essay, this is a necessary question and yet a misleading one. It is necessary because we have to ask who is participating in the digital economy before we can pass a judgment on it. It is misleading because it implies that all we need to know is how to locate the knowledge workers within a "class," and knowing which class it is will give us an answer to the political potential of the Net as a whole. If we can prove that knowledge workers are the avant-garde of labor, then the Net becomes a site of resistance;[17] if we can prove that knowledge workers wield the power in informated societies, then the Net is an extended gated community for the middle classes.[18] Even admitting that knowledge workers are indeed fragmented in terms of hierarchy and status won't help us that much; it will still lead to a simple system of categorization, where the Net becomes a field of struggle between the diverse constituents of the knowledge class.

The question is further complicated by the stubborn resistance of "knowledge" to quantification: knowledge cannot be exclusively pinned down to specific social segments. Although the shift from factory to office work, from production to services is widely acknowledged, it just isn't clear why some people qualify and some others do not.[19] The "knowledge worker" is a very contested sociological category.

A more interesting move, however, is possible by not looking for the knowledge class within quantifiable parameters and concentrating instead on "labor." Although the notion of class retains a material value that is indispensable to make sense of the experience of concrete historical subjects, it also has its limits: for example, it "freezes" the subject, just like a substance within the chemical periodical table, where one is born as a certain element (working-class metal) but then might become something else (middle-class silicon) if submitted to the proper alchemical processes (education and income). Such an understanding of class also freezes out the flows of culture and money that mobilize the labor force as a whole. In terms of Internet use, it gives rise to the generalized endorsements and condemnations that I have described above and does not explain or make sense of the heterogeneity and yet commonalities of Internet users. I have therefore found it more useful to think in terms of what the Italian autonomists, and especially Maurizio Lazzarato, have described as *immaterial labor*. For Lazzarato the concept of immaterial labor refers to *two different aspects* of labor:

> On the one hand, as regards the "informational content" of the commodity, it refers directly to the changes taking place in workers' labor processes … where the skills involved in direct labor are increasingly skills involving cybernetics and computer control (and horizontal and vertical communication). On the other hand, as regards the activity that produces the "cultural content" of the commodity, immaterial labor involves a series of activities that are not normally recognized as "work"—in other words, the kinds of activities involved in defining and fixing cultural and artistic standards, fashions, tastes, consumer norms, and, more strategically, public opinion.[20]

Immaterial labor, unlike the knowledge worker, is not completely confined to a specific class formation. Lazzarato insists that this form of labor power is not limited to highly skilled workers but is a form of activity of every productive subject within postindustrial societies. In the highly skilled worker, these capacities are already there. However, in the young worker, the "precarious worker," and the unemployed youth, these capacities are "virtual," that is they are there but are still undetermined. This means that immaterial labor is a virtuality (an undetermined capacity) that belongs to the postindustrial productive subjectivity as a whole. For example, the obsessive emphasis on education of 1990s governments can be read as an attempt to stop this virtuality from disappearing or from being channeled into places that would not be as acceptable to the current power structures. In spite of all the contradictions of advanced capital and its relation to structural unemployment, postmodern governments do not like the completely unemployable. The potentialities of work must be kept alive, the unemployed must undergo continuous training in order both to be monitored and kept alive as some kind of postindustrial reserve force. Nor can they be allowed to channel their energy into the experimental, nomadic, and antiproductive life-styles which in Britain have been so savagely attacked by the Criminal Justice Act in the mid-1990s.[21]

However, unlike the post-Fordists, and in accordance with his autonomist origins, Lazzarato does not conceive of immaterial labor as purely functional to a new historical phase of capitalism:

> The virtuality of this capacity is neither empty nor ahistoric; it is rather an opening and a potentiality, that have as their historical origins and antecedents the "struggle against work" of the Fordist worker and, in more recent times, the processes of socialization, educational formation, and cultural self-valorization.[22]

This dispersal of immaterial labor (as a virtuality and an actuality) problematizes the idea of the "knowledge worker" as a class in the "industrial" sense of the word. As a collective quality of the labor force, immaterial labor can be understood to pervade the social body with different degrees of intensity. This intensity is produced by the processes of "channeling" a characteristic of the capitalist formation which distributes value according to its logic of profit.[23] If knowledge is inherently collective, it is even more so in the case of the postmodern cultural economy: music, fashion, and information are all produced collectively but are selectively compensated. Only some companies are picked up by corporate distribution chains in the case of fashion and music; only a few sites are invested in by venture capital. However, it is a form of collective cultural labor that makes these products possible even as the profit is disproportionately appropriated by established corporations.

From this point of view, the well-known notion that the Internet materializes a "collective intelligence" is not completely off the mark. The Internet highlights the existence of networks of immaterial labor and speeds up their accretion into a collective entity. The productive capacities of immaterial labor on the Internet encompass the work of writing/reading/managing and participating in mailing lists/Web sites/chatlines. These activities fall outside the concept of "abstract labor," which Marx defined as the provision of time for the production of value regardless of the useful qualities of the product.[24] They witness an investment of desire into production of the kind cultural theorists have mainly theorized in relation to consumption.

This explosion of productive activities is undermined for various commentators by the minoritarian, gendered, and raced character of the Internet population. However, we might also argue that to recognize the existence of immaterial labor as a diffuse, collective quality of postindustrial labor in its entirety does not deny the existence of hierarchies of knowledge (both technical and cultural) which prestructure (but do not determine) the nature of such activities. These hierarchies shape the degrees to which such virtualities become actualities; that is, they go from being potential to being realized as processual, constituting moments of cultural, affective, and technical production. Neither capital nor living labor want a labor force that is permanently excluded from the possibilities of immaterial labor. But this is where their desires stop from coinciding. Capital wants to retain control over the unfolding of these virtualities and the processes of valorization. The relative abundance of cultural/technical/affective production on the Net, then, does not exist as a free-floating postindustrial Utopia but in full, mutually constituting interaction with late capitalism, especially in its manifestation as global-venture capital.

Collective Minds

The collective nature of networked, immaterial labor has been simplified by the Utopian statements of the cyberlibertarians. Kevin Kelly's popular thesis in *Out of Control*, for example, is that the Internet is a collective "hive mind." According to Kelly, the Internet is another manifestation of a principle of self-organization that is widespread throughout technical, natural, and social systems. The Internet is the material

evidence of the existence of the self-organizing, infinitely productive activities of connected human minds.[25] From a different perspective Pierre Levy draws on cognitive anthropology and poststructuralist philosophy to argue that computers and computer networks are sites that enable the emergence of a "collective intelligence." According to Eugene Provenzo, Levy, who is inspired by early computer pioneers such as Douglas Engelbart, argues for a new humanism "that incorporates and enlarges the scope of self-knowledge and collective thought."[26] According to Levy, we are passing from a Cartesian model of thought based on the singular idea of *cogito* (I think) to a collective or plural *cogitamus* (we think).

> What is collective intelligence? It is a form of *universally distributed intelligence,* constantly enhanced, coordinated in real time, and resulting in the effective mobilization of skills. . . . The basis and goal of collective intelligence is the mutual recognition and enrichment of individuals rather than the cult of fetishized or hypostatized communities.[27]

Like Kelly, Levy frames his argument within the common rhetoric of competition and flexibility that dominates the hegemonic discourse around digitalization: "The more we are able to form intelligent communities, as open-minded, cognitive subjects capable of initiative, imagination, and rapid response, the more we will be able to ensure our success in a highly competitive environment."[28] In Levy's view, the digital economy highlights the impossibility of absorbing intelligence within the process of automation: unlike the first wave of cybernetics, which displaced workers from the factory, computer networks highlight the unique value of human intelligence as the true creator of value in a knowledge economy. In his opinion, since the economy is increasingly reliant on the production of creative subjectivities, this production is highly likely to engender a new humanism, a new centrality of man's [*sic*] creative potentials.

Especially in Kelly's case, it has been easy to dismiss the notions of a "hive mind" and a self-organizing Internet-as-free-market as euphoric capitalist mumbo jumbo. One cannot help being deeply irritated by the blindness of the digital capitalist to the realities of working in the high-tech industries, from the poisoning world of the silicon chips factories to the electronic sweatshops of America Online, where technical work is downgraded and worker obsolescence is high.[29] How can we hold on to the notion that cultural production and immaterial labor are collective on the Net (both inner and outer) without subscribing to the idealistic cyberdrool of the digerati?

We could start with a simple observation: the self-organizing, collective intelligence of cybercultural thought captures the existence of networked immaterial labor, but also neutralizes the operations of capital. Capital, after all, is the unnatural environment within which the collective intelligence materializes. The collective dimension of networked intelligence needs to be understood historically, as part of a specific momentum of capitalist development. The Italian writers who are identified with the post-Gramscian Marxism of autonomia have consistently engaged with this relationship by focusing on the mutation undergone by labor in the aftermath of the factory. The notion of a self-organizing "collective intelligence" looks uncannily like one of their central concepts, the "general intellect," a notion that the autonomists "extracted" out of the spirit, if not the actual wording, of Marx's *Grundrisse*. The "collective intelligence" or "hive mind" captures some of the spirit of the "general intellect," but removes the autonomists' critical theorization of its relation to capital.

In the autonomists' favorite text, the *Grundrisse*, and especially in the "Fragment on Machines," Marx argues that "knowledge—scientific knowledge in the first place, but not exclusively—tends to become precisely by virtue of its autonomy from production, nothing less than the principal productive force, thus relegating repetitive and compartmentalized labor to a residual position. Here one is dealing with knowledge ... which has become incarnate ... in the automatic system of machines."[30] In the vivid pages of the "Fragment," the "other" Marx of the *Grundrisse* (adopted by the social movements of the 1960s and 1970s against the more orthodox endorsement of *Capital*), describes the system of industrial machines as a horrific monster of metal and flesh:

> The production process has ceased to be a labor process in the sense of a process dominated by labor as its governing unity. Labor appears, rather,

merely as a conscious organ, scattered among the individual living workers at numerous points of the mechanical system; subsumed under the total process of the machinery itself, as itself only a link of the system, whose unity exists not in the living workers, but rather in the living, (active) machinery, which confronts his individual, insignificant doings as a mighty organism.[31]

The Italian autonomists extracted from these pages the notion of the "general intellect" as "the ensemble of knowledge ... which constitute[s] the epicenter of social production."[32] Unlike Marx's original formulation, however, the autonomists eschewed the modernist imagery of the general intellect as a hellish machine. They claimed that Marx completely identified the general intellect (or knowledge as the principal productive force) with fixed capital (the machine) and thus neglected to account for the fact that the general intellect cannot exist independently of the concrete subjects who mediate the articulation of the machines with each other. The general intellect is an articulation of fixed capital (machines) *and* living labor (the workers). If we see the Internet, and computer networks in general, as the latest machines—the latest manifestation of fixed capital—then it won't be difficult to imagine the general intellect as being well and alive today.

The autonomists, however, did not stop at describing the general intellect as an assemblage of humans and machines at the heart of postindustrial production. If this were the case, the Marxian monster of metal and flesh would just be updated to that of a world-spanning network where computers use human beings as a way to allow the system of machinery (and therefore capitalist production) to function. The visual power of the Marxian description is updated by the cyberpunk snapshots of the immobile bodies of the hackers, electrodes like umbilical cords connecting them to the matrix, appendixes to a living, all-powerful cyberspace. Beyond the special effects bonanza, the box-office success of *The Matrix* validates the popularity of the paranoid interpretation of this mutation.

To the humanism implicit in this description, the autonomists have opposed the notion of a "mass intellectuality," living labor in its function as the determining articulation of the general intellect. Mass intellectuality—as an ensemble, as a social body—"is the repository of the indivisible knowledges of living subjects and of their linguistic cooperation. . . . An important part of knowledge cannot be deposited in machines, but . . . it must come into being as the direct interaction of the labor force."[33] As Virno emphasizes, mass intellectuality is not about the various roles of the knowledge workers, but is a *"quality* and a distinctive sign of the *whole* social labor force in the post-Fordist era."[34]

The pervasiveness of the collective intelligence within both the managerial literature and Marxist theory could be seen as the result of a common intuition about the quality of labor in informated societies. Knowledge labor is inherentiy *collective,* it is always the result of a collective and social production of knowledge.[35] Capital's problem is how to extract as much value as possible (in the autonomists' jargon, to "valorize") out of this abundant, and yet slightiy intractable, terrain.

Collective knowledge work, then, is not about those who work in the knowledge industry. But it is also not about employment. The acknowledgment of the collective aspect of labor implies a rejection of the equivalence between labor and employment, which was already stated by Marx and further emphasized by feminism and the post-Gramscian autonomy.[36] Labor is not equivalent to waged labor. Such an understanding might help us to reject some of the hideous rhetoric of unemployment which turns the unemployed person into the object of much patronizing, pushing, and nudging from national governments in industrialized countries. (Accept any available work or else. . . .) Often the unemployed are such only in name, in reality being the life-blood of the difficult economy of "under-the-table," badly paid work, some of which also goes into the new media industry.[37] To emphasize how labor is not equivalent to employment also means to acknowledge how important free affective and cultural labor is to the media industry, old and new.

Ephemeral Commodities and Free Labor

There is a continuity, and a break, between older media and new media in terms of their relationship to cultural and affective labor. The continuity seems to lie in their common reliance on their public/users as productive subjects. The difference lies both in the mode of production and in the ways in which power/knowledge works in the two types. In spite of different national histories (some of which stress public service more than others), the television industry, for example, is relatively conservative: writers, producers, performers, managers, and technicians have definite roles within an industry still run by a few established players. The historical legacy of television as a technology for the construction of national identities also means that television is somehow always held more publicly accountable.

This does not mean that old media do not draw on free labor, on the contrary. Television and print media, for example, make abundant use of the free labor of their audiences/readers, but they also tend to structure the latter's contribution much more strictly, both in terms of economic organization and moralistic judgment. The price to pay for all those real-life TV experiences is usually a heavy dose of moralistic scaremongering: criminals are running amok on the freeways and must be stopped by tough police action; wild teenagers lack self-esteem and need tough love. If this does not happen on the Internet, why is it then that the Internet is not the happy island of decentered, dispersed, and pleasurable cultural production that its apologists claimed?

The most obvious answer to such questions came spontaneously to the early Internet users who blamed it on the commercialization of the Internet. E-commerce and the progressive privatization were blamed for disrupting the free economy of the Internet, an economy of exchange that Richard Barbrook described as a "gift economy"[38] Indeed maybe the Internet could have been a different place than what it is now. However, it is almost unthinkable that capitalism could stay forever outside of the network, a mode of communication that is fundamental to its own organizational structure.

The outcome of the explicit interface between capital and the Internet is a digital economy that manifests all the signs of an acceleration of the capitalist logic of production. It might be that the Internet has not stabilized yet, but it seems undeniable that the digital economy is the fastest and most visible zone of production within late capitalist societies. New products and new trends succeed each other at anxiety-inducing pace. After all, this is a business where you need to replace your equipment/ knowledges and possibly staff every year or so.

At some point, the speed of the digital economy, its accelerated rhythms of obsolescence, and its reliance on (mostly) "immaterial" products seemed to fit in with the postmodern intuition about the changed status of the commodities whose essence was said to be *meaning* (or lack of) rather than *labor* (as if the two could be separable).[39] The recurrent complaint that the Internet contributes to the disappearance of reality is then based *both* in humanistic concerns about "real life" *and* in the postmodern nihilism of the recombinant commodity.[40] Hyperreality confirms the humanist nightmare of a society without humanity, the culmination of a progressive taking over of the realm of representation. Commodities on the Net are not material and are excessive (there is too much of it, too many Web sites, too much clutter and noise) with relation to the limits of "real" social needs.

It is possible, however, that the disappearance of the commodity is not a material disappearance but its visible subordination to the quality of labor behind it. In this sense the commodity does not disappear as such; rather, it becomes increasingly ephemeral, its duration becomes compressed, and it becomes more of a process than a finished product. The role of continuous, creative, innovative labor as the ground of market value is crucial to the digital economy. The process of valorization (the production of monetary value) happens by foregrounding the quality of the labor that literally animates the commodity.

In my opinion, the digital economy challenges the postmodern assumption that labor disappears while the commodity takes on and dissolves all meaning. In particular, the Internet is about the extraction of value out of continuous, updateable work, and it is extremely labor intensive. It is not enough to produce a good Web site, you need to update it continuously to maintain interest in it and fight off obsolescence. Furthermore, you need updateable equipment (the general intellect is always an assemblage of humans and their machines), in its turn propelled by the intense collective labor of programmers, designers, and workers. It is as if the acceleration of production has pushed to the point where commodities, literally, turn into translucent objects. Commodities do not so

much disappear as become more transparent, showing throughout their reliance on the labor that produces and sustains them. It is the labor of the designers and programmers that shows through a successful Web site, and it is the spectacle of that labor changing its product that keeps the users coming back. The commodity, then, is only as good as the labor that goes into it.

As a consequence, the sustainability of the Internet as a medium depends on massive amounts of labor (which is not equivalent to employment, as we said), only some of which is hypercompensated by the capricious logic of venture capitalism. Of the incredible amount of labor that sustains the Internet as a whole (from mailing list traffic to Web sites to infrastructural questions), we can guess that a substantial amount of it is still "free labor."

Free labor, however, is not necessarily exploited labor. Within the early virtual communities, we are told, labor was really free: the labor of building a community was not compensated by great financial rewards (it was therefore "free," unpaid), but it was also willingly conceded in exchange for the pleasures of communication and exchange (it was therefore "free," pleasurable, not imposed). In answer to members' requests, information was quickly posted and shared with a lack of mediation that the early Netizens did not fail to appreciate. Howard Rheingold's book, somehow unfairly accused of middle-class complacency, is the most well-known account of the good old times of the old Internet, before the Net-tourist overcame the Net-pioneer.[41]

The free labor that sustains the Internet is acknowledged within many different sections of the digital literature. In spite of the volatile nature of the Internet economy (which yesterday was about community, today is about portals, and tomorrow who knows what), the notion of users' labor maintains an ideological and material centrality that runs consistently throughout the turbulent succession of Internet fads. Commentators who would normally disagree, such as Howard Rheingold and Richard Hudson, concur on one thing: the best Web site, the best way to stay visible and thriving on the Web, is to turn your site into a space that is not only accessed, but somehow built by its users.[42] Users keep a site alive through their labor, the cumulative hours of accessing the site (thus generating advertising), writing messages, participating in conversations, and sometimes making the jump to collaborators. Out of the fifteen thousand volunteers that keep AOL running, only a handful turned against it, while the others stayed on. Such a feature seems endemic to the Internet in ways that can be worked on by commercialization, but not substantially altered. The "open source" movement, which relies on the free labor of Internet tinkers, is further evidence of this structural trend within the digital economy.

It is an interesting feature of the Internet debate (and evidence, somehow, of its masculine bias) that users' labor has attracted more attention in the case of the open source movement than in that of mailing lists and Web sites. This betrays the persistence of an attachment to masculine understandings of labor within the digital economy: writing an operating system is still more worthy of attention than just chatting for free for AOL. This in spite of the fact that in 1996 at the peak of the volunteer moment, over thirty thousand "community leaders" were helping AOL to generate at least $7 million a month.[43] Still, the open source movement has drawn much more positive attention than the more diffuse user labor described above. It is worth exploring not because I believe that it will outlast "portals" or "virtual communities" as the latest buzzword, but because of the debates it has provoked and its relation to the digital economy at large.

The open source movement is a variation of the old tradition of shareware and freeware software which substantially contributed to the technical development of the Internet. Freeware software is freely distributed and does not even request a reward from its users. Shareware software is distributed freely, but implies a "moral" obligation for the user to forward a small sum to the producer in order to sustain the shareware movement as an alternative economic model to the copyrighted software of giants such as Microsoft. Open source "refers to a model of software development in which the underlying code of a program—the source code, a.k.a. the crown jewels—is by definition made freely available to the general public for modification, alteration, and endless redistribution."[44]

Far from being an idealistic, minoritarian practice, the open source movement has attracted much media and financial attention. Apache, an open source Web server, is the "Web-server program of choice for more than half of all publicly accessible Web servers."[45] In 1999, open source conventions are anxiously attended by venture capitalists, who have been informed by the digerati that the open source movement is a necessity "because you must go open-source to get access to the benefits of the open-source development community—the near-instantaneous bug-fixes, the distributed intellectual resources of the Net, the increasingly large open-source code base."[46] Open source companies such as Cygnus have convinced the market that you do not need to be proprietary about source codes to make a profit: the code might be free, but tech support, packaging, installation software, regular upgrades, office applications, and hardware are not.

In 1998, when Netscape went "open source" and invited the computer tinkers and hobbyists to look at the code of its new browser, fix the bugs, improve the package, and redistribute it, specialized mailing lists exchanged opinions about its implications.[47] Netscape's move rekindled the debate about the peculiar nature of the digital economy. Was it to be read as being in the tradition of the Internet "gift economy"? Or was digital capital hijacking the open source movement exactly against that tradition? Richard Barbrook saluted Netscape's move as a sign of the power intrinsic in the architecture of the medium:

> The technical and social structure of the Net has been developed to encourage open cooperation among its participants. As an everyday activity, users are building the system together. Engaged in "interactive creativity," they send emails, take part in listservers, contribute to newsgroups, participate within on-line conferences and produce Websites. . . . Lacking copyright protection, information can be freely adapted to suit the users' needs. Within the hi-tech gift economy, people successfully work together through ". . . an open social process involving evaluation, comparison and collaboration."[48]

John Horvarth, however, did not share this opinion. The "free stuff" offered around the Net, he argued, "is either a product that gets you hooked on to another one or makes you just consume more time on the net.

After all, the goal of the access people and telecoms is to have users spend as much time on the net as possible, regardless of what they are doing. The objective is to have you consume bandwidth."[49] Far from proving the persistence of the Internet gift economy, Horvarth claimed Netscape's move is a direct threat to those independent producers for whom shareware and freeware have been a way of surviving exactly those "big boys" that Netscape represents:

> Freeware and shareware are the means by which small producers, many of them individuals, were able to offset somewhat the bulldozing effects of the big boys. And now the bulldozers are headed straight for this arena.
>
> As for Netscrape [*sic*], such a move makes good business sense and spells trouble for workers in the field of software development. The company had a poor last quarter in 1997 and was already hinting at job cuts. Well, what better way to shed staff by having your product taken further by the freeware people, having code-dabbling hobbyists fix and further develop your product? The question for Netscrape now is how to tame the freeware beast so that profits are secured.[50]

Although it is tempting to stake the evidence of Netscape's layoffs against the optimism of Barbrook's gift economy, there might be more productive ways of looking at the increasingly tight relationship between an "idealistic" movement such as open source and the current venture mania for open source companies.[51] Rather than representing a moment of incorporation of a previously authentic moment, the open source question demonstrates the overreliance of the digital economy as such on free labor, both in the sense of not financially rewarded and willingly given. This includes AOL community leaders, the open source programmers, the amateur Web designers, mailing list editors, and the NetSlaves willing to "work for cappuccinos" just for the excitement and the dubious promises of digital work.[52]

Such a reliance, almost a dependency, is part of larger mechanisms of capitalist extraction of value which are fundamental to late capitalism as a whole. That is, such processes are not created outside capital and then reappropriated by capital, but are the results

of a complex history where the relation between labor and capital is mutually constitutive, entangled and crucially forged during the crisis of Fordism. Free labor is a desire of labor immanent to late capitalism, and late capitalism is the field that both sustains free labor *and* exhausts it. It exhausts it by subtracting selectively but widely the means through which that labor can reproduce itself: from the burnout syndromes of Internet start-ups to underretribution and exploitation in the cultural economy at large. Late capitalism does not appropriate anything: it nurtures, exploits, and exhausts its labor force and its cultural and affective production. In this sense, it is technically impossible to separate neatly the digital economy of the Net from the larger network economy of late capitalism. Especially since 1994, the Internet is always and simultaneously a gift economy *and* an advanced capitalist economy. The mistake of the neoliberalists (as exemplified by the *Wired* group), is to mistake this coexistence for a benign, unproblematic equivalence.

As I stated before, these processes are far from being confined to the most self-conscious laborers of the digital economy. They are part of a diffuse cultural economy which operates throughout the Internet and beyond. The passage from the pioneeristic days of the Internet to its "venture" days does not seem to have affected these mechanisms, only intensified them and connected them to financial capital. Nowhere is this more evident than in the recent development of the World Wide Web.

Enter the New Web

In the winter of 1999, in what sounds like another of its resounding, short-lived claims, *Wired* magazine announces that the old Web is dead: "The Old Web was a place where the unemployed, the dreamy, and the iconoclastic went to reinvent themselves . . . The New Web isn't about dabbling in what you don't know and failing—it's about preparing seriously for the day when television and Web content are delivered over the same digital networks."[53]

The new Web is made of the big players, but also of new ways to make the audience work. In the "new Web," after the pioneering days, television and the Web converge in the one thing they have in common: their reliance on their audiences/users as providers of the cultural labor that goes under the label of "real-life stories." Gerry Laybourne, executive of the Web-based media company Oxygen, thinks of a hypothetical show called *What Are They Thinking?* a reality-based sketch comedy based on stories posted on the Web, because "funny things happen in our lives everyday."[54] As Bayers also adds, "until it's produced, the line separating that concept from more puerile fare dismissed by Gerry, like *America's Funniest*, is hard to see."[55]

The difference between the puerile fare of *America's Funniest* and user-based content seems to lie not so much in the more serious nature of the "new Web" as compared to the vilified output of television's "people shows" (a term that includes docusoaps, docudramas, and talk shows). From an abstract point of view there is no difference between the ways in which people shows rely on the inventiveness of their audiences and the Web site reliance on users' input. People shows rely on the activity (even amidst the most shocking sleaze) of their audience and willing participants to a much larger extent than any other television programs. In a sense, they manage the impossible, creating monetary value out of the most reluctant members of the postmodern cultural economy: those who do not produce marketable style, who are not qualified enough to enter the fast world of the knowledge economy, are converted into monetary value through their capacity to perform their misery.

When compared to the cultural and affective production on the Internet, people shows also seem to embody a different logic of relation between capitalism (the media conglomerates that produce and distribute such shows) and its labor force—the beguiled, dysfunctional citizens of the underdeveloped North. Within people's shows, the valorization of the audience as labor and spectacle always happens somehow within a power/knowledge nexus that does not allow the *immediate* valorization of the talk show participants; you cannot just put a Jerry Springer guest on TV on her own to tell her story with no mediation (indeed, that would look too much like the discredited access slots of public service broadcasting). Between the talk show guest and the apparatus of valorization intervenes a series of knowledges that normalize the dysfunctional subjects through a moral or therapeutic discourse and a more traditional institutional

organization of production. So after the performance, the guest must be advised, patronized, questioned, and often bullied by the audience and the host, all in the name of a perfunctory, normalizing morality.

People shows also belong to a different economy of scale: although there are more and more of them, they are still relatively few when compared to the millions of pages on the Web. It is as if the centralized organization of the traditional media does not let them turn people's productions into pure monetary value. People shows must have morals, even as those morals are shattered by the overflowing performances of their subjects.

Within the Internet, however, this process of channeling and adjudicating (responsibilities, duties, and rights) is dispersed to the point where practically anything is tolerated (sadomasochism, bestiality, fetishism, and plain nerdism are not targeted, at least within the Internet, as sites that need to be disciplined or explained away). The qualitative difference between people's shows and a successful Web site, then, does not lie in the latter's democratic tendency as opposed to the former's exploitative nature. It lies in the operation, within people's shows, of moral discursive mechanisms of territorialization, the application of a morality that the "excessive" abundance of material on the Internet renders redundant and even more irrelevant. The digital economy cares only tangentially about morality. What it really cares about is an abundance of production, an immediate interface with cultural and technical labor whose result is a diffuse, nondialectical contradiction.

Conclusion

My hypothesis that free labor is structural to the late capitalist cultural economy is not meant to offer the reader a totalizing understanding of the cultural economy of new and old media. However, it does originate from a need to think beyond the categories that structure much Net debate these days, a process necessarily entailing a good deal of abstraction.

In particular, I have started from the opposition between the Internet as capital and the Internet as the anticapital. This opposition is much more challenging than the easy technophobia/technophilia debate. The question is not so much whether to love or hate technology, but an attempt to understand whether the Internet embodies a continuation of capital or a break with it. As I have argued in this essay, it does neither. It is rather a mutation that is totally immanent to late capitalism, not so much a break as an intensification, and therefore a mutation, of a widespread cultural and economic logic.

In this context, it is not enough just to demystify the Internet as the latest capitalist machination against labor. I have tried to map a different route, an immanent, flat, and yet power-sensitive model of the relationship between labor, politics, and culture. Obviously I owe much of the inspiration for this model to the French/Italian connection, to that line of thought formed by the exchanges between the Foucault/Deleuze/Guattari axis and the Italian Autonomy (Antonio Negri, Maurizio Lazzarato, Paolo Virno, Franco Berardi), a field of exchanges formed through political struggle, exile, and political prosecution right at the heart of the postindustrial society (Italy after all has provided the model of a post-Fordist economy for the influential flexible specialization school). On the other hand, it has been within a praxis informed by the cybernetic intelligence of English-speaking mailing lists and Web sites that this line of thought has acquired its concrete materiality.

This return to immanence, that is, to a flattening out of social, cultural, and political connections, has important consequences for me. As Negri, Haraway, and Deleuze and Guattari have consistently argued, the demolition of the modernist ontology of the Cartesian subject does not have to produce the relativism of the most cynical examples of postmodern theory. The loss of transcendence, of external principles which organize the social world from the outside, does not have to end up in nihilism, a loss of strategies for dealing with power.

Such strategies cannot be conjured by critical theory. As the spectacular failure of the Italian Autonomy reveals,[56] the purpose of critical theory is not to elaborate strategies that then can be used to direct social change. On the contrary, as the tradition of cultural studies has less explicitly argued, it is about working on what already exists, on the lines established by a cultural and material activity that is already happening. In this sense this essay does not so much propose a theory as it identifies a *tendency* that already exists in the Internet literature and on-line exchanges. This tendency is not the truth of the digital economy; it is necessarily partial just as it tries to hold to the need for an overall perspective on an immensely complex range of cultural and economic phenomena. Rather than retracing the holy truths of Marxism on the changing body of late capital, free labor embraces some crucial contradictions without lamenting, celebrating, denying, or synthesizing a complex condition. It is, then, not so much about truth-values as about relevance, the capacity to capture a moment and contribute to the ongoing constitution of a nonunified collective intelligence outside and in between the blind alleys of the silicon age.

Notes

This essay has been made possible by research carried out with the support of the "Virtual Society?" program of the Economic and Social Research Council (ESRC) (grant no. L132251050). I share this grant with Sally Wyatt and Graham Thomas, Department of Innovation Studies, University of East London.

1. Lisa Margonelli, "Inside AOL's 'Cyber-Sweatshop,'" *Wired*, October 1999, 138.
2. See Paolo Virno and Michael Hardt, *Radical Thought in Italy: A Potential Politics* (Minneapolis: University of Minnesota Press, 1996); and Toni Negri, *The Politics of Subversion: A Manifesto for the Twenty-first Century* (Cambridge: Polity, 1989) and *Marx beyond Marx: Lessons on the "Grundrisse"* (New York: Autonomedia, 1991). The quote is from Negri, *Politics of Subversion*, 92.
3. Donna Haraway, *Simians, Cyborgs, and Women: The Reinvention of Nature* (London: Routledge, 1991), 159.
4. Paul Gilroy, *The Black Atlantic: Modernity and Double Consciousness* (London and New York: Verso, 1993), 40.
5. Manuel Castells, *The Rise of the Network Society* (Cambridge, Mass.: Blackwell, 1996), 395.
6. In discussing these developments, I will also draw on debates circulating across Internet sites. On-line debates in, for example, nettime, telepolis, rhizome and c-theory, are one of the manifestations of the surplus value engendered by the digital economy, a hyper-production that can only be partly reabsorbed by capital.
7. See Richard Barbrook, "The Digital Economy," (posted to *nettime* on 17 June 1997; also at www.nettime.org; "The High-Tech Gift Economy," in *Readme! Filtered by Nettime: ASCII Culture and the Revenge of Knowledge*, ed. Josephine Bosma et al. (Brooklyn, N.Y.: Autonomedia,

1999), 132–38. Also see Anonymous, "The Digital Artisan Manifesto" (posted to *nettime* on 15 May 1997).

8. Barbrook, "The High-Tech Gift Economy," 135.

9. Ibid., 137

10. Don Tapscott, *The Digital Economy* (New York: McGraw-Hill, 1996), xiii.

11. Ibid., 35; emphasis added.

12. Ibid., 48.

13. For a discussion of the independent music industry and its relation to corporate culture see David Hesmondalgh, "Indie: The Aesthetics and Institutional Politics of a Popular Music Genre," *Cultural Studies* 13 January 1999): 34–61. Angela McRobbie has also studied a similar phenomenon in the fashion and design industry in *British Fashion Design: Rag Trade or Image Industry?* (London: Routledge, 1998).

14. See the challenging section on work in the high-tech industry in Bosma et al., *Readme!*

15. Martin Kenney, "Value-Creation in the Late Twentieth Century: The Rise of the Knowledge Worker," in *Cutting Edge: Technology, Information Capitalism and Social Revolution*, ed. Jim Davis, Thomas Hirsch, and Michael Stack (London: Verso, 1997), 93; also see in the same anthology Tessa Morris-Suzuki, "Capitalism in the Computer Age," 57–71.

16. See Darko Suvin, "On Gibson and Cyberpunk SF," in *Storming the Reality Studio*, ed. Larry McCaffery (London: Durham University Press, 1991), 349–65; and Stanley Aronowitz and William DiFazio, *The Jobless Future: Sci-Tech and the Dogma of Work* (Minneapolis: University of Minnesota Press, 1994). According to Andrew Clement, information technologies were introduced as extensions of Taylorist techniques of scientific management to middle-level, rather than clerical, employees. Such technologies responded to a managerial need for efficient ways to manage intellectual labor. Clement, however, seems to connect this scientific management to the workstation, while he is ready to admit that personal computers introduce an element of autonomy much disliked by management. See Andrew Clement, "Office Automation and the Technical Control of Information Workers," in *The Political Economy of Information*, ed. Vincent Mosco and Janet Wasko (Madison: University of Wisconsin Press, 1988.

17. Barbrook, "The High-Tech Gift Economy."

18. See Kevin Robins, "Cyberspace or the World We Live In," in *Fractal Media: New Media in Social Context*, ed. Jon Dovey (London: Lawrence and Wishart, 1996).

19. See Frank Webster, *Theories of the Information Society* (London and New York: Routledge, 1995).

20. Maurizio Lazzarato, "Immaterial Labor," in *Marxism beyond Marxism*, ed. Saree Makdisi, Cesare Casarino,

and Rebecca E. Karl for the Polygraph collective (London: Routledge, 1996), 133.

21. The Criminal Justice Act (CJA) was popularly perceived as an antirave legislation, and most of the campaign against it was organized around the "right to party." However, the most devastating effects of the CJA have struck the neotribal, nomadic camps, basically decimated or forced to move to Ireland in the process. See Andrea Natella and Serena Tinari, eds., *Rave Off* (Rome: Castelvec-chi, 1996).

22. Lazzarato, "Immaterial Labor," 136.

23. In the two volumes of *Capitalism and Schizophrenia*, Gilles Deleuze and Félix Guattari described the process by which capital unsettles and resettles bodies and cultures as a movement of "decoding" ruled by "axiomatisation." Decoding is the process through which older cultural limits are displaced and removed as with older, local cultures during modernization; the flows of culture and capital unleashed by the decoding are then channeled into a process of axiomatization, an abstract moment of conversion into money and profit. The decoding forces of global capitalism have then opened up the possibilities of immaterial labor. See Gilles Deleuze and Félix Guattari, *Anti-Oedipus: Capitalism and Schizophrenia* (London: Athlone, 1984); and *A Thousand Plateaus: Capitalism and Schizophrenia* (London: Athlone, 1988).

24. See Franco Berardi (Bifo), *La nefasta utopia di potere operaio* (Rome: Castelvecchi/DeriveApprodi, 1998), 43.

25. See Kevin Kelly, *Out of Control* (Reading, Mass.: Addison Wesley, 1994).

26. Eugene Provenzo, foreword to Pierre Levy, *Collective Intelligence: Mankind's Emerging World in Cyberspace* (New York: Plenum, 1995), viii.

27. Levy, *Collective Intelligence*, 13.

28. Ibid., 1.

29. See Little Red Henski, "Insider Report from UUNET" in Bosma et al., *Readme!* 189–91.

30. Paolo Virno, "Notes on the General Intellect," in *Marxism beyond Marxism*, 266.

31. Karl Marx, *Grundrisse* (London: Penguin, 1973), 693.

32. Paolo Virno, "Notes on the General Intellect," in *Marxism beyond Marxism*, 266.

33. Ibid., 270.

34. Ibid., 271.

35. See Lazzarato, "New Forms of Production," in Bosma et al., *Readme!* 159–66; and Tessa Morris-Suzuki, "Robots and Capitalism," in *Cutting Edge*, 13–27.

36. See Toni Negri, "Back to the Future," in Bosma et al., *Readme!* 181–86; and Haraway, *Simians, Cyborgs, Women*.

37. Andrew Ross, *Real Love: In Pursuit of Cultural Justice* (London: Routledge, 1998).

38. See Barbrook, "The High-Tech Gift Economy."

39. The work of Jean-François Lyotard in *The Postmodern Condition* is mainly concerned with *knowledge*, rather than intellectual labor, but still provides a useful conceptualization of the reorganization of labor within the productive structures of late capitalism. See Jean-François Lyotard, *The Postmodern Condition: A Report on Knowledge*, trans. Geoff Bennington and Brian Massumi (Minneapolis: University of Minnesota Press, 1989).

40. See Arthur Kroker and Michael A. Weinstein, *Data Trash: The Theory of the Virtual Class* (New York: St. Martin's, 1994).

41. See Howard Rheingold, *The Virtual Community: Homesteading on the Electronic Frontier* (New York: Harper Perennials, 1994).

42. See Howard Rheingold, "My Experience with Electric Minds," in Bosma et al., *Readme!* 147–50; also David Hudson, *Rewired: A Brief (and Opinionated) Net History* (Indianapolis: Macmillan Technical Publishing, 1997). The expansion of the Net is based on different types of producers adopting different strategies of income generation: some might use more traditional types of financial support (grants, divisions of the public sector, in-house Internet divisions within traditional media companies, businesses' Web pages which are paid as with traditional forms of advertising); some might generate interest in one's page and then sell the user's profile or advertising space (freelance Web production); or some might use innovative strategies of valorization, such as various types of e-commerce.

43. See Margonelli, "Inside AOL's 'Cyber-Sweatshop.'"

44. Andrew Leonard, "Open Season," in *Wired*, May 1999, 140. Open source harks back to the specific competencies embodied by Internet users in its pre-1994 days. When most Net users were computer experts, the software structure of the medium was developed by way of a continuous interaction of different technical skills. This tradition still survives in institutions like the Internet Engineering Task Force (IETF), which is responsible for a number of important decisions about the technical infrastructure of the Net. Although the IETF is subordinated to a number of professional committees, it has important responsibilities and is also open to anybody who wants to join. The freeware movement has a long tradition, but it has also recently been divided by the polemics between the free software or "copyleft" movement and the open source movement, which is more of a pragmatic attempt to make freeware a business proposition. See debates on-line at www.gnu.org and www.salonmag.com.

45. Leonard, "Open Season."

46. Ibid., 142.

47. It is an established pattern of the computer industry, in fact, that you might have to give away your product if you want to reap the benefits later on. As John Perry Barlow has remarked, "Familiarity is an important asset in the world of information. It may often be the case that the best thing you can do to raise demand for your product is to give it away." See John Perry Barlow, "Selling Wine without Bottles: The Economy of Mind on the Global Net," in *High Noon on the Electronic Frontier: Conceptual Issues in Cyberspace*, ed. Peter Ludlow (Cambridge: MIT Press, 1996), 23. Apple started it by giving free computers to schools, an action that did not determine, but certainly influenced, the subsequent stubborn presence of Apple computers within education; MS-Dos came in for free with IBM computers.

48. Barbrook, "The High-Tech Gift Economy," 135–36.

49. John Horvarth, "Freeware Capitalism," posted on *nettime*, 5 February 1998.

50. Ibid.

51. Netscape started like a lot of other computer companies: its founder, Marc Andreessen, was part of the original research group who developed the structure of the World Wide Web at the CERN laboratory, in Geneva. As with many successful computer entrepreneurs, he developed the browser as an offshoot of the original, state-funded research and soon started his own company. Netscape was also the first company to exceed the economic processes of the computer industry, inasmuch as it was the first successful company to set up shop on the Net itself. As such, Netscape exemplifies some of the problems that even the computer industry meets on the Net and constitutes a good starting point to assess some of the common claims about the digital economy.

52. Ross, *Real Love*.

53. Chip Bayers, "Push Comes to Show," in *Wired*, February 1999, 113.

54. Ibid., 156.

55. Ibid.

56. Berardi, *La nefasta Utopia*.

SECTION V

MEDIA/IDENTITY

Introduction

This section traces the contours of scholarship on media and identity. All of the essays follow the poststructuralist insight that there is no "true" self: our identities are socially constituted through discourses and practices that often involve media culture. Categories such as male and female have no fixed or essential characteristics; they are rather defined and performed within socio-historical contexts. Likewise, media play an important role in defining the meaning of ethnicity, race, class, and sexual orientation, providing the symbolic material for identification as well as the construction of selfhood through difference. The selections presented here exemplify theoretical as well as empirical analyses of media's relationship to the processes through which we are constructed as subjects and perform identities in relation to the power dynamics and material conditions of particular historical moments.

Stuart Hall's 1996 overview "Who Needs Identity" traces and synthesizes critical scholarship on identity, including the work of Louis Althusser, Michel Foucault, and Judith Butler. Combining Marxism and psychoanalysis, Althusser (1968) proposed the term interpellation to characterize how people are hailed as subjects through unconscious processes; recognizing oneself (however temporarily) in the terms of dominant ideologies sutures our sense of self to the power dynamics of capitalist societies. While he moved beyond the reductionism of earlier Marxist critique by suggesting that subjects are constituted as subjects through discursive processes, Althusser has been critiqued for perpetuating another type of psychoanalytic reductionism by failing to historicize this process.

Michel Foucault's analysis of the subject as produced through and within discourse (2000) helped overcome this by showing how "normalizing regimes of truth" come to bear on the materiality of the body through practices of discipline, confession and self-policing. For Foucault, subjects are not "duped" by ideologies, as much as they are enticed to produce themselves in accordance with particular norms and political objectives. In his later work on technologies of the self, Foucault emphasized more fully the role of culture (as a type of training) in everyday practices of self-constitution and self-shaping. Unlike Althusser's focus on the unconscious, this approach—which has gained influence in critical media studies in recent years—envisions personhood as a technical process.

Hall concludes by presenting the enormously impactful work of Judith Butler, one of the pioneers of queer theory. As Hall points out, Butler's analysis of the "complex transactions between the subject, the body and identity" in works such as Gender Trouble: Feminism and the Subversion of Identity (1990) and Bodies That Matter: On the Discursive Limits of Sex (1993) emphasizes the discursive construction of the subject as well as the materiality of this process: "sex produces the body as it governs." Upsetting any notion of a natural or essential subject, as well as feminist identity politics (which presume the universality and unity of the category woman), Butler situates the "materialization of the body as an effect of power," and in so doing emphasizes the performative nature of language and subjectivity. It is in performing the cultural script of femininity (rather than through processes of interpellation) that female subjects are constituted and regulated.

In "Under Western Eyes: Media, Empire, Otherness," a chapter from their 1995 book *Spaces of Identity: Global Media, Electronic Landscapes and Cultural Boundaries*, David Morley and Kevin Robbins theorize the role of the media in the process of "cultural encounter" in the wake of accelerated global cultural flows. Drawing from Edward Said's groundbreaking book *Orientalism* (1979), which argues that the exotic and subaltern "otherness" of the East has been conceived on the basis of what it is presumed to lack (modernity, rationality, universality), Morley and Robbins argue that television accentuates and encourages this process. With the rise of cable networks such as CNN and increased reporting on global affairs, TV viewers in the West have become "armchair" imperialists and anthropologists, surveying the "world of all those 'Others' who are represented to us on the screen," they suggest. The screen functions as an interface for witnessing the world's events from a safe distance, a viewing position that, for them, involves not only images from afar but the psychic processes of viewers. Taking television coverage of the first U.S. invasion of Iraq in the early 1990s as a case study, they argue that Orientalism cannot be challenged simply by replacing negative images with positive ones, as the Other has become "central to our own psychic fantasies and defenses, mediated through the screen."

In the 2007 essay "What's Your Flava? Race and Postfeminism in Media Culture" Sarah Banet-Weiser examines the proliferation of difference within the specific context of late industrial capitalism in the United States, "a moment that has been characterized in racial terms as a multicultural or post-race society and in gendered terms as a postfeminist culture." Since the 1990s, she argues, mediated categories of gender and racial identity have been highly ambiguous, inflected with hip multicultural sensibility and the assumption of individual empowerment, yet simultaneously suggesting that gender and racial inequalities no longer exist. Banet-Weiser questions this "posting" logic, arguing that that race and ethnicity, along with girl power, only matter when they are marketable. Taking the pan-ethnic *Dora the Explorer* franchise as an example, she unravels an important paradox. If difference is everywhere apparent and celebrated by commercial media, it is also commodified. In a hyper-commercial and increasingly branded culture, she argues, political identity is subsumed into consumer culture.

Judith Halberstam's 2001 essay "Oh Behave! Austin Powers and the Drag Kings" extends her influential theory of female masculinity to comic film, showing how lesbian drag king culture has seeped into mainstream media culture. If gender functions as a "copy for which there is no original," as Judith Butler contends, dominant masculinity can also be seen as the result of repeated and scripted notions. For Halberstam, "king comedies" such as the *Austin Powers* series make visible this process, adopting the conventions of the drag king performance by mimicking and parodying white male masculinity and, in the process, highlighting the way in which most masculinity "copies and models itself on an ideal that it can never replicate." More optimistic than other theorists of commodification, Halberstam argues that her goal is not to suggest that "straight men learn how to parody masculinity from butch women and then take that parody to the bank," but rather to map subultural influence. Toward this end, she reconsiders Dick Hebdige's account of the hegemonic absorption of marginalized subcultures by capitalism and suggests that some subcultures "do not fade away" once they are plundered. Lesbian drag king culture and its uptake by Hollywood, Halberstam contends, presents an opportunity to retheorize the "lines of affiliation" between the marginal and the dominant.

In "Trash, Class and Cultural Hierarchy," a chapter from her 2002 book *The Money Shot: Trash, Class and the Making of TV Talk Shows*, Laura Grindstaff discusses the construction and performance of class identity in daytime talk shows, an early example of the trend toward reality programming. Unlike most theorists of identity, who tend to focus on the analysis of media texts, Grindstaff's analysis is grounded in an ethnographic study of the production process. Working as an intern at a popular show, Grindstaff observed ritualized interactions between producers and participants, and brought her research to bear on the ethics of casting ordinary people as stereotypically uneducated, loud and "trashy" working class talk show guests.

Part of Grindstaff's analysis concerns the behind-the-scenes labor of producing "emotional states in others," a process that greatly influences the micro melodramas played out on national television. However, Grindstaff rejects an essentialist notion of class as a position determined by one's place in the capitalist mode of production. Drawing from post-structural theory she theorizes class as the product of discourse and cultural capital, as well as socio-economics. One of the many interesting things about Grindstaff's contribution is her suggestion that class, like other axes of identity, is also performed according to script. Daytime talk shows—similar to all factual and fictional media—operate as a "theatrical context" that scripts and fictionalizes the performance of ordinary people. The category of "white trash" often ascribed to talk show participants is neither natural nor inevitable—it is the result of racial and cultural hierarchies and "performed" by participants within the ratings-driven logic of commercial television. While daytime talk shows—like current reality shows—trade on the promise of authenticity, their terms of participation often require lower-income people to actively perform a kind of "poorface." In this sense, white trash identity as constituted by reality television involves a complex mixture of agency and manipulation, Grnidstaff contends.

In his 2010 contribution "The Promotion and Presentation of the Self: Celebrity as a Marker of Presentational Media", P. David Marshall discusses celebrity culture as a "pedagogical aid" in the discourse of the self. For some time consumers have looked to the stars for guidance on self-fashioning. Celebrity thus plays a role in the broadening of practices of self-production, Marshall contends. However, in the context of new media, the ability to represent celebrity as a moniker of "identity, individuality and the consumer self may be waning." Marshall identifies a historical shift from representational to presentational culture, in which celebrities re-present and re-construct themselves via social media, offering a template for the production of the online self that comes more from celebrity gossip than from idealized images of the stars.

Drawing from the work of sociologist Erving Goffman, he explores the pedagogical role of celebrity at a conjuncture when the "props and accoutrements of the stage can now be translated to the Facebook site" and social media interpersonalize the representation of public and private worlds. What does self-making and identity entail at a time when the online "posting" is rapidly becoming a dominant mode of self-expression? If celebrity has always guided and shaped self-making practices, as Marshall suggests, the way in which celebrities re-present themselves via social media may provide some insights.

References

Althusser, Louis, "Ideology and Ideological State Apparatuses," in *Lenin and Philosophy and Other Essays* (New York: Monthly Review Press, 1971), p. 128–186.

Butler, Judith, *Gender Trouble: Feminism and the Subversion of Identity* (New York: Routledge, 1990).

Butler, Judith, *Bodies that Matter: On the Discursive Limits of Sex* (New York: Routledge, 1993).

Foucault, Michel, "The Subject & Power," in *Power*, ed. James D. Faubion (New York: The Free Press, 2000), p. 326–347.

Said, Edward, *Orientalism* (New York: Vintage Books, 1979).

25.
WHO NEEDS 'IDENTITY'?
Stuart Hall

There has been a veritable discursive explosion in recent years around the concept of 'identity', at the same moment as it has been subjected to a searching critique. How is this paradoxical development to be explained? And where does it leave us with respect to the concept? The deconstruction has been conducted within a variety of disciplinary areas, all of them, in one way or another critical of the notion of an integral, originary and unified identity. The critique of the self-sustaining subject at the centre of post-Cartesian western metaphysics has been comprehensively advanced in philosophy. The question of subjectivity and its unconscious processes of formation has been developed within the discourse of a psychoanalytically influenced feminism and cultural criticism. The endlessly performative self has been advanced in celebratory variants of postmodernism. Within the anti-essentialist critique of ethnic, racial and national conceptions of cultural identity and the 'politics of location' some adventurous theoretical conceptions have been sketched in their most grounded forms. What, then, is the need for a further debate about 'identity'? Who needs it?

There are two ways of responding to the question. The first is to observe something distinctive about the deconstructive critique to which many of these essentialist concepts have been subjected. Unlike those forms of critique which aim to supplant inadequate concepts with 'truer' ones, or which aspire to the production of positive knowledge, the deconstructive approach puts key concepts 'under erasure'. This indicates that they are no longer serviceable – 'good to think with' – in their originary and unreconstructed form. But since they have not been superseded dialectically, and there are no other, entirely different concepts with which to replace them, there is nothing to do but to continue to think with them – albeit now in their detotalized or deconstructed forms, and no longer operating within the paradigm in which they were originally generated (cf. Hall, 1995). The line which cancels them, paradoxically, permits them to go on being read. Derrida has described this approach as thinking at the limit, as thinking in the interval, a sort of double writing. 'By means of this double, and precisely stratified, dislodged and dislodging writing, we must also mark the interval between inversion, which brings low what was high, and the irruptive emergence of a new 'concept', a concept that can no longer be and never could be, included in the previous regime' (Derrida, 1981). Identity is such a concept – operating 'under erasure' in the interval between reversal and emergence; an idea which cannot be thought in the old way, but without which certain key questions cannot be thought at all.

A second kind of answer requires us to note where, in relation to what set of problems, does the *irreducibility* of the concept, identity, emerge? I think the answer here lies in its centrality to the question of agency and politics. By politics, I mean both the significance in modern forms of political movement of the signifier 'identity', its pivotal relationship to a politics of location – but also the manifest difficulties and instabilities which have characteristically affected all contemporary forms of 'identity polities'. By 'agency' 1 express no desire whatsoever to return to an unmediated and transparent notion of the subject or identity as the centred author of social practice, or to restore an approach which 'places its own point of view at the origin of all historicity – which, in short, leads to a transcendental consciousness' (Foucault, 1970, p. xiv). I agree with Foucault that what we require here is 'not a theory of the knowing subject, but rather a theory of discursive practice'. However, I believe that what this decentring requires – as the evolution of Foucault's work clearly shows – is not an abandonment or abolition of 'the subject' but a reconceptualization – thinking it in its new, displaced or decentred position within the paradigm. It seems to be in the attempt to rearticulate the relationship between subjects and discursive practices that the question of identity recurs – or rather, if one prefers to stress the process of subjectification to discursive practices, and the politics of exclusion which all such subjectification appears to entail, the question of *identification*.

Identification turns out to be one of the least well-understood concepts – almost as tricky as, though preferable to, 'identity' itself; and certainly no guarantee against the conceptual difficulties which have beset the latter. It is drawing meanings from both the discursive and the psychoanalytic repertoire, without being limited to either. This semantic field is too complex to unravel here, but it is useful at least to establish its relevance to the task in hand indicatively. In common sense language, identification is constructed on the back of a recognition of some common origin or shared characteristics with another person or group, or with an ideal, and with the natural closure of solidarity and allegiance established on this foundation. In contrast with the 'naturalism' of this definition, the discursive approach sees identification as a construction, a process never completed – always 'in process'. It is not determined in the sense that it can always be 'won' or 'lost', sustained or abandoned. Though not without its determinate conditions of existence, including the material and symbolic resources required to sustain it, identification is in the end conditional, lodged in contingency. Once secured, it does not obliterate difference. The total merging it suggests is, in fact, a fantasy of incorporation. (Freud always spoke of it in relation to 'consuming the other' as we shall see in a moment.) Identification is, then, a process of articulation, a suturing, an over-determination not a subsumption. There is always 'too much' or 'too little' – an over-determination or a lack, but never a proper fit, a totality. Like all signifying practices, it is subject to the 'play', of *différance*. It obeys the logic of more-than-one. And since as a process it operates across difference, it entails discursive work, the binding and marking of symbolic boundaries, the production of 'frontier-effects'. It requires what is left outside, its constitutive outside, to consolidate the process.

From its psychoanalytic usage, the concept of identification inherits a rich semantic legacy. Freud calls it 'the earliest expression of an emotional tie with another person' (Freud, 1921/1991) In the context of the Oedipus complex, however, it takes the parental figures as both love-objects and objects of rivalry, thereby inserting ambivalence into the very centre of the process. 'Identification is, in fact, ambivalent from the very start' (1921/1991:134). In 'Mourning and Melancholia', it is not that which binds one to an object that exists, but that which binds one to an abandoned object-choice. It is, in the first instance, a 'moulding after the other' which compensates for the loss of the libidinal pleasures of primal narcissism. It is grounded in fantasy, in projection and idealization. Its object is as likely to be the one that is hated as the one that is adored; and as often taken back into the unconscious self as 'taking one out of oneself'. It is in relation to identification that Freud elaborated the critical distinction between 'being' and 'having' the other. 'It behaves like a derivative of the first, oral phase of organization of the libido, in which the object that we long for is assimilated by eating and is in that way annihilated as such' (1921/1991:135). 'Identifications viewed as a whole', Laplanche and Pontalis (1985) note 'are in no way a coherent relational system. Demands coexist within an agency like the super-ego, for instance, which are diverse, conflicting and disorderly. Similarly, the ego-ideal is composed of identifications with cultural ideals that are not necessarily harmonious' (p. 208).

I am not suggesting that all these connotations should be imported wholesale and without translation into our thinking around 'identity', but they are cited to indicate the novel repertoires of meaning with which the term is now being inflected. The concept of identity deployed here is therefore not an essentialist, but a strategic and positional one. That is to say, directly contrary to what appears to be its settled semantic career, this concept of identity does *not* signal that stable core of the self, unfolding from beginning to end through all the vicissitudes of history without change; the bit of the self which remains always-already 'the same', identical to itself across time. Nor – if we translate this essentializing conception to the stage of cultural identity – is it that 'collective or true self hiding inside the many other, more superficial or artificially imposed "selves" which a people with a shared history and ancestry hold in common' (Hall, 1990) and which can stabilize, fix or guarantee an unchanging 'oneness' or cultural belongingness underlying all the other superficial differences. It accepts that identities are never unified and, in late modern times, increasingly fragmented and fractured; never singular but multiply constructed across different, often intersecting and antagonistic, discourses, practices and positions. They are subject to a radical historicization, and are constantly in the process of change and transformation. We need to situate the debates about identity within all those historically specific developments and practices which have disturbed the relatively 'settled' character of many populations and cultures, above all in relation to the processes of globalization, which I would argue are coterminous with modernity (Hall, 1996) and the processes of forced and 'free' migration which have become a global phenomenon of the so-called 'postcolonial' world. Though they seem to invoke an origin in a historical past with which they continue to correspond, actually identities are about questions of using the resources of history, language and culture in the process of becoming rather than being: not 'who we are' or 'where we came from', so much as what we might become, how we have been represented and how that bears on how we might represent ourselves. Identities are therefore constituted within, not outside representation. They relate to the invention of tradition as much as to tradition itself, which they oblige us to read not as an endless reiteration but as 'the changing same' (Gilroy, 1994): not the so-called return to roots but a coming-to-terms-with our 'routes'. They

arise from the narrativization of the self, but the necessarily fictional nature of this process in no way undermines its discursive, material or political effectivity, even if the belongingness, the 'suturing into the story' through which identities arise is, partly, in the imaginary (as well as the symbolic) and therefore, always, partly constructed in fantasy, or at least within a fantasmatic field.

Precisely because identities are constructed within, not outside, discourse, we need to understand them as produced in specific historical and institutional sites within specific discursive formations and practices, by specific enunciative strategies. Moreover, they emerge within the play of specific modalities of power, and thus are more the product of the marking of difference and exclusion, than they are the sign of an identical, naturally-constituted unity – an 'identity' in its traditional meaning (that is, an all-inclusive sameness, seamless, without internal differentiation).

Above all, and directly contrary to the form in which they are constantly invoked, identities are constructed through, not outside, difference. This entails the radically disturbing recognition that it is only through the relation to the Other, the relation to what it is not, to precisely what it lacks, to what has been called its *constitutive outside* that the 'positive' meaning of any term – and thus its 'identity' – can be constructed (Derrida, 1981; Laclau, 1990; Butler, 1993). Throughout their careers, identities can function as points of identification and attachment only *because* of their capacity to exclude, to leave out, to render 'outside', abjected. Every identity has at its 'margin', an excess, something more. The unity, the internal homogeneity, which the term identity treats as foundational is not a natural, but a constructed form of closure, every identity naming as its necessary, even if silenced and unspoken other, that which it 'lacks'. Laclau (1990) argues powerfully and persuasively that 'the constitution of a social identity is an act of power' since,

> If ... an objectivity manages to partially affirm itself it is only by repressing that which threatens it. Derrida has shown how an identity's constitution is always based on excluding something and establishing a violent hierarchy between the two resultant poles – man/woman, etc. What is

peculiar to the second term is thus reduced to the function of an accident as opposed to the essentiality of the first. It is the same with the black-white relationship, in which white, of course, is equivalent to 'human being'. 'Woman' and 'black' are thus 'marks' (i.e. marked terms) in contrast to the unmarked terms of 'man' and 'white'.

(Laclau, 1990:33)

So the 'unities' which identities proclaim are, in fact, constructed within the play of power and exclusion, and are the result, not of a natural and inevitable or primordial totality but of the naturalized, overdetermined process of 'closure' (Bhabha, 1994; Hall, 1993).

If 'identities' can only be read against the grain – that is to say, specifically *not* as that which fixes the play of difference in a point of origin and stability, but as that which is constructed in or through *différance* and is constantly destabilized by what it leaves out, then how can we understand its meaning and how can we theorize its emergence? Avtar Brah (1992:143), in her important article on 'Difference, diversity and differentiation', raises an important series of questions which these new ways of conceptualizing identity have posed:

> Fanon notwithstanding, much work is yet to be undertaken on the subject of how the racialized 'other' is constituted in the psychic domain. How is post-colonial gendered and racialized subjectivity to be analyzed? Does the privileging of 'sexual difference' and early childhood in psychoanalysis limit its explanatory value in helping us to understand the psychic dimensions of social phenomena such as racism? How do the 'symbolic order' and the social order articulate in the formation of the subject? In other words, how is the link between social and psychic reality to be theorized?'
>
> (1992:142)

What follows is an attempt to begin to respond to this critical but troubling set of questions.

In some recent work on this topic, I have made an appropriation of the term identity which is certainly not widely shared and may not be well understood. I use 'identity' to refer to the meeting point, the point of *suture*, between on the one hand the discourses and

practices which attempt to 'interpellate', speak to us or hail us into place as the social subjects of particular discourses, and on the other hand, the processes which produce subjectivities, which construct us as subjects which can be 'spoken'. Identities are thus points of temporary attachment to the subject positions which discursive practices construct for us (see Hall, 1995). They are the result of a successful articulation or 'chaining' of the subject into the flow of the discourse, what Stephen Heath, in his path-breaking essay on 'Suture' called 'an intersection' (1981:106). 'A theory of ideology must begin not from the subject but as an account of suturing effects, the effecting of the join of the subject in structures of meaning.' Identities are, as it were, the positions which the subject is obliged to take up while always 'knowing' (the language of consciousness here betrays us) that they are representations, that representation is always constructed across a 'lack', across a division, from the place of the Other, and thus can never be adequate – identical – to the subject processes which are invested in them. The notion that an effective suturing of the subject to a subject-position requires, not only that the subject is 'hailed', but that the subject invests in the position, means that suturing has to be thought of as an *articulation*, rather than a one-sided process, and that in turn places *identification*, if not identities, firmly on the theoretical agenda.

The references to the term which describes the hailing of the subject by discourse – interpellation – remind us that this debate has a significant and uncompleted pre-history in the arguments sparked off by Althusser's 'Ideological state apparatuses' essay (1971). This essay introduced the notion of interpellation, and the speculary structure of ideology in an attempt to circumvent the economism and reductionism of the classical Marxist theory of ideology, and to bring together within one explanatory framework both the materialist function of ideology in reproducing the social relations of production (Marxism) and (through its borrowings from Lacan) the symbolic function of ideology in the constitution of subjects. Michele Barrett, in her recent discussion of this debate, has gone a considerable way to demonstrating 'the profoundly divided and contradictory nature of the argument Althusser was beginning to make' (Barrett, 1991:96; see also Hall, 1985:102: 'The two sides of the difficult problem of ideology were fractured in that essay and, ever since, have been assigned to different poles'). Nevertheless, the ISAs essay, as it came to be known, has turned out to be a highly significant, even if not successful, moment in the debate. Jacqueline Rose, for example, has argued in *Sexuality in the Field of Vision* (1986), that 'the question of identity – how it is constituted and maintained – is therefore the central issue through which psycho-analysis enters the political field'.

> This is one reason why Lacanian psychoanalysis came into English intellectual life, via Althusser's concept of ideology, through the two paths of feminism and the analysis of film (a fact often used to discredit all three). Feminism because the issue of how individuals recognize themselves as male or female, the demand that they do so, seems to stand in such fundamental relation to the forms of inequality and subordination which it is feminism's objective to change. Film because its power as an ideological apparatus rests on the mechanisms of identification and sexual fantasy which we all seem to participate in, but which – outside the cinema – are for the most part only ever admitted on the couch. If ideology is effective, it is because it works at the most rudimentary levels of psychic identity and the drives.
>
> (Rose, 1986:5)

However, if we are not to fall directly from an economistic reductionism into a psychoanalytic one, we need to add that, if ideology is effective, it is because it works at *both* 'the rudimentary levels of psychic identity and the drives' *and* at the level of the discursive formation and practices which constitute the social field; and that it is in the articulation of these mutually constitutive but not identical fields that the real conceptual problems lie. The term identity – which arises precisely at the point of intersection between them – is thus the site of the difficulty. It is worth adding that we are unlikely ever to be able to square up these two constituents as equivalents – the unconscious itself acting as the bar or cut between them which makes it 'the site of a perpetual postponement or deferral of equivalence' (Hall, 1995) but which cannot, for that reason, be given up.

Heath's essay (1981) reminds us that it was Michael Pêcheux who tried to develop an account of discourse within the Althusserian perspective, and who in effect, registered the unbridgeable gap between the first and the second halves of Althusser's essay in terms of 'the heavy absence of a conceptual articulation elaborated between *ideology* and the *unconscious*, (quoted in Heath, 1981:106). Pêcheux tried 'to describe with reference to the mechanisms of the setting in position of its subjects' (Heath, 1981:101–2), using the Foucauldian notion of discursive formation as that which 'determines what can and must be said'. As Heath put Pêcheux's argument:

> Individuals are constituted as subjects through the discursive formation, a process of subjection in which [drawing on Althusser's loan from Lacan concerning the specular character of the constitution of subjectivity] the individual is identified as subject to the discursive formation in a structure of misrecognition (the subject thus presented as the source of the meanings of which it is an effect). Interpellation names the mechanism of this structure of misrecognition, effectively the term of the subject in the discursive and the ideological, the point of their correspondence.
>
> (1981:101–2)

Such 'correspondence', however, remained troublingly unresolved. Interpellation, though it continues to be used as a general way of describing the 'summoning into place' of the subject, was subjected to Hirst's famous critique. It depended, Hirst argued, on a recognition which, in effect, the subject would have been required to have the capacity to perform *before* it had been constituted, within discourse, as a subject. 'This something which is not a subject must already have the faculties necessary to support the recognition that will constitute it as a subject' (Hirst, 1979:65). This argument has proved very persuasive to many of Althusser's subsequent readers, in effect bringing the whole field of investigation to an untimely halt.

The critique was certainly a formidable one, but the halting of all further inquiry at this point may turn out to have been premature. Hirst's critique was effective in showing that all the mechanisms which constituted the subject in discourse as an interpellation, (through the speculary structure of misrecognition modelled on the Lacanian mirror phase), were in danger of presupposing an already constituted subject. However, since no one proposed to renounce the idea of the subject as constituted in discourse as an effect, it still remained to be shown by what mechanism which was not vulnerable to the charge of presupposition this constitution could be achieved. The problem was postponed, not resolved. Some of the difficulties, at least, seemed to arise from accepting too much at face value, and without qualification, Lacan's somewhat sensationalist proposition that *everything* constitutive of the subject not only happens through this mechanism of the resolution of the Oedipal crisis, but happens in the same moment. The 'resolution' of the Oedipal crisis, in the over-condensed language of the Lacanian hot-gospellers, *was* identical with, and occurred through the equivalent mechanism as, the submission to the Law of the Father, the consolidation of sexual difference, the entry into language, the formation of the unconscious as well – after Althusser – as the recruitment into the patriarchal ideologies of late capitalist western societies! The more complex notion of a subject-in-process is lost in these polemical condensations and hypothetically aligned equivalences. (Is the subject racialized, nationalized and constituted as a late-liberal entrepreneurial subject in this moment too?)

Hirst, too, seems to have assumed what Michele Barrett calls 'Althusser's Lacan'. However, as he puts it, 'the complex and hazardous process of formation of a human adult from "a small animal" does not necessarily correspond to Althusser's mechanism of ideology . . . *unless the Child* . . . remains in Lacan's mirror phase, or unless we fill the child's cradle with anthropological assumptions' (Hirst, 1979). His response to this is somewhat perfunctory. 'I have no quarrel with Children, and I do not wish to pronounce them blind, deaf or dumb, merely to deny that they posses the capacities of *philosophical* subjects, that they have the attributes of "knowing" subjects independent of their formation and training as social beings.' What is at issue here is the capacity for self-recognition. But it is an unwarrantable assumption to make, that 'recognition' is a purely cognitive let alone 'philosophical' attribute, and unlikely that it should appear in the child at one fell swoop, in a before/after

fashion. The stakes here seem, unaccountably, to have been pitched very high indeed. It hardly requires us to endow the individual 'small animal' with the full philosophical apparatus to account for why it may have the capacity to 'misrecognize' itself in the look from the place of the other which is all we require to set the passage between the Imaginary and the Symbolic in motion in Lacan's terms. After all, following Freud, the basic cathexing of the zones of bodily activity and the apparatus of sensation, pleasure and pain must be already 'in play' in however embryonic a form in order for any relation of any kind to be established with the external world. There is already a relation to a source of pleasure – the relation to the Mother in the Imaginary – so there must be already something which is capable of 'recognizing' what pleasure is. Lacan himself noted in his essay on 'The Mirror Stage' that 'The child, at an age when he is for a time, however short, outdone by the chimpanzee in instrumental intelligence, can nevertheless already recognize his own image in a mirror.' What is more, the critique seems to be pitched in a rather binary, before/after, either/or logical form. The mirror stage is not the *beginning* of something, but the *interruption* – the loss, the lack, the division – which initiates the process that 'founds' the sexually differentiated subject (and the unconscious) and this depends not alone on the instantaneous formation of some internal cognitive capacity, but on the dislocating rupture of the look from the place of the Other. For Lacan, however, this is already a fantasy – the very image which places the child divides its identity into two. Furthermore, that moment only has meaning in relation to the supporting presence and the look of the mother who guarantees its reality for the child. Peter Osborne notes (1995) that in *The Field Of The Other* Lacan (1977) describes the 'parent holding him up before the mirror', with the child looking towards the Mother for confirmation, the child seeing her as a 'reference point . . . not his ego ideal but his ideal ego' (p. 257). This argument, Osborne suggests, 'exploits the indeterminacy inherent in the discrepancy between the temporality of Lacan's description of the child's encounter with its bodily image in the mirror as a "stage" and the punctuality of his depiction of it as a scene, the dramatic point of which is restricted to the relations between two "characters" alone: the child and its bodily image'. However, as Osborne says, either it represents a critical addition to the 'mirror stage' argument – in which case, why is it not developed? Or it introduces a different logic whose implications remain unaddressed in Lacan's subsequent work.

The notion that nothing of the subject is there until the Oedipal drama is an exaggerated reading of Lacan. The assertion that subjectivity is not fully constituted until the Oedipal crisis has been 'resolved' does not require a blank screen, *tabula rasa*, or a before/after conception of the subject, initiated by a sort of *coup de théâtre*, even if – as Hirst rightly noted – it leaves unsettled the problematic relationship between 'the individual' and the subject. (What *is* the individual 'small animal' that is not yet a subject?)

One could add that Lacan's is only one of the many accounts of the formation of subjectivity which takes account of unconscious psychic processes and the relation to the other, and the debate may look different now that the 'Lacanian deluge' is somewhat receding and in the absence of the early powerful impulsion in that direction which we were given by Althusser's text. In his thoughtful recent discussion of the Hegelian origins of this concept of 'recognition' referred to above, Peter Osborne has criticized Lacan for 'the way in which the child's relation to the image is absolutized by being abstracted from the context of its relations to others (particularly, the mother)', while being made ontologically constitutive of 'the symbolic matrix in which the I is precipitated in a primordial form ...' and considers several other variants (Kristeva, Jessica Benjamin, Laplanche) which are not so confined within the alienated misrecognition of the Lacanian scenario. These are useful pointers beyond the impasse in which this discussion, in the wake of 'Althusser's Lacan', has left us, with the threads of the psychic and the discursive spinning loose in our hands.

Foucault, I would argue, also approaches the impasse with which Hirst's critique of Althusser leaves us, but so to speak from the opposite direction. Ruthlessly attacking 'the great myth of interiority', and driven both by his critique of humanism and the philosophy of consciousness, and by his negative reading of psychoanalysis, Foucault also undertakes a radical historicization of the category of the subject. The subject is produced 'as an effect' through and within discourse, within specific discursive formations, and has no existence, and certainly no transcendental continuity or identity from one subject position to another. In his 'archaeological' work (*Madness and Civilization, The Birth of the Clinic, The Order of Things, The Archaeology of Knowledge*), discourses construct subject positions through their rules of formation and 'modalities of enunciation'. Powerfully compelling and original as these works are, the criticism levelled against them in this respect at least seems justified. They offer a formal account of the construction of subject positions within discourse while revealing little about why it is that certain individuals occupy some subject positions rather than others. By neglecting to analyse how the social positions of individuals interact with the construction of certain 'empty' discursive subject positions, Foucault reinscribes an antinomy between subject positions and the individuals who occupy them. Thus his archaeology provides a critical, but one-dimensional, formal account of the subject of discourse. Discursive subject positions become *a priori* categories which individuals seem to occupy in an unproblematic fashion. (McNay, 1994: 76–7). McNay cites Brown and Cousins's key observation that Foucault tends here to elide 'subject positions of a statement with individual capacities to fill them' (Brown and Cousins, 1980: 272) – thus coming up against the very difficulty which Althusser failed to resolve, by a different route.

The critical shift in Foucault's work from an archaeological to a genealogical method does many things to render more concrete the somewhat 'empty formalism' of the earlier work, especially in the powerful ways in which power, which was missing from the more formal account of discourse, is now centrally reintroduced and the exciting possibilities opened up by Foucault's discussion of the double-sided character of subjection/subjectification (*assujettisement*). Moreover, the centring of questions of power, and the notion that discourse itself is a regulative and regulated formation, entry into which is 'determined by and constitutive of the power relations that permeate the social realm' (McNay, 1994: 87), brings Foucault's conception of the discursive formation closer to some of the classical questions which Althusser tried to address through the concept of 'ideology' – shorn, of course, of its class reductionism, economistic and truth-claiming overtones.

In the area of the theorization of the subject and identity, however, certain problems remain. One implication of the new conceptions of power elaborated in this body of work is the radical 'deconstruction' of the body, the last residue or hiding place of 'Man', and its 'reconstruction' in terms of its historical, genealogical and discursive formations. The body is constructed by, shaped and reshaped by the intersection of a series of disciplinary discursive practices. Genealogy's task, Foucault proclaims, 'is to expose the body totally imprinted by history and the processes of history's destruction of the body' (1984: 63). While we can accept this, with its radically 'constructivist' implications (the body becomes infinitely malleable and contingent) I am not sure we can or ought to go as far as his proposition that 'Nothing in man – not even his body – is sufficiently stable to serve as a basis for self-recognition or for understanding other men.' This is not because the body *is* such a stable and true referent for self-understanding, but because, though this may be a 'misrecognition', it is precisely how the body has served *to function as the signifier of the condensation of subjectivities in the individual* and this function cannot simply be dismissed because, as Foucault effectively shows, it is not true.

Further, my own feeling is that, despite Foucault's disclaimers, his invocation of *the body* as the point of application of a variety of disciplinary practices tends to lend this theory of disciplinary regulation a sort of 'displaced or misplaced concreteness' – a residual materiality – and in this way operates discursively to 'resolve' or appear to resolve the unspecified relationship between the subject, the individual and the body. To put it crudely, it pins back together or 'sutures' those things which the theory of the discursive production of subjects, if taken to its limits, would irretrievably fracture and disperse. I think 'the body' has acquired a totemic value in post-Foucauldian work precisely because of this talismanic status. It is almost the only trace we have left in Foucault's work of a 'transcendental signifier'.

The more well-established critique, however, has to do with the problem which Foucault encounters with theorizing resistance within the theory of power

he deploys in *Discipline and Punish* and *The History of Sexuality*; the entirely self-policing conception of the subject which emerges from the disciplinary, confessional and pastoral modalities of power discussed there, and the absence of any attention to what might in any way interrupt, prevent or disturb the smooth insertion of individuals into the subject positions constructed by these discourses. The submission of the body through 'the soul' to the normalizing regimes of truth constitutes a powerful way of rethinking the body's so-called 'materiality' (which has been productively taken up by Nikolas Rose, and the 'governmentality' school, as well as, in a different mode, by Judith Butler in *Bodies That Matter*, 1993). But it is hard not to take Foucault's own formulation seriously, with all the difficulties it brings in its train: namely, that the subjects which are constructed in this way are 'docile bodies'. There is no theorized account of how or why bodies should not always-for-ever turn up, in place, at the right time (exactly the point from which the classical Marxist theory of ideology started to unravel, and the very difficulty which Althusser reinscribed when he normatively defined the function of ideology as 'to reproduce the social relations of production'). Furthermore, there is no theorization of the psychic mechanism or interior processes by which these automatic 'interpellations' might be produced, or – more significantly – fail or be resisted or negotiated. Powerful and productive as this work undoubtedly is, then, it remains the case that here 'Foucault steps too easily from describing disciplinary power as a *tendency* within modern forms of social control, to positing disciplinary power as a fully installed monolithic force which saturates all social relations. This leads to an overestimation of the efficacy of disciplinary power and to an impoverished understanding of the individual which cannot account for experiences that fall outside the realm of the "docile" body' (McNay, 1994: 104.)

That this became obvious to Foucault, even if it is still refused as a critique by many of his followers, is apparent from the further and distinctive shift in his work marked by the later (and incomplete) volumes of his so-called 'History of Sexuality' (*The Use of Pleasure*, 1987; *The Care of the Self*, 1988, and as far as we can gather, the unpublished – and from the point of view of the critique just passed, the critical – volume on 'The Perversions'). For here, without moving very far from his insightful work on the productive character of normative regulation (no subjects outside the Law, as Judith Butler puts it), he tacitly recognizes that it is not enough for the Law to summon, discipline, produce and regulate, but there must also be the corresponding production of a response (and thus the capacity and apparatus of subjectivity) from the side of the subject. In the critical Introduction to *The Use of Pleasure* Foucault lists what by now we would expect of his work – 'the correlation between fields of knowledge, types of normativity and forms of subjectivity in particular cultures' – but now critically adds

> the practices by which individuals were led to focus attention on themselves, to decipher, recognize and acknowledge themselves as subjects of desire, bringing into play between themselves and themselves a certain relationship that allows them to discover, in desire, the truth of their being, be it natural or fallen. In short, with this genealogy, the idea was to investigate how individuals were led to practice, on themselves and on others, a hermeneutics of desire.
>
> (1987: 5)

Foucault describes this – correctly, in our view – as 'a third shift, in order to analyze what is termed "the subject". It seemed appropriate to look for the forms and modalities of the relation to self by which the individual constitutes and recognizes himself *qua* subject.' Foucault, of course, would not commit anything so vulgar as actually to deploy the term 'identity', but I think, with 'the relation to self' and the constitution and recognition of 'himself' (*sic*) qua subject we are approaching something of the territory which, in the terms established earlier, belongs to the problematic of 'identity'.

This is not the place to trace through the many productive insights which flow from Foucault's analysis of the truth-games, the elaboration of ethical work, of the regimes of self-regulation and self-fashioning, of the 'technologies of the self' involved in the constitution of the desiring subject. There is certainly no single switch to 'agency', to intention and volition, here (though there are, very centrally, the

practices of freedom which prevent this subject from ever being simply a docile sexualized body).

But there is the *production* of self as an object in the world, the practices of self-constitution, recognition and reflection, the relation to the rule, alongside the scrupulous attention to normative regulation, and the constraints of the rules without which no 'subjectification' is produced. This is a significant advance, since it addresses for the first time in Foucault's major work the existence of some interior landscape of the subject, some interior mechanisms of assent to the rule, as well as its objectively disciplining force, which saves the account from the 'behaviourism' and objectivism which threatens certain parts of *Discipline and Punish*. Often, in this work, the ethics and practices of the self are most fully described by Foucault as an 'aesthetics of existence', a deliberate stylization of daily life; and its technologies are most effectively demonstrated in the practices of self-production, in specific modes of conduct, in what we have come from later work to recognize as a kind of *performativity*.

What I think we can see here, then, is Foucault being pushed, by the scrupulous rigour of his own thinking, through a series of conceptual shifts at different stages in his work, towards a recognition that, since the decentring of the subject is not the destruction of the subject, and since the 'centring' of discursive practice cannot work without the constitution of subjects, the theoretical work cannot be fully accomplished without complementing the account of discursive and disciplinary regulation with an account of the practices of subjective self-constitution. It has never been enough – in Marx, in Althusser, in Foucault – to elaborate a theory of how individuals are summoned into place in the discursive structures. It has always, also, required an account of how subjects are constituted; and in this work, Foucault has gone a considerable way in showing this, in reference to historically-specific discursive practices, normative self-regulation and technologies of the self. The question which remains is whether we also require to, as it were, close the gap between the two: that is to say, a theory of what the mechanisms are by which individuals as subjects identify (or do not identify) with the 'positions' to which they are summoned; as well as how they fashion, stylize, produce and 'perform' these positions, and why they never do so completely, for once and all time, and some never do, or are in a constant, agonistic process of struggling with, resisting, negotiating and accommodating the normative or regulative rules with which they confront and regulate themselves. In short, what remains is the requirement to think this relation of subject to discursive formations *as an articulation* (all articulations are properly relations of 'no necessary correspondence', i.e. founded on that contingency which 'reactivates the historical' cf. Laclau, 1990:35).

It is therefore all the more fascinating that, when finally Foucault *does* make the move in this direction (in work which was then tragically cut short), he was prevented, of course, from going to one of the principal sources of thinking about this neglected aspect – namely, psychoanalysis; prevented from moving in that direction by his own critique of it as simply another network of disciplinary power relations. What he produces instead is a discursive *phenomenology* of the subject (drawing perhaps on earlier sources and influences whose importance for him have been somewhat underplayed) and a genealogy of the *technologies of the self.* But it is a phenomenology which is in danger of being overwhelmed by an overemphasis on intentionality – precisely because it cannot engage with *the unconscious.* For good or ill, that door was already foreclosed.

Fortunately it has not remained so. In *Gender Trouble* (1990) and more especially in *Bodies That Matter* (1993), Judith Butler has taken up, through her concern with 'the discursive limits of "sex" ' and with the politics of feminism, the complex transactions between the subject, the body and identity, through the drawing together in one analytic framework insights drawn from a Foucauldian and a psychoanalytic perspective. Adopting the position that the subject is discursively constructed and that there is no subject before or outside the Law, Butler develops a rigorously argued case that

> sex is, from the start, normative; it is what Foucault has called a 'regulatory ideal'. In this sense, then, sex not only functions as a norm, but is part of a regulatory practice that produces (through the repetition or iteration of a norm which is without origin) the bodies it governs, that is, whose

regulatory force is made clear as a kind of productive power, the power to produce – demarcate, circulate, differentiate – the bodies it controls . . . 'sex' is an ideal construct which is forcibly materialized through time.

> (Butler, 1993:1)

Materialization here is rethought as an effect of power. The view that the subject is produced in the course of its materialization is strongly grounded in a performative theory of language and the subject, but performativity is shorn of its associations with volition, choice and intentionality and (against some of the misreadings of *Gender Trouble*) re-read 'not as the act by which a subject brings into being what she/he names but rather as that reiterative power of discourse to produce the phenomena that it regulates and constrains' (Butler, 1993:2).

The decisive shift, from the viewpoint of the argument being developed here, however, is 'a linking of this process of "assuming" a sex with the question of *identification*, and with the discursive means by which the heterosexual imperative enables certain sexed identifications and forecloses and/or disavows other identifications' (Butler, 1993:5). This centring of the question of identification, together with the problematic of the subject which 'assumes a sex', opens up a critical and reflexive dialogue in Butler's work between Foucault and psychoanalysis which is enormously productive. It is true that Butler does not provide an elaborate theoretical meta-argument for the way the two perspectives, or the relation between the discursive and the psychic, are 'thought' together in her text beyond a suggestive indication: 'There may be a way to subject psychoanalysis to a Foucauldian redescription even as Foucault himself refused that possibility.' At any rate

> this text accepts as a point of departure Foucault's notion that regulatory power produces the subjects it controls, that power is not only imposed externally but works as the regulatory and normative means by which subjects are formed. The return to psychoanalysis, then, is guided by the question of how certain regulatory norms form a 'sexed' subject in terms that establish the indistinguishability of psychic and bodily formation.

> (1993:23)

However, Butler's relevance to the argument is made all the more pertinent because it is developed in the context of the discussion of gender and sexuality, framed by feminism, and so is directly recurrent both to the questions of identity and identity politics, and to the questions which Avtar Brah's work posed earlier about the paradigmatic function of sexual difference in relation to other axes of exclusion. Here Butler makes a powerful case that all identities operate through exclusion, through the discursive construction of a constitutive outside and the production of abjected and marginalized subjects, apparently outside the field of the symbolic, the representable – 'the production of an "outside", a domain of intelligible effects' (1993:22) – which then returns to trouble and unsettle the foreclosures which we prematurely call 'identities'. She deploys this argument with effect in relation to the sexualizing and the racializing of the subject – an argument which requires to be developed if the constitution of subjects in and through the normalizing regulatory effects of racial discourse is to acquire the theoretical development hitherto reserved for gender and sexuality (though, of course, her most well-worked example is in relation to the production of these forms of sexual abjection and lived unintelligibility usually 'normalized' as pathological or perverse).

As James Souter (1995) has pointed out, 'Butler's internal critique of feminist identity politics and its foundationalist premises questions the adequacy of a representational politics whose basis is the presumed universality and unity of its subject – a seamless category of women.' Paradoxically, as in all other identities treated politically in a foundational manner, this identity 'is based on excluding "different" women . . . and by normatively prioritizing heterosexual relations as the basis for feminist politics'. This 'unity', Souter argues, is a 'fictive unity', 'produced and restrained by the very structures of power through which emancipation is sought'. Significantly, however, as Souter also argues, this does *not* lead Butler to argue that all notions of identity should therefore be abandoned because they are theoretically flawed. Indeed, she takes the speculary structure of identification as a critical part of her argument. But she acknowledges that such an argument *does* suggest 'the necessary limits of identity politics'.

In this sense, identifications belong to the imaginary; they are phantasmatic efforts of alignment, loyalty, ambiguous and cross-corporeal cohabitations, they unsettle the 1; they are the sedimentation of the 'we' in the constitution of any 1, the structuring present of alterity in the very formulation of the 1. Identifications are never fully and finally made; they are incessantly reconstituted, and, as such, are subject to the volatile logic of iterability. They are that which is constantly marshalled, consolidated, retrenched, contested and, on occasion, compelled to give way.

(1993:105)

The effort, now, to think the question of the distinctiveness of the logic within which the racialized and ethnicized body is constituted discursively, through the regulatory normative ideal of a 'compulsive Eurocentrism' (for want of a different word), cannot be simply grafted on to the arguments briefly sketched above. But they have received an enormous and original impetus from this tangled and unconcluded argument, which demonstrates beyond the shadow of a doubt that the question, and the theorization, of identity is a matter of considerable political significance, and is only likely to be advanced when both the necessity and the 'impossibility' of identities, and the suturing of the psychic and the discursive in their constitution, are fully and unambiguously acknowledged.

References

Althusser, L. (1971) *Lenin and Philosophy and Other Essays*, London: New Left Books.

Barrett, M (1991) *The Politics of Truth*, Cambridge: Polity.

Bhabha, H. (1994) 'The Other Question', in *The Location Of Culture*, London: Routledge.

Brah, A. (1992) 'Difference, diversity and differentiation', in J. Donald and A. Rattansi (eds), *Race, Culture and Difference*, London: Sage (126–45).

Brown, B. and Cousins, M. (1980) 'The linguistic fault', *Economy and Society*, 9(3).

Butler, J (1990) *Gender Trouble*, London: Routledge.

Butler, J. (1993) *Bodies That Matter*, London: Routledge.

Derrida, J. (1981) *Positions*, Chicago: University of Chicago Press.

Foucault, M. (1970) *The Order of Things*, London: Tavistock.

Foucault, M. (1972) *The Archaeology of Knowledge*, London: Tavistock.

Foucault, M. (1977) *Discipline and Punish*, Harmondsworth: Penguin.

Foucault, M. (1981) *The History of Sexuality Volume 1*, Harmondsworth: Penguin.

Foucault, M. (1987) *The Use of Pleasure*, Harmondsworth: Penguin.

Foucault, M. (1988) *The Care of the Self*, Harmondsworth: Penguin.

Foucault, M. (1984) 'Nietzsche, genealogy, history', in P. Rabinow (ed.), *The Foucault Reader*, Harmondsworth: Penguin.

Freud, S (1921/1991) *Group psychology and the analysis of the ego*, in *Civilization, Society and Religion, Vol. 12 Selected Works*, Harmondsworth: Penguin.

Gilroy, P. (1994) *The Black Atlantic: Modernity and Double Consciousness*, London: Verso.

Hall, S. (1985) 'Signification, representation and ideology: Althusser and the post-structuralist debates'. *Critical Studies in Mass Communication*, 2(2).

Hall, S. (1990) 'Cultural identity and diaspora', in J. Rutherford (ed.), *Identity*, London: Lawrence & Wishart.

Hall, S. (1993) 'Cultural identity in question', in S. Hall, D. Held and T. McGrew (eds), *Modernity and its Futures*, Cambridge: Polity.

Hall, S. (1995) 'Fantasy, identity, politics', in E. Carter, J. Donald and J. Squites (eds). *Cultural Remix: Theories of Politics and the Popular*, London: Lawrence & Wishart.

Hall, S. (1996) 'When was the post-colonial?', in L. Curti and I. Chambers (eds), *The Post-Colonial in Question*, London: Routledge.

Heath, S. (1981) *Questions of Cinema*, Basingstoke: Macmillan.

Hirst, P. (1979) *On Law and Ideology*, Basingstoke: Macmillan.

Laclau, E. (1990) *New Reflections on the Revolution of Our Time*, London: Verso.

Lacan, J. (1977) *Ecrits*, London: Tavistock.

Lacan, J. (1977) *The Four Fundamental Concepts of Psychoanalysis*, London: Hogarth Press.

Laplanche, J. and Pontalis, J.-B. (1985) *The Language of Psychoanalysis*, London: Hogarth Press.

McNay, L. (1994) *Foucault: A Critical Introduction*, Cambridge: Polity Press.

Osborne, P. (1995) *The Politics of Time*, London: Verso.

Rose, J. (1986) *Sexuality in the Field of Vision*, London: Verso.

Souter, J. (1995) 'From *Gender Trouble* to *Bodies That Matter*', unpublished manuscript.

26.
UNDER WESTERN EYES
Media, Empire and Otherness
David Morley and Kevin Robbins

The helicopter landed with the body in a metal casket, which revolutionary guards carried on their shoulders a short distance to the grave. But then the crowd surged again, weeping men in bloody headbands, and they scaled the barriers and overran the gravesite.

The voice said, Wailing chanting mourners. It said, Throwing themselves into the hole.

Karen could not imagine who else was watching this. It could not be real if others watched. If other people watched, if millions watched, if these millions matched the number on the Iranian plain, doesn't it mean we share something with the mourners, know an anguish, feel something pass between us, hear the sigh of some historic grief? ... If others saw these pictures, why is nothing changed, where are the local crowds, why do we still have names and addresses and car keys?

(Don DeLillo, *Mao II*)

Already by action we maintain a living relationship with a real object; we grasp it, we conceive it. The image neutralises this real relationship, this primary conceiving through action.

(Emmanuel Levinas, 1983)

Media Imperialism

One of the distinguishing characteristics of the present period is the role played by improved systems of physical transportation and by various forms of symbolic communication in linking the different parts of the world together. It has been observed that the role of geographical distance in human affairs is much diminished (Meyrowitz, 1985), and that 'time-space compression' is constitutive of our supposedly postmodern condition (Jameson, 1985; Harvey, 1989). These might be seen as no more than extrapolations of Marshall McLuhan's well-worn adage about the contribution of communications media to the construction of a 'global village'. However, as many of McLuhan's critics have emphasised, this is no mere technological phenomenon, not least in so far as the media technologies in question have a very particular (Western or Euro-American) point of origin and are controlled by identifiable interests (Walt Disney, News Corporation, Berlusconi, Time Warner, Bertelsmann or whatever), engendering a largely one-way 'conversation', in which the West speaks and the Rest listen.

All of this clearly points to the need to pay close attention to the role of the media in this process of cultural encounter. How are we to understand this influence of the media? Within media studies, there is a longstanding tradition which has addressed the issue in terms of 'media imperialism'. In the work of, for example, Armand Mattelart *et al.* (1984), Herbert Schiller (1969) and Jeremy Tunstall (1977), there has been considerable analysis of the cultural consequences of the West's long-exercised control over the world's media systems. The flaw in this body of work, however, has been in its reliance on a simplistic 'hypodermic' model of media effects – a model, long discredited within the mainstream of media studies, in which it is assumed that media products have direct and necessary cultural 'effects' on those who consume them. This is not to fall prey to any kind of foolish presumption that the media do not exercise profound forms of cultural influence, but it is to insist that the ways in which they have influence over their audiences are rather more complex than any hypodermic model can allow (Morley, 1992), and it is to insist that, in analysing the implication of the media for transcultural encounters, we must adequately deal with that complexity.

We referred earlier to the debates which went on throughout the 1980s over the almost global popularity of the American television series *Dallas*. As we noted, by the mid-1980s *Dallas* had become the privileged hate symbol for all those who saw the worldwide popularity of the programme as an indication of the growing threat to the variety of world cultures that was posed by American dominance over the world's media industries.

The problem with this argument, or assertion, is that all the subsequent audience research on the consumption of *Dallas*, in different cultural contexts, far from demonstrating any automatic 'media effects', has tended, rather, to demonstrate that viewers from different cultural backgrounds 'read' the programme in quite different ways, depending on their own cultural contexts. Thus, Ien Ang (1985) demonstrates how many Dutch women interpreted the programme ironically, through the grid of their own feminist agenda. Eric Michaels (1988) showed how Australian Aboriginals reinterpreted *Dallas* through their particular conceptions of kinship so as to produce quite different readings from those intended by the programme's makers. And, most exhaustively, Tamara Liebes and Elihu Katz (1991) have demonstrated the ways in which viewers from American, Russian, North African and Japanese backgrounds came to see quite different things in the programme and took quite different 'messages' from their encounter with *Dallas*. However, against this Gripsrud (1995) makes the important point that, while these ethnographic findings concerning varieties of reception in different contexts are of considerable interest (as counter-evidence to any simple-minded theory of 'hypodermic' media effects), we would be foolish to conclude that the continuing world dominance of the

Hollywood film and television production base is therefore of no consequence.

Certainly, one should not overestimate the freedom of the media consumer to make whatever he or she likes of the material transmitted. Even if they could, their choice of materials to reinterpret would still be limited to the 'menu' constructed by powerful media organisations. Moreover, such programmes are usually made in such a way as to 'prefer' one reading over another (Hall, 1981) and to invite the viewer to 'take' the message in some particular way, even if such a 'reading' can never be guaranteed. Clearly, we should not respond to the deficiencies in the hypodermic model of media effects by romanticising the consumption process and cheerfully celebrating the 'active' viewer as a kind of semiotic guerrilla, continuously waging war on the structures of textual power (Curran, 1990). We must balance an acceptance that audiences are in certain respects active in their choice, consumption and interpretation of media texts, with a recognition of how that activity is framed and limited, in its different modalities and varieties, by the dynamics of cultural power.

Equally, we should not fall into any technologically determinist argument Even if media technologies have, historically, been developed and controlled by the powerful countries of the West, they are, none the less, always capable of being appropriated and used in other ways than those for which they were intended. Eliut Flores (1988), for example, describes how expatriate Puerto Rican families in New York use video conferencing facilities (designed for business applications) during evenings and weekends, when rates are low, to substitute for an air trip 'home'. Similarly, Stephen Greenblatt describes certain uses of modern video technology in Bali in which the technology is in effect incorporated into traditional rituals, to the extent that it is unclear who is assimilating whom in the process through which the villagers incorporate a sophisticated version of international capitalism's representational machinery into their own patterns of activity. We should resist a priori ideological determinism, he argues, and recognise that cultures have 'fantastically powerful assimilative mechanisms ... that work like enzymes to change the ideological composition of foreign bodies'. In this example, video technology is by no means 'unequivocally and irreversibly the bearer of the capitalist ideology that was the determining condition of [its] . . . creation' (Greenblatt, 1992: 4). In a similar vein, Daniel Miller (1992), one of the few anthropologists who has offered any direct analysis of processes of media consumption, in an analysis of the viewing of the American series *The Young and the Restless* in Trinidad, helpfully offers the concept of 'indigenisation' (on the model of digestion, incorporation and assimilation) as a way of understanding how 'local' cultures are continually refashioned out of elements initially produced elsewhere. Criticising the traditional model in which authentic local cultures are seen as being invaded by 'foreign' and 'corrupting' influences, Miller suggests we should accept an alternative approach in which 'authenticity' is defined a posteriori, as a matter of local consequences rather than of local (or 'foreign') origins.

So far, we have been concerned principally with debates about the consequences of Western media for other cultures. In addressing this issue, we have kept to the terms of a fairly conventional model of communications, which many authors (for example, Baudrillard, 1988; Harvey, 1989) would argue is, in fact, inadequate to our present situation. In their view, the condition of so-called 'postmodernity' is in fact characterised by a new ordering of experience and the creation of a new sense of place, a complex process in which the media play a particularly vital role.

Culture, Geography and Media

The central issue here concerns the effects of modern media in constructing new geographies. Already apparent in some of the examples we have given is the fact that the media have consequences for the way we imagine space and place. Doreen Massey (1991a) has argued that places themselves should no longer be seen as internally homogeneous, bounded areas, but as 'spaces of interaction' in which local identities are constructed out of resources (both material and symbolic) which may well not be at all local in their origin, but are none the less 'authentic' for all that.

In an anthropological context, James Clifford (1992) takes up the same issue, noting that 'villages', inhabited by 'natives' and conceived as bounded sites of residence which stand as metonyms for a whole culture, have long been the focus of anthropological fieldwork. Against this traditional preoccupation of anthropology, however, he emphasises that cultures are not 'in' places in any simple sense. The focus on 'rooted', 'authentic' or 'native' culture and experience fails to address 'the wider world of intercultural import-export in which the ethnographic encounter has always already enmeshed'. Clifford supports Arjun Appadurai's contention that 'natives, people confined to and by the places to which they belong, groups unsullied by contact with a larger world, have probably never existed' (Appadurai, 1988: 39). We should work, Clifford argues, not only with a model of eccentric natives, conceived in their multiple external connections, but with a notion of places as sites of travel encounters as much as sites of residence. Clifford suggests that we should be attentive to 'a culture's farthest range of travel, while *also* looking at its centres; to the ways in which groups negotiate themselves in external as much as internal relations; to the fact that culture is also a site of travel for others and that one group's core is another's periphery'. This is to argue for a multi-locale ethnography of both 'travelling-in-dwelling' and 'dwelling-in-travelling', when it comes to those 'permanently installed in the wanderground between here and there', those facing the question not so much of where they are from, as of where they are between (Clifford, 1992: 107–9). Clifford's arguments are well supported by those of Gupta and Ferguson (1992), who argue that 'people have undoubtedly always been more mobile and identities less fixed than the static and typologising approaches of classical anthropology would suggest', not least because that conventional anthropological approach allowed the 'power of topography to conceal successfully the topography of power' (ibid.: 8–9).

Eric Wolf makes the fundamental criticism that, on the whole, the 'concept of the autonomous, self-regulating and self-justifying society and culture has trapped anthropology inside the bounds of its own definitions' (1982; 18). His point is that the methodological tail of anthropology's commitment to 'fieldwork' has too much wagged the discipline's theoretical dog, in terms of the basic model of what constitutes a 'society' or a 'culture'. As 'fieldwork' has become a hallmark of anthropological method, heuristic considerations have often been improperly converted into theoretical postulates about society and culture. As Wolf argues, 'limitations of time and energy in the field dictate limitations in the number and locations of possible observations and interviews, demanding concentration of effort on an observable place and on a corps of specifiable informants' (ibid.: 13–14) – which is then treated relatively unproblematically as a metonym of the larger 'society' or 'culture' being studied. As far as he is concerned, the problem with the study of the 'living cultures' of specified populations in 'locally delimited habitats' is that the model wrongly presumes an a priori closure in its conception of its unit of study. In the context of centuries of imperialism and cross-cultural contact, we would do better to think of human societies as open systems 'inextricably involved with other aggregates, near and far, in weblike, netlike connections' (Alexander Lesser, quoted in ibid.: 19).

The conventional model of cultural exchange, then, presumes the existence of a pure, internally homogeneous, authentic, indigenous culture which becomes subverted or corrupted by foreign influences. The reality, however, is that every culture has, in fact, ingested foreign elements from exogenous sources, with the various elements gradually becoming 'naturalised' within it. As Said argues, 'the notion that there are geographical spaces with indigenous, radically "different" inhabitants who can be defined on the basis of some religion, culture or racial essence, proper to that geographical space is a highly debatable idea' (quoted in Clifford, 1988: 274). As argued earlier (cf. Appadurai, 1990; Bhabha, 1987; Hall, 1987), cultural hybridity is, increasingly, the normal state of affairs in the world, and in this context, any attempt to defend the integrity of indigenous or authentic cultures easily slips into the conservative defence of a nostalgic vision of the past.

Let us consider more carefully how the media are implicated in this transformation of both real and imaginative geographies. At its simplest, the point was well expressed some sixty years ago by the art historian Rudolf Arnheim, who speculated that the principal social consequences of television followed from the fact that it is 'related to the motor car and the aeroplane – as a means of transport for the mind'; as such, it 'renders the object on display independent of its port of origin, making it unnecessary for spectators to flock together in front of an original' (quoted in Rath, 1985: 199). If, in days of old, explorers and anthropologists set off on long journeys into the unknown to bring us back written accounts of the strange customs of exotic Others in distant places, today we are all ethnographers to the extent that all kinds of Others are exposed to our gaze (nightly on the regular television news and hourly on CNN) in the form of electronic representation on the television screens in our own living rooms. These days we have only to sit on the couch and press a button to behold the Other or the Exotic.

As early as 1946, Max Read recognised how media technologies can shape our perceptions of social reality:

> The radio not only reports history, it seems to make it. The world seems to originate from the radio. People still see things and events, but they become real only after the radio has reported the event and the newspaper has run a picture of it. The radio apperceives, registers and judges for people. Our souls are immediately connected to the radio and no longer to our own sensory organs. People no longer have an inner history, an inner continuity, the radio today is our history, it validates our existence.
>
> (quoted in Kaes, 1989: 197)

In a classic article, Donald Horton and Richard Wohl argued that through the new mass media, remote people are met 'as if they were in the circle of one's peers' in a 'seeming face-to-face relationship', a 'simulacrum of conversational give and take which may be called para-social interaction' (1956: 215). In a more recent extension of this perspective, the German psychoanalyst Claus-Dieter Rath (1985: 203) has argued that, increasingly, we all live within a 'television geography', where what counts is the space of electronic transmission, which often cuts across national borders, as we view television representations of 'planetary affairs which we face privately in our cosy living rooms' (Rath, 1989: 88). On occasion, these televisual forms of para-social contact can be celebratory – sometimes literally, as when a recent papal ruling concluded that, for the sick and the ill who are unable to go to church, the celebration of mass 'live', through television, was valid (though it was not if recorded and time-shifted on video because of the consequent loss of 'immediacy'). At other times, the contact may be felt to be intrusive, as was the case with the American television series *Julia*, one of the first to show black people in leading roles on prime-time American television, where the producers received a number of irate letters from white viewers, complaining that, having succeeded in physically keeping blacks out of their neighbourhoods, they did not want to come home and find them 'invading' their living rooms through the television screen (Bodroghkozy, 1992).

On occasion, even trauma can be transmitted through this para-social kind of interaction. In 1990, in response to claims made by relatives of those who died in the televised tragedy at Hillsborough football ground, the Liverpool High Court ruled that people who suffer psychological illness after watching live television coverage of tragedies involving close relatives are eligible to claim damages in the same way as those witnessing the events *in situ* (*The Guardian*, 1 August 1990). Indeed, the judge pointed out that a television watcher might be even more traumatised, by virtue of the camera's ability to bring into sharp focus events that might not be as clear to an observer of the real event. The point is that television,

> allows us to share the literal time of persons who are elsewhere. It grants us ... *instantaneous* ubiquity. The telespectator of a lunar landing becomes a vicarious astronaut, exploring the moonscape at the same time ... as the astronauts themselves. The viewer of a live transmission, in fact can in some respects see better than those immediately on the scene.
>
> (Stam, 1983: 24)

In this respect television 'transforms us into "armchair imperialists"; through its all encompassing viewpoint, we become "audio-visual masters of the world"'(ibid.: 25).

This is a situation rife with its own ironies. *The Guardian*'s Southern Africa correspondent, David

Beresford, offers a telling account of the transformed meaning of 'being there' geographically, in relation to news events in the contemporary media environment on the occasion of his own attempt to report Nelson Mandela's speech on his release from prison in April 1990. For Beresford, being physically 'on the spot', but merely one of hundreds of reporters, jostling for position, unfortunately entailed being unable either to see or hear Mr Mandela. Beresford recounts this as an experience of both 'being there and not being there', where being the 'man on the spot' had the perverse effect of making him unable to witness the images and hear the words being clearly relayed, via the well-positioned television cameras, to the global audience at home.

In a similar vein, Joshua Meyrowitz has offered a fascinating analysis of the impact of electronic media on social behaviour, in transforming the 'situational geography of human life'. Meyrowitz's concern is for the way in which electronic media have undermined the traditional relationship between physical setting and social situation to the extent that we are 'no longer "in" places in quite the same way' we once were, or thought we were (1989: 333). The media, he argues, make us 'audiences to performances that happen in other places and give us access to audiences who are not physically present' (1985: 7). Meyrowitz's central contention is that these new media redefine notions of social 'position' and 'place', divorcing experience from physical location. Thus, '*Live Aid* was an event that took place nowhere but on television' (1989: 333), the ultimate example of the freeing of communications experience from social and physical constraints. The electronic media have transformed the relative significance of live and mediated encounters, bringing 'information and experience to everyplace from everyplace' as state funerals, wars or space flights become 'dramas that can be played on the stage of almost anyone's living room' (1985: 118).

In this way, the media create new 'communities' across their spaces of transmission, bringing together otherwise disparate groups around the common experience of television, and bringing about a cultural mixing of here and there. Television thereby becomes the basis of common experiences and interactions: 'to watch television is to look into the common experience and to see what others are watching' (ibid.: 145–7). Thus, the millions who watched the assassination of Kennedy

> were in a 'place' that is no place at all ... the millions of Americans who watch television every evening ... are in a 'location' that is not defined by walls, streets or neighbourhoods but by evanescent 'experience' ... more and more, people are living in a national [or international] information-system rather than in a local town or city.
>
> (ibid.: 146)

It is in this sense that the electronic media are transforming our sense of locality and relocating us in terms of the 'generalised elsewhere' of distant places and 'non-local' people. As Lidia Curti puts it:

> In every country the media pose the problem of the shifting boundaries between the national and the foreign, otherness and sameness, repetition and difference. *Italia TV* shows sharply how different countries mingle and blend on the national screen, in a flow of fictions ... it highlights how *Dallas* is naturalised in ... Naples, how California-ness can become part of the imaginary of a Southern Italian housewife, how the proximity of a poor Roman 'bargata' to a petty bourgeois household in Rio, to a mansion in Denver, Colorado is made acceptable and plausible, by its appearing on the same flat screen in the same household in close succession.
>
> (1988: 16–17)

Through the electronic media we have seen the construction of a new experience of virtual space and place and of virtual community. It is with virtual reality that we now have to come to terms. As Christopher Coker has suggested, 'the impact of television lies not at the level of opinion and concepts, but [at the level of] "sense ratios" and patterns of perception. A profound structural change in the world has been brought about in human relations in terms of scale, models and habits' (1992: 197).

Living in a Mediated World

The media now make us all rather like anthropologists, in our own living rooms, surveying the world of all those 'Others' who are represented to us on the screen. Edward Said (1978) has argued against any comforting notion that technically improved communications media will necessarily improve inter-cultural relations, claiming that the media have, if anything, increased regressive tendencies. Indeed, he goes on, one aspect of the electronic postmodern world is that there has been a reinforcement of the stereotypes by which the Orient is viewed: 'So far as the Orient is concerned, standardisation and cultural stereotyping have intensified the hold of the nineteenth-century academic and imaginative demonology of the "mysterious Orient" ' (ibid.: 26).

Seeing by way of the media may even be an obstacle to understanding. Paul Hartmann and Charles Husband (1972) long ago offered good evidence that, largely as a result of media images of black people, racism in Britain is strongest in areas where white people have less day-to-day contact with them and are thus more dependent on media images for their knowledge of blacks (indeed, largely as a result of media obsessions with 'numbers' in debates about race, the average white person overestimates the number of black people in Britain by a factor of ten).

We are all largely dependent on the media for our images of non-local people, places and events, and the further the 'event' from our own direct experience, the more we depend on media images for the totality of our knowledge. It is at this point that the question of media representations of Otherness relates directly to the growing debate within anthropology concerning the ethics of anthropological depictions of the Other. In the light of the contributions of Clifford and Marcus (1986), Marcus and Fischer (1986) and Said (1978), many anthropologists have begun to address the Foucauldian version of the question of representation – as always involving a relation of power, as well as a relation of knowledge, between representer and represented (whether or not the Other concerned is wearing 'exotic' tribal dress). Put crudely, the question is, of course, 'who are we to represent them?' (Rabinow, 1986). As James Clifford (1986: 13) insists, we must always be sure to ask: 'Who speaks? When and where? With or to whom? Under what institutional and historical constraints?' At its strongest, the case is put by authors such as the late Bob Scholte, who suggested that anthropology as a whole may simply be 'a way Europeans have invented of talking about their darker brethren or sisters' (1987: 35–6). 'Ethnography' itself is a word that carries a heavy ideological burden, in so far as, if its denotative meaning can be defined innocently as 'the description of peoples', connotatively the implication is always that the 'peoples' to be described are Others – non-whites, non-Europeans, non-Christians: 'Them' (Fabian, 1990: 758). Trinh Minh-Ha explores the metaphor of anthropology's attempt to 'grasp the marrow of native life' as itself a cannibalistic rite, arguing that today 'the only possible ethnology is the one which studies the anthropophagous [metaphorically cannibalistic] behaviour of the white man' (1989: 73).

The point of the analogy is that just as, historically, it is Western anthropology that has arrogated to itself the right to represent the 'native', so today, given the largely one-way nature of the flow of international communications, it is the Western media which arrogate to themselves the right to represent all non-Western Others, and thus to provide 'us' with the definitions by which 'we' distinguish ourselves from 'them'. To extend, and complicate, our central metaphor, the television screen on which the Other is represented to (and for) us functions at a number of different levels. If, in one sense, screening means that 'they' are made present to 'us' in representation, it is also the case that the image of 'them' is screened in the different sense of being filtered, with only certain selected images getting through. At the same time, in a psychic sense, the screen is not only the medium through which images are projected for us, but also the screen onto which we project our own fears, fantasies and desires concerning the Others against whom our identities are defined and constructed. If this is a routine process, at particular moments of crisis, its operations can be highlighted, as basic dilemmas are thrown into dramatic relief, under the glare of the world media spotlight

The crucial question, then, is 'who are we who are screening them?' The reflexive question is the vital one:

The viewer experiences events, not at first hand, but through perception. What he perceives will inevitably trigger an individual response to the nature of identity. There is a vital connection between what the world imposes and the mind demands, receives and shapes. Everything seen on the screen says something about ourselves. It challenges us to respond, to relate what we see to what we are. It compels us to validate our own identity.

(Coker, 1992: 197)

What we have to come to terms with are our watching technologies and the watching behaviour they make possible. What should concern us is how, through the screen, we devour images of the Other. The screen is implicated in the construction of the fundamental antimonies of 'self-us-good' versus 'Other-them-bad'. Kobena Mercer (1990: 69) has referred to the 'sheer difficulty of living with difference', and Paul Hoggett (1992: 352) to the fundamental psychic dilemma in which 'unity without difference' is the only form of unity tolerable to the troubled psyche. We are not suggesting that any of this is new. Tzvetan Todorov's masterly analysis of the representation of the Other by the Spanish, in the process of conquest and colonisation of the 'New World', addresses the same fundamental dilemma. On the one hand, the Spaniards can conceive of the Indians as human, and therefore as 'identical' to themselves and having equal rights, in which case they are then ripe for the 'assimilation' of Spanish values; alternatively, they can recognise difference, but that is then immediately translated into the terms of superiority and inferiority, into the belief that the Indians are sub-human, and therefore into a justification for their enslavement. As Todorov puts it, 'what is denied is the existence of a human subject truly other, someone capable of being not merely an imperfect state of oneself'; what is at stake is 'the failure to recognise the Indians, and the refusal to admit them as a subject having the same rights as oneself, but different. Columbus discovered America but not the Americans' (Todorov, 1984: 42, 49).

Under Western Eyes

Nowadays, our 'discoveries' of Otherness are made not so often by means of long and perilous sea crossings as by use of the remote-control, as we flick between the varieties of exotica on offer on different television channels. In televisual encounters, however, we find many of the same fundamental processes in play, the same compulsion to split Good from Evil in some absolute way, the same inability to tolerate difference without relegating the different to the sub-human or inhuman category of the 'monster'. This we saw very clearly when the Gulf War was brought under Western eyes. In the media presentation of the war, Saddam Hussein was portrayed as representing all the forces of irrational barbarism that must be contained and controlled by the forces of reason and sanity. It was up to Europe and its civilisational off-spring, America, to slay the dragon, to vanquish the alien: the UN crusaders had to take on the 'beast of Baghdad' and his 'empire of terror'. Reason, suppos-edly universal reason, had to be made to prevail. The problem, of course, is that it is all too easy to project all the evil outwards, and then to believe that all is well in our own community. The demonisation of the enemy and the accusations against the Evil Other for their criminality and bestiality were related to the desire to purify our own culture and civilisation. To see the Evil Other as the embodiment of irrationality was to be certain of our own rational cause and motives. The symbolic damnation of Saddam-Hitler revealed, then, a great deal about the fears, anxieties and guilt at the heart of Western modernity and rationality.

It is important to attend to the media dimension of such events. This is, not least, because it was as an experience mediated by CNN that most people out-side Iraq were put into some kind of relation to, and given some form of knowledge of, the actual events that took place. Our principal interest here lies in the role of various media in constructing a sense of the reality (or otherwise) of events in one place for people in other places. On a visit to the United States during the Gulf War, Judith Williamson observed:

> It is the unreality of anywhere outside the US, in the eyes of its citizens, which must frighten any foreigner. Like an infant who has yet to learn there are other centres of self, this culture sees others merely as fodder for its dreams and nightmares. . . . It isn't that Americans don't *care* (God knows,

they care) but that, for most of them, other lands and other people cannot be imagined as real.

(1991: 21)

Having earlier criticised 'hypodermic' theories of media effects at the social or cultural levels, we have no intention of reinstating such a theory at the psychic level (see Morley, 1992, ch. 2, for a critique of such tendencies in cultural theory). However, we would argue that in order to explore adequately the unconscious dynamics in play in the reception of media materials, we do need recourse to concepts derived from a psychoanalytic perspective (cf. Robins, 1993, for an elaboration of this perspective).

The intensive encounter with other cultures, brought about by imperialist expansion, has always been one of the driving forces defining the modern West. The historian Albert Hourani argues that some-thing new in history was 'created by the vast expan-sion of the European mind and imagination so as to appropriate all existing things' (1980: 13). In its quest to appropriate the world, the West learned to define its own uniqueness against the Other, against 'non-Europe'. If the political reality has always been one of conflict and disunity, the construction of an imagi-nary Orient helped to give unity and coherence to the idea of the West. This Orient was, moreover, a mirror in which Europe (and subsequently America) could see its own supremacy reflected. In learning to account for its difference from non-Europe, it also had to account for this supremacy, for the unquestion-able success it had had in imposing its hegemony on 'Inferior' cultures.

Fundamental to both its difference and its inher-ent superiority, it seemed, was the principle of reason It was on the basis of reason, embodied in modern science and technology, that Europe had triumphed throughout the world and had made itself the univer-sal point of reference. This reason it came to see as the basis of a universal culture; the justification for its claim to define universal values, to define its values as universal. Modernity was defined against pre-modernity, reason against irrationality and super-stition; and this divide was, as we know, then mapped onto a symbolic geography that counterposes the West and its Orient. *Its* Orient, because if 'the West' did not exist, then the Orient could not exist either. It is 'the West' that has given both existence and identity to 'the Orient'. And the existence and identity it has bestowed is one of constitutive inferiority and deficit. Oriental culture is defined as a subaltern culture, conceived through the very process of its subjugation and subordination to the universal culture. And it is a culture defined by what it lacks (modernity, rationality, universality); its 'Otherness' is defined in terms of the backwardness, the irrationality and the particularity of its values. This confrontation, as Edward Said (1978) has so powerfully demonstrated, has assumed its most intense and confrontational form in the encounter with Islam.

Hourani describes how the encounter with the West has led to a sense of secondariness in modern Arab and Islamic identity: 'It is no longer to have a standard of values of one's own, not to be able to create but only to imitate; and so not even to imitate correctly, since that also needs a certain originality' (1946: 70–1). In the face of self-proclaimed Western universalism, Islamic and Arabic culture was shaken to its foundations. Within the terms of this self-proclaiming universal culture, moreover, there could be no escape from this degradation. Islam was inferior in its very essence. Under Western eyes (though contrary to historical evidence) it was constituted as a conservative culture, a culture of dogmatism and fanaticism. History and progress were possible only in the West. Islam, by contrast, was a static culture, an eternally medieval and feudal culture: it was the culture of impossible modernisation. And it could not be otherwise because the very difference and supremacy of the West were constructed around this image of Arab and Islamic Otherness. 'Our' civilisation was defined against 'their' barbarism; 'our' beauty against 'their' bestiality. If that irrational culture had access to our rationality and science, what would be the implications for the Western sense of difference and uniqueness? If that backward culture would modernise itself where should we then find the mirror to reflect our superiority?

This unthinkable predicament of modernity in the Orient was what confronted the West at the time of the Gulf War. In that war, Saddam Hussein was assaulting the norms that have defined Western uniqueness and superiority; he was violating the boundaries that have differentiated rationality and irrationality, Western modernity and the pre-modern Orient. He armed himself with the munitions of modernity, not only with conventional arms but also with an arsenal of nuclear, biological and chemical weapons. But, according to the Western myth, he was by nature – by his Arab and Oriental nature – irrational. When equipped with the scientific instruments of warfare, Saddam's inherent irrationality could only become explosive; with modern technologies he was a monstrous and psychotic force. The armies of Reason then had to suppress this crazed, monstrous Unreason.

The media presented Saddam as the embodiment of evil, of all that 'we' are not, in terms which stand diametrically opposed to our civilisation and culture. He was 'imagined' as absolutely and monstrously 'Other'. To see him in this way made it possible – made it logical and rational – to set fire to the night skies of Iraq. But Saddam used our weapons, the weapons that we sold him, and he used them, like us, in a rational and calculating way. Saddam embodied the aspirations and logic of modernity; he was modernity as it now exists in that part of the world. Saddam was a mirror – a distorting mirror perhaps, but a mirror none the less – reflecting an image of us. The West did not like what it saw in that mirror. But let us be clear about just what it is that it was seeing: it was the monstrous side of its own modernity; it was the irresistible spread of its own project, a project that has been marked by both rationality and violence. Saddam was not an alien monster, a monster against modernity, but rather a monster born of modernity, a monster within modernity.

Many commentators have described the creation of a Frankenstein's monster in Iraq. Like Mary Shelley's creature, Saddam was a monster created through the global spread of modernity. In him, too, our fear of modernity's monstrous aspect was projected onto an elemental hatred of the 'Other'. Saddam had to be seen as a member of a race apart. If Iraq was to be seen as in the process of modernisation, then it had to be an alien kind of modernity that could never be acceptable to the civilised world. Like Frankenstein's monster, Saddam Hussein had to be banned from civilisation. Only through his exclusion could reason be reclaimed in the name of universal progress and humanity.

And so the 'smart' technologies of Western reason were mobilised to smash the 'Other'. And courtesy of the latest media technology, we could sit in front of our television screens, safe at home, and watch, as in a video game, as the bombs homed in on their targets. The media then allowed us a kind of para-social, thrilled involvement in the obliteration of the monstrous Other.

Western Screen, Western Psyche

Writing from a psychoanalytic perspective, Paul Hoggett describes how all human beings carry a primordial fear, a persistent dread, a sense of imminent catastrophe, within themselves:

> So what is this fear, what is this catastrophe that stalks us like a crazy dog? We cannot say because we cannot name it. But it is there, right in our guts, and as soon as we find the means to do so we seek to represent it, despite the fact that it cannot be represented. We construct an endless series of misrepresentations all of which share one essential quality, the quality of otherness, of being not-me.
>
> (1992: 345–6)

Whatever the political realities, the Gulf War offered itself as an occasion, a rich opportunity, to rid ourselves, for a while at least, of this 'crazy dog' through the projection of our fears outwards. This time the 'not-me' we used to embody the sense of catastrophic danger was Saddam Hussein vilified as child-molester, rapist, murderer and monster. His scuddish evil, George Bush assured the Western world, confirmed us as the guardians of enlightened and civilised values. In so far as Saddam symbolised the forces of irrationality, it became possible for us to imagine ourselves as all reason. To protect our new-found peace of mind, it seemed both reasonable and inevitable that we should attack the 'new Hitler'. Now that the 'crazy dog' of our fears had a name we would 'cut it off' and 'kill it'.

What is, of course, significant about a world historical event like the Gulf War is how individual fantasies are drawn into a collective strategy of psychic defence. The collective expulsion of fear becomes the basis for reaffirming group solidarity. Membership of a social group, of a society, is never an easy or an uncomplicated matter: belonging to it is associated with feelings of discomfort, from indifference to resentment and anxiety. At particular historical moments, however, such tensions are eased, as the collectivity reasserts itself through what, following Didier Anzieu (1984), we might call the working of the 'group illusion'. The group discovers its common identity at the same time as its individual members are able to avow that they are all identical in their fears, and then that they are consensual in the defensive violence and hatred they direct against the threat that is 'not-us.' It is a moment in which the individual can fuse with the group: for a time, at least, the defence of individual identity can be displaced onto the collectivity. And for as long as danger and threat can be projected from its midst, the group experiences a sense of exultation through its new-found wholeness and integrity. It was this exultation that infused the *esprit de corps* of the coalition nations in the Gulf War. What it reflected was the pleasure of experiencing harmonious community and in joining in righteous struggle (the just crusade). It was, however, like so many times before, predicated on a consensual misrepresentation: on the illusory belief that the dangers and threats were all simply 'out there' and that the crazy dog really was Saddam.

In an essay on the Gulf War – one that can be read as both symptom and diagnosis – Lloyd deMause (1990), an American psycho-historian, suggests that, prior to the conflict, American national culture had been characterised by feelings of guilt, depression and sinfulness – partly linked to the 'Vietnam Syndrome'. He describes this condition as a 'shared emotional disorder'. In this context, the Gulf War could be seen as a cleansing and purifying experience, through which, in George Bush's words, America could finally 'kick the Vietnam Syndrome'. What the war offered was the possibility of renewal and revitalisation: America could rediscover its moral purpose and emotional wholeness. Of course, there is a simplification in this account of the Gulf War as a kind of morality play. But there is also a persuasive truth in it. For a moment, a brief moment, this epic spectacle sustained a sense of national integrity and moral regeneration. The Gulf War was to purify

America by exorcising an 'evil' – which was projected as being outside ('in a desolate Middle Eastern desert').

Television was fundamental to this process. We have drawn attention to the group processes at work, rather than invoking the more conventional agenda of the media as public sphere, because we are, for the moment, more concerned with the emotional and libidinal, rather than the rational, dimensions of collective behaviour. In most discussions of Gulf War television, there was a tendency to privilege the informational role of television, and to overlook the significance of the screen and the screening process for the psyche-at-war. As the conflict developed, however, the television screen played a crucial role, first in projecting our fears outwards and creating the image of external threat, and then in mobilising defensive violence against that threat. It was perhaps in the form of the television audience (the audience-as-group) that the 'group illusion', functioning as a defensive mechanism against persecutory anxieties, manifested itself most powerfully. The screen mediated between the dangers we imagined out there and the fear, anger and aggression we were feeling inside (Robins, 1993).

The nature and functioning of the screen are crucial. The screen can allow us to witness the world's events while, at the same time, protecting us – keeping us separate and insulated – from the reality of the events we are seeing. It can expose audiences to the violence and catastrophe of war while they still remain safe in their living rooms. But how do we learn to live with this violence? To ask this question is to consider the mechanisms through which we manage to screen ourselves from evil. Our exposure to the violence of the Gulf War was through the mediation of the screen, as a 'media event'. The screen is a powerful metaphor for our times: it symbolises how we now exist in the world, our contradictory condition of engagement and disengagement. Increasingly we confront moral issues through the screen, and the screen confronts us with increasing numbers of moral dilemmas. At the same time, however, it screens us from those dilemmas. It is through the screen that we disavow or deny our human implication in moral realities.

'To suffer is one thing', writes Susan Sontag, 'another thing is living with the photographed images of suffering, which does not necessarily strengthen conscience and the ability to be compassionate' (1979:20). Yet, through the distancing force of images, frozen registrations of remote calamities, we have learned to manage our relationship to suffering. The photographic image at once exposes us to, and insulates us from, actual suffering. It does not, and cannot, of itself implicate us in the real and reciprocal relations necessary to sustain moral and compassionate existence. Cinema, too, has kept the viewer at a distance from the consequences of violent action. Screen violence is routinely presented 'as a ritual, distant experience, like listening to news of a tragedy in a place you've never heard of' (Leith, 1993). With video screens and electronic images, this moral chasm has been made wider. As we have become exposed to, and assaulted by, images of violence on a scale never before known, we have also become more insulated from the realities. It may no longer be a question of whether this strengthens conscience and compassion, but of whether it is actually undermining and eroding it. If we are to come to terms with this moral condition, we must consider the nature of our engagement with screen culture.

To the ordinary audience member, the screen affords access to experiences of the unfamiliar and the extreme, the fantastic, aberrant and frightening. In this respect the screen has the potential to extend and amplify human awareness and sensibility. And, of course, this can be liberating. But it can also be very problematical. The screen also encourages a morbid voyeurism. So the screen affords access to experiences beyond the ordinary. But experience and awareness for what, we might ask. What does it mean to be 'fascinated' by a missile-eye perspective on death? What does it mean to become quickly 'bored' by pictures of slaughter and suffering? What does it mean to turn to horror movies to satisfy a 'need to be terrified'? The spectator-self can rove almost at random from one visual sensation to the next; a cruising voyeur. The screen exposes the ordinary viewer to harsh realities, but it also tends to screen out the harshness of those realities. It has a certain moral weightlessness. It grants sensation without demanding responsibility. It can involve us in a spectacle without engaging us in the complexity of its reality. This clearly satisfies basic needs and desires. Through its capacity to project frightening and threatening experiences, we can say that the screen provides a space in which to master anxiety, and allows us to rehearse our fantasies of omnipotence to overcome this anxiety.

Screening Bosnia

More recently, as a horrific sequel to the Gulf massacre, we have seen another war filling our screen time. This time in Europe itself, we have seen the horrors of concentration camps, massacre, rape and terror. As Branka Magas puts it, 'the year 1992, scheduled to be a milestone on the road to European unity, has seen Sarajevo and other Bosnian cities slowly bombarded to pieces and their inhabitants starved before the television eyes of the world' (1992: 102). This is a war that is closer to the quick of our own lives here in the west end of Europe. 'The crisis of Bosnia', as Akbar Ahmed says, 'is the crisis of Europe itself' and 'in failing to salvage Bosnia, it is clear that Europe is failing to salvage itself' (1992: 14). This war is closer, dangerously closer, to home.

Writing from Croatia, Slavenka Drakulić movingly describes her own experience of the war how, from being a distant reality, an external event, it entered into her soul and changed her life. 'All last year', she writes,

> war was a distant rumour, something one managed to obscure or ignore – something happening to other people, to people in Knin or Slavonia on the outskirts of the republic, but never to us in the centre, in Zagreb. We were busy with our private lives, with love, careers, a new car. War was threatening us, but not directly, as if we were somehow protected by that flickering TV screen – we might just as well have been in Paris or Budapest.
> (1993a: 18)

For some time, it was possible to keep the war at a distance, to see it only as 'familiar media images':

> While it still seemed so far away, it had a mythical quality. Everyone knew about its existence, but not many people had seen it and the stories we heard sounded so horrible and exaggerated that it

was difficult to believe them. Everyone read reports, listened to the news and looked at the television images but its mythical dimension remained preserved by the distance – the majority of us had no direct experience.
> (Drakulić, 1993b: xiv)

But it was not possible to go on screening out the reality of the conflict: 'For a long time we have been able to fend off the ghost of war, now it comes back to haunt us, spreading all over the screen of our lives, leaving no space for privacy, for future, for anything but itself' (Drakulić, 1993a: 18). Living in the war zone has meant coming to live with war and coming to be profoundly changed by it.

Outside the war zone, we are still protected by the flickering screen; the mythical dimension of the war is still preserved through the distancing effect of the screen images. Beyond that zone, there is a sense of comfort in the knowledge that the war is not only happening to other people but that it is happening to another kind of people. In Western Europe, the war is seen as an atavistic affair, being acted out by primitive and tribal populations. Arjun Appadurai describes how, in anthropological theory, places become associated with what he calls 'gatekeeping concepts', that is to say 'concepts that seem to limit anthropological theorising about the place in question, and that define the quintessential and dominant questions of interest in the region. . . . The point is that there is a tendency for places to become showcases for specific issues over time' (1986: 357–8). This is not, of course, restricted to theoretical anthropology. And, in the case of the Balkans, what limits our understanding is the ideologically conceived association of this unfortunate region with the passions of ethnic hatred and primordial violence. Our cherished reason may then recoil, as we witness what to us are irrational and incomprehensible acts of savagery. This is a mad place, we say, and these are mad people, unlike us.

The fear is that the madness might be contagious. 'New tribalism threatens to infect us all', proclaims a recent article in *The Guardian* (Hutton, 1993). 'In the place of evil empires', as Paula Franklin Lytle (1992: 304) observes, 'are resurgent nationalisms, and the terms used to describe them are images of infection and disease'. The point about this kind of imagery is that it interprets events in the former Yugoslavia as pathological and as the consequence of some kind of catastrophic natural force. The Balkans are seen 'as a body infected by nationalism, rather than as a war possibly amenable to any form of mediation or intervention' (ibid.: 316). The viral metaphor excuses Western inaction or ineffectiveness. More than this, it comes to legitimate a policy of disengagement and withdrawal: 'In the absence of an effective vaccine the alternative response to viral contagion is quarantine' (ibid.: 306). We must be screened from the infecting body.

The television screen may well be the key mechanism through which this distancing has been achieved. Press coverage has also drawn attention to the 'shocking images' of ethnic cleansing: 'Now the grim results are finally showing up on television screens and the front pages of newspapers. Pictures sear the conscience of the world'. And yet, it goes on, 'the response of the outside world so far – a lot of hand-wringing and a few relief supplies for one besieged city, Sarajevo – looks pathetically inadequate' (*Newsweek*, 17 August 1993: 8). The television images do not necessarily involve us in the plight of those distant Others: what they may rather do is to bring us voyeuristically, and perhaps even cognitively, closer, whilst maintaining an emotional distance and detachment. The screen is then a separation, a shield, a protection.

In considering what he calls 'the postmodern call of the other reaching towards us from the mediatised image', Richard Kearney poses the crucial question: 'Are not those of us who witness such images (as well as those who record and transmit them through the communications network) obliged to respond not just to surface reflections on a screen but to the call of human beings they communicate?' (1988a: 387–8). Most of us know what we would want to answer individually. We are also aware of what our collective response has ended up being. How are we to explain the uses of the screen that seem to preclude moral response and engagement?

At one level, of course, we can see it in terms of a mutation in television journalism which is associated with an increasing 'analytical paralysis' in its account of the world (Ferro, 1993). According to Paolo Carpignano and his colleagues, we have seen the demise of journalistic authority and the creation of a state of affairs in which 'information has created a world rich in events but devoid of shared experience' (1990: 36).

But it is more than just the transformation in media technologies and journalistic techniques that is at issue. There is something more fundamental at work in the process of screen mediation, something that is more than a technological matter. The journalistic organisation of the 'world as a show' responds to individual and collective psychological demands. In this respect, it can be said that 'the media are used by the unconscious mind as an auxiliary system [the screen], which stabilises and takes care of the personal and direct relationships which are too painful and lie between dream and reality' (Dufour and Dufour-Gompers, 1985: 320). In looking at the television screen, the watcher can say to himself or herself:

> I see that these anxieties, hatreds, killings and destructions are not me.... I can see that these hungers for power and these continual confrontations are not me.... I see that these inhibited, distorted sexual appetites are not me ... in a word, all this craziness is not me.
>
> (ibid.: 321)

The television screen can be seen as functioning, then, in terms of psychic defence and screening. What we must take into account is how the imaginary institution of television can become a collective mechanism of defence.

What needs to be understood, as much as what is actually happening in the Balkans, is what is going on in the TV audience, watching the war from a safe distance. We are invited, by the nature of the TV coverage to take up the position of the 'armchair anthropologist', gazing at the 'Other' on the screen, in the living room. We must recognise that, in so far as this war is 'viewed' as something (mythical) happening to 'Other' people, this can make its viewers insensitive to their own psychic investments in the material viewed. We must be attentive, then, not only to the ethics of everyday depictions, but also to the psychic investments we make in such depictions. We have organised our collective fantasies around the idea of 'the Balkans as the Other of the West', but in so doing we have failed to see how, 'far from being the Other of Europe, ex-Yugoslavia was rather Europe itself in its Otherness, the screen on to which Europe projected its own repressed reverse' (Žižek, 1992). What should concern us is how the screen helps us to organise reality in the cause of our own psychic fantasies and defences.

In all of this, the relation to the 'mediated' and the 'real' is a complex one. It could certainly be argued that the airlift of wounded children from Sarajevo in August 1993 was a real event almost entirely shaped by the media. The strategy seemed mainly designed to boost the standing of the Western powers in their own voters' eyes, by virtue of the 'good publicity' generated through the consequent photo-opportunities for politicians to pose with 'rescued' children. However, when it became clear that strictly medical priorities would mean that the first plane-load of evacuees would contain, not only sick children, but also some severely wounded adults, the British popular media were outraged, running headlines complaining of Muslim duplicity in 'tricking' the Western charities and doctors. The presence of wounded Muslim adults among the evacuees was certainly taken to represent a kind of 'pollution' of the Western crusade on behalf of innocent children. It seems that wounded Muslim children were predominantly seen as part of the universal 'race' of children, and thus deserving of help, whereas wounded adults were predominantly seen as Muslims, and thus represented 'matter out of place' on a Western crusade. The cynicism of the British Government in the whole episode, its attempt to exploit this tragic situation for political publicity, was perhaps best summed up in the words of a UN representative, Sylvana Foa (*The Guardian*, 14 August 1993): 'Does this mean Britain only wants to help children? Maybe it only wants children under six, or blond children, or blue-eyed children?' Our own analysis would lead us to believe that her question, even if rhetorical, is none the less pertinent for that.

'What can happen next, is this the end of the horror?' asks Slavenka Drakulić (1993b: xiii) in a letter to her publisher in London. 'No, I am afraid that we will have to live with this war for years. But you too will have to live with it, and it will change you, not immediately, but over time.' For the moment we are still watching the flickering screen. For the moment, we still have names and addresses, and car-keys. But, in Sarajevo, it was reported (*The Guardian*, 26 August 1993) that the price of an almost new Volkswagen Golf had fallen to around $150, as few people could get hold of the petrol needed to run a car: in which context, what price car-keys?

References

Ahmed, A. (1992), *Postmodernism and Islam*, London: Routledge.

Ang, I. (1985), *Watching Dallas*, London: Methuen.

Anzieu, D. (1984), *The Group and the Unconscious*, London: Routledge & Kegan Paul.

Appadurai, A. (1986), 'Theory in anthropology: center and periphery', *Comparative Studies in Society and History*, 28(2): 356–61.

Appadurai, A. (1988), 'Putting hierarchy in its place', *Cultural Anthropology*, 3(1): 36–49.

Appadurai, A. (1990), 'Disjuncture and difference in the global cultural economy', in M. Featherstone (ed.) *Global Culture*, London: Sage.

Baudrillard, J. (1988), *Selected Writings*, edited by M. Poster, Cambridge: Polity Press.

Bhabha, H. (1987), 'Interrogating identity', in L. Appignanesi (ed.) *Postmodernism and the Question of Identity*, London: Institute or Contemporary Arts.

Bodroghkozy, A. (1992), 'Is this what you mean by color TV?', in L. Spigel and D. Mann (eds) *Private Screenings*, Minneapolis: University of Minnesota Press.

Carpignano, P., Andersen, R., Aronowitz, S. and Difazio, W. (1990), 'Chatter in the age of electronic reproduction: talk television and the "public mind"', *Social Text*, 25/26: 33–55.

Clifford, J. (1986), 'Introduction: partial truths', in J. Clifford and G. Marcus (eds) *Writing Culture*, Berkeley: University of California Press.

Clifford, J. (1988), *The Predicament of Culture: Twentieth Century Ethnography, Literature and Art*, Cambridge, Mass.: Harvard University Press.

Clifford, J. (1992), 'Travelling cultures', in L. Grossberg *et al.* (eds) *Cultural Studies*, London: Routledge.

Clifford, J. and Marcus, G. (eds) (1986), *Writing Culture*, Berkeley: University of California Press.

Coker, C. (1992), 'Post-Modernity and the end of the cold war: has war been disinvented?', *Review of International Studies*, 18(3): 189–98.

Curran, J, (1990), 'The "new revisionism" in mass communications research', *European Journal of Communication*, 5(2–3): 135–64.

Curti, L. (1988), 'Imported Utopias', unpublished paper, Instituto Orientale, Naples.

DeLillo, D. (1985), *White Noise*, London: Picador.

deMause, L. (1990), 'The Gulf War as mental disorder', *The Nation*, 11 March: 301–8.

Drakulić, S. (1993a), *Balkan Express: Fragments from the Other Side of War*, London: Hutchinson.

Drakulić, S. (1993b), *How We Survived Communism and Even Laughed*, London: Vintage.

Dufour, Y. R. and Dufour-Gompers, N. (1985), 'Journalists, anxiety and media as an intra-psychic screen', *Israel Journal of Psychiatry and Related Sciences*, 22(4): 315–24.

Fabian, J. (1990), 'Presence and representation: the other and anthropological writing', *Critical Inquiry*, 16: 753–72.

Ferro, M. (1993), 'Médias et intelligence du monde', *Le Monde diplomatique*, January: 32.

Flores, E. (1988), 'Mass media and the cultural identity of the Puerto Rican people'. Paper presented to the Conference of the International Association for Mass Communications Research, Barcelona, July.

Franklin Lytle, P. (1992), 'US policy toward the demise of Yugoslavia: the "virus of nationalism"', *East European Politics and Societies*, 6(3): 303–18.

Greenblatt, S. (1992), *Marvellous Possessions: The Wonder of the New World*, Oxford: Oxford University Press.

Gripsrud, J. (forthcoming), *The 'Dynasty' years*, London: Routledge.

Gupta, A. and Ferguson, J. (1992), 'Beyond culture: space, identity and the politics of difference', *Cultural Anthropology*, 7: 6–23.

Hall, S. (1981), 'Encoding/decoding in TV discourse', in S. Hall, D. Hobson, A. Lowe and P. Willis (eds) *Culture, Media, Language*, London: Hutchinson.

Hall, S. (1987), 'Minimal selves', in L. Appignanesi (ed.) *Postmodernism and the Question of Identity*, London: Institute of Contemporary Arts.

Hartmann, C. and Husband, P. (1972), 'Race and the British media', in D. McQuail (ed.) *The Sociology of Mass Communication*, Harmondsworth: Penguin.

Harvey, D. (1989), *The Condition of Postmodernity*, Oxford: Basil Blackwell.

Hoggett, P. (1992), 'A place for experience: a psychoanalytical perspective on boundary, identity and culture', *Environment and planning D: Society and Space*. 10: 345–56.

Horton, D. and Wohl, R. R. (1956), 'Mass communication and para-social interaction: observations on intimacy at a distance', *Psychiatry*, 19: 215–29.

Hourani, A. (1946), *Syria and Lebanon: A Political Essay*, London: Oxford University Press.

Hourani, A. (1980), *Europe and the Middle East*, London: Macmillan.

Hutton, W. (1993), 'New tribalism threatens to infect us all,' *The Guardian*, 1 February.

Jameson, F. (1985), 'Postmodernism and consumer society', in H. Foster (ed.) *Postmodern Culture*, London: Pluto.

Kaes, A. (1989), *From Hitler to Heimat*, Cambridge, Mass.: Harvard University Press.

Kearney, R. (1988a), *The Wake of Imagination*, London: Hutchinson.

Leith, W. (1993), 'The kind of violence lovers hate', *The Independent on Sunday*, 3 January.

Levinas, E. (1983), 'Beyond intentionality', in A. Montefiore (ed.) *Philosophy in France Today*, Cambridge: Cambridge University Press.

Liebes, T. and Katz, E. (1991), *The Export of Meaning: Cross-Cultural Readings of Dallas*, Oxford: Oxford University Press.

Magas, B. (1992), 'The destruction of Bosnia-Herzegovina', *New Left Review*, 196: 102–12.

Marcus, G. and Fischer, M. (1986), *Anthropology as Cultural Critique, Chicago:* University of Chicago Press.

Massey, D. (1991a), 'A global sense of place', *Marxism Today*, June 1991.

Mattelart, A., Delcourt, X. and Mattelart, M. (1984), *International Image Markets*, London: Comedia.

Mercer, K. (1990), 'Welcome to the jungle', in J. Rutherford (ed.) *Identity: Community, Culture Difference*, London: Lawrence & Wishart.

Meyrowitz, J. (1985), *No Sense of Place*, Oxford: Oxford University Press.

Meyrowitz, J. (1989), 'The generalised elsewhere', *Critical Studies in Mass Communication*, 6(3): 326–34.

Michaels, E. (1988), 'Hollywood iconography: a Warlpiri reading', in P. Drummond and R. Paterson (eds) *Television and its Audience*, London: British Film Institute.

Miller, D. (1992), 'The Young and the Restless in Trinidad: a case of the local and the global in mass consumption', in R. Silverstone and E. Hirsch (eds), *Consuming Technologies*, London: Routledge.

Minh-Ha, Trinh T. (1989), *Woman, Native, Other*, Bloomington: Indiana University Press.

Morley, D. (1992), *Television, Audiences and Cultural Studies*, London: Routledge.

Rabinow, P. (1986), 'Representations are social facts', in J. Clifford and G. Marcus (eds) *Writing Culture*, Berkeley: University of California Press.

Rath, C.-D. (1985), 'The invisible network', in P. Drummond and R. Paterson (eds) *Television in Transition*, London: British Film Institute.

Rath, C.-D. (1989), 'Live television and its audiences', in E. Seiter, H. Borchers, G. Kreutzner and E.-M. Warth (eds) *Remote Control*, London: Routledge.

Robins, K. (1993), 'The war, the screen, the crazy dog and poor mankind', *Media Culture and Society*, 15(2): 321–7.

Said, E. (1978), *Orientalism*, Harmondsworth: Penguin.

Said, E. (1984), 'Reflections on exile', *Granta*, 13: 157–72.

Schiller, H. I. (1969), *Mass Communications and American Empire*, New York: Beacon Press.

Scholte, R. (1987), 'The literary turn in contemporary anthropology', *Critique of Anthropology*, 7(1): 33–47.

Sontag, S. (1979), *On Photography*, Harmondsworth: Penguin.

Stam, R. (1983), 'Television news and its spectator', in E. Kaplan (ed.) *Regarding Television*, vol. 2, New York: American Film Institute.

Todorov, T. (1984), *The Conquest of America: the Question of the Other*, New York: Harper & Row.

Tunstall, J. (1977), *The Media are American*, London: Constable.

Williamson, J. (1991), 'Mad bad Saddam', *The Guardian*, 31 January.

Wolf, E. (1982), *Europe and the People Without History*, Berkeley: University of California Press.

Žižek, S. (1992), 'Ethnic dance macabre', *The Guardian*, 28 August.

27.
WHAT'S YOUR FLAVA?

Race and Postfeminism in Media Culture

Sarah Banet-Weiser

In the spring of 2003, an advertisement appeared on the children's cable television channel Nickelodeon for the Mattel toy company's recent doll line, Flavas. This ad features young girls of various races and ethnicities playing with female Barbie-type dolls characterized by ambiguous ethnic identities—with "neutral" skin color and vague facial features, the dolls could easily be Latina, African American, Asian, or white. What is clear is that the dolls are urban: they wear clothing that is hip and trendy, they carry boom boxes, and they are sold in boxes with a cardboard backdrop that resembles a concrete wall covered with graffiti. On toymania.com, a Web-based toy outlet, Mattel issued the following press release the week the dolls appeared in stores.

EL SEGUNDO, Calif.—July 29, 2003—Flava, according to "Hip Hoptionary: The Dictionary of Hip Hop Terminology" by Alonzo Westbrook, means personal flavor or style. With the nationwide introduction of Flavas (pronounced FLAY-vuhz) this week, the first reality-based fashion doll brand that celebrates today's teen culture through authentic style, attitude and values, Mattel (™) has created a hot hip-hop themed line that allows girls to express their own personal flava.

Born in the world of music and fashion, the hip-hop movement has evolved into a cultural phenomenon and celebrates fearless self-expression through freestyle dance, hip-hop music, street sport and signature fashions. Flavas, for girls ages 8–10, is the hottest doll line to embrace this latest tween trend encouraging girls to show their inner flava to the outer world.[1]

The Flavas marketing campaign featured not only ads, such as the one on Nickelodeon, which featured hip-hop music and trendy dance moves, but also a sponsorship of the pop singer Christina Aguilera's tour, a singer that Mattel claims "personifies the idea of fearless self-expression." Despite the fact that the word *flava*, the culture of hip-hop, and the idea of street style all signify racially in contemporary American culture, the racial identity of the dolls is never mentioned in the ads or the press release. While this could have been an interesting opportunity for Mattel to explore issues of different skin color among African Americans, as there is a dark-skinned doll and a light-skinned doll, or racial issues in and between Latinos and African Americans, race in this context is just a flava, a street style, an individual characteristic, and a commercial product.

Like race, gender identity is constructed in the present "postfeminist" cultural economy as a "flava," a flexible, celebratory identity category that is presented in all its various manifestations as a kind of product one can buy or try on. Signified by the hip consumer slogan "girl power," postfeminist gender identity is a slippery category precisely because of the ways in which it intervenes in productive ways in traditional ideological frameworks even as it works in other ways to shore up those same frameworks. For example, Nickelodeon is widely lauded for its efforts to champion girls in what has been a historically male-dominated televisual landscape. Proudly cele-brating its contributions to girl power, Nickelodeon forced the attention of parents and young people to the connection between these two concepts, "girl" and "power," a connection that has become normal-ized within the discourses of consumer culture. In the contemporary cultural climate, in other words, the empowerment of girls is now something that is more or less taken for granted by both children and parents and has certainly been incorporated into commodity culture, evidenced by consumer goods ranging from T-shirts to lunch boxes to dolls proclaiming that "Girls rule!" Like other brands in contemporary media cul-ture, Nickelodeon taps into this commodity-driven empowerment by targeting aspects of personal iden-tity (such as gender and race) as a way to be inclusive; in fact, Nickelodeon's brand identity is crafted around the way in which the network is different from other children's media in the way it "empowers" children through (among other things) its commitment to gen-der and ethnic representation.

On the other hand, Nickelodeon's ability to claim that diversity matters has proved strategic from a busi-ness standpoint, positioning the network as "different" in the competitive field of children's television. In other words, despite the lofty goals of the channel to empower children, Nickelodeon's carefully crafted industry identity as the "diversity channel" and a champion for girls is a lucrative business strategy. Within the world of children's television, representa-tions of race and gender work as a kind of cultural capital, in terms of which it increases the political and social clout of a network to be able to claim that it is "diverse."[2] As is well known, historically there has been a dearth of diverse characters on children's television (in terms of both race and gender), and the few that have been represented have been depicted in highly stylized and stereotypical ways.[3] However, in the cur-rent media economy it no longer makes commercial sense to ignore girls or people of color as important characters. Nickelodeon has capitalized on the histori-cal invisibility and exclusion of diverse characters and has framed this history as part of a shrewd business strategy. In this way, its decision to create diverse pro-gramming is often discussed in such nonspecific terms as "good business," thus distancing the channel from the political implications of embracing diversity.

These two identity categories—race as a "flava" and girl power—function together in the current media environment to produce categories of identity that are defined by ambiguity rather than specificity, ambivalence rather than political certainty. These mediated forms of race and gender are produced within the specific context of late industrial capital-ism in the United States, a moment that has been characterized in racial terms as a multicultural or post-race society and in gendered terms as a post-feminist culture. My concerns in this essay focus on television programming within this "postrace" and "post-feminist" culture and are twofold. First, I explore how these two features of contemporary American media culture function together as a productive kind of tension or ambivalence. The tension resides within the acknowledgment that race and gender are impor-tant identity categories to consider in terms of repre-sentation, while at the same time the acknowledgment itself works to repudiate this very importance. Angela McRobbie, writing about how this works within post-feminism, argues that contemporary popular culture is effective in the "undoing of feminism" precisely by appearing to participate in an inclusion of feminist ideologies.[4] I argue that a similar dynamic occurs with recent popular representations of race and ethnicity. Within the contemporary climate, television and media products seem to acknowledge the historical racist landscape of television not only by featuring programming with casts that include people of color but also by incorporating non-white narratives in ads, programs, and merchandise. Yet these particular rep-resentations and narratives of race and ethnicity are marketed by media corporations as cool, authentic, and urban and have proven to be incredibly lucrative economic tools for marketing to broad, especially white, audiences. Contemporary marketers, selling clothing brands such as Tommy Hilfiger and soft drinks such as Sprite, have efficiently capitalized on the connection of "cool" with images and narratives of the urban so that popular culture is rife with what Herman Gray describes as the *proliferation* of difference.[5] This redefinition of the urban stands in contrast to media representations in the United States of the "urban" in the 1980s and early 1990s, which predominantly signified the dangerous "other" and indeed functions to render irrelevant and repudiate those earlier concerns about racist imagery. The representation of the "urban," like the representation of girl power, is associated with the ideological notion that contemporary American society is a multicultural, postfeminist one in which racial difference and gender discrimination are no longer salient. Race, like gender, comes to us in the contemporary context as a commodity, and as such the ideologies shaping these representational politics are necessarily rethought and recast.

Second, I examine how the contemporary definitions of *postfeminism* and *postracial culture* are framed around generational differences. In terms of gender representation, this generational difference appears most often in ideological struggles between second-wave feminism and postfeminism. This particular generational divide revolves most centrally around a general assumption (one that is supported by commercial popular culture) that the goals of feminism have been accomplished and are now history, rendering it unnecessary to continue rehashing old political issues. Regarding postracial culture, these generational differences have a more specific economic angle. That is, in what Christopher Smith calls the "New Economy" of the late twentieth century and early twenty-first the tropes of the urban and hip-hop culture are used as means to designate a particular national perspective on diversity. Despite the material realities of poverty, unemployment, and general institutionalized racism in the United States, a contemporary ideology about race casts it as a style, an aesthetic, a hip way of being. Indeed, Smith identifies the 1990s New Economy as one in which "hip-hop evolved from being the symbolic anathema of the dominant commercial apparatus to serving as one of its most strategically effective symbolic instruments."[6] Like commodity feminism or what Bonnie Dow has identified as "prime-time feminism," the commodification of the urban works to diffuse the politics from this particular racial formation, resulting in a kind of racial ambivalence that dominates the representational landscape.[7] Given the contemporary representational context, what are the consequences when race or gender becomes cultural capital—a "competency" or mode of consumption within the world of media entertainment?

I see these shifts in gender and race representation as located within the struggles between generations so

that representation itself becomes an arsenal in a kind of cultural territory war. Within this particular battlefield, the struggles of the past to represent women and people of color are read through a nostalgic lens as an "old school" kind of politics. Indeed, contemporary manifestations of "girl power" and the "urban" render the language of sexism and disenfranchisement as old-fashioned and even quaint. The dismissal of the language and the politics associated with it is characteristic of "new school" politics, where commodity culture is situated not in opposition to those politics but rather provides the very means to exploit and represent these dynamics of race and gender. To demonstrate how this works in television programming, I offer a brief analysis of a very successful Nickelodeon program, *Dora the Explorer*, and argue that Dora, the intrepid, seven-year-old, Latina heroine of the show, is poised as a global citizen in the New Economy. Before I turn to Dora, however, the generational differences in how girl power and the urban are understood and used by media audiences need to be explored.

Generational Differences: Grumpy Old Women and a New Generation of Feminists

In her discussion of contemporary forms of popular culture, McRobbie identifies the 1990s and the early twenty-first century as a "postfeminist cultural space." This space, she argues, is a context in which "we have a field of transformation in which feminist values come to be engaged with, and to some extent incorporated across, civil society in institutional practices, in education, in the work environment, and in the media."[8] However, this engagement most often results in a denial of those very same feminist values so that postfeminist popular culture is more accurately antifeminist in its trajectory. Postfeminism, understood in this manner, is thus a different political dynamic than third wave feminism, which is positioned more overtly as a kind of feminist politics, one that extends the historical trajectory of first-and second-wave feminism to better accommodate contemporary political culture and the logic of consumer citizens. Postfeminism, on the other hand, is as McRobbie puts it, "feminism taken into account," a process in which feminist values and ideologies are acknowledged only to be found dated and passé and thus negated.

Importantly, McRobbie sees this process of repudiation taking place in the popular media,

> where a field of new gender norms emerges (e.g., *Sex and the City, Ally McBeal*) in which female freedom and ambition appear to be taken for granted, unreliant on any past struggle (an antiquated word), and certainly not requiring any new, fresh political understanding, but instead merely a state into which young women appear to have been thrown, or in which they find themselves, giving rise to ambivalence and misgiving.[9]

Part of young female identity in this contemporary context means to engage this media narrative about new gender norms not in a traditional, politically engaged way but rather in what McRobbie calls a "ritualistic denunciation." This denunciation occurs when feminism is acknowledged but in a trivialized fashion, shelved as something that may have been useful in the past but is clearly out of date in today's world.

This denunciation of feminism thus informs the ways in which postfeminism situates issues of gender within commercial and popular culture. This commercial embrace of postfeminism is often invoked as the crucial difference between it and other feminisms because postfeminism is understood as more representative for a new generation of women. This struggle over the "ownership" of the politics of feminism seems to be the primary lens through which contemporary feminisms are understood. Indeed, one of the most impassioned discourses involving feminism lately has not been generated by differing political platforms or a specific egregious act of discrimination against women but from the arguments, contradictions, and general disavowals between different manifestations of feminisms. Within the contemporary context there are different feminisms (just as many different feminisms made up the broad second-wave feminist movement in the United States). Thus, the political focus of postfeminism is vastly different from that of third-wave feminism for the former eschews gender politics as rather old-fashioned and dreary and the latter refigures gender politics in a commercially bounded culture. There is clearly a lack of generational cohesion between the various

feminisms, making it difficult to figure out one's position within feminism. And yet, as Lisa Hogeland points out, different generations are not a significant explanation. The alternative, recognizing problems within feminism, means confronting the "unevenness" of the movement itself and the "fundamental differences in our visions of feminism's tasks and accomplishments."[10] One of these differences concerns media visibility. In part because of the proliferation of media images of strong, independent female characters, many contemporary feminists seem to regard consumer culture as a place of empowerment and as a means of differentiating themselves from second-wave feminists (although empowerment itself is read differently by postfeminists and third-wave feminists). Second-wave feminism has thus tended to be critical of the misogyny of popular consumer culture.

The embrace of consumer culture is the site for tension around the concept of the individual within feminisms as well. One of the key differences between the "cultural space of postfeminism" and second-wave feminist politics in the United States and the United Kingdom is the focus on female individualism and individual empowerment. As McRobbie points out, postfeminism shifts feminism into the past—not just the ideas and values of feminism but the emancipatory politics and community activism of feminism as well.[11] Key to this shift is the fact that in work that claims to be postfeminist there is what McRobbie calls a "double failure," for, "In its over-emphasis on agency and the apparent capacity to choose in a more individualized society, it has no way of showing how subject formation occurs by means of notions of choice *and* assumed gender equality coming together to actually ensure adherence to new unfolding norms of femininity."[12]

This move toward focusing on individual empowerment rather than coalition politics or structural change forces consideration of several questions. Once feminism is represented as a commodity in precisely the mainstream it has traditionally challenged, can we still talk about it as political? Can the social elements of feminism be represented and enacted within the context of popular culture's relentless celebration of the individual or is popular culture by design hostile to feminism? Are we simply living in, as Naomi Klein claims, a "Representation Nation," where visibility in the media takes precedence over "real" politics?[13] Again, for those who consider themselves to be third-wave feminists, such as Jennifer Baumgardner and Amy Richards, the argument is made that this kind of media visibility is absolutely crucial to politics.[14] For those who position themselves as postfeminists, this kind of media visibility is precisely the evidence needed to "prove" that there is no longer a need for feminist politics. And yet, as Bonnie Dow argues, while the liberal feminist politics of equal opportunity and equal pay for equal work has been somewhat normalized (although the material reality of this politics is not always or even often achieved), it is also the case that the process of mainstreaming an oppositional politics often functions as a hegemonic strategy to diffuse that very politics. In other words, the normalization of feminism has prevented it from existing as a discrete politics; rather it emerges as a kind of slogan or generalized "brand."[15]

However, for third-wave feminism, this normalization of feminism within the media and popular culture has encouraged an embrace of feminism as political; as Baumgardner and Richards argue, the young women who make up the third wave were "born with feminism simply in the water," a kind of "political fluoride" that protects against the "decay" of earlier sexism and gender discrimination.[16] The struggle for "positive" representations in the media is certainly not over, but we also do not experience the same media that we did even ten years ago, when, as Susan Douglas contends, the most pervasive media story remained "structured around boys taking action, girls waiting for the boys, and girls rescued by the boys."[17] There has been a clear historical trajectory of incorporating feminist ideologies into mainstream popular culture, ranging, as Dow points out, from the 1970s television show *One Day at a Time* to shows in the 1980s and 1990s such as *Murphy Brown* and *Designing Women*.

As a contemporary social and political movement, then, feminism itself has been rescripted (though not necessarily disavowed) so as to allow its smooth incorporation into the world of commerce and corporate culture—what Robert Goldman calls "commodity feminism."[18] This commodity feminism has resulted in a complex dynamic that is directly concerned not only with general gender issues but also with issues of cultural territory. As part of a general self-identification, second-wave feminism is at times overly romanticized in terms of its commitment to social protest politics, and there seems to be a kind of reluctance on the part of second-wave feminists to rethink and redefine politics according to the stated needs and desires of contemporary feminism (Susan Brownmiller, in a now infamous *Time* magazine interview about third-wave feminists and postfeminists, claimed that "they're just not movement people").[19] Part of this reluctance to rethink contemporary feminism concerns the ways in which gender identity is also always about racial identity; perhaps because of the commercial "urban" context of many contemporary feminists, the intersectionality of race and gender has been acknowledged in ways that challenge the exclusionary history of second-wave feminism. For many third-wave feminists, the territorialism that surrounds some of the current politics of feminism seems to be about salvaging the term *feminism* (and presumably the politics that grounds and historicizes it). Baumgardner and Richards, Barbara Findlen, and Naomi Wolf, for example, participate in this kind of salvation project, the project of not necessarily appropriating a historical concept of feminism but widening its borders to include more contemporary manifestations of the politics.[20] While in theory this makes sense, and certainly these authors at times do justice to the legacies of feminisms, Baumgardner and Richards also insist that "underneath all of these names and agendas is the same old feminism."[21] However, it is precisely *not* the same old feminism that structures the politics of third-wave feminism. The insistence that it is stems from a range of sentiments, from nostalgic yearnings for "real" social protest movements to respectful acknowledgments of political practices that open up economic and social opportunities to a sheer base desire to "belong" to something. Without discounting these sentiments, it is also the case that lingering in this generational battle between second- and third-wave feminism has paralyzed the debate and prevented the further development and refinement of a feminist praxis and material feminist politics. In turn, this paralysis has allowed for a more conservative postfeminism to become dominant in media representation, so much so that feminist politics—be it second-wave, third-wave, or some other version—is rendered obsolete in the contemporary historical moment of hip empowerment.

The complexity of the current feminist landscape means that the idea that "we" all share a feminist politics, that we all "want the same thing," is highly problematic, as it clearly connects to history. Not only does this propagate the mistake made by many second-wave feminists, who insisted on a universal feminist standpoint, but it also functions as a kind of refusal to identify what it is we all apparently want.[22] In other words, if "we" all want the same thing in feminism, what is it: a liberal version of equality, a more radically configured understanding of liberation from patriarchy, or simply a more frequent and "positive" media appearance? And, if this is true, does contemporary feminism address other factors of identity, such as race and sexuality, in ways that challenge the exclusive nature of second-wave feminism? This struggle over territory has encouraged feminisms to exist primarily as part of a turf war. The politics of feminism is quite obviously different for different generations, and third-wave feminists and postfeminists are produced in a very different cultural and political context than were the feminists of the twentieth century. It then becomes impossible to combine contemporary manifestations of feminisms into a singular "movement"; rather, feminisms exist in the present context as a politics of contradiction and ambivalence. Rather than dismissing this politics as an elaborate corporate masquerade, one that intends to encourage an ever more vigorous consumer body politic at the expense of social change, it makes more sense to theorize how power functions in contradictory ways within the context of consumerism.

One way to do this is to situate postfeminism as an ironic configuration of power, a configuration that, as McRobbie points out, skillfully uses the language of feminist cultural studies "against itself."[23] The ironic use of oppositional language and counterhegemonic practices within mainstream commodity culture has been widely theorized. For instance, Naomi Klein understands today's brand culture to be using the language of identity politics as an effective means through which brand loyalty can be assured; Malcolm Gladwell has theorized the economic importance of "cool" in the contemporary political economy; and Joseph Heath and Andrew Potter have argued that

countercultural values have always been, ironically, "intensely entrepreneurial" (in fact, as they point out, the commodification of rebellion reflects "the most authentic spirit of capitalism").[24] McRobbie theorizes a similar kind of dynamic within postfeminist consumer culture, where much of contemporary advertising and popular culture uses a particular kind of irony when representing women, as if to suggest that the "problem" of objectification of women's bodies is one of history; women "get it" about objectification, and *because* of this understanding it is acceptable—indeed, even ironically empowering—to objectify women's bodies in the most blatantly demeaning ways. Thus, popular media function as a kind of critique of mainstream culture through the strategies of irony, camp, and a kind of postmodern cynicism—but within a conventional narrative framework. Current advertising uses this kind of self-reflexivity to both critique and ultimately sell products.[25]

Thus, one of the factors that characterize a contemporary postfeminist generation is this group's finely honed sense of irony. Decades of economic seesawing, progressively more sophisticated marketing strategies, and gradually more blurry boundaries between consumption habits and political and cultural beliefs have produced, among other things, a generation that is savvy, "smart," and generally perceived to be disaffected or cynical about culture. This general ideology makes it difficult to sustain an "old-fashioned" feminist politics that involves understanding women as victims of patriarchy, the theorizing of structural impediments in terms of employment and child care, or even more general assumptions about the various ways in which women are oppressed because *they are* women in the contemporary climate. In other words, the cynicism of the current generation is not only directed toward consumer culture but also toward historical political formations such as feminism.

Part of this has to do with the fact that irony as politics is a much more personal kind of politics than a more activist, public politics. As Jeffrey Sconce says about "smart films" of the 1990s, "American smart cinema has displaced the more activist emphasis on the 'social politics' of power, institutions, representation and subjectivity so central to 1960s and 1970s art cinema (especially in its 'political' wing), and replaced it by concentrating, often with ironic disdain, on the 'personal politics' of power, communication, emotional dysfunction and identity in white middle-class culture."[26] The consumer culture that Klein characterizes as "ironic consumption" seems to evacuate politics from the landscape in one sense because of the intense focus on personal identity. And it is this focus on personal identity and the rhetoric of choice that characterizes not only postfeminist culture but also the "New Economy" of race, where representations of personal success and media visibility seem to provide enough evidence that historical struggles over the enfranchisement of minorities and minority communities were crucial interventions but are no longer necessary in the current media economy.

No More *Cosby Show*: Generational Struggles over Race in the New Economy

In his incisive study of race representation (and specifically the representation of African Americans) on American television, Herman Gray delineates televisual depictions of race as a series of discursive practices that were particularly relevant in the 1980s. He identifies these practices as three interconnected strategies: assimilationist, or invisibility, where blacks are either simply not represented or represented as white people; pluralist, or "separate but equal," where blacks are represented on television but as a discrete niche or target group; and multiculturalist, or diversity, where Gray sees the "struggle for blackness" taking place in complex and often contradictory ways.[27] The influx of racial representations in the 1980s media landscape did not necessarily reflect a progressive political consciousness about the politics of race but were the result of a convergence of political and cultural dynamics, including the increase of niche channels on cable television, the rise of brand culture, the marketing tool of lifestyle demographics, and the conservative politics of the Reagan administration. In the 1980s, it became palatable—indeed, fashionable—to be multicultural and multiracial (under certain constraints and conditions). Black representation in 1980s media was part of a conservative appropriation of discourses of "political correctness" as a specific element in brand identity development in a burgeoning brand environment and came to represent cultural capital in this context.

As Gray, Justin Lewis, Sut Jhally, and others have argued, the American sitcom *The Cosby Show*, a hit in the 1980s under the guidance of Bill Cosby and featuring an all African American cast, represents a culturally and politically significant moment in television representations of race. In fact, Gray argues that it is impossible to understand contemporary representations of blackness without a consideration of what he calls "the Cosby Moment."[28] He locates the impetus for *The Cosby Show* (as well as other programs that featured African American characters) within a context in which the cultural definition of *diversity* as a specific marketing tool was beginning to be realized in corporate America. This emergent moment is crucial to consider when theorizing the contemporary context of race and representation, but, as with the generational differences between twentieth- and twenty-first-century feminisms, there is a generational distinction not only between the representations of race on television in the 1980s and the early twenty-first century but also in what these representations mean for a larger political formation.

In other words, what Gray regards as a "struggle for blackness" that took place over representational issues of the 1980s is a different kind of struggle in the context of the early twenty-first century. To "struggle" for blackness assumes a kind of stable identity for blackness itself—something tangible and "authentic" and worth struggling over. The struggle to which Gray referred was not simply about a politics of inclusion within the media but more generally a politics of inclusion within all areas of American cultural and civic life. In the current media moment, media representations of people of color are much more commonplace precisely because of the kinds of struggles Gray details and because the connections between media visibility and American cultural life are formulated primarily within consumption practices. Thus, as a way to extend Gray's historical analysis, I see a slightly different practice occurring within the current representational landscape, a practice that might be called "postracial" or "urbanized."

Indeed, a more overt connection of race with marketing dominated in the 1990s, especially marketing the "urban" to young, white, middle-class

Americans. This was a different kind of urban than the images of urban black underclass that constituted most of the representations of people of color on 1980s American television. However, the urban image that was increasingly part of the 1990s televisual landscape also contrasted with the wholesome, "positive," Cosby image of the 1980s. Leon Wynter sees this more recent movement or shift in representation as resulting in what he calls "Transracial America," which is a "vision of the American Dream in which we are liberated from the politics of race to openly embrace any style, cultural trope, or image of beauty that attracts us regardless of its origin."[29] Of course, the notion that through a process of urbanization we have been liberated from the politics of race is clearly an illusion, but it is the case that this politics has been reframed within brand culture. Popular discourses of race and images of nonwhites have become cultural capital in the contemporary marketing world, so that, as Gray discusses, there is a proliferation of difference rather than an absence of diversity. This practice can be seen on television channels such as Nickelodeon, where programs feature "diverse characters and themes."[30] Nickelodeon, like other contemporary media companies, uses newly shaped economic models and an ethnically nonspecific, "transracial" style as a way to appeal to increasingly diverse and segmented audiences without alienating specific groups. As with postfeminist representations, the "problem" of diversity in the current climate is no longer one of invisibility and, indeed, no longer about "separate but equal" doctrine or pluralism. On the contrary, capitalism and brand culture, through the relentless narrowing of marketing niches by means of gender, sexual identity, and ethnic and racial identity, has *provided for* rather than prevented a kind of diversity. That is to say, particular definitions of diversity are recognized as significant by media outlets such as Nickelodeon because diverse images, like images of girl power, sell well in a segmented political economy. The definition of *diversity* that has the most economic potential in the current climate is one that relies on a hip, cool, urban, "postracial" style.

The danger, of course, in labeling any kind of shift in discourse or practice "post" is that this prefix implies that whatever it modifies is somehow *over*— postfeminism, for instance, suggests (and at times insists) not only that feminism is passé but also, more obliquely, that whatever goals feminism sought have been accomplished. As Sarah Projansky has argued, one form of postfeminism clearly invokes a linear, historical trajectory, insisting that if we are in an age of postfeminism then we cannot also be in a moment of feminism—the two cannot coexist within linear logic.[31] However, to call this moment in late capitalism postracial is not to suggest that race and race relations are somehow irrelevant but rather to think seriously about recent shifts in capitalism that contain and market race and diversity in the media using new strategies. More traditional cultural definitions of race have been repackaged in the New Economy in ways that further disconnect race as a commodity from race as a material and social reality. The representation of race in current media is, on the whole, "positive" and is significant to how race is interpreted and navigated in cultural politics.[32] Because of historical interventions and social change, there is clearly more public awareness concerning "negative stereotypes" of people of color. Yet the various ways in which cultural definitions of race and diversity signify a market orientation toward the "urban" has further consolidated the ways in which race is produced as a particular commodity more than a more traditional kind of engaged politics. This kind of diversity thus functions according to the logic of a different political economic model than the one that supports Gray's discussion of television images.

What has occurred in the more than twenty years since the 1984 premiere of *The Cosby Show* is that media representations of people of color have proliferated but the connection between individual and group empowerment gained by media visibility and progressive change in poverty levels, unemployment, policy, and education continues to be illusive. Words such as *identity* and *multiculturalism* were, in the 1980s, codewords for race; in the early-twenty-first century, these same terms are code words (especially for the consumer market) for "hip," "urban," and "cool." Race, like gender, as a political identity has been appropriated (at least in part) in the dominant culture through the brand identity of the urban and postfeminism. Within this context, I do not want to romanticize a definition *politics* as something stable and immediately meaningful—or, conversely, to vilify brand identity as exclusively superficial and ephemeral —but I do want to shift the cultural frame through which youth empowerment is understood.

Visions of Power: Empowerment within a Postfeminist, Postracial, Media Culture

As I've briefly discussed in this essay, one of the interesting, as well as disturbing, consequences of the increasing mainstream visibility of identity politics and multiculturalism is not simply that people of color and girls "matter" publicly through their media and policy presence but also that these groups became the target for corporate America in terms of cultivating specific marketing niches. Because of the historical connection between empowerment and media visibility within this contemporary context, empowerment cannot be theorized as separate from market strategies but is rather a *constitutive* element in these strategies. Empowerment is thus discursively figured in at least two ways in this historical moment: as media visibility and market demographic. It is true, however, that there is a particular lack of substance that supports these representations for the number of people of color living below the poverty line in the United States continues to increase, women continue to make only 78 cents to the dollar of their male counterparts, and sexism and racism seem to be as institutionalized as ever.

There is, however, no lack of the *image* of diversity and gender within media culture; images of savvy, urban individuals and empowered girls function as lucrative commodities in the media marketplace. Advertisements feature young, urban, hip people of all races and genders, the soundtracks of ads and television programs often include urban music (such as hip-hop or rap), words associated with hip-hop culture such as *bling* and *dawg* are frequently used in family television, and casts that feature strong, independent young girls in youth television are more the rule than the exception. The taboo long associated with media representations of people of color is no longer salient. As Wynter points out, "As this taboo melts in the marketplace, whether as a reflection of social reality or in spite of it, the underlying energy of desire associated with racial prohibition is being liberated for exploitation by commercial marketers."[33]

This, of course, raises the question of the nature of this liberation. The process whereby images of diversity are liberated from the racist practice of invisibility only to be used for a different set of purposes yet still rooted within the capitalist structure of the media deserve examination. In other words, McRobbie's proposition that postfeminism is "feminism taken into account" can be amended in the contemporary American context to include "diversity taken into account"—and, like feminism, an institutional kind of diversity is situated within this formulation as something belonging to history.

Thus, while the contemporary visual landscape certainly shares some similarities with that of the 1980s, when the economic and political context made it profitable to include particular representations of people of color and women within popular culture, the political economic landscape has clearly shifted. Race and gender have become even more important commodities within media culture and thus have achieved a sort of status within media consumer culture. However, as I've been arguing, not just any representation of race or gender will do in the contemporary U.S. media context; rather, the *kind* of ethnicity and the *particular* gender identity need to be specified. Specific images of ethnicity and gender function effectively as marketing tools within this cultural economy and are used to sell products by appealing to consumers who self-identify as empowered individuals or are "ethnic identified."[34] Race and gender within the current media culture are inextricably tied to dynamics of the market, where segmented marketing strategies and more localized capitalist ventures lead to a consumer-based valorization of self-identity.

This commercially defined articulation of identity needs to be distinguished from other means of self-construction within the social and political world, but the distinction itself is one that is in flux and continually negotiated. That is, when a media audience is "empowered" by images of race and gender, there is no linear connection to empowering communities. Rather, the connection is based on a notion of agency that is consumer driven and thus has consequences primarily in terms of consumption habits and even specific purchases made—a T-shirt that reads "Girls Rule!" perhaps, or a CD by the popular hip-hop artist

50 Cent. The current moment is thus characterized by ambivalence rather than specificity, where an ambivalent identity category such as urban or girl power becomes dominant and is the entry point to a commercially defined "postfeminist" or "postracial" society. As Eric King Watts and Mark P. Orbe argue in their essay about the commodification of race in Budweiser television commercials, this ambivalence is experienced by media audiences as a kind of "spectacular consumption" that works, in this specific case, in particular ways to contain race representations: "As the market economy seeks to regulate and integrate 'authentic' difference, white American ambivalence toward blackness is paradoxically both assuaged by its 'universality' and heightened by its distinctiveness."[35] This focus on the universality of racially or gender-specific images marks an interesting shift from the logic of clearly defined niche markets (i.e., the African American market, the female market, etc.) to one that is more ambiguous yet still clearly "diverse."

Dora the Explorer: The Global Individual

> Finally the idea emerged to have the star be a little girl with a sidekick partner, but it wasn't until a Nickelodeon executive attended a Children Now diversity seminar in 1998 that the doors opened for Dora. Did someone say abre?[36]

While spectacular consumption works in a contradictory way to both challenge and reify dominant ideologies of race and gender in Budweiser ads, hip-hop videos, and prime-time television, I'd like to turn briefly to the children's cable channel Nickelodeon to examine the representations of postfeminism and urbanization on kids' TV. Children's television in the United States has typically been more diverse than prime-time television, primarily because of the assumed pedagogical function of shows such as *Sesame Street, Blue's Clues*, and *Dora the Explorer*.[37] Indeed, the twenty-first-century context of postfeminism and the present celebration of urban images have encouraged a lineup of children's shows that feature strong, smart girls and multicultural casts.

The use of diversity as a part of social identity, and as a more abstract narrative theme, is an important element in Nickelodeon's claim to empower kids and address its child audience as active cultural citizens. Diversity, for Nickelodeon, is part of the network's brand identity. Like other brands in contemporary culture, Nickelodeon targets aspects of personal identity such as race as a way to be inclusive. In fact, its brand identity is crafted around the way it "empowers" children through (among other things) a commitment to gender and ethnic representation.

The ability to claim that diversity matters to Nickelodeon has thus given the network a way to stand out in the competitive field of children's television. In a recent report on diversity within children's television, the media advocacy group Children Now featured an article written by Nickelodeon's then-president, Herb Scannell, on the network's success with diversity.[38] As Scannell puts it, "One of the questions we are frequently asked by the media and the advocacy community is why we've been able to present a more diverse screen when other networks are often criticized for their lack of diversity. I can only speak for Nickelodeon when I say that it really boils down to our core mission of serving all kids."[39] Scannell explicitly connects the channel's images of diversity to Nickelodeon's claims to "respect" kids, thus building up cultural capital not only with advocacy groups such as Children Now but also with parents, educators, and others in the television industry. Indeed, within the world of children's television, racial and ethnic identity works as a kind of cultural capital, and it increases the political and social clout of a network to be able to claim that it is "diverse." As cultural capital, Nickelodeon's mission to respect kids and provide a safe and secure environment connects specifically to representation. The network's claim to empower kids overtly references the historical invisibility and exclusion of people of color that has plagued television since its inception, and the inclusion of diverse casts and characters is explicitly recognized by the network as part of its mission to "respect" kids. As with the channel's commitment to girls, Nickelodeon has pledged to air diverse programming, created shows that feature nonwhite characters, and developed programming that directly invokes racial or ethnic themes. Diverse programming is, as we have seen, often discussed as "good business," thus distancing the channel from the political implications of embracing diversity.

Dora the Explorer is one of these programs. Produced for Nick Jr. (Nickelodeon's preschool lineup), the show embodies some of the contradictory discourses of race and gender celebrated within a contemporary popular culture context. Dora is an animated, seven-year-old Latina with dark skin and brown eyes who speaks both English and Spanish throughout the show. In every episode, the narrative revolves around solving a puzzle or mystery (such as how to find a frog's lost voice or how to save a baby jaguar) and encourages interactive behavior on the part of the audience. The program itself is structured like a computer game, so there is a cursor that "clicks" on the right answer when Dora asks the audience for help. There are pauses in the program when Dora looks at the audience, waiting for viewers to reply to her questions about the daily mystery, thus encouraging a kind of active engagement on the part of the preschool audience.

The emphasis on audience interaction is, of course, typical of many contemporary children's programs for which the creators have researched the pedagogical potential of television. It also speaks to a more general cultural shift—signified by postfeminism among other things—that recognizes media audiences as active, savvy consumers. Textually, the tropes of postfeminism and urbanization are evident in the overall aesthetics of the show, including featuring an intelligent girl as a lead character and celebrating a kind of racial "authenticity" through the physical representation of Dora, the names of the other characters on the show, and the general representational style of the program. The show features both human and animal characters, most of whom are recognizably Latino, in either physical representation or linguistic behavior. Dora's parents, Mami and Papi, her grandmother, Abuela, and her cousin, Diego, all speak Spanish and English, and animals on the program are gendered and racialized (e.g., as Benni the Bull, Isa the Iguana, and Tico the Squirrel). The home in which Dora resides with her parents is Spanish in style, an adobe building with a red tile roof. While the plot themes of the show are often developmental and pedagogical, the narrative of Dora also frequently references Latino culture, traditions, and styles, though not necessarily in an ethnically or geographically specific manner. All the episodes follow the same format,

in which Dora solves a mystery by following a series of clues, guided by her anthropomorphized "backpack" and "map," and the clues often are framed within an ambiguous Latin American lens. So, for instance, the Latin American rain forest is a frequent destination on Dora's quest to solve mysteries, a Christmas episode features a Mexican parade called a *parranda*, and characters on the show play salsa music to celebrate Dora's successes. One episode, "El Coqui," based on a famous Puerto Rican legend, involves Dora and a *coqui* (frog) who has lost his voice and will not be able to sing unless he gets back to his island. Dora and the frog eventually make their way to the island, assisted by a bird named Señor Tucan, allowing the frog to reunite with his friends and family.[40]

The weaving of the Puerto Rican legend into the show and, more specifically, incorporating themes of migration and exile culture as the primary narrative of the episode along with Latino dances and music, are ways to employ the strategy of being racially specific but ethnically nonspecific. In the most recent episodes of the program, this strategy continues to be honed and deployed. Perhaps most overtly, the expansion of Dora's extended and immediate family has added new dimensions to her postfeminist, "pan-Latino" persona. The show's producers have added two siblings to the family, twins, and in new episodes Dora is charged with taking care of the babies. The babies, like Dora, are drawn as Latino characters and are spoken to in Spanish as often as they are in English. Dora's status as a big sister is a frequent theme of current programs (as well as a new theme for toy manufacturing), and the program has smoothly incorporated a nurturing element into Dora's adventurous personality. The babies often accompany Dora on her adventures, allowing the show's producers to both create new thematic ideas for the show and add further elements to its postfeminist framing. Dora teaches the babies to speak English and Spanish, Spanish lullabies are now part of the show, and Dora's family is featured more centrally. Another way in which the show celebrates a particular notion of "difference" occurs with the addition of Dora's bilingual eight-year-old cousin, Diego Marquez, who was introduced in *Dora the Explorer* as someone who helps animals in danger, now has his own show, *Go Diego*

Go!, which is also part of Nickelodeon's preschool programming package. The program continues the theme of Dora through its celebration of "authentic" Latin American culture: the animals that Diego rescues are all indigenous creatures to Latin American rain forests, each show contains references to Latin American folktales and traditions, and Spanish is intermingled with English throughout each episode.

Diego's character furthers the initial strategy of *Dora the Explorer* where postfeminist culture and the celebration of "difference" function as effective ways to both target and create a particular community of consumers. Dora's character, as well as Diego's and others on the show, are depicted in such a way that race and ethnicity *matter*, though in particular ways, as a kind of "authentic" pleasure and an unproblematic embrace of "difference." Race, in this context, is not rendered invisible, but it is also not presented as specific and particular. Rather, Dora, like Diego, represents a marketable global citizen. Dora is pan-Latino intentionally so that as a Latina she has a wide appeal for her young audiences across the world. Indeed, her "Latinidad" has been expertly commodified in dozens of toys, books, clothes, and food items that appeal to a wide demographic of consumers, including, but certainly not limited to, American Latinos. In an article entitled "Adorable Dora Is Opening the Doors of Diversity," the producers of the show comment specifically on her panethnic representation: " 'With Dora, Nickelodeon found a heroine that appeals to kids of all ethnic backgrounds'... [said producer Gifford,] recalling one Chinese child who said, 'She's just like me; she speaks another language.' The creators purposely do not specify Dora's ethnic background, preferring that she have a pan-Latino appeal, and revised her original green eyes to brown after content supervisor Dolly Espinal pointed out that a majority of Latinos have brown eyes and that it was important to celebrate that."[41] The difference embodied by the character of Dora allows for an ethnically informed style of politics, yet it is, in McRobbie's terms, difference "taken into account" yet not necessarily acted on. Challenging racist stereotypes by creating a new one fit for the current political and cultural economy, Dora operates as part of a strategy that motivates a commercially defined notion of diversity. As Arlene Dávila points out in her study about

marketing aimed at Latinos, "To sell themselves and their products, those in [the advertising] industry have not only drawn from existing stereotypes . . . but have also positioned themselves as the 'politically correct' voice with which to challenge stereotypes and educate corporate clients about Hispanic language and culture."[42] Nickelodeon's self-identity as the "diversity station" utilizes a similar kind of strategy through which it gains cultural capital by offering diverse representations to its young audience.

Within the current market environment, a dual process of challenging and reinforcing racial stereotypes in the media is necessary in order to maintain an "ethnic" niche in the market.[43] Yet in programs such as *Dora the Explorer*, which confront stereotypes as they simultaneously reformulate them for a shifted market, the stereotype that is reconstituted is one that is not necessarily intended for an ethnic niche market but is meant to appeal to a broader (more "global") audience. Using this strategy, Nickelodeon can claim that the network is committed to diversity despite the fact that this progressive ideology works as a more general market imperative. This strategy works hand in hand with postfeminist politics, where Dora, as a strong, smart, female character, is clearly a product of a culture that recognizes the importance of "positive" gender representations yet does not call attention to any kind of feminist politics other than the politics of representation. Thus, the challenges to dominant stereotypes that *Dora the Explorer* poses are framed within normative social conventions so that the challenge is contained and made palatable for a media audience. What this means, at least for Dora, is to utilize Latino "themes" as part of the program but in a safe way so as not to alienate Nickelodeon's predominantly white, middle-class cable audience.

In the case of Nickelodeon, as demonstrated by *Dora the Explorer*, diversity is less about a specific identity in terms of ethnicity than about an identity as an empowered consumer-citizen. Indeed, the show's cocreator and executive producer, Chris Gifford, claimed he had "empowering children in mind" when he created *Dora*.[44] The construction of Dora as a global citizen whose ethnicity is specific but whose appeal is racially nonspecific makes her what one consultant, Carlos Cortes, calls "a crossover phenomenon and the product of a slow evolution in television."[45] This "evolution" in television is indicated by the construction of ethnic markets, an increasingly diverse body of consumers, and the emergence of a cool, more "multicultural" approach to making television shows that corresponds to a general youth market. Another element of this television evolution is signaled by postfeminism, which similarly celebrates the "empowered" consumer-citizen.

Conclusion

Within the current media environment, itself a product of a post-civil-rights society, race functions as an ambivalent category in which, on the one hand, race remains an important issue in terms of representation—shown by featuring people of color more prominently (as demonstrated by the Flava dolls) and crafting story lines that focus on race and race relations. On the other hand, the plethora of images of urban and cool people of color in advertising, television programs, and music videos (among other popular culture artifacts) implies that representational visibility no longer has the same urgency. Indeed, the implication is that race itself no longer matters in the same way it once did but is now simply an interesting way to feature the authentic, cool, or urban or develop a theme in a reality show. This postracial television economy is the legacy of diverse programs such as *Sesame Street* and *The Cosby Show*, but it engages these earlier representations of race within new economic models in which the connection between enfranchisement and "positive" images of diversity no longer has the meaning it did in the media context of the 1970s and 1980s. These new economic models also inform the production of postfeminist popular culture, in which "feminism taken into account" is the dominant narrative, effectively framing feminism as history even as a commodified version of feminist ideas and values is normalized.

It is not my aim to resolve these tensions or expose postfeminism or the "urban" as a commercial hoax. It is my goal, rather, to theorize how the contradictory media representations of girl power and urbanization function as a particular kind of politics and as such work to constitute audiences as particular kinds of cultural citizens. The same problems and distinctions that formulate the current postfeminist

and postracial cultural space also constitute consumer citizenship: nostalgia, an imagined golden past, superficiality, a focus on the individual, rhetorics of choice reframed in terms of consumer purchases, and so on. Like consumer citizenship, postfeminist and postracial culture is profoundly, indeed necessarily ambivalent.

Notes

1. Press release, Flava Dolls, Mattel, Inc., www.Toymania.com, retrieved February 2004. Unfortunately for Mattel, Flava Dolls were not a big hit with girls age nine to eleven, and shortly after their release in toy stores across the United States Mattel stopped production. However, clearly this style of toy remains significant, as another brand of similar dolls, Bratz Dolls, produced by MGA entertainment, are immensely popular in the United States. Bratz Dolls are also multiethnic and, according to a fan Web site, are "known for having fun, detailed accessories and play sets which reflect their 'cool' (and somewhat materialistic) lifestyle—discos, karaoke and sushi bars, salons and spas, limousines, retro cafes, malls are all available" (collectdolls.about.com, retrieved June 2005).

2. Pierre Bourdieu theorized cultural capital as knowledge, or a kind of competence, about styles and genres that are socially valued and confer prestige on those who have mastered them. He distinguished between economic capital, which refers to the quantity of material goods and income commanded by an individual, and cultural capital, which refers to a kind of competency derived from education, familiarity with a legitimized cultural tradition, and modes of consumption. For more on this, see Bourdieu, *Distinction*.

3. For more on this subject, see Buckingham, *After the Death of Childhood*; Buckingham, *The Making of Citizens*; Seiter, *Sold Separately*; and Gray, *Watching Race*.

4. See McRobbie, "Notes on Postfeminism and Popular Culture."

5. Gray, *Cultural Moves*. As Gray argues, this proliferation of images does not necessarily connect with a more equitable legal system or a lessening of racist practices in the United States. In fact, the increasing presence of images of African Americans often obscures the ways in which a racist society functions.

6. Smith, "I Don't Like to Dream about Getting Paid."

7. Dow, *Prime-Time Feminism*.

8. McRobbie, "Notes on Postfeminism and Popular Culture," 5.

9. Ibid., 6.

10. Hogeland, "Against Generational Thinking; or, Some Things That 'Third Wave' Feminism Isn't," 107.

11. McRobbie discusses this shift to a more "lifestyle" type of politics in "Notes on Post-feminism and Popular Culture."

12. Ibid., 10–11.

13. Klein, *No Logo*.

14. Baumgardner and Richards, *Manifesta*.

15. The awareness of feminist accomplishments in the areas of employment, wages, and policy led to a widespread adoption of the adage "I'm not a feminist, but . . ." As Susan Douglas argues, the comma in this statement is hugely significant, marking the contradictions involved in feminist politics: "The comma says that the speaker is ambivalent, that she is torn between a philosophy that seeks to improve her lot in life and a desire not to have to pay too dearly for endorsing that philosophy" (*Where the Girls Are*, 270).

16. Baumgardner and Richards, *Manifesta*, 83.

17. Douglas, *Where the Girls Are*, 293.

18. Goldman, *Reading Ads Socially*.

19. Bellafante, "It's All about Me!" 57.

20. Baumgardner and Richards, *Manifesta*; Findlen, *Listen Up*; Wolf, *Fire with Fire*.

21. Baumgardner and Richards, *Manifesta*, 80.

22. See Hartsock, *The Feminist Standpoint Revisited and Other Essays*.

23. McRobbie, "Notes on Postfeminism and Popular Culture."

24. See Klein, *No Logo*; Gladwell, "The Coolhunt"; and Heath and Potter, *The Rebel Sell*.

25. See, for example, Gladwell, "The Coolhunt"; Klein, *No Logo*; and Quart, *Branded*.

26. Sconce, "Irony, Nihilism, and the American 'Smart' Film," 352.

27. Gray, *Watching Race*. While Gray recognizes the historical trajectory of these discourses, he also acknowledges that all three practices continue simultaneously.

28. Gray, *Watching Race*, 79.

29. Wynter, *American Skin*, 135.

30. Scannell, "Why Not Diversity?"

31. Projansky, *Watching Rape*.

32. See Wynter, *American Skin*, and Smith, "I Don't Like to Dream about Getting Paid."

33. Wynter, *American Skin*, 17.

34. By this, I do not mean "authentic" ethnicity (i.e., a physical relationship with ethnic identity and history) but rather a more diffused embrace of ethnic identity and the urban.

35. Watts and Orbe, "The Spectacular Consumption of 'True' African American Culture, 3.

36. Cabrera, "Adorable Dora Is Opening the Doors of Diversity."

37. Although these programs take an explicit political position on diversity, and federal regulations in the United States dictate that at least three hours a week of children's television must be "educational," there are certainly plenty of programs that are not diverse. Indeed, the enormous market for licensed character products lends itself to rigid stereotypes because simplistic hegemonic images are easier to package and sell—they have a clearer market identity.

38. The network leadership of Nickelodeon has changed since this article was written; in January 2006, Herb Scannell resigned as president of Nickelodeon and was succeeded by Cyma Zarghami.

39. Scannell, "Why Not Diversity?"

40. *Dora the Explorer*, "El Coqui."

41. Cabrera, "Adorable Dora."

42. Dávila, *Latinos, Inc.*

43. This dual function of stereotypes is not unique to Dora, of course, but is characteristic of stereotyping more generally. For more on this, see Bhabha, "The Other Question."

44. Cabrera, "Adorable Dora."

45. Ibid.

References

Baumgardner, Jennifer, and Amy Richards. *Manifesta: Young Women, Feminism, and the Future*. New York: Farrar, Straus and Giroux, 2000.

Bellafante, Gina. "It's All about Me!" *Time*, 29 June 1998.

Bhabha, Homi. "The Other Question." *Screen* 24:6 (1983): 18–36.

Bourdieu, Pierre. *Distinction: A Social Critique of the Judgement of Taste*. Cambridge, Mass.: Harvard University Press, 1987.

Buckingham, David. *After the Death of Childhood: Growing Up in the Age of Electronic Media*. London: Polity Press, 2000.

Cabrera, Yvette. "Adorable Dora Is Opening the Doors of Diversity." *Orange County Register*, 13 September 2002.

Dávila, Arlene. *Latinos, Inc.: The Marketing and Making of a People*. Berkeley: University of California Press, 2001.

Douglas, Susan. *Where the Girls Are: Growing Up Female with the Mass Media*. New York: Times Books, 1994..

Dow, Bonnie J. *Prime-Time Feminism: Television, Media Culture, and the Woman's Movement since 1970*. State College: Pennsylvania University Press, 1996.

Gladwell, Malcolm. "The Coolhunt." In *The Consumer Society Reader*, ed. Juliet B. Schor and Douglas B. Holt. New York: New Press, 2000.

Goldman, Richard. *Reading Ads Socially*. New York: Routledge, 1992.

Gray, Herman. *Cultural Moves: African Americans and the Politics of Representation*. Berkeley: University of California Press, 2005.

——. *Watching Race: Television and the Struggle for Blackness*. Minneapolis: University of Minnesota Press, 1995.

Hartsock, Nancy. *The Feminist Standpoint Revisited and Other Essays*. Colorado: Westview, 1998.

Hogeland, Lisa. "Against Generational Thinking; or, Some Things That 'Third Wave' Feminism Isn't." *Women's Studies in Communication* 24 (2001):107.

Klein, Naomi. *No Logo: No Space, No Choice, No Jobs*. New York: Picador, 2002.

McRobbie, Angela. "Notes on Postfeminism and Popular Culture: Bridget Jones and the new Gender Regime." In *All about the Girl: Culture, Power, and Identity*, ed. Anita Harris. London: Routledge, 2004.

Quart, Alyssa, *Branded: The Buying and Selling of Teenagers*. New York: Perseus, 2003.

Scannell, Herb. "Why Not Diversity?" *Children Now*, summer 2002. Newsletter.

Seiter, Ellen. *Sold Separately: Parents and Children in Consumer Culture*. New Brunswick, N.J.: Rutgers University Press, 1995.

Smith, Christopher Holmes. "'I Don't Like to Dream about Getting Paid': Representations of Social Mobility and the Emergence of the Hip-Hop Mogul." *Social Text* 77 (winter 2003): 69–98.

Watts, Eric, and Mark Orbe. "The Spectacular Consumption of 'True' African American Culture: 'Whassup' with the Budweiser Guys?" *Critical Studies in Media Communication* 19:1 (2002):1–20.

Wynter, Leon. *American Skin: Pop Culture, Big Business, and the End of White America*. New York: Crown, 2002.

28.
OH BEHAVE!

Austin Powers and the Drag Kings

Judith Halberstam

That ain't no woman! It's a man, man!

—Austin Powers

There has been much ink spilled in the popular media and in popular queer culture about the intimate relations between gay men and straight women. The "fag hag" role has become a staple feature of popular film, and at least part of the explanation for how gay male culture and gay male images have so thoroughly penetrated popular film and TV cultures lies in the recognized and indeed lived experience of bonds between "queens" and "girls." There is no such parallel between lesbians and straight men. While the dynamic between lesbians and hetero-males could change significantly in the next few decades as more and more lesbians become parents and raise sons, for the moment there seem to be no sit-coms on the horizon ready to exploit the humorous possibilities of interactions between a masculine woman and her butch guy pal. This is not to say that no relations exist between the way lesbians produce and circulate cultures of masculinity and the way men do. However, these relations are for the most part submerged and mediated and difficult to read.

This essay will trace the strange and barely discernible influence of lesbian drag-king cultures on hetero-male comic film. My contention will not be that straight men learn how to parody masculinity from butch women and then take that parody to the bank; rather, I will try to map circuits of subcultural influence across a wide range of textual play. I take for granted Dick Hebdige's formulation of subcultures as marginalized cultures that are quickly absorbed by capitalism and then robbed of their oppositional power,[1] but I will expand on Hebdige's influential reading of subcultures by arguing that some subcultures do not simply fade away as soon as they have been plundered for material. Furthermore, I emphasize the utility of tracking precisely when, where, and how the subculture is "beamed up" into the mainstream. Tracing the mysterious process by which, say, a performance in a queer nightclub or a genre of queer humor or a specific mode of parody has been observed, appreciated, and then reproduced is not simple and has much to offer future studies of the ever more complex lines of affiliation between the marginal and the dominant. One obvious way to trace the difference between the dominant and the marginal in this instance is to see who becomes rich from certain performances of male parody and who never materially benefits at all. Yet profit is not ultimately the best gauge of success, and it may well be that by tracing a cultural phenomenon back to its source, we restore a different kind of prestige to the subculture and honor its creativity in the process.

King Comedies

For abject English masculinity films, 1997 was a banner year: *The Full Monty* (dir. Peter Cattaneo) and *Austin Powers: International Man of Mystery* (dir. Jay Roach) both took American audiences by surprise. *The Full Monty*, for example, was made for only $3 million, but within a few months it had made twice that much at the box office. Both of these "king comedies," as I like to call them, using *king* as a more precise term than *camp*, were built around the surprising vulnerabilities of the English male body and psyche. Indeed, the king comedy attempts to exploit not the power but the frailty of the male body for the purpose of generating laughs at the hero's expense. King comedies also capitalize on the humor that comes from revealing the derivative nature of dominant masculinities, and so they trade heavily in the tropes of doubling, disguise, and impersonation. So while *Austin Powers* parodically reenacts a long tradition of secret-agent films and raids the coffers of sexist British humor from Benny Hill to the *Carry On* comedies, *The Full Monty* forces its lads to relearn masculinity the hard way—from women.

What models of masculinity do *Austin Powers* and *The Full Monty* draw on? What is their appeal to American audiences in particular, and what visions of Englishness and English manliness circulate through these very different comedies? Furthermore, what cultural changes allowed mainstream parodies of dominant masculinity to flourish in the 1990s? What are the main features of the king-comedy genre, and what kinds of subcultural histories subtend it? Can we read kinging and king comedy as equivalent to camp? If camp, on some level, describes an ironic relation between femaleness and the performance of femininity, can "king" describe the distance between maleness and the performance of masculinity in comic terms?

King comedies emerge out of very specific traditions of masculine humor, but in their present incarnation they can also be linked to the recent explosion of active drag-king cultures. Not surprisingly, mainstream comedies about masculinity never articulate their indebtedness to these subcultural and queer comedic representations; accordingly, we have to re-create and actively imagine the possible routes of transmission that carry drag-king humor from the queer club to the mainstream blockbuster movie. In his book *Disidentifications*, José Esteban Muñoz allows for such re-creations of routes of transmission by way of the term *counterpublics*, or "communities and relational chains of resistance that contest the dominant public sphere."[2] Counterpublics, in Muñoz's work on performances by queers of color, validate and produce minoritarian public spheres while offering a potent challenge to the white heteronormativity of majoritarian public spheres. Drag-king culture, I believe, constitutes just such a counterpublic space, where white and heteronormative masculinities can be contested and where minority masculinities can be produced, validated, fleshed out, and celebrated.

In my work on drag kings I have tried to identify the specificity of drag-king acts and distinguish them from drag-queen acts by using the term *kinging*. As I explain in my drag-king chapter of *Female Masculinity*, to "king" a role can involve a number of modes of performance, from earnest repetition to hyperbolic re-creation and from quiet understatement to theatrical layering.[3] My hope was there, and remains here, that we can recognize a genre of cultural work in drag-king performances that is not exactly commensurate with what we call "camp" and yet has similar effects. Camp has been written about widely as a critical comic style deployed by Euro-American gay male and drag-queen cultures but present in other nongay cultural forms. Esther Newton, in particular, traces camp back to drag-queen performances, where specific use is made of "incongruity, theatricality and humor" to denaturalize gender.[4] Obviously, however, while camp may have originated in and may be peculiar to drag-queen cultures, it also travels as a cultural style and allows for a gay counterpublic site to influence and ironize the depiction of femininity in mainstream venues. In other words, just as camp shows up in many sites that are not gay, as an aesthetic mode detached from one type of identity, so we might expect kinging to exceed the boundaries of lesbian and transgender subcultures and to circulate independently of the drag-king act itself. In relation to the king comedies, we need not trace one-to-one instances of transmission between drag-king cultures and filmmakers and producers; what we can trace is a particular kingy effect in otherwise mainstream representations.

We find moments of king humor in both auteur comedy (Jerry Lewis or Woody Allen) and ensemble comedy, featuring a duo or trio (Abbott and Costello, Laurel and Hardy, the Marx Brothers); in each case, male fragility or male stupidity has been tapped as a primary source of humor. In much male comedy, indeed, a weak or vulnerable male is paired with a more robust specimen of manhood. Sometimes, as in

Laurel and Hardy, both forms of manhood are shown to be lacking and futile, but often, as in a Jerry Lewis and Dean Martin routine, the bumbling guy makes the straight guy less formal, and the straight guy makes his idiot companion more appealing. Sometimes it is difficult to see or appreciate the kingy effect of the classic comedy act until it is reproduced in a counterpublic sphere. So, for example, Laurel and Hardy may not immediately shout male parody, and yet, when we see Beryl Reid and Susannah York dressing up as Laurel and Hardy in *The Killing of Sister George*, the kingy effect comes to the surface. Much as the image of a gay man impersonating Bette Davis makes Davis herself into a camp icon, the image of lesbians impersonating Laurel and Hardy can transform them into king icons.

Whereas camp reads dominant culture at a slant and mimics dominant forms of femininity in order to produce and ratify alternative drag femininities that revel in irony, sarcasm, inversion, and insult, kinging reads dominant male masculinity and explodes its effects through exaggeration, parody, and earnest mimicry. It may be helpful to use images to establish some of the methods of drag-king performance. In "Mo B. Dick with Muscles," Del LaGrace Volcano's photographic method allows us to visualize the dragking technique of "de-authentication". The mirror scene is one that LaGrace returns to repeatedly in his work. Here the mirror is a clue that what we are looking at is not to be read as "real," and yet the image of Mo B. flexing is a classic pose of authenticity. The muscle pose is complemented by the basketball T-shirt, but even as the shirt seemingly affirms maleness, it also deconstructs it, because "DRAG KING" is inscribed across the back. As the viewer searches for clues to the "authentic gender" of the body in sight, the photograph frames the project of authenticity as flawed and unproductive. Instead, LaGrace revels in the proliferation of clues and red herrings all in the same location.

Another strategy favored by LaGrace can be called "masculine supplementarity". Now we move from the drag king and his mirrored self to the drag king ("Tomcat") coupled with what could be a drag queen or a bio-woman ("Tits"). The "tits" on the "woman" here both affirm and destabilize Tomcat's masculinity. On the one hand, they allow us to see

him as obviously not female; on the other hand, his size in relation to the much larger female allows him to be read as not male. Ultimately, however, the woman's hyperfemininity supplements the masculinity that the drag king's own image lacks. In many ways, the contrast between Mike Myers and Elizabeth Hurley as Austin Powers and Vanessa Kensington in *Austin Powers* depends on masculine supplementarity. He anxiously announces and emphasizes his masculinity even as she towers over him and makes visible his masculine lack. Austin's lack of sex appeal is supplemented and veiled by Vanessa's desire *nonetheless*.

In "The Geezers," one drag king is coupled with another to enhance or emphasize the realness of the drag masculinity. Doubling, as we will see, is a major trope in *Austin Powers*, and in both the dominant and the subcultural arenas, it invokes a homoerotic aesthetic. Doubling, however, is different from cloning or impersonating, as we see in this image of Elvis Herselvis and an Elvis Herselvis impersonator. White masculinity in particular becomes more performative when it is not simply multiplied but, as we see here, replicated imperfectly. We might consider the Mini-Me clone in *Austin Powers 2* as the mainstream version of this standard drag-king move, whereby a form of masculinity that is already defined in terms of impersonation (Elvis, for example) is impersonated. I want to name one last drag-king strategy of masculine performance now: indexical representation. The cover of *The Drag King Book* uses one of the "realness" kings as a cover and as *the* cover. Without the title that runs across his middle, the viewer would not know that this masculine icon was a drag king—so we can refer to a strategy of indexical naming that reminds the viewer or reader at various moments that he or she is watching or viewing a representation of a representation. Mike Myers uses precisely this mode of indexing in a clever sight gag in *Austin Powers*. In one scene Austin walks around a room nude while Vanessa, seated in the foreground and oblivious to his presence, holds up various objects (a sausage, a magnifying glass, a pen) that simultaneously conceal and prosthetically extend his penis. In this penis concealment/replacement sequence, the naked body of the male is both on display and under construction; while the gaze of the camera at Austin's nude body should confirm at least that this body is phallic, in fact it suggests once again that the body requires a prosthetic supplement. Like a drag-king strip act that culminates in the exposure not of the female body but of the dildo, this scene suggests that masculinity and indeed maleness are no less constructed on the body than in the clothing.

Drag-king parodies of particularly white masculinity are perhaps the most popular form of drag-king performance at present. In the past, male impersonation might have been much more oriented toward the production of an effect of male credibility (Storme Delaverie of the Jewel Box Revue, for example). The latest wave of drag-king cultures, however, has reveled in the humor of male mimicry and the power of male parody. At a drag-king show nowadays, comedic acts outnumber sexy acts ten to one, and while certainly this has something to do with the influence of drag-queen models of camp performance, it also implies the spectators' desire for a deconstruction of maleness rather than a reconstruction of masculinity elsewhere. Much of the humor of these parodies revolves around exposing the dated look of latter-day sex gods (like Tom Jones or Elvis or Donny Osmond) and emphasizing the prosthetic nature of male sexual appeal by using overstuffed crotches, chest rugs, and wigs.

In my own work on "female masculinity," I have tried to provide full accounts of the histories, forms, and cultures of these "counterfeit" masculinities—masculinities that are produced subculturally and that challenge the primacy, authenticity, and originality of dominant masculinities—and I want to continue that work here by tracking the effect of the rise of mimic genders on those bodies that still imagine themselves to be "original." So while we may grant the reversal of original and copy in queer theoretical formulations of heterosexuality and homosexuality, the question I want to tackle here is how drag-king performances (copies, supposedly) influence the representation of male performativity (original, supposedly).

Drag king shows draw large crowds of both straight and gay spectators, and they have also attracted quite a bit of media interest. Mainstream magazine articles on drag kings have commented on the altogether unusual and hilarious spectacle of ridicule directed at dominant masculinity, yet the general interest in drag-king theater has not translated into anything like mainstream visibility. Drag-king shows and clubs may well have been fixtures in places like New York City and San Francisco for five years or more, but there still seems to be only a small market beyond the lesbian club circuit for parodies of male midlife crisis, performances of bloated male pride, and drag-king stand-up comedy routines. The reverse sexism of the drag-king shows has, not surprisingly, simply failed to sell. But while marketing people assume that mainstream audiences will not tolerate the active ridicule of male sex symbols by queer male impersonators, there is no such assumption about the appeal of men parodying masculinity. Of course, the tolerance for male parodies of masculinity depends on a long history of male comedy in which male insufficiency is first played for laughs and then rescued from a future of constant boyhood or else explicit effeminacy by the mechanism of compulsory heterosexuality. The transition from inadequate but humorous boy to sufficient and funny man is made by coding humor as either an intellectual skill (as in Woody Allen films) or a mark of attractive male vulnerability (as in Jerry Lewis films). In the new king comedies, however, humor is neither a skill nor a gift; rather, it is an effective tool for exposing the constructedness of male masculinity.

Many of the king comedies in the theaters today, surprisingly, seem to have learned some lessons in gender trouble and even show signs of recognizing what students in cultural studies programs across the country already know so well: that, in Judith Butler's influential phrase, gender functions as a "copy for which there is no original."[5] While this phrase has become a standard academic formulation for rethinking the relations between heterosexual and homosexual embodiment and performance in the late twentieth century, we may still be a little shocked to find evidence of a self-conscious recognition of performativity in mainstream culture itself. Still, the king comedies that I am most interested in here all show dominant masculinity to be the product of repeated and scripted motions; furthermore, they highlight the ways that most masculinity copies and models itself on an ideal that it can never replicate.

The king comedy derives much of its humor from an emphasis on small penises and a general concern with male anxiety and fragility: in this respect, it seems to call for a psychoanalytic reading. Yet while psychoanalysis has usefully detailed the forms and methods of male empowerment, only rarely does it provide tools for the examination of male vulnerability. Because of the emphasis on the drama of castration in psychoanalysis, we are left with remarkably limited, and humorless, ways of thinking about male vulnerability—indeed, in a phallic economy, one either has the phallus or lacks it; one either masters castration anxiety or is mastered by it. In either case, the drama of castration is tragic rather than comic. The king comedy, however, takes castration anxiety to new levels, or rather new depths, and in the process manages to find and produce more nuanced models of male masculinity. For example, it may build on not castration but phallic renunciation, and much of its humor may well derive from exposing the elaborate mechanisms that prop up seemingly normative masculinity. Traditional psychoanalytic formulations of male comedy tend to read the comic male body as tainted by fallibility and femininity: the funny man, in other words, has often been marked in explicit ways as simply hysterical, in all senses of the word. The comic hero—think here of Jerry Lewis—is some combination of twitches and spasms, pratfalls and stutters; he spits, he trips, he cries, he screams. Yet by marking the funny man as flawed and hysterical, instead of (say) seductive and hyperbolic, we simply read him back into the phallic economy of having or lacking.

Psychoanalytic critics talk about masculine comedy in terms of oedipal and pre-oedipal genres. In an oedipal comedy, the overgrown boy (think here of Jim Carrey or Adam Sandler) resists adult manhood and indeed seems inadequate to its demands: the plot involves the boy's accession to maturity, which is marked by the beginning of a heterosexual romance with an acceptable female love object; the love object may find the boy humorous but not ridiculous, and this distinction allows him access to the illusion of mastery. Pre-oedipal comedy, by contrast, tends to avoid excessive individuation and to revel in the farcical humor of undirected play; Keystone Kops and Buster Keaton films are examples of this kind of comedy, which almost refuses narrative coherence.[6] The king comedies actively resist, in various ways, the narrative conditions of both oedipal and pre-oedipal

comic convention. In *Austin Powers* and *The Full Monty*, the comic heroes neither struggle to resist adulthood nor struggle to achieve it; on the contrary, in both films our heroes have become men and have discovered that manhood does not allay the fear of castration: it confirms it! In fact, in each film the comic hero has to grapple with the serious limitations of male masculinity in a world where feminism has empowered women, changes in the workplace have altered dominant conceptions of masculinity, and queer models of gender seem far more compelling and successful than old-fashioned heterosexual models of gender polarity. Confronted by the failure of the masculine ideal, the male hero must accept economic and emotional disappointment and learn to live with the consequences of a shift of power that has subtly but completely removed him from the center of the universe. While contemporary oedipal comedies like the gross-out films released in the late 1990s (*American Pie* and *Big Daddy*, for example) continue to invest in fantasies of robust and normative masculinities that have both national and racial dimensions (American manhood in one and white fatherhood in the other), the king comedies expose the anxious male posturing of these films as the aftershocks of a seismic shift that has already taken place. The humor in *The Full Monty* in particular depends on some recognition of the toll taken by postimperial decline on the psyches of white males in England in the 1980s and 1990s. And the ridiculous but lovable character of Austin Powers derives at least in part from a serious reconsideration of the waning appeal of stereotypical English masculinity in a postcolonial and multiracial Britain.

The Full Monty

The Full Monty, starring Robert Carlyle, takes place in the aftermath of the decline of Sheffield's steel industry. The film refers clearly to the effects of changes in the workplace on the meaning of male masculinity. After a promotional short predicting a rosy future for Sheffield, "a city on the move" in the early 1970s, the film jumps ahead twenty-five years, when the steelworks have closed. Steel, in this film, is a metaphor for past models of masculinity, for masculinities dependent on "hard bodies," to use Susan Jeffords's term, but the decline of the steelworks also serves as a grim reminder of the ravages of Thatcherism on British nationalized industry.[7] Many men in Sheffield are out of work, while their girlfriends, wives, and mothers in the service industries still have jobs. The economic disparity between the blue-collar men who are now unemployed and the blue-collar women who have retained their service jobs shifts significantly and irrevocably the coordinates and meanings of gender and sexuality. When a Chippendales show comes to town, some local lads decide that they too should try to make some money as strippers. Amazingly, the process of developing a show throws the men into dilemmas that we almost never associate with masculinity but that have come to define femininity: the men worry about their bodies, their clothes, their ability to dance, their desirability.

The film opens with a series of assaults on male privilege: the film's protagonist, Gaz, is unemployed and struggling to make custody payments to his ex-wife in order to maintain a relationship with his son. Dave, his mate, has, in the words of his wife, "given up" and resigned himself to "redundancy" at work and at home. Gerald, Gaz and Dave's former boss, cannot bring himself to tell his wife that he is out of work, so he leaves as if for work every morning and heads to the job center, desperately hoping to find work before she finds out that their money is gone. The conventional masculine roles of father, husband, and breadwinner are all under serious pressure; masculinity is defined from the outset as a category threatened on all sides by redundancy.

As Gaz and Dave return home one evening after a hard day of trying to steal scrap metal from the old factory, they encounter a long line of women waiting to be admitted to a working men's club where the Chippendale dancers are performing. Gaz sneaks into the men's bathroom through a window to survey the "women-only" scene inside. But before he has a real chance to take in the scene of hundreds of women whooping at a male stripper, three women make their way toward the men's room, hoping to avoid a line for the toilet. Gaz slips into a stall and watches what transpires through a hole in the door. While he occupies the seemingly traditional position of the Peeping Tom, what he sees changes radically the gendered roles of spectatorship. At first Gaz takes pleasure in watching the women transform the men's room into a

women's room by applying makeup in the mirror. He watches them watching themselves. Right before his eyes, however, the scene changes abruptly from a feminine scene of display to a masculine scene of activity when one of the women hikes up her skirt and pees at the urinal, to the delight of her friends. Rather than simply conform to a psychoanalytic model of either castration or female phallicism, this scene, I think, registers a refusal of several gender logics: first, it refuses to mark maleness as the place of sexualized voyeurism; second, it suggests the effects of even casual invasions of male space by women. Finally, the framing of the shot—which locates a man hiding behind a door, two women in front of a mirror, and another woman at a urinal—predicts the politics of the gaze that will be elaborated in the film and will culminate in the film's final shot.

The growing redundancy of old forms of gender relations and of masculinity is underscored in *The Full Monty* by this abrupt, irreversible reconfiguration of the male gaze. In Hollywood cinema, the male gaze structures the look of the viewer and allows the male spectator to identify with activity in the scene and to desire the female who is positioned as the object of his gaze and desire. The masculine woman in this scene, the woman at the urinal, restructures the male gaze by insisting that it be routed through alternative modes of masculinity. Thus Gaz can peer voyeuristically at the women in the mirror only if he also looks at the woman at the urinal. His struggle, here and in other key scenes of watching and being watched, indicates how thoroughly male-female relations have been transformed by changes at the level of economy and labor practices. It would be inaccurate, however, to say that the lack of economic power exercised by the working-class men of Sheffield castrates them; rather, it allows them to see themselves, instead of women, as the subjects who represent and figure lack.

When Gaz reports to his friends at the job center what he has witnessed in the men's room, their responses record unfamiliar forms of male paranoia that are inflected less by rage at women than by a sense of the impending redundancy of heteronormative maleness once masculinity circulates through different bodies. Gaz himself suggests, "When women start pissing like us, that's it. We're finished, Dave, extincto." Another man adds, "They're turning into us." "A few years," Gaz continues, "and men won't exist, except in zoos or summat. I mean, we're not needed no more, are we? Obsolete, dinosaurs, yesterday's news." The theme of male self-deprecation reaches its nadir when Dave and Gaz find a man trying to kill himself in his car. The rescue and resuscitation of the suicidal character, Lomper, is unsentimental, and yet it precipitates a strong fraternity among men in trouble. The fraternity crosses class lines when the lads recruit Gerald, their former foreman, to be their dance instructor. His ballroom dancing skills, once the mark of a refined and respectable masculinity, now become the basis for a new male collectivity inspired by disenchantment and exclusion but productive of a new model of maleness centered on masculine display and vulnerability.

The dance fraternity grows when Gaz and his friends begin auditions for their stripper troupe and find two more members: a black man named Horse and a gay man named Guy. *The Full Monty* hints at alternative constructions of masculinity and associates them through these characters with race and sexuality. The character of Horse, despite his name, departs from the stereotype of a black masculinity anchored by a huge phallus; rather, it is the gay man, generically called Guy, who assumes the role of alpha male in the group. Furthermore, when Guy begins a relationship with Lomper, their alternative version of masculinity only persuades the other men that dominant masculinity (like the dying steel industry) is a bankrupt form.

The film ultimately suggests that when men and women reverse places socially, financially, and even culturally, the effects are not all bad. Women with power, we discover, do not behave simply like men; they cultivate their own relations to masculinity and femininity, and they encourage the men around them to do the same. Similarly, disempowered men may easily fall into conventional concerns about impotence, but they also learn lessons in objectification. In a hilarious scene at Gerald's, where the men first try stripping in front of each other, a whole array of issues about embodiment comes up. When Dave confesses that he feels fat and out of shape, Gerald shoots back, "Fat, David, is a feminist issue." The men proceed to give Dave and each other advice about

dieting and working out. The fact that this scene takes place in the "posh" suburban home of the former foreman also recalculates the class differentials in the group and the relationships between men and domesticity. Just as we find women in the men's room at the working men's club, so we find men at home during the day discussing body issues.

One final scene suggests how new conceptions of masculinity can and indeed must be routed through feminism and the female body. Gaz has Dave steal a copy of *Flashdance* to give the dancers some sense of what good dancing should look like. But as the video begins, Dave peers at the screen in disgust at Jennifer Beals, dancer by night, welding by day in a factory. The spectacle of the female dancer as welder, like the image of the woman at the urinal, challenges once more the idea of woman as an object of display but also creates the uncanny image of a female masculinity that the men must now emulate. Masculinity throughout *The Full Monty* is precisely welded together from a collectivity of minority masculinities. This film about men under pressure sets new standards for the depiction of masculinity in mainstream film, and it ends by referencing the taboo representation of male nudity. In its final flourish, it reveals that minority masculinities can expose mainstream masculinity as a dangerous myth of potency, invulnerability, and violence. The final shot, which should constitute the money shot of "the full monty," actually refuses to make the visibility of the phallus into the totality of maleness; the finale of the strip show is filmed from the back of the stage, and a freeze frame captures the six naked men from behind and the crowd of screaming women full on. The *full monty*, then, includes the female voyeur looking and the male body on display; moreover, this scene echoes in form and content the earlier one of the woman at the urinal. In both scenes we only see the phallic subject from behind, and in both scenes the gaze of the male voyeur is routed through the gaze of women. The two scenes together make up "the full monty."

We can link this final shot in *The Full Monty* to the use of reaction shots in *Austin Powers*. As we will see next, in *Austin Powers* masculinity may not be learned from women, but it is modeled on a drag-king aesthetic.

Austin Powers: International Man of Mystery

In Mike Myers's first and classic *Austin Powers* film, our hero leaves behind the shagadelic revels of 1967 and enters a thirty-year cryogenic sleep in order to pursue the nefarious Dr. Evil (also Myers) through time and space. When he awakens, various British intelligence agents and his future partner, the delectable Vanessa Kensington, welcome Austin to the 1990s. Vanessa also warns him promptly that "a lot has changed in thirty years, Austin." Undaunted, Austin responds: "As long as people are still having premarital sex with many anonymous partners while at the same time experimenting with mind-expanding drugs in a consequence-free environment, I'll be sound as a pound!" Of course, Austin finds that safe sex and enforced monogamy are only the most obvious signifiers of what has changed since the groovy sixties in London. Confronting the brave new world into which he awakes, Austin discovers slowly that the time warp that propelled him into the future has also transformed him into a dinosaur whose own brand of English masculinity has come and gone. Inspired by the prospect of being the last of his kind, Austin dives into the nineties still wearing his Union Jack Y-fronts and hoping against hope that he can still find lots of willing "birds" to shag.

In a self-conscious nod to its own time-loop conceit, *Austin Powers* tries to carry forward into the 1990s the comic English masculinity from the 1960s and 1970s. Part Peter Sellers from *Casino Royale*, part Benny Hill or Frankie Howard, the character of Austin Powers is both a loving tribute to and a fond critique of the repulsive and lascivious "carry on" heroes of 1970s British comedy. The *Carry On* comedies of the 1960s and 1970s created a comic universe on the thin, very thin, premise of the ubiquitous appeal of the randy white Englishman, embodied most often in these films by Sid James. The *Carry On* comedies paired James, however, with a rather flaming counterpart played by Kenneth Williams, whose signature line, "Stop messing about," is echoed in Austin's naughty and nasal "Oh behave!" While Williams spends his time in these films running from matrons and other overpowering females (mostly played by Hattie Jacques), the James character usually tries to ditch his wife while propositioning busty nurses and curvaceous ingenues. These two forms of masculinity are depicted as interdependent: Williams's homoeroticism is tolerated by James, while James's homophobia is actively encouraged by Williams. In *Austin Powers* Myers brings these two "carry on" masculinities into one body with interesting and queer results. Inheriting James's randy disposition, Austin also channels Williams through his campy overuse of double entendres. By combining these two "carry on" roles, indeed, Myers exposes English masculinity as a peculiar combination of camp and compulsory heterosexuality.

While I will return later to the implications of this parody of national manhood, I want to focus here on the queerness of Austin's masculine affect and the drag-king effect of his mode of male parody. I do so precisely because the film does not reference these sources for its humor, even as it is positively meticulous in telegraphing to its audience the mainstream historical sources.[8] Austin's clothing, his fashion photography career, and his overall camp affect suggest that his imperfect masculinity owes much to gay male models of manhood, but his non-phallic, emphatically prosthetic, and endearingly cloddish attentions to women make his sexual identity look butch or kingy rather than "faggy." Furthermore, Austin's prosthetic masculinity is matched in the film by the fabulous prosthetic femininity of the "fembots," robotic killer females sent to shoot Austin. The fembots serve to locate an automated femininity that ensures that femaleness cannot be the signifier of the "natural" in the film. The drag-king effect becomes even more readable when Myers takes his parody of English masculinity beyond camp and adds phallic renunciation to the mix. As we see in the infamous penis-enlarger scene, Myers's particular genius lies in his ability to transform the rather unappealing and misogynist English comic masculinities of the 1960s into a new form of abject comic masculinity that bears a close resemblance to queer and sub-cultural forms of male parody.

In a film in which penis jokes are second only to jokes about flatulence, the penis-enlarger scene is the ultimate acknowledgment of the failure of the phallus. I want to read this scene closely to demonstrate the kingy effect of both phallic renunciation and what Myers refers to as "comedy torture." In some remarks about his comedic method in *Austin Powers*, Myers speaks of the effect of taking a joke much further than it should go.[9] Comedy torture, he says, comes from repeating something until it stops being funny and then repeating it some more until it becomes funny again. The line between comic and no longer comic is of course a thin one, but repeatedly in *Austin Powers* Myers finds exactly the right balance among repetition, overkill, torture, and comedy. In this scene a joke that points to Austin's failed phallic masculinity is repeated until it becomes the source of a new masculine power accessed through abjection.

In brief, the penis-enlarger scene begins when Austin goes to collect his belongings after being awakened from his long sleep and welcomed to the 1990s. Austin is handed his things piece by piece by a cloakroom guard, who presents him, finally, with a Swedish penis-enlarger. "That's not mine," Austin says to Vanessa. The officer now gives Austin "one credit card receipt for Swedish-made penis-enlarger signed by Austin Powers." Again Austin protests, "I'm telling you, baby, that's not mine!" The guard continues, "One warranty card for Swedish-made penis-enlarger pump, filled out by Austin Powers." Austin again protests, "I don't even know what this is! This sort of thing ain't my bag, baby." Then the guard clinches the scene: "One book, 'Swedish-Made Penis-Enlargers and Me: This Sort of Thing Is My Bag, Baby' by Austin Powers."

Here we witness Austin's castration under Vanessa's withering gaze. In this scene Austin reclaims his "kit," the bundle of accessories that were crucial to his sex appeal in the 1960s: the male-symbol necklace and crushed velvet suit with black pointy boots suggest the swinger, the sexy man about town, but the Swedish penis-enlarger suggests that the accessories are not the superficial markers of an invisible phallic potency; instead, they cover over a phallic lack. Austin is revealed by the law (represented by the guard) and in front of the desirable woman as lacking the equipment for phallic success, and as hopelessly sexist at a moment when women simply expect more. But rather than wilt or rebuild his masculinity in normative ways, Austin works his loser status up into an alternative mode of masculinity throughout the film. Danger may be his middle name, but his last name, Powers, speaks to the refusal of the logic of castration. This is

not to say that Austin repudiates lack; he revels in it. This point is driven home by the rivalry between Austin and his nemesis, Dr. Evil; in a parody of conventional spy film rivalries, in which two men compete for phallic mastery, Austin and Dr. Evil achieve equal levels of incompetence. Dr. Evil may float around the earth in a phallically promising spaceship called Big Boy, but when he comes down to earth, he too finds that he is hopelessly and permanently out-of-date. The incompetence of Dr. Evil, matched only by Austin's spectacular knack for losing, ensures that this will be a film with no winners.

Furthermore, Austin's lack of phallic authority does not diminish his ability to attract Vanessa's attention. The penis-enlarger scene, then, is proof positive that her attraction to Austin does not depend on phallic endowment. In fact, Austin becomes attractive to her precisely because he lacks it and therefore has to try harder, has to seduce her through laughter rather than phallic mastery. In one scene, for example, Vanessa declares her absolute abhorrence of Austin's randy attentions and tells him: "Mr. Powers, I would never have sex with you, ever! If you were the last man on earth and I was the last woman on earth, and the future of the human race depended on our having sex, simply for procreation, I still would not have sex with you!" To which Austin responds quickly: "What's your point, Vanessa?" He refuses to understand her rejection of him, refuses phallic mastery, but also playfully turns the intensity and hyperbole of her rejection into a potential for further comic interaction.

Vanessa's responses to Austin are recorded in minute detail in this film. As if to emphasize the subtle but momentous shift in gender dynamics that the film reveals, the comic power of the penis-enlarger scene depends absolutely on a series of reaction shots from Vanessa. For example, as Austin plays out the comedy torture of repudiating and then accepting the penis-enlarger as his own, as his "bag, baby," Vanessa responds with a range of reactions, from amused, to disdainful, to amused again, to imperious, and finally to seduced. The director, Jay Roach, has commented that the film could easily have been 10 percent comic action and 90 percent comic reaction shots.[10] This cinematic emphasis on the reaction shot here, as in *The Full Monty*, reverses the formula of the masculinist action film, in which very little time is spent on reaction; the reaction shot, of course, records and actively engages the presence of an other, and in this film it acknowledges rather than obliterates the comedic contribution of the mostly female other to the comic success of the film. Vanessa plays earnest to Austin's superficial, knowing to his ignorant, competent to his inept, and prim to his lascivious. She is not simply his opposite or his stooge; she is a filter for the audience's own responses, and, again as in *The Full Monty*, she provides a powerful image of female voyeurism.

Abject English Masculinity

In terms of his dependence on the reaction of others, his camp femininity, and his demonstrably prosthetic, presumably charming, butch masculinity, Austin Powers is marked irredeemably as queer. And with his foppish clothes and fake chest hair, his penis-enlarger and off-color jokes, he represents a variation of drag-king masculinity. Austin's name, however, specifies his masculinity by linking Englishness (the Austin Healey car) to power and suggesting that white English masculinity, perhaps more than most masculinities, relies heavily on prosthetics, tricks, and bad jokes. As I have suggested, *Austin Powers* also continually recalls its debts to other generic traditions (the spy film, British comedy), and its hero is marked throughout as a winner from the sixties who becomes a loser in the nineties. Through the mechanism of the time loop, *Austin Powers* remarks on and indeed participates in the recent English nostalgia for the sixties, a decade not remembered as one step removed from the ravages of World War II and the decline of empire but glorified as the good old days, when England had just "won the war."

By making the sixties into the fab world of swingers, *Austin Powers* participates fully in the romance of this golden age. Yet by remarking throughout on Austin's obvious repulsiveness—his bad teeth being a metonym for unappealing white English masculinity—the film seems aware of the cultural agenda at work in harking back to an all-white England and erasing other memories of the sixties. While the romance with a depoliticized sixties is somewhat understandable in the context of the anxieties generated by a

multiracial and postcolonial England in the nineties, what is the appeal of the British sixties to American audiences? Specifically through the *Austin Powers* films, American audiences have invested heavily in the idea of England as a place untouched by civil rights strife and racial disharmony; *Austin Powers's* shagadelic vision of sixties' love fests replaces the more threatening history of a postimperial Britain torn by race riots and struggling with the pernicious anti-immigration legislation inspired by Enoch Powell's new populism. Furthermore, the advertising campaigns that accompanied the second *Austin Powers* film, *The Spy Who Shagged Me*, continued to sell England to American tourists as the land of the Fab Four, Carnaby Street, and Monty Python.

In 1999, in yet another summer comedy, American audiences lapped up yet another version of an idyllic England, a place emptied of people of color and rich in traditional values: this time the film was *Notting Hill*. This comedy of errors tells of an American slave to celebrity (Julia Roberts) who tries to escape into the anonymity of a bustling London neighborhood. Hugh Grant reprises his role from *Four Weddings and a Funeral* as the bumbling lover whose masculinity is understated, restrained, and quintessentially English. In *Notting Hill* he is contrasted favorably to the muscle-bound, bad-boy, American masculinity of Roberts's ex-boyfriend, played by Alec Baldwin, and his appeal continues to rely on what one critic has called "the social tactics of niceness, compliance and liberal tolerance."[11] Grant's "nice" model of manliness aspires to represent both Old World charm and New World sensitivity to women's issues. Setting the romance between the new woman and the "new" old man in Notting Hill also wipes out the memory of Notting Hill as the site of race riots and holds fast to the idea of England as a place that balances properly the charge of keeping a tradition alive while remaining in touch with contemporary culture. That Grant's character works in a charming old bookstore, a travel bookstore in fact, only completes the imperial fantasy of a Great Britain whose "greatness" resides in a learned cultural tradition that must be preserved in England and imported elsewhere by any means necessary.

Mike Myers, of course, is no Hugh Grant, in the sense that he deliberately pokes fun at this fantasy of

English masculinity. In the first *Austin Powers* film, Myers creates a wicked parody out of the American romance with white English manliness. The film's appeal, even charm, lies precisely in its acknowledgment of a sea change in sexual mores and in gender norms, a sea change, moreover, that leaves Austin's once dominant mode of masculine narcissism exposed to ridicule at every turn. No longer the international man of mystery from the sixties, in the nineties Austin becomes a lovable loser. But in 1999's overmarketed sequel, *The Spy Who Shagged Me*, his abject masculinity is recuperated and turned into potency once more. Even before the release of *The Spy Who Shagged Me*, Myers's mug appeared on numerous billboards selling Virgin Atlantic ("Shagatlantic, yeah Baby!"), Heineken beer, and other products. What, we might ask, happened between 1997 and 1999 to make *Austin Powers* into a marketing dream? How and why did the rotten-toothed antihero in need of a Swedish penis-enlarger morph from dated and dateless in the first film to hip and clueless in the second?

In many ways, the second *Austin Powers* film attempted to rewrite or reroute the cultural chain of transmission that begins with queer parodies of masculinity in drag-king comedies, passes into subcultural visibility through extensive press coverage (and more limited exposure for films like *Pecker*, by John Waters), and ends with male parodies of male masculinity consumed by mass audiences. In *The Spy Who Shagged Me*, not even the British *Carry On* comedies and spy farces occupy the position of original. Instead, the second *Austin Powers* movie retells the first one, meticulously repeating every clever joke and thereby making those jokes seem original. The difference between the two films reveals the ways that mainstream culture absorbs and disarms the subcultural material on which it depends. The first *Austin Powers* film tries to disarm both hero and villain in the espionage set piece, whereas the second makes hero and villain equally attractive and powerful. In the first film Austin fights to save the world for free love; in the second he saves it for multinational capitalism. The first *Austin Powers* movie clearly and humorously acknowledges and articulates a feminist critique of sexism that completely changes the constitutive forms of male masculinity. In the sequel Austin's sexism is no longer a mark of his anachronism; it has become his comic signature.

But this is not to say that *The Spy Who Shagged Me* is totally irredeemable. Cloning and doubling in the sequel remain as an echo of the powerful humor of the first film. In *The Spy Who Shagged Me*, Austin clones himself through a malfunctioning time machine; at the same time, Dr. Evil, not satisfied with his legitimate offspring, Scott, creates a clone of himself in miniature. "I shall call him Mini-Me," Dr. Evil says, in one of the film's few highlights. The presence of the clone self-consciously refers to the kingy effect of "repetition ad nauseam" and allows for a forceful critique of masculine authenticity. There is also another evil character in *The Spy Who Shagged Me*, an obese Scotsman called Fat Bastard, who is again played by Myers; the cumulative impact of having Myers in three of the main roles is to make masculinity into merely another of the film's special effects. Myers's monopolization of the male roles (with the exception of Mini-Me, played by Verne Troyer) seems to quote Eddie Murphy's virtuoso comic performances in *The Nutty Professor*, where Murphy plays the nerdy professor; his alter ego, Buddy Love; and Love's entire family (both Buddy Love and Austin Powers are also marked by grandiose allegorical names). Murphy's *Nutty Professor*, of course, is already a remake of the Jerry Lewis film. Lewis's film uses the trope of cloning to suggest that a perfect masculinity can emerge from the combination of two extreme forms—the nerd and the cad—but in Murphy's remake, the practice of cloning becomes a fascinating meditation on racial stereotypes as fetish figures for all of black masculinity.

The Spy Who Shagged Me refuses the Lewis method of resolving masculinity into a perfect whole; it offers us in many ways a counterpart to Murphy's clever representation of the stereotypes of black masculinity. If Murphy tries to expose both the pleasure and the danger of racial stereotyping, Myers tries to disarm white masculinity of the power it draws from racial stereotyping. In *The Spy Who Shagged Me*, the effect of cloning allows white masculine failure and ineptitude to spread across the entire narrative and breaks down all claims to masculine and white authenticity.

One scene explicitly registers the historical debt that seemingly authentic white masculinity owes to performative black masculinity: Dr. Evil and Mini-Me perform a rap duet that samples not only Grover Washington's "Just the Two of Us" but also Will Smith's version of the Washington original. In one comic move, Myers reveals the structure of "evil" white masculinity as homoerotic, narcissistic, and culturally derivative. The spectacle of Dr. Evil and Mini-Me rapping and dancing to a romantic duet both creates a drag-king effect in which one form of masculinity is expressed through and layered over another, and articulates the cultural debt that white heteromasculinity owes to the gay, black, and butch masculinities that it absorbs and erases.

The scene also reminds us that, significantly, *The Spy Who Shagged Me* has moved from England to America in location as well as in the cultural archive it draws from. For example, when we first see her, Austin's love object in the second film, Felicity Shagwell, is dancing to Lenny Kravitz's remake of "American Woman"; later, when Austin and Ms. Shagwell drive off together, he notes that the English countryside looks an awful lot like southern California, and references to American products like Starbucks coffee litter the script. Self-conscious as it may be, the Americanization of king comedy, in the case of this film, severely diminishes the set of opportunities that the film offers for the representation of masculine abjection. In terms of its box office success, its marketing tie-ins, and its mainstream appeal, *The Spy Who Shagged Me* has clearly relinquished the more subculturally informed aspects of the original and opted instead to feed into the gross-out comedy market seeking to fill the theater with teenage boys chortling at shit jokes. So the king method of repetition ad nauseam meets a sorry end by reneging on its promise of nonphallic mastery and humorous seduction. By the end of *The Spy Who Shagged Me*, we are no longer in the realm of king comedy, drag-king parody, subversive repetition, masculine abjection: Austin does not have to work hard to get the girl, he is no longer bewildered by the abrupt time zone shifts, nor is he playing off an English sensibility of white male decline; instead, he is an American imperial master of his domain. No longer a comic king, he has become another American king of comedy.

Conclusion

In this essay I have tried to trace the evolution of a sensibility that we can call kinging, which links mainstream critiques of normative masculinity with subcultural forms of parody, tribute, and satire. While refusing to trace a one-to-one or cause-and-effect relationship between mainstream culture and queer subcultural productions, I have argued that, like camp, kinging works through indirect and mediated influence. If camp can as easily be found in classic Hollywood film, 1960s drag-queen performances, and contemporary fashion shows, then we should also attend to the multiple sites in which the kingy distance between maleness and masculinity becomes visible with comic effects. I am also trying to allow for distinctions between mainstream comedies that prop up dominant masculinities and king comedies that aim at disarming them. The *Austin Powers* phenomenon illustrates for me not only the power of the kinging effect but also how short-lived the subversive ripples may be. While the first *Austin Powers* film revels in the phallic incompetence of its comic hero, the second film reduces his masculine abjection by cloning him and transforming him into a sex machine who temporarily loses his mojo. While the first film is marked by its cultural debt to other locations of king comedy, the second film, as sequel, turns the first one into an original. The mechanism of mainstreaming can be seen in precisely the way that the two films create a neat circuit of transmission that cuts out the subcultural, and even the historical, influences altogether. Significantly, then, the punch line in *The Spy Who Shagged Me* is not from a low-budget spy film, a drag-king performance, or even a *Carry On* comedy; it comes from the Tom Cruise blockbuster romance *Jerry Maguire*. Dr. Evil is reunited with Mini-Me after a near disaster, and he mimics Cruise telling his romantic partner in sign language, "You complete me." This gesture, hilarious as it is, unfortunately fails to parody *Jerry Maguire* and shows how far we have come from the king comedy acknowledgment that gender is a "copy with no original." This combo of Dr. Evil completed by his Mini-Me clone takes the sting out of king comedy and reminds the queer spectator that, once again, the joke is on us.

But as the summer's gross-out comedies give way to the winter's mawkish dramas, we can at least take comfort in our knowledge that *Austin Powers, The Full Monty*, and other king comedies have borrowed liberally from butch or non-male or penisless models of masculinity and have resigned themselves to a world in which the phallus is always fake, the penis is always too small, and the injunction to the masculine subject is not to "be" but to "behave." The work that falls to us, then, is constantly to recall the debts that the successful king comedies would rather forget, to remember, in other words, that behind every good king comedy is a great drag king.

Notes

1. Dick Hebdige, *Subculture: The Meaning of Style* (London: Methuen, 1979).

2. José Esteban Muñoz, "Pedro Zamora's *Real World* of Counterpublicity: Performing an Ethics of the Self," in *Disidentifications: Queers of Color and the Performance of Politics* (Minneapolis: University of Minnesota Press, 1999), 146.

3. Judith Halberstam, *Female Masculinity* (Durham: Duke University Press, 1998), 231–66.

4. Esther Newton, *Mother Camp: Female Impersonators in America* (1972; rpt. Chicago: University of Chicago Press, 1979), 106.

5. Judith Butler, "Imitation and Gender Insubordination," in *Inside/Out: Lesbian Theories, Gay Theories*, ed. Diana Fuss (New York: Routledge, 1991), 21.

6. See Andrew S. Horton, introduction to *Comedy/Cinema/Theory*, ed. Andrew S. Horton (Berkeley: University of California Press, 1991), 10–11.

7. Susan Jeffords, *Hard Bodies: Hollywood Masculinity in the Reagan Era* (New Brunswick, N.J.: Rutgers University Press, 1994).

8. There are even Web sites listing the multiple references to other spy films, English comedies, and James Bond spoofs in the *Austin Powers* films. One Web site (www.frankwu.com/AP2.html) meticulously traces every joke back to its source. Thanks to Lauren Berlant for directing me to this site.

9. *Austin Powers: International Man of Mystery*, DVD version, New Line Cinema, 1997.

10. Ibid.

11. Jonathan Rutherford, *Forever England: Reflections on Race, Masculinity, and Empire* (London: Lawrence and Wishart, 1997), 140.

29.
TRASH, CLASS, AND CULTURAL HIERARCHY
Laura Grindstaff

Part of the larger trend toward reality programming, daytime talk shows have proved to be one of the most controversial television genres of our times. When friends and acquaintances first learned that I was conducting this research, they responded with a predictable mixture of fascination and distaste—it was as if I had infiltrated a cult or an underground drug ring. And most took for granted that I would approach talk shows much as one might approach a cult or an underground drug ring: as a social problem in need of a solution.

I have not done that in this book. Instead, I have been concerned with the ways in which talk shows make stars and experts out of ordinary people and, in the process, produce ordinariness as something both similar to yet distinct from conventional stardom and expertise. I have been interested less in the question of how specific topics and issues are represented on talk shows, or in who watches them and why, than in the work that producers do in translating taken-for-granted, class-based assumptions about ordinary people into extraordinary performances onstage. Key to this translation is the assumption that ordinariness is associated with emotion (the body) and with the private life world of personal relations, while expertness is associated with rationality (the mind) and the public realm of social relations. At the same time, talk shows trouble these distinctions, elevating laypeople to expert status, and prioritizing forms of expertise that are themselves rooted in personal experience to varying degrees.

In many ways, the work of producing a talk show has much in common with other forms of media production. Like journalists, producers have beat territories that they cover on a regular basis, deadlines that they have to meet, and routine channels for securing participants. They must orient simultaneously to the constraints of the media organization (the need for certain kinds of stories told in certain kinds of ways) and to the constraints of the outside world (the availability, willingness, and performative competence of guests, ordinary and expert alike). Like the producers of late-night celebrity talk, producers of daytime talk must generate lively interaction among participants in order to deliver good television. This is partly a function of the topic itself, partly a function of the strategic juxtaposition of panelists, and partly a function of backstage preparation and coaching. At the same time, because of what ordinariness signifies, lively interaction looks somewhat different on daytime talk shows than it does elsewhere on television, and its orchestration poses some unique challenges to producers behind the scenes. Significantly, the things that they do to elicit a dramatic money shot—targeting people experiencing a conflict or crisis, orchestrating surprises and confrontations—can lead to a volatile production context and exacerbate the tension between scriptedness and spontaneity that producers love to hate.

As we have seen, producing the money shot requires a certain amount of emotional labor from producers. As Hochschild (1983) observes, the commodification of emotion occurs whenever feelings enter the marketplace and are bought and sold as an aspect of labor power. In effect, producers are buying the emotional performances of guests with their own commodified displays of sympathy and friendship, in combination with more tangible rewards like television exposure and free vacations. Sometimes these displays are genuinely felt, but often they are not since the conditions of workplace speedup tend to foster a disjuncture between display and feeling—what Hochschild calls *emotive dissonance*. Speedup demands that workers "make personal human contact at an inhuman speed" (Hochschild 1983, 126), and producers respond by falling back on surface acting, relying on situations in which underlying conflict is already built into the topic, and foregrounding the material benefits of participating in their interactions with guests. Emotive dissonance is further encouraged by the cultural and socioeconomic distance between producers and guests, especially at trashy shows like *Randy*. As the profile of guests shifted from middle to lower class, and as the money shot consequently grew more hardcore, it became increasingly difficult for producers to empathize with guests, both for personal and for professional reasons.

For Hochschild, emotion management in commercial contexts is largely a middle-class phenomenon, most prevalent in quasi-professional occupations (nursing, social work, bill collecting, insurance, sales, etc.) that require extended personal contact with the public and that involve the production of a particular emotional state in others.[1] Middle-class women tend to dominate these occupations, according to Hochschild, because they are taught from a young age to be more cooperative and to adapt to the needs of others and because the general economic subordination of women means that women often make a special resource out of feeling, both on and off the job. For women, deep acting has high "secondary gains," and thus, as with others of low status, it is in women's interests to be good actors (Hochschild 1983, 167). But men do institutionalized emotion work, too, albeit of a different sort. Whereas women often manage feeling in the service of "making nice," men are more likely to manage feeling in order to persuade, enforce rules, or secure compliance (see Hochschild 1983, 162–98). By any of these criteria, talk-show producers, women and men alike, are emotional laborers par excellence. They simply reverse

the normal functioning of the work, which is to discourage rather than to encourage "a scene."

If managing emotion is construed as a largely middle-class phenomenon, one in which women play a central role, the work of performing or embodying emotion is presented on daytime talk shows as a largely working- or lower-class phenomenon, also one in which women play a central—although increasingly a less central—role. In contrast to the performances of experts, who are understood to be more distanced and dignified participants, it falls to "just folks" to display the feeling that producers so carefully cultivate, to deliver the scene that in everyday (non-televised) life emotional labor is supposed to diffuse or prevent. The link between class and the particular type of emotional expressiveness that talk shows promote is clear enough in the way the genre changed over time and in the current distinction between classy and trashy variants. Classy shows like *Diana*, featuring more serious topics, are devoted to a more or less tasteful version of the money shot. They bear the imprint of the self-help recovery movement and the rise of popular psychology as well as of mainstream feminism and other identity-based social movements of the 1960s and 1970s. Trashy shows like *Randy*, on the other hand, which prioritize conflict and confrontation, overlay these same influences with a distinctly tabloid brand of emotional display, one that is perceived by critics to be excessive, transgressive, and out of control. Trashy shows produce a hardcore version of the money shot, and they garner high ratings because they "shock and amaze," much like the nineteenth-century freak show. They shock and amaze not so much because they exhibit anomalous bodies, however. When friends tell me that they cannot believe that real people actually get up there and do those things on national television, they are marveling at the transgression of taken-for-granted codes governing normative public conduct. Part of what I have tried to do in this book, then, is examine how producers normalize and make routine that transgression.

I also examine why real people do in fact get up there and do those things on national television, what happens to them along the way, and how they think about their participation. Guests are by no means uniformly pleased with their experience or with the strategies employed by producers to elicit from them the right sort of performance. Just as the circus side-show raised important ethical questions about the exploitation of human freaks, talk shows raise similar questions about the manipulation and exploitation of guests. Even when guests have no specific complaints about their experience, there is a larger question about the nature of their representation and how that representation is received by others. In the course of my research, I worried about the ethical dimensions of producers' work (and, by implication, my own). I still worry, for the issues involved are complicated and, to my thinking, not easily resolved. But, since this chapter is the final segment of this particular "show" and it's time for the "host" to wrap things up, it is to the matter of exploitation that I now turn.

Generally speaking, there have been two inter-twined concerns about daytime talk shows as voiced by critics in the media: the specific ways in which guests are manipulated and deceived by producers and the more generalized exploitation assumed to inhere in the act of airing one's dirty laundry in public—the former most strongly emphasized in the immediate aftermath of the *Jenny Jones* murder, the latter a more diffuse and longstanding concern that grew in direct proportion to the genre's increasing levels of sensationalism. Critics are right when they suggest that producers have an instrumental stance toward guests and their problems, that, as much as hosts or producers might stress educational, informa-tional, or therapeutic goals, talk shows are making entertainment out of ordinary people's lives, using their transgressions and hardships to garner ratings. Critics are also right when they point out that, for the most part, ordinary guests are drawn from trailer parks and tenements rather than country clubs or penthouse suites. As Barbara Ehrenreich (1995) has observed, you will not find investment bankers bicker-ing on *Ricki Lake* or see Montel Williams recommend-ing therapy to sobbing professors. But whether this is "class exploitation pure and simple," as she con-cludes, is a rather more complicated question. By what right do scholars and critics sit in judgment of the guest who bickers with her in-laws, admits to cheating on her spouse, or discloses the details of her acrimonious divorce on national television? More to the point, is it possible to separate a concern with

exploitation from middle-class notions of appropriate conduct and good taste?

Manipulation and Mass Mediation

The issue of manipulation on talk shows is far from simple or clear-cut. Manipulation occurs at both the individual and the structural levels, and, while some forms are relatively easy to identify and condemn, others are not. A certain amount of manipulation or deception is inherent in talk-show production since part of what producers do is convince people to tell their stories on television and then package those stories in ways that enhance their dramatic, unusual, or spectacular effect. Every phase of the process involves the transformation of an old reality into a new one. As a producer once said to me, "Asking a producer to describe manipulation is like asking a fish to describe the aquarium." Certainly, it is unethical for producers to lie to guests, make prom-ises that they have no intention of keeping, or lure guests onto a show under false pretenses. Such tactics have drawn considerable fire from critics in and outside the industry and made potential guests wary of participating. Producers, not surprisingly, deny these practices and insist that honesty is not only good ethics but good producing as well since it ensures a stronger bond with guests and, therefore, greater compliance. Nevertheless, producers can avoid outright deception and still not be completely forthright with guests or adequately prepare them for their performance.

The *Jenny Jones* murder was an indirect warning signal to the industry about the acceptable limits of deception in the service of obtaining a dramatic money shot. At the same time, the failure to ade-quately inform guests is not always or necessarily deliberate since the genre is predicated on spontane-ity and live-audience participation (and hence may involve unanticipated events) and since producers themselves may not know in advance all the details of a show. Even when they do know, the pace of produc-tion prevents them from reviewing every element with each and every guest—in fact, producers are trained *not* to "overrehearse" guests. Moreover, as we have seen, whether guests feel manipulated or deceived can have less to do with what actually happens to them onstage, objectively speaking, and more to do with a goodness of fit between expectation and outcome.[2] For producers and guests alike, there is a fine line between being informed and being uninformed, between honesty and deception, between exaggeration and outright distortion. Producers who encourage guests to exaggerate their emotions or prioritize the more sensational aspects of their stories do so in the name not of deception but of producing good television; this *requires* a certain level of manipulation. For their part, some guests exaggerate their emotions or embellish their stories with little or no encouragement from producers because they, too, know what constitutes good television within the parameters of the genre and are eager to prove their performative competence. Carried to an extreme, this can lead to deception of another sort: the deception of audiences by fake guests, which may or may not involve the complicity of producers.

There are many manipulative aspects to the production of daytime talk shows. As Gamson (1996) notes, talk shows can be a dangerous place to speak and a difficult place to get heard. But focusing on extreme instances of manipulation, as critics are wont to do, both reproduces the sensationalism that critics despise and ignores the ways in which manipulation is systemic, built into the routines and practices of the production process. It also masks the degree to which manipulation and mediation are fundamentally intertwined. The media do not simply reflect reality "out there." By definition, they mediate, even when, or perhaps especially when, it is real life that is purportedly being revealed. The ways in which talk shows mediate the experiences of ordinary people are not random or haphazard but systematic and patterned; talk shows institutionalize certain kinds of manipulation. In doing so, however, they have much in common with other forms of media—in particular the news. Paul Willis (1994, 38) has noted the sense of "colossal misinterpretation" often felt by people who find themselves or their experiences the subject of news reports. From the outside, the news may appear to have a certain "straightforward reasonableness," he writes, "but for those involved in the real events being reported, there is a characteristic, if muted, sense of colossal misinterpretation. The continuity of real

events has been sacrificed in the media to the continuity of much larger myths about the real."

The news media construct these myths in much the same way talk shows do: by decontextualizing issues and events, privileging individual solutions to complex, social problems, creating drama by juxtaposing opposing viewpoints, and emphasizing deviance, conflict, and violence over normal consensual relations.[3] Both talk shows and news media also require participants to speak in sound bites, perhaps the biggest point of frustration for the guests I interviewed, ordinary and expert alike. One industry veteran estimated, in fact, that the pressure to "cut the exposition and get to the sound bite" accounts for upwards of 80 percent of the manipulation on talk shows. Guests complain that the genre is too much show and too little talk, that the format precludes them from telling their stories as they feel their stories deserve to be told. They are right about this, but the problem is not unique to talk shows and is arguably much worse in the news. As one of my expert guests observed, he has greater opportunity to articulate and explain his point of view on talk shows, limited as the opportunity might be, than he does on the CBS evening news. "I could be on a national network news program for fifteen to twenty seconds," he said, "and I've been on [a talk show] for an hour! So which one is tabloid, which one is ethical? Well, from my point of view, I'd rather be on [a talk show]."

Like daytime talk, other forms of media are self-referential or "incestuous," recycling ideas, information, sources, and contacts. Almost all mass-media organizations seek to maximize profits, and most media professionals believe that a dramatic personal narrative will affect audiences in a way that abstract generalizations and statistical data cannot. It is for this reason that virtually all media texts—especially televisual ones—deliver their own particular versions of the money shot. All good television is built around moments of dramatic revelation. All television, from news and documentary to soap opera and sports, aims to stimulate people visually, give people a look, let people see for themselves—hence the importance of slow motion and the close-up. Indeed, to the extent that television is itself a visual discourse better suited to expressive than to informational content, devoted to making public and visible what would otherwise remain private and invisible (see Meyrowitz 1985), it can be seen as a kind of machine for producing the money shot. How else to explain the incessant news coverage of President Clinton's affair with Monica Lewinsky? Not since the coverage of John Wayne Bobbitt have I heard so much public discussion about a man's penis. There were moments when the biggest difference between *Larry King Live* and *Jerry Springer* was the fact that all the guests on King's show were white men with perfect teeth.

Desire for the money shot was the driving force behind the long-running *Candid Camera*, which deliberately placed ordinary people in extraordinary situations in order to provoke them into losing their cool, and it is the reason why shows like *The Real World* and *Survivor* do not just throw together a random collection of participants but carefully select a particular mix that will yield maximum dramatic potential (see Marsh 2000; Zurawik 2000). Desire for the money shot is what prompts Barbara Walters to ask, regardless of topic or interview subject, "So how does that make you *feel?*" and it is also what compels reporters to interrogate people immediately after they have experienced a terrible shock or tragedy—a form of ambushing if ever there was one. Randy himself made this point in our interview: "For ten years, I used to anchor the news, and every day we would jam a microphone in the face of someone who didn't ask to be on the air—someone coming out of the courthouse, out of a scandal—or you go into their homes, and you ask them a question. Sometimes they're humiliated, sometimes you embarrass their families, but you do it anyway—and we say it's OK because it's the news."

Critics are also concerned that talk shows blur the boundary between fact and fiction, that they deceive audiences and compromise truth for the sake of ratings. This is a charge to which industry insiders are particularly sensitive, especially when it comes to the matter of fake guests—after all, real stories told by ordinary people are the bedrock of the genre. Over and over, I witnessed staffers at both *Diana* and *Randy* deliberately reject people who appeared overly eager to get on TV, whose lives seemed to fit every topic under the sun, or whose stories kept changing from one day to the next. At the same time, the structural demands of the workplace can mitigate *against*

authenticity. Producers desire real guests with real problems, people who are not slick or practiced, who express genuine emotion, who are not media savvy, and who have never been on a talk show before. But these are also the guests who, in some ways, pose the greatest challenge to producers, for the very qualities that make them real make them more difficult to manage in routine ways. The pressure of deadlines, the nature of the topics, and the performances required of guests can push producers toward people who *are* media savvy, have had prior talk-show experience, and may even be actors faking their stories. Thus, the blurring of fact and fiction has structural causes and is not a conspiracy but a practicality.

At the same time, even the "realest" of guests are inserted into a theatrical context that fictionalizes their performances to some degree, and fictionalizing of this sort occurs in news, documentary, and reality programming, too—in the selection and juxtaposition of images, the choice of music and narration, the presence of cutaways and reaction shots, the artful shaping of story lines, and the things people say (and possibly lie about) on camera. As Randy said about news reporting, "When I did the news, how many times did people lie to me? Every day if I interviewed a politician." Likewise, a former cast member of *The Real World* admits that he was not "entirely himself" on the set and that neither were the other participants. Even if they had been, the final portrait might well have conveyed something else. According to Marsh (2000), the amount of raw footage shot on *The Real World* is so vast that each twenty-two-minute episode takes an entire month to assemble. She describes the show as "a cut and paste version of reality" exhibiting a "surprising degree of manipulation." "[They get] the footage they need for the ends they want" (76), one cast member told her. Former participants on *Big Brother* have lodged similar complaints in the press, claiming that they were "manipulated into stereotypes" and had become "pawns in a game" (McCann 2000). These charges would no doubt sound familiar to vérité filmmaker Craig Gilbert, as they are remarkably like those of the family members featured in his PBS documentary series *An American Family*, on which *The Real World* is based (see Gilbert 1988a, 1988b).[4]

The most significant feature that talk shows share with other media, however, is the tendency to deny ordinary people routine access unless they engage in exceptional behavior. Talk shows are by no means alone in this regard. Because ordinary people exist largely outside the official channels and established routines of newsmaking and the entertainment industry, they must do and say *extra*ordinary things to gain entry. Gans (1979) noted long ago that experts and officials constitute between 70 and 80 percent of all individuals appearing in the U.S. domestic news media, both print and electronic, while ordinary people obtain about a fifth of the available time or space. Aside from a small percentage who are voters or survey respondents, these ordinary people are newsworthy precisely because they are disruptive or deviant. Not being naturally newsworthy for *who they are* (as is the case with celebrities and other elites), ordinary people gain access to media more because of *what they do*, and notions of unusualness, disruptiveness, and deviance play a crucial role in determining this access (see also Hall et al. 1978; Sigal 1986; Langer 1998). Thus, the tendency of media critics to distance daytime talk as the "other"—as if talk shows were the only discourse "othering" ordinary people—is more than a little disingenuous. Talk shows simply exaggerate or throw into high relief the manipulative practices of other media forms.[5] News coverage of daytime talk shows—focused almost exclusively on murder, deception, and fraud—is itself good evidence of their common ground. Talk shows are especially maligned, however, because their strategies of manipulation are particularly visible, because they sometimes take manipulation to unacceptable levels, and, most important, because of the kind of ordinary people they target and the nature of the performances that these people are asked to give.

Ethics and Exploitation

The kind of ordinary people that talk shows target and the nature of the performances that they are asked to give bring me to the second ethical concern mentioned earlier: the issue of class exploitation. For some critics, the problem with daytime talk shows is not so much that producers deceive or manipulate guests but that they go after the most vulnerable and disenfranchised, making entertainment out of lives distorted by poverty and hardship. According to

Ehrenreich (1995, 92), "[Guests] are so needy—of social support, of education, of material resources and self-esteem—that they mistake being the center of attention for being actually loved and respected." While this characterization is clearly biased toward shows on the trashy end of the continuum, it is true that such shows do not attract just anybody. I once heard the executive producer of *Jerry Springer* say that his guests represent a "cross section of the American public." This is absurd, for the guests on *Springer* are no more a cross section of the American public than are the guests on *Nightline*.[6] Certain groups of people are more vulnerable to experiencing the kinds of problems that trashy talk shows capitalize on, and certain groups of people are more willing to bring these problems on national television.

The case of Sonny and her daughter, Jordan, is illustrative. They appeared on a *Springer* show about teen prostitution, along with several other family members. Jordan is nineteen, has a baby daughter, is pregnant with a second child, and has been working intermittently as a prostitute since the age of thirteen. She is currently living with her sixty-four-year-old boyfriend, who provides her with expensive cars, clothes, and whatever else she wants, including (so family members claim) drugs and clients. It was Jordan who first contacted producers in response to a plug. Initially, the show was supposed to feature a confrontation between the elderly boyfriend and Sonny, the mom. Sonny was to accuse the boyfriend of being a pedophile and a pimp and to tell him to "get the hell out of my daughter's life" or risk arrest for solicitation. But the boyfriend got cold feet and disappeared from his hotel room the morning of the taping. So producers quickly reframed the confrontation, substituting Jordan's uncle Casey (Sonny's stepbrother) for the other man. Bisexual, addicted to crack, and allegedly a prostitute himself, Casey told producers that his very first girlfriend—a call girl murdered by a serial killer—actually helped Jordan secure her first trick. He admitted that he, too, introduced his niece to "trustworthy" clients on occasion, but only to save her a fate like the girlfriend's. He claimed that Sonny, the mom, secured Jordan tricks for the same reason. So the conflict was between Sonny and her stepbrother, Casey, each accusing the other of prostituting Jordan.

Ehrenreich's assertion that talk shows take lives distorted by poverty and hold them up as entertaining exhibits rings painfully true here. Yet the show itself represents but the tip of the iceberg when it comes to the hardships that some guests face. Now thirty-seven and on permanent disability because of multiple sclerosis, Sonny never knew her biological father and was raised by her alcoholic mother and stepfather. A white woman, Sonny says she was raped at the age of seventeen by a black man and conceived Jordan as a result, but, because she refused to give the child up for adoption, her family accused her of being a "nigger lover" and disowned her. Stepbrother Casey was the only one who stood by her. Sonny then entered a bad marriage with an abusive white husband, whose sister was also a prostitute. Sonny is currently divorced, living with her mother, and, before going on disability, worked as a housekeeper in a large hotel. She says that she did her best raising Jordan but has never been able to control the girl. As she put it, "Sometimes you have choices of where you live, and how your kids are raised, and what they're raised around. I had no choices because this family is into drugs, and prostitution, and everything else—that's what Jordan's had to get around."

The lives of certain other guests were no less difficult. Winona, who went on *Randy* to be confronted by her two daughters for child abuse, was adopted as an infant and raised in a well-to-do but strict religious home. As a teenager, she was sent away to boarding school, where she was gang-raped, became pregnant as a result, and was forced to give the baby up for adoption. She later married an abusive man and became severely depressed and alcoholic. Now in her late forties, Winona lives in the rural South; she has no steady income and no telephone. For her part, Anitra went on *Jenny Jones* to confront her siblings, who accused her of being a bad mother because her only daughter had been molested by her boyfriend and subsequently placed in foster care. Anitra describes her own childhood as "traumatic." Her mother was an exotic dancer, and the two were constantly on the road, living mostly out of cheap hotels.

Is it ethical for producers to put such individuals onstage? Does it matter if they are consenting adults, willing participants, regular talk-show viewers? If they have prior talk-show experience? To paraphrase a former *Geraldo* producer, tricking guests into going on a talk show is like tricking people into swimming: if they've ever seen water, they know that they are going to get wet. The particular circumstances surrounding a guest matter, of course. People who are, say, suffering from psychiatric disorders are probably not in the best position to make a decision about whether to appear on national television, regardless of how much or how little they watch talk shows. The same goes for those normal guests whose experience of loss, betrayal, victimization, or abuse is acute, recent, or overwhelming. For producers (or, worse yet, these guests' friends and family members) to capitalize on their vulnerability seems clearly unethical and exploitative.

But what about guests who are more or less mentally stable or whose conflicts and problems are not fresh or raw but ongoing and longstanding? What about guests who, in the absence of being duped or deceived by producers, *choose* to air their dirty laundry on television? What about guests who are simply poor or lower class? Are they, too, atypically vulnerable such that we can speak of their participation on talk shows as exploitative? What if guests themselves do not see it this way? In an essay about the ethics of nineteenth-century freak shows, Gerber (1996) asks by what right we sit in judgment of such people as the fat lady who displays herself for profit. The same question obviously applies to certain guests on trashy talk shows. In both cases, as Gerber points out, one runs the risk of condescension.

In the case of freak-show exhibits, people with physical anomalies faced extreme ostracism and stigmatization, which effectively limited their opportunities for work and social interaction. This larger context of oppression leads Gerber to conclude that choice on the part of human exhibits was so constrained that freak shows can never be seen as anything but exploitative. Is this how we should think about the choices of Sonny or Winona? Even individuals who have everything going for them often make poor choices, and *Randy* guests could hardly be said to have everything going for them. Nor does a person need to experience exploitation consciously in order for it to exist. Whether one considers talk shows exploitative might depend not only on the attitude or motivation of specific guests but on the attitude of audience members toward the genre as a whole. On the other hand, unlike sideshow freaks, talk-show guests do not earn a living from their performances, and, if a guest wants to participate and has not been coerced by producers, what right do critics have to insist that she is being exploited, regardless of what audiences think? How paternalistic are we willing to be? Talk shows are not some special arena of victimization here. Choice can never be other than a relative concept, for, in a society characterized by structural inequality, the choices of those at the bottom are never as free as the choices of those at the top.

There are no right answers to these questions. Some producers I interviewed actually insisted that putting stories of conflict and abuse on television was a positive thing for society. Tyler, formerly with *Jerry Springer*, said that television had an ethical responsibility to portray all kinds of reality, not just the reality represented by *Leave It to Beaver* or *Ozzie and Harriet*.

"Is everything in life good?" she asked me. "No. The reality is most people are miserable. This is not an Ozzie-and-Harriet world, and any talk show that tries to make life look like *Ozzie and Harriet* is being irresponsible. Because there are both sides. There are the happinesses, the joys, the overcoming tremendous odds, that sort of thing. But there's also the misery and the conflict and the hatred that is such a big part of humanity. And I think it would be extremely irresponsible of television to portray only the happy side of life."

Saul Feldman made a similar point when he compared daytime talk shows to the sitcom *Friends*, suggesting that the latter was as exploitative as any talk show. At least a talk show is relatively honest in its portrayal, he said. "The people are not attractive necessarily; they are not well dressed; they're not wealthy; they're maybe not even very literate or thoughtful." By contrast, *Friends* is full of beautiful people leading beautiful lives, people who never seem to work yet always have plenty of money, people whose biggest worry is, in Feldman's words, "getting laid." And *Friends* has millions more viewers than even the top-rated talk show. "Now, what kind of influence does that have on all these viewers, week after week after week, to see those images of wealth and privilege?"

Of course, *no* television show presents life as it really is, talk shows no less than sitcoms. The problem with such arguments is that a show like *Randy* does not simply portray life's hardships. It portrays a narrow range of hardships (mostly sexual and family conflict) represented by a narrow range of people (mostly poor or working class) who perform these conflicts in narrow, predictable ways—ways that rarely foster an empathetic response from audiences. The experiences of guests are too decontextualized for empathy. *Randy* producers tend to "cut the exposition and get to the sound bite" in such a way as to preclude most everything but a brief spurt of trashy behavior. As a result, it is difficult to relate to guests and their problems; there seems to be no sensible way of responding save to laugh or feel contempt. Thus, even if we agree that the media should portray the bad as well as the good in life, it is important to ask what kind of badness gets represented, who represents it, how, and with what consequences. At the same time, it is important to reiterate that producing the money shot is not a deliberate act of class exploitation on the part of producers necessarily but is mandated and made possible by a variety of institutional and generic needs as well as by a more general media structure that excludes many populations from public visibility and, therefore, feeds them willingly, if ambivalently, into a genre that exaggerates their lower status.[7]

As Seen on TV

Talk shows appear especially exploitative if one does not see media exposure (particularly *that* kind of media exposure) as a fair trade-off for whatever consequences guests incur by participating. People often wonder why guests do it, why they are seemingly complicit in their own degradation. This wonderment is clearly directed more toward guests on the *Randy* end of the continuum since classy shows typically are not degrading (at least not in the same way or to the same degree) and the motivations of their guests are easier to understand. Guests on trashy shows tend to have less legitimate motivations: they may have an ax to grind, a secret to reveal, or a score to settle; they may have acting or modeling aspirations, enjoy the trappings of celebrity, want a free vacation, or just want to be seen on TV. Of all these reasons, it is the desire for television exposure that most confounds critics. Unlike the participants on the primetime reality-based shows *The Real World, Road Rules,* or *Survivor*, talk-show guests raise not only the question of why ordinary people want media celebrity but also the question of why they are willing to accept it on such unflattering terms.

As with the issue of exploitation, there are both individual and structural explanations to consider. One answer, implied in the discussion presented above, is that guests are so poor or needy or screwed up that they mistake media attention for compassion and respect. Another possibility is that some guests do not see anything wrong with discussing their personal lives or expressing their emotions on television. "Everybody has problems," Lori, a *Randy* guest, told me, "and there's nothing wrong with expressing them on television in front of other people." Moreover, guests understand at some level that they are playing roles and thus can distance themselves from their own trashy behavior, displacing it onto the larger theatrical context. Even Joanne, a *Randy* guest who went on the show to express her "real, natural, gut feelings" toward a woman she despised, was playing a role and a stock one at that: the *genuinely outraged guest*. She knew that producers wanted her to express raw emotion onstage, and she complied. Generally speaking, the degree to which guests are self-conscious about their role-playing appears to increase as the characters they play grow more melodramatic or cartoonish; guests seem to have an easier time dissociating self from role when the level of exaggeration is high.

But the most obvious explanation, and one that does not by definition exclude the rest, is that guests who desire television exposure want to leave a mark on the world, however small or fleeting or disdained. Guests do not say this in so many words, but I believe it to be true and not so difficult to understand. Most people want to feel that who they are and what they do matter to others. They want to be noticed; they want recognition or validation; they want to be part of something larger than themselves. The desire to leave a mark is surely common to all classes and strata of society, even if the specific avenues for fulfilling it are not. Professors write books; politicians author laws; athletes win medals; directors make films; artists make art; activists effect social change. Some ways of making one's mark on the world are clearly more

prestigious and far-reaching than others. The elite or truly gifted leave entire legacies and dynasties behind them. Their actions become part of the "official" historical record, their names memorialized on monuments and museums, buildings and street signs, parks, rivers, and towns.

Most ordinary guests on daytime talk shows have more modest aims and arenas of influence. Those on a show like *Randy* do not hold official titles or professional jobs. They have little connection to, or experience with, the production of official knowledge, whether in the realm of science, art, politics, or law. Universities, Wall Street, Congress—these institutions are not necessarily perceived as relevant to, or part of, their everyday lives. But television is. Television is a discourse that they know. Many of them, in fact, know it quite intimately, at least as consumers, for television viewing is inversely correlated with social class. Writing a book or authoring a law is not really on the map for most *Randy* guests. But starring in a talk show is. And, at some level, it does not much matter that the role is a negative or unflattering one, for the larger goal is simply to participate in the discourse and be part of the scene. As with many of the audience members I saw asking questions at tapings, and in contrast to experts, such guests could be said to exemplify a ritual as opposed to a transmission model of communication (see Carey 1989), where the mere act of conveying a message is more important than what, specifically, gets said.

It is very likely that guests on *Randy, Ricki Lake*, or *Jenny Jones* would prefer media exposure on more dignified terms. Guests, even those who respond to plugs, need a lot of persuasion. The better part of producers' emotional labor at *Randy* is spent convincing people to do the show or to follow through with their initial impulse to volunteer. No doubt, such folks would prefer starring roles in *The Real World, Road Rules*, or *Survivor*. But most talk-show guests are not hip and attractive enough for these shows. Moreover, they would have to compete with thousands of other people and do much more than make a telephone call to apply. Despite the less prestigious nature of talk shows, guests allow themselves to be persuaded to go on them because they want to be part of television and because, unless they break the law and appear on *Cops*, they see few other options for fulfilling this desire.

Talk-show guests are clearly not the only ordinary people seeking television exposure these days. Thirty-five thousand eager applicants submitted audition tapes to MTV in 1999, hoping to get on *The Real World*. Since its debut in 1992, the show has chronicled forty-five months in the lives of sixty-three young adults, capturing a marriage, an abortion, a gay commitment ceremony, a drunk-driving episode, a physical assault, and "thousands of bitchy spats" (Marsh 2000, 71). As one former participant told Marsh, "Everyone in my cast wanted to go into entertainment, and they were all using the show as a springboard" (76). Likewise, it is not for the prize money alone that people agree to be stranded together in remote locations, suffer physical exhaustion, and engage in a wilderness version of smarmy office politics, as they are in *Survivor*. Nor was it just greed that compelled Darva Conger to compete with fifty other women for the privilege of marrying a total stranger on FOX's *Who Wants to Marry a Multi-Millionaire*—and then attempt to reclaim her dignity by giving dozens of television interviews and posing nude in *Playboy*, all the while pleading to be left alone (as she put it in her interview on *Good Morning America*, "I'm a private person, and I just want my life back"). Twenty-three million viewers tuned in to watch the TV marriage, while the final *Survivor* episode clocked a record 58 million, the most-watched program of 2000 next to the Superbowl. (More people watched *Survivor* than even the Academy Awards—which some commentators took as proof that viewers prefer watching ordinary people compete for money rather than celebrities compete for Oscars.) Of course, once an ordinary person stars in a primetime series and is watched by 58 million viewers, the line between ordinariness and stardom begins to break down. Cast members from the middlebrow reality shows appear routinely on morning and late-night talk shows, grace the covers of mass-circulation magazines, do commercial endorsements, travel the college lecture circuit, and are represented by agents and publicists. (In Britain, where *Big Brother* was a hit, the show's best-known contestant is said to be worth £1 million in endorsements annually.)[8] So great is the media attention paid to the participants on reality shows that I would not be surprised if celebrities start passing themselves off as ordinary people in order to get on TV rather than the other way around.

Media coverage or exposure is a powerful form of validation in our culture, for ordinary people no less than celebrities, experts, politicians, and activists of various sorts. As Larry Gross (1994, 143) puts it, "Representation in the mediated 'reality' of our mass culture is in itself power . . . [and] those who are at the bottom of the various hierarchies will be kept in their place in part through their relative invisibility." Yet, when people do gain visibility, it is only by submitting to the implicit rules of the media industry, by conforming to journalistic notions of what constitutes a good story, a dramatic event, or a compelling performance. This submission is required of all media participants, not just ordinary people on daytime talk shows. How many experts on *Nightline* actually *like* debating international politics in thirty-second sound bites? How many black actors on television *prefer* stereotypical bit parts as sidekicks or comic relief? How many white women *opt* to play the passive love interest rather than the take-charge protagonist in the latest Hollywood film? Clearly, even experts and celebrities are manipulated and constrained by media discourse in systematic—and unequal—ways. To paraphrase Gamson (1996), seizing the microphone is a complicated sort of power in a media culture because the voice that emerges is never only yours: if you speak, you must prepare to be used. To this I would add that not all ways of being used are equal and that, the more invisible within mainstream media—by virtue of one's political activities and convictions, physical attractiveness, education/credentials, occupation, age, class status, sexuality, race, or gender—the "higher" the price of admission is likely to be.

When a category of people without a lot of power and resources suddenly gains visibility in popular discourse after having been largely ignored, the resulting portrait is rarely multifaceted or complex—at least initially. We have seen this principle at work with carnival freak shows, but there are other examples as well. Kano (2001) documents how, when women were first admitted to the kabuki theater in Japan, they had to enact ultrastereotypical versions of femininity in order to convey the notion of femaleness, which, up to that point, had been the purview of male actors.

Ironically, when real women took over, their biological status was not enough; they had to play exaggerated, male-defined versions of themselves.

Minstrel shows provide another clear example in relation to racialized representations of African Americans. One of the earliest points of entry of black culture into American popular entertainment, minstrel performances—which initially featured white actors performing in blackface—were hardly an accurate representation of blackness. With few exceptions, and in both comic and sentimental variants, minstrel shows were stereotypically racist, positioning African Americans as inferior to whites. Even when African American actors became part of the minstrel tradition, their physiognomic status as *racial other* apparently was not "other" enough, for their roles were no less stereotypical, and they too performed in blackface (see Lott 1993; Lhamon 1998). The parallel here to the participation of the lower classes on trashy daytime talk shows is clear: when real nonexpert, noncelebrity people play the role of ordinary guest, their actual ordinariness cannot stand on its own and be presented as such but must be re-presented as a stereotypical facsimile of lower-class life. Indeed, talk shows are often compared to freak shows, but they are also like modern-day minstrel shows, with guests performing in "poorface."

Consequently, the issue of realness and authenticity in relation to guests on daytime talk shows is not strictly limited to the case of the aspiring actor faking her story *but rather extends to the real ordinary guest as well.* In the world of daytime talk shows, excessive emotional and bodily displays operate implicitly as markers of class difference, not because they come naturally to guests necessarily (if they did, producers would not spend so much time preparing guests for their roles), but because they are consistent with existing cultural stereotypes and thus are actively constituted as such through the backstage activities of the production process. Only by conforming to these markers do ordinary people have routine access to national television in the first place. Far from being neutral, then, the representation of "just folks" on daytime talk shows is shaped by their larger invisibility in media discourse as well as by the implicit rules and practices of the discourse itself. Talk shows are not and never have been a forum for expressing

the interests and urgencies of ordinary people *as* ordinary people since the very conditions that subtend their entry into television transform them into something else.

Trash, Class, and Distinction

In the case of trashy shows, the existing cultural stereotype to which guests are made to conform—that something else that they become—is perhaps best summed up by the pejorative label *white trash*. Of all people without a lot of power and resources in our culture, few are disparaged with quite the same sense of impunity as white trash. As Jim Goad (1997) puts it, "White trash are open game. The trailer park has become the media's cultural toilet, the only acceptable place to dump one's racist inclinations." From *The Beverly Hillbillies* to *Deliverance*, white trash have been stereotyped as stupid, lazy, shiftless, licentious, alcoholic, and prone to violence and inbreeding. Such stereotypes are uniquely American, the result of a complex racial history as well as the general failure to recognize social class as a central category of identity and consciousness outside the extremes of rich and poor.

On the one hand, as Bettie (1995, 140) notes, the phrase *poor white trash* upholds the existing racial hierarchy by suggesting that color, poverty, and degenerate lifestyle go together so naturally that, when white folks behave this way, "their whiteness needs to be named." White trash are traitors to their race because they are not "doing whiteness" properly. On the other hand, in bringing together two attributes normally separated in popular discourse—whiteness and poverty—the term foregrounds the class diversity among whites (reminding us that, while class privilege is associated with whiteness, it is not essential to it) and *belies* the ideology of white supremacy: if whites are naturally so superior, then how do you explain white trash (Wray and Newitz 1997)? *White trash* thus challenges the presumed superiority of whiteness, as well as the myth of upward mobility that goes with it, by making explicit the existence of class difference, and the operation of class inequality, per se.

In both cases, the primary function of invoking the term *white trash* is to solidify for the middle and upper classes a sense of cultural and intellectual superiority. According to Wray and Newitz (1997), white-trash stereotypes both serve as a useful way of blaming the poor for being poor and help distance middle- and upper-class whites from their guilt and animosity toward racial minorities by substituting a safe target believed to embody many of the same racist assumptions. *White trash* creates a new racial other, which, like racial others of old, is linked to notions of uncivilized savagery and thus occupies the primitive side of the primitive/civilized divide (see Newitz 1997; Torgovnik 1991).[9] As such, as Hartigan (1997, 51) points out, *white trash* is not simply a stereotype or a false preconception; rather, "it delineates a discourse of difference whereby class identities are relationally formulated." The white middle classes rely on the attributes embodied by *white trash* to distinguish themselves from the lower orders, in effect saying, *We are not that.* Like *primitive* and *civilized, trashy* and *classy* are oppositional and relational, helping define and reinforce one another.

For all these reasons, *trashy* as used in the talk-show context is not just about class, nor is it coterminous with the term *poor white.* While the latter denotes a specific socioeconomic status, *trashy* connotes an interlocking set of despised behavioral, cultural, and aesthetic qualities that can be applied to a broader spectrum of individuals—within a limited degree across color and, as the case of *The Beverly Hillbillies* proves, despite actual material circumstances. Recall the description of *Randy* guests provided by Brian, a *Diana* producer: "White trash, black trash, Hispanic—any kind of, like, low-caliber people. Physical violence is such a routine part of their lives. . . . It's, like, they fight all the time, and they're half drunk, I don't think you'd even need to offer them money to do it." Indeed, any guests who look, talk, or behave a certain way can be labeled *white trash* or *trailer trash* regardless of whether they are poor, white, or living in a trailer park because the term *white trash* contains such an excess of meanings, functioning to mark symbolic boundaries between groups rather than simply differences of race or class per se. As we know from Durkheim (1965), symbolic boundaries presuppose both inclusion ("us," desirable) and exclusion ("them," undesirable), and they survive only if they are repeatedly defended by members of the more powerful group. Of course, most *Randy* guests *are* in fact

lower- or working-class whites, but, in and of itself, this is not what makes them trashy, and this is not why critics object to their performances.

It is certainly a problem that a show like *Randy* makes white trash out of ordinary people, that it produces a cartoonish version of lower classness cut from the cloth of *The Beverly Hillbillies* rather than, say, *The Waltons.* Yet it is not just a concern with negative stereotyping that prompts critics to disparage the genre. Indeed, the vast majority of critics in the mainstream media rarely mention stereotyping at all, instead, like producers, reading the trashy performances of guests as authentic expressions of their natural inclinations. Nor are the majority of critics concerned about the potential manipulation of guests (although some are) or even about class exploitation (although, again, some are). Barbara Ehrenreich notwithstanding, the denigration of daytime talk shows appears to be motivated less by a concern with the material circumstances of guests than by a concern to enforce symbolic boundaries, a sense of distinction, what Bourdieu (1984) calls the *aesthetic disposition*—the separation of culture from nature such that the *nature* against which *culture* is constructed is whatever is deemed low, vulgar, coarse, common, generic, easy, etc. Bourdieu argues that culture is used to distinguish among social classes, but the political dimensions of this function are naturalized as matters of aesthetics or taste. Tastes are a practical affirmation of seemingly inevitable (because seemingly natural) cultural difference, which is why aesthetic intolerance can be, and often is, quite strong.

Talk shows undoubtedly got trashier as they got more personal and emotionally expressive, and they undoubtedly linked these qualities with lower-class folks in stereotypical and derogatory ways. In the binary organization that opposes mind to matter, culture to nature, and textuality to orality, *the body* is the domain in which the lower classes—and other others—have been allowed and encouraged to operate. Like women generally, blacks and white ethnic groups have been considered creatures of feeling, naturally inclined toward emotional display.[10] On the other hand, why should emotional and bodily displays be considered trashy? Concepts of aesthetic merit and appropriate conduct are *not* natural or universal; they reflect dominant class interests. The outcry against *Jerry Springer* is good evidence of this, and the fact that lots of lower-class people probably hate the show does not change the fundamentally class-based nature of the response.

For Bourdieu, the body is the most indisputable materialization of class taste as well as its most explicit battleground. Biological or physical differences are underlined and symbolically accentuated by differences in bearing, gesture, and behavior that express a whole relation to the social world. Culturally legitimate bodies reflect the bourgeois aesthetic that privileges restraint, control, distance, and discipline over excess, impulse, and sensuality, and certain bodies—those that defy social norms of proper size, dress, manner, speech, etc.—are by definition in violation of that aesthetic. At the same time, the signs that constitute the body and its distance from nature themselves appear grounded in nature so that "the legitimate use of the body is perceived as an index of moral uprightness, while its opposite, a 'natural' body, is seen as an index of 'letting oneself go,' a culpable surrender to facility" (Bourdieu 1984, 193).[11]

What is at stake in the struggle for distinction, then, as Bourdieu so aptly demonstrates, is the ability to establish a perceived distance from, and mastery over, the body and its material existence. The association of the lower classes with the body is both an embodied manifestation of class difference, grounded in historical-material reality, and the ideological means by which difference as hierarchy is justified. Middle-class disgust with daytime talk shows helps reproduce the hierarchy when it confuses the characterization of talk shows as overly emotional and excessive with a negative, moral evaluation of those characteristics.[12]

The taste-class nexus is, in turn, connected to the separation of public from private space. Like the aesthetic disposition, *the private*—a product of history, culture, and ideology—is defined naturally in moral terms. The private is constructed as sacred, inviolable, and exclusive. It is the space of bodily processes, intimate functions, the backstage preparation of self. So, when private matters spill out into public discourse—especially those private matters branded shameful, dirty, or polluting—it is perceived as a moral breech. The immorality lies not so much in the specific contents of private life as in the violation of the public/private boundary itself, the intrusion of the contents of one sphere into the space of the other. (As Bourdieu [1984, 56] puts it, "The most intolerable thing for those who regard themselves as the possessors of legitimate culture is the sacrilegious reuniting of tastes which taste dictates shall be separated.") Like the aesthetic dimensions of taste, the moral dimensions of privacy work to naturalize social and material privilege. In the United States, privacy and access to privacy—including, especially, private goods and services—are connected explicitly to wealth. Many poor people in this country know that when you depend for your existence on public assistance, there is no aspect of your private life—including your sexual and reproductive life—that is off-limits to public scrutiny, public surveillance, and public control. Ehrenreich (1995, 92) herself recognizes this when she observes, "It is easy enough for those who can afford spacious homes and private therapy to sneer at their financial inferiors and label their pathetic moments of stardom vulgar." If she had a talk show, she says, it would feature a different cast of characters and a different category of crimes: "CEOs who rake in millions while their employees get downsized" and "senators who voted for welfare and Medicaid cuts." This is a great idea, but booking guests would be quite a challenge since the ability to keep one's "private" affairs off-limits to public scrutiny is partly what constitutes the eliteness of elites to begin with.

Like distinctions between public and private space, class distinctions between culture and nature did not arise in a historical vacuum. Norms of emotional control and bodily discipline, so fundamental to bourgeois sensibility, emerged in the United States alongside larger social, economic, and cultural transformations during the latter half of the nineteenth century. During this period, massive immigration and a lack of established social traditions—in combination with the rise of a new monied class eager to distinguish itself from those below—made civility nothing less than a moral imperative (see Kasson 1990; Levine 1900). And, because industrialization and urbanization created sharp discontinuities between public and private life, drawing together in intimate proximity strangers of diverse backgrounds, one's personal conduct *in public* was of special concern. As etiquette manuals exhorted tact and respect for privacy, individuals attempted to be as inconspicuous and self-effacing in public as possible. This was especially true for upper-class white women, whose participation in public life was precarious, and for whom the stakes of transgression were high. According to Kasson (1990), laughing, loud or boisterous talk, demonstrations of affection, or expressions of anger were branded vulgar and indecent, considered proof of one's inferior breeding, as were staring, bodily contact, and other expressions of familiarity or overinvolvement in the affairs of others. Underlying these exhortations was an increasingly instrumental stance toward feeling, consistent with the greater demands for emotional control and the growing disgust for bodily functions evident in Western societies from the fifteenth century on (Elias 1994).

In the United States, the segmentation of the individual epitomized by rising standards of emotional control and the separation of private from public space paralleled the increasing segmentation of society, including a more rigid separation of elite from popular culture. In the antebellum period, the boundaries between different forms of art, entertainment, and performance were relatively fluid: minstrel shows shared the stage with Shakespearean drama, and mastodon bones were exhibited alongside paintings and sculpture (Levine 1988). But all this changed as culture underwent a process that Levine calls *sacralization*, whereby certain forms of high art, music, and performance were removed from their popular origins (in effect, rescued from the marketplace) and enshrined in official institutions controlled by wealthy patrons (see also DiMaggio 1982a, 1982b). Sacralization had profound implications not only for the content of cultural forms but also for venue, clientele, the reasons audiences attended, and the ways audiences were expected to behave: as people mounted the scale to high or refined art, they were expected to behave in a more refined (i.e., restrained) manner themselves. Sacralization thus changed the norms of engagement between actor and spectator, increasing the distance and hierarchy between them, and eroding "a communal and amateur spirit of participation in which the lower classes played a vital role" (Kasson 1990, 255). Eventually, the rules of middle-class gentility became the norm of public conduct

for everyone, and even the popular entertainments such as cabaret and vaudeville were similarly transformed. This was but one aspect of a more general process of professionalization in the late nineteenth century in which the systems of taste and canons of behavior embraced by elites—legal, political, economic, medical, and scientific as well as artistic and cultural—were increasingly separated from and elevated above the tastes and behaviors of the masses.[13]

Laura's Final Thought

Generally speaking, the commercialization of leisure that occurred at the turn of the twentieth century and the full-scale mass mediation of culture that followed had a leveling effect on distinctions between high and low culture (see Crane 1992). As a result, our notions of cultural hierarchy are more fluid today than they were in the past. Yet cultural hierarchy per se has not disappeared, and the struggle for distinction continues to be played out within the realm of mass culture itself in the ongoing debates between the serious and the tabloid media. Whereas the former have aligned themselves with the framework and trappings of science, the latter are excessive, sensational, and contradictory and draw heavily on the codes of melodrama. The tabloid media are focused on the personal and the proverbial, evoking a world in which notions of general morality are shared by all human beings regardless of social position and in which emotions play a deep and fundamental role (see Gripsrud 1992; Fiske 1992). This reflects in mediated form the character of working-class knowledge itself, which is said to focus on the immediacies of home, family, and neighborhood and emphasize concreteness, subjectivity, and orality (see Hoggart 1957). By contrast, the serious media emphasize knowledge that is abstract, rational, and impersonal. They traffic in public, not private, affairs, focus mostly on the doings of officials and other elites, and speak in the language of "truth," "fact," and "objectivity" (see Schudson 1978; Campbell 1991). Within the terms of this discourse, the print media have generally had a superior claim to scientific adequacy and are associated with literacy, whereas the visual image has been generally characterized as "soft" and linked with femininity or with the illiteracy of marginalized classes (Campbell 1991).

Historically, daytime talk shows have existed somewhere between the two forms, both reinscribing and blurring the boundaries between expert and ordinary, reason and emotion, public and private, serious and tabloid. Over time, as talk shows as a whole grew more sensational, a trashy/classy distinction developed internal to the genre itself, one that reproduced on a smaller scale many of the same boundaries. This "tabloid turn" is part and parcel of a more general popularization of the media landscape, in which even the serious media are said increasingly to resemble a daytime talk show. Some scholars and critics see this as a threat to democracy and civilization, symptomatic of a deep and possibly irreparable cultural failing (see Postman 1985; Mitroff and Bennis 1989; Ewen 1989). Randy remarked to me that more Americans know the words to the *Brady Bunch* theme song than to the national anthem. Kipnis (1996) notes that more people watch daytime talk shows than vote. If these things are true, then perhaps we really are "amusing ourselves to death," as Postman (1985) laments.

But, if more people watch daytime talk shows than vote, presumably this also has something to with the meanings that the genre makes available and with the meanings attached to the act of watching itself. In the case of *Randy*, this may involve little more than the gawk factor said to characterize the nineteenth-century freak show, where witnessing the difference of others serves to reassure spectators of their own superiority. But, on other shows, as Kipnis (1996) points out, underneath the marital sniping and tales of injustice are some serious questions: How do you act ethically when your desires conflict with someone else's? What is the personal price of conformity versus the social violence exacted on nonconformity? Is human nature at bottom selfish or benevolent? Such questions have a general relevance to viewers' lives, even if the particular circumstances or experiences of guests do not. Producers at *Diana* had a mandate to provide information that viewers could relate to and use, and perhaps they did this. At the same time, like the tabloid media more generally, talk shows are less about dispensing information in the classic town-hall sense and more about drawing moral boundaries through stories of hardship, transgression, and conflict. Like ritual, the stories can be valued as much for the sameness of the responses that they elicit as for

the quality or variety of information that they yield; the repetition allows audiences and guests alike to "enter into the game" using a familiar formula or code (Bourdieu 1984; Bird 1992). For this reason, the specific talk that occurs is subordinate to the larger performative context in which the talk is embedded, something that guests themselves, especially professional experts, do not always understand (not surprisingly since experts by definition have been trained to operate according to the logic of a different code). According to Meyrowitz (1985), the emphasis of television on expressive over informational content reflects the inherent bias of electronic versus print-based media, a bias that talk shows throw into high relief. In Meyrowitz's words, "Talk shows do not succeed because of talk … the 'learning' in these programs comes from the 'truth' and 'reality' inherent in human behavior and experience" (103).[14]

If more people watch talk shows than vote, I would also venture to guess that more people volunteer to be on talk shows—and other forms of television—than volunteer to get involved in their own communities or in official party politics. But to say that the mass media create apathy and lead people away from traditional forms of civic engagement is to miss an important point. People, especially the young and the poor, are not necessarily apathetic about politics because they watch too much television or because the "unreality" promoted by the media has become "our primary mode of reference" (Mitroff and Bennis 1989, 10). They are apathetic because they see official party politics as an insider game that has little direct relevance to their lives. Bourdieu and others have noted that one's investment in, and ability to influence the destiny of, an institution varies according to one's status within it. To explain the relation between status and political involvement, one must consider more than the objective capacity to understand or produce political discourse. One must also consider the subjective (and socially encouraged) sense of being entitled to be concerned with politics in the first place, of being authorized to talk politics, and of feeling at home with, *even caring to have*, this authorization. Not surprisingly, political participation in the United States is higher among men than among women, among older people than among younger, and among the upper classes than among the lower.

What is interesting about daytime talk shows is that they *do* afford a certain kind of political engagement with the world, but on popular rather than elite terms. The discourse of talk shows is not the discourse of the *New York Times*, for the popular aesthetic demands that its cultural forms have a local relevance and use, a certain perceived continuity with everyday life. I was reminded of this recently when I attended a rally protesting sexual violence against women. During the open-mike portion of the program in which survivors of sexual assault share their experiences of victimization with the audience, a woman in her mid-fifties revealed that she had been molested by her father as a child. Back then, she told the crowd, no one ever spoke of matters like incest; it was as if they did not exist. She first learned about incest from watching daytime talk shows. As she put it, "It was not until I heard those women talking on television did I understand that I was not alone or that there was a name for what had happened to me." To be sure, the emphasis of the media here on the private and the personal can be read as tabloidization, but it can also be read as bringing issues of import into the life worlds of ordinary people.[15] Of course, the meanings and messages of popular culture are not always or only progressive, and they may just as easily perpetuate as challenge oppressive social arrangements. Popular culture is not simply a space outside elite discourse for celebrating the culture of the masses or paying homage to a romanticized notion of class resistance. Rather, to paraphrase Bird (1992), popular culture is the symbolic order within which subordinate classes live their subordination.

There are serious problems with talk shows, as I have tried to document in this book. They give ordinary people a voice, but only a certain kind of voice, only under certain conditions, and only according to certain rules. In Foucauldian terms, they extend the visibility of marginalized groups, but the nature of this visibility simultaneously creates fresh opportunities for marginalization. At the same time, the critical condemnation of the genre as trashy and debased is not any less classifying than the genre's initial stereotypical association of emotional and physical expressiveness with ordinary people. However much a matter of consensus, this condemnation further contributes to the marginalization of guests when it confuses

middle-class notions of civility with morality and when it takes for granted a set of cultural codes in which divisions of taste mask and reinforce divisions of class. There are serious problems with talk shows, but there are serious problems with the "respectable" media, too, and even more serious problems with society at large. It is therefore important not to scapegoat talk shows for the activities and practices common to the media more generally or to use talk shows (or the media more generally) as a way of *not* talking about society's most pressing social problems. Certain talk shows might take advantage of people in poverty or distress, but they do not create out of whole cloth the conditions of hardship under which many guests live. Indeed, it is telling that those who *do* bear some responsibility for these conditions—politicians who oppose increased spending for welfare and public education, for instance—are among the genre's most ardent critics, as if to suggest that the real problem is the cartoonish display of poverty on television rather than the actual fact of poverty itself. There is no one factor responsible for the perceived decline of American culture, but, if I believed in such a decline and wanted someone or something to blame, talk shows are not the first place I would look.

Notes

1. As Hochschild notes, a great many jobs place emotional burdens on workers, regardless of class (which is one reason why *work* is defined as work and not play). For example, when work is boring and deskilled, as it is for the data processor or the factory seamstress, one may have to suppress feelings of anger, boredom, or frustration. But, while this is an emotional burden, it is not in itself emotional labor, for what is made into a commodity or resource is one's physical rather than one's emotional capacity. This is not to suggest that emotional labor is exclusively middle class. Consider, for example, the work of the personal servant, the prostitute, the Park Avenue doorman, or the waitress. These people, too, must do emotion work as a routine part of the job, especially when their clients or customers have greater status than they themselves do. Yet Hochschild is most concerned with forms of emotion work that have been removed from the private domain and placed in the public arena, where feeling is processed, standardized, and subject to hierarchic control by institutional mechanisms. And most jobs of this sort, she

insists, tend to be filled by members of the middle class. Hochschild suggests a connection here to class differences in socialization since middle-class parents tend to discipline their children via appeals to feeling and to managing feeling, whereas working-class parents tend to focus more on controlling behavior—differences in socialization that amount to different degrees of training for the commodification of emotion in commercial contexts (see Hochschild 1983, 156–61; see also Kohn 1963; Bernstein 1974).

2. Complicating this scenario is the fact that, when guests *do* feel manipulated because they have been unexpectedly humiliated or ridiculed, producers are often not the only ones responsible, at least from an ethical standpoint, for producers could never orchestrate a surprise confrontation without the complicity of the person who wants to do the confronting.

3. These patterns have been documented by, among others, Cohen and Young (1973), Tuchman (1978), Gans (1979), Gitlin (1980), Hartley (1982), and Manoff and Schudson (1986).

4. Gilbert wanted to document the "typical" American family in their natural setting in order to explore, as he put it to the Louds, both the ordinariness and the universality of their everyday lives. The cameras rolled every day, all day, for seven months, and the footage was assembled into twelve one-hour segments for broadcast on public television. Not only did the family agree to participate, but they approved a rough cut of each episode. But the press following the broadcast was largely negative, characterizing the Louds as shallow and dysfunctional, and the family blamed Gilbert for "setting them up" (see Gilbert 1988a, 1988b).

5. Langer (1992, 1998) makes much the same point about the similarities between the serious and the tabloid ("unworthy") news, arguing that they are different in degree, not in kind. As he writes, "The unworthy news may get its bad name, not because of its popularity or shameless persistence in bulletins, but because it is unruly, more openly acknowledging and flaunting devices and constructions which the serious news suppresses and hides. Perhaps, in the end, this is why the lament is so harsh on this kind of news, because it is what news is, only more so" (1992, 128).

6. A study of *Nightline* by Hoynes and Croteau (1989) showed that, in the late 1980s, 90 percent of *Nightline* guests were men and 83 percent were white. Professionals, government officials, and corporate representatives together accounted for 80 percent of all guests, while public-interest representatives, labor leaders, and racial/ethnic leaders together accounted for only 6 percent of all guests.

7. Thanks to Joshua Gamson (personal communication, July 1997) for helping clarify this point.

8. This estimate comes from an article in the *London Daily Telegraph* (see Leonard 2000).

9. Here, again, we have significant parallels to black minstrelsy, for, if *white trash* represents a discourse about class inflected with racial overtones, minstrel shows represented a discourse of race inflected with class overtones. According to Lott (1993, 68), "Blackface in a real if partial sense, *figured* class. Its languages of race so invoked ideas about class as to provide displaced maps or representations of working-classness." Lott suggests that there was a historical logic in glossing working-class whites as black, given the degree to which large portions of both groups shared a common culture in the North, and given that many popular racial slurs (*coon, buck*) referred to whites as well as to blacks. In Lott's words, "Blackface quickly became a sort of useful shorthand in referring to working men." This was true in England as well, where American minstrel shows gained wide popularity. As Lott writes, quoting F. C. Wemyss, a historian of the period, "It is said of T. D. Rice's English tour that his burlesque skits were 'vulgar even to grossness,' and captivated 'the chimney sweeps and apprentice boys of London, who wheeled about and turned about and jumped Jim Crow, from morning until night, to the annoyance of their masters, but the great delight of the cockneys.'"

10. Women are said to be more "embodied" than men not only because of their presumed greater emotionality but also because of their historic role in the reproduction and maintenance of bodies (bearing, feeding, washing, clothing, and sheltering bodies), their connection to private, domestic space (where the reproduction of bodies occurs), and the larger cultural tendency to define women in sexual rather than intellectual or cognitive terms. For different but related reasons, this same presumed lack of emotional control and "rootedness in the body" has been attributed to people of color.

11. In the contemporary moment, this "surrender to facility" is linked strongly to fatness, which in turn is linked explicitly and implicitly to the lower classes. In her brilliant 1996 essay "Life in the Fat Lane," Laura Kipnis suggests that our culture treats fat people with an unparalleled viciousness that generally goes unchallenged because the "index of moral uprightness" signified by fat bodies appears so natural and universal. Body type, Kipnis argues, is linked both factually and stereotypically to social class, with fatness—and the discriminatory behavior that accompanies it—increasing as one goes down the economic scale. Fat people are less likely to be hired, less likely to be promoted if hired, and

less likely to marry up socially or economically—and this is especially true for fat women. According to Kipnis, psychological studies of body image suggest that fat is linked to a range of things that people fear and despise, including loss of control, infantile regression, failure, self-loathing, laziness, sloth, and passivity. She writes, "Substitute 'welfare class' for 'fat' here and you start to see that the phobia of fat and the phobia of the poor are heavily cross-coded" (1996, 101). The irony in this is not only that we live in a culture that encourages overconsumption while punishing all bodily evidence of it but that fat people (read poor people) come to stand as its privileged signifier. "The burden of fat is not only of pounds," Kipnis concludes. "It's the sorry fate of being trapped in a body that conveys such an excess of meanings" (102). The equation between fatness and social class appears to be borne out on daytime talk shows, which is one of the few places on television where fat people are given representation.

12. Fiske (1989, 103–27) makes a similar observation about the highbrow criticism of supermarket tabloids.

13. Moreover, at a time when the ranks of the masses were more and more made up of recent immigrants and migrant blacks, the emerging ideology separating elite from popular culture began to assume ethnic and racial dimensions. Levine reminds us that the terms *highbrow* and *lowbrow* have their origins in the nineteenth-century practice of craniometry, a "science" that purported to distinguish intelligence levels on the basis of racial classifications: the closer to Western and Northern Europe a people's origins were, the higher their brows and thus the more intelligent they were said to be. Adjectives such as *high, low, legitimate,* and *vulgar* thus cluster around a set of values that not only define and distinguish culture vertically but also are inseparable from other social hierarchies.

14. This is exactly what Randy meant when he told me that his was not an informational show, "other than what you learn by seeing how people relate to one another." Indeed, for Meyrowitz, *all* television programs that depict the behavior of people are about the same thing: "human gesture, feeling, and emotion" (1985, 108). And, while the bias toward expressive content clearly renders television less effective than print-based media in conveying complex ideas and critical analysis (a core concern for critics), the bias has also democratized media consumption. Meyrowitz (1985, 107–8) observes that groups of people who are excluded from the public forum created by print (and now the Internet) because they lack the requisite entry skills can nevertheless participate in the public arena created by television. In contrast to reading and writing, television viewing involves an access code that is barely a code at all: the expressive quality of television makes almost any program accessible to the average viewer.

15. The same point is made by Bird (2000) in discussing the trend toward "personalization" in the tabloid media. At the same time, she warns against personalization as the only way to engage audiences, especially if the personal is disconnected from a larger social or political context. For a discussion of the role of the personal story in informing audiences about global issues, see Tomlinson (1997). For a discussion of tabloid media more generally, see Sparks and Tulloch (2000).

References

Bernstein, Basil, 1974. *Class, Codes, and Control.* London: Routledge & Kegan Paul.

Bettie, Julie. 1995. "Class Dismissed? Roseanne and the Changing Face of Working-Class Iconography." *Social Text* 45 (winter): 125–49.

Bird, Elizabeth, 1992. *For Enquiring Minds: A Cultural Study of Supermarket Tabloids.* Knoxville: University of Tennessee Press.

Bird, Elizabeth. 2000. "Audience Demands in a Murderous Market: Tabloidization in US Television News." In *Tabloid Tales: Global Debates over Media Standards*, ed. Colin Sparks and John Tulloch, 213–28. New York: Rowman & Littlefield.

Bourdieu, Pierre. 1984. *Distinction: A Social Critique of the Judgment of Taste.* Cambridge: Harvard University Press.

Campbell, Richard. 1991. "Word vs. Image: Elitism, Popularity, and TV News." *Television Quarterly* 25, no. 2:73–81.

Carey, James, 1989. *Communication as Culture.* New York: Unwin Hyman.

Cohen, Stanley, and Jock Young, 1973. *The Manufacture of News.* Beverly Hills, Calif.: Sage.

Crane, Diana, 1992. "High Culture versus Popular Culture Revisited: A Reconceptualization of Recorded Cultures." In *Cultivating Differences: Symbolic Boundaries and the Making of Inequality*, ed. Michele Lamont and Marcel Fournier, 58–74. Chicago: University of Chicago Press.

DiMaggio, Paul, 1982a. "Cultural Entrepreneurship in Nineteenth-Century Boston, Part I: The Creation of an Organizational Base for High Culture in America." *Media, Culture, and Society* 4:33–50.

——. 1982b. "Cultural Entrepreneurship in Nineteenth-Century Boston, Part II: The Classification and Framing of American Art." *Media, Culture, and Society* 4:303–22.

Durkheim, Emile. 1965. *The Elementary Forms of Religious Life.* Translated by Joseph Ward Swain. New York: Free Press.

Ehrenreich, Barbara. 1995. "In Defense of Talk Shows." *Time*, 4 December, 92.

Elias, Norbert. 1994. *The Civilizing Process*. Translated by Edmund Jephcott. Cambridge, Mass.: Blackwell.

Fiske, John. 1989. *Understanding Popular Culture*. Boston: Unwin Hyman.

——. 1992. "Popularity and the Politics of Information." In *Journalism and Popular Culture*, ed. Peter Dahlgren and Colin Sparks, 45–63. Newbury Park, Calif.: Sage.

Gamson, Joshua. 1996. "Do Ask, Do Tell." *Utne Reader*, January/February, 79–83.

Gans, Herbert. 1979. *Deciding What's News*. New York: Pantheon.

Gerber, David. 1996. "The Careers of People Exhibited in Freak Shows: The Problem of Volition and Valorization." In *Freakery: Cultural Spectacles of the Extraordinary Body*, ed. Rosemarie Garland Thomson, 38–54. New York: New York University Press.

Gilbert, Craig. 1988a. "Reflections on an American Family I." In *New Challenges for Documentary*, ed. Alan Rosenthal, 191–201. Berkeley and Los Angeles: University of California Press.

——. 1988b. "Reflections on an American Family II." In *New Challenges for Documentary*, ed. Alan Rosenthal, 289–307. Berkeley and Los Angeles: University of California Press.

Gitlin, Todd. 1980. *The Whole World Is Watching: Mass Media in the Making and Unmaking of the New Left*. Berkeley and Los Angeles: University of California Press.

Goad, Jim. 1997. *The Redneck Manifesto: How Hillbillies, Hicks, and White Trash Became America's Scapegoats*. New York: Simon & Schuster.

Gripsrud, Jostein. 1992. "The Aesthetics and Politics of Melodrama." In *Journalism and Popular Culture*, ed. Peter Dahlgren and Colin Sparks, 84–95. Newbury Park, Calif.: Sage.

Gross, Larry. 1994. "What's Wrong with This Picture?" In *Queer Words, Queer Images: Communication and the Construction of Homosexuality*, ed. R. Jeffrey Ringer, 143–156. New York: New York University Press.

Hall, Stuart, Chas Critcher, Tony Jefferson, John Clarke, and Brian Roberts. 1978. *Policing the Crisis*. New York: Holmes & Meier.

Hartigan, John. 1997. "Name Calling: Objectifying 'Poor Whites' and 'White Trash' in Detroit." In *White Trash: Race and Class in America*, ed. Matt Wray and Annalee Newitz, 41–56. New York: Routledge.

Hartley, John. 1982. *Understanding News*. London: Methuen.

Hochschild, Arlie Russell. 1983. *The Managed Heart: Commercialization of Human Feeling*. Berkeley and Los Angeles: University of California Press.

Hoggart, Richard. 1957. *The Uses of Literacy*. New York: Oxford University Press.

Hoynes, William, and David Croteau. 1989. *Are You on the* Nightline *Guest List? An Analysis of 40 Months of* Nightline *Programming*. A special report prepared for Fairness and Accuracy in Reporting.

Kano, Ayako. 2001. *Acting Like a Woman in Modern Japan: Theater, Gender, and Nationalism*, New York: Palgrave.

Kasson, John. 1990. *Rudeness and Civility: Manners in Nineteenth Century Urban America*, New York: Hill & Wang.

Kipnis, Laura. 1996. *Bound and Gagged: Pornography and the Politics of Fantasy in America*. New York: Grove.

Kohn, Melvin. 1963. "Social Class and the Exercise of Parental Authority." In *Personality and Social Systems*, ed. Neil Smelser and William Smelser, 297–313. New York: Wiley.

Langer, John. 1992. "Truly Awful News on Television." In *Journalism and Popular Culture*, ed. Peter Dahlgren and Colin Sparks, 113–29. Newbury Park, Calif.: Sage.

——. 1998. *Tabloid Television: Popular Journalism and the "Other News."* London: Routledge.

Leonard, Tom. 2000. "Why the Tabloids Are Turning." *London Daily Telegraph*, 7 September, 21.

Levine, Lawrence. 1988. *Highbrow Lowbrow: The Emergence of Cultural Hierarchy in America*. Cambridge: Harvard University Press.

Lhamon, W.T., Jr. 1998, *Raising Cain: Blackface Performance from Jim Crow to Hip Hop*. Cambridge: Harvard University Press.

Lott, Eric, 1993. *Love and Theft: Blackface Minstrelsy and the American Working Class*. New York: Oxford University Press.

Manoff, Karl, and Michael Schudson, eds. 1986. *Reading the News*. New York: Pantheon.

Marsh, Katherine. 2000. "What Is Real? Deep behind the Scenes of the New Season of MTV's *The Real World*." *Rolling Stone*, June, 71–79, 141.

McCann, Paul. 2000. "Stars of Real-Life TV Attack 'Distorted' Footage." *Times* (London), 13 November, on-line edition.

Meyrowitz, Joshua. 1985. *No Sense of Place: The Impact of Electronic Media on Social Behavior*. New York: Oxford University Press.

Mitroff, Ian, and Warren Bennis. 1989. *The Unreality Industry: The Deliberate Manufacturing of Falsehood and What It Is Doing to Our Lives*. New York: Carol Publishing Group.

Newitz, Annalee. 1997. "White Savagery and Humiliation; or, A New Racial Consciousness in the Media." In *White Trash: Race and Class in America*, ed. Matt Wray and Annalee Newitz, 131–54. New York: Routledge.

Postman, Neil. 1985. *Amusing Ourselves to Death: Public Discourse in the Age of Show-business*. New York: Penguin.

Schudson, Michael. 1978. *Discovering the News: A Social History of American Newspapers*. New York: Basic.

Sigal, Leon 1986. "Who? Sources Make the News." In *Reading the News*, ed. Karl Manoff and Michael Schudson, New York: Pantheon.

Sparks, Colin, and John Tulloch, eds. 2000. *Tabloid Tales: Global Debates over Media Standards*. New York: Rowman & Littlefield.

Torgovnik, Marianna. 1991. *Gone Primitive*. Chicago: University of Chicago Press.

—— 1978. *Making News: A Study in the Construction of Reality*. London: Free Press.

Willis, Paul. 1994. "Women in Sport in Ideology." In *Women, Sport, and Culture*, ed. Susan Birrell and Cheryl Cole, 31–46. Champaign, Ill.: Human Kinetics.

Wray, Matt, and Annalee Newitz, eds. 1997. *White Trash: Race and Class in America*. New York: Routledge

Zurakwik, David. 2000. "We Become the Watchful Big Brother, Big Sister: From 'Survivors' on a Tropical Island to a British Family Living without Running Water and McDonald's 'Reality Television' Gives Us the Chance to Test Our Voyeuristic Sensibilities." *Baltimore Sun*, 31 May, 1E.

30.
THE PROMOTION AND PRESENTATION OF THE SELF

Celebrity as Marker of Presentational Media

P. David Marshall

Introduction

Over the last 15 years, there have been two moments where the regular decrying of the vacuity of celebrity culture appeared to gain some traction. One can recall the outrage of fellow celebrities after Diana's death in 1997 and the chorus of the famous proclaiming that the hounding of celebrities must stop: the invasion of privacy had just crossed well beyond the boundary of propriety and entered into the illegality of harassment (Roberts 1997). Similarly, in post 9-11 America in particular, there was the month in 2001 of the new sobriety in popular culture where celebrity represented everything that was excessively insignificant. Adding to the new sobriety was the parade of celebrities led by George Clooney and Tom Hanks presenting their serious support for the real heroes of America – the fire-fighters and the police who gave their lives to save others while the Twin Towers collapsed (Beach 2001). In both these cases, celebrity culture represented a new unwanted excess that needed to be reined into the structure of a civil society. And in both these cases, apart from a temporary chastising blip, celebrity culture continued and perhaps even intensified in new ways and permutations.

The question I want to answer here is why: why does celebrity and celebrity culture continue to hold its fascination? A corollary question I want to address is, given the shifted structure of media and entertainment industries in the twenty-first century, what do celebrities continue to address that is so essential to contemporary culture? These questions have to be prefaced by the fact that the lament contained in these two moments detailed above is not anomalous. It is ever-present and helps to maintain the duality with which we hold the overwhelming production of celebrity: collectively, we disdain the public focus on celebrity at the same time as we continue to watch, discuss and participate and thereby ensure the maintenance of a celebrity industry.

The first dimension of an answer to the questions is that celebrity has been and is increasingly a pedagogical tool and specifically a pedagogical aid in the discourse of the self. For much of the twentieth century, celebrities served as beacons of the public world. They helped define the *Zeitgeist* of any particular moment – 'a structure of feeling' that relied in part on its mediation through film, radio, popular music and television. Thus, the stories of how women's hairstyles of the 1920s, 1930s and 1940s were determined by the screen icons of the Hollywood industry in the United States represents a basic example of how their representations moved into the cultural world. Similarly, Clarke Gable's singlet or JFK's hatless inauguration also shaped sartorial style, at least in the United States. There are examples of the power of screen icons to embody a mood – James Dean, for instance, through his role in *Rebel without a Cause* (1955), embodied a general fear of the angst in 1950s youth culture. The examples of this representative power of celebrities are legion as well as diverse. The impact of music videos in the 1980s, for instance, provided a panoply of styles and attitude that migrated transnationally with surprising force. Certain celebrities were able to capitalise on these changes in origins and powers of representation. For example, Madonna became an expert at translating subcultural style for its wider mediation through popular music, performance and music videos for more than two decades. In turn, her appropriation of subcultural style percolated through popular culture and fashion.

The pedagogy of the celebrity has served very particular purposes throughout the twentieth century. Celebrity taught generations how to engage and use consumer culture to 'make' oneself. In a number of treatises on advertising and consumer culture, cultural critics have identified how the individual had to be taught how to consume and to recognise the value of consumption for their own benefit (for example, Leiss *et al.* 2005, Story 1999, Toland and Mueller 2003). Instead of making clothes, it was much easier to have them made for you and use wages – as Ewen (1975) has explained as wage slavery – to capture the latest fashion and the most recent style. Shops provided the pathways to a consumer world which represented possibility and potential as much as a participation in a wider and connected culture (Schudson 1984) that was cross-linked with entertainment culture and its stars. What is less developed in these critiques of consumer culture is that pedagogic work performed to transform a more traditional culture into a consumer culture was very much dependent upon celebrities and their capacity to embody the transformative power writ large of consumer culture. Also generally missing in the studies of advertising and consumer culture was a further key element in that this transformation of the individual into consumer is not the shift to consumption from production but a shift to a wider and more pervasive *production* of the self. The production of the self implies the mutability of the production process, as it is built from the array of possible forms of consumption and expression that these types of consumption provided for the individual.

Because of celebrity's centrality in what can be defined as self-production, the elaborate celebrity gossip can be seen as providing a continuity of discourse around the presentation of the self for public consumption. The pedagogy of the celebrity in the twentieth century can be read as a very elaborate morality tale that mapped a private world into a public world. What we have described above is the ideal self that celebrities were able to proffer and ultimately led to their capacity to effectively sell a wide variety of products. This reading of celebrity identifies only a partial story of how celebrities taught the world. The narratives of divorce, of drunkenness, of aspects of personal lawlessness, of violence, of affairs and of misbehaving offspring, among many other stories, served to articulate a different public sphere than that constructed through the official histories of a culture. Implied in the celebrity discourse of gossip was an interpersonal dimension – what was often defined in newspaper coverage as the human feature – of the organisation of our culture. Gossip, in particular, circulated around celebrities as an explanation of personality that went beyond their onscreen personae and moved them into a public 'community' of recognisable figures who revealed at least part of their private experiences to heighten the affective connection to an audience.

Gossip has been studied from a number of perspectives. On one level, gossip has represented a form of social cohesion, a means by which group membership is enacted, reclaimed, and produced forms of exclusion (Gluckman 1963). De Backer, for instance, divides gossip into two functions: reputation gossip, where the status of a person is redrawn based on the information circulated in a community, and strategy learning gossip, where one learns social cues and preferred behaviour through the information gleaned about others (2005, in de Backer *et al.* 2007, p. 335). Other studies have focused upon how, among adolescents in particular, there is a form of reinforcement within a group of attitudes through gossip exchanges (Eder and Enke 1991). One of the key features of gossip as a discourse is that it is a structure of speech engagement or conversation that speaks about others specifically when they are not present.

This non-presence of the object of the gossip has actually made celebrity gossip perhaps one of the easiest and readily available forms of gossip. In the studies of celebrity gossip, researchers of 1970s' and 1980s' American tabloid gossip refer to the way in which it helps to produce social order in the populace through its representations of the problems and unhappiness of the rich and famous, despite their wealth and the adulation they attract from others

(Levin *et al.* 1988). The use of celebrity gossip, then, is an extension of the uses of gossip in a community as a form of social control. Celebrity gossip, however, slips the yoke of the local and has often allowed debates to move seamlessly into a national or in some cases international debate while at the same time dealing with issues related to intimacy, family, and what has been regarded as the personal and private realm. What has to be understood about celebrity gossip throughout the twentieth century is that it has operated on two levels:

- first, there has been the reportage that has appeared as a form of information for readers in tabloids, newspapers, television programmes and magazines – in other words, it is structured and highly mediated; and
- secondly, there has been the deployment of celebrity gossip through personal conversation and evaluation that constantly moves the highly mediated into the interpersonal dimensions of everyday interchange. The movement of this kind of celebrity gossip information into the interpersonal is accentuated precisely because of the often personal nature of the information presented about celebrities.

Celebrity gossip is one of the principal components of an elaborate celebrity discourse that continued and intensified for most of the last century. It was a discourse that spanned from the official and the sanctioned to the transgressive and the titillating, with many layers and levels of revelation between these two ends of the spectrum of what constituted the public self of the celebrity. Critically, it was used by an audience to make sense of the intersection of their public and private worlds and how that intersection related to the production of the self. De Backer *et al.* have identified how celebrity gossip can operate for younger people as a form of social learning – in other words, as a way to work out how they should dress, act and engage (De Backer *et al.* 2007, pp. 345–346). Their study also revealed that with older adults, celebrities were used in what can be called parasocial activities: the celebrity is integrated as if they are part of a social network for conversation purposes, but their parasociality means that this integration into the interpersonal is entirely one way, where the celebrity is obviously not truly part of the social network, but only in a mediated form (De Backer *et al.* 2007, pp. 340, 347–348).

On the surface, to understand the continued resonance and value of celebrity discourse in a changed media culture appears difficult. After all, celebrities are a production of the self specifically dependent upon a very elaborate and powerful media culture. They are elemental components of *representational culture* (Marshall 2006, pp. 636–637). With their dependence upon television, film, radio and the press for their influence even at this parasocial level, it would appear that the dispersal quality of on-line culture and its transformation of the power of traditional media to represent and embody interests and desires, celebrity as a moniker of identity, individuality and the consumer self may also be waning. However, what can be identified in this century-long discourse are some specific elements which are incredibly valuable to the emergence of on-line culture. I will highlight each of these elements and then explain how they are elemental to the production of the on-line self. In order to unpack the production of the on-line self and how it is informed by celebrity culture, I am going to use the way that particular celebrities are presenting themselves in this era of *presentational culture* to, in a very real sense, re-present and re-construct themselves with the benefit of this continued negotiation of the self that celebrity culture has articulated, leading up to the emergence of on-line culture and identity.

The Technological and Cultural Change: Social Networks to Presentational Media

Some of the key changes in the way that we find, explore and share entertainment and information have produced this shifted constitution of our culture. It is not that television and film as examples of representational media do not continue to produce quite profound structure for our culture; it is more accurate to say that that influence is just less profound and less relentlessly omnipresent and perhaps more remediated through on-line pathways. Key changes have happened relatively recently. In the last half-decade, internet usage in all its manifestations is now challenging and in some cases surpassing television viewing in many countries in Australasia, North America and Europe (Gorman, 2008, Nielsen, 2008; Microsoft, 2009).[1] From the early part of this century, a very profound change in on-line use was developing. Social network sites began to develop that were built on forms of social exchange, such as internet relay chat, e-mail and instant messaging, and partially blended with the kinds of social interchange that had emerged with weblogs, or blogs. Certain countries such as Korea embraced particular forms of social media – in their case, the Mini-Hompy from Cyworld – that began to be used by more than a fraction of youth culture and became a pervasive form of interpersonal, and what could be called social, communication (TechCrunch 2009). Various forms of social networks developed in other parts of the world, loosely modelled on constructing and networking groups of friends into patterns of continuous engagement and sharing. Simultaneously massive multiplayer on-line games grew from the late 1990s that also produced environments for constructing circles of friends that would band together in pursuit of certain game objectives as well as converse in in-character and out-of-character modes. Since 2004, there have been various social network sites that have become the channel through which these rings of social and friendship exchanges have flourished, some designed for children, but most designed for young adult usage. Friendster and MySpace both have occupied important places in the development of social networks in the English-speaking world. Facebook has captured a very large number of users, and like its Korean counterpart has pervaded the culture from its origins in university life to now encompassing a comprehensive connection to all demographic groups (Facebook 2009). More recently, Twitter has been able to capture a slightly different constitution of connection through its short messaging, linking to other sites of interest and becoming part of a more mobile on-line culture. Professional networking sites such as LinkedIn have developed simultaneously to other sharing and exhibition sites such as YouTube for video, Flickr for images and Digg and Delicious for broader on-line information sharing and following.

On-line social network sites are interesting for what they allow the user to do – what are often called a technology's 'affordances'. They are very much connected to a desire to produce (Burnett and Marshall 2003, pp. 70–78, Marshall 2004, pp. 10–11), as they have simplified the process of constructing a website and ensuring that that website has some sort of audience – a constitution of a public – for any user. It is these two dimensions – a form of cultural production and a form of public engagement and exchange – that make social networks simultaneously a media *and* communication form. What makes them very much connected to celebrity is that as much as they are about an exchange and dissemination of thoughts and links to other media and on-line sources, they are a constitutive and organic production of the self. That self-production is the very core of celebrity activity and it now serves as a rubric and template for the organisation and production of the on-line self which has become at the very least an important component of our presentation of ourselves to the world.

Performance of the Self

Performance is a critical component in any public figure's identity. For the politician, as strong and popular as his/her policies might be, the actual performance in a public forum is often a factor in how policies are received by a public. Celebrities perform in their primary art form – as actors, musicians, singers, athlete – as well as the extra-textual dimensions of interviews, advertisements/commercial endorsements, award nights and premieres. These elements of performance are the professional or producerly elements that are closest to their status as, or at least as conveyors of, cultural commodities.

There remain other dimensions of performance of their public everyday lives. Celebrities are under constant and regular surveillance and thus their more mundane and sometimes more personal activities are the subject of a gaze. The gaze provided by the paparazzi and distributed to magazines, television programmes and on-line sites makes their often everyday activities a kind of performance to be read further.

Erving Goffman wrote about the presentation of the self and its performative qualities from a sociological perspective more than 50 years ago. In his now highly influential *The presentation of self in everyday life*, Goffman (1959) studied gestures and the way an individual composed a version of him/herself for the world. Performance of the self was a conscious act of the individual and required careful staging to maintain the self – a composed and norm-driven construction of character and performance:

> The whole machinery of self-production is cumbersome, of course, and sometimes breaks down, exposing its separate components: back region control; team collusion; audience tact; and so forth. But, well oiled, impressions will flow from it fast enough to put us in the grips of one of our types of reality – the performance will come off and the firm self accorded each performed character will appear to emanate intrinsically from its performer.
> (Goffman 1959, cited in Lamert and Branaman 1997, p. 23)

What we are witnessing now is the staging of the self as both character and performance in on-line settings. The props and accoutrements of the stage can now be translated to the various profiles, images and messages that are part of a Facebook site. Goffman draws upon Park's insight that the definitional origin of 'person' is a mask (1959, cited in Lamert and Branaman 1997, p. 97), and what is constructed via Facebook but equally through Twitter is a construction of character for a kind of ritual of the performance of the self. It is highly conscious of a potential audience as much as it is a careful preening and production of the self.

For celebrities, as they begin to reconstruct their personae for on-line use, interesting insights are already in play. For the actor Vin Diesel on Facebook it is very important that he reveals something of his professional self in a kind of collaboration of his private self. There is a performance of connection to his 'fans', as one of the Facebook affordances is to have levels and layers of friends. His profile indicates that he has 7,018,079 fans (Diesel 2009) and his 28 September postings indicate that he wanted to share something from a:

> special lunch meeting where my father said something so dead on . . . He said . . . 'Confidence is the

most important thing that you can teach someone . . . if you can teach them confidence, you don't have to teach them anything else' . . . Thanks for the love.
>
> (Diesel 2009)

Interspersed with these 'personal' posts are the associated images of a lunch meeting and other images, video and production stills. Diesel is constructing a carefully managed Facebook persona that actually indicates that the studio is at least part of its construction. At the same time he personalises his posts, which indicates the use of his Facebook site as a kind of publicly accessible diary – a performance of the actor's everyday life.

The Widening Dimension of the Public Self

In the book *Fame games*, one of the chapters deals specifically with the accidental celebrity. The research for that chapter was focused upon the moment when a private individual was suddenly caught in the glare of overwhelming media and by implication public interest (Turner *et al.* 2000, pp. 110–114). The private individual, then, was catapulted into the public spotlight in a media feeding frenzy. Although the intention of that particular research was to identify the way that this was managed by certain individuals and agents, the related point was how the public sphere in the era of representational media was actually much tighter and more centrally controlled and perhaps manipulated. Also, it was also apparent that constructing a public self was not what most people would think was worth producing. Something has changed in the era of social media and presentational culture, and it is worth exploring what appears to be a widening of the public sphere.

Graeme Turner has called this change the 'demotic turn' (Turner 2004, pp. 82–85, 2010), where the media are drawn more and more to the everyday and perhaps the ordinary as a form of extraordinary discourse that is a ritualisation of media openness rather than any democratic turn in the media. Certainly, reality television shows where carefully auditioned audience members become the object of this relatively new form of docudrama identify the demotic in contemporary culture.

What needs to be nuanced into this reading of the public world is the expanding desire of the populace to be part of a public, but a far different public sphere than that perhaps articulated by Habermas, that formed to legitimise a certain organisation of power (1988, 1992). Through social media, the public self is presented through a new layer of interpersonal conversation that in its mode of address bears little relationship to its representational media past.

Celebrity use of social media articulates this change. There have already been massive campaigns by individuals to produce followers that would rival the largest of television networks. The most famous of these was conducted by the actor Ashton Kutcher, who worked tirelessly on constructing an on-line Twitter presence and challenged CNN to match his number of followers. Indeed, Kutcher passed the 1 million followers mark before CNN: what this campaign underlined was the capacity of an individual to produce a very large media and communication event (Petersen 2009). It also revealed the capacity of an individual, albeit an already well-known personality, to produce this effect through a combination of media and interpersonal communication.

Other campaigns by celebrities are worthy of note in their movement between representational media and the need for presentational structures in social media. Christina Applegate crusaded to save her television show from being cancelled by constructing a social network army of interest (Stechyson 2009). As she explained, social network sites allow a much more direct connection to fans and can be mobilised quite rapidly. Britney Spears, who does not suffer from a lack of coverage in representational media, has constructed a YouTube channel called Britney TV that houses all her videos (Spears 2009a). Like many other social media users, Britney has engaged in making herself a subscriber-structured identity through YouTube.

Celebrities are allowing themselves to expose their lives further in order to gain a following and an audience. Neil Diamond, definitively a very popular singer and songwriter from a different era, has invested heavily in a Twitter identity and is working on constructing a particularised public identity in this stage of his career. He has cultivated a paternal and godfather relationship to other younger musicians on-line, discusses his own life and music regularly and has allowed his fans to observe and follow his posts. Here is an example of his posts over the last year that identify his connection to a new generation of performers:

(@joshproban Hi Josh. Hope you liked the TV show. Keep making those great records. All the best, Neil7:23 PM Aug 18th from web in reply to joshgroban@jonasbrothers Congratulations on your #1 album! 11:46 AM Jun 26th from web Caught Chris Cornell at Webster Hall in NYC on Sat. Night. Love his voice and the band really rocked. I wish he'd have done Kentucky Woman.7:30 AM Apr 10th from Twitterrific.

(Diamond 2009)

In a parallel stream, MCHammer has used social media for a public reconstruction of his fame and has constructed a following of more than 1.5 million on Twitter to reinsert himself in a differently constituted public. Interlaced with his religious messages he replies to tweets from fans and fellow celebrities, and re-tweets comments from others about himself. Below are examples of these two constructions of the self from MC Hammer's Twitter page:

He did It Again !! Woke Us Up !!! Have A Great Day!!! God Bless 1:35 AM Oct 31st from web

http://twitpic.com/oqp5r – Who knew one of my childhood heroes @Mchammer would be one of coolest dudes ever and know us (via @benjaminmadden)10:12 AM Nov 9th from Tweetie in reply to benjaminmadden.

(Hammer 2009)

Celebrities are engaging in often very sophisticated uses of on-line and social media to produce a different presence. It is an investment in a public self that acknowledges that this engagement has widened to millions of users who generally predated the expanding army of celebrity social media users. The public self, whether through the activities of known personalities or by other social media users, is a recognition that these sites and the exchanges that develop on them are extensions in the production of the self and are vital to the maintenance of one's identity. What is different about this engagement is its interpersonalisation of the public world. Conversation is at the epicentre of postings and is the fibre that holds social networks together over time. The public self is constantly worked upon and updated in its on-line form to both maintain its currency and to acknowledge its centrality to the individual's identity, which is dependent upon its network of connections to sustain the life of the on-line persona.

The Intercommunicative Self

One of the key elements of celebrity culture and discourse for the last century is its different forms of address. As described above, celebrities presented themselves in their cultural forms as performers, but they also were presented in interview structures and in celebrity gossip settings. All these forms are precursors for the interplay of media and communication that is part of constructing the on-line self. The layered structure of producing the celebrity self for a form of public display and consumption becomes a precursor for the production of the on-line self.

In on-line culture, it is a spectrum of communication registers that produces an array of connected forms. The term 'intercommunication' can be defined as the layering of forms in an inter-related structure that moves between types of interpersonal communication that are integrated with highly mediated presentations. Intercommunication acknowledges a shifted public sphere where the interpersonal is overlaid onto its flows of interpretation and meaning from the outset. Intercommunication as a concept helps us to understand this new mix of representational and presentational culture and how they are interconnected in complex and intricate ways.

The intercommunicative self identifies that, at least in on-line cultures such as social network sites, we are engaged in a multi-layered form of communication that kneads mediated forms with conversation, that allows photos to be the starting-point for reactions and discussions, and that produces, partly because of expediency and partly for the desire to remain connected to someone or a group of people, very simplistic and phatic forms of communication that invite response. The intercommunicative self

provides links to YouTube videos or samples of popular music or interesting articles that are extensions of the self's identity that are articulated through friends. The intercommunicative self also acknowledges the necessity of linking one's own identities into some sort of pattern, from Twitter to Facebook, from YouTube and Flickr to MySpace, from blogs to Digg.

Celebrities have quickly embraced the forms of intercommunication through their on-line personae, and because of the resources that they devote to constructing themselves as valuable commodities are able to maintain these profiles. For instance, the rapper and television personality Snoop Dogg ensures that both his Facebook and Twitter sites are alive with material for his fans. Twitter cross-lists to Facebook and is used to maintain the presence of Snoop Dogg, and further aligns with his official website. His presence is very calculated to promote his concerts and his music, and ensures that there is at least a connection to his followers no matter where they search on-line (Dogg 2009a, 2009b). Artists such as Lily Allen have made sure that their Tweets are re-tweeted to appear on their more official Facebook sites, and thereby enliven the connection between Allen and her fans with the regularity of posts, even engaging in debates with fans as to the morality of downloading music (Allen 2009).[2] Demi Moore and Ashton Kutcher are famous for their use of images through Twitpics that are emerging from their private lives in order to construct and control a complete persona, thereby bypassing the traditional media. Kutcher's posting of a picture of the backside of Demi in her underwear is particularly noteworthy as an example of celebrity actively playing between different intercommunicative registers in his public distribution of what could only be thought of as a private moment (Kells 2009, Kutcher 2009).

The Parasocial Self

The intercommunicative dimension of on-line social networking identifies the new need for celebrities to stay connected in some way to this shifted relationship to an audience and a public. It demands an engagement that was, in the past, at least partially handled by the ancillary press of the celebrity industry, but now implicates the celebrity themselves in the interpersonal flow of communication. None the less, celebrities are at the forefront along with their fans in terms of an etiquette of engagement. The parasocial self is a pragmatic understanding that it is impossible to communicate individually with thousands and millions; and yet in this shifted on-line culture some effort has to be made. Thus celebrities are not fully fledged friends with all the people that may follow them but superficially, at least, they are. All social network users have to determine privacy settings, openness to follow others as much as they are followed, and a kind of moral code about presenting as themselves or allowing others to present on their behalf.

The level of engagement with friends as fans is often related to the relative power of the celebrity's position in representational culture. Thus Oprah Winfrey, who has one of the most successful talkshows both nationally and internationally, was very concerned with expanding her reach into the Twitterverse and raced to achieve followers in the first half of 2009 (Winfrey 2009). She has minimal reply to the massive number of followers she has garnered and follows very few. Similarly, Ashton Kutcher and Demi Moore, the celebrity royalty of Twitter, only follow 261 and 113, respectively (Kutcher 2009, Moore 2009). They do, however, make an effort to reply to fans' messages. They also promote others and maintain the exchange of information that has made Twitter so attractive. For example, Ashton Kutcher posted this rather 'normal' tweet which resembles countless users of Twitter in its relaying of a link that indicates interest:

> AK very cool project by David Lynch http://bit.
> ly/fj2YP 11:14 AM Aug 21st from Tweet-Deck.
> (Kutcher 2009)

Others, such as Kathy Griffin, construct their comic persona in interpersonal language, but never reply or re-tweet: in a sense, she is maintaining a broadcast model of communication through conversational messages. She has 209,671 followers and follows no one. Her posts maintain the jocular and the informative:

> If u watch the 'My Life on the D List' finale tonight on Bravo, I'll blow you. It's that simple. Oh, and I

think I'm pregnant. 8:52 AM Aug 10th from web Dear Seacrest, EMMY voting ends tomorrow. I voted for u. Did u vote for me??? Love, Kathy Griffin-Johnston2:30 PM Aug 27th from web.

> (Griffin 2009)

In this new parasocial connection between an audience of users and the celebrity, there are difficult boundaries to traverse. For some stars it is very obvious that a publicist has written the posts. What is emerging is a first-person and third-person relationship to posts. Thus, Mariah Carey assiduously structures her personal posts in the first person and when they are not, her posts are listed in the third person. Here are two Tweets which identity the duality of conversational discourse of star and persona:

> I believe I had the worst toothache today and I'm not in ny so its a definite situation! Anyway, thanks to all my friends for the support!!!
>
> Let's take MC straight to the top! Cast your vote for OBSESSED on VH1's Top 20 Video countdown @ http://tinyurl.com/32ssp2 (MC.com/gina).

> (Carey 2009)

Rob Thomas, of Matchbox 20, splits his 'identity' between publicist posts on Facebook and personal posts on Twitter (Thomas 2009a, 2009b). Britney Spears' on-line Twitter persona resembles that of Mariah Carey, where the first- and third-person address is employed (Spears 2009b). Where trouble emerges is when people pretend that they are writing their posts as the on-line persona becomes routinised into publicity structures. One of the dimensions of on-line personae is that the depictions are believed to be closer to the real than other representations. Thus, a giant sense of betrayal occurred when it was revealed that someone was impersonating the Dalai Lama (Campbell 2009), or that Hugh Jackman was not in fact managing and posting on his Twitter account (Petersen 2009). In the era of social media and presenting and producing the self, the search for the true and the real continues in a manner similar to the way celebrity gossip was a channel in the twentieth century to the more authentic star (Dyer 1979).

Fans continue to try to strip away the veneers of performance and publicity to find these true versions of celebrities, and the on-line world constructs the parasocial interpersonal pathways for an apparent intensified connection. The reading of the 'true' public self through the celebrity is now linked to an audience/user pedagogic function of constructing and producing the self, as well as the continuing celebrity effect of producing emulative desire in an audience.

The Private Self for Public Presentation

There are new categories needed to describe the different ways in which the self is presented in on-line culture and, by implication, to a wider public. Social networking can reveal the private self, but in its design it has the potential of complete revelation to a wider public world. Interwoven into this mixture of private self and public world is the interpersonal register of on-line communication. What is emerging are three ways of looking at on-line production of the public version of the private self.

On one level, there is the *public self*. This is the official version that in celebrity parlance would be the industrial model of the individual. It would identify release dates of recordings and films, premieres and appearances, performance videoclips, the path to get tickets for specific appearances and events and biographical profiles of the most fawning nature. Official websites produce this effect, but because social networking defines the way users often find information there is a tendency to use Facebook as a quasi-official version of the public self. For high-profile celebrities, as discussed above, these kinds of sites are managed by their publicity assistants and work to maintain the public persona as a valued cultural commodity.

The second level of presentation is the *public private self*. It is in this version of the self that the celebrity engages, or at least appears to engage, in the world of social networking. It is a recognition of the new notion of a public that implies some sort of further exposure of the individual's life. Twitter has become the vehicle of choice in maintaining a public private self for many celebrities. Its affordances limit the compulsion to respond and the possibility of short textual bursts that identify thought or location of a particular celebrity. Moreover, the currency of Twitter is that it is much more connected to mobile delivery and thus gives the sensation of immediacy. For some celebrities the self-negotiation of the public private self wrests control of the economy of their public persona in a way that resembles the 1950s breakdown of the film studio system, and the emergence of the star at the centre of film culture. The value of the public private self is still being determined, as individuals construct their versions of what parts of their lives they are willing to convey to an on-line public.

The third level is the *transgressive intimate self*. In answer to a question after his high-impact back-to-school speech in September 2009, President Barack Obama warned against putting something on Facebook that you might regret later, because 'Whatever you do, it will be pulled up later in your life' (cited Pace 2009). The transgressive intimate on-line version of the self is the one motivated by temporary emotion; but it is also the kind of information/image that passes virally throughout the internet because of its visceral quality of being closer to the core of the being. Elizabeth Taylor's Twitter posts exposed her grief-stricken self in response to Michael Jackson's death (Taylor 2009). What may have appeared appropriate for one's closest friends is, in this case, shared with hundreds of thousands who pass it on virally to millions. The movement of the transgressive intimate self travels quickly back into the representative media culture as well as entertainment reports on celebrities. These transgressive moments are also clustered in on-line celebrity sites such as those of Perez Hilton, Harvey Levin and Jason Binn, who are regularly trawling Tweets and Facebook sites for moments of transgressive behaviour (Binn 2009, Hilton 2009, Levin 2009). Transgression remains a beacon in on-line or off-line form for fans and audiences to see a persona's true nature exposed and the event/moment for intercommunicative sharing, comment and discussion. It is thus an accelerated pathway to notoriety and attention both in the wider world of on-line culture for all users and very visibly for celebrities whose behavioural transgressions expressed in interpersonal registers move swiftly into the powerful viral on-line juggernaut.

Conclusion: The Increasing Value to Produce the Self

Twelve years after the publication of *Celebrity and power* (Marshall 1997), it remains an intriguing question what makes celebrity culture prosper, proliferate and continue to have a kind of powerful influence. This article has tried to grapple and ultimately answer that perplexing question. On one hand, we are in the middle of a quite dramatic change in the organisation and legitimation of our culture in all its manifestations. Our celebrity system has been deeply embedded and wedded to what I have called a representational regime where culture and politics have relied upon a media filtering system to organise and hierarchise what is valuable, significant and important. It has produced a system of 'representatives', some of which are celebrities who embody our public discourse.

On-line culture has led to a partial – and by no means complete – dispersal of that representative system and we are living in cultures that are partly organised through the representational structures which remain dominant, but also partly organised through what I am calling a presentational culture and regime. Of course, all these grand claims are constituted differently in various parts of the world, but there is some similarity in Europe, North America and parts of Asia in this development. Celebrity culture is intriguingly poised between these two cultures – representational and presentational – because of its power to express cultural desire and will in significant ways.

What this article identifies is that celebrity culture has been a very elaborate discourse on the individual and throughout the twentieth century it has served a certain pedagogical function. Its capacity to train populations to consumer culture only partially captures the educative power of celebrity culture. More profoundly, celebrity culture articulates a way of thinking about individuality and producing the individual self through the public world.

The longer historical trajectory of celebrity discourse maps this increasing focus on the production of the self that has been partially designed to identify the power of individuals in the process of cultural production, as well as the ideological importance to identify individual power in an era of democratic capitalism.

The new dimension of this discourse on individuality provided by celebrity is its articulation with the demands and exigencies of on-line culture which operates as the expanding source of presentational culture. Past celebrity discourse, with its textual and more significantly extra-textual dimensions that revealed an interrelation between the public self and the private self, has served as the template for the production of the on-line self. Moreover, because of this expertise in producing the public self, observing the way celebrities are constructing their on-line identities isolates on the various facets of the new public self that is now a form of production engaged in by the vast users of the various and interconnected on-line social networks.

Acknowledgements

The author would like to acknowledge the assistance of Kim Barbour in the preparation of this article along with the preliminary research assistance of Katie Freund and Rebecca Walker.

Notes

1. Internet usage in Australia surpassed television viewing time in early 2008 (Nielsen 2008). Microsoft currently predicts that this change will also occur in Europe by June 2010 (Microsoft 2009), and it can be expected that this trend will spread throughout the world.
2. Lily Allen has now left Twitter, although her Twitter page is still available to view on-line. Her final post on 28 September 2009 reads 'I am a neo-luddite, goodbye' (Allen 2009).

References

Allen, L., 2009. *lilyroseallen* [Twitter]. Available from: http://twitter.com/lilyroseallen [Accessed 29 September 2009].

Beach, M., 2001. Song of unity – tearful stars raise $230m in US telethon. *Sunday Telegraph* (Sydney, Australia). 23 September, 5 ed. p. World 1.

Binn, J., 2009. *JasonBinn* [Twitter]. Available from: http://twitter.com/JasonBinn [Accessed 14 September 2009].

Burnett, R. and Marshall, P.D., 2002. *Web theory*. London: Routledge.

Campbell, I.G., 2009. *All A-Twitter about the Dalai Lama* [on-line]. Social Science Research Network. Available from: http://ssrn.com/abstract=1340724 [Accessed 09 November 2009].

Carey, M., 2009. *MariahCarey* [Twitter]. Available from: http://twitter.com/MariahCarey [Accessed 31 August 2009].

De Backer, C, 2005. *Like Belgian chocolate for the universal mind: interpersonal and media gossip from an evolutionary perspective*. PhD thesis, Ghent University, Belgium.

De Backer, C, Nelissen, M., Vyncke, P., Braeckman, J. and Mcandrew, F., 2007. Celebrities: from teachers to friends. *Human Nature*, 18 (4), 334–354.

Diesel, V., 2009. *Vin Diesel* [Facebook]. 25 September. Available from: http://www.facebook.com [Accessed 25 September 2009].

Diamond, N., 2009. *NeilDiamond* [Twitter]. Available from: http://twitter.com/NeilDiamond [Accessed 31 August 2009].

Dogg, S., 2009a. *Snoop Dogg* [Facebook]. Available from: http://www.facebook.com [Accessed 01 September 2009].

Dogg, S., 2009b. *snoopdogg* [Twitter]. Available from: http://twitter.com/snoopdogg [Accessed 29 September 2009].

Dyer, R., 1979. *Stars*. London: Educational Advisory Service, British Film Institute.

Eder, D. and Enke, J.A., 1991. The structure of gossip: opportunities and constraints on collective expression among adolescents. *American Sociological Review*, 56 (4), 494–508.

Ewen, S., 1975. *Captains of consciousness: advertising and the social roots of consumer culture*. New York: McGraw-Hill.

Facebook, 2009. *Statistics* [on-line]. Facebook. Available from: http://www.facebook.com/press/info.php?statistics [Accessed 10 November 2009].

Gluckman, M., 1963. Gossip and scandal. *Current Anthropology*, 4 (3), 307–316.

Goffman, E., 1959. *The presentation of self in everyday life*. New York, Doubleday.

Gorman, S., 2008. *Nielsen finds strong TV-internet usage overlap* [on-line]. Reuters. Available from: http://www.reuters.com/article/televisionNews/idUSTRE49U7SC20081031 [Accessed 10 November 2009].

Griffin, K. 2009. *officialkathyg* [Twitter]. Available from: http://twitter.com/officialkathyg [Accessed 31 August 2009].

Habermas, J., 1992. *The structural transformation of the public sphere: an inquiry into a category of bourgeois society*. Cambridge: Polity Press.

Habermas, J., 1988. *Legitimation crisis*. London: Heinemann Educational.

Hammer, MC. 2009. *MCHammer* [Twitter]. Available from: http://twitter.com/MCHammer [Accessed 31 August 2009].

Hilton, P., 2009. *PerezHilton* [Twitter]. Available from: http://twitter.com/PerezHilton [Accessed 14 September 2009].

Kells, T., 2009. Ashton Kutcher, Demi Moore, get cheeky on Twitter, punk paparazzi. *NowPublic*. Weblog [on-line] 23 March. Available from: http://www.nowpublic.com/culture/ashton-kutcher-demi-moore-get-cheeky-twitter-punk-paparazzi [Accessed 09 November 2009].

Kutcher, A., 2009. *aplusk* [Twitter]. Available from: http://twitter.com/aplusk [Accessed 29 September 2009].

Lamert, C. and Branaman, A., eds, 1997. *The Goffman reader*. Malden, MA: Blackwell.

Leiss, W., Kline, S. and Jhally, S., eds, 2005. *Social communication in advertising: persons, products, and images of well being*. New York: Routledge.

Levin, H., 2009. *HarveyLevinTMZ* [Twitter]. Available from http://twitter.com/HarveyLevinTMZ [Accessed 31 August 2009].

Levin, J., Mody-Desbareau, A. and Arluke, A., 1988. The gossip tabloid as agent of social control. *Journalism Quarterly*, 65 (2), 514–517.

Marshall, P.D., 2006. New media, new self: the changing power of the Celebrity. *In*: P.D. Marshall, ed. *The celebrity culture reader*. London: Routledge, 634–644.

Marshall, P.D., 2004. *New media cultures*. London: Hodder Arnold/Oxford.

Marshall, P.D., 1997. *Celebrity and power: fame in contemporary culture*. Minneapolis, MN: University of Minnesota Press.

Moore, D., 2009. *mrskutcher* [Twitter]. Available from http://twitter.com/mrskutcher [Accessed 29 September 2009].

Nielsen, 2008. *Aussie internet usage overtakes TV viewing for the first time* [news release, on-line]. Available from http://www.nielsen-online.com/pr/pr_080318_AU.pdf [Accessed 11 November 2009].

Pace, J., 2009. *Obama cautions kids about Facebook* [on-line]. AOL News. Available from: http://news.aol.com/article/president-obama-gives-school-speech-to/657798 [Accessed 12 November 2009].

Parr, B., 2009. *MySpace's U.S. traffic falls off a cliff* [on-line]. Mashable: The Social Media Guide. Available from: http://mashable.com/2009/10/12/myspace-traffic-plummets/ [Accessed 10 November 2009].

Petersen, A.H., 2009. 'We're making our own paparazzi': Twitter and the construction of star authenticity. *Flow – A Critical Forum on Television and Media Culture*, 9 (14) [on-line], Available from: http://flowtv.org/?p=3960 [Accessed 10 June 2009].

Roberts, R., 1997. The princess and the press: a dance ending in death. *Washington Post*, 4 September, p. D1.

Sandison, N., 2009. *European internet consumption to overtake TV in 14 months* [on-line]. BrandRepublic. Available from: http://www.brandrepublic.com/News/897321/European-internet-consumption-overtake-traditional-TV-14-months/ [Accessed 10 November 2009].

Schonfield, E., 2009. *Twitter finds growth abroad with 58.4 million global visitors in September* [on-line]. TechCrunch. Available from: http://www.techcrunch.com/2009/10/26/twitter-finds-growth-abroad-with-58–4-million-global-visitors-in-september/ [Accessed 10 November 2009].

Schudson, M., 1984. *Advertising, the uneasy persuasion: its dubious impact on American society.* New York: Basic Books.

Spears, B., 2009a. *Britney TV* [YouTube]. Available from: http://www.youtube.com/user/BritneyTV?blend=2&ob=1 [Accessed 25 September 2009].

Spears, B., 2009b. *britneyspears* [Twitter]. Available from: http://twitter.com/britneyspears [Accessed 31 August 2009].

Stechyson, N., 2009. CELEBS A-TWITTER: Networking tool a boon – and bane – for the rich and famous [online]. CanWest Newsservice. Available from: http://www2.canada.com/news/celebs+twitter/1651693/story.html?id=1651693 [Accessed 25 June, 2009].

Story, J., 1999. *Cultural consumption and everyday life.* London: Edward Arnold, 1999.

Taylor, E., 2009. *DameElizabeth* [Twitter]. Available from: http://twitter.com/DameElizabeth [Accessed 31 August 2009].

TechCrunch, 2009. *CrunchBase: cyworld* [on-line]. Techcrunch. Available from: http://www.crunchbase.com/company/cyworld [Accessed 10 November 2009].

Thomas, R., 2009a. *Rob Thomas* [Facebook]. Available from: http://www.facebook.com [Accessed 31 August 2009].

Thomas, R., 2009b. *ThisIsRobThomas* [Twitter]. Available from http://twitter.com/ThisIsRob-Thomas [Accessed 31 August 2009].

Toland, K. and Mueller, B., 2003. *Advertising and societies: global issues.* New York: Peter Lang.

Turner, G., Bonner, F., and Marshall, P.D., (2000). *Fame games: the media production of the Australian celebrity.* Melbourne: Cambridge University Press.

Turner, G., 2010. *Ordinary people and the media: the demotic turn.* London: Sage.

Turner, G., 2004. *Understanding celebrity.* London: Sage.

Winfrey, O., 2009. *Oprah* [Twitter]. Available from: http://twitter.com/oprah [Accessed 31 August 2009].

SECTION VI

MEDIA/AUDIENCE

Introduction

This section situates the media audience as an object of critical analysis. Cultural studies influenced audience research emerged in the 1980s as a response to both the pessimism of screen theory, which was based on the critic's reading of unconscious processes and texts, as well as the positivist limited effects and uses and gratifications traditions of the social sciences. While Stuart Hall's influential 1980 essay "Encoding/Decoding" was a theoretical treatise rather than a research study per se, it paved the way for empirical reception research informed by cultural theory, feminism and critical race theory. David Morley's pioneering 1980 *Nationwide Audience* study, which took the encoding/decoding model as the basis for measuring the varied ideological responses of TV news viewers, exemplified one strand of critical audience research.

Janice Radway's equally formative study *Reading the Romance: Women, Patriarchy and Popular Literature* (1984) considers women's interpretations of the ideologies circulated in romance novels. However, she also investigates practices of media use, which leads her to characterize romance reading as a "declaration of independence" from feminized domestic labor. Both Morley and Radway have had an enormous influence on the subsequent scholarship on television, music, film and magazine viewers and readers. Indeed, during the 1980s and 1990s, critical media studies was focused on audiences, and this focus became a contentious debate, with some scholars suggesting that ordinary people actively use popular commercial media to negotiate and sometimes resist dominant power relations (a position associated most strongly with the cultural studies scholar John Fiske) and others suggesting that the concept of the active audience was overblown.

Ien Ang's "On the Politics of Empirical Audience Research," a chapter from her 1996 book *Living Room Wars*, deftly synthesizes an impressive swatch of critical audience research, while also reflecting on the conundrums of empirical study, based in part on her own experience as an audience researcher. Ang differentiates mainstream and critical audience studies, noting in particular the tension between liberal pluralist conceptions of society that see individuals as autonomous and "unhindered by cultural powers," and cultural studies approaches that, building on poststructuralist insights, envision people as "always-already implicated in, and necessarily constrained by the web of relationships and structures which constitute them as social subjects."

For Ang, the latter approach need not involve stripping individuals of agency, but it does require situating the "negotiations" of subjects as audiences within the material conditions they find themselves in. Ang challenges the equation of audience activity with empowerment and questions the impetus to find the "truth" about audiences—even as she continues to advocate what she calls an ethnographic approach. Calling for a more modest approach, she argues that the best thing to come out of audience studies is open-minded and grounded analyses: "The critical promise of the ethnographic attitude resides in its potential to make and keep our interpretations sensitive to concrete specifications, to the unexpected, to history," she contends.

Lawrence Grossberg theorizes fandom as a sensibility or mode of engagement distinct from other types of media consumption his 1991 essay "Is There a Fan in the House? The Affective Sensibility of Fandom." Grossberg's focus is on music, not visual culture, and unlike much audience research in the wake of Hall's "Encoding/Decoding" he focuses on affect rather than meaning making and ideology. According to Grossberg, if the sensibility of the consumer operates by producing structures of pleasure, the category of the fan is different: "The fan's relationship to cultural texts operates in the domain of affect or mood." One of the first media scholars to study the affective dimensions of audiencehood, Grossberg takes rock and roll as a site for theorizing popular media as a "crucial ground" for constructing mattering maps, or investments that, because they are excessive, go beyond ideological challenge. While his focus is not on the pleasure or meaning of the text, Grossberg shares some of the optimism associated with proponents of the active audience. For him, fandom matters because it buffers the conditions of everyday life and sustains the energy needed for social change. When fans invest in a song or a band, they are empowered to keep going, to "continue struggling to make a difference," Grossberg contends.

In "The Oppositional Gaze," a chapter from her 1992 book *Black Looks: Race and Representation*, bell hooks interrogates the theory of the male gaze, a key concept in feminist film studies. While screen scholars like Laura Mulvey theorized the power dynamics of looking from the sole perspective of gender and assumed that the category of woman was universal, hooks reminds readers that white and Black women are positioned differently in and by Hollywood film. Likewise, if the "gaze" is said to perpetuate sexual objectification, it has also been a site of resistance for colonized Black people, a device for inter-rogating the gaze of the Other, looking back and at one another and "naming what we see." For hooks, agency results from necessity: Black female spectators, she argues, have had to develop looking relations within a "cinematic context that constructs our presence as an absence ... so as to perpetuate white supremacy." For hooks the "oppositional gaze" is a dimension of resistance to class, race and gender oppression that is not limited to media consumption but extends to everyday practices of identification and resistance that oppose the dominant order.

Jack Bratich's 2005 contribution "Amassing the Multitude: Revisiting Early Audience Studies" reviews the history of audience research with the goal of taking the field in new directions. His voluminous survey of mainstream and critical research makes several contributions. First, Bratich historicizes the "problema-tization" of the audience from the earliest propaganda studies to the moral panics of the 1950s to the contestation of the audience as a category, understood less as a common sense reality than a fiction used by industry and scholars alike. Second, he shows that the history of audience research is marked by "attempts to measure, identify, understand and target" an elusive object, a point that Michael Hardt and Antonio Negri (2001) also make about the relationship between capital and attempts to measure, contain and name the "multitude."

Bringing their theorization of the multitude into media studies, Bratich calls for a shift away from the study of the audience to the study of audience power or the "mediated multitude." Audience power, he explains, is less about people watching, reading or listening to mediated texts than it is about "creative processes of meaning making, the appropriation and circulation of affects, and the engagement of these capacities"—in other words the collective invention of values, signification and affects. Moving beyond existing debates over the audience, Bratich's approach highlights people's dispersed role in producing as well as consuming media culture.

Mark Andrejevic's 2002 essay "The Work of Being Watched: Interactive Media and the Exploitation of Self-Disclosure" brings a concern with work and surveillance into the study of audiences. Blending politi-cal economy and Foucault's understanding of panopticism (1995), Andrejevic's scholarship focuses on new media interactivity, from filling out marketing surveys online to discussing TV programs on fan forums and social networking sites. Challenging any notion that expanded opportunities to interact with media through new technologies represent a democratization of media or a subversion of its economic and cul-tural power, Andrejevic argues what is actually happening is that labor is being offloaded onto consumers who effectively participate in their own surveillance and target marketing.

The work of being watched closely intersects with what Andrejevic calls the 21st century confessional —self-expression and individualization—as it incites us to do the work of "making ourselves into niches" with customized marketing pitches and specialized programming. The capacity to interact online does not extend the empowerment ascribed to the "active audience" as much as it enlists viewers and users in broader shifts in late capitalist production and the extension of work into leisure. Providing a counterpoint to celebratory analysis of new media, Andrejevic suggests that the audience has become the unpaid workforce of the 21st century.

Mizuko Ito's 2006 essay "Japanese Media Mixes and Amateur Cultural Exchange" approaches the alternative economies of new media fandom, particularly Japanese animation media mixes that combine analog and digital media forms. Drawing from Henry Jenkin's influential work on participatory culture (1992, 2005) she provides an alternative to Andrejevic's more cautious model, arguing that children's engagement with media mixes provides "evidence that they are capable not only of critical engagement and creative production, but also of entrepreneurial participation in the exchange systems and economies that they have developed around media mix content." However, Ito does not suggest that new media technologies have created "a new network of participatory media culture." Rather, new media fandom builds on existing fan cultures and activities—Yugioh media mixes, for example, involve participatory activities such as remixing, customization and peer-to-peer exchange, but these interactive practices depend on an existing fandom buttressed by a cross-reference to a TV anime series, a card game, video games, occasional movie releases and character merchandise.

While Andrejevic characterizes the synergy between interactive media users and commercial industry as a form of exploitation, Ito grounds her analysis of otaku fan subcultures as a form of amateur cultural production and community building, as "niche communities of disenfranchised youth who are mobilizing through the internet to create communities of interest that challenge elite and adult sensibilities."

References

Hall, Stuart, "Encoding/decoding," in *Culture, Media, Language*, ed. Stuart Hall, David Rowe and Dorothy Hobson (New York: Routledge, 1980), p. 128–138.

Foucault, Michel, *Discipline & Punish* (New York: Vintage, 2nd ed., 1995).

Hardt, Michael and Negri, Antonio, *Empire* (Cambridge, MA: Harvard University Press, 2001).

Jenkins, Henry, *Textual Poachers: Television Fans and Participatory Culture* (New York: Routledge, 1992).

Jenkins, Henry, *Convergence Culture: Where Old and New Media Collide* (New York: NYU Press, 2005).

Morley, David, *Nationwide Audience* (London: British Film Institute, 1980).

Radway, Janice, *Reading the Romance: Women, Patriarchy and Popular Literature* (Durhan, NC: University of North Carolina Press, 1991).

31.
ON THE POLITICS OF EMPIRICAL AUDIENCE RESEARCH

Ien Ang

In his pioneering book, *The 'Nationwide' Audience*, David Morley situates his research on which the book reports as follows:

> The relation of an audience to the ideological operations of television remains in principle an empirical question: the challenge is the attempt to develop appropriate methods of empirical investigation of that relation.
>
> (Morley 1980a: 162)

Although this sentence may initially be interpreted as a call for a methodological discussion about empirical research techniques, its wider meaning should be sought in the theoretical and political context of Morley's work. To me, the importance of *The 'Nationwide' Audience* does not so much reside in the fact that it offers an empirically validated, and thus 'scientific', account of 'the ideological operations of television', nor merely in its demonstration of some of the ways in which the television audience is 'active'. Other, more wide-ranging issues are at stake – issues related to the *politics* of research.

Since its publication in 1980, *The 'Nationwide' Audience* has played an important role in media studies. The book occupies a key strategic position in the study of media audiences – a field of study that went through a rapid development in the 1980s. It seems fair to say that this book forms a major moment in the growing popularity of an 'ethnographic' approach on media audiences – Morley himself has termed his project an 'ethnography of reading' (1981: 13). This type of qualitative empirical research, usually carried out in the form of in-depth interviews with a small number of people (and at times supplemented with some form of participant observation), is now recognized by many as one of the best ways to learn about the differentiated subtleties of people's engagements with television and other media.

This 'ethnographic' approach has gained popularity in both 'critical' media studies and 'mainstream' mass communications research (see, e.g., Hobson 1980 and 1982; Lull 1980 and 1988; Radway 1984; Ang 1985; Jensen 1986; Lindlof 1987; Liebes and Katz 1990). A sort of methodological consensus has emerged, a common ground in which scholars from divergent epistemological backgrounds can thrive. On the one hand, qualitative methods of empirical research seem to be more acceptable than quantitative ones because they offer the possibility to avoid what C. Wright Mills (1970) has termed abstracted empiricism – a tendency often levelled at the latter by 'critical' scholars. On the other hand, some 'mainstream' audience researchers are now acknowledging the limitations on the kind of data that can be produced by large-scale, quantitative survey work, and believe that ethnographically oriented methods can overcome the shortcomings observed. Given this enthusiastic, rather new interest in qualitative research methods, I would like to reflect upon its general implications for our understanding of television audiences. What kind of knowledge does it produce? What can this manner of doing empirical research on audiences mean? In short, what are the politics of audience 'ethnography'?[1]

In exploring these questions, I want to clarify some of the issues that are at stake in developing a *critical* perspective in empirical audience studies. The term 'critical' as I would like to use it here refers first of all to a certain intellectual-political *orientation* towards academic practice: whatever its subject matter or methodology, essential to doing 'critical' research would be the adoption of a self-reflective perspective, one that is, first, conscious of the social and discursive nature of any research practice, and, second, takes seriously the Foucauldian reminder that the production of knowledge is always bound up in a network of power relations (Foucault 1980). By characterizing 'critical' research in this way, that is, as an orientation rather than as a fixed 'paradigm', I aim to relativize the more rigid ways in which 'critical' and 'mainstream' research have often been opposed to one another.

Formally speaking, positions can only be 'critical' or 'mainstream' in relation to other positions within a larger discursive field. The two terms thus do not primarily signify fixed contents of thought, but their status within a whole, often dispersed, field of statements, claims and knowledges, what Foucault calls a 'regime of truth'. The relations of force in that field can change over time: what was once 'critical' (or marginal) can become part of the 'mainstream'; what was once 'mainstream' (or dominant) can lose its power and be pushed aside to a marginal(ized) position. Furthermore, as Larry Grossberg (1987) has usefully remarked, the term 'critical' can bear uneasy arrogant connotations: after all, is there any scholar whose work is not 'critical' in some sense?

This does not mean, of course, that the distinction is totally devoid of any substantive bearings. In media studies, for instance, the 'critical' tradition, whose beginnings can be located in the work of the Frankfurt School, has generally derived its philosophical and political inspiration from European schools of thought such as Marxism and (post)structuralism. In terms of research problematics, 'critical' media researchers have mainly been concerned with the analysis of the ideological and/or economic role of the media in capitalist and patriarchal society. Furthermore, the epistemological underpinnings of this kind of work are generally characterized by a strident anti-positivist and anti-empiricist mentality.[2]

This distrust of positivist empiricism on the part of 'critical' theorists, however, does not necessarily imply an *inherent* incompatibility between 'critical' and empirical research, as is often contended by 'mainstream' scholars.[3] Indeed, if doing 'critical' research is more a matter of intellectual-political orientation than of academic paradigm building, then no fixed, universal yardstick, theoretical or methodological, for what constitutes 'critical' knowledge is possible. On the contrary, in my view what it means to be critical needs to be assessed and constantly reassessed in every concrete conjuncture, with respect to the concrete issues and directions that are at stake in any concrete research field. In other words, I am proposing an *open* and *contextual* definition of 'critical' research, one that does not allow itself to rest easily on pre-existent epistemological foundations but, on the contrary, is reassessed continuously according to the ways in which it contributes to our understanding of the world. In the following, I hope to clarify some of the implications of this perspective on doing 'critical' research for an evaluation of the current developments in audience studies as I indicated above.

More concretely, what I will discuss and try to elaborate in this chapter is what I take as the political and theoretical specificity of the *cultural studies* approach as a 'critical' perspective, from which David Morley, coming from the Birmingham Centre for Contemporary Cultural Studies, has developed his work (see Hall *et al.* 1980; Streeter 1984; Fiske 1987b). I will set this perspective on audience studies against some developments in and around the uses and gratifications approach, where an interest in 'ethnographic' methods has been growing recently. In doing this I will not be able to discuss the wide range of concrete studies that have been made in this area. Rather I will restrict myself, somewhat schematically and all too briefly, to the more programmatic statements and proposals pertaining to the identity and the future development of the field, and evaluate them in the light of what I see as important for a critical cultural studies approach. Furthermore, it is not my intention to construct an absolute antagonism between the two approaches. Rather, I would like to highlight some of the differences in preoccupation and perspective, in order to specify how ethnographic or ethnographically oriented studies of media audiences can contribute to a 'critical' approach in the sense I have outlined. Before doing this, I will first give a short sketch of the intellectual arena in which Morley intervened.

The Problem of the Disappearing Audience

The 'Nationwide' Audience appeared at a time when critical discourse about film and television in Britain was heavily preoccupied with what Morley (1980a: 161), following Steve Neale, calls an 'abstract text/ subject relationship', formulated within a generally (post)structuralist and psychoanalytic theoretical framework. In this discourse, primarily developed in the journal *Screen*, film and television spectatorship is almost exclusively theorized from the perspective of the 'productivity of the text'. As a consequence, the role of the viewer was conceived in purely formalist terms: as a position inscribed in the text. Here, the subject-in-the-text tends to collapse with 'real' social subjects. In this model, there is no space for a dialogical relationship between texts and social subjects. Texts are assumed to be the only source of meaning; they construct subject positions which viewers are bound to take up if they are to make sense of the text. In other words, the reading of texts is conceived in 'Screen theory' as entirely dictated by textual structures.

It is this model's textual determinism that fuelled Morley's dissatisfaction. Theoretically, it implied an ahistorical, asocial and generalist conception of film and TV spectatorship. Methodologically, the analysis of textual structures alone was considered to be sufficient to comprehend how viewers are implicated in the texts they encounter. Politically, this model left no room for manoeuvre for television viewers. They are implicitly conceived as 'prisoners' of the text. It was against this background that Morley decided to undertake an empirical investigation of how groups of viewers with different social positions read or interpret one particular text: an episode of the British TV magazine programme *Nationwide*. One of the most important motivations of Morley's intervention, then, was to overcome the textualism of *Screen* theory's discourse, in which the relation of text and subject is dealt with 'as an *a priori* question to be deduced from a theory of the ideal spectator "inscribed" in the text' (Morley 1980a: 162). By looking at how one text could be decoded in different ways by different

groups of social subjects, Morley's intention, in which he was successful, was to demonstrate that encounters between texts and viewers are far more complex than the textualist theory would suggest; they are overdetermined by the operation of a multiplicity of forces – certain historical and social structures, but also other texts – that simultaneously act upon the subjects concerned.[4] What *The 'Nationwide' Audience* explores is the notion that the moment of decoding should be considered as a relatively autonomous process in which a constant struggle over the meaning of the text is fought out. Textual meanings do not reside in the texts themselves: a certain text can come to mean different things depending on the interdiscursive context in which viewers interpret it.

The significance of Morley's turn towards empirical research of the television audience should be assessed against this critical background. It is first of all a procedure that is aimed at opening up a space in which watching television can begin to be understood as a complex cultural practice full of dialogical negotiations and contestations, rather than as a singular occurrence whose meaning can be determined once and for all in the abstract. Doing empirical research, then, is here used as a strategy to break out of a hermetically closed theoreticism in which an absolute certainty about the ideological effectivity of television is presumed. Thus, when Morley says that the relation of an audience to television 'remains an empirical question', what he is basically aiming at is to open up critical discourse on television audiences, and to sensitize it for the possibility of struggle in the practices of television use and consumption – a struggle whose outcome cannot be known in advance, for the simple reason that encounters between television and audiences are always historically specific and context-bound.

Academic Convergence?

The 'Nationwide' Audience has generally been received as an innovative departure within cultural studies, both theoretically and methodologically. If *Screen* theory can be diagnosed as one instance in which critical discourse on television suffered from 'the problem of the disappearing audience' (Fejes 1984), Morley's project represents an important acknowledgement within cultural studies that television viewing is a practice that involves the active production of meanings by viewers. But the book has not only made an impact in cultural studies circles. Curiously, but not surprisingly, it has also been welcomed by adherents of the uses and gratifications approach, one of the most influential 'mainstream' strands of audience research in mass communication scholarship. These scholars see books such as Morley's as an important step on the part of 'critical' scholars in their direction, that is, as a basic acceptance of, and possible contribution to, a refinement of their own basic axiomatic commitment to 'the active audience'. At the same time, some uses and gratifications researchers, for their part, have now incorporated some of the insights developed within the 'critical' perspective into their own paradigm. For example, they have adopted semiologically informed cultural studies concepts such as 'text' and 'reader' in their work. This move indicates an acknowledgement of the symbolic nature of negotiations between media texts and their readers which they, in their narrow functionalist interest in the multiple relationships between audience 'needs' and media 'uses', had previously all but ignored. ... As Jax Blumler, Michael Gurevitch and Elihu Katz admit:

> Gratifications researchers, in their paradigmatic personae, have lost sight of what the media are purveying, in part because of an over-commitment to the endless freedom of the audience to reinvent the text, in part because of a too rapid leap to mega-functions, such as surveillance or self-identity.
>
> (Blumler *et al.* 1985: 272)

On top of this conceptual rapprochement, they have also expressed their delight in noticing a methodological 'concession' among 'critical' scholars: at last, so they exclaim, some 'critical' scholars have dropped their suspicion of doing empirical research. In a benevolent, rather fatherly tone, Blumler, Gurevitch and Katz, three senior ambassadors of the uses and gratifications approach, have thus proclaimed a gesture of 'reaching out' to the other 'camp' (1985: 275). Therefore the prospect is evoked of a merger of the two approaches, to the point that they may ultimately fuse into a happy common project in which the perceived hostility between the two 'camps' will have been

unmasked as academic 'pseudo-conflicts'. As one leading gratifications researcher, Karl Erik Rosengren, optimistically predicts: 'To the extent that the same problematics are empirically studied by members of various schools, the present sharp differences of opinion will gradually diminish and be replaced by a growing convergence of perspectives' (1983: 203).[5]

However, to interpret these recent developments in audience studies in terms of such a convergence is to simplify and even misconceive what is at stake in the 'ethnographic turn' within cultural studies. For one thing, I would argue that cultural studies and uses and gratifications research only superficially share 'the same problematics', as Rosengren would have it. Also, what separates a 'critical' from a 'mainstream' perspective is more than merely some 'differences of opinion', sharp or otherwise. Rather, it concerns fundamental differences not only in epistemological but also in theoretical and political attitudes towards the aim and status of doing empirical work in the first place.

The academic idealization of joining forces in pursuit of a supposedly common goal as if it were a neutral, scientific project is a particularly depoliticizing strategy, because it tends to neutralize all antagonism and disagreement in favour of a forced consensus. If I am cautious and a little wary about this euphoria around the prospect of academic convergence, it is not my intention to impose a rigid and absolute, eternal dichotomy between 'critical' and 'mainstream' research. Nor would I want to assert that Morley's project is entirely 'critical' and the uses and gratifications approach completely 'mainstream'. As I have noted before, the relationship between 'critical' and 'mainstream' is not a fixed one; it does not concern two mutually exclusive, antagonistic sets of knowledge, as some observers would imply by talking in terms of 'schools', 'paradigms' or even 'camps'. In fact, many assumptions and ideas do not, in themselves, intrinsically belong to one or the other perspective. For example, the basic assumption that the audience is 'active' (rather than passive) and that watching television is a social (rather than an individual) practice is currently accepted in both perspectives. There is nothing spectacular about that.[6] What matters is how this idea of 'activeness' is articulated with a more general theory of social agency and power. Also, I would suggest that the idea that texts can generate multiple meanings because readers/ viewers can 'negotiate' textual meanings is not in itself a sufficient condition for the declared convergence. For example, Tamar Liebes has suggested that 'the focus of the convergence is on the idea that the inter-action between messages and receivers takes on the form of negotiation, and is not predetermined' (1986:1). However, as I will try to show below, what makes all the difference is the way in which 'negotia-tion' is conceived. After all, 'not predetermined' does not mean 'undetermined'; on the contrary.

While uses and gratifications researchers generally operate within a liberal pluralist conception of society where individuals are seen as ideally free, that is, unhin-dered by external powers, in cultural studies, following Marxist/(post)structuralist assumptions, people are conceived as always-already implicated in, and neces-sarily constrained by, the web of relationships and structures which constitute them as social subjects. This doesn't mean that they are stripped of agency like preprogrammed automatons, but that that agency itself, or the 'negotiations' subjects undertake in constructing their lives, is *over*determined (i.e. neither predetermined nor undetermined) by the concrete conditions of exis-tence they find themselves in. Following Hall (1986b: 46), 'determinacy' here is understood in terms of the setting of limits, the establishment of parameters, the defining of the space of operations, rather than in terms of the absolute predictability of particular outcomes. This is what Hall (1986c) calls a 'Marxism without guarantees', a non-determinist theory of deter-mination, or, to put it simply, a recognition of the virtual truism that 'people make their own history but under conditions not of their own making'.

How complex structural and conjunctural deter-minations of viewership and audiencehood should be conceived remains therefore an important point of divergence between 'critical' and 'mainstream' stud-ies. Finally, it is also noteworthy to point out that, while uses and gratifications researchers now seem to be 'rediscovering the text', researchers working within a cultural studies perspective seem to be moving away from the text. This is very clear in Morley's sec-ond book, *Family Television* (1986), on which I will comment later. In fact, it becomes more and more dif-ficult to delineate what 'the television text' is in a media-saturated world.

In other words, in evaluating whether we can really speak of a paradigmatic convergence, it is not enough to establish superficially similar research questions, nor to take at face value a shared acknowledgement of the usefulness of certain methods of inquiry. Of course, such commonalities are interesting enough and it would be nonsense to categorically discard them. I do think it is important to avoid a dogmatism or antagonism-for-the-sake-of-it, and to try to learn from others wherever that is possible. But at the same time we should not lose sight of the fact that any call for a convergence itself is not an innocent gesture. It tends to be done from a certain point of view, and therefore necessarily involves a biased process in which certain issues and themes are highlighted and others sup-pressed. And it is my contention that an all too hasty declaration of convergence could lead to neglecting some of the most important distinctive features of cultural studies as a critical intellectual enterprise.

A difference in conceptualizing the object of study is a first issue that needs to be discussed here. As I have already suggested, in a cultural studies per-spective 'audience activity' cannot and should not be studied nominalistically, decontextualized from the larger network of social relationships in which it occurs. The aim of cultural studies is not a matter of dissecting 'audience activity' in ever more refined variables and categories so that we can ultimately have a complete and generalizable formal 'map' of all dimensions of 'audience activity' (which seems to be the drive behind the uses and gratifications project; e.g. Levy and Windahl 1984, 1986). Rather, the aim, as I see it, is to arrive at a more historicized and contex-tualized insight into the ways in which 'audience activity' is articulated within and by a complex set of social, political, economic and cultural forces. In other words, what is at stake is not the understanding of 'audience activity' as such as an isolated and iso-latable object of research, but the embeddedness of 'audience activity' in a complex network of ongoing cultural practices and relationships.

As a result, an audience researcher working within a cultural studies sensibility cannot restrict herself or himself to 'just' studying audiences and their activi-ties (and, for that matter, relating those activities with other variables such as gratifications sought or obtained, dependencies, effects, and so on). She or he will also engage herself/himself with the structural and cultural *processes* through which the audiences she or he is studying are constituted and being constituted. Thus, one essential theoretical point of the cultural studies approach of the television audience is its foregrounding of the notion that the dynamics of watching television, no matter how heterogeneous and seemingly free, are always related to the operations of forms of social power. It is in this light that we should see Morley's decision to do research on viewers' decodings: it was first of all motivated by an interest in what he in the quote at the beginning of this chapter calls 'the ideological operations of television'.

It is important then to emphasize that the reference to 'the active audience' does not occupy the same theoretical status in the two approaches. From a cultural studies point of view, evidence that audiences are 'active' cannot simply be equated with the rather triumphant, liberal pluralist conclusion, often displayed by gratificationists, that media consumers are 'free' or even 'powerful' – a conclusion which allegedly undercuts the idea of 'media hegemony'. The question for cultural studies is not simply one of 'where the power lies in media systems' (Blumler *et al.* 1985: 260) – i.e. with the audience or with the media producers – but rather how relations of power are organized within the heterogeneous practices of media use and consumption. In other words, rather than constructing an opposition between 'the' media and 'the' audience, as if these were separate ontological entities, and, along with it, the application of a distributional theory of power – i.e. power conceived as a 'thing' that can be attributed to either side of the opposing entities – cultural studies is interested in understanding media consumption as a site of cultural struggle, in which a variety of forms of power are exercised, with different sorts of effects.[7] Thus if, as Morley's study has shown, viewers decode a text in different ways and sometimes even give oppositional meanings to it, this should be understood not as an example of 'audience freedom', but as a moment in that cultural struggle, an ongoing struggle over meaning and pleasure which is central to the fabrication) of everyday life.

I hope to have made it clear by now that in evaluating the possibility or even desirability of a paradigmatic convergence, it is important to look at how 'audience activity' is theorized or interpreted, and how research 'findings' are placed in a wider theoretical framework. So, if one type of 'audience activity' which has received much attention in both approaches has been the 'interpretive strategies' used by audiences to read media texts (conceptualized in terms of decoding structures, interpretive communities, patterns of involvement, and so on), how are we to make sense of those interpretive strategies? The task of the cultural studies researcher, I would suggest, is to develop *strategic interpretations* of them, different not only in form and content but also in scope and intent from those offered in more 'mainstream' accounts.[8] I will return to this central issue of interpretation below.

Beyond Methodology

A troubling aspect about the idea of (and desire for) convergence, then, is that it tends to be conceptualized as an exclusively 'scientific' enterprise. Echoing the tenets of positivism, its aim seems to be the gradual accumulation of scientifically confirmed 'findings'. It is propelled by the hope that by seeking a shared agreement on what is relevant to study and by developing shared methodological skills, the final scientific account of 'the audience' can eventually be achieved. In this framework, audience research is defined as a specialized niche within an academic discipline (e.g. 'mass communication'), in which it is assumed that 'the audience' is a proper object of study whose characteristics can be ever more accurately observed, described, categorized, systematized and explained until the whole picture is 'filled in'. In other words, this scientific project implicitly claims in principle (if not in practice) to be able to produce total knowledge, to reveal the full and objective 'truth' about 'the audience'. The audience here is imagined as, and turned into, an object with researchable attributes and features (be it described in terms of preferences, uses, effects, decodings, interpretive strategies, or whatever) that can be definitively known – if only researchers of different breeding would stop quarrelling with each other and unite to work harmoniously together to accomplish the task.[9]

From such a point of view, the question of *methodology* becomes a central issue. After all, rigour of method has traditionally been seen as the guarantee *par excellence* for the 'scientific' status of knowledge. In positivist social science, the hypothetico-deductive testing of theory through empirical research, quantitative in form, is cherished as the cornerstone of the production of 'scientific' knowledge. Theory that is not empirically tested or that is too complex to be moulded into empirically testable hypotheses has to be dismissed as 'unscientific'. These assumptions, which are more or less central to the dominant version of the uses and gratifications approach as it was established in the 1970s, are now contested by a growing number of researchers who claim that reality cannot be grasped and explained through quantitative methods alone. Stronger still, they forcefully assert that to capture the multidimensionality and complexity of audience activity the use of qualitative methods – and thus a move towards the 'ethnographic' – is desperately called for (cf. Lull 1986; Jensen 1987; Lindlof and Meyer 1987).

From a 'scientific' point of view, it is this methodological challenge that forms the condition of possibility of the perceived convergence. However, although I think that the struggle for legitimization of qualitative research is a very important one, I do believe that it is not the central point for critical cultural studies. This is the case because, as the struggle is defined as a matter of methodology, its relevance is confined to the development of audience research as an *academic* enterprise. Of course, this development is in itself interesting given the decades-long hegemony of positivism and the quantifying attitude in audience research. Furthermore, the growing influence of alternative 'paradigms' such as ethnomethodology and symbolic interactionism should certainly be welcomed. The problem with many 'mainstream' claims about the usefulness of qualitative methods, however, is that they are put forward in the name of 'scientific progress', without questioning the epistemological distinction between Science and common-sense which lies at the heart of positivism. The aim still seems to be the isolation of a body of knowledge that can be recognized as 'scientific' (in its broadest meaning), the orientation being one towards the advancement of an academic discipline, and, concomitantly, the technical improvement of its instruments of analysis.

A cultural studies perspective on audience research cannot stop short at this level of debate. For a critical cultural studies, it is not questions of

methodology, nor 'scientific progress' that prevail. On the contrary, we should relativize the academic commitment to increasing knowledge *per se*, and resist the temptation of what Stuart Hall (1986b: 56) has called the 'codification' of cultural studies into a stable realm of established theories and canonized methodologies. In this respect, the territorial conflict between 'mainstream' and 'critical' research, quantitative and qualitative methods, humanistic and social-scientific disciplines, and so on, should perhaps not bother us too much at all in the first place. As James Carey once remarked, '[p]erhaps all the talk about theory, method, and other such things prevents us from raising, or permits us to avoid raising, deeper and disquieting questions about the purposes of our scholarship' (1983:5). And indeed: why are we so interested in knowing about audiences in the first place? In empirical audience research, especially, it is important to reflect upon the politics of the knowledge produced. After all, scrutinizing media audiences is not an innocent practice. It does not take place in a social and institutional vacuum. As we all know, historically, the hidden agenda of audience research, even when it presents itself as pure and objective, has all too often been its commercial or political usefulness. In other words, what we should reflect upon is the *political* interventions we make when studying audiences – political not only in the sense of some external societal goal, but, more importantly, in that we cannot afford to ignore the political dimensions of the process and practice of the production of knowledge itself. What does it mean to subject audiences to the researcher's gaze? How can we develop insights that do not reproduce the kind of objectified knowledge served up by, say, market research or empiricist effects research? How is it possible to do audience research which is 'on the side' of the audience?[10] These are nagging political questions which cannot be smoothed out by the comforting canons of epistemology, methodology and Science.

Of course it is not easy to pin down what such considerations would imply in concrete terms. But it could at least be said that we should try to avoid a stance in which 'the audience' is relegated to the status of exotic 'other' merely interesting in so far as 'we', as researchers, can turn 'them' into 'objects' of study, and about whom 'we' have the privileged position of acquiring 'scientific' knowledge.[11] To begin with, I think, critical audience studies should not strive and pretend to tell 'the truth' about 'the audience'. Its ambitions should be much more modest. As Grossberg has suggested, 'the goal of [critical research] is to offer not a polished representation of the truth, but simply a little help in our efforts to better understand the world' (1987: 89). This modesty has less to do with some sort of false humility than with the basic acknowledgement that every research practice unavoidably takes place in a particular historical situation, and is therefore in principle of a partial nature. As Hammersley and Atkinson have provocatively put it, 'all social research takes the form of participant observation: it involves participating in the social world, in whatever role, and reflecting on the products of that participation' (1983: 16). The collection of data, either quantitative or qualitative in form, can never be separated from its interpretation; it is only through practices of interpretive theorizing that unruly social experiences and events related to media consumption become established as meaningful 'facts' about audiences. Understanding 'audience activity' is thus caught up in the discursive representation, not the transparent reflection, of diverse realities pertaining to people's engagements with media.

These considerations lead to another, more politicized conception of doing research. It is not the search for (objective, scientific) Truth in which the researcher is engaged, but the construction of *interpretations*, of certain ways of understanding the world, always historically located, subjective and relative. It is the decisive importance of this interpretive moment that I would like to highlight in exploring the possibilities of a critical audience studies.[12]

In positivism, the necessarily worldly nature of interpretation is repressed, relegated to the refuted realm of 'bias'. It is assumed to follow rather automatically – i.e. without the intervention of the subjective 'whims' of the researcher – from the controlled process of 'empirical testing of theory'. An apparent innocence of interpretation is then achieved, one that is seemingly grounded in 'objective social reality' itself. In fact, the very term 'interpretation' would seem to have definite negative connotations for positivists because of its connection with 'subjectivism'. And even within those social science approaches in which the interpretive act of the researcher – i.e. the

moment of data analysis that comes after data collection – is taken more seriously, interpretation is more often than not problematized as a technical rather than a political matter, defined in terms of careful inference making rather than in terms of discursive constructions of reality.

It should be recognized, however, that because interpretations always inevitably involve the construction of certain representations of reality (and not others), they can never be 'neutral' and merely 'descriptive'. After all, the 'empirical', captured in either quantitative or qualitative form, does not yield self-evident meanings; it is only through the interpretive framework constructed by the researcher that understandings of the 'empirical' come about. No 'theory' brought to bear on the 'empirical' can ever be 'value-neutral'; it is always 'interested' in the strong sense of that word. Here, then, the thoroughly political nature of any research practice manifests itself. What is at stake is a *politics of interpretation*: '[T]o advance an interpretation is to insert it into a network of power relations' (Pratt 1986: 52).

Of course, this also implies a shift in the position of the researcher. She or he is no longer a bearer of the truth, but occupies a 'partial' position in two senses of the word. On the one hand, she or he is no longer the neutral observer, but is someone whose job it is to produce historically and culturally specific knowledges that are the result of equally specific discursive encounters between researcher and informants, in which the subjectivity of the researcher is not separated from the 'object' s/he is studying. The interpretations that are produced in the process can never claim to be definitive: on the contrary, they are necessarily incomplete (for they always involve simplification, selection and exclusion) and temporary. 'If neither history nor politics ever comes to an end, then theory (as well as research) is never completed and our accounts can never be closed or totalized' (Grossberg 1987: 89). On the other hand, and even more important, the position of the researcher is also more than that of the professional scholar: beyond being a capable interpreter she or he is also inherently a political and moral subject. As an intellectual s/he is responsible not only to the Academy, but to the social world s/he lives in as well, consciously or unconsciously so. It is at the interface of 'ethics' and 'scholarship' that the researcher's interpretations take on their distinctive political edge (cf. Rabinow 1986).

Of course, all this entails a different status for empirical research. Material obtained by ethnographic fieldwork or depth-interviews with audience members cannot simply be treated as direct slices of reality, as in naturalist conceptions of ethnography. Viewers' statements about their relation to television cannot be regarded as self-evident facts. Nor are they immediate, transparent reflections of those viewers' 'lived realities' that can speak for themselves. What is of critical importance, therefore, is the way in which those statements are made sense of, that is, interpreted. Here lies the ultimate political responsibility of the researcher. The comfortable assumption that it is the reliability and accuracy of the methodologies being used that will ascertain the validity of the outcomes of research, thereby reducing the researcher's responsibility to a technical matter, is rejected. In short, to return to Morley's opening statement, audience research is undertaken because the relation between television and viewers is an empirical *question*. But the empirical is not the privileged domain where the *answers* should be sought. Answers – partial ones, to be sure, that is, both provisional and committed – are to be constructed, in the form of interpretations.[13]

Towards Interpretive Ethnography

I would now like to return to Morley's work, and evaluate its place in the research field in the light of my reflections above. To be sure, Morley himself situates his work firmly within the academic context. And parallel to the recent calls for convergence and cross-fertilization of diverse perspectives, Morley seems to have dropped his original antagonistic posture. For example, while in *The 'Nationwide' Audience* he emphasizes that 'we need to break fundamentally with the "uses and gratifications" approach' (1980a: 14),[14] in *Family Television,* he simply states that this new piece of research draws 'upon some of the insights' of this very approach (1986: 15). The latter book is also in a more general sense set in a less polemical tone than the first one: rather than taking up a dissident's stance against other theoretical perspectives, which is a central attribute of *The 'Nationwide' Audience, Family Television* is explicitly presented as a study that aims to combine the perspectives of separate traditions in order to overcome what Morley calls an 'unproductive form of segregation' (ibid.: 13). Furthermore, both books have been written in a markedly conventional style of academic social science, structured according to a narrative line which starts out with their contextualization within related academic research trends, followed by a methodological exposition and a description of the findings, and rounded off with a chapter containing an interpretation of the results and some more general conclusions. In both books Morley's voice is exclusively that of the earnest researcher; the writer's 'I', almost completely eliminated from the surface of the text, is apparently a disembodied subject solely driven by a disinterested wish to contribute to 'scientific progress'.[15]

Morley's academistic inclination tends to result in a lack of clarity about the critical import and political relevance of his analyses. For example, the relevance of *Family Television* as a project designed to investigate at the same time two different types of questions regarding television consumption – questions of television use, on the one hand, and questions of textual interpretation, on the other – is simply asserted by the statement that these are 'urgent questions about the television audience' (Morley 1986: 13). But why? What kind of urgency is being referred to here? Morley goes on to say that it is the analysis of the domestic viewing context as such which is his main interest, and that he wishes to identify the multiple meanings hidden behind the catch-all phrase 'watching television'. Indeed, central to *Family Television*'s discourse are, as Hall remarks in his introduction to the book, the notions of variability, diversity and difference:

> We are all, in our heads, several different audiences at once, and can be constituted as such by different programmes. We have the capacity to deploy different levels and modes of attention, to mobilise different competences in our viewing. At different times of the day, for different family members, different patterns of viewing have different 'saliences'. Here the monolithic conceptions of the viewer, the audience or of television itself have been displaced – one hopes forever – before the new emphasis on difference and variation.
>
> (Hall 1986a: 10)

Yet when taken in an unqualified manner it is exactly this stress on difference that essentially connects Morley's project with the preoccupations of the gratificationists. After all, it is their self-declared distinctive mission to get to grips with 'the gamut of audience experience' (Blumler *et al.* 1985: 271). For them too, the idea of plurality and diversity is pre-eminently the guiding principle for research. A convergence of perspectives after all?

Despite all the agreements that are certainly there, however, a closer look at the ramifications of Morley's undertaking reveals other concerns than merely the characterization and categorizing of varieties within viewers' readings and uses of television. Ultimately, it is not difference as such that is of main interest in Morley's work. To be sure, differences are not just simple facts that emerge more or less spontaneously from the empirical interview material; it is a matter of interpretation what are established as *significant* differences – significant not in the formal, statistical sense of that word, but in a culturally meaningful, interpretive sense. In cultural studies, then, it is the meanings of differences that matter – something that can only be grasped, interpretively, by looking at their contexts, social and cultural bases, and impacts. Thus, rather than the classification of differences and varieties in all sorts of typologies, which is a major preoccupation of a lot of uses and gratifications work, cultural studies would be oriented towards more specific and conjunctural understandings of how and why varieties in experience occur – a venture, to be sure, that is a closer approach to the ethnographic spirit.

In *Family Television*, for example, Morley has chosen to foreground the pattern of differences in viewing habits that are articulated with gender. What Morley emphasizes is that men and women clearly relate in contrasting ways to television, not only as to programme preferences, but also in, for example, viewing styles. The wives interviewed by Morley tend to watch television less attentively, at the same time doing other things such as talking or doing some housework. The husbands, in contrast, state a clear preference for viewing attentively, in silence, without interruption, 'in order not to miss anything' (Morley 1986: chapter 6). These differences are substantiated and highlighted by Morley's research as empirical facts, but he is careful to avoid considering these as

essential differences between men and women. As Charlotte Brunsdon has noted, it seems possible

> to differentiate a male – fixed, controlling, uninterrupted gaze – and a female – distracted, obscured, already busy – manner of watching television. There is some empirical truth in these characterizations, but to take this empirical truth for explanation leads to a theoretical short-circuit.
>
> (Brunsdon 1986: 105)

Indeed, in mainstream sociological accounts, gender would probably be treated as a self-evident pregiven factor that can be used as 'independent variable' to explain these differences. Male and female modes of watching television would then be constituted as two separate, discrete types of experience, clearly defined, fixed, static 'objects' in themselves as it were.[16] Such an empiricist account not only essentializes gender differences, but also fails to offer an understanding of how and why differentiations along gender lines take the very forms they do.

In contrast to this, both Morley and Brunsdon start out to construct a tentative interpretation which does not take the difference between male and female relations to television as an empirical given. Neither do they take recourse to psychological notions such as 'needs' or 'socialization' – as is often done in accounts of gender differences, as well as in uses and gratifications research – to try to understand why men and women tend to watch and talk about television in the disparate ways they do. In their interpretive work Morley and Brunsdon emphasize the structure of domestic power relations as constitutive for the differences concerned. The home generally has different meanings for men and women living in nuclear family arrangements: for husbands it is the site of leisure, for wives it is the site of work. Therefore, television as a domestic cultural form tends to be invested with different meanings for men and women. Television has for men become a central symbol for relaxation; women's relation to television, on the other hand, is much more contradictory. Brunsdon has this to say on Morley's research:

> The social relations between men and women appear to work in such a way that although the

men feel ok about imposing their choice of viewing on the whole of the family, the women do not.
The women have developed all sorts of strategies
to cope with television viewing they don't particularly like. The men in most cases appear to feel it
would be literally unmanning for them to sit quiet
during the women's programmes. However, the
women in general seem to find it almost impossible to switch into the silent communion with the
television set that characterises so much male
viewing.

(Brunsdon 1986: 104)

Women's distracted mode of watching television,
then, does not have something to do with some
essential femininity, but is a result of a complex of
cultural and social arrangements which makes it difficult for them to do otherwise, even though they
often express a longing to be able to watch their
favourite programmes without being disturbed. Men,
on the other hand, can watch television in a concentrated manner because they control the conditions to
do so. Their way of watching television, Brunsdon
concludes, 'seems not so much a masculine mode,
but a mode of power' (1986: 106).

What clearly emerges here is the beginning of
an interpretive framework in which differences in
television-viewing practices are not just seen as
expressions of different needs, uses or readings, but
are connected with the way in which particular social
subjects are structurally positioned in relation to each
other. In the context of the nuclear family home,
women's viewing patterns can only be understood in
relation to men's patterns; the two are in a sense constitutive of each other. Thus, if watching television is
a social and even collective practice, it is not a harmonious practice.[17] Because subjects are positioned
in different ways towards the set, they engage in a
continuing struggle over programme choice and programme interpretation, styles of viewing and textual
pleasure. What kind of viewer they become can be
seen as the outcome of this struggle, an outcome,
however, that is never definitive because it can always
be contested and subverted. What we call 'viewing
habits' are thus not a more or less static set of behaviours inhabited by an individual or group of individuals; rather they are the temporary result of a

neverending, dynamic and conflictual process in
which 'the fine-grained interrelationships between
meaning, pleasure, use and choice' are shaped (Hall
1986a: 10).

Morley's empirical findings, then, acquire their relevance and critical value in the context of this emerging theoretical understanding. And of course it could
only have been carried out from a specific interpretive
point of view. Needless to say, the point of view taken
up by Morley and Brunsdon is a feminist one, that is, a
worldly intellectual position that is sensitive to the
micro-politics of male/female relationships. Television
consumption, so we begin to understand, contributes
to the everyday construction of male and female subjectivities through the relations of power, contradiction and struggle that men and women enter into in
their daily engagements with the TV sets in their
homes. At this point, we can also see how Morley's
research enables us to begin to conceive of 'the ideological operations of television' in a much more radical way than has hitherto been done. The relation
between television and audiences is not just a matter
of discrete 'negotiations' between texts and viewers.
In a much more profound sense the process of television consumption – and the positioning of television
as such in the culture of modernity – has created new
areas of constraints and possibilities for structuring
social relationships, identities and desires. If television
is an 'ideological apparatus', to use that old-fashioned-
sounding term, then this is not so much because its
texts transmit certain 'messages', but because it is a
cultural form through which those constraints are
negotiated and those possibilities take shape.

But, one might ask, do we need empirical research,
or, more specifically, ethnographic audience research,
to arrive at such theoretical understandings? Why
examine audiences empirically at all? After all, some
critical scholars still dismiss the idea of doing empirical audience research altogether, because, so they
argue, it would necessarily implicate the researcher
with the strategies and aims of the capitalist culture
industry (e.g. Modleski 1986: xi–xii). Against this
background, I would like to make one last comment
on Morley's work here. Due to his academistic posture Morley has not deemed it necessary to reflect
upon his own position as a researcher. We do not get
to know how he found and got on with his

interviewees, nor are we informed about the way in which the interviews themselves took place. One of the very few things we learn about this in *Family Television* is that he gave up interviewing the adults and the young children at the same time, reportedly 'because after an initial period of fascination the young children quite quickly got bored' (Morley 1986: 174)! But what about the adults? What were the reasons for their willingness to talk at such length to an outsider (or was David Morley not an outsider to them)? And how did the specific power relationship pervading the interview situation affect not only the families, but also the researcher himself? These are problems inherent to conducting ethnographic research that are difficult to unravel. But that does not mean that audience researchers should not confront them, and, eventually, draw the radical and no doubt uncomfortable conclusions that will emerge from that confrontation. We can think of Valerie Walkerdine's provocative and disturbing query:

> Much has been written about the activity of watching films in terms of scopophilia. But what of that other activity, [. . . .] this activity of research, of trying so hard to understand what people see in films? Might we not call this the most perverse voyeurism?
>
> (Walkerdine 1986: 166)

It is, of course, important for us to recognize the inherent symbolic violence of any kind of research. However, we cannot renounce our inevitable complicity simply by not doing research at all, empirical or otherwise. Indeed, such a retreat would only lead to the dangerous illusion of our own exemption from the realities under scrutiny, including the realities of living with the media – as if it were possible to keep our hands clean in a fundamentally dirty world. It is precisely for this reason that I believe that, in the expanding field of audience studies, an ethnographic approach can and does have a distinct critical value. Ethnographic work, in the sense of drawing on what we can perceive and experience in everyday settings, acquires its critical edge when it functions as a reminder that reality is always more complicated and diversified than our theories can represent, and that there is no such thing as 'audience' whose characteristics can be set once and

for all.[18] The critical promise of the ethnographic attitude resides in its potential to make and keep our interpretations sensitive to concrete specificities, to the unexpected, to history; it is a commitment to submit ourselves to the possibility of, in Paul Willis's words, 'being "surprised", of reaching knowledge not prefigured in one's starting paradigm' (1980: 90). What matters is not the certainty of knowledge about audiences, but an ongoing critical and intellectual engagement with the multifarious ways in which we constitute ourselves through media consumption. Or, as in the words of Stuart Hall: 'I am not interested in Theory, I am interested in going on theorizing' (1986b: 60).

Notes

1. It should be noted that the term 'ethnography' is somewhat misplaced in this context. Within anthropology, ethnography refers to an in-depth field study of a culture and its inhabitants in their natural location, which would require the researcher to spend a fair amount of time in that location, allowing her/him to acquire a nuanced and comprehensive insight into the dynamics of the social relationships in the culture under study, and enabling her/him to produce a 'thick description' of it. Most qualitative studies of media audiences do not meet these requirements. In Morley's *Nationwide* study, for example, the informants were extracted from their natural viewing environment and interviewed in groups that were put together according to socio-economic criteria. In a looser sense, however, the use of the term 'ethnographic' can be justified here in so far as the approach is aimed at getting a thorough insight into the 'lived experience' of media consumption.

2. It should be stressed, however, that the 'critical' tradition is not a monolithic whole: there is not one 'critical theory' with generally shared axioms, but many different, and often conflicting, 'critical perspectives', e.g. political economy and cultural studies.

3. Thus, the dichotomization of 'critical' and 'empirical' schools in communication studies, particularly in the United States, should be considered with some flexibility. See, e.g., the famous 'Ferment in the Field' issue of the *Journal of Communication* (1983).

4. The direct theoretical inspiration of Morley's research was the so-called encoding/decoding model as launched by Stuart Hall, which presented a theoretical intervention against '*Screen* theory'. See Hall (1980a, 1980b). Morley himself has elaborated on the

'interdiscursive' nature of encounters between text and subjects. See Morley (1980b).

5. See also Tamar Liebes (1986) and Kim Christian Schrøder (1987). Such an insistence upon convergence is not new among 'mainstream' communication researchers. For example, Jennifer Slack and Martin Allor have recalled how in the late 1930s Lazarsfeld hired Adorno in the expectation that the latter's critical theory could be used to 'revitalize' American empiricist research by supplying it with 'new research ideas'. The collaboration ended only one year later because it proved to be impossible to translate Adorno's critical analysis into the methods and goals of Lazarsfeld's project. Lazarsfeld has never given up the idea of a convergence, however (Slack and Allor 1983: 210).

6. Note, for instance, the striking similarities between the following two sentences, one from a uses and gratifications source, the other from a cultural studies one: 'There seems to be growing support for that branch of communications research which asserts that television viewing is an active and social process' (Katz and Liebes 1985: 187); 'Television viewing, the choices which shape it and the many social uses to which we put it, now turn out to be irrevocably active and social process' (Hall 1986a: 8).

7. In stating this I do not want to suggest that cultural studies is a closed paradigm, nor that all cultural studies scholars share one – say, Foucauldian – conception of power. For example, the Birmingham version of cultural studies, with its distinctly Gramscian inflection, has been criticized by Lawrence Grossberg for its lack of a theory of pleasure. An alternative, postmodernist perspective on cultural studies is developed in Grossberg (1983).

8. Strategic interpretations, that is, interpretations that are 'political' in the sense that they are aware of the fact that interpretations are always concrete interventions into an already existing discursive field. They are therefore always partial in both senses of the word (i.e. partisan and incomplete), and involved in making sense of the world in specific, power-laden ways. See Mary Louise Pratt (1986).

9. Rosengren expresses this view in very clearcut terms, where he reduces the existence of disagreements between 'critical' and 'mainstream' researchers to 'psychological reasons' (1983: 191).

10. I have borrowed this formulation from Virginia Nightingale (1986: 21–2). Nightingale remarks that audience research has generally been 'on the side' of those with vested interests in influencing the organization of the mass-media in society, and that it is important to develop a research perspective that is 'on the side' of the audience. However, it is far from simple to

work out exactly what such a perspective would mean. The notion of the 'active audience', for example, often put forward by uses and gratifications researchers not just as an object of empirical investigation but also as an article of faith, as an axiom to mark the distinctive identity of the 'paradigm', is not in itself a guarantee of a stance 'on the side of the audience'. In fact, the whole passive/active dichotomy in accounts of audiences has now become so ideologized that it all too often serves as a mystification of the real commitments behind the research at stake.

11. Reflections on the predicaments and politics of research on and with living historical subjects have already played an important role in, for example, feminist studies and anthropology, particularly ethnography. At least two problems are highlighted in these reflections. First, there is the rather awkward but seldom discussed concrete relation between researcher and researched as concrete subjects occupying differential social positions, more and less invested with power; second, there is the problem of the discursive form in which the cultures of 'others' can be represented in non-objectifying (or, better, less objectifying) ways. See, e.g., Angela McRobbie (1982); James Clifford (1983); James Clifford and George Marcus (1986); Lila Abu-Lughold (1991). Researchers of media audiences have, as far as I know, generally been silent about these issues. However, for a thought-provoking engagement with the problem, see Valerie Walkerdine (1986).

12. See, for a more general overview of the interpretive or hermeneutic turn in the social sciences, Paul Rabinow and William M. Sullivan (1979). A more radical, Foucauldian conception of what they call 'interpretive analytics' is developed by Hubert Dreyfuss and Paul Rabinow (1982).

13. A concise and useful criticism of empiricist mass communication research is offered by Robert C. Allen (1985: chapter 2).

14. Morley's main objection to the uses and gratifications approach concerns 'its psychologistic problematic and its emphasis on individual differences of interpretation' (1983: 117). Elsewhere Morley even more emphatically expresses his distance from the uses and gratifications approach: 'Any superficial resemblance between this study of television audience and the "uses and gratifications" perspective in media research is misleading' (ibid.).

15. Note that in positivist epistemology intersubjectivity is considered as one of the main criteria for scientific 'objectivity'. One of the myths by which the institution of Science establishes itself is that scientific discourse is a process without a subject. Hence the normative rule that the concrete historical subject of scientific practice,

the researcher, should be interchangeable with any other so as to erase all marks of idiosyncratic subjectivity.

16. All sorts of cautious qualifications as to the generalizability of such 'findings', so routinely put forward in research reports so that the validity of the given typifications are said to be limited to certain demographic or subcultural categories (e.g. the urban working class), do not in principle affect this reification of experiential structures.

17. An image of the television audience as consisting of harmonious collectivities is suggested by Elihu Katz and Tamar Liebes, when they describe the process of decoding a television programme as an activity of 'mutual aid' (1985). While this idea is useful in that it highlights the social nature of processes of decoding, it represses the possibility of tension, conflict and antagonism between different decodings within the same group.

18. For epistemological deconstructions of the category of 'audience' as object of power/knowledge, see Briankle G. Chang (1987); Martin Allor (1988); Ang (1991).

References

Abu-Lughold, L. (1991) 'Writing Against Culture', in R.G. Fox (ed.) *Recapturing Anthropology*, Sante Fe, NM: School of American Research Press.

Allen, R.C. (1985) *Speaking of Soap Operas*, Chapel Hill/London: University of North Carolina Press.

Allor, M. (1988) 'Relocating the Site of the Audience', *Critical Studies in Mass Communication*, 5(3): 217–33.

Ang, I. (1985) *Watching Dallas: Soap Opera and the Melodramatic Imagination*, London/New York: Methuen.

—— (1991) *Desperately Seeking the Audience*, London/New York: Routledge.

Blumler, J.G., Gurevitch, M. and Katz, E. (1985) 'Reaching Out: A Future for Gratifications Research', in K.E. Rosengren, L.A. Wenner and P. Palmgreen (eds) *Media Gratifications Research: Current Perspectives*, Beverly Hills, CA: Sage.

Carey, J. (1983) 'Introduction', in M.S. Mander (ed) *Communications in Transition*, New York: Praeger.

Chang, B.G. (1987) 'Deconstructing the Audience: Who Are They and What Do We Know About Them?', in M.L. McLaughlin (ed.) *Communication Yearbook 10*, Beverly Hills CA: Sage.

Clifford, J. (1983) 'On Ethnographic Authority', *Representations* 1 (Spring) 2: 118–46.

Clifford, J. and Marcus, G.E. (eds) (1986) *Writing Culture: The Poetics and Politics of Ethnography*, Berkeley/Los Angeles/London: University of California Press.

Dreyfuss, H. and Rabinow, P. (1982) *Michel Foucault: Beyond Structuralism and Hermeneutics*, Chicago: University of Chicago Press.

Fejes, F. (1984) 'Critical Communications Research and Media Effects: The Problem of the Disappearing Audience', *Media, Culture and Society* 6: 219–32.

Fiske (1987b) 'British Cultural Studies and Television', in R.C. Allen (ed.) *Channels of Discourse*, Chapel Hill/London: University of North Carolina Press.

Foucault, M. (1980) *Discipline and Punishment*, trans. A. Sheridan, Harmondsworth : Penguin.

Grossberg, L. (1983) 'Cultural Studies Revisited and Revised', in M.S. Mander (ed.) *Communications in Transition*, New York: Praeger.

—— (1987) 'Critical Theory and the Politics of Empirical Research', in M. Gurevitch and M.R. Levy (eds) *Mass Communication Review Yearbook 6*, Newbury Park, CA: Sage.

Hall, S. (1980a) 'Encoding/Decoding', in S. Hall, D. Hobson, A. Lowe and P. Willis (eds) *Culture, Media, Language*, London: Hutchinson.

—— (1980b) 'Recent Developments in Theories of Language and Ideology: A Critical Note', in S. Hall, D. Hobson, A. Lowe and P. Willis (eds) *Culture, Media, Language*, London: Hutchinson.

—— (1982) 'The Rediscovery of "Ideology": Return of the Repressed in Media Studies', in M. Gurevitch, T. Bennett and J. Woollacott (eds) *Culture, Society, and the Media*, London/New York: Methuen.

—— (1986a) 'Introduction', in D. Morley, *Family Television: Cultural Power and Domestic Leisure*, London: Comedia/Routledge.

—— (1986b) 'On Postmodernism and Articulation: An Interview with Stuart Hall', *Journal of Communication Inquiry* 10(2): 45–60.

—— (1986c) 'The Problem of Ideology – Marxism without Guarantees', *Journal of Communication Inquiry* 10(2): 5–27.

Hall, S., Hobson, D., Lowe, A. and Willis, P. (eds) (1980) *Culture, Media, Language*, London: Hutchinson.

Hammersley, M. and Atkinson, P. (1983) *Ethnography: Principles in Practice*, London/New York: Tavistock.

Hobson, D. (1980) 'Housewives and the Mass Media', in S. Hall, D. Hobson, A. Lowe and P. Willis (eds) *Culture, Media, Language*, London: Hutchinson.

—— (1982) *Crossroads: The Drama of a Soap Opera*, London: Methuen.

Jensen, K.B. (1986) *Making Sense of the News*, Århus: University of Århus Press.

—— (1987) 'Qualitative Audience Research: Towards an Integrative Approach to Reception', *Critical Studies in Mass Communication* 4: 21–36.

Katz, E. and Liebes, T. (1985) 'Mutual Aid in the Decoding of *Dallas*: Preliminary Notes from a Cross-Cultural Study', in P. Drummond and R. Paterson (eds) *Television in Transition*, London: BFI.

Levy, M.R. and Windahl, S. (1984) 'Audience Activity and Gratifications: A Conceptual Clarification and Exploration', *Communication Research* 11: 51–78.

—— (1986) 'The Concept of Audience Activity', in K.E. Rosengren, L. Wenner and P. Palmgreen (eds) *Media Gratifications Research*, Beverly Hills: Sage.

Liebes, T. (1986) 'On the Convergence of Theories of Mass Communication and Literature Regarding the Role of the Reader', paper presented to the Sixth International Conference on Culture and Communication, October.

—— (1990) *The Export of Meaning: Cross-Cultural Readings of Dallas*, New York: Oxford University Press.

Lindlof, T.R. (ed.) (1987) *Natural Audiences*, Norwood, NJ: Ablex.

Lindlof, T.R. and Meyer, T.P. (1987) 'Mediated Communication as Ways of Seeing, Acting, and Constructing Culture: The Tools and Foundations of Qualitative Research', in T.R. Lindlof (ed.) *Natural Audiences*, Norwood, NJ: Ablex Publishing Company.

Lull, J. (1980) 'The Social Uses of Television', *Human Communication Research* 6(3): 198–209.

—— (1986) 'The Naturalistic Study of Media Use and Youth Culture', in K.E. Rosengren, L.A. Wenner and P. Palmgreen (eds) *Media Gratifications Research: Current Perspectives*, Beverly Hills, CA: Sage.

—— (ed.) (1988) *World Families Watch Television*, Newbury Park, CA: Sage.

McRobbie, A. (1982) 'The Politics of Feminist Research: Between Talk, Text and Action', *Feminist Review* 12 (October): 46–57.

Mills, C. W. (1970) *The Sociological Imagination*, Harmondsworth: Penguin.

Modleski, T. (1986) ' Introduction', in T. Modleski (ed.) *Studies in Entertainment: Critical Approaches to Mass Culture*, Bloomington/Indianapolis: Indiana University Press.

Morley, D. (1980a) *The 'Nationwide' Audience: Structure and Decoding*, London: BFL.

—— (1980b) ' Texts, Readers, Subjects', in S. Hall, D. Hobson, A. Lowe and P. Willis (eds) *Culture, Media, Language*, London: Hutchinson.

—— (1981) ' "The Nationwide Audience" – A Critical Postscript', *Screen Education* 39 (Summer): 3–14.

—— (1983) ' Cultural Transformations: The Politics of Resistance', in H. Davies and P. Walton (eds) *Language, Image, Media*, Oxford: Basil Blackwell.

—— (1986) *Family Television: Cultural Power and Domestic Leisure*, London: Comedia/Routledge.

Nightingale, V. (1986) 'What's Happening to Audience Research?', *Media Information Australia*, 39 (February): 21–2.

Pratt, M.L. (1986) 'Interpretive Strategies/Strategic Interpretations: On Anglo-American Reader-Response Criticism', in J. Arac (ed.) *Postmodernism and Politics*, Minneapolis: University of Minnesota Press.

Rabinow, P. (1986) 'Representations Are Social Facts: Modernity and Post-Modernity in Anthropology', in J. Clifford and G.E. Marcus (eds) *Writing Culture: The Poetics and Politics of Ethnography*, Berkeley/Los Angeles/London: University of California Press.

Rabinow, P. and Sullivan, W.M. (eds) (1979) *Interpretive Social Science*, Berkeley/Los Angeles/London: University of California Press.

Radway, J. (1984) *Reading the Romance: Women, Patriarchy, and Popular Literature*, Chapell Hill: University of North Carolina Press.

Rosengren, K.E. (1983) 'Communication Research: One Paradigm, or Four?', *Journal of Communication* 33: 185–207

Schrøder, K.C. (1987) 'Convergence of Antagonistic Traditions? The Case of Audience Research', *European Journal of Communication* 2(1): 7–31.

Slack, J.D and Allor, M. (1983) 'The Political and Epistemological Constituents of Critical Communication Research', *Journal of Communication* , 33(3): 208–18.

Streeter, T. (1984) 'An Alternative Approach to Television Research: Developments in British Cultural Studies in Birmingham', in W.D. Rowland Jr and B. Watkins (eds) *Interpreting Television*, Beverly Hills, CA: Sage.

Walkerdine, V. (1986) 'Video Replay: Families, Films and Fantasy', in V. Burgin, J. Donald and C. Kaplan (eds) *Formations of Fantasy*, London/New York: Methuen.

32.
IS THERE A FAN IN THE HOUSE?

The Affective Sensibility of Fandom

Lawrence Grossberg

There is something odd about 'fans.' I remember when I began teaching university classes on rock-and-roll. A number of colleagues tried to sabotage them, by arguing that such forms of culture did not belong in the university curriculum. When this argument was defeated, they took a different strategy: they argued that, as a fan of rock, I was not the appropriate person to teach the class. While I disagreed with their implicit assumption that fans could not have any critical distance, I was fascinated by their insight that, somehow, being a fan entails a very different relationship to culture, a relationship which seems only to exist in the realm of popular culture. For example, while we can consume or appreciate various forms of 'high culture' or art, it makes little sense to describe someone as a fan of art. How, then, do we understand what it means to be a fan? The easiest answer, one that I reject, is that it is all a matter of what forms of and relationships to culture are legitimated within the existing relations of power. This assumes that it is all a matter of status and that there are no real distinctions that mark the 'fan.'

How then do we look for those distinctions? One way would be to consider what differences if any define the sorts of texts that fans are fans of. Or in other words, we can try to understand what makes popular culture popular? The question seems innocent enough but, as soon as we begin to look for an answer, we are confronted only by ambiguity and uncertainty. What is it, after all, that we are attempting to explain? Is it a matter of aesthetic or moral criteria which define the differences between popular texts

and other forms of cultural texts (for example, high culture, mass culture, folk culture)? But history has shown us that texts move in and out of these categories (for example, what was popular can become high art), and that a text can exist, simultaneously, in different categories. There are no necessary correspondences between the formal characteristics of any text and its popularity, and the standards for aesthetic legitimacy are constantly changing. Is it then a matter of where the text comes from, of how and by whom it is produced? But again, there are too many exceptions to this assumed correlation. The mode by which a text is produced, or the motivations behind it, do not guarantee how it is placed into the larger cultural context nor how it is received by different audiences. So perhaps the answer to our question is the most obvious one: what makes something popular is its popularity; it is, in other words, a matter of taste. This formulation begins to point us away from the texts, and toward the audiences of popular cultures. But, in the end, it does not help us very much, for the same questions remain, albeit in different forms: how much popularity? whose tastes? and what do different tastes signify?

A second approach attempts to begin by characterizing the particular sorts of people who become fans, and the basis on which their relationship to popular culture is constructed. In this model, it is often assumed that popular culture appeals to the lowest and least critical segments of the population. These audiences are thought to be easily manipulated and distracted (not only from 'serious' culture but also from real social concerns), mobilized solely to make a profit. The various forms of popular culture appeal to the audience's most debased needs and desires, making them even more passive, more ignorant and non-critical than they apparently already are. Fans are simply incapable of recognizing that the culture they enjoy is actually being used to dupe and exploit them. A second, related view of fans assumes that they are always juveniles, waiting to grow up, and still enjoying the irresponsibility of their fandom.

For many years, the only alternative to this image of fans as cultural dopes came from various arguments that divided the audience for popular culture into two groups: the larger segment is still assumed to be cultural dopes who passively consume the texts of popular culture. But there is another segment, much smaller and more dispersed, who actively appropriate the texts of specific popular cultures, and give them new and original significance. For example, one small part of the audience for comic books or popular music might approach such forms as art; or another group might take them to be the expression of their own lived experience. And still others may use them to resist the pressures of their social position and to construct new identities for themselves. According to this 'subcultural' model, any of these groups would be considered fans; fans constitute an elite fraction of the larger audience of passive consumers. Within this model, the fan is able to discriminate between those forms of popular culture which are 'authentic' (that is, which really are art, which really do represent their experience, etc.) and those which are the result of the efforts of the commercial mainstream to appropriate these forms and produce tainted versions for the larger audience. Thus, the fan is always in constant conflict, not only with the various structures of power, but also with the vast audience of media consumers. But such an elitist view of fandom does little to illuminate the complex relations that exist between forms of popular culture and their audiences. While we may all agree that there is a difference between the fan and the consumer, we are unlikely to understand the difference if we simply celebrate the former category and dismiss the latter one.

We have to acknowledge that, for the most part, the relationship between the audience and popular texts is an active and productive one. The meaning of a text is not given in some independently available set of codes which we can consult at our own convenience. A text does not carry its own meaning or politics already inside of itself; no text is able to guarantee what its effects will be. People are constantly struggling, not merely to figure out what a text means, but to make it mean something that connects to their own lives, experiences, needs and desires. The same text will mean different things to different people, depending on how it is interpreted. And different people have different interpretive resources, just as they have different needs. A text can only mean something in the context of the experience and situation of its particular audience. Equally important, texts do not define ahead of time how they are to be used or what functions they can serve. They can have different uses for different people in different contexts. The same text can be a source of narrative romance, sexual fantasy, aesthetic pleasure, language acquisition, identity or familial rebellion. Given contemporary recording technology (whether audio or video), a text can be remade and even remixed to conform to the audience's expectations and desires. How a specific text is used, how it is interpreted, how it functions for its audience – all of these are inseparably connected through the audience's constant struggle to make sense of itself and its world, even more, to make a slightly better place for itself in the world.

Audiences are constantly making their own cultural environment from the cultural resources that are available to them. Thus, audiences are not made up of cultural dopes; people are often quite aware of their own implication in structures of power and domination, and of the ways in which cultural messages (can) manipulate them. Furthermore, the audience of popular culture cannot be conceived of as a singular homogeneous entity; we have to take seriously the differences within and between the different fractions of the popular audience.

This view of an active audience only makes it more difficult for us to understand the nature of fandom, for if all consumers are active, then there is nothing against which to measure the fan. Such views cannot explain the significance of the fact that some people pay attention to particular texts, in ways that demand particular sorts of interpretations, or that some texts are granted an importance and perhaps even a power denied to others. We need a different approach, then, to the question of fandom and popular culture. If we cannot locate a viable response in either the nature of the cultural forms or the audience, then perhaps it is necessary to look at the relations that exist between them. But we have to consider the relationship without falling back into theories which privilege either the text or the audience by giving one the power to determine the relationship. For even if it is true that audiences are always active, it does not follow that they are ever in control.

The relations between culture and audiences cannot be understood simply as the process by which people appropriate already existing texts into the already constituted context of their social position, their experience or their needs. Nor can it be described in terms which suggest that the audience is simply passively acceding to the predetermined nature of the text. In fact, both audiences and texts are continuously remade – their identity and effectiveness reconstructed – by relocating their place within different contexts. The audience is always caught up in the continuous reconstruction of cultural contexts which enable them to consume, interpret and use texts in specific ways. It is these 'specific ways' that concern us here.

Audiences never deal with single cultural texts, or even with single genres or media. Culture 'communicates' only in particular contexts in which a range of texts, practices and languages are brought together. The same text can and often will be located in a number of different contexts; in each, it will function as a different text and it will likely have different relations to and effects on its audience. For example, a typical context of rock-and-roll – and there are many of them at a single moment – brings together musical texts and practices, economic and race relations, images of performers and fans, social relations (for instance, of gender, of friendship), aesthetic conventions, styles of language, movement, appearance and dance, media practices, ideological commitments and, sometimes, media representations of rock-and-roll itself. It is within such contexts that the relations between audience members and cultural forms are defined.

We can call the particular relationship that holds any context together, that binds cultural forms and audiences, a 'sensibility.' A sensibility is a particular form of engagement or mode of operation. It identifies the specific sorts of effects that the elements within a context can produce; it defines the possible relationships between texts and audiences located within its spaces. The sensibility of a particular cultural context (an 'apparatus') defines how specific texts and practices can be taken up and experienced, how they are able to effect the audience's place in the world, and what sort of texts can be incorporated into the apparatus. Different apparatuses produce and foreground different sensibilities. This assumes that human life is multidimensional, and texts may, in various contexts, connect into certain dimensions more powerfully than others. There is, in fact, more to the organization of people's lives than just the distribution or structure of meaning, money and power.

I want now to describe the dominant sensibilities of contemporary popular culture in order to identify the sensibility within which fandom is located. Just as the same text can exist in different contexts and thus, different sensibilities, so too can different audience members. The different sensibilities are not mutually exclusive; people always exist in different sensibilities, and their relations to a particular set of cultural practices (for instance, rock-and-roll) may be defined by an overlapping set of sensibilities. Nevertheless, it may be useful to make some basic distinctions here.

The sensibility of the consumer operates by producing structures of pleasure. Of course, pleasure is itself a complex phenomenon, and there are many different relations operating in this notion of consumption: there is the satisfaction of doing what others would have you do, the enjoyment of doing what you want, the fun of breaking the rules, the fulfillment – however temporary and artificial – of desires, the release of catharsis, the comfort of escaping from negative situations, the reinforcement of identifying with a character, and the thrill of sharing another's emotional life, and so on. All of these are involved in the 'normal' and common relationship to popular culture and the mass media. We are engaged with forms of popular culture because, in some way and form, they are entertaining; they provide us with a certain measure of enjoyment and pleasure.

I am suggesting that our most common relationship to popular culture is determined by the cultural production of pleasures. But again, this consumerist sensibility rarely operates in total isolation. It is quite usual, for example, to find that such pleasures depend upon the production of other sorts of effects. The culture of the mass media often depends upon the production of meanings and, more specifically, of ideological representations. Ideology refers to the structures of meaning within which we locate ourselves. That is, ideologies are the maps of meaning which we take for granted as the obviously true pictures of the way the world is. By defining what is natural and commonsensical, ideologies construct the ways we experience the world. A consumerist sensibility might, in specific instances, be connected to ideological sensibilities, either by making certain experiences pleasurable, or through the pleasures of ideological reinforcement. Nevertheless, I still believe that the real source of the popularity of the culture of the mass media lies, not in its ideological effects, but in its location within a consumerist sensibility emphasizing the production of pleasure. We can find some evidence for this claim in the existence of a variant of the consumer relation, one that we might call the 'hyperconsumerist' sensibility. This describes the seemingly compulsive consumption of mass media, regardless of whether any actual single text provides pleasure. That is, hyperconsumerism describes the situation in which the very activity of consuming becomes more important, more pleasurable, more active as the site of the cultural relationship, than the object of consumption itself (for instance, 'couch potatoes,' collectors, and so on).

The category of the fan, however, can only be understood in relation to a different sensibility. The fan's relation to cultural texts operates in the domain of affect or mood. Affect is perhaps the most difficult plane of our lives to define, not merely because it is even less necessarily tied to meaning than pleasure, but also because it is, in some sense, the most mundane aspect of everyday life. Affect is not the same as either emotions or desires. Affect is closely tied to what we often describe as the feeling of life. You can understand another person's life: you can share the same meanings and pleasures, but you cannot know how it feels. But feeling, as it functions here, is not a subjective experience. It is a socially constructed domain of cultural effects. Some things feel different from others, some matter more, or in different ways, than others. The same experience will change

drastically as our mood or feeling changes. The same object, with the same meaning, giving the same pleasure, is very different as our affective relationship to it changes. Or perhaps it is more accurate to say that different affective relations inflect meanings and pleasures in very different ways. Affect is what gives 'color,' 'tone' or 'texture' to our experiences.

Perhaps this can be made clearer if we distinguish two aspects of affect: quantity and quality. Affect always defines the quantitatively variable level of energy (activation, enervation) or volition (will); it determines how invigorated we feel in particular moments of our lives. It defines the strength of our investment in particular experiences, practices, identities, meanings, and pleasures. In other words, affect privileges volition over meaning. For example, as one ad campaign continuously declares, 'Where there's a will there's an "A".' But affect is also defined qualitatively, by the inflection of the particular investment, by the nature of the concern (caring, passion) in the investment, by the way in which the specific event is made to matter to us.

Within an affective sensibility, texts serve as 'billboards' of an investment, but we cannot know what the investment is apart from the context in which it is made (that is the apparatus). While critics generally recognize that meanings, and even desires, are organized into particular structures or maps, they tend to think of mood as formless and disorganized. But affect is also organized; it operates within and, at the same time, produces maps which direct our investments in and into the world; these maps tell us where and how we can become absorbed – not into the self but into the world – as potential locations for our self-identifications, and with what intensities. This 'absorption' or investment constructs the places and events which are, or can become, significant to us. They are the places at which we can construct our own identity as something to be invested in, as something that matters.

These mattering maps are like investment portfolios: there are not only different and changing investments, but different forms, as well as different intensities or degrees of investment. There are not only different places marked out (practices, pleasures, meanings, fantasies, desires, relations, and so on) but different purposes which these investments can play, and different moods in which they can operate.

Mattering maps define different forms, quantities and places of energy. They tell us how to use and how to generate energy, how to navigate our way into and through various moods, and how to live within emotional and ideological histories. This is not to claim that all affective investments are equal or even equivalent; there are, at the very least, qualitative and quantitative differences among them.

The importance of affect derives, not from its content, but from its power over difference, its power to invest difference. Affect plays a crucial role in organizing social life because affect is constantly constructing, not only the possibility of difference, but the ways specific differences come to matter. Both ideology and pleasure depend on defining and privileging particular terms within various relations of difference. But it is affect which enables some differences (for instance, race, and gender) to matter as markers of identity rather than others (foot length, angle of ears, eye color) in certain contexts and power relations. While we might notice these latter sorts of things on certain occasions, we would think it ridiculous to imagine a world in which they mattered. Those differences which do matter can become the site of ideological struggle, and to the extent that they become common-sense social investments, they are landmarks in the political history of our mattering maps.

Through such investments in specific differences, fans divide the cultural world into Us and Them, but the investment in – and authority of – any identity may vary within and across apparatuses. In fact, as individuals and as members of various social groups, there are many axes along which we register our difference from others – some are physical categories, some are sociological, some are ideological and some are affective. We are women, black, short, middle-class, educated, and so on. Any particular difference, including that marked out by being a rock fan, is always augmented and reshaped by other differences. At different points and places in our lives, we reorder the hierarchical relations among these differences. We redefine our own identity out of the relations among our differences; we reorder their importance, we invest ourselves more in some than in others. For some, being a particular sort of rock fan can take on an enormous importance and thus come to constitute a dominant part of the fan's identity (this is how we often think of subcultures). For others, it remains a powerful but submerged difference that colors, but does not define, their dominant social identities.

The most obvious and frightening thing about contemporary popular culture is that it matters so much to its fans. The source of its power, whatever it may seem to say, or whatever pleasures one may derive from it, seems to be its place on people's mattering maps, and its ability to place other practices on those maps. For the fan, certain forms of popular culture become taken for granted, even necessary investments. The result is that, for the fan, specific cultural contexts become saturated with affect. The relations within the context are all defined affectively, producing a structure of 'affective alliances.' And the apparatus, as an affective alliance, itself, functions as a mattering map within which all sorts of activities, practices and identities can be located. It is in their affective lives that fans constantly struggle to care about something, and to find the energy to survive, to find the passion necessary to imagine and enact their own projects and possibilities. Particular apparatuses may also provide the space within which dominant relations of power can be challenged, resisted, evaded or ignored.

Consequently, for the fan, popular culture becomes a crucial ground on which he or she can construct mattering maps. Within these mattering maps, investments are enabled which empower individuals in a variety of ways. They may construct relatively stable moments of identity or they may identify place which, because they matter, take on an authority of their own. Fans actively constitute places and forms of authority (both for themselves and for others) through the mobilization and organization of affective investments. By making certain things or practices matter, the fan 'authorizes' them to speak for him or her, not only as a spokesperson but also as surrogate voices (as when we sing along to popular songs). The fan gives authority to that which he or she invests in, letting the object of such investments speak for and as him or her self. Fans let them organize their emotional and narrative lives and identities. In this way, they use the sites of their investments as so many languages which construct their identities. In so far as a fan's investments are dispersed, his or her identity is similarly dispersed. But in so far as fandom organizes these investments – both structurally (as a mattering) and intensively (as different quantities) – so it establishes different moments of relative authority, moments which are connected affectively to each other (for example, the investment in rock may make an investment in certain ideological positions more likely although it can never guarantee them). The fan need not – and usually does not – have blind faith in any specific investment site, but he or she cannot give up the possibility of investment as that which makes possible a map of his or her own everyday life and self.

The image of mattering maps points to the constant attempt, whether or not it is ever successful, to organize moments of stable identity, sites at which we can, at least temporarily, find ourselves 'at home' with what we care about. The very notion of a fan assumes the close relationship between identity and caring; it assumes that identity matters and that what matters – what has authority – is the appropriate ground of stable identity. But mattering maps also involve the lines that connect the different sites of investment; they define the possibilities for moving from one investment to another, of linking the various fragments of our identity together. They define not only what sites (practices, pleasures, and so on) matter, but how they matter. And they construct a lived coherence for the fan.

Moreover, the affective investment in certain places (texts, identities, pleasures) and differences demands a very specific ideological response, for affect can never define, by itself, why things should matter. That is, unlike ideology and pleasure, it can never provide its own justification, however illusory such justifications may in fact be. The result is that affect always demands that ideology legitimate the fact that these differences and not others matter, and that within any difference, one term matters more than the other. This is accomplished by linking specific mattering maps to an ideological principle of excessiveness. Because something matters, it must have an excess which explains the investment in it, an excess which ex post facto not only legitimates but demands the investment. Whatever we invest ourselves into must be given an excess which outweighs any other consideration. The more powerful the affective investment in difference is, the more powerfully must that difference be ideologically and experientially legitimated, and the greater the excess which differentiates it. This excess, while ideologically

constructed, is always beyond ideological challenge, because it is called into existence affectively. The investment guarantees the excess.

For example, what defines rock's difference – what makes it an acceptable and, for its fans, absolutely necessary investment – is simply the fact that it matters. It offers a kind of salvation which depends only on our obsession with it. It constructs a circular relation between the music and the fan: the fact that it matters makes it different; it gives rock an excess which can never be experienced or understood by those outside of the rock culture. And this excess in turn justifies the fan's investment in it. Rock refers, in this sense, to the excess which is granted the music by virtue of our investment in it. By virtue of the fact that rock matters, rock is granted the excess which justifies its place on our mattering maps, and its power to restructure those maps. Thus it is not so much that rock has a 'real' difference but, rather, the fact that it matters calls its difference into existence. Consequently, the ideology and even the pleasure of rock are always secondary to, or at least dependent upon, the fan's assumption of rock's excess, an excess produced by the ways rock is placed in the fan's everyday life. The place of rock defines possible mattering maps, maps which specify the different forms, sites and intensities of what can matter, maps which chart out affective alliances. Rock positions not only the elements of rock culture, but other aspects of everyday life. It can determine how other things matter. Thus, for example, within rock's mattering maps, entertainment matters but in a very different way from rock, as something to be consumed and to produce pleasure. Rock works by offering the fan places where he or she can locate some sense of his or her own identity and power, where he or she can invest his or her self in specific ways.

But how are we to understand rock's excess? Rock, like any other culture of fandom, is organized around a particular ideology of excess, an ideology which distinguishes certain kinds of musical–cultural practices and certain kinds of 'fans' (although the two dimensions do not always correspond). This ideology not only draws an absolute distinction between rock and 'mere' entertainment, it says that it is the excess of the difference – its authenticity – that enables rock to matter. Every fan – of whatever forms of popular culture – exists within a comparable ideology of authenticity, although the difference need not operate in just the same way, and the ideological grounds of authenticity may vary considerably. This ideological difference has taken many forms, which are not necessarily the same: the center vs the margin, rock vs pop, the mainstream vs the periphery, commercial vs independent, coopted vs resistant. Moreover, the same distinction can be applied in very different ways to describe the same musics. In different rock apparatuses, the difference can be explained in different ways; for example, the line can be justified aesthetically or ideologically, or in terms of the social position of the audiences, or by the economics of its production, or through the measure of its popularity, or the statement of its politics. In all of these cases, the line serves, for the fan, 'properly' to distribute rock cultures. On the one side, entertainment, on the other, something more – an excess by virtue of which even mere fun can become a significant social statement. The excess links the social position and experience of musicians and fans with rock's ability to redefine the lines of social identity and difference. That is, the excess marks the rock fan's difference. Rock fans have always constructed a difference between authentic and coopted rock. And it is this which is often interpreted as rock's inextricable tie to resistance, refusal, alienation, marginality, and so on.

However, we must be careful, for sometimes 'authenticity' is used to refer to a single definition of authenticity. But there are many forms of authenticity, even within rock culture. One need only compare the various contemporary performers who might qualify as authentic rockers: Springsteen, U2, REM, Tracy Chapman, Sting, Prince, Public Enemy, Talking Heads and even the Pet Shop Boys. In general, it is possible to isolate three versions of this ideological distinction. The first, and most common, is usually linked to hard rock and folk rock. It assumes that authentic rock depends on its ability to articulate private but common desires, feelings and experiences into a shared public language. The consumption of rock constructs or expresses a 'community.' This romantic ideology displaces sexuality and makes desire matter by fantasizing a community predicated on images of urban mobility, delinquency, bohemianism and artistry. The second, often linked with dance and black music, locates authenticity in the construction of a rhythmic

and sexual body. Often identifying sexual mobility and romance, it constructs a fantasy of the tortured individual struggling to transcend the conditions of their inadequacy. The third, often linked with the self-consciousness of pop and art rock, is built on the explicit recognition of and acknowledgment that the difference that rock constructs (and which in turn is assigned back to rock) is always artificially constructed. That is, the difference does not exist outside of the consumption of rock itself. Such music, which is increasingly seen as 'avant garde' or 'postmodern,' celebrates style over music, or at least it equates the two. But despite its self-conscious negation of both romantic transcendence and transcendental sexuality, it still produces real and significant differences for its fans.

I do not mean to suggest that the category of the 'fan' exists in the same way in every historical situation. The fan can only be understood historically, as located in a set of different possible relations to culture. In fact, everyone is constantly a fan of various sorts of things, for one cannot exist in a world where nothing matters (including the fact that nothing matters). In fact, I think that what we today describe as a 'fan' is the contemporary articulation of a necessary relationship which has historically constituted the popular, involving relationships to such diverse things as labor, religion, morality and politics. Thus, there is no necessary reason why the fan relationship is located primarily on the terrain of commercial popular culture. But it is certainly the case that for the vast majority of people in advanced capitalist societies, this is increasingly the only space where the fan relationship can take shape. It is in consumer culture that the transition from consumer to fan is accomplished. It is here, increasingly, that we seek actively to construct our own identities, partly because there seems to be no other space available, no other terrain on which, we can construct and anchor our mattering maps. The consumer industries increasingly appeal to the possibilities of investing in popular images, pleasures, fantasies and desires. The fact that we relate to these appeals, as either consumers or fans, does not guarantee our subjugation to the interests or practices of the commercial sector. One can struggle to rearticulate effective popular appeals but I think it is also true that the consumer, however active, cannot remake the conditions of their subordination through their act of consumption.

The fan, however, is a different matter altogether. For the fan speaks from an actively constructed and changing place within popular culture. Moreover, because the fan speaks for and to the question of authority, and from within an ideology of excess (which constructs a certain critical distance), the politics of the fan never entails merely the celebration of every investment or every mattering map. The fan's relation to culture in fact opens up a range of political possibilities and it is often on the field of affective relations that political struggles intersect with popular concerns. In fact, the affective is a crucial dimension of the organization of political struggle. No democratic political struggle can be effectively organized without the power of the popular. It is in this sense that I want to say that the relationship of fandom is a potentially enabling or empowering one, for it makes it possible to move both within and beyond one's mattering maps.

Empowerment is an abstract possibility; it refers to a range of effects operating at the affective level. It is not synonymous with pleasure (for pleasure can be disempowering and displeasure can be empowering); nor does it guarantee any form of resistance to or evasion of existing structures of power, although it is a condition of the possibility of resistance. Empowerment refers to the reciprocal nature of affective investment: that is, because something matters (as it does when one invests energy in it), other investments are made possible. Empowerment refers to the generation of energy and passion, to the construction of possibility. Unlike the consumer, the fan's investment of energy into certain practices always returns some interest on the investment through a variety of empowering relations: in the form of the further production of energy (for example, rock dancing, while exhausting, continuously generates its own energy, if only to continue dancing); by placing the fan in a position from which he or she feels a certain control over his or her life (as a recent ad proclaimed, 'shopping puts me on top of the world'); or by making fans feel that they are still alive (as Tracy Chapman sings, 'I had a feeling I could be someone').

In all of these cases, fans are empowered in the sense that they are now capable of going on, of continuing to struggle to make a difference. Fans' investment in certain practices and texts provides them with strategies which enable them to gain a certain amount of control over their affective life, which further enables them to invest in new forms of meaning, pleasure and identity in order to cope with new forms of pain, pessimism, frustration, alienation, terror and boredom. Such empowerment is increasingly important in a world in which pessimism has become common sense, in which people increasingly feel incapable of making a difference, and in which differences increasingly seem not to matter, not to make any difference themselves. Fandom is, at least potentially, the site of the optimism, invigoration and passion which are necessary conditions for any struggle to change the conditions of one's life. At this level, culture offers the resources which may or may not be mobilized into forms of popular struggle, resistance and opposition. The organization of struggles around particular popular languages depends upon their articulation within different affective economies, that is, upon the different investments by which they are empowered and within which they empower their fans. While there is no guarantee that even the most highly charged moments will become either passive sites of evasion or active sites of resistance, without the affective investments of popular culture the very possibility of such struggles is likely to be drowned in the sea of historical pessimism.

33.
THE OPPOSITIONAL GAZE

Black Female Spectators

bell hooks

When thinking about black female spectators, I remember being punished as a child for staring, for those hard intense direct looks children would give grown-ups, looks that were seen as confrontational, as gestures of resistance, challenges to authority. The "gaze" has always been political in my life. Imagine the terror felt by the child who has come to understand through repeated punishments that one's gaze can be dangerous. The child who has learned so well to look the other way when necessary. Yet, when punished, the child is told by parents, "Look at me when I talk to you." Only, the child is afraid to look. Afraid to look, but fascinated by the gaze. There is power in looking.

Amazed the first time I read in history classes that white slave-owners (men, women, and children) punished enslaved black people for looking, I wondered how this traumatic relationship to the gaze had informed black parenting and black spectatorship. The politics of slavery, of racialized power relations, were such that the slaves were denied their right to gaze. Connecting this strategy of domination to that used by grown folks in southern black rural communities where I grew up, I was pained to think that there was no absolute difference between whites who had oppressed black people and ourselves. Years later, reading Michel Foucault, I thought again about these connections, about the ways power as domination reproduces itself in different locations employing similar apparatuses, strategies, and mechanisms of control. Since I knew as a child that the dominating power adults exercised over me and over my gaze was

never so absolute that I did not dare to look, to sneak a peep, to stare dangerously, I knew that the slaves had looked. That all attempts to repress our/black peoples' right to gaze had produced in us an overwhelming longing to look, a rebellious desire, an oppositional gaze. By courageously looking, we defiantly declared: "Not only will I stare. I want my look to change reality." Even in the worse circumstances of domination, the ability to manipulate one's gaze in the face of structures of domination that would contain it, opens up the possibility of agency. In much of his work, Michel Foucault insists on describing domination in terms of "relations of power" as part of an effort to challenge the assumption that "power is a system of domination which controls everything and which leaves no room for freedom." Emphatically stating that in all relations of power "there is necessarily the possibility of resistance," he invites the critical thinker to search those margins, gaps, and locations on and through the body where agency can be found.

Stuart Hall calls for recognition of our agency as black spectators in his essay "Cultural Identity and Cinematic Representation." Speaking against the construction of white representations of blackness as totalizing, Hall says of white presence: "The error is not to conceptualize this 'presence' in terms of power, but to locate that power as wholly external to us—as extrinsic force, whose influence can be thrown off like the serpent sheds its skin." What Franz Fanon reminds us, in *Black Skin, White Masks,* is how power is inside as well as outside:

. . . the movements, the attitudes, the glances of the Other fixed me there, in the sense in which a chemical solution is fixed by a dye. I was indignant; I demanded an explanation. Nothing happened. I burst apart. Now the fragments have been put together again by another self. This "look," from—so to speak—the place of the Other, fixes us, not only in its violence, hostility and aggression, but in the ambivalence of its desire.

Spaces of agency exist for black people, wherein we can both interrogate the gaze of the Other but also look back, and at one another, naming what we see. The "gaze" has been and is a site of resistance for colonized black people globally. Subordinates in relations of power learn experientially that there is a critical gaze, one that "looks" to document, one that is oppositional. In resistance struggle, the power of the dominated to assert agency by claiming and cultivating "awareness" politicizes "looking" relations—one learns to look a certain way in order to resist.

When most black people in the United States first had the opportunity to look at film and television, they did so fully aware that mass media was a system of knowledge and power reproducing and maintaining white supremacy. To stare at the television, or mainstream movies, to engage its images, was to engage its negation of black representation. It was the oppositional black gaze that responded to these looking relations by developing independent black cinema. Black viewers of mainstream cinema and television could chart the progress of political movements for racial equality *via* the construction of images, and did so. Within my family's southern black working-class home, located in a racially segregated neighborhood, watching television was one way to develop critical spectatorship. Unless you went to work in the white world, across the tracks, you learned to look at white people by staring at them on the screen. Black looks, as they were constituted in the context of social movements for racial uplift, were interrogating gazes. We laughed at television shows like *Our Gang* and *Amos 'n' Andy,* at these white representations of blackness, but we also looked at them critically. Before racial integration, black viewers of movies and television experienced visual pleasure in a context where looking was also about contestation and confrontation.

Writing about black looking relations in "Black British Cinema: Spectatorship and Identity Formation in Territories," Manthia Diawara identifies the power of the spectator: "Every narration places the spectator in a position of agency; and race, class and sexual relations influence the way in which this subjecthood is filled by the spectator." Of particular concern for him are moments of "rupture" when the spectator resists "complete identification with the film's discourse." These ruptures define the relation between black spectators and dominant cinema prior to racial integration. Then, one's enjoyment of a film wherein representations of blackness were stereotypically degrading and dehumanizing co-existed with a critical practice that restored presence where it was negated. Critical discussion of the film while it was in progress or at its conclusion maintained the distance between spectator and the image. Black films were also subject to critical interrogation. Since they came into being in part as a response to the failure of white-dominated cinema to represent blackness in a manner that did not reinforce white supremacy, they too were critiqued to see if images were seen as complicit with dominant cinematic practices.

Critical, interrogating black looks were mainly concerned with issues of race and racism, the way racial domination of blacks by whites overdetermined representation. They were rarely concerned with gender. As spectators, black men could repudiate the reproduction of racism in cinema and television, the negation of black presence, even as they could feel as though they were rebelling against white supremacy by daring to look, by engaging phallocentric politics of spectatorship. Given the real life public circumstances wherein black men were murdered/lynched for looking at white womanhood, where the black male gaze was always subject to control and/or punishment by the powerful white Other, the private realm of television screens or dark theaters could unleash the repressed gaze. There they could "look" at white womanhood without a structure of domination overseeing the gaze, interpreting, and punishing. That white supremacist structure that had murdered Emmet Till after interpreting his look as violation, as "rape" of white womanhood, could not control black male responses to screen images. In their role as spectators, black men could enter an imaginative space of phallocentric power that mediated racial negation. This gendered relation to looking made the experience of the black male spectator radically different from that of the black female spectator. Major early black male independent filmmakers represented black women in their films as objects of male gaze. Whether looking through the camera or as spectators watching films, whether mainstream cinema or "race" movies such as those made by Oscar Micheaux, the black male gaze had a different scope from that of the black female.

Black women have written little about black female spectatorship, about our moviegoing practices. A growing body of film theory and criticism by black women has only begun to emerge. The prolonged silence of black women as spectators and critics was a response to absence, to cinematic negation. In "The Technology of Gender," Teresa de Lauretis, drawing on the work of Monique Wittig, calls attention to "the power of discourses to 'do violence' to people, a violence which is material and physical, although produced by abstract and scientific discourses as well as the discourses of the mass media." With the possible exception of early race movies, black female spectators have had to develop looking relations within a cinematic context that constructs our presence as absence, that denies the "body" of the black female so as to perpetuate white supremacy and with it a phallocentric spectatorship where the woman to be looked at and desired is "white." (Recent movies do not conform to this paradigm but I am turning to the past with the intent to chart the development of black female spectatorship.)

Talking with black women of all ages and classes, in different areas of the United States, about their filmic looking relations, I hear again and again ambivalent responses to cinema. Only a few of the black women I talked with remembered the pleasure of race movies, and even those who did, felt that pleasure interrupted and usurped by Hollywood. Most of the black women I talked with were adamant that they never went to movies expecting to see compelling representations of black femaleness. They were all acutely aware of cinematic racism—its violent erasure of black womanhood. In Anne Friedberg's essay "A Denial of Difference: Theories of Cinematic Identification" she stresses that "identification can

only be made through recognition, and all recognition is itself an implicit confirmation of the ideology of the status quo." Even when representations of black women were present in film, our bodies and being were there to serve—to enhance and maintain white womanhood as object of the phallocentric gaze.

Commenting on Hollywood's characterization of black women in *Girls on Film*, Julie Burchill describes this absent presence:

> Black women have been mothers without children (Mammies—who can ever forget the sickening spectacle of Hattie MacDaniels waiting on the simpering Vivien Leigh hand and foot and enquiring like a ninny, "What's ma lamb gonna wear?") ... Lena Horne, the first black performer signed to a long term contract with a major (MGM), looked gutless but was actually quite spirited. She seethed when Tallulah Bankhead complimented her on the paleness of her skin and the non-Negroidness of her features.

When black women actresses like Lena Horne appeared in mainstream cinema most white viewers were not aware that they were looking at black females unless the film was specifically coded as being about blacks. Burchill is one of the few white women film critics who has dared to examine the intersection of race and gender in relation to the construction of the category "woman" in film as object of the phallocentric gaze. With characteristic wit she asserts: "What does it say about racial purity that the best blondes have all been brunettes (Harlow, Monroe, Bardot)? I think it says that we are not as white as we think." Burchill could easily have said "we are not as white as we want to be," for clearly the obsession to have white women film stars be ultra-white was a cinematic practice that sought to maintain a distance, a separation between that image and the black female Other; it was a way to perpetuate white supremacy. Politics of race and gender were inscribed into mainstream cinematic narrative from *Birth of A Nation* on. As a seminal work, this film identified what the place and function of white womanhood would be in cinema. There was clearly no place for black women.

Remembering my past in relation to screen images of black womanhood, I wrote a short essay,

"Do you remember Sapphire?" which explored both the negation of black female representation in cinema and television and our rejection of these images. Identifying the character of "Sapphire" from *Amos 'n' Andy* as that screen representation of black femaleness I first saw in childhood, I wrote:

> She was even then backdrop, foil. She was bitch—nag. She was there to soften images of black men, to make them seem vulnerable, easygoing, funny, and unthreatening to a white audience. She was there as man in drag, as castrating bitch, as someone to be lied to, someone to be tricked, someone the white and black audience could hate. Scapegoated on all sides. *She was not us.* We laughed with the black men, with the white people. We laughed at this black woman who was not us. And we did not even long to be there on the screen. How could we long to be there when our image, visually constructed, was so ugly. We did not long to be there. We did not long for her. We did not want our construction to be this hated black female thing—foil, backdrop. Her black female image was not the body of desire. There was nothing to see. She was not us.

Grown black women had a different response to Sapphire; they identified with her frustrations and her woes. They resented the way she was mocked. They resented the way these screen images could assault black womanhood, could name us bitches, nags. And in opposition they claimed Sapphire as their own, as the symbol of that angry part of themselves white folks and black men could not even begin to understand.

Conventional representations of black women have done violence to the image. Responding to this assault, many black women spectators shut out the image, looked the other way, accorded cinema no importance in their lives. Then there were those spectators whose gaze was that of desire and complicity. Assuming a posture of subordination, they submitted to cinema's capacity to seduce and betray. They were cinematically "gaslighted." Every black woman I spoke with who was/is an ardent moviegoer, a lover of the Hollywood film, testified that to experience fully the pleasure of that cinema they had to close

down critique, analysis; they had to forget racism. And mostly they did not think about sexism. What was the nature then of this adoring black female gaze—this look that could bring pleasure in the midst of negation? In her first novel, *The Bluest Eye*, Toni Morrison constructs a portrait of the black female spectator; her gaze is the masochistic look of victimization. Describing her looking relations, Miss Pauline Breedlove, a poor working woman, maid in the house of a prosperous white family, asserts:

> The onliest time I be happy seem like was when I was in the picture show. Every time I got, I went, I'd go early, before the show started. They's cut off the lights, and everything be black. Then the screen would light up, and I's move right on in them picture. White men taking such good care of they women, and they all dressed up in big clean houses with the bath tubs right in the same room with the toilet. Them pictures gave me a lot of pleasure.

To experience pleasure, Miss Pauline sitting in the dark must imagine herself transformed, turned into the white woman portrayed on the screen. After watching movies, feeling the pleasure, she says, "But it made coming home hard."

We come home to ourselves. Not all black women spectators submitted to that spectacle of regression through identification. Most of the women I talked with felt that they consciously resisted identification with films—that this tension made moviegoing less than pleasurable; at times it caused pain. As one black woman put, "I could always get pleasure from movies as long as I did not look too deep." For black female spectators who have "looked too deep" the encounter with the screen hurt. That some of us chose to stop looking was a gesture of resistance, turning away was one way to protest, to reject negation. My pleasure in the screen ended abruptly when I and my sisters first watched *Imitation of Life*. Writing about this experience in the "Sapphire" piece, I addressed the movie directly, confessing:

> I had until now forgotten you, that screen image seen in adolescence, those images that made me stop looking. It was there in *Imitation of Life*, that

comfortable mammy image. There was some-thing familiar about this hard-working black woman who loved her daughter so much, loved her in a way that hurt. Indeed, as young southern black girls watching this film, Peola's mother reminded us of the hardworking, churchgoing, Big Mamas we knew and loved. Consequently, it was not this image that captured our gaze; we were fascinated by Peola.

Addressing her, I wrote:

> You were different. There was something scary in this image of young sexual sensual black beauty betrayed—that daughter who did not want to be confined by blackness, that "tragic mulatto" who did not want to be negated. "Just let me escape this image forever," she could have said. I will always remember that image. I remembered how we cried for her, for our unrealized desiring selves. She was tragic because there was no place in the cinema for her, no loving pictures. She too was absent image. It was better then, that we were absent, for when we were there it was humiliating, strange, sad. We cried all night for you, for the cin-ema that had no place for you. And like you, we stopped thinking it would one day be different.

When I returned to films as a young woman, after a long period of silence, I had developed an opposi-tional gaze. Not only would I not be hurt by the absence of black female presence, or the insertion of violating representation, I interrogated the work, cul-tivated a way to look past race and gender for aspects of content, form, language. Foreign films and U.S. independent cinema were the primary locations of my filmic looking relations, even though I also watched Hollywood films.

From "jump," black female spectators have gone to films with awareness of the way in which race and racism determined the visual construction of gender. Whether it was *Birth of A Nation* or Shirley Temple shows, we knew that white womanhood was the racialized sexual difference occupying the place of stardom in mainstream narrative film. We assumed white women knew it to. Reading Laura Mulvey's pro-vocative essay, "Visual Pleasure and Narrative

Cinema," from a standpoint that acknowledges race, one sees clearly why black women spectators not duped by mainstream cinema would develop an oppositional gaze. Placing ourselves outside that pleasure in looking, Mulvey argues, was determined by a "split between active/male and passive/female." Black female spectators actively chose not to identify with the film's imaginary subject because such identi-fication was disenabling.

Looking at films with an oppositional gaze, black women were able to critically assess the cinema's construction of white womanhood as object of phal-locentric gaze and choose not to identify with either the victim or the perpetrator. Black female spectators, who refused to identify with white womanhood, who would not take on the phallocentric gaze of desire and possession, created a critical space where the binary opposition Mulvey posits of "woman as image, man as bearer of the look" was continually decon-structed. As critical spectators, black women looked from a location that disrupted, one akin to that described by Annette Kuhn in *The Power of The Image:*

> . . . the acts of analysis, of deconstruction and of reading "against the grain" offer an additional pleasure—the pleasure of resistance, of saying "no": not to "unsophisticated" enjoyment, by our-selves and others, of culturally dominant images, but to the structures of power which ask us to consume them uncritically and in highly circum-scribed ways.

Mainstream feminist film criticism in no way acknowledges black female spectatorship. It does not even consider the possibility that women can con-struct an oppositional gaze via an understanding and awareness of the politics of race and racism. Feminist film theory rooted in an ahistorical psychoanalytic framework that privileges sexual difference actively suppresses recognition of race, reenacting and mir-roring the erasure of black womanhood that occurs in films, silencing any discussion of racial difference— of racialized sexual difference. Despite feminist criti-cal interventions aimed at deconstructing the category "woman" which highlight the significance of race, many feminist film critics continue to structure their discourse as though it speaks about "women" when in actuality it speaks only about white women. It seems ironic that the cover of the recent anthology *Feminism and Film Theory* edited by Constance Penley has a graphic that is a reproduction of the photo of white actresses Rosalind Russell and Dorothy Arzner on the 1936 set of the film *Craig's Wife* yet there is no acknowledgment in any essay in this collection that the woman "subject" under discussion is always white. Even though there are photos of black women from films reproduced in the text, there is no acknowledgment of racial difference.

It would be too simplistic to interpret this failure of insight solely as a gesture of racism. Importantly, it also speaks to the problem of structuring feminist film theory around a totalizing narrative of woman as object whose image functions solely to reaffirm and reinscribe patriarchy. Mary Ann Doane addresses this issue in the essay "Remembering Women: Psychical and Historical Construction in Film Theory":

This attachment to the figure of a degeneralizible Woman as the product of the apparatus indicates why, for many, feminist film theory seems to have reached an impasse, a certain blockage in its theorization . . . In focusing upon the task of delineating in great detail the attributes of woman as effect of the apparatus, feminist film theory participates in the abstraction of women.

The concept "Woman" effaces the difference between women in specific socio-historical contexts, between women defined precisely as historical subjects rather than as *a* psychic subject (or non-subject). Though Doane does not focus on race, her comments speak directly to the problem of its erasure. For it is only as one imagines "woman" in the abstract, when woman becomes fiction or fantasy, can race not be seen as significant. Are we really to imagine that feminist theorists writing only about images of white women, who subsume this specific historical subject under the totalizing category "woman," do not "see" the whiteness of the image? It may very well be that they engage in a process of denial that eliminates the necessity of revisioning conventional ways of thinking about psychoanalysis as a paradigm of analysis and the need to rethink a body of feminist film theory that is firmly rooted in a denial of the reality that

sex/sexuality may not be the primary and/or exclusive signifier of difference. Doane's essay appears in a very recent anthology, *Psychoanalysis and Cinema* edited by E. Ann Kaplan, where, once again, none of the theory presented acknowledges or discusses racial difference, with the exception of one essay, "Not Speaking with Language, Speaking with No Language," which problematizes notions of orientalism in its examination of Leslie Thornton's film *Adynata*. Yet in most of the essays, the theories espoused are rendered problematic if one includes race as a category of analysis.

Constructing feminist film theory along these lines enables the production of a discursive practice that need never theorize any aspect of black female representation or spectatorship. Yet the existence of black women within white supremacist culture problematizes, and makes complex, the overall issue of female identity, representation, and spectatorship. If, as Friedberg suggests, "identification is a process which commands the subject to be displaced by an other; it is a procedure which breeches the separation between self and other, and, in this way, replicates the very structure of patriarchy." If identification "demands sameness, necessitates similarity, disallows difference"—must we then surmise that many feminist film critics who are "over-identified" with the mainstream cinematic apparatus produce theories that replicate its totalizing agenda? Why is it that feminist film criticism, which has most claimed the terrain of woman's identity, representation, and subjectivity as its field of analysis, remains aggressively silent on the subject of blackness and specifically representations of black womanhood? Just as mainstream cinema has historically forced aware black female spectators not to look, much feminist film criticism disallows the possibility of a theoretical dialogue that might include black women's voices. It is difficult to talk when you feel no one is listening, when you feel as though a special jargon or narrative has been created that only the chosen can understand. No wonder then that black women have for the most part confined our critical commentary on film to conversations. And it must be reiterated that this gesture is a strategy that protects us from the violence perpetuated and advocated by discourses of mass media. A new focus on issues of race and representation in the field of film theory could critically intervene on the historical repression reproduced in some arenas of contemporary critical practice, making a discursive space for discussion of black female spectatorship possible.

When I asked a black woman in her twenties, an obsessive moviegoer, why she thought we had not written about black female spectatorship, she commented: "We are afraid to talk about ourselves as spectators because we have been so abused by 'the gaze'." An aspect of that abuse was the imposition of the assumption that black female looking relations were not important enough to theorize. Film theory as a critical "turf" in the United States has been and continues to be influenced by and reflective of white racial domination. Since feminist film criticism was initially rooted in a women's liberation movement informed by racist practices, it did not open up the discursive terrain and make it more inclusive. Recently, even those white film theorists who include an analysis of race show no interest in black female spectatorship. In her introduction to the collection of essays *Visual and Other Pleasures*, Laura Mulvey describes her initial romantic absorption in Hollywood cinema, stating:

> Although this great, previously unquestioned and unanalyzed love was put in crisis by the impact of feminism on my thought in the early 1970s, it also had an enormous influence on the development of my critical work and ideas and the debate within film culture with which I became preoccupied over the next fifteen years or so. Watched through eyes that were affected by the changing climate of consciousness, the movies lost their magic.

Watching movies from a feminist perspective, Mulvey arrived at that location of disaffection that is the starting point for many black women approaching cinema within the lived harsh reality of racism. Yet her account of being a part of a film culture whose roots rest on a founding relationship of adoration and love indicates how difficult it would have been to enter that world from "jump" as a critical spectator whose gaze had been formed in opposition.

Given the context of class exploitation, and racist and sexist domination, it has only been through resistance, struggle, reading, and looking "against the grain," that black women have been able to value our process of looking enough to publicly name it. Centrally, those black female spectators who attest to the oppositionality of their gaze deconstruct theories of female spectatorship that have relied heavily on the assumption that, as Doane suggests in her essay, "Woman's Stake: Filming the Female Body," "woman can only mimic man's relation to language, that is assume a position defined by the penis-phallus as the supreme arbiter of lack." Identifying with neither the phallocentric gaze nor the construction of white womanhood as lack, critical black female spectators construct a theory of looking relations where cinematic visual delight is the pleasure of interrogation. Every black woman spectator I talked to, with rare exception, spoke of being "on guard" at the movies. Talking about the way being a critical spectator of Hollywood films influenced her, black woman filmmaker Julie Dash exclaims, "I make films because I was such a spectator!" Looking at Hollywood cinema from a distance, from that critical politicized standpoint that did not want to be seduced by narratives reproducing her negation, Dash watched mainstream movies over and over again for the pleasure of deconstructing them. And of course there is that added delight if one happens, in the process of interrogation, to come across a narrative that invites the black female spectator to engage the text with no threat of violation.

Significantly, I began to write film criticism in response to the first Spike Lee movie, *She's Gotta Have It*, contesting Lee's replication of mainstream patriarchal cinematic practices that explicitly represents woman (in this instance black woman) as the object of a phallocentric gaze. Lee's investment in patriarchal filmic practices that mirror dominant patterns makes him the perfect black candidate for entrance to the Hollywood canon. His work mimics the cinematic construction of white womanhood as object, replacing her body as text on which to write male desire with the black female body. It is transference without transformation. Entering the discourse of film criticism from the politicized location of resistance, of not wanting, as a working-class black woman I interviewed stated, "to see black women in the position white women have occupied in film forever," I began to think critically about black female spectatorship.

For years I went to independent and/or foreign films where I was the only black female present in the theater. I often imagined that in every theater in the United States there was another black woman watching the same film wondering why she was the only visible black female spectator. I remember trying to share with one of my five sisters the cinema I liked so much. She was "enraged" that I brought her to a theater where she would have to read subtitles. To her it was a violation of Hollywood notions of spectatorship, of coming to the movies to be entertained. When I interviewed her to ask what had changed her mind over the years, led her to embrace this cinema, she connected it to coming to critical consciousness, saying, "I learned that there was more to looking than I had been exposed to in ordinary (Hollywood) movies." I shared that though most of the films I loved were all white, I could engage them because they did not have in their deep structure a subtext reproducing the narrative of white supremacy. Her response was to say that these films demystified "whiteness," since the lives they depicted seemed less rooted in fantasies of escape. They were, she suggested, more like "what we knew life to be, the deeper side of life as well." Always more seduced and enchanted with Hollywood cinema than me, she stressed that unaware black female spectators must "break out," no longer be imprisoned by images that enact a drama of our negation. Though she still sees Hollywood films, because "they are a major influence in the culture"—she no longer feels duped or victimized.

Talking with black female spectators, looking at written discussions either in fiction or academic essays about black women, I noted the connection made between the realm of representation in mass media and the capacity of black women to construct ourselves as subjects in daily life. The extent to which black women feel devalued, objectified, dehumanized in this society determines the scope and texture of their looking relations. Those black women whose identities were constructed in resistance, by practices that oppose the dominant order, were most inclined to develop an oppositional gaze. Now that there is a growing interest in films produced by black women and those films have become more accessible to viewers, it is possible to talk about black female spectatorship in relation to that work. So far, most

discussions of black spectatorship that I have come across focus on men. In "Black Spectatorship: Problems of Identification and Resistance" Manthia Diawara suggests that "the components of 'difference'" among elements of sex, gender, and sexuality give rise to different readings of the same material, adding that these conditions produce a "resisting" spectator. He focuses his critical discussion on black masculinity.

The recent publication of the anthology *The Female Gaze: Women as Viewers of Popular Culture* excited me, especially as it included an essay, "Black Looks," by Jacqui Roach and Petal Felix that attempts to address black female spectatorship. The essay posed provocative questions that were not answered: Is there a black female gaze? How do black women relate to the gender politics of representation? Concluding, the authors assert that black females have "our own reality, our own history, our own gaze—one which sees the world rather differently from 'anyone else.'" Yet, they do not name/describe this experience of seeing "rather differently." The absence of definition and explanation suggests they are assuming an essentialist stance wherein it is presumed that black women, as victims of race and gender oppression, have an inherently different field of vision. Many black women do not "see differently" precisely because their perceptions of reality are so profoundly colonized, shaped by dominant ways of knowing. As Trinh T. Minh-ha points out in "Outside In, Inside Out": "Subjectivity does not merely consist of talking about oneself . . . be this talking indulgent or critical."

Critical black female spectatorship emerges as a site of resistance only when individual black women actively resist the imposition of dominant ways of knowing and looking. While every black woman I talked to was aware of racism, that awareness did not automatically correspond with politicization, the development of an oppositional gaze. When it did, individual black women consciously named the process. Manthia Diawara's "resisting spectatorship" is a term that does not adequately describe the terrain of black female spectatorship. We do more than resist. We create alternative texts that are not solely reactions. As critical spectators, black women participate in a broad range of looking relations, contest, resist, revision, interrogate, and invent on multiple levels.

Certainly when I watch the work of black women filmmakers Camille Billops, Kathleen Collins, Julie Dash, Ayoka Chenzira, Zeinabu Davis, I do not need to "resist" the images even as I still choose to watch their work with a critical eye.

Black female critical thinkers concerned with creating space for the construction of radical black female subjectivity, and the way cultural production informs this possibility, fully acknowledge the importance of mass media, film in particular, as a powerful site for critical intervention. Certainly Julie Dash's film *Illusions* identifies the terrain of Hollywood cinema as a space of knowledge production that has enormous power. Yet, she also creates a filmic narrative wherein the black female protagonist subversively claims that space. Inverting the "real-life" power structure, she offers the black female spectator representations that challenge stereotypical notions that place us outside the realm of filmic discursive practices. Within the film she uses the strategy of Hollywood suspense films to undermine those cinematic practices that deny black women a place in this structure. Problematizing the question of "racial" identity by depicting passing, suddenly it is the white male's capacity to gaze, define, and know that is called into question.

When Mary Ann Doane describes in "Woman's Stake: Filming the Female Body" the way in which feminist filmmaking practice can elaborate "a special syntax for a different articulation of the female body," she names a critical process that "undoes the structure of the classical narrative through an insistence upon its repressions." An eloquent description, this precisely names Dash's strategy in *Illusions*, even though the film is not unproblematic and works within certain conventions that are not successfully challenged. For example, the film does not indicate whether the character Mignon will make Hollywood films that subvert and transform the genre or whether she will simply assimilate and perpetuate the norm. Still, subversively, *Illusions* problematizes the issue of race and spectatorship. White people in the film are unable to "see" that race informs their looking relations. Though she is passing to gain access to the machinery of cultural production represented by film, Mignon continually asserts her ties to black community. The bond between her and the young black woman singer Esther Jeeter is affirmed by caring gestures of affirmation, often expressed by eye-to-eye contact, the direct unmediated gaze of recognition Ironically, it is the desiring objectifying sexualized white male gaze that threatens to penetrate her "secrets" and disrupt her process. Metaphorically, Dash suggests the power of black women to make films will be threatened and undermined by that white male gaze that seeks to reinscribe the black female body in a narrative of voyeuristic pleasure where the only relevant opposition is male/female, and the only location for the female is as a victim. These tensions are not resolved by the narrative. It is not at all evident that Mignon will triumph over the white supremacist capitalist imperialist dominating "gaze."

Throughout *Illusions*, Mignon's power is affirmed by her contact with the younger black woman whom she nurtures and protects. It is this process of mirrored recognition that enables both black women to define their reality, apart from the reality imposed upon them by structures of domination. The shared gaze of the two women reinforces their solidarity. As the younger subject, Esther represents a potential audience for films that Mignon might produce, films wherein black females will be the narrative focus, Julie Dash's recent feature-length film *Daughters of the Dust* dares to place black females at the center of its narrative. This focus caused critics (especially white males) to critique the film negatively or to express many reservations. Clearly, the impact of racism and sexism so over-determine spectatorship—not only what we look at but who we identify with—that viewers who are not black females find it hard to empathize with the central characters in the movie. They are adrift without a white presence in the film.

Another representation of black females nurturing one another *via* recognition of their common struggle for subjectivity is depicted in Sankofa's collective work *Passion of Remembrance*. In the film, two black women friends, Louise and Maggie, are from the onset of the narrative struggling with the issue of subjectivity, of their place in progressive black liberation movements that have been sexist. They challenge old norms and want to replace them with new understandings of the complexity of black identity, and the need for liberation struggles that address that complexity. Dressing to go to a party, Louise and Maggie claim the "gaze." Looking at one another, staring in mirrors, they appear completely focused on their encounter with black femaleness. How they see themselves is most important, not how they will be stared at by others. Dancing to the tune "Let's get Loose," they display their bodies not for a voyeuristic colonizing gaze but for that look of recognition that affirms their subjectivity—that constitutes them as spectators. Mutually empowered they eagerly leave the privatized domain to confront the public. Disrupting conventional racist and sexist stereotypical representations of black female bodies, these scenes invite the audience to look differently. They act to critically intervene and transform conventional filmic practices, changing notions of spectatorship. *Illusions, Daughters of the Dust*, and *A Passion of Remembrance* employ a deconstructive filmic practice to undermine existing grand cinematic narratives even as they retheorize subjectivity in the realm of the visual. Without providing "realistic" positive representations that emerge only as a response to the totalizing nature of existing narratives, they offer points of radical departure. Opening up a space for the assertion of a critical black female spectatorship, they do not simply offer diverse representations, they imagine new transgressive possibilities for the formulation of identity.

In this sense they make explicit a critical practice that provides us with different ways to think about black female subjectivity and black female spectatorship. Cinematically, they provide new points of recognition, embodying Stuart Hall's vision of a critical practice that acknowledges that identity is constituted "not outside but within representation," and invites us to see film "not as a second-order mirror held up to reflect what already exists, but as that form of representation which is able to constitute us as new kinds of subjects, and thereby enable us to discover who we are." It is this critical practice that enables production of feminist film theory that theorizes black female spectatorship. Looking and looking back, black women involve ourselves in a process whereby we see our history as counter-memory, using it as a way to know the present and invent the future.

References

Burchill, Julie. *Girls on Film*. New York: Pantheon, 1986.

de Lauretis, Teresa. *Technologies of Gender: Essays on Theory, Film, and Fiction*. Bloomington, IN: Indiana University Press, 1987.

Diawara, Manthia. "Black British Cinema: Spectatorship and Identity Formation in Territories." *Public Culture*, Vol. 1, No. 3 (Summer 1989).

——"Black Spectatorship: Problems of Identification and Resistance." *Screen*, Vol. 29, No. 4 (1988).

Doane, Mary Ann. "Remembering Women: Psychical and Historical Constructions in Film Theory." In *Psychoanalysis and Cinema*, edited by E. Ann Kaplan. London: Routledge, 1990.

——"Woman's Stake: Filming the Female Body." In *Feminism and Film Theory*, edited by Constance Penley. New York: Routledge, 1988.

Fanon, Franz. *Black Skin, White Masks*. New York: Monthly Review, 1967.

Foucault, Michel. *Language, Counter-memory, Practice: Selected Essays and Interviews*. Edited by Donald F. Bouchard, translated by Bouchard and Sherry Simon. Ithaca, NY: Cornell University Press, 1977.

——*Power/Knowledge: Selected Interviews and Other Writings*. Edited by Colin Gordon, translated by Gordon et al. New York: Pantheon, 1980.

Friedberg, Anne. "A Denial of Difference: Theories of Cinematic Identification." In *Psychoanalysis & Cinema*, edited by E. Ann Kaplan. London: Routledge, 1990.

Gamman, Lorraine and Margaret Marshment. *Female Gaze: Women as Viewers of Popular Culture*. Seattle, WA: Real Comet Press, 1989.

Kaplan, E. Ann, ed., *Psychoanalysis & Cinema: AFI Film Readers*, New York: Routledge, 1989.

Kuhn, Annette. *Power of the Image: Essays on Representation and Sexuality*. New York: Routledge, 1985.

Minh-ha, Trinh. "Outside In, Inside Out." In *Questions of Third World Cinema*, edited by Jim Pines. London: British Film Institute, 1989.

Mulvey, Laura. *Feminism and Film Theory*. New York: Routledge, 1988.

——*Visual and Other Pleasures*. Bloomington, IN: Indiana University Press, 1989.

Penley, Constance. *Feminism and Film Theory*. New York: Routledge, 1988.

34.
AMASSING THE MULTITUDE

Revisiting Early Audience Studies

Jack Bratich

The field of audience studies goes on because its object is a fugitive. It should not be surprising, then, that proclamations about the end of the audience are commonplace. The gradual erosion over the past few decades of ontological questions in audience studies and cultural studies has contributed to these pronouncements. A few decades ago, the "audience" was a relatively unproblematic term (Dahlgren, 1998). The fugitive audience may have been difficult to research and hard to measure, but it was still a common-sense reality. The audience was out there; it was just a matter of sharpening the research tools to understand it. Now, however, the audience is a contested term. The goal of research is not to accumulate better knowledge of an object out there, but to ask what kind of knowledge is possible and desirable (Dahlgren, 1998).

To pursue the question "whither the audience?" this article uses Michael Hardt and Toni Negri's (2000, 2004) social theory of subjectivity to focus on three early models and discourses (propaganda, marketing, and moral). I ask, what does a conceptual shift from audience to "audience power" or mediated multitude do to the field of audience research? After this theoretical clearing, I propose a number of research agendas that would further this project.[1]

Audience, Method, Ontology: Audience as Problematization

Pertti Alasuutari (1999) laid out what he called the three generations of reception studies (within cultural studies/media studies). For Alasuutari, cultural studies' historical trajectory has shifted from a focus on texts to one on audiences. The first crucial moment was Stuart Hall's essay "Encoding/ Decoding" and the voluminous research that followed this model. The second generation was characterized by the method of audience ethnography, which displaced the controlled settings for investigating the variety of decodings (e.g., Ang, 1991, 1996; Fiske, 1987, 1994; Morley, 1992,1996; Radway, 1984; Silverstone, 1990, 1996). The third generation, constructionist, breaks with the emphasis on empirical audiences altogether and examines media culture and its discourses (especially as these discourses produce and require a conception of the audience).

It is this last iteration that has deontologized the audience. As Grossberg, Wartella, and Whitney (1998) argued, "the audience as such does not actually exist except as idealization" (p. 208). Martin Allor (1988) has elaborated the multiplicity of sites and functions the audience can have in research. John Hartley (1992) argued that the audiences are "invisible fictions. . . . [They] may be imagined empirically, theoretically or politically, but in all cases the product is a fiction that serves the imagining institutions. In no case is the audience 'real' or external to its discursive construction" (Hartley, p. 105). Tony Bennett (1996) has elaborated this, specifically examining how cultural studies' notion of the active audience is pedagogically mobilized to authorize critics in the name of empowering readers.

In these challenges to audience ontology, audiences are seen not as empirical actors to be examined in their concrete activity, but as discursive constructs, as effects of a variety of programs, institutions, and measuring instruments. Constructionism is a metatheoretical approach that treats audience as signifier and subject position rather than referent and autonomous subject. Doing media studies in this frame entails "interrogating the systems that produce regimes of representations" (Cruz & Lewis, 1994, p. 5). To study audiences is to study the discourses that take audiences as their object. The method here would be discourse analysis.

This article partially emerges from this constructionist framework, adding that audiences are a product of what Foucault (1988, 1997a, 1997b) called "problematization." According to Foucault (1988), a problematization is

> not the representation of a pre-existing object, nor the creation by discourse of an object that does not exist. It is the totality of discursive and nondiscursive practices that introduces something into the play of true and false and constitutes it as an object for thought.
>
> (p. 257)

A problematization takes a variety of practices, habits, and experiences and isolates them into an object of concern or discussion. Sometimes this takes the literal form of a "problem" or threat (such as youth audiences in relation to sexual or violent imagery); other times the problematization creates a source of anxiety or worry. In each case, lots of time, energy, and resources are spent isolating and analyzing an object.

Furthermore, problematizations are not simply idealizations or abstract linguistic postulates. As a number of Foucauldian researchers have argued, problematizations are the conceptual "carvings out" that make reality intelligible and thus enable practices to "take place" (Bratich, 2003; Burchell, 1991; Dean, 1996; Foucault, 1997; Rabinow, 1997). Very material practices follow from (and produce more) problematizations. In the present case, the audience is an anchor and alibi for a variety of decisions. Problematizing audiences constitutes a fundamental part of public policy, educational initiatives, corporate production, cultural programming, research funding, even the interpersonal protocols of families in the domestic sphere.

Audience as Mediated Multitude/Audience Power

This constructivist approach is crucial, as it both wards off the traps of naïve empiricism and shifts attention to the discursive investment in creating, knowing, and modifying the audience. In other words, it directs our perspective to knowledge production and power relations in the cultural field.

However, this position is not sufficient in allowing a thorough understanding of the audience question. As a supplement we can turn to the methodological strategy proposed by Hardt and Negri (2000) in *Empire*. They employed a two-pronged method, what they call the "critical-deconstructive" and the "constructive/ethico-political" (p. 47). The former aims to "subvert the hegemonic languages and social structures" by examining the dominant discourses and hegemonic problematizations as such (pp. 47–48). This corresponds to the third generation of cultural reception studies above, as it works on the terrain of the discursive production of the category audience. A discourse analysis of the hegemonic languages that problematize the audience would be the method here.

The second component is the constructive and ethico-political, which for Hardt and Negri (2000) means entering the terrain of the ontological. Whereas the first approach may offer a glimpse into alternative practices and processes (by critically exposing the exclusions performed by discourses), this second approach *begins* with those "alternative" practices. This entails a shift in perspective: considering history from the point of view of the "res gestae, the power of the multitude to make history" (p. 47). This res gestae refers to "the subjective forces acting in the historical context … a horizon of activities, resistances, wills and desires" that resists hegemonic orders while also creating new possibilities (p. 48).

In other words, the second methodological approach examines the material dynamics of subjective, "self-valorizing" practices and productive processes. It is this milieu of subjectivity that spurs dominant codes to create their problematizations, in the first place. Rather than give priority to the series of problematizations, the ontological-constructive perspective begins with the notion that any hegemonic discourse "selects, limits, and constricts the possibilities of a more expansive field of social practices" (Dyer-Witheford, 1999, p. 176). This expansive field of potentialities, what Negri (1999) called "constituent power," produces meaning and is only partially captured in representation and problematization.

In the case of audiences, it means we need to look at the production of subjectivity that constitutes audience practices on their own terms. It entails examining audiences as constituent power (*potentia*: "local, immediate, actual force of constitution") and not simply constituted power (*potestas*: "centralized, mediating, transcendental force of command; Hardt, 1991, p. xiii). The method requires an ontology of audiences to complement the critical deconstructive approach. Rather than assume that the discursive production of subject positions exhausts the field of audience study, the ontological approach seeks to examine the material field of practices performed by the referent of the term audiences, however elusive that referent may be.

I am not arguing, then, for a banishing of the constructionist framework in order to get back to the audiences themselves. One way to state this is to say the double method looks both at what audiences do (their practices) and what is done to them in representation (the problematizations). However, this oversimplifies the matter and requires further clarification. "Looking at what audiences do" assumes the stability of the term audience, which the social constructionist and earlier cultural studies approaches undermine. We may rephrase the matter in the following way: The audience is a problematization, a conceptual capture of a variety of communicative practices and mediated processes of subjectivity. The ontological realm, then, is not one belonging to the audience, but to these mediated subjective forces. Production itself, in the form of meanings, desires, pleasures, and self-value, constitutes media subjectivity. The audience is "produced," but also refers to production as such in a communicative context. It is only when a discourse or program stabilizes these forces into an object of concern or study that an audience appears.

Audience can thus be said to be the end result of conceptual capture, or constituted power. Constituent power, on the other hand, has a less precise analogue. For Hardt and Negri (2000, 2004), constituent power is embodied in what they call the "multitude." As a concept, the multitude is as amorphous and fugitive as the becoming it tries to name. It names a collective process of production, one that embodies the res gestae and the creative capacities of co-operative social forces, as well as a self-valorizing relation (what they call *homo homo* and *vis viva*).

As for the audience's constituent power, one could call it a mediated multitude, media subjectivity, or something like "audience power." Audience power requires some initial elucidation. First, it should be recognized as a shortened form of audience constituent power. Second, although the Italian notion for this is potentia, I choose to use audience power over audience potential. "Potential" still seems to retain the connotations of "untapped," "latent," or "nascent" activity. This does not resonate with the productive processes I am attributing to mediated multitude (a closer term would be Gilles Deleuze's notion of the virtual). The word "power" still has some of these qualities (as in "capacity") while also carrying a differential and relational quality (as in Foucault's notion of a force acting on another force). Finally, the term "audience power" can be used as long as we remember that audience is itself not a subject, but the name for the media/human assemblage (in fact, it may be best to think of it as hyphenated: audience-power).

Audience power refers to the creative processes of meaning making, the appropriation and circulation of affects, and the enhancement of these very capacities. It does not simply refer to people watching, reading, or listening to mediated texts (no matter how active the consumption). In the traditional transmission model of communication, for instance, the audience is assumed to refer to people who are at the endpoint of the chain of media communication. Audience constituent power, however, does not come after production (located elsewhere). It highlights the collective invention of values, significations, and affects—in other words, the very production of culture itself. Audience power refers to a configuration of humans and communication technologies in which the capacities of production (both semiotic and somatic) are enhanced. Thus audience power entails a fundamental modification of Negri's more abstract version of constituent power. Audience power is actualized only through the mediation of communications technologies. Only later, as a reaction to these processes, does an audience appear, via a problematization that places these productive powers at the end of the communication chain.

There is another version of audience power that bears mention here, namely Dallas Smythe's (1981) germinal essay, "On the Audience Commodity and Its Work." Smythe proposed a focus on the audience as commodity. This meant demystifying the myth of free time and foregrounding the creative activities of audiences as labor, in which leisure time was spent exerting effort for advertisers. Although he introduced the notion of audience power to media studies, he really only treated it from the perspective of its already commodified form. In other words, while foregrounding the productive power of the mediated multitude, Smythe's audience labor has already been expropriated into the commodity-form. As Negri and the other autonomist thinkers have argued, the primacy of subjective labor power would need to precede objective capture.

These methodological issues are crucial for this article because much of recent audience studies has relied on the critical, deconstructionist approach. This article retains elements of this approach (by focusing on three problematizing discourses), but recognizes concrete media subjects' activities as the immanent horizon from which problematizations are formed. My intervention in audience studies thus draws from Hardt and Negri's call for a methodological shift in perspective, one that turns to the ontology of subjective practices in order to open up a different interpretation of audiences and audience studies as a field. It means studying audiences, and especially studying audience studies, from the perspective of constituent power, the motor that provokes discourses of power/knowledge to take action. In essence, this shift means taking Hardt and Negri's analysis of living labor as productive process and transposing it to the cultural field. Placing this subjective figure of the multitude into cultural and media studies may provide a conceptual clearing for a new set of issues around media, culture, and power

Amassing the Audience: Early Formations of Managing the Multitude

The audience has been in crisis since it was generated. The history of audience research is marked by

attempts to measure, identify, understand, and target the elusive object. These techniques continually renew themselves, providing consistency to a tradition in the very failure and refinement of conceptual capture. This trajectory of continual crisis is, according to Hardt and Negri (2000), a key marker of the history of Western political thought and practice. For Hardt and Negri, modernity is marked by a series of attempts to measure, contain, and name the "multitude." Modernity has instituted a series of sovereign names (nation, people, folk) that attempt to transform immanence into transcendence, and through this sovereignty machine "the multitude is in every moment transformed into an ordered totality" (p. 87).

With regard to the audience, I argue that this crisis of modernity also marks the perpetual crisis in audience studies. The very emergence of the notion of the audience inaugurates a series of conceptual captures of the mediated multitude, especially via the term "mass." How did audiences become masses, or more accurately, how did media subjects become "audiences as masses"? As Raymond Williams (1961) argued, there are "no masses, there are only ways of seeing people as masses" (p. 20). He took this nominalism one step further, by claiming that we interpret masses "according to some convenient formula . . . it is the formula, not the mass, which it is our real business to examine" (p. 20). This is similar to the notion that rather than chasing the real referent of the concept, we need to examine the discursive and nondiscursive constructions and mobilizations of the category.

Rise of Social Sciences and the Mass

Mass communications arose as a latecomer in the lineage of the social sciences. The rise of mass culture produced new approaches and objects of study in other social sciences before a full-fledged field of mass communications emerged. The audience was not originally a precise object of measurement or of systematic study. It was hardly an object at all, dispersed as it was across a range of discourses and disciplines. Early problematizations of the audience were primarily speculative, performed by social observers, press agents, and critics. Some of the early attempts at observing/reflecting on audiences included pundits' reflections on the rise of the "penny press" in the 1830s, especially around the issues of the potential benefits for the public of increasing the reach of communication, especially to immigrants. Soon thereafter, Alexis de Tocqueville's musings on the American character included his observation that an increase in mass communication would lead to an increase in conformity, thus linking the audience to issues of democracy and creativity. Finally, in the 1880s, the rise of women's magazines emerged from an early conception of a demographic, in which media managers began to think of their mass-mediated products in terms of a "typology of readerships" (Mattelart & Mattelart, 1998, p. 12).

By the turn of the 20th century, however, the discipline of sociology began to take a more systematic approach to media. Mass media were seen as a necessary component of the newly emerging social formation, as the "nervous system" of the social body (where society was modeled as an "organism," see Mattelart, 1994, p. 36). Methods employed by social research to regulate this organism were designed to "manag[e] the multitudes" (Mattelart & Mattelart, 1998, p. 11; Mattelart, 1994).The rise of statistics was linked to a desire to understand and manage sprawling populations (Hacking, 1990; Mattelart, 1996; Rose, 1999). Given the mobile and free-floating character of Western subjects in the late 19th century, statistical instruments made judicial and demographic flows measurable, and thus manageable (Mattelart, 1996). These unruly flows were conceptually tamed via the statistical unit of analysis: the "average man." This averageness gave a center of gravity to the normal, fused the moral order with the physical order, and reduced social dynamics to a series of calculable effects and types. Early audience measurement was indebted to these instruments, seeking to statistically track and commodify these flows (see Meehan, 1990).

The treatment of audience as mass also grew out of the field of collective psychology. Such classic works as Gustav Le Bon's *The Crowd* laid the groundwork for a social psychology of collectives. Although ostensibly a theory of human nature (in which humans are primarily ruled by passions and emotion rather than rational choice), this science of crowds was rooted in social theory. The mass, an anonymous, amorphous aggregate, was linked to large-scale industrialization, the mobility of populations, the

concentration of populations into urban spaces, the interlinking of sites via transportation innovations, and the rise of cultural forms corresponding to these developments (Cruz & Lewis, 1994; Mattelart, 1994; Simpson, 1994; Williams, 1961). Cities became defined as sites of mixture, of the breakdown of ethnic tradition and order, and of an emerging conformity (Cruz & Lewis, 1994; Lears, 1983; Leiss, Kline, & Jhally, 1997; Marchand, 1985). In addition, the mass was an outcome of the rise of education and new technologies of transmission (Williams, 1961).

This amorphous collective also represented the threat of mental, moral, and physical contagion. As Williams (1961) argued, masses became a new word for mob. Much like the mob and the crowd, masses were essentially ruled by irrational impulses, were easily excited, and led to conformity in conduct. This was a heavily gendered analysis, as these characteristics painted collectives as "feminine," thus anchoring representations of the feminine in the populace, and vice versa (Huyssen, 1986; Modleski, 1986; Petro, 1986; Soderlund, 2002). However, mobs and crowds were defined as temporary assemblies that gathered at specific times and places, usually surrounding an event. The masses were abstract: They were always threatening with mixtures, posing dangers of crossing boundaries, and loosening traditional bonds. The mass referred to a more routinized and normalized state of affairs and was thus an abstract and virtual category. As a permanent crisis and continuous threat, this disruption had to be managed.

The conceptualization of the audience-as-mass emerged from this broader set of problematizations. Social, political, and economic upheavals, and the attendant production of new subjectivities (citizens, laborers, religious leaders, activists) all created a milieu that finds a countermovement in new measurement techniques and objects of study. Sociology, especially, began to train its eye on the socius itself, analyzing its components and dynamics. The place of media in this emerging configuration of masses and space increasingly became an object of scrutiny and research. With the breakdown in cultural traditions, the massive mingling of immigrants and mobility of nomadic labor, and the skepticism toward traditional institutions, media were considered a major force in creating a national society (Anderson,

1991). Logically, the audience became a paramount concern.

For some, like the early Chicago School researchers Robert Park and Charles Horton Cooley, media subjectivities alleviated some shortcomings of modernization (Mattelart, 1994). Park found that newspapers promoted assimilation among urban immigrants and thus acted as an antidote to the disintegrating function of modernization. Cooley, also studying newspapers, found them to enhance variety, and thus remedy fears of mass conformity brought about by the impersonal, anonymous city. This "positive" role for mass media included gathering up mobile and dispersed populations, creating a national identity, and educating and informing citizens. In sum, mass media ameliorated the pernicious effects of mass society.

At the same time, other researchers argued that media contributed to those pernicious effects. Mass media exacerbated the problem of modernization, especially the loss of community through impersonal media technologies, where audiences replace citizens/community members. Thus we see a fundamental ambivalence in the mass media/audience problematic. Media could be harmonizing or disaggregating, "centripetal" or "centrifugal" (Carey, 1969; McQuail, 1994; cited in Grossberg, Wartella, & Whitney, 1998). Mass media, in the Deweyian sense of being both source of and corrective for loss of democracy, could thus produce audience subjects that either inhibited or promoted good citizenship.

Even while seemingly contradictory, these varying positions indicate an overall concern for and anxiety over the audience. All are grappling with questions like, how powerful is the newly developing mass media? How important is communication to a democracy? How can communication subvert it? What is the media's role in governing and citizenship? What is the capacity of media to affect mobile, dispersed, and varied populations? Within these questions, the audience-as-citizen is fundamental. What can people do with media? What "people" are constituted via media (here we can read the history of concerns over media and populism, the public, and partisanship)? To put it succinctly, the capacity of actors to produce effects *with* media was just as important as the effects on people *by* media. Whether media were envisioned as centripetal or centrifugal, as unifier or divider, this

early ambivalence spoke to the power of mediated masses, of media subjects as contributing to or blocking new arrangements of culture and economy. The early systematic reflections on audience, within the sociology of media, thus recognized the vital yet ambivalent qualities of audience powers.

Propaganda Studies: The Vulnerable and Reactive Audience

A few decades later, with the emergence of mass communications as a field of study, this recognition of the power of media subjects takes on a different ambivalence. In this era, the audience/mass gets defined as vulnerable (a passive recipient of influences) and as active polluter (of hierarchies and values). First, we turn to the audience as vulnerable to propaganda.

With the success of the Woodrow Wilson-appointed Creel Committee, designed to disseminate propaganda during WWI, and the accepted belief, at least among pundits, that the Germans were defeated primarily through "the paper war," propaganda became increasingly an object of fear and admiration (Mattelart, 1994; Simpson, 1994). Simultaneously, the call by Walter Lippman in the 1920s for a scientific approach to mass media research unleashed new ideas and techniques for addressing the audience/mass: public opinion, propaganda analysis, techniques of persuasion, and marketing research. The interwar years increasingly saw a public fear of manipulation, a concern over the power of media to mobilize opinion. What was once the democratic promise for the Chicago School (reaching enormous numbers of dispersed populations), now became an issue of persuasion and manipulation. Studies like Harold Lasswell's *Propaganda Technique in the World War* (1927) and *Psychopathology and Politics* (1930) were fueled by the will to improve American propaganda as well as defend vulnerable audiences from external forces (Mattelart, 1994; Simpson, 1994).

Within propaganda analysis, media subjects were defined as passive and often unknowing recipients of persuasive messages. However, this passivity was not simply a description of a numb or paralyzed audience. It must be remembered that propaganda researchers had two main objectives regarding the homefront: to defend the citizenry against pernicious foreign communication and to mobilize the same citizenry via domestic state communication. This dual goal of propaganda—to protect from foreign effects and to provoke domestic effects—acknowledged audience power as an increasing component of warfare.

The audience/mass was identified with a set of passions, impulses, and irrational desires. Audiences were considered easily provoked, mobilized, and excited. If anything, audience powers were *rendered* passive, even conceptually pacified. It may not make sense even to use "passive" as a modifier, however, and certainly not to describe the resulting subject of mass media (like the narcotized couch potato figure that later dominated images of passivity). Instead, audiences were identified via their highly charged capacity to be activated. Rather than thinking of audiences as passive, they are more accurately described as reactive. This difference is crucial, as it begins to recognize the capacities of media subject, even if it is the capacity to be affected. The force produced by a human/media assemblage (audience power) was something to be respected, cultivated, and activated for particular policy objectives.

It may seem odd to characterize the propaganda framework as one that acknowledged audience power. After all, many communications scholars associate the early persuasion research with the hypodermic needle model of media effects. This direct-effects tradition carries with it the image of a strong media power and a weak audience passively receiving messages. Although this may be the case, it characterizes the persuasion discourse only after it has already performed a conceptual maneuver in response to the threat and promise of audience powers. Media, already immersed in and inseparable from the capacities of audiences, had to be separated and extracted as an autonomous instrument. Propaganda research, confronting the immanence of media in a milieu of active production, tried to isolate media power as an instrument to use on that milieu. The "hypodermic needle" was an object of fear when used by malevolent others and of desire when used by benevolent selves. Audiences were not neutralized victims, but useful resources: vulnerable and pliable, yes; passive and inert, no.

The problematization was formulated in this grammar: a subject (propaganda or propagandists), an instrument (media), and an object (audiences). Yet this formula is itself a technique designed to organize, re-channel, and harness audience constituent power. Audiences are capable of significant production, which begets the desire to make that production serve policy objectives.

The heyday of direct-effects research thus emerged in a context that defined the mass audience as easily stimulated, activated, and agitated—small wonder, given the mobilizing powers attributed to wartime photojournalism and ad campaigns (Wombell, 1986). In addition, labor organizers' successful use of media spurred Ivy Lee to inaugurate counter-campaigns that scholars consider the origin of public relations (see Ewen, 1996; Stauber & Rampton, 1995). Given the significance of labor organizing and the proliferation of oppositional and local media during these decades, it is no surprise that the audience would come to connote a heightened capacity for action.

Effects-oriented studies that followed, most famously associated with Robert Merton and Carl Hovland, especially during World War II, revolved around experimenting with these audience powers, with what would and would not work to activate audiences. The study, and fine-tuning, of motivational radio programs and films for soldiers and citizens (like Frank Capra's *Why We Fight* film series (1943–1945) spoke to the belief in the immense power of audiences to act. Eruptions of audience activity such as that accompanying the *War of the Worlds* (Welles) broadcast in 1938 fascinated researchers for generations. Cantril, Gaudet, and Herzog's (1940) famous Princeton study attempted to delineate which elements of the audience body filtered the messages and which ones were eager to accept the reality effect of the program.

The classic works defining the limited-effects tradition (like Lazarsfeld et al.'s *People's Choice* and Robert Merton's *Mass Persuasion)* all sought mitigating factors in media reception, either internal to the media subject, like selective exposure and retention, or in other subjects, like opinion leaders. For both direct- and limited-effects researchers, the target was similar: understanding and directing dispersed, fragmented, and undecided populations. They managed multitudes while not always relying on media to do the brunt of the work.

The variations in audience reception so enthralled researchers that the limited-effects tradition remains the bedrock of the empirical approach. The audience as mass came to be defined through its variations and heterogeneity instead of through an equation with a homogeneous and amorphous mob. Thus, the work that criticized the direct-effects model retained this fundamental problematization of audience powers as reactive. Rather than finding audiences passive (as lack of activity), they were characterized by the capacity to be affected, the *power* to be activated.

Although audience power was recognized through testing, this experimentation was performed within a functionalist paradigm (Mattelart & Mattelart, 1998). The empirical tradition recognized media subjects and sought to understand constituent audience power in order to reabsorb it into the social body. This functionalist approach experimented with all of the powers of the audience as a way to manage possible deviations and reorient these capacities toward the homeostatic tendency of the social body.

What is important here is to recognize that even in the canonical moment when the audience-as-mass was positioned as hopelessly and fundamentally passive, the problematization of audiences spoke to the anxieties over audience power. At stake fundamentally was the capacity of subjects to be acted upon, and then to act, in their relation with media. So, whereas this era is canonically defined by its belief in the great power of media, it can just as well be described as the anxiety over the great power of media subjects.

Marketing: The Desiring Audience

While propaganda discourses defined the audience-mass as needing protection and activation, another contemporary discourse, marketing, focused only on the latter. Much of early audience research was motivated by marketing objectives and performed in advertising agencies. The fusion of selling and communication that came to define advertising agencies in the early 1900s meant the fusion of two subjects: the audience (of advertising media) and the consumer (see Leiss, Kline, & Jhally, 1997).[2]

The rise of the consumer society was dependent upon the ability to activate media subjects for particular purposes. Audience power was mobilized to alter conceptions of the self from producers to consumers. The consumer was a historically emergent subject that was not simply a buyer of particular products. As many researchers have noted, consumption became a way of being in which desires were channeled toward the self, and identity itself was wrapped up in consuming (Ewen, 1976; Lears, 1983; Leiss, Kline, & Jhally, 1997; Marchand, 1985). When it shifted its textual techniques from information-heavy, product-oriented pitches to transformational promises for the buyer, advertising did more than define particular needs and desires. It trained audiences to think of themselves primarily as consumers, as individuals with desires that could be resolved in the sphere of consumption. Audience power was rerouted and transformed into consumer power.

The development of market research into audiences is important for our purposes here in a number of ways. First, it demonstrates the practical application of problematizations. Scrutinizing audiences as objects by articulating them to consumption shows how seemingly abstract definitional changes have effectivity in the social sphere. Second, this meaning-made-practical was crucial to the general shift in the locus of social control from work to leisure and from effort to pleasure (Mattelart, 1994). That is, the multitude was recognized to have a set of capacities outside of the labor power captured in the factory. Leisure is not, thus, only a tool for reproducing and replenishing labor power, but itself becomes a target of social management. This shift can be seen as increasing the sites for the deployment of power—what Hardt and Negri (2000), following Foucault, call the context of "biopower"—as well as being part of the early development of the "diffuse factory" (Lazzarato, 1996) or "social factory" (Dyer-Witheford, 1999, p. 81; Tronti, 1980).

Finally, what market researchers have demonstrated is another early appreciation of the audience as capable of being activated. As others have noted, advertising and marketing have not operated primarily via an external manipulation, but have studied audiences in their concrete specificity (Balnaves & O'Regan, 2002; Jhally, 1987; Marchand, 1985). Audiences were problematized as a set of desires (e.g., aspirations for self, family, society; imagination of the good life, an optimistic future, and their own place in it) and the capacities to satisfy those desires. These desires and wills preexisted the marketing "audience," being bound, for instance, to traditional institutions like church, family, state, communal mores, ethnic rituals, and customs. Advertisers, rather than imposing their will on passive audiences, tapped into and redirected these immanent capacities.

With the increasing reliance on psychological techniques of persuasion, marketers further understood audiences to be producers of affect. These subjects' capacities were "exercised" and redirected via images and persuasive techniques. The early history of public relations was also marked by this recognition of audience power. The influence of Freudian thought on early PR advocates, such as like Walter Lippman and Edward Bernays, resulted in defining humans as essentially irrational and driven by the unconscious. Lippman, for instance, made it clear that audiences were not passive; in fact, audience appetites were such that they needed exercising via images (Ewen, 1996, pp. 154–158).

Of course, this tapping and channeling selected some desires over others, exacerbated some while denying others, created new ones (e.g., anxieties over modernization, self-identity, and courtship), and provided alienating and self-defeating solutions. The immanent capacities of audience power were led to the particular resolution in the commodity form, but this was only the goal and endpoint. While ultimately channeling these impulses toward consumption, early marketers nonetheless could produce the audience-consumer only by recognizing and addressing the generative powers of media subjects.[3]

In each of the above problematizations of the audience as mass (the vulnerable audience of propaganda and the desiring audience of consumer society), media subjects were defined through their irrationality, as a bundle of emotions, impulses, and desires. Rather than dismiss these accounts for not cultivating the innate capacities for informed and reasoned choice, however, we can at least acknowledge that their problematizations rested on a belief in the powers of the mass. Whether positioned as a threat or a resource, subjects were acknowledged to be able to produce their own sense, to activate desires through a relation to media, and to enhance their own power with media. However, this audience constituent

power was acknowledged, then countered, by the propaganda and market frameworks, which sought to transform these impulses for their own interests, winnowing audience potentialities into prescribed pathways. The response to audience constituent power ultimately dampened and froze the capacities in their self-valorizing open-endedness and potentiality.

Moral Panics Framework: The Vulnerable, Yet Threatening, Audience

Continuing the propaganda framework's concern over the "vulnerable" audience, the "moral panics" framework signifies the most conspicuous of problematizations (Cohen, 2002; Soderlund, 2002). This framework has come to inform much of media-effects research, especially the research that has contributed to public policies and debates over the triad youth-violence-sex.

This media-effects tradition is consistently taken up in the public domain as evidence of media power, as proof of the need to protect and manage the vulnerable audience (often a special population, especially children and juveniles). Regardless of the scholarly debates over the validity of media-effects research, when this tradition is taken up in popular controversies, it becomes a truth-producing discourse, at least as an authoritative source for cultural debates and public policies.

Moral frameworks are invoked when media images and sounds are blamed for alleged spikes in youth excess, typically sexual or violent in nature. Marilyn Manson/Columbine and Chucky/James Bulger are perhaps the most spectacular examples in recent memory, but the link between image and violence has a long history in media culture. We might even say that the genealogy of media culture is intertwined with moral panics about that fusion.[4]

Perhaps the most famous example of this moral discourse in media history is the Payne Fund Study of the 1920s. The rapid diffusion of cinema led critics and moralists to probe this social force. This multivolume study was commissioned to analyze, among other things, the impact of cinema on knowledge of other cultures, on attitudes toward violence, and on delinquent behavior. Critics wanted to know: Was this booming cultural phenomenon destroying parental authority? Was it promoting immorality, ignorance, and rebelliousness?

The various experiments conducted in the Payne Fund Studies produced a variety of conclusions, but this variation was ignored in favor of a general conclusion in public discourse that linked frequency of movie attendance to antisocial behavior. Criticisms by media researchers for many of the studies' sloppy scientific work had little impact. As another example of problematizations of audiences having pragmatic effects, the Payne Fund study significantly contributed to the context of moral hysteria from which emerged the film industry's early production code and ratings system. This context, as film scholars have noted (Gunning, 1988; Ross, 1999), involved problem behavior both in and out of the theater.

Later studies also operated on this moral framework. Frederick Wertham's 1955 study, *Seduction of the Innocent*, examined the influence of comic books on juvenile delinquency, focusing on residents of a juvenile detention center. This 1950s research found that the excitement conveyed by the subjects about representations of criminal and deviant behavior provoked and encouraged mimicry among the readers. In the late 1960s, the NIMH continued this concern with juvenile delinquency when it produced a report to the U.S. Supreme Court connecting deviant behavior with television viewing. Although the report provided ambivalent and nuanced conclusions, the public only homed in on the evidence for a link and demanded Senate hearings on the matter. In 1990s Britain, the Newson Report linked the viewing of violent films (video nasties) to antisocial behavior among children, examined in great detail by Barker (1997).

Common to these moral frameworks is the concern over youth and deviance. Whether focusing on children or juveniles, what is at stake here is an audience whose deviant behavior is isolated, in keeping with the functionalist paradigm, and correlated with media consumption. The response to this crisis is a call to protect endangered populations from pernicious influences. However, this distinction between powerful media and victimized populations obscures the fact that the threat is not media per se but the audiences themselves. The studies problematize the audience as having the capacities to disrupt the norms of cultural initiation and disciplinary

regulations. These are the constituent powers that the discourses seek to curtail, while the studies locate these constituent powers in media influence.

Defining media as the problem betrays the scenario of competing discourses of protection. In the moral panics frame, the smooth transition from child to adult, from family to school to military is interrupted. Discourses of moral upbringing and character education are losing hold, while "cultural authority" is transferred to mass-produced and mass-distributed texts (Zelizer, 1992). Which agents and discourses will be authorized to perform passage rites: educators, family, church, the state? Or popular culture? The context for these studies and their problematizations includes a breakdown in traditional forms of upbringing and the need to eliminate potential competitors as threats.

The media become defined as a surrogate trainer of morals and proper subjectivities, in the case of younger children, and the substitute initiator of cultural members into adulthood, in the case of juveniles. Media are blamed, and the audience is determined to want protection from that media influence, to be seduced by another set of stories and discourses. The problematized audience wants to return to disciplinary institutions and practices and pleads for a guide. By problematizing the audience as vulnerable and reactive, rather than active, the discourses of protection were able to empower themselves as active agents of intervention into media subjectivity. Struggling with their own waning authority, these discourses found renewal in the taming of the threat to that authority. In this way, audiences "are produced institutionally in order for the various institutions to take charge of the mechanisms of their own survival" (Hartley, 1992, p. 105).

Whereas scapegoating media is one tactic of rejuvenation here, it is only at the level of a competing discourse of initiation. Viewing the scene from the perspective of audience power adds another layer of analysis. In terms of audience power, it is much more significant that active media subjects (in this case youth) were transformed into helpless victims of media power and thus in need of further guidance and assistance. Audience power here is reduced to the activity of emitting SOS signals. Once again, a problematization of the audience as vulnerable transforms audience power into two agents: active media power and pacified audience. Media subjects are reduced to dangerous deviant behavior, rendered objects of a moral gaze, and their capacities are activated as subjects in need of intervention.

Problematizing the Audience-Mass and the Multitude

We can now return to Raymond Williams's claim that critical work should examine the formulas through which masses are interpreted. Problematizing the audience as mass serves a variety of material interests and produces practical effects. From the most explicit political sense of moral regulation and censorship to the strategic interests of propaganda and public relations to the transformation of citizens into consumers, the mass audience circulates in discourses of power and representation.

In these discourses, audiences are both passive and highly excitable, mute and excessively articulating. Discourses seek to bolster themselves via protecting the mass (the propaganda and moral frameworks) or via activating certain potentialities in that mass (the propaganda and market frameworks). Problematizing the audience as a vulnerable mass thus requires a selection process, a displaced recognition of the mediated multitude, and a rechanneling of power towards the problematizing discourse. Defining the problem in this manner raises and denies the immanent forces of media subjects, splitting this constituent power into two constituted powers: (a) a determining agency (the media) and (b) a determined object (the audience). Both of these new powers become positions within the problematizing discourse and a target of numerous applications (protection, regulation, and mobilization).

In sum, these three discourses transformed the multitude into a mass. As Michael Hardt argued:

> The masses and mob are most often used to name an irrational and passive social force, dangerous and violent because so easily manipulated. The multitude, in contrast, is an active social agent—a multiplicity that acts. It is in fact the foundation of all social creativity.
> (Hardt & Dumm, 2004, p. 173)

For audience studies, this does not mean simply placing one term (audience as multitude) for another (audience as masses). To bring in the concept multitude is to undermine audience as a category, which, after all, names only the mediated multitude as *constituted* power. It is not the case that 100 years ago audiences were masses, and now we have audiences as multitudes. These are two concepts that address the creative productive practices of media subjectivities. The multitude, as concept, is more just and appropriate to the creative powers of that force.

Early conceptions of the audience-as-mass were representations that, when faced with a mediated multitude, attempted to pacify and activate these forces through problematization. It matters little at this stage what those affects, meanings, and desires actually were (their content). The fact that the capacity to produce them posed such a disruptive force that they needed pacification is enough to warrant attention. Emerging out of a milieu of social scientific techniques designed to manage unruly subjects, these audience discourses acknowledged audience constituent power, only to defuse or rechannel it.

These discourses themselves were reactive, operating only on a terrain composed of media subjects. These discourses sought to split audience power from itself, dividing constituent power into constituted powers. The audience-as-mass thus contains the traces of all these powers. To return to Hardt and Negri's double method: The problematization of the audience in these discourses does indeed produce an object (á la the constructionist model). At the same time, these problematizations are reactive and selective forces that capture already existing practices in specific ways. The field of media subjective processes is primary and constitutes the terrain of the ontological.

Proposals for Future Work

Empirical Research

This essay has operated in a conceptual realm, seeking to clear theoretical ground by unsettling certain assumptions in audience studies. It has worked at the level of the constitution of problematizations themselves, but an ontology of audience power can be successful only via the difficult empirical work of locating and recovering practices of the mediated multitude. Although I have occasionally mentioned some examples of audience power (e.g., early labor organizers' use of the press, rowdy cinema-going practices), much research could be done to add to this empirical layer. Indeed, a lot of this work has already been done in media history (e.g., Douglas, 1987) on the importance of early amateur ham operators to radio's emergence); it would just be a matter of reorienting these examples through the filter of audience power. In addition, contemporary research on alternative media practices has provided a wealth of examples (see Critical Art Ensemble, 2001; Dyer-Witheford, 1999; Klein, 2000; Kline, Dyer-Witherford, & de Peuter, 2003; McCaughey & Ayers, 2003; Rushkoff, 1996a, 1996b). It would mean not just finding examples of audience production (e.g., community press or fanzines) but examples that alter the notion of production itself.

Active Audience Model

This article focuses on early audience problematizations. How have subsequent discourses and their sovereign names (like "public," "identity," and "popular") addressed audience power? Perhaps the most compelling lineage would be the active audience model in cultural studies. Some might even say that calling audiences a multitude may be simply dressing up the active audience in new, loftier garb. There are indeed many similarities among the projects, and I find great resonance with De Certeau's (1984, 1986) writing on the heterological practices of consumption here, as well as his subsequent cultural studies uptake by John Fiske, Ien Ang, Virginia Nightengale, Janice Radway, Jacqueline Bobo, and others. The issues surrounding wandering or dispersed audience subjects are of particular relevance (Grossberg, 1988; Radway, 1988). Some initial differences with this tradition can be sketched here.

The active audience tradition essentially sought to displace and correct previous notions of the passive audience via analyzing what concrete audiences do. They revived the productive capacities of media subjects but within the already given problematic of the audience. That is, productivity was inscribed within constituted power, after a problematization has

occurred. My analysis is directed at the level of the problematizations themselves, reinscribing productivity prior to the moment of constituted power, in the constituent power captured by the term audience.

In the active audience model, the endpoints of two chains, the communication chain (audience) and economic chain (consumption), are assumed and combined. Activity is located in the fusion of these given positions, where decoding as a consumer has many degrees of freedom, but still within the structured constraints. Perhaps this can be traced to the ambivalence even in Hall's (1980) germinal essay, "Encoding and Decoding," in which he sought to give decoding a separate set of conditions, while retaining the essential spatial arrangement of the transmission model. Similarly, De Certeau sought to give consumption its own history and economy, but often retained the notion that this autonomy was a secondary reaction to production performed elsewhere. What would happen if activity and productivity preceded these chains, even acting as catalysts for their reactive emergence?

Contemporary Problematizations

The audience as mass emerged in an historical context in the U.S. that included gathering populations in urban centers, dispersion within a national border, the rise of industrialized mass production techniques, the admixture of cultures and traditions in concentrated settings, the expansion of market relations, and the concomitant extension of disciplinary institutions across these spaces (factory, school, army, hospital). Given current globalized conditions, as well as the technological developments in information and communication networking, what are the current discourses that problematize audiences? In an age in which communications and information technologies have integrated into everyday life, what specificity does the audience have? Haven't media become less a mass entity than a mobile, variegated, converged, and niched set of practices?

Current research on media convergence, mobile technologies, and networked media all make the question of the audience paramount. The fugitive audience has not disappeared per se, instead dispersing in scattered and masked forms in other research. The audience is everywhere being studied, but rarely named as such. Audiences are problematized as mobile, interactive, and highly technologized media subjects in a variety of disciplines and fields, including organizational communication, computer-mediated communication, library studies, telecommunications, information science, social network analysis, distance education, media literacy, and technology studies, to name a few.

Studies of cell phone uses and gratifications, pedagogic applications of emerging technologies, and the new mediated arrangements of kinship, identity, and leisure time all belong to this new style of problematization. Examples of this range from the impact of instant messaging on youth identity, to the influence of interactive websites on public journalism, to the networked labor practices in the new office space, to the effect of new technologies on diasporic identity. Smart mobs, electronic democracy, netiquette, new media literacy, virtual communities, and a host of other topics have emerged in which audiences as technologized media subjects have become central, even if not named as such, or named as users, interfacers, players, consumers, targets, participants, and so on. The topics of subjective interconnection, mobility, and global dispersion have come to the foreground of much communication research and, I argue, constitute the new audience studies.

Studying these new problematizations could still benefit from Hardt and Negri's autonomist toolbox. One could take up their arguments in *Empire* (2000) and *Multitude* (2004) that the integration of information technologies, communication processes, and strategies of biopolitical control has created a set of subjects who are increasingly interconnected, nomadic, and flexible. Jodi Dean's (2002, 2004) focus on communicative capitalism would supplement the more sprawling argument of Hardt and Negri. The audience, as media subject at the intersection of these social forces, becomes problematized in its continuous modulation, in its technological hybridity, and in its increasing mobility. Drawing also from Deleuze's (1990a, 1990b) writings on Societies of Control (which he also dubs Societies of Communication) and the growing governmentality studies literature (e.g., Balnaves & O'Regan's, 2002, "Governing the Audience") could augment this approach.

Conclusion: The Active (End of the) Audience

Within audience studies, the contemporary pronouncements about the audience's disappearance ultimately have a degree of truth value. They speak to the demise of a particular problematization of the mediated multitude. What has withered is not audience constituent power—if anything, that is intensifying with networked technologies. Rather, what is waning is the constituted power of "audience," and the discourses that historically have produced it as object. This passing has opened up new ways of conceptualizing audience studies and its fugitive object.

Whereas the method of much audience research, including the constructionist approach, entailed analyzing audience powers from the perspective of constituted power, the diminution of that power allows a shift in perspective. This article has tried to follow Hardt and Negri in the broader shift in perspective about historical subjectivity via turning audience problematization on its head: Traditionally we have analytically placed media power first and audiences second. With the waning (and scattering) of the term audience, we can reverse the polarities: active audience power, reactive discourses. As the active subject of production, the "wellspring of skills, innovation, and cooperation" (Dyer-Witheford, 1999, p. 65), audience power is self-valorizing. Ultimately, media industries, and the problematizing discourses, need the audience. The audience, as mediated multitude, does not need media industries in order to produce culture, nor the problematizing discourses in order to produce value.

Within this methodological shift, the audience is no longer tied to its problematized representation, but returned to the milieu of immanent creative forces. It is this sphere of audience powers that motors those problematizations in the first place, as well as offers the site and resource for new potentials of becoming and collectivity. Among these potentials remains the question of whether audience power has the antagonistic will to struggle that could motor future cultural production, and what forms these powers will take.

Notes

1. The essay concentrates on *media* audiences. This is crucial to note, as other research fields have a different tradition of problematizing the audience. In the performance

studies tradition, the history of the audience revolves around the live audience, in which the site of performance and material copresence comes to define the audience (see Butsch, 2000). The unruly corporeal audiences produce their own attending counterdiscourses and problematizations, and their history deserves a separate analysis.

2. Cruz and Lewis (1994) have noted this early tension between marketing (the malleable audience) and propaganda (the vulnerable audience) as a fundamental ambiguity of the early audience.

3. On top of this redirecting, market researchers ideologized the audience power as "consumer sovereignty" in which audience-consumers operate under rational (at times irrational) choice theory. This early appreciation for immanence also led to later manifestations of consumer research, such as the ease with which "critical consumer studies" celebrates "active audiences" and clings tenaciously to the uses and gratifications model of consumer behavior.

4. Loosely borrowing the term "moral panics" from Stanley Cohen (2002), I note here the close link between panics over youth and panics over media. It is difficult to think of them in isolation, at least since the beginning of the 20th century.

References

Alasuutari, P. (1999). Introduction: Three phases of reception. In P. Alasuutari (Ed.), *Rethinking the media audience* (pp. 1–21). London: Sage.

Allor, M. (1988) Relocating the site of the audience. *Critical Studies in Mass Communication, 5*, 217–233.

Anderson, B. (1991). *Imagined communities: Reflections on the origin and spread of nationalism*. New York: Verso.

Ang, I. (1991). *Desperately seeking audiences*. London: Routledge.

Ang, I. (1996). *Living room wars*. New York: Routledge.

Balnaves, M., & O'Regan, T. (2002). Governing audiences. In M. Balnaves, T. O'Regan, & J. Sternberg (Eds.), *Mobilising the audience* (pp. 10–28). St. Lucia, Australia: University of Queensland Press.

Barker, M. (1997). The Newson report. In M. Barker & J. Petley (Eds.), *Ill effects* (pp. 12–31). London: Routledge.

Bennett, T. (1996). Figuring audiences and readers. In J. Hay, L. Grossberg, & E. Wartella (Eds.), *The audience and its landscape* (pp. 145–60). Boulder, CO: Westview Press.

Bratich, J. (2003). Making politics reasonable: Conspiracism, subjectification, and governing through styles of thought. In J. Bratich, C. McCarthy, & J. Packer (Eds.), *Foucault, cultural studies, and governmentality* (pp. 67–100). Albany: State University of New York Press.

Burchell, G. (1991). Peculiar interests: Civil society and governing "the system of natural liberty." In G. Burchell, C. Gordon, & P. Miller (Eds.), *The Foucault effect: Studies in governmentality* (pp. 119–150). Chicago: University of Chicago Press.

Butsch, R. (2000). *The making of American audiences*. Cambridge, UK: Cambridge University Press.

Cantril, H., Gaudet, H., & Herzog, H. (1940). *The invasion from Mars*. Princeton, NJ: Princeton University Press.

Carey, J. (1969). The communications revolution and the professional communicator. In P. Halmos (Ed.), *The sociology of mass-media communicators* (pp. 23–38). Keele, UK: Keele University.

Cohen, S. (2002). *Folk devils and moral panics: The creation of the mods and rockers* (3rd ed.). New York: Routledge.

Critical Art Ensemble. (2001). *Digital resistance: Explorations in tactical media*. New York: Autonomedia.

Cruz, J., & Lewis, J. (1994). Introduction. *Viewing, reading, listening: Audiences and cultural reception*. Boulder, CO: Westview Press.

Dahlgren, P. (1998). Critique: Elusive audiences. In R. Dickinson, R. Harindranath, & R. O. Linné (Eds.), *Approaches to audiences* (pp. 298–310). London: Arnold.

Dean, J. (2002). *Publicity's secret*. Ithaca, NY: Cornell University Press.

Dean, J. (2004). The networked empire: Communicative capitalism and the hope for politics. In P. Passavant & J. Dean (Eds.), *Empire's new clothes: Reading Hardt and Negri* (pp. 265–288). New York: Routledge.

Dean, M. (1996). Foucault, government, and the enfolding of authority. In A. Barry, T. Osborne, & N. Rose (Eds.), *Foucault and political reason* (pp. 209–230). Chicago: University of Chicago Press.

De Certeau, M. (1984). *The practice of everyday life* (S. Rendall, Trans.). Berkeley: University of California Press.

De Certeau, M. (1986). *Heterologies: Discourses on the other* (B. Massumi, Trans.). Minneapolis: University of Minnesota Press.

Deleuze, G. (1990a). Control and becoming. In *Negotiations* (M. Joughin, Trans.; pp. 169–176). New York: Columbia University Press.

Deleuze, G. (1990b). Postscript on control societies. In *Negotiations* (M. Joughin, Trans.; pp. 177–182). New York: Columbia University Press.

Dyer-Witheford, N. (1999). *Cyber-Marx: Cycles and struggles in high technology capitalism*. Urbana: University of Illinois Press.

Ewen, S. (1976). *Captains of consciousness: Advertising and the social roots of the consumer culture*. New York: McGraw-Hill.

Ewen, S. (1996). *PR! A social history of spin*. New York: Basic Books.

Fiske, J. (1987): *Television culture*. London: Routledge

Fiske, J. (1994). Audiencing: Cultural practice and cultural studies. In N. K. Denzin & Y. S. Lincoln (Eds.), *Handbook of qualitative research* (pp. 189–198). Thousand Oaks, CA: Sage.

Foucault, M. (1988). The concern for truth. In L. D. Kritzman (Ed.), *Foucault, politics, philosophy, culture* (pp. 255–267). New York: Routledge.

Foucault, M. (1997a). Polemics, politics, and problematizations. In P. Rabinow (Ed.), *Foucault, ethics: Subjectivity and truth* (pp. 111–120). New York: New Press.

Foucault, M. (1997b). Preface to the *History of sexuality* (Vol. 2). In P. Rabinow (Ed.), *Foucault, ethics: Subjectivity and truth* (pp. 199–206). New York: New Press.

Grossberg, L. (1988). Wandering audiences, nomadic critics. *Cultural Studies, 2*, 377–391.

Grossberg, L., Wartella, E., & Whitney, C. (1998). *MediaMaking*. Thousand Oaks, CA: Sage.

Gunning, T. (1988). From the opium den to the theatre of morality: Moral discourse and the film process in early American cinema. *Art and Text, 30*, 30–40.

Hacking, I. (1990). *The taming of chance*. New York: Cambridge University Press.

Hall, S. (1980). Encoding/decoding. In D. Hobson, A. Lowe, & P. Willis (Eds.), *Culture, media, language*. London: Hutchinson.

Hardt, M. (1991). Translator's foreword: The anatomy of power. In A. Negri, *The savage anomaly*. Minneapolis: University of Minnesota Press.

Hardt, M., & Dumm, T. (2004). Sovereignty, multitudes, absolute democracy: A discussion between Michael Hardt and Thomas Dumm about Hardt and Negri's *Empire*. In P. Passavant & J. Dean (Eds.), *Empire's new clothes*. New York: Routledge.

Hardt, M., & Negri, A. (2000). *Empire*. Cambridge, MA: Harvard University Press.

Hardt, M., & Negri, A. (2004). *Multitude*. Cambridge, MA: Harvard University Press.

Hartley, J. (1992). *Tele-ology: Studies in television*. London: Routledge.

Huyssen, A. (1986). *After the great divide: Modernism, mass culture, postmodernism*. Bloomington: Indiana University Press.

Jhally, S. (1987). *The codes of advertising: Fetishism and the political economy of meaning in the consumer society*. New York: St. Martin's Press.

Klein, N. (2002). *No logo*. New York: St. Martin's Press.

Kline, S., Dyer-Witheford, N., & De Peuter, G. (2003). *Digital play: The interaction of technology, culture, and marketing*. Montreal, Canada: McGill-Queen's University Press.

Lasswell, H. (1927). *Propaganda technique in the world war*. London: Kegan Press.

Lasswell, H. (1930). *Psychopathology and politics*. New York: Viking Press.

Lazarsfeld, P., Berelson, B., & Gaudet, H. (1944). *The people's choice: How the voter makes up his mind in a presidential campaign*. New York: Duell, Sloan, & Pearce.

Lazzarato, M. (1996). Immaterial labour. In P. Virno & M. Hardt (Eds.), *Radical thought in Italy: A potential politics*. Minneapolis: University of Minnesota Press.

Lears, J. (1983). From salvation to self-realization: Advertising and the therapeutic roots of the consumer culture, 1880–1930. In R. Fox & J. Lears (Eds.), *The culture of consumption: Critical essays in American history, 1880–1980*. New York: Pantheon Books.

Leiss, W., Kline, S., & Jhally, S. (1997). *Social communication in advertising*. New York: Routledge.

Marchand, R. (1985). *Advertising the American dream: Making way for modernity, 1920–1940*. Berkeley: University of California Press.

Mattelart, A. (1994). *Mapping world communication: War progress culture* (S. Emanuel & J. Cohen, Trans.). Minneapolis: University of Minnesota Press.

Mattelart, A. (1996). *The invention of communication* (S. Emanuel, Trans.). Minneapolis: University of Minnesota Press.

Mattelart, A., & Mattelart, M. (1998). *Theories of communication*. London: Sage.

McCaughey, M., & Ayers, M. (2003). *Cyberactivism*. New York: Routledge.

McQuail, D. (1994). *Mass communication theory: An introduction*. Thousand Oaks, CA: Sage.

Meehan, E. (1990). Why we don't count: The commodity audience. In P. Mellencamp (Ed.), *Logics of television* (pp. 117–137). Indianapolis: Indiana University Press.

Merton, R. (1946). *Mass persuasion: The social psychology of a war bond drive*. New York: Harper.

Modleski, T. (1986). Femininity as mas(s)querade: A feminist approach to mass culture. In C. MacCabe (Ed.), *High theory, low culture* (pp. 37–52). Manchester, UK: Manchester University Press.

Morley, D. (1992). *Television, audiences, and cultural studies*. London: Routledge.

Morley, D. (1996). The geography of television: Ethnography, communications, and community. In J. Hay, L. Grossberg, & E. Wartella (Eds.), *The audience and its landscape* (pp. 317–342). Boulder, CO: Westview Press.

Negri, A. (1999). *Insurgencies: Constituent power and the modern state*. Minneapolis: University of Minnesota Press.

Petro, P. (1986). Mass culture and the feminine: The "place" of television in film studies. *Cinema Journal, 25*, 5–21.

Rabinow, P. (1997). Introduction. In P. Rabinow (Ed.), *Foucault, ethics: Subjectivity and truth* (pp. xi–xlv). New York: New Press.

Radway, J. (1984). *Reading the romance: Women, patriarchy and popular literature*. Chapel Hill: University of North Carolina Press.

Radway, J. (1988). Reception studies: Ethnography and the problems of dispersed audiences and nomadic critics. *Cultural Studies, 2*, 359–376.

Rose, N. (1999). *Powers of freedom: Reframing political thought*. New York: Cambridge University Press.

Ross, S. J. (1999). *Working-class Hollywood: Silent film and the shaping of class in America*. Princeton, NJ: Princeton University.

Rushkoff, D. (1996a). *Media virus! Hidden agendas in popular culture*. New York: Ballantine Books.

Rushkoff, D. (1996b). *Playing the future: How kids' culture can teach us to thrive in an age of chaos*. New York: HarperCollins.

Silverstone, R. (1990). Television and everyday life: Towards an anthropology of the television audience. In M. Ferguson (Ed.), *Public communication: The new imperatives* (pp. 173–189). London: Sage.

Silverstone, R. (1996). From audiences to consumers: The household and the consumption of communication and information technologies. In J. Hay, L. Grossberg, & E. Wartella (Eds.), *The audience and its landscape* (pp. 281–296). Boulder, CO: Westview Press.

Simpson, C. (1994). *Science of coercion: Communication research and psychological warfare 1945–1960*. New York: Oxford University Press.

Smythe, D. (1981). *Dependency road: Communications, capitalism, consciousness, and Canada*. Norwood, NJ: Ablex.

Soderlund, G. (2002). *Sex panics and city papers in America, 1907–1917: Mass media and public controversy over the traffic in women*. Unpublished dissertation, University of Illinois.

Stauber, J., & Rampton, S. (1995). *Toxic sludge is good for you: Lies, damn lies, and the public relations industry*. Monroe, ME: Common Courage Press.

Tronti, M. (1980). The strategy of refusal. In S. Lotringer & C. Marazzi (Eds.), *Italy: Autonomia/post-political politics* (pp. 36–61). New York: Semiotext(e).

Welles, Orson. (1938, October 30). *The War of the Worlds*. [Radio broadcast]. New York: Columbia Broadcasting System, Mercury Theater.

Wertham, F. (1955). *Seduction of the innocent*. London: Museum Press.

Williams, R. (1961). *Culture and society*. London: Random House.

Wombell, P. (1986). Face to face with themselves. In P. Holland, J. Spence, & S. Watney (Eds.), *Photography/Politics: Two* (pp. 84–81). London: Comedia/Photography Workshop.

Zelizer, B. (1992). *Covering the body: The Kennedy assassination, the media, and the shaping of collective memory*. Chicago: University of Chicago Press.

35.
THE WORK OF BEING WATCHED
Interactive Media and the Exploitation of Self-Disclosure
Mark Andrejevic

During the halcyon days of the high-tech economy—at the dawn of the new millennium—an entrepreneurial-minded former employee of the AirTouch corporation decided to change his name to DotComGuy and live his life on-line. For the former Mitch Maddox (a.k.a. DotComGuy) the decision was more than just a lifestyle decision; it was a business decision. By living his life in front of 25 cameras installed in his house and yard, DotComGuy hoped to demonstrate the benefits of e-commerce, ordering everything he needed on-line so that he wouldn't have to leave his home for a year. As an on-line advertisement for e-commerce—an entrepreneurial Truman Burbank—DotComGuy hoped to turn his Website into a for-profit corporation that would generate enough money to support his handlers and earn him a $98,000 paycheck for his year-long stint in the DotCompound.

The plan started swimmingly—Dot-ComGuy's stunt resulted in media coverage that drew sponsors and captured the attention of viewers, who generated more than a million hits a day for his Website during its first few months (personal interview with Mitch Maddox, Sept. 16, 2000). By the end of the year, the euphoria over the on-line economy had been replaced by a healthy dose of skepticism, and as the NASDAQ, headed south, so did Dot-ComGuy's fortunes. On New Year's Day 2001, DotComGuy left the compound behind and forfeited his $98,000 payday, keeping as payment only those products that the company had purchased or received for promotional purposes (Copeland, 2001). DotComGuy's venture may have failed as a business enterprise, but it succeeded in drawing attention to an important aspect of the emerging online economy: the productivity of comprehensive surveillance.

DotComGuy understood that while he was in the DotCompound, he was *working* 24-hours-a-day. Even when he was sleeping, the image of Maddox tucked into bed in his Dallas home was surrounded with banner ads and the names of sponsors, some of which were posted on the walls of his house. It was for the work he was performing by subjecting himself to online surveillance that DotComGuy was to receive his $98,000 payday. That he failed to turn a profit doesn't alter the economic fact upon which his entrepreneurial venture was based: that the emerging online economy increasingly seeks to exploit the work of being watched. DotComGuy may have failed to capitalize on this labor as an entrepreneur, but major corporations continue to attempt to exploit the economic potential of this labor on a much larger scale.

Some 15 years ago, Jhally and Livant (1986), inspired by the work of Dallas Smythe (1977; 1981), argued that communication theory needed to take seriously the notion that audiences were working when they were watching television. This paper seeks to develop their argument a bit further—to update it, as it were, for an era of new-media interactivity—by highlighting the emerging significance of the work not just of watching, but of *being* watched. The two complement each other, insofar as the development of interactive media allows for the rationalization of viewing and consumption in general, thanks to devices like interactive television that watch us while we watch. In the era of "reality" TV, wherein networks are winning ratings battles by enlisting people to submit their lives to comprehensive scrutiny, the claim that being watched is a form of value-generating labor ought not to be a particularly surprising one. We are not just facing a world in which a few select members of the audience are entering the celebrity ranks and cashing in on their 15 minutes of fame, but one in which non-celebrities—the remaining viewers—are being recruited to participate in the labor of being watched to an unprecedented degree by subjecting the details of their daily lives to increasingly pervasive and comprehensive forms of high-tech monitoring. Their viewing habits, their shopping habits, even their whereabouts are subject not just to monitoring but to inclusion in detailed marketing databases, thanks to the advent of computer-based forms of interactive media. This observation has become a commonplace in the popular literature on new media and has generated plenty of discussion on the fate of personal privacy in the on-line economy (see, for example, Garfinkel, 2000; Rosen, 2000; Whitaker, 1999). The consensus seems to be that the development of interactive media and of computer processing and storage power enable the increasing economic exploitation of comprehensive forms of consumer monitoring. In response, organizations like the Electronic Privacy Information Center (EPIC) have organized to advocate for consumer privacy rights and protection from creeping corporate surveillance.

The drawback of much of the discussion about privacy, as authors including Lyon (1994) and Gandy (1993) have suggested, is that the attempt to defend privacy rights has a disconcerting tendency to work as much in the interest of the corporations doing the monitoring as in that of the individuals being monitored. The development of demographic databases relies heavily on the protection accorded to private property, since these databases are profitable in large part because the information they contain is proprietary. As Lyon (1994) puts it "Privacy grows from the same modern soil as surveillance, which is another reason for doubting its efficacy as a tool of counter-surveillance" (p. 21).

As an alternative to the popular portrayal of the proliferation of corporate surveillance in terms of the incredible shrinking private sphere, this essay suggests an approach influenced by the concerns of political economy and the analysis of disciplinary panopticism. Conceived as a form of labor, the work of being watched can be critiqued in terms of power and differential access to both the means of surveillance and the benefits derived from their deployment. The operative question is not whether a particular conception of privacy has been violated but, rather: what are the relations that underwrite entry into a relationship of surveillance, and who profits from the work of being watched? Such an analysis draws its inspiration from Robins and Webster's (1999) assessment of the Information Revolution as "a matter of differential (and unequal) access to, and control over, information resources" (p. 91). Gandy (1993), quoting Klaus Lenk, cuts to the heart of the matter:

> The real issue at stake is not personal privacy, which is an ill-defined concept, greatly varying according to the cultural context. It is power gains of bureaucracies, both private and public, at the expense of individuals and the non-organized sectors of society.
>
> (p. 52)

Foucault's (1975/1977) discussion of disciplinary surveillance offers an approach to the question of power that seems particularly relevant to the development of the online economy since it focuses not so much on the repressive force of panopticism, but its productive deployment. The potential of the online economy that has recently attracted so much speculation—both financial and cultural—is predicated in large part on the anticipated productivity of generalized network surveillance. The power in question is not the static domination of a sovereign Big Brother, but that of a self-stimulating incitement to productivity: the multiplication of desiring subjects and subjects' desires in accordance with the rationalization of consumption. In this context, the production of ever more refined and detailed categories of desiring subjectivities serves, as Butler's (1997) analysis suggests, as a site for the reiteration of existing conditions and relations of power.

The starting point for an analysis of surveillance as exploitation is the assertion that just as workplace monitoring contributes to the rationalization of production, so on-line surveillance contributes to the rationalization of consumption. The attempt to extend the monitoring reach of corporate managers via the internet serves to compel personal disclosure by replacing non-monitored forms of consumption with monitored interactive transactions. The following sections attempt to trace the outlines of the process whereby the work of being watched comes to serve as a means of rationalizing not just what Jhally and Livant (1986) call the work of watching, but the process of on-line consumption in general. The goal is to offer an alternative approach to the debate over on-line privacy in the era of new-media interactivity. Not only is the privacy defense aligned with the process it ostensibly contests, but, practically speaking, it has failed to provide effective resistance to encroaching surveillance. Indeed, opponents of corporate surveillance seem unable to provide a compelling rationale for privacy protection in an era when consumers remain surprisingly willing to surrender increasingly comprehensive forms of personal information in response to offers of convenience and customization.

Perhaps some awareness of the way in which the new "transparency" exacerbates informational asymmetries and power imbalances, serving as a form of marketplace discipline, might provide stronger grounds for a critique of the proliferation of corporate surveillance. Such a critique might also help challenge the promotion of interactive technologies (and the forms of consumption and production they facilitate) as inherently democratic and empowering. This essay seeks to provide one starting point for such a challenge by exploring how the promise of interactivity functions as an invitation to engage in the work of being watched. The remaining sections of the essay trace the development of the productive role of surveillance from its deployment in the workplace to its extension into the realm of online consumption, drawing on the example of interactive TV, especially TiVo, to illustrate the importance of interactive media to the rationalization of e-commerce.

Productive Surveillance

The productivity of surveillance, for the purposes of this article, can be understood as being always parasitic upon another form of labor. For example,

Braverman's (1974) discussion of the pioneering work of Frederick Taylor in developing a system of workplace rationalization in the late 19th and early 20th centuries highlights the reliance of what Taylor called "scientific management" upon comprehensive forms of workplace monitoring. Taylor's description of how he succeeded in dramatically increasing the productivity of steel workers starts off with a description of the role of surveillance in deciding which workers would be targeted. Managers observed the entire workforce for four days before choosing several workers upon whom to focus their efforts: "A careful study was then made of each of these men. We looked up their history as far back as practicable and thorough inquiries were made as to the character, habits, and the ambition of each of them" (Taylor, as quoted in Braverman, 1974, p. 104). The selected worker's training consisted in his being supervised by a manager who observed his every action, timing him with a stopwatch, and dictating the laborer's actions down to the most specific detail. The result of all this monitoring and managing was that the productivity of the day laborer, whom Taylor refers to in his case study as "Schmidt," almost quadrupled. The activity of being watched wasn't productive on its own, but coupled with another form of labor, it helped multiply the latter's productivity. Over time, the recognition of the productivity of surveillance helped to institutionalize the rationalization of production based on ever more detailed forms of workplace monitoring, including Gilbreth's famous time and motion studies.

Among those who write about surveillance, Foucault (1975/1977; 1976/1978) has powerfully thematized its productive aspect, which all too often gets short shrift in the critical literature on surveillance. For example, Giddens's (1981) discussion of the police power of the surveillance state, as well as the various discussions of disciplinary surveillance offered by Norris and Armstrong (1999), Lyon (1994), and Gandy (1993), retain strong overtones of what Foucault describes as the insistence in the West on "seeing the power it exercises as juridical and negative rather than technical and positive" (1980, p. 121). This tendency is also reflected in the public debate over online privacy, which centers on the "invasion" of privacy and the oppressive surveillance capacity of the state. The emphasis is upon the ways in which disciplinary surveillance creates "docile bodies" and not upon the more suggestive aspect of Foucault's analysis: the spiraling cycle of productivity incited by disciplinary regimes: the fact that docile bodies are not rendered inert, but stimulated. As Foucault puts it in *Discipline and Punish* (1975/1977): "Let us say that discipline is the unitary technique by which the body is reduced as a 'political' force at the least cost and maximized as a useful force" (p. 221). Docility and pacification are certainly among the goals of discipline, but the real power of surveillance is a relentlessly productive and stimulating one:

> The Panopticon ... has a role of amplification; although it arranges power, although it is intended to make it more economic and effective, it does so not for power itself ... its aim is to strengthen the social forces—to increase production, to develop the economy ... to increase and multiply.
> (1977, p. 208)

This power—and not the sterile juridical "repressive" gaze of Big Brother—is what attracts the interest and the capital of the online economy.

In contemporary terms, productive disciplinary power stimulates the proliferation of desiring subjectivities through the multiplication of consumption categories: the endless sub-categorization and specification of individualized sets of tastes and preferences. Recording and measuring, specifying and naming, these are the current watchwords of the marketing industry, which doesn't "set boundaries" for consumption, but extends its various forms, "pursuing them to lines of indefinite penetration" (Foucault 1976/1978, p. 47). For example, the proponents of mass customization (Negroponte, 1995; Pine, 1993; Gates 1996) imagine the possibilities of specifying desire ever more narrowly based not just on consumers' past preferences and socio-economic backgrounds, but on the details of the moment: location, the time of day, the weather. As in the case of sexuality, the elaboration and proliferation of desire is achieved through subjection to a discursive regime of self-disclosure whose contemporary cultural manifestations include not just the mania for interactivity, but the confessional culture of a talk show nation, and, most recently, the ethos of willing submission to comprehensive surveillance associated with the booming reality TV trend.

The power of Foucault's approach is that it extends its consideration of the productive role of panoptic surveillance beyond the realm of the workplace. The accumulation of bodies—their organization and deployment not just within the factory walls, but in the "privacy" of homes and bedrooms—is a necessary corollary to the accumulation of capital (and vice versa). As Foucault puts it, capitalism "would not be possible without the controlled insertion of bodies into the machinery of production and the adjustment of the phenomena of population to economic processes" (1975/1977, p. 141). Disciplinary surveillance does not just underwrite subjection to the proliferation of desire, it also—and not incidentally—enhances economic productivity.

Foucault's account of the productive role of desire thus provides a useful rejoinder to those who engage in what Schiller (1988) describes as a "Sisyphean attempt to distinguish productive from unproductive labor in terms of a hypostasized set of productive activities" (p. 36). The information economy—including that designed to stimulate consumption via the accumulation, manipulation, and deployment of information derived from consumer surveillance—is economically productive, and the labor associated with it can be identified by its status as a value-generating activity. The stimulation and rationalization of consumer desire is a practical corollary to the rationalization of production proper. As Harvey (1999), following Marx, puts it, "production and consumption relate to each other so that 'each of them creates the other in completing itself, and creates itself as the other'" (p. 80). For example, as historians, marketers, and social critics alike have recognized (Marchand, 1985; Sloan, 1963; Robins & Webster, 1999), the development of consumer society required techniques for stimulating consumption to keep pace with the increasing volume and variety of products made available by the technological and managerial advances associated with the industrial revolution. These techniques went far beyond management of the workplace proper, and relied upon detailed monitoring of consumer habits and life-styles. Gathering this information was the work of market researchers and advertisers—work that is becoming increasingly important in the era of niche markets and customized products and services. Interactive technologies, as the business world has come to recognize (Mougayar, 1998), allow for much of this work to be offloaded onto consumers, who increasingly provide detailed information about themselves as they consume. The economic value of this information means not just that it can be bought and sold, but that consumers are often compensated for their participation in producing it.

Rationalizing the Work of Watching

Jhally and Livant (1986) describe another form of labor for which consumers are "paid": the work of watching. Building on their approach, this section takes the argument a step further by exploring the way in which the work of *being watched* contributes to the rationalization of the work of watching. Jhally and Livant's analysis is straightforward: audiences perform work by viewing advertising in exchange for "payment" in the form of programming content. The viewing of advertising is productive because it helps "speed up the selling of commodities, their circulation from production to consumption. ... Through advertising, the rapid consumption of commodities cuts down on circulation and storage costs for industrial capital" (p. 125). In these terms, watching advertising might be understood as an activity in which, as Harvey (1999) puts it, the process of consumption completes itself in the process of production.

For the purposes of a consideration of the labor of *being* watched, the crucial point made by Jhally and Livant (1986) is that the goal of media management is to rationalize the work of watching—to "make the audience watch harder" (p. 133), just as Taylor made Schmidt quadruple his daily productivity. One strategy for rationalization is niche marketing, which Jhally and Livant describe as "the specification and fractionation of the audience" that leads to "a form of 'concentrated viewing' in which there is (from the point of view of advertisers) little wasted watching" (p. 133). As in the case of Schmidt, what is needed is detailed information about the audience labor force: both its background and its behavior. The commodification of this information has already been institutionalized as the secondary market in ratings, whose growth accompanied that of the electronic mass

media. The labor of *being* watched goes hand-in-hand with the work of watching: viewers are monitored so advertisers can be ensured that this work is being done as efficiently as possible. Ratings, in this context, are informational commodities that generate value because they help to rationalize the viewing process. They become what Mosco (1996), following Meehan, describes as "cybernetic" commodities: "feedback" commodities produced through consumption or interaction (p. 151).

Within the context of the mass media, the labor of being watched faced certain limitations, both structural and cultural. Watching advertising may be a form of work, according to Jhally and Livant, but it does not take place within a centralized space that would allow broadcasters to stand over viewers with a stopwatch, as in the case of the scientific management of the factory labor force. Indeed, a certain expectation of privacy outside the workplace is one of the hurdles that those who would rationalize the work of being watched need to overcome. The fact that we accept surveillance more readily in the workplace is a function of the characteristic spatio-temporal differentiation associated with wage labor in modernity, according to Giddens (1981): "Two opposed modes of time-consciousness, 'working time' and 'one's own' or 'free time', become basic divisions within the phenomenal experience of the day" (p. 137). Surveillance, within this schema, is associated with time that is not free, but which is subject to the asymmetrical power relations of the workplace, underwritten by the workers' subordination to those who control the space of production.

The productive potential of the labor of being watched is further limited by the structure of the mass media, which are only capable of exploiting the logic of market fractionation up to a point. It is desirable to isolate an affluent demographic, but to continue to subdivide the audience beyond a certain point would be counter-productive, not least because the existing technology is not well-suited to individualized programming. At the same time, detailed monitoring has tended to be relatively costly and has relied to a large extent on the consent of the monitored. Thus, the television industry has, until recently, contented itself with the relatively small sample offered by the Nielsen ratings, rather than attempting more detailed and comprehensive approaches to managing the work of watching. However, the advent of interactive, networked forms of content delivery promises to overcome these limitations and to develop the potential of the work of being watched to its fullest.

Interactive Surveillance in the Digital Enclosure

The emerging model of the on-line economy is explicitly based on the strategy for rationalizing and disciplining the labor of viewing—and of consumption in general—so as to make it more productive. The goal is to replace mass marketing and production with customized programming, products, and marketing. In the business literature (Mougayar, 1998; Pine, 1993), this paradigm is described as "mass customization": the ability to produce mass quantities of products that are, at the same time, custom-tailored to niche markets and, at the extreme, to specific individuals. Described as the advent of flexible production in response to increasingly volatile market conditions, mass customization represents the enhanced capacity of interactive technology to exploit the productive potential of market segmentation. Viewed as a strategy for promoting consumption, niche marketing is not a demand-driven phenomenon, instigated by the sudden, inexplicable volatility of consumer preferences, but rather, as Harvey (1990) suggests, a supply-side response to the saturation of the mass market.

In the media market, as well as in other segments of the economy, the promise of interactive communication technologies is to surpass the structural limitations that prevented the exploitation of increasingly compact market niches. If the advent of cable television allowed for market segmentation up to a point, the development of digital delivery allows for its extension down to the level of the individual viewer. Bill Gates (1996), for example, anticipates a world in which not just the timing and choice of programs will be customized, but in which the content and the advertising can be adapted to viewer preferences, allowing individuals to choose the type of ending they want, the setting of the movie, and even the stars (who can be "customized" thanks to digitization). Similarly, customized advertising would ensure that every ad is tailored to the demographics of its recipient. A similar

logic could be extended to products other than media programming. For example, computerization, according to Gates (1996), will allow "Increasing numbers of products—from shoes to chairs, from newspapers and magazines to music albums" to be "created on the spot to match the exact specifications of a particular person" (p. 188). Half a decade after Gates made these predictions, *Wired* magazine, in its April, 2001 "Megatrends" issue declared "personal fabrication on demand" to be one of the top emerging trends of the new millennium (p. 172).

The attempt to develop increasingly customized programming and products foregrounds the economic importance of what might be described as the 21st century digital confessional: an incitement to self-disclosure as a form of self-expression and individuation. Interactive (cybernetic) media promote this self-disclosure insofar as they offer the potential to integrate the labor of watching with that of *being* watched. The cybernetic economy thus anticipates the productivity of a digital form of disciplinary panopticism, predicated not just on the monitoring gaze, but on the vast array of digital data made available by interactive and convergent communication technologies.

The accumulation of detailed demographic information allows not only for the customization of products and programming, but also for customized pricing. Whereas mass production was reliant on the aggregation of individual demand curves, customization allows for the dis-aggregation of demand curves, and thus for the possibility that producers can extract some of the "surplus" previously realized by consumers. Amazon.Com's recent experiments in "variable pricing" anticipated this dis-aggregation by attempting to charge customers different prices for the same product, based on demographic information gleaned on-line from purchasers' "cookies" (Grossman, 2000).

Digital Enclosure

The current deployment of the Internet for e-commerce may be viewed as an attempt to achieve in the realm of consumption what the enclosure movement achieved in the realm of production: an inducement to enter into a relationship of surveillance-based rationalization. The process of digital enclosure can be defined, in these terms, as the process whereby activities formerly carried out beyond the monitoring capacity of the Internet are enfolded into its virtual space. The process is still very much in its early stages, but is heavily underwritten by investments in new media technologies (Schiller, 1999) and by the enthusiastic and breathless predictions of cyber-futurists that continue to make their way into the mass media. Lester (2001) notes that entrance into what I call the digital enclosure is often voluntary (at least for the moment), but he coins an interesting term to suggest that consumers are compelled to go on-line for an increasing array of transactions by "the tyranny of convenience" (p. 28). The current trend suggests that over time, alternatives to this "tyranny" may be increasingly foreclosed. The result is that consumption and leisure behaviors will increasingly migrate into virtual spaces where they can double as a form of commodity-generating labor. If the latest work of a popular author or musical group is available *only* on-line, consumers are compelled to enter a virtual space within which very detailed forms of surveillance can take place. Electronic databases can keep track not only of who is reading or listening to what, but when and where.

The exploitation of the labor of being watched is thus crucially reliant upon public acceptance of the penetration of digital surveillance into the realm of "free" time. That this acceptance may not be immediately forthcoming is reflected in surveys like the 1999 *Wall Street Journal* NBC poll cited by Lester (2001) for its finding that "privacy is the issue that concerns Americans most about the twenty-first century, ahead of overpopulation, racial tensions, and global warming" (p. 27). Lawmakers have recognized the importance to the digital economy of assuaging these concerns and are attempting to pass legislation to ensure consumers a certain degree of "privacy protection" (Labaton, 2000, p. Al). The problem with such legislation from a business standpoint, and perhaps one of the reasons it tends to get bogged down in committees, is that it threatens to dry up the flow of surveillance-generated information that is the life-blood of the economy it ostensibly enables.

The more promising approach, from a corporate perspective, has been to attempt to reposition surveillance as a form of consumer control. The popular reception of the Internet as a means of democratizing mediated interaction and surpassing the one-way,

top-down mass media certainly works in favor of this attempt. Thus, the claims of the cyber-celebrants, such as George Gilder's (1994) oft-cited prediction that "The force of microelectronics will blow apart all the monopolies, hierarchies, pyramids, and power grids of established industrial society" (p. 180) line up neatly with the corporate promise that the interactive digital market is "a customer's paradise," presumably because the "customer is in control" (Mougayar, 1998, p. 176). Casting the net slightly wider, it is worth investigating the extent to which the celebration of the progressive potential of interactivity in some strands of media theory helps to promote the advantages of entry into the digital enclosure. The more we view this enclosure as a site for the potential revitalization of community (Rheingold, 1993) and democracy (Brady, 1998; Kellner, 1999), the more inviting it appears. Similarly, as Robins and Webster (1999) suggest, the celebration of the information age as a post-industrial resolution to the depredations of industrial society helps background the fundamental continuity of the "information era" within the exploitative relations of industrial capitalism. My intent is not to dismiss the progressive potential of interactive media outright, but rather to note how neatly their uncritical promotion lines up with the interests of those who would deploy the interactive capability of new media to exploit the work of being watched.

In short, the promise of the "revolutionary" potential of new media bears a marked similarly to the deployment of the supposedly subversive potential of sex that Foucault (1976/1978) outlines in his discussion of the "repressive hypothesis." When, for example, the *New York Times* informs its readers that the advent of interactive digital television is "the beginning of the end of another socialistic force in American life: the mass market" (Lewis, 2000), it contributes to the deployment of what might be called "the mass society repressive hypothesis." The latter underwrites the ostensibly subversive potential of interactivity even as it stimulates the productivity of consumer labor. The most familiar version of this hypothesis suggests that mass production worked to stifle the forms of individuation and self-expression that will be fostered in the upcoming digital revolution: that the incitement to divulge our consumption-related behavior (and what else is there, from a marketing perspective?) paradoxically represents a subversion of the totalitarian, homogenizing forces of the mass market. As in the case of the deployment of the repressive hypothesis, the promised subversion turns out to be an incitement to multiply the very forms of self-disclosure that serve the disciplinary regime they purportedly subvert. As Marchand (1985) suggests, the promise of individuation—of the self-overcoming of mass homogeneity—was a strategy of the regime of mass society *from its inception*. Mass society's ostensible self-overcoming becomes a ruse for the incitement to self-disclosure crucial to the rationalization of what undoubtedly remains a form of mass consumption.

The Example of TiVo

Recent developments in television technology can perhaps provide a more concrete example of how the work of being watched is deployed to rationalize the work of watching. The emergence of digital VCR technology, including TiVo, Replay TV, and Microsoft's Ultimate TV, anticipates the way in which the digital enclosure overcomes the limitations of the mass media while enhancing their productivity. The rudimentary data generated by Nielsen Media Research, based on a sample of some 5,000 homes, may have been good enough for the standardized advertising fare offered by pre-interactive television, but it clearly cannot provide the information necessary to custom-tailor advertising to the 105 million households with television sets in the United States. As Daryl Simm, the former head of worldwide media programming for Procter & Gamble, and the current head of media at the Omnicom conglomerate recently put it,

> The measurement we use today is very crude. . . . It's an average measurement of the number of viewers watching an individual program that does not even measure the commercial break. When you think about improvements in measuring viewing habits, you think not about incremental changes but great leaps.
>
> (Lewis, 2000, p. 41)

The developers of digital VCR technology are looking to make that leap. For home viewers, digital VCRs offer several advantages over their analog ancestors: they can record several shows at the same time; they store dozens of hours of programming which can be retrieved at a moment's notice; and they automatically record programs in response to key-word requests. From the advertisers' perspective, digital VCRs offer a highly detailed form of demographic monitoring. As a rather celebratory piece about TiVo in *The New York Times* put it,

> While the viewer watched television, the box would watch the viewer. It would record the owner's viewing habits in a way that TV viewing habits have never been recorded. . . . Over time, the box would come to know what the viewer liked maybe even better than the viewer himself.
>
> (Lewis, 2000, p. 38)

Even as it retrieves programming for viewers, the digital VCR doubles as a monitoring device in the service of the system's operators, creating a detailed "time and motion study" of viewing habits that can be sold to advertisers and producers. In the panoptic register, the digital VCR becomes an automated consumption confessional: an incitement to divulge the most intimate details of one's viewing habits.

In this respect, the digital VCR represents a preliminary attempt to bring the activity of television viewing within the monitoring reach of the digital enclosure. The enticement to consumers is that of convenience and customization (perhaps even self-expression). As Lewis (2000) puts it, "Over time, the viewer would create, in essence, his own private television channel, stored on a hard drive in the black box, tailored with great precision to his interests" (p. 38). There is a degree of truth to the claim of convenience: devices like TiVo will allow viewers to more easily store and record those programs they want to watch. This is, perhaps, the compensation viewers receive in exchange for providing detailed information about their viewing habits. They will also be able to skip through commercials in 30-second intervals, but this advantage is being rendered obsolete by the integration of advertising content into the program itself (Elliott, 2000).

Drawing on the promotional strategy of the digital economy, celebrants of the new technology have adopted the "revolutionary" promise that new media will transfer control to viewers and consumers as a means of promoting their products. One of the early advertising spots for TiVo, for example, featured two bouncers throwing a network executive through his plate glass window, enacting the de-throning of centralized corporate control. This image corresponds with the description in *The New York Times* of TiVo as a challenge to the mass market and top-down, centralized planning. According to this account, when viewed through the lens of the new "freedom" that TiVo ostensibly offers consumers, "The entire history of commercial television suddenly appears to have been a Stalinist plot erected, as it has been, on force from above rather than choice from below" (Lewis, 2000, p. 41). This retelling of history promotes interactive technologies as one more force bringing about what Shapiro (1999) calls "The control revolution," whereby "new technology is allowing individuals to take power from large institutions such as government, corporations, and the media. To an unprecedented degree, we can decide what news and information we're exposed to" (p. xi).

Disturbingly, this perspective is not unique to mainstream news outlets and business-oriented futurism, as evidenced by the fact that *Adbusters*, the "hip," alternative magazine of media criticism and culture jamming, hailed TiVo as a technology that "struck true fear into the hearts of the transnational bosses," because it "sticks it to every broadcast advertiser" (Flood, 2001, p. 17). The *Adbusters* article goes on to claim that TiVo is among those new-media technologies that herald "something revolutionary. Something almost purely democratic. Something essentially non-commercial, driven not by price but by value. At long last, the people—could it be true?—would have control of what they wanted to hear and see" (2001, p. 17). In this portrayal of the revolutionary promise of the new technology, the champions of subversive chic close ranks with their ostensible foes: neo-liberal propagandists like Wriston (1992) and Gilder (1994).

Perhaps not surprisingly—given the anticipated role of TiVo in allowing for comprehensive demographic monitoring—the "transnational bosses" aren't quivering in their boots. Rather, they have been investing whole-heartedly in the technology that will purportedly undermine their fiefdom. In 1999, Time

Warner, Disney, NBC and CBS invested a combined total of more than $100 million in digital VCR technology (Lewis, 2000, pp. 40–41). Either the prognosticators of democratic utopia are overly optimistic or the "transnational bosses" of industry are working overtime against their own interests. History, combined with the market potential of interactive monitoring, tends to side with the bosses against the revolutionary promise. This tendency is not inherent in the technology itself, which, as Lessig (1999) points out, lends itself to diverse uses depending on how it is configured and deployed. Rather it is a reflection of the imperatives of the decisions we make about how to use those technologies and upon the pressures exerted by those in a position to develop and implement the Internet of the future. The increasing privatization of the network infrastructure combined with the recent spate of merger activity designed to exploit the commercial potential of the Internet suggests those applications that promise to be commercially successful (economically profitable} will likely take top priority.

All of which should come as no surprise to those familiar with the history of electronic media in the United States—a history that has largely been the story of technological developments adapted to commercial ends. Often, as the critical history compiled by Solomon and McChesney (1993) suggests, this story has followed a pattern whereby non-commercial and community-oriented uses are displaced by commercial applications as the medium is developed over time. Despite the claims of those who herald the subversive potential of the Internet—whether in the realm of theory or popular culture—there is little evidence to suggest the Internet will enact a radical departure from this pattern. On the contrary, applications originally heralded as subversive of centralized corporate control, such as Napster and Freenet, are already being tailored to serve commercial purposes. If it is not difficult to imagine how interactive media could help promote more democratic forms of mediated communication, it is even easier to envision their role in allowing for ever more sophisticated techniques for the exploitation of the work of being watched.

Whether or not TiVo and its competitors are ultimately successful, they are helping to forge the commercial paradigm of interactive media as a means of inducing viewers to watch more efficiendy. Subscribers to TiVo— or to the next generation of interactive television—will help lead the way into a digital enclosure wherein the work of watching can be as closely monitored as was the manual labor overseen by Frederick Taylor. The compilation of detailed demographic profiles of viewers will be facilitated by computer storage and retrieval techniques so as to ensure "wasted" watching will be kept to a minimum. The celebrants of mass customization envision this will take place in two ways: first, advertising will be tailored to match the demographics of each household and, eventually, of individual viewers; second, the line between content and advertising will continue to blur to the point of extinction.

If, as Gates (1996) suggests, every item of clothing, every location, and every product in a television show can—within the context of an interactive medium—double as both an advertising appeal and a clickable purchase point, *all* viewing counts as work in the sense outlined by Jhally and Livant (1986). Indeed, all activity of virtually any kind that can be monitored within this enclosure becomes work, as in the example of Mitch Maddox's DotCom-pound. In the case of interactive television, the added convenience of customization may well work to maximize not just the relative time devoted to the work of watching, but overall viewing time. The Replay Corporation has already found that "its customers watch, on average, three hours more television each week than they did before they got the box" (Lewis, 2000, p. 40).

The model of interactive television is generalizable to an increasing variety of activities that take place within the digital enclosure—and, to the extent that monitoring is involved, more and more activities seem to fall under the umbrella of consumption. The work of being watched can, in other words, help to rationalize the entire spectrum of consumption-related activities that have traditionally taken place beyond the monitoring gaze of the workplace. The general outlines of a commercial model for interactive media can thus be gleaned from the example of TiVo. Its main components are: customization (the disaggregation of demand curves, the direct linkage between a specific act of production and a targeted act of consumption), interactivity (the ability to monitor consumers in the act of consumption), off-loading labor to consumers (who perform the work of

generating their own demographic information), and the development of an on-going relationship with consumers (that allows for the exploitation of demographic information gathered overtime).

Perhaps not surprisingly, several elements of this business model can be discerned in the development of a recent, supposedly subversive media technology: that of the music file-sharing utility Napster. As *Wired* magazine recently noted in a short aside to its celebratory coverage of the revolutionary potential of "peer-to-peer" networking, Napster represents a forward-looking business model for the on-line economy: "the system keeps customer relationships in-house, but outsources the lion's share of infrastructure back to a captive audience. It's . . . clear that a better music-industry strategy would be not to ban Napster's technology, but to make it their own" (Kuptz, 2000, p. 236). The German publishing giant Bertelsmann, with a major presence in the recording industry, clearly agrees, as evidenced by its decision to enter into a partnership with Napster. This arrangement should not be viewed as an aberration or a "sellout" on the part of Napster—whose ostensible assault on the record industry was not a subversion of market logic per se, but one more example of the "creative destruction" that Schumpeter (1947) famously attributed to the process of capitalist development: the replacement of an older business paradigm by a newer one.

Like TiVo, Napster-style technology allows for the comprehensive documentation of on-line consumption: it enables not only the monitoring of music selections downloaded by users, but, potentially, the retrieval of their entire on-line music inventory. It may well offer companies like Bertelsmann the ability to peer into subscribers' virtual CD-cabinets and eventually to catalogue their actual listening habits in order to market to them more effectively. Just as TiVo offloads the work of market research to consumers who add to their profile of preferences with every program they select, Napster potentially offloads this work to users who share files on-line. Moreover, as the *Wired* article notes, the Napster model also offloads infrastructure to consumers, whose home computers become the repository for the music files traded on-line. Napster technology makes possible the future envisioned by Gates (1996), wherein subscribers will be able to download music to portable digital devices and to pay according to how often they plan to listen to an individual track. In this respect the future of online music and television delivery envisioned by the industry represents the application of mediated inter-activity to the emerging paradigm of surveillance-based customization. The result is the promise that consumers will be able to perform the work of being watched with even greater efficiency.

Conclusion

Rumors of the death of privacy in the 21st century have been greatly exaggerated. The increasingly important role of on-line surveillance in the digital economy should be construed not as the disappear-ance of privacy per se, but as a shift in control over personal information from individuals to *private* cor-porations. The information in question—behavioral habits, consumption preferences, and so on—is emphatically not being publicized. It is, rather, being aggregated into proprietary commodities, whose economic value is dependent, at least in part, upon the fact that they are privately owned. Such commod-ities are integral to the exploitation of customized markets and the administration of the "flexible" mode of production associated with mass customization. Making markets more efficient, according to this model, means surpassing the paradigm of the mass market and its associated inefficiencies, including the cost of gathering demographic information, of storing inventory, and of attempting to sell a mass-produced product at a standardized price. Interactive media combined with the development of computer memory and processing speed allow for the compre-hensive forms of surveillance crucial to the scientific management of consumption within the digital enclosure.

Like the factory workers of the early 20th century, the consumers of the early 21st century will be sub-jected to more sophisticated monitoring techniques and their attendant forms of productive discipline. The intended result is the stimulation of the forces of consumption—the indirect complement of the enhanced productivity associated with network tech-nology. If the effort expended in shopping feels more and more like labor, if we find ourselves negotiating ever more complex sets of choices that require more

sophisticated forms of technological literacy, the digi-tal economy is poised to harness the productive power of that labor through the potential of interactivity.

At the same time, it is worth pointing out the potentially productive contradiction at the heart of the promise of the digital "revolution". If indeed its promise is predicated on the subversion of the very forms of market control it serves, this promise invokes a moment of critique. This is the flip side of Foucault's assertion of the subject as the site of the reiteration of conditions of power. It is the critical moment her-alded by Butler's (1997) assertion that "Where condi-tions of subordination make possible the assumption of power, the power assumed remains tied to those conditions, but in an ambivalent way" (p. 13). Subjection/subjectification suggests that the condi-tions of power are not reproduced "automatically" but can be contested by the very forms of subjectivity they produce. From this perspective, it is telling that in the celebratory discourse of the digital revolution, centralized forms of market control are re-presented as homologous with their former opponent: totalitar-ian, centralized planning. Intriguing avenues for resis-tance open up in an era when the *New York Times* can liken the television network system to Stalinism. Such critiques might do well to start with the premises appealed to by the digital revolution: that there is a need for greater shared control of the economic and political processes that shape our lives in an age of seemingly dramatic technological transformation. Even if the promise of interactivity as a form of de-centralization and shared control fails to be realized (as is suggested by the flurry of record-breaking merger activity in recent years), its implicit assess-ment of the shortcomings of mass society serves as a potential purchase point for a critique of the very rationalization it enables. In this respect, the realiza-tion that the promise of interactivity bases its appeal on perceived forms of exploitation (that ought to be overcome) lines up with Foucault's observation that where there is power, there is also, always, the poten-tial for resistance.

Of central interest from a critical perspective, therefore, is the extent to which the marketers of the digital revolution continue to base its appeal upon the interpellation of an "active," empowered consumer. As consumers start to realize that their activity feels more like labor (filling out online surveys, taking the time to "design" customized products and services) and less like empowerment, it is likely that the explicit appeal to shared control will be replaced by the emerging trend toward automated, autonomous forms of "convenient" monitoring. This is the direction anticipated by futurists like Negroponte (1995) and the planners behind the MIT "Project Oxygen," whose goal is to make computers as invisible and ubiquitous as air. Their approach represents a retreat from the version of the "active" consumer associated with explicitly participatory forms of data gathering that characterized some of the early experiments in interactivity (the "design your own sneaker" or "write a review of this book" approach). Instead, the goal is the proliferation of an increasingly invisible, automated, and autonomous network. The agency of the active consumer is displaced onto what Negroponte (1995) calls "the digital butler." Interactivity will likely be increasingly reformulated as inter-*passivity* insofar as the goal is to make the monitoring process as unobtrusive as possible. The call to "action" will be displaced onto the ubiquitous technology, whose autonomy is designed to replace that of the consumer/viewer. Perhaps an early incarnation of this unobtrusive form of monitoring is the browser "cookie." Designed to increase convenience by allowing a site to remember a particular visitor so that customized settings don't have to be reconfigured, the "cookie" doubles as a digital butler for marketers, providing detailed browsing information about online consumers. It is hard not to imagine that the same would be true of other forms of digital butlers, whose allegiance remains rather more ambiguous than Negroponte implies. As these services become increasingly invisible and fade into the background, the increasingly monitored and transparent consumer comes to the fore.

In the face of the emergence of increasingly ubiquitous and invisible forms of monitoring, the appeal to privacy is often enlisted as a form of resistance. This type of resistance is rendered problematic by the fact that what is taking place—despite the recurring claim that the end of privacy is upon us—is the extensive *appropriation* of personal information. More information than ever before is being privatized as it is collected and aggregated so that it can be re-sold as a

commodity or incorporated into the development of customized commodities. The enclosure and monopolization of this information reinforces power asymmetries in two ways: by concentrating control over the resources available for the production of subjects' desires and desiring subjects, and by the imposition of a comprehensive panoptic regime. The digital enclosure has the potential to become what Giddens (1981), following Goffman, terms a "total institution." The good news, perhaps, is that once the red-herring of the "death" of privacy is debunked, the enclosure of personal information can be properly addressed as a form of exploitation predicated on unequal access to the means of data collection, storage, and manipulation. A discussion of surveillance might then be couched in terms of conditions of power that compel entry into the digital enclosure and submission to comprehensive monitoring as a means of stimulating and rationalizing consumption. The way in which the promise of participation is deployed as an incentive to submit to the work of being watched might be further illuminated by the extension of models of "concertive control" (Papa, Auwal, & Singh, 1997; Tompkins & Cheney, 1985) to the realm of consumer labor. Additionally, such a discussion would necessarily address the questions of who controls the means of surveillance and to what ends, how this power is reproduced through subjection to interactive monitoring, who benefits from the work of being watched, and who is compelled to surrender control over personal information in exchange for a minimum "wage" of convenience or customization. For too long, the discussion of mediated interactivity has tended to assume that as long as the Internet allowed unfettered interactivity, questions of network control and ownership were rendered moot by the revolutionary potential of the technology itself. Perhaps it is not too much to hope that an understanding of the relation of interactivity to disciplinary surveillance and, thus, to the labor of being watched might work to counter the unwonted euphoria of the utopian cyber-determinists and to refocus the question of the fate of collective control over personal information. Otherwise, we may all find ourselves toiling productively away in the DotCompound, narrowcasting the rhythms of our daily lives to an ever smaller and more exclusive audience of private corporations.

References

Bedell, D. (2000, March 2). FTC to survey e-commerce sites on how they use customers' data. *The Dallas Morning News*, p. 1F.

Braverman, H. (1974). *Labor and monopoly capital*. New York: Monthly Review Press.

Bryan, C. (1998). Electronic democracy and the civic networking movement. In R. Tsagarou-sianou, D. Tambini, & C. Bryan (Eds.), *Cyberdemocracy: Technology, cities, and civic networks* (pp. 1–17). London: Routledge.

Butler, J. (1997). *The psychic life of power*. Palo Alto: Stanford University Press.

Choney, S. (2001, March 27). Juno may not charge, but it's no free lunch. *The San Diego Union-Tribune*, p. 2.

Copeland, L. (2001, Jan. 3). For DotComGuy, the end of the online line. *The Washington Post*, p. C2.

Elliott, S. (2000, Oct. 13). TiVo teams up with the Omnicom Group to tell the world about digital video recorder. *The New York Times*, p. C4.

Flood, H. (2001, March/April). Linux, TiVo, Napster … information wants to be free. You got a problem with that? *Adbusters*, No. 34, 17.

Foucault, M. (1976/1977). *Discipline and punish: The birth of the prison* (A. Sheridan, Trans.). New York: Vintage Books.

Foucault, M. (1976/1978). *The history of sexuality: An introduction* (Vol. I) (R. Hurley, Trans.). New York: Vintage Books.

Foucault, M. (1980). *The Foucault reader* (P. Rabinow, Ed.). New York: Pantheon Books.

Gandy, O. (1993). *The panoptic sort: A political economy of personal information*. Boulder, CO: Westview.

Garfinkel, S. (2000). *Database nation: The death of privacy in the 21st century*. Cambridge: O'Reilly.

Gates, B. (1996). *The road ahead*. New York: Penguin.

Giddens, A. (1981). *A contemporary critique of historical materialism*. Berkeley: University of California Press.

Gilder, G. (1994). *Life after television: The coming transformation of media and American life*. New York: Norton.

Grossman, W. (2000, Oct. 26). Shock of the new for Amazon customers. *The Daily Telegraph* (London), p. 70.

Harvey, D. (1999). *The limits to capital*. London: Verso.

Harvey, D. (1990). *The condition of postmodernity*. Cambridge: Blackwell.

Jhally, S., & Livant, B. (1986). Watching as working: The valorization of audience consciousness. *Journal of Communication, 36*, 124–143.

Kellner, D. (1999). Globalisation from below? Toward a radical democratic technopolitics. *Angelaki, 4*, 101–111.

Kuptz, J. (2000, October). Independence array. *Wired*, 236–237.

Labaton, S. (2000, May 20). U.S. is said to seek new law to bolster privacy on Internet. *New York Times*, p. A1.

Lessig, L. (1999). *Code: And other laws of cyberspace*. New York: Basic Books.

Lester, T. (2001, March). The reinvention of privacy. *The Atlantic Monthly*, 27–39.

Lewis, M. (2000, Aug. 13). Boombox. *The New York Times Magazine*, 36–67.

Lyon, D. (1994). *The electronic eye: The rise of surveillance society*. Minneapolis: University of Minneapolis Press.

Marchand, R. (1985). *Advertising the American dream: Making way for modernity, 1920–1940*. Berkeley: University of California Press.

Mosco, V. (1996). *The political economy of communication*. London: Sage.

Mougayar, W. (1998). *Opening digital markets*. New York: McGraw-Hill.

Negroponte, N. (1995). *Being digital*. New York: Alfred A. Knopf.

Norris, C., and Armstrong, G. (1999). *The maximum surveillance society: The rise of CCTV*. Oxford: Berg.

Papa, M. J., Auwal, M.A., & Singhal, A. (1997, September). Organizing for social change within concertive control systems: Member identification, empowerment, and the masking of discipline. *Communication Monographs, 64*, 219–249.

Pine, J. (1993). *Mass customization: The new frontier in business competition*. Cambridge, MA: Harvard University Press.

Rheingold, H. (1993). *Virtual community*. Reading, MA: Addison-Wesley.

Robins, K., & Webster, F. (1999). *Times of the technoculture: From the information society to the virtual life*. London: Routledge.

Rosen, J. (2000). *The unwanted gaze: The destruction of privacy in America*. New York: Random House.

Schiller, D. (1999). *Digital capitalism*. Cambridge, MA: The MIT Press.

Schiller, D. (1988). How to think about information. In V. Mosco & J. Wasko (Eds.), *The Political Economy of Information* (pp. 27–43). Madison: University of Wisconsin Press.

Schumpeter, J. (1947). *Capitalism, socialism, and democracy*. New York: Harper & Brothers.

Shapiro, A. (1999). *The control revolution: How the Internet is putting individuals in charge and changing the world we know*. New York: PublicAffairs.

Sloan, A. (1963). *My years with General Motors*. Garden City, NY: Doubleday.

Smythe, D. (1981). *Dependency road: Communications, capitalism, consciousness, and Canada*. Toronto: Ablex.

Smythe, D. (1977). Communications: Blindspot of western Marxism. *Canadian Journal of Political and Social Theory, 1*, 1–27.

Tompkins, P.K., & Cheney, G. (1985). Communication and unobtrusive control in contemporary organizations. In R.D. McPhee & P.K. Tompkins (Eds.), *Organizational communication: Traditional themes and new directions* (pp. 179–210). Newbury Park, CA: Sage.

Whitaker, R. (1999). *The end of privacy: How total surveillance is becoming a reality.* New York: New Press.

Wriston, W. (1992). *The twilight of sovereignty: How the information revolution is transforming our world.* New York: Scribner.

36.
JAPANESE MEDIA MIXES AND AMATEUR CULTURAL EXCHANGE

Mizuko Ito

In research about young people's relationship to media, there is growing recognition that children are capable of active and critical engagement and interpretation, rather than uncritical and passive viewing of mass media messages. For example, in his introduction to his reader on children's culture, Jenkins (1998) argues against the view of children as innocent victims "in favor of works that recognize and respect their social and political agency" (p. 3). Similarly, Kinder (1999) suggests that "children's reactions to media culture tend to be more active, variable, and negotiated than is usually realized" (p. 19). When translated to educational practice, this recognition has led to what Buckingham (2003) calls a "new paradigm" in media education that seeks less to protect children from the harmful effects of media than to promote understanding and participation in media cultures. These new approaches to media education take children's existing knowledge of and pleasures in media culture as a starting point, with the aim of developing critical practices of reflection and active media production. Buckingham also suggests that "the participatory potential of new technologies—and particularly of the internet—has made it much more possible for young people to undertake creative media production" (p. 14).

Digital technologies enter the conversation about children, media, and media literacy in the context of offering new tools and environments for children to author their own perspectives in media worlds. Although it is crucial to question hyperbole and technical determinist rhetorics when evaluating the promises of these new technologies, it is also important for research to grasp foundational changes to children's lives that are accompanying their growing engagement with digital media. As Valentine and Holloway (2001) suggest, there are problems with both those who are exclusively boosters and the debunkers of new technologies (see also Buckingham, 2000). My own perspective is that digital media broaden the base of participation in certain long-standing forms of media engagement. This includes the growing accessibility to tools of media production, as well as more diverse Internet-enabled means for communicating about and trafficking in cultural content. In this chapter, I focus on the latter, the peer-to-peer exchange surrounding a particular genre of new media: Japanese animation media mixes that rely on a combination of various analog and digital media forms. I argue that children's engagement with these media mixes provides evidence that they are capable not only of critical engagement and creative production, but also of entrepreneurial *participation* in the exchange systems and economies that they have developed around media mix content.

I describe two cases from my fieldwork in Tokyo from 1998 to 2000, where I tracked young people's engagement with current media mixes. I focus on media engagement that involves new forms of peer-to-peer participation and exchange to highlight young people's political and economic entrepreneurism. After first describing my conceptual framework for understanding media fandom and participatory media cultures, I describe the cultural and historical backdrop to the Japanese media *otaku* as an example of particularly activist forms of media engagement. My two ethnographic cases are, first, the creation, collection, and exchange of Yugioh cards, and, second, amateur girls' comics.

Participatory Media Cultures

Studies of fan groups have provided ample fodder for understanding media engagement that involves not only active and negotiated interpretation, but also rich social exchange and alternative cultural production. Even before the advent of digital authoring tools and internet exchange, fans appropriated mainstream cultural icons and narratives to organize communities of shared interest and create their own fan fictions, music videos, and music (Bacon-Smith, 1991; Jenkins, 1992; Penley, 1997; Tulloch & Jenkins, 1995). In other words, fans invoke what Jenkins (1992) calls a *participatory* media culture that blurs the distinction between production and consumption. Fans not only consume professionally produced media, but also produce their own meanings and media products. Jenkins' model of participatory culture includes this productive activity, as well as the ongoing social exchange that is at the core of robust fan activities—fans will develop interpretations and alternative readings of shows in group viewing situations and, historically, exchange fan-produced art, zines, videos, and audiotapes in conventions and through the mail.

Fan-level peer-to-peer organization has expanded in tandem with technological changes. VCR and photocopier technologies enabled alternative production and reproduction, stimulating the fan cultures of the 1970s and 1980s, the fan zines, filk (folk) songs, and remixed music videos that the first wave of fan researchers documented in their ground-breaking studies. Now the internet has emerged as a privileged technology of social organization and exchange as fans communicate over blogs and bulletin boards, share media over file-sharing sites, and sell amateur works over auction sites such as eBay. This lateral, peer-to-peer social organization represents both an evolution of existing fan groups, as well as an expansion of fanlike cultural activity to a broader demographic. In many ways, fan groups epitomize the kinds of niche communities of interest that are

thriving on the internet and, in turn, have driven the evolution of new forms of internet technology and social organization.

Historically, this kind of organized fan activity has been a subcultural and marginalized cultural domain and, in the United States, mostly comprised of adults. Although audience and reader studies have documented how even relatively casual engagement involves active and negotiated interpretive positions in relation to media texts (e.g., Ang, 1996; Morley, 1992; Radway, 1991), fan studies have been distinctive in documenting a more activist and productive stance toward the content of mainstream media. Casual consumers generally see this stance as obsessive, infantilized, and cut off from normative realities. Although this tension between casual/mainstream and participatory/fan media cultures is resilient, there is also clearly a growing cadre of consumers who are crossing the line toward more activist forms of engagement. Even a quick search on the internet for any popular media content will reveal dozens of fan-oriented discussion groups and informational sites with hundreds of participants of varying ages. Ethnographies of fandoms in the pre-internet era document a higher threshold for participation, where people had to travel to conventions or develop local interpersonal networks to engage in this participatory media culture. Now having an internet-connected computer enables easy access to a rich archive of fan communication and content. This accessibility is particularly significant in the case of children and youth, who are generally not able to travel to local gatherings and national conventions but may have online access.

The point is *not* that the new technology of the internet has somehow created a burgeoning network of participatory media cultures. Rather, these networks have expanded over the internet because existing fan cultures and activities have driven and taken up new technological capabilities. In other words, the new technologies of internet communication and exchange are produced by old fan activity as much as they are productive of new forms of social and cultural practice. In this approach, I draw from social studies of the technology that see the internet as growing out of existing social contexts as well as producing new ones (e.g., Hine, 2000; Lessig, 1999; Miller & Slater, 2000). This relationship between emergent technologies and existing media cultures and practices is particularly evident within a subset of international media fandoms—those associated with Japan-origin manga, anime, and games. Although these types of fandoms have only recently become internationally visible as part of Japan's newfound "gross national cool" (McGray, 2002), they are grounded in a much older tradition of media connoisseurship associated with Japan's *otaku* cultures. After providing an introduction to *otaku* culture, I describe in more detail two cases of children and youth participatory media cultures that are evidence of the spread of *otaku*-like media culture across different age groups and countries.

Media Mixes, *Otaku* Cultures, and Media Literacy

Although English-language research literature on Japanese manga and anime-related fandom is just beginning to emerge (Kinsella, 2000; McLelland, 2001; Napier, 2000), these types of media have been a significant force in both Japan and abroad for over three decades. Outside of Japan, *Pokémon* forced the recognition of Japanese anime into the mainstream in the 1990s (Tobin, 2004), providing a popular counterpoint to the longer term growth of adult anime fandom in other parts of Asia, the United States, and Europe. In Japan, vibrant manga (comics) and anime (animation) cultures originated in the 1960s as child- and youth-identified media and have grown into a multigenerational and transnational phenomenon. My primary reference point for this chapter is Japanese *otaku* cultures and my research in Japan. But in keeping with the transnational spread of these cultures, I also include some observations from my U.S.-based research on media engagement of American children and online fan communication.

Japan-origin manga, anime, and game content are heterogeneous, spanning multiple media types and genres, yet still recognized as a cluster of linked cultural forms. Because of the absence of a single overarching media type or genre, I use the native industry term *media mix* to describe the linked character-based media types of games, anime, and manga. Manga are generally (but not always) the primary texts of these media forms. They were the first component of the contemporary mix to emerge in the postwar period in the 1960s and 1970s, eventually providing the characters and narratives that go on to populate games, anime, and merchandise. Although electronic gaming was in a somewhat separate domain through the 1980s, by the 1990s, it was well integrated with the overall media mix of manga and anime characters, aided by the popularity of game-origin characters such as Mario and Pikachu. In this chapter, my focus is on this overall media mixed ecology and the ways in which digital media are amplifying certain dimensions of the mix. In other words, I see the move toward new media as an interaction between long-standing and emergent media forms, rather than a shift from old analog to new digital media. I spend most of my time discussing the low-tech media of trading cards and comic books, but I hope to make clear how these analog media forms are being newly inflected through digitally enabled sociality.

The same period of rapid economic growth and cultural renewal that gave birth to Japan's contemporary media mix also gave birth to youth cultures that responded to the new material affluence and media culture. During the 1960s, young people flocked to manga as a new form of culture that fit their generational identity. Kinsella (1998) writes, "By spending hours with their noses buried in children's manga books obtuse students demonstrated their hatred of the university system, of adults, and of society as a whole" (p. 291). Young people developed new sensibilities that responded to consumer brands, rich media environments, and new urban street cultures that were not available to the wartime generation of their parents. Soon they were labeled as *shinjinrui* or *the new breed*. A subset of these young media consumers went on to create distinctive participatory fan cultures. In the 1980s, the term *otaku* was coined and popularized to describe these media-obsessed youth who took manga and anime as their primary cultural referents.

According to *otaku* scholar and apologist Okada (2000), the term originated in the beginning of the 1980s as a polite term of address between upper crust college students who were fans of emergent anime cultures. The term was transformed into a label for a social group by columnist Akio Nakamori, who published a column on "*Otaku* Research" in a manga magazine in 1983. In 1989, a full-blown moral panic (Cohen, 1972) about *otaku* arose after the arrest of Miyazaki Tsutomu. He had abducted, murdered, and mutilated four girls, and *otaku* media were blamed for providing the inspiration for his sociopathic acts. Photos and footage of his bedroom, crammed with manga and videotapes, many of the Lolita-complex and pornographic variety, flooded the popular press, and Miyazaki became the posterboy of the *otaku* subculture. After this, the term came to be used and recognized by the mainstream as a stigmatizing label for somebody who is obsessed with media mix content and out of touch with everyday social reality.

Mainstream perception of *otaku* bears at least a family resemblance to how Trekkies have been stereotyped in the United States (Jenkins, 1992). An important difference, however, between English-language terms such as *fan* or *Trekkie* and the term *otaku* is that the Japanese term invokes a broader set of cultural connotations not restricted to a particular social group, set of activities, or media type, genre, or artist. *Otaku-kei* or *otaku*-variety cultural style is part of a general palette of Japanese popular cultural reference. A publication or an anime series might be described as *otaku-kei* even if it is in mainstream distribution. Similarly, people can engage with a wide variety of cultural activities in an *otaku*-like way. Colloquially, the term gets used to describe a specific subculture of youth who are fans of media mixes, but also as a general term for collection and connoisseurship. For example, one might call somebody a *wine otaku* or a *fishing otaku*. In this, the term is probably closer to *geek* or *nerd* than to *fan*. It is a term that has come to connote a general sociocultural logic or gestalt, which takes as its core a sense of connoisseurship, attention to esoterica, media mixing, and amateur cultural production.

Okada (2000) argues against the stigmatizing use of the term *otaku* and offers a counterdefinition: "I believe *otaku* are a new breed born in the 20th century 'visual culture era.' In other words, *otaku* are people with a viewpoint based on an extremely evolved sensitivity toward images" (p. 14). Further, he argues that the uses of the term in such labels as *fishing otaku* or *anime otaku* are fundamentally incorrect, and that one defining feature of the *otaku* sensibility is that they do not obsess over a single media genre or type, but rather read across genres and media forms.

Anime are certainly the home ground for *otaku*-ism. But games, special effects, Western films, and manga also include works which rank high on the *otaku* scale. And actually, these works influence one another. The *otaku* sensibility comes from recognizing and enjoying these as genre cross-overs.

(p. 43)

In the 1990s, the term started to be taken up with mostly positive valences overseas to refer to enthusiasts of Japanese media mixes, particularly anime. In its premier 1993 issue, *Wired* magazine featured an article on *otaku* as "the incredibly strange mutant creatures who rule the universe of alienated Japanese zombie computer nerds." More recently, science fiction writer Gibson (2001) described *otaku* as "passionate obsessives," and English-language anime fan sites proudly adopt the term as a form of self-address.

I believe that Okada's approach and the recent transnational popularity of the term represents a valuable native view of *otaku* culture and is a useful corrective to the penumbra of connotations that resulted from the moral panics over the Miyazaki incident. At the same time, I would argue for a view of *otaku* that locates the subculture within a resilient set of cultural and social structural dynamics, rather than just the internal definitions that Okada provides. Viewed anthropologically, the more stigmatizing meanings attached to *otaku* by the mainstream culture are not simply misunderstandings, but structurally determined outcomes of challenges that *otaku* represent to mainstream logics of cultural production, capitalism, gender, and age categories. As Okada suggests, the *otaku* sensibility has grown out of contemporary media cultures, pushing back at their dominant cultural logics and power dynamics. *Otaku* sensibilities were born from the specific sociocultural contexts of Japan, but have also proved to have appeal well beyond Japan's borders. Specifically, *otaku* culture destabilizes certain key sociocultural categories: the distinction between professional and amateur cultural production, the commodity form of media, age-based boundaries for media consumption, and normative forms of gender and sexuality. I return to these broader structural dynamics in the conclusion of my chapter after first turning to my two ethnographic cases.

The *Yugioh* Knowledge and Card-trading Economy

During the period of my fieldwork in Japan, the most popular forms of play among boys centered around *Yugioh*, a media mix series that rose from the ashes of *Pokémon* to become a major force both in Japan and overseas. Like *Pokémon*, *Yugioh* relies on cross-referencing among serialized manga, a TV anime series, a card game, video games, occasional movie releases, and a plethora of character merchandise. The series centers on a boy, Mutoh Yugi, a game master who gets involved in various adventures with a small cohort of friends and rivals. The narrative, first rendered in manga and then anime, focuses on long sequences of card game duels, stitched together by an adventure narrative. Yugi and his friends engage in a card game derivative of the U.S.-origin game *Magic the Gathering*, and the series is devoted to fantastic duels that function to explicate the detailed esoterica of the games, such as the strategies and rules of game play, the properties of the cards, and the fine points of card collecting and trading. Compared with *Pokémon*, where games were only loosely tied to the narrative media by character identification, with *Yugioh* the gaming comprises the central content of the narrative.

As part of my research, I talked to parents and played with children who engaged with *Yugioh* as part of their everyday local peer relations. I was also a regular at specialty card shops that hosted weekly *Yugioh* tournaments, and I was able to befriend an older group of *Yugioh* aficionados who engaged in more deeply *otaku*-like forms of engagement with *Yugioh*. Although these two groups of *Yugioh* players—children engaged in play at or near home, and older players congregating at specialty shops—represent different degrees of game expertise and knowledge networks, both groups exhibit similar types of enthusiasm and investments in both collecting cards and knowledge. In other words, across a spectrum of *Yugioh* players, all evidenced certain forms of *otaku*-like engagement in a participatory media culture. Both the "core" community of older *Yugioh* players and the larger mass of kid *Yugioh* players can be located on a shared cultural continuum.

In the case of a media mix such as *Yugioh*, the participatory dimensions of media culture lie at the

core, rather than being something "poached" at the margins as is the case for most TV and cinema content (Jenkins, 1992). Building on the lessons of *Pokémon*, *Yugioh* card game play has been designed around the premise that learning will happen in a group social setting, rather than as a relation between child and machine or child and text. As Sefton-Green (2004) writes with respect to *Pokémon*, *Yugioh* play involves a "knowledge industry." It is nearly impossible to learn how to play the card game rules and strategy without the coaching of more experienced players. My research assistants and I spent several weeks with the *Yugioh* starter pack, poring through the rule book and the instructional videotape, trying to figure out how to play. It was only after several game sessions with some 9- to 10-year-olds, followed by some coaching from some of the more patient adults at the card shops, that we slowly began to understand the basic game play as well as some of the fine points of collection—how cards are acquired, valued, and traded.

Among children, this learning process is part of their everyday peer relations, as they congregate after school in homes and parks, showing off their cards, hooking up their Game Boys to play against one another, and trading cards and information. We found that children generally develop certain conventions of play among their local peer group, negotiating rules locally, often on a duel-by-duel basis. They will collectively monitor the weekly manga release in *Shonen Jump* magazine, often sharing copies among friends. In addition to the weekly manga about Yugi, the magazine also features information about upcoming card releases, tournaments, and tournament results. The issues featuring the winning decks of tournament duelists are often the most avidly studied. When children get together with their collections of *Yugioh* cards, there is a constant buzz of information exchange and deal-cutting, as children debate the merits of different cards and seek to augment both their play deck and their broader card collection. Players build a personalized relationship to the media mix content by collecting their own set of cards and virtual monsters and combining them into a deck or battle team that reflects a unique style of play. Buckingham and Sefton-Green (2004) write that with *Pokémon* "activity—or agency—is an indispensable part of the process rather than something that is exercised *post hoc*" (p. 19). *Yugioh* card game play similarly requires active participation as a precondition of media engagement.

In the case of the older *Yugioh* aficionados, the productive and participatory dimensions are even more pronounced, leading to the construction of alternative economies of knowledge and card exchange. *Yugioh otaku* are avid fans of *Yugioh* and rely on the mainstream media and toy industry to produce the content that is central to their activity. At the same time, they engage in tactics and entrepreneurial activities that push back at the dominant meanings of the narrative and game content, as well as at the structures of commodity capitalism. When a new series of cards is released, they are the first to purchase the whole series, posting the new cards in the series on their web sites and trying them out for playability. Any ambiguity in play dynamics and rules is immediately identified and reported to the company. On one of my evenings at a card shop, a group of gamers were talking about how they had telephoned the official Konami gamers line repeatedly to complain about the play dynamic of a particular card.

The buying, selling, and trading of postmarket single cards after the card pack has been opened are largely at the level of peer-to-peer exchange. The industries that produce *Yugioh* get no direct benefit from the millions of card trades and purchasing among children, at specialty card shops, and among card collectors on the internet and at conventions. Konami has been rumored to have tried unsuccessfully to pressure some card shops to stop the sale of single cards. Although by far the bulk of *Yugioh* card exchange is noncommercial, for serious Internet traders and specialty shops, the sale of single cards is a significant source of income. Card collectors scour the shelves of convenience stores on the night of a new series release, using special methods to identify packs with rare cards that they will add to their collections and auction on the internet. Although looked down on by all card *otaku* I spoke to, there is also a vibrant industry of counterfeit *Yugioh* cards that are often sold on street corners or at festivals, drawing throngs of appreciative children.

Although fan studies have documented the participatory dimensions of engagement with TV, film, and print media, media mixes are more consciously designed for player level customization, remix, and social interaction. The format of media mixes like *Yugioh* builds on the sensibilities of children who grew up with the interactive and layered formats of video games as a fact of life, bringing this subjectivity to bear on other media forms. *Pokémon* decisively inflected children's video game culture toward personalization and recombination, demonstrating that children can master highly esoteric content, customization, remixing, and a pantheon of hundreds of characters. These participatory dimensions—collecting, remixing, customizing, revaluing, and reframing within a social context of peer-to-peer exchange—are central to an *otaku*-like approach to media engagement.

Doujinshi and *Shojo* Fan Cultures

Although gaming *otaku* cultures have been largely dominated by boys, girls have had a leadership role in the cultures of *doujinshi* (amateur manga), an arena of *otaku* practice that is in many ways more challenging to mainstream sensibilities than the peer-to-peer exchanges of *Yugioh* cards. Like the case of *Yugioh* card exchange, manga production by girls spans a range between casual engagement by young girls and average consumers and *otaku*-identified practices that are much more activist and entrepreneurial.

Manga have been a major source of subcultural cultural capital since the postwar period, particularly from the 1970s onward. The period of high-speed economic growth in Japan from the 1960s through the 1970s transformed existing graphical arts into modern mass cultural production industries. Through the course of the 1970s and 1980s, manga slowly became recognized as a legitimate cultural product that could take up difficult intellectual and political topics as well as provide light entertainment. The Japanese manga industry is unique in that it comprises about 38% of all print publications in Japan (Schodt, 1996) and spans a much wider range of genres and topics than in other countries. Topics taken up by manga include fictional and nonfictional topics that are generally not published in comic books elsewhere (e.g., adult-oriented pornography, stories of businessmen, childrearing, mah jong, sports, and historical fiction). Today, manga are enjoyed by all age groups in Japan and are generally the primary literacy experiences for children. Manga are such a central fixture of Japanese childhood that one editor asked me with puzzlement after our interview, "What do American children *do* without manga?"

As part of my fieldwork with children in Japan, I made regular visits to a public children's center that runs an afterschool program for elementary-school-age children. I spent most of my time in the arts and crafts room and the library on the second floor, foraying down to the first-floor gym only during the occasional Yugioh tournaments hosted there. The library had a substantial collection of novels and reference books, but also stocked the latest manga magazine for elementary-age boys and girls, as well as well-thumbed archives of popular series that are later released in paperback book format. In the library, there was always an array of children sprawled on the floor and on the sofas with manga in hand. In the arts and crafts room, they copied and traced their favorite manga characters from coloring books or drew them from memory in their notebooks. When there was not a structured activity in the arts and crafts room, small groups of girls would often be drawing their own pictures of characters from popular anime. *Pokémon* and *Hamtaro* characters were the most popular, and girls would often delight in showing me and other girls how skilled they were at drawing a particular *Pokémon* or hamster from the pantheon.

The children frequenting this center were mostly first and second graders (6- to 8-year-olds) just beginning to use the visual culture of manga as part of their own form of personal expression. When I spoke to older girls and women in other contexts, many described how this early drawing practice evolved into "pencil manga" or the drawing of manga frames and narratives in the late elementary through high school years. For those who came on to be more serious or fan-identified, they might aspire to become a professional manga artist or participate in the vibrant *doujinshi* scene. In this sense, there is a continuity between the informal and everyday practices of growing up in a manga-saturated childhood and the more hard-core or *otaku* practices of aspiring to be a manga artist. At the same time, the identity shift from a girl who can draw manga characters to an *otaku* who aspires to writing her own manga is a shift from

a normative to an alternative or subcultural identity. Just as in the case of *Yugioh* fandom, where *otaku* knowledge and card economies are bifurcated from mainstream economies, "regular" girls do not participate beyond the reading of manga and casual drawing of favorite characters.

One event I attended traced the boundary zones between the subjectivity of manga readership, fandom, and production. In 2001, I attended a summer festival organized by *Ribon* magazine, the most popular manga magazine for lower elementary school-age girls. Readers of the magazine applied with postcards to a lottery to be selected to attend the festival, and the large hall in central Tokyo was packed with girls and young women. The highlight of the event was a panel of four of the magazine's most popular artists. All four described how they had started drawing manga in elementary school, eventually moving to pencil manga, and had their first manga work published while they were in high school. The MC of the event said that the most common question that readers have for the artists is, "How did you get so good at drawing?" He introduced a prerecorded sequence of the most popular artists giving tips on drawing and character development. The audience was assumed to be young aspiring artists. In the back of all manga magazines are regular announcements inviting readers to submit their own manga to competitions designed to identify new talent. The successful works are published with fanfare together with the more established artists who run regular series in any given magazine. Although only the most dedicated of readers go on to submit their own manga to a competition of this sort, the magazines interpellate all readers as potential manga writers, simultaneously citing and constructing the shared cultural frame that manga writing is a commonplace form of literacy and expression.

These types of events and competitions represent the officially sanctioned interface zones between mainstream publishing and the amateur and aspiring artist, but this is just the tip of the iceberg of the girls' amateur manga movement. In tandem with the growth of the manga industry, the *otaku* base of manga readership also grew. In the early 1970s, with the advent of photocopying and cheap offset printing, amateur manga and fan fiction became a viable medium for what came to be called "mini communications" or "minicomi," in contrast to mass communication (Kinsella, 2000). Aided by the relatively relaxed copyright regime of Japanese publishers, this amateur manga movement flourished in the late 1970s and 1980s. Comic Market, the premier convention for *doujinshi*, began in 1974, growing from a small annual gathering to become the largest convention of any kind in Japan. By the mid-1990s, up to 300,000 *doujinshi* aficionados would flock to the largest convention center in Tokyo for the now biannual meeting. In addition to Comic Market, numerous other smaller gatherings are organized regularly around the country focused on region or specific manga genre or title.

Historically, amateur manga contained a large number of original works and represented a way for an aspiring artist to break into mainstream publishing. With the broadening base of participation, however, works derivative of professional content became the overwhelming majority. *Doujinshi* written for women by women that depict romance between *bishounen* (beautiful boys) appropriated from mainstream manga represented the first major wave of popular *doushinshi* writing in the 1970s and 1980s. More recently, the *bishoujo* (beautiful girl) and *Lolicom* (Lolita complex comics) genres written by men for men have become popular. Both of these genres of *doujinshi* are scorned by the mainstream because of their often explicit and offbeat sexual content, the fact that the works are derivative, and because they generally lack any substantive narrative development (see Kinsella, 1998, 2000; McLelland, 2001).

After the arrest of Miyazaki in 1989, the ensuing moral panic engulfed the *doujinshi* scene. Kinsella (2000) writes, "Amateur manga culture was repeatedly linked to Miyazaki, creating what became a new public perception, that young people involved with amateur manga are dangerous, psychologically-disturbed perverts" (p. 128). By the early 1990s, *doujinshi* artists and purveyors became subject to police harassment, where bookshops were raided and artists were brought in for questioning. This public discourse was taken up by young people as well as the older generation (Kinsella, 2000). "Young people themselves, were persuaded that amateur manga subculture was a serious social problem, rather than a 'cool' youth activity that they might like to enter into"

(Kinsella, 2000, p. 137). In my fieldwork in Japan, I found these attitudes alive and well over a decade after the Miyazaki incident. Although the young people staffing the booths at the Comic Market were quite happy to chat with me about their works, they balked at the idea of doing a follow-up interview. The operators of the Comic Market continue to be vigilant about negative press and publicizing participants' identities. Cameras and video cameras are banned on the Comic Market floor. Others I spoke to involved with *doujinshi* or related activities often kept their activities hidden from their classmates and family, attesting to the continued social stigma attached to these subcultures.

With the spread of the Internet in the late 1990s, the dynamics of *doujinshi* exchange are changing substantially. As with the case of *Yugioh* card trafficking, *doujinshi* are ideal collectors' items to be exchanged via internet auction sites and homepages run by the artists. A quick search on popular Japanese auction sites will bring up thousands of *doujinshi* for sale, ranging from the equivalent of hundreds of U.S. dollars to just a few. This internet trafficking in *doujinshi* and related information has made these cultural products much more accessible to a broader demographic both within and outside Japan (McLelland, 2001). In the Comic Market convention catalog from summer 2000, one of the organizers editorializes about the "out of control boom in net auctions" (Unamu, 2000, p. 1314). Unlike professionalized and mass distributed comics, *doujinshi* were traditionally only available at conventions like the Comic Market or a handful of specialty shops in urban centers stocking only a fraction of the comics that you would see at a large-scale event. Now with net distribution, rare and niche publications can be easily bought and sold. The author of the Comic Market editorial ponders the pluses and minuses of having works sold on the net for much higher prices than sold on the Comic Market floor, the emergence of people who seem to be buying and selling *doujinshi* to make a living, people auctioning off their spots on the Comic Market floor, and the emergent grey zone of auctioneers who photocopy rare *doujinshi* and sell them on auction sites. He concludes:

At the rate things are going, people are going to start auctioning their staff IDs and armbands. But for the generation who started going to Comic Market after it moved to the Ariake site, and were already contacting each other with mobile phones, this is just a normal state of affairs. Even if the older folks complain about a declining morality, there is nothing we can do. We need to look ahead and say this is the current state of affairs. Now how should we respond to it?

(p. 1319)

The jury is still out as to the long-term prospects of the burgeoning *doujinshi* activities on the internet, but clearly the trend is toward moving more and more of the *doujinshi* traffic online. This is particularly true of foreign readers of Japanese *doujinshi* who gain access to these publications almost exclusively through inter-net sales (McLelland, 2001). Some of these sites even offer scanlations (scanned translations) into English. Due to the sexually explicit nature of many *doujinshi*, controversy continues to abound as to the appropriate-ness of the traffic in these publications, particularly among the teens who both produce and purchase these works. In many ways, the internet has proved to be an ideal medium for bringing together marginal and niche communities of interest that are highly dispersed. At the same time, the net has become a vehicle for making these subcultures visible and subject to scrutiny by an unsympathetic mainstream. At one U.S. anime fan con-vention I attended, a high school student lamented that she felt uncomfortable reading manga in front of her friends because they assumed that she was reading pornography, even though she was not interested in those genres of manga. Although only one sector of an immense and diverse format of publication, the image of manga as focusing on sex and violence has even been exported overseas as a mainstream perception.

Amateur Cultural Production

For my purposes here, the most significant aspects of *doujinshi* production and exchange are not the par-ticulars of how the communities have shifted to online and transnational spaces. Rather, I am interested in how *doujinshi* production and exchange, even in the pre-internet era, represent the activist participatory media cultures that are proliferating in tandem with the spread of digital media. In a sense, they are prototypical of niche communities of disenfranchised youth who are mobilizing through the internet to create communities of interest that challenge elite and adult sensibilities. In her studies of *doujinshi* and "cute" girl culture central to much of manga and anime, Kinsella (1995) suggests that these cultures operate from a position of disenfranchisement vis-à-vis the mainstream. *Doujinshi*, in particular, have working-class origins, and Kinsella (2000) suggests that "this is one of the very few cultural and social forums in Japan (or any other industrialized country), which is not managed by privileged and highly edu-cated classes of society" (p. 110).

It is possible that the intense emphasis placed, firstly, on educational achievement, and secondly, on acquiring a sophisticated cultural taste, in Japan since the 1960s, has also stimulated the involvement of young people excluded from these officially recognized modes of achievement, with amateur manga subculture.

(Kinsella, 2000, p. 111)

Although it is probably clear that I share with *otaku* cultures an appreciation for peer-based and bottom-up forms of media production and exchange, my view of these subcultures is not univocally celebratory. I have questioned the implicit technical determinism in both cautionary and celebratory visions of the digital generation, and I acknowledge that contradictory ten-dencies emerge from the heterogeneous uptake of diverse digital technologies. The profound unease that educated elites experience when confronted with the "junk culture" of *Yugioh* and *doujinshi* is evidence of the persistent tension between high-brow educational agendas and subaltern youth activism (see Seiter, 1993). We may celebrate the active nature of youth media engagement, but we may not be prepared to cede control or provide validation to bottom-up kid cultures interested in the esoterica of fantasy game play or Lolita porn. As an ethnographer interested in educational reform, my own stance has been that we need to first understand and appreciate the social and political dynamics represented by these expanding subaltern networks before we can arrive at principled interventions that do not simply reinscribe the distinc-tions between high and low, kid and adult cultures.

The cultural movements I have described—*otaku* media subcultures, card trafficking, and amateur manga—are all examples of participatory media cultures that predate the so-called "digital age." They grow out of resilient dynamics of stratification by age, gender, and class. At the same time, these practices are merging with new digital technologies of production and exchange to expand the range and possibilities of amateur cultural production. My goal in this chapter has been to describe a certain politics of engagement with media cultures that are not specific to media type, but have strong affinities with the recombinant and peer-to-peer forms of media and communication that have been increasingly supported by digital technologies. The broadening base of participation in *otaku* culture, as well as their transnational spread, are evidence of the synergistic relationship between these niche subcultures and the networked ecologies of the internet. In Japan, as elsewhere, those engaged in hard-core fan and *otaku* activities are a relatively small proportion of overall media consumers. At the same time, the communicative environment of the internet, interactive media formats, as well as the industry paradigm represented by Japanese media mixes encourage these types of practices and subjectivities among even casual readers and players. My effort, in other words, has been to highlight continuities as much as ruptures between new and old media and between marginal and mainstream consumers.

The cases I have described may seem irrelevant and exotic, but I would argue for their growing salience in the international media ecology. Although this is speculative, I feel that the transnational spread of Japanese-origin media mixes and the tropes of *otaku* culture are evidence of the resonance between *otaku* subjectivities and digital cultures. Clearly this spread has been uneven and restricted to technologically privileged and non-mainstream media consumers overseas. At the same time, the spread of a subculture of this sort from a cultural margin to Euro-American cultural centers is enough to have raised a wave of well-circulated writing about Japan's "gross national cool" and "soft" power (Faiola, 2003; McGray, 2002; Solomon, 2003). I am not suggesting an exclusively Japanese national original to *otaku* fandoms, but rather a new transnational cross-pollination among participatory media cultures of diverse national stripes. My cases are examples of the unique alchemy when marginal subcultures and subaltern groups combine with distributed and heterogeneous media networks and ecologies. Although the cultural identities of niche media cultures are diverse, they are probably part of a shared technocultural trend that challenges modern distinctions between production and consumption, and between child and adult subjectivity.

Given that stratification by class and age seem unlikely to disappear anytime soon, subaltern groups of amateur media producers will continue to thrive in the shadows of mainstream media production, pushing back at their dominant logics and narratives. For those shut out of dominant and professionalized adult subjectivities by factors such as age or class identity, these shadow exchanges and amateur reputation systems offer an alternative economy of value and productive participation. If we place these amateur practices along a global-local scale that contrasts large-scale cultural production and individual-scale cultural consumption, we can see that they lie in the intermediary zone that we might call a community scale of interaction. Cultural content is being exchanged and engaged with at a scale that is larger than intimate and personal communication, but not at the scale of mass media transmission. This is the scale of perhaps a dozen to several hundred people where there is some kind of named relation among participants, emergent leadership, and ongoing community exchange. Although lacking access to professional media networks, these amateur networks are viable subeconomies where young people gain a sense of expertise, deep knowledge, and validation from knowledgeable peers. In other words, these are expert communities, although not professionalized ones.

I would like to conclude with a question. Is it possible to legitimate amateur cultural production and exchange as a domain of learning and identity production for young people? Institutionally and culturally, amateurism is a marginalized domain, associated with volunteers, starving artists, and hobbyists. Yet it is clearly also an arena that supports vibrant learning communities and forms of productive activity that differ from the power dynamics of schooling.

If we shift from the domain of entertainment to education, many of the distinctions between cultural producers and consumers also apply to knowledge producers and consumers, which in the academy we distinguish as faculty and students or teachers and learners. Amateur fan cultural production shares many structural similarities to community-level learning that has been the subject of ethnographic studies of apprenticeship and other small-scale learning communities. This is a layer of social organization that supports identities like the assistant, apprentice, or graduate student—people who do not occupy the professional identity category, but who still perform productive labor in that community, rather than being passive consumers of knowledge (see also Lave & Wenger, 1991). Although the roguish practices I have described may seem distant from our current ideas of media education, perhaps they provide some hints for supporting practices that are driven by the motivations of young people's participation in media and peer networks, complicating our long-standing distinctions between who are the producers and who are the consumers of knowledge and culture.

References

Ang, I. (1996). *Living room wars: Rethinking media audiences in a postmodern world*. New York: Routledge.

Bacon-Smith, C. (1991). *Enterprising women: Television fandom and the creation of popular myth*. Philadelphia: University of Pennsylvania Press.

Buckingham, D. (2000). *After the death of childhood: Growing up in the age of electronic media*. Cambridge: Polity.

Buckingham, D. (2003). *Media education: Literacy, learning, and contemporary culture*. Cambridge: Polity.

Buckingham, D., & Sefton-Green, J. (2004). Structure, agency, and pedagogy in children's media culture. In J. Tobin (Ed.), *Pikachu's global adventure: The rise and fall of Pokémon* (pp. 12–33). Durham, NC: Duke University Press.

Cohen, S. (1972). *Folk devils and moral panics*. London: MacGibbon & Kee.

Faiola, A. (2003, December 27). Japan's empire of cool. *Washington Post*, p. A01.

Gibson, W. (2001, April 1). Modern boys and mobile girls. *The Observer*. Retrieved November 15, 2005, from http://observer.guardian.co.uk/life/story/0,6903,466391,00.html

Hine, C. (2000). *Virtual ethnography*. London: Sage.

Jenkins, H. (1992). *Textual poachers: Television fans and participatory culture*. New York: Routledge.

Jenkins, H. (1998). Introduction: Childhood innocence and other modern myths. In H. Jenkins (Ed.), *The children's culture reader* (pp. 1–37). New York: New York University Press.

Kinder, M. (1999). Kids' media culture: An introduction. In M. Kinder (Ed.), *Kids' media culture* (pp. 1–12). Durham, NC: Duke University Press.

Kinsella, S. (1995). Cuties in Japan. In L. Skov & B. Moeran (Eds.), *Women, media, and consumption in Japan* (pp. 220–254). Honolulu: University of Hawaii Press.

Kinsella, S. (1998). Japanese subculture in the 1980s: Otaku and the amateur manga movement. *Journal of Japanese Studies, 24*, 289–316.

Kinsella, S. (2000). *Adult manga: Culture and power in contemporary Japanese society*. Honolulu: University of Hawaii Press.

Lave, J., & Wenger, E. (1991). *Situated learning: Legitimate peripheral participation*. Cambridge: Cambridge University Press.

Lessig, L. (1999). *Code and other laws of cyberspace*. New York: Basic Books.

McGray, D. (2002, June/July). Japan's gross national cool. *Foreign Policy*. Retrieved July 13, 2005, from http://www.douglasmcgray.com/articles.html

McLelland, M. (2001). Local meanings in global space: A case study of women's "Boy Love" Web sites in Japanese and English. *Mots Pluriels, 19*. Retrieved July 13, 2005, from http://www.arts.uwa.edu.au/MotsPluriels/MP1901mcl.html

Miller, D., & Slater, D. (2000). *The Internet: An ethnographic approach*. New York: Berg.

Morley, D. (1992). *Television, audiences, and cultural studies*. New York: Routledge.

Napier, S. J. (2000). *Anime: From Akira to Princess Mononoke*. New York: Palgrave.

Okada, T. (2000). *Otaku-gaku Nyuumon* [Introduction to otaku studies]. Tokyo: Ohta Shuppan.

Penley, C. (1997). *Nasa/Trek: Popular science and sex in America*. New York: Verso.

Radway, J. A. (1991). *Reading the romance: Women, patriarchy, and popular literature*. Chapel Hill: University of North Carolina Press.

Schodt, F. L. (1996). *Dreamland Japan: Writings on modern manga*. Berkeley, CA: Stonebridge.

Sefton-Green, J. (2004). Initiation rites: A small boy in a Poké-World. In J. Tobin (Ed.), *Pikachu's global adventure: The rise and fall of Pokémon* (pp. 141–164). Durham, NC: Duke University Press.

Seiter, E. (1993). *Sold separately: Parents and children in consumer culture*. New Brunswick, NJ: Rutgers University Press.

Solomon, C. (2003, June 1). Inspired by the film they inspired. *Los Angeles Times*, p. E24.

Tobin, J. (Ed.). (2004). *Pikachu's global adventure: The rise and fall of Pokémon*. Durham, NC: Duke University Press.

Tulloch, J., & Jenkins, H. (1995). *Science fiction audiences: Watching Doctor Who and Star Trek*. New York: Routledge.

Unamu, H. (2000). Nazono Burokku-cho Misutaa S no Kachiku Yahoo [Mystery block chief Mister S domestic yahoo]. *Comic Market 58 Catalog* (pp. 1314–1319).

Valentine, S., & Holloway, G. (2001). *Cyberkids: Children in the information age*. New York: Routledge.

SECTION VII

MEDIA/CITIZENSHIP

Introduction

This section considers the various ways that critical scholars have conceptualized the relationship between media and citizenship. Jürgen Habermas's concept of the public sphere (1962) is often the starting point for considering media's relationship to democracy. Defined as a space for deliberation outside the control of the market and the state, the public sphere has been updated to account for the role of media, both in constituting imagined communities of citizen-subjects and in circulating the information and dialogue upon which the ideal of deliberative democracy is said to depend. Other scholars are less convinced that the public sphere as conceived this way is possible or desirable, given its historical association with propertied, white, educated men. Just as women and minorities were excluded from the public sphere of the pre-electronic era, the media forms (such as serious newspapers and news reports) valued by proponents of the mediated public sphere tend to correlate with the dispositions and cultural capital of educated white masculinity. It is for this reason that more scholars have begun to assess the popular media as a site for citizenship formation—with mixed results.

Some have built on theories of governmentality (Foucault, 1991; Miller, 1993; Bennett, 1998) to conceptualize media as a technology for guiding and shaping citizen-subjects within socio-political contexts. This approach differs from the focus on the public sphere in that it assumes that governing through freedom is subject to individualized practices of self-regulation, especially at an historical juncture when personal responsibility and lifestyle choices overshadow collectivity and the nation as sites of civic action. Citizenship is also approached from the perspective of media policy and law, including the impact of deregulation on public interest expectations and objectives such as diversity in hiring practices and content.

In his overview essay "Mediating Democracy," a chapter from his 1995 book *Television and the Public Sphere*, Peter Dahlgren reflects on democracy as a model and ideal, tracing the role of interaction among citizens in the political process back to ancient Greece. He considers Habermas' theory of the public sphere as well as the criticisms it has engendered, and this synthesis provides the backdrop for mapping the media's role in the public sphere (or better, spheres). Dahlgren usefully charts four areas of concern for scholars—media institutions (policy issues around media institutions and their output), media representation (what gets represented, and the role of the media in constructing the space of the public sphere), social structure (to what extent is a centralized or pluralist public sphere better) and socio-cultural interaction (collective sense-making practices and modes of participation). Despite its limitations, Dahlgren finds utility in the concept of the public sphere, especially as theorized by alternative philosophers. Anticipating developments of the 1990s and beyond, however, he also concedes that citizenship is increasingly being defined in consumerist terms that require quite different modes of analysis.

Stuart Cunningham's 2001 essay "Popular Media as Public 'Sphericules' for Diasporic Communities" takes research on Asian disasporic communities as the basis for adapting theories of the public sphere to better suit culturally plural and highly mediated societies. He traces the debate between media scholars who see the public sphere as fundamentally compromised by commercial media culture and those who envision such media as the venue for what exists of the public sphere, an approach exemplified by John Hartley's conception of the "mediasphere" (2006). As a way of moving beyond this dualism, Cunningham points to the proliferation of diasporic public sphericules that forge affective connections through commercialized niche media while also connecting indigenous and migrant groups. Referencing Chinese, Vietnamese and aboriginal popular media in Australia, he suggests that narrowcast cultural spaces reconfigure essentialist notions of community and confound dualisms—such as public-private, and information-entertainment—that define scholarship on the public sphere.

Jeffrey Jones' 2006 essay "A Cultural Approach to the Study of Mediated Citizenship" questions the assumption pervasive in much scholarship that popular media negatively affect the political process and culture and discourage civic engagement. This position, most famously associated with the work of Robert Putnam, is based on flawed assumptions, Jones contends, including the notion that the interaction between politicians and the news media is the most important sphere of political communication, a position that leads to a focus on "serious" news and a dismissal of entertainment media as a distraction. Jones also questions the model of the "informed citizen," which is based on the idea that media's principal contribution to democracy is disseminating "useful" political information. Against these "instrumental and transmission views," Jones advocates a cultural approach to the construction of citizenship that emphasizes the intimate role that media play in our everyday lives. From talk radio to fake news shows, popular media consumption is integral to political identities and varied understandings of community, nation and society, he contends.

Lauren Berlant's influential 1993 essay "The Theory of Infantile Citizenship," which later appeared in her book *The Queen of America Goes to Washington City: Essays on Sex and Citizenship* (1997) takes a different approach to cultural studies of citizenship. Citing an episode of *The Simpsons* entitled "Mr. Lisa Goes to Washington" and other film, literary and televisual examples, she traces what she calls an "imaginary children's public sphere" and the centrality of frequently gendered and classed forms of infantile citizenship to the construction of U.S. national culture. In this oft-repeated narrative, a pilgrimage to Washington provides the basis for a childish disruption of the norms of the nation's capital, in which the "citizen's insistent stupidity has enormous power to unsettle, expose and reframe the machinery of national life." For Berlant, the recurring trope of infantile citizenship performs the ideological work of negotiating tensions between utopia and history, childlike innocence and cynical reason. The upshot of every pilgrimage to Washington narrative links the "abstract national to the situated local, underinformed, abjected and idealistic citizen," she contends, confirming the necessity of the knowledge that the media provide to the child consumer "who has no interest in touring Washington in order to feel occasionally 'free.' "

In the 2009 essay "Makeover Television, Governmentality and the Good Citizen," Laurie Ouellette and James Hay also emphasize the importance of popular media to citizenship formation. Extending theories of governmentality to media studies, they analyze reality television as a "technology of citizenship" that guides and shapes normative citizenship in the post-welfare era. Situating the proliferation of makeover-themed entertainment within the broader context of privatization, public sector downsizing and welfare reform, they argue that television has become an increasingly visible node of dispersed practices of governing that depend as much or more on private entities and self-regulation as official government, politicians and state intervention. These practices of governing hinge less on the construction of "informed citizens"—an ideal associated with a waning stage of liberal democracy—than with the making of self-enterprising citizens who make use of cultural resources (such as television) to maximize their own fates and futures. Reality television, with its focus on transforming the self, provides the perfect conduit for neoliberal understandings of good citizenship, they suggest.

Finally, Hector Amaya's 2010 contribution "Citizenship, Diversity, Law and *Ugly Betty*" also addresses the impact of neoliberalism on media culture. Focusing on the policy realm, Amaya shows how deregulation, the waning of earlier public interest discourses, and the unraveling of affirmative action policies have coincided with commercial television's embrace of "diversity" as a selling point. Amaya critiques a variety of legal prescriptions that "directly impinge on the formation of the citizen"—including labor laws, international law and global finance policies, "which lay the ground for asymmetrical immigration between Latin American nations and the U.S."

Situating the legal production of citizenship within the corporate liberalism of the commercial media, he shows how the ABC television network's version of the telenovela *Ugly Betty*—which features a character who is an undocumented immigrant and has been heralded as evidence of ABC's commitment to diversity—disavows the systemic marginalization of Latino labor. The definition of diversity that has emerged in the deregulated media environment, Amaya contends, is rooted more in corporate interests than in social justice. Whereas "legal remedies enacted during the Civil Rights movement were meant to change the way industries, including media, reconstituted themselves," he contends, something was fundamentally lost in the "translation between Civil Rights law and corporate structures."

References

Bennett, Tony, *Culture: A Reformer's Science* (Thousand Oaks, CA: Sage, 1998).

Berlant, Lauren, *The Queen of America Goes to Washington City: Essays on Sex and Citizenship* (Durham, NC: Duke University Press, 1997).

Foucault, Michel, "Governmentality," in *The Foucault Effect: Studies in Governmentality*, eds. Graham Burchell, Colin Gordon and Peter Miller (Chicago: University of Chicago Press, 1991), p. 87–104.

Habermas, Jürgen, *Structural Transformation of the Public Sphere* (Cambridge: Polity Press, 1962, trans. 1989).

Hartley, John, *Popular Reality: Journalism, Modernity, Popular Culture* (London: Arnold, 1996).

Miller, Toby, *The Well-Tempered Self: Citizenship, Culture and the Postmodern Subject* (Baltimore: Johns Hopkins University Press, 1993).

37.
MEDIATING DEMOCRACY
Peter Dahlgren

In today's world, democracy remains precarious and vulnerable. We can point to many factors which contribute to this, among the more obvious being declining economies and their political fall-out, an environment threatened by the fundamental premises of our civilization, a chaotic international system where the status of the nation-state is increasingly problematical, and where the distinction between the military and criminal use of organized violence is often blurred. Many in the West who cheered the collapse of the Soviet system saw the triumph of both capitalism and liberal democracy. At this historical juncture, global capitalism clearly has no serious competitor. However, what this means for the well being of humanity and for the planet is arguable. What it means for democracy is also problematic. If the tension between democracy and capitalism has long been with us, in the contemporary situation the threats to democratic development cannot be seen as emanating exclusively from the logic of the market.

While private corporations function beyond popular democratic control, many allegedly democratic regimes bypass both their electorates and representative assemblies. Even with the most noble of intentions, the process of government has become paralysingly difficult. Many decisions which governments face require a degree of knowledge or even expertise far beyond the grasp of most citizens. In many countries, citizens, in turn, are increasingly withdrawing from the official political arena, leaving its management to 'the political class', which Hobsbawm (1994) describes as 'a special-interest group of professional politicians, journalists, lobbyists and others whose occupations ranked at the bottom of the scale of trustworthiness in sociological inquiries.' Such depoliticization includes on the one hand the affluent, who have the private means and influence to pursue and satisfy their interests, and on the other, those among the majority who increasingly feel they have nothing to gain from participating in a game they view as rigged against them.

Some of the forces undermining democracy are explicit, active and obvious, while others are more implicit or passive. Some antidemocratic forces may be unwitting: the consequences of human intentionality cannot always be predicted. Yet, though one may in darker moments wonder if democracy in the future will be seen as a temporary parenthesis in the history of civilization, we also find continual as well as new and unexpected manifestations of democracy's power to inspire. Not least as a far-reaching and compelling issue on the contemporary societal agenda, democracy is very much alive. It remains an historical accomplishment, continuously needing to be regenerated. We cannot take it for granted or assume that it will live its own life, yet rumours of its death are premature. Drawing lessons from the revolutions of 1989, Hobsbawm (1994) in a paraphrase quips 'the 20th century showed that one can rule against all the people for some of the time, some of the people all of the time, but not all the people all of the time.'

For better or worse, democracy is also one of our most pervasive and all-purpose hurrah words. The powerful publicly extoll it, the vast majority support it;

few people will publicly admit to being against it. The invocation of democracy can serve as a ritual of collective belonging, joining people from virtually all social sectors in a common cause. It would seem that this allegiance to democracy creates such an all-encompassing 'us' that one is hard put to point to a 'them' – an 'other' who stands opposed to it. The only catch, of course, is that democracy can mean quite different things to different people; the vision it embodies is far from unitary. Moreover, as societal and political conditions change, so too can the definitions of democracy – criteria found to be too ambitious can be modified.

The health of democracy in the course of the twentieth century has more and more been linked to the health of systems of communication, though of course democracy cannot be reduced to issues of the media. However, the dynamics of democracy are intimately linked to the practices of communication, and societal communication increasingly takes place within the mass media. In particular, it is television which has gained a prominent position within the political systems of the modern world. Concern for democracy automatically necessitates a concern about television, to which I turn in the two following chapters.

In this chapter, I begin with reflections on democracy as a model and as an ideal, based on some of the more recent literature. Thereafter, I briefly take up Habermas' much discussed theory and model of the public sphere. It is now well over three decades old, yet continues to inspire thinking about the relationship between the media and democracy. Then I review some of the major issues which have arisen in the criticisms levelled against it, thematizing the major points of contention. I will be returning to a number of these themes later in the book. Much of the debate around the public sphere has taken the form of media policy discussions. This is of the utmost importance and must continue. However, accompanying this frame must be a broader understanding of the social structural and sociocultural dimensions of the public sphere, and how these condition its possibilities and limits.

Desiring Democracy

The concept of democracy has an evocative rhetoric which embodies so many of our desires for the good society. Yet, as with many objects of desire, closer inspection can generate complication. Citing Dunn, Arnason (1990) speaks of two basic directions in democratic theory today: one which is 'dismally ideological', representing a conservative functionalization, and another which is 'fairly blatantly Utopian', which he sees as a romantic radicalism. This polarity certainly captures some of the theoretic tension: in the first case, for example, in mainstream political science we have a declining level of ambition regarding the criteria for democracy, where necessity becomes virtue. Thus, democracy is no longer seen as a system expressing the will of the people, but rather one which offers consumer choice in the rotation of élites. That this system seems to lead to declining levels of citizen participation is even hailed as an attribute of its success, in that it enhances its stability (Simonds, 1989, develops this view). Moreover, there is a closure at work, whereby the concept of democracy becomes identical with the current political systems of liberal capitalist societies. The Utopian antithesis, of course, is easily revealed to rest on a cheerful mixture of wishful thinking and sociological near-sightedness.

Rather than choosing between the two extremes, we would do well, carefully and flexibly, to situate ourselves between them. If we reject the identity logic that says what we now see is by definition the realization of democracy, we can still judiciously retain and expand upon that which is worth saving within the present arrangements. Indeed, looking further to the philosophical tradition of liberal democracy, many on the left (for example, Held, 1993; Keane, 1988; Mouffe, 1992b) emphasize the importance of preserving many of its ideals, the argument being that their implementation in practice would result in truly radical consequences. Thus, the left too can see in the tradition of liberal democracy important elements for setting limits on state power and for generally handling conflicts of interest and social antagonisms. Democratic procedures become a way to organize and mediate the varying competing interests, projects, and values within plural societies, while at the same time the perceived limits of the liberal tradition are identified and contested.

In addition, if the Utopian version at times loses contact with the problems of social reality, the importance of a vision – of a horizon – should not be undervalued. I will return to the theme of Utopian horizons later, but regarding the romantic view of democracy, I would just say that it is often associated with what is called its direct or participatory version. As a model for the political systems of advanced industrial societies it cannot, of course, be taken seriously. Even the small worlds of university democracy require mechanisms of representation: is there any faculty member prepared to sit on all the committees which are of relevance to him or her? Oscar Wilde once quipped that the problem with socialism is that it would take up too many free evenings; the same can be said for democracy in general.

Ideally we should have a blend of direct and representational mechanisms, as Held (1989) argues. Not only do elements of direct democracy, which involve face-to-face relations, enhance the responsiveness of the system itself, but – assuming they are sufficiently widespread – they also provide 'training grounds' for anchoring democracy in the experiences of lived reality. This sociocultural dimension, which encompasses values and a sense of identity as a citizen, is important both for the vitality of democracy as a system and the dynamics of the public sphere.

There are other difficulties as we probe deeper into democracy. Chaney (1993:115) takes up the built-in tension which appears when intellectuals talk about 'the people'. The rhetoric of political mobilization, whereby intellectuals incorporate themselves with the people, structures a dubious collective self-consciousness, for the people also remain to some extent an 'Other', an object of ethnographic curiousity. Simonds (1989) goes further, suggesting that when the people do make progressive political choices, they are lauded for their clear-sightedness and commitment; but when they manifest reactionary tendencies, they are portrayed by intellectuals as being duped by ideology, manipulated by the media, and seduced by politicians. In other words, the people are deemed free agents only when they happen to choose correctly, and are seen as victims, tools of sinister powers, when they veer towards reactionary politics. Now of course 'the people' manifest the philosophical ping-pong of free will versus determinism as much and as little as anybody else, including intellectuals. The problem is that the rhetoric of democracy, which celebrates the formation of popular will and the power of the people,

must also live with the insight that the majority may not always choose the enlightened path. A system which is fundamentally democratic may be deemed good on that formal criterion, but there is no guarantee that the decisions arrived at will be an expression of the 'good society'. There is always the ominous dark side of democracy; it does not ensure peace and light. In Eastern Europe today, for example, as many xenophobic and populist policies win acclaim, there must be a good number of former dissident intellectuals who feel disappointed by 'the people' whose liberty they struggled to achieve.

It is just this kind of democracy, without guarantees and without foundations, that Keane (1991) writes about. This agnostic view can be seen as a largely procedural version of democracy. It is not assumed that democracy is infallible: bad decisions cannot be precluded, but rather what is crucial is that any decision taken can, in principle, be reversed. Also, while democracy is generally understood to provide mechanisms for arriving at agreements, perhaps more importantly it must also offer mechanisms for handling disagreements, which in turn may warrant reversals of previous decisions. Democracy requires systems of rules and commitments to abide by them, but beyond that does not *per se* ensure that any particular set of values will prevail.

A similar agnosticism is reflected in Mouffe's (1993) arguments that we must free ourselves from the thought that we will ever reach a point in history characterized by pervasive social harmony. Expanding on themes she and Laclau developed earlier (Laclau and Mouffe, 1985), she asserts that there is no end to the political, no juncture awaiting us which will not be characterized by conflicts and antagonisms. In a similar vein, we will never arrive at a fully realized democracy, a millenium where everyone participates in will formation and where unanimity prevails (Mouffe, 1992a:Introduction). This is because social interests, as well as individual and collective identities, are relational and contextual; they are never static. New situations give rise to new interests and identities, new constellations of cooperation and antagonism. The varied conflicts emerging in the aftermath of the collapse of communism give ample evidence of this.

The challenge of such a perspective requires a sober balancing act, to acknowledge the Sysiphus-like character of our condition and *still* not give up on a moral vision. As Garnham (1992) pointedly comments in his evaluation of Habermas' notion of the public sphere, what we have here is not Utopianism but, on the contrary, a tragic view of life. Such a view understands and comes to terms with human limitations, the vicissitudes of history, and the misplaced hubris of certain strands of modern thought. It tries to generate 'a garden', knowing that it is in perpetual struggle with a wilderness which can encroach both from within and without. In regard to democracy more generally, Mouffe says that we should not dream about the disappearance of political conflict, but rather that political adversaries can meet each other in dialogue and not view each other as enemies to be liquidated. Like Keane and Held, Mouffe takes a procedural view of democracy, emphasizing the need for a common democratic culture expressed through loyalty to democratic values. Again, this is something which cannot be a trait of the system or a feature of structure; it must be anchored in the microworlds of people's everyday values and experience.

In western society, a fixation of the formal political system as the exclusive centre of politics continues to exist and continues to frame the common understanding of democracy. Yet, as Beck (1992), Eder (1993) and others point out, there is a growing loss of power by centralized political systems; changes in social structure are bringing about new forms of political culture. An unravelling of centralized systems politics correlates with transitions whereby many formerly non-political topics become, if not politicized, at least 'sub-political' or 'quasi-political'. The obvious manifestations of this, but not the only ones, are contemporary social movements, such as those of various feminist and ecological orientations. These developments tie in with another important yet difficult polarity with regard to democracy that many theorists (for example, Held, 1989; Keane, 1988; Cohen and Arato, 1992) have recently taken up, namely the relationship between the state and civil society, with particular emphasis on the status and position of civil society.

The concept of civil society is a contested one among contemporary theorists. Tester (1992), for example, sees civil society essentially as an incoherent expression of the antinomies of modernism: while it

served to kindle people's imaginations for a while, the idea of civil society disassembles with the failing self-confidence of modernity. In Tester's acerbic words, civil society today can feed our imagination only 'to the extent that it can continue to provide easy and comforting answers to easy and irrelevant questions' (Tester 1992:176). Walzer (1992), on the other hand, sees civil society as an absolutely essential 'space of uncoerced human association and also the set of relational networks – formed for the sake of family, faith, interest and ideology – that fill this space' (Walzer 1992:89). It is this line of thinking, further developed by Cohen and Arato (1992), which I find fruitful and to which I will return later in the book. For Walzer, civil society must serve as a buffer against single-minded and reductionistic visions of the good life, including political community, economic production, market activity and nationalism. Against their singularity, civil society stands as 'the realm of fragmentation and struggle but also of concrete and authentic solidarities' (Walzer 1992:97). It is the domain of association which exists basically for the sake of sociability, rather than for any goal of social formation.

An interesting aspect of Walzer's formulation is that he sees a paradox in civil society's relation to the state and to politics generally. He warns against seeing civil society in exclusively apolitical terms, yet civil society must not be reduced to the interaction of citizens within the state: 'Only a democratic state can create a democratic civil society; only a democratic civil society can sustain a democratic state' (Walzer 1992:104). Thus, citizens' political power is necessary, but not sufficient; there must be a viable social dimension beyond the political. While Walzer sees this as a paradox which he feels unable fully to resolve, one can also see this as an important theoretical step: treating the boundary between the political and the sociocultural in a fluid manner, seeing it as permeable and contestable, may well prove to be a crucial feature of democracy's future.

It is the interplay between the state and civil society which both Held (1989) and Keane (1988) emphasize. Each side, as Walzer suggests, is a precondition for the democratization of the other. This necessitates what Held calls the need for a 'double democratization'; our democratic desire requires a dual focus – a struggle on two fronts. Civil society is not to be reduced to a political arena, yet its democratization is a political project. It does not derive from or express any natural 'authentic humanity' and can certainly function in many repressive ways. It may well tend to hinder the conditions for political reflection and participation. If the state is too weak, it cannot foster democratization of civil society. If it is too strong, it becomes too interventionist; without a viable civil society, the state becomes too all-encompassing. The democratization of civil society has to do with the development of a democratic culture or mentality within the context of everyday life. Yet in the face of the state, civil society remains relatively powerless. The concept of civil society highlights among other things the inseparable links between the socio-cultural and the political. A rigid distinction between them, writes Hohendahl (1992:108), 'will necessarily constrain our understanding of those concerns that come under the category of the good life'.

At the level of theory, civil society has a particular relationship to the public sphere. In brief, civil society constitutes the sociocultural preconditions for a viable public sphere. The two categories are inseparable, but not identical: much of civil society, such as the whole realm of family relations, has little to do with the public sphere directly. Also, the public sphere encompasses the media, which are not easily situated within civil society. For now I want to turn my attention directly to the public sphere.

The Public Sphere as Historical Narrative

Notions of what is termed the public sphere, or public space, which thematize the role of interaction among citizens in the political process, can be traced back to the ancient Greeks. Notions of what is 'public' are of course premised on conceptions of what constitutes the 'private'. The public/private polarity has several overlapping historical strands, as I take up in Chapter 4. In recent modern political thought, however, the idea of 'public' in relation to the processes of democracy has been given ambitious formulations in the work of many writers; among the most prominent are Dewey (1954/1923), Arendt (1958), and Habermas (1989/1962). The concept is by no means identical in these three authors; they work out of different traditions and their approaches vary. The functions and

problematics of the mass media, for example, are explicitly central to Dewey and Habermas, but not to Arendt. There are similarities and differences in their political, sociological and historical horizons, but it is Habermas' version which is the most fruitful, despite a number of serious difficulties. Thus, my focus here will be on his concept of the public sphere and the response it has evoked. Specifically, my emphasis will be on his notion of the political public sphere, rather than the more broad cultural public sphere, where literature and the arts circulate. I will also consider some of his ideas regarding communicative rationality, which can be seen to extend and modify his earlier thinking on the public sphere. While I will focus on Habermas, the three authors can be and have been fruitfully compared; a recent effort in this regard, with an hermeneutic perspective on citizenship, is found in Alejandro (1993).

In this section I will first briefly summarize Habermas' (1989/1962) theory of the public sphere. This will only be a compressed synopsis; a comprehensive overview of this topic, containing many commentaries, is found in Calhoun (1992). From there I will review the major criticisms that have been levelled against it. Finally, I will present a scheme of four dimensions as a conceptual aid approaching the public sphere analytically.

In ideal terms, Habermas conceptualizes the public sphere as that realm of social life where the exchange of information and views on questions of common concern can take place so that public opinion can be formed. The public sphere 'takes place' when citizens, exercising the rights of assembly and association, gather as public bodies to discuss issues of the day, specifically those of political concern. Since the scale of modern society does not allow more than relatively small numbers of citizens to be physically co-present, the mass media have become the chief institutions of the public sphere. Yet Habermas' concept of the public sphere insists on the analytic centrality of reasoned, critical discourse. The public sphere exists, in other words, in the active reasoning of the public. It is via such discourse that public opinion is generated, which in turn is to shape the policies of the state and the development of society as a whole.

Of course this is not how society today actually operates. Habermas tells a story; it is a rather melancholic historical narrative in two acts. In the first act he portrays a fledgling bourgeois public sphere emerging under liberal capitalism in the eighteenth century. This 'category' of the public sphere is historically specific to the societal arrangements of Britain, France and Germany in this period. Prior to this, in the Middle Ages, there was no social space which could be called 'public' in contrast to 'private'; powerful feudal lords (as well as the Church) may have displayed themselves and their power to the populace, but this did not in any way constitute a public sphere in Habermas' sense. With the demise of feudalism, and the growth of national states, parliaments, commerce, the middle classes and, not least, printing, a public sphere began to take root in certain societies of Western Europe. This public sphere consisted of certain segments of the educated, propertied strata (almost exclusively male), and operated via such media as intellectual journals, pamphlets and newspapers, as well as in such settings as salons, coffee houses and clubs. This exchange of factual information, ongoing discussion and often heated debate was a new phenomenon, to which Habermas attributes much significance.

The second act traces the decline of the bourgeois public sphere in the context of advanced industrial capitalism and the social welfare state of mass democracy. With mass democracy, the public loses its exclusivity: its socio-discursive coherence comes apart as many less educated citizens enter the scene. The state, to handle the growing contradictions of capitalism, becomes more interventionist; the boundaries between public and private, both in political economic terms and in cultural terms, begin to dissipate. Large organizations and interest groups become key political partners with the state, resulting in a 'refeudalization' of politics which greatly displaces the role of the public. The increasing prevalence of the mass media, especially where the commercial logic transforms much of public communication into PR, advertising and entertainment, erodes the critical functions of the public. The public becomes fragmented, losing its social coherence. It becomes reduced to a group of spectators whose acclaim is to be periodically mobilized, but whose intrusion in fundamental political questions is to be minimized.

The story of the decline of the public sphere is still very much with us, continuously being replayed in updated versions by researchers and commentators. On the other hand, the gloomy portrayal of the modern public sphere's demise has been rejected in more optimistic corners as overstating the case. From yet other corners, Habermas' affirmative historical picture of the rise of the bourgeois public sphere has been contested. Some may even question the utility of the notion of the public sphere itself. However, I find the concept still to be a valid and helpful one. It points to those institutional constellations of the media and other fora for information and opinion – and the social practices around them – which are relevant for political life. That these institutional constellations and practices may be anaemic does not *per se* mean they are irrelevant.

The political public sphere constitutes a space – a discursive, institutional, topographical space – where people in their roles as citizens have access to what can be metaphorically called societal dialogues, which deal with questions of common concern: in other words, with politics in the broadest sense. This space, and the conditions for communication within it, are essential for democracy. This nexus of institutions and practices is an expression of public culture – visible and accessible sets of societal meanings and practices – and at the same time presupposes a public culture. One could say that a functioning public sphere is the fulfilment of the communicational requirements of a viable democracy. And like the concept of democracy, to use the notion of the public sphere does not suggest that what we see today is its consummate embodiment. Again, we would be advised to try to position ourselves between 'dismally ideological' and 'blatantly Utopian' views.

Habermas' intellectual roots lie with the Frankfurt School, and his theses about the public sphere became inspirational for much critical media research. But as Peters (1993) points out, his basic understanding of democracy and the public sphere are not totally remote from the Anglo-American liberal tradition and its notion of the marketplace of ideas. The liberal discourses (that is, the 'classic', not 'neo-liberal' ones) on media and democracy normally do not use the category 'public sphere', but they nonetheless underscore the citizens' need for useful and relevant journalism. With access to reliable information from a variety of perspectives, and a diversity of opinions on current affairs, citizens will arrive at their own views on important issues and thus prepare themselves for political participation. Both the public sphere and the marketplace of ideas can be seen as normative and very idealized pictures, easily contrasted with current realities.

But there are differences as well. Habermas situates the bourgeois public sphere within the history of capitalism, the rise of the interventionist state, and the emergence of the culture industries, emphasizing not least the difficult conditions which democracy requires and how the modern media can obstruct those conditions. Thus, we should not lose sight of the fact that the public sphere retains an anchoring in critical theory, and to use the term incorporates the media within a critical perspective on democracy (see, for example, Dahlgren and Sparks, 1991). If the shortcomings of the marketplace of ideas at best tends to generate calls for reforms in the conditions and operations of journalism, the disparity between the model and reality of the public sphere goes further. It evokes wide-ranging critical reflection on social structure, the concentration of power, cultural practices, and the dynamics of the political process.

Many have written on the inspirational quality of Habermas' text, lauding the weight he gives to the modern media, the historical perspective on their evolution, and, not least, his emphatic reminder of the twin dangers of state power and corporate control over the logic of their operations. Criticisms from many angles have also been forthcoming; many have pointed to the ambiguous status of the entire concept of the public sphere in Habermas' book, arguing that it appears both as a normative ideal to be strived for and as a manifestation of actual historical circumstances in early bourgeois Europe. In other words, how are we to view those social features in the late eighteenth and early nineteenth centuries whereby a relatively small group of economically and politically privileged men communicated with each other within the context of a small, budding press and the settings of salons, coffee houses and exclusive societies? Was this a genuine public sphere or merely an exercise in bourgeois self-delusion? Should we see this only as an emancipatory space or should we also see it in terms of Foucault's

perspective, as Verstraeten (1994) suggests: he makes the point that we can also look at the public sphere's social disciplining and exclusionary functions which stand in contrast to its liberatory aspects.

However, if we allow that the public sphere was not merely an ideological misconception but contained at least the germ of something new and progressive (which Habermas argues for by contrasting the bourgeois public sphere with previous historical versions of what constituted publicness), it was in any case very much grounded in a notion of small-scale print media and rational, conversational interaction among a small sector of, at that time, much smaller populations. Where does that leave us in the age of massive-scale societies and electronic media? If the public sphere today is so dominated by the mass media, what does this suggest for the viability of the larger analytical category of civil society? If we do not simply equate the public sphere with the mass media, there remain many questions for democracy about the nature and extent of face-to-face communication.

Feminists have criticized not only the actual exclusion of women in the bourgeois public sphere, but also Habermas' failure to make a critical point of this in his evaluation. Such feminist encounters with Habermas' work (see especially Fraser, 1987, 1992) merge with the larger critical feminist projects illuminating the gender partiality within the public/private distinction of liberal theory and within political philosophy more generally; at bottom this project has to do with reconstructing the concept of democracy in the light of feminist analysis (see Pateman, 1987, 1988, 1992; Nicholson, 1992; Phillips, 1991,1993; Bock and James, 1992; Jónasdóttir, 1991; Brown, 1988; Elshtain, 1993). Feminist as well as other writers have taken up the overly rationalistic view of human communication in Habermas' work. This rationalist quality of Habermas' understanding of discourse becomes more explicit and central in his later work, particularly in his major theoretical contribution from the early 1980s, *The Theory of Communicative Action* (1984, 1987). It is understandable that critics take into account the perspectives from this later study, and commentaries on Habermas' view of communication often connect the two phases of his work.

Habermas (1992a) responded to these and many other criticisms of his *Structural Transformation of the*

Public Sphere (1989/1962) in the context of a conference. He expressed appreciation for the interest and
critical insights of the contributors, while reminding
them that the book came out in the early 1960s. He
self-critically assured his colleagues that were he to
write the book today, he would make many changes,
yet felt justified in asserting its continued usefulness,
despite its limitations. It is hard not to agree. If the
concept of the public sphere is one which hovers
between philosophical and historical groundings, as
one of the conference contributors (Hohendahl,
1992) suggested, we can perhaps turn this into a
strength. We can take the idea – the vision of a public
sphere – as inspirational, yet accept that there is no
single universal model which is possible or even suitable for all historical circumstances. The task becomes
to try to devise new forms and strategies. If modesty
must prevail on our social and historical analyses, we
should allow ourselves to be ambitious and expansive
in our conceptual and normative thinking.

Four Dimensions

As we can already see, critical encounters with
Habermas' conception of the public sphere have come
from a variety of directions. I cannot attend to all the
issues here; for example, one question to which many
have pointed has to do with his historical interpretation
which ignores alternative public spheres which functioned parallel with the bourgeois one. But by synthesizing a number of key points in the commentaries – I
make particular use of texts by Garnham (1992), Peters
(1993), Fraser (1992), Thompson (1990) – we can conveniently sort the critical themes and questions into
four areas: media institutions, media representation,
social structure and sociocultural interaction. This in
turn offers us a framework for conceptualizing four
analytic dimensions of the public sphere. Each dimension serves as an entry port to sets of issues about the
public sphere, both theoretical and conceptual questions as well as empirical and evaluative ones about its
actual functioning. No one dimension stands on its
own; all four interlock with each other and constitute
reciprocal conditions for one another.

The dimension of media institutions, their organization, financing, regulation, and the dimension of
media representation, chiefly in regard to journalistic

coverage, are the two which generally receive most
attention. Both figure at the centre of considerable
policy debate. The dimension of social structure
points to the broader horizon of factors which constitute the historical conditions and institutional milieu
of the public sphere. These structural elements from
the broader institutional arrangements of society
include social stratification, power alignments, and,
not least, the state. Economic, political and legal
aspects are included here. Also, the nature and quality
of the entire educational system, and its place in the
social order, becomes relevant in this regard. This is a
topic I cannot pursue here, but the role of education
in shaping the analytic and communicative competencies of the citizenry is crucial for the character of
the public sphere, despite the inevitable ideological
dimensions of schooling. Finally, sociocultural interaction refers to non-mediated face-to-face encounters between citizens, to relevant aspects of
subjectivity and identity processes, and also to the
interface of media and citizens, that is, the processes
of reception. Civil society composes the space for
much of the public sphere beyond the media; without
attention to this interactionist dimension of the public
sphere, the whole conceptual foundation of democracy is undermined.

The dimension of social structural factors defines
not least the 'political ecology' of the media, setting
boundaries for the media's institutional and organizational profile, as well as for the nature of the information and forms of representation and expression
which may circulate. Obviously the social structural
dimension also impacts on the patterns of sociocultural interaction. Thus, social structure complexly
constitutes a set of conditions for the public sphere
which can also be charted via the three other dimensions. Social structure is no doubt the dimension
which is conceptually the most difficult to deal with,
since it is potentially so vast. In fact, at some point in
the analysis, social structure must be put in brackets if
we are not to not lose our specific focus on the public
sphere. However, its role must not be lost from view.
That the public sphere cannot be seen as a space
operating in isolation from all other social, political
and economic domains, as if it were a self-contained
entity, is one of Habermas' central points. To understand the public sphere under any specific historical

circumstances requires taking into account the larger societal figurations which both comprise its space and constitute the preconditions for its functioning.

A society where democratic tendencies are weak and the structural features of society are highly inegalitarian is not going to give rise to healthy institutional structures for the public sphere. Such structural features translate into mechanisms whereby the basic patterns of power and social hierarchy detrimentally shape the character of the public sphere. These mechanisms operate by institutionally *delimiting* the public sphere as such; for instance, the state, together with vested interests, can pursue media policies which hinder the flow of relevant information and constrict the range of opinion. Alternatively, such mechanisms may operate *through* the public sphere to hinder democratic development, for example 'news plants', disinformation, trivialization. Further, power and social hierarchy can shape the public sphere at the level of interaction, impacting on the sites and settings where such contact takes place.

Media Institutions

Policy issues around media institutions and their output are of course the most tangible and immediate expression of political attention to the public sphere. Such policy issues include the organization, financing, and legal frameworks of the media. The legal frameworks encompass not only questions of ownership, control, procedures for licensing, rules for access, and so on, but also the freedoms and the constraints on communication. The public sphere's entwinement with the state and with society's overall political situation comes most clearly to the fore in the case of broadcasting. Such policy is shaped to a great extent by forces and actors located within the state and the economy; progressive policy efforts attempt to steer this influence in democratically productive directions, and also aim to enhance the influence of the public itself in shaping broadcasting (Raboy, 1994).

Habermas' image of the public sphere lurks beneath the surface of many progressive interventions into media policy issues (see Raboy, 1991; Raboy, 1994); however, all such efforts do not have to depend on his conceptualizations. The loosely defined movement for democratic communication and information

(see, for example, Splichal and Wasko, 1993), which has been active at local levels as well as in the international debates over the New World Information Order during the past two decades, emphasizes a similar vision of the public sphere, even if its vocabulary differs somewhat. As Wasko and Mosco put it:

> Thus the concept of democractic communications is two-fold . . .:
>
> 1. *democratization* of media and information technologies, or participatory and alternative media forms and democratic uses of information technologies; and
>
> 2. *democratization through* media and information technologies, or media strategies of various social movements and groups devoted to progressive issues and social change.
>
> (1992:7)

In Europe, the most explicit appropriation of Habermas' public sphere concept has been within the British debates where it has been utilized as a platform from which to defend public service broadcasting. There was a strong effort from the left to associate public service broadcasting with the realization of the public sphere, and to portray commercial broadcasting and the market model of financing as a serious threat to it (Garnham, 1983; Scannell, 1989; R. Collins, 1993). However, critiques of public service broadcasting were also forthcoming, even from the left. Across Western Europe, these institutions were perceived as paternalistic in their programme output, they tended to ignore the growing pluralistic and multicultural character of their own societies, and they were generally stagnant and in need of creative renewal.

However, in the 1980s the ideological bathwater was accompanied by the critical baby when the political climate began to support policies which strived to subvert the very principles and goals of public service. The commitment to serve and represent the interests of *all* the citizenry was increasingly displaced by policies that aimed to introduce and/or expand the commercial broadcasting sector. For the most part this has not enhanced the development of democracy. While there is of course much variation among the different countries, it can be said that, generally, the increased commercialization of television has not augmented the diversity of programming, whether judged in terms of form or content. On the contrary, programming has tended to follow the classic logic of homogenization and has been aimed at the large, general market, with the output of all channels becoming increasingly standardized (see, for example, Achille and Bueno, 1994 for a discussion of these trends).

In Sweden, for example, the public service channels still retain programmes aimed at specialized groups within society, but they also feel they must compete with the commercial channels. They do this by using some programming which is largely identical to the broadly popular fare of the commercial channels, thereby further reducing the overall diversity available. The immediate policy danger is that, with increased homogenization, the public will begin asking why they should pay a licence fee for channels that provide an output not significantly different from that of those which are supported by advertising. The long-term dilemma is that the remaining diversity becomes replaced by mere repetitive abundance, and that abundance will be low on programming which strengthens the public sphere.

The ideational reconstruction of public broadcasting as a goal is at present greatly hampered by the prevailing political climate which puts the tradition of the social democratic welfare state on the defensive and believes that social policy issues are best resolved by market forces. However, there are further practical difficulties ahead, aside from the political climate. The economics of public service are highly problematic in a period where costs continue to rise rapidly, and where a political ceiling seems to have been reached on the size of licence fees. Along with the need for the internal institutional renewal mentioned above, there is also the problem that public service broadcasting is so strongly linked to the nation-state. As a political unit, the nation-state is by no means on its death bed, but the growth of transnational economic and financial flows, coupled with migration and other forms of globalization, have contributed to eroding much of its former sphere of power. As many have noted, the nation-state is in some ways both too small and too large a unit to deal effectively with many of the newer historical realities.

Technological innovation in transnational television cannot be ignored: how should public service television position itself *vis-à-vis* the growth of satellite channels? There have been calls taking the public service model into the international arena and developing a pan-European public sphere based on non-commercial broadcasting (for example, Venturelli, 1993). However, the historical, sociological and political obstacles to a European public sphere based on public service television are not to be underestimated, as Schlesinger (1994) and Hjarvard (1993) clearly demonstrate. Not least is the question of what is the political entity to which the viewers of European television would be the polity? The European Union is hardly a political institution where popular will is invited and mediated to a responsive decision-making body. Transplanting the public sphere to a global context also involves enormous financial as well as regulatory considerations. Porter (1993), for example, takes up some of the complicated legal issues surrounding the rights of viewers which are involved in transfrontier television.

We should recall that the traditional arguments in support of public service broadcasting were premised in part on the airwaves being a scarce resource, and thus requiring state regulation. This logic becomes somewhat eclipsed in the new media environment, where technologies are not dependent on a space in the spectrum. Also, traditional media like the press must be incorporated into policy thinking which aims at enhancing the public sphere. Public service broadcasting still must play a central role, but the ideal of the public sphere requires a broader perspective which can encompass the entire media landscape (see Curran, 1991, for an ambitious attempt in this direction). Thus, the state has less to say about broadcasting specifically, as it allows television and radio to be run by private concerns, but must instead tackle the overall structural media situation, such as issues of concentration and cross ownership. In a sense, what is needed is re-regulation, to counteract the negative aspects of market forces and to optimize the positive role they can play.

Media Representation

The dimension of representation directs our attention to media output. It is concerned with what the media portray, how topics are presented, the modes of discourse at work, and the character of debates and discussion. In empirical terms the concern is largely with journalism, as it is broadly understood – news reporting is but one of several journalistic genres. Representation has to do with both the informational and extra-informational aspects of media output, such as the symbolic and rhetorical. Moreover, as I take up in a later chapter, all the non-journalistic media output takes on relevance as a semiotic environment of the journalistic material, as well as of our everyday lives more generally. Analysing what comes out of the media has been the dominant focus of media research through the decades, and the wide-ranging variety of methodological tools and analytic constructs mobilized for this purpose is generally familiar to researchers.

The dimension of representation in the public sphere points to such basic questions as *what* should be selected for portrayal and *how* should it be presented. The answers to these basic questions, which lie at the core of the journalistic profession, can only have rather broad, guide-line formulations; new events, ongoing developments and historical circumstances demand that the answers always remain tentative. The criteria relating to media representations should only have an 'until further notice' character, since they must respond to an ever-changing social reality. Ideally, within journalism, self-monitoring and self-reflection would always be simmering just below the surface, ready to be actualized. We know from the sociology of newswork, however, that the organizational practices of journalism – like all other bureaucratic structures – tend to deflect such problematization and strive to 'routinize the unexpected' (see Tuchman, 1978).

All media representation potentially can become an object of critical analysis – from whatever perspective one is working from. Research which shares the organizational frames of reference of journalism can focus on the quality of coverage of particular issues, invoking such criteria as objectivity and bias. Though in academic quarters these seem to be increasingly eclipsed by newer analytical strategies (see Hackett, 1984), fundamental issues of truth and accuracy can never become wholly irrelevant. The media themselves can be manipulated by powerful and organized sources, which can result in distortions and disinformation. (Ericson, et al., 1989). Alternatively, from a critique of ideology perspective there is much to be said about media representation; from Baudrillardian theory one can explore the theme of simulacra, and so on. For television analysis in particular, there are now a number of methodological trajectories (see Allen, 1992).

Also, we should bear in mind that television representation is not just constructed portrayals, visual stories about what is happening in the world. As Scannell (1991) reminds us, television's representations consist to a great extent of talk. This talk is public talk, usually taking place in a studio. It consists of people talking among themselves, but its 'communicative intentionality' is such that it is aimed at the television audience beyond the studio. Indeed, it seems at present that 'talk television' is expanding, no doubt partly in response to economic factors (it is a relatively inexpensive format), and figures prominently in the growing popularization of television journalism.

From the standpoint of the public sphere, there is a need for continual monitoring of what goes on in the media, analysing specific cases and routine representations, while at the same time it is important not to lose sight of the larger, more theoretical issues. Perhaps most central is the question of whether representation via the media is in itself at all compatible with the notion of a public sphere. Peters (1993) takes this up as a difficulty in Habermas, whose public sphere model is very wedded to the notion of face-to-face interaction. Despite the centrality of the early press to Habermas' understanding of the bourgeois public sphere, he reveals a distrust of mediated representation, a sense that it is an obstacle to discursive rationality and communicative authenticity. We can safely assume that the mass media are not about to fade from the scene – and in fact they continue to grow – and that just as representation in democracy is unavoidable, so is representation in communication. Neither by itself necessarily means the demise of civilization, even though both generate special problems. The question is how we can make best use of representation for democratic purposes.

Other commentaries on Habermas have taken up the issue of the desirability and feasibility of shared discourse rules in media representations, that is, the tension between universalistic and particularistic communicative logics. Should there be one overarching mode of discursive reason, one key code of communicative logic which is to prevail above all others, or is a multiplicity of different, but equal modes to be fostered? This may seem like a rather academic issue, but in the context of multicultural and multilingual societies, where identity politics are gaining in importance, it raises very concrete questions not only about modes of media discourse but also flows into policy issues in culture and education, as well as the criteria for citizenship (see Taylor, 1992).

A related but perhaps even more pointed issue has to do with rational/analytic versus affective/aesthetic modes of communication, a topic which takes on particular relevance with regard to television. There is often a questionable assumption at work, whereby politics is analytically associated with rationality, and entertainment is seen exclusively as pertaining to emotionality. Controversial questions arise: Can television communicate in a 'rational' manner (however that may be defined)? Should it always strive to? Does it inevitably portray even the most serious issues of public concern largely in terms of emotionality? Is the 'entertainment bias' in television so strong that it unavoidably trivializes everything it touches, as some diatribes claim (for example, Postman, 1985)? And even if we assume that there are 'good journalistic programmes', (again, however this may be defined) on television, can they really be very meaningful if they are surrounded by programming and advertising whose chief aims are to capture and hold our attention by providing escapist pleasure? In other words, would a few oases of rationality make much difference in a media culture, the chief characteristics of which are arational?

Social Structures

Returning to Habermas' model, commentators have raised a number of theoretical questions to do with the public sphere's structural dimension. A fundamental one, which Garnham (1992) emphasizes, has to do with scale and boundaries. He makes the indisputable point that there must a coherence, a goodness of fit, between political entities and the scale and boundaries of the public sphere. The difficulties of attaining this in the modern world via policy strategies should be obvious. However, it is precisely this evolution of political realities which must be incorporated into policy considerations: how to structure a public sphere which is congruent with the processes of political decision making and the consequences of the decisions taken. In terms of democratic theory, Held (1993) discusses how, currently, global realities are increasingly problematizing traditional conceptions of political boundaries and entities, and the challenge that this implies for how we are to view the structures and processes of democracy. Held and many other commentators note especially the processes of globalization, whereby some of the traditional structures, functions and *raisons d'être* of the nation-state are being eclipsed by transnational processes, regional developments and local decentralization.

Another issue has to do with fitting the public sphere to the complex social structures of modern society. In short, is it better with a centralized or a pluralistic model of the public sphere? Can everyone be accommodated within one and the same public sphere, or is such a goal oppressive? Can factors such as class, gender and race, and their cultural correlates, be disregarded? Such differences begin with the fundamental features of social structure. These are not easily bridged by media discourses. Or should precisely such bridging be seen as a goal of a centralized public sphere? It is alleged that arguing for a 'one size fits all' public sphere subordinates minorities to the discursive and social power of dominant groups. The counter argument is that political decisions taken within a political entity objectively can affect everyone within it, regardless of their subjective positions, and to construct separatist public sphere enclaves is to foster discursive ghettos which are detrimental to democracy.

Now, few would argue that everyone should or even can always participate in the same societal conversation, and it may be in part a semantic question whether one argues for a single large pluralistic public sphere which connects many smaller discrete arenas or whether one posits that a multiplicity of many smaller public spheres is what constitutes the public sphere as a whole. However, the two formulations may well capture differing emphases or perspectives, and the tension between the whole and the parts remains a central policy problematic. Public spheres must arise partly out of necessity, in response to particular circumstances. Media institutions are, in theory, accessible to constructive policy intervention – if, of course, the political interest can be mobilized. Social structure, however, reflects the slowly shifting complexities of a societal totality which increasingly defies both coherent conceptualization and decisive steering. If the public sphere generally, like democracy, is viewed as a political accomplishment, it will be understood that its boundaries, even its forms, must remain at some level open and contestable.

Interaction: Social Bonds and Social Construction

If we think in terms of the 'space' in which 'public sphering' gets done, we can readily see that while the media constitute much of this space (as discursive, semiotic space), the space of the public sphere is – and must be – larger than that of media representations. It must also include sociocultural interaction. This dimension takes us into the realm of people's encounters and discussions with each other, with their collective sense-making and their cultural practices. The processes and setting of media reception are also a part of this dimension of interaction: the interface between media and its audiences. Reception studies are normally cast in terms of people making sense of the output, however, I would also underscore the importance of basic functions such as comprehension and recall (see Höijer, 1992). Beaud (1994) problematizes the whole idea of a televisual public sphere, given the apparent amnesia among viewers which he sees deriving from televisual discourse.

Even if television in many cases is a totally individual affair, the experiences gained from viewing are carried over into social interaction. And where viewing is a social activity, done together with others, talk about the programming can take place simultaneously with the transmission as well as directly afterwards. Thus, while most viewing still takes place in the home, which is traditionally seen as a private space, this domestic site of 'mediated publicness' is where talk about public matters may begin – hence my assertion that reception is often a first step of interaction. Finally, interaction has to do not only with what gets said between people, but also the processes

of intersubjectivity and identity which arise in this interaction, and which in turn shape a sense of belonging and a capacity for participation in society.

While reception analysis is prominently on the media research agenda, interaction is the dimension of the public sphere which has often been given somewhat short shrift in terms of theoretical attention. Mediacentric perceptions tend at times to ignore the issue of what takes place between citizens. It is useful to compare Habermas with a liberal American writer such as Dewey (1954/1923), whose thinking on the distinction between audience and public is echoed in the influential work of the Chicago School of sociology (McIntyre, 1987). Both Habermas and Dewey argue that a 'public' should be conceptualized as something other than just a media audience.

A public, according Habermas and Dewey, exists as discursive interactional processes; atomized individuals, consuming media in their homes, do not comprise a public, nor do they tend to contribute much to the democratization of civil society. There are of course strong interests in society which have a stake in defining 'the public' in terms of aggregate statistics of individual behaviour and opinion; such approaches certainly do have their uses from the standpoints of marketing, the official political system, and not least from that of media institutions themselves. However, from the standpoints of democracy, it is imperative not to lose sight of the classic idea that democracy resides, ultimately, with citizens who engage in talk with each other.

The theme of interaction is hardly a new one: the early sociological formulations about the processes and effects of mass communication underscored the 'two step flow' and the notion of intermediary 'opinion leaders' (see Katz and Lazarsfeld, 1955). Obviously not all social interaction can be treated as manifestations of a well-functioning public sphere; there must be a focus on politics and current affairs – a quality of publicness attained by people interacting in their roles as citizens. Even if we find it harder these days to mark boundaries and maintain distinctions, the public sphere must have politics as its chief horizon, even if we allow that this category is always potentially in tension with the prepolitical and the cultural.

For convenience, we can specifiy three areas of analytic concern within the interactional dimension of the public sphere: discursive, spatial, and communal. The discursive has to do with the nature of the talk which circulates between citizens. (This category would also include non-verbal forms of interpersonal communication.) There are many topics which can be raised in regard to the discursive aspects of interaction; perhaps most relevant for the public sphere is the question of discursive resources and repertoires: what are the ways of meaning-making at work within given sectors of the populace and what bearing do they have on political competence? This evokes in part the discussion above on universalistic versus particularistic discourse rules in media representations; regardless of possible inherent suppressive aspects of the dominant modes of political communication, if one does not have access to them or at least to their translatable equivalence, one is excluded from the processes of democratic participation.

The spatial refers to the sites and settings of social interaction. Where do people meet as citizens? What factors foster or hinder their interaction in these spaces? The nature of urban/suburban architecture, the fear of crime, home media technology and other factors become relevant in this regard. Such themes take us into several subfields of sociology, urban anthropology, as well as social geography. The spatial is seldom separable from the discursive: both together serve to define contexts and occasions. Thus, in terms of the media, Sennett (1977) sees them as reinforcing the retreat to domestic space and contributing to the decline of public culture. That much public space and interaction is dedicated to consumer practices and discourses becomes significant for the public sphere, since the role of citizen is displaced by that of the consumer; the cultural assumptions surrounding shopping malls, for example, do not make them prime settings for the public sphere.

Space is of course conceptual as well as strictly topographical. Certainly the newer electronic interactive media offer a new version of social space. The experimental electronic town meetings on cable systems have been one manifestation of this newer space. Another manifestion is the public network which is set up as an ever-present citizen resource: The Public Electronic Network (PEN) in Santa Monica, California, is the first such publicly funded electronic network, and initial evaluation suggests that one of its advantages may be that it facilitates interaction between people who would not normally have much contact with each other when they share the same physical space (van Tassel, 1994). Still more dramatic is the expansion of the Internet, with its data bases, e-mail, electronic bulletin boards and other forms of virtual reality. This cyberspace, the most placeless of spaces, can be put to many uses which can contribute to the public sphere, and no doubt its relevance will continue to grow. However, the battles for political control and economic exploitation of the Internet are already well under way. (For an American introduction to the Internet, written in a popular style which also takes up the issues of citizenship and the public sphere, see Rheingold, 1994.) However, despite all the possible democratic uses and advantages of virtual reality, I would still argue that a democratic public sphere, and a democratic social order more generally, cannot exist exclusively in cyberspace: there must be face-to-face interaction as well.

The communal aspect refers to the nature of the social bonds between citizens. Sennett (1977) has argued that in the modern era, the 'ideology of intimacy', has contributed to the demise of public culture: public space becomes dead space because we have the expectation that the most desirable or valid form of relations between people is one of closeness. Yet the stranger is (increasingly) perceived as a possible threat. This tendency undercuts the opportunities for people to meet as citizens and exchange views. The nature of what the social bond should be between citizens has been a point of contention within political philosophy, but it is clear that some minimal form of collective identity, what Vico (quoted in Shotter, 1993a: 54) calls the *sensus communis*, is required. Even if it is de-emphasized, no democratic order will work without some shared sense of commonality among its members. Talk both manifests and presupposes some kinds of social bond between citizens.

I would make one final but important theoretic point regarding the dimension of interaction: talk is constructive. It is the foundation of the social order of everyday life, as the various social interactionist theorists have argued (Shotter, 1993a, offers a vigorous argument of the thesis of social construction via conversation). Interaction has traditionally been seen as fundamental to human existence, and rightly so. Even our identities, our 'selves', emerge via social interaction (see Burkitt, 1991). Through talk, the social world is linguistically constructed and maintained, albeit in dialectical interplay with the more structural features of society. Interaction is what makes the category of subjectivity come socially alive: subjectivity becomes a moment – a partial element – of what are fundamentally processes of inter-subjectivity.

Talk can generate the unforeseen. From a constructivist perspective, talk represents the ongoing production of the social world, the perpetual making, circulating and remaking of meaning. It is not simply the expression of fixed inner subjective states, but rather the mutual creation of intersubjectivity, whose outcome is never fully predetermined. Our minds are not like computers, with the same inert data available for retrieval in any circumstance. The common notion of opinion as simply something existing in people, to be captured by multiple choice questions, is indeed misguided, for it ignores the dynamics whereby meaning circulates, is acted upon, and revised, to result in political interpretation and will formation (see Herbst, 1993, for a recent overview of popular perspectives on the concept of public opinion; Price, 1992, discusses the evolution and some of the current difficulties of the concept; and Steiner, 1994, presents three authors who take fresh critical looks at public opinion). We must view our inner realities as always partially potential: they become actualized through concrete interaction with other people. While our subjectivities tend to follow patterns, they can never be seen as predetermined.

Thus in terms of the public sphere, there must be interaction to permit and foster the *processes* of political sense-making. The centrality of social interaction through talk, and the concept of the public as discursive interaction which takes place in particular settings, must inform any theorizing about the public sphere (see also Lenart, 1994, for an update on the social science approach to social interaction as a factor between the individual and media impact).

Subjectivity, Identity, Interaction

Sociocultural interaction has many facets, and I have mentioned that I see subjectivity and identity as two important aspects. At a common sense level,

subjectivity has to do with what goes on in people's heads and this is of obvious relevance for the public sphere: opinions and attitudes, values and norms, knowledge and information, frames of reference and schemes of relevance, world views, and so on, are all pertinent. These and related notions, which can be expressed in a variety of vocabularies from different traditions, are central features in the processes by which citizens participate in the communicative dynamics of democracy.

At another level, we may consider the general forms of collective subjectivity that prevail within various groups and classes in society at certain times. Certain world views, frames of reference, ideological understandings, and so on are sufficiently widespread and deeply embedded in various sectors of the population that they constitute important cultural patterns for those collectivities. Such forms of mass subjectivity may well be linked to contemporary trends in media output. More specifically, we might find that certain media discourses foster or hinder certain subject positions, and that these textual subject positions, inscribed in media discourses, actually do have some correlation with social subjects. Thus, the discourses of advertising, which permeate the semiotic environment of the public sphere, encourage consumption and invite a consumerist subject position, which certainly manifests itself in a general way in social subjectivity. Ours is a consumer culture, even if most advertising campaigns do not attain the intended success and even if many people are cynical about commercialism; the commodification of everyday practices and social relations is beyond dispute (see Willis, 1991, for an interesting analysis of the interface of advertising discourses and daily life).

Even the nature of the mass mediated public sphere itself can be examined from the standpoint of what forms of subjectivity it fosters. People do not simply emerge out of their private spheres as fully-fashioned individuals – as wholly competent citizens – and then leap into the public sphere. The media, not least those elements directly relevant to the public sphere, contribute to the shaping of subjectivity. The issue of ideology is always hovering in the wings, awaiting its cue.

The work of Negt and Kluge (1993/1972) can be seen in this light. Their book is more than just a commentary on Habermas; it represents a full-scale theoretical alternative. The very title of their book, *The Public Sphere and Experience*, defines a central dynamic. The original German word, *Erfahrung*, does not resonate with full equivalence in the English term 'experience'; the latter carries with it – among other things – empiricist associations, as Hansen (1993) points out in a text which also appears as a foreword to the English translation of Negt and Kluge's book. She writes that '*Erfahrung* is seen as the matrix that mediates individual perception and social horizons of meaning' (Hansen, 1993:188). Now, while the Marxism of Negt and Kluge remains within the older analytic framework of a philosophy of consciousness, and while nuances inevitably get skewed in translation, I would suggest that the term 'subjectivity' corresponds at least in part with the dimension that they emphasize. Thus, the public sphere, and the media more generally, can be understood in terms of their role in the organization of collective and individual subjectivity.

In addition, subjectivity also includes a particular aspect which is of importance for the public sphere, namely that of identity. Our sense of who we are, to ourselves and to others, takes on relevance for the public sphere because it shapes the way in which we participate, and may well determine if we participate or not. Specifically, this has to do with the nature of our identity as citizens, and what this means in the practical circumstances of political discussion and activity. For active participants in the public sphere, how, for example, do they balance their identities as citizens, which implies some sort of universality and commitment to the common good, to a 'civic culture', with the particular identities which emerge from pursuing specific interests? Or, from a different angle, the public sphere is not just a 'marketplace of ideas' or an 'information exchange depot', but also a major societal mechanism for the production and circulation of culture, which frames and gives meaning to our identities. How do the identities thus fostered relate to the vision of democracy?

More pointedly, if we link the pervasive commodification of public culture with the notion of citizenship as an identity, we see how, at the level of political ideology, forces on the right have been defining citizenship precisely in consumerist terms. I would suggest that one of the chief ideological tensions

today is situated in this force field; what is at stake is whether people's identities as citizens can largely be reduced to and framed in consumer terms or whether some sense of the political – beyond market logics – can be retained in people's conceptions of citizenship.

These brief glimpses of the four dimensions of the public sphere should suggest something of the vast array of issues involved. If Habermas' theoretical step in conceptualizing the public sphere was an immensely valuable step, no one, not even Habermas himself, would argue that we should remain fully within those initial formulations. We must see the public sphere partly as an ideal we aim for a direction charted. It always remains (in the best of cases) a political accomplishment, ever in need of renewal, and we should avoid clutching an historically frozen model. It is an historically contingent space, negotiated and contested, situated at the interface of an array of vectors. It is structured by macrosocietal factors and shaped by the mass media, especially television. Yet, it is also socio-culturally constructed by the discursive practices of civil society.

References

Achille, Y. and Bueno, J.J. (1994) *Les télévisions publiques en quête d'avenir*. Grenoble: Presses Universitaires de Grenoble.

Alejandro, R. (1993) *Hermeneutics, Citizenship and the Public Sphere*. Albany: State University of New York Press.

Allen, R.C. (ed.) (1992) *Channels of Discourse, Reassembled*. London: Routledge.

Arendt, H. (1958) *The Human Condition*. Chicago: University of Chicago Press.

Arnason, J.P. (1990) 'The theory of modernity and the problematic of democracy' in P. Beilharz, G. Robinson and J. Rundell (eds), *Between Totalitarianism and Postmodernism: A Thesis Eleven Reader*. London: MIT Press.

Beaud, P. (1994) ' "Medium without message? Public opinion, in spite of all" '. *Réseaux: The French Journal of Communication* 2(2).

Beck, U. (1992) *Risk Society*. London: Sage.

Bock, G. and James, S. (eds) (1992) *Beyond Equality and Difference: Citizenship. Feminist Politics and Female Subjectivity*. London: Routledge.

Brown, Wendy (1988) *Manhood and Politics: A Feminist Reading in Political Theory*. Totowa, NJ: Rowman and Littlefield.

Burkitt, I. (1991) *Social Selves*. London: Sage.

Calhoun, C. (ed.) (1992) *Habermas and the Public Sphere*. London: MIT Press.

Chaney, D. (1993) *Fictions of Collective Life: Public Drama in Late Modern Culture*. London: Routledge.

Cohen, J. and Arato, A. (1992) *Civil Society and Political Theory*. London: MIT Press.

Collins, R. (1993) 'Public service versus the market ten years on: reflections on Critical Theory and the debate on broadcasting policy in the UK'. *Screen* 34(3).

Curran, J. (1991) 'Mass media and democracy: a reappraisal' in J. Curran and M. Gurevitch (eds), *Mass Media and Society*. London: Edward Arnold.

Dahlgren, Peter and Sparks, Colin (eds) (1991) *Communication and Citizenship*. London: Routledge.

Dewey, J. (1954/1923)) *The Public and its Problems*. Chicago: Swallow Press.

Eder, K. (1993) *The New Politics of Class: Social Movements and Cultural Dynamics in Advanced Societies*. London: Sage.

Elshtain, J.B. (1993) *Public Man, Private Woman: Women in Social and Political Thought*. 2nd edn. Princeton, NJ: Princeton University Press.

Ericson, R.V., Baranek, B.M. and Chan, J.B.L. (1989) *Negotiating Control: A Study of News Sources*. Milton Keynes: Open University Press.

Fraser, N. (1987) 'What's critical about critical theory? The case of Habermas and gender' in S. Benhabib and D. Cornell (eds), *Feminism as Critique*. Cambridge: Polity Press.

Fraser, N. (1992) 'Rethinking the public sphere: a contribution to the critique of actually existing democracy' in C. Calhoun, (ed.), *Habermas and the Public Sphere*. London: MIT Press.

Garnham, N. (1983) 'Public service versus the market'. *Screen* 5(1).

Garnham, N. (1992) 'The media and the public sphere' in C. Calhoun (ed.), *Habermas and the Public Sphere*. Cambridge, MA and London: MIT Press.

Habermas, J. (1984, 1987/1981) *The Theory of Communicative Action*. 2 vols. Cambridge: Polity Press.

Habermas, J. (1989/1962) *Structural Transformation of the Public Sphere*. Cambridge: Polity Press.

Habermas, J. (1992a) 'Further reflections on the public sphere' in C. Calhoun (ed.), *Habermas and the Public Sphere*. London: MIT Press.

Hackett, R.A. (1984) 'Decline of a paradigm? Bias and objectivity in news media studies'. *Critical Studies in Mass Communication* 1(3).

Hansen, M. (1993) 'Unstable mixtures, dilated spheres: Negt and Kluge's *The Public Sphere and Experience*, twenty years later'. *Public Culture* 5:179–212.

Held, D. (1989) *Political Theory and the Modern State*. Cambridge: Polity Press.

Held, D. (1991) 'Between state and civil society: citizenship' in G. Andrews (ed.), *Citizenship*. London: Lawrence and Wishart.

Held, D. (1993) 'Democracy: from city states to a cosmopolitan order?' in D. Held (ed.), *Prospects for Democracy*. Cambridge: Polity Press.

Herbst, S. (1993) 'The meaning of public opinion: citizens' constructions of political reality'. *Media, Culture and Society* 15(3).

Hjarvard, S. (1993) 'Pan-European television news: towards a European political public sphere?' in P. Drummond, et al., (eds), *National Identity and Europe: The Television Revolution*. London: British Film Institute.

Hobsbawm, E. (1994) *Age of Extremes: The Short Twentieth Century 1914–1991*. London: Michael Joseph. (Quoted in *The Independent on Sunday*. 'The Sunday Review', 16 Oct., 1994, pp. 9–11).

Hohendahl, P. (1992) 'The public sphere: models and boundaries' in C. Calhoun (ed.), *Habermas and the Public Sphere*. London: MIT Press.

Höijer, B. (1992) 'Socio-cognitive structures and television reception'. *Media, Culture and Society* 14:583–603.

Jónasdóttir, A.G. (1991) *Love, Power and Political Interests*. Örebro, Sweden: University of Örebro Press.

Katz, E. and Lazarsfeld, P. (1955) *Personal Influence*. Glencoe, IL: Free Press.

Keane, J. (1988) *Democracy and Civil Society*. London: Verso.

Keane, J. (1991) *The Media and Democracy*. Cambridge: Polity Press.

Laclau, E. and Mouffe, C. (1985) *Hegemony and Socialist Strategy*. London: Verso.

Lenart, S. (1994) *Shaping Political Attitudes: The Impact of Interpersonal Communication and Mass Media*. London: Sage.

McIntyre, J.S. (1987) 'Repositioning a landmark: the Hutchins Commission and freedom of the press'. *Critical Studies in Mass Communication* 4:136–60.

Mouffe C. (ed.) (1992a) *Dimensions of Radical Democracy*. London: Verso.

Mouffe, C. (1992b) 'Democratic citizenship and the political community' in C. Mouffe (ed.), *Dimensions of Radical Democracy*. London: Verso.

Mouffe, C. (1993) *The Return of the Political*. London: Verso.

Negt, O. and Kluge, A. (1993/1972) *The Public Sphere and Experience*. Minneapolis: University of Minnesota Press.

Nicholson, L. (1992) 'Feminist theory: the private and the public' in L. McDowell and R. Pringle (eds), *Defining Women*. Cambridge: Polity Press/Open University.

Pateman, C. (1987) 'Feminist critiques of the public/private dichotomy' in A. Phillips (ed.), *Feminism and Equality*. Oxford: Blackwell.

Pateman, C. (1988) 'The fraternal social contract' in J. Keane (ed.), *Civil Society and the State*. London: Verso.

Pateman, C. (1992) 'The patriarchal welfare state' in L. McDowell and R. Pringle (eds), *Defining Women*. Cambridge: Polity Press/Open University Press.

Peters, J.D. (1993) 'Distrust of representation: Habermas on the public sphere'. *Media, Culture and Society* 15(4).

Phillips, A. (1991) *Engendering Democracy*. Cambridge: Polity Press.

Phillips, A. (1993) *Democracy and Difference*. Cambridge: Polity Press.

Porter, V. (1993) 'The consumer and transfrontier television'. *Consumer Policy Review* 3(3).

Postman, N. (1985) *Amusing Ourselves to Death*. New York: Viking.

Price, V. (1992) *Public Opinion*, London: Sage.

Raboy, M. (1991) 'L'économie politique des médias et le nouvel espace public de la communication' in M. Beauchamp (ed.), *Communication Publique et Société*. Boucherville, Québec: Gaëtan Morin.

Raboy, M. (1994) 'The role of the public in broadcast policy-making and regulation: lessons for Europe from Canada'. *European Journal of Communication* 9:5–23.

Rheingold, H. (1994) *Virtual Community: Homesteading on the Electronic Frontier*. New York: Harper Perennial.

Scannell, P. (1989) 'Public service broadcasting and modern public life'. *Media, Culture and Society* 11:135–66.

Scannell, P. (ed.) (1991) *Broadcast Talk*. London: Sage.

Schlesinger, P. (1994) 'Europe's contradictory communicative space'. *Dædalus*. Spring.

Sennett, R. (1977) *The Fall of Public Man*. New York: Knopf.

Shotter, J. (1993a) *Conversational Realities*. London: Sage.

Simonds, A. (1989) 'Ideological domination and the political information market'. *Theory and Society* 18:181–211.

Splichal, S. and Wasko, J. (eds) (1993) *Communication and Democracy*. Norwood, NJ: Ablex.

Steiner, L. (ed.) (1994) 'Review and criticism: public opinion paradigms'. *Critical Studies in Mass Communication* 11:274–306.

van Tassel, J. (1994) 'Yakety yak, do talk back!'. Wired: January.

Taylor, C. (1992) *The Ethics of Authenticity*. Cambridge, MA: Harvard University Press.

Tester, K. (1992) *Civil Society*. London: Routledge.

Thompson, J.P. (1990) *Ideology and Modern Culture*. Cambridge: Polity Press.

Tuchman, G. (1978) *Making News*. New York: Free Press.

Venturelli. S.S. (1993) 'The imagined transnational public sphere in the European Community's broadcast philosophy: implications for democracy'. *European Journal of Communication* 8:491–518.

Verstraeten, H. (1994) 'The media and the transformation of the public sphere'. Unpublished paper, Centre for Media Sociology, Free University Brussels.

Walzer, M. (1992) 'The civil society argument' in C. Mouffe (ed.), *Dimensions of Radical Democracy*, London: Verso.

Wasko, J. and Mosco, V. (eds) (1992) *Democratic Communications in the Information Age*, Toronto: Garamond Press and Norwood, NJ: Ablex.

Willis, S. (1991) *A Primer for Daily Life*. London: Routledge.

38.
POPULAR MEDIA AS PUBLIC 'SPHERICULES' FOR DIASPORIC COMMUNITIES

Stuart Cunningham

The research team that authored *Floating Lives: The Media and Asian Diasporas* (Cunningham and Sinclair, 2000) mapped the mediascapes of Asian diasporic communities against the background of the theoretical and policy territory of understanding media use in contemporary, culturally plural societies. In this article, I will take further than *Floating Lives* the nature of the public spheres activated around diasporic media as a specific form of public communication, by engaging with public sphere debates and assessing the contribution that the research conducted for *Floating Lives* might make to those debates.

The public sphere, in its classic sense advanced in the work of Jürgen Habermas (1989 [1962]), is a space of open debate standing against the state as a special subset of civil society in which the logic of 'democratic equivalence' is cultivated. The concept has been used regularly in the fields of media, cultural and communications studies to theorize the media's articulation between the state and civil society. Indeed, Nicholas Garnham claimed in the mid-1990s that the public sphere had replaced the concept of hegemony as the central motivating idea in media and cultural studies (Garnham, 1995). This is certainly an overstatement, but it is equally certain that, almost 40 years since Habermas first published his public sphere argument, and almost 30 years since it was first published in outline in English (Habermas, 1974), the debate continues strongly over how progressive elements of civil societies are constructed and how media support, inhibit or, indeed, are coterminous with such self-determining public communication.

The debate is marked out at either end of the spectrum by those, on the one hand, for whom the contemporary western public sphere has been tarnished or even fatally compromised by the encroachment of particularly commercial media and communications (for example, Schiller, 1989). On the other hand, there are those for whom the media have become the main, if not the only, vehicle for whatever can be held to exist of the public sphere in such societies. Such 'media-centric' theorists in these fields can hold that the media actually *envelop* the public sphere:

The 'mediasphere' is the whole universe of media … in all languages in all countries. It therefore completely encloses and contains as a differentiated part of itself the (Habermasian) public sphere (or the many public spheres), and it is itself contained by the much larger semiosphere … which is the whole universe of sense-making by whatever means, including speech … it is clear that television is a crucial site of the mediasphere and a crucial mediator between general cultural sense-making systems (the semiosphere) and specialist components of social sense-making like the public sphere. Hence the public sphere can be rethought not as a category binarily contrasted with its implied opposite, the private sphere, but as a 'Russian doll' enclosed within a larger mediasphere, itself enclosed within the semiosphere. And within 'the' public sphere, there may equally be found, Russian-doll style, further counter-cultural, oppositional or minoritarian public spheres.

(Hartley, 1999: 217–18)

Hartley's topography has the virtue of clarity, scope and heuristic utility, even while it remains provocatively media-centric. This is mostly due to Hartley's commitment to the strictly textual provenance of public communication, and to his greater interest in Lotman's notion of the semiosphere than Habermas' modernist understanding that the public sphere stands outside and even against its 'mediatization'.

I will complicate that topography by suggesting that minoritarian public spheres are rarely subsets of classic nationally bound public spheres but are none the less vibrant, globalized but very specific spaces of self- and community-making and identity (see, for example, Husband, 1998). I agree with Hartley, however, in his iconoclastic insistence that the commercial realm must be factored into the debate more centrally and positively than it has been to date. Diasporic media entrepreneurs and producers are mostly uninterested in or wary of the state, in part because the copyright status of much of their production is dubious.

I will also stress another neglected aspect of the public sphere debate developed by Jim McGuigan (1998: 92) – the 'affective' as much as 'effective' dimension of public communication, which allows for an adequate grasp of entertainment in a debate dominated by ratiocinative and informational activity. McGuigan speaks of a 'rather softer' conception of the public sphere than is found in the work of Habermas and others (1998: 98) and develops these ideas around the significance of affective popular politics expressed through media mobilization of western responses to poverty and aid campaigns. Underdeveloped, though, and tantalisingly so, is the role played by the entertainment content of the media in the formation and reproduction of public communication (McGuigan, 1998: 98, quoting Garnham, 1992: 274). This is the domain on which such strongly opposed writers as McGuigan and Hartley might begin to at least share an object of study.

Todd Gitlin has posed the question as to whether we can continue to speak of the ideal of *the* public sphere as an increasingly complex, polyethnic, communications-saturated series of societies develop around the world. Rather, what might be emerging are numerous public 'sphericules': 'does it not look as though the public sphere, in falling, has shattered into a scatter of globules, like mercury?' (Gitlin, 1998: 173). Gitlin's answer is the deeply pessimistic one of seeing the future as the irretrievable loss of elements of a modernist public commonality.

The spatial metaphor of fragmentation, of dissolution, of the centre not holding, assumes that there is a singular nation-state to anchor it. Thinking of public sphericules as constituted beyond the singular nation-state, as *global narrowcasting of polity and culture*, assists in restoring them to a place – not necessarily counter-hegemonic but certainly culturally plural and dynamically contending with western forms for recognition – of undeniable importance for contemporary, culturally plural societies and any media, cultural and communication studies claiming similar contemporaneity.

There are now several claims for such public sphericules. One can speak of a feminist public sphere and international public sphericules constituted around environmental or human rights issues. They may take the form of 'subaltern counterpublics', as Nancy Fraser (1992) calls them, or they may be termed taste cultures, such as those formed around gay style (which doesn't of course exclude them from acting as 'counterpublics'). As John Hartley and Allen McKee put it in *The Indigenous Public Sphere* (2000: 3), these are possibly peculiar examples of public spheres because they are not predicated on any nation that a public sphere usually expresses – they are the 'civil societies' of nations without borders, without state institutions and without citizens. These authors go on to suggest that such public spheres might stand as a model for developments in late modern culture generally, with do-it-yourself citizenship based on culture, identity and voluntary belonging rather than based on rights derived from, and obligations to, a state.

My present argument is in part a contribution to the elaboration of just such a project. However, there are still undeniably relations of dominance, and 'mainstreams' and 'peripheries'; the metaphor is not simply a series of sphericules, overlapping to a greater or lesser extent. Although this latter explanatory model goes some distance in explaining the complexity of overlapping taste cultures, identity formations, social commitments and specialist understandings that constitute the horizon of many if not most citizens/consumers in post-industrial societies, there are broad consensuses and agenda-setting capabilities that cannot be gainsaid in enthusiasm for embracing *tout court* a 'capillary' model of power. The key, as Hartley and McKee identify, is the degree of control over the meanings created about and within the sphericule (2000: 3,7) and by which this control is exercised.

In contrast to Gitlin, then, I argue that ethno-specific global mediatized communities display in microcosm elements we would expect to find in 'the' public sphere. Such activities may constitute valid and indeed dynamic counter-examples to a discourse of decline and fragmentation, while taking full account of contemporary vectors of communication in a globalizing, commercializing and pluralizing world.

Ongoing public sphere debates in the field, then, continue to be structured around dualisms which are arguably less aids than inhibitors of analysis: dualisms such as public-private, information-entertainment, cognition-affect or emotion, public versus commercial culture and – the 'master' dualism – public sphere in the singular or plural. What follows is no pretence at a Hegelian *Aufhebung* (transcendence) catching up these dualisms in a grand synthesis, but rather a contribution to a more positive account of the operations of media-based public communication – in this case, ethno-specific diasporic sphericules – which place a different slant on highly generalized debates about globalization, commercialization and the fate of public communication in these contexts.

The Ethno-specific Mediatized Sphericule

First, they are indeed 'sphericules'; that is, they are social fragments that do not have critical mass. Nevertheless, they share many of the characteristics of the classically conceived public sphere – they provide a central site for public communication in globally dispersed communities, stage communal difference and discord productively, and work to articulate insider ethno-specific identities – which are by definition 'multi-national', even global – to the wider 'host' environments.

The audience research for *Floating Lives* was conducted in communities in Australia. Although

Australia is, in proportional terms, the world's second-largest immigrant nation next to Israel, the relatively low numbers of any individual group (at present, more than 150 ethnic groups speaking over 100 different languages) has meant that a critical mass of a few dominant Non-English Speaking Background (NESB) groupings has not made the impact that Hispanic peoples, for example, have made in the United States. No one non-Anglo Celt ethnic group has, therefore, reached 'critical mass' in terms of being able to operate significantly as a self-contained community in the nation. For this reason, Australia offers a useful laboratory for testing notions of diasporic communities that need to be 'de-essentialized', adapted to conditions where ethnicities and sub-ethnicities jostle in ways that would have been unlikely or impossible in their respective homeland settings or where long and sustained patterns of immigration have produced a critical mass of singular ethnicities.

Sinclair et al.'s (2000) study of the Chinese in *Floating Lives* posits that the sources, socioeconomic backgrounds and circumstances of Chinese immigrant arrivals in Australia have been much more diverse than those of Chinese communities in the other great contemporary immigrant-receiving countries such as the United States, Canada, Britain and New Zealand, or earlier immigrant-receiving countries in Southeast Asia, South America, Europe and Africa. To make sense of 'the' Chinese community is to break it down into a series of complex and often interrelated sub-groupings based on geographical origin – mainland (PRC), Southeast Asia (Indonesia, Malaysia and Singapore), Taiwan, Indochina (Vietnam, Laos, Cambodia), Hong Kong – together with overlapping language and dialect use.

Similarly, Cunningham and Nguyen's (2000) Vietnamese study shows that there are significant differences among quite a small population along axes of generation, ethnicity, region of the home country, education and class, and recency of arrival and conditions under which arrival took place. And for the Fiji Indians in Manas Ray's work (2000), if it was legislated racial discrimination that compelled them to leave Fiji, in Australia they find themselves 'othered' by, and othering, the mainland Indian groupings who contest the authenticity of Fiji Indian claims to rootedness in Indian popular culture.

The formats for diasporic popular media owe much to their inscription within such 'narrowcast' cultural spaces and share many significant attributes: karaoke, with its performative, communal and de-aestheticized performative and communal space (Wong, 1994); the Vietnamese variety music video and 'Paris/Sydney/Toronto by Night' live show formats; and the typical 'modular' Bollywood film and accompanying live and playback music culture.

Against the locus of examination of the 'diasporic imagination' as one of aesthetically transgressive hybridity produced out of a presumed 'ontological condition' occupied by the migrant subject, these are not necessarily aesthetically transgressive or politically progressive texts. Their politics cannot be read off their textual forms, but must be grasped in the use to which they are put in the communities. In *Floating Lives* we see these uses as centring on popular culture debates – where communities contend around the politics, identity formations and tensions of hybrid popular forms emerging to serve the diasporas.

Much diasporic cultural expression is a struggle for survival, identity and assertion, and it can be a struggle as much enforced by the necessities of coming to terms with the dominant culture as it is freely assumed. And the results may not be pretty. The instability of cultural maintenance and negotiation can lead, at one extreme, to being locked into a time warp with the fetishized homeland – as it once might have been but no longer is or can be; and, at the other, to assimilation to the dominant host culture and a loss of place in one's originary culture. It can involve insistent reactionary politics and extreme overcommercialization (Naficy [1993: 71] cites a situation in 1987 when Iranian television in Los Angeles was scheduling more than 40 minutes advertising an hour) because of the need to fund expensive forms of media for a narrowcast audience; and textual material of excoriating tragedy (the [fictional] self-immolation and [actual] atrocity scenarios played out in some, respectively, Iranian and Croatian videos), as recounted by Naficy and by Kolar-Panov (1997).

Second, there is explanatory pay-off in pursuing the specificity of the ethno-specific public sphericule in comparison with other emergent public spheres. Like the classic Habermasian bourgeois public sphere of the café society of 18th- and 19th-century France

and Britain, they are constituted as elements of civil society. However, our understanding of civil society is formulated out of its dualistic relationship to formal apparatuses of political and juridical power. Ethno-specific sphericules constitute themselves as potentially global civil societies that intersect with state apparatuses at various points (immigration law, multicultural public policy and, for the irredentist and the exilic, against the regimes that control homeland societies). It follows that ethno-specific public sphericules are not congruent with international taste cultures borne by a homogenizing global media culture. For diasporic groupings *were* parts of states, nations and polities and much of the diasporic polity is about the process of remembering, positioning and, by no means least, constructing business opportunities around these pre-diasporic states and/or nations.

It is out of these realities that the assumption grows that ethnic minoritarian publics contribute to the further fragmentation of the majoritarian public sphere, breaking the 'social compact' that subsumes nation and ethnicity within the state; a process that has been foundational for the modern nation state. Irredentist politics and 'long-distance' nationalism, where the prime allegiance continues to be to an often-defunct state or regime, are deemed non-progressive by most commentators – classically captured by Susan Sontag in her celebrated essays on the Cubans in Florida. However, a focus on the popular culture of diasporas and its place in the construction of public sphericules complicates these assumptions, as it shows that a variety of voices contend for recognition and influence in the micro-polity, and great generational renewal can arise from the vibrancy of such popular culture.

Sophisticated cosmopolitanism and successful international business dealing sit alongside long-distance nationalism – the diasporic subject is typically a citizen of a western country, who is not stateless and is not seeking the recognition of a separate national status in their 'new' country, like the prototypal instances in the European context such as the Basques, the Scots or the Welsh. These sphericules are definitively transnational, even global in their constitution but are not the same as emerging transnational polities and cultures of global corporate culture, world-spanning non-governmental organizations and international bodies of governments.

Perhaps the most consistent relation, or non-relation, that diasporic media have with the various states into which they are introduced concerns issues of piracy. This gives another layer to the notion of civil cultures standing against the state, where 'public' is irreducible to 'official' culture. Indeed, given that significant amounts of the cultural production exist in a paralegal penumbra of copyright breach and piracy, there is a strong desire on the part of the entrepreneurs who disseminate such products to keep their distance from organs of the state. It is apparent that routinized piracy makes of much diasporic media a 'shadow system', as Kolar-Panov (1997: 31) dubs such minority video circuits as they are perceived from outside. They operate 'in parallel' to the majoritarian system, with few industry linkages.

Third, they reconfigure essentialist notions of community and reflex anti-commercialism. These sphericules are communities in a sense that goes beyond the bland homogeneous arcadia that the term community usually connotes. On the one hand, the ethno-specific community assumes an importance that is greater by far than the term usually implies in mainstream parlance, as the community *constitutes* the markets and audiences for the media services – there is almost no cross-over or recognition outside the specific community in most cases of diasporic cultural production. The 'community' therefore becomes an economic calculus, not only a multicultural demographic instance. The community is to an important extent constituted *through* media (see Hartley and McKee, 2000: 84) in so far as media performance is one of the main reasons to meet together, and there is very little else available as a mediator of information and entertainment. These media and their entrepreneurs and audiences work within a de-essentialized community and its differences as a condition of their practice and engagement.

Diasporic media are largely commercially driven media but are not fully fledged markets. They are largely constituted in and through a commercial culture but this is not the globalizing, homogenizing commercialism that has been posed by neo-Marxist political economists as threatening cultural pluralism, authenticity and agency at the local level. With notable exceptions such as global Chinese popular cultural forms such as cantopop and Hong Kong cinema,

which has experienced significant cross-over into both dominant and other emerging contemporary cultural formations, and the Indian popular Bhangra music and Bollywood cinema which is still more singularly based in Indian homeland and diasporic audiences, this is small business commercialism that deals with the practical specificities of cultural difference at the local level as an absolute precondition of business viability.

The spaces for ethno-specific public communication are, fourth, media-centric, and this affords new configurations of the information–entertainment dualism. Given the at times extreme marginalization of many diasporic groupings in public space and their lack of representation within leaderships of influence and persuasion in the dominant forums of the host country, ethno-specific media become, by default, the main organs of communication outside of certain circumscribed and defined social spaces, such as the Chinatowns, Koreatowns, the little Saigons, the churches and temples, or the local video, spice and herb parlours.

The ethno-specific sphericule is mediacentric but, unlike the way that mediacentricity can give rise to functionalist thinking (media are the cement that forms and gives identity to the community), it should be thought of rather as 'staging' difference and dissension in ways that the community *itself* can manage. There are severe constraints on public political discourse among, for example, refugee-based communities such as the Vietnamese. The 'compulsive memorialisation' (Thomas, 1999: 149) of the pre-communist past of Vietnam and the compulsory anti-communism of the leadership of the Vietnamese community are internalized as unsavoury to mainstream society. As part of the pressure to be the perfect citizen in the host society (Hage, 1998: 10), there is considerable self-censorship in the expression of public critical opinion. This filtering of political partisanship for external consumption is also turned back on itself in the community, with attempts by members of the community to have the rigorous anti-communist refugee stance softened (by the mid-1990s, only 30 percent of the Vietnamese community in Australia were originally refugees) met with harsh rebuke. In this situation, Vietnamese entertainment formats, discussed below, operate to create a space where political and cultural identities can be processed in a self-determining way, where voices other than the official, but constitutive of community sentiment, can speak.

Mediacentricity also means, in this context, a constant blurring of the information–entertainment distinction, giving rise to a positive sense of a 'tabloidized' sphericule wherein McGuigan's affective as well as effective communication takes on another meaning. The information–entertainment distinction – usually maintained in the abundance of available media in dominant cultures – is blurred in the diasporic setting. As there is typically such a small diet of ethno-specific media available to these communities, they are mined deeply for social cues (including fashion, language use and so on), personal gossip, public information as well as singing along to the song or following the fictional narrative. Within this concentrated and contracted informational and libidinal economy, 'contemporary popular media as guides to choice, or guides to the attitudes that inform choices' (Hartley, 1999: 143) take on a thoroughly continuous and central role in information and entertainment for creating a negotiated *habitus*.

The Vietnamese

The Vietnamese are by far the largest refugee community in Australia. For most, 'home' is a denigrated category while 'the regime' continues in power, and so media networks, especially music video, operate to connect the dispersed exilic Vietnamese communities. As Cunningham and Nguyen (2000) argue in our chapter in *Floating Lives*, there are obviously other media in play (community newspapers, Hong Kong film and video products) but music video carries especial significance and allows a focus on the affective dimension of public communication. Small business entrepreneurs produce low-budget music videos mostly out of southern California (but also Paris), which are taken up within the fan circuits of the United States, Australia, Canada, France and elsewhere. The internal cultural conflicts in the communities centre on the felt need to maintain pre-revolutionary Vietnamese heritage and traditions; find a negotiated place in a more mainstreamed culture; or engage in the formation of distinct hybrid identities around the

appropriation of dominant western popular cultural forms. These three cultural positions or stances are dynamic and mutable, but the main debates are constructed around them, and are played out principally within variety music video formats.

Although by no means exhausting the media diet of the Vietnamese diaspora, live variety shows and music videos are undeniably unique to it, as audio-visual media made specifically by and for the diaspora. These media forms bear many similarities to the commercial and variety-based cultural production of Iranian television in Los Angeles studied by Naficy in his benchmark *The Making of Exile Cultures* (1993), not least because Vietnamese variety show and music video production is also centred on the Los Angeles conurbation. The Vietnamese grouped there are not as numerous or as rich as Naficy's Iranians and so have not developed the business infrastructure to support the range and depth of media activity recounted by Naficy. The business infrastructure of Vietnamese audiovisual production is structured around a small number of small businesses operating on very low margins.

To be exilic means not, or at least not 'officially', being able to draw on the contemporary cultural production of the home country. Indeed, it means actively denying its existence in a dialectical process of mutual disauthentification (Carruthers, 2001). The Vietnam government proposes that the *Viet Kieu* (the appellation for Vietnamese overseas which carries a pejorative connotation) are fatally westernised. Ironically, the diasporic population makes a similar counter-charge against the regime, proposing that the homeland population has lost its moral integrity through the wholesale compulsory adoption of an alien western ideology – Marxism-Leninism.

Together, the dispersed geography and the demography of a small series of communities frame the conditions for 'global narrowcasting' – that is, ethnically specific cultural production for widely dispersed population fragments centripetally organized around their disavowed state of origin. This makes the media, and the media use, of the Vietnamese diaspora fundamentally different from those of the Indian or Chinese diasporas. The last revolve around massive cinema and television production centres in the 'home' countries that enjoy international cachet.

By contrast, the fact that the media uses of the Vietnamese diaspora are globally oriented but commercially marginal ensures that they flourish outside the purview of state and major commercial vectors of subvention and trade.

These conditions also determine the small business character of the production companies. These small enterprises run at low margins and are constantly undercut by piracy and copying of their video products. They have clustered around the only Vietnamese population base that offers critical mass and is geographically adjacent to the much larger ECI (entertainment-communications-information) complex in Southern California. There is evidence of internal migration within the diaspora from the rest of the United States, Canada and France to Southern California to take advantage of the largest overseas Vietnamese population concentration and the world's major ECI complex.

During the course of the 20 and more years since the fall of Saigon and the establishing of the diaspora through flight and migration, a substantial amount of music video material has been produced. Thuy Nga Productions, by far the largest and most successful company, organizes major live shows in the United States and franchises appearance schedules for its high-profile performers at shows around the global diaspora. It has produced more than 60 two- to three-hour videotapes since the early 1980s, as well as a constant flow of CDs, audio-cassettes and karaoke discs, in addition to documentary specials and re-releases of classic Vietnamese movies. The other companies, between them, have also produced hundreds of hours of variety music video.

Virtually every overseas Vietnamese household views this music video material, most regularly attend the live variety performances on which the video material is based, and a significant proportion have developed comprehensive home libraries. The popularity of this material is exemplary, cutting across the several axes of difference in the community: ethnicity, age, gender, recentness of arrival, educational level, refugee or immigrant status, and home region. It is also widely available in pirated form in Vietnam itself, as the economic and cultural 'thaw' that has proceeded since the government's so-called Doi Moi policies of greater openness has resulted in extensive penetration of the homeland by this most international of Vietnamese forms of expression. As the only popular culture produced by and specifically for the Vietnamese diaspora, these texts attract an emotive investment in the overseas communities which is as deep as it is varied. The social text that surrounds, indeed engulfs, these productions is intense, multi-layered and makes its address across differences of generation, gender, ethnicity, class and education levels and recentness of arrival.

The key point linking attention to the textual dynamics of the music videos and media use in the communities is that each style cannot exist without the others, because of the marginal size of the audience base. From the point of view of *business* logic, each style cannot exist without the others. Thus, at the level of both the individual show/video and company outputs as a whole, the organizational structure of the shows and videos reflects the heterogeneity required to maximize the audience within a strictly narrowcast range. This is a programming philosophy congruent with 'broadcasting' to a globally spread, narrowcast demographic: 'the variety show form has been a mainstay of overseas Vietnamese anti-communist culture from the mid seventies onwards' (Carruthers, forthcoming).

In any given live show or video production, the musical styles might range from precolonial traditionalism to French colonial era high modernist classicism, to crooners adapting Vietnamese folksongs to the Sinatra era and to bilingual cover versions of *Grease* or Madonna. Stringing this concatenation of taste cultures together are comperes, typically well-known political and cultural figures in their own right, who perform a rhetorical unifying function:

> Audience members are constantly recouped via the show's diegesis, and the anchoring role of the comperes and their commentaries, into an overarching conception of shared overseas Vietnamese identity. This is centred on the appeal to ... core cultural values, common tradition, linguistic unity and an anti-communist homeland politics.
>
> (Carruthers, 2001)

Within this overall political trajectory, however, there are major differences to be managed. The stances evidenced in the video and live material range on a continuum from 'pure' heritage maintenance and ideological monitoring; to mainstream cultural negotiation; through to assertive hybridity. Most performers and productions seek to situate themselves within the mainstream of cultural negotiation between Vietnamese and western traditions. However, at one end of the continuum there are strong attempts both to keep the original folkloric music traditions alive and to keep the integrity of the originary anti-communist stance foundational to the diaspora, through very public criticism of any lapse from that stance. At the other end, Vietnamese-American youth culture is exploring the limits of hybrid identities through the radical intermixing of musical styles.

The Fiji Indians

In a remarkably short time, essentially since the coups of the late 1980s which pushed thousands of Fiji Indians out of Fiji and into diaspora around the Pacific Rim in cities such as Vancouver, Auckland and Sydney, the community in Sydney has fashioned a vibrant popular culture based on consumption and celebration of Hindi filmdom and its associated music, dance and fashion cultures. It is an especial irony that a people 'extracted' from mainland Indian polity and culture a century or more ago – for whom the relationship with the world of Hindi film is a purely imaginary one – should embrace and appropriate such a culture with far greater strength than those enjoying a much more recent connection to the 'homeland'.

Manas Ray's analysis of the Fiji Indian public sphericule in *Floating Lives* (2000) is structured around a comparison with the expatriate Bengalis. The two groups are contrasted on a caste, class and cultural consumption basis, and Ray stresses that, given that there is no critical mass of sub-ethnicities within the Indian diaspora in Australia, cultural difference is definitional. The Bengalis are seen as locked into their history as bearers of the Indian project of modernity which they assumed centrally under the British Raj. The once-unassailed centrality that the educated, Hindu Bengali gentry, the *bradralok*, had in the political and civic institutions of India has been challenged in the decades since independence by the subaltern classes:

It is from this Bengal that the *bradralok* flees, either to relatively prosperous parts of India or, if possible, abroad – to the affluent west, taking with them the dream of a nation that they were once so passionate about and the cultural baggage which had expressed that dream.

(Ray, 2000: 142–3)

The Bengali diaspora, argues Ray, frames its cultural life around the high culture of the past, which has become a 'fossilized' taste culture (2000: 143).

In startling contrast to the Fiji Indian community, which is by far the highest consumer of Hindi films, for the Indian Bengalis, Indian-sourced film and video is of little interest and is even the subject of active disparagement. The literature and other high cultural forms, which once had 'organic links to the independence movement and to early post-independence hardship and hope', have fossilized into a predictable and ageing taste culture that is remarkably similar whether the Bengali community is in Philadelphia, Boston, London, Düsseldorf, Dubai or Sydney (Ray, 2000: 143). The issues of inter-generational deficit as the young turn to western youth culture are evident.

The politics of popular culture are fought out across the communal fractions and across the generations. The inter-communal discord between mainland Indians and Fiji Indians, which are neither new nor restricted only to Australia – where many mainland Indians continue to exhibit deeply entrenched casteist attitudes and Fiji Indians often characterized mainland Indians with the same kind of negativity they were wont to use for ethnic Fijians – are often played out around media and film culture. There are elements of fully blown popular culture debates being played out. At the time of a particularly vitriolic controversy in 1997, the editor of the mainland *Indian Post* argued that while the Fiji Indians are 'good Hindus' and 'they are the people who spend', their 'westernised ways' and 'excessive attachment to filmy culture' bring disrepute to the Indian community as a whole (Dello, 1997). The resolution to these kinds of issues is often found in the commercial reality that Fiji Indians are the main consumers of the products and services advertised in mainland Indian shops!

Despite virtual slavery in the extraction period and uprootedness in the contemporary period, the affective dimension of the Fiji Indian public spheri-cule is deeply rooted in Hindu belief and folklore. The central text of Hinduism, 'The Ramayan', thus was used to heal the wounds of indenture and provide a cultural and moral texture in the new settlement. A strong emotional identification to the Ramayan and other expressions of the Bhakti movement – a con-strained cultural environment, continued degradation at the hands of the racist white regime, a disdain for the culture of the ethnic Fijians, a less hard-pressed post-indenture life and, finally, a deep-rooted need of a dynamic, discursive site for the imaginative recon-struction of motherland – were all factors which, together, ensured the popularity of Hindi films once they started reaching the shores of Fiji. This was because Hindi film deployed the Ramayan exten-sively, providing the right pragmatics for 'continual mythification' of home (Ray, 2000: 156).

As a result, second-generation Fiji Indians in their twice-displaced settings of Sydney, Auckland or Vancouver have developed a cultural platform that, although not counter-hegemonic, is markedly differ-ent from their western host cultures. In contrast, 'the emphasis of the first generation Indian Bengali dias-pora on aestheticised cultural forms of the past offers to second generation very little in terms of a home country popular youth culture with which they can identify' (Ray, 2000: 145).

References

Carruthers, Ashley (2001) 'National Identity, Diasporic Anxiety and Music Video Culture in Vietnam', in Yao Souchou (ed.) *House of Glass: Culture, Modernity and the State in Southeast Asia*. Singapore: Institute of Southeast Asian Studies.

Cunningham, Stuart and John Sinclair, eds (2000) *Floating Lives: The Media and Asian Diasporas*, pp. 91–135. St Lucia: University of Queensland Press (and Boulder, CO: Rowman & Littlefield, 2001).

Cunningham, Stuart and Tina Nguyen (2000) 'Popular Media of the Vietnamese Diaspora', in Stuart Cunningham and John Sinclair (eds) *Floating Lives: The Media and Asian Diasporas*. St Lucia: University of Queensland Press (and Boulder, CO: Rowman & Littlefield, 2001).

Dello, Sanjay (1997) Interview with Manas Ray, Sydney, May.

Fraser, Nancy (1992) 'Rethinking the Public Sphere: A Contribution to the Critique of Actually Existing Democracy', in C. Calhoun (ed.) *Habermas and the Public Sphere*, pp. 109–42. Cambridge, MA: MIT Press.

Garnham, Nicholas (1992) 'The Media and the Public Sphere', in C. Calhoun (ed.) *Habermas and the Public Sphere*, pp. 359–76. Cambridge, MA: MIT Press

Garnham, Nicholas (1995) 'The Media and Narratives of the Intellectual', *Media, Culture & Society* 17(3): 359–84.

Gitlin, T. (1998) 'Public Sphere or Public Sphericules?', in T. Liebes and J. Curran (eds) *Media, Ritual and Identity*, pp. 175–202. London: Routledge.

Habermas, J. (1974) '"The Public Sphere', *New German Critique* 1(3): 49–55.

Habermas, J. (1989[1962]) *The Structural Transformation of the Public Sphere: An Inquiry in a Category of Bourgeois Society*. Cambridge: Polity Press.

Hage, Ghassan (1998) *White Nation: Fantasies of White Supremacy in a Multi-cultural Society*. Annandale: Pluto Press; and West Wickham: Comerford and Miller.

Hartley, John (1999) *Uses of Television*. London: Routledge.

Hartley, John and Allen McKee (2000) *The Indigenous Public Sphere*. Oxford: Oxford University Press.

Husband, Charles (1998) 'Differentiated Citizenship and the Multi-ethnic Public Sphere', *Journal of International Communication* 5(1/2): 134–48.

Kolar-Panov, D. (1997) *Video, War and the Diasporic Imagination*. London: Routledge.

McGuigan, Jim (1998) '"What Price the Public Sphere?', in Daya Kishan Thussu (ed.) *Electronic Empires: Global Media and Local Resistance*, pp. 91–107. London: Arnold.

Naficy, Hamid (1993) *The Making of Exile Cultures: Iranian Television in Los Angeles*. Minneapolis: University of Minnesota Press.

Ray, Manas (2000) 'Bollywood Down Under: Fiji Indian Cultural History and Popular Assertion', in Stuart Cunningham and John Sinclair (eds) *Floating Lives: The Media and Asian Diasporas*, pp. 136–84. St Lucia: University of Queensland Press (and Boulder, CO: Rowman & Littlefield, 2001).

Schiller, H. (1989) *Culture Inc.: The Corporate Takeover of Public Expression*. New York: Oxford University Press.

Sinclair, John, Audrey Yue, Gay Hawkins, Kee Pookong and Josephine Fox (2000) 'Chinese Cosmopolitanism and Media Use', in Stuart Cunningham and John Sinclair (eds) *Floating Lives: The Media and Asian Diasporas*, pp. 35–90. St Lucia: University of Queensland Press (and Boulder, CO: Rowman & Littlefield, 2001).

Thomas, Mandy (1999) *Dreams in the Shadows: Vietnamese-Australian Lives in Transition*. St Leonards: Allen & Unwin.

Wong, Deborah (1994) '"I Want the Microphone": Mass Mediation and Agency in Asian-American Popular Music', *TDR (The Drama Review)* 38(3): 152–67.

39.
A CULTURAL APPROACH TO THE STUDY OF MEDIATED CITIZENSHIP

Jeffrey P. Jones

Citizens in Western societies have experienced the explosive growth and diffusion of media technologies and their increasingly central location in our public and private lives. The potential number of places in which we now attend to, even brush up against, various forms of political information, symbols, and narratives are astounding. These engagements with politics are not segregated as separate activities for the duty-bound "good citizen." Instead, they are interspersed and concomitant with the flow and rhythms of routine activities in daily life.[1] Nor are these engagements necessarily related to the intentional acquisition of political information. Instead, these encounters with mediated politics are often related to pedestrian pursuits of pleasure, distraction, curiosity, community, sociability, and even happenstance. And although much attention has been given of late to the potentialities of new media technologies for a revival of democratic participation (Meikle 2002; Rheingold 2002; McCaughey and Ayers 2003; Gillmor 2004), it is this intermixing of old media and new media—taken both individually and as a whole—and the political content that is made available through them that deserves our attention. For it is within this saturated media environment that political culture is shaped and maintained in late-modern society, and hence, an important starting place if we seek to understand media's role in contemporary meanings of citizenship.

Yet despite the changes that have occurred in the mediation between citizen and state, much of the discussion of mediation continues to be focused on supposed ways in which media negatively affect the political process (specifically) and political culture (in general). What typically motivates such criticisms is the need to account for the decline of traditional measures of democratic vitality in Western societies, such as voting, political party affiliation, political knowledge, trust in leaders, and voluntary activism. The ubiquity of media, its popularity as a central source for popular understanding of politics, and its increasing centrality to the act of governance itself results in media becoming a natural place to look for the "cause" of these "effects." Robert Putnam's (2000) argument that television is a leading source of civic disengagement is perhaps one of the more popular manifestations of what is known as the "media malaise" thesis. Beyond Putnam, however, are numerous scholarly claims that comprise this thesis, ranging from a focus on media content (such as negativity, conflictual framing, horse race coverage, and tabloidization), to institutional limitations (such as pack journalism and the "miscast institution" of the press), to media's supposed detrimental effects on citizens (such as the illusion of participation, lack of trust in government, amusement and distraction, and cynicism).[2] And although assessments of new media technologies such as the Internet are often accompanied by claims of democratic revival, there is no shortage of dystopian views that suggest the possible negative effects of new media on the polity, such as fragmented communication, loss of shared experience, personalized information, polarization, and the withering of community (Freie 1998; Sunstein 2002).

Underlying these arguments, however, are three central but flawed assumptions that, despite the inclusion of other foci and approaches to political communication in the past three decades, continue to dominate the study of mediated citizenship. The first is that the most important sphere of political communication occurs in the interactions between politicians/government officials and the news media.[3] The Fourth Estate is seen as the central and most legitimate institution in a democracy to keep a check on power, to uncover facts, to seek truth, and to present reality in a fair and unbiased manner. Furthermore, the press maintains a formal and routine relationship to political power, with regularized, institutional-based interactions, including regulatory oversight, office space, supplied content (e.g. press conferences and interviews), and so on. The news media are therefore seen as the most important players in the creation and/or representation of political reality, even leading some scholars to consider it the fourth branch of government (Cook 1998).

To be sure, these functions are vital to successful self-governance. Nevertheless, this persistent focus on news media has weaknesses. It leads to dismissals of other, more popular sources of political information and content as illegitimate (derisively labeled "infotainment" or "soft news"). Entertainment media are seen as distractions from the serious duty of the informed citizen. Yet recent scholarship in America and Europe has demonstrated, to the contrary, that citizens who employ a variety of popular media in their encounters with politics (such as fictional narratives, humorous talk shows, popular music, etc.) actually derive meaningful engagement with the political process (Corner and Pels 2003; Baym 2005; Jones 2005a; van Zoonen 2005). Furthermore, news stories are simply one type of narrative, while entertainment media provide yet another (and indeed, often do a better job in offering complex narratives because storytelling is what the entertainment industry does so well). Thus, it is important to recognize that different media can, and often do, present different narratives about politics. Even narratives within a single medium (say television, for instance) can have great variance, levels of quality, and appeal. Outright dismissals of popular content about politics miss this fact.

Another weakness of the focus on news is that it ignores the citizens or consumers of media themselves. What we now see is that people are, for better

or worse, increasingly turning away from news as their primary source of engagement with the political world.[4] Young people, in particular, utilize other sources of information than broadcast news or print journalism, such as entertainment media and the Internet (Mindich 2005). Both broadcast and print journalism, furthermore, are in a state of crisis in the United States (Kovach and Rosenstiel 2001; Hachten 2005). With declining readership and viewership, the institution is economically challenged by dwindling advertising revenues as well as increased costs of production (Roberts, Kunkle, and Layton 2001; Seeyle 2005a). Recent scandals related to professional norms and ethics (from story fabrication by Jayson Blair at the *New York Times* and Stephen Glass at *The New Republic* to poor fact checking on President Bush's Air National Guard records by Dan Rather at *CBS News*) have contributed to a decline in trust with news media consumers (Johnson 2003; Hachten 2005, 102–12). Concurrently, with new media technologies such as blogs and search engine portals, citizens are questioning the top-down, gatekeeper role of news media, and instead increasingly desire a more active role in the determination and construction of what constitutes news and who gets to make it (Gillmor 2004; Seelye 2005b). Finally, the press's timidity in questioning and thwarting overt propaganda efforts by the Bush administration (as both the *New York Times* and *Washington Post* offered *mea culpa* for their lack of serious reporting on assertions and evidence by the Bush administration in the run-up to the Iraq war) also weakens the news media's claim to serving as effective and trustworthy watchdogs to power (Younge 2004; Seeyle 2005c). In short, these numerous factors suggest a more urgent need to look to other locations beyond news for citizen engagement with mediated politics.

The second yet related assumption dominating the study of mediated citizenship is that the primary function of media in political communication is the provision of useful political "information." Michael Schudson's (1998) history of American civic life has demonstrated how a model of citizenship developed in the Progressive Era—that of the "Informed Citizen"—continues to foster the normative expectation that the media's central role or obligation is to provide information that allows citizens to be fully informed on political matters of the day. Only through an informed citizenry, the argument goes, can self-governance be truly realized. The role for mass media in a democracy, then, is to supply citizens with the substantive and thorough information they need to fulfill that role. When media stray from this function—for instance, in the provision of entertaining content—they are decried for subverting the needs of the citizenry. Scholars who criticize the decline of quality journalism contribute to this assumption that citizens are being denied that which they need the most: a certain brand of information about politics deemed more important than others (Scheuer 1999; Bennett 2001).

But is "information" about politics the primary thing that citizens want from media? Or is the supposed benefit of information—knowledge or education about issues, parties, politicians, and legislation—the primary benefit they seek in their interactions with mediated politics? Certainly trustworthy and unbiased information about politics is a necessary and important ingredient of citizenship. Yet scholars of symbolic interactionism and political language have long noted the significant role of political symbols, rituals, myths, metaphors, and other significations in constituting public life (Burke 1966; Barthes 1972; Edelman 1988; Kertzer 1988; Lakoff 1996). As Bruce Gronbeck argues, "Symbolic life *is* life—is the world we actually inhabit as collective beings. Politics may shuffle money, votes, territory, and other material entities, but politics *itself* is a symbolic process wherein cultural entities—myths, ideologies, values, attitudes, beliefs—are evoked, rearranged, and ordered in ways that produce political decisions. Politics thus is not *about* symbolic matters but is in essence symbolic" (1990, 212; original emphasis).

Information acquisition is primarily an instrumental approach that the rational citizen employs in certain situations. But the citizen is also just as likely to embrace political material that expresses, reifies, confirms, or celebrates the core beliefs and values he or she connects to the state, or those things that affirm his or her identity as a citizen. For instance, the fact that citizens have made Fox News—with its overt ideological bias, manipulative patriotic displays, spectacle performances by cheerleading pundits, and jingoistic rhetoric—the highest rated cable news show in America suggests that perhaps some of them want

or desire more from political communication than just "information." Similarly, while the documentary film *Fahrenheit 9/11* was director Michael Moore's effort to inform citizens of the corruption and vacuousness of the Bush presidency (and, in turn, sway voters' opinions), the tremendous popularity of the film suggests that the film also served the important communal function of expressing, reifying, and confirming the frustrations of many citizens on the political left who were opposed to the Iraq war and Republican leadership (as well as providing a similar rallying point for the political right to mobilize against what they considered leftist propaganda) (Jones 2005b).

The third assumption that dominates the study of media and politics is the belief that political engagement is primarily a physical activity first and foremost. As political scientist Norman Nie put it some 30 years ago, "If citizens are home watching television or its future counterpart, they cannot be out participating in politics" (quoted in Peterson 1990, 244). Even the literature on new media and their relationship to politics emphasizes the avenues for direct political action (i.e. mobilization, fundraising, discussion) that can and do occur through these new channels of communication. Yet, what *other* roles exist when we say a citizen "engages" politics? Does media material that leads to significant cognitive activities—say, the development of schemas or mental maps about political reality—actually count as "engagement" *per se* (Kertzer 1988, 77–101; Graber 2001; Marcus, Neuman, and MacKuen 2000; Lakoff 2004)? What to make of the building blocks we use for constructing these maps of the political and social world outside our direct experience (or as Kenneth Burke would have it, the " 'clusters' or 'equations' in [a person's] particular 'psychic economy' "; Burke 1969, 114)? From where do we obtain the reservoir of images and voices, heroes and villains, sayings and slogans that we draw upon in making sense of politics, and how are they involved in the creation of political "reality"? As George Herbert Mead has argued, "language does not simply symbolize a situation or object which is already there in advance; it makes possible the existence or the appearance of that situation or object, for it is a part of the mechanism whereby that situation or object is created" (quoted in Pranger 1968, 156). An examination of the variety of media that supply such materials seems fundamental in this regard.

Furthermore, what role for consumption? As our lives are more commonly defined and lived as consumers, and as consumption becomes a central means through which we establish our identities (including its increasingly important influence in social institutions such as the family, religion, and education), how does consumerism affect or structure our engagement with the state (Scammell 2003)? Physical engagement is important, but what of the forces and factors that *precede* political action? Finally, how do the broader aspects of political culture, the activities that influence and shape our self-conceptions as citizens, affect our desires, hopes, fears, and expectations of what political life has to offer?

All three assumptions, then, are based on an instrumental orientation toward media, one that allows rational actors to *use* media to transmit "messages over distance for the purpose of control," as James Carey most famously described this "transmission view" or transport model of communicative *interaction* (Carey 1989, 15). That is, communicative actions are seen as a means to an end—to persuade, to inform, to learn, and so on. As one survey of the field of political communication summarized, "the field's center or mainstream continues to be devoted to studying the strategic uses of communication to influence public knowledge, beliefs, and action on political matters and to regard the political campaign as the paradigmatic instance of the subject" (Nimmo and Swanson 1990, 9). These dominating assumptions are the result of just such a transmission view of political communication: that citizens garner information through news media that will in turn influence how they interact with politics behaviorally (i.e. ultimately, how they vote). Hence, political communication is, in essence, a strategic enterprise (for both rhetors and consuming citizens).

As will be discussed later, this is contrasted by a ritual view of communication where individuals engage in communication as a form of social *integration*; that is, communication "not out of self-interest nor for the accumulation of information but from a need for communion, commonality and fraternity" (Holmes 2005, 123). To comprehend the place and role of media in shaping political culture and contemporary citizenship, we would do well to add to the logocentric, instrumental orientation of political communication research a *cultural* approach that can account for the wide variety of mediated relationships—both interactive and integrative—that citizens employ in their engagements with political life.

Unlike instrumental or transmission views, a cultural approach foregrounds the intimate role that media play in our lives—the myriad ways in which media are used and integrated into our daily routines, or what Todd Gitlin calls the "wraparound presence" of media (2002, 10); how this type of usage affects our understandings of and commitments to democracy; how the variety of narratives that comprise different media address needs we have as citizens and consumers; how we understand and make sense of the world through this media plentitude; and how these opportunities for engagement shape our identities as citizens.

This cultural approach is an empirical (rather than normative) undertaking. The intent is to describe the way that citizenship is now partly constituted by and through media, and how such mediation is central to understanding the citizen's relationship to the state. This article, therefore, seeks to chart a different course by offering four propositions that highlight the important role that media play in shaping citizenship. The four propositions are: *media are plural*; *mediums affect meanings*;[5] *mediation occurs beyond information acquisition*; and *we live in a culture of political engagement*.

Media are Plural

The study of media and politics is still dominated by a monolithic conception of what constitutes "the media"—that is, the news. Almost all leading textbooks in the field maintain this distinction, concentrating their discussions primarily on news media (Alger 1995; McNair 1995; Woodward 1997; Perloff 1998; Purvis 2000; Bennett 2001; Paletz 2002; Jamieson and Waldman 2003). This focus—on what amounts to the institutionalized interaction of elites (e.g. politicians and journalists)—is a limited one, and one that may disregard the relationship that many people maintain with the sphere of elite actions. As Murray Edelman contends, "To hear or read the news is to live intermittently in a world one does not touch in daily life; and not to read it ordinarily makes little difference … Most experiences that make life joyful, poignant, boring, or worrisome are not part of the news" (1988, 35).

Instead, we should also examine media and politics from the bottom up—that is, from the perspective of those who utilize numerous and multiple forms of media in their interactions with the world of politics. To understand how citizens make sense of political reality, we must first recognize that there is a profusion of media, almost all of which carry some form of political content. Our accountings of how media shape contemporary civic culture should lead us to examine traditional (or old) media, new media, and alternative media *as a whole*. Not only should we study television, radio, film, and print media (newspapers, magazines, books, newsletters), but also their concurrent existence alongside new media (cell phones, websites, discussion boards, email, blogs and vlogs), alternative media,[6] fax machines, music, comics, direct mail, videotapes and DVDs, satellite transmissions, photocopies, billboards, and so on (Ganley 1992). For it is this intermixing of media forms that most closely approximates the way in which citizens employ communication technologies in their daily lives.

Even within one media form, we should examine the sheer variety of political engagement that occurs. Radio, for instance, connects citizens to the political world through talk radio, public radio, commercial music stations, Christian radio, satellite radio, low-power FM, pirate or rebel radio, and short-wave radio (such as the right-wing Patriot movement broadcasts in the United States) (Hilliard and Keith, 1999). Determining the specific types of radio that citizens choose from (as well as their frequency of usage) is fundamentally important to understanding *how* citizens employ radio in their engagements with politics. Similarly, when we discuss "the press," we must recognize the enormous range of sources that are included in that designation. Although many citizens read the newspaper, either a national or local daily, many also have the opportunity to engage with politics via suburban and alternative weeklies, the alternative press (black, gay, ethnic), magazines (ideological and general interest), or even the international press and newswires (available online). And within a particular press organ, the types of political material available

can vary widely, from reportage and opinion-editorials to letters to the editor, cartoons, and photographs.

Some discussions of media and politics certainly account for this variety of form and content (Bucy and Gregson 2002; Moy and Pfau 2000; Nimmo and Combs 1983). But if we are to take a bottom-up approach in understanding mediated citizenship, the recognition of this great variety of political content should direct our attention to what audiences derive from these multiple forms—what mix of serious and humorous, ideological and non-partisan, informative and mythological, local and national, mainstream and marginal they consume, and why. It should lead us to see the complexity of preferences audiences display for certain types of political material, and what type of sources they find valuable, trustworthy, or pleasurable. Moreover, citizens have unequal or differential access to such media, and as such often utilize that which is most easily or cheaply at their disposal. We thus should focus on the detailed political constitution of what some scholars call our "media ensemble," the particular assemblage of media routinely employed that, in this instance, structures our primary engagements with politics in media (Bausinger 1984).

The conservative movement in the United States, for instance, has recognized the power inherent in employing a variety of media forms to project the movement's message and extend its penetration by enveloping audiences in a consistent message that reverberates across media channels. Conservative activist and direct mail fundraiser Richard Viguerie, with David Franke, recently documented the movement's success in this regard in their book, *America's Right Turn: How Conservatives Used New and Alternative Media to Take Power* (Viguerie and Franke 2004). Viguerie and Franke speak openly about the ways in which conservatives have intentionally employed talk radio, cable television, newsletters, advertising, magazines, books, direct mail, faxes, and the Internet to create a movement that now controls every branch of government at the federal level in the United States.

A separate study of Christian right media also shows how evangelicals have used AM radio stations, cable and local television access channels, news services, think tanks, bookstores, the postal service, telephone lines, and the Internet to disseminate their messages linking Christian beliefs to direct political action, mobilization, and fundraising. Through the process of "recycling," Christian media operatives realize that a particular story serves "multiple needs, media formats, and potential listener/viewerships," and therefore they exploit every channel available for saturated coverage (Lesage 1998, 27). Lest one think that these studies only describe top-down communication strategies of a well-funded and highly coordinated ideological movement, Hilliard and Keith offer evidence of similar usage of disparate media forms (such as "mail-order book services, computer bulletin boards, gun shows, Bible camps, pamphlets, periodicals, and short-wave radio broadcasts") by widely dispersed users at the grassroots level of the radical right (1999, 89). In short, what these three studies illuminate is how conservatives and right-wing radicals have recognized the great panoply of media forms that citizens employ in their daily lives and have, in turn, exploited these consumptive habits and relationships with media in their reach for political power.

These studies, therefore, should be extended beyond partisan and religious formations to examine how citizens uncommitted to such defined ideological perspectives employ a similar array of media forms through their own patterns of media consumption. In the area of television studies, scholars have examined television in everyday life (Silverstone 1994; Gauntlett and Hill 1999; Lembo 2000); but in regards to analyses of political content in media, we have not looked across media forms with much regularity to consider the interplay of everyday life and political consumption.[7] In a single given day, a citizen might engage in all of the following activities that offer a mediated relationship to the conventional political arena through differing texts about politics: read a newspaper in the morning over breakfast, watch a morning news show while getting dressed, listen to talk radio in the car while driving to work, read politically charged emails, scan a news magazine in the office lobby, hear a political protest song in the car, see a political advertisement on a billboard on the way home, watch a political drama on DVD during the evening hours, then turn to a satirical faux television news show while getting ready for bed, only to retire for the evening by reading a political biography. An examination of the interplay between these activities will probably illuminate how this complex intermixing of media affects average citizen understandings of and

relationship to politics. Why does this matter? Because, as the next proposition argues, each form of media contains different narratives about politics, and as such, provide different meanings to be used in the construction of political reality by citizens.

Mediums Affect Meanings

Just as political content is available through multiple and varied media technologies, the particular narratives found there offer a range of interpretations of the political world. Why this is so, of course, has to do with differences in the political economy of production and distribution, standardized or popularized narrative conventions and form, authorship, audience expectations, and numerous other factors that media scholars routinely discuss. But as medium theory would also have us understand, important distinctions exist between media because of qualities resident in the mediums themselves.

Joshua Meyrowitz argues that three central metaphors shape how we should view communication mediums—medium as vessel or conduit, medium as language or grammar, and medium as environment. First, to view the medium as vessel, we study the content of media and the effects that derive from that content. Applying this to mediated politics on television, for instance, we note that the medium carries a variety of content related to politics. News, as noted earlier, is the most obvious, but other varieties include pundit talk shows (*Crossfire*), humorous talk shows (*The Daily Show with Jon Stewart*), documentaries (*Frontline*), fictional dramas (*The West Wing*), sitcoms (*Spin City*), political satire (*Saturday Night Live*), and video feeds (C-SPAN). The resulting narratives about politics that each of these forms provide can produce significant variation in meanings about political reality (even within the same medium and genre). One study, for instance, compared the narratives about the Bill Clinton-Monica Lewinsky scandal constructed on a pundit television talk show (*This Week*) with those formulated on a humorous talk show (*Politically Incorrect with Bill Maher*). It found that the discussants arrived at very different conclusions about the scandal and what should be done about it—outcomes that were structured (although not determined) by the show's format, the compositional variety of participants in the discussions, and the means of sense-making employed by those participants (Jones 2005a, 141–57).

Another study compared the narratives formulated by a satirical, fake news program (*The Daily Show*) with those created by a real news show (CNN), both covering the same campaign events in the 2004 US presidential election. Although both shows imparted information about the campaign, the overall interpretive meaning offered to the viewer differed greatly—not because one was "objective" and the other satirical (or subjective), but largely because of the types of campaign imagery and rhetoric that the programs focused on and interrogated, even though both programs aired clips from the same event, and therefore had similar content (Jones 2006). In short, not only do different media encode political reality in different ways, but the narrative content that comprises even a single medium such as television (or genres within it) can lead to quite different understandings of politics for citizens. A cultural approach to mediated citizenship emphasizes the need to investigate these various forms of political content.

Second, when examining media based upon its language or grammar (such as its visual or aural qualities, its type fonts or size, its usage of dissolves, zooms, or angles, etc.), we recognize that the rudimentary features comprising how a medium "speaks" also affect the ways in which the medium constructs or leads the user to "make sense" of a particular reality. Differences in a medium's grammar result in different types of "perception, comprehension, emotional reaction, and behavioral responses" in audiences (Meyrowitz 1999). Students of political communication have long recognized that audience interpretations of a politician's performance can be quite different when experienced, for instance, on radio rather than television (with the 1960 Kennedy-Nixon debate as one of the most famous in this regard). More recently, Donnalyn Pompper (2003) has examined the narratives of *The West Wing*—and argues that the dramatic television form is better suited for offering viewers certain insights into the executive branch than is news. Viewers, she maintains, develop a stronger connection to politics via dramatic narratives because they assume a subjective positioning, seeing into the motivations and desires, frailties and faults of the characters involved in political decision-making. Hence, the particular dramatic grammar of television

(i.e. lightening, close-ups, point-of-view shots, music, etc.) formulates narratives that engage the viewing public in ways that journalism most often does not. Liesbet van Zoonen offers data on audiences for *The West Wing* that corroborates Pompper's arguments. She concludes that popular or entertainment-based representations of politics have a particular appeal for viewers, affecting how they judge political performance and political processes beyond the television environment (van Zoonen 2005, 123–41).

Third, by examining the medium as environment, we foreground the differing relationships that people maintain in their interactions with a medium and the particular biases resident in its technological features. As Meyrowitz argues, this includes "the type of sensory information the medium can and cannot transmit; the speed and degree of immediacy of communication; unidirectional vs. bidirectional vs. multidirectional communication; simultaneous or sequential interaction; the physical requirements for using the medium; and the relative ease or difficulty of learning to use the medium to code or decode messages" (1999). A citizen's act of expressing a political opinion via a letter to the editor of the local newspaper versus his/her entering a political chat room on the Internet to do the same thing are very different means of political participation, largely structured by the media he/she has chosen to employ. Both the newspaper and the Internet allow for participation, yet each environment differs in how that interaction will proceed because of factors such as regulated/unregulated access to publication, timing/temporality of the participatory act, continuous and open feedback from other readers, length and space limitations, and so on. Similarly, the political messages included in the lyrics of a popular song will be received and interpreted in quite different fashion to the latest "kiss-and-tell" book by a former government official. The former has greater potential to engage the listener's affective and pathos-centered desires, whereas the latter is more likely to appeal to his or her rational and logos-centered sensibilities (although for different people this may not always be the case). In other words, music and print are not just different in their grammatical make-up, but also in the way the medium itself engages the user.[8]

Another example of media as environment is how a citizen can make sense of the Enron scandal from a documentary film versus reports on television news as the scandal is unfolding. A film such as *Enron: The Smartest Guys in the Room* (2005), using interviews, news clips, and graphics, lays out the contours and intricacies of the scandal in 109 minutes. It establishes the narrative of good guys and bad guys, and in the process transforms a set of complex financial dealings into a "story" of human fallibility. While the overall narrative imparted by a film and a television news report might be similar, the medium through which the story is told nevertheless affects the overall message and audience's interpretive experience. From the documentary's sequential storytelling, length, temporal appearance, and muckraking conventions to the audience's cost in attending, focused attention, and expectations of documentary form—each contributes to the medium's particular interpretive effects (Nichols 1991, 3–31).

In sum, medium theory directs our attention to the fact that the medium does matter in how politics is communicated. As James Carey argues,

> The exploitation of a particular communications technology fixes particular sensory relations in members of society. By fixing such a relation, it determines a society's world view; that is, it stipulates a characteristic way of organizing experience. It thus determines the forms of knowledge, the structure of perception, and the sensory equipment attuned to absorb reality,
>
> (quoted in Holmes 2005, 39)

The "sense" that citizens therefore make of political communication is partially structured by the medium itself. And it is not just the variety of political content that matters, but also the means through which that content is received. With the numerous types of communication technologies available to citizens today, the meanings of politics at any given time are wide-ranging and unstable.

Mediation Occurs Beyond Information Acquisition

As noted, the traditional focus of political communication on news media has also tended to emphasize the importance of "information" as the central component

of mediated citizenship. But as proponents of the ritual view of communication argue, there are many reasons why citizens engage in communicative acts that are either unrelated or tangential to the desire to be informed. Ritual acts of communication facilitate a sense of identification, community/sociability, security/control, expression, pleasure/entertainment, distraction, and even possession. A cultural approach to mediated citizenship foregrounds the ways in which citizens utilize media for these ends, as well as how certain media facilitate these feelings or behaviors more than others.

Public access television, for instance, is almost meaningless if one views it as a significant source for political information that extends beyond the ideological status quo of two-party rule in the United States (primarily because of its structural and financial limitations in most cities). But for the citizens who produce such programming, one study reports, it offers a feeling of empowerment, a sense that they do indeed "own" the airwaves in some fashion, and that they have a measure of control over television programming, however minimal (Linder 1999). Similarly, those who engage in the practice of "culture jamming"—where the ideology of capitalism is interrupted and subverted through the manipulation of advertising codes and symbols—are probably not changing anyone's mind about whether they should drink Absolut vodka or purchase Nike shoes. Culture jammers are, however, staking a claim that they too have the right to possess and control their cultural environment, even as they violate property or trademark law in the process (Branwyn 1997; Harold 2004).

A study of the "shadow campaign" occurring in popular culture during the 2004 US presidential election also highlights the functions of popular media forms (such as films, music, television and radio programs, books, etc.) beyond the instrumental intentionality of those who produced the material. The vast array of overtly political documentary films originating on the political left and right during the campaign, for instance, exemplifies how the films served as more than just rhetorical arguments of support for or detraction from the political candidates. These films also had the effect of provoking dialog, offering different ways of thinking about the candidates and the world, advancing additional issues not raised by the campaigns, and providing a means through which viewers could establish a sense of belonging and/or connections to the community of other concerned, frustrated or partisan citizens (Jones, 2005b).

In this way, then, a ritual view of communication focuses our attention on the important integrative aspects of media. As numerous studies have demonstrated, media remind citizens of their place in a community, nation, or society. Media serve as "priests" in offering civil religious "sacraments" during times of conflict, trouble, or mourning (Hallin and Gitlin 1992; Dayan and Katz 1992; Marvin and Ingle 1999). It alerts citizens when core values are threatened, and notifies them when they should rise up like patriots to defend those values (Thelen 1996). It offers a rich symbolic universe that, perhaps more often than not, taps into affective feelings, emotions, and beliefs having more political resonance with citizens than logic-centered appeals (Comstock and Scharrer 2005).

Finally, citizen desire for entertainment, pleasure, and distraction when attending to media are accounted for in a cultural approach as well. Engaging politics through media need not be the proverbial equivalent of eating one's vegetables. With a dramatic increase in new forms of entertainment-centered programming on television that deals with the formal political arena, audiences are offered many different formats—some more pleasurable than others—for consuming political narratives. One study of audiences for humorous political talk shows on television, for instance, reports that audiences watch precisely because it informs *while* offering feelings of enjoyment or pleasure not available on traditional, pundit-based talk shows (Jones 2005a).

Recent scholarly work, particularly in Europe, has begun to explore the relationship that exists between the types of affective politics I am describing here and the more rationalistic conceptions of citizenship that continue to dominate the study of political communication. John Corner and Dick Pels argue that the aesthetics of political representation have changed, with voters more attuned to notions of celebrity and style in their judgments of politicians and their character. The visual and emotional literacy that is the basis of these judgments arises from what they call the "post-ideological lifestyle choices" derived from consumerism, celebrity, and entertainment (Corner

and Pels 2003, 7). The ways that politicians therefore use media to exploit this, or the types of media used by citizens as they attend to politics in these ways, becomes increasingly significant. Hence, both affective appeals and affective voter assessments become incorporated into what is often conceived as a realm of political activity that should be dominated by rational thought and action.

We Live in a Culture of Political Engagement

A cultural approach to understanding mediated citizenship foregrounds the relationships that citizens maintain with the enormous array of media forms available to them. This emphasis on mediation, therefore, recognizes that daily citizen engagement with politics is more frequently *textual* than organizational or "participatory" in any traditional sense. That is, the most common and frequent form of political activity comes, for most people, through their choosing, attending to, processing, and engaging myriad media texts about the formal political process of government and political institutions as they conduct their daily lives.[9] As discussed earlier, those engagements may be instrumental in nature—intentional encounters, segregated from other activities, focused on the attainment of information, perhaps even ideologically derived or centered. Conversely, those engagements may be cursory and haphazard, enmeshed in daily routines, associated with pursuits of pleasure, and existing far afield from ideological or partisan concerns. They may derive from the rational pursuit of self-interest, the need for social integration, or both. In either case, media provide the central means for citizens' understanding of and connection to the political world.

And that is the point. Politics today is as ubiquitous as advertising. It just as likely comes into our lives uninvited as otherwise. We engage politics everywhere, all the time, and media are central to that engagement. Some of it grabs our attention and some of it does not. Some of it sticks and some of it does not. If a technological device can communicate with people, we can be assured that politicians are going to communicate to citizens through it. But citizens themselves are also going to try to make sense of and participate in the political world through those devices as well. Email is a case in point. Somehow the gods of solicitation learn our virtual whereabouts, and, before we know it, appeals for our beliefs, money, commitments, and efforts are on our screen. But so are the random, yet frequent mailings from friends and colleagues that appeal to other aspects of our citizenship. They are angry or hopeful missives on contemporary political affairs. They are file attachments offering hilarious renderings of politicians and their foibles in Photoshop political art. They are links to video clips of political parody that we ourselves feel the need to send to others.

We must recognize, therefore, that our political culture has changed as well, a culture in which everyday life and politics are now intimately intertwined *because* of media. Political culture is, by one definition, "the realms of experience, imagination, values and dispositions that provide the settings within which a political system operates, shaping the character of political processes and political behaviour. It is the elements of political culture that, among other things, interconnect the 'official' world of professional politics with the world of everyday experience and with the modes of 'the popular' variously to be found within work and leisure" (Corner and Pels 2003, 3). A cultural approach foregrounds the ways in which popular media shape public experiences with and dispositions toward politics, including our civic values and democratic imaginations.[10] To do so is to recognize that this shaping occurs through many different media forms (beyond news) that offer a variety of meanings, each with the potential for multiple means of individual and communal interaction (beyond information acquisition).

What political engagement means, therefore, has changed as well (beyond voting and institution-based activities). A cultural approach to citizenship emphasizes the mediated nature of that engagement. It highlights the agency of direct political action available to citizens *through* media (as emphasized in the literature on new media and alternative media, yet also seen in the earlier examples regarding conservative and Christian usage of multiple media forms for political engagement). But it also recognizes the continued importance of political messages and symbolizations that citizens routinely use to make sense of politics in older, still-dominant forms of media (as emphasized in

the literature on mass media, political psychology, and rhetorical studies). As Marc Howard Ross explains, a "cultural analysis of politics takes seriously the post-modern critique of behavioral political analyses and seeks to offer contextually rich inter-subjective accounts of politics which emphasize how political actors understand social and political actions" (2000, 33). In short, a focus on the mediation of contemporary citizenship highlights the ontological and epistemological dimensions of our mediated public lives.

This does not mean, however, that this culture of engagement necessarily provides a means of overcoming the structured differences in power, access, and legitimacy that certain institutions, voices, and discourses occupy in society. Political economists will rightly point out that mediated citizenship is dominated by large media conglomerates. Access to, representation in, and diversity of media are, and will continue to be, structured by relations of inequality (Golding and Murdock 1999, 159). Whether the blossoming of new media technologies will provide citizens with powerful countervailing means of communication efficacy is yet to be seen. Similarly, official voices and discourses will continue to find their way into newer or more popular forms of communication, as witnessed, for instance, by the Bush administration's attempts in 2001–2002 to use popular media forms (such as prime-time television dramas, MTV, and reality programming) as a way to sell its "War on Terror" to citizens through non-traditional channels of political communication (Jones 2005a, 6–7).

Nevertheless, as this argument has attempted to demonstrate, the multiple and varied means of cultural production and dissemination now available to citizens through new, alternative, and popular media—as well as traditional media forms—opens avenues for engagement that cannot be totally dominated or determined by the interests of capital or state (if only, at least, in the open, interpretive nature of popular narratives themselves). And as I have also argued, central to contemporary culture is the "lived with" nature of media and its dominant (and dominating) presence in our lives. Perhaps this torrent of media images and messages will blind citizens to the important locations of power and governmental action that ultimately shape their lives. What we can conclude, however, is that the means through which citizens construct the "reality" of politics and the state—and their relationship to it—will be influenced greatly by their daily, routinized engagements with the multiple media forms at their disposal.

Notes

1. As Todd Gitlin notes, media form "an accompaniment *to* life that has become a central experience *of* life" (2002, 17; original emphasis).
2. See Norris (2000, 3–21) for a survey and critique of this thesis.
3. Two prominent examples are found in recent scholarly treatments of the state of political communication. In the *Journal of Communication's* special issue on "the state of the art in communication theory and research," Doris Graber's quantitative analysis of political communication research appearing in top discipline journals highlights the continued dominance of news as a central focus of academic research (2005, 483). In Lynda Lee Kaid's (2004) recent update to the classic *Handbook of Political Communication*, research on news media is the only mass-mediated form of political communication that receives its own section and numerous chapters devoted to it. In short, although European scholars have more actively embraced the "cultural turn" in the study of all forms of communication, including politics, that change has come much more slowly in US scholarship.
4. In 2002, the Pew Research Center reported that audiences for network news, network news magazines programs, CNN, and local news had fallen from 26 percent to 54 percent between 1993 and 2003. See Pew Research Center for the People and the Press, "Public's News Habits Little Changed Since September 11" (retrieved 25 September 2005, from http://people-press.org/reports/display.php3?ReportID = 156).
5. Throughout this article, the term "medium" (as developed and employed by media ecologists and proponents of medium theory) is used to highlight Marshall McLuhan's conception that "media technologies carry distinct temporal and spatial specificities to which correspond definite frameworks of perception" (Holmes 2005, 39). The usage of differing communication mediums, then, will have differential effects on citizens' relationship to the political world.
6. Because "alternative media" is a term used to represent a wide variety of politically conscious, non-mainstream media forms, Couldry and Curran use the term to refer to "media production that challenges, at least implicitly, actual concentrations of media power, whatever form those concentrations may take in different locations" (2003, 7).

7. See Shaun Moores (2000) for an examination of the integration of various media forms into everyday life.
8. For a discussion of the epistemology of oral, written, and electronic forms of communication, see Ong (1982). For an application of such thinking to television, see Postman (1985).
9. Gronbeck makes a similar argument when he asserts that it is the task of political communication scholars to understand how politics is partly the negotiation over meaning making "wherein political subjects do battle with their leaders via texts and intertextual associations for control of the political environment" (1990, 212).
10. See Dahlgren (2000) for a discussion of what he calls our "civic culture," or the "cultural attributes prevalent among citizens that can in various ways facilitate democratic life." See Jones for an application of the concept of civic culture to the medium of television (2005a, 187–96).

References

Alger, Dean E. 1995. *The media and politics.* 2nd ed. New York: Wadsworth.

Barthes, Roland. 1972. *Mythologies.* New York: Hill and Wang.

Bausinger, H. 1984. Media, technology and daily life. *Media, Culture and Society* 6:343–51.

Baym, Geoffrey. 2005. *The Daily Show:* Discursive integration and the reinvention of political journalism. *Political Communication* 22:259–76.

Bennett, Lance. 2001. *News: The politics of illusion.* 4th ed. New York: Longman.

Branwyn, Gareth. 1997. *Jamming the media: A citizen's guide.* San Franciscom Calif.: Chronicle Books.

Bucy, Eric P., and Kimberly S. Gregson. 2002. Media participation: A legitimizing mechanism of mass democracy. *New Media & Society* 3:357–80.

Burke, Kenneth. 1966. *Language as symbolic action.* Berkeley: University of California Press.

——. 1969. *A grammar of motives.* Berkeley: University of California Press.

Carey, James. 1989. *Communication as culture: Essays on media and society.* Boston, Mass.: Unwin Hyman.

Comstock, George, and Erica Scharrer. 2005. *The psychology of media and politics.* New York: Elsevier Academic Press.

Cook, Timothy E. 1998. *Governing with the news: The news media as a political institution.* Chicago, Ill.: University of Chicago Press.

Corner, John, and Dick Pels, eds. 2003. *Media and the restyling of politics.* Thousand Oaks, Calif.: Sage.

Couldry, Nick, and Curran James, eds. 2003. *Contesting media power: Alternative media in a networked world.* Lanham, Md.: Rowman and Littlefield.

Dahlgren, Peter. 2000. Media, citizenship and civic culture. In *Mass media and society*, edited by James Curran and Michael Gurevitch. London: Arnold.

Dayan, Daniel, and Elihu Katz. 1992. *Media events: The live broadcasting of history*. Cambridge, Mass.: Harvard University Press.

Edelman, Murray. 1988. *Constructing the political spectacle*. Chicago, Ill.: University of Chicago Press.

Freie, John. 1998. *Counterfeit community*. Lanham, Md.: Rowman and Littlefield.

Ganley, Gladys D. 1992. *The exploding power of personal media*. Norwood, N.J.: Ablex.

Gauntlett, David, and Annette Hill. 1999. *TV living: Television culture and everyday life*. London: Routledge.

Gillmor, Dan. 2004. *We the people: Grassroots journalism, by the people, for the people*. Sebastopol, Calif.: O'Reilly.

Gitlin, Todd. 2002. *Media unlimited: How the torrent of images and sounds overwhelm our lives*. New York: Henry Holt and Company.

Golding, Peter, and Graham Murdock. 1999. Culture, communications, and political economy. In *News: A reader*, edited by Howard Tumber. New York: Oxford University Press.

Graber, Doris A. 2001. *Processing politics: Learning from television in the Internet age*. Chicago, Ill.: University of Chicago Press.

———. 2005. Political communication faces the 21st century. *Journal of Communication* 55 (September):479–507.

Gronbeck, Bruce E. 1990. Popular culture, media, and political communication. In *New directions in political communication*, edited by David L. Swanson and Dan Nimmo. Newbury Park, Calif.: Sage.

Hachten, William A. 2005. *The troubles of journalism*. 3rd ed. Mahwah, N.J.: Lawrence Erlbaum Associates.

Hallin, Dan C, and Todd Gitlin. 1992. Agon and ritual: The Gulf War as popular culture and as television drama. *Political Communication* 10:411–24.

Harold, Christine L. 2004. Pranking rhetoric: "Culture jamming" as media activism. *Critical Studies in Media Communication* 21:189–211.

Hilliard, Robert L., and Michael C. Keith. 1999. *Waves of rancor: Tuning in the radical right*. London: M.E. Sharpe.

Holmes, David. 2005. *Communication theory: Media, technology and society*. Thousand Oaks, Calif.: Sage.

Jamieson, Kathleen Hall, and Paul Waldman. 2003. *The press effect: Politicians, journalists, and the stories that shape the political world*. New York: Oxford University Press.

Johnson, P. 2003. Trust of media keeps on slipping. *USA Today*, 28 May.

Jones, Jeffrey P. 2005a. *Entertaining politics: New political television and civic culture*. Lanham Md.: Rowman and Littlefield.

———. 2005b. The shadow campaign in popular culture. In *The 2004 presidential campaign: A communication perspective*, edited by Robert E. Denton, Jr. Lanham, Md.: Rowman and Littlefield Publishers.

———. 2006. "Fake" news versus "real" news as sources of political information: The Daily Show and postmodern political reality. In *Politicotainment: Television's take on the real*, edited by Kristina Riegert. New York: Peter Lang Publishers.

Kaid, Lynda Lee, ed. 2004. *Handbook of political communication research*. Mahwah, N.J.: Lawrence Erlbaum.

Kertzer, David. 1988. *Ritual, power and politics*. New Haven, Conn.: Yale University Press.

Kovach, Bill, and Tom Rosenstiel. 2001. *The elements of journalism: What newspeople should know and the public should expect*. New York: Crown Publishers.

Lakoff, George. 1996. *Moral politics: What conservatives know that liberals don't*. Chicago, Ill.: University of Chicago Press.

———. 2004. *Don't think of an elephant! Know your values and frame the debate*. White River Junction, Vt.: Chelsea Green Publishing.

Lembo, Ron. 2000. *Thinking through television*. Cambridge: Cambridge University Press.

Lesage, Jessica. 1998. Christian media. In *Media, culture, and the religious right*, edited by Linda Kintz and Jessica Lesage. Minneapolis: University of Minnesota Press.

Linder, Laura R. 1999. *Public access television: America's electronic soapbox*. Westport, Conn.: Praeger.

Marcus, George E., W. Russell Neuman, and Michael MacKuen. 2000. *Affective intelligence and political judgment*. Chicago, Ill.: University of Chicago Press.

Marvin, Carolyn, and David W. Ingle. 1999. *Blood sacrifice and the nation: Totem rituals and the American flag*. Cambridge: Cambridge University Press.

McCaughey, Martha, and Michael D. Ayers, eds. 2003. *Cyberactivism: Online activism in theory and practice*. London: Routledge.

McNair, Brian. 1995. *An introduction to political communication*. London: Routledge.

Meikle, Graham. 2002. *Future active: Media activism and the Internet*. London: Routledge.

Meyrowitz, Joshua. Understandings of media (three images of media). *ETC.: A Review of General Semantics* 56.1 (Spring 1999):44(9). *InfoTrac OneFile*, Thomson Gale, Old Dominion University Library, 18 October 2005.

Mindich, David T. Z. 2005. *Tuned out: Why Americans under 40 don't follow the news*. New York: Oxford University Press.

Moores, Shaun. 2000. *Media and everyday life in modern society*. Edinburgh: Edinburgh University Press.

Moy, Patricia, and Michael Pfau. 2000. *With malice toward all?: The media and public confidence in democratic institutions*. Westport, Conn.: Praeger.

Nichols, Bill. 1991. *Representing reality*. Bloomington: Indiana University Press.

Nimmo, Dan, and James E. Combs. 1983. *Mediated political realities.* New York: Longman.

——, and David L. Swanson. 1990. The field of political communication: Beyond the voter persuasion paradigm. In *New directions in political communication,* edited by David L. Swanson and Dan Nimmo. Newbury Park, Calif.: Sage.

Norris, Pippa. 2000. *The virtuous circle: Political communication in post-industrial societies.* Cambridge: Cambridge University Press.

Ong, Walter. 1982. *Orality and literacy: The technologizing of the word.* New York: Routledge.

Paletz, David L. 2002. *The media in American politics: Contents and consequences* 2nd ed. New York: Longman.

Perloff, Richard M. 1998. *Political communication: Politics, press, and public in America.* Mahwah, N.J.: Lawrence Erlbaum Associates.

Peterson, Steven A. 1990. *Political behavior: Patterns in everyday life.* Newbury Park, Calif.: Sage.

Pompper, Donnalyn. 2003. *The West Wing:* White House narratives that journalism cannot tell. In *The West Wing: The American presidency as television drama,* edited by Peter C. Rollins and John E. O'Connor. Syracuse, N.Y.: Syracuse University Press.

Postman, Neil. 1985. *Amusing ourselves to death.* New York: Penguin Books.

Pranger, Robert J. 1968. *Action, symbolism, and order: The existential dimensions of politics in modern citizenship.* Nashville, Tenn.: Vanderbilt University Press.

Purvis, Hoyt. 2000. *The media, politics, and government.* New York: Wadsworth.

Putnam, Robert D. 2000. *Bowling alone: The collapse and revival of American community.* New York: Simon & Schuster.

Rheingold, Howard. 2002. *Smart mobs: The next social revolution.* New York: Basic Books.

Roberts, Gene, Thomas Kunkle, and Charles Layton. 2001. *Leaving readers behind: The age of corporate newspapering.* Fayetteville, Ark.: University of Arkansas Press.

Ross, Marc Howard. 2000. The relevance of culture for the study of political psychology. In *Political psychology: Cultural and crosscultural foundations,* edited by Stanley A. Renshon and John Duckitt. New York: New York University Press.

Scammell, Margaret. 2003. Citizen consumers: Towards a new marketing of politics? In *Media and the restyling of politics,* edited by John Corner and Dick Pels. Thousand Oaks, Calif.: Sage.

Scheuer, Jeffrey. 1999. *The sound-bite society: Television and the American mind.* New York: Four Walls Eight Windows.

Schudson, Michael. 1998. *The good citizen: A history of American civic life.* New York: The Free Press.

Seelye, Katharine Q. 2005a. At newspapers, some clipping. *New York Times,* 10 October, C1.

——. 2005b. Why newspapers are betting on audience participation. *New York Times,* 4 July.

——. 2005c. Survey on news media finds wide displeasure. *New York Times,* 27 June.

Silverstone, Roger. 1994. *Television and everyday life.* London: Routledge.

Sunstein, Cass. 2002. *Republic.com.* Princeton, N.J.: Princeton University Press.

Thelen, David. 1996. *Becoming citizens in the age of television.* Chicago, Ill.: University of Chicago Press.

van Zoonen, Liesbet. 2005. *Entertaining the citizen: When politics and popular culture converge.* Lanham, Md.: Rowman and Littlefield.

Viguerie, Richard A., and David Franke. 2004. *America's right turn: How conservatives used new and alternative media to take power.* Chicago, Ill.: Bonus Books.

Woodward, Gary C. 1997. *Perspectives on American political media.* Boston, Mass.: Allyn and Bacon.

Younge, G. 2004. Washington Post apologizes for underplaying WMD scepticism. *The Guardian* (London), 13 August, 2.

40.
THE THEORY OF INFANTILE CITIZENSHIP
Lauren Berlant

When Americans make the pilgrimage to Washington they are trying to grasp the nation in its totality. Yet the totality of the nation in its capital city is a jumble of historical modalities, a transitional space between local and national cultures, private and public property, archaic and living artifacts, processes of nation making that bridge the national history that marks the monumental landscape and the everyday life temporalities of federal and metropolitan cultures. That is to say, it is a place of national *mediation,* where a variety of nationally inflected media come into visible and sometimes incommensurate contact. As a borderland between these domains, Washington tests the very capacity of anyone who visits there: this test is a test of citizenship competence. Usually made in tandem with families or classes of students, the trip to the capital makes pedagogy a patriotic performance, one in which the tourist "playing at being American" is called on to coordinate the multiple domains of time, space, sensation, exchange, knowledge, and power that represent the scene of what we might call "total" citizenship.[1] To live fully both the ordinariness and the sublimity of national identity, one must be capable not just of imagining but of managing being American.

To be able to feel less fractured than the nation itself would be, indeed, a privilege. Audre Lorde tells a story of her family's one visit to Washington in 1947.[2] Lorde's parents claim to be making the trip to commemorate their two daughters' educational triumphs, in an eighth grade and a high school graduation. The truth is, though, that Lorde's sister Phyllis was barred from accompanying her graduating class on its celebratory visit to Washington because Washington was a southern, segregated city, not at all "national" in the juridical or patriotic sense. The Lorde family refuses to acknowledge racism as the impetus for its own private journey: rather, the very denial that racism is a national system motivates their performance as American tourists. For at every moment the family encounters its unfreedom to enter certain spaces of private property, the parents refuse to acknowledge the irony that, although "public" monuments like the Lincoln Memorial allow African-Americans like Audre Lorde and Marian Anderson access to a public sphere of symbolic national identification, the very ordinary arrangements of life in America, eating and sleeping, are as forbidden to the Lorde family in Washington as America itself is to those without passports. This is to say that in Washington the bar of blackness effectively splits the national symbolic from the possessive logics of capitalist culture, even as each nonetheless dominates the American public sphere.

Still, they schedule their visit to Washington on Independence Day, and when Lorde bitterly remarks on her patriotic exile from America, symbolized in the apartheid of its most local abridgment, and in particular in a waitress's refusal of the family's desire to celebrate the nation's birthday by eating ice cream they had paid for *inside* of a restaurant, she describes it as the line she steps over from childhood to something else, a different political, corporeal, sensational, and aesthetic "adulthood": "[T]he waitress was white, and the counter was white, and the ice cream I never ate in Washington D.C. that summer I left childhood was white, and the white heat and the white pavement and the white stone monuments of my first Washington summer made me sick to my stomach."[3] Lorde's "education" in national culture provoked a nauseated unlearning of her patriotism – "Hadn't I written poems about Bataan?" she complains, while resolving, again, to write the president, to give the nation another chance to not betray her desire for it – and this unlearning, which is never complete, as it involves leaving behind the political faith of childhood, cleaves her permanently from and to the nation whose promises drew her parents to immigrate there and drew herself to identify as a child with a horizon of national identity she was sure she would fulfill as an adult citizen.

That was 1947. Stephen Heath has argued recently that transformations in the production of political consciousness that have taken place in the context of developments in global media culture have made the category "citizen" archaic, and many worthy theorists of television in particular agree that the ruptural force of its technologies and logics of capital has unsettled norms of signifying national culture and political agency.[4] It is now a commonplace in television criticism that television promotes the annihilation of memory and, in particular, of historical knowledge and political self-understanding. It may be an ontology and ideology of "liveness," common sense, banality, distraction, catastrophe, interminable "flow": it may be the implicitness of capital in generating an ideology of "free" entertainment (which makes the consumption of commercial, "free/floating" anxieties about power, history, and identity the metaproblem *and* the critical promise of the medium), it may be the global lexicon of images that has come to dominate the pseudomulticultural scene of consumption, or – perhaps – some combination of these.[5] But because in all areas of its mode of production television encounters, engages, and represents citizenship, and because it underscores the activity of animating and reflecting on as well as simply having a national identity, the problem of generating memory and knowledge in general becomes fraught with issues of national pedagogy, of representing what counts as patriotism and what counts as criticism to the public sphere of consumers itself.[6]

If, as I have described, the pilgrimage to Washington is already all about the activity of national pedagogy, the production of national culture, and the constitution of competent citizens, then the specificity of mass mediation in the dissemination of national knowledges redoubles and loops around the formation of national identity. There is nothing archaic about citizenship – its signs and cadences are changing. Margaret Morse (1990) argues that television enters history by annexing older forms of national self-identity, cultural literacy, and leisure. It does this to reacclimate continuously consumer identifications during transitions in media-saturated national and international public spheres: in these conditions of specifically uneven development, the work of media in redefining citizenship and framing what can legitimately be read as national pedagogy becomes more, not less, central to any analysis of political identity in postmodern American culture.

This is to say that the definitional field of citizenship – denoting either simple membership in a political identity category or a reflexive operation of agency and criticism – is precisely what is under contestation, as the norms of signifying in what we might call "mass nationality" change the face of power in America (e.g., in the public discussion over town halls versus other modes of national "expert" culture). In addition, the problem of harnessing publicity to struggles within national culture predates the televisual moment – just as *Mr. Smith Goes to Washington* predates *Adventure in Washington, Born Yesterday*, and more recent narratives like *The Distinguished Gentleman*. These intertexts and many others structured by pilgrimages to Washington all foreground the problem, place, and promise of media in the business of making nationality; they all contain montages and plots that show both the potential for agentive citizenship and the costs of the mediated dispersal of critical national identifications. Television's role in constructing the hegemony of the national must thus be understood as a partial, not a determining, moment in a genealogy of crises about publicity and the production of "national" subjects.[7]

This essay explores the genre of the pilgrimage to Washington, focusing not on a news or a biographical event but on an episode of the popular weekly cartoon television show "The Simpsons," entitled "Mr.

Lisa Goes to Washington." This project is about how different modes of national and mass cultural memory specifically intersect in America. As intertexts to this episode, the essay will gesture toward the other tourist/citizenship pilgrimages this episode revises, notably *Mr. Smith Goes to Washington.* Deploying the typical codes of the narrative trope, they hold that the state of America can be read in the manifestations of infantile citizenship and in the centrality to national culture of an imaginary children's public sphere.[8]

Lisa Simpson wins a trip to Washington ("all expenses paid") by writing a "fiercely pro-American" patriotic essay for a contest that her father, Homer Simpson, discovers in a complementary copy he receives of *Reading Digest.* The family stays at the Watergate, encounters Barbara Bush in the bathtub at the White House, visits the mint, and generates commentary on national monuments. Then Lisa accidently witnesses graft (securing the destruction of her beloved hometown national park by logging interests – signaling the realpolitik, the will-to-dominate-nature of the Reagan-Bush era). Lisa then tears up her prize-winning essay, substituting for it a new essay about how Washington "stinks." Losing her patriotic simplicity, she loses the national jingoism contest. A Senate page, seeing her loss of faith in democracy, calls his senator for help, and within two hours the FBI has the crooked congressman in jail: he rapidly becomes a born-again Christian. On witnessing the evidence of the effects of her muckraking, Lisa exclaims, at the end of the show, "The system works!" We will return to the question of systems later.

I have described the aspects of this plot that are repeated in the other pilgrimage-to-Washington narratives. Someone, either a child or an innocent adult described as an "infant," goes to Washington: the crisis of her/his innocence/illiteracy emerges from an ambivalent encounter between America as a theoretical ideality and America as a site of practical politics, mapped onto Washington, D.C. All of the "children" disrupt the norms of the national locale: their "infantile citizenship" operates the way Oskar Negt and Alexander Kluge (1992) predict it would, eliciting scorn and cynicism from "knowing" adults who try to humiliate them and admiration from these same adults, who can remember with nostalgia the

time that they were "unknowing" and thus believed in the capacity of the nation to be practically utopian.

As it is, citizen adults have learned to "forget" or to render as impractical, naive, or childish their utopian political aspirations, in order to be politically happy and economically functional. Confronting the tension between utopia and history, the infantile citizen's insistent stupidity thus gives her/him enormous power to unsettle, expose, and reframe the machinery of national life. Thus the potential catastrophe of all visits to Washington: can national identification survive the practical habitation of everyday life in the national locale? Can the citizen/tourist gain the skills for living nationally without losing faith in nationality to provide the wisdom and justice in promises? Is the utopian horizon of national identity itself a paramnesia or a Zizekian "fantasy" that covers over impossible contradictions and lacks in national culture?[9] The stakes in a text's answer to these questions have everything to do with the scene of "adult" or "full" citizenship in its historical imaginary.

The transition in Audre Lorde's life from patriotic childhood to a less defined but powerful rage at the travesty everyday life makes of national promises for justice indeed marks a moment in the education of an American citizen that marks both personal and fictional narratives of the pilgrimage to Washington whose intertextual topography will be the subject of this essay. When cinematic, literary, and televisual texts fictively represent "Washington" as "America," they thus both theorize the conditions of political subjectivity in the United States and reflect on the popular media's ways of constructing political knowledge in a dialectic of infantile citizenship and cynical reason. To extricate the politics of this dialectic on behalf of a history of citizenship, my strategy here will be to work from the negative pedagogical to the utopian, mass-mediated horizons of national identity practice.

Incompetent Citizens and Junk Knowledges, American-Style

"Mr. Lisa Goes to Washington" shares with *Born Yesterday, The Distinguished Gentleman*, and other "Washington" narratives a rhetoric of citizenship that locates the utopian possibilities of national identity in terroristic, anarchic, and/or comic spectacles of someone's personal *failure* to be national. The "scene" of citizenship is revealed by way of events that humiliate a citizen, disclosing him/her as someone incapable of negotiating the semiotic, economic and political conditions of his/her existence in civil society. And just as the dirty work of representing the detritus of a white, bourgeois national culture will almost inevitably go to the citizens whose shameful bodies signify a seemingly natural incapacity to become (masters of the) abstract, the plot of "Mr. Lisa Goes to Washington" is embedded not in Lisa's story but in the gross activities of the failed father, Homer Simpson.

The show opens with Homer opening his junk mail. He is reading what the mail says and yelling at the letters in minor sarcastic outrage at their mistakes (e.g., one is addressed to "Homer Simpsoy") and their pseudopromises of wealth with no risk or labor. Yet, for all of his cynical knowledge, he also makes a grave optimistic reading error. Rapacious and desiring to the point of senselessness, Homer takes a representation of a "check" in a Publisher's Clearing House-like contest as a real representation of money. He goes to the bank to cash the million-dollar pseudocheck – that says phrases like "void void void" and "This is not a check" – and is devastated to find the "deal" "queered." Homer continues, throughout the episode, to show himself incompetent in the face of money – indeed, in a scene toward the end, he makes the very same error with another check. When the eventual winner of the patriotism contest symbolically shares his prize with Lisa, a prize represented by what the young man calls an "oversized novelty check," Homer yells from the audience, "Give her the check!" and then, amidst everyone's laughter, protests, "I wasn't kidding." Though at every moment money appears in the show Homer has no control over the differences between its symbolic and exchange value – unlike Bart, who understands and exploits to his great pleasure the ambiguity of the word "expense" in "all expenses paid" – Homer is constantly surprised and betrayed at his constant "discovery" that even in Washington money is not "free."

What Homer does well instead is to drool and moan and expose himself compulsively like an idiot relegated to his insipid appetites. Immediately after his humiliation by the advertising check, he becomes,

literally, the "butt" of more jokes about freedom and about money: having proved his inadequacy to owning money in late capitalism by miscasting the contest check as a negotiable one, he stands up and shows the "Simpsons" audience the top, cracked part of his exposed rear. Like a bald spot or an unzipped fly, the crack of the butt winks at the cruel superior public that knows how to use money, knows how to distinguish between real and false checks, and can stick to a decorous hierarchy of desires, needs, and appetites, while regulating its body. Homer has no capacity to think abstractly, or to think: as when he drools on the head of a worker at the mint and then sputters "lousy, cheap country!" when they refuse to give out free samples of money.

There are many other instances of Homer's humiliation by the tacit text of bourgeois nationalism in this episode, as he tries to enter as a master public language and knowledges. His working-class brutishness is disclosed, for example, in the scene of Lisa's triumph at the "Veterans of Popular Wars" contest. When a contest judge feels suspicious of young Lisa having written such a beautiful essay, she opines, "Methinks I smell the sickly scent of the daddy," and decides to interview Homer, who becomes entirely aphonic and grunting in the face of her series of questions. Lisa gets extra points for having survived descending from such a brute. Later, snorting down "free" food at the convention in Washington, Homer again loses language at a moment when he explicitly attests to his love of the vocabulary-builder sections of *Reader's Digest:* he asks but is unable to retain the information clarifying this chain of signs: "V (Very) I (Important) P (Person)." Why should he? for he is none of these things. With none of the social competences of a person who has knowledge about money or the world, he demonstrates what George Lipsitz has called the "infantile narcissism" of consumer self-addiction: "Who would have thought," he says to Lisa, "that reading or writing would pay off!"[10]

"Have . . . You Ever Run Into Any Problems Because of Your Superior Ability?"

When Homer "loses" the million dollars, his wife, Marge, consoles him by showing him the "free" *Reader's Digest* they have received in the mail. Like

Billie Dawn learning to negotiate the topography of power through print and other national media in *Born Yesterday*, Homer becomes a regular public intellectual while he reads the magazine: he pulls the children away from a "period" film they are watching on television about the Anglo-American theft of land from Native-American nations (which depicts a white preacher telling an "Indian chief" that the tribe's homeland will be more valuable if they abandon and irrigate it) and reads them a true-life adventure story; he is caught reading on the job at the nuclear power plant by Mr. Burns, who asks his assistant, "Who is that bookworm, Smithers? . . . His job description clearly specifies an illiterate!"; and he reads "Quotable Notables" as a substitute for eating lunch. But when Homer reads that the patriotic essay contest is for children, he loses interest in the magazine and throws it out. This is when "Mr. Lisa" takes over the plot: fishing as usual through the garbage of her family's affections to gain some emotional capital, she becomes, as Bart says, ". . . the pony to bet on."

In what does Lisa's smartness and competence consist? When she first attempts the patriotic essay, she tries dutifully to quote Ben Franklin or to extract inspiration from a diagram showing how a bill becomes law. But, quoting *Mr. Smith*, "Mr. Lisa" comes to derive her power from association with a kind of "natural" national property whose value is in its non-circulation in a system of exploitation and profit: the public domain called Springfield National Park. "America, inspire me," she says to the park, and a bald eagle straight from the national seal alights in front of her. This collaboration of the national symbolic and nature enkindles Lisa, and the show provides a montage of such speeches by our "patriots of tomorrow" in which her speech takes top honors.

As a backdrop to this little speech-making montage, the "nation" imagined by its youth is visually signified by a pastel national map marked by the kinds of local-color images that airport postcards often sport, by some regional accents, and by the homely spun-out puns and metaphors of American children:

1. Nelson Muntz ("Springfield"), "Burn, Baby Burn": So burn that flag if you must! But before you do, you'd better burn a few other things!

You'd better burn your shirt and your pants! Be sure to burn your TV and your car! Oh yeah, and don't forget to burn your house! Because none of those things would exist without six red stripes, seven white stripes, and a helluva lotta stars!!

2. Anonymous girl (Rosemount, Minnesota), "Recipe for a Free Country": Recipe for a Free Country: Mix one cup liberty, with three teaspoons of justice. Add one informed electorate. Baste well with veto power. . . . Stir in two cups of checks, sprinkle liberally with balances.

3. Anonymous boy (Mobile, Alabama), "The American Nonvoter": My back is spineless. My stomach is yellow. I am the American nonvoter.

4. Anonymous boy (Queens, New York), "Ding-Dong": Ding dong. The sound of the Liberty Bell. Ding. Freedom. Dong. Opportunity. Ding. Excellent Schools. Dong. Quality Hospitals.

5. Lisa Simpson (Springfield, T.A.): "The Roots of Democracy": When America was born on that hot July day in 1776, the trees in Springfield Forest were tiny saplings, trembling towards the sun, and as they were nourished by Mother Earth, so too did our fledgling nation find strength in the simple ideals of equality and justice. Who would have thought such mighty oaks or such a powerful nation could grow out of something so fragile, so pure. Thank you.

There is a certain regularity to what counts as a patriotic essay: the range of tonalities and rhetorical modes notwithstanding, fiercely patriotic citizenship always requires the deployment of analogies that represent the threat of imaginary violence to the national body – of the biosphere; the citizen; the conceptual, mappable nation. Even the feminine essay, "Recipe for a Nation," carries the implied warning that bad citizenship together with bad government is a form of bad nutrition that threatens the body politic. The national stakes of keeping these domains of the social in at least linguistic conjunction are comically telegraphed throughout the episode: the ultimate contest winner, Vietnamese immigrant Trong Van Din, says, "That's why, whenever I see the Stars and

Stripes, I will always be reminded of that wonderful word: flag!"

But why does Lisa win? Is she simply smarter or more creative than the other kids? She wins with her essay, "The Roots of Democracy," because she uses not just analogy but a national allegory that links organically the nation's natural growth to the emergence of its political facticity. In addition, her speech is itself an allegory of infantile citizenship, for the nation grows out of "something so fragile, so pure," so young. No secular or human power has yet affected its course: apparently, in the national/world "system" natural value prevails, assuring that in the infinite "tomorrow" all systems will exist in the space of America. In this, her "intelligence" is articulated in excess to the jingoism of ordinary Americans – in this episode, these are figured by white, decorous persons carrying protest-style placards bearing messages like "Everything's A-OK," "No Complaints Here," and "Things Are Fine" in front of the White House.

Thus, when Lisa gets to Washington, she feels supremely national, symbolic, invulnerable, intellectual. Although her superiority to other kids derives simply from her capacity to sustain a metaphor, and although in Washington she makes pranks and acts like a kid, she also seeks there an affirmation of her idealized self-image: learning early that the reason people go to national conferences is to find confirming images of their ideal selves, she asks the other kid finalists, "Have either of you ever run into any problems because of your superior ability?" and hugs them when they confirm, saying plaintively, "Me, too!" Her capacity to reflect on language and power marks her as the national Simpson in this episode, even as the public surely knows that it is Bart, not Lisa, who has captured the minds and money of consumers who identify with his bratty tactical disruptions and exploitations of the bourgeois public sphere. Her already-confirmed failure as a commodity outside of the show surely follows her around every episode in which she imagines that she might find a place for her "superior talents" in the national system. In this regard, she is Homer's twin, not his opposite: their excesses to the norms of body and language mark them each precisely as American failures, citizens unfit to profit from their

drives and talents in a national symbolic and capitalist system.

The End of National Fantasy: "The System Works!"

However, while each of the Simpsons is finding and revelling in her/his level of national competence, the federal nation is itself operating and corrupting both the natural and the capital forms that inspire the Simpson family. National corruption is tacitly everywhere in the show: the family stays at the Watergate; their bank advertises itself as "not a savings and loan"; Homer scoffs, "Yeah, right," at a sign in the White House bowling alley that claims Nixon bowled 300 back-to-back games there; Teddy Kennedy sits quietly at the Kennedy Center award ceremony, looking formless and dissipated; Lisa's congressman is shown cynically exploiting her for a photo opportunity (a form of presidential mass mediation invented, naturally, by Nixon).

But when Lisa witnesses graft that threatens to despoil the natural beauty of Springfield National Park, the tacit knowledge of national corruption the show figures via "Nixonia" becomes itself the ground of a new figuration of nationality that she produces. This requires, in two stages, recourse to a genealogy of national forms through which criticism and patriotism have been traditionally routed and mediated. The transformation of consciousness, sensuality, causality, and aesthetics she experiences is, again, typical of this genre, in which the revelation of the practical impossibility of utopian nationalism produces gothic, uncanny, miraculating effects in the affects of the persons whose minds are being transformed by "true," not idealized, national knowledges.

In stage one of Lisa's transfiguration, she immerses herself in the national symbolic, preparing to give her patriotic speech by visiting a constellation of Washington monuments. The payoff she sees takes place at the "Winnifred Beecher Howe" memorial, raised in fictive tribute to "an early crusader for women's rights [who] led the Floor Mop Rebellion of 1910," who later "appeared on the highly unpopular 75 cent piece." Howe's motto, I Will Iron Your Sheets When You Iron Out the Inequities in Your Labor Laws, marks the overdetermined and absurd space of

Lisa's imaginary relation to American nationality. It is not only the absurd notion that America would honor a labor activist who foregrounds the exploitation of women as workers, not the incommensurateness of sheets/labor laws, nor, merely, the wild ungoverned state of Howe's statuesque body, in its messy housewife regalia, nor Lisa's sighing adoration of this spectacle. The violent, nationally authored insult this absurdity hides in sarcasm is reduced, finally, to mere sexual grossness: in the afterglow of the congressman's sale of his favors to the lobbyist at the memorial, they look at Howe and say, on parting, "Woof woof!" and "What a pooch!"

Lisa is heartbroken: "How can I read my essay now, if I don't believe my own words?" She looks up from the reflecting pool at the Lincoln Memorial and feels that "Honest Abe" will "show me the way." But the memorial is overcrowded with Americans obsessed with the same possibility. They crowd around, projecting questions to Lincoln's stony, wise, iconic face; the questions range from, "What can I do to make this a better country?" to "How can I make my kid brush more?" and "Would I look good with a mustache?" Lisa, crowded out in the cacophony of national-popular need, goes to Jefferson's memorial, where the statue yells at her in ressentiment that his own accomplishments are underappreciated by the American people. She leaves quickly and goes to sit on the Capitol steps. There, magically, federal workers in their white-collar suits are transformed into pigs with skins engraved in the mode of dollar bills, sitting at troughs gorging themselves on dollar bills, wiping their mouths on the flag. This mutation of the cartoon places this episode in a genealogy of critical editorial cartooning, especially where national criticism takes the form of petty sarcasm; moreover, the gluttonous snorting of the pigs refers to Homer's own grotesque greedy excesses, thus reframing the class hierarchies and incompetences of national culture that the Simpsons embody into translations of the patriarchal corruptions of the national symbolic and the federal system themselves.

It turns out, in short, that Lisa was not that smart. I have described how America is split into a national and a capitalist system in "Mr. Lisa Goes to Washington." But this simple description is for infants, just as Bart's opening punishment on the blackboard, "Spitballs are not free speech," reduces the problem of protecting costly speech to a joke, a joke that once again allegorizes the conceptual problematic of freedom and its media by locating politics in a disgusting body. Lisa's response to the revelation of graft is to not become an adult, that is, to disidentify with the horizon of the politically-taken-for-granted whom the nation seeks to dominate. Her first response is to become abjected to America, by visiting Lincoln and soliciting his pedagogy. We have seen there, comedically, how the overidentification with national icons evacuates people's wisdom from the simplest judgments of everyday life; failing this identification, Lisa next invents a countercartoon aesthetic: she changes her title from "The Roots of Democracy" to "Cesspool of the Potomic."

But this first explosion of the affect, causal norms, monumental time, vision, sensation, and aesthetics of American citizenship is followed by yet another dislocation. This montage sequence takes place at the moment the Senate page beholds Lisa's crisis of faith in democracy. He telephones a senator; the FBI entraps the corrupt congressman, on videotape; the Senate meets and expels him; George Bush signs the bill; a newspaper almost instantly reports the congressman's imprisonment and conversion to a bornagain consciousness. Lisa says, "The system works!"

As in the telephone, telegraph, newspaper popular media montage sequence of *Mr. Smith Goes to Washington*, "The Simpsons" produces national criticism through another countertransformation of time, space, and media that involves shifting from the lexicon of patriotic monumentality and classical national representation to accelerating postmodern media forms: video, microchip bugs, cameras, late-edition daily newspapers. In addition, here the FBI's mastery of the media establishes it as the guardian of America, much as in the extraordinary 1933 film *Gabriel over the White House:* in contrast to the corrupt and lazy print media of *Mr. Smith*, "The Simpsons," and dozens of other pilgrimage-to-Washington films, global media formations are the real citizen-heroes here. Televisual technology itself becomes the representative of the "average man" who rises above his station, protected by FBI agents who seek to clean out and preserve all sorts of purity: of language (the FBI agent uses a southern drawl in his criminal guise and reverts to a television announcer's pure generic intonations in his "real" persona as the police), of region, and of the purity of the stream of faith that connects residents of the "mythical" Springfield, T.A., to the nation that represents America in Washington.

In two minutes of television time, and two hours of accelerated chronological time, then, the system cleans itself out, and the cesspool itself becomes born again, returns "home" to the discourse of national growth. Nothing complicated about this. The performance of mass media-dominated national political culture reveals a system of national meaning in which *allegory is the aesthetic of political realism* at every moment of successful national discourse, one in which the narrative of that discourse itself, at a certain point of metarepresentation, becomes a conceit that erases aggregate memory as it produces knowledge of the nation as a thing in itself. The competent citizen knows this and learns how conveniently and flexibly to read between the lines, thus preserving both domains of utopian national identification and cynical practical citizenship. This temporalizing mode of resolving questions about the way power dominates bodies, value, exchanges, dreams in the national public sphere is typical of the pilgrimage genre: for the resolution in time takes over what might slowly and unevenly happen in space were the system to be publicly engaged and remarked on in its own incoherence and unevenness. As it is, when Lisa says, "The system works!" she embodies the "patriot of tomorrow," because through the randomness we have witnessed she continues to believe a system exists, that "bills" motivated by democratic virtue do, indeed, become law. But to which system does she refer?

"Spitballs Are Not Free Speech"

In "Mr. Lisa," as in every fictive pilgrimage to Washington, national monuments, traditional symbolic narratives, print, radio, and television news coexist with other popular phenomena: here the right-wing cultural agenda of the Reagan-Bush era is everywhere in the narrative, including in its recourse to sarcasm as a form of criticism and in the tacitness of the Nixon intertext, which "reminds" without interfering with the pleasure of the narrative of a televisual moment when the nation thought it possible to

imagine a patriotic mass-mediated *criticism*. It is not just that television histories, children's textbooks, *Reader's Digest*, FBI surveillance video, national parks, and national spaces are here brought into conjunction, constituted as the means of production of modern citizenship. It is not even just that the Bushes themselves are portrayed here as benign patriarchs – for this might be coded as the text's return to the modality of wishful resolution that seems to mark the crisis of *having* national knowledge inevitably produced by the pilgrimage.

But the very multiplicity of media forms raises the question of the genres of patriotism itself, modes of collective identification that have become the opposite of "protest" or "criticism" for a generation of youths who have been drafted to vitalize a national fantasy politics unsupported by a utopian or even respectable domestic political agenda. The construction of a patriotic youth culture must be coded here as a postmodern nationalist mode of production: in this light, Bill Clinton's recent appearances on "Mister Rogers' Neighborhood," MTV, and so on involve merely one more extension of the national aura to the infant citizens of the United States, who are asked to identify with a "youthful" idealism untempered by an even loving critical distance.

This is to say that Lisa's assertion that the system works counts as even a parodic resolution to her epistemic murk because consciousness that a system exists at all has become what counts as the ideal pedagogical outcome of contemporary American politics: thus, in the chain that links the fetus, the wounded, the dead, and the "children" as the true American "people," the linkage is made through the elevation of a zero-sum mnemonic, a consciousness of the nation with no imagination of agency – apart perhaps from voting, here coded as a form of consumption. In other words, national knowledge has itself become a modality of national amnesia, an incitement to forgetting that leaves simply the patriotic trace, for real and metaphorically infantilized citizens, that confirms that the nation exists and that we are in it. Television is not the cause of this substitution of the fact (that the nation exists) for the thing (political agency) but is one of many vehicles where the distilling operation takes place and where the medium itself is installed as a necessary switch point between any locales and any national situation.

Let me demonstrate this by contrasting the finales of *Mr. Smith* and "Mr. Lisa." It is a crucial and curious structure of infantile citizenship plots that the accumulation of plot leads to an acceleration and a crisis of knowledge relieved not by modes of sustained criticism but by amnesia and unconsciousness. At the end of *Mr. Smith*, Jefferson Smith, played by Jimmy Stewart, is defeated by capitalists' manipulation of the law, property rights, and the media. Smith, who has been filibustering and improving on what discursive virtue might look like in the Senate, is confronted by a wagon load of telegrams embodying a manufactured public opinion mobilized against Smith and his cause; Smith, dispirited and depleted, faints on the Senate floor. His loss of spirit drives a senator (Claude Rains) to attempt suicide and to confess everything: in the film's final moments, a hubbub lead by Jean Arthur claims victory over corruption, and the mob dances out of the chambers into, presumably, the streets. The film, in other words, leaves Mr. Smith lying there on the Senate floor, unconscious. It might be interesting to speculate about what he would think when he awoke: would he think the system had worked? How could he, when so many systems were at play?

In contrast, it might seem that Lisa's violation by capital logic produces consciousness: but her belief in the "system" is renewed by the condensation of time and power the television-style media produce for her. By the end the field of waste and excess that has dominated the scene of patriotism makes her forget not just what she knew but what she did not know: and we realize, on thinking back to her speech, that at no point did Lisa know anything about America. She could be inspired by the national symbolic and by the corruptions of capital; she is moved aesthetically by nature's nation and also by the boorish appetites of both professional and ordinary men; she is not at all transformed by her experience of Washington, though she remembers she had experiences there.

The infantile citizen has a memory of the nation and a tactical relation to its operation. But no version of sustained agency accompanies the national system here. It provides information but no memory-driven access to its transformative use: it is not surprising, in this context, that the two commercials between the opening credits and the narrative proper — for the U.S. Army and for an episode of "In Living Color" that featured the violent heterosexualization of a gay film critic — promote the military life and the Cold War, to the suppression of American gay identity on behalf of national boyhood and heterosexual national manhood; it is not surprising, in this context, that I could pull the script of this episode from a "Simpsons" bulletin board using Internet, a computer network derived from a U.S. Defense Department system that currently frames much of the information about scientific and military culture across the telephone lines daily. Just as every pilgrimage-to-Washington narrative deploys information and scientific technologies to link the abstract national to the situated local, underinformed, abjected, and idealistic citizen, so too this system confirms its necessity at every moment for the production of the knowledge that American media perform for the child/consumer who has no "interests" but in touring Washington in order to feel occasionally "free."

Yet a distinguished tradition of collective popular resistance to national policy has taken the form of marches on Washington: dispossessed workers, African-Americans, gays, lesbians, queers, pro- and antichoice activists, feminists, veterans of popular and unpopular wars, for example. These collective activities invert the small-town and metropolitan spectacle of the "parade" honoring local citizens into national acts, performances of citizenship that predict votes and make metonymic "the people" whom representatives represent, but they also claim a kind of legitimate mass political voice uniquely performed outside of the voting booth. On the one hand, mass political marches resist, without overcoming, the spectacular forms of identification that dominate mass national culture — through individualizing codes of celebrity, heroism, and their underside, scandal — for only in times of crisis are Americans solicited to act en masse as citizens whose private patriotic identifications are indeed *not enough* to sustain national culture at a particular moment. On the other hand, we might note as well the problem mass political movements face in translating their activities into the monumentalizing currency of national culture: in this light, we witness how an impersonation or an icon of political struggle can eclipse the movement it represents, for instance in the image of Martin

Luther King on the mall; in the image of the subaltern citizen in the body of the fetus; or in the image, dominating national culture as we speak, of the infantile citizen, too helpless to do anything but know, without understanding, what it means that the "system" of the nation "freely" exists, like "free" television itself.

Notes

Much thanks to Michael Warner and the great audience at the Society for Cinema Studies for their critical engagement with this paper/project.

1. See Anderson (1983) and Caughie (1990).
2. See Lorde (1982:68–71).
3. *Ibid.*, 71.
4. See Heath (1990:278–79).
5. For the main arguments for the pervasiveness of televisual amnesia or information fatigue, see Mellencamp, ed. (1990:222–39). See also Feuer (1983).
6. The ongoing pedagogic/civic activity of television is more widely appreciated on the right, and the saturated moral domination of the medium by conservatives has been central to the right-wing cultural agenda of the Reagan-Bush era. What counts as "public" access "public" television has undergone massive restrictive redefinition under the pressure of a certain pseudorepresentative form of "public" opinion, whose virtue is established by reference to a supposedly nonideological or noninterest group-based politics of transcendence that must be understood as fundamentalist in its imagination of a nation of pure, opinionated minds. For overviews and thoughtful reconsiderations on the left, see Lipsitz (1990); Morse (1990); Rasula (1990); Schwoch, White, and Reilly, eds. (1992).
7. This essay is a much shortened version of a longer investigation of pilgrimages to Washington in history/narrative, as one relay into thinking through whether there is, in fantasy or in instrumental practice, something called a "national" culture. The texts mentioned in this paragraph are crucial intertexts to the theory of infantile citizenship.
8. See Negt and Kluge (1992).
9. See Zizek (1989:87–129).
10. Lipsitz (1990:70–71).

Literature Cited

Anderson, Benedict. 1983. *Imagined Communities: Reflections on the Origins and Spread of Nationalism*. London: Verso.

Caughie, John. 1990. "Playing at Being American." Pages 44–58 in Mellencamp, ed.

Feuer, Jane. Playing at Being American. "The Concept of Life Television: Ontology as Ideology." Pages 12–21 in E. Ann Kaplan, ed., *Regarding Television: Critical Approaches – an Anthology*. Washington, D.C.: University Publications of America.

Heath, Stephen. 1990. "Representing Television." Pages 278–79 in Mellencamp, ed.

Lipsitz, George. 1990. *Time Passages: Collective Memory and American Popular Culture*. Minneapolis: University of Minnesota Press.

Lorde, Audre. 1982. *Zami: A New Spelling of My Name*. Trumansburg, N.Y.: Crossing Press.

Mellencamp, Patricia, ed. 1990. *Logics of Television: Essays in Cultural Criticism*. Bloomington: Indiana University Press.

Morse, Margaret. 1990. "An Ontology of Everyday Distraction: The Freeway, the Mall, and Television." Pages 193–221 in Mellencamp, ed.

Negt, Oskar, and Alexander Kluge. 1992. "Selections from *The Proletariat Public Sphere*." *Social Text* 35/36:28–32.

Rasula, Jed. 1990. "Nietzsche in the Nursery: Naive Classics and Surrogate Parents in Postwar American Cultural Debates." *Representations* 29 (Winter): 50–77.

Schwoch, James, Mimi White, and Susan Reilly, eds. 1992. *Media Knowledge: Readings in Popular Culture, Pedagogy, and Critical Citizenship*. Albany, N.Y.: SUNY Press.

Zizek, Slavej. 1989. *The Sublime Object of Ideology*. New York: Verso.

41.
MAKEOVER TELEVISION, GOVERNMENTALITY AND THE GOOD CITIZEN

Laurie Ouellette and James Hay

In June 2006, ABC TV encouraged families to 'get healthy' in conjunction with its new reality series, *Shaq's Big Challenge*. Each week, NBA champion Shaquille O'Neal worked with a 'dream team' of nutritionists, coaches, medical experts and physical trainers to improve the bodies – and the lives – of six overweight middle school children while the cameras rolled. As the kids endured the physical and emotional challenges of Shaq's transformational 'boot camp', the basketball star consulted with local school districts and government officials to develop a suggested 'wellness program' for the State of Florida, where the series was filmed. Television viewers were encouraged to implement their own lifestyle makeovers in partnership with the *Big Challenge* website, where they could generate customized health report cards, replay material from the television broadcast and download resources for getting themselves and their children into shape. While *Shaq's Big Challenge* was packaged as reality entertainment, it was also promoted as an effort to transform the way 'we approach the health of a nation – one child, one community, one state at a time, until we truly are a happier, healthier, fitter America'. In this paper, we analyse the changing relationship between television and social welfare implied by this mission statement, and show how the impulse to remake television viewers into active and healthy citizens speaks to the 'reinvention' of government in neoliberal capitalist democracies such as the United States.

Practical instruction by experts in the care and improvement of the self, the family, and home – the basic elements of makeover television – is hardly new. In the early twentieth century, progressive social workers sought to disseminate the 'science of right living' to working-class and immigrant populations, believing that positive changes of habit and conduct would improve the quality of life for these groups, and stabilize society as a whole.[1] With the growth of the culture industries – movies, magazines, radio and eventually television – pedagogies of self and lifestyle transformation were situated within the cultural economy of serial entertainment and advertising.[2] What has changed is the 'political rationality' of the makeover as a resource for achieving the changing demands of citizenship: Today, we contend, the impetus to facilitate, improve and makeover people's health, happiness and success through television programming is tied to distinctly 'neoliberal' reasoning about governance and social welfare.

The spirit of personal reinvention endemic to the current spate of makeover television has gained visibility and social currency as part of the reinvention of government as a decentralized network of entrepreneurial ventures on the one hand, and the diffusion of personal responsibility and self-enterprise as ethics of 'good' citizenship on the other.[3] 'Reinventing government' is a technical term used by policy analysts and advocates since the late 1980s to refer to the re-conception of the public sector as the primary administrator of social assistance (Osbourne and Gaebler 1992).[4] As the liberal capitalist state is reconfigured into a network of public–private partnerships, and social services from education to medical care

are outsourced to commercial firms, citizens are also called upon to play an active role in caring for and governing themselves through a burgeoning culture of entrepreneurship.[5] Within this context, cultural technologies such as television, which have always played an important role in the formation of idealized citizen subjects, become instrumental as resources of self-achievement in different and politically significant ways.

Reality television, which has proliferated in the context of deregulation, welfare reform and other attempts to reinvent government, has become the quintessential technology of citizenship of our age. Our book *Better Living through Reality TV: Television and Post-welfare Citizenship* (2008) analyses this development in the United States, showing how reality-based entertainment enacts experiments in governance and 'civic laboratories' for testing, refining and sharpening people's abilities to conduct themselves in accordance with the new demands being placed on them.[6] As Anna McCarthy demonstrates in her seminal study of *Candid Camera* (2004), television's capacity to govern through entertaining 'real-life' human experiments was mobilized as early as the 1950s, but only now are social and political conditions ripe to position television as a resource for achieving 'post-welfare' citizenship. Not only does reality television provide an experimental training ground for the government of the enterprising self, it has also adopted an active and visible role in coordinating non-state resources (money, expertise, outreach) for achieving the ethic of self-sufficient citizenship promoted by neoliberal regimes. In this sense, reality television is being inserted into the reinvention of government in complex, everyday, constitutive ways.

Reality television governs less through the dissemination of ideology than through the enactment of participatory games and lifestyle tutorials that guide, test and supposedly enhance subjects' capacity to play an active role in shaping uncertain outcomes – to govern themselves through freedom, not control, in the language of political philosophy. As an early adopter of what scholars now call convergence culture, much reality television extends the experimentalism and participatory flair of its programming to viewers at home, so that the 'programme' in the old

sense of broadcast media becomes the entry point into a broader menu of customizable entertainment and self-fashioning opportunities and requirements. Contrary to the stereotypical equation of television watching with passivity, the contemporary viewer – like the contemporary citizen – is increasingly expected to purposefully navigate the array of multimedia resources that television coordinates.

Makeover television has achieved a visible role in the new circuitry of citizenship formation afforded by reality entertainment. Utilizing techniques from behavioural experiments and self-tests to lifestyle instruction and role modelling, programmes such as *Shaq's Big Challenge* diffuse and amplify the government of everyday life, utilizing the cultural power of television (and its convergence with new media) to evaluate and guide the behaviours and routines of ordinary people, and, more importantly, to teach us how to perform these techniques on ourselves. Makeover programmes enact the promised freedoms as well as the apparent burdens of enterprising citizenship on screen, utilizing coaches, lifestyle experts and motivators to transform floundering individuals into successful self-managers. At the same time, makeover programmes challenge a wide range of citizens organized by lifestyle clusters to expand their capacities, work harder on themselves, and exploit the resources of self-care made available to them. We are all called upon by the governing logic of our times to play the makeover game, and television – through the regularity of its programming as well as its interactivity – has played a powerful role in inserting the imperative to make and remake ourselves as citizens into the fabric of everyday life.

Television and the 'State of Welfare'

Before elaborating on makeover television, a discussion of our terminology and theoretical orientation will be helpful. Our work applies critical theories of governmentality to media culture, particularly reality television. The term governmentality, as developed by philosopher Michel Foucault and his followers, refers to the processes through which individuals shape and guide their own conduct – and that of others – with certain aims and objectives in mind (Foucault 1991; Gordon 1991; Burchell 1996; Rose

1996; Cruikshank 1999; Dean 1999). Scholars of governmentality look beyond the formal institutions of official government to also emphasize the proliferation and diffusion of the everyday techniques through which individuals and populations are expected to reflect upon, work on and organize their lives and themselves as an implicit condition of their citizenship. These techniques do not emanate directly from the state, nor can they be traced to any singular power centre. Rather, techniques of governmentality are circulated in a highly dispersed fashion by social and cultural intermediaries and the institutions (schools, social work, the medical establishment) that authorize their expertise. Television, along with other popular media, are an important – if much less examined – part of this mix in that they too have operated as technologies called upon to assist and shape citizens 'who do not need to be governed by others, but will govern themselves, master themselves, care for themselves' (Rose 1996, 45).[7]

Because governmental practices and rationalities are never stable, attempts to map and analyse them must be contextual, geographic and historical. Our focus is on the neoliberal present, by which we mean the bipartisan effort to 'reinvent' government (particularly in the United States) and to remodel the welfare state through dispersed networks of privatization and self-responsibilization. While we are charting television's crucial contribution to this remodelling, we are not implying that welfare no longer exists, nor are we pitting neoliberal strategies of governing at a distance against a romanticized view of the state as public welfare administer. We use the term 'post-welfare' citizenship to indicate the re-privatized arrangements, political reasoning, and individualized responsibilities demanded by the reinvention of government in the United States, but we also understand welfare in a broader sense, as a mutating but nonetheless integral component of liberal rule. Reality television, for better or worse, has come to play an important role in the transformation of welfare by helping to reconstitute the way it is conceptualized and practised in the United States.

Foucault's chronicle of the birth of the liberal state showed how its ability to govern relied on nascent social and cultural technologies for cultivating the perceived health and wellness – i.e. the welfare – of the citizenry (Rabinow 1997; Faubion 2000). The dispersion of technologies of governance, as a matter of guiding and shaping habits and behaviours through expertise, provided the initial basis for state power as well as the origins of modern welfare as a dispersed strategy of governing populations outside state apparatuses through religious institutions, charities, clinics and asylums.[8] What Nikolas Rose (1996) calls a 'state of welfare' emerged in the twentieth century to provide publicly coordinated and administered public services, including education, health care, public assistance, social work and mental hygiene. Technologies of governing through welfare that had developed privately were brought more squarely under the control of state bureaucracies, partly as a means of 'civilizing' the industrial working classes, notes Rose. Yet this move also represented a progressive move towards social democracy to the extent that the autonomous individual of liberal rule was recast as a 'citizen with rights to social protection and social education in return for duties of social obligation and social responsibility' (Rose 1996, 49).

Since the 1980s, the social contract implied by the 'state of welfare' has been the target of vigorous attempts to reinvent the public sector – in part because state involvement in welfare is seen as a breech of liberalism's emphasis on governing at a distance. Particularly in the United States, public-sector welfare programmes are claimed to have bred passive and dependent citizens who do not respond to market incentives.[9] The 'reinvented' state is still concerned to ensure the health and wellness of the population as the basis of its capacity to rule, however. As Wendy Brown (2003) points out, it now relies on a combination of overt and indirect strategies to produce citizens who are self-sufficient as well as self-governing.[10] Harsh penal policies (i.e. 'Three Strikes You're Out') and welfare-to-work schemes exemplify the former; the Bush Administration's 'Compassion Agenda' and Get Fit Campaign illustrate the latter. Today, however, the state relies primarily on the private sector rather than public bureaucracies to produce 'good' citizens. Acting more as a supporter and less as an 'overseer', the United States has offloaded much of the responsibility of governing onto public–private partnerships and depends more than ever before on cultural technologies such as television to translate what Rose calls the 'goals of authorities' into guidelines for enterprising living (Rose 1996, 58). Reality television's experiments, tests, challenges, and instructions have flourished within this context.

Reality television does more than evaluate and advise the conduct of citizens: increasingly, it also plays a visible role in stitching public service into privatized networks of self-care. This is especially evident in the United States, where commercial television networks have partnered with private and non-governmental entities to provide charity and social services (*Extreme Makeover: Home Edition, Three Wishes*) to cultivate volunteerism (*American Idol Gives Back*) and to coordinate an array of privatized self-help resources. Television is thus quite literally helping to produce a privatized system of welfare, one that is significantly more aligned with a market logic than was the case in the 'state of welfare' and the earlier stage of welfare that preceded it. Under neoliberalism, civic well-being is increasingly both commodified (produced for profit) and tied to entrepreneurial imperatives, while 'lifestyle maximization' (Rose 1996, 57–9) is joined to (and often supersedes) the nation and electoral politics as the domain through citizenship is tested and achieved. Within this context, expertise becomes authorized by corporate and business sectors, with coaches, motivational speakers, corporate sponsors, and celebrities taking over the dispersed governmental work once performed by social workers, educators and other professionals.

The reinvention of government also provides the necessary context for understanding television's own changing ethic of public service. Whether operated as a public service or regulated in the public interest, this ethic has become increasingly controversial due to its affiliation with the old 'state of welfare'. The state's role in overseeing the provision and diversity of broadcasting in the name of public enlightenment and citizenship training was authorized by the discourse of 'social rights and responsibilities' discussed by Rose. The ideal citizen cultivated by broadcasting was expected to serve the goals of the nation (and earn her/his enfranchisement). In the United States, this approach to public service reached its zenith in the 1960s, when the Public Broadcasting System was created to operate as a technology of public education and citizenship (Ouellette 2002). Since the 1980s, deregulation and market competition have largely freed commercial broadcasters from the unprofitable, and (particularly in the United States) unrealized expectations of serving the 'public good' so defined; these same forces have forced public broadcasters in Europe to accommodate a wider range of consumer choices and lifestyles.

While these developments have not eliminated education as the basis of citizenship formation through television, they have reconfigured and repurposed institutions and technologies of education: Today, televised instruction is more apt to be articulated to lifestyle governance and everyday regimes of self-care facilitated through interactive reality entertainment. The skills, problem-solving techniques, step-by-step demonstrations, intimate feedback, motivational support mechanisms and suggestions for everyday application offered by the makeover genre, as one dimension of this shift, are more useful to current strategies of governing than is the residual public service ethic. The new curriculum is also more profitable than earlier incarnations of citizenship education by television – not only because it renders learning more inclusive and pleasurable, but because in a climate that demands enterprising skills and dispositions of all citizens, the civic training it provides has become a desirable commodity.

Television has also linked public education to new models of social service provision. While the earlier public service ethic emphasized the transmission of 'enlightenment' and civility through well-conceived programmes, today's reality entertainment is increasingly inserted into privatized social networks and resources of citizenship that transcend television viewing. Makeover television's civic engagement lies in its ability to bind work on the self to the reinvention of government; its role as a facilitator for customizing programmes of self-care makes it an attractive partner for a policy agenda that seeks to deputize private administrators of welfare.

The Makeover as Life Intervention

The political rationalities we are describing can be glimpsed across makeover sub-genres, from style transformation programmes to home and gardening television. For example, Katherine Sender (2006) shows how the lifestyle and fashion training provided by *Queer Eye for the Straight Guy* also encourages citizens to take personal responsibility for the unstable job market. However, they are particularly acute in the *life intervention*, the term we use to describe helping ventures that mobilize resources to help ordinary people overcome problems in relation to children (*Supernanny*), pets (*Dog Whisperer*), sexuality (*Sex Inspectors*), unemployment (*Starting Over*), addiction (*Intervention*), hygiene (*How Clean is Your House?*), health and fitness (*Honey We're Killing the Kids*), safety (*It Takes a Thief*), and finance (*Suze Orman*). Life interventions address risks, problems and challenges, guiding and shaping citizens within television's cultural economy. As commercial ventures, the governing capacities of reality television's life interventions are realized (particularly within the United States) within a market logic that values entrepreneurialism, mass customization and profit accumulation. Similar to the reinvented state, the format relies on a range of partners (corporate sponsors, advertisers, clinics, professional associations and non-profit agencies) to enact its helping missions. As social service, life interventions operate within networks of support, offering serialized entertainment and popular instruction, often tailored to specific demographics and lifestyle clusters. While television as a social institution carries out its work independently of official government, the state plays a supportive role in this new strand of programming by activating the spirit of public–private cooperation in which the life intervention has thrived.

Because television in the United States is now a largely unregulated enterprise, life interventions pursue civic and public service goals within the logic of cultural commerce and its allegiance to ratings, advertising, product placement revenue, format licensing and merchandising tie-ins. In this sense, they are perfectly compatible with the logic of entrepreneurial government. The programmes deploy a continuum of governing strategies, from detainment in a private facility to self-help strategies that liken running one's life to managing a business. Their aims run the gamut from instilling good behaviour in children to improving health and longevity to avoiding toxic relationships to achieving self-esteem as a path

to professional growth. What unites the life intervention as a politically significant strand of makeover television is a concern to facilitate care of the self as a strategy of freedom and empowerment. No matter how controlling some of the techniques used can appear (i.e. hidden-camera surveillance, public humiliation, detainment), the impetus is not really to display cruelty and punishment as a means of deterring misbehaviour, as Foucault hypothesized of the pre-modern spectacle of torture in public. The political rationality of the life intervention is to enact the reasoning that people who are floundering can and must be taught to develop and maximize their capacities for normalcy, happiness, material stability, and success rather than rely on a public 'safety net'.

Life interventions circulate techniques for a government of the self that complement the value now being placed on choice, personal accountability and self-empowerment as ethics of neoliberal citizenship. In an era when the state has offloaded much of the responsibility of facilitating the welfare of the citizenry to individuals and the private sector, reality television's efforts to help people improve their 'quality of life' plays another governing role as well. As Brown points out, the 'withdrawal of the state from certain domains, and privatization of certain state functions does not amount to a dismantling of government, but is a technique of governing – rational economic action suffused throughout society replaces express state rule or provision' (2003, n.p.). As neoliberal regimes shift the 'regulatory competence of the state onto responsible, rational individuals' with the aim of encouraging them to 'give their lives a specific entrepreneurial form', the scope and strategies of citizenship training change. The capacity to make enterprising lifestyle choices in matters of health, security, consumption, family and household takes on more urgency in a political climate where individuals are expected to maximize their interests as a condition of self-rule.

Central to the enterprising 'government of the self' enacted by television's life interventions is the convergence between television and the Web. Convergence allows television viewers to acquire, customize, and personalize the helping resources offered through the cultural economy of television, and to participate in the lifestyle clusters served by makeover programming and its websites. Interactivity provides a framework for enacting entrepreneurial citizenship in both senses. While the reinvention of the self is performed with the help of motivators and guides who administer the rules and techniques, it is performed on the self in the name of personal empowerment and can provide an entry point into group membership based on similar lifestyle challenges. While television provides the everyday framework for supervising the development of personal regimens, viewers are encouraged to take matters into their own hands, using the interactive resources available to them (or not).

Motivating Healthy Citizens

Life interventions geared to changing people's diet, exercise regimens and nutrition habits have proliferated on cable channels such as Discovery, The Learning Channel and Fit TV, a network entirely devoted to teaching consumers how to develop a lifestyle based on home exercise, rational grocery shopping and healthy eating. The major commercial broadcast networks have also developed how-to health and fitness makeover programmes such as *The Biggest Loser* and *Shaq's Big Challenge* that insert television into a circuit of resources for caring for oneself and improving one's lifestyle. This development has occurred at a time when the US government is concerned about obesity and other costly health 'problems' allegedly caused by improper lifestyles, but is unwilling to intervene in ways that might compromise a deregulatory ethos and reliance on privatized networks of welfare administration. Unlike the Progressive Era, when social workers promoted national legislative reforms as well as education and individual compliance, today's helping culture is focused mainly on maximizing personal responsibility (doing it yourself) as a path to self-regulation and empowerment. When public interest organizations do push for policy action, they are cast as proponents of a nanny state that seeks to regulate freedom of choice. During the 2004 House Government Reform Committee's hearings on 'The Supersizing of America', for example, Marshall Manson of the conservative Center for Individual Freedom criticized the Center for Science in the Public Interest for pushing

'extreme' measures such as regulating the food sold in schools and 'mandated labeling of restaurants with detailed nutrition information'. Linking such regulatory possibilities to the curtailing of market incentive and 'free choice', Manson told the committee:

> Our democracy is founded on the idea that individuals have basic freedoms. Among these, certainly, is the right to choose what we put on our plates and in our goblets ... anti-food extremists like CSPI would gladly take away that freedom and mandate our diet in order to save us from ourselves. It is time for these zealous advocates to understand that it is not the federal government's job to save us from ourselves by making our choices for us.
>
> (2004)

For Mason, the state's role is not to oversee but to support 'responsible decision-making' in consumers who are not only free to manage their own health but are also expected to do so. George W. Bush's Steps to a Healthier US, a programme designed to encourage 'simple improvements in physical activity, diet and behavior' as a means of controlling chronic disease, is an example of how the new approach reconstitutes welfare. Steps to a Healthier US is sponsored by the Presidential Program on Physical Fitness and Sport, which dates to the Kennedy administration but is now administered through more than 600 'partnerships' with corporations, non-profits and local governments. Similarly, the President's Fitness Challenge was created in 2002 as a network of corporate, non-profit and regional/municipal partners, including major sports and athletic businesses, food companies (Burger King, Coca-Cola, General Mills) and television networks (including ESPN and the Cartoon Network). These partnerships between government, corporations, and non-profits are how the state currently supports health as a dimension of welfare – not as a publicly administered 'entitlement' but as a personal responsibility to be achieved through individualized networks of support.[11]

Like other initiatives promoted by the Bush administration, including the Citizen Corp., the Faith-based and Community Initiative, and the short-lived campaign for privatizing Social Security, the Fitness

Challenge is about reinventing government and enabling citizens to manage their personal welfare. The Steps to a Healthier US similarly seeks to make-over the mission of the Department of Health, Education, and Welfare (HEW): instead of breeding passive and dependent citizens, HEW's new role is to mobilize private providers and supporters with a stake in personal fitness. Inserting HEW within the culture of entrepreneurialism, the Challenge's injunction to 'Get Fit' cast the network of corporate partners as coaches motivating their subjects to succeed by tak-ing advantage of their resources. As a mantra for empowering citizens to take control of their own wel-fare, the expression 'You're It; Get Fit' cast the private sector and individual citizens as the primary line of defence against unhealthy behaviours that might lead to physical illness and a life of dependency. This pro-gramme and similar efforts to embed social welfare in privatized networks of personal responsibility have changed the economic and political value of the makeover as a technology of citizenship.

At a jogging event inaugurating his Fitness Challenge, Bush claimed that it is part of a larger ini-tiative '. . . to help Americans live longer, better, and healthier lives. And the good news is this: when it comes to your health, even little steps can make a big difference.' These steps may have referred to the jog-gers surrounding him at the event, but they also referred to the everyday measures through which each citizen is now expected to work on herself, and to the various non-state institutions – including cor-porate sponsors – who administer resources to them. The website for the President's Challenge differenti-ates between non-profit 'advocates' and corporate providers, including Dasani Water, Starbucks and a long list of brands (Pepsi, Coke, Burger King, Kellogg, and General Mills) whose association with the net-work rearticulates their social value away from unhealthy consumption and towards a new-and-improved regime of personal makeover. The website also distinguishes between different lifestyles – kids, teens, adults and seniors – and assigns to each a dif-ferent set of fitness resources and techniques. Here, as with television's life interventions, the achievement of health through the marketing and education of lifestyle clusters is a process open to consumer customization through television and Web resources.

Bush's recruitment of television networks to the Challenge is also significant in light of television's per-ceived association with passivity and a sedentary life-style. In recent years, a number of high-profile programmes have challenged that association by enlisting television as a resource in helping people get healthy and lose weight. In 2005, NBC broadcast *The Biggest Loser*, providing the services of nutritionists and personal trainers to people who agreed to slim down on television, and offering a cash prize to the person who shed the most body fat. Cameras documented the contestants as they carried out intense physical exer-cise regimes, learned about nutrition and developed balanced and 'disciplined' eating habits. Evoking Foucault's discussion of the care of the self in ancient Greece (1986) where the feast was one of many rituals for testing one's capacity for self-control, the cast was regularly tempted with vast displays of decadent foods to test their determination and willpower. At the end of each episode, the 'outcome' of these physical and mental activities was measured live on television in a dramatic weighing ceremony.

Television viewers were invited to stage their own lifestyle intervention by slimming down and 'getting healthy'. NBC constructed an interactive website complete with nutritional guides, dieting tips, sample recipes and menus, customizable exercise regimes and weight loss tools, including a body mass index calculator. Tie-in merchandise – including workbooks and the *Biggest Loser* exercise DVD – was available for purchase, and participants were urged to join the *Biggest Loser* email club and sign up for informative podcasts. Finally, for people on the go there was also the much-promoted *Biggest Loser* wireless service. For only $2.99 per month, anyone with a mobile phone could sign up to receive a daily health tip, an exercise pointer or inspirational message. In extending these body and health management resources and tech-niques to individuals, the network fused popular entertainment (weight loss as competitive game) and self-shaping activities with current dynamics of governing and the demand for citizens to make use of privatized networks of support and accept account-ability for the consequences of their lifestyle choices.

On *Honey We're Killing the Kids*, which originated on the BBC and was shown in the United States on The Learning Channel, a nutritionist shows how 'everyday choices can have long-term impacts on children, and offers both the motivation and the know-how to help turn families lives around'. Armed with scientific research and a team of advisors, she aims to change the 'bad habits' of a family in a period of just three weeks. The parents, who are often scolded for smoking and overeating, are shocked into a lifestyle regime change by the accusation they're 'killing their kids' by letting them eat too much junk food and watch video games and watch television instead of exercising. Digitally aged images of the children at 40 show the ill effects of their current habits, and the parents are told their children are 'at risk' of developing obesity and other health problems. In teaching care of the self, the programme objectifies the child-subject, turning him/her into an undesirable stranger. Not surprisingly, the parents usually agree to cooperate with the new 'rules, guidelines and techniques' for improving their children's health and lifestyle.

The programme follows the generic template of many television life interventions. The diagnostician arrives at the home, observes the family, diagnoses their nutritional problems and introduces a new lifestyle regimen. Cameras capture some initial resistance as well as the eventual mastering of the healthy lifestyle that the subjects come to desire as their own. At the end of each episode, the objective 'outcome' of the regimen is demonstrated by new digitalized photographs that show the children ageing in a healthier manner and the parents promise to enforce the new diet and exercise programme once the diagnostician has moved on to assist other needy families.[12]

Repetition and redundancy do not diminish the importance of *Honey We're Killing the Kids* as a form of citizenship training. In fact, repetition is crucial to the creation of a personal 'programme' as a technical everyday regimen of self-care. This programme teaches personal responsibility, risk-avoidance and choice by diagnosing and rehabilitating cases of 'ignorance' and self-neglect, and allowing the television viewer at home to identify as normal in comparison. At the same time, the programme coordinates resources for the health-conscious: television viewers are invited to seek out and master the skills required to create a healthy lifestyle on the programme's website, which includes interactive resources, games and merchandising tie-ins.

Honey We're Killing the Kids operates as a technology of citizenship, helping to solve the crisis of obesity by issuing a 'critical wake-up call for parents'. Reformers like Manson have no problem with television programmes adopting this role, because their authority to administer new forms of welfare is sanctioned not by the state but by the commercial logic of supply and demand and its ability to capitalize on welfare as outreach and instruction. The programme exemplifies television's contemporary utility for ensuring the health outcomes of the population, illustrating Rose's argument that while healthy bodies are still a 'public value and political objective' of the state, we no longer need public bureaucracies to 'enjoin healthy habits of eating … with compulsory inspection, subsidized incentives to eat or drink correctly and so forth'. In the new context of public–private cooperation and personally regulated consumption, 'individuals will want to be healthy, experts will instruct them on how to be so, and entrepreneurs will exploit and enhance this market for health. Health will be ensured through a combination of the market, expertise, and a regulated autonomy' (Rose 1998, 162).

Like many television interventions, *Honey We're Killing the Kids* puts the impetus to succeed in health and in life on individuals, offering a regimen for personal change but overlooking inequalities related to the price of healthy food, lack of low-cost health care, and a sharpening class system that makes fast food an attractive option for many people. *Shaq's Big Challenge* also emphasizes the transformation of extreme behaviours to teach healthy living to a wide range of citizens. More explicitly than *Honey We're Killing the Kids*, this programme also stitches welfare into private–public partnerships of support that include not only television but also local school districts and professional sports. *Shaq's* intervention is, in this sense, more specifically tied to the reinvention of government in the United States. However, it allows a broader range of governmental tactics and outcomes (such as private citizens and celebrities calling on public schools to remove fast food) than does Manson's free-market approach to personal responsibilization, thus demonstrating the contingency – and the stakes of political engagement – *within* neoliberalism as a governing rationality.

The first episode reintroduces the audience to one of the National Basketball Association's most recognizable and beloved players. Shaquille O'Neal has agreed to help seven children overcome obesity, a 'big problem' he ascribes to a combination of poor diet, inactivity, and lack of motivation. Some of the children are also depicted as immersed in unregulated television-watching, video game playing and Web surfing, and these activities are also targeted as 'causes' of an unhealthy lifestyle. Shaq's role as motivator and welfare facilitator is to break the children's presumed dependency on unhealthy food as well as entertainment regimens, moving the kids out of their sedentary lifestyles and onto the playing field valorized by professional sports. Over the course of the first season, he emerges as a paragon of tough love who combines gentleness and discipline to help children whose futures appear bleak if they fail to learn how to take steps towards fitness and self-care.

Shaq has relied on his own entrepreneurial instincts to locate and assemble a 'dream team' of professional coaches, motivators, doctors and lifestyle specialists to assist with the boot camp. Like other television diagnosticians (Dr. Phil, finance advisor, Suze Orman, *Queer Eye*'s Carson Kressley, or Cesar Milan, the 'dog whisperer'), these experts facilitate and monitor the children's gradual progress out of obesity; they also operate as agents of surveillance on Shaq's behalf, recording slip-ups such as a 'lack of discipline' during workouts. While much of the action hinges on the ultra-disciplinary boot camp, the team also educates the parents to become 'coaches' at home and works with local school officials and neighbours to create an extended 'support network' for the children.

While *Shaq's Big Challenge* is not formally affiliated with the White House, the programme repeatedly invokes the President's Physical Fitness Test as the standard against which to measure the children's progress. The programme combines the conventions of the contest and the civic laboratory to verify who is an active, motivated and entrepreneurial citizen and to affirm the current rationality of 'challenging' citizens to help themselves through television. The interactivity afforded by the Web is crucial to this affirmation, not only in the sense of extending the logic of the boot camp to the customizable menu made available through the Web but also in guiding television viewers towards presumably 'healthy' forms of media engagement.[13] Not unlike Shaq's regimen for moving sedentary kids into physical activity, the life intervention is about moving passive television viewers into the role of resourceful, enterprising and active citizens.

ABC's role in enacting an alternative to the 'state of welfare' was stressed throughout the series. In the first episode, Shaq discusses the problem of childhood obesity with Jeb Bush, the governor of Florida. In this climate of outsourcing welfare and emphasizing personal responsibility, O'Neal must justify to the governor the rationality of a venture (the Fitness Challenge) already sponsored by the President, the governor's brother. This provides the basis for differentiating television's helping ventures from stigmatized state regulations and welfare programmes. To combat the extent to which many public schools – including those in Florida – have cut mandatory physical education and allowed fast food companies to set up shop in cafeterias, the basketball star and his team also consult with school officials to create a 'suggested' wellness regimen, exemplifying the spirit of public–private partnership. This spirit is also extended through media convergence, in that ABC positions *Shaq's Biggest Challenge* as both entertainment and community outreach on its website, while the site created by the programme's producers links the programme to the website for Bush's fitness initiatives. Both sites operate as self-described 'download centers' that facilitate the regulation of obesity and other health risks through the management of individual choice, providing, for example, scorecards of 'daily drills', membership information, personal pledge cards, and tips for combating everyday 'snack attacks' (a play on sportscasters' idiom for stopping a 'Shaq attack' on the basketball court). In this way, they make membership in Shaq's programme tantamount to a form of healthy citizenship in a nation where a citizenship test is a President's Challenge.

Conclusion

Reality television, as we have shown, has instrumentalized the personal makeover as a technology of citizenship in new ways. No longer outside the logic of public service, these popular non-scripted entertainment formats have become the domains through which television contributes to the reinvention of government, the reconstitution of welfare and the production of a self-sufficient citizenry. Critical questions remain: how do we evaluate television's efforts to insert itself into diffuse, privatized networks of self-fashioning and care? How do the generic conventions of makeover television intersect with new ways of delivering and administering social welfare? How might citizens hold television accountable as a form of social service? What does it mean when celebrities, television executives and casting agents take over the role of public officials or social workers? And, how might critical media and cultural studies intervene in this process?

Because our analysis considers television as operating within changing programmes and networks of government, rather than merely as an 'ideological apparatus', we want to emphasize that television does not represent or distort welfare as much as it produces new formations of welfare by providing citizens with the resources that currently valorize their freedom and empowerment. In this context, we might reasonably ask from television the practical questions asked of other 'customer-oriented' social service providers: how are the subjects treated? Is the application process reasonable and fair? What are the outcomes of the interventions? This approach can only get us so far, however. We are still left with the contradictions and potentially devastating consequences of relegating public service, including social welfare, to private networks of support. Who provides for people who don't have access to privatized welfare networks, including the technologies of instruction, customization and self-fashioning facilitated through television and convergence culture? If television aims to make citizens/consumers more productive of their own welfare, how has this process also contributed to the growing class of people who, lacking access to resources, eventually are deemed unproductive or 'disabled' and thus a new problem for a healthy economy?

Michael Moore's documentary *Sicko* (2007) foregrounds this latter contradiction, documenting widespread instances when privatized health care in the United States has been unwilling to provide for citizens who lack the financial resources to participate in that system. The film's title refers ironically to the regime of truth that has 'rationalized' the current governmental arrangement between the state, the insurance industry, and private health care providers, and to an increasing population whose health is put at risk by this arrangement. Moore chronicles the disparity between the US health care system (whose emphasis on financial profit has left citizens without medical care) and socialist democratic strategies of health care provision in Canada and Western Europe. In some respects, the premise of the television makeover – particularly the life interventions we are examining – are simply other instances of the tendency in the United States that Moore's film represents. Yet reality television's impetus to help produce 'healthy' citizens also complicates Moore's approach to activism in several ways.

One is that the countries valorized by *Sicko* have also increasingly reinvented television (as public service) around makeovers and interventions similar to those shown in the United States. Some of these formats originated in European countries with national health care systems, indicating an impetus to create healthy citizens in new ways across the different cultural economies of national broadcasting systems. While the transnationalism of makeover television may indicate the global turn towards neoliberal strategies of governing at a distance, socialized medicine and public health care are, as Moore points out, still operational outside the United States – at least for now. Public services and a governing rationality that values self-enterprise and personal responsibility coexist outside the United States, complicating any causal understanding of market privatization as a causal factor in the transformation of welfare and demonstrating the geographic complexities of the dynamics charted here.

While Moore's film draws attention to a growing portion of US citizens who lack health care, his political economic critique neglects the productive valence of the new system of welfare implemented in the United States since the 1990s. Television's life interventions promote health and wellness through privatized and entrepreneurialized networks of support, calling on each individual to achieve citizenship as an obligation to him/herself. This system has lethal effects, as Moore documents, but it also allows politicians to claim that 'something is being done' – and conversely to blame unmotivated citizens when the system fails. It comes as no surprise that the US Congress, while downscaling and outsourcing virtually every other welfare programme, has authorized the public subsidy of digital converters so that television remains technically available to all (Labaton 2005). Television has become one of the cultural instruments through which healthy citizenship – for better or worse – is accomplished. Likewise, the object of political intervention for those seeking an *alternative* to neoliberalism can include both the political economic failures of the current rationality of government (as Moore documents) and the cultural technologies such as television through which 'resources' of self-empowerment and care are made available to citizens. We have taken the latter approach by documenting how reality television's interventionist forms of civic and personal instruction simultaneously speak to the broader reinvention of government and complicate any conclusion that there is *no* welfare in the United States. By taking these ventures seriously, and attending to their nuances and specificities, we might better understand the remodelling of welfare and the remaking of citizens.

Acknowledgements

The authors would like to thank Mark Andrejevic, Gareth Palmer, Anna McCarthy and an anonymous reviewer for helpful comments on some of the arguments developed in this essay.

Notes

1. For the history of social work in the United States see Ehrenreich (1985); for a study of professional expertise as a related technology of governing see Ehrenreich and English (1978).
2. For the role of magazines in demonstrating self and lifestyle pedagogies within the cultural economy of consumerism see Ohmann (1998) and Lears (1983). For early US television's engagement in self and lifestyle instruction see Leibman (1995), Watts (2006) and Cassidy (2005).
3. See Osbourne and Gaebler's influential *Reinventing Government: How the Entrepreneurial Spirit is Transforming*

the Public Sector (1992) for the changing rationalities of governing that we are describing here. President Bill Clinton endorsed the book, claiming it 'should be read by every elected official in America. Those of us who want to revitalize government . . . have to reinvent it. This book gives us a blueprint.'
4. We elaborate in more detail how this term is useful for thinking about contemporary television in *Better Living through Reality TV* (2008).
5. For a useful summary of the move to make social services (as a dimension of the public sector) accountable to an entrepreneurial ethic see Rom (1999). Several critics have also observed reality television's parallel encouragement of a self-governing culture of entrepreneurialism. Gareth Palmer (2004), for example, has noted similarities between makeover television and the 'personal development movement', showing how both resonate with notions of entrepreneurial citizenship.
6. Our use of the term 'civic laboratories' is indebted to Tony Bennett's (2005) use of the term to describe the civic training provided by museum culture.
7. Rose (1998, 1999) has traced the dispersion of technologies of governance in a number of important studies. For an influential discussion of the role of culture in governing see also Bennett (1998).
8. Foucault discusses the relation between 'welfare states', governmentality, and the biopolitical in 'Security, Territory, Population' (1997b, 67–71). He discusses the relation between liberalism and neoliberalism in 'The Birth of Biopolitics' (1997a, 72–9). Foucault analyses early programmes for 'social health' in 'The Politics of Health in the Eighteenth Century' (2000b, 90–105). He discusses the state's role in administering 'social medicine' in 'The Birth of Social Medicine' (2000a, 134–56). The 'right to health' in contemporary France is discussed in 'The Risks of Security' (2000c, 365–81).
9. The 'genealogy' of welfare dependency as a regime of truth, and the gendering of the dependent welfare citizen, is charted in Fraser and Gordon (1997). The racialization of the female welfare subject is charted in Gilens (2000).
10. For an excellent analysis of the changing 'state of welfare' see also Clarke (2004).
11. We draw from material found on the 'Healthy US' website, the remarks of George Bush at his Fitness Challenge, the President's Challenge website 'You're It, Get Fit', and the website for the President's Council on Physical Fitness, with links to the Department of Health and Human Services.
12. Our discussion of *Honey We're Killing the Kids* is elaborated in *Better Living through Reality TV*.
13. For more on interactivity as viewer labour see Andrejevic (2004).

References

Andrejevic, Mark. 2004. *Reality TV: The work of being watched*. New York and Oxford: Rowman & Littlefield.

Bennett, Tony. 1998. *Culture: A reformer's science*. London: Sage.

———. 2005. Civic laboratories: Museums, culture object-hood, and the governance of the social. *Cultural Studies* 19, no. 5: 521–47.

Brown, Wendy. 2003. Neoliberalism and the end of liberal democracy. *Theory & Event* 7, no. 1. http://muse.jhu.edU/journals/theory_and_event/v007/7.1 brown.html

Burchell, Graham. 1996. Liberal government and techniques of the self. In *Foucault and political reason: Liberalism, neo-liberalism and rationalities of government*, ed. A. Barry, T. Osborne, and N. Rose, 19–36. Chicago: University of Chicago Press.

Bush, George W. 2002. Remarks by the President at Fitness Challenge. The White House. http://www.whitehouse.gov/news/releases/2002/06/20020622-2.html

Cassidy, Marsha. 2005. *What women watched: Daytime television in the 1950s*. Austin: University of Texas Press.

Clarke, John. 2004. *Changing welfare, changing states: New directions in social policy*. London: Sage.

Cruikshank, Barbara. 1999. *The will to empower: Democratic citizens and other subjects*. Ithaca, NY: Cornell University Press.

Dean, Mitchell. 1999. *Governmentality: Power and rule in modern society*. London: Sage.

Ehrenreich, John. 1985. *The altruistic imagination: A history of social work and social policy in the United States*. Ithaca, NY: Cornell University Press.

Ehrenreich, Barbara, and Deirdre English. 1978. *For her own good: 150 years of the experts' advice to women*. New York: Doubleday.

Faubion, James, ed. 2000. *Power*. New York: New Press.

Foucault, Michel. 1986. *The care of the self: The history of sexuality volume 3*. New York: Vintage.

———. 1991. Governmentality. In *The Foucault effect: Studies in governmentality*, ed. G. Burchell, C. Gordon, and P. Miller, 87–104. Chicago: University of Chicago Press.

———. 1997a. The birth of biopolitics. In *Ethics: Subjectivity & truth*, ed. P. Rabinow, 72–9. New York: New Press.

———. 1997b. Security, Territory, Population. In *Ethics: Subjectivity & truth*, ed. P. Rabinow, 67–71. New York: New Press.

———. 2000a. The birth of social medicine. In *Power*, ed. J. Faubion, 134–56. New York: New Press.

———. 2000b. The politics of health in the eighteenth century. In *Power*, ed. J. Faubion, 90–105. New York: New Press.

———. 2000c. The risks of security. In *Power*, ed. J. Faubion, 365–81. New York: New Press.

Fraser, Nancy, and Linda Gordon. 1997. A genealogy of 'dependency': Tracing a keyword of the US welfare state. In *Justice interruptus: Critical reflections on the 'post-socialist' condition*, ed. N. Fraser, 121–50. New York: Routledge.

Gilens, Martin. 2000. *Why Americans hate welfare: Race, media, and the politics of antipoverty policy*. Chicago: University of Chicago Press.

Gordon, Colin. 1991. Governmental rationality: An introduction. In *The Foucault effect*, ed. G. Burchell, C. Gordon, and P. Miller, 1–54. Chicago: University of Chicago Press.

Labaton, Stephen. 2005. Transition to digital gets closer. *New York Times*, 20 December. http://www.nytimes.com/2005/12/20/technology/20digital.html

Lears, Jackson. 1983. From salvation to self-realization: Advertising and the therapeutic roots of the consumer culture 1880–1930. In *The culture of consumption*, ed. R. Wrightman Fox and J. Lears, 1–38. New York: Pantheon.

Leibman, Nina C. 1995. *Living room lectures: The fifties family in film and television*. Austin: University of Texas Press.

Manson, Marshall. 2004. Written testimony to the House Government Reform Committee Hearing on 'The Supersizing of America'. 3 June, http://www.cfif.org/htdocs/legislative_issues/state_issues/supersizing_america.htm

McCarthy, Anna. 2004. Stanley Milgram, Allen Funt, and me: Postwar social science and the 'first wave' of reality TV. In *Reality TV: Remaking television culture*, ed. S. Murray and L. Ouellette, 19–39. New York: New York University Press.

Ohmann, Richard. 1998. *Selling culture: Magazines, markets and class at the turn of the century*. New York: Verso.

Osbourne, David, and Ted Gaebler. 1992. *Reinventing government: How the entrepreneurial spirit is transforming the public sector*. New York: Plume.

Ouellette, Laurie. 2002. *Viewers like you? How public TV failed the people*. New York: Columbia University Press.

Ouellette, Laurie, and James Hay. 2008. *Better living through reality TV: Television and post-welfare citizenship*. Maiden, MA: Blackwell.

Palmer, Gareth. 2004. The new you: Class and transformation in lifestyle television. In *Understanding reality television*, ed. S. Holmes and D. Jermyn, 173–90. London: Routledge.

Rabinow, Paul, ed. 1997. *Ethics: Subjectivity & truth*. New York: New Press.

Rom, Mark Carl. 1999. From welfare state to Opportunity, Inc. *American Behavioral Scientist* 43, no. 1: 155–76.

Rose, Nikolas. 1996. Governing 'advanced' liberal democracies. In *Foucault and political reason: Liberalism, neo-liberalism and rationalities of government*, ed. A. Barry, T. Osborne, and N. Rose, 37–64. Chicago: University of Chicago Press.

———. 1998. *Inventing ourselves: Psychology, power and person-hood.* Cambridge: Cambridge University Press.

———. 1999. *Governing the soul: The shaping of the private self.* 2nd ed. London: Free Association Books.

Sender, Katherine. 2006. Queens for a day: *Queer Eye for the Straight Guy* and the neoliberal project. *Critical Studies in Media Communication* 23, no. 2: 131–51.

Watts, Amber. 2006. *Queen for a Day:* Remaking consumer culture one woman at a time. In *The great American makeover: Television, history, nation,* ed. D. Heller, 141–58. New York: Palgrave.

Websites

ABC Television. Shaq's Big Challenge official website. http://abc.go.primetime/shaqsbigchallenge/index

'Healthy US' website, http://www.whitehouse.gov/infocus/fitness/

President's Council on Physical Fitness, http://www.fitness.gov/

Shaq's Big Challenge. Family Challenge website. ShaqsFamilyChallenge.com

You're It, Get Fit website, http://www.presidentschallenge.org/

42.
CITIZENSHIP, DIVERSITY, LAW AND *UGLY BETTY*

Hector Amaya

Early in the first season of *Ugly Betty* (ABC) we learn that Betty's father, Ignacio Suarez (played by Cuban-American actor Tony Plana) is having some problems with his Health Maintenance Organization (HMO). He is ill; his medicine has run out, but he does not want to ask the HMO for a new prescription. In the episode 'Fey's Sleigh Ride', Betty (America Ferrera) must go in person to the pharmacy where she discovers that her father has been using a fake social security number. Up to this point in the narrative, Ignacio has been depicted as an unusual man and father. He is the primary care-giver to his two daughters: he cooks for them, stays at home, and shows kindness and emotional wisdom not typically associated with an older working-class Latino male. He has been made sympathetic through softening (or perhaps feminizing) his masculinity. But the plot throws a monkey-wrench in the narrative when we discover that he is an undocumented immigrant, one who has committed what the legal and immigration system tried to define as a felony. Perhaps because of this sympathetic representation of an undocumented immigrant, perhaps because the show casts Latinas/os in key production, writing and acting positions, *Ugly Betty* is seen in the media world as a great example of good media corporate ethics. However, *Ugly Betty* is the only one-hour show centered on and at least partly produced by Latinas/os on prime-time English-speaking US television. Ironically, by its very existence, the show has helped ABC maintain a respectable reputation regarding diversity programming. In its exceptionality, and in the discursive positioning of the show as good

corporate ethics, *Ugly Betty* illustrates current understandings of diversity and labor in today's deregulated media environment.

Using Latina/o media and citizenship studies, in this article I will show that current ideas of diversity and labor are constitutive of *Ugly Betty*'s exceptionality. That is, *Ugly Betty*'s circulation as an exemplar of media ethics relies on the systematic marginalization of Latino labor in the industry and in legal frameworks of citizenship, as well as on a definition of diversity tuned more to corporate interests than to social justice. After decades of legal and activist efforts, it remains difficult for Latinas/os to participate in mainstream English-language media. This is the result of a complex of cultural practices and law, including a broad array of laws that produce differentiated citizenship experiences.

If citizenship is understood as the theoretical lens that addresses belonging and law, then Latino citizenship is at stake in the discursive positioning of *Ugly Betty*. In this article, I look at citizenship in ways that are not typically discussed in media studies. Although most media studies research on citizenship references the law, often this is done only tangentially or within the language of reform (e.g. media reform scholarship). For instance, analyses of cultural citizenship do the work of fleshing out systematic (if not structural) inequality where formal/legal equality is declared (notably, race/ethnicity, gender/sex and disability), yet they typically leave to the side what Nicholas de Genova calls: 'the legal *production* of citizenship' (2005: 2). With this term, de Genova refers to the 'calculated interventions by which particular laws have effectively generated' the category of the citizen and its companion, the 'illegal' non-citizen. De Genova is not referring only to citizenship law (e.g. the Fourteenth Amendment or immigration law), but to the full array of legal prescriptions that directly impinge on the formation of the citizen, including local and federal labor laws, international law and global financial policies, which lay the ground for asymmetrical immigration between Latin American nations and the United States. Like de Genova, I see citizenship and law as mutually constituted. Going further, I see the legal production of citizenship embedded in what Thomas Streeter (1996) calls 'corporate liberalism', a notion that speaks to the deep influence of capitalist logic on the egalitarian philosophy of liberalism, and to the framing of political values (which are central to the three fields) in the language of capital. On this, Thomas Streeter writes:

> [Commercial] broadcasting is a child of the collection of habits of thought some scholars call liberalism, understood not as a point on the political spectrum, but as a form of dominant social consciousness ... in particular, [liberalism] involves the hope that the process of buying and selling can complement or help create freedom and democracy for individuals, especially when integrated through the rule of law.
>
> (1996: 9)

In the case of *Ugly Betty*, corporate liberalism impacts the legal production of citizenship by defining the show through media legal frameworks that normalize definitions of diversity and corporate civics that are unlikely to improve the overall social standing of Latinas/os and other minorities.

In engaging the question of media's racial composition, in this article I argue that the current environment of media deregulation is a constitutive part of the discourse surrounding *Ugly Betty* as an example of diversity, because deregulation has legally and culturally normalized differentiated citizenship experiences in media industries, and given shape to the set of political and cultural constraints and possibilities that the show represents to ABC in particular and the industry in general. The differentiated citizenship

experiences I reference begin at the level of labor rights of Latinas/os, which have been eroded since the 1970s. So, when I refer to deregulation, I am mostly concerned with the continuous erosion of Equal Employment Opportunity and affirmative action (EEO/AA) measures in media industries. Differentiated citizenship experiences rooted in labor have cultural ripples that affect the citizenship experience of all Americans, who consume a universe of media texts that are always already discriminatory.

After a brief description of the show, the following section expands on the claim of differentiated citizenship experience and labor structures. First, I explore the relationship of labor laws to media industries, concluding with a snapshot of Latino labor involvement in contemporary media. This snapshot reveals an appalling reality, which I problematize by reference to theories of corporate values and labor. My point here is consistent with the position of most people writing on media labor: left to their own devices, media corporations reproduce existing values. But values are embodied ethics, hence, in the process of reproducing values corporations reproduce embodied structures of specific racial, class and gender characteristics. Corporations are hardly innocent and in the next section I explore the discursive efforts by corporations to transform the legal expectations of the 1960s efforts for labor equality into the neoliberal standard of self-regulation. This is most evident in the way the discourse of diversity has changed from one connoting racial justice to one connoting market savvy and potential for profit in an age of media segmentation. The last section details how a show like *Ugly Betty* fits within this latter, toothless notion of diversity, and hence how the show came to exist and circulate as an exemplar of media corporate civics through the embracing of diversity.

Normalizing Exclusion: Labor, Law and Citizenship

It should not be surprising that one of the few positive fictional representations in mainstream English-language television of an undocumented Latino was found in *Ugly Betty*. The show, much like Ignacio, has a complex transnational history that spans several countries. It began in Colombia, passed through Mexico and ended up in the US, first as an imported narrative aired by Univision and, now, in its English version, as an immigrant story. A hugely successful *telenovela* in its original version (the Mexican version of *Ugly Betty – La Fea Mas Bella* – is a ratings success at Univision, typically taking several spots in the top-ten highest rated shows in Spanish-language television), *Yo Soy Betty La Fea* has become an international phenomenon, re-created several times in only a few years. Chiefly another retelling of 'The Ugly Duckling' story, all the versions of *Yo Soy Betty La Fea* tell the story of a young, homely woman who wishes to pursue a career in fashion where she is an outcast because of her physical appearance (Rivero, 2003). In the Latin American versions, Betty's wit, intelligence and integrity help her succeed and win her boss's heart.

The American version, *Ugly Betty*, is an unusual televisual text. It is written, produced and starred in partly by Latinas/os. However, just as Latinas/os are often coded as partly foreign, regardless of whether they have lived in the United States for generations, this rare Latino show is heavily coded as immigrant for several reasons. Its script, parts of which have traveled across borders, has been modified by making Betty and her family immigrants who must endure not only the challenges of class (as in the Colombian version), but also the challenges of race, ethnicity and nationality. Also, the people in charge of bringing it to non-Latino audiences identify themselves as immigrants, and they refer to the show as an immigrant story. Silvio Horta, one of the show's three key executive producers and the person most responsible for its American adaptation, is a Cuban-American who, in his speech when receiving the 2007 Golden Globe for Best Television Series (Musical or Comedy), described the show as an 'immigrant' effort. On the business side of things, Salma Hayek, a Mexican-American international media star, was one of those most responsible for convincing ABC to pick up the series and continues her involvement as executive producer and invited guest.

Because *Ugly Betty* is coded as immigrant, it manifests the tensions between the national and transnational, tensions that are more evident when considering the nationally bound legal systems that shape labor alongside the show's transnational textualization and international distribution. In this section

I explore the legal field's relation to media industries through the lens of employment and lay out the worrisome shape of the television industrial field. Readers versed in race and cultures of production in the United States will be familiar with the data, but I restate it here for the benefit of the rest. I aim to emphasize labor as constitutive of citizenship and argue that labor discrimination is one of the most efficient means used in neoliberal governmentality to constitute unequal citizenship experiences.

When discussing the legal production of citizenship, de Genova is mostly concerned with labor and the manipulation of Mexican-American workers by mainstream economic and legal structures in Chicago. His concern with labor and citizenship is hardly unusual. As Evelyn Nakano Glenn (2002) and Linda Bosniak (2002) have noted, citizenship has been given shape throughout our history through legal definitions of labor. It is partly though this relationship of labor and law that we have constituted differentiated experiences of citizenship for the working class, women, African-Americans, Asian-Americans and Latinas/os. Although slavery as a legal framework, or the '*bracero*' program as international labor policy, no longer exist, labor laws continue to produce differentiated citizenship experiences, and this is particularly true in media. Labor regulation in media industries is magnified by the economic, cultural and political might of our media system, which has the unusual ability to influence government and society by constructing the cultural frameworks that will serve to interpret political and legal behavior. Whoever controls our media system is also in partial control of the constitution of citizenship.

Media control cannot be exercised without government intervention. For instance, *Ugly Betty* airs on ABC, a television network that belongs to Disney, which, like other profitable media corporations, has been successful at interacting with governmental and legal structures. According to Robert McChesney (2004) and Paul Starr (2004), media like ABC have always existed within close proximity of political structures in at least two ways. First, they exist as industries tightly regulated by government, which monitors ownership patterns, holdings and mergers, technological infrastructure, market performance (competitiveness) and media's relation to the public good. As McChesney states: '[T]he U.S. media system – even its most "free market" sectors – is the direct result of explicit government policies and in fact would not exist without those policies' (2004: 17). Second, media industries shape the democratic process by influencing the types of knowledge the citizenry has about the political world, thus helping legitimize or put into question the political and legal worlds. McChesney and Starr help us understand that the relative harmony between the political and media worlds, their multiple connections and interdependences, has profound implications for the political health of the nation.

During the 1960s it finally became evident that our political structures were sick and during that decade the government set the basis for the regulation of labor in all industries, including media, based on the principles of the Civil Rights Act of 1964. The Equal Employment Opportunity Commission (EEOC), created to monitor discrimination in the workplace, was part of the Civil Rights Act and constituted one of the Act's achievements, but also one of its biggest compromises. The EEOC's official history acknowledges that the agency was toothless from 1965 to 1971; as a testament to the influence of corporations and industry in federal policy, the EEOC was created on the condition that it would only 'receive, investigate, and conciliate complaints' (EEOC, 2007). The EEOC could not enact remedies until later in the 1970s. Other research shows that corporate influence on these government agencies has led to weak enforcement labor law or inefficient way of using legal sanctions (Bullock and Lamb, 1984; Leonard, 1985). Our social ills were partly due to media, as the Kerner Commission argued. According to this document, media news organizations contributed to the racial unrest by failing to convey the urgency of racial problems. This failure, the report continued, was based on the fact that television: 'is almost totally white in both appearance and attitude' (Brooks et al., 2003: 125). As Chon Noriega (2000: 20), among others, has observed, this conclusion placed employment and representation at the center of racial unrest, in a sense acknowledging the political and social power of media, and the necessity to regulate it more closely. During the following years, the media industries became regulated by different

government agencies with the goal of implementing a remedy to labor inequality, chiefly through the EEOC and the FCC (Brainard, 2004: 45–46; Rodriguez, 1999: 62–3). Media also became the logical target of much civic activism. Noriega suggests a three-part historiography of this effort by Latino organizations. From 1968 to 1977, he notes, Latino media activists used the state's civil rights institutions to demand labor and representational justice. Between 1974 and 1984, Latinos made direct demands on the television industry, but relied on public 'funding sources for production'. Since 1981, Latino media activism has taken on a corporate logic and has demanded from state and industry ' "consumer sovereignty" in commercial *and* public broadcasting'. In Noriega's view, during this time, activists '[staked] a moral and economic claim to the Chicano citizen-consumer' (2000: 25).

By in large, legal and activist efforts have failed. Latino numbers in English-language media industries remain dismally low (Keller, 1994; Mayer, 2003; Noriega, 2000; Ramirez Berg, 2002; Rodriguez, 1999). Simply, Latinas/os have a hard time getting access to mainstream media jobs. In journalism, Latinos account for 4 percent of personnel in print news, and 6 percent of news staffers in English-language television (NAHJ, 2007). Bob Papper (2003: 21) has found that Latinos account for only 1.5 percent of radio news-staffers and, in television, for only 4.4 percent of news directors. The lack of Latino personnel in news has a predictable effect on coverage. Federico Subervi's latest report on Latino representation in television news media shows that stories about Latinas/os account for only 0.82 percent in the major television networks and CNN (2005: 4). In mainstream, English-speaking television, Latinos accounted for 6.5 percent of prime-time characters and 6 percent of opening credit characters in 2003 (Children Now, 2004). This is a significant improvement from 1999, when Latino prime-time representation was around 2 percent, but still unsatisfactory if we consider census figures in the US and California. As the US Census (2007) figures indicate, at this moment, Latinas/os have surpassed African-Americans as the most numerous racial/ethnic minority in the nation and account for more than 14.8 percent of the population in general, and 35.5 percent in California, the state where most media is produced. This lack of representation in media work is worrisome, not only because it represents the exclusion of Latinas/os from the enormous wealth that media industries generate, but, as importantly, because it has laid the basis for culturally normalizing Latino disenfranchisement. Referring back to Delgado and Stefancic (1998), the 'Latino condition' is largely caused by legal disenfranchisement in most significant spheres of life, including, I add, media employment.

Latino lack of representation in media industries has been normalized partly because of hiring practices that tend to work under what organizational demographers call the 'similarity-attraction paradigm' (people tend to hire and promote others like themselves), partly because post-Reaganism has succeeded in eroding EEO/AA provisions and partly because organizations have never fully believed in the value of racial justice. In a social system such as media organizations, Nan Lin (2001) notes, some values are interpreted as commonsensical and are internalized by most members of the system. He calls them 'persuasive' values. Other resources come through 'coercion', a 'process by which fellow actors are forced to recognize the merit of a resource or face certain sanction or punishment' (2001: 30). Resources that become valued because of coercion (e.g. racial justice) are often not understood as holding intrinsic merit. Given the history media corporations have with the values of racial/sexual equality, it is safe to assume that these have been perceived mostly as coercive values.[1] Not surprisingly, researchers and civil rights state organizations have found that media corporations have tried, and too often succeeded, at cheating EEO/AA law, sidestepping their legal responsibilities, and lobbying against racial (and sexual) justice policies. Either by using the 'two-fer' (a woman of color that a media corporation would report twice, as woman and non-white employee), inflating their numbers of hires of color, isolating these hires from the advancement track or placing them in highly visible but relatively powerless positions, media organizations have reacted to the values of racial/sexual justice in chauvinist but predictable ways (Brooks et al., 2003: 127; United States Civil Rights Commission, 1977: 93–7; Wilson and

Gutierrez, 1995). In doing so, they have normalized different ways of experiencing citizenship: one reserved for communities of people who, in their embodied selves, can convey persuasive values and another for those whose embodiment conveys coercive values.

Perhaps the biggest impact corporations have had on legal remedies for racial discrimination in labor was reframing the ideas of racial justice within corporatist and managerial logics (Edelman, 1992). This is the context for the current state of affairs: a media industry that, four decades after the formation of the EEO/AA, still lacks racial and sexual equality (Brooks et al, 2003: 123–46). Regarding EEO/AA, media and government have produced a state of deregulation. This does not mean that the idea of diversity is not current or popular in contemporary organizations, but rather, as I illustrate, that diversity has been redefined in ways that weaken its applicability to the goal of racial/sexual justice.

Diversity in a State of Deregulation

For the last couple of decades, the work of Lauren Edelman has shown the ways in which civil rights legal prescriptions, including labor justice laws (e.g. EEO/AA), have been adopted by organizations, corporations and the managerial class. She notes that EEO/AA law is particularly open to mediation by organizations because it is ambiguous, has weak enforcement and emphasizes procedural over substantive effects. Title VII of the 1964 Civil Rights Act, for instance, makes it unlawful to discriminate, but fails to define the term. It is weakly enforced because the EEOC's goal is first to conciliate between employer and employee, the process is lengthy and costly, and it has one of the lowest rates of success of legal suits (plaintiffs win only 21 percent of cases). To make matters worse, the courts today emphasize process over substance. For instance, compliance with Title VII is widely interpreted as being based on whether employers followed hiring processes that encourage diversity, rather than actual hires. So, if employers made a 'good faith effort' to achieve EO goals, they are home safe (1992: 1536–41). In Edelman's view, EEO/AA law is mediated by organizations in ways that minimize their effect on long-held cultural beliefs and managerial processes. The means by which organizations can do both is by creating offices, positions and rules that visibly show the public and law enforcers that they are complying with the law.

Media organizations are not exceptions, as the amount of EEO/AA initiatives and postings show. Most media corporations now have diversity officers, diversity initiatives and so on. Fox has an office of 'Diversity Development' that proudly displays the racial variety of shows like *House* (Omar Epps's photograph is on the front page), *24* and its multi-racial cast and the diversity jewel, *K-Ville*, with Anthony Anderson's proud face legitimating these practices and goals.[2] The ABC Television Group has a program for developing talent that prominently displays in its 2007 calendar a 'Native American Actors Mixer' in January, an 'African American Heritage Ceremony' and a 'Hispanic Symposium Multicultural Day' in February.[3] NBC has created what they call 'DiverseCity NBC', a web space that showcases the diversity that exists already in NBC's programming, and that also functions as a space agents and casting executives can use to locate 'unsigned talent'.[4] Media leaders often argue that 'diversity' is one of their key goals. Fox Entertainment President Peter Liguori has stated:

> We think, as a network, [diversity is] the moral thing to do. And it's the right business thing to do. When you look at the top 10, top 20 shows out there, they're diverse. For TV and certainly for Fox to be vibrant, relevant and authentic, we need to be reflective of the general population.

In a similar vein, Anne Sweeney, President of the Disney-ABC Television Group, declared for *Variety*: 'The more textured, the more real, the more authentic our writing and directing staffs are and our on-air talent, the more successful we'll be, because we are reflecting the real world around us, not just the bubble world' (Toledo, 2007). Because many of these initiatives, with these stated goals, have been going on for some time, there is reason to believe that they are not having quite the desired effect, which supports what Edelman theorizes: 'Organizations create EEO/AA structures, then, largely as gestures to their legal environments; these structures are designed to secure

legitimacy and minimize the threat of liability' (1992: 1545; Edelman et al., 2001: 1590).

Although these network initiatives are meant to bring these organizations into compliance with EEO/AA legal environment, they exist within a discursive framework of diversity that no longer has as its goal racial/sexual justice, a value widely perceived as coercive. Instead, the new managerial discourse of diversity, which Edelman notes has changed since the 1980s (Edelman et al., 2001: 1589), recasts diversity as a legal prescription of a different sort. Typically, today's discourse of diversity has expanded to include diversity of all sorts, including diversity of thought, religion, lifestyle, dress and the like (2001: 1616). As important, diversity has become a matter of organizational success, a new managerial tactic that tries to create wealth for the organization (2001: 1618). In this discourse, different types of employees have different ways of thinking and working, and different background knowledge, thus providing organizations with more ways of succeeding in a changing world and a new economy. Fox's office of 'Diversity Development' justifies this initiative with precisely this language. Not surprisingly, the most frequently cited reason to embrace diversity in this managerial rhetoric is profit.

In this deregulated environment, a show like *Ugly Betty* becomes evidence of media industry's compliance with current legal expectations of diversity. Sylvia Franklin (2007: 19), in perfect corporate media liberal lingo, follows this rationale when she writes for *Television Weekly* regarding *Ugly Betty*: 'diversity pays'. She is referring to the ratings and critical success of *Ugly Betty* and other shows like *Grey's Anatomy* and *Lost*, which also have diverse casts, in front of and behind the camera. In today's media world, Franklin's definition, rooted in managerial rhetoric, has become the standard view of a diversity that can be embraced by profit-seeking organizations. As Charo Toledo (2007), *Variety*'s writer declares, ABC's diverse line-up has made it a success with Latinas/os. Six of the top-ten highest rated shows among Latinas/os (18–49 rating) are shown on ABC. Although perhaps privately these people may indeed believe that opening media to Latinas/os is a matter of basic justice, in public speeches they seem to consistently stick to the script and justify their own positive behaviors as profitable. Such discourse of diversity is also reproduced by media activists working closely with the industry. For instance, Alex Nogales is the President CEO of the National Hispanic Media Coalition, a wonderful organization that brings together Latino media workers and helps them enter into the industry's social networks. Nogales, in receiving an award from Southwest Airlines, justified diversity in terms of profit. In his speech, he noted: 'ABC is the biggest model for everyone to follow. ... Diversifying led to their success in ratings with hit shows like *Ugly Betty* and *Grey's Anatomy*' (in Ruano, 2007: 52). *Ugly Betty* also presents itself as a text that is extremely conscious of the extended notion of diversity by including in its storylines transsexual, gay, immigrant, illegal, black, Latino and so-called 'ugly' characters, all of whom have been understood as diverse by viewers and/or critics.

According to Edelman et al., the managerial view of diversity has '[arisen] in response to the decline of political support for affirmative action and civil rights law' (2001: 1626). As troublesome, there is evidence that this definition of diversity is now mirrored in legal communities. The most visible case is the Supreme Court decision on university admissions at the University of Michigan. The rationale in that case framed diversity as a resource valued in universities because it provides a benefit to the existing university population (Harvey, 2007: 57). The Supreme Court here, in a move that betrays the principles of legal frameworks created during the civil rights era, disregards the standard of racial justice and substitutes it with a standard that benefits the majority.

Embracing *Ugly Betty*

Ugly Betty has succeeded in circulating in the public sphere partly because it exemplifies a type of media ethics and positive corporate civic behavior hegemonic at a time when the notion of diversity is linked to new profit opportunities. Here, ethics is bound in a complex way to good capitalism, which substitutes the state as the primary grantor of citizenship rights. This is a perfect example of corporate liberalism, under which diversity becomes morphed from a term rooted in the racial and sexual struggles of the civil rights movement, to an ethnocentric term that is valued because of the benefits it can provide to the majority who identify with our current racial

patriarchy. In the media corporate world, diversity becomes a cross-cultural marketing strategy that aims to strengthen a media network's chances of victory in the ratings war. In mainstream politics and law, as our Supreme Court now believes, diversity should be valued only if it represents a net gain for the political majority, which in the current racial formation means net gains for the white, heterosexual, patriarchal, middle and upper classes. In this section I explore further how diversity itself became the corporate tactic to tackle ratings, signaling a moment in our political culture where the social space often referred to as the public sphere becomes, under this definition of diversity and these conditions of citizenship, neatly occupied by the values and ethical concerns of corporations.

Streeter (1996) argues that our broadcasting regulatory structure, led by the Federal Communications Commission, increasingly abides by the utilitarian, individualistic and capitalist rules of corporate liberalism, and suggests that the current legal field regulating media is under its spell. This is not only evident to scholars, but also to Latino media activists who have adapted to speak this language. As Noriega and Dávila posit, many Latinas/os have understood that to share in the privilege of media access they have to stop using the argument that diversity is a stand-alone resource, and utilize it, instead, in addition to, or, as a frame for, corporatist logic. It is because of corporatist logic that *Ugly Betty* is able to enter ABC's line-up, and it is capitalism that eventually authorizes this show to speak about citizenship and some of the laws that constitute it.

The most important corporate reasons for ABC developing this show have to do with the show's ability to plug into promising Latino textual forms and demographic potential. Regarding textuality, the show borrows from *telenovelas*. The *telenovela*, as format (long series, with scripted endings) and narrative style (melodrama, with over-the-top situations), has been made famous around the world by Latin American television, especially by Televisa in Mexico, Venevisa in Venezuela and Globo in Brazil. In Latin America and in the US Spanish-language media market (e.g. Univision and Telemundo, Azteca America and Galavision), *telenovelas* are the prime-time. Their success is sustained and international. Hoping to replicate this success, all American English-language television networks are developing *telenovela-*influenced series. The most advanced projects – and the ones that got airtime – are Fox's MyNetworkTV programs *Desire* and *Fashion House* and ABC's *Ugly Betty* ('Domestic Drama . . .', 2006: 16). Part of the appeal of *telenovelas* is related to narrative style and conventions, which have typically produced stories that have multi-generational audiences. As CBS senior vice-president of daytime programs Barbara Bloom stated, these are 'Programs [that] 'I can watch with my 16-year-old daughter, and my mother' ('Domestic Drama . . .', 2006: 16). The attraction of multi-generational audiences is not necessarily related to embracing 'family values' or some kind of wholesome view of what television ought to be. The attraction of multi-generational shows is that this viewing practice may slowdown network viewership erosion due to age-based market fragmentation (Potter, 2004). Since the introduction of cable in the 1970s, the networks' audience has dwindled. Today, the four English-language networks (CBS, NBC, ABC and Fox) average a 41 percent share during regular broadcast season, and a 30 percent share during the summer (in 2007, the four networks averaged only a 27 percent share) (Consoli and Crupi, 2007). Multi-generational shows may increase their share and revenue. The economic challenges faced by the networks due to losing viewers also forces them to rely more than ever on their ability to market their programming internationally and through different media. The *telenovela* scores high on both standards. *Telenovelas* are products that can be sold internationally, as Globo, Venevisa and Televisa have shown, and that can be repackaged in different formats such as DVDs and video-on-demand (VOD) (Whitney, 2007: 26). Already *Ugly Betty* has been hugely successful internationally, with ABC having no difficulty placing it in national markets as dissimilar as Germany, Britain, Dubai and Spain. The show has also been selected to be delivered on VOD and DVD (Hopewell and de Pablos, 2006: 14; Jaafar, 2007: 20).

The format's attraction, and the potential international success of *telenovelas*, are part of the backstory to the development of *Ugly Betty*. Another part is the growing importance and wide recognition of the size of the Latino market and the mainstreaming

of *Latinidad*. As Arlene Dávila (2000), and Isabel Molina and Angharad Valdivia (2004: 206) have commented, Latinas/os are the 'It' market. Partly this is because of demography. As stated before, Latinos are the fastest-growing minority in the nation, have surpassed African-Americans as the most important minority numerically, and, if census projections are correct, will only become more important as times goes by. Latino wealth is also rapidly increasing. Since 1990, Latino wealth has been compounding at a rate of 8.2 percent, almost doubling the wealth growth of non-Latinos (4.9 percent). Their buying power has grown from $220 billion in 1990, to $687 billion in 2004, and will grow to a projected $923 billion by 2009 (Humphreys, 2006: 6). Because of this, marketers and advertisers who specialize in targeting Hispanics are thriving. As Dávila (2002: 24–38) has shown, for more than five decades, professionals in the business of crafting markets have, sometimes painstakingly, given shape to a Hispanic market that can be described to advertisers in terms of ethnicity, language, international (where do Latinos come from?) and national geographies (e.g. California and Texas, or the growing Latino concentration in the south), and cultural specificity. Today, these marketers are harvesting the benefits of this ground work.

The Hispanic market is not equal to the Latino communities it claims to represent. It is constructed through an array of archetypes, cultural stereotypes, and profit-driven exaggerations. For instance, Hispanic marketers have often suggested that Latinos/Hispanics favor Spanish-language media, yet millions of middle- and upper middle-class Latinos (who are one of the most marketable segments of the Latino community, and who have often lived in the US for generations) do not speak Spanish (Dávila, 2002:60–3).[5] Highlighting the importance of Spanish, however, has allowed these marketers to market their services and linguistic expertise: Hispanic marketers speak Spanish; most advertisers and mainstream marketers do not. This Spanish-centric view of the Hispanic market is eroding and *Ugly Betty* is evidence of this. The show proves that cross-linguistic, trans-cultural marketing strategies are increasingly feasible. One of the target audiences for the show, according to ABC, is bilingual Latinos who are both viewers of *Betty la Fea* from Univision and *Ugly Betty* from ABC.

As a nod to this audience, in the season finale of *Ugly Betty* season 2, Betty, who travels to Mexico in order to try to fix her father's migration status, meets her look-alike cousin played by Angélica Vale, the Mexican actress who plays Betty in Televisa's version of the *telenovela* (Ayala, 2007). ABC's tactic seems successful if we consider that *Ugly Betty* attracts 800,000 Latina/o viewers every week. This same bilingual Hispanic market is also attractive to Univision, which this fall will air a Spanish-language adaptation of ABC's hit *Desperate Housewives*. (This remapping of Univision's audiences came only months after Univision was acquired by TPG Capital, LP, Thomas H. Lee Partners and Haim Saban, two equity firms and an Egyptian media mogul).

For the show to be successful, ABC needed to target more viewers than bilingual Latinas/os. The show had to have cross-over appeal and, so far, ABC has not been disappointed. The 'it'-ness of Latinas/os, which is symbolized by the star personas of Hayek, Jennifer Lopez, Martin Sheen (*The West Wing*), Edward James Olmos (*Battlestar Galactica*), Jimmy Smits (*Cane*, 2007; *The West Wing*), Shakira, and, now, Ferrara, is perhaps reaching a point where Latinas/os, as characters and narrative centers, can go mainstream. The ratings consistently have shown that, in the highly competitive Thursday 8pm (EST) slot, *Ugly Betty* is a winner with the most coveted demographics.

Because today more advertisers believe in the strength of the Hispanic market, television, which typically has been inhospitable to Latinas/os, may see a gradual change. If discourse around *Ugly Betty* is any indication, these changes will be defined partly in terms of diversity. But this is not the diversity of the civil rights era, but a social and economic tactic aimed at attracting new profits, new markets, and securing success for mainstream media in a Latinized future. In making this point, I am not arguing that such view of diversity cannot have a positive impact on Latino representation and employment in mainstream media. Rather, I believe that the re-casting of diversity as a self-serving economic tactic damages Latinas/os for several reasons: it precludes Latinas/os from using the language of justice; it forces Latina/o narratives to become 'universal' rather than particular; and it reconstitutes current stratifications between citizens and communities. At the root of this notion of

diversity is a tension between racial ethics (doing the right thing for racial/ethnic equality) and profit. Almost invariably, media makers will only espouse an ethics that can also be profitable and very rarely will risk economic loses for a principle, however important this may be. This balancing act between ethics and profit has become normalized to the point that the inherent contradiction of having a principle that can only be embraced when it is economically convenient is never vocalized by media insiders or the press that reports on them.

Conclusion

Because *Ugly Betty* makes us laugh, it is perhaps easy to forget how unusual it is for Latinas/os to share in the privilege of broadcasting narratives. It is equally easy to forget that most mainstream media, at all times, is dominated by the views of citizens, and not just any citizens. The bulk of those working in media industries, at all levels, are white, male, upper middle class, and aware of it. As the numbers show, with their cold, factual poise, English-language media is in the hands of a community of embodied individuals that reconstitutes itself.

Legal remedies enacted during the civil rights movement were meant to change the way industries, including media, reconstituted themselves and had the goal of avoiding conscious discriminatory labor practices. But something was lost in translation between civil rights law and corporate structures. Beginning in the 1980s, the Reagan era of neoliberal policies and the language of diversity management transformed the discourse of diversity from one connoting racial justice to one connoting profit. Following the logic of this discourse, media corporations have created many diversity initiatives, all with the goal of fitting the legal environment of compliance with EEO/AA prescriptions, but only when this compliance can be translated into economic success. Everybody loves *Ugly Betty*. Latinas/os, immigrants and media professionals. It is the latest example that diversity can indeed be profitable, and the latest opportunity for a mostly white structure to embrace mainstream racial protocols without giving up structural privileges.

I began by referencing de Genova's notion of the 'legal production of citizenship' and argued that media helps produce differentiated citizenship experiences. These two ideas are interrelated at media's structural level. On the one hand, media is always participating in the legal construction of citizenship, even when shows do not denotatively address it. I argue this because our mainstream media industries allow people to access social, economic and political capital, and participating in them is thus a significant privilege for the participants. On the other hand, this privilege is reserved for some, which makes media a veritable political system. In this system, resources are allocated based on race, sexuality and class. This political role, which is given shape by labor regulation, jeopardizes the access of Latinas/os to other political roles that media plays in our society. Because of labor laws, Latinas/os cannot use mainstream media as a way of exercising cultural citizenship and thus are partly banned from the public sphere (Flores and Benmayor, 1997). Because of the current toothless legal environment of EEO/AA compliance, Latinas/os cannot influence, through media, our political structures, legal interpretations and discourses (McChesney, 2004; Starr, 2004). These political roles of media are granted legitimacy by a legal system that, through deregulation, has legitimized labor inequality in media industries and is closing the avenues by which to address these issues. The legal production of citizenship is thus constituted partly through labor regulation of media.

According to Streeter and Dávila, the influence of corporate liberalism on our political system has given form to a type of citizenship discursively regimented by corporate logic. Consumer rights stand in for political rights. Beyond this, I believe that changes in the discourse of diversity are evidence of more complex interiorizations of corporate citizenship. In naturalizing the notion that diversity should produce profit and benefit the majority (*Ugly Betty*, University of Michigan), we redefine the legal and political elements of our subjectivity, circumscribing ethics to capitalism. Because our experiences as citizens are manifestations of legal structures and because the legal field is so entwined with corporate logic, our political value becomes equal to our ability to generate profit for the majority. This is a highly racially conservative and alienating political schema that forces individuals to define their political worth based on

majoritarian values. Central to these values is the idea that broadcasting televisual texts should speak to the majority, thus sidelining the argument that to have a just society, the majority must substantially learn about the other. This idea is at play in the public discussions of *Ugly Betty* and other Latino programming. Ferrera, extremely happy and proud of having won a Golden Globe, explained to the press that Betty's story is 'universal'. Horta has repeated this notion in several occasions (Garvin, 2006). Nina Tassler, who oversaw the development of *Cane* (another Latino-focused program) at CBS, has similarly stated: 'This series illustrates our overall philosophy about diversity. It's the quintessential American dream. In its specificity, it becomes universal. We have to tell universal stories, and this is an American family' (Braxton, 2007). To be universal is to de-specify race/class/and origin and highlight majoritarian values, fantasies and narratives. For whites, this is the norm. For non-whites, this is cross-marketing.

Notes

1. Most industries and organizations have reacted similarly to the media industries. For resistance to EEOC and affirmative action, see the work of James Coleman (1984: 84–8) and Christopher Stone (1975).
2. See Fox's office of diversity at: http://www.fox.com/diversity/
3. See ABC's Talent Development site at: http://abctalentdevelopment.com/default.htm
4. See DiverseCity NBC at: http://www.diversecitynbc.com/
5. For a discussion of the different uses of the terms 'Latino' and 'Hispanic', see Dávila (2000: 15).

References

Ayala, N. (2007) '"Betty" Finds Herself in Mexico: A Wink to the Hispanic Market Played Out on ABC's *Ugly Betty* Finale', *Marketing y Medios* 10 May.

Bosniak, L. (2002) 'Citizenship and Work', *North Carolina Journal of Law and Commerce Regulation* 23: 497–506.

Brainard, L.A. (2004) *Television: The Limits of Deregulation*. Boulder, CO: Lynne Rienner.

Braxton, G. (2007) 'White Still a Primary Color: Black, Latino and Asian Groups Feel Multicultural Momentum at the Networks Has Been Lost', *Los Angeles Times* 6 June: 1E.

Brooks, D., G. Daniels and C.A. Hollifield (2003) 'Television in Living Color: Racial Diversity in the Local Commercial Television Industry', *Howard Journal of Communications* 14: 123–46.

Bullock, C.S. III and C.M. Lamb (eds) (1984) *Implementation of Civil Rights Policy*. Monterey, CA: Brooks/Coleman.

Children Now (2004) *Fall Colors: Prime Time Diversity Report 2003*, URL (consulted June 2007): http://publications.childrennow.org/publications/media/fallcolors_2003.cfm

Coleman, J. (1984) 'Introducing Social Structure into Economic Analysis', *American Economic Review* 74(2): 84–8.

Consoli, J. and A. Crupi (2007) 'Broadcast's Summer Ratings Swoon as Cable Blooms', *Mediaweek* 6 August, URL (consulted September 2007): http://www.mediaweek.com/mw/news/recent_display.jsp?vnu_content_id=1003621417

Dávila, A. (2000) 'Talking Back: Hispanic Media and U.S. Latinidad', *Centro Journal* 12(1): 36–47.

Dávila, A. (2002) *Latinos Inc.: The Marketing and Making of a People*. Berkeley, CA: University of California Press.

De Genova, N. (2005) *Working the Boundaries: Race, Space, and 'Illegality' in Mexican Chicago*. Durham, NC: Duke University Press.

Delgado, R. and J. Stefancic (1998) *The Latino/a Condition: A Critical Reader*. New York: New York University Press.

'Domestic Drama: Hugely Popular Internationally, *Telenovelas'* Cat Fights and Contretemps are Trying to Find a Primetime Niche on English-language TV', *Media Week* 16(32) Sept.

Edelman, L.B. (1992) 'Legal Ambiguity and Symbolic Structures: Organizational Mediation of Civil Rights Law', *American Journal of Sociology* 97(6): 1531–76.

Edelman, L.B., H.S. Erlanger and J. Lande (1993) 'Internal Dispute Resolution: The Transformation of Civil Rights in the Workplace', *Law & Society Review* 27(3): 497–534.

Edelman, L.B., S.R. Fuller and I. Mara-Drita (2001) 'Diversity Rhetoric and the Managerialization of Law', *American Journal of Sociology* 106(6): 1589–641.

EEOC (2007) *35 Years of Ensuring the Promise of Opportunity*, URL (consulted June 2007): http://www.eeoc.gov/abouteeoc/35th/prel965/index.html

Flores, W. and R. Benmayor (eds) (1997) *Latino Cultural Citizenship: Claiming Identity, Space and Rights*. Boston, MA: Beacon Press.

Franklin, S. (2007) 'Actors Do the Right Thing', *Television Week* 5 February: 19.

Garvin, G. (2006) '*Ugly Betty* Producer Grows into His role', *Miami Herald* 28 September: Lifestyle Section.

Glenn, E.N. (2002) *Unequal Freedom: How Race and Gender Shaped American Citizenship and Labor*. Cambridge, MA: Harvard University Press.

Harvey, D. (2007) 'A Preference for Equality: Seeking the Benefits of Diversity Outside the Educational Context', *BYU Journal of Public Law* 21(1): 55–82.

Hopewell, J. and E. de Pablos (2006) 'U.S. Skeins Top Spain's Wish List', *Variety* 25–31 December: 14.

Humphreys, J. (2006) 'The Multicultural Economy 2006', *GBEC* (*Selig Center for Economic for Economic Growth*) 66(3): 1–15.

Jaafar, A. (2007) 'Imports Dominate, But Domestics Swell', *Variety* 16–22 April: 20.

Leonard, J.S. (1985) 'What Promises Are Worth: The Impact of Affirmative Action Goals', *Journal of Human Resources* 20: 3–20.

Lin, N. (2001) *Social Capital: A Theory of Social Structure and Action*. Cambridge: Cambridge University Press.

Keller, G.D. (1994) *Hispanics and United States Film: An Overview and Handbook*. Tempe, AZ: Bilingual Review/press.

Mayer, V. (2003) *Producing Dreams, Consuming Youth: Mexican Americans and Mass Media*. New Brunswick, NJ: Rutgers University Press.

McChesney, R. (2004) *The Problem of the Media: U.S. Communication Politics in the Twenty-first Century*. New York: Monthly Review Press.

Molina Guzmán, I. and A.N. Valdivia (2004) 'Brain, Brow, and Booty: Latino Iconicity in U.S. Popular Culture', *Communication Review* 7: 205–21.

NAHJ (2007) *Parity Project*. National Association of Hispanic Journalists, URL (consulted June 2007): http://www.nahj.org/parityproject/parityproject.shtml

Noriega, C.A. (2000) *Shot in America: Television, the State, and the Rise of Chicano Cinema*. Minneapolis, MN: University of Minnesota Press.

Papper, B. (2003) 'Women and Minorities: One Step Forward Two Steps Backward', *Communicator* July/August: 20–5.

Potter, D. (2004) 'The End of Sweeps?', *American Journalism Review* 26(2): 64.

Ramírez Berg, C. (2002) *Latino Images in Film: Stereotypes, Subversion, and Resistance*. Austin, TX: University of Texas Press.

Rivero, Y. (2003) 'The Performance and Reception of Televisual "Ugliness" in *Yo Soy Betty la Fea*', *Feminist Media Studies* 3(1): 65–81.

Rodriguez, A. (1999) *Making Latino News: Race, Language and Class*. Thousand Oaks, CA: Sage.

Ruano, E. (2007) 'Advocating Change; Leadership Landing Presented by Southwestern Airlines', *Latino Leaders* 8(5): 52–4.

Starr, P. (2004) *The Creation of the Media: Political Origins of Modern Communications*. New York: Basic Books.

Stone, C. (1975) *Where the Law Ends: The Social Control of Corporate Behavior*. New York: Harper and Row.

Streeter, T. (1996) *Selling the Air: A Critique of the Policy of Commercial Broadcasting in the United States*. Chicago: University of Chicago Press.

Subervi, F. (2005) *Network Brownout Report 2005: The Portrayal of Latinos and Latino Issues on Network Television News, 2004, with a Retrospect to 1995: Quantitative and Qualitative Analysis of the Coverage*. Austin, TX: NAHJ.

Toledo, C. (2007) 'Alphabet Spells Hope for Diverse America', *Daily Variety* 27 July: A1.

US Census Bureau (2007) *American FactFinder*, URL (consulted July 2007): http://factfinder.census.gov/servlet/ACSSAFFFacts?_submenuId=factsheet_0&_sse=on

United States Civil Rights Commission (1977) *Window Dressing on the Set: Women and Minorities in Television*, Washington, DC: Report of the United States Civil Rights Commission.

Whitney, D. (2007) 'ABC-Cox Deal Paves Way for Series on VOD; Hits to Be Available On-demand in Test, but No Fast-forwarding Allowed', *Television Week* 14 May: 26.

Wilson, C. and F. Gutiérrez (1995) *Race, Multiculturalism and the Media: From Mass to Class Communication*. London: Sage.

PERMISSIONS

Section I: Media/Culture

1. "The Culture Industry: Enlightenment as Mass Deception" from *The Dialectic of Enlightenment* by Max Horkheimer and Theodor W. Adorno, edited by Gunzelin Schmid Noerr, translated by Edmund Jephcott. Copyright © 1944 by Social Studies Association, NY. New edition copyright © 1969 S. Fisher Verlag GmbH, Frankfurt am Main; English translation copyright © 2002 Stanford University. Used by permission of Stanford University Press, www.sup.org.

2. Tania Modleski, "Mass-Produced Fantasies for Women," in *Loving with a Vengeance* (New York: Routledge, 1982), p. 11–34. Copyright © 1982, 2008 by Tania Modleski.

3. "Popular Culture: This Ain't No Sideshow" from *Time Passages: Collective Memory and American Popular Culture* by George Lipsitz. (Minneapolis: University of Minnesota Press, 1990). Originally published as "This Ain't No Sideshow" in *Critical Studies in Mass Communication*, Vol. 5, No. 2 (June 1988), 147–61. Copyright © 1988, SCA.

4. 'Eyes Wide Shut: Capitalism, Class, and the Promise of Black Media," from *Pimpin' Ain't Easy* by Beretta Smith-Shomade. Copyright © 2007 by Routledge.

5. "Disjuncture and Difference in the Global Cultural Economy" by Arjun Appadurai. In *Theory, Culture & Society* (SAGE, London, Newbury Park and New Delhi), Vol. 7 (1990), 295–310. Copyright © 1990 by SAGE. Reprinted by permission of SAGE.

6. "The Practice of Everyday (Media) Life: From Mass Consumption to Mass Cultural Production" by Lev Manovich. In *Critical Inquiry*, Vol. 35 (Winter 2009), 319–31. Copyright © 2008 by The University of Chicago. All rights reserved. Reprinted by permission of the University of Chicago Press.

Section II: Media/Technology

7. "The Turn Within: The Irony of Technology in a Globalized World." by Susan Douglas *American Quarterly*, Vol. 58, No. 3 (2006), 619–638. Copyright © 2006 The American Studies Association. Reprinted with permission of The Johns Hopkins University Press.

8. "The Work of Art in the Age of Mechanical Reproduction" from *Illuminations* by Walter Benjamin, copyright ©1955 by Suhrkamp Verlag, Frankfurt a.M., English translation by Harry Zohn copyright © 1968 and renewed 1996 by Houghton Mifflin Harcourt Publishing Company, reprinted by permission of Houghton Mifflin Harcourt Publishing Company.

9. "Reading Music, Reading Records, Reading Race" by Lisa Gitelman. In *Musical Quarterly*, Vol. 81, No. 2 (Summer 1997), 265–90. Copyright © 1997, Oxford University Press. Reprinted by permission of Oxford University Press.

10. "The Domestic Economy of Television Viewing in Postwar America" by Lynn Spigel. In *Critical Studies in Mass Communication*, Vol. 6, No. 4 (December 1989), 337–54. Copyright © 1989, SCA.

11. "From Screen to Site" by Anna McCarthy. In *October*, Vol. 98 (Fall 2001), 93–111. Copyright © 2001 by October Magazine, Ltd. and the Massachusetts Institute of Technology. Reprinted by permission of the MIT Press.

12. "The Mobile Phone: Towards New Categories and Social Relations" by Leopoldina Fortunati. In *Information, Communication & Society* Vol. 5, No. 4 (2002), 513–528. Copyright © 2002 by Taylor & Francis Ltd.

Section III: Media/Representation

13. "The Word of Representation" by Stuart Hall, reproduced by permission of SAGE Publications, London,

Section IV: Media/Industry

Section V: Media/Identity

Section VI: Media/Audience

Section VII: Media/Citizenship

INDEX